To lift 1,000 pounds, you need about 65,000 cubic feet of hot air!

Parachute Valve

Burners

Propane Tanks (Inside)

A balloon uses about **1,800** square yards of nylon fabric,

3 miles of thread,

and $\frac{1}{2}$ **mile** of reinforcing nylon webbing.

CALIFORNIA
HSP Math

Visit *The Learning Site!*
www.harcourtschool.com

Printed in the United States of America

ISBN 13: 978-0-15-354171-1
ISBN 10: 0-15-354171-7

3 4 5 6 7 8 9 10 751 16 15 14 13 12 11 10 09 08

Mathematics Advisor

Richard Askey
Professor of Mathematics, Emeritus
University of Wisconsin
Madison, Wisconsin

Senior Authors

Evan M. Maletsky
Professor Emeritus
Montclair State University
Upper Montclair, New Jersey

Joyce McLeod
Visiting Professor, Retired
Rollins College
Winter Park, Florida

Authors

Angela G. Andrews
Assistant Professor, Math Education
National-Louis University
Lisle, Illinois

Juli K. Dixon
Associate Professor of Mathematics Education
University of Central Florida
Orlando, Florida

Karen S. Norwood
Associate Professor of Mathematics Education
North Carolina State University
Raleigh, North Carolina

Tom Roby
Associate Professor of Mathematics
Director, Quantitative Learning Center
University of Connecticut
Storrs, Connecticut

Janet K. Scheer
Executive Director
Create-A-Vision
Foster City, California

Jennie M. Bennett
Mathematics Teacher
Houston Independent School District
Houston, Texas

Lynda Luckie
Director, K–12 Mathematics
Gwinnett County Public Schools
Suwanee, Georgia

Vicki Newman
Classroom Teacher
McGaugh Elementary School
Los Alamitos Unified School District
Seal Beach, California

Robin C. Scarcella
Professor and Director, Program of Academic English and ESL
University of California, Irvine
Irvine, California

David G. Wright
Professor
Department of Mathematics
Brigham Young University
Provo, Utah

Program Consultants and Specialists

Russell Gersten
Director, Instructional Research Group
Long Beach, California
Professor Emeritus of Special Education
University of Oregon
Eugene, Oregon

Michael DiSpezio
Writer and On-Air Host, JASON Project
North Falmouth, Massachusetts

Tyrone Howard
Assistant Professor
UCLA Graduate School of Education Information Studies
University of California at Los Angeles
Los Angeles, California

Lydia Song
Program Specialist, Mathematics
Orange County Department of Education
Costa Mesa, California

Rebecca Valbuena
Language Development Specialist
Stanton Elementary School
Glendora, California

Whole Numbers and Decimals

1 Place Value, Addition, and Subtraction 2

2 Place Value: Understand Decimals 36

Number Theory and Fraction Concepts

5 Number Theory 118

6 Fraction Concepts 142

MATH ON LOCATION

The Harcourt Learning Site: www.harcourtschool.com
Multimedia Math Glossary www.harcourtschool.com/hspmath

Fraction Operations

9 Add and Subtract Mixed Numbers 218

10 Multiply and Divide Fractions 236

MATH ON LOCATION

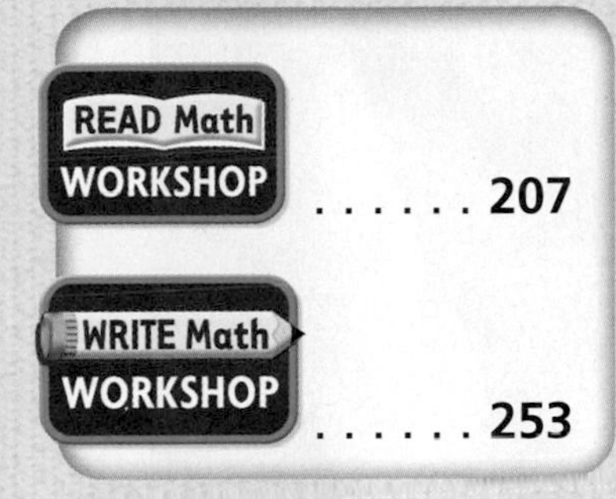

GO ONLINE Technology

Harcourt Mega Math: Chapter 7, p. 182; Chapter 8, p. 203; Chapter 10, p. 252; Extra Practice, pp. 190, 212, 230, 260
The Harcourt Learning Site: www.harcourtschool.com
Multimedia Math Glossary www.harcourtschool.com/hspmath

Decimal Operations

13 Divide Decimals 314

MATH ON LOCATION

GO ONLINE Technology

The Harcourt Learning Site: www.harcourtschool.com
Multimedia Math Glossary www.harcourtschool.com/hspmath

Algebra and Percent

16 Percent 402

MATH ON LOCATION

GO ONLINE Technology

Harcourt Mega Math: Chapter 14, p. 356; Chapter 15, p. 392; Chapter 16, p. 408; Extra Practice, pp. 368, 396, 424
The Harcourt Learning Site: www.harcourtschool.com
Multimedia Math Glossary www.harcourtschool.com/hspmath

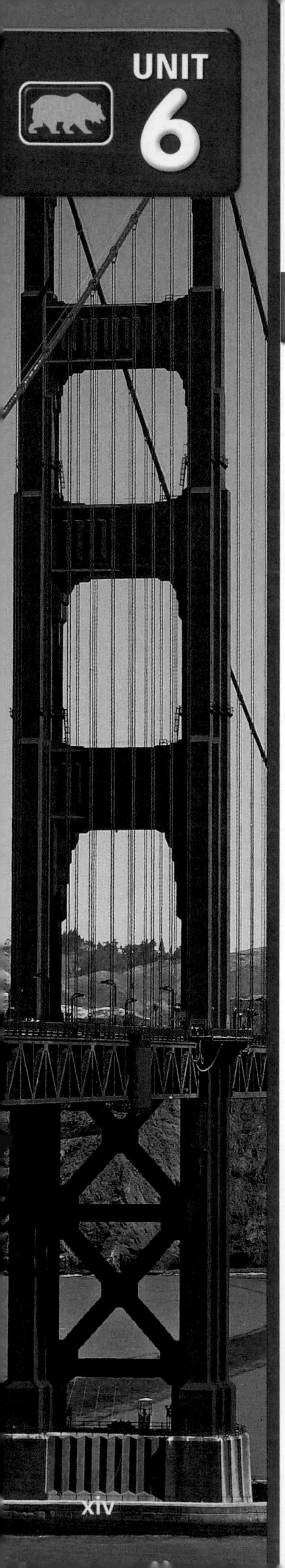

Geometry

GO ONLINE Technology

Harcourt Mega Math: Chapter 17, p. 438; Chapter 18, p. 470; Extra Practice, pp. 460, 490, 512
The Harcourt Learning Site: www.harcourtschool.com
Multimedia Math Glossary www.harcourtschool.com/hspmath

Measurement

20 Measurement and Perimeter 522

21 Area 544

22 Surface Area and Volume 572

MATH ON LOCATION

GO ONLINE Technology

Harcourt Mega Math: Chapter 20, p. 525; Chapter 21, p. 550; Chapter 22, p. 582; Extra Practice, pp. 538, 566, 586
The Harcourt Learning Site: www.harcourtschool.com
Multimedia Math Glossary www.harcourtschool.com/hspmath

Data and Graphs

23 Analyze Data 596

24 Display and Interpret Data 622

Student Handbook

MATH ON LOCATION

Harcourt Mega Math: Chapter 24, p. 630; Extra Practice, pp. 616, 638
The Harcourt Learning Site: www.harcourtschool.com
Multimedia Math Glossary www.harcourtschool.com/hspmath

TALK, READ, and WRITE About Math

Mathematics is a language of numbers, words, and symbols.

This year you will learn ways to communicate about math as you **talk**, **read**, and **write** about what you are learning.

The line graph shows the average maximum temperature during the year at the airport in San Diego, California.

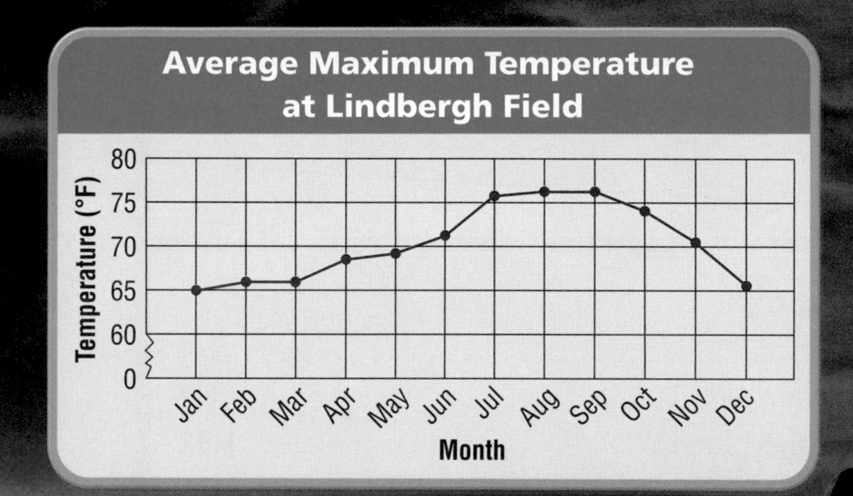

TALK Math

Talk about the line graph.

1. What do the words *average* and *maximum* in the title tell you about the data?
2. What do the numbers along the left side of the graph represent?
3. What is the interval on the graph scale?
4. What can you tell about the data by looking at the line on the graph?

READ Math

Read the data on the graph.

5. Which months have the highest temperatures?

6. What is the greatest temperature difference between any two months?

7. Which two months have a difference of 4°F in the average temperatures?

8. How much greater is the temperature in November than in December?

WRITE Math

Write a problem about the graph.

This year you will write many problems. When you see **Pose a Problem**, you look at a problem on the page and use it to write your own problem.

In your problem you can
- change the numbers or some of the information.
- exchange the known and unknown information.
- write an open-ended problem that can have more than one correct answer.

These problems are examples of ways you can pose your own problem. Solve each problem.

Problem What is the difference in the average temperatures of May and August?

- **Change the numbers or information**
  What is the difference in the average temperatures of January and April?
- **Exchange the known and unknown information**
  Which two months have a difference of 3°F in the average temperatures?
- **Open-Ended**
  Which two consecutive months have a difference of 1°F in the average monthly temperatures?

Pose a Problem Choose one of three ways to write a new problem. Use the information on the bar graph.

UNIT 1

Whole Numbers and Decimals

Math on Location

1

▲ At this contact center, employees take about 2,000,000 customized computer system orders each month.

2

▲ Parts sized precisely to thousandths of an inch move along systems of conveyors in the assembly building.

3

▲ The different parts move on a roller conveyor to where they are divided and sent to different packing areas.

VOCABULARY POWER

TALK Math

What math is used in the **Math on Location**? How can you compare two parts that are less than one-hundredth of an inch?

READ Math

REVIEW VOCABULARY You learned the words below when you learned about operations with whole numbers and decimals. How do these words relate to **Math on Location**?

decimal point a symbol used to separate the ones place and the tenths place in a decimal

product the answer to a multiplication problem

quotient the number, not including the remainder, that results from dividing

WRITE Math

Copy and complete a diagram like the one below. Use what you know about multiplication and division to fill in the answers.

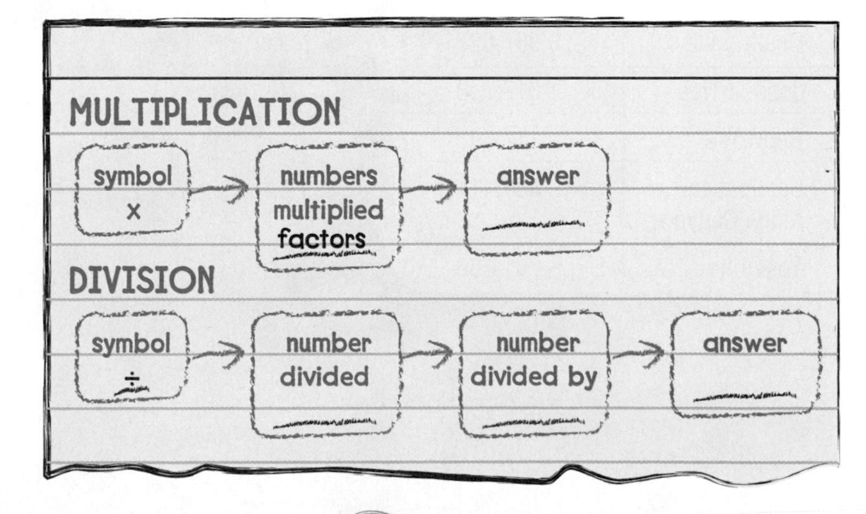

Technology
Multimedia Math Glossary link at
www.harcourtschool.com/hspmath

1 Place Value, Addition, and Subtraction

The Big Idea The position of a digit determines its value; addition and subtraction of multi-digit numbers is based on basic facts and base-ten and place value concepts.

Investigate

Choose three parks from the table that you would like to visit. Write their areas from least to greatest. How much greater is the area of the largest park you chose than the area of the smallest?

California National Parks

Name	Size (in acres)
Death Valley	3,367,627
Joshua Tree	1,017,748
Redwood	112,598
Sequoia and Kings Canyon	864,411
Yosemite	761,266

CALIFORNIA FAST FACT

The National Park Service maintains 23 different units in California. They include national parks, monuments, historical sites, and recreation areas.

GO ONLINE Technology Student pages are available in the Student eBook.

Show What You Know

Check your understanding of important skills needed for success in Chapter 1.

▶ Place Value Through Hundred Thousands

Write the value of the underlined digit.

1. $32\underline{8},406$ **2.** $\underline{4}19,003$ **3.** $16,\underline{2}97$ **4.** $152,4\underline{1}9$

5. $4\underline{5}6,107$ **6.** $9,3\underline{4}2$ **7.** $\underline{2}04,593$ **8.** $\underline{3}8,452$

▶ Round to Thousands

Round each number to the nearest thousand.

9. 837 **10.** 6,409 **11.** 13,526 **12.** 70,143

13. 4,810 **14.** 238,456 **15.** 42,718 **16.** 354,630

▶ Add and Subtract up to 4-Digit Numbers

Find the sum or difference.

17. $\begin{array}{r} 258 \\ +437 \\ \hline \end{array}$ **18.** $\begin{array}{r} 984 \\ -562 \\ \hline \end{array}$ **19.** $\begin{array}{r} 739 \\ -271 \\ \hline \end{array}$ **20.** $\begin{array}{r} 3,926 \\ +1,451 \\ \hline \end{array}$

21. $\begin{array}{r} 4,025 \\ +2,933 \\ \hline \end{array}$ **22.** $\begin{array}{r} 8,059 \\ -5,426 \\ \hline \end{array}$ **23.** $\begin{array}{r} 1,294 \\ +\ 638 \\ \hline \end{array}$ **24.** $\begin{array}{r} 9,162 \\ -2,543 \\ \hline \end{array}$

25. $67 + 45 + 83$ **26.** $134 + 72 + 250$

27. $563 - 209$ **28.** $7,652 - 3,114$

VOCABULARY POWER

CHAPTER VOCABULARY

algebraic expression
Associative Property of Addition
billion
Commutative Property of Addition
compensation
difference
estimate
inverse operations
millions
numerical expression
overestimate
period
round
sum
variable

WARM-UP WORDS

billion 1,000 million; written as 1,000,000,000

estimate a number close to an exact amount

overestimate an estimate that is greater than the exact answer

Place Value Through Billions

OBJECTIVE: Read and write whole numbers to billions.

Quick Review

Write the number that is 1,000 more than the given number.

1. 336
2. 1,230
3. 1,580
4. 3,975
5. 8,627

Vocabulary

billion

Learn

PROBLEM Picture 1 billion pennies. How much space would they fill? One **billion** is 1,000 million. You can write 1 billion as 1,000,000,000.

Look at the pictures to understand the space filled by 1 billion pennies.

About 1,000 pennies could fill a small vase.

About 1,000,000 pennies could fill a car trunk.

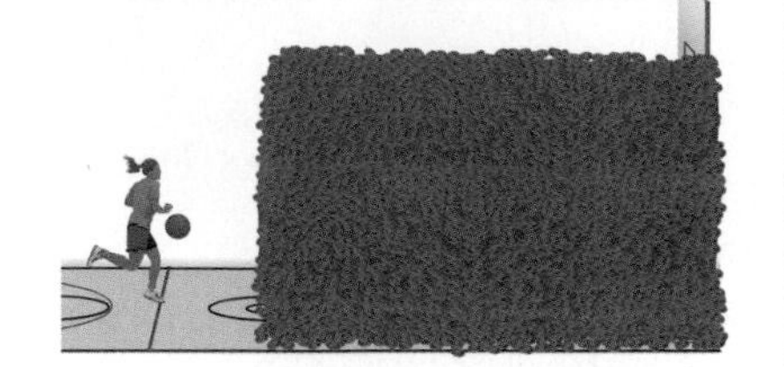

About 1,000,000,000 pennies could fill half a basketball court to a height of 10 feet.

You can use a place-value chart to find the value of a digit.

Example **What is the value of the digit 2 in 3,205,000?**

MILLIONS			THOUSANDS			ONES		
Hundreds	Tens	Ones	Hundreds	Tens	Ones	Hundreds	Tens	Ones
		3,	2	0	5,	0	0	0
		3 × 1,000,000	2 × 100,000	0 × 10,000	5 × 1,000	0 × 100	0 × 10	0 × 1
		3,000,000	200,000	0	5,000	0	0	0

The digit 2 is in the hundred thousands place, so its value is 200,000.

- What is the value of the digit 5 in 3,205,000?

ERROR ALERT

Remember when writing a number in expanded form, you do not need to write the values for places that have the digit 0.
Example: 305
Expanded Form: 300 + 5

A number can be written in standard form, word form, and expanded form.

Standard Form: 13,181,260,000

Word Form: thirteen billion, one hundred eighty-one million, two hundred sixty thousand

Expanded Form: 10,000,000,000 + 3,000,000,000 + 100,000,000 + 80,000,000 + 1,000,000 + 200,000 + 60,000

NS 1.0 Students compute with very large and very small numbers, positive integers, decimals, and fractions and understand the relationship between decimals, fractions, and percents. They understand the relative magnitudes of numbers. *also* **MR 1.1, MR 2.3, MR 2.4, MR 3.0, MR 3.1, MR 3.2**

Place-Value Patterns

As you move to the left in a place-value chart, the value of the place is multiplied by 10.

Suppose you had 1,000,000 pennies. How many stacks could you make if you put 100 pennies in each stack?

ONE WAY Use a place-value chart.

Step 1

Write the numbers in a place-value chart.

BILLIONS			MILLIONS			THOUSANDS			ONES		
Hundreds	Tens	Ones	Hundreds	Tens	Ones	Hundreds	Tens	Ones	Hundreds	Tens	Ones
					1,	0	0	0,	0	0	0
									1	0	0

×10 ×10 ×10 ×10

Step 2

Count the number of places in each number.

1,000,000 → 4 more places than 100

10 × 10 × 10 × 10 = 10,000

1,000,000 is 10,000 times greater than 100.

So, you could make 10,000 stacks of 100 pennies each.

ANOTHER WAY Use place-value patterns.

1,000,000	1 million	1 × 1,000,000
1,000,000	10 hundred thousands	10 × 100,000
1,000,000	100 ten thousands	100 × 10,000
1,000,000	1,000 thousands	1,000 × 1,000
1,000,000	10,000 hundreds	10,000 × 100

So, 1,000,000 is 10,000 times greater than 100.

- Using place value, what are some other ways to rename 6,000? 900,000?

Guided Practice

1. How can you use the place-value chart to find the value of the digit 4.

BILLIONS			MILLIONS			THOUSANDS			ONES		
Hundreds	Tens	Ones	Hundreds	Tens	Ones	Hundreds	Tens	Ones	Hundreds	Tens	Ones
	3	8,	7	5	2,	4	9	1,	0	5	0

Write the value of the underlined digit.

2. 1,3$\underline{6}$8,034
3. 10$\underline{1}$,123,020
✓4. 8,$\underline{6}$87,104,902
5. $\underline{2}$43,903,804,391

Write the number in two other forms.

✓6. 2,000,000,000 + 20,000,000 + 3,000,000 + 30,000 + 500 + 6
7. sixty billion, four hundred three million, nine hundred six
8. 2,910,000
9. 8,007,500,000
10. 1,890,001
11. 3,900,945,000
12. 4 ten thousands
13. 37 ten thousands
14. **TALK Math** How many pennies are shown at the right–1,000 pennies, 1,000,000 pennies, or 1,000,000,000 pennies? **Explain.**

Independent Practice and Problem Solving

Write the value of the underlined digit.

15. 1$\underline{2}$6,568,657,0003
16. 3,$\underline{5}$83,007,165
17. $\underline{9}$,848,012,112
18. 3,20$\underline{5}$,772,994

Write the number in two other forms.

19. 4,000,000,000 + 60,000,000 + 5,000,000 + 40,000 + 200 + 8
20. 50,000,000,000 + 7,000,000,000 + 9,000,000 + 700,000 + 50,000
21. eighty billion, three hundred twenty million, four hundred thirty
22. five hundred forty-five thousand, nine hundred ninety-nine
23. 562,000
24. 7,000,145
25. 12,042,514
26. 5,316,295,000
27. 800 hundred thousands
28. 7,000 ten thousands
29. 20 ten millions
30. 5 ten millions

Algebra Write the missing number for each ■.

31. 70,000,000 = ■ × 100
32. 600,000,000 = ■ × 1,000
33. 900,000,000,000 = ■ × 10,000
34. 400,000,000 = ■ × 100,000

USE DATA For 35–36, use the table.

35. How does the nickel mass change from 1 nickel to 10 nickels to 100 nickels?
36. What is the mass of 1,000 nickels? **Explain.**
37. **Reasoning** There are 100 pennies in \$1, 1,000 pennies in \$10, and 10,000 pennies in \$100. How many pennies are in \$1,000?

Nickel Mass

Number of Nickels	Mass (in grams)
1	5
10	50
100	500

Extra Practice on page 30, Set A

38. What's the Error? Matt wrote the number four million, three hundred five thousand as 4,350,000. Describe Matt's error.

39. WRITE Math **Explain** which one of the following numbers cannot be a product of multiplying 1,087 repeatedly by 10.

10,870; 180,700; 1,087,000

Achieving the Standards

40. John bought 5 packs of collector cards. Each pack has 8 cards. How many cards did John buy? (Grade 4 O-π NS 3.2)

41. The referee tosses a quarter to decide which football team kicks first. What is the probability of tossing tails? (Grade 4 SDAP 2.2)

42. Test Prep What is the value of the underlined digit in 34<u>8</u>,912,605?

A 800,000,000 **C** 8,000,000

B 80,000,000 **D** 800,000

43. Kathy has 60 beads that she wants to separate into 12 equal groups. How many beads will she have in each group? (Grade 4 NS 4.1)

44. Test Prep In the number 875,693,214, which digit is in the ten millions place?

A 8

B 7

C 9

D 1

Problem Solving and Reasoning

NUMBER SENSE You have learned about our place-value system, which is the base-10 system. It uses the digits 0 to 9.

BASE 10					
Hundred thousands	Ten thousands	Thousands	Hundreds	Tens	Ones
	7	2,	0	0	5

Computer programmers use a base-2 system. The base-2 system uses only the digits 0 and 1.

Example **What base-10 number is equivalent to the base-2 number 101?**

BASE 2					
Thirty-twos	Sixteens	Eights	Fours	Twos	Ones
			1	0	1

$(4 \times 1) + (2 \times 0) + (1 \times 1)$ ← Multiply each place value by the digit 0 or 1 in the chart.

$4 + 0 + 1$ ← Add to find the base-10 value.

5 So, 101 in the base-2 system is equal to 5 in the base-10 system.

Find the base-10 value of each base-2 number.

1. 110 **2.** 1010 **3.** 111 **4.** 1011

LESSON 2

Compare and Order Whole Numbers

OBJECTIVE: Use place value and number lines to compare and order whole numbers.

Quick Review

Compare. Write $<$, $>$, or $=$.

1. 132 ● 140
2. 1,541 ● 2,038
3. 17,008 ● 17,008
4. 5,612 ● 5,613
5. 62,100 ● 62,001

Learn

PROBLEM The United States Mint's 50 State Quarters program began in 1999. How does the number of minted Pennsylvania quarters compare with the number of minted Delaware quarters?

774,824,000 coins minted

707,332,000 coins minted

662,228,000 coins minted

939,932,000 coins minted

1,346,624,000 coins minted

ONE WAY **Use place value to compare. Start at the left. Compare the digits in each place-value position until the digits are different.**

Step 1	Step 2
Compare the hundred millions. 707,332,000 ↓ same 774,824,000	Compare the ten millions. 707,332,000 ↓ $7 > 0$ 774,824,000

So, 774,824,000 $>$ 707,332,000, and 707,332,000 $<$ 774,824,000. There were more Delaware quarters minted than Pennsylvania quarters.

ANOTHER WAY **Use a number line to compare.**

Compare 99,638 and 100,204.

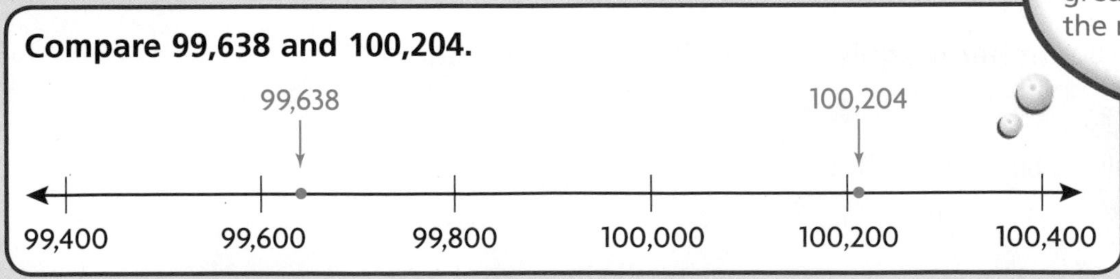

So, 99,638 $<$ 100,204.

Math Idea
On a number line, the greater number is to the right.

NS 1.0 Students compute with very large and very small numbers, positive integers, decimals, and fractions and understand the relationship between decimals, fractions, and percents. They understand the relative magnitudes of numbers. *also* **NS 1.1, MR 2.3, MR 2.4, MR 3.0, MR 3.2**

Order Whole Numbers

The Maryland quarter was released in 2000, and the New York quarter was released in 2001. Order from least to greatest the numbers of Connecticut, Maryland, and New York quarters minted.

1,234,732,000

1,275,040,000

1,346,624,000

ONE WAY Use place value.

Step 1

Compare the billions.

1,234,732,000
1,275,040,000
1,346,624,000 same

Step 2

Compare the hundred millions.

1,234,732,000
1,275,040,000 $2 < 3$
1,346,624,000 ← greatest

Step 3

Compare the other two numbers at ten millions.

1,234,732,000 ← least
1,275,040,000 $3 < 7$
1,346,624,000

So, the states listed in order of quarters minted from least to greatest are Maryland, New York, and Connecticut.

ANOTHER WAY Use a number line.

A Order from least to greatest.

1,002; 1,091; 997

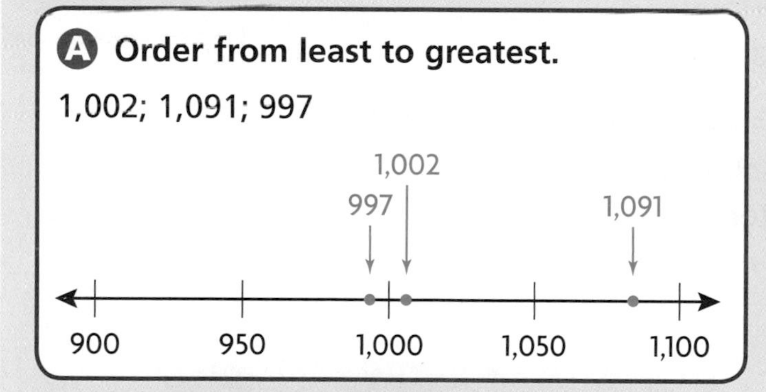

So, $997 < 1,002 < 1,091$.

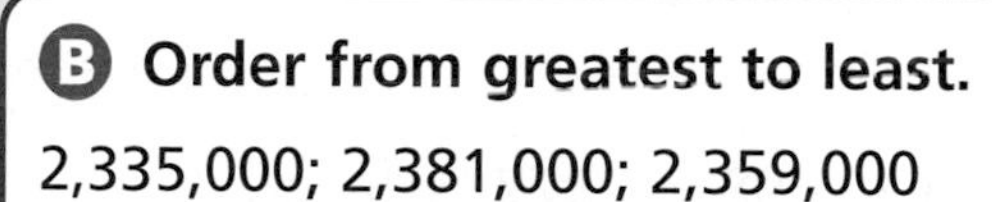

B Order from greatest to least.

2,335,000; 2,381,000; 2,359,000

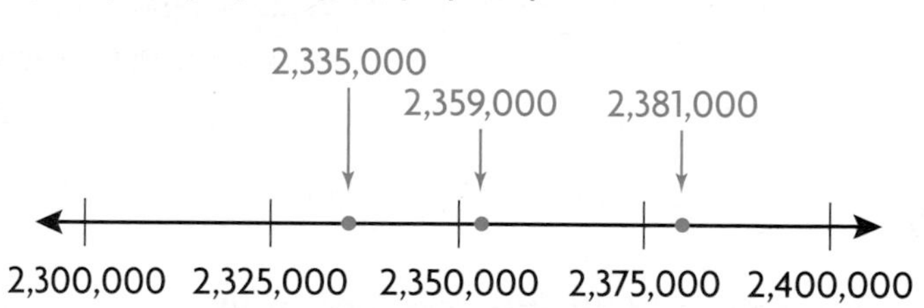

So, $2,381,000 > 2,359,000 > 2,335,000$.

Guided Practice

1. Use the place-value chart to compare the two numbers. What is the greatest place-value position where the digits differ?

THOUSANDS			ONES		
Hundreds	Tens	Ones	Hundreds	Tens	Ones
5	4	2,	9	0	0
5	4	4,	7	2	0

Compare. Write <, >, or = for each ●.

2. 32,403 ● 32,304
3. 102,405 ● 102,405
✓4. 2,306,821 ● 2,310,084

Name the greatest place-value position where the digits differ. Name the greater number.

5. 2,318; 2,328
6. 93,462; 98,205
✓7. 664,592,031; 664,598,347

Order from least to greatest.

8. 36,615; 36,015; 35,643
9. 5,421; 50,231; 50,713
10. 707,821; 770,821; 700,821

11. **TALK Math** Do you think it is easier to use place value or a number line to compare and order numbers? **Explain** your choice.

Independent Practice and Problem Solving

Compare. Write <, >, or = for each ●.

12. 8,942 ● 8,492
13. 603,506 ● 603,506
14. 7,304,552 ● 7,430,255
15. 1,908,102 ● 1,890,976
16. 530,240 ● 540,230
17. 10,670,210 ● 10,670,201

Order from least to greatest.

18. 503,203; 530,230; 305,320
19. 561,682,500; 561,862,500; 561,628,600
20. 1,092,303; 1,173,303; 1,292,210
21. 97,395; 98,593; 97,359

Order from greatest to least.

22. 85,694; 82,933; 85,600
23. 21,390,208; 21,309,280; 21,309,820
24. 5,505,055; 5,402,987; 5,577,001
25. 696,031; 966,301; 696,103

Algebra Find the missing digit to make each statement true.

26. $35{,}938 < 35{,}9\blacksquare0 < 35{,}941$
27. $134{,}862 > 134{,}8\blacksquare0 > 134{,}857$

USE DATA For 28–29, use the table.

28. In comparing the numbers of coins minted, what is the greatest place value where the digits differ?

29. **WRITE Math** **Explain** how to order the numbers of coins minted from least to greatest.

Turban Head Ten-Dollar Coins

Year	Number of Coins Minted
1795	5,583
1796	4,416
1797	3,615

CD ROM Technology
Use Harcourt Mega Math, Fraction Action, *Number Line Mine*, Level B.

 Extra Practice on page 30, Set B

Achieving the Standards

30. How many books were read in all? (Grade 4 SDAP 1.3)

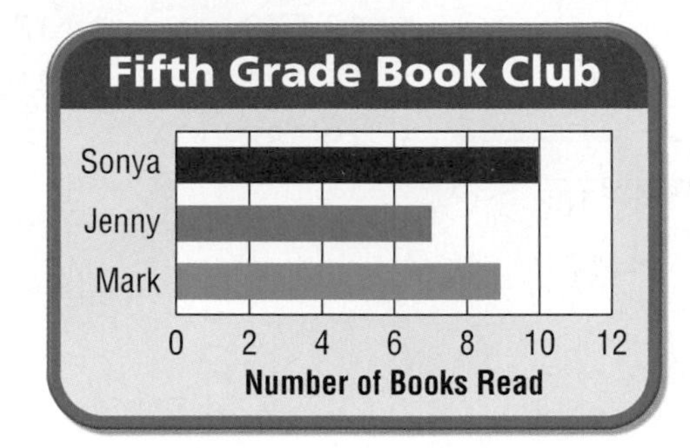

31. What is the value of the underlined digit in 15,149? (NS 1.0, p. 4)

32. What number makes the statement true?
$2{,}000{,}000 = 20 \times$ ■ (NS 1.1, p. 4)

33. **Test Prep** What is the missing digit in the statement below?

46,726 < 46,7 ■ 0 < 46,741

A 0 **B** 1 **C** 2 **D** 3

34. **Test Prep** Which list shows the numbers in order from greatest to least?

A 8,107,450; 8,071,504; 8,059,631

B 8,059,631; 8,071,504; 8,107,450

C 8,071,504; 8,059,631; 8,107,450

D 8,107,450; 8,059,631; 8,071,504

Problem Solving and Reasoning

VISUAL THINKING You can use a number line to find the distance between two points.

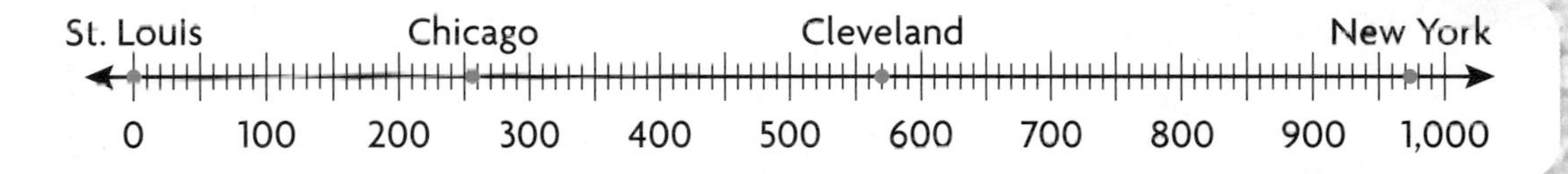

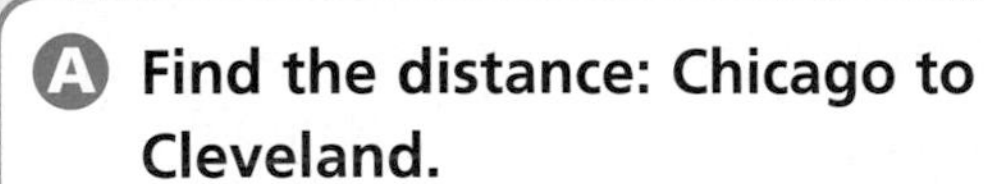

A **Find the distance: Chicago to Cleveland.**

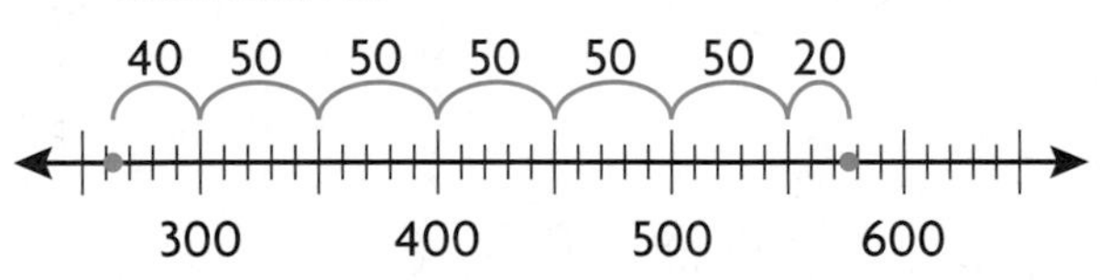

So, the distance is 310 miles.

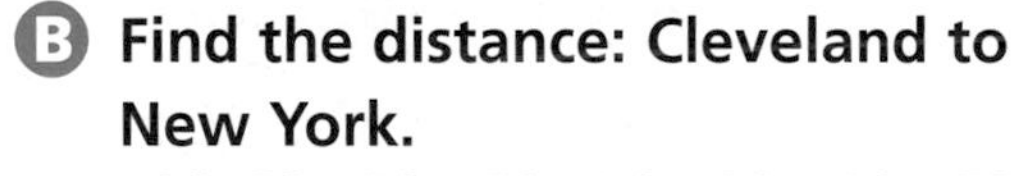

B **Find the distance: Cleveland to New York.**

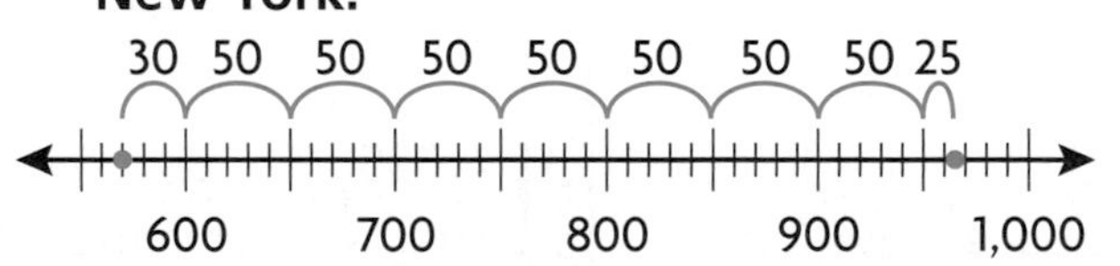

So, the distance is 405 miles.

Find the distance between each pair of points.

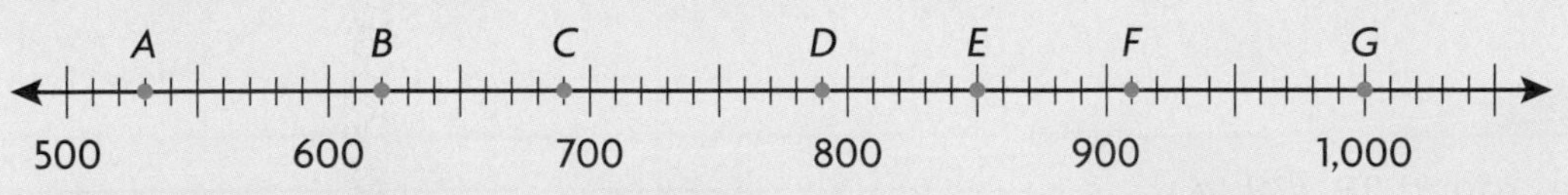

1. *A* and *B*; *A* and *C*

2. *D* and *E*; *C* and *D*

3. *D* and *G*; *C* and *E*

4. *A* and *D*; *C* and *F*

5. **Explain** how you can use the number line to compare the distance between points *B* and *C* and points *B* and *D*.

LESSON 3

Round Whole Numbers

OBJECTIVE: Round whole numbers to a given place value.

Quick Review

Tell whether the number is closer to 10,000 or 20,000.

1. 13,579
2. 18,208
3. 15,781
4. 11,627
5. 19,488

Learn

PROBLEM A newspaper reported that 53,855 people attended a baseball game at Yankee Stadium. During the game, a TV sportscaster rounded that number to 50,000. Is the sportscaster's estimate reasonable? Why?

Rounding a number means replacing it with an approximate number. A rounded number is often easier to compute.

ONE WAY **Use a number line.**

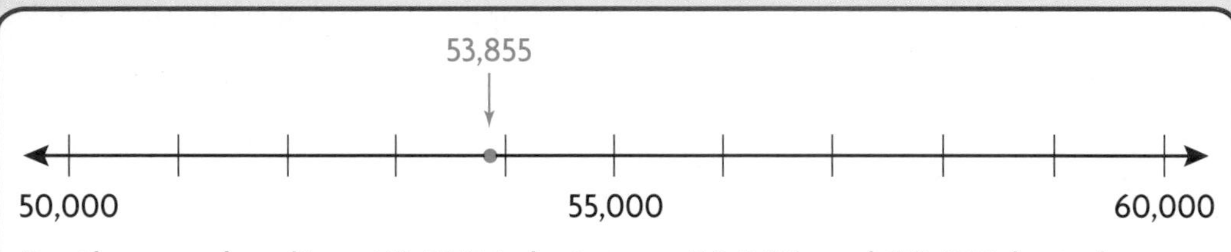

On the number line, 53,855 is between 50,000 and 60,000 but closer to 50,000.

So, the sportscaster's estimate was reasonable.

ANOTHER WAY **Use place value.**

Round 4,835,971 to the place of the underlined digit.

A Million

4,835,971 (4 underlined)
↓
5,000,000

$8 > 5$ Round up.

4,835,971 rounded to the nearest million is 5,000,000.

B Hundred thousand

4,835,971 (8 underlined)
↓
4,800,000

$3 < 5$ Round down.

4,835,971 rounded to the nearest hundred thousand is 4,800,000.

C Ten thousand

4,835,971 (3 underlined)
↓
4,840,000

$5 = 5$ Round up.

4,835,971 rounded to the nearest ten thousand is 4,840,000.

Remember

When rounding, look at the digit to the right of the place to which you are rounding.

- If that digit is 5 or greater, round up.
- If that digit is less than 5, round down.
- Change each digit after the place being rounded to 0.

Guided Practice

1. Use the number line to round 38,778 to the nearest thousand.

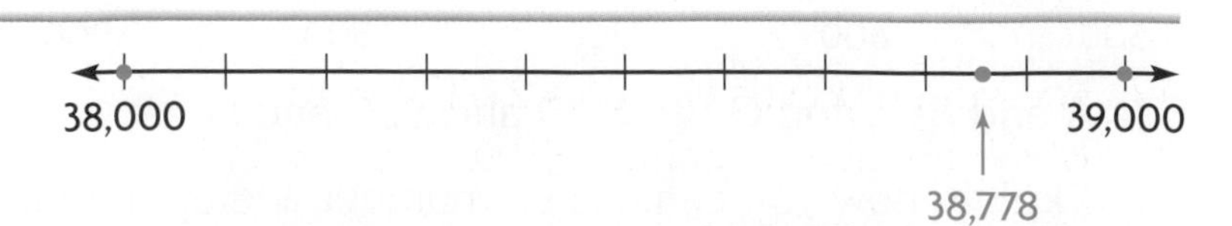

NS 1.1 Estimate, round, and manipulate very large (e.g., millions) and very small (e.g., thousandths) numbers. *also* MR 1.0, MR 2.3, MR 2.4, MR 3.2

Round each number to the place of the underlined digit.

2. $6\underline{7},348$
3. $141,\underline{7}42$
4. $\underline{8},304,952$
5. $1\underline{2},694,022$
6. $\underline{3}6,402,695$

7. TALK Math **Explain** why rounding 428,024 and 425,510 to the nearest ten thousand results in the same number.

Independent Practice and Problem Solving

Round each number to the place of the underlined digit.

8. $6\underline{7}5,345,803$
9. $\underline{3},981$
10. $26,\underline{9}39,676$
11. $500,35\underline{7},836$
12. $56,\underline{4}69$
13. $\underline{2}4,508,349$
14. $792,\underline{4}06,314$
15. $\underline{2}76,405,651$

Name the place to which each number was rounded.

16. 56,037 to 60,000
17. 919,919 to 900,000
18. 65,308,976 to 65,309,000

Round 4,813,726 to the place named.

19. millions
20. hundred thousands
21. thousands
22. ten thousands

USE DATA For 23–25, use the table.

23. The total attendance of two basketball teams, rounded to the nearest ten thousand, are the same. Name the two teams.

24. **What's the Error?** Travis says that the total attendance at the Syracuse games, rounded to the nearest thousand, is 413,000. Is he correct? If not, what is his error?

25. WRITE Math A rounded number for the distance between two cities is 540 miles. What are the highest and the lowest numbers that round to 540? **Explain.**

2005 NCAA Men's Basketball

School	Total Attendance
Syracuse	413,605
Connecticut	234,109
Illinois	245,807
Michigan State	221,383
Ohio State	233,169

Achieving the Standards

26. A square patio is 8 meters on each side. What is its perimeter? (Grade 4 MG 1.4)

27. Write $<$, $>$, or $=$ to compare 15,109 and 15,190. (NS 1.0, p. 8)

28. The sum of x plus y equals 21. If $x = 13$, which equation can be used to find the value of y? (Grade 4 NS 2.1)

29. **Test Prep** What number rounded to the nearest million is 30,000,000?

A 28,065,402

B 29,405,477

C 29,612,300

D 30,755,141

Extra Practice on page 30, Set C

LESSON 4

Estimate Sums and Differences

OBJECTIVE: Use rounding to estimate sums and differences.

Quick Review

Round each number to the place of the underlined digit.

1. 178,902
2. 34,998
3. 2,503,499
4. 901,694
5. 5,500,000

Vocabulary

estimate   underestimate

overestimate

Learn

PROBLEM California has 58 counties. About how many more people live in Los Angeles County than in Orange County?

You can solve the problem by finding an estimate. An **estimate** is a number close to an exact amount.

California Counties

County	2004 Population
Los Angeles	9,937,739
Orange	2,987,591
San Diego	2,931,591

Example 1 Use rounding.

Step 1

Round the numbers to the nearest million.

$$\begin{array}{rcr} 9{,}937{,}739 & \rightarrow & 10{,}000{,}000 \\ -\,2{,}987{,}591 & \rightarrow & -\,3{,}000{,}000 \\ \hline \end{array}$$

Step 2

Subtract.

$$\begin{array}{r} 10{,}000{,}000 \\ -\,3{,}000{,}000 \\ \hline 7{,}000{,}000 \end{array}$$

So, about 7,000,000 more people live in Los Angeles County.

Example 2 Use an overestimate and an underestimate.

An **overestimate** is greater than the exact answer.
An **underestimate** is less than the exact answer.

A high school football team pays $6,717 for uniforms. It also pays $3,477 for a blocking sled and $5,400 for jackets. About how much does the team spend? Find a range to estimate.

To overestimate, round up.

$$\begin{array}{rcrl} \$6{,}717 & \rightarrow & \$\ 7{,}000 & \text{Round up.} \\ \$3{,}477 & \rightarrow & \$\ 4{,}000 & \\ +\,\$5{,}400 & \rightarrow & +\,\$\ 6{,}000 & \\ \hline & & \$17{,}000 & \end{array}$$

An overestimate is $17,000.

To underestimate, round down.

$$\begin{array}{rcrl} \$6{,}717 & \rightarrow & \$\ 6{,}000 & \text{Round down.} \\ \$3{,}477 & \rightarrow & \$\ 3{,}000 & \\ +\,\$5{,}400 & \rightarrow & +\,\$\ 5{,}000 & \\ \hline & & \$14{,}000 & \end{array}$$

An underestimate is $14,000.

So, a range in which the answer will be is $14,000 to $17,000.

Guided Practice

1. Round to the nearest ten thousand. Then estimate. 143,209 + 789,324

2. Find a range by using an overestimate and an underestimate. 4,529 + 1,523 + 2,773

NS 1.1 Estimate, round, and manipulate very large (e.g., millions) and very small (e.g., thousandths) numbers. *also* **MR 2.3, MR 2.4, MR 3.1, MR 3.2**

Estimate the sum or difference.

✓**3.** 4,829 − 2,325 ✓**4.** 25,902 + 18,188 + 3,502 **5.** 312,300 + 429,301

6. **TALK Math** Look at your overestimate and underestimate in Exercise 2. Which is closer to the exact answer? **Explain** how you know.

Independent Practice and Problem Solving

Estimate the sum or difference.

7. $\begin{array}{r} 249 \\ +387 \\ \hline \end{array}$ **8.** $\begin{array}{r} 24{,}619 \\ +45{,}998 \\ \hline \end{array}$ **9.** $\begin{array}{r} 67{,}209 \\ -28{,}584 \\ \hline \end{array}$ **10.** $\begin{array}{r} \$51{,}922 \\ +\$39{,}104 \\ \hline \end{array}$ **11.** $\begin{array}{r} 560{,}051 \\ +237{,}845 \\ \hline \end{array}$

12. 8,793,972 − 4,239,981 **13.** 6,382,011 + 950,429 **14.** 488,352 − 290,128

15. 66,207 + 24,914 + 6,937 **16.** 569,203,123 − 43,192,291 **17.** 6,204 + 4,589

Find a range to estimate the sum.

18. 254 + 746 + 832 **19.** 3,822 + 7,916 **20.** 3,491,812 + 4,721,874

21. 6,845 + 1,391 **22.** 973 + 235 **23.** 4,357 + 5,891 + 8,622

USE DATA **For 24–25, use the table.**

24. About how many more people went to Angels games than to Giants games?

25. Find a range to estimate the total of all the teams' attendance.

26. **WRITE Math** **What's the Question?** Kenny bought two bicycles for $270 each. The sales tax on each bike was about $15. The answer is about $600.

2005 California Major-League Baseball Home Game Attendance

Team	Total Attendance
Angels	3,404,686
Athletics	2,109,298
Dodgers	3,603,680
Giants	3,140,781

Achieving the Standards

27. Find the value of the expression $(4 \times 3) + 12 - 8$. (Grade 4 O–n AF 1.2)

28. What is the mode for the data set 4, 8, 3, 7, 9, 4, 5? (Grade 4 SDAP 1.2)

29. What is the value of the underlined digit in $\underline{4}52{,}302$? (NS 1.0, p. 4)

30. Round 45,782,106 to the nearest hundred thousand. (NS 1.1, p. 12)

31. **Test Prep** City bus passes were used by 28,769 people in one week. During the next week, 35,204 people used passes. About how many more people used bus passes the second week?

A 6,000 **C** 10,000

B 8,000 **D** 20,000

Extra Practice on page 30, Set D

LESSON

5 Add and Subtract Whole Numbers

OBJECTIVE: Add and subtract whole numbers.

Quick Review

Estimate the sum or difference.

1. $379 + $298
2. 14,668 − 8,015
3. $2,359 − $1,131
4. 74,952 + 3,883
5. 20,141 + 912 + 11,018

Vocabulary

inverse operations

Learn

PROBLEM Michigan's land area is 56,804 square miles. Its water area is 39,912 square miles. Find the total area of Michigan.

Example 1

Add. 56,804 + 39,912

Estimate. 60,000 + 40,000 = 100,000

```
  1 1
 56,804   Start with the ones.
+39,912   Regroup as needed.
 96,716
```

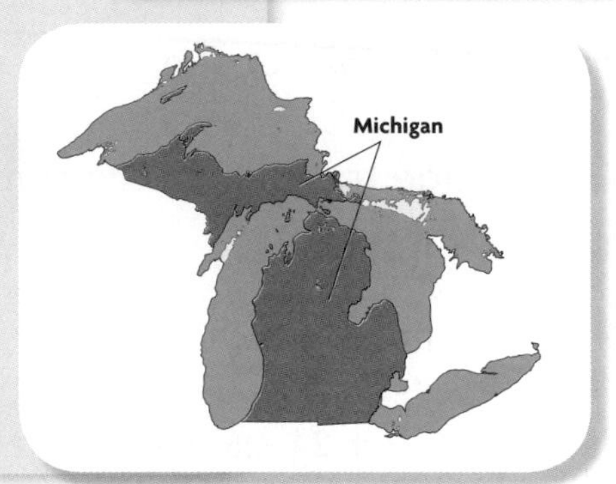

So, the total area of Michigan is 96,716 square miles. This is close to the estimate of 100,000, so it is reasonable.

New York State has an area of 54,556 square miles. Its neighbor, New Jersey, has an area of 8,721 square miles. How much greater is New York's area than New Jersey's?

Example 2

Subtract. 54,556 − 8,721

Estimate. 50,000 − 10,000 = 40,000

```
    13
  4 3̸ 15
  5̸4̸,5̸56   Start with the ones.
−  8,721   Regroup as needed.
  45,835
```

So, New York's area is 45,835 square miles greater than New Jersey's area. Since 45,835 is close to the estimate of 40,000, it is reasonable.

- Explain the regrouping in Example 2.

NS 1.0 Students compute with very large and very small numbers, positive integers, decimals, and fractions, and understand the relationship between decimals, fractions, and percents. They understand the relative magnitudes of numbers. *also* **NS 1.1, MR 2.1, MR 2.3, MR 2.4, MR 3.2**

Add and Subtract Greater Numbers

The area of North America is 8,260,174 square miles. The area of South America is 6,765,422 square miles. How much greater is the area of North America than the area of South America?

Example 3

You can compute the answer by using paper and pencil.

Subtract. 8,260,174 − 6,765,422

Estimate. 8,000,000 − 7,000,000 = 1,000,000

```
  8,260,174   Start with the ones.
− 6,765,422   Regroup as needed.
  1,494,752
```

Inverse operations are operations that undo each other. The inverse relationship allows you to check addition by using subtraction and to check subtraction by using addition.

How can you check your answer for Example 3 above?

Guided Practice

Copy and complete to find the sum or difference.

1. 32,146 + 18,219 = ■0,■65

2. 516,828 − 198,756 = ■1■,0■2

3. 6,941 + 9,387 = 1■,■2■

4. 702,418 − 319,295 = ■■3,12■

Estimate. Then find the sum or difference.

5. 3,794 + 2,073

6. 54,042 + 21,394

7. 409,232 − 403,243

✓8. 3,593,209 − 1,254,155

✓9. 789,039 + 325,155

10. **TALK Math** **Explain** how to find 92,010 − 61,764.

Independent Practice and Problem Solving

Estimate. Then find the sum or difference.

11. $4{,}596 + 9{,}293$

12. $39{,}515 + 69{,}036$

13. $109{,}958 - 102{,}989$

14. $480{,}084 + 515{,}765$

15. $2{,}308{,}027 - 1{,}456{,}328$

16. $8{,}023{,}154 + 731{,}636$

17. $129{,}993 + 74{,}875$

18. $67{,}846 - 38{,}559$

19. $1{,}009{,}875 - 872{,}945$

20. $6{,}693{,}071 + 2{,}381{,}305 + 1{,}043{,}829$

21. $43{,}831 + 8{,}375 + 30{,}294$

22. $4{,}801{,}123 - 1{,}956{,}627$

23. $100{,}230 - 76{,}834$

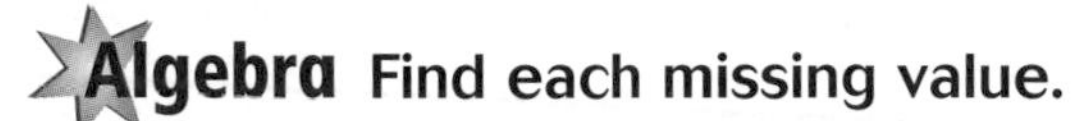

Algebra **Find each missing value.**

24. ■ − 2,346 = 9,638

25. 93,010 − ■ = 61,871

26. ■ + 197,794 = 200,010

27. **Reasoning** How can you use inverse operations to check your answers in Problems 24–26?

USE DATA **For 28–31, use the table.**

Great Lakes Facts

Lake	Water Surface Area (in sq mi)
Superior	31,700
Michigan	22,300
Ontario	7,340
Erie	9,910
Huron	23,000

28. How many more square miles of surface area does Lake Superior have than Lake Erie?

29. What is the total water surface area of the Great Lakes?

30. The maximum depth of Lake Erie is 210 feet. Find the maximum depth of Lake Superior if its maximum depth is 1,122 feet greater than that of Lake Erie.

31. **WRITE Math** **What's the Question?** Tami and Paul compared the water surface areas of two lakes. The answer is 24,360 square miles.

Achieving the Standards

32. Which of the following numbers are prime? (Grade 4 NS 4.2)

2, 6, 14, 19, 27

33. What is 409,537 rounded to the nearest thousand? (NS 1.1, p. 12)

34. **Test Prep** Which is 628,315 greater than 547,906?

A 1,761,221

B 1,716,212

C 1,176,221

D 1,176,211

35. What number makes this sentence true?
(8 − 6) × 4 = 2 × ■ (Grade 4 AF 2.2)

36. **Test Prep** The Summit Theater sold 35,890 tickets. The Capital Theater sold 43,741. How many more tickets did the Capital Theater sell?

A 6,851

B 7,851

C 8,951

D 12,151

Extra Practice on page 31, Set E

WRITE Math WORKSHOP

Write to Explain

Pennsylvania ranks fifth in the United States for producing apples. In 2002, there were nearly 3,000,000 apple trees in 373 orchards in Pennsylvania. How many of those trees were 21 years old or less in 2002? **Explain** how to solve the problem.

There are important things you can do when explaining how to solve a problem. Writing a good explanation means learning how to carefully describe a process.

Pennsylvania's Apple Trees 2002

Age (in yr)	Number of Trees
1–3	394,021
4–6	478,455
7–21	1,322,786
22+	619,177

First I read the problem and saw that I did not have to use the information in the first two sentences.

Then I looked at the table and saw that I needed to add three of the numbers to find the number of trees 21 years old or less in 2002.

I added the numbers of trees in the age groups less than 22 years to find the total that are 21 years old or less:

394,021 + 478,455 + 1,322,786 = 2,195,212.

The answer, 2,195,262, is reasonable because the estimate is about 2,200,000.

Tips

- Include only information needed.
- Write complete sentences, using transition words such as *first* and *then*.
- Break the explanation into steps to make it clear.
- Use math vocabulary to describe how to solve the problem.
- Draw a picture or a diagram if needed.
- Check that the answer is reasonable.

Problem Solving Explain how to solve the problem.

1. The Kane family is traveling on a 1,238-mile trip from New York City to Miami. The first day, the Kanes traveled 405 miles, and the second day 390 miles. How many more miles must the Kane family travel to reach Miami? **Explain** how to solve.
2. Larry scored 62,309 on a computer game. Justin scored 9,548 fewer points than Larry. Kyle's score was 10,283 points higher than Justin's. What was Kyle's score? **Explain** how to solve.

LESSON 6

MENTAL MATH

Addition and Subtraction

OBJECTIVE: Use mental math to add and subtract.

Quick Review

1. 35 + 87
2. 61 − 45
3. 32 + 56 + 21
4. 90 − 46
5. 99 + 37

Vocabulary

Commutative Property of Addition

Associative Property of Addition

compensation

Learn

PROBLEM A skateboard store ran a three-day sale. It sold 14 skateboards on Monday, 31 on Tuesday, and 56 on Wednesday. How many skateboards were sold during the sale?

Some problems can be solved mentally by using properties. The **Commutative Property of Addition** is that if the order of addends changes, the sum stays the same. The **Associative Property of Addition** is that the way addends are grouped does not change the sum.

Example 1 Use the Commutative Property.

14 + 31 + 56 = 14 + 56 + 31	Use the Commutative Property.
= 70 + 31	Use mental math.
= 101	

So, 101 skateboards were sold during the sale.

Example 2 Use the Associative Property.

36 + (104 + 105) = (36 + 104) + 105	Use the Associative Property.
= 140 + 105	Use mental math.
= 245	

Compensation is a mental-math strategy you can use for addition and subtraction.

Example 3 Use compensation to add.

Change one addend to a multiple of 10. Then adjust the other addend by subtracting to keep the balance.

328 + 546 = (328 + 2) + (546 − 2)	Add 2 to 328 to get 330.
= 330 + 544	Then subtract 2 from 546.
= 874	

Example 4 Use compensation to subtract.

Make the second number a multiple of 10. Then adjust the first number by subtracting to keep the balance.

565 − 243 = (565 − 3) − (243 − 3)	Subtract 3 from 243 to get 240.
= 562 − 240	Then subtract 3 from 565.
= 322	

NS 1.0 Students compute with very large and very small numbers, positive integers, decimals, and fractions and understand the relationship between decimals, fractions, and percents. They understand the relative magnitudes of numbers. *also* **MR 2.3, MR 2.4, MR 3.2**

Guided Practice

1. Copy and complete. Name the property.

$19 + 52 + 31 = 19 + 31 + ■$
$= 50 + 52$
$= ■$

2. Copy and complete.

$148 - 125 = (148 - 5) - (125 - ■)$
$= 143 - ■$
$= ■$

3. **TALK Math** **Explain** how you can use compensation to find $128 + 56$.

Independent Practice and Problem Solving

Use the properties and mental math strategies to find the sum or difference.

4. $83 + 37$
5. $42 - 17$
6. $384 - 239$
7. $898 - 617$
8. $(218 + 462) + 112$
9. $328 + 256 + 802$
10. $772 + 848$
11. $469 + 752$
12. $662 - 328$
13. $751 - 737$
14. $137 + 458$
15. $(617 + 927) + 403$
16. $(7 + 19) + 13$
17. $36 + (58 + 44)$
18. $671 - 328$
19. $944 - 726$

USE DATA For 20, 21, and 23, use the table.

Skateboards Bought

Month	Number
April	52
May	18
June	47
July	72

20. Use mental math to find the total number of skateboards bought. Explain your answer.
21. Was the number of skateboards bought in April and May greater than or less than the number of skateboards bought in July? Use mental math to explain.
22. ***FAST FACT*** The first contest in skateboarding history was held in Hermosa Beach, CA, in 1963. How many years before 2009 was the first contest held?
23. **WRITE Math** **Explain** how you can use mental math to find how many more skateboards were bought in July than in May.

Achieving the Standards

24. Write 4,097,310 in word form. (NS 1.0, p. 4)
25. What is the value of $(9 \times 3) + (7 + 3)$? (Grade 4 O— AF 1.2)
26. Which is greater, 4.09 or 4.1? (Grade 4 O— NS 1.2)
27. **Test Prep** Name the property used.
$(64 + 15) + 55 = 64 + (15 + 55)$
   - **A** Associative
   - **B** Commutative
   - **C** Identity
   - **D** Order

Extra Practice on page 31, Set F

ALGEBRA

Addition and Subtraction Expressions

OBJECTIVE: Write and find the value of addition and subtraction expressions.

Quick Review

Use mental math to add or subtract.

1. 23 + 17
2. 40 + 50
3. 46 − 26
4. 110 − 15
5. 532 + 28

Vocabulary

numerical expression
algebraic expression
variable

Learn

PROBLEM The coaster Superman: The Escape has a top speed of 100 miles per hour, and the coaster Goliath has a top speed of 85 miles per hour. Write a numerical expression for the difference of the top speeds of the two coasters. Then find the value of the expression.

A **numerical expression** is a mathematical phrase that uses only numbers and operation symbols. It does not have an equal sign.

Example 1

Step 1 **Write an expression.**

Superman The Escape	−	Goliath
↓		↓
100	−	85

Step 2 **Find the value of the expression.**

100 − 85 → Subtract.
15

100 − 85 is the expression for the difference in the top speeds of the two coasters. The value of the expression is 15. So, the value is the difference in the top speeds of the two coasters.

Expressions can contain one operation or more than one operation.

More Examples **Write a numerical expression. Then find the value.**

A twelve more than 38

38 + 12
38 + 12 Add.
50

B fifty-two less than 400

400 − 52
400 − 52 Subtract.
348

C five less than the sum of 70 and 2

(70 + 2) − 5
(70 + 2) − 5 Add.
72 − 5 Subtract.
67

🔑 **AF 1.2** Use a letter to represent an unknown number; write and evaluate simple algebraic expressions in one variable by substitution. *also* **AF 1.0, MR 2.3, MR 2.4, MR 3.2**

Algebraic Expressions

Some expressions are algebraic expressions. An **algebraic expression** is an expression that includes at least one variable. A **variable** is a letter or symbol that stands for one or more numbers.

READ Math

You might see the expression "some number and 5 more" written in other ways. Here are some examples:

- a number plus 5
- a number increased by 5
- the sum of some number and 5.

All of the expressions above can be shown as the algebraic expression $t + 5$.

Example 2

The fifth grade classes are planning a field trip to the zoo. Five adults are going with each class. Each class travels on its own bus. Write an algebraic expression for the number of people on each bus.

The expression needs to say "number of students in a class and 5 more."

Let s = the number of students in a class.

$s + 5$

number of students → s; 5 adults → 5

So, $s + 5$ is the algebraic expression for the number of people on each bus.

To find the value of an algebraic expression, replace the variable with a given value. Then find the value of the expression.

Example 3 **Find the value of the expression $b - 9$ if $b = 12$ and if $b = 23$.**

$b - 9$	Write the expression.
$12 - 9$	Replace the variable, b, with 12.
3	Find the value.

So, if $b = 12$, the value of $b - 9$ is 3.

$b - 9$	Write the expression.
$23 - 9$	Replace the variable, b, with 23.
14	Find the value.

So, if $b = 23$, the value of $b - 9$ is 14.

Guided Practice

Tell what operation you would use to write each expression. Then write the expression.

1. 4 more than 19
2. 12 less than 33
3. 8 increased by a number

Write a numerical expression. Then find the value. Tell what the value represents.

4. Lee had $12 and received $10 more as a gift.
5. Julie saved $52. Then she spent $8.
6. Shawn collected 32 baseball cards, bought 12 more, and then sold 4.

Define the variable. Then write an algebraic expression.

7. There was a crowd of people in line to see the movie. The doors opened and allowed 75 people in.

8. It is always 10°F cooler at the lake than in our apartment.

9. All Serena's necklaces had 10 silver beads and colorful clay beads.

10. TALK Math **Explain** how to find the value of $n - 26$ if $n = 54$.

Independent Practice and Problem Solving

Write a numerical expression. Then find the value. Tell what the value represents.

11. Julie is walking on level 3 of a treadmill. She increases the level by 2.

12. Marcus had an average of 94. After a test, his average decreased by 5.

13. Sandra bought 15 cards, sent 4 cards, and then bought 7 more.

14. The difference of 23 and 8

15. Seventeen plus 32

16. The sum of 22 and 18 decreased by 9

Define the variable. Then write an algebraic expression.

17. Each student added 3 points to his or her score.

18. During the shoe sale, the price of shoes was reduced by $3.

19. Mr. Forni made 2 extra copies with each order of posters.

20. Some number subtracted from 112

21. Thirty-nine increased by some number

22. Some number plus 23

Find the value for each expression.

23. $15 - n$ if $n = 3$

24. $36 + n$ if $n = 14$

25. $b + 3$ if $b = 12$

26. $a - 6$ if $a = 18$

27. $m + 180$ if $m = 312$

28. $90 - t$ if $t = 38$

USE DATA For 29–31, use the table.

29. Riders on the coaster Tidal Wave, feel a force that is n more than the force riders feel on the coaster X. Write an expression for the force riders feel on Tidal Wave.

30. At 2 g-forces, you feel twice as heavy as when you stand still. If you weigh 94 pounds, how heavy will you feel at 2 g-forces?

31. Riders on the coaster *Rattler* feel a force of 3.5 g-forces, or 3.5 times the force of gravity. How much more force do riders feel on Tidal Wave than on Rattler?

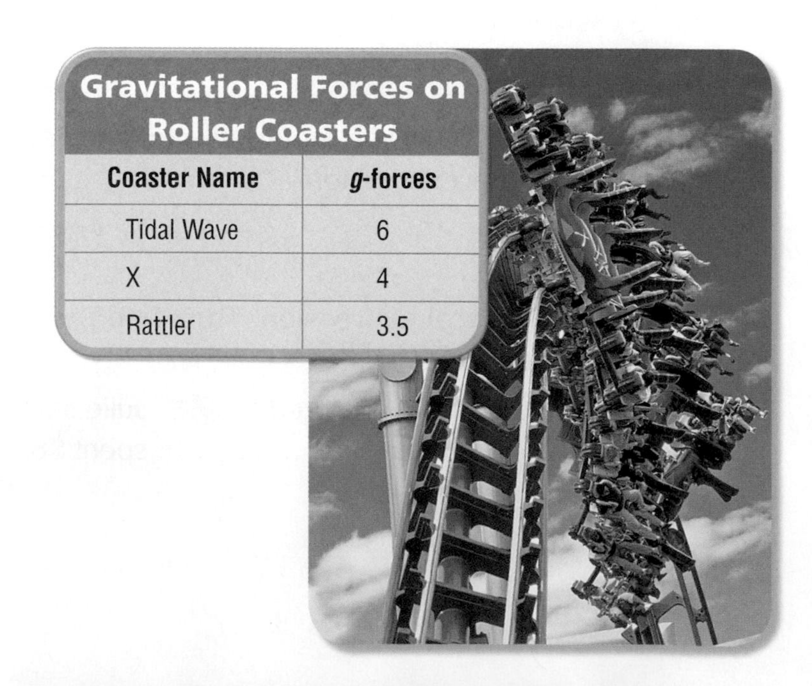

Gravitational Forces on Roller Coasters

Coaster Name	*g*-forces
Tidal Wave	6
X	4
Rattler	3.5

Extra Practice on page 31, Set G

32. **Algebra Reasoning** Write an expression for the pattern. Then use the expression to find the next number in the pattern.

5, 13, 21, 29, ■

33. **WRITE Math** Elena bought a shirt for \$38. She saved *c* dollars by buying it on sale. **Explain** what the expression $38 - c$ represents.

Achieving the Standards

34. A store sold 813 games on Monday, 1,022 games on Tuesday, and 1,270 games on Wednesday. How many games did the store sell in 3 days? (NS 1.0, p. 16)

35. **Test Prep** Tim had 80 CDs. He traded in 20 for 15 new ones. Which expression shows the number of CDs he has now?

A $80 - 20 + 15$
B $80 + 20 - 15$
C $80 - 20$
D $20 - 15$

36. **Test Prep** Which shows a way to write the expression $r + 68$ in words?

A 68 more than a number
B 68 less than a number
C a number less than 68
D a number decreased by 68

37. The coaster Superman The Escape cost about twenty million dollars to build. Write this number in standard form. (NS 1.0, p. 4)

Problem Solving connects to Science

Why do planets follow a roughly circular orbit? It is because of the gravitational attraction between the mass of each planet and the mass of the sun. This force of attraction between planets and the sun keeps planets in their orbits.

Each planet has a different gravitational attraction. The greater the planet's gravitational attraction, the more you would weigh on that planet's surface.

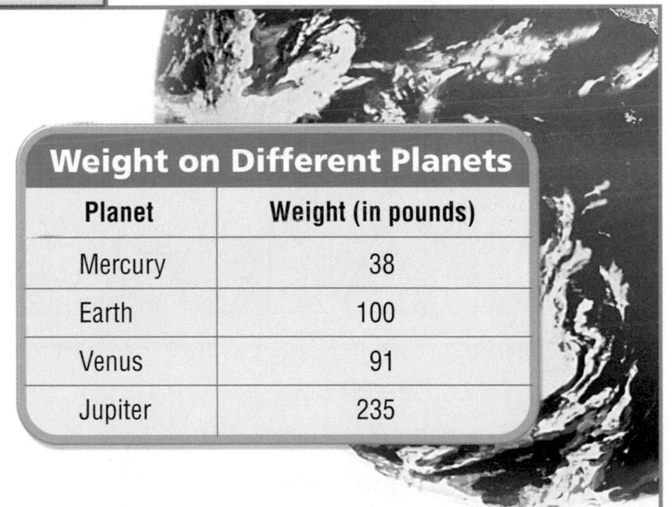

Weight on Different Planets

Planet	Weight (in pounds)
Mercury	38
Earth	100
Venus	91
Jupiter	235

Example **Write a numerical expression and find the value. Then name the planet described.**

If you weigh 100 pounds on Earth, your weight on this planet would be 9 pounds less.

$100 - 9$ ← numerical expression
91 ← value

So, you would weigh 91 pounds on Venus.

1. If you weigh 38 pounds on Mercury, your weight would be 62 pounds greater on this planet.
2. If you weigh 100 pounds on Earth, your weight on this planet would be the same as the sum of 91 and 144.
3. If you weigh 91 pounds on Venus, your weight would decrease by 53 pounds on this planet.

Problem Solving Workshop
Strategy: Find a Pattern

OBJECTIVE: Solve problems by using the strategy *find a pattern*.

Learn the Strategy

Patterns are all around us. There are color patterns, number patterns, and geometric patterns. Finding a pattern can help you see how information in a problem is related. You can use different types of patterns and their rules to solve different types of problems.

A pattern can have numbers.

Mara planted 13 flowers in one row, 11 flowers in the next row, and 9 in the next. If she continues this pattern, how many rows of flowers will Mara plant?

13, 11, 9

13, 11, 9, 7, 5, 3, 1

−2 −2 −2 −2 −2 −2

A rule for the pattern is subtract 2.

A pattern can repeat.

Gordon is painting a border on a wall. This is his work so far.

What shape will Gordon paint next?

What is a pattern?

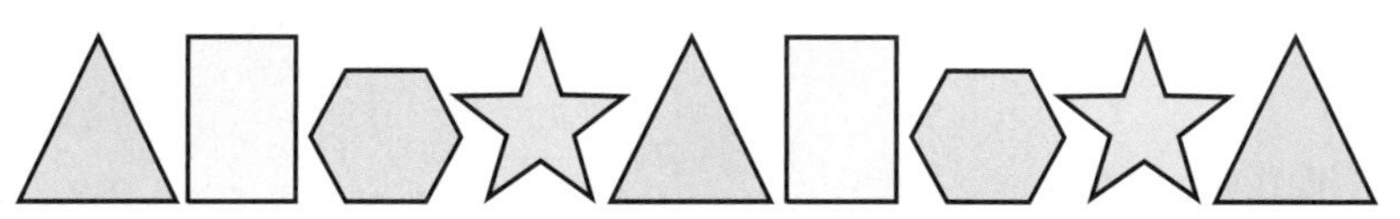

A pattern can grow.

If the pattern continues, how many tiles will be in the sixth tile design?

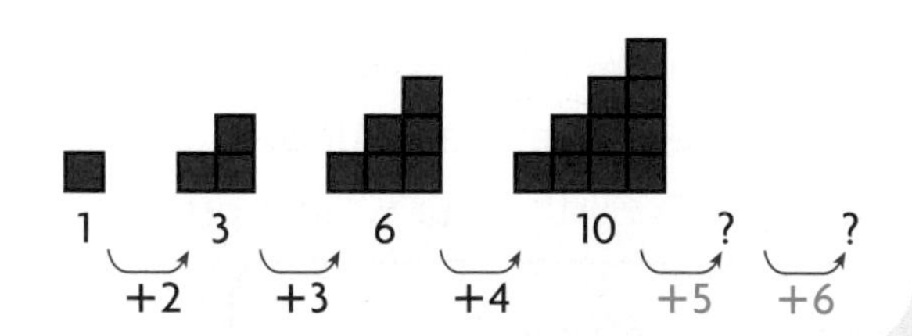

TALK Math

Describe some other patterns that you have seen.

NS 1.0 Students compute with very large and very small numbers, positive integers, decimals, and fractions and understand the relationship between decimals, fractions, and percents. They understand the relative magnitudes of numbers. *also* **MR 1.0, MR 1.1, MR 1.2, MR 2.0, MR 2.3, MR 2.4, MR 3.0, MR 3.1, MR 3.2, MR 3.3**

Use the Strategy

PROBLEM A coast redwood tree can produce 100,000 to 1,000,000 seeds per year. If one coast redwood tree produces 1,000,000 seeds, about how many pounds will the seeds weigh?

Read to Understand

- **What information is given?**
- **Use graphic aids using the information you are given.**

Plan

- **What strategy can you use to solve the problem?**

  You can *find a pattern* to solve the problem.

Solve

- **How can you use the strategy to solve the problem?**

  Think: How do the number of seeds change as the number of pounds increase?

  Look at the numbers in the table. Extend the pattern to 1,000,000 seeds.

Coast Redwood Tree Seeds		
Weight (in pounds)	Approximate Number of Seeds	
1	125,000	**+125,000**
2	250,000	**+125,000**
3	375,000	

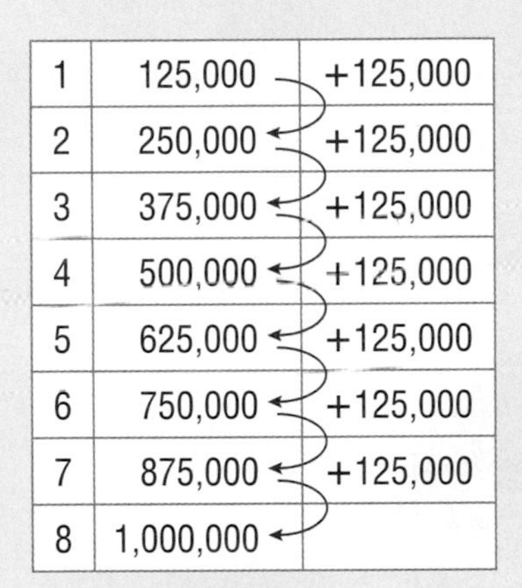

1	125,000	+125,000
2	250,000	+125,000
3	375,000	+125,000
4	500,000	+125,000
5	625,000	+125,000
6	750,000	+125,000
7	875,000	+125,000
8	1,000,000	

So, 1,000,000 seeds will weigh about 8 pounds.

Check

- **How can you check your answer?**
- **How else could you solve the problem?**

Guided Problem Solving

Read to Understand
Plan
Solve
Check

1. Ally saved $75 to make and maintain a garden. After one week of the gardening season, she had $68 left. After 2 weeks, she had $61 left, and after 3 weeks, she had $54. How much will Ally have left after 7 weeks?

   First, look for a pattern and write a rule. 75, 68, 61, 54 — A rule is subtract 7.

   Then, extend the pattern to 7 weeks. 75, 68, 61, 54, ■, ■, ■ — **Think:** 54 − 7 = ■, and so on.

   Finally, find the amount Ally has left.

2. The Garcia family is on a 40-kilometer hiking trip in the Redwood National Forest. By the end of the first day, the Garcias had hiked 8 kilometers. By the end of the second day, they had hiked a total of 16 kilometers, and by the end of the third day, they had hiked 24 kilometers in all. If the pattern continues, how many days will it take the Garcias to finish the hike?

3. **What if** the Garcias had hiked only 4 kilometers by the end of the first day, a total of 8 kilometers by the end of the second day, and a total of 12 kilometers by the end of the third day? How many days would it take them to finish the hike?

Problem Solving Strategy Practice

4. The Redwood Club is making a quilt. So far, the quilt has this design. If the pattern continues, what design will the twelfth row of the quilt have?

USE DATA For 5–6, use the graph.

5. Coast redwood trees can grow more than one foot each year. If the tree shown in the graph continues its growth pattern, how tall will it be in 2010?

6. WRITE Math If the growth pattern continues, when will this tree be more than 100 feet tall? **Explain** how you know.

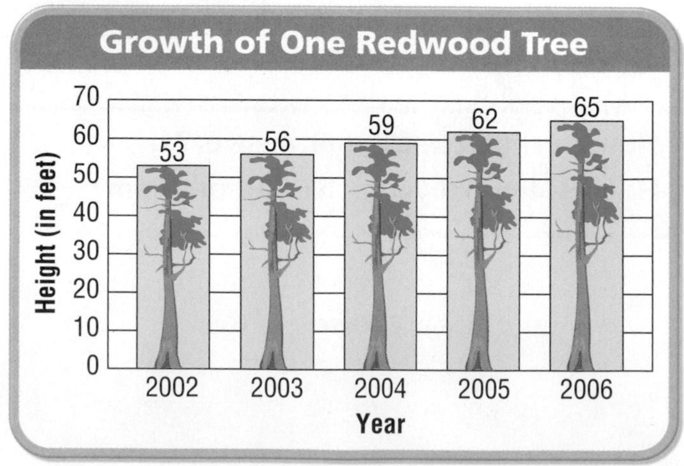

Mixed Strategy Practice

USE SCIENCE DATA For 7–10, use the table.

7. Robin and Terry are using a map to prepare for a hiking trip. They can hike on easy, moderate, or strenuous trails to see each of the trees. How many possible choices do they have if they want to see all the trees?
8. The sixth-largest sequoia in California is Stagg in Alder Creek. Its volume is 9,951 cubic feet less than the largest sequoia. What is the volume of Stagg?
9. **Pose a Problem** Use the information in the table to write a problem. **Explain** how to find the answer to your problem.
10. **Open-Ended** Display one set of the data in the table in a different way. **Explain** your choice of display.
11. Natalie made this pattern of dots.

    Natalie continued her pattern, adding one dot to each of the "legs." How many dots will there be in the seventh figure?

Choose a STRATEGY

- Draw a Diagram or Picture
- Make a Model
- Make an Organized List
- Find a Pattern
- Make a Table or Graph
- Predict and Test
- Work Backward
- Solve a Simpler Problem
- Write an Equation
- Use Logical Reasoning

Giant Sequoia Trees

Tree	Height (to the nearest ft)	Volume (in cubic feet)
General Sherman	275	52,508
Washington	255	47,850
General Grant	268	46,608
The President	241	45,148
Lincoln	256	44,471

CHALLENGE YOURSELF

The Pasadena City Hall, built in 1927, is the tallest building in Pasadena, California, but it is shorter than all the giant sequoias listed in the table.

12. The height of the Pasadena City Hall shares two digits with the height of the third-tallest tree in the table. The General Sherman tree is about 70 feet taller than City Hall. How tall is the Pasadena City Hall? **Explain** how you found your answer.
13. The tallest building in California is located in Los Angeles. Rounded to the nearest hundred feet, its height is 800 feet greater than only one of the trees in the table when their heights also are rounded to the nearest hundred feet. The ones digit in the building's height is 8, and the tens digit is 1. How tall is California's tallest building? **Explain** how you found your answer.

Extra Practice

Set A Write the value of the underlined digit. (pp. 4–7)

1. $2\underline{4},404,485$
2. $14,0\underline{3}0,315$
3. $\underline{1},084,303,220$
4. $9,\underline{2}04,503,661$
5. $14,\underline{3}36,872$
6. $1\underline{6},603,582,495$

Write the number in two other forms. (pp. 4–7)

7. 300,000 + 60,000 + 5,000 + 800 + 70 + 9
8. 50,000,000 + 5,000,000 + 50,000 + 500 + 5
9. six billion, eight million, ninety-seven thousand, three hundred four
10. two billion, thirty-seven million, fourteen thousand, ninety-seven
11. 4,061,002
12. 80,046,300

Set B Compare. Write <, >, or = for each ●. (pp. 10–11)

1. 62,023 ● 63,032
2. 2,401,393 ● 2,104,933
3. 13,114,591 ● 13,114,951
4. 54,304,125 ● 45,304,125
5. 823,158 ● 823,158
6. 693,103,430 ● 693,103,340
7. There were 37,884 people who attended a tennis tournament last year. This year, 36,799 people attended. In which year did fewer people attend the tennis tournament?
8. Jordan scored 4,872 points in a video game. Mike scored 4,921 points. Who scored the greater number of points?

Set C Round each number to the place of the underlined digit. (pp. 12–13)

1. $63,49\underline{4},506$
2. $76\underline{1},584,204$
3. $1\underline{1},586,988$
4. $6,3\underline{9}3,958$
5. $\underline{2}6,591,000$
6. $4,\underline{1}92,295$
7. $899,9\underline{9}2$
8. $\underline{1},999,204$
9. $64,0\underline{2}3,111$

Set D Estimate the sum or difference. (pp. 14–15)

1. $\begin{array}{r} 321 \\ +652 \\ \hline \end{array}$
2. $\begin{array}{r} 19,592 \\ +43,596 \\ \hline \end{array}$
3. $\begin{array}{r} 75,293 \\ -\ 9,501 \\ \hline \end{array}$
4. $\begin{array}{r} 64,381 \\ -12,944 \\ \hline \end{array}$
5. $\begin{array}{r} 314,992 \\ -275,841 \\ \hline \end{array}$
6. $\begin{array}{r} 693,932 \\ +529,000 \\ \hline \end{array}$
7. $\begin{array}{r} 266,749 \\ -135,699 \\ \hline \end{array}$
8. $\begin{array}{r} 699,083 \\ +\ 74,999 \\ \hline \end{array}$

CD ROM **Technology**
Use Harcourt Mega Math, The Number Games, *Tiny's Think Tank*, Levels A, B, C.

Set E Estimate. Then find the sum or difference. (pp. 16–19)

1. $\begin{array}{r} 10{,}135 \\ +\ 12{,}858 \\ \hline \end{array}$

2. $\begin{array}{r} 168{,}930 \\ +\ 929{,}856 \\ \hline \end{array}$

3. $\begin{array}{r} 92{,}000 \\ -\ 63{,}580 \\ \hline \end{array}$

4. $\begin{array}{r} 120{,}049 \\ +\ 81{,}852 \\ \hline \end{array}$

5. $\begin{array}{r} 1{,}090{,}991 \\ -\ 327{,}193 \\ \hline \end{array}$

6. $\begin{array}{r} 61{,}942 \\ +\ 9{,}835 \\ \hline \end{array}$

7. $\begin{array}{r} 84{,}125 \\ -\ 60{,}938 \\ \hline \end{array}$

8. $\begin{array}{r} 206{,}398 \\ -\ 187{,}489 \\ \hline \end{array}$

9. Jerry has put together 3,921 pieces of a puzzle. He has 1,579 pieces left in the box. How many pieces in all are in the puzzle?

10. A male elephant at the zoo weighs 13,894 pounds. A female elephant weighs 12,907 pounds. How much more does the male elephant weigh?

Set F Use mental math strategies to find the sum or difference. (pp. 20–21)

1. $26 + 84$
2. $2{,}321 + 497$
3. $255 - 119$
4. $16 + (29 + 44)$
5. $604 - 337$
6. $(66 + 93) + 37$
7. $1{,}872 - 623$
8. $14 + 23 + 17$
9. $96 - 28$
10. $522 - 188$
11. $186 + (224 + 179)$
12. $779 - 535$

13. A collector card booth at the flea market sold 485 cards on Friday. On Saturday, 721 cards were sold at the booth. How many more cards were sold on Saturday?

14. Shelly planted an herb garden using 24 basil plants, 47 rosemary plants, and 16 dill plants. How many plants did Shelly use in her garden?

Set G Write a numerical expression. Then find the value. Tell what the value represents. (pp. 24–25)

1. Brian caught 4 fish. The next day he caught 5 more.
2. The difference of 37 and 14.
3. Emma borrowed 6 library books. She returned 3 and borrowed 4 more.

Define the variable. Then write an algebraic expression.

4. Marilyn's bracelet has 12 gold beads and some pearls.
5. Some number increased by 58.
6. The temperature in Clay's classroom is 5° less than the temperature outside.

Find the value for each expression.

7. $12 + n$ for $n = 9$
8. $x - 15$ for $x = 34$
9. $h + 152$ for $h = 94$

Chapter 1 Review/Test

Check Vocabulary and Concepts

Choose the best term from the box.

VOCABULARY
overestimate
periods
underestimate
variable

1. A number in the billions has four __?__. (NS 1.1, p. 4)
2. A __?__ is a letter or symbol that stands for one or more numbers. (AF 1.2, p. 22)
3. An estimate that is less than the actual answer is called an __?__. (NS 1.1, p. 14)

Check Skills

Write each number in two other forms. (NS 1.1, pp. 4–7)

4. six million, nine hundred eighteen thousand, seven hundred sixty-two
5. 9,000,000,000 + 70,000,000 + 3,000,000 + 100,000 + 90,000 + 400 + 3
6. 560,034,107

Compare. Write <, >, or = for each ●. (NS 1.0, pp. 8–11)

7. 489,384 ● 894,384
8. 920,090 ● 902,900
9. 76,941,497 ● 76,941,497

Round each number to the place of the underlined digit. (NS 1.1, pp. 12–13)

10. $6\underline{7},339$
11. $6,\underline{8}91,543$
12. $62\underline{3},971,764$
13. $770,6\underline{4}1,785$

Estimate. Then find the sum or difference. (NS 1.1, pp. 14–15)

14. $\begin{array}{r} 89,044 \\ +73,491 \\ \hline \end{array}$
15. $\begin{array}{r} 600,921 \\ -321,650 \\ \hline \end{array}$
16. $\begin{array}{r} 824,377 \\ -799,562 \\ \hline \end{array}$
17. $\begin{array}{r} 4,583,100 \\ +3,902,145 \\ \hline \end{array}$
18. $\begin{array}{r} 3,941,042 \\ -2,953,161 \\ \hline \end{array}$

Find the value for each expression. (🔑 AF 1.2, pp. 22–25)

19. $19 + k$ for $k = 7$
20. $d - 9$ for $d = 44$
21. $76 - a$ for $a = 22$
22. $x - 28$ for $x = 91$

Check Problem Solving

Solve. (NS 1.0, MR 1.1, pp. 26–29)

23. Kip made $15 after one week of mowing lawns. At the end of the second week, Kip had a total of $30. After the third week, Kip had $45. If this pattern continues, how much will Kip have earned after 8 weeks?
24. Rosa is making a beaded bracelet using this pattern unit: 3 red beads, 2 pink beads, and one white bead. If she repeats the pattern 6 times, how many pink beads will she have used?
25. WRITE Math Troy drew a pattern of 4 dots, 8 dots, 12 dots and then 16 dots. He says he should draw 24 dots next. **Explain** Troy's error and tell how many dots he should draw next.

GO ONLINE **Technology** Use *Online Assessment.*

Enrich • Other Ways to Add and Subtract

Fitness Fun!

Field Day at Stewart Elementary includes Grades 3, 4, and 5. There were 237 Grade 3 students, 369 Grade 4 students, and 409 Grade 5 students.

Kickoff

A Partial-Sums Method for Addition

How many students at Stewart Elementary participated in Field Day?

$$237 + 369 + 409 = ?$$

Add hundreds.	$200 + 300 + 400 =$	900
Add tens.	$30 + 60 + 0 =$	90
Add ones.	$7 + 9 + 9 =$	+ 25
Add partial sums.		1,015

So, 1,015 students participated in Field Day at Stewart Elementary.

B Counting-Up Method for Subtraction

How many more Grade 5 students than Grade 3 students participated in Field Day?

$$409 - 237 = ?$$

Start with the smaller number.	237	
Count up to the next ten.	+ 3 →	3
	240	
Count up to the next hundred.	+ 60 →	60
	300	
Count up to match hundreds.	+ 100 →	100
	400	
Count up to the larger number.	+ 9 →	+ 9
	409	172
Find the sum of the numbers you added.		↑

So, 172 more Grade 5 students than Grade 3 students participated in Field Day.

Game

Use the partial-sums or counting-up method to find the sum or difference.

1. $185 + 427$
2. $376 + 152 + 827$
3. $386 - 228$
4. $802 - 655$
5. $29 + 305 + 912$
6. The cafeteria served 567 lunches on Wednesday and 492 lunches on Thursday. How many lunches were served on both days?

Recap

WRITE Math Use the method from page 16 and the partial-sums method to find 325 + 107 + 416. Which method do you prefer? **Explain.**

Achieving the Standards
Chapter 1

Number Sense

1. Which of these is the number 4,003,012? (Grade 4 NS 1.1)

   A four thousand, three hundred, twelve

   B four million, three hundred, twelve

   C four million, three thousand, twelve

   D four billion, three million, twelve

2. The largest national park is in Alaska and is 8,323,148 acres. What is this value rounded to the nearest thousand acres? (Grade 4 NS 1.3)

   A 8,300,000 C 8,324,000

   B 8,323,000 D 8,330,000

Test Tip **Decide on a plan.**

See item 3. Writing the number in expanded form first may help you write the number in standard form.

3. The new sports complex cost three million, five hundred dollars to build. What is this number in standard form? (Grade 4 NS 1.1)

   A $300,500,000

   B $3,500,000

   C $3,000,500

   D $300,500

4. WRITE Math In the United States, the total land area is 3,537,437 square miles and the total water area is 181,272 square miles. **Explain** how to estimate the total land and water area for the United States to the nearest hundred thousand square miles. (Grade 4 NS 2.1)

Algebra and Functions

5. What is the value of the expression below? (Grade 4 AF 1.2)

$$7 \times (6 - 2)$$

   A 28

   B 45

   C 63

   D 126

6. What is the value of y if $x = 12$? (Grade 4 AF 1.5)

$$x = y + 8$$

   A 1 C 4

   B 3 D 9

7. The table below shows how many pounds are in each bag of dog food.

Dog Food			
Number of Bags	2	4	6
Number of Pounds	20	40	60

   If Greg buys n bags of dog food, which expression represents the number of pounds he buys? (Grade 4 AF 1.1)

   A $n + 3$

   B $n \times 3$

   C $n + 10$

   D $n \times 10$

8. WRITE Math **Explain** how a and b in this number sentence below are related. (Grade 4 AF 2.1)

$$a + 38 = b + 38$$

Measurement and Geometry

9. On line segment AB, point A is at (3,6) and point B is at (3,10).

Which number sentence shows how to find the length of line segment AB? (Grade 4 MG 2.3)

A $3 + 3 = 6$ **C** $10 - 3 = 7$

B $3 + 6 = 9$ **D** $10 - 6 = 4$

10. Max drew the coordinate grid shown below.

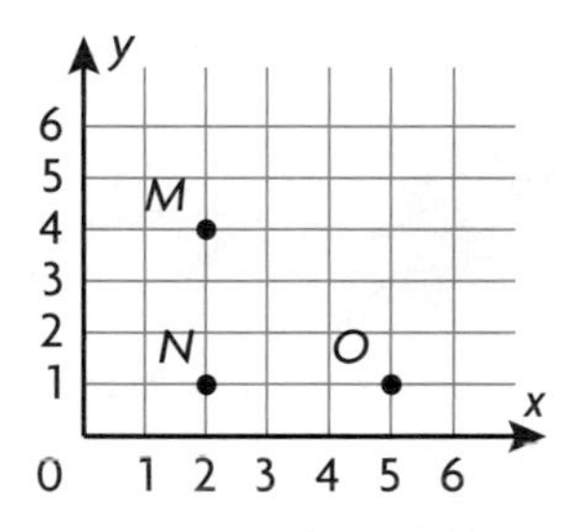

He will plot point P so that $MNOP$ is a square. Where should Max plot point P? (Grade 4 MG 2.0)

A (4,4) **C** (4,5)

B (5,4) **D** (5,2)

11. WRITE Math **Explain** how to classify the triangle as *equilateral*, *isosceles*, or *scalene*. (Grade 4 MG 3.7)

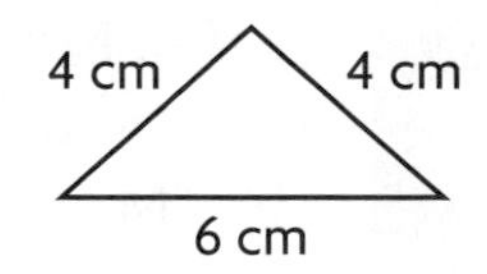

Statistics, Data Analysis, and Probability

12. Which statement is true about the data shown in the graph below? (SDAP 1.0)

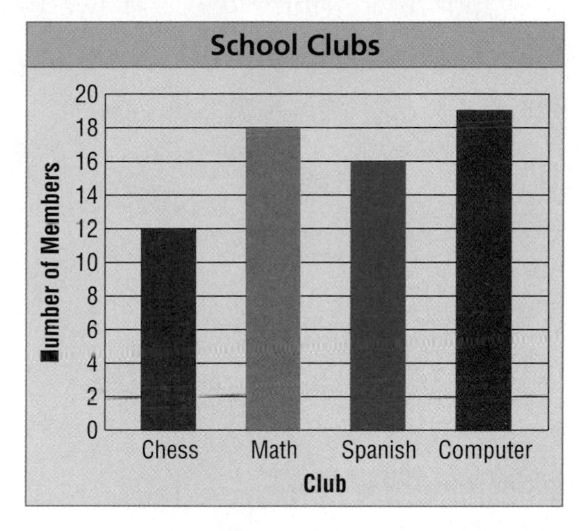

A There are 3 more students in the Computer Club than in the Math Club.

B There are 3 more students in the Computer Club than in the Spanish Club.

C There are 30 students in both the Computer Club and the Chess Club.

D There are 37 students in both the Computer Club and the Spanish Club.

13. Jill recorded her friends' heights in inches. (SDAP 1.1)

66, 64, 64, 67, 63, 60

What is the mode of these numbers?

A 63 **C** 65

B 64 **D** 66

14. WRITE Math **Explain** how to find the median of the following set of numbers. (SDAP 1.1)

3, 8, 5, 9, 7, 4

2 Place Value: Understand Decimals

The Big Idea The place values to the right of the decimal point in the base-ten system name numbers less than one.

Investigate

You want to buy a new computer. The table below shows the speeds of different processors that are available for your purchase. Choose and compare the speed of two different processors. Which processor provides the greater speed?

Computer Processors

Processor	Speed (GHz)
Intel Pentium 4	3.8
Intel Xeon	2.8
Intel Core Duo	1.83
AMD Anthlon 64	2.4
PowerPC G5	1.9

CALIFORNIA FAST FACT

In 1958, Robert Noyce developed the first silicon chip—a miniaturized electrical circuit on a silicon wafer. Noyce would later be nicknamed the "Mayor of Silicon Valley."

GO ONLINE **Technology** Student pages are available in the Student eBook.

Show What You Know

Check your understanding of important skills needed for success in Chapter 2.

▶ Compare and Order Whole Numbers

Compare. Write $<$, $>$, or $=$ for each ●.

1. 572 ● 800 **2.** 635 ● 599 **3.** 706 ● 760 **4.** 3,926 ● 3,906

5. 3,404 ● 3,440 **6.** 52,008 ● 52,100 **7.** 90,523 ● 90,098 **8.** 146,025 ● 146,025

Write the numbers in order from least to greatest.

9. 4,032; 4,203; 3,402; 4,320

10. 25,046; 25,406; 50,256; 45,620

11. 73,801; 38,710; 187,039

12. 182,950; 208,109; 102,985

▶ Decimal Models

Write as a decimal.

13. 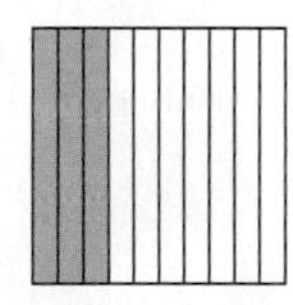

14. 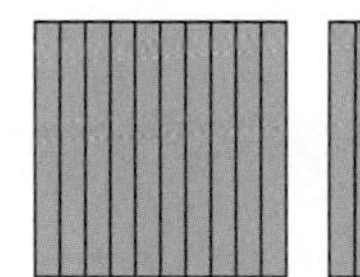

15. 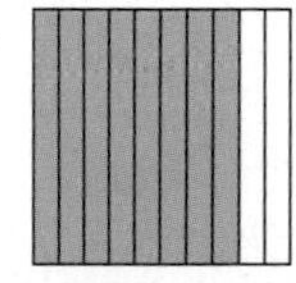

16. 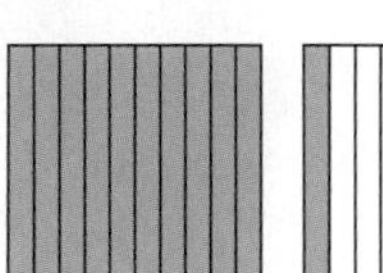  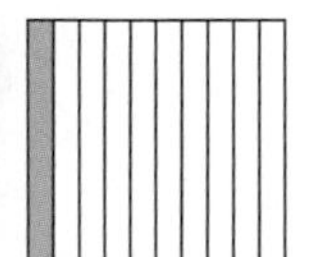

17. 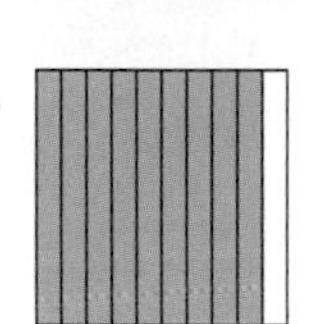

18. 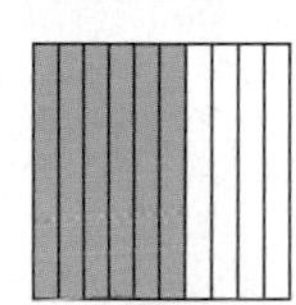

Write the numbers in two other forms.

19. four and seven tenths

20. 10 + 0.3

21. 200 + 5 + 0.9

22. 5.2

VOCABULARY POWER

CHAPTER VOCABULARY

decimal
equivalent decimals
hundredth
tenth
thousandth

WARM-UP WORDS

hundredth one of one hundred equal parts

thousandth one of one thousand equal parts

equivalent decimals decimals that name the same number or amount

1 Decimal Place Value

OBJECTIVE: Read and write decimals through hundredths.

Quick Review

Mr. Hense drove twelve thousand, four hundred eighty miles last year. Write the distance in standard form.

Vocabulary

hundredth

Learn

A decimal names wholes and parts of a whole. A **hundredth** is one of one hundred equal parts. The models below show the decimal 0.52, or 52 hundredths.

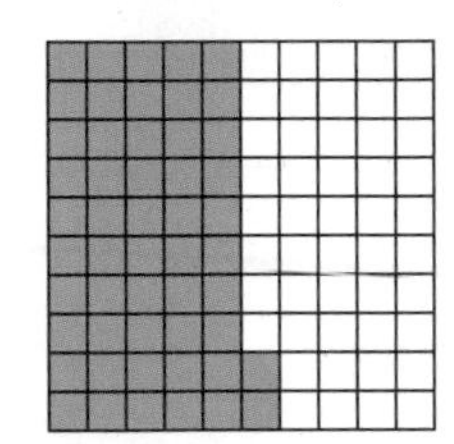

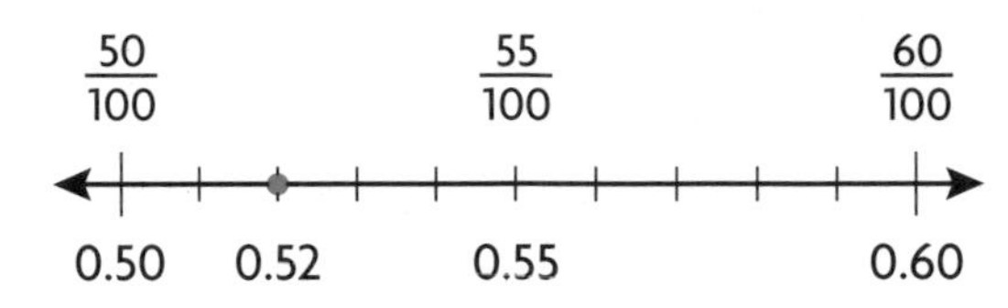

Write: 0.52 or $\frac{52}{100}$ **Read:** fifty-two hundredths

PROBLEM President Lincoln was the tallest President of the United States. He was 1.92 meters tall. What is the value of the digit 2 in 1.92?

Example 1 Use a place-value chart.

Ones	Tenths	Hundredths
1	9	2
1 × 1	9 × 0.1	2 × 0.01
1	0.9	0.02

← The value of each place of a decimal is ten times the value of the place to its right.

So, the value of the digit 2 is 2 hundredths, or 0.02.

You can write a decimal in standard form, in word form, and in expanded form.

Example 2 Write 5.87 in two other forms.

Standard Form: 5.87 **Word Form:** five and eighty-seven hundredths

Expanded Form: 5 + 0.8 + 0.07

ERROR ALERT

Remember to include the word *and* for the decimal point when reading or writing in word form a decimal greater than one.

Guided Practice

1. Copy and complete to find the value of each digit.

Ones	Tenths	Hundredths
2	6	8
2 × 1	■ × ■	■ × ■
2	■	■

NS 1.0 Students compute with very large and very small numbers, positive integers, decimals, and fractions and understand the relationship between decimals, fractions, and percents. They understand the relative magnitudes of numbers. *also* **MR 2.3, MR 2.4, MR 3.2**

Write the value of the underlined digit.

2. 1.9$\underline{3}$ **3.** 0.$\underline{7}$6 **4.** 0.$\underline{3}$9 ✓**5.** 8.6$\underline{1}$ ✓**6.** 7.$\underline{9}$2

7. TALK Math **Explain** how to use a model to show the decimal 0.36.

Independent Practice and Problem Solving

Write the value of the underlined digit.

8. 0.$\underline{6}$2 **9.** 8.0$\underline{3}$ **10.** 1.$\underline{4}$9 **11.** 2$\underline{5}$.94 **12.** 0.4$\underline{5}$

13. 3.2$\underline{7}$ **14.** 0.4$\underline{3}$ **15.** 0.$\underline{8}$1 **16.** 6.5$\underline{4}$ **17.** 16.$\underline{2}$1

Write each number in two other forms.

18. 0.87 **19.** 0.29 **20.** 3.36 **21.** 8.17

22. 1 + 0.06 **23.** 10 + 4 + 0.05 **24.** 5 + 0.4 + 0.03 **25.** 10 + 2 + 0.04

26. fifteen and seventy-three hundredths **27.** one and thirty-seven hundredths

USE DATA For 28–30, use the table.

28. Write the height of President James Madison in word form.

29. **Reasoning** There are 10 decimeters in a meter. Write George Washington's height in decimeters in expanded form.

30. WRITE Math President Zachary Taylor was one and seventy-three hundredths meters tall. Which other U.S. President was the same height as President Taylor? **Explain** how you know.

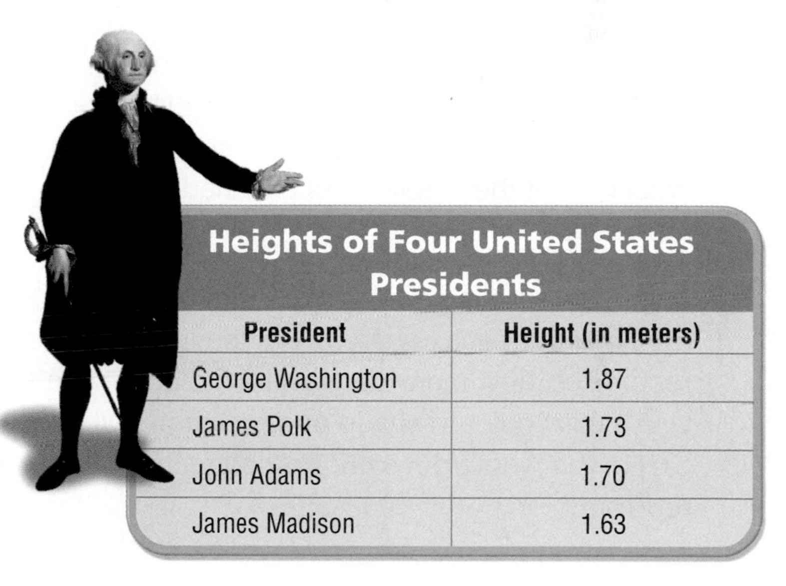

Heights of Four United States Presidents

President	Height (in meters)
George Washington	1.87
James Polk	1.73
John Adams	1.70
James Madison	1.63

Achieving the Standards

31. 4,520,990 − 970,620 (NS 1.1, p. 16)

32. Los Angeles Airport handled 1,913,676 tons of cargo in 2004. What is this value rounded to the nearest thousand tons?
(NS 1.1, p. 12)

33. Write the number 4,009,721 in word form.
(NS 1.0, p. 4)

34. **Test Prep** Which shows the standard form of three and five hundredths?

A 3500 **C** 3.5

B 30.5 **D** 3.05

Extra Practice on page 52, Set A

CD ROM **Technology**
Use Harcourt Mega Math, Fraction Action, *Number Line Mine*, Level M.

LESSON 2 HANDS ON

Model Thousandths

OBJECTIVE: Use models to understand, read, and write decimals to thousandths.

Quick Review

Write each in word form.

1. 0.3
2. 1.9
3. 0.72
4. 2.28
5. 4.06

Vocabulary

thousandths

Investigate

Materials ■ decimal square ■ color pencils ■ straightedge

You can make a model to understand decimals to **thousandths**.

A Start with a decimal square. The decimal square represents one whole.

B Divide the square into 10 equal rectangles. Shade one of the rectangles. What part of the whole does this shaded rectangle represent?

C Divide each rectangle into 10 equal squares. How many parts will the model have? Use a second color to shade one of the squares. What part of the whole does the shaded square represent?

D Divide one of the squares into 10 equal rectangles. If each square is divided into 10 equal rectangles, how many parts will the model have? Use a third color to shade one rectangle. What part of the whole does the shaded rectangle represent?

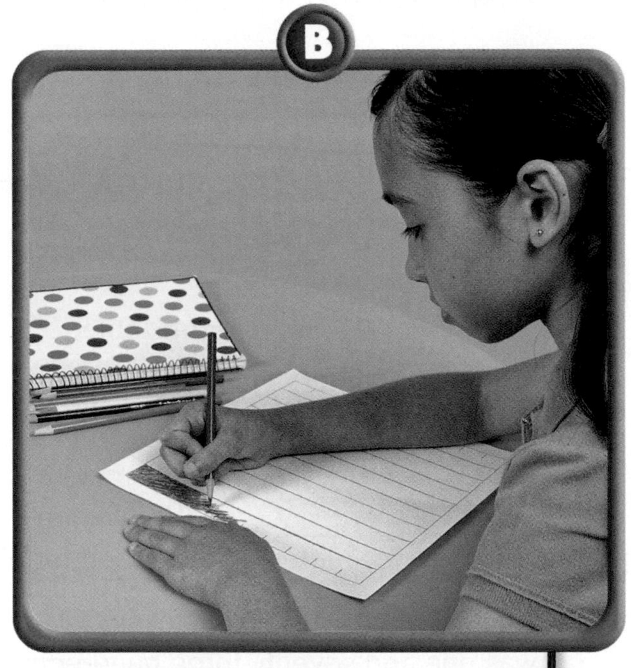

Draw Conclusions

1. Which part of your model shows one tenth, and which shows one hundredth? Explain how they are different.
2. Which part of your model shows one thousandth? Explain how you know.
3. Compare your model with those of other classmates. What can you conclude? Explain.
4. **Analysis** How can you use a decimal square to show 0.251? Explain.

NS 1.0 Students compute with very large and very small numbers, positive integers, decimals, and fractions and understand the relationship between decimals, fractions, and percents. They understand the relative magnitudes of numbers. *also* **MR 2.0, MR 2.3, MR 2.4, MR 3.2**

Connect

You can also use a place-value chart to find the value of each digit in a decimal.

Ones	. Tenths	Hundredths	Thousandths
2	2	2	2
2×1	2×0.1	2×0.01	2×0.001
2	0.2	0.02	0.002

← value

Math Idea
The value of each place of a decimal is ten times the value of the place to its right.

The number shown in the place-value chart is 2.222.

You can write a decimal in standard form, in expanded form, and in word form.

Standard Form: 3.756

Expanded Form: $3 + 0.7 + 0.05 + 0.006$

Word Form: three and seven hundred fifty-six thousandths

TALK Math
Explain how you can use patterns in place value to understand decimals.

Practice

Write the decimal shown by the shaded part.

1. 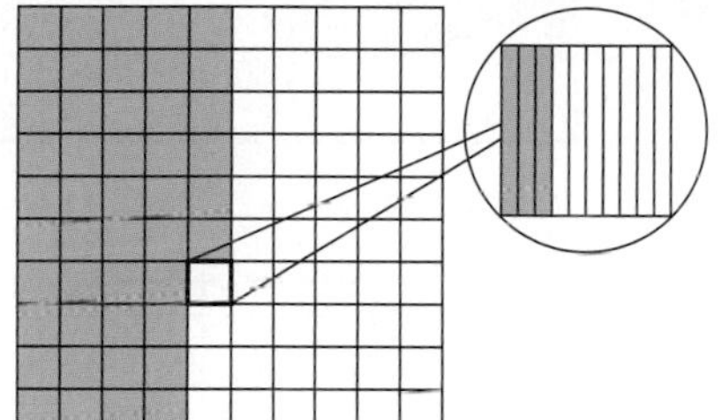

✓2. 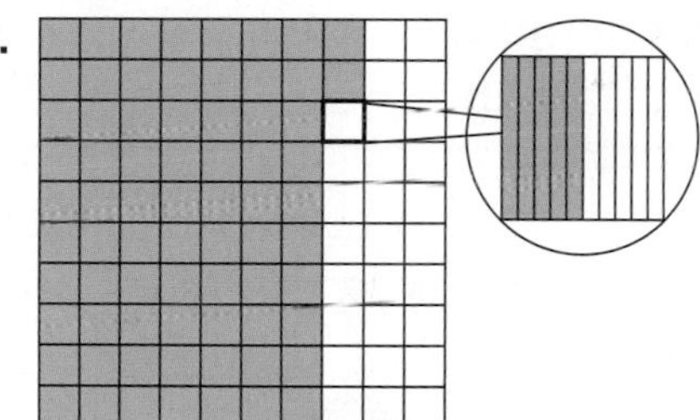

Write the value of the underlined digit.

3. $0.5\underline{3}7$
4. $0.05\underline{9}$
5. $1.\underline{4}07$
6. $2.00\underline{6}$
✓7. $1.01\underline{4}$
8. $1.72\underline{5}$
9. $0.0\underline{8}9$
10. $3.\underline{5}06$
11. $0.\underline{2}46$
12. $2.15\underline{9}$

Write each number in two other forms.

13. two and three thousandths
14. 0.093
15. $3 + 0.4 + 0.07 + 0.001$
16. 6.553
17. $5 + 0.08 + 0.009$
18. eighty-six thousandths
19. **WRITE Math** **Explain** how to use a place-value chart to show the value of each digit in a decimal to thousandths.

LESSON 3

Equivalent Decimals

OBJECTIVE: Identify and write equivalent decimals.

Learn

PROBLEM The whooping crane is the tallest bird in North America. An adult whooping crane can reach a height of 1.5 meters. Write an equivalent decimal for 1.5.

Quick Review

1. 3.■ = $3\frac{4}{10}$
2. 1.9 = $1\frac{■}{10}$
3. 7.■ = $7\frac{52}{100}$
4. 9.84 = $9\frac{■}{100}$
5. 12.■ = $12\frac{3}{10}$

Vocabulary

equivalent decimals

Equivalent decimals are different names for the same number or amount. In the place-value chart below, zeros have been placed to the right of the digit 5 to make equivalent decimals.

Ones	.	Tenths	Hundredths	Thousandths
1	.	5		
1	.	5	0	
1	.	5	0	0

So, the decimals 1.50 and 1.500 are equivalent to 1.5.

Math Idea
You can add zeros to the right of the last digit in a decimal without changing the value of the decimal.

You can use models to determine if two decimals are equivalent.

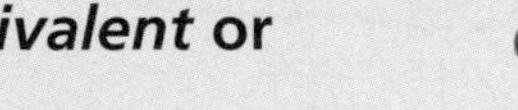

Examples Draw a model for each decimal. Write *equivalent* or *not equivalent* to describe each pair of decimals.

A 0.3 and 0.30

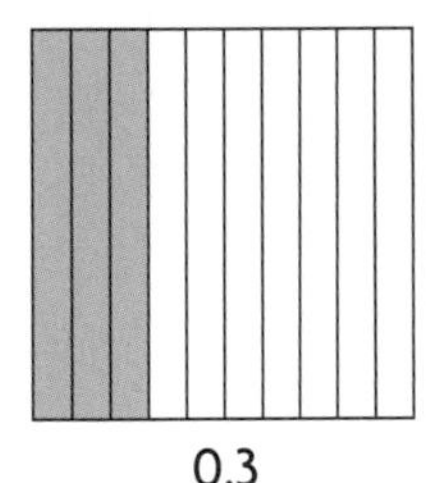

0.3

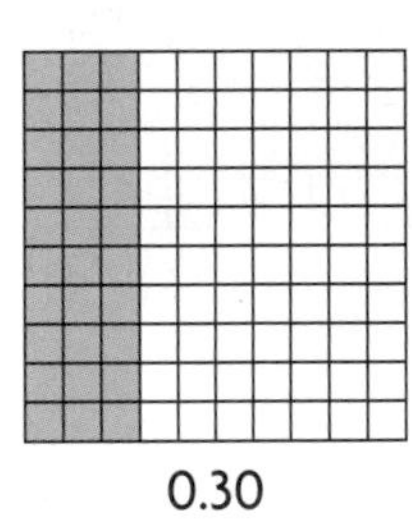

0.30

The shaded area for both models is the same size. So, 0.3 is equivalent to 0.30.

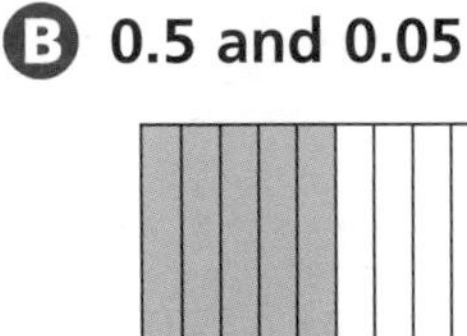

B 0.5 and 0.05

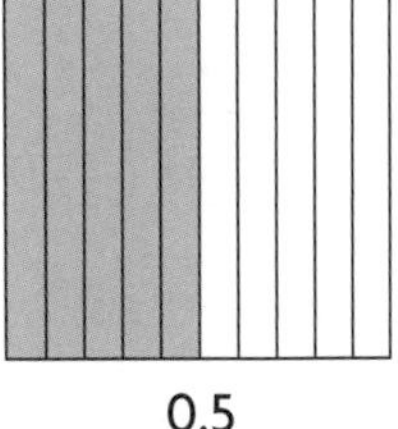

0.5

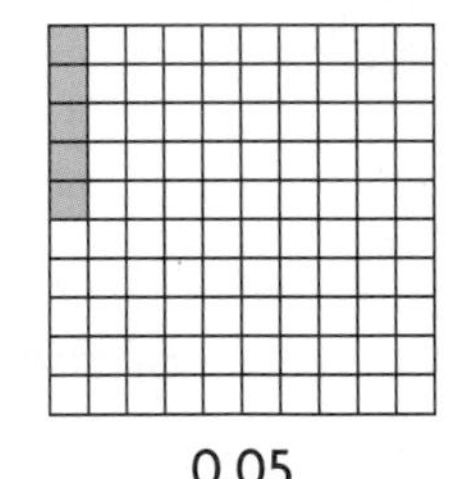

0.05

The shaded area for both models is **not** the same size. So, 0.5 is **not** equivalent to 0.05.

- Ten hundredths are equivalent to one tenth. How many tenths are equivalent to 1? Use a model to explain your answer.

Guided Practice

1. Make a model for 0.4 and 0.40. Then explain how the models help you decide if the decimals are equivalent. Are the decimals equivalent?

NS 1.0 Students compute with very large and very small numbers, positive integers, decimals, and fractions and understand the relationship between decimals, fractions, and percents. They understand the relative magnitudes of numbers. *also* **MR 2.3, MR 2.4, MR 3.2**

Write *equivalent* or *not equivalent* to describe each pair of decimals.

2. 3.7 and 3.70
3. 0.06 and 0.006
4. 8.90 and 8.09
5. 2.5 and 2.5
6. 0.52 and 0.520
7. 7.8 and 7.08
8. 0.9 and 0.09
9. 0.42 and 0.420
10. TALK Math **Explain** how you can determine if 1.206 is equivalent to 1.026.

Independent Practice and Problem Solving

Write *equivalent* or *not equivalent* to describe each pair of decimals.

11. 2.09 and 2.90
12. 5.003 and 5.03
13. 12 and 12.0
14. 9.01 and 9.010
15. 3.26 and 3.260
16. 4.01 and 4.011
17. 6.004 and 6.04
18. 7.08 and 7.80

Write an equivalent decimal for each number.

19. 0.09
20. 1.430
21. 0.6
22. 2.400
23. 5.08
24. 0.700
25. 4.08
26. 8.90

Write the two decimals that are equivalent.

27. 6.03
6.300
6.030
28. 0.041
0.0401
0.0410
29. 1.006
1.600
1.6000
30. 0.5900
0.059
0.59

USE DATA For 31–33, use the table.

31. Write two equivalent decimals for the mass of the demoiselle crane.
32. Which two cranes have an equivalent mass? Are the heights of these two cranes equivalent?
33. WRITE Math **What's the Question?** The blue crane has an average height of 1.23 meters. The answer is sandhill.

Cranes' Average Height and Mass

Kind of Crane	Height (in meters)	Mass (in kilograms)
Sandhill	1.23	4.55
Wattled	1.85	6.36
Demoiselle	0.92	2.50
Sarus	1.85	6.36

Achieving the Standards

34. Which expression has the greater value, $3 + (8 \times 4)$ or $(3 + 8) \times 4$? (Grade 4 AF 1.2)
35. Estimate the sum 638,299 + 196,500. (NS 1.1, p. 14)
36. What is six tenths written as a decimal? (NS 1.0, p. 36)
37. **Test Prep** Jamie hiked 2.75 miles to the waterfall. Which decimal is equivalent to 2.75?
    - A 2.075
    - B 2.705
    - C 2.750
    - D 2.755

Extra Practice on page 52, Set B

LESSON 4

Change to Tenths and Hundredths

OBJECTIVE: Understand and write decimals as fractions and mixed numbers with tenths and hundredths.

Quick Review

Write an equivalent decimal.

1. 0.3
2. 0.45
3. 1.090
4. 3.270
5. 0.800

Learn

PROBLEM The Round Lake Loop Trail in Plumas County, CA, touches nine mountain lakes. This popular trail is 3.75 miles long. What is the trail length written as a mixed number?

ONE WAY **Use a decimal model.**

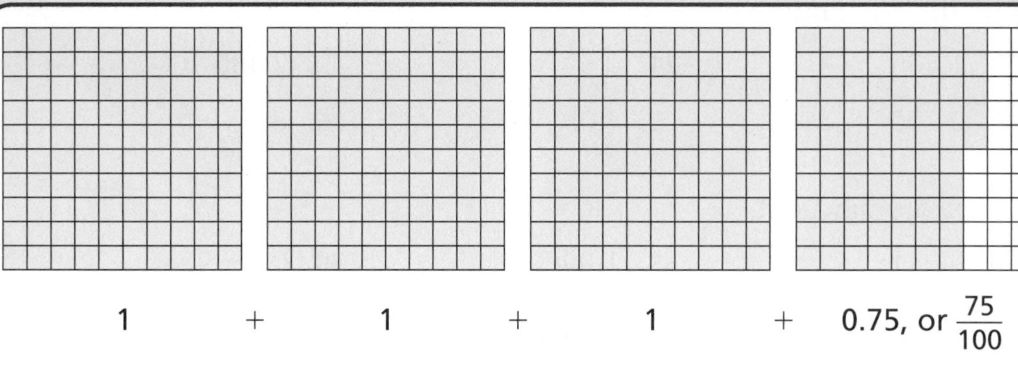

Think: 3.75 is made up of 3 wholes and 0.75 of a whole.

So, written as a mixed number, the trail length is $3\frac{75}{100}$ miles.

Remember
A mixed number is represented by a whole number and a fraction.

ANOTHER WAY **Use place value.**

Write 2.5 as a mixed number with hundredths.

2.5 = 2.50	Write an equivalent decimal showing hundredths.
2.50 = two and fifty hundredths	Write the decimal in word form.
$= 2\frac{50}{100}$	Write the mixed number.

So, written as a mixed number with hundredths, 2.5 is $2\frac{50}{100}$.

More Examples

A **Write 0.80 as a fraction with tenths.**

0.80 = 0.8 equivalent decimals

0.8 = eight tenths

$= \frac{8}{10}$

B **Write 0.62 as a fraction with hundredths.**

0.62 = sixty-two hundredths

$= \frac{62}{100}$

NS 1.2 Interpret percents as part of a hundred; find decimal and percent equivalents for common fractions and explain why they represent the same value; compute a given percent of a whole number. *also* **NS 1.0, MR 2.3, MR 2.4, MR 3.1, MR 3.2**

Guided Practice

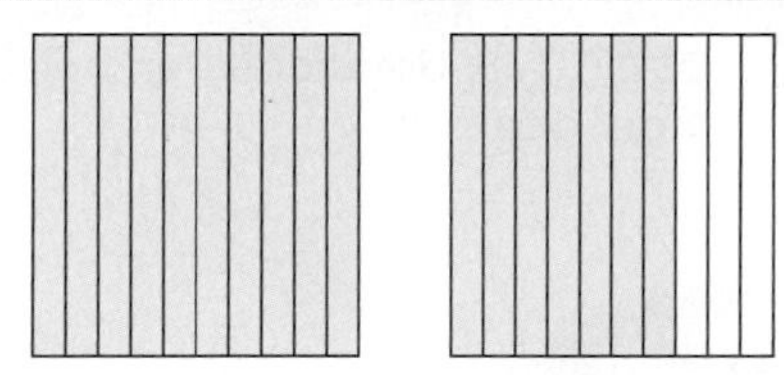

1. Look at the model at the right. Write a decimal and a mixed number for the model.

Write each decimal as a fraction or mixed number with tenths and with hundredths.

2. 0.3
3. 0.80
4. 5.6

5. **TALK Math** **Explain** how writing a decimal in word form helps you write a fraction or a mixed number with tenths or hundredths.

Independent Practice and Problem Solving

Write each decimal as a fraction or mixed number with tenths and with hundredths.

6. 1.4
7. 0.6
8. 3.20
9. 2.6
10. 0.70
11. 0.8
12. 5.2
13. 11.30
14. 4.6
15. 0.90

Algebra Complete.

16. $1.45 = 1\frac{■}{100}$
17. $3.97 = 3\frac{■}{100}$
18. $2.3 = 2\frac{3}{10} = 2\frac{■}{100}$

USE DATA For 19–21, use the sign.

19. The Yellow Creek Trail is $1\frac{50}{100}$ miles long. Which trail is the same length as the Yellow Creek Trail? **Explain** how you know.

20. **Pose a Problem** A lap around a track is $\frac{1}{4}$ mile. Using this fact and the data, write a problem about an equivalent decimal.

21. **WRITE Math** **What's the Error?** Grass Lake Trail has the same length as another trail that is $3\frac{8}{100}$ miles. Describe the error in this statement.

Achieving the Standards

22. What is the mode of this set of numbers?
7, 3, 10, 7, 5, 7, 3 (Grade 4, SDAP 1.2)

23. What decimal does the point on the number line represent? (NS 1.5, p. 38)

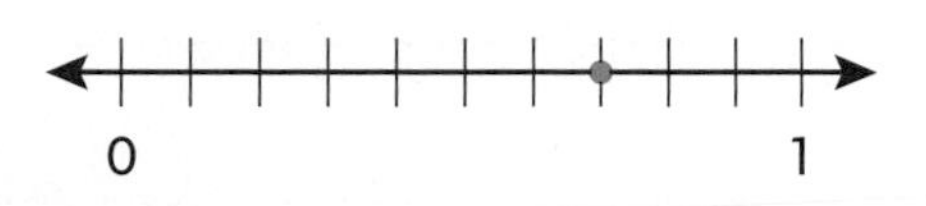

24. If $m = 280$, what is the value of $423 - m$?
(Grade 4, AF 1.1)

25. **Test Prep** Which shows 2.30 as a mixed number?

A $\frac{3}{10}$

B $2\frac{3}{100}$

C $2\frac{30}{10}$

D $2\frac{30}{100}$

Extra Practice on page 52, Set C

Compare and Order Decimals

OBJECTIVE: Use models and place value to compare and order decimals.

Quick Review

Write *equivalent* or *not equivalent* to describe each pair.

1. 0.06 and 0.60
2. 3.5 and 3.50
3. 4.09 and 4.090
4. 5.201 and 5.021
5. 0.78 and 0.780

Learn

PROBLEM An entomologist, a scientist who studies insects, is comparing the lengths of two ladybird beetles, also called ladybugs. The ladybugs are 0.528 and 0.534 centimeter long. Which ladybug has the greater length?

ONE WAY **Use a number line.**

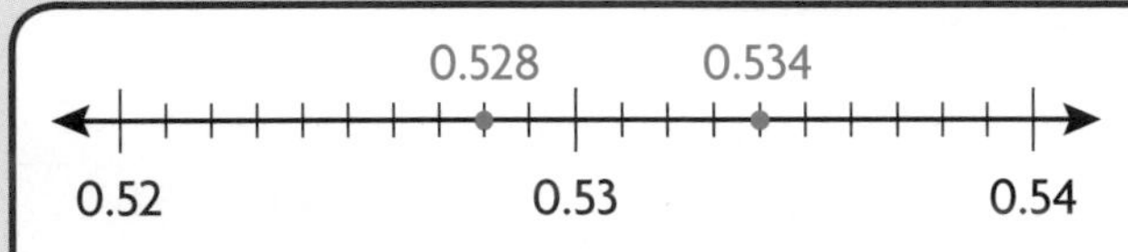

Since 0.534 is to the right of 0.528, 0.534 > 0.528.

Remember
On a number line, the greater number is to the right.

So, the ladybug that is 0.534 centimeter long has the greater length.

ANOTHER WAY **Use place value. Compare 3.25 and 3.254.**

Step 1	Step 2	Step 3	Step 4
Line up the decimal points. Begin at the left. Compare the ones.	Compare the tenths.	Compare the hundredths.	To compare thousandths, write an equivalent decimal for 3.25. Then compare.
3.25 3.254 same	3.25 3.254 same	3.25 3.254 same	3.250 3.254 0 < 4

So, 3.25 < 3.254, or 3.254 > 3.25.

Example **Use place value. Order 4.137, 4, and 4.19 from least to greatest.**

Step 1	Step 2	Step 3
Line up the decimal points. Write equivalent decimals.	Begin at the left. Compare the digits until they are different.	Continue comparing.
4.137 4.000 4.190	4.137 4.000 ← 0 < 1 4.190 4.000 is least.	4.137 3 < 9 4.190 ← 4.190 is greatest.

So, the order is 4, 4.137, 4.19.

NS 1.5 Identify and represent on a number line decimals, fractions, mixed numbers, and positive and negative integers. *also* **NS 1.0, NS 1.1, MR 2.3, MR 2.4, MR 3.2**

Guided Practice

1. Copy the number line. Locate 0.72 and 0.7 on the number line. Then, compare the decimals.

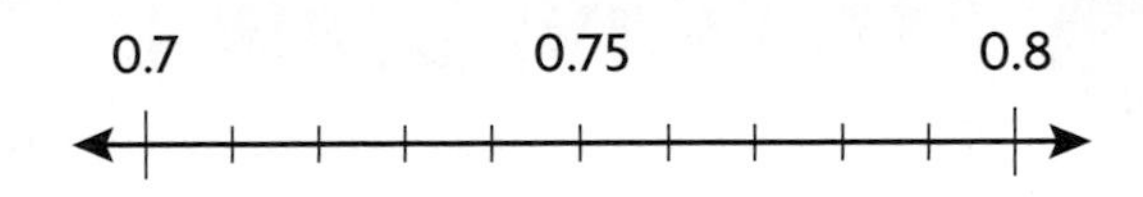

Compare. Write $<$, $>$, or $=$ for each ●.

2. 5.43 ● 5.432
3. 0.28 ● 0.208
4. 9.39 ● 9.9

5. **TALK Math** **Explain** how to use place value to order 1.567, 1.571, and 1.556 from greatest to least.

Independent Practice and Problem Solving

Compare. Write $<$, $>$, or $=$ for each ●.

6. 0.972 ● 0.98
7. 4 ● 0.79
8. 3.602 ● 3.082
9. 10.3 ● 1.898
10. 6.7 ● 6.701
11. 0.749 ● 0.769

Order from least to greatest.

12. 0.123, 0.32, 0.113, 0.2
13. 6.0, 6.498, 6.52, 6.490
14. 5.6, 9, 6.8, 8.005

Algebra **Find all of the digits that can replace each ■.**

15. $9.7■7 < 9.770$
16. $0.28■ > 0.284$
17. $2.356 > 2.■83$

USE DATA **For 18–20, use the table.**

18. Which beetle is the longest? Which beetle is the shortest?
19. **Reasoning** Suppose another beetle was measured with a length of 0.84 centimeter. Between which two beetles' lengths does the length of this beetle fall?
20. **WRITE Math** Order the lengths of the beetles in the table from least to greatest. **Explain** how you ordered the lengths.

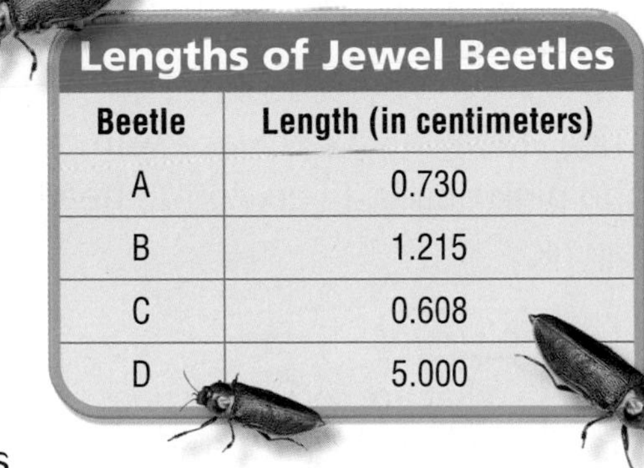

Lengths of Jewel Beetles

Beetle	Length (in centimeters)
A	0.730
B	1.215
C	0.608
D	5.000

Achieving the Standards

21. What kinds of lines form right angles where they intersect? (Grade 4, MG 3.1)
22. Write whether 1.3 and 1.30 are equivalent or *not* equivalent. (NS 1.1, p. 42)
23. $5 \times 1{,}000 = ■$ (Grade 4, NS 1.0)
24. **Test Prep** Taylor received the following scores in a diving competition. The lowest score is to be tossed out. Which score will be tossed out?

A 8.400
B 8.175
C 9.075
D 8.250

Extra Practice on page 52, Set D

Problem Solving Workshop
Strategy: Draw a Diagram

OBJECTIVE: Solve problems by using the strategy *draw a diagram.*

Learn the Strategy

Drawing a picture or a diagram can help you understand a problem and can make the solution visible. You can use different types of diagrams for different types of problems.

A diagram can show order or position.

Harold is 1.63 meters tall, Britney is 1.59 meters tall, and Ryan is 1.71 meters tall.

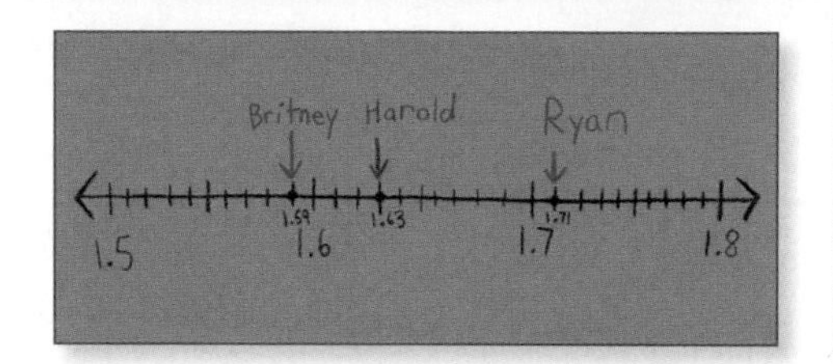

A diagram can show size.

The mass of a bag of apples is about 1.5 kg more than three times the mass of a bag of oranges. The total mass of the bags is 3.5 kg.

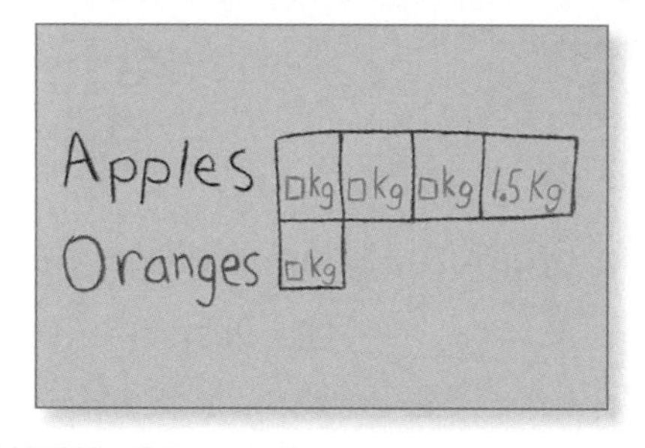

A diagram can show a pattern.

Erica is making a necklace with purple and pink beads. Every fourth bead is pink.

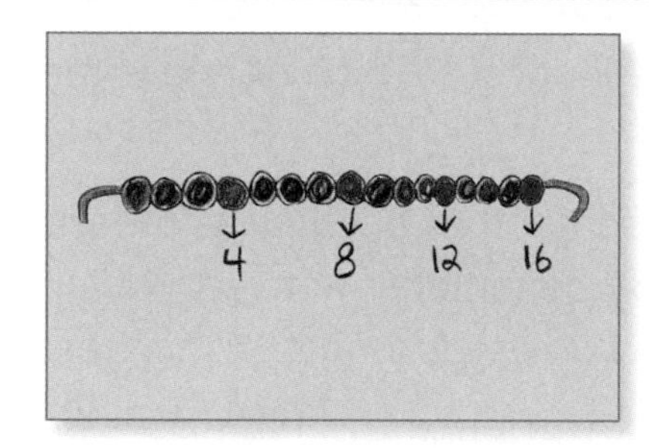

What are some questions that can be answered by using each of the diagrams shown above?

To draw a diagram, carefully follow the information given in the problem. Keep the diagram simple. Label the parts to show what they represent.

NS 1.0 Students compute with very large and very small numbers, positive integers, decimals, and fractions and understand the relationship between decimals, fractions, and percents. They understand the relative magnitudes of numbers *also* **O-π NS 1.5, MR 1.0, MR 2.0, MR 2.3, MR 2.4, MR 3.0, MR 3.2, MR 3.3**

Use the Strategy

PROBLEM Jessica's family members recorded the number of kilometers they traveled each day on their vacation. On Monday the family traveled 87.3 kilometers; on Tuesday, 88.75 kilometers; on Wednesday, 87.6 kilometers; and on Thursday, 88.4 kilometers. On which day did Jessica's family travel the greatest distance?

Read to Understand
Plan
Solve
Check

Read to Understand

- **How can you summarize what you are asked to find?**
- **What information is given?**

Plan

- **What strategy can you use to solve the problem?**
  You can draw a diagram to solve the problem.

Solve

- **How can you use the strategy to solve the problem?**
  Draw a number line to compare the distances.

Draw a number line from 87.0 to 89.0.

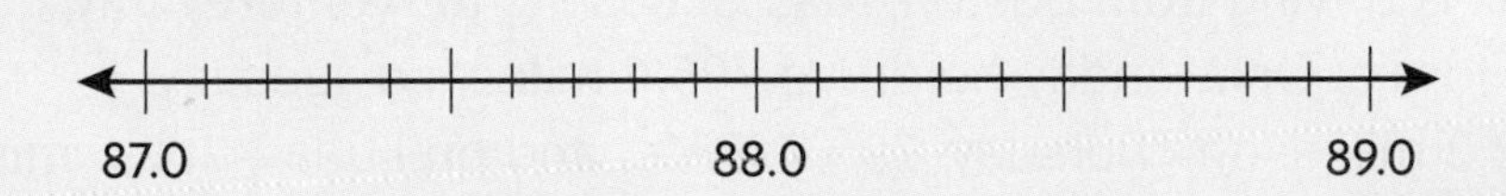

Locate each number on the number line.

A number line shows the numbers from least to greatest.

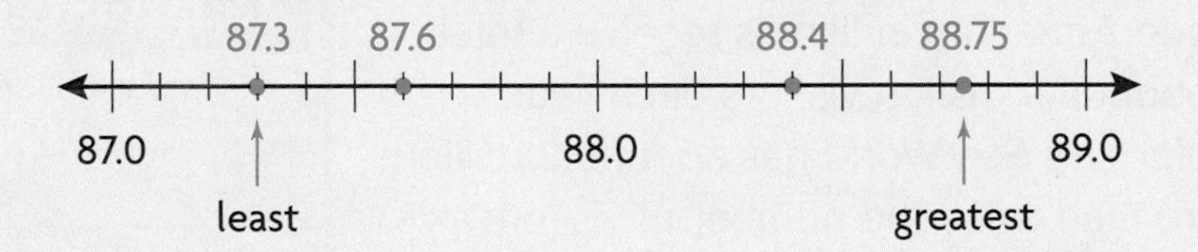

On a number line, the greatest number is at the right.

So, Jessica's family traveled the greatest distance on Tuesday.

Check

- **What other ways could you solve the problem?**
- **How do you know the answer is correct?**

Guided Problem Solving

Read to Understand
Plan
Solve
Check

1. Jessica's family stopped for lunch at noon each day. Before lunch on Monday, the family traveled 45.91 kilometers; on Tuesday, 44.83 kilometers; on Wednesday, 45.48 kilometers; and on Thursday, 44.38 kilometers. On which morning did the family travel the least distance before lunch?

   First, draw a number line.

   Then, locate each number on the number line.

   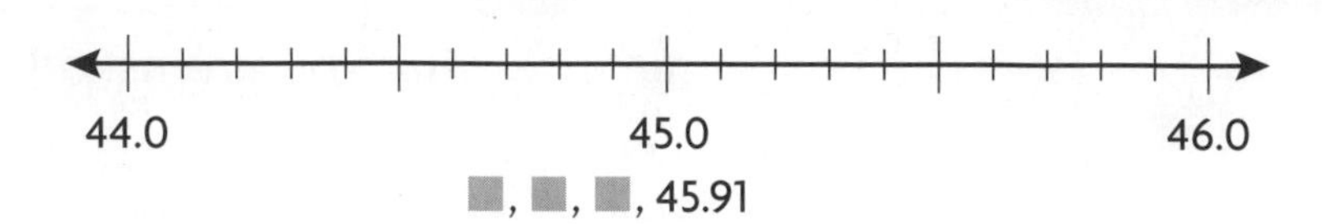

   Finally, use the number line to order the distances from least to greatest.

   ■, ■, ■, 45.91

2. **What if** Jessica's family had traveled 44.95 kilometers before lunch on Monday? On which morning would the family have traveled the greatest distance before lunch?

3. Jessica, her brother Sam, her mother Nan, and her father Bill are the first four people in line at lunch. Sam is not first in line. Jessica has at least two people ahead of her. Bill is third. Give the order from first to last.

Problem Solving Strategy Practice

Draw a diagram to solve.

4. Felix is driving from Boston, Massachusetts to Monterey Bay, California. On Monday he drove 795.6 miles; on Tuesday, 822.2 miles; on Thursday, 799.7 miles; and on Friday, 782.5 miles. On which day did Felix drive the greatest distance?

USE DATA For 5–7, use the table.

5. Sea World in California and the John G. Shedd Aquarium in Illinois receive a total of about 5.9 million visitors each year. California's Sea World has about 0.2 million more than twice the number of visitors as the Shedd Aquarium. About how many people visit the John G. Shedd Aquarium in Illinois each year?

Aquariums in the United States

Aquarium	Estimated Number of Visitors Each Year (in millions)
National Aquarium, MD	1.6
Sea World, CA	4.0
Monterey Bay Aquarium, CA	1.8

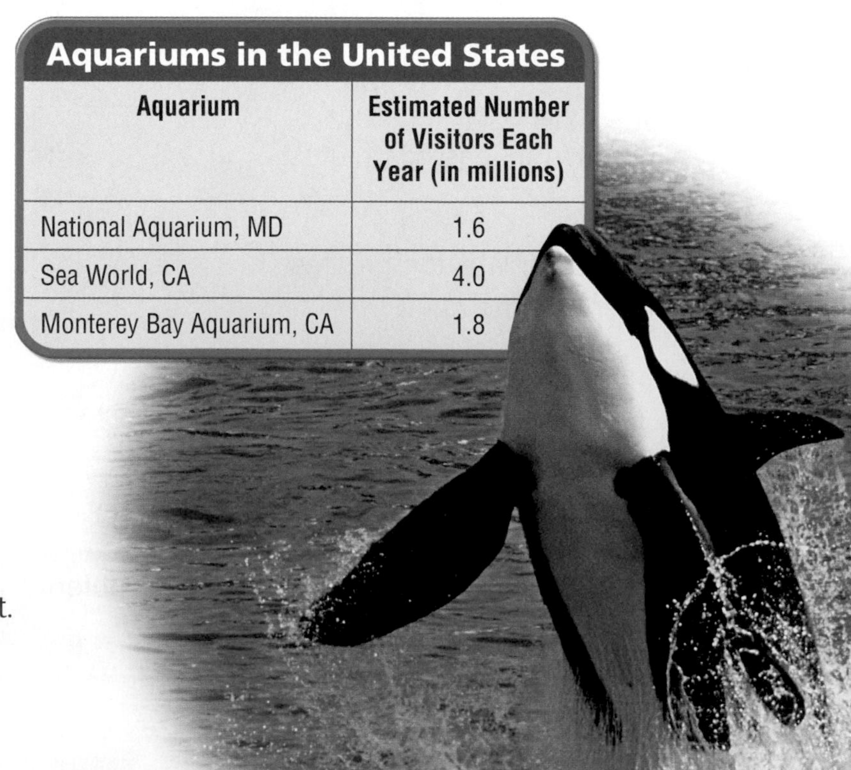

6. Which of the aquariums has the greatest number of visitors? Which of the aquariums has the least number of visitors?

7. **WRITE Math** Describe how using a diagram can help you write the number of visitors at each aquarium in order from least to greatest.

Mixed Strategy Practice

USE DATA For 8–11, use the map and the bus schedule.

8. The bus schedule from Chicago to Cincinnati is shown below. Which route takes the least amount of time?

9. Four buses are traveling from Chicago to Cincinnati. Bus A is on the red route, which takes the least amount of time. Bus B is on the yellow route, which arrives in Cincinnati at 11:30 P.M. Bus C is on the orange route, which takes 7.25 hours. Bus D is on a route that takes 8.5 hours. Name the route number and route color for each bus.

10. Mr. Jackson lives in Gary, IN, and works in Chicago, IL. He drives from home to the office and then home again 5 times a week. About how many miles does Mr. Jackson travel to and from work each week?

11. **Pose a Problem** Look back at Problem 10. Write a similar problem by changing the number of times Mr. Jackson drives to work.

CHALLENGE YOURSELF

The red route is the shortest route at 303.38 miles long and the yellow route is the longest route at 355.05 miles long.

12. The green route's length is between the lengths of the red and orange routes. The length of the green route has the same hundreds, tens, and tenths digits as the length of the orange route. The ones digit is 3 less and the hundredths digit is 4 more than these digits in the length of the orange route. What is the green route's length?

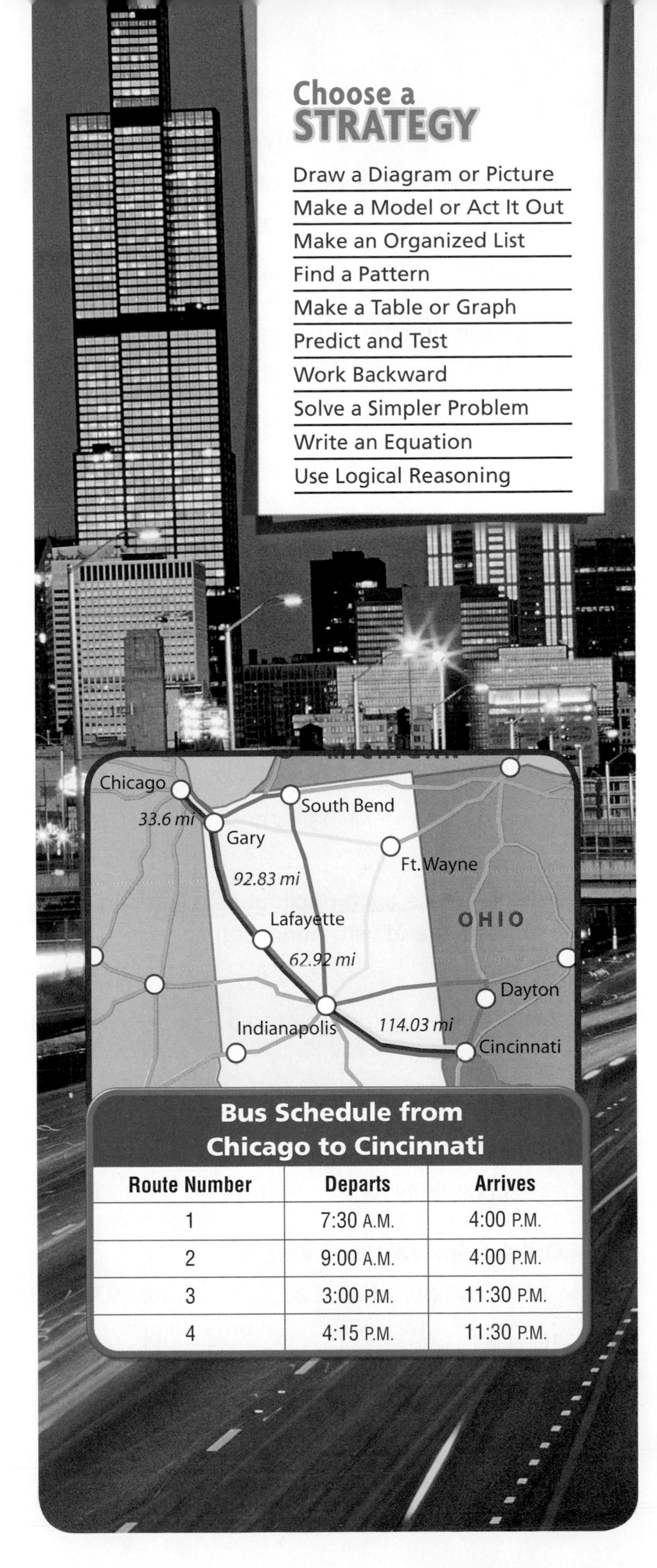

Bus Schedule from Chicago to Cincinnati

Route Number	Departs	Arrives
1	7:30 A.M.	4:00 P.M.
2	9:00 A.M.	4:00 P.M.
3	3:00 P.M.	11:30 P.M.
4	4:15 P.M.	11:30 P.M.

Extra Practice

Set A Write the value of the underlined digit. (pp. 38–39)

1. 0.$\underline{4}$5 2. 5.0$\underline{9}$ 3. 2.$\underline{8}$3 4. 1$\underline{4}$.90
5. 6.0$\underline{6}$ 6. 0.$\underline{7}$1 7. 1$\underline{2}$.56 8. 23.9$\underline{4}$

Write the number in two other forms.

9. 0.33 10. 0.72 11. 1.98 12. 9.26
13. $2 + 0.9 + 0.01$ 14. $20 + 3 + 0.06$ 15. $7 + 0.5 + 0.04$ 16. $8 + 0.9 + 0.01$
17. forty-four hundredths 18. three and seven hundredths

Set B Write *equivalent* or *not equivalent* to describe each pair of decimals. (pp. 42–43)

1. 4.6 and 4.06 2. 7.030 and 7.03 3. 15 and 15.0 4. 1.008 and 1.08
5. 6.013 and 6.13 6. 9.13 and 9.31 7. 8.40 and 8.400 8. 4.15 and 4.150

Write an equivalent decimal for each number.

9. 0.02 10. 3.580 11. 0.9 12. 6.600 13. 5.07
14. 0.100 15. 4.600 16. 3.09 17. 14.70 18. 0.4

Set C Write each decimal as a fraction or mixed number with tenths and with hundredths. (pp. 44–45)

1. 0.9 2. 1.6 3. 0.20 4. 4.50 5. 0.90
6. 0.3 7. 12.80 8. 0.10 9. 5.6 10. 11.40

Set D Compare. Write <, >, or = for each ●. (pp. 46–47)

1. 0.163 ● 0.16 2. 0.83 ● 5 3. 4.049 ● 4.712
4. 5.068 ● 5.608 5. 3.801 ● 3.8 6. 20.4 ● 2.089

Order from least to greatest.

7. 1.78, 1.36, 1.696, 1.8 8. 0.62, 0.584, 0.221, 0.3 9. 8.3, 6.9, 10, 9.001
10. 1.34, 1.09, 1.4, 1.343 11. 0.287, 0.276, 0.285, 0.274 12. 7.3, 7.003, 7.303, 7.323

CD ROM **Technology**
Use Harcourt Mega Math, Fraction Action, *Number Line Mine*, Levels P, Q.

PRACTICE GAME

Decimal Challenge

Players

2–4 players

Materials

- 4 sets of symbol cards (<, >, =)
- Number cube labeled 1, 1, 1, 2, 2, 3
- Game pieces

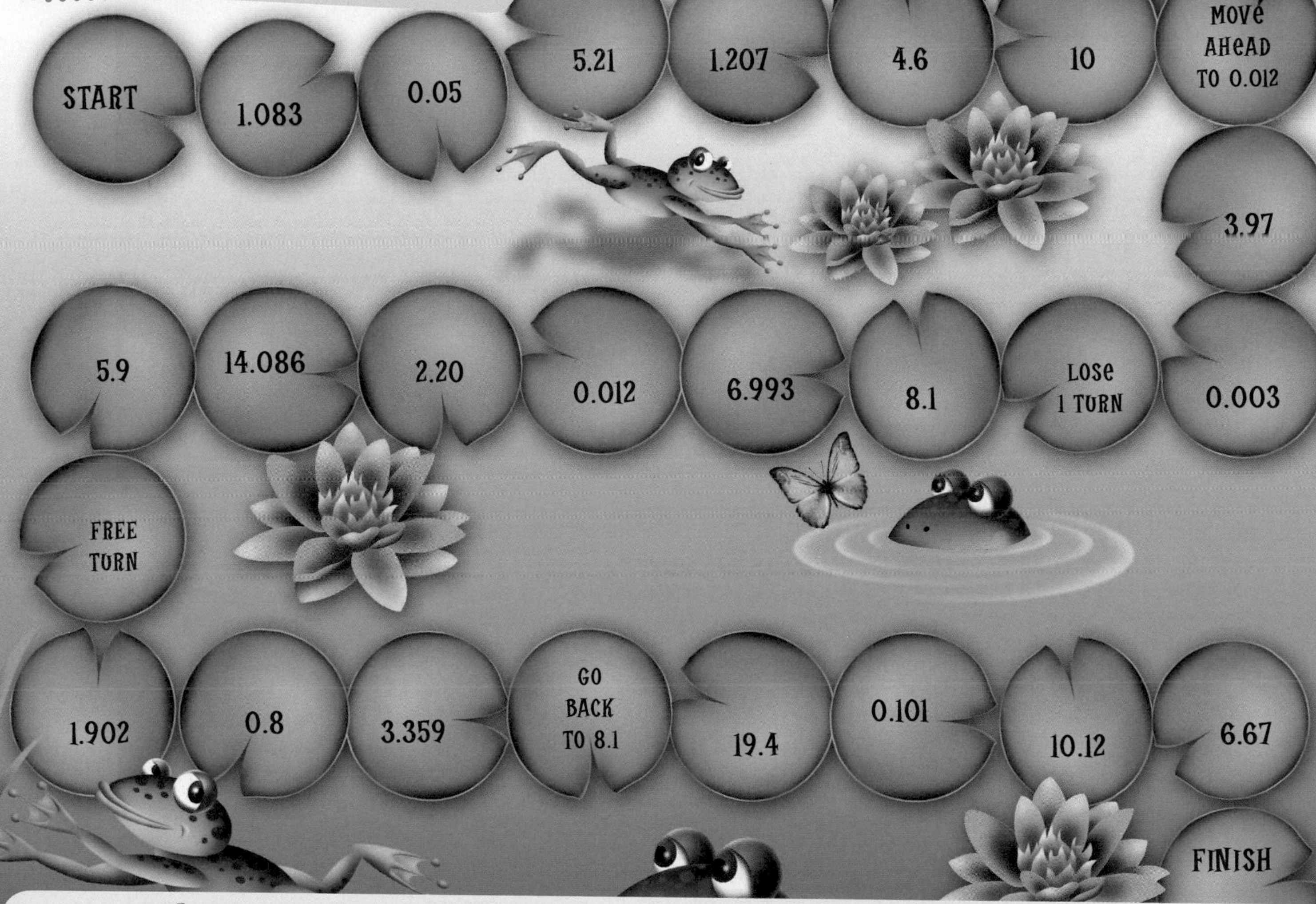

Compare!

- Players shuffle the symbol cards and place them facedown in a pile.
- Each player selects a different game piece and places it on *START*.
- Players take turns tossing the number cube and moving that many spaces on the board.
- On their turns, players draw a symbol card. Depending on the card, they must think of a decimal that is greater than, less than, or equal to the decimal they landed on.
- If a player gives an incorrect answer, he or she loses a turn.
- The first player to reach *FINISH* wins.

Chapter 2 Review/Test

Check Vocabulary and Concepts

Choose the best term from the box.

VOCABULARY
hundredth
thousandth
equivalent decimals

1. The standard form for one _?_ is 0.01. (NS 1.0, p. 38)
2. Decimals that name the same amount are called _?_. (NS 1.0, p. 42)

Check Skills

Write the value of the underlined digit in each number. (NS 1.0, pp. 38–39)

3. $0.\underline{2}3$
4. $0.00\underline{6}$
5. $0.\underline{1}09$
6. $2.7\underline{8}$

Write each number in two other forms. (NS 1.0, pp. 38–39)

7. 1.3
8. 0.4 + 0.07
9. 0.926
10. 2.055

Write an equivalent decimal for each number. (NS 1.0, pp. 42–43)

11. 0.5
12. 2.690
13. 0.01
14. 3.400

Write each decimal as a fraction or mixed number showing tenths and hundredths. (NS 1.0, pp. 44–45)

15. 0.5
16. 2.7
17. 0.80

Compare. Write <, >, or = for each ●. (NS 1.0, pp. 46–47)

18. 0.23 ● 0.246
19. 9 ● 0.935
20. 6.778 ● 6.07

Order from least to greatest. (NS 1.0, pp. 46–47)

21. 1.6, 1.75, 1.461, 1.09
22. 0.33, 0.289, 0.314, 0.4

Check Problem Solving

Solve. (NS 1.0, MR 1.2, MR 2.3, pp. 48–51)

23. Sean took 3 steps forward, 6 steps backward, 9 steps forward, and 4 steps backward. Finally, he took 8 steps forward. What is Sean's position now?
24. Pat swam 25.2 meters on Monday, 18.6 meters on Tuesday, 31.5 meters on Friday, and 29 meters on Saturday. On which day did she swim the greatest distance?
25. **WRITE Math** Abel, Suzi, Jackson, and Lance each won blue, red, white, and yellow ribbons at the science fair. Abel won the yellow ribbon. Suzi did not win the red or the white ribbon. Jackson did not win the white ribbon. Draw a diagram to show which ribbon each student won.

GO ONLINE **Technology** Use *Online Assessment.*

Enrich • Ten-Thousandths

The Tiniest Insect

The Fairyfly wasp is the tiniest insect in the world. The insect is so small that it can fly through the eye of a needle! Scientists estimate that the wingspan of the Fairyfly wasp is 0.0067 inch. What is the value of the digit 7 in 0.0067?

You can use a place-value chart to find the value.

Ones	Tenths	Hundredths	Thousandths	Ten-thousandths
0	0	0	6	7
$0 \times 0 = 0$	$0 \times 0.1 = 0$	$0 \times 0.01 = 0$	$6 \times 0.001 = 0.006$	$7 \times 0.0001 = 0.0007$

So, the value of the digit 7 is 7 ten-thousandths, or 0.0007.

You can write decimals in different forms.

Examples Write 0.0067 in different forms.

A Standard Form: 0.0067

B Word Form: sixty-seven ten-thousandths

C Expanded Form:

- $0.006 + 0.0007$
- $(6 \times 0.001) + (7 \times 0.0001)$

Try It

What is the value of the underlined digit?

1. $1.388\underline{2}$
2. $0.\underline{7}514$
3. $6.094\underline{0}$
4. $0.00\underline{1}2$
5. $10.000\underline{9}$
6. $2.8\underline{1}83$
7. $0.0\underline{6}01$
8. $19.734\underline{1}$
9. $0.00\underline{4}1$
10. $5.\underline{5}762$
11. $24.008\underline{9}$
12. $8.22\underline{9}8$

Write each number in two other forms.

13. 0.0034
14. 0.2169
15. 1.0005
16. 3.1008
17. 2.0032
18. 0.0701
19. 4.0066
20. 10.0004
21. $0.001 + 0.0006$
22. $0.4 + 0.05 + 0.0007$
23. one and ninety-six ten-thousandths
24. two thousand thirty-five ten-thousandths

Think About It

WRITE Math **Explain** how you would compare the numbers 2.9075 and 2.9073.

Achieving the Standards

Chapters 1–2

Number Sense

1. What is the area of Fresno County, rounded to the nearest million acres? (NS 1.0)

Area of California Counties	
County	**Area (in acres)**
Alpine	475,640
Fresno	3,851,140
San Diego	2,896,320

A 2,000,000 acres C 3,900,000 acres

B 3,000,000 acres D 4,000,000 acres

2. Imperial County has 307 square miles of water. Yuba County has 13 square miles of water. How much more water does Imperial County have than Yuba County? (NS 1.0)

A 284 square miles C 307 square miles

B 294 square miles D 384 square miles

3. Long Beach has a population of 461,522. The population of Oakland is 399,484. San Francisco has a population of 776,733. Which correctly compares the populations of Oakland and San Francisco? (NS 1.0)

A $461{,}522 > 399{,}484$

B $399{,}484 < 776{,}733$

C $776{,}733 > 461{,}522$

D $776{,}733 < 399{,}484$

4. WRITE Math **Explain** how you would order the populations of Long Beach, Oakland, and San Francisco from *least* to *greatest*. (NS 1.0)

Algebra and Functions

5. Brenna wrote the expression below.

$$(27 + 8) - (3 \times 4)$$

What is the value of the expression? (Grade 4 O-n AF 1.2)

A 128 C 23

B 28 D 7

6. The letters *a* and *b* represent numbers. If $a + 500 = b + 500$, which statement is true? (Grade 4 O-n AF 2.1)

A $a = b$ C $a < b$

B $a > b$ D $a = b + 500$

7. Mr. Vega drew the diagram below of his classroom. Which equation represents the area (*A*) of the classroom in square feet? (Grade 4 AF 1.4)

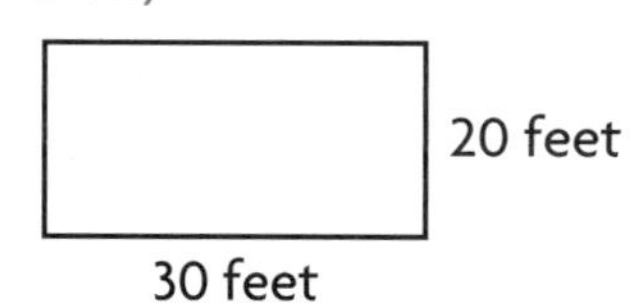

A $A = 20 \times 30$

B $A = (2 \times 20) + (2 \times 30)$

C $A = 2 \times (20 + 30)$

D $A = 20 + 30$

8. WRITE Math **Explain** the steps you would take to solve the expression $19 + (20 \div 4)$. (Grade 4 O-n AF 1.2)

Measurement and Geometry

Decide on a plan.

See item 9. You can draw the triangle. Use simpler measures of 15 centimeters, 25 centimeters, and 15 centimeters.

9. A city park has the shape of a triangle. The sides measure 150 meters, 250 meters, and 150 meters. What kind of triangle is the park? **(Grade 4 MG 3.7)**

A acute **C** equilateral

B obtuse **D** isosceles

10. Which pair of lines is perpendicular? **(MG 2.1)**

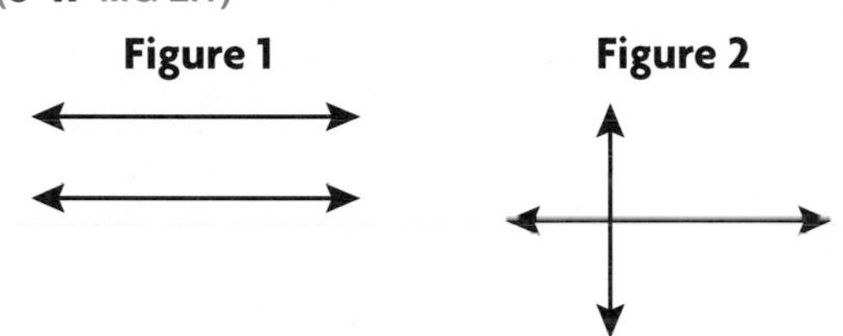

Figure 3

A Figure 1

B Figure 2

C Figure 3

D Figures 1 and 3

11. **WRITE Math** **Explain** how you would find the area of a square if its perimeter is 32 inches. **(MG 1.0)**

Statistics, Data Analysis, and Probability

12. A fifth-grade class conducted a survey about favorite foods. The bar graph shows the results.

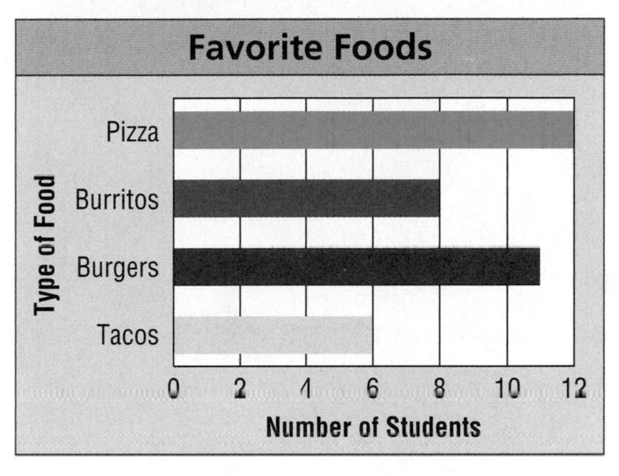

How many more students like pizza than tacos? **(SDAP 1.2)**

A 18

B 9

C 6

D 2

13. Leo tosses a cube numbered 1–6. What is the probability that he will toss an odd number? **(Grade 4 SDAP 2.2)**

A $\frac{1}{6}$ **C** $\frac{1}{2}$

B $\frac{1}{3}$ **D** 1

14. **WRITE Math** **Explain** how you would add the following data to the bar graph in item 12: Nine students like chicken best. **(Grade 4 SDAP 1.1)**

3 Multiply Whole Numbers

The Big Idea Multiplication of multi-digit whole numbers is based on place value and the basic multiplication facts.

CALIFORNIA FAST FACT

18th century English explorers named the Macaroni penguin because of its yellow crest feathers. The feathers looked much like those worn in fancy young men's hats called *macaronis*.

Investigate

You are a scientist studying penguin populations. You have noticed that the population of Adelie penguins is about 4 times greater than the population of Southern Rockhopper penguins. Choose two species of penguins. Estimate how many times greater one population is than the other.

Penguin Populations Worldwide

Species	Estimated Population (in pairs)
Adelie	2,500,000
Northern Rockhopper	350,000
Southern Rockhopper	650,000
Macaroni	9,000,000
Gentoo	320,000

Technology
Student pages are available in the Student eBook.

Show What You Know

Check your understanding of important skills needed for success in Chapter 3.

▶ Multiply Basic Facts and Multiples of 10

Find the product.

1. 90×7

2. 40×6

3. 50×7

4. 20×8

5. 30×9

6. 60×6

7. 80×4

8. 70×8

9. 5×40

10. 9×60

11. 6×30

12. 80×3

▶ Multiply 2-Digit Numbers

Find the product.

13. 14×6

14. 23×4

15. 19×5

16. 31×8

17. 56×3

18. 97×2

19. 37×9

20. 69×4

21. 72×5

22. 86×7

23. 63×5

24. 96×3

25. 62×2

26. 76×3

27. 48×7

28. 88×4

VOCABULARY POWER

CHAPTER VOCABULARY

array
basic fact
Distributive Property
estimate
multiple
partial product
pattern
product
overestimate
regroup
round
underestimate

WARM-UP WORDS

Distributive Property the property that states that multiplying a sum by a number is the same as multiplying each addend in the sum by the number and then adding the products

multiple the product of a given whole number and another whole number

estimate to find a number that is close to the exact amount

LESSON 1

MENTAL MATH

Patterns in Multiples

OBJECTIVE: Multiply basic facts using mental math and patterns of zeros.

Quick Review

1. 5×10
2. 6×20
3. 9×40
4. 80×3
5. 7×70

Learn

PROBLEM A colony of Macaroni penguins may contain thousands of nests. The colony population is found by counting the nests. Suppose a Macaroni penguin colony has 12,000 nests, each with two adults and one chick. About how many penguins are there in the colony?

▲ The Macaroni penguin got its name because its head feathers look like the hat made famous by the song "Yankee Doodle".

Example Multiply. $3 \times 12{,}000$

You can use basic facts and patterns in factors that are multiples of 10 to find products.

$3 \times 12 = 36$ basic fact

$3 \times 120 = 3 \times 12 \times 10 = 360$ basic fact times 10

$3 \times 1{,}200 = 3 \times 12 \times 100 = 3{,}600$ basic fact times 100

$3 \times 12{,}000 = 3 \times 12 \times 1{,}000 = 36{,}000$ basic fact times 1,000

So, the colony has about 36,000 Macaroni penguins in all.

- Count the number of zeros in a factor that is a multiple of 10. How is it related to the number of zeros in the product?

More Examples Use basic facts and a pattern.

A
$4 \times 5 = 20$
$4 \times 50 = 200$
$4 \times 500 = 2{,}000$
$4 \times 5{,}000 = 20{,}000$

B
$6 \times 8 = 48$
$6 \times 80 = 480$
$6 \times 800 = 4{,}800$
$60 \times 800 = 48{,}000$

Math Idea
You can use mental math to find the product. Start with the basic fact. Then count the number of zeros in the multiple of 10. Add the same number of zeros to the end of the product.

Guided Practice

Find the missing numbers.

1. $4 \times 4 = \blacksquare$
   $4 \times 40 = \blacksquare$
   $40 \times 40 = \blacksquare$
2. $5 \times 2 = \blacksquare$
   $5 \times 20 = \blacksquare$
   $5 \times 200 = \blacksquare$
3. $2 \times 3 = \blacksquare$
   $2 \times 30 = \blacksquare$
   $20 \times 30 = \blacksquare$
4. ✓ $8 \times 7 = \blacksquare$
   $8 \times 70 = \blacksquare$
   $8 \times 700 = \blacksquare$

Find the product.

5. 3×40
6. 2×500
7. 60×70
8. 80×100
9. ✓ $3 \times 3{,}000$

10. **TALK Math** **Explain** how 5×7 and patterns of zeros can help you find the product of a very large number like $500 \times 70{,}000$.

NS 1.1 Estimate, round, and manipulate very large (e.g., millions) and very small (e.g., thousandths) numbers. *also* **AF 1.2, MR 1.1, MR 2.3, MR 2.4, MR 2.5, MR 3.2**

Independent Practice and Problem Solving

Find the product.

11. 40×80 **12.** 8×200 **13.** 3×400 **14.** 9×700 **15.** 10×500

16. 11×100 **17.** 60×300 **18.** 90×120 **19.** $7 \times 6{,}000$ **20.** $1{,}100 \times 12$

Algebra **Find the missing number.**

21. $3 \times 7{,}000 = ■$ **22.** $50 \times ■ = 4{,}500$ **23.** $■ \times 600 = 5{,}400$ **24.** $8 \times 3{,}000 = ■$

25. $70 \times 80 = ■$ **26.** $20 \times ■ = 8{,}000$ **27.** $■ \times 500 = 3{,}000$ **28.** $■ \times 50 = 200$

USE DATA **For 29–31, use the krill facts.**

29. Krill lay eggs, or spawn, several times in one season. If a krill lays eggs 4 times, about how many eggs will it lay?

30. Suppose a penguin eats about 5 pounds of krill a day. About what number of krill does the penguin eat in 100 days? (Hint: 1 pound = 16 ounces.)

31. **Reasoning** Researchers discovered a large group of krill that was more than 30,000 feet long. About how long is 30,000 feet, measured in the number of krill?

32. WRITE Math **Explain** how you can tell without multiplying that $700 \times 60{,}000$ and $7{,}000 \times 6{,}000$ have the same value.

Krill are small, shrimplike crustaceans that swim in the water like swarms of insects.

Krill Facts
• Krill are a major source of food for sea animals and birds.
• Adult Antarctic krill are about 2 inches long.
• 30 Antarctic krill weigh about 1 ounce.
• A krill lays about 8,000 eggs at a time.

Achieving the Standards

33. What is the outlier in this set of numbers? (Grade 4 SDAP 1.2)

21, 25, 8, 20, 23, 22

34. What is the value of $n - 15$ for $n = 40$? (AF 1.2, p. 22)

35. What is 4,096 rounded to the nearest hundred? (NS 1.1, p. 12)

36. **Test Prep** There are 90 rows of strawberry plants in a field. Each row contains 600 plants. How many strawberry plants are in the field?

A 54 **C** 5,400

B 540 **D** 54,000

Extra Practice on page 78, Set A

LESSON 2

Estimate Products

OBJECTIVE: Estimate products by rounding and using the expanded form of numbers.

Quick Review

1. 3×600
2. $5 \times 3{,}000$
3. 70×900
4. 80×50
5. 90×400

Learn

PROBLEM A company wants to buy 58,000 board feet of lumber to build 4 houses. Mr. Nelson has 23 acres of land. Each acre has enough trees to make an average of about 3,245 board feet of lumber. Does Mr. Nelson have enough trees to sell the company to build the 4 houses?

You do not need to know the exact number of board feet of lumber in 23 acres, so you can estimate.

A board foot is a cubic unit of wood that usually measures 1 foot by 1 foot by 1 inch, but it can also be 144 cubic inches of wood of any shape.

Example Estimate. 3,245 × 23

Step 1

Round both factors to the greatest place value.

$$\begin{array}{c} 23 \times 3{,}245 \\ \downarrow \quad\quad \downarrow \\ 20 \times 3{,}000 \end{array}$$

Step 2

Use the basic fact and patterns of multiples of 10 to find the estimate.

$$\begin{aligned} 20 \times 3{,}000 &= 2 \times 10 \times 3 \times 1{,}000 \\ &= 6 \times 10{,}000 \\ &= 60{,}000 \end{aligned}$$

So, since Mr. Nelson has enough trees to make about 60,000 board feet of lumber, he could sell them to the company.

- Is 60,000 an overestimate of 23 × 3,245 or an underestimate? Explain.

More Examples

A Basic fact and a multiple of 10

$$\begin{array}{c} 6 \times 593 \\ \downarrow \\ 6 \times 600 = 3{,}600 \end{array}$$

B Basic fact and two multiples of 10

$$\begin{array}{c} 480 \times 422 \\ \downarrow \quad\quad \downarrow \\ 500 \times 400 = 200{,}000 \end{array}$$

C Basic fact with greater numbers

$$\begin{array}{c} 90{,}189 \times 794 \\ \downarrow \quad\quad \downarrow \\ 90{,}000 \times 800 = 72{,}000{,}000 \end{array}$$

D Nearest dollar

$$\begin{array}{c} 16 \times \$12.95 \\ \downarrow \\ 16 \times \$13.00 = \$208.00 \end{array}$$

NS 1.1 Estimate, round, and manipulate very large (e.g., millions) and very small (e.g., thousandths) numbers. *also* AF 1.2, MR 1.1, MR 2.3, MR 2.4, MR 2.5, MR 3.2

Guided Practice

Estimate the product.

Step 1	Step 2
1. $28 \times 3{,}125$ $\downarrow \quad \downarrow$ $■ \times 3{,}000$	$■ \times 3{,}000 = ■ \times 10 \times 3 \times ■$ $= ■ \times 10{,}000$ $= ■$

2. 76×41 **3.** 122×67 **4.** $\$9.65 \times 18$ ✓**5.** 32×723 ✓**6.** 48×612

7. TALK Math **Explain** why you can sometimes estimate instead of finding an exact answer.

Independent Practice and Problem Solving

Estimate the product.

8. 53×22 **9.** 96×51 **10.** 37×13 **11.** 626×94 **12.** $82 \times \$5.86$

13. 28×491 **14.** 76×927 **15.** $5{,}678 \times 31$ **16.** $29 \times 7{,}059$ **17.** $2{,}492 \times 65$

18. $1{,}682 \times 73$ **19.** $2{,}351 \times 505$ **20.** $589 \times 3{,}208$ **21.** $\$21.07 \times 29$ **22.** $32 \times 89{,}075$

USE DATA For 23–25, use the table.

23. The Conservation Society raised $17,000 to buy 38 magnolia trees for a city park. Estimate to find whether the group raised enough money to buy the trees.

24. The Conservation Society has $6,000 to spend on oleander bushes to plant along a bike trail. Estimate to find whether it has enough money to buy the bushes.

25. **Pose a Problem** Look back at Problem 23. Write a similar problem by changing the type of plant and the numbers.

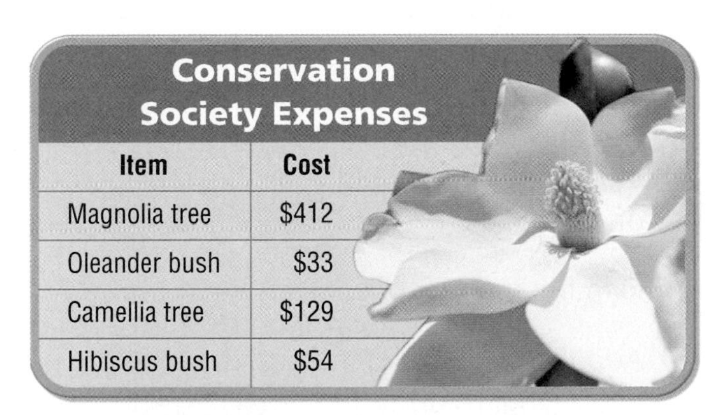

Conservation Society Expenses

Item	Cost
Magnolia tree	$412
Oleander bush	$33
Camellia tree	$129
Hibiscus bush	$54

26. WRITE Math Estimate the product $2{,}788 \times 48$. Explain whether it is an overestimate or an underestimate.

Achieving the Standards

27. Which decimal number is greater, 3.092 or 3.598? (NS 1.0, p. 46)

28. Classify the pair of lines as parallel or perpendicular. (Grade 4 MG 3.1)

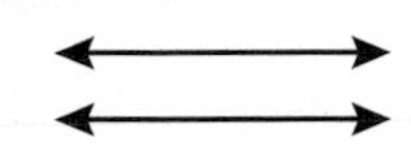

29. $40 \times 6{,}000 =$ (NS 1.1, p. 60)

30. **Test Prep** An airplane flies about 960 miles from Los Angeles to Seattle. Estimate the number of miles there are in 34 trips from Los Angeles to Seattle.

A 3,000 miles **C** 34,000 miles

B 24,000 miles **D** 44,000 miles

Extra Practice on page 78, Set B

LESSON 3 HANDS ON

The Distributive Property

OBJECTIVE: Model multiplication using the Distributive Property.

Quick Review

1. 6×7
2. 4×8
3. 9×50
4. 7×30
5. 8×80

Vocabulary

Distributive Property

Investigate

Materials ■ cm grid paper ■ scissors

The **Distributive Property** states that multiplying a sum by a number is the same as multiplying each addend in the sum by the number and then adding the products.

For example:

$6 \times 18 = 6 \times (10 + 8) = (6 \times 10) + (6 \times 8)$

You can use a grid and the Distributive Property to solve multiplication problems.

A Draw an array on grid paper to find 12×27.

B Break apart one of the factors to make two smaller arrays. Cut the array into two smaller arrays whose products you know. One array should show the multiplication of tens, and the other array should show the multiplication of ones.

C Find the product of each array.

D Add the products of the arrays to find the product of the original array.

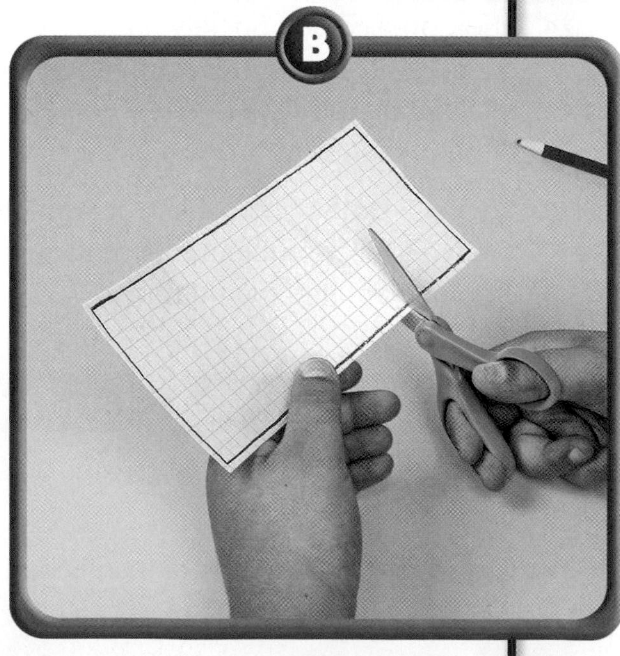

Draw Conclusions

1. How do the arrays illustrate the Distributive Property?
2. Does it matter which factor you break apart when using the Distributive Property? Use the model to explain.
3. **Analysis** Could you have broken apart the factor in another way than breaking it into tens and ones? Would they have made it easier or harder to find the product 12×27? Explain.

AF 1.3 Know and use the distributive property in equations and expressions with variables.
also MR 1.2, MR 2.0, MR 2.3, MR 2.4, MR 3.2

Connect

You can use the Distributive Property to multiply without using arrays.

Step 1

Multiply 13×29.

Write the greater factor in expanded form.

$13 \times 29 = 13 \times (20 + 9)$

Step 2

Use the Distributive Property.

$13 \times 29 = 13 \times (20 + 9)$

$= (13 \times 20) + (13 \times 9)$ Multiply to find the partial products.

$= 260 + 117$ Add the partial products.

$= 377$

So, $13 \times 29 = 377$.

In the model, the array is broken into two parts. In Step 2 above, the expanded form of one factor is multiplied by the other factor to form two partial products.

TALK Math

How does multiplying the expanded form of the number make finding the product easier?

Practice

Find the product.

1. 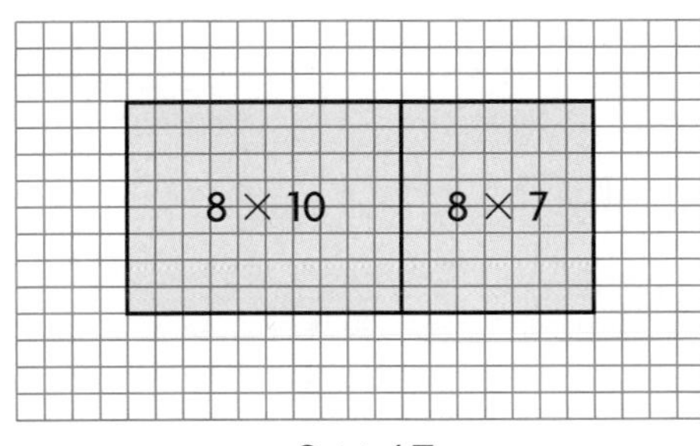

8×17

2. 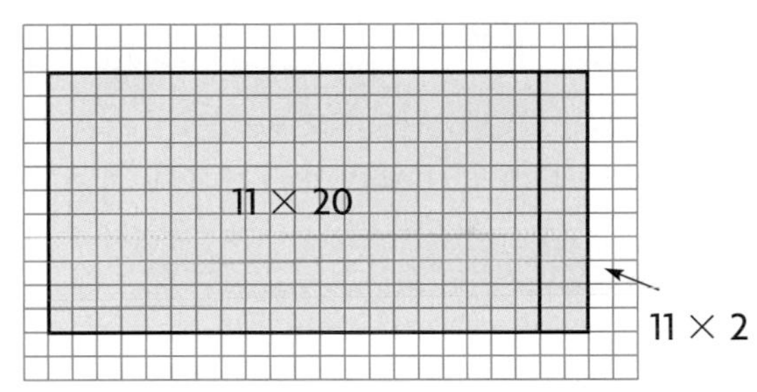

11×22

Draw a model to find the product using the Distributive Property.

3. 6×14
4. 3×25
5. 5×37
6. 11×16

Use the Distributive Property to find the product. Show your work.

7. 7×15
8. 9×54
9. 34×8
10. 5×75
11. 6×23
12. 8×36
13. 9×82
14. 11×43
15. 56×12
16. 44×14
17. 15×27
18. 18×35

Algebra **Use the Distributive Property to solve for *n*.**

19. $7 \times 98 = (7 \times 90) + (7 \times n)$
20. $3 \times 45 = (3 \times n) + (3 \times 5)$
21. $n \times 13 = (9 \times 10) + (9 \times 3)$
22. $4 \times 56 = (4 \times 60) - (4 \times n)$

23. **WRITE Math** How does using the Distributive Property make the product easier to find?

LESSON 4

Multiply by 1-Digit Numbers

OBJECTIVE: Multiply by a 1-digit number.

Quick Review

Estimate the product.

1. 4×672
2. 335×3
3. $1,806 \times 7$
4. $5 \times 7,891$
5. $8,288 \times 4$

Learn

PROBLEM An airline flies six 747 jets from New York to Paris every day. If each flight carries an average of 238 passengers, how many passengers fly on this airline from New York to Paris every day?

The cruising altitude of a 747 jet is 35,000 feet. The flying time from Paris to New York is about 7 hours 55 minutes.

ONE WAY **Use the Distributive Property.**

Example **Multiply.** 6×238 **Estimate.** $6 \times 200 = 1,200$

Remember that the Distributive Property states that multiplying a sum by a number is the same as multiplying each addend in the sum by the number and then adding the products.

Step 1

Write the greater factor in expanded form.

$6 \times 238 = 60 \times (200 + 30 + 8)$

Step 2

Multiply each addend by 6.

$6 \times 238 = 6 \times (200 + 30 + 8)$

$= (6 \times 200) + (6 \times 30) + (6 \times 8)$ Multiply to find the partial products.

$= 1,200 + 180 + 48$ Add the partial products.

$= 1,428$

Compare the product to the estimate. Since 1,428 is close to 1,200, it is a reasonable answer.

So, the airline flies an average of 1,428 passengers from New York to Paris each day.

READ Math

The expression 6×238 can be read in different ways:

- 6 groups of 238
- the product of 6 and 238
- 6 times 238

NS 1.0 Students compute with very large and very small numbers, positive integers, decimals, and fractions and understand the relationship between decimals, fractions, and percents. They understand the relative magnitudes of numbers. *also* **NS 1.1, AF 1.3, AF 1.5, MR 1.2, MR 2.1, MR 2.3, MR 2.4, MR 3.2**

ANOTHER WAY Use place value and regrouping.

Step 1	Step 2	Step 3
Multiply the ones. $6 \times 8 = 48$ ones Regroup.	Multiply the tens. 6×3 tens $= 18$ tens Add the 4 regrouped tens. 18 tens + 4 tens = 22 tens	Multiply the hundreds. 6×2 hundreds $= 12$ hundreds Add the 2 regrouped hundreds. 12 hundreds + 2 hundreds = 14 hundreds
$\begin{array}{r} \scriptstyle 4 \\ 238 \\ \times \quad 6 \\ \hline 8 \end{array}$	$\begin{array}{r} \scriptstyle 2\,4\; \\ 238 \\ \times \quad 6 \\ \hline 28 \end{array}$	$\begin{array}{r} \scriptstyle 2\,4\; \\ 238 \\ \times \quad 6 \\ \hline 1{,}428 \end{array}$

- How is multiplying with regrouping like using the Distributive Property? How is it different?

More Examples

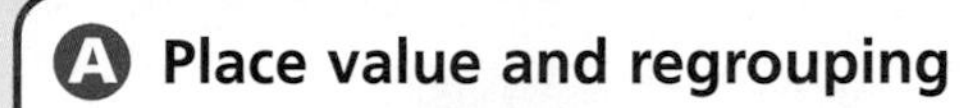

A Place value and regrouping

$$\begin{array}{r} \scriptstyle 1\;\;2\;\; \\ 5{,}628 \\ \times \quad\; 3 \\ \hline 16{,}884 \end{array}$$

B Place value and regrouping

$$\begin{array}{r} \scriptstyle 3\;\;\;2\,4\;\; \\ 44{,}036 \\ \times \qquad 8 \\ \hline 352{,}288 \end{array}$$

C Distributive Property

$$\begin{aligned} 7 \times 9{,}184 &= 7 \times (9{,}000 + 100 + 80 + 4) \\ &= (7 \times 9{,}000) + (7 \times 100) + (7 \times 80) + (7 \times 4) \\ &= 63{,}000 + 700 + 560 + 28 \\ &= 64{,}288 \end{aligned}$$

Math Idea
To multiply a greater number by a 1-digit number, use the same method you use for a 2- or 3-digit number. Just repeat the steps for all of the digits in the greater number.

Guided Practice

Copy and complete.

1. $4 \times 283 = 4 \times (200 + 80 + ■)$
$= (4 \times 200) + (■ \times 80) + (4 \times 3)$
$= 800 + ■ + 12$
$= ■$

2. $5 \times 769 = ■ \times (■ + 60 + 9)$
$= (5 \times ■) + (5 \times ■) + (5 \times ■)$
$= ■ + 300 + ■$
$= ■$

Estimate. Then find the product.

3. 36×7 **4.** 497×3 **5.** 208×8 ✓**6.** 556×4

7. 821×5 **8.** 4×915 **9.** $3{,}006 \times 9$ ✓**10.** $9{,}682 \times 2$

11. **TALK Math** **Explain** how to find the digit in the hundreds place of the product of 731×7.

Independent Practice and Problem Solving

Estimate. Then find the product.

12. 32×4
13. 85×5
14. 709×2
15. 573×4
16. 625×3
17. 423×7
18. 716×5
19. $11{,}808 \times 8$
20. $32{,}045 \times 6$
21. $42{,}531 \times 9$
22. 632×4
23. 709×9
24. $4{,}625 \times 3$
25. $5{,}473 \times 2$
26. $5 \times 3{,}954$
27. $1{,}739 \times 8$
28. $8{,}576 \times 7$
29. $34{,}253 \times 6$

Algebra Solve for the missing number.

30. $6 \times 5{,}396 = ■$
31. $8 \times 5{,}179 = ■$
32. $5 \times 42{,}736 = ■$
33. $7 \times 135{,}819 = ■$

USE DATA For 34–40, use the table.

Round-trip Airfares from New York, NY

Destination	Cost in Dollars
Detroit, MI	239
Chicago, IL	140
London, England	591
Paris, France	883
Tokyo, Japan	1,237
Sydney, Australia	1,329

34. How much would it cost a family of four to fly round-trip from New York to Detroit?
35. The Bayport Dance Team is flying from New York to a contest in Chicago. There are 6 dancers and 3 chaperones. How much will the plane tickets cost in all?
36. Zach drove from New York to Detroit and back. He paid $452 for gas and a one-night stay at a hotel. How much less would Zach have paid if he had flown round-trip from New York to Detroit in one day?
37. Mr. Abrams went on several business trips. Flying from New York, he went to Sydney and Chicago once, to Tokyo and Paris twice, and to London four times. What was the total cost of Mr. Abrams's plane tickets?
38. The weight of a passenger's suitcase on a certain airline cannot be greater than 44 pounds. If a family of three brought two suitcases per person that weighed 44 pounds each, what is the total weight of their luggage?
39. How many times could a person fly round-trip from New York to Chicago before the cost was greater than the cost to fly from New York to Sydney, Australia, one time?
40. How much more does it cost 3 people to fly round-trip from New York to Tokyo than to fly from New York to Paris?
41. **WRITE Math** **What's the Error?** Paxton wrote $5 \times 2{,}047 = (5 \times 20) + (4 \times 4) + (4 \times 7)$. Describe his error. Then write the equation correctly.

CD ROM
Technology
Use Harcourt Mega Math, The Number Games, *Up, Up, and Array,* Level J.

 Extra Practice on page 78, Set C

Achieving the Standards

42. Write a rule for the table using an equation with the variables x and y. (Grade 4 🔑 AF 1.5)

Input	x	6	15	18	23	28
Output	y	13	22	25	30	35

43. Write 0.7 as a fraction whose denominator is a hundredth. (NS 1.2, p. 44)

44. A restaurant supply store charges \$76 for one table. About how much would 38 tables cost? (NS 1.1, p. 62)

45. **Test Prep** What is the cost of 6 train tickets if 1 ticket costs \$349?

A \$698 **C** \$2,070

B \$1,047 **D** \$2,094

46. **Test Prep** Which expression has the same value as $5 \times (900 + 60 + 4)$?

A $5 \times 900{,}604$

B $4{,}500 + 60 + 4$

C $4{,}500 + 300 + 20$

D $45 + 30 + 20$

Problem Solving and Reasoning

NUMBER SENSE Carl Friedrich Gauss, a mathematician, was born in Germany in 1777. A famous story is told about Gauss when he was 10 years old.

Gauss's teacher asked Gauss and his classmates to add the numbers from 1 to 100. The teacher was surprised when, in only moments, Gauss came up with the correct answer of 5,050.

Here is one way Gauss could have answered the question.

Carl Friedrich Gauss

$1 + 100 = 101$ Start with the greatest and the least numbers.
$2 + 99 = 101$ Continue to add the next greatest and next least numbers.
$3 + 98 = 101$ The sum of each pair is 101.
⋮

$49 + 52 = 101$
$50 + 51 = 101$ This is the last pair because they are consecutive addends with a sum of 101. There are 50 pairs. The first addend of each sum counts the number of pairs.

There are 50 sums of 101, so multiply 50×101. $50 \times 101 = 5{,}050$

Use the method above to find the sum of the numbers.

1. from 1 to 50 **2.** from 1 to 80 **3.** from 1 to 200 **4.** from 1 to 500

LESSON 5

Multiply by 2-Digit Numbers

OBJECTIVE: Multiply by a 2-digit number.

Quick Review

1. 48 × 4 **2.** 5 × 23
3. 85 × 4 **4.** 50 × 70
5. 839 × 2

Learn

PROBLEM Ana lives in San Francisco, California, and plans to cycle to Cape May, New Jersey. She wants to take a few side trips along the way. She plans to travel about 36 miles each day for 124 days. How many miles in all is Ana planning to cycle?

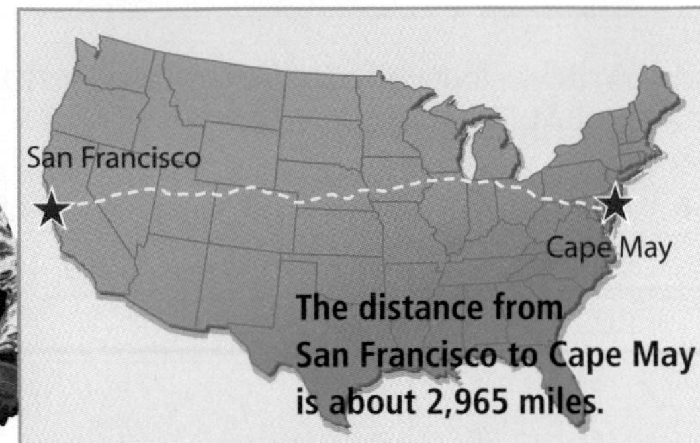
San Francisco
Cape May
The distance from San Francisco to Cape May is about 2,965 miles.

Example **Multiply.** 36 × 124 **Estimate.** 40 × 120 = 4,800

Step 1

Multiply by the ones.

```
  12
  124
×  36
  744 ← 6 × 124
```

Step 2

Multiply by the tens.

```
   1
  12
  124
×  36
  744
 3720 ← 30 × 124
```

Step 3

Add the partial products.

```
    1
   12
   124
×   36
   744  ⎫ partial
+ 3720  ⎭ products
 4,464
```

So, Ana plans to cycle 4,464 miles. Since it is close to the estimate of 4,800, it is a reasonable answer.

- In Step 2, why does the partial product of 3,720 have a zero in the ones place?

More Examples

A Money

```
     5
     3
  $208
×   74
   832 ← 4 × 208
+14560 ← 70 × 208
$15,392
```

B 4-digit factor

```
   1 53
     32
  8,164
×    95
  40820 ← 5 × 8,164
+734760 ← 90 × 8,164
775,580
```

C Two 3-digit factors

```
     2
     6
    11
    619
  × 372
   1238 ← 2 × 619
  43330 ← 70 × 619
+185700 ← 300 × 619
230,268
```

- In Example A, what happens to the regrouped digits 3 and 5, since there is a zero in the factor?

NS 1.0 Students compute with very large and very small numbers, positive integers, decimals, and fractions and understand the relationship between decimals, fractions, and percents. They understand the relative magnitudes of numbers. *also* **MR 2.1, MR 2.3, MR 2.4, MR 3.2**

Guided Practice

Find the missing numbers.

1. $\begin{array}{r} 453 \\ \times\ 17 \\ \hline 3171 \\ +4530 \\ \hline 7{,}701 \end{array}$ $\begin{array}{l} \\ \\ \leftarrow 453 \times ■ \\ \leftarrow 453 \times ■ \\ \\ \end{array}$

2. $\begin{array}{r} 608 \\ \times\ 29 \\ \hline 5472 \\ +12160 \\ \hline 17{,}632 \end{array}$ $\begin{array}{l} \\ \\ \leftarrow ■ \times ■ \\ \leftarrow ■ \times ■ \\ \\ \end{array}$

3. $\begin{array}{r} 571 \\ \times\ 38 \\ \hline 4568 \\ +17130 \\ \hline ■■■■■ \end{array}$ $\begin{array}{l} \\ \\ \leftarrow ■ \times ■ \\ \leftarrow ■ \times ■ \\ \\ \end{array}$

Estimate. Then find the product.

4. $\begin{array}{r} 221 \\ \times\ 19 \\ \hline \end{array}$

5. $\begin{array}{r} 308 \\ \times\ 36 \\ \hline \end{array}$

6. $\begin{array}{r} 416 \\ \times\ 54 \\ \hline \end{array}$

✓7. $\begin{array}{r} \$533 \\ \times\ 85 \\ \hline \end{array}$

✓8. $\begin{array}{r} 688 \\ \times\ 67 \\ \hline \end{array}$

9. **TALK Math** **Explain why** the second partial product is always greater than the first partial product when you multiply a 3-digit number by a 2-digit number.

Independent Practice and Problem Solving

Estimate. Then find the product.

10. $\begin{array}{r} 295 \\ \times\ 53 \\ \hline \end{array}$

11. $\begin{array}{r} 604 \\ \times\ 72 \\ \hline \end{array}$

12. $\begin{array}{r} 724 \\ \times\ 46 \\ \hline \end{array}$

13. $\begin{array}{r} \$4{,}151 \\ \times\ \ \ 81 \\ \hline \end{array}$

14. $\begin{array}{r} 307 \\ \times 197 \\ \hline \end{array}$

15. 22×348

16. 436×50

17. $25 \times 1{,}803$

18. $52 \times 7{,}009$

19. 938×254

20. While Brandon is cycling, his heart rate rises to 185 beats per minute for 25 minutes. During this 25-minute time period, how many times does Brandon's heart beat?

21. Sandra trained for a bike race by riding 108 miles per day, 4 days a week, for 8 weeks. What is the total number of miles that Sandra rode while training?

22. **WRITE Math** **What's the Question?** A cyclist on a bike with 27-inch wheels travels about 85 inches for each revolution the wheels make. The wheels make 325 revolutions. The answer is 27,625 inches.

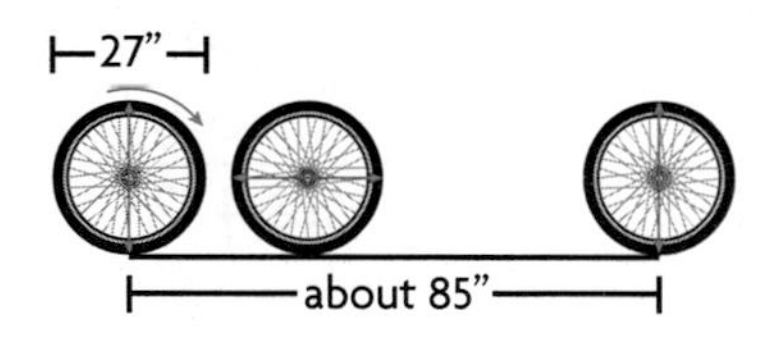

Achieving the Standards

23. The perimeter of a square garden is 196 yards. What is the length of each side? (Grade 4 MG 1.4)

24. Ivette ran 3.6 miles on Tuesday and 3.48 miles on Wednesday. On which day did Ivette run the greater distance? (NS 1.0, p. 46)

25. What number makes the sentence $4 \times 29 = (4 \times n) + (4 \times 9)$ true? (O‑π AF 1.2, AF 1.3, p. 64)

26. **Test Prep** How much does a store make if it sells 57 computers at $1,348 each?

    A $16,176
    B $67,400
    C $76,836
    D $86,476

Extra Practice on page 79, Set D

LESSON 6

Practice Multiplication

OBJECTIVE: Practice multiplication by 1- and 2-digit numbers.

Quick Review

1. 90×40
2. 40×61
3. 74×5
4. 96×27
5. 30×405

Learn

PROBLEM The weight of a male African elephant can be as much as 93 times the weight of an adult man. If an average adult man weighs about 172 pounds, how much might a male African elephant weigh?

▲ The trunk of an African elephant contains more than 40,000 muscles.

Example

Multiply. 93×172 **Estimate.** $90 \times 200 = 18{,}000$

Step 1

Multiply by the ones.

$$\begin{array}{r} {}^{2} \\ 172 \\ \times\ 93 \\ \hline 516 \end{array}$$

Step 2

Multiply by the tens.

$$\begin{array}{r} {}^{6\,1} \\ {}^{2} \\ 172 \\ \times\ 93 \\ \hline 516 \\ 15480 \\ \hline \end{array}$$

Step 3

Add the partial products.

$$\begin{array}{r} {}^{6\,1} \\ {}^{2} \\ 172 \\ \times\ 93 \\ \hline 516 \\ +\,15480 \\ \hline 15{,}996 \end{array}$$

So, a male African elephant may weigh as much as 15,996 pounds. This is close to the estimate of 18,000, so the answer is reasonable.

More Examples

A Multiply by 1 digit.

$$\begin{array}{r} {}^{5\ \ 7} \\ 3{,}608 \\ \times\quad 9 \\ \hline 32{,}472 \end{array}$$

B Multiply by 2 digits.

$$\begin{array}{r} {}^{2\ 1\,1} \\ {}^{4\ 3\,2} \\ 2{,}754 \\ \times\quad 36 \\ \hline 16524 \\ +\,82620 \\ \hline 99{,}144 \end{array}$$

ERROR ALERT

When you multiply by tens, put a zero in the ones place to align place values.

C Use the Distributive Property.

$$\begin{aligned} 20 \times 324 &= 20 \times (300 + 20 + 4) \\ &= (20 \times 300) + (20 \times 20) + (20 \times 4) \\ &= 6{,}000 + 400 + 80 \\ &= 6{,}480 \end{aligned}$$

- In Example A, what happens to the regrouped digit 7 since there is a zero in the factor?

NS 1.0 Students compute with very large and very small numbers, positive integers, decimals, and fractions and understand the relationship between decimals, fractions, and percents. They understand the relative magnitudes of numbers. *also* **NS 1.1, NS 2.5, MR 1.1, MR 2.1, MR 2.3, MR 2.4, MR 2.6, MR 3.2**

Guided Practice

1. Copy each step of the problem at the right. Then tell what is happening in each step.

Step 1	Step 2	Step 3
$500 \times 7 = 3{,}500$ 528×7	(regrouped 1 5) 528×7 96	(regrouped 1 5) 528×7 3,696

Estimate. Then find the product.

2. 201×5
3. 4×655
4. 33×312
5. 420×29
6. 874×36
7. TALK Math **Explain** why place value is important when multiplying.

Independent Practice and Problem Solving

Estimate. Then find the product.

8. 168×6
9. 432×8
10. $3{,}587 \times 9$
11. $15{,}882 \times 4$
12. $149{,}516 \times 8$
13. 576×31
14. $1{,}008 \times 55$
15. $81 \times 6{,}102$
16. $64 \times 54{,}092$
17. $73 \times 132{,}396$

USE DATA For 18–19, use the table.

18. How many pounds of food does a male lion eat in one year? (Hint: 1 year = 365 days.)
19. How many more pounds of food does a hippopotamus eat in 6 weeks than a gorilla?
20. WRITE Math **Sense or Nonsense?** Nicky says that the product of a 3-digit number and a 2-digit number will be a 4- or 5-digit number. Does Nicky's statement make sense? Why or why not?

Animal Diets

Animal	Daily Food (in pounds)
Gorilla	40
Hippopotamus	150
Lion (male)	15

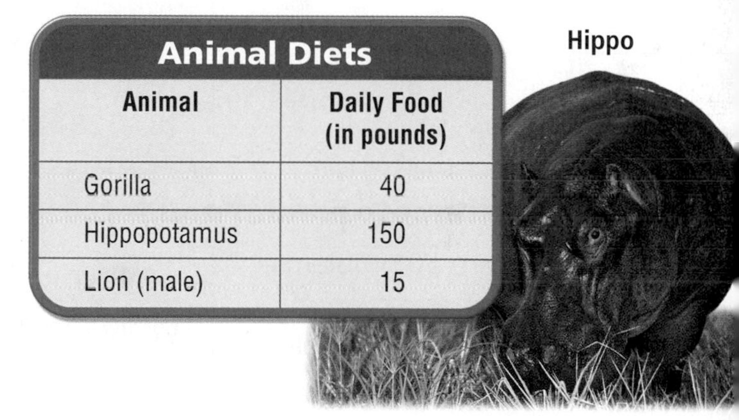
Hippo

Achieving the Standards

21. What digit is in the millions place in the number 146,378,920? (NS 1.1, p. 1)
22. Maria is reading a book with 98 pages. She reads 15 pages every day for 6 days. How many pages does Maria have left to read? (Grade 4 NS 3.0)
23. What is the mode for this set of numbers? (Grade 4 SDAP 1.2)

    2, 8, 3, 3, 5, 2, 6, 2, 1, 8, 2

24. **Test Prep** Admission to a natural history museum is $16 per person. Which is the total amount of money that 2,473 visitors paid for admission in one day?

    A $17,311
    B $36,158
    C $39,558
    D $39,568

Extra Practice on page 79, Set E

Problem Solving Workshop
Strategy: Predict and Test

OBJECTIVE: Solve problems using the strategy *predict and test.*

Learn the Strategy

Sometimes, you may not be sure how to solve a problem. At other times, there may be several ways to solve a problem but you are not sure which is the best. You can predict a solution to the problem, and then test and revise the solution until your answer is correct.

Use estimation and number sense to predict and test.

The product of 28 and a number is 504. What is the number?

Estimate: I can round 28 to 30. What can I multiply by 30 that gives me a product close to 500?
$30 \times 16 = 480$

Think: To get a product that ends with 4, 28 must be multiplied by a number that ends with 3 or 8. The number must be close to the estimate, 16.

Predict: 13 or 18.

Test: $13 \times 28 = 364$, which is too low.
$18 \times 28 = 504$, so 18 is the solution to the problem.

Use patterns to predict and test.

There are 50 problems on a test. For every correct answer, 2 points are given. For each incorrect answer, 1 point is subtracted. Tina scored 91 points on the test. How can Tina find out the number of problems that she missed?

Predict		Test		
Correct	Incorrect	Score	Pattern	
50	0	$(50 \times 2) - 0 = 100$		too high
49	1	$(49 \times 2) - 1 = 97$	subtract 3	too high
48	2	$(48 \times 2) - 2 = 94$	subtract 3	too high
47	3	$(47 \times 2) - 3 = 91$	subtract 3	correct

Tina can predict the number of answers that she missed by making a table to find a pattern. Each incorrect answer subtracts 3 points. Tina can subtract 3 points from 100 until it matches her score. Then she can use her table to find the number of problems she missed.

Revise your prediction when your guess is not the solution. Reread the problem and find a method that will help you make a prediction that is closer to the actual answer.

TALK Math

How do you revise your prediction if your tested solution is too large or too small?

NS 1.0 Students compute with very large and very small numbers, positive integers, decimals, and fractions and understand the relationship between decimals, fractions, and percents. They understand the relative magnitudes of numbers. *also* **MR 1.0, MR 1.2, MR 2.1, MR 2.6, MR 3.0, MR 3.1, MR 3.3**

Use the Strategy

Read to Understand
Plan
Solve
Check

PROBLEM Jack is taking swimming lessons and soccer lessons while he is at camp. So far, Jack has paid \$116. If swimming lessons cost \$8 each and soccer lessons cost \$15 each, how many of each type of lesson has Jack taken?

Read to Understand

- **Summarize what you are asked to find.**
- **What information is not given?**

Plan

- **What strategy can you use to solve the problem?**
  You can predict and test to help you solve the problem.

Solve

- **How can you use the strategy to solve the problem?**
  Make a table to show your predictions and tests. Your table should have enough rows to make several predictions. Start by estimating and using number sense. Ten swimming lessons cost \$80, ten soccer lessons cost \$150, and ten of each cost \$230. Five of each lesson would cost half as much, or \$115.

Predict	Test	Revise
5 swimming lessons, 5 soccer lessons	$(5 \times \$8) + (5 \times \$15) =$ $\$40 + \$75 = \$115$	too low but very close; try one less swimming lesson and one more soccer lesson
4 swimming lessons, 6 soccer lessons	$(4 \times \$8) + (6 \times \$15) =$ $\$32 + \$90 = \$122$	too high; try adjusting the numbers the other way
6 swimming lessons, 4 soccer lessons	$(6 \times \$8) + (4 \times \$15) =$ $\$48 + \$60 = \$108$	too low; only \$8 off, need 1 more swimming lesson
7 swimming lessons, 4 soccer lessons	$(7 \times \$8) + (4 \times \$15) =$ $\$56 + \$60 = \$116$	correct

So, Jack has taken 7 swimming lessons and 4 soccer lessons.

Check

- **How can you check your answer?**
- **Does your answer make sense for the problem?**

Guided Problem Solving

Read to Understand
Plan
Solve
Check

1. Sherri is going to a water sports adventure camp. She is learning how to scuba dive and water ski. Scuba-diving lessons cost $75 per day and water-skiing lessons cost $56 per day. So far, Sherri has paid $505. How many of each type of lesson has Sherri taken?

First, predict the number of scuba-diving lesson and the number of water-skiing lessons that she has taken.

Then, test the prediction by comparing the cost to $505.

Finally, revise your prediction if necessary. Repeat until your solution fits the information given in the problem.

Predict	Test	Revise
4 scuba, 4 water skiing-lessons	$(4 \times \$75) + (4 \times \$56) = \$524$	too high; try one less scuba lesson
3 scuba, 4 water skiing-lessons	$(3 \times \$75) + (4 \times \$56) = \$449$	too low; think: how much greater than $449 is $505?
■	■	?

2. **What if** Sherri had spent $580 on scuba-diving and water-skiing lessons? How many of each type of lesson would she have taken?

3. Lloyd is making wallets and bookmarks at camp. Bookmark kits cost $3, and wallet kits cost $8. Lloyd spent $34 on kits. How many bookmarks and how many wallets is he planning to make?

Problem Solving Strategy Practice

Predict and test to solve.

USE DATA For 4–6, use the table.

4. Chase did a different combination of activities at camp on Monday and Tuesday. He did three different activities each day. He paid $12 for activities on Monday and $17 for activities on Tuesday. What activities did Chase do each day?

5. **Reasoning** Amanda did two different types of activities each day Monday through Saturday. The following chart shows the amount she paid each day. Which two activities did Amanda do each day?

Day	M	T	W	T	F	S
Amount	$7	$13	$12	$9	$11	$8

Camp Activities

Activity	Cost
Swimming	$4 per day
Archery	$3 per day
Horseback riding	$8 per day
Diving	$5 per day

6. WRITE Math Describe three ways that a camper could spend $15 or less for 3 days of activities, doing one activity each day.

Mixed Strategy Practice

USE DATA For 7–12, use the information in the table.

7. Dave is going to performing arts camp for 2 weeks. He has $511 saved, and his father will contribute $250. How much more money will Dave need to save for two weeks of camp?

8. Cynthia is attending computer camp for one week. She will pay the weekly camp cost and she needs to buy supplies. She needs to buy 10 blank CDs for $1 each, a package of computer paper for $5, and a set of headphones for $12. How much money in all does Cynthia need?

9. Sheryl decided not to go to astronaut camp because it was so expensive. She wants to go to surfing camp instead. For how many weeks can she go to surfing camp in place of one week of astronaut camp?

10. **Pose a Problem** Look back at Problem 8. Write a similar problem by changing the type of camp, the supplies needed, and the numbers.

11. **Open-Ended** Hector's grandmother gave him $2,000 to go to summer camp. Describe different ways that Hector could spend the money to go to different camps for different amounts of time.

12. Josh earned 3 times as many merit badges at scout camp as Joey. Joey earned 3 fewer merit badges than Troy. Troy earned 6 merit badges. How many merit badges did Josh and Joey each earn?

CHALLENGE YOURSELF

While Nick is at camp, he sends a postcard to his mother and father every two days and a postcard to his grandmother every five days.

13. Nick has sent a total of 9 postcards. What is the least number of days that Nick could have been at camp?

14. If Nick spends the entire month of July at camp, on how many days will he send a postcard to his parents and his grandmother on the same day? **Explain** how you found your answer.

Choose a STRATEGY

- Draw a Diagram or Picture
- Make a Model or Act It Out
- Make an Organized List
- Find a Pattern
- Make a Table or Graph
- Predict and Test
- Work Backward
- Solve a Simpler Problem
- Write an Equation
- Use Logical Reasoning

Summer Camps

Type of Camp	Weekly Cost
Astronaut	$1,635
Computer	$1,333
Performing arts	$625
Surfing	$314

Extra Practice

Set A Use mental math to find the product. (pp. 60–61)

1. 30×60
2. 9×400
3. 5×700
4. 10×600
5. 40×800
6. 9×50
7. 20×80
8. 40×120
9. $8 \times 7{,}000$
10. $5 \times 6{,}000$
11. 70×300
12. 50×80
13. $2 \times 9{,}000$
14. $30 \times 1{,}300$
15. $90 \times 6{,}000$
16. $5{,}000 \times 14$
17. Mr. Kent ordered 8 boxes of pencils. There are 70 pencils in each box. How many pencils did he order?
18. Each package of tacks contains 120 tacks. How many tacks are in 30 packages?

Set B Estimate the product. (pp. 62–63)

1. 42×23
2. 98×61
3. 34×17
4. $\$823 \times 39$
5. 72×512
6. 871×29
7. $4{,}862 \times 32$
8. $68 \times 5{,}123$
9. $23 \times 6{,}198$
10. $\$46 \times 58$
11. 18×47
12. 429×88
13. 31×759
14. $53 \times 3{,}827$
15. $19 \times 1{,}762$
16. $42 \times 23{,}891$
17. A card shop ordered 48 boxes of cards. Each box has 112 cards. About how many cards did the store order?
18. A store sold 272 day planners. Each day planner cost $12. About how much did the store earn for the planners?

Set C Find the product. Estimate to check. (pp. 66–69)

1. $\begin{array}{r} 73 \\ \times\ 6 \\ \hline \end{array}$
2. $\begin{array}{r} 49 \\ \times\ 3 \\ \hline \end{array}$
3. $\begin{array}{r} 502 \\ \times\ 8 \\ \hline \end{array}$
4. $\begin{array}{r} 639 \\ \times\ 2 \\ \hline \end{array}$
5. $\begin{array}{r} 391 \\ \times\ 7 \\ \hline \end{array}$
6. $\begin{array}{r} 452 \\ \times\ 6 \\ \hline \end{array}$
7. $\begin{array}{r} 2{,}186 \\ \times\ 9 \\ \hline \end{array}$
8. $\begin{array}{r} 5{,}063 \\ \times\ 7 \\ \hline \end{array}$
9. $3{,}926 \times 4$
10. $4{,}192 \times 8$
11. 823×4
12. 9×265
13. 470×6
14. 3×748
15. 902×5
16. $6 \times 2{,}695$
17. Claire sold 6 books of raffle tickets. Each book contains 32 raffle tickets. How many raffle tickets did she sell altogether?
18. Travis read all 8 books in a detective series. If each book has 245 pages, how many pages did he read in all?

CD ROM **Technology**
Use Harcourt Mega Math, The Number Games, *Tiny's Think Tank*, Levels K, V.

Set D Find the product. Estimate to check. (pp. 70–73)

1. 384×17
2. 503×24
3. 236×32
4. $\$1,963 \times 78$
5. 402×86
6. 209×46
7. 716×34
8. 185×16
9. 811×57
10. $\$2,084 \times 63$
11. 582×43
12. $5,004 \times 13$
13. 90×835
14. 193×36
15. $14 \times 2,607$
16. 41×738
17. 833×60
18. $19 \times 4,601$
19. $27 \times 3,018$
20. 19×278
21. Mr. Carter rides his bike 135 mi each week. How many miles does he ride in 52 weeks?
22. Paint Plus sold 392 gallons of paint at $27 for each gallon. How much were the total sales for the paint?

Set E Find the product. Estimate to check. (pp. 74–75)

1. 248×7
2. 396×4
3. $2,764 \times 5$
4. $6,952 \times 3$
5. $7,245 \times 6$
6. 219×37
7. 824×15
8. 412×40
9. $4,009 \times 28$
10. $3,016 \times 52$
11. $2,715 \times 9$
12. 847×62
13. 72×58
14. $2,716 \times 29$
15. $20 \times 2,145$
16. 452×37
17. $1,040 \times 72$
18. $63 \times 5,009$
19. $51 \times 4,082$
20. $9 \times 1,278$
21. There are 5 boxes of paper in a delivery. Each box has 450 sheets of paper. How many sheets of paper are in the delivery?
22. A company releases 3,275 newsletters each week. How many newsletters will the company release in 8 weeks?

Chapter 3 Review/Test

Check Vocabulary and Concepts

For 1, choose the better term from the box.

VOCABULARY
Distributive Property
partial product

1. The __?__ states that multiplying a sum by a number is the same as multiplying each addend in the sum by the number and then adding the products. **(AF 1.3, p. 64)**

2. Explain how you can use the Distributive Property to make it easier to find a product. **(NS 1.0, pp. 64–65)**

Check Skills

Find the product. **(NS 1.0, pp. 60–61)**

3. 80×20
4. 6×90
5. 70×500
6. $4 \times 3{,}000$
7. 400×30

Estimate the product. **(NS 1.1, pp. 62–63)**

8. 38×61
9. 56×878
10. $2{,}183 \times 49$
11. 91×327
12. $\$19.78 \times 27$

Estimate. Then find the product. **(NS 1.0, NS 1.1, pp. 66–69, 70–73)**

13. $\begin{array}{r} 56 \\ \times \ 8 \\ \hline \end{array}$
14. $\begin{array}{r} 782 \\ \times \ \ 5 \\ \hline \end{array}$
15. $\begin{array}{r} 918 \\ \times \ \ 3 \\ \hline \end{array}$
16. $\begin{array}{r} 438 \\ \times \ 29 \\ \hline \end{array}$
17. $\begin{array}{r} 723 \\ \times 158 \\ \hline \end{array}$

18. 428×7
19. $5 \times 3{,}105$
20. 268×73
21. 85×39
22. $42 \times 6{,}002$

Check Problem Solving

Solve. **(NS 1.0, NS 1.1, MR 3.2, pp. 74–77)**

23. At the book fair, hard cover books cost \$7 each and paperback books cost \$2 each. Dorothy spent \$40 on books at the fair. How many of each type of book did she buy?

24. Mr. Lindon spent \$129 to buy tickets to the concert. The tickets cost \$18 for adults and \$15 for children. How many of each type of ticket did he buy?

25. **WRITE Math** Estimate the product of 93×62. **Explain** how you can tell if the estimate is greater than or less than the actual product.

GO ONLINE **Technology** Use *Online Assessment.*

Enrich • Distributive Property

Compatible Numbers

Students are looking at fossils arranged in 4 display cases. Each case holds 140 fossils. How many fossils are there?

You can use **compatible numbers** and the Distributive Property to find the product mentally.

Find 4×140.

$4 \times 140 = 4 \times (100 + 40)$	Break apart 140 into compatible numbers. **Think:** $140 = 100 + 40$
$= (4 \times 100) + (4 \times 40)$	Use the Distributive Property. Multiply mentally.
$= 400 + 160$	Add mentally.
$= 560$	

So, there are 560 fossils.

Another Example

Find 6×48.

$6 \times 48 = 6 \times (m - n)$	Break apart 48 into compatible numbers.
$= (6 \times m) - (6 \times n)$	**Think:** $48 = 50 - 2$. Let $m = 50$ and $n = 2$.
$= (6 \times 50) - (6 \times 2)$	Use the Distributive Property. Multiply mentally.
$= 300 - 12$	Subtract mentally.
$= 288$	

Try It

Use compatible numbers and the Distributive Property to find the product mentally.

1. 2×156
2. 3×197
3. 5×210
4. 8×525
5. 6×395
6. 4×550
7. 2×176
8. 4×485
9. **Challenge** Sticker books in the museum gift shop cost \$6.50 each. How much do 4 sticker books cost?

WRITE Math **Explain** how you would find $3 \times 9{,}998$ mentally.

Achieving the Standards
Chapters 1–3

Number Sense

Eliminate choices.

See Item 1. Find the answer choices that compare only the populations of California and Texas. Then choose the correct comparison.

1. Which compares the populations of California and Texas? (Grade 4, O–π NS 1.2)

2000 State Populations	
State	**Population**
Texas	20,851,820
Ohio	11,353,140
California	33,871,648

A $33{,}871{,}648 > 20{,}851{,}820$

B $33{,}871{,}648 < 20{,}851{,}820$

C $33{,}871{,}648 > 11{,}353{,}140$

D $20{,}851{,}820 < 11{,}353{,}140$

2. A farmer plants 4608 artichoke plants in 8 equal rows. How many artichoke plants are in each row? (Grade 4, O–π NS 3.4)

A 576 **C** 586

B 581 **D** 601

3. Which is the decimal equivalent of $\frac{3}{10}$? (O–π NS 1.2)

A 3.0 **C** 0.03

B 0.3 **D** 0.003

4. WRITE Math **Explain** how you could estimate the total number of artichoke plants in Item 2. (Grade 4, O–π NS 1.1)

Measurement and Geometry

5. Which solid figure has 6 faces? (Grade 4 MG 3.6)

A square pyramid **C** cone

B cube **D** triangular prism

6. Will is making a copy of the California flag. Each side of the star on the flag measures 4 inches.

What is the perimeter of the star? (Grade 4 MG 1.0)

A 28 inches **C** 36 inches

B 32 inches **D** 40 inches

7. Look at the triangle.

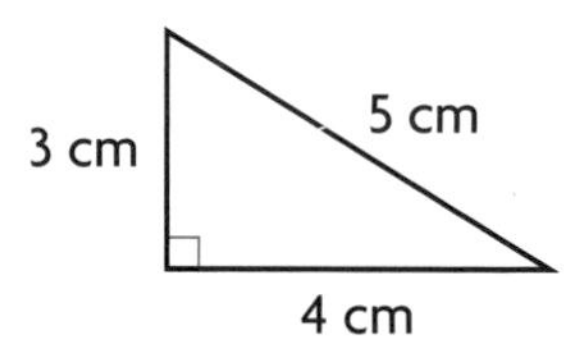

Which classifies the triangle? (Grade 4 MG 3.7)

A equilateral; right

B equilateral; acute

C scalene; right

D isosceles; right

8. WRITE Math **Explain** how you would find the area of a flag that is 6 feet long and 4 feet wide. (Grade 4 MG 1.4)

Algebra and Functions

9. If $f = 7$, what is the value of $28 - f$? (O-π AF 1.2)

   A 4 **C** 21

   B 11 **D** 35

10. Look at the input/output table.

Input	Output
x	y
12	6
24	12
36	18
48	■

   Which is the unknown number? (Grade 4 O-π AF 1.5)

   A 96

   B 60

   C 24

   D 20

11. At 10:00 A.M., the temperature was 25°F. By noon, the temperature had risen some degrees. Which expression shows the temperature at noon? (O-π AF 1.2)

   A $25 - t$

   B $25 + t$

   C $t - 25$

   D $25 \times t$

12. WRITE Math **Explain** how you could use the Distributive Property to find 3×46. (AF 1.3)

Statistics, Data Analysis, and Probability

13. Mrs. Boyd's fifth-grade class went on a field trip to San Diego, California. The Venn diagram shows the tourist attractions visited by the students.

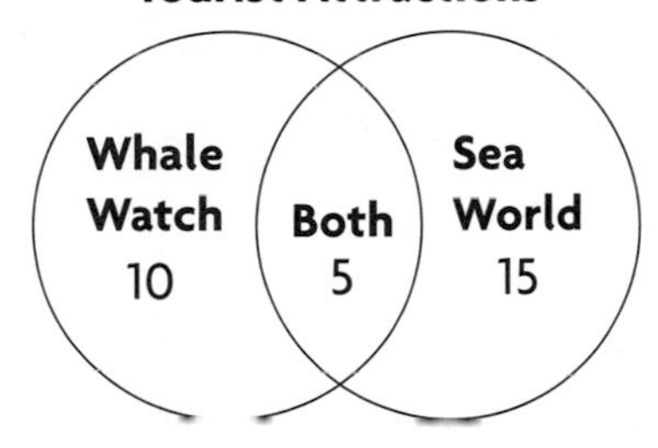

   How many students are in the class? (Grade 4 SDAP 1.0)

   A 5 **C** 25

   B 20 **D** 30

14. Look at the table below.

Magazine Sales	
Week	Number of Subscriptions
1	1240
2	989
3	3205
4	2754

   How many more magazines were sold in week 3 than week 4? (SDAP 1.0)

   A 1551 **C** 551

   B 1441 **D** 451

15. WRITE Math **Explain** how you would display information from a tally table in a frequency table. (Grade 4 SDAP 1.1)

4 Divide by 1- and 2-Digit Divisors

The Big Idea Division of a multi-digit number by a 1- or 2-digit number is based on place value and the basic multiplication and division facts.

Investigate

For the Rose Parade, bands will place between 6 and 11 band members in each row. Choose a band from the graph. Divide the band into rows using an equal number of members in each row. What is the greatest number that can be placed in equal rows? The least number?

2006 Rose Parade High School Bands

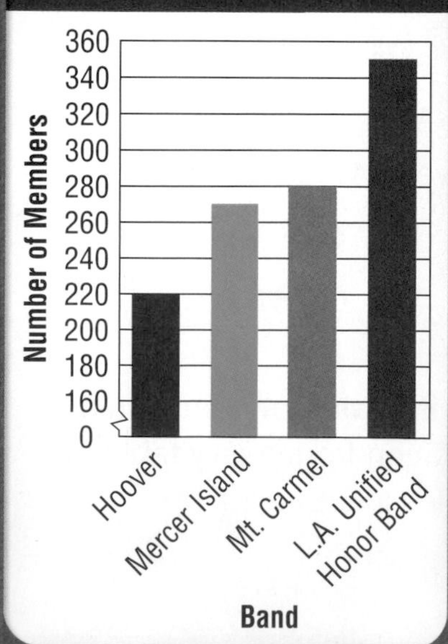

CALIFORNIA FAST FACT

The first marching band to appear in the Rose Parade of 1891 had fewer than 20 members. In 2006, the largest performing band had more than 600 members.

GO ONLINE Technology
Student pages are available in the Student eBook.

Show What You Know

Check your understanding of important skills needed for success in Chapter 4.

▶ Estimate Quotients

Estimate the quotient.

1. $4\overline{)130}$ **2.** $6\overline{)230}$ **3.** $3\overline{)280}$ **4.** $5\overline{)340}$

5. $8\overline{)500}$ **6.** $9\overline{)520}$ **7.** $4\overline{)390}$ **8.** $7\overline{)640}$

9. $400 \div 6$ **10.** $370 \div 6$ **11.** $610 \div 8$ **12.** $200 \div 3$

▶ Place the First Digit

Name the position of the first digit of the quotient.

13. $5\overline{)428}$ **14.** $2\overline{)361}$ **15.** $7\overline{)403}$ **16.** $9\overline{)572}$

17. $3\overline{)645}$ **18.** $4\overline{)793}$ **19.** $8\overline{)622}$ **20.** $6\overline{)917}$

▶ Multiply by 1- and 2-Digit Numbers

Find the product.

21. 78×6 **22.** 413×9 **23.** 826×5 **24.** 673×8

25. 329×12 **26.** 168×33 **27.** $2{,}716 \times 25$ **28.** $3{,}118 \times 34$

VOCABULARY POWER

CHAPTER VOCABULARY

algebraic expression
compatible numbers
dividend
divisor
evaluate
numerical expression
quotient
variable

WARM-UP WORDS

compatible numbers numbers that are easy to compute mentally

evaluate to find the value of a numerical or algebraic expression

quotient the number, not including the remainder, that results from dividing

LESSON 1

Estimate with 1-Digit Divisors

OBJECTIVE: Estimate quotients by using compatible numbers and rounding.

Quick Review

1. 15 ÷ 3
2. 24 ÷ 4
3. 32 ÷ 8
4. 49 ÷ 7
5. 54 ÷ 6

Vocabulary

compatible numbers

Learn

PROBLEM Tractor trailer trucks move cars from factories to dealerships. A truck can hold 9 cars. Last month, a dealership sold 405 cars. About how many truckloads of cars were sold?

You can round or use compatible numbers to estimate quotients.

Compatible numbers are numbers that are easy to compute mentally.

ONE WAY **Use compatible numbers. Estimate.** 405 ÷ 9

Step 1 Find multiples of 9.

9, 18, 27, 36, 45, 54, 63, 72, 81

Look at the beginning digits. Since 40 is between 36 and 45, use 36 and 45 as compatible numbers.

Step 2 Use 2 sets of compatible numbers to estimate the quotient.

405 ÷ 9
↓ ↓
360 ÷ 9 = 40

or

405 ÷ 9
↓ ↓
450 ÷ 9 = 50

Use the same place value in the estimate as in the original equation.

ANOTHER WAY **Use rounding and patterns in multiples of 10.**

Step 1

Round the dividend and the divisor to the first digit, each multiplied by the nearest power of 10.

405 ÷ 9
↓ ↓
400 ÷ 10

Step 2

Divide. 400 ÷ 10

Think: What can I multiply by 10 to get a product of 400?

10 × ■ = 400
■ = 40

400 ÷ 10 = 40

So, between 40 and 50 truckloads of cars were sold.

More Examples

A **Use compatible numbers.**

236 ÷ 4
↓ ↓
200 ÷ 4 = 50

or

236 ÷ 4
↓ ↓
240 ÷ 4 = 60

B **Use rounding.**

267 ÷ 3
↓ ↓
300 ÷ 3 = 100

NS 1.1 Estimate, round, and manipulate very large (e.g., millions) and very small (e.g., thousandths) numbers. *also* **NS 1.0, NS 2.2, MR 2.1, MR 2.3, MR 2.4, MR 3.2**

Guided Practice

1. Estimate 624 ÷ 8 using compatible numbers. 560 ÷ 8 = ■ 640 ÷ 8 = ■

Estimate the quotient.

2. $9\overline{)333}$ 3. $6\overline{)148}$ 4. $7\overline{)455}$ ✓5. $6\overline{)216}$ ✓6. $8\overline{)598}$

7. **TALK Math** **Explain** how you know that 40 is an overestimate for 351 ÷ 9.

Independent Practice and Problem Solving

Estimate the quotient.

8. $2\overline{)704}$ 9. $5\overline{)430}$ 10. $8\overline{)208}$ 11. $4\overline{)296}$ 12. $6\overline{)534}$

13. 268 ÷ 6 14. 894 ÷ 3 15. 324 ÷ 9 16. 832 ÷ 4 17. 595 ÷ 7

USE DATA For 18–20, use the table.

18. A motorcycle repair shop received a shipment of motors that included 7 Wind Rider motors. About how much does each Wind Rider motor weigh?

19. There are 6 Open Road motors in the shipment. About how much does each Open Road motor weigh?

20. The shipment included 6 Strada Sprint motors. About how much more does an Open Road motor weigh than a motor for a Strada Sprint?

21. **WRITE Math** **Explain** how to estimate 478 ÷ 7 using two sets of compatible numbers.

Motorcycle Motors Shipment by Total Weight

Kind of Motorcycle Motor	Total Weight (in pounds)
Open Road	936
Strada Sprint	684
Wind Rider	945

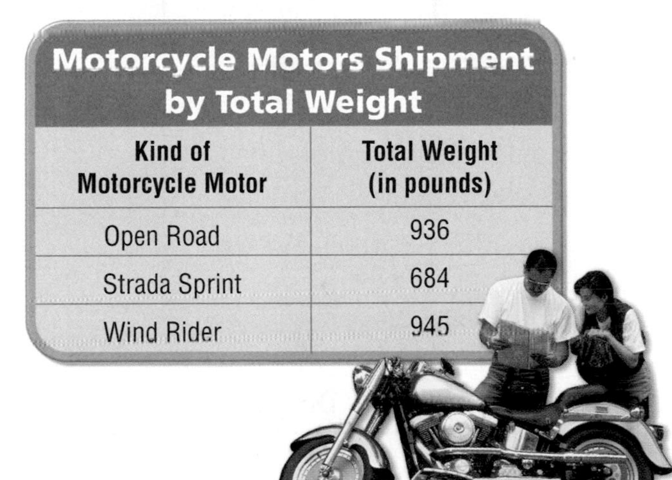

Achieving the Standards

22. 56 × 1,858 = (NS 1.1, p. 70)

23. Mikela has 2 hamsters, Bear and Fluff. Bear weighs 0.31 kilogram and Fluff weighs 0.27 kilogram. Which hamster weighs less? (NS 1.1, p. 46)

24. Estimate the product. (NS 1.1, p. 62)

 820 × 8,100

25. **Test Prep** Mr. Stone drove 458 miles in 3 days. If he drove about the same number of miles each day, how far did Mr. Stone drive in 1 day?

 A about 200 miles

 B about 150 miles

 C about 100 miles

 D about 90 miles

Extra Practice on page 108, Set A

LESSON 2

Divide by 1-Digit Divisors

OBJECTIVE: Divide 3-digit and 4-digit dividends by 1-digit divisors.

Quick Review

1. 5×9
2. 4×70
3. 6×60
4. 8×300
5. 7×800

The California gold rush began in 1848.

Learn

PROBLEM In 1854, a gold nugget weighing 195 pounds was found in Carson Hill, California. Suppose the gold nugget was melted down and made into 5 gold bricks. How many pounds would each gold brick weigh?

ONE WAY **Use estimation to place the first digit.**

Divide. $195 \div 5$.

Step 1

Estimate.

$5\overline{)150}$ = 30 or $5\overline{)200}$ = 40

So, place the first digit in the tens place.

$5\overline{)195}$ with ■ in the tens place

Step 2

Divide the 19 tens.

$$\begin{array}{r} 3 \\ 5\overline{)195} \\ -15 \\ \hline 4 \end{array}$$

Divide. $5\overline{)19}$
Multiply. 5×3
Subtract. $19 - 15$
Compare. $4 < 5$

Step 3

Bring down the 5 ones.
Divide the 45 ones.

$$\begin{array}{r} 39 \\ 5\overline{)195} \\ -15\downarrow \\ \hline 45 \\ -45 \\ \hline 0 \end{array}$$

Divide. $5\overline{)45}$
Multiply. 5×9
Subtract. $45 - 45$
Compare. $0 < 5$

So, each gold brick would weigh 39 pounds.

More Examples Divide.

A $8\overline{)4,872}$

Estimate: $4,800 \div 8 = 600$

$$\begin{array}{r} 609 \\ 8\overline{)4,872} \\ -48 \\ \hline 7 \\ -0 \\ \hline 72 \\ -72 \\ \hline 0 \end{array}$$

Since $7 < 8$, write 0 in the quotient in the tens place.

Check ✓

$$\begin{array}{r} \overset{7}{6}09 \\ \times\ \ 8 \\ \hline 4,872 \end{array}$$

B $9\overline{)1,700}$

Estimate: $1,800 \div 9 = 200$

$$\begin{array}{r} 188 \text{ r}8 \\ 9\overline{)1,700} \\ -9 \\ \hline 80 \\ -72 \\ \hline 80 \\ -72 \\ \hline 8 \end{array}$$

Check ✓

$$\begin{array}{r} 1\overset{7}{8}\overset{7}{8} \\ \times\ \ 9 \\ \hline 1,692 \end{array}$$

$$\begin{array}{r} 1,\overset{1}{6}\overset{1}{9}2 \\ +\ \ 8 \\ \hline 1,700 \end{array}$$

Remember
The remainder is the amount left over when a number cannot be divided evenly.

To check your answer, multiply the quotient by the divisor. Then add the remainder to get the dividend.

ANOTHER WAY Use place value to place the first digit.

Divide. 637 ÷ 7.

Step 1	Step 2	Step 3
Look at the hundreds.	Divide the 63 tens.	Bring down the 7 ones. Divide the 7 ones.
$7\overline{)637}$ 6 < 7, so look at the tens. $7\overline{)637}$ 63 > 7, so use 63 tens. Place the first digit in the tens place.	$\begin{array}{r} 9 \\ 7\overline{)637} \\ -63 \\ \hline 0 \end{array}$ Divide. $7\overline{)63}$ Multiply. 9×7 Subtract. $63 - 63$ Compare. $0 < 7$	$\begin{array}{r} 91 \\ 7\overline{)637} \\ -63 \\ \hline 07 \\ -7 \\ \hline 0 \end{array}$ Divide. $7\overline{)7}$ Multiply. 1×7 Subtract. $7 - 7$ Compare. $0 < 7$

So, the quotient is 91.

More Examples Divide.

C $5\overline{)2,654}$

$$\begin{array}{r} 530 \text{ r4} \\ 5\overline{)2,654} \\ -25 \\ \hline 15 \\ -15 \\ \hline 04 \end{array}$$

D $7\overline{)3,702}$

$$\begin{array}{r} 528 \text{ r6} \\ 7\overline{)3,702} \\ -35 \\ \hline 20 \\ -14 \\ \hline 62 \\ -56 \\ \hline 6 \end{array}$$

Check ✓

$$\begin{array}{r} 528 \\ \times \quad 7 \\ \hline 3,696 \end{array} \qquad \begin{array}{r} 3,696 \\ + \quad 6 \\ \hline 3,702 \end{array}$$

- Explain how you would check the answer to Example C.

Guided Practice

1. Use the estimate to find the position of the first digit of the quotient for $4\overline{)236}$.

   Estimate: $200 \div 4 = 50$.

Name the position of the first digit of the quotient. Then find the first digit.

2. $3\overline{)579}$
3. $5\overline{)1,035}$
4. $6\overline{)282}$
5. $8\overline{)1,766}$
6. $4\overline{)1,027}$

7. **TALK Math** **Explain** how you can tell without dividing whether a 3-digit number divided by a 1-digit number will have a quotient of 2 or 3 digits.

Independent Practice and Problem Solving

Name the position of the first digit of the quotient. Then find the first digit.

8. $5\overline{)275}$ **9.** $8\overline{)624}$ **10.** $3\overline{)468}$ **11.** $2\overline{)810}$ **12.** $8\overline{)2,546}$

13. $7\overline{)966}$ **14.** $4\overline{)3,220}$ **15.** $9\overline{)1,157}$ **16.** $6\overline{)6,723}$ **17.** $7\overline{)8,567}$

Divide. Check by multiplying.

18. $2\overline{)518}$ **19.** $6\overline{)618}$ **20.** $8\overline{)736}$ **21.** $4\overline{)1,716}$ **22.** $5\overline{)1,875}$

23. $3\overline{)223}$ **24.** $5\overline{)693}$ **25.** $4\overline{)762}$ **26.** $8\overline{)2,012}$ **27.** $2\overline{)1,729}$

28. $693 \div 9$ **29.** $2,203 \div 4$ **30.** $341 \div 2$ **31.** $3,632 \div 6$ **32.** $8,524 \div 7$

Algebra Write the missing number for each ■.

33. $564 \div 8 =$ ■ **34.** ■ $\div 3 = 317$ r2 **35.** ■ $\div 5 = 66$ r4 **36.** $685 \div$ ■ $= 97$ r6

USE DATA For 37–38, use the table.

37. If the Welcome gold nugget were turned into 3 gold bricks, how much would each brick weigh?

38. **Pose a Problem** Look back at Problem 37. Write a similar problem by changing the numbers and information. Then solve the problem.

39. There are 246 students going on a field trip to pan for gold. If each van holds 9 students, how many vans are needed? How many students will ride in the van that isn't full?

40. There are 420 students on a field trip. If there is 1 adult chaperone for every 8 students, how many chaperones have a full group of 8 students? How many students will be with the chaperone who has less than a full group?

41. WRITE Math **Explain** how you know where to place the first digit of the quotient in $374 \div 4$.

Large Gold Nuggets Found

Name	Weight	Location
Welcome Stranger	2,284 troy ounces	Australia
Welcome	2,217 troy ounces	Australia
Willard	788 troy ounces	California

Gold and other precious metals are measured in troy ounces.

Technology CD ROM
Use Harcourt Mega Math, The Number Games, *Up, Up, and Array,* Levels M, N, and O.

Extra Practice on page 108, Set B

Achieving the Standards

42. A computer keyboard has 114 keys. How many keys would 100 computer keyboards have? **(NS 1.0, p. 60)**

43. Vincent is 37 years old. His sister, Maggie, is 9 years younger. How old is Maggie? Write a numerical expression. Then find the value. **(AF 1.2, p. 22)**

44. Elena had $45. She spent some of her money to buy a sweater. Then Elena bought a snack for $6. Write an algebraic expression to show how much she had left. **(AF 1.2, p. 22)**

45. **Test Prep** One carton can hold 8 boxes of cereal. How many cartons are needed for 128 boxes of cereal?

A 1,024 **C** 16
B 17 **D** 8

46. **Test Prep** For a bake sale, a fifth-grade class made 324 cupcakes. The class put the cupcakes in packages of 5. How many cupcakes remained?

A 1,260 **C** 64
B 64 r4 **D** 4

Problem Solving and Reasoning

VISUAL THINKING The puzzles below are called number pyramids. You can use multiplication and division formulas to solve the puzzles.

To find the number in the top box, use the formula $A \times B = C$

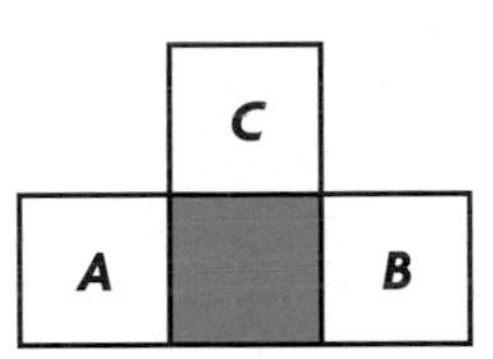

To find the number in the lower right box, use the formula $C \div A = B$

Example

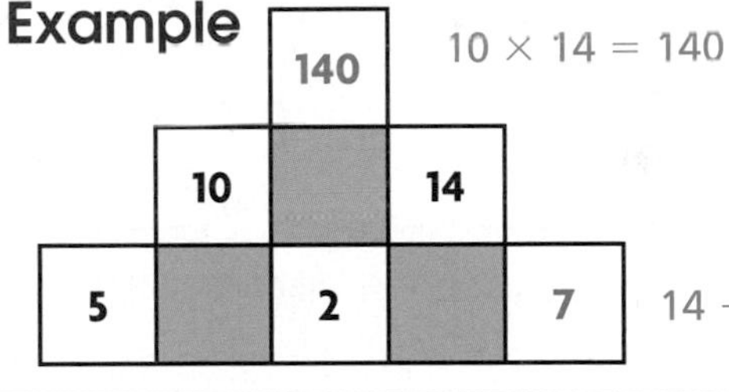

$10 \times 14 = 140$

$14 \div 2 = 7$

Copy and complete the number pyramids. Use the multiplication and division formulas.

1.

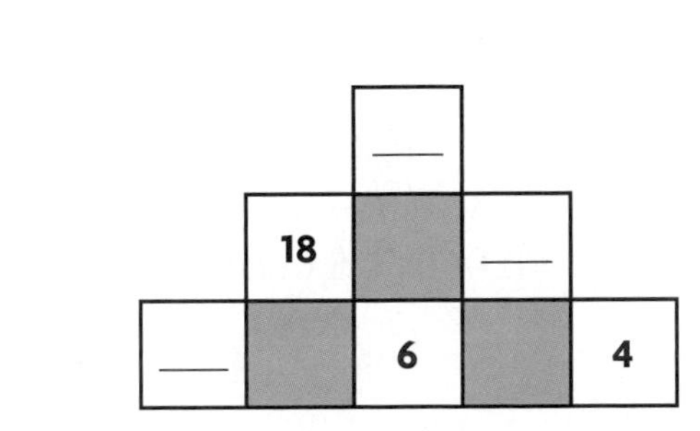

2.

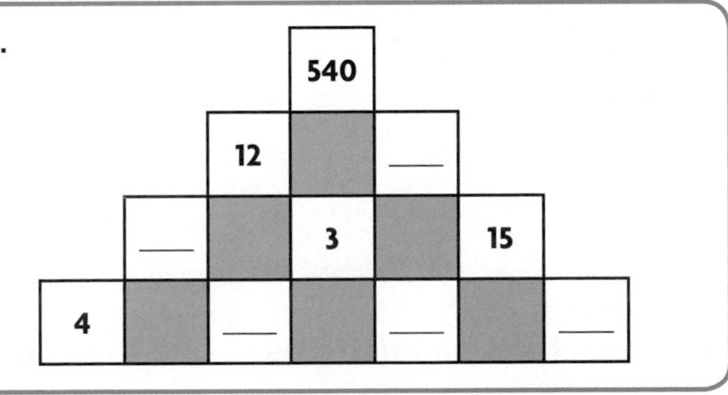

LESSON 3

ALGEBRA

Patterns in Division

OBJECTIVE: Use patterns to divide.

Quick Review

1. $10 \div 2$
2. $18 \div 3$
3. $24 \div 4$
4. $15 \div 5$
5. $32 \div 8$

Learn

PROBLEM A fifth-grade class wrote a book about the history of its school. The book has 40 sheets of paper. The class has 8,000 sheets of paper to make copies of the book. How many copies can the class make?

To find the quotient, you can start with a basic division fact and look for a pattern.

Math Idea

If the dividend increases by a power of 10, then the quotient increases by a power of 10.

Example **Divide.** $8{,}000 \div 40$

$8 \div 4 = 2$ ← basic fact
$80 \div 40 = 2$
$800 \div 40 = 20$
$8{,}000 \div 40 = 200$

So, the class made 200 copies.

More Examples

A
$27 \div 3 = 9$ ← basic fact
$270 \div 3 = 90$
$2{,}700 \div 3 = 900$
$27{,}000 \div 3 = 9{,}000$

B
$\$35 \div 5 = \$7$ ← basic fact
$\$350 \div 50 = \$7$
$\$3{,}500 \div 50 = \$70$
$\$35{,}000 \div 50 = \$700$

C
$6 \div 1 = 6$ ← basic fact
$6{,}000 \div 10 = 600$
$6{,}000 \div 100 = 60$
$6{,}000 \div 1{,}000 = 6$

- Explain the difference between the patterns in Example B and Example C.

Guided Practice

Find the missing numbers.

1. $9 \div 3 = 3$
   $90 \div 3 = 30$
   $900 \div 3 = n$
   $9{,}000 \div 3 = 3{,}000$

2. $24 \div 6 = 4$
   $240 \div 6 = 40$
   $2{,}400 \div 6 = 400$
   $24{,}000 \div 6 = n$

3. $40 \div 5 = n$
   $400 \div 50 = n$
   $4{,}000 \div 500 = n$
   $40{,}000 \div 5{,}000 = n$

Use basic facts and patterns to find the quotient.

4. $80 \div 2$
5. $140 \div 20$
✓6. $\$3{,}200 \div 8$
✓7. $36{,}000 \div 60$

NS 2.2 Demonstrate proficiency with division, including division with positive decimals and long division with multidigit divisors. *also* AF 1.2, MR 1.1, MR 2.3, MR 2.4, MR 3.2

8. TALK Math **Explain** why the quotient decreases as the number of zeros in the divisor increases.

Independent Practice and Problem Solving

Use basic facts and patterns to find the quotient.

9. $20 \div 10$
10. $180 \div 9$
11. $\$160 \div 40$
12. $420 \div 7$
13. $300 \div 50$
14. $640 \div 80$
15. $810 \div 9$
16. $540 \div 60$
17. $1,200 \div 4$
18. $\$1,000 \div 10$
19. $5,600 \div 70$
20. $3,600 \div 90$
21. $49,000 \div 70$
22. $60,000 \div 2$
23. $40,000 \div 20$
24. $\$25,000 \div 50$

Compare. Use <, >, or = for each ●.

25. $560 \div 80$ ● $5,600 \div 8$
26. $3,000 \div 5$ ● $300 \div 5$
27. $32,000 \div 40$ ● $3,200 \div 4$

28. A school ordered 40 cartons of paper weighing a total of 2,000 pounds. How much does 1 carton of paper weigh?

29. One carton holds 10 reams of paper, which is 5,000 sheets of paper. How many sheets of paper are in 1 ream?

30. A company is buying 4 laser printers for \$800. If each printer comes with a \$25 mail-in rebate, what is the cost of a single printer?

31. It takes about 3 trees to make 24,000 sheets of paper. About how many sheets of paper can be made out of one tree?

32. **Algebra** How would you find the value of n for $2,400 \div n = 80$?

33. WRITE Math **What's the Error?** Mela says that $66,000 \div 6$ is 1,100. What is her error?

Achieving the Standards

34. A garden measures 8 feet by 12 feet. What is the area of the garden in square feet? **(Grade 4 MG 1.4)**

35. The Rose Bowl stadium in Pasadena, California, has a capacity of 92,542 people. Round the stadium's capacity to the nearest thousand. **(NS 1.1, p. 12)**

36. $18 \times 39 =$ **(Grade 4 O━ NS 3.3)**

37. A hotel owner spends \$20,000 on 40 new television sets. How much does she spend on each television set if each costs the same amount?

A \$400
B \$500
C \$4,000
D \$5,000

Extra Practice on page 108, Set C

Estimate with 2-Digit Divisors

OBJECTIVE: Estimate quotients when dividing by 2-digit numbers.

Quick Review

1. 16 ÷ 2
2. 28 ÷ 4
3. 30 ÷ 5
4. 72 ÷ 8
5. 36 ÷ 12

Learn

PROBLEM The Transamerica Pyramid in San Francisco, California, is 853 feet tall and has 48 floors. If each floor is the same height, about how tall is each floor?

You can use compatible numbers to estimate quotients.

Example 1 Estimate. 853 ÷ 48

853 ÷ 48
↓ ↓
850 ÷ 50 = 17   850 and 50 are compatible numbers since 85 ÷ 5 = 17.

So, each floor is about 17 feet tall.

You can also estimate a quotient by using two sets of compatible numbers to find two different reasonable estimates.

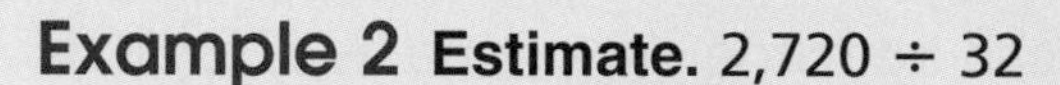

Example 2 Estimate. 2,720 ÷ 32

Think: 2,720 is between 2,700 and 3,000.

Use 2,700.

2,720 ÷ 32
↓ ↓
2,700 ÷ 30 = 90 ← 2,700 and 30 are compatible numbers since 27 ÷ 3 = 9.

Use 3,000.

2,720 ÷ 32
↓ ↓
3,000 ÷ 30 = 100 ← 3,000 and 30 are compatible numbers since 3 ÷ 3 = 1.

So, two reasonable estimates for 2,720 ÷ 32 are 90 and 100.

- Do you think that the estimate of 100 for 2,720 ÷ 32 is an overestimate or an underestimate? Explain.

Guided Practice

1. Estimate 149 ÷ 43 using two sets of compatible numbers.

   120 ÷ 40 = ■   or   ■ ÷ 40 = 4

Write two sets of compatible numbers for each. Then give two possible estimates.

2. $22\overline{)94}$
3. $68\overline{)523}$
4. $81\overline{)705}$
5. $43\overline{)2,326}$
6. $23\overline{)1,260}$

NS 1.1 Estimate, round, and manipulate very large (e.g., millions) and very small (e.g., thousandths) numbers. *also* **NS 2.2, MR 2.1, MR 2.3, MR 2.4, MR 2.5, MR 3.2**

Estimate the quotient.

7. $33\overline{)291}$ 8. $49\overline{)427}$ 9. $85\overline{)\$618}$ 10. $91\overline{)1{,}805}$ 11. $31\overline{)6{,}468}$

12. TALK Math **Explain** whether 60 or 70 is a more reasonable estimate for $4{,}158 \div 58$.

Independent Practice and Problem Solving

Write two sets of compatible numbers for each. Then give two possible estimates.

13. $42\overline{)396}$ 14. $56\overline{)413}$ 15. $71\overline{)580}$ 16. $21\overline{)1{,}716}$ 17. $59\overline{)4{,}636}$

18. $\$375 \div 63$ 19. $2{,}302 \div 34$ 20. $4{,}337 \div 74$ 21. $\$3{,}426 \div 47$ 22. $8{,}199 \div 77$

Estimate the quotient.

23. $19\overline{)228}$ 24. $25\overline{)\$595}$ 25. $27\overline{)914}$ 26. $96\overline{)831}$ 27. $31\overline{)6{,}468}$

28. $462 \div 83$ 29. $1{,}319 \div 41$ 30. $5{,}535 \div 74$ 31. $33{,}842 \div 36$ 32. $48{,}574 \div 53$

USE DATA **For 33–35, use the picture.**

33. About how many meters tall is each floor of the Chrysler Building?

34. Estimate the difference between the number of meters in each floor of the Columbia Center and the Aon Center.

35. **Reasoning** George ran for 45 minutes. Lily ran for 3,180 seconds. Who ran for the shorter amount of time?

36. WRITE Math **Explain** how you know the quotient $298 \div 31$ will be between 9 and 10.

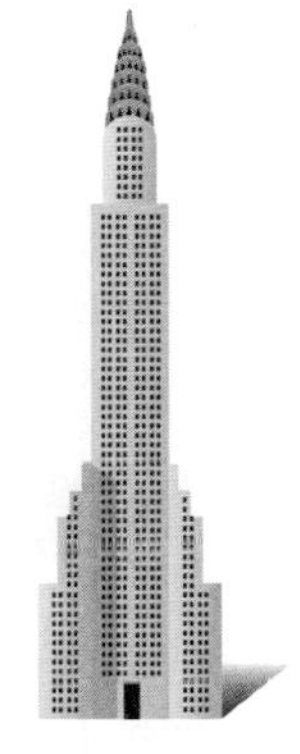

319 meters
77 floors
Chrysler Building
New York City

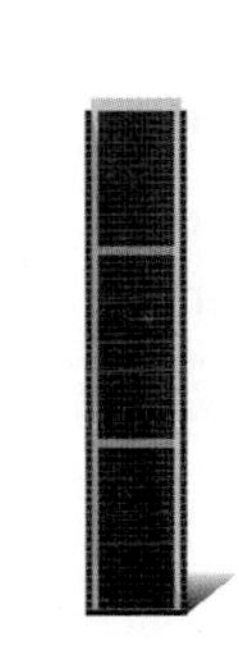

262 meters
62 floors
Aon Center
Los Angeles

295 meters
76 floors
Columbia Center
Washington

Achieving the Standards

37. What is the mode of the data set? (Grade 4 SDAP 1.2)

 74, 73, 82, 73, 65, 78, 81, 73, 82

38. The supermarket had a delivery of 132 cases of milk. If there were 18 gallons of milk in each case, how many gallons of milk were delivered? (NS 1.1, p. 70)

39. What number is represented by n?
 $9 \times n = 144$ (Grade 4 NS 1.1)

40. Joli built a tower out of building cubes. It was 640 centimeters tall. The height of each cube was 16 centimeters. What was the height of Joli's tower measured in building cubes?

 A 10 cubes **C** 40 cubes
 B 16 cubes **D** 400 cubes

Extra Practice on page 108, Set D

LESSON 5

Divide by 2-Digit Divisors

OBJECTIVE: Divide by 2-digit numbers.

Quick Review

1. 4×30
2. 6×19
3. 25×10
4. 46×20
5. 60×16

Learn

PROBLEM On average, each person in the United States eats 23 pounds of pizza every year. Based on this fact, how many years would it take one person in the United States to eat 1,000 pounds of pizza?

To solve the problem, you can divide by using place value.

Surveys of kids between the ages of 3 and 11 show that they prefer pizza for lunch and dinner to all other foods.▼

Example 1 Use place value.

Divide. $1000 \div 23$ $\quad 23\overline{)1000}$

Step 1

Estimate to place the first digit in the quotient.

23 is about 25.

$$\begin{array}{r} 40 \\ 25\overline{)1000} \end{array}$$

So, place the first digit of the quotient in the tens place.

Step 2

Divide the 100 tens by 23.

$$\begin{array}{r} 4 \\ 23\overline{)1,000} \\ -92 \\ \hline 8 \end{array}$$

Divide. $23\overline{)1,000}$
Multiply. 23×4
Subtract. $100 - 92$
Compare. $8 < 23$

Step 3

Bring down the 0 ones.
Divide 80 by 23.

$$\begin{array}{r} 43 \text{ r}11 \\ 23\overline{)1,000} \\ -92\downarrow \\ \hline 80 \\ -69 \\ \hline 11 \end{array}$$

Divide. $23\overline{)80}$
Multiply. 23×3
Subtract. $80 - 69$
Compare. $11 < 23$

Step 4

To check your answer, multiply the quotient by the divisor. Then add the remainder.

$$\begin{array}{r} 43 \\ \times 23 \\ \hline 129 \\ +860 \\ \hline 989 \end{array}$$

$989 + 11 = 1000$

So, it would take more than 43 years to eat 1,000 pounds of pizza.

NS 2.2 Demonstrate proficiency with division; including division with positive decimals and long division with multidigit divisors. *also* **NS 1.0, NS 1.1, MR 1.1, MR 2.1, MR 2.3, MR 2.4, MR 3.2**

Example 2 Use place value.

How many years would it take the average person in the United States to eat 1,158 pounds of pizza?

A **Divide.** $1{,}158 \div 23$ $\quad 23\overline{)1{,}158}$

Step 1

Estimate to place the first digit in the quotient.

$$\begin{array}{r} 50 \\ 20\overline{)1{,}000} \end{array}$$

So, place the first digit of the quotient in the tens place.

Step 2

Divide the 115 tens.

$$\begin{array}{r} 5 \\ 23\overline{)1{,}158} \\ -115 \\ \hline 0 \end{array}$$

Divide. $23\overline{)1{,}158}$
Multiply. 23×5
Subtract. $115 - 115$
Compare. $0 < 23$

Step 3

Bring down the 8 ones.
Divide the 8 ones.

$$\begin{array}{r} 50 \text{ r}8 \\ 23\overline{)1{,}158} \\ -115\downarrow \\ \hline 08 \\ -0 \\ \hline 8 \end{array}$$

Divide. $23\overline{)08}$
Multiply. 23×0
Subtract. $08 - 0$
Compare. $8 < 23$

So, it would take the average person in the U.S. more than 50 years to eat 1,158 pounds of pizza.

B $2{,}394 \div 63$ $\quad 63\overline{)2{,}394}$

Estimate. $\begin{array}{r} 40 \\ 60\overline{)2{,}400} \end{array}$

$$\begin{array}{r} 38 \\ 63\overline{)2{,}394} \\ -189\downarrow \\ \hline 504 \\ -504 \\ \hline 0 \end{array}$$

Check ✓

$$\begin{array}{r} {\scriptstyle 2} \\ 63 \\ \times 38 \\ \hline 504 \\ +1890 \\ \hline 2{,}394 \end{array}$$

C $1{,}506 \div 22$ $\quad 22\overline{)1{,}506}$

Estimate. $\begin{array}{r} 60 \\ 25\overline{)1{,}500} \end{array}$

$$\begin{array}{r} 68 \text{ r}10 \\ 22\overline{)1{,}506} \\ -132\downarrow \\ \hline 186 \\ -176 \\ \hline 10 \end{array}$$

Check ✓

$$\begin{array}{r} {\scriptstyle 1} \\ 68 \\ \times 22 \\ \hline 136 \\ +1360 \\ \hline 1{,}496 \end{array}$$

$1{,}496 + 10 = 1{,}506$

Guided Practice

1. Copy and complete the problem below to find $328 \div 31$.

Estimate: $\begin{array}{r} ■■ \\ 30\overline{)300} \end{array}$

$$\begin{array}{r} ■■ \text{ r}18 \\ 31\overline{)328} \\ -31\downarrow \\ \hline 18 \\ -\ \ 0 \\ \hline 18 \end{array}$$

Divide.

2. $18\overline{)648}$ 3. $22\overline{)929}$ ✓4. $53\overline{)2,369}$ ✓5. $62\overline{)3,774}$ 6. $47\overline{)7,395}$

7. TALK Math **Explain** how you would find $2,044 \div 28$.

Independent Practice and Problem Solving

Divide. Check your answer.

8. $24\overline{)744}$ 9. $46\overline{)874}$ 10. $39\overline{)975}$ 11. $73\overline{)584}$ 12. $57\overline{)855}$

13. $37\overline{)862}$ 14. $82\overline{)964}$ 15. $56\overline{)2,492}$ 16. $91\overline{)3,276}$ 17. $89\overline{)8,969}$

18. $916 \div 41$ 19. $707 \div 96$ 20. $298 \div 12$ 21. $1,117 \div 53$ 22. $2,816 \div 56$

Algebra Write the missing number for each ■.

23. $263 \div 13 =$ ■ r3 24. ■ $\div 35 = 3$ r24 25. $648 \div$ ■ $= 24$ 26. $416 \div 67 = 6$ r■

USE DATA For 27–30, use the list.

Each year, the average person in the U.S. eats...
• 68 quarts of popcorn
• 53 pounds of bread
• 19 pounds of apples
• 14 pounds of turkey
POPCORN

27. How many years would it take for the average person in the U.S. to eat 855 pounds of apples?

28. How many pounds of bread would the average person in the U.S. eat in 25 years?

29. How many quarts of popcorn would 6 average people in the U.S. eat in 5 years?

30. **Reasoning** Will the average person in the U.S. eat more pounds of turkey in 20 years or more pounds of apples in 15 years?

31. WRITE Math **Sense or Nonsense** The average person in the U.S. will eat more than 40,000 pounds of bread in his or her lifetime.

Achieving the Standards

32. One acre is 4,480 square yards. How many square yards are in 8 acres? (NS 1.0, p. 66)

33. What is the value of the expression $78 + n$ for $n = 67$? (AF 1.2, p. 22)

34. A parking garage holds 650 cars. The garage has 8 levels. About how many cars can each level hold? (NS 1.1, p. 88)

35. **Test Prep** A skyscraper has 48 floors with a total of 1,248 windows. Each floor has the same number of windows. How many windows does each floor have?

A 26

B 96

C 260

D 288

 Extra Practice on page 109, Set E

Up, Up, and Away!

Summarize

Over the years, many hot-air balloon distance records have been set. The first time that the Atlantic Ocean was crossed in a propane-fueled hot-air balloon was in 1987. This flight covered a distance of 2,900 miles and took the two pilots 33 hours. In 1991 the same two pilots crossed the Pacific, a distance of 6,700 miles, in 47 hours. In 1999, the first flight around the world covered a distance of 26,542 miles and took about 472 hours. Which balloon flight had the fastest average speed in miles per hour?

When you summarize, you restate the most important information in a shortened form to understand what you have read.

ONE WAY **Rewrite the paragraph in a shortened form.**

Summary: Several distance records have been set in hot-air balloons. In 1987, the record was 2,900 miles in 33 hours; in 1991, it was 6,700 miles in 47 hours; and in 1999, it was 26,542 miles in 472 hours. Which balloon flight had the fastest average speed?

ANOTHER WAY **Use a table for important information.**

Hot-Air Balloon Distance Records		
Year	**Distance Traveled (miles)**	**Time (in hours)**
1987	2,900	33
1991	6,700	47
1999	26,542	472

- The title of the table tells the main idea of the word problem.
- The table shows the information needed to solve the problem.

Problem Solving Summarize to understand the problem.

1. Solve the problem above.
2. Hot-air balloons once used helium gas. In 1978, the *Double Eagle II* used helium gas to cross the Atlantic, a distance of 3,120 miles, in 137 hours. Three years later, the *Double Eagle V*, crossed the Pacific Ocean, setting a new distance record of 3,535 miles. The flight took 84 hours. Which balloon flight had the faster average speed in miles per hour? Solve the problem.

Correcting Quotients

OBJECTIVE: Correct the quotient if the estimate is too high or too low.

Quick Review

Compare. Use <, >, or =.

1. 37 ● 35 **2.** 16 ● 19
3. 55 ● 55 **4.** 28 ● 48
5. 92 ● 29

Learn

PROBLEM An art class is using 336 crayons. All of the crayons are from 48-crayon boxes. How many boxes of crayons does the art class have?

Example **Divide.** $336 \div 48$ $48\overline{)336}$

Estimate. $300 \div 50 = 6$ or $350 \div 50 = 7$

Step 1

Divide, using your first estimate.

$48\overline{)336}$ quotient 6	Divide.	$336 \div 48$
-288	Multiply.	48×6
48	Subtract.	$336 - 288$
	Compare.	$48 = 48$

Since $48 = 48$, the estimate of 6 is too low.

Step 2

Correct the quotient. Divide, using your second estimate.

$48\overline{)336}$ quotient 7	Divide.	$336 \div 48$
-336	Multiply.	48×7
0	Subtract.	$336 - 336$
	Compare.	$0 < 48$

So, the art class has 7 boxes of crayons.

More Examples **Divide.**

A $536 \div 64$ $64\overline{)536}$

Estimate. $540 \div 60 = 9$ or $480 \div 60 = 8$

Divide.

$$\begin{array}{r} 9 \\ 64\overline{)536} \\ -576 \end{array}$$

$576 > 536$

The estimate of 9 is too high.

Correct the quotient.

$$\begin{array}{r} 8 \text{ r}24 \\ 64\overline{)536} \\ -512 \\ \hline 24 \end{array}$$

B $4{,}563 \div 37$ $37\overline{)4{,}563}$

Estimate. $4{,}400 \div 40 = 110$ or $4{,}800 \div 40 = 120$

Divide.

$$\begin{array}{r} 11 \\ 37\overline{)4{,}563} \\ -37 \\ \hline 86 \\ -37 \\ \hline 49 \end{array}$$

$49 > 37$

The estimate of 110 is too low.

Correct the quotient.

$$\begin{array}{r} 123 \text{ r}12 \\ 37\overline{)4{,}563} \\ -37 \\ \hline 86 \\ -74 \\ \hline 123 \\ -111 \\ \hline 12 \end{array}$$

- Explain how you know that an estimate of 5 is too low for $115 \div 19$.

NS 2.2 Demonstrate proficiency with division, including division with positive decimals and long division with multidigit divisors. *also* **NS 1.1, MR 2.1, MR 2.3, MR 2.4, MR 2.5, MR 3.2**

Guided Practice

1. Use compatible numbers to estimate the quotient.

   $74\overline{)528}$ $\quad 490 \div 70 = ■ \quad ■ \div 70 = 8$

Write *too high, too low,* or *just right* for each estimate.

2. $\begin{array}{r}400\\4\overline{)1{,}546}\end{array}$
3. $\begin{array}{r}30\\27\overline{)810}\end{array}$
4. $\begin{array}{r}90\\34\overline{)2{,}831}\end{array}$
5. ✓ $\begin{array}{r}20\\16\overline{)416}\end{array}$
6. ✓ $\begin{array}{r}50\\67\overline{)3{,}350}\end{array}$
7. TALK Math **Explain** how you know if an estimated quotient is too low or too high.

Independent Practice and Problem Solving

Write *too high, too low,* or *just right* for each estimate.

8. $\begin{array}{r}20\\26\overline{)541}\end{array}$
9. $\begin{array}{r}30\\53\overline{)1{,}592}\end{array}$
10. $\begin{array}{r}9\\38\overline{)327}\end{array}$
11. $\begin{array}{r}10\\43\overline{)688}\end{array}$
12. $\begin{array}{r}60\\67\overline{)4{,}873}\end{array}$

Choose the better estimate to use for the quotient. Write *a or b*.

13. $29\overline{)117}$ **a.** 3 **b.** 4
14. $18\overline{)786}$ **a.** 30 **b.** 40
15. $75\overline{)3{,}300}$ **a.** 40 **b.** 50

Divide.

16. $15\overline{)975}$
17. $37\overline{)264}$
18. $22\overline{)6{,}837}$
19. $59\overline{)126}$
20. $83\overline{)5{,}146}$
21. $2{,}135 \div 42$
22. $452 \div 31$
23. $1{,}067 \div 97$
24. $8{,}610 \div 82$
25. $592 \div 74$
26. Liz needs to buy 675 candles for a wedding reception. Each package contains 24 candles. How many packages should Liz buy?
27. A car repair shop ordered 192 ounces of a special hand cleaner. The cleaner comes in 16-ounce containers that costs $4 each. How much did the order cost?
28. WRITE Math **Explain** how you know that $785 \div 21$ will have a quotient that is less than 40.

Achieving the Standards

29. Write an algebraic expression for 85 less than some number. Use *n* for the number. (O-n AF 1.2, p. 22)
30. Alexis can type 55 words per minute. At this rate, how many words can Alexis type in 10 minutes? (NS 1.1, p. 60)
31. $231 \div 82 =$ (NS 2.2, p. 96)
32. **Test Prep** The Box of Socks Company packs 18 pairs of socks in a box. How many boxes are 810 pairs of socks packed in?

    A 40

    B 45

    C 50

    D 56

Extra Practice on page 109, Set F

Practice Division

OBJECTIVE: Practice division by 1- and 2-digit divisors.

Quick Review

1. $5\overline{)155}$
2. $7\overline{)287}$
3. $4\overline{)368}$
4. $6\overline{)426}$
5. $8\overline{)648}$

Learn

PROBLEM A cube can be made from 6 square cards. How many cubes can be made out of 1,896 cards?

Example 1 Divide. 1,896 ÷ 6 $6\overline{)1,896}$

Step 1

Estimate to place the first digit.

$$\begin{array}{r} 300 \\ 6\overline{)1,800} \end{array}$$

So, place the first digit of the quotient in the hundreds place.

Step 2

Divide the 18 hundreds.

$$\begin{array}{r} 3 \\ 6\overline{)1,896} \\ -18 \\ \hline 0 \end{array}$$

Step 3

Divide the 9 tens.

$$\begin{array}{r} 31 \\ 6\overline{)1,896} \\ -18 \\ \hline 9 \\ -6 \\ \hline 3 \end{array}$$

Step 4

Bring down the 6 ones. Divide the 36 ones.

$$\begin{array}{r} 316 \\ 6\overline{)1,896} \\ -18 \\ \hline 9 \\ -6 \\ \hline 36 \\ -36 \\ \hline 0 \end{array}$$

So, 316 cubes can be made out of 1,896 cards. Since the answer is close to the estimate of 300, it is reasonable.

More Examples Divide.

A $18\overline{)419}$

Estimate. 400 ÷ 20 = 20

$$\begin{array}{r} 23 \text{ r5} \\ 18\overline{)419} \\ -36 \\ \hline 59 \\ -54 \\ \hline 5 \end{array}$$

B $9\overline{)753}$

Estimate. 720 ÷ 9 = 80

$$\begin{array}{r} 83 \text{ r6} \\ 9\overline{)753} \\ -72 \\ \hline 33 \\ -27 \\ \hline 6 \end{array}$$

C $76\overline{)6,847}$

Estimate. 7,200 ÷ 80 = 90

$$\begin{array}{r} 90 \text{ r7} \\ 76\overline{)6,847} \\ -684 \\ \hline 07 \\ -00 \\ \hline 7 \end{array}$$

- What is 5,029 ÷ 7? Check your answer by multiplying.

NS 2.2 Demonstrate proficiency with division, including division with positive decimals and long division with multidigit divisors. *also* **NS 1.1, MR 2.1, MR 2.2, MR 2.3, MR 2.4; MR 2.5, MR 3.0, MR 3.2, MR 3.3**

Guided Practice

1. Estimate to place the first digit of the quotient for 232 ÷ 5. ■ ÷ 5 = ■

Divide. Multiply to check your answer.

2. $3\overline{)177}$
3. $28\overline{)2{,}688}$
4. $4\overline{)353}$
5. $41\overline{)3{,}085}$

6. **TALK Math** **Explain** how you can use division to find the missing number in $9 \times n = 1{,}332$.

Independent Practice and Problem Solving

Divide. Multiply to check your answer.

7. $8\overline{)2{,}744}$
8. $9\overline{)5{,}047}$
9. $25\overline{)15{,}325}$
10. $44\overline{)310{,}375}$
11. 9,088 ÷ 3
12. 12,422 ÷ 6
13. 45,090 ÷ 9
14. 74,608 ÷ 12

Algebra **Write the missing number for each ■.**

15. 532 ÷ ■ = 28
16. 2,493 ÷ 9 = ■
17. 863 ÷ 23 = 37 r■

USE DATA **For 18–20, use the table.**

Making Origami Cranes and Boxes

- By using a certain computer program, you can fold an origami box in about 4 minutes.
- Using the same computer program, you can fold an origami crane in about 10 minutes.

18. Using the method taught by the computer program, how many origami boxes can be folded in 336 minutes?
19. Malik spent 1,250 minutes making paper cranes for his sister's wedding. What is the greatest number of cranes Malik could have made?
20. **WRITE Math** **What's the Question?** Jed used the computer program to learn how to fold origami boxes. The answer is 106 origami boxes.

Achieving the Standards

21. Luis makes 4 stacks of cards. Each stack has 23 cards in it. How many cards does Luis use? (Grade 4 NS 3.0)
22. Gen has \$42.72. She earned \$19.50 for pet sitting. How much money does Gen have now? (Grade 4 NS 2.1)
23. Find the value of n.
$250 + n = 528$. (Grade 4 AF 1.1)
24. **Test Prep** A school cafeteria used 1,300 flour tortillas in one week. There are 24 tortillas in a package. How many packages of tortillas did the cafeteria use?

A 6

B 24

C 54

D 55

Extra Practice on page 109, Set G

Problem Solving Workshop
Skill: Interpret the Remainder

OBJECTIVE: Solve problems by using the skill *interpret the remainder.*

▶ This footpath is part of the Appalachian Trail.

Use the Skill

PROBLEM The Appalachian Trail is a 2,160-mile-long footpath that goes from Maine to Georgia. The Jacksons want to hike about 11 miles per day along 1,000 miles of the trail. Each of the division problems below uses this information.

When you solve a division problem with a remainder, the way you interpret the remainder depends on the situation and the question.

A The quotient stays the same. Drop the Remainder.

On how many days will the Jacksons hike at least 11 miles?

```
      90 r10
11)1,000
   -99
     10
     -0
     10
```

The miles left over are not enough for another 11-mile day. So, they will hike at least 11 miles for 90 days.

B Increase the quotient by 1.

How many days will it take to hike the entire 1,000 miles?

To hike the remaining miles will take 1 more day. So, it will take 91 days to hike the entire 1,000 miles.

C Use the remainder as the answer.

If the Jacksons hike 11 miles each day except the last day, how many miles will they hike on the last day?

The remainder is 10. So, they will hike 10 miles on the last day.

D Use the quotient and the remainder written as a fraction.

If the Jacksons' average hiking speed for 11 miles is 3 miles per hour, about how long will it take for them to hike 11 miles?

```
   3 2/3  ← Write the remainder as a fractional part of the
3)11        divisor. Use the remainder as the numerator
  -9        and the divisor as the denominator.
   2
```

So, it will take the Jacksons about $3\frac{2}{3}$ hours to hike 11 miles.

NS 2.2 Demonstrate proficiency with division, including division with positive decimals and long division with multidigit divisors. *also* MR 1.0, MR 2.0, MR 2.3, MR 2.4, MR 3.0, MR 3.1, MR 3.2, MR 3.3

Think and Discuss

Read to Understand
Plan
Solve
Check

Tell how you would interpret the remainder. Then give the answer.

A warehouse has 1,235 books to be shipped. Each shipping carton can hold 9 books.

a. How many cartons will be full?

b. How many cartons are needed for all of the books?

c. How many books will be in the last carton?

Guided Problem Solving

1. Amy and her family want to bike on Missouri's Katy Trail. They will bike a total of 224 miles along the Missouri river, and want to bike only 9 miles per day. On how many days will Amy and her family bike exactly 9 miles? How many days will their trip last in all?

First, divide to find the quotient and remainder. $9\overline{)224}$

Then, decide whether to use the remainder in your answer.

2. What if Amy's family wanted to bike only 165 miles at a rate of 9 miles per day? How long would it take for them to bike the entire distance? How many miles would they bike on the last day?

3. A total of 75 fifth-grade students are going on a field trip to a local park. The school is providing minivans to take the students to the park. If each minivan holds 9 students, how many minivans are needed?

Mixed Applications

4. Andrew is going hiking with 4 friends. He is making trail mix to take on the hike. He is using 5 ounces of peanuts, 6 ounces of cashews, and 12 ounces of raisins. If each hiker got the same amount of trail mix, how much would be left over?

5. A music store wants to hire a salesperson to work on weekends. The salesperson would work 10 hours on Saturday and 8 hours on Sunday. If the rate of pay is $8 per hour, how much would the salesperson earn each weekend?

6. WRITE Math Mrs. Smith wants to give each of her 36 students a certificate for a job well done. If there are 8 certificates in one package, is it reasonable to say that Mrs. Smith will need to buy 4 packages of certificates? **Explain.**

7. A restaurant can seat 228 people inside and 88 people outside on its patio. If each table inside can seat 6 people and each table outside can seat 4 people, how many tables are inside and outside the restaurant?

LESSON 9

Algebra: Multiplication and Division Expressions

OBJECTIVE: Write and evaluate expressions.

Quick Review

1. $45 + 16$
2. $33 - 18$
3. 7×8
4. $64 \div 8$
5. 123×5

Vocabulary

evaluate

Learn

PROBLEM Ann rents a bike for $5 per hour. Write an algebraic expression to represent the cost of renting a bike. Then evaluate the algebraic expression if Ann rents the bike for 4 hours.

When you **evaluate** an expression, you find its value. To evaluate an algebraic expression, you replace the variable with a given number, and then find the value of the numerical expression.

Example

Step 1

Write an algebraic expression to represent the cost of hourly bike rental.

$5 \times h$ ← hours rented

Step 2

Evaluate the algebraic expression.

$5 \times 4 = 20$ ← Replace h with 4.

So, it will cost Ann $20 to rent the bike for 4 hours.

More Examples Evaluate the algebraic expression.

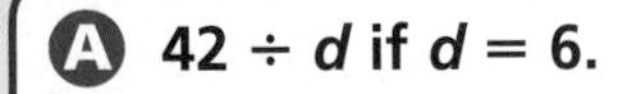

A $42 \div d$ if $d = 6$.

Step 1

Replace the variable d with 6.

$42 \div 6$

Step 2

Evaluate the expression.

$42 \div 6$
7

B $50m$ if $m = 12$.

Step 1

Replace the variable m with 12.

50×12

Step 2

Evaluate the expression.

50×12
600

READ Math

Each of these expressions can be read as "seven multiplied by n."

$7 \times n$ $\quad 7 \cdot n$

$7(n)$ $\quad 7n$

Guided Practice

1. Twenty-eight students are divided into equal groups. Choose the expression at the right that represents the number of students in each group. Then find how many students are in each group if there are 7 groups.

$28 + n$ $\quad 28 \div n$

$28n$ $\quad 28 - n$

AF 1.2 Use a letter to represent an unknown number; write and evaluate simple algebraic expressions in one variable by substitution. *also* **AF 1.0, NS 2.2, MR 2.3, MR 2.4, MR 3.2**

Write an algebraic expression for each phrase.

2. 18 books on each of x shelves
3. 63 CDs more than s
4. 56 students in m equal groups

Evaluate each expression if $n = 4$.

5. $n + 49$
6. $16 - n$
7. $21 \times n$
8. $36 \div n$
9. $137n$

10. TALK Math **Explain** how to evaluate the algebraic expression $27w$ if $w = 10$.

Independent Practice and Problem Solving

Write an algebraic expression for each phrase.

11. 6 groups of y items
12. r divided into 8 equal groups
13. 3 less than w

Evaluate each expression if $a = 7$ and $c = 22$.

14. $18 + a$
15. $c - 3$
16. $32 \times a$
17. $84 \div a$
18. $8c$

USE DATA For 19–21, use the table.

Service	Cost (in dollars)
Campsite rental (per day)	30
Firewood bundle (per bundle)	10
Bike rental (per hour)	5
Canoe rental (per hour)	10

PARK SERVICE COSTS

19. Sue wants to go canoeing for h hours. Write an algebraic expression to represent how much her canoe trip will cost.

20. Glenn bought b bundles of firewood. How much did his bundles cost in all? Write and evaluate an algebraic expression for $b = 3$.

21. **Reasoning** Lita has paid for bike rental for 5 hours. She has biked for n hours. For how many more hours can she bike? Write and evaluate an algebraic expression for $n = 3$.

22. WRITE Math **Explain** the difference between $x \div 9$ and $9 \div x$.

Achieving the Standards

23. In how many different ways can you write 19 as the product of two numbers? (Grade 4 NS 4.2)

24. 312×23 (NS 1.1, p. 70)

25. What is the name of a triangle that has exactly 2 equal sides? (Grade 4 MG 3.0)

26. **Test Prep** Jude has 16 pencils to share among r students. Which algebraic expression shows how many pencils each student will have?

A $16 - r$

B $16 + r$

C $16r$

D $16 \div r$

Extra Practice on page 109, Set H

Extra Practice

Set A Estimate the quotient. (pp. 86–87)

1. $2\overline{)510}$
2. $4\overline{)216}$
3. $8\overline{)3{,}684}$
4. $5\overline{)3{,}105}$
5. $455 \div 7$
6. $862 \div 9$
7. $7{,}124 \div 2$
8. $9{,}365 \div 4$

Set B Name the position of the first digit of the quotient. Then find the first digit. (pp. 88–91)

1. $2\overline{)724}$
2. $5\overline{)260}$
3. $4\overline{)1{,}248}$
4. $9\overline{)3{,}779}$
5. $6\overline{)7{,}592}$
6. $4\overline{)624}$
7. $2\overline{)804}$
8. $5\overline{)3{,}955}$

Divide. Check by multiplying.

9. $4\overline{)624}$
10. $2\overline{)804}$
11. $3\overline{)1{,}119}$
12. $5\overline{)4{,}603}$
13. $296 \div 2$
14. $510 \div 3$
15. $9{,}234 \div 9$
16. $1{,}523 \div 4$
17. Ellie bought 7 same-size bags of mulch for her garden. The total weight was 175 pounds. How much did each bag weigh?
18. A florist packaged 1,125 tulip bulbs. He put 9 bulbs in each package. How many packages of bulbs did he make?

Set C Use basic facts and patterns to find the quotient. (pp. 92–93)

1. $40 \div 20$
2. $280 \div 7$
3. $\$120 \div 60$
4. $200 \div 10$
5. $320 \div 8$
6. $\$400 \div 50$
7. $210 \div 3$
8. $540 \div 90$
9. $1{,}600 \div 4$
10. $\$5{,}000 \div 10$
11. $4{,}200 \div 70$
12. $1{,}800 \div 30$
13. $21{,}000 \div 3$
14. $64{,}000 \div 80$
15. $\$45{,}000 \div 9$
16. $16{,}000 \div 20$
17. The drama club collected $360 from the sale of 90 tickets. If all the tickets were the same price, what was the price of each ticket?
18. Seats in a theater are arranged in 80 rows. There are 1,600 seats. How many seats are in each row?

Set D Estimate the quotient. (pp. 94–95)

1. $18\overline{)210}$
2. $36\overline{)\$795}$
3. $72\overline{)265}$
4. $61\overline{)3{,}884}$
5. $263 \div 49$
6. $305 \div 56$
7. $5{,}999 \div 27$
8. $\$1{,}853 \div 51$

Technology
Use Harcourt Mega Math, The Number Games, *Up, Up, and Array,* Levels L, M, N, Q, R.

Set E Divide. Check your answer. (pp. 96–99)

1. $22\overline{)836}$
2. $38\overline{)608}$
3. $54\overline{)486}$
4. $18\overline{)446}$
5. $15\overline{)630}$
6. $82\overline{)256}$
7. $65\overline{)572}$
8. $45\overline{)126}$
9. $804 \div 67$
10. $450 \div 12$
11. $381 \div 74$
12. $826 \div 13$
13. $14\overline{)965}$
14. $23\overline{)280}$
15. $51\overline{)831}$
16. $65\overline{)687}$
17. A produce stand owner put 460 jars of apple butter on shelves. There were 92 jars on each shelf. How many shelves were used?
18. There are 378 pumpkins displayed in rows. There are 54 pumpkins in each row. How many rows are there?

Set F Which estimate is better to use for the quotient? Choose *a* or *b*. (pp. 100–101)

1. $63\overline{)352}$ **a.** 5 **b.** 6
2. $46\overline{)5,798}$ **a.** 110 **b.** 120
3. $43\overline{)3,192}$ **a.** 70 **b.** 80

Divide.

4. $48\overline{)336}$
5. $21\overline{)950}$
6. $34\overline{)192}$
7. $58\overline{)453}$
8. Teachers at Park Elementary need 180 rulers. Each package contains 12 rulers. How many packages should they buy?
9. A toy company packs 18 of the same game in one box. In how many boxes would 288 games be packed?

Set G Divide. Multiply to check your answer. (pp. 102–103)

1. $5\overline{)171}$
2. $4\overline{)516}$
3. $2\overline{)175}$
4. $3\overline{)1,437}$
5. $7\overline{)4,567}$
6. $93\overline{)812}$
7. $62\overline{)1,643}$
8. $84\overline{)2,536}$
9. $3\overline{)3,012}$
10. $52\overline{)4,715}$
11. $56\overline{)2,072}$
12. $43\overline{)3,609}$
13. $907 \div 5$
14. $380 \div 76$
15. $5,236 \div 44$
16. $1,608 \div 24$

Set H Write an algebraic expression. Evaluate each expression if $a = 5$ and $c = 12$. (pp. 106–107)

1. 128 divided into p groups
2. t divided into 6 equal groups
3. 12 groups of c items
4. 16 less than y
5. $19 + a$
6. $a \div 5$
7. $c \times 20$
8. $105 \div a$
9. $c + 39$
10. $8a$
11. $132 \times a$
12. $12 - c$

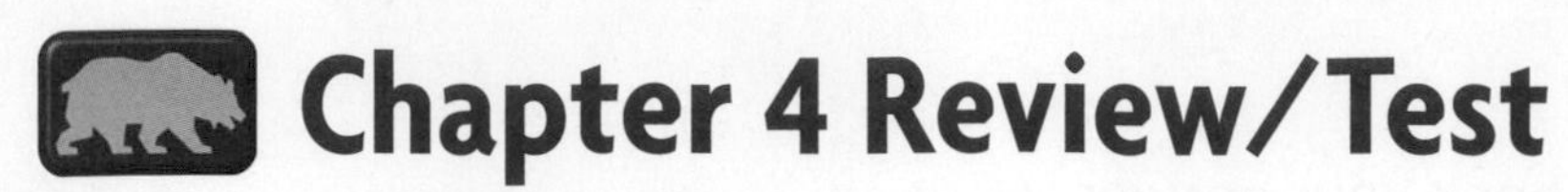

Chapter 4 Review/Test

Check Vocabulary and Concepts

Choose the best term from the box.

VOCABULARY
compatible numbers
evaluate
variables

1. You ___?___ an expression when you find its value. (AF 1.2, p. 106)
2. Numbers that are easy to compute mentally are called ___?___. (NS 1.1, p. 86)

Check Skills

Estimate the quotient. (NS 1.1, pp. 86–87, 94–95)

3. $5\overline{)275}$
4. $2\overline{)5,032}$
5. $345 \div 7$
6. $3,782 \div 4$
7. $18\overline{)170}$
8. $63\overline{)\$2,541}$
9. $168 \div 52$
10. $3,982 \div 39$

Find the quotient. (NS 2.2, pp. 92–93)

11. $60 \div 30$
12. $240 \div 8$
13. $\$4,500 \div 90$
14. $17,000 \div 10$

Divide. (NS 2.2, pp. 96–99, 100–101, 102–103)

15. $6\overline{)372}$
16. $3\overline{)6,105}$
17. $462 \div 9$
18. $8,253 \div 4$
19. $3\overline{)309}$
20. $3\overline{)2,516}$
21. $21\overline{)315}$
22. $75\overline{)5,328}$
23. $594 \div 28$
24. $893 \div 47$
25. $4,082 \div 68$
26. $5,304 \div 51$

Evaluate each expression for $a = 3$ or $c = 18$. (AF 1.2, pp. 106–107)

27. $2 + a$
28. $c - 12$
29. $21 \times a$
30. $99 \div a$
31. $5c$

Check Problem Solving

Solve. (NS 2.2, MR 1.0, MR 2.4, pp. 104–105)

32. A total of 105 students are going on a field trip. There must be one chaperone for each group of 5 students. How many chaperones are needed for the trip?

33. WRITE Math Suppose 108 students were going on the field trip. **Explain** how to determine the number of chaperones needed if there is one chaperone for each group of 5 students.

GO ONLINE **Technology** Use *Online Assessment.*

Enrich • Divide by 12

Mod 12

Standard time divides a 24 hour day into two groups of 12 hours. Military time does not divide a day into two groups. Instead, military time is given as part of a 24 hour day.

PROBLEM A military air show is scheduled to begin at 16:00. What time does the air show start, expressed in standard time?

One Way

You can use a standard, 12-hour clock face to find the time. Begin at zero and count around the clock 16 places. After passing all twelve A.M. hours, you will land at 4 o'clock P.M.

Another Way

You also can use **modular arithmetic** to find the time.

Modular arithmetic uses a repeating cycle of numbers and remainders to express a value. When the numbers reach a certain value, called the modulus, they repeat. The number 16 expressed in mod 12 is the same as the remainder left after dividing 16 by 12.

$16 \div 12 = 1$ r4 $\longrightarrow$ 16 mod 12 = 4

So, the show will begin at 4 P.M.

Examples

A Ricki went to sleep at 21:00. What is her bedtime in standard time?

21 mod 12 $\longrightarrow$ $21 \div 12 = 1$ r9 $\longrightarrow$ She went to bed at 9 P.M.

B John has 39 collector cards. How would you express 39 in mod 12?

39 mod 12 $\longrightarrow$ $39 \div 12 = 3$ r3 $\longrightarrow$ So, 39 mod 12 is 3.

Try It

Express each value in mod 12. Show your work.

1. 87 **2.** 117 **3.** 200 **4.** 14:00 **5.** 62

6. WRITE Math **Explain** how you would use modular arithmetic to express 11 P.M. in military time.

Unit Review/Test
Chapters 1–4

Multiple Choice

1. What is 5,309.348 rounded to the nearest hundred? (NS 1.1, p. 12)

   A 5,300

   B 5,309

   C 5,309.35

   D 5,309.3

2. The total area of the state of California is 163,707 square miles. What is this value rounded to the nearest thousand square miles? (NS 1.1, p. 12)

   A 163,000

   B 163,700

   C 164,000

   D 200,000

3. A zoo had 8,872 visitors on Saturday. On Sunday, 9,305 people visited the zoo. How many people visited the zoo over the two days? (NS 1.1, p. 16)

   A 17,177

   B 18,177

   C 18,179

   D 18,277

4. What is 0.3 written as a fraction? (O-π NS 1.2, p. 38)

   A $\frac{1}{3}$

   B $\frac{1}{4}$

   C $\frac{1}{2}$

   D $\frac{3}{10}$

5. Which point on the number line *best* represents 0.28? (O-π NS 1.5, p. 38)

   A 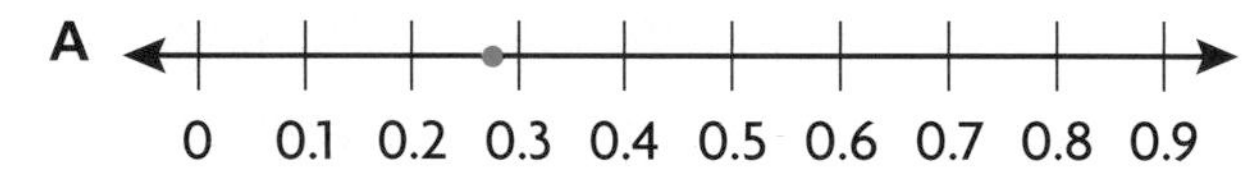

   B 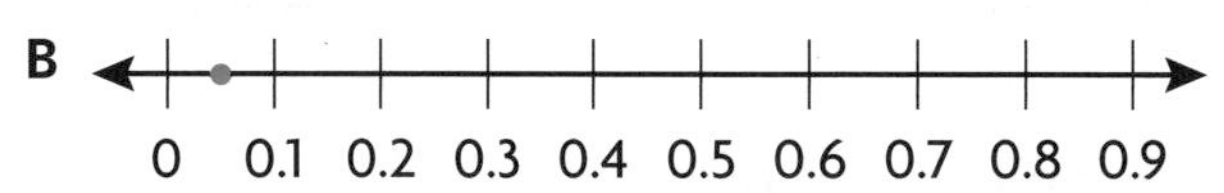

   C 0 0.1 0.2 0.3 0.4 0.5 0.6 0.7 0.8 0.9

   D 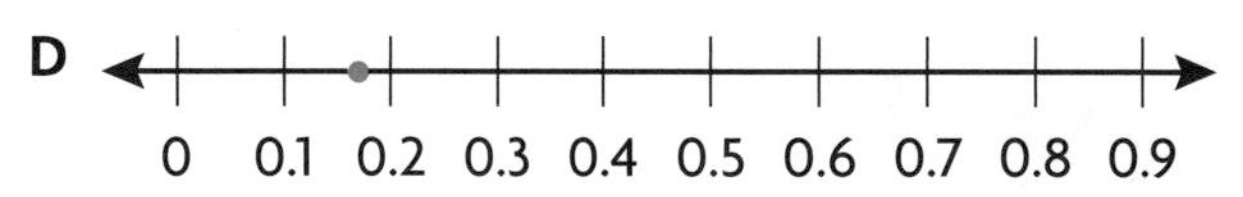

6. $4,302 \div 18 =$ (O-π NS 2.2, p. 96)

   A 23

   B 228

   C 239

   D 339

GO ONLINE **Technology** Use *Online Assessment.*

7. Find the quotient: 24,912 divided by 48. (O—π NS 2.2, p. 96)

A 19

B 519

C 525

D 629

8. What value for *y* makes this equation true? (AF 1.3, p. 106)

$$9 \times y = 162$$

A 15

B 17

C 18

D 20

9. What situation could be described by the expression $s \div 3$? (O—π AF 1.2, p. 106)

A Tim had *s* amount of marbles, then won 3 more marbles.

B Tim had *s* amount of marbles, then won 3 times as many marbles.

C Tim had *s* amount of marbles, then gave 3 marbles to his friend.

D Tim had *s* amount of marbles, then shared them equally with 3 friends.

Short Response

10. Write an equivalent decimal and fraction for the model shown. (O—π NS 1.2, p. 42)

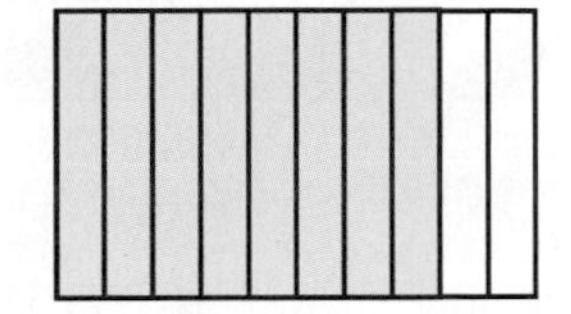

11. An auditorium has 18 rows of chairs. Each row has 21 chairs each. About how many chairs are in the auditorium? (NS 1.1, p. 70)

12. Copy the numbers below. Next to each number, write the letter that represents the quantity on the number line. (O—π NS 1.5, p. 38)

1.3 0.5 3.6 2.4

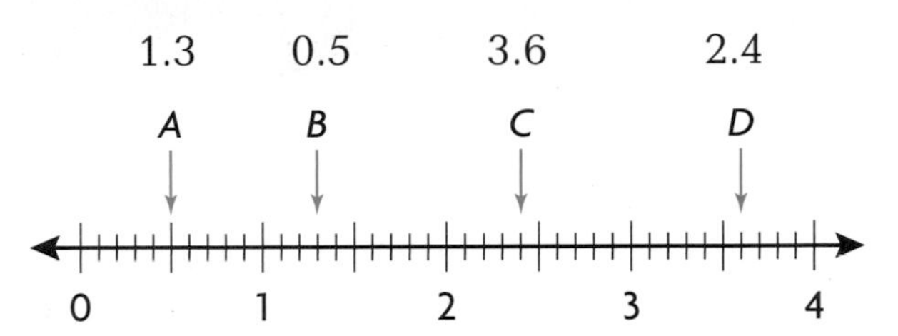

Extended Response WRITE Math

13. At a soccer camp, the number of players has increased each year as shown in the table. What might be the pattern for the number of players from one year to the next? How many soccer players do you predict will attend the camp in year 6? **Explain.** (O—π AF 1.5, p. 26)

Year	Soccer Players
1	150
2	175
3	200
4	225

14. The problem below shows part of the quotient for $864 \div 24$. How many tens does the digit in the tens place of the quotient show? What digit is missing? **Explain** how to find it. (O—π NS 2.2, p. 96)

$$\begin{array}{r} 3\blacksquare \\ 24\overline{)864} \\ -72 \\ \hline 144 \\ -144 \\ \hline 0 \end{array}$$

California

Problem Solving

from THE WORLD ALMANAC FOR KIDS

Racing in California

California Speedway

Many racing fans travel to the closest speedway to cheer on their favorite driver and car. Different kinds of cars, and even trucks and motorcycles, are raced in different competitions throughout the year. Drivers and their teams can earn millions of dollars!

The California Speedway near Fontana, California opened in 1997. It has a 2-mile track and hosts races as long as 500 miles. The grandstand can hold 92,100 fans as they watch the cars race up to 200 miles per hour.

FACT·ACTIVITY

For 1–5, use the data on this page.

1. Whose earnings have a zero in the hundred thousands place?
2. Order the drivers' earnings from greatest to least.
3. Estimate how much more money Driver 4 made than Driver 1.
4. What is the difference in earnings between Driver 2 and Driver 3?
5. **Pose a Problem** Write a problem like question 3. Choose at least one different driver.

Earnings Won at the California Speedway

Driver	Earnings
Driver 1	$5,840,067
Driver 2	$5,963,574
Driver 3	$5,934,504
Driver 4	$6,036,554

ALMANAC **Fact**

The California Speedway keeps fans informed with 338 speakers, 20 assisted hearing devices, and 750 television monitors.

500,000 Steps

How many steps do you walk in a day? California Speedway promotes better health for families and children in Southern California by challenging people to take 500,000 steps between racing seasons.

Families and children can use a *pedometer*, a device that measures the number of steps taken, to track their progress. Early in the program, a race-car driver had already walked 34,785 steps, a sports reporter had walked 39,835 steps, and a race-car executive had taken 48,221 steps.

FACT • ACTIVITY

Answer the questions.

1. Order the steps walked from greatest to least.
2. How many more steps does the race-car driver need to take to reach the goal of 500,000?
3. Track your own progress.
   - Measure out 10 feet. Count the number of steps you take while walking the 10 feet. Use this to help you estimate your steps.
   - Estimate the number of steps you take in a day. Now estimate how many steps you take in a week. How long will it take you to reach the goal of 500,000 steps?
   - Count your steps to school. Compare your data with your classmates. Who takes more steps to school? How many more? Write a number sentence to show the results.

UNIT 2

Number Theory and Fraction Concepts

Math on Location

1 ▲ Beats of 3, 4, or 8 per measure form repeating patterns or rhythms on electronic drums.

2 ▲ Like patterns of factors, the rhythm is combined with another recorded, but different, rhythm.

3 ▲ Electronic equipment displays the recorded rhythms as patterns that can be viewed.

VOCABULARY POWER

TALK Math

What math is used in music in the **Math on Location**? How can you determine when two different rhythm patterns will share a single beat?

READ Math

REVIEW VOCABULARY You learned the words below when you learned about factors and fractions. How do these words relate to **Math on Location**?

common factor a number that is a factor of two or more numbers

factor a number that is multiplied by another number to find a product

mixed number a number represented by a whole number and a fraction

WRITE Math

Copy and complete the table below. Use what you know about patterns.

Question	Rhythms
How many beats in 7 measures?	2 beats per measure: 2, 4, 6, 8, 10, 12, 14, 16, 18
When do two different rhythms share beats?	2, 3 beats per measure: 2, 4, 6, 8, 10, 12, 14, __, __ 3, 6, 9, 12, __, __, __
When do two different rhythms share beats?	3, 4 beats per measure: 3, 6, 9, __, __, __, __, __ 4, 8, __, __, __, __, __

CHAPTER

5 Number Theory

The Big Idea The study of number theory builds understanding of factors, exponents, and prime and composite numbers.

CALIFORNIA FAST FACT

Since 1959, the championship game of the Little League World Series has been played at Howard J. Lamade Stadium in Williamsport, Pennsylvania.

Investigate

The table shows some of the highest-scoring championship games since the Little League World Series began in 1947. Choose 3 games. Write the prime factorization for both scores of each game. Do the scores share any of the same prime factors?

Little League World Series Highest Scoring Championship Games

Year	Winner	Score	Runner-Up
1998	New Jersey	12–9	Japan
1987	Taiwan	21–1	California
1971	Taiwan	12–3	Indiana
1959	Michigan	12–0	California
1947	Williamsport, PA	16–7	Lock Haven, PA

Technology
Student pages are available in the Student eBook.

Show What You Know

Check your understanding of important skills needed for success in Chapter 5.

▶ Multiplication and Division Facts

Find the product.

1. 3×7 **2.** 4×2 **3.** 8×5 **4.** 6×4

5. 7×9 **6.** 3×8 **7.** 5×9 **8.** 9×6

9. 2×5 **10.** 8×8 **11.** 7×4 **12.** 2×9

Find the quotient.

13. $16 \div 4$ **14.** $20 \div 5$ **15.** $30 \div 6$ **16.** $24 \div 3$

17. $49 \div 7$ **18.** $32 \div 8$ **19.** $56 \div 7$ **20.** $54 \div 9$

21. $12 \div 2$ **22.** $36 \div 4$ **23.** $81 \div 9$ **24.** $15 \div 5$

▶ Factors

Write all the factors for each number.

25. 10 **26.** 23 **27.** 20 **28.** 12

29. 17 **30.** 36 **31.** 72 **32.** 50

33. 42 **34.** 37 **35.** 28 **36.** 66

VOCABULARY POWER

CHAPTER VOCABULARY

base
composite number
exponent
factor tree
perfect square
prime factorization
prime number
square number
square root

WARM-UP WORDS

composite number a number having more than two factors

prime number a number that has exactly two factors: 1 and itself

base a number used as a repeated factor

LESSON 1 HANDS ON

Hands On: Prime and Composite Numbers

OBJECTIVE: Identify factors and tell whether a number is prime or composite.

Quick Review

Write *true* or *false*.

1. 5 is a factor of 15.
2. 4 is a factor of 18.
3. 7 is a factor of 27.
4. 8 is a factor of 32.
5. 9 is a factor of 54.

Vocabulary

prime number **composite number**

Investigate

Materials ■ data table ■ counters

A **prime number** has exactly two factors, 1 and itself. A **composite number** is a number that has more than two factors.

You can use counters to represent whole numbers and their factors.

A Draw a table like the one shown at the right. Include numbers from 1 to 20. The number 1 is neither prime nor composite.

Number	Arrays	Factors
1	1 × 1	1
2	2 × 1, 1 × 2	1, 2
3	3 × 1, 1 × 3	1, 3
4		

B Use the counters to represent numbers from 2 to 20. For each number, make every array possible. Record your results in the table.

C For 6, you can make four different arrays: 6 × 1, 3 × 2, 2 × 3, 1 × 6. The factors of 6 are 1, 2, 3, and 6. Record this data in the table.

6 × 1

3 × 2

2 × 3

1 × 6

D Repeat Steps A, B, and C for the other numbers. Complete the table.

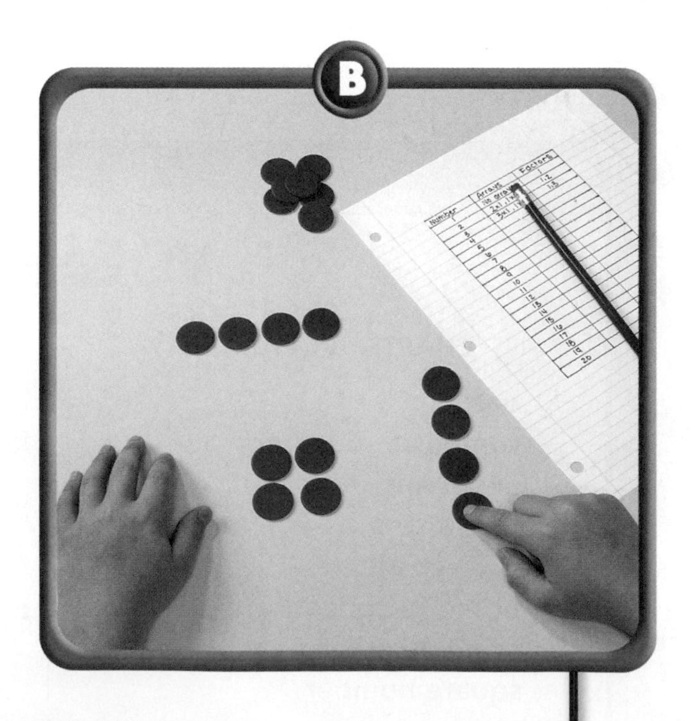

Draw Conclusions

1. Look at your table. Which numbers from 2 to 20 are prime numbers?
2. Which numbers from 2 to 20 are composite numbers?
3. **Comprehension** How can you use counters to determine whether a number greater than 20 is prime or composite? Explain.

NS 1.4 Determine the prime factors of all numbers through 50 and write the numbers as the product of their prime factors by using exponents to show multiples of a factor (e.g., $24 = 2 \times 2 \times 2 \times 3 = 2^3 \times 3$)
also **MR 1.1, MR 2.0, MR 2.3, MR 2.4, MR 3.2**

Connect

You can use the sieve of Eratosthenes to find prime numbers. This method for identifying primes was invented over 2,200 years ago by the Greek mathematician Eratosthenes. Copy the table. Follow the steps to circle all prime numbers from 1 to 60.

1	2	3	4	5	6	7	8	9	10
11	12	13	14	15	16	17	18	19	20
21	22	23	24	25	26	27	28	29	30
31	32	33	34	35	36	37	38	39	40
41	42	43	44	45	46	47	48	49	50
51	52	53	54	55	56	57	58	59	60

Remember

A multiple is the product of a given whole number and another whole number.

Step 1

Cross out 1, since it is not a prime number.

Step 2

Circle 2, since it is a prime. Cross out all multiples of 2.

Step 3

Circle the next number that is not crossed out. Then cross out all of its multiples.

Step 4

Repeat Step 3 until all numbers are either circled or crossed out.

- **Reasoning** Why are the multiples of any number not prime numbers?

TALK Math

Explain why the numbers that are not crossed out in the table are prime numbers.

Practice

Write prime or composite. You may use counters or draw arrays.

1. 25 **2.** 23 ✓**3.** 32 ✓**4.** 36

5. 48 **6.** 53 **7.** 71 **8.** 60

9. 95 **10.** 97 **11.** 144 **12.** 103

ERROR ALERT

- 1 is neither prime nor composite.
- 2 is a prime number.

13. True or false: the product of two prime numbers is a prime number. Explain. Use an example.

14. The combination to Erica's lock is 24, 35, and the greatest prime number between 30 and 40. What is the third combination number?

15. WRITE Math **Explain** why all prime numbers greater than 2 are odd numbers.

Problem Solving Workshop
Strategy: Make an Organized List

OBJECTIVE: Solve problems by using the strategy *make an organized list*.

Learn the Strategy

Making an organized list can help you look at data in different ways. You can use different types of lists to analyze different types of data.

An organized list can show all possibilities.

At Antonio's Pizza Place, you can choose from two types of crust and three different toppings. Antonio made a tree diagram to show all the possible pizzas you can order.

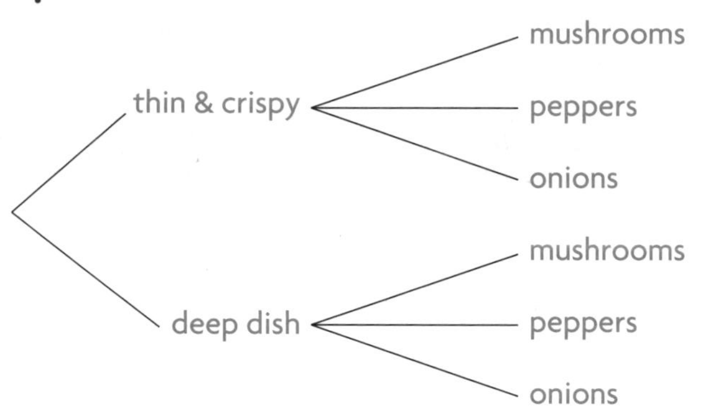

An organized list can help you sort information.

During the month of July, Emilee has gymnastics practice every other day and a gymnastics meet every Saturday. On July 7, she has practice and a meet. She made a list to see when both activities would occur on the same day.

Practice is every other day.

1, 3, 5, **7**, 9, 11, 13, 15, 17, 19, **21**, 23, 25, 27, 29, 31

The first gymnastics meet is on July 7. Since there are 7 days in a week, list multiples of 7.

7, 14, **21**, 28

TALK Math

What additional questions can be answered by using each of the lists above?

Recording work in an organized way makes it easier to discover relationships and patterns among data.

NS 1.4 Determine the prime factors of all numbers through 50 and write the numbers as the product of their prime factors by using exponents to show multiples of a factor (e.g., $24 = 2 \times 2 \times 2 \times 3 = 2^3 \times 3$).
also **MR 1.0, MR 1.1, MR 2.0, MR 2.3, MR 2.4, MR 3.2, MR 3.3**

Use the Strategy

PROBLEM For an art project, each student is making a rectangular mosaic design with 1-inch-square tiles. Students can use 22 tiles, 28 tiles, or 31 tiles in their designs. How many different rectangles can a student make with 22 tiles? with 28 tiles? with 31 tiles?

Read to Understand

- Visualize the problem situation.
- What information is given?

Plan

- **What strategy can you use to solve the problem?**
  You can make an organized list to solve the problem.

Solve

- **How can you use the strategy to solve the problem?**
  List the data in a table to show all the possible rectangles.

Step 1

List the number of tiles that can be used in the mosaic design.

Step 2

For each number of tiles used, list all the possible rectangles.

Number of Tiles	Rectangles
22	1×22, 2×11
28	1×28, 2×14, 4×7
31	1×31

So, with 22 tiles students can make 2 different rectangles. With 28 tiles students can make 3 different rectangles, and with 31 tiles students can make only 1 rectangle.

Check

- **Look back at the problem. Do the answers make sense for the question in the problem? Explain.**

Guided Problem Solving

Read to Understand
Plan
Solve
Check

1. The students in design class are drawing floor plans on graph paper. They know that on their drawings, 1 square unit is equivalent to 1 square yard. In their plans, the rectangular spaces such as rooms, hallways, and closets must have areas of 5 square units, 9 square units, and 16 square units. How many possible rectangles can the students choose from?

   First, copy the table and list the areas for the rectangular spaces.

   Then, list all the possible rectangles that can be formed.

   Finally, count the number of rectangles.

Area of Space (in sq units)	Rectangular Spaces
5	
9	
16	

2. **What if** the students could increase the area of each space by one square unit? How would the number of possible rectangles change?

3. Toni and Hector are weaving pot holders using the colors red, white, green, and blue. If they use only two colors for each pot holder, how many ways can they combine two colors?

Problem Solving Strategy Practice

Use an organized list to solve.

4. Students at art camp must turn in a sketch every 3 days and a finished painting every 7 days. During the first 30-day period, when would the students have both assignments due on the same day?

5. Elliott is building a model. The top level has 1 block, and the next level has 3 blocks. The third level has 6 blocks and the fourth level has 10 blocks. If this pattern continues, how many blocks will be in the seventh level?

For 6–9, use the table of sculpture supplies to solve.

6. Each sculpture student can choose a tool, a material, and a finish from the list. How many choices do the students have?

7. If they can choose only a material and a tool, how many choices do they have?

8. Derek owns a complete set of tools. He only needs to choose the material and the finish. What are his choices?

9. Three students are doing a sculpture together. Ana does not want to use plaster and Rob does not want to use clay. Sheila wants to use paint. What material and finish did the students use?

Sculpture Supply List

Tool	Material	Finish
Hammer	Clay	Glaze
Scraper	Plaster	Paint
Sandpaper	Wood	
Paintbrush		

Mixed Strategy Practice

10. There are 7 art classes offered in the enrichment program. A class can have no more than 20 students. If there are 89 students in the program now, how many more can join?

11. Cara made twice as many bracelets as Keith, and Paulo made 7 more than Cara. If Paulo made 15 bracelets, how many bracelets did Keith make?

12. There are 12 boys and 6 girls in Mr. Smith's art class. If he puts the same number of boys at each table and the same number of girls at each table, what is the greatest number of boys and girls he can have at a table if each table can seat 6?

Choose a STRATEGY

- Draw a Diagram or Picture
- Make a Model or Act It Out
- Make an Organized List
- Find a Pattern
- Make a Table or Graph
- Predict and Test
- Work Backward
- Solve a Simpler Problem
- Write an Equation
- Use Logical Reasoning

USE DATA For 13 and 14, use the graph.

13. Copy and complete the graph. Use the clues below to find the missing data in the graph.

Clue 1: The most students are in drawing class.

Clue 2: Design class has twice as many students as in sculpture class.

Clue 3: Crafts is the second-largest class.

Clue 4: There are $\frac{1}{3}$ as many students in jewelry class as in sculpture class.

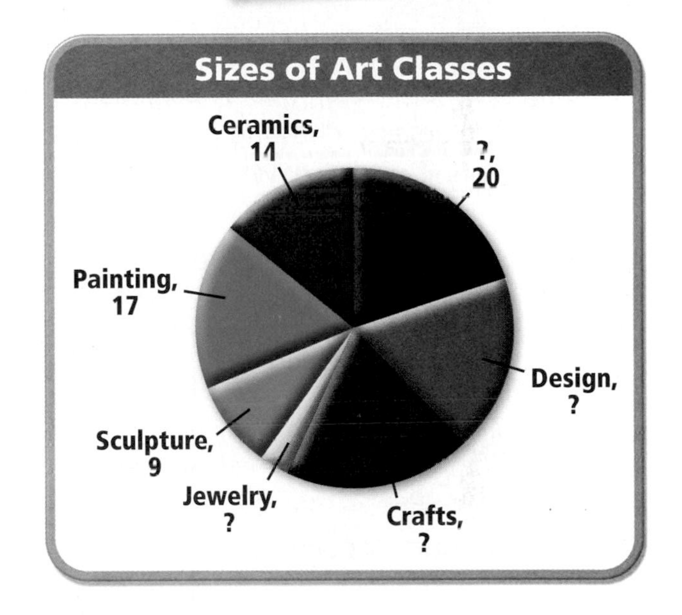

14. **Open-Ended** Next year the art classes will have a total of 125 students. Based on the clues in Problem 13, predict about how many students could be in each art class next year.

15. **Pose a Problem** Look back at Problem 13. Write a similar problem by changing the size of the ceramics class and the drawing class. Then solve the problem.

16. **WRITE Math** Write the numbers 2 to 15. Cross out all multiples of 2, not including 2. Cross out all multiples of 3, but not including 3. **Describe** the list of numbers that is left.

CHALLENGE YOURSELF

Before starting a project, the crafts teacher counted all the beads. She found that there were 235 purple beads, 180 red beads, 231 green beads, 198 yellow beads, and 203 blue beads.

17. A bracelet pattern requires two colors in groups of 3 and 11. Which two groups of beads can be divided evenly by both 3 and 11? **Explain** how you know.

18. Two colors of beads are divisible by one and themselves, and two other prime numbers. Which colors are these?

LESSON 3

Introduction to Exponents

OBJECTIVE: Write and evaluate powers of 10.

Quick Review

Find each product.

1. $3 \times 3 \times 3$
2. $2 \times 2 \times 2 \times 2 \times 2$
3. $5 \times 5 \times 5$
4. $4 \times 4 \times 4 \times 4$
5. $6 \times 6 \times 6$

Vocabulary

base exponent

Learn

You can represent numbers by using exponents. In exponent form, numbers have a base and an exponent. The **base** is a number used as a repeated factor. The **exponent** is a number that shows how many times the base is used as a factor.

$$1{,}000 = \underbrace{10 \times 10 \times 10}_{\text{3 factors}} = \underset{\text{base}}{10}^{3 \leftarrow \text{exponent}}$$

READ Math

The second and third powers have special names.

- Read 10^2 as "ten squared" or "the second power of 10".
- Read 10^3 as "ten cubed" or "10 to the third power".

PROBLEM In the United States, oil is used for many things including fuel, fertilizers, medicines, plastics, insulation, computers, asphalt, ink, glue, and chewing gum. Every 42 seconds, about 10^4 barrels of oil are used. What is the value of 10^4?

Example Find the value of 10^4.

Step 1

Identify the exponent and base.

10^4 ← exponent; 10 ← base

Read: "the fourth power of ten."

Step 2

Write the base as repeated factors.

$$\underbrace{10 \times 10 \times 10 \times 10}_{\text{4 factors}}$$

Step 3

Multiply.

$10 \times 10 \times 10 \times 10 = 10{,}000$

So, about 10,000 barrels of oil are used every 42 seconds.

More Examples

A **Find the value of 10^5.**

$10^5 = 10 \times 10 \times 10 \times 10 \times 10$ ← ten is used as a factor 5 times.

$= 100{,}000$

B **Write 1,000 in exponent form.**

$10 \times 10 \times 10$ ← Write as factors of 10.

$10 \times 10 \times 10$ ← Count the factors: 3.

10^3 ← Write in exponent form.

Hybrid cars use a combination of gasoline and electric power. They get about 50 miles to a gallon of gas. In comparison, a traditional gas-powered car gets about 25 miles to a gallon of gas.▼

NS 1.3 Understand and compute positive integer powers of nonnegative integers; compute examples as repeated multiplication *also* **MR 2.3, MR 2.4, MR 3.2.**

Guided Practice

1. Look at the expression at the right. If you wrote it in exponent form, what would be the base? What would be the exponent?

$$10 \times 10 \times 10$$

Write in exponent form. Then find the value.

2. 10×10
3. $10 \times 10 \times 10 \times 10$
4. $10 \times 10 \times 10 \times 10 \times 10$
5. $10 \times 10 \times 10$
6. **TALK Math** **Explain** how to find the value of 10^8.

Independent Practice and Problem Solving

Find the value.

7. 10^5
8. 10^7
9. 10^8
10. 10^6

Write in exponent form.

11. 100
12. 10,000
13. 100,000
14. 1,000,000

Algebra **Find the value of *n*.**

15. $10^7 = n$
16. $10 = 10^n$
17. $10 \times 10 \times 10 = 10^n$
18. $10^6 = n$

USE DATA For 19–22, use the table.

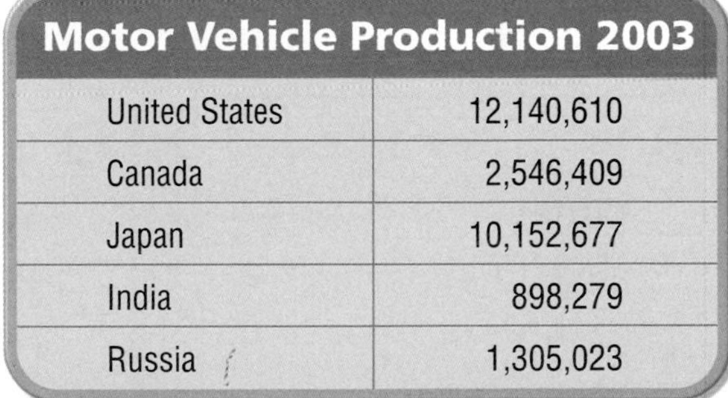

Motor Vehicle Production 2003	
United States	12,140,610
Canada	2,546,409
Japan	10,152,677
India	898,279
Russia	1,305,023

19. Which country produced a number of motor vehicles that is closest to 10^7?
20. Is the total number of motor vehicles produced by all 5 countries greater than or less than 10^8?
21. Which country produced less than 10^6 motor vehicles?
22. **WRITE Math** Is the number of motor vehicles produced in India closer to 10^5 or 10^6? **Explain** how you found the answer.

Achieving the Standards

23. Is the number 14 prime or composite? (NS 1.4, p. 120)
24. $25{,}194 \div 38 =$ (NS 1.0, p. 96)
25. What is the missing factor? (NS 1.0, p. 60)

$10 \times \blacksquare = 300$

26. **Test Prep** Which number represents $10 \times 10 \times 10 \times 10 \times 10 \times 10 \times 10 \times 10$?

A 10^0 **B** 10^8 **C** 8^{10} **D** 10^{10}

Extra Practice on page 136, Set A

Exponents and Square Numbers

OBJECTIVE: Write and evaluate repeated factors in exponent form and identify square numbers.

Learn

PROBLEM A frog egg starts as a single cell and then splits into 2 cells. Each of the two cells splits again. This process continues. After splitting 5 times, there are $2 \times 2 \times 2 \times 2 \times 2$ cells. Write this number in exponent form.

Exponents can be written with bases other than 10.

Quick Review

Write the missing factor.

1. $5 \times ■ = 25$
2. $3 \times ■ = 9$
3. $10 \times ■ = 100$
4. $6 \times ■ = 36$
5. $9 \times ■ = 81$

Vocabulary

square number

perfect square

square root

Example 1 Write $2 \times 2 \times 2 \times 2 \times 2$ in exponent form.

Step 1

Count the number of times the base is repeated.

repeated 5 times

$2 \times 2 \times 2 \times 2 \times 2$

exponent is 5

Step 2

Write the exponent and the base together.

2^5 ← exponent

base

So, $2 \times 2 \times 2 \times 2 \times 2$ can be written in exponent form as 2^5.

Example 2 Write each in exponent form and in words.

A $3 \times 3 \times 3 \times 3$

Write: 3^4

Read: the fourth power of three or three to the fourth power

B $5 \times 5 \times 5$

Write: 5^3

Read: the third power of five, or five cubed

C 8×8

Write: 8^2

Read: the second power of eight, or eight squared

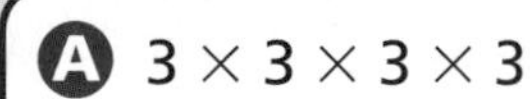

Example 3 Write each in exponent form and in words.

D 27

$27 = 3 \times 3 \times 3 = 3^3$

Read: the third power of three, or three cubed

E 49

$49 = 7 \times 7 = 7^2$

Read: the second power of seven, or seven squared

Math Idea

The zero power of any number, except zero, is 1.

$6^0 = 1$

NS 1.3 Understand and compute positive integer powers of nonnegative integers; compute examples as repeated multiplication *also* **MR 2.3, MR 2.4, MR 3.2.**

Square Numbers

A **square number**, sometimes called a **perfect square**, is the product of a number and itself. A square number can be represented with the exponent 2.

Example: 25 = 5×5 or 5^2
↑
square number

Activity

Materials ■ square tiles

You can use square tiles to learn about square numbers.

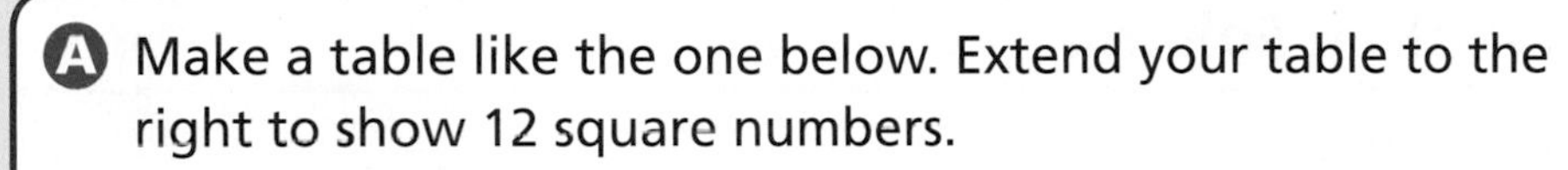

A Make a table like the one below. Extend your table to the right to show 12 square numbers.

B Use the square tiles to make an array of each square number. Record the number of tiles you used in all.

C Complete your table. Show arrays with up to 12 tiles on each side.

Square Numbers

Model				
Equal Factors	1×1	2×2	3×3	
Base	1	2	3	
Exponent Form	1^2	2^2		
Standard Form	1	4		

- Are square numbers all even, all odd, or both even and odd?
- **Analysis** Compare the last digit of a square number to its base. What pattern do you see?
- **Reasoning** Would the square of 137 be an even or odd number? **Explain** how you know without finding 137×137.

Guided Practice

1. What number in exponent form does this expression represent? $5 \times 5 \times 5 \times 5$

Technology
Use Harcourt Mega Math, Ice Station Exploration, *Arctic Algebra*, Levels V, W, X.

Write in exponent form and then write in words.

2. 6×6 **3.** $4 \times 4 \times 4$ **4.** $7 \times 7 \times 7 \times 7$ ✓**5.** $3 \times 3 \times 3 \times 3 \times 3 \times 3$

Find the value.

6. 3^3 **7.** 9^2 **8.** 8^3 **9.** 11^2 ✓**10.** 6^4

Compare. Write $<$, $>$, or $=$ for each ●.

11. 3^2 ● 2^3 **12.** 3^3 ● 4^3 **13.** 8^2 ● 2^6 **14.** 5^3 ● 6^2

15. TALK Math **Explain** how to express $6 \times 6 \times 6 \times 6$ in exponent form and find its value.

Independent Practice and Problem Solving

Write in exponent form. Then find the value.

16. $9 \times 9 \times 9$ **17.** $2 \times 2 \times 2 \times 2 \times 2$ **18.** $8 \times 8 \times 8 \times 8$ **19.** $5 \times 5 \times 5 \times 5 \times 5 \times 5$

Find the value.

20. 7^2 **21.** 3^4 **22.** 2^8 **23.** 12^3 **24.** 5^3

25. 6^2 **26.** 4^5 **27.** 19^0 **28.** 10^4 **29.** 9^3

Compare. Write $<$, $>$, or $=$ for each ●.

30. 2^4 ● 4^2 **31.** 3^5 ● 2^7 **32.** 9^3 ● 4^5 **33.** 5^6 ● 4^7

Algebra Find the value of *n*.

34. $2^4 = 4^n$ **35.** $3^4 = n^2$ **36.** $4^3 = n^2$ **37.** $8^2 = 4^n$

For 38–41, use the pattern in the table.

Frog Cells

Number of Splits	Cells	Exponent Form
Start	1	2^0
1	2	2^1
2	4	2^2
3	8	2^3

38. A frog egg has split several times so it now has 128 cells. How many times has it split?

39. What number in exponent form represents the number of eggs after a frog egg splits 9 times? How many cells would a frog egg have after splitting 9 times?

40. How many times will a frog egg need to split so it first has more than 1,000 cells?

41. **Pose a Problem** Use the information in the table to write a problem involving exponents. Have a classmate solve the problem.

42. WRITE Math Is 7^8 greater than 6^8? **Explain** how you know without doing any multiplying.

 Extra Practice on page 136, Set B

Achieving the Standards

43. Round 154,872 to the nearest thousand. (NS 1.1, p. 12)

44. What are the factors of 15? (Grade 4 NS 4.1)

45. Is the number 3 prime or composite? (Grade 4, O━π NS 4.2)

46. Test Prep Which number is less than 5^4?

A 4^5 **C** 7^4

B 3^5 **D** 10^4

47. Test Prep Which is the greatest square number that is even and less than 200?

A 10^2 **C** 15^2

B 14^2 **D** 16^2

Problem Solving and Reasoning

NUMBER SENSE Each square number has a square root. A **square root** is the base that was multiplied by itself to get a square number.

3 is the square root of 9, because $3^2 = 9$.

4 is the square root of 16, because $4^2 = 16$.

Find the square roots of 1, 4, and 9.

Step 1	Step 2
Break down each square number into repeated factors.	The square root is the base of each square number.
$1 = 1 \times 1 = 1^2$	The square root of 1 is 1.
$4 = 2 \times 2 = 2^2$	The square root of 4 is 2.
$9 = 3 \times 3 = 3^2$	The square root of 9 is 3.

Find the square root of each number.

1. 25 **2.** 49 **3.** 100 **4.** 144

5. 36 **6.** 64 **7.** 81 **8.** 121

9. What are the square numbers between 100 and 200? Find the square root of each of those square numbers.

LESSON 5

Prime Factorization

OBJECTIVE: Find and write the prime factorization of a number using exponents.

Quick Review

Write *prime* or *composite*.

1. 17
2. 70
3. 49
4. 93
5. 89

Vocabulary

prime factorization

factor tree

Learn

Remember

A **prime** number has exactly two factors, 1 and itself. A **composite** number has more than two factors.

All composite numbers can be written as the product of prime factors. This is called the **prime factorization** of the number.

PROBLEM The math club members write messages to each other in code. Each member's name is represented by a number. To identify someone in a message, you must find the prime factorization of the number. Kira received a message from 12. Who is 12?

Secret Chart of Prime Factorizations	
Kira	3×5
Alec	$2 \times 2 \times 2$
Grace	2×7
Sara	$2 \times 2 \times 3$
Alberto	5×2

You can use a diagram called a **factor tree** to find the prime factorization of a number. Since there is only one prime factorization of a number, you can start with any pair of factors of the number. Continue factoring until only prime factors are left.

ONE WAY

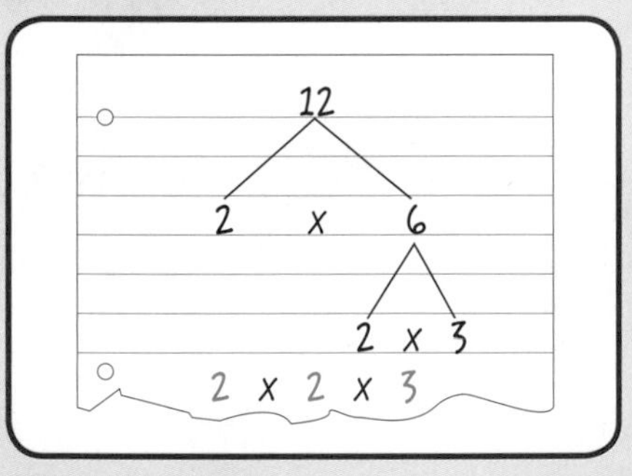

ANOTHER WAY

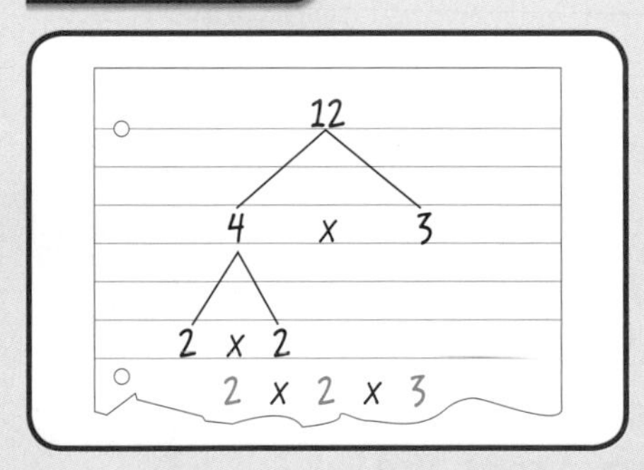

The prime factorization of 12 is $2 \times 2 \times 3$. Look at the Secret Chart. So, Sara is 12.

Examples Find the prime factorization.

A

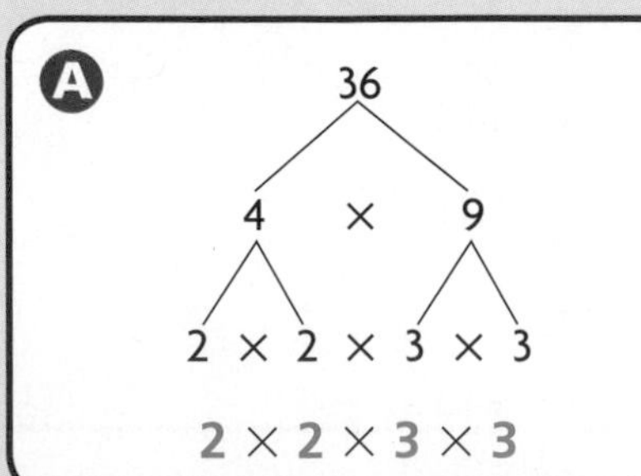

B

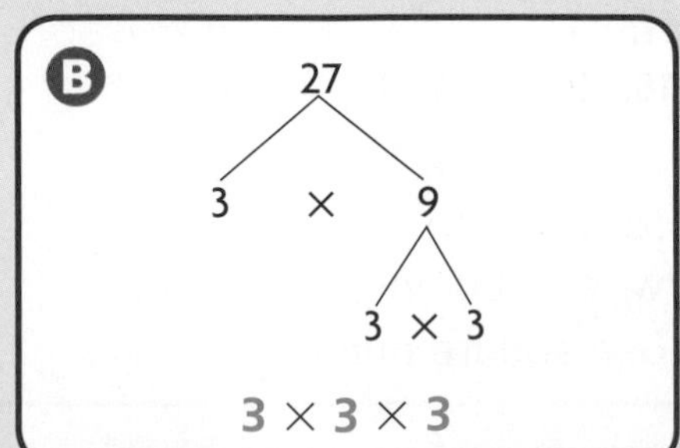

C

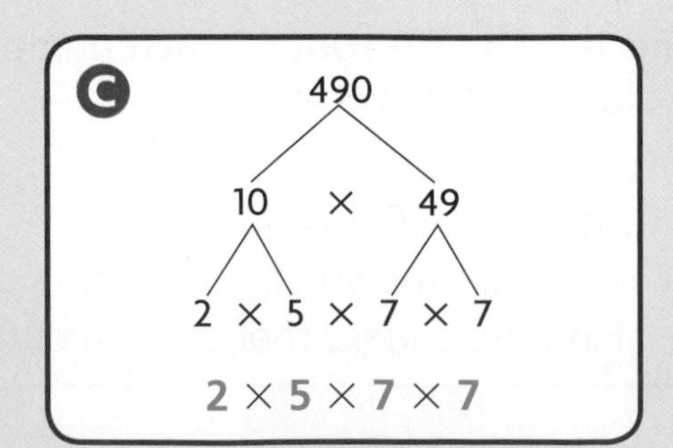

NS 1.4 Determine the prime factors of all numbers through 50 and write the numbers as the product of their prime factors by using exponents to show multiples of a factor (e.g., $24 = 2 \times 2 \times 2 \times 3 = 2^3 \times 3$). *also* **NS 1.3, MR 2.3, MR 2.4, MR 3.2**

Exponents in Prime Factorization

Sometimes you can use exponents to write the prime factorization of a number.

When a prime factor is repeated in a factorization, use the prime as the base and use the number of times it is repeated as the exponent.

$81 = \underbrace{3 \times 3 \times 3 \times 3}_{\text{factors}}$ ← 3 is a factor four times.

$81 = 3^4$ ← exponent; 3 is the base

Example

$8 = \underbrace{2 \times 2 \times 2}$

$8 = 2^3$

B

$45 = \underbrace{3 \times 3} \times 5$

$45 = 3^2 \times 5$

C

$128 = \underbrace{2 \times 2 \times 2} \times \underbrace{4 \times 4}$

$128 = 2^3 \times 4^2$

Notice that in Example B, the exponent of 1 is not written.

- **Explain** how to write $3 \times 3 \times 3 \times 7$ using exponents.

Guided Practice

1. Draw a factor tree to find the prime factorization of 28. Write the prime factors.

Find the prime factorization. You may use a factor tree.

2. 18
3. 70
4. 54
5. 8
6. 12
7. 16
8. 50
9. 36
10. 81
11. 125

Rewrite the prime factorization using exponents.

12. $2 \times 3 \times 3$
13. $5 \times 2 \times 5 \times 2 \times 5$
14. $3 \times 7 \times 3 \times 11 \times 3$
15. $3 \times 5 \times 3 \times 5 \times 13$
16. $3 \times 3 \times 17 \times 3$
17. $5 \times 3 \times 3 \times 11 \times 11 \times 3$

Find the number for each prime factorization.

18. 3^4
19. $2 \times 2 \times 7 \times 2 \times 7$
20. $5^2 \times 3^4$
21. $3 \times 2 \times 13 \times 3$
22. 2×3^2
23. $7^2 \times 2^4$
24. $17 \times 2 \times 2 \times 2$
25. $11^2 \times 3$

26. **TALK Math** **Explain** how to find the prime factorization of 100 and express it using exponents.

Independent Practice and Problem Solving

Find the prime factorization. You may use a factor tree.

27. 48 **28.** 66 **29.** 63 **30.** 72 **31.** 9

32. 98 **33.** 96 **34.** 65 **35.** 56 **36.** 121

Rewrite the prime factorization using exponents.

37. $19 \times 2 \times 2$ **38.** $2 \times 3 \times 5 \times 2 \times 5$ **39.** $11 \times 3 \times 2 \times 11 \times 2$

40. $3 \times 3 \times 3 \times 3 \times 7$ **41.** $5 \times 5 \times 5 \times 5$ **42.** $2 \times 7 \times 2 \times 7 \times 7 \times 7$

Find the number for each prime factorization.

43. 2^4 **44.** $5 \times 3 \times 3 \times 5$ **45.** $7^3 \times 2^2$ **46.** $2 \times 2 \times 13 \times 2$

47. 3×11^2 **48.** $5^3 \times 3^2$ **49.** $13^2 \times 2$ **50.** $2 \times 2 \times 2 \times 2 \times 2$

Algebra **Write a number for n that solves the equation.**

51. $5^2 \times n = 75$ **52.** $343 = 7^n$ **53.** $3^2 \times n^2 = 144$ **54.** $2^n = 128$

For 55–58, use the table.

The Crypto Lock Company has lock dials that look like clocks. The factors of the lock number tell the combination of the lock. Combination numbers are listed in order from least to greatest.

Crypto Lock Company

Lock	Lock Number	Factors
Ace	84	■, ■, ■, ■
Deluxe	140	■, ■, ■, ■
Super	■	■, ■, ■, ■
Mega	441	3, 3, 7, 7

55. The factors of the Ace 84 Lock are all prime. What four prime factors give the combination of the Ace 84 lock?

56. What are the four primes that unlock the Deluxe 140 lock?

57. None of the four prime factors in the Super Lock's combination are repeated. What is the greatest possible lock number the Super Lock could have? The lowest possible lock number?

58. **Pose a Problem** Use the information in the table to write a problem. Have a classmate solve it.

59. WRITE Math If a number is the product of a prime and a composite number, what is the fewest number of prime factors it could have? Explain.

Achieving the Standards

60. The 58 fifth graders are planning a field trip to a museum. The tickets cost a total of $522. How much does each ticket cost? (O-π NS 2.2, p. 96)

61. **Test Prep** Which numbers are two of the prime factors of 78?

A 13 and 2

B 2 and 6

C 39 and 4

D 6 and 13

62. A diagonal divides a rectangle into two right triangles. The area of the rectangle is 30 square inches. What is the area of each triangle? (Grade 4 SDAP 1.4)

63. Julie made a pie for her family and cut the pie into 8 equal slices. Julie's family ate 5 slices of the pie. What fraction of the pie did her family eat? (Grade 4, NS 1.7)

64. **Test Prep** What is the least number that is the product of two different primes that are squared?

Problem Solving and Reasoning

NUMBER SENSE Computer security systems use large composite numbers as codes. Each composite number is the product of two secret primes. If you can find the primes, you can crack the code. The secret primes that computers use are *very large*, and could involve 100 digit numbers. These secret prime factors are just about impossible to find—even for a computer!

Example Make your own secret computer security code.

Step 1	Step 2	Step 3
Find two large primes. Examples: 61 ← prime 103 ← prime	Multiply the primes to get a composite number. Example: $61 \times 103 = 6{,}283$	Trade composite numbers with a classmate. Can you crack each other's code?

1. Greg's composite number is 2,419. He identified one prime as 41. What is the other prime?

2. Sunil's composite was 8,633. Both primes were less than 100 and greater than 88. What were they?

3. **Reasoning** Rita's composite was 5,069. She identified one prime as 37. Is the second prime greater or less than 100? Explain.

Extra Practice

Set A Find the value. (pp. 126–127)

1. 10^3
2. 10^4
3. 10^2
4. 10^9

Write in exponent form.

5. 1,000
6. 10,000,000
7. 10
8. 100,000
9. A 2005–2006 survey found that there are about 10^7 pet reptiles in the United States. What is the value of 10^8?
10. More than 10^9 cell phones were in use worldwide in 2005. What is the value of 10^9?

Set B Find the value. (pp. 128–131)

1. 3^2
2. 4^6
3. 2^6
4. 5^4
5. 9^4
6. 1^7
7. 8^4
8. 7^4
9. 6^1
10. 12^0

Compare. Write <, >, or = for each ●.

11. 3^2 ● 2^4
12. 2^6 ● 5^2
13. 1^3 ● 2^1
14. 7^2 ● 8^2
15. 3^6 ● 9^3
16. Lee folds a piece of paper into 2 parts. He does this 3 times. Then Lee unfolds the paper. How many parts did he make?
17. Lee folds another piece of paper to form 32 parts. How many times in all did Lee fold the paper?

Set C Find the prime factorization. You may use a factor tree. (pp. 132–135)

1. 10
2. 14
3. 45
4. 175
5. 64
6. 30
7. 210
8. 75

Rewrite the prime factorization using exponents.

9. $3 \times 3 \times 3$
10. $11 \times 5 \times 2 \times 2$
11. $2 \times 7 \times 3 \times 7$
12. $2 \times 5 \times 5 \times 3$
13. $3 \times 13 \times 3 \times 2$
14. $2 \times 2 \times 2 \times 2$

Find the number for each prime factorization.

15. 4^4
16. $3^3 \times 5^3$
17. $3 \times 3 \times 5 \times 13$
18. 2×11^3
19. $7^3 \times 4^0$
20. $3 \times 3 \times 3 \times 7 \times 7$
21. $2 \times 2 \times 3 \times 19$
22. $2^2 \times 3^3 \times 23^1$

CD ROM Technology
Use Harcourt Mega Math, Ice Station Exploration, *Arctic Algebra* Levels O, U, V, W.

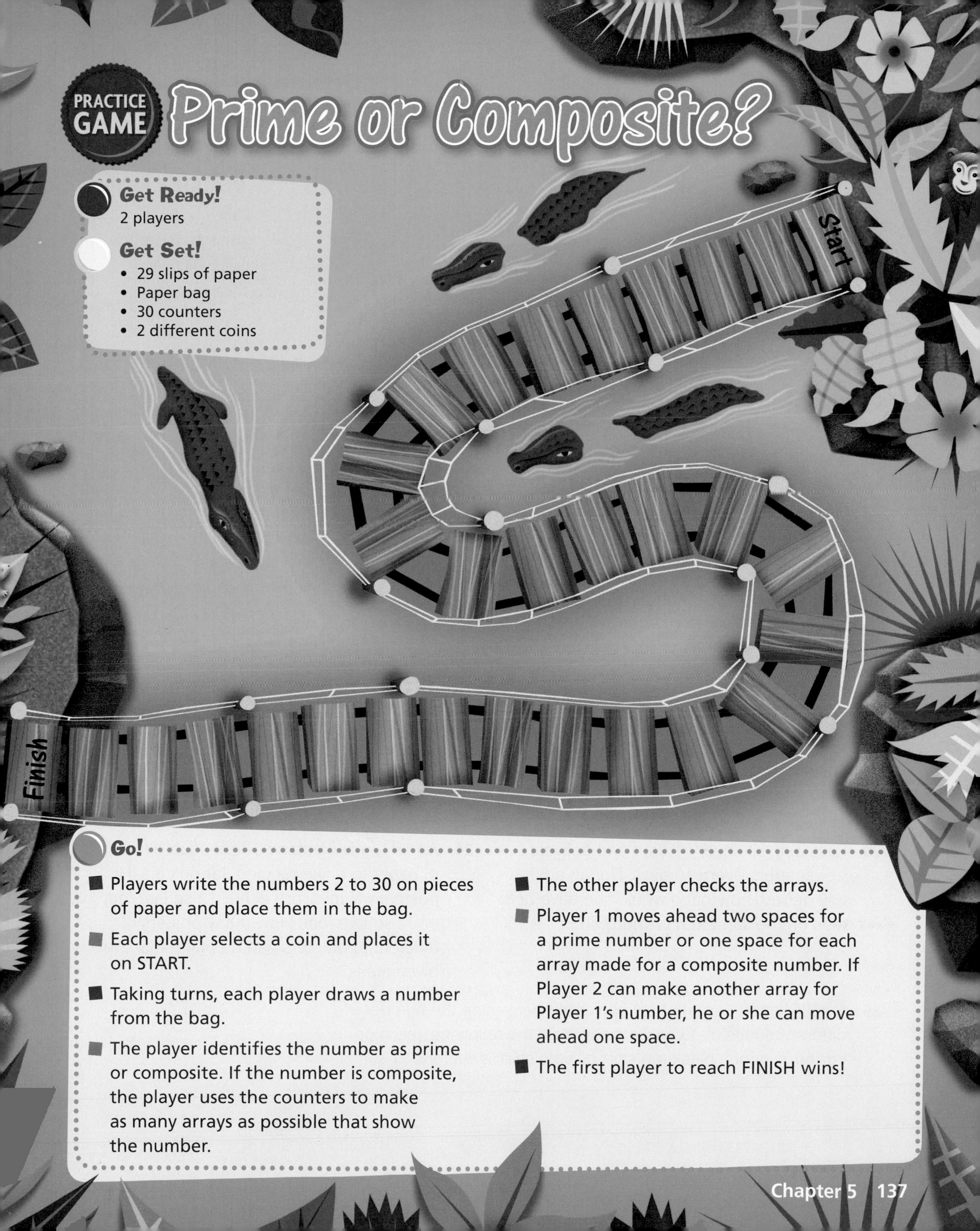

PRACTICE GAME

Prime or Composite?

Get Ready!
2 players

Get Set!
- 29 slips of paper
- Paper bag
- 30 counters
- 2 different coins

Go!
- Players write the numbers 2 to 30 on pieces of paper and place them in the bag.
- Each player selects a coin and places it on START.
- Taking turns, each player draws a number from the bag.
- The player identifies the number as prime or composite. If the number is composite, the player uses the counters to make as many arrays as possible that show the number.
- The other player checks the arrays.
- Player 1 moves ahead two spaces for a prime number or one space for each array made for a composite number. If Player 2 can make another array for Player 1's number, he or she can move ahead one space.
- The first player to reach FINISH wins!

Chapter 5 Review/Test

Check Vocabulary and Concepts

Choose the best term from the box.

VOCABULARY
base
prime factorization
prime number
square number

1. A _?_ is a whole number greater than 1 that has exactly two factors, one and itself. (NS 1.4, p. 120)
2. In 10^2, the 2 shows how many times the _?_ is used as a factor. (NS 1.3, p. 126)
3. The _?_ of 8 is 2^3. (1.4, p. 132)

Check Skills

Find the value. (NS 1.3, pp. 126–127, 128–131)

4. 10^5
5. 10^3
6. 10^7
7. 10^2
8. 2^2
9. 4^2
10. 18^1
11. 1^9

Compare. Write <, >, or = for each ●. (NS 1.3, pp. 126–127, 128–131)

12. 2^5 ● 2^4
13. 1^6 ● 25^1
14. 2^4 ● 4^2
15. 5^4 ● 12^2

Rewrite the prime factorization using exponents. (NS 1.4, pp. 132–135)

16. $3 \times 3 \times 5 \times 2$
17. $5 \times 7 \times 7 \times 2 \times 2 \times 2$
18. $11 \times 2 \times 3 \times 3 \times 2$

Find the prime factorization of the number. Use exponents when possible. (NS 1.4, pp. 132–135)

19. 15
20. 12
21. 80
22. 54

Check Problem Solving

Solve. (NS 1.4, MR 2.2, pp. 122–125)

23. Rikki babysits every 4 days and delivers newspapers every 10 days. During a 60-day period, how often would she have both jobs on the same day? When?
24. An artist will combine 1-foot square sheets of paper to make rectangular posters. His posters will measure either 12 square feet or 32 square feet. How many posters of different perimeters can he make with the given areas?
25. WRITE Math **Explain** how you could determine the number of different outfits that can be made from the following: jeans or corduroy pants; black tee-shirt or polo shirt; sweater or T-shirt.

GO ONLINE **Technology** Use *Online Assessment.*

Enrich • Scientific Notation

SOLAR SYSTEM TRAVELER

Scientific notation is a way to express a very large number as the product of two factors. The first factor is a number greater than 1 and less than 10. The second factor is a power of 10 expressed as a exponent.

Get On Board

Earth lies about 93,000,000 miles from the Sun. Follow these steps to express this distance in scientific notation.

1. Put a decimal point at the end of the number.
   93,000,000.
2. Count the number of places the decimal point must be moved to the left to form a number greater than 1 but less than 10. This number is the first factor.
   9.3000000. ⟶ 9.3
   7 places
3. The second factor is a power of 10. Its exponent is the number of places you moved the decimal point.
   9.3×10^7

Warm Up

A Write 475,000 in scientific notation.
475,000. ⟶ 4.75×10^5
5 places

B Write 640,000,000 in scientific notation.
640,000,000. ⟶ 6.4×10^8
8 places

Take Off

Write each number in scientific notation.

1. 47,000,000,000 **2.** 38,000 **3.** 910,000,000 **4.** 1,600,000

5. 520,000,000,000 **6.** 173,000 **7.** 219,000,000 **8.** 67,000

Touch Down

WRITE Math **Explain** how you would write 7.8×10^5 in standard form.

Achieving the Standards
Chapters 1–5

Number Sense

1. A group of 15 children is going to an amusement park for a birthday party. Each child will receive 25 tokens to use at the arcade. How many tokens will the children use in all? (NS 1.0)

   A 40 **C** 375

   B 225 **D** 400

Test Tip Understand the problem.

See item 2. The problem has a remainder. You have to decide whether to drop the remainder, increase the quotient by 1, or use the remainder as the answer.

2. There are 460 campers and counselors at the Tall Pines Summer Camp. Each table in the dining hall can seat 12 people. How many tables are needed to seat everyone? (O‑π NS 2.2)

   A 40 **C** 38

   B 39 **D** 4

3. What is the prime factorization of 81? (O‑π NS 1.4)

   A $3 \times 3 \times 3 \times 3 = 3^4$

   B $3 \times 3 \times 3 = 3^3$

   C $9 \times 3 \times 3 = 9 \times 3^2$

   D 27×3

4. WRITE Math **Explain** how you can choose compatible numbers to estimate the quotient $5{,}329 \div 62$. (O‑π NS 1.1)

Algebra and Functions

5. Which number is represented by n? (Grade 4 AF 1.1)

   $$6 \times n = 162$$

   A 22 **C** 28

   B 27 **D** 32

6. What value of p makes this equation true? (AF 1.3)

   $$6 \times 43 = (6 \times 40) + (6 \times p)$$

   A 3

   B 4

   C 40

   D 43

7. Four students each evaluated the expression $(12 + 6) - (n \times 2)$; for $n = 4$.

Jasmine	$(12 + 6) - (4 \times 2) = 28$
Michael	$(12 + 6) - (4 \times 2) = 26$
Aliyah	$(12 + 6) - (4 \times 2) = 16$
Dwayne	$(12 + 6) - (4 \times 2) = 10$

   Who evaluated it correctly? (Grade 4 O‑π AF 1.2)

   A Jasmine **C** Aliyah

   B Michael **D** Dwayne

8. WRITE Math A rectangle has an area of 48 square inches. The width of the rectangle is 6 inches. **Explain** how you can use the formula $A = l \times w$ to find the length of the rectangle. (Grade 4 AF 1.4)

Measurement and Geometry

9. Look at the figure below.

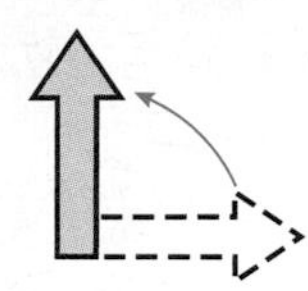

How many degrees has the figure been turned? **(Grade 4 MG 3.5)**

A 90°

B 180°

C 270°

D 360°

10. Which statement is true about the figures shown below? **(Grade 4 MG 3.3)**

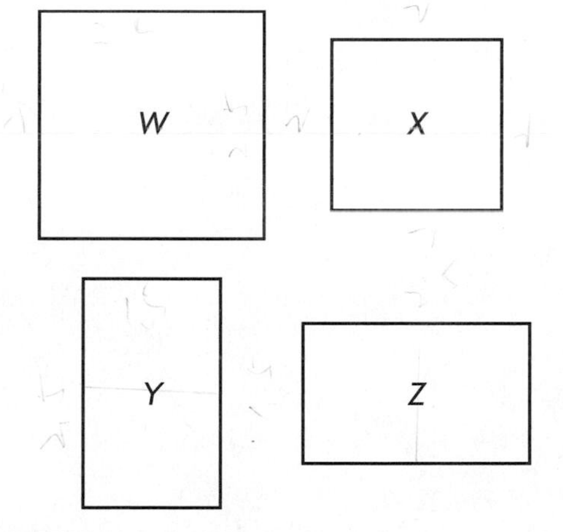

A Figures *W* and *X* appear congruent.

B Figures *Y* and *Z* appear congruent.

C Figures *X* and *Y* appear congruent.

D Figures *X* and *Z* appear congruent.

11. **WRITE Math** **Explain** how you can tell if a figure has line symmetry. **(Grade 4 MG 3.4)**

Statistics, Data Analysis, and Probability

12. For a science project, Amanda recorded the temperature each hour from 9:00 A.M. to 3:00 P.M. Which type of graph would be *best* to display the data? **(SDAP 1.2)**

A circle graph

B pictograph

C line plot

D line graph

13. Look at the frequency table below.

Favorite Ice Cream Flavor	
Flavor	**Number of Votes**
Vanilla	𝍸 𝍸 |||
Chocolate	𝍸 𝍸 𝍸
Strawberry	𝍸 ||

How many people were surveyed? **(SDAP 1.2)**

A 29

B 30

C 35

D 40

14. What is the mode of the data? **(SDAP 1.2)**

12, 11, 9, 6, 9, 18, 8, 15

A 9

B 10

C 11

D 12

15. **WRITE Math** Two line graphs each show the growth of a different plant. The horizontal axes on both graphs show time, and the vertical axes show plant growth. After 5 weeks, the plants are the same height. What do you know about the points on each graph at 5 weeks? **Explain.** **(SDAP 1.0)**

6 Fraction Concepts

The Big Idea Fractions and mixed numbers can be expressed in equivalent forms and can be compared and ordered.

CALIFORNIA FAST FACT

The L.A. Philharmonic Orchestra was formed in 1919 with 94 musicians. It first performed before an audience of 2,400 at Trinity Auditorium in downtown Los Angeles.

Investigate

Today, the L.A. Philharmonic Orchestra consists of 106 musicians. The largest section is stringed instruments. Choose 2 stringed instruments from the graph. Write each instrument's number of musicians as a fraction, in simplest form, of the total number of musicians.

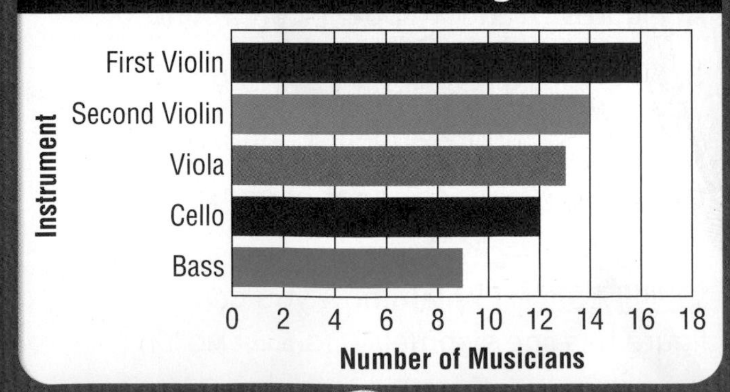

GO ONLINE **Technology** Student pages are available in the Student eBook.

Show What You Know

Check your understanding of important skills needed for success in Chapter 6.

▶ Understand Fractions

Write the fraction for the shaded part.

1. 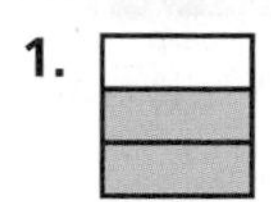
2. 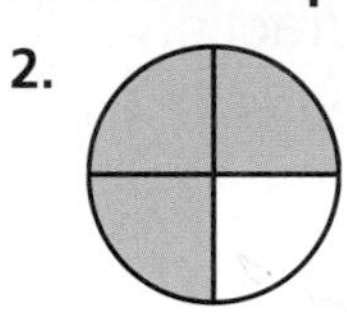
3. 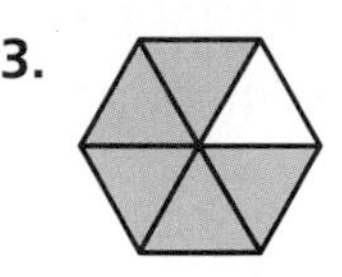
4. 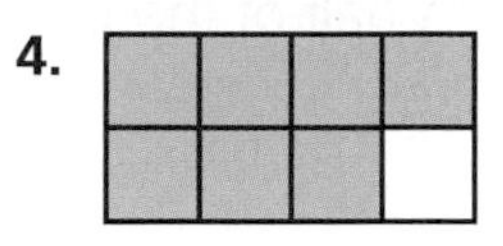

Write in words.

5. $\frac{2}{5}$
6. $\frac{1}{7}$
7. $\frac{4}{9}$
8. $\frac{1}{3}$

▶ Understand Mixed Numbers

Write a mixed number for each picture.

9. 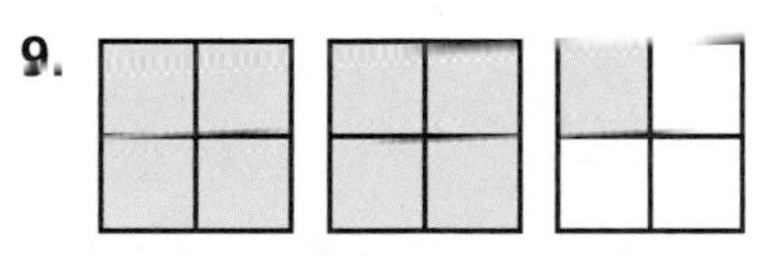
10. 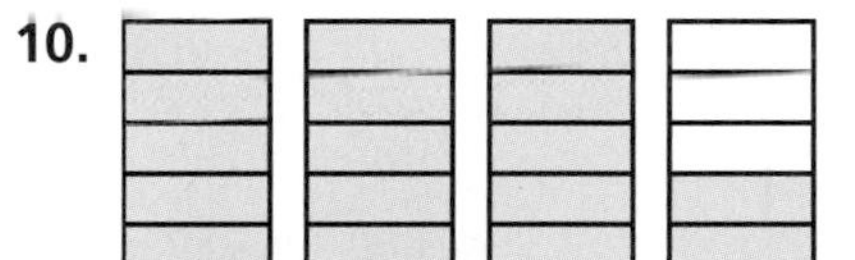
11. 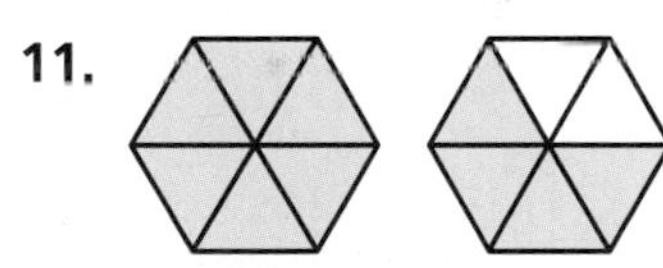

▶ Compare Fractions

Compare the fractions. Write <, >, or = for each ●.

12. $\frac{1}{4}$ ● $\frac{1}{3}$
13. $\frac{2}{4}$ ● $\frac{4}{8}$
14. $\frac{2}{3}$ ● $\frac{1}{2}$
15. $\frac{1}{2}$ ● $\frac{3}{8}$

VOCABULARY POWER

CHAPTER VOCABULARY

benchmark fractions
common multiple
equivalent fractions
greatest common factor (GCF)
mixed number
simplest form

WARM-UP WORDS

equivalent fractions fractions that name the same number or amount

simplest form A fraction is in simplest form when the numerator and denominator have only 1 as their common factor.

greatest common factor (GCF) the greatest factor that two or more numbers have in common

Equivalent Fractions

OBJECTIVE: Identify and write equivalent fractions.

Quick Review

Model each fraction.

1. $\frac{1}{4}$
2. $\frac{2}{3}$
3. $\frac{3}{5}$
4. $\frac{1}{8}$
5. $\frac{4}{12}$

Vocabulary

equivalent fraction

Learn

PROBLEM Eva wants to share $\frac{1}{2}$ of a cake with two friends. She divides half of the cake into three equal parts. Write two fractions to represent the part of the cake she is sharing with her friends.

Activity **Materials** ■ pattern blocks

You can use pattern blocks to model fractions.
Let the hexagon equal 1 whole.

Step 1

Cover a hexagon with a trapezoid to show $\frac{1}{2}$.

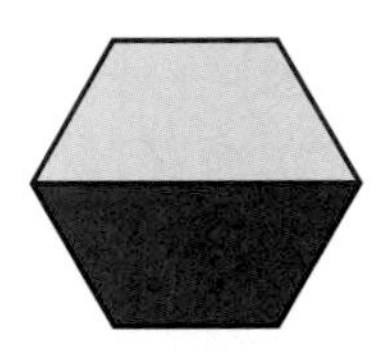

Step 2

Cover another hexagon with triangles to show $\frac{3}{6}$.

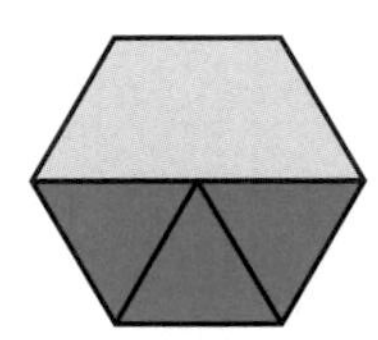

Step 3

Compare the two hexagons.

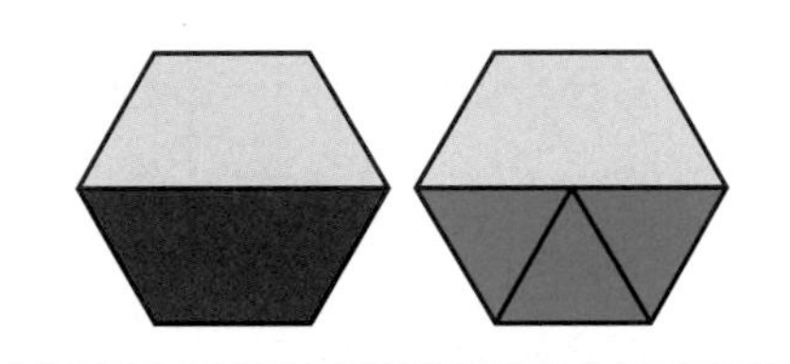

So, both $\frac{3}{6}$ and $\frac{1}{2}$ represent the part of the cake Eva is sharing with her friends.

The fractions $\frac{1}{2}$ and $\frac{3}{6}$ are called equivalent fractions. **Equivalent fractions** are fractions that name the same number or amount. On the number lines at the right, the fractions $\frac{1}{3}$ and $\frac{2}{6}$ are equivalent fractions because they are the same distance from 0.

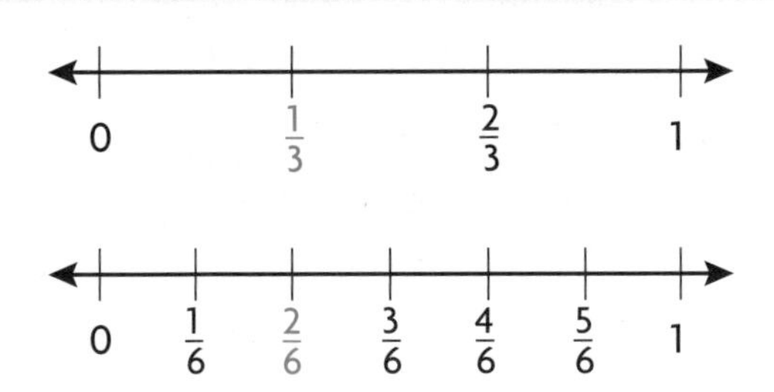

You can also find equivalent fractions by multiplying or dividing the numerator and the denominator by the same number. A fraction with the same numerator and denominator is equal to 1.

ONE WAY **Use multiplication.**

$$\frac{6}{8} = \frac{6 \times 2}{8 \times 2} = \frac{12}{16}$$

So, $\frac{6}{8} = \frac{12}{16}$.

ANOTHER WAY **Use division.**

$$\frac{6}{8} = \frac{6 \div 2}{8 \div 2} = \frac{3}{4}$$

So, $\frac{6}{8} = \frac{3}{4}$.

🔑 **NS 1.5** Identify and represent on a number line decimals, fractions, mixed numbers, and positive and negative integers. *also* **NS 1.0,** 🔑 **NS 1.2, MR 2.3, MR 2.4, MR 3.2**

Guided Practice

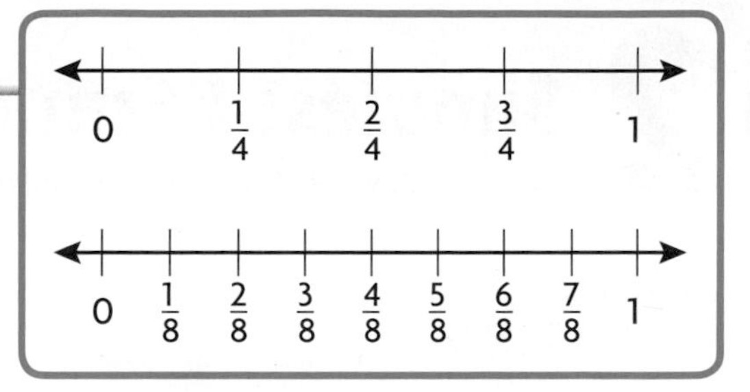

Use the number lines to name an equivalent fraction for each.

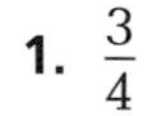

1. $\frac{3}{4}$ 2. $\frac{2}{8}$ 3. $\frac{2}{4}$ 4. $\frac{6}{8}$

Write an equivalent fraction.

5. $\frac{1}{4}$ 6. $\frac{5}{10}$ 7. $\frac{1}{3}$ 8. $\frac{5}{8}$ ✓9. $\frac{2}{5}$ ✓10. $\frac{5}{6}$

11. TALK Math **Explain** how to find an equivalent fraction for $\frac{6}{10}$.

Independent Practice and Problem Solving

Write an equivalent fraction.

12. $\frac{1}{5}$ 13. $\frac{6}{10}$ 14. $\frac{3}{6}$ 15. $\frac{6}{9}$ 16. $\frac{3}{8}$ 17. $\frac{5}{15}$

18. $\frac{1}{9}$ 19. $\frac{3}{10}$ 20. $\frac{3}{12}$ 21. $\frac{10}{12}$ 22. $\frac{2}{3}$ 23. $\frac{12}{16}$

Tell which fraction is *not* equivalent to the others.

24. $\frac{3}{4}, \frac{2}{3}, \frac{8}{12}$ 25. $\frac{2}{5}, \frac{4}{10}, \frac{3}{15}$ 26. $\frac{2}{6}, \frac{1}{4}, \frac{1}{3}$ 27. $\frac{3}{4}, \frac{5}{6}, \frac{6}{8}$

Use the picture for 28–30.

28. Mark has these 24 marbles. Write four equivalent fractions to show how many of the marbles are blue.

29. What if Mark trades the six green marbles for six more blue marbles? Write three equivalent fractions to show how many blue marbles he has now.

30. WRITE Math Mark said that $\frac{1}{4}$ of his marbles are green. He said that was the same as $\frac{2}{8}$ of his marbles. Was Mark right? **Explain.**

Achieving the Standards

31. How many angles does a pentagon have? (Grade 4 MG 3.0)

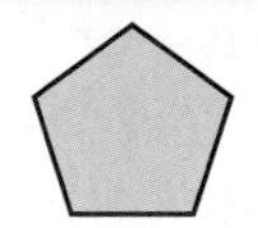

32. Find the quotient. 42,780 ÷ 46 (NS 2.2, p. 96)

33. Use exponents to write the prime factorization of 32. (NS 1.4, p. 134)

34. **Test Prep** Which fraction is the same as $\frac{1}{3}$?

A $\frac{1}{6}$ C $\frac{3}{5}$

B $\frac{4}{12}$ D $\frac{2}{3}$

Extra Practice on page 164, Set A

LESSON 2

Simplest Form

OBJECTIVE: Write fractions in simplest form.

Quick Review

Write an equivalent fraction.

1. $\frac{1}{4}$ 2. $\frac{5}{7}$ 3. $\frac{3}{8}$
4. $\frac{4}{10}$ 5. $\frac{2}{3}$

Vocabulary

simplest form

greatest common factor (GCF)

Learn

PROBLEM The United States is divided into regions. Ten states are in the Northeast region. That is $\frac{10}{50}$ of the states. What is $\frac{10}{50}$ in simplest form?

A fraction is in **simplest form** when the numerator and denominator have 1 as their only common factor. You can divide by common factors to find the simplest form of $\frac{10}{50}$.

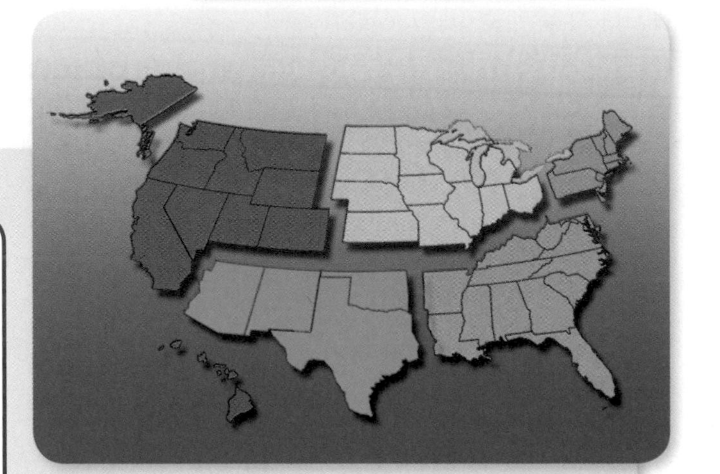

Example 1

Divide both the numerator and denominator by a common factor of 10 and 50.

Try 2. $\frac{10 \div 2}{50 \div 2} = \frac{5}{25}$ ← not in simplest form

Try 5. $\frac{5 \div 5}{25 \div 5} = \frac{1}{5}$ ← The numerator and denominator have 1 as their only common factor.

So, $\frac{10}{50}$ in simplest form is $\frac{1}{5}$.

Of the 50 states, $\frac{1}{5}$ of them are in the Northeast region.

More Examples

A $\frac{15}{24}$

$\frac{15 \div 3}{24 \div 3} = \frac{5}{8}$ simplest form

$\frac{15}{24}$ in simplest form is $\frac{5}{8}$.

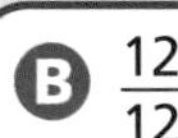

B $\frac{12}{12}$

$\frac{12 \div 12}{12 \div 12} = \frac{1}{1}$

$\frac{1}{1} = 1$ simplest form

$\frac{12}{12}$ in simplest form is $\frac{1}{1}$ or 1.

C $\frac{45}{60}$

$\frac{45 \div 5}{60 \div 5} = \frac{9}{12}$

$\frac{9 \div 3}{12 \div 3} = \frac{3}{4}$ simplest form

$\frac{45}{60}$ in simplest form is $\frac{3}{4}$.

- When do you have to divide by a common factor more than once to write a fraction in simplest form?

NS 2.3 Solve simple problems, including ones arising in concrete situations, involving the addition and subtraction of fractions and mixed numbers (like and unlike denominators of 20 or less), and express answers in the simplest form. *also* **NS 1.0, MR 2.0, MR 2.3, MR 2.4, MR 3.0, MR 3.2, MR 3.3**

Use the Greatest Common Factor

For the fraction $\frac{30}{50}$, the common factors of the numerator and denominator are 1, 2, 5, and 10. When you divide the numerator and denominator by 1, 2 or 5, the fraction is not in simplest form.

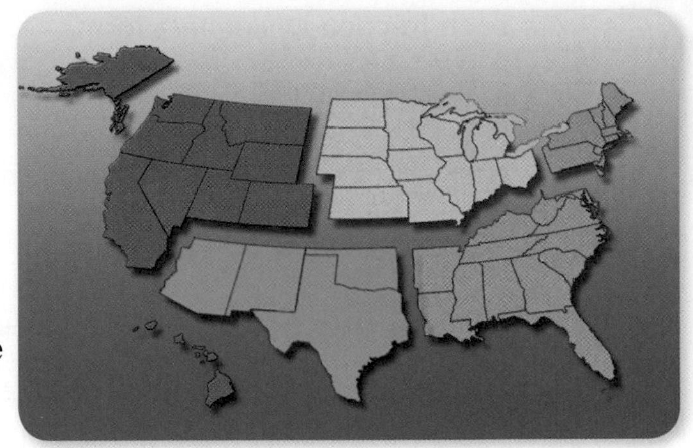

You can divide the numerator and the denominator by the greatest common factor, also known as the greatest common divisor, to write a fraction in simplest form in one step. The **greatest common factor (GCF)** is the greatest factor that two or more numbers have in common.

Example 2

The Southeast, Southwest, Midwest regions and Hawaii, make up $\frac{30}{50}$ of the United States. Write $\frac{30}{50}$ in simplest form.

Step 1

Find the greatest common factor of 30 and 50.

30: 1, 2, 3, 5, 6, 10, 15, 30
50: 1, 2, 5, 10, 25, 50

The GCF is 10.

Step 2

Divide the numerator and denominator by the greatest common factor.

$\frac{30 \div 10}{50 \div 10} = \frac{3}{5}$ ← simplest form

So, $\frac{30}{50}$ written in simplest form is $\frac{3}{5}$.

More Examples

A **Write $\frac{35}{49}$ in simplest form.**

$\frac{35 \div 7}{49 \div 7} = \frac{5}{7}$ 7 is the only common factor other than 1 for 35 and 49.

So, $\frac{35}{49}$ in the simplest form is $\frac{5}{7}$.

B **Write $\frac{18}{36}$ in simplest form.**

$\frac{18 \div 18}{36 \div 18} = \frac{1}{2}$ Divide the numerator and denominator by the greatest common factor.

So, $\frac{18}{36}$ in the simplest form is $\frac{1}{2}$.

Guided Practice

Complete to write each fraction in simplest form.

1. $\frac{9}{12} = \frac{9 \div ■}{12 \div 3} = \frac{■}{4}$
2. $\frac{4}{20} = \frac{4 \div 4}{20 \div ■} = \frac{1}{■}$
3. $\frac{5}{11} = \frac{5 \div ■}{11 \div 1} = \frac{■}{11}$

Name the greatest common factor of the numerator and denominator.

4. $\frac{5}{12}$
5. $\frac{5}{10}$
6. $\frac{25}{45}$
7. $\frac{6}{9}$
8. $\frac{3}{12}$
9. $\frac{12}{18}$

Write each fraction in simplest form.

10. $\frac{4}{8}$ 11. $\frac{6}{10}$ 12. $\frac{5}{5}$ 13. $\frac{7}{9}$ 14. $\frac{24}{36}$ 15. $\frac{10}{14}$

16. **TALK Math** **Explain** how you would find the simplest form of $\frac{12}{36}$ using the greatest common factor.

Independent Practice and Problem Solving

Name the greatest common factor of the numerator and denominator.

17. $\frac{10}{30}$ 18. $\frac{4}{22}$ 19. $\frac{11}{13}$ 20. $\frac{9}{18}$ 21. $\frac{12}{42}$ 22. $\frac{18}{24}$

Write each fraction in simplest form.

23. $\frac{30}{45}$ 24. $\frac{5}{5}$ 25. $\frac{6}{16}$ 26. $\frac{24}{32}$ 27. $\frac{18}{30}$ 28. $\frac{3}{7}$

29. $\frac{14}{16}$ 30. $\frac{20}{100}$ 31. $\frac{12}{25}$ 32. $\frac{16}{32}$ 33. $\frac{15}{75}$ 34. $\frac{48}{54}$

35. $\frac{2}{6}$ 36. $\frac{12}{15}$ 37. $\frac{25}{100}$ 38. $\frac{8}{20}$ 39. $\frac{24}{26}$ 40. $\frac{9}{30}$

Algebra Complete.

41. $\frac{1}{2} = \frac{■}{6}$ 42. $\frac{3}{4} = \frac{9}{■}$ 43. $\frac{■}{20} = \frac{1}{4}$ 44. $\frac{2}{■} = \frac{10}{15}$ 45. $\frac{4}{12} = \frac{■}{3}$

USE DATA For 46–49, use the graph.

46. What fraction of the 50 states are part of the Southeast region? Write the fraction in simplest form.

47. What fraction of the 50 states are in either the Southwest or the Northeast regions? Write the fraction in simplest form.

48. **FAST FACT** Only five states border the Gulf of Mexico. What fraction of the states is this? Write the fraction in simplest form.

49. **WRITE Math** **What's the Question?** Six twenty-fifths of the 50 states make up this region.

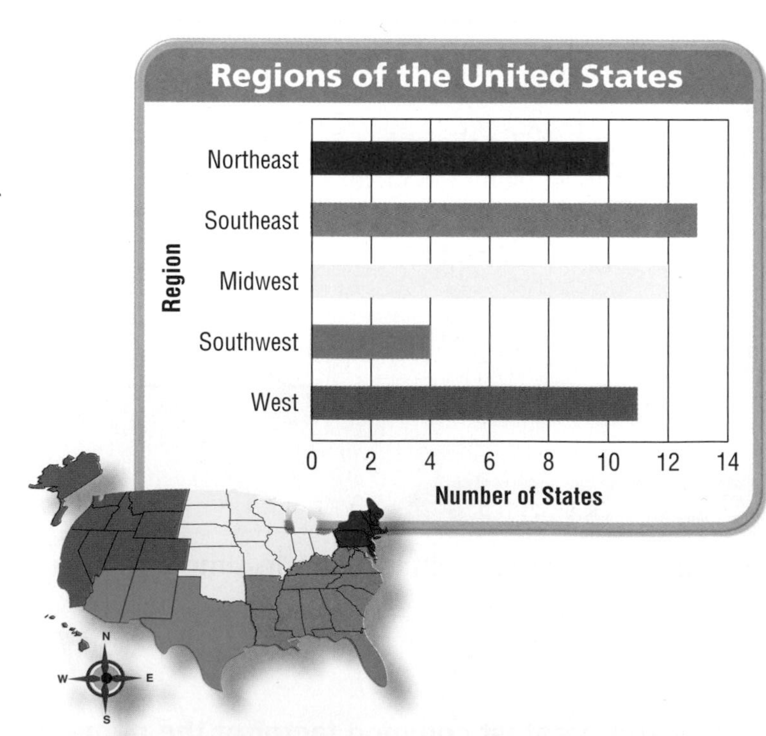

Technology
Use Harcourt Mega Math, Fraction Action, *Fraction Flare Up*, Level E.

 Extra Practice on page 164, Set B

Achieving the Standards

50. Troy had some CDs. He gave 4 to his brother. Write an expression with a variable to model the situation. (AF 1.2, p. 22)

51. Jessie's classroom is 25 feet wide and 30 feet long. What is the classroom's perimeter? (Grade 4 MG 1.4)

52. What mixed number is shown by the model? (Grade 4 NS 1.7)

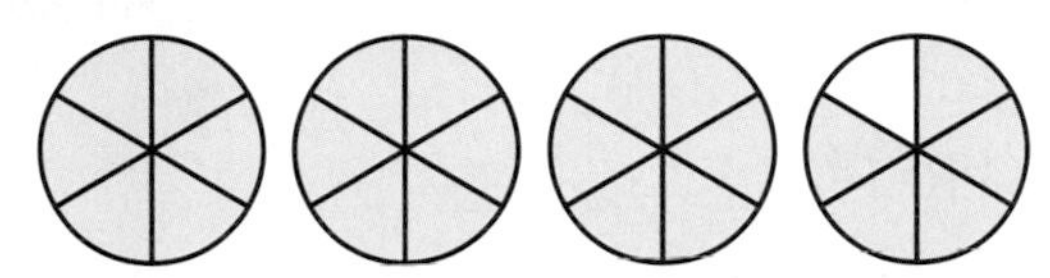

53. **Test Prep** Which fraction is NOT equivalent to $\frac{2}{3}$?

A $\frac{4}{6}$ **C** $\frac{2}{5}$

B $\frac{8}{12}$ **D** $\frac{12}{18}$

54. **Test Prep** Today, 10 of 22 students bought lunch. What fraction of the students bought lunch? Write the fraction in simplest form.

Problem Solving and Reasoning

VISUAL THINKING You can use a Venn diagram to show common factors.

The Venn diagram at the right shows the factors and common factors for 12 and 30. The common factors appear where the two circles overlap.

1. What are the factors for 12? What are the factors for 30? What are the common factors for 12 and 30?
2. How can you use the Venn diagram to find the greatest common factor for 12 and 30? What is the greatest common factor?
3. Draw Venn diagrams to show the factors and common factors for the following pairs of numbers. Identify the greatest common factor for each pair.

   a. 18 and 24 **b.** 20 and 30

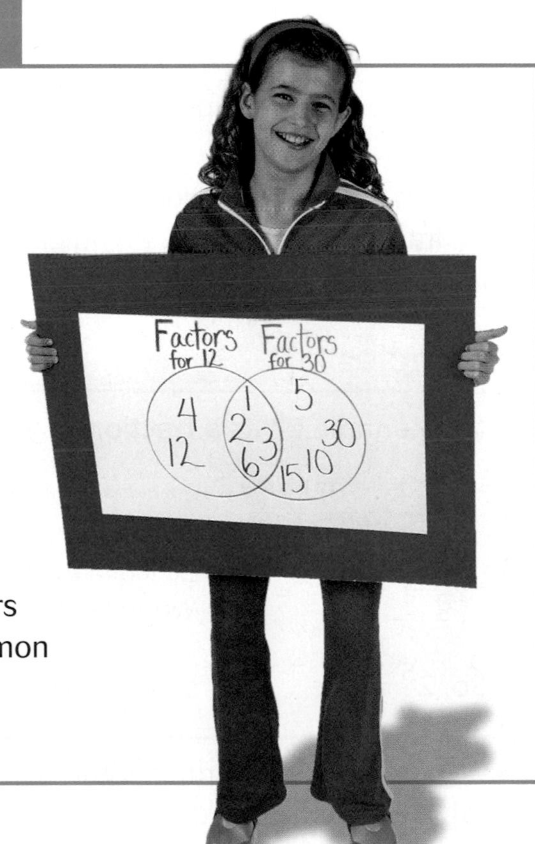

LESSON 3

Understand Mixed Numbers

OBJECTIVE: Rename fractions greater than 1 as mixed numbers and mixed numbers as fractions greater than 1.

Quick Review

Write each fraction in simplest form.

1. $\frac{4}{4}$
2. $\frac{10}{14}$
3. $\frac{10}{25}$
4. $\frac{4}{8}$
5. $\frac{9}{12}$

Vocabulary

mixed number

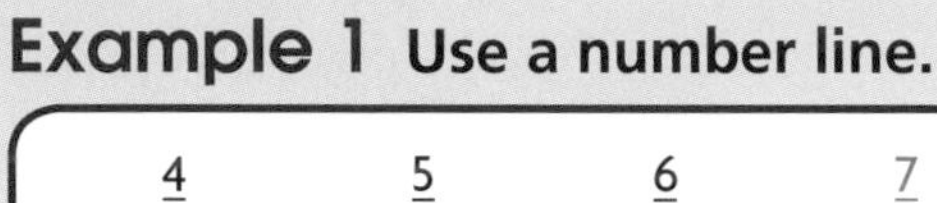

Learn

A **mixed number** is made up of a whole number and a fraction. A mixed number can be renamed as a fraction greater than 1. A fraction greater than 1 is sometimes called an *improper fraction*.

PROBLEM Ricardo is making fruit punch. He starts with one cup of orange juice. Then he adds $\frac{3}{4}$ cup more. He uses $1\frac{3}{4}$ cups of orange juice in all. $1\frac{3}{4}$ is a mixed number. How many $\frac{1}{4}$ cups of orange juice does Ricardo use in his fruit punch?

Example 1 Use a number line.

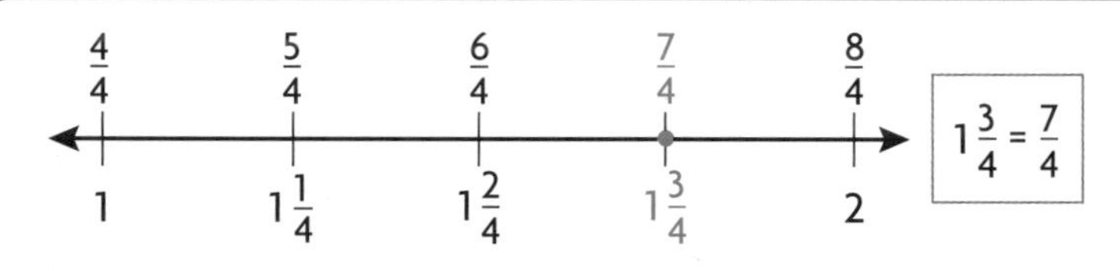

So, Ricardo uses $\frac{7}{4}$ cups of orange juice in his fruit punch.

You can use multiplication and addition to rename a mixed number as a fraction greater than 1. You can use division to rename a fraction greater than 1 as a mixed number.

Examples

A Rename $2\frac{5}{8}$ as a fraction.

$2 = \frac{(8 \times 2)}{8} = \frac{16}{8}$ Write the whole number as a fraction using the denominator, 8.

$2\frac{5}{8} = \frac{16 + 5}{8} = \frac{21}{8}$ Write the number of eighths as a fraction greater than 1.

So, $2\frac{5}{8} = \frac{21}{8}$.

B Rename $\frac{21}{8}$ as a mixed number.

$$\begin{array}{r} 2 \\ 8\overline{)21} \\ -16 \\ \hline 5 \end{array} \rightarrow 2\frac{5}{8}$$

Divide the numerator by the denominator. Use the remainder and the divisor to write a fraction.

So, $\frac{21}{8} = 2\frac{5}{8}$.

- When a mixed number is changed to a fraction, what is always true about the numerator and the denominator?

NS 1.5 Identify and represent on a number line decimals, fractions, mixed numbers, and positive and negative integers. *also* **NS 1.0, MR 2.0, MR 2.3, MR 2.4, MR 3.2**

Guided Practice

Use the number line. Write each fraction as a mixed number. Write each mixed number as a fraction.

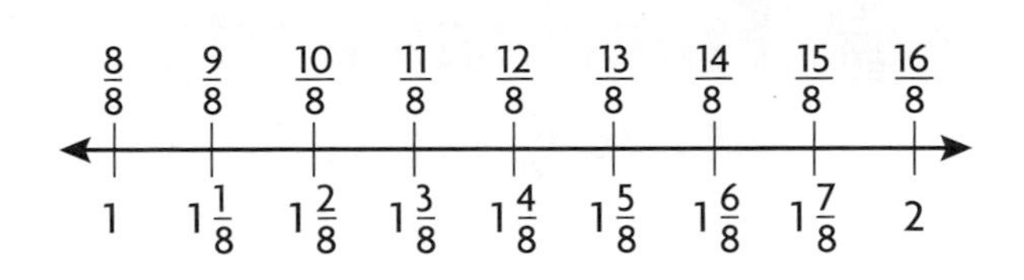

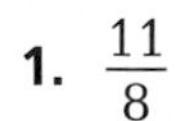

1. $\frac{11}{8}$ **2.** $1\frac{1}{8}$ **3.** $1\frac{5}{8}$

Write each mixed number as a fraction. Write each fraction as a mixed number.

4. $\frac{11}{4}$ **5.** $\frac{6}{5}$ **6.** $2\frac{7}{9}$ **7.** $3\frac{2}{3}$ ✓**8.** $\frac{23}{10}$ ✓**9.** $4\frac{2}{5}$

10. TALK Math **Explain** how you can rename a mixed number as a fraction greater than 1.

Independent Practice and Problem Solving

Write each mixed number as a fraction. Write each fraction as a mixed number.

11. $1\frac{3}{5}$ **12.** $2\frac{1}{3}$ **13.** $\frac{9}{4}$ **14.** $\frac{11}{10}$ **15.** $\frac{13}{6}$ **16.** $1\frac{3}{7}$

17. $\frac{8}{3}$ **18.** $3\frac{5}{6}$ **19.** $7\frac{1}{2}$ **20.** $\frac{47}{15}$ **21.** $\frac{25}{4}$ **22.** $2\frac{7}{12}$

USE DATA Use the recipe for 23–25.

23. Cal is making one batch of energy squares. How many $\frac{1}{3}$-cups of honey will he use?

24. What is the amount of bran cereal in the recipe written as a fraction?

25. WRITE Math Cal has a $\frac{1}{2}$-cup measure. How many times must he fill it to measure out the right amount of peanut butter? **Explain.**

Achieving the Standards

26. Keisha bought a bicycle for \$475. She also bought pedals for \$95. Did she pay more or less than \$600? (Grade 4 NS 3.0)

27. Write the fraction $\frac{12}{30}$ in simplest form. (NS 2.3, p. 146)

28. Compare the fractions. Write $<$, $>$, or $=$.
$\frac{3}{4}$ ● $\frac{1}{4}$ (Grade 4 NS 1.9)

29. **Test Prep** Which fraction is the same as $2\frac{3}{5}$?

A $\frac{5}{5}$ **B** $\frac{11}{5}$ **C** $\frac{12}{5}$ **D** $\frac{13}{5}$

Extra Practice on page 164, Set C

LESSON 4

Compare and Order Fractions and Mixed Numbers

OBJECTIVE: Compare and order fractions and mixed numbers.

Quick Review

Tom had 12 fruit bars. He gave 6 bars to Mark and 2 bars to Marge. Write two equivalent fractions to describe the fraction of fruit bars that are left.

Vocabulary

common multiple

Learn

PROBLEM Greg and Sayre are ushers for a symphony orchestra. Greg plans to usher at $\frac{2}{3}$ of the concerts. Sayre plans to usher at $\frac{3}{4}$ of the concerts. Who will usher at more concerts? Compare $\frac{2}{3}$ and $\frac{3}{4}$.

ONE WAY Use fraction bars to compare.

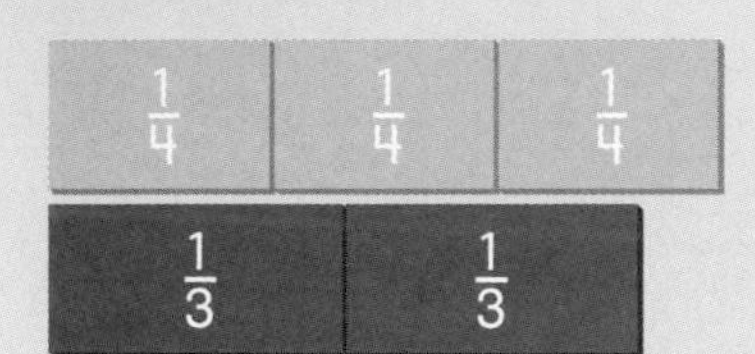

$\frac{3}{4} > \frac{2}{3}$

ANOTHER WAY Find like denominators.

Step 1

Write the multiples of the denominators and then find a common multiple. When a number is a multiple of two or more numbers, it is a **common multiple**.

Multiples of 3: 3, 6, 9, 12, 15, 18, 21, 24
Multiples of 4: 4, 8, 12, 16, 20, 24

12 and 24 are common multiples of the denominators, also known as common denominators.

Step 2

Use equivalent fractions and rename each fraction using a common denominator.

$\frac{3}{4}$ can be renamed as $\frac{3 \times 3}{4 \times 3} = \frac{9}{12}$ or $\frac{3 \times 6}{4 \times 6} = \frac{18}{24}$

$\frac{2}{3}$ can be renamed as $\frac{2 \times 4}{3 \times 4} = \frac{8}{12}$ or $\frac{2 \times 8}{3 \times 8} = \frac{16}{24}$

Step 3

Compare the numerators of the renamed fractions.

Since $9 > 8$, or $18 > 16$, $\frac{3}{4} > \frac{2}{3}$.

So, Sayre will be an usher at more concerts.

Remember

To compare fractions with like denominators, you need only to compare the numerators. Since $5 > 2$, $\frac{5}{8} > \frac{2}{8}$.

NS 1.0 Students compute with very large and very small numbers, positive integers, decimals, and fractions and understand the relationship between decimals, fractions, and percents. They understand the relative magnitude of numbers. *also* **MR 1.2, MR 2.0, MR 2.3, MR 2.4, MR 3.2**

Order Fractions and Mixed Numbers

Tony ushered at $\frac{5}{6}$ of the concerts. Maria ushered at $\frac{4}{9}$ of the concerts, and Tanya ushered at $\frac{2}{3}$ of the concerts. Order the fractions $\frac{5}{6}$, $\frac{4}{9}$, and $\frac{2}{3}$ from least to greatest to find who ushered at the least number of concerts.

Example 1 Order Fractions

Step 1

Find a common denominator for 6, 9, and 3.

6: 6, 12, 18, 24, 30
9: 9, 18, 27, 36
3: 3, 6, 9, 12, 15, 18, 21

A common denominator is 18.

Step 2

Rename as equivalent fractions with a denominator of 18.

$$\frac{5 \times 3}{6 \times 3} = \frac{15}{18}$$

$$\frac{4 \times 2}{9 \times 2} = \frac{8}{18}$$

$$\frac{2 \times 6}{3 \times 6} = \frac{12}{18}$$

Step 3

Compare the numerators. Put them in order from least to greatest.

Since $8 < 12 < 15$,

$$\frac{8}{18} < \frac{12}{18} < \frac{15}{18}.$$

The order from least to greatest is $\frac{4}{9}$, $\frac{2}{3}$, $\frac{5}{6}$

So, Maria ushered at the least number of concerts.

- How can you order unit fractions from least to greatest?

You can use the common denominators to order mixed numbers. First, compare the whole numbers. Then compare the fractions.

Example 2 Order Mixed Numbers

Order $2\frac{2}{3}$, $3\frac{1}{6}$, $2\frac{3}{4}$ from greatest to least.

Step 1

Compare the whole numbers.

$$2\frac{2}{3} \quad 3\frac{1}{6} \quad 2\frac{3}{4}$$

Since $3 > 2$, $3\frac{1}{6}$ is the greatest.

Step 2

Use common denominators to compare the other two fractions— $\frac{2}{3}$ and $\frac{3}{4}$.

$$2\frac{2}{3} = 2\frac{8}{12} \qquad 2\frac{3}{4} = 2\frac{9}{12}$$

Since $9 > 8$, $2\frac{9}{12} > 2\frac{8}{12}$.

So, the order from greatest to least is $3\frac{1}{6}$, $2\frac{3}{4}$, $2\frac{2}{3}$.

- If you were ordering mixed numbers that all had different whole numbers, which parts of the mixed numbers would you compare?

Guided Practice

Compare the fractions. Write <, >, or = for each.

1. 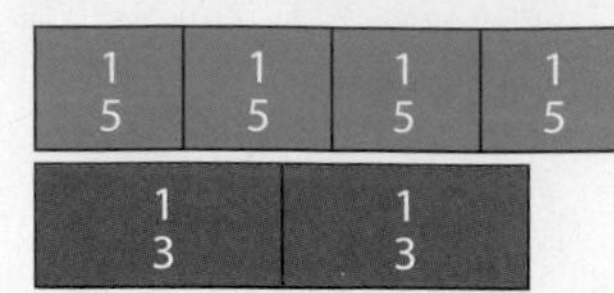 $\frac{2}{3} \bullet \frac{4}{5}$

2. 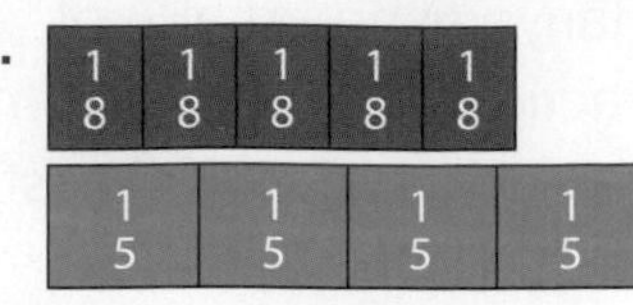 $\frac{4}{5} \bullet \frac{5}{8}$

Compare. Write <, >, or = for each.

3. $\frac{1}{3} \bullet \frac{2}{3}$
4. $\frac{2}{5} \bullet \frac{3}{8}$
5. $3\frac{1}{4} \bullet 2\frac{13}{15}$
6. $1\frac{3}{4} \bullet 1\frac{9}{12}$
7. $5\frac{7}{21} \bullet 5\frac{3}{7}$
8. **TALK Math** **Explain** how to order the unit fractions $\frac{1}{6}$, $\frac{1}{2}$, and $\frac{1}{3}$ from least to greatest.

Independent Practice and Problem Solving

Compare. Write <, >, or = for each.

9. $\frac{1}{2} \bullet \frac{1}{3}$
10. $\frac{3}{4} \bullet \frac{6}{8}$
11. $\frac{5}{7} \bullet \frac{3}{5}$
12. $\frac{2}{11} \bullet \frac{1}{4}$
13. $3\frac{5}{7} \bullet 3\frac{7}{14}$

Write in order from least to greatest.

14. $\frac{1}{2}, \frac{3}{4}, \frac{1}{4}$
15. $\frac{3}{8}, \frac{1}{8}, \frac{7}{8}$
16. $1\frac{3}{8}, 1\frac{1}{4}, 1\frac{5}{6}$
17. $2\frac{2}{3}, 3\frac{1}{8}, 2\frac{3}{5}$
18. $1\frac{1}{4}, \frac{7}{8}, 2\frac{1}{5}$

Use the table for 19–21.

19. Janine collects animal-shaped flutes called ocarinas. List her flutes in order from longest to shortest.
20. Janine buys a turtle-shaped ocarina that is $6\frac{7}{8}$ inches long. Which flute in her collection has a greater length?
21. **WRITE Math** **Explain** how to determine which ocarina is between $6\frac{1}{2}$ inches and $6\frac{3}{4}$ inches long.

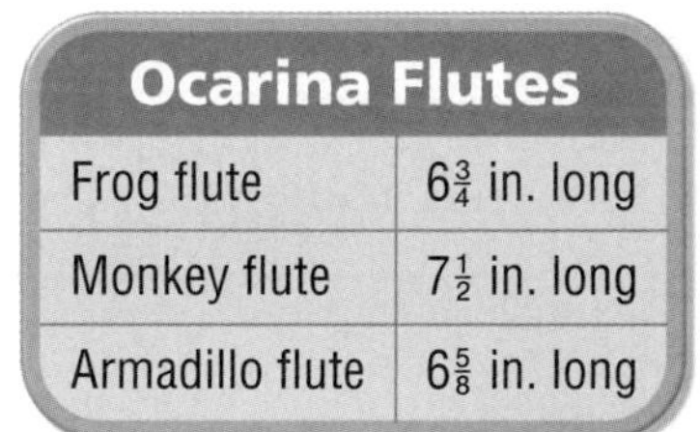

Ocarina Flutes	
Frog flute	$6\frac{3}{4}$ in. long
Monkey flute	$7\frac{1}{2}$ in. long
Armadillo flute	$6\frac{5}{8}$ in. long

Achieving the Standards

22. If $y = 8$, what is the value of $22.5 - y$? (AF 1.2, p. 22)
23. What is the prime factorization of 30? (NS 1.4, p. 132)
24. What is the decimal 0.3 written as a fraction? (NS 1.2, p. 38)
25. **Test Prep** Ken practiced his trumpet $1\frac{2}{3}$ hours on Monday. He practiced $1\frac{5}{6}$ hours on Tuesday, and $1\frac{4}{9}$ hours on Wednesday. On which day did he practice the longest?

    A Monday
    B Tuesday
    C Wednesday
    D Thursday

Extra Practice on page 165, Set D

Water Planet

READ Math WORKSHOP

Reading Skill **Visualize**

Earth's water moves through the environment as part of the water cycle. Most of the water is salt water located in the oceans and seas. The rest of the water is fresh water. The chart below shows the different places where the Earth's fresh water is located. Where is most of the Earth's fresh water located?

About $\frac{3}{4}$ of Earth's surface is covered with water.

Earth's Fresh Water		
Ice caps and glaciers	Groundwater	Lakes, rivers, and water in soil and air
$\frac{47}{56}$	$\frac{1}{7}$	$\frac{1}{56}$

You can solve some problems by visualizing them. When you visualize a problem, you picture the problem in your mind.

Step 1 Read the problem carefully and visualize it.

Step 2 Think about how best to show the problem. You might draw a picture or make a chart or graph. You might use a model, such as fraction bars or counters.

← Fresh Water 28 mL

← Salt Water 972 mL

If all the Earth's water could be held in a 1-liter bottle, the contents would be divided like this.

Problem Solving Visualize to solve the problem.

1. Solve the problem above.
2. Where is the least amount of Earth's fresh water located?
3. Compare the amount of fresh groundwater to the amount of fresh water in ice caps and glaciers.

Problem Solving Workshop
Strategy: Make a Model

OBJECTIVE: Solve problems by using the strategy *make a model*.

Learn the Strategy

Making a model can help you solve a problem. There are different types of models for different types of math problems.

A model can show fractions.

Joe asked his friends Matt and Ellen to help him paint his room. Each person was painting the same size wall. By lunchtime Joe had painted $\frac{3}{8}$ of his wall. Matt had painted $\frac{2}{3}$ of his wall, and Ellen had painted $\frac{3}{5}$ of her wall. Who had painted the greatest part of his or her wall?

Use fractions bars to show how much wall each person painted. Compare the fraction bars.

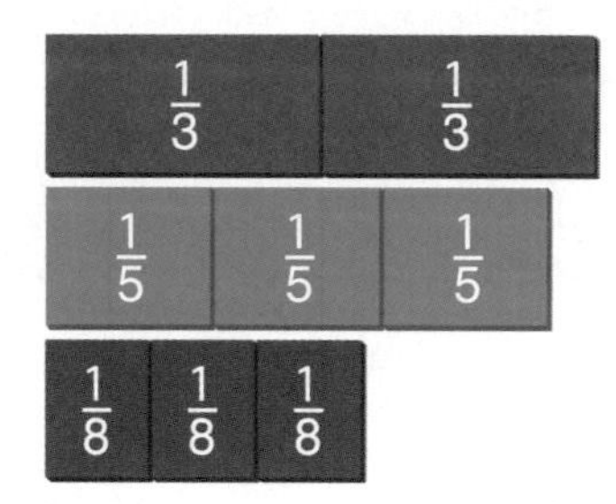

A model can help you estimate.

Enrollment at Bakersville Elementary School increased to 445. About how many students attend the school? Round your answer to the nearest hundred.

Locate 445 on the number line. Find the hundred that is closest to 445.

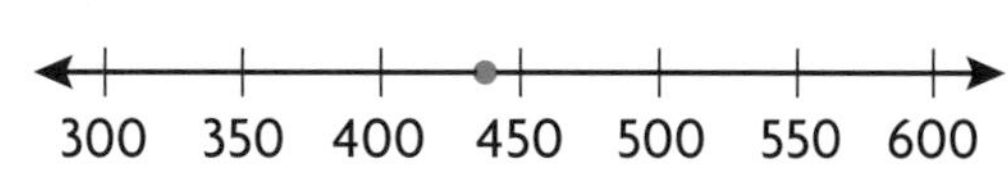

A model can show decimals.

Ira needs 0.8 meter of denim cloth to make a backpack. How many meters of denim cloth does Ira need to make 3 backpacks?

Shade 0.8 three times.

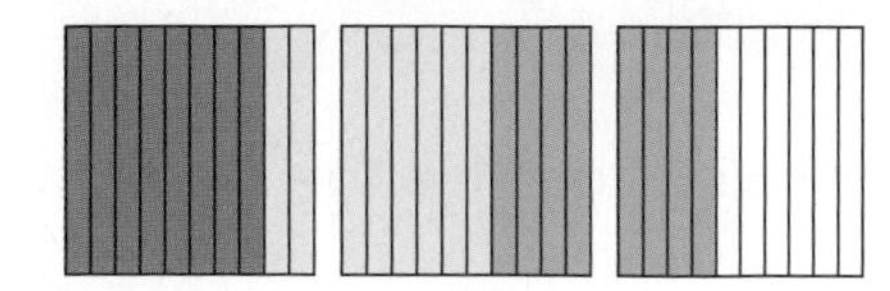

TALK Math

What other types of math problems can you model with a number line?

NS 1.0 Students compute with very large and very small numbers, positive integers, decimals, and fractions and to understand the relationship between decimals, fractions, and percents. They understand the relative magnitudes of numbers. *also* **MR 1.0, MR 2.0, MR 2.3, MR 2.4, MR 3.0, MR 3.1, MR 3.2, MR 3.3**

Use the Strategy

PROBLEM Shelly and her friends are playing horseshoes at a family picnic. Mike's horseshoe lands $1\frac{5}{6}$ feet from the stake. Tonya tosses her horseshoe $2\frac{1}{4}$ feet from the stake. Rico's is $1\frac{7}{12}$ feet from the stake. Shelly's lands $1\frac{2}{3}$ feet from the stake. Whose horseshoe was closest to the stake? Whose horseshoe was farthest from the stake?

Read to Understand

- **Identify the details in the problem.**
- **What information is given?**

Plan

- **What strategy can you use to solve the problem?**

  You can use make a model to help you solve the problem.

Solve

- **How can you use the strategy to solve the problem?**

  Compare the whole-number parts of the mixed numbers.

$\mathbf{1}\frac{5}{6}$, $\mathbf{2}\frac{1}{4}$, $\mathbf{1}\frac{7}{12}$, $\mathbf{1}\frac{2}{3}$ Since $\mathbf{2} > \mathbf{1}$, $2\frac{1}{4}$ feet is the greatest distance.

Use fraction bars to compare the fractional parts of the other mixed numbers.

$\frac{1}{12}$	$\frac{1}{12}$	$\frac{1}{12}$	$\frac{1}{12}$	$\frac{1}{12}$	$\frac{1}{12}$	$\frac{1}{12}$

$\frac{1}{3}$	$\frac{1}{3}$

$\frac{1}{6}$	$\frac{1}{6}$	$\frac{1}{6}$	$\frac{1}{6}$	$\frac{1}{6}$

Since $\frac{7}{12}$ is the shortest, $1\frac{7}{12}$ feet is the least distance.

So, Rico's horseshoe was closest to the stake, and Tonya's was farthest.

Check

- **What other models could you use to solve the problem?**

Guided Problem Solving

Read to Understand
Plan
Solve
Check

1. Some of Shelly's friends decided to have a jumping contest. Who jumped the longest distance? Who jumped the shortest distance?

   First, compare the whole-number parts of the mixed numbers.

   $$3\frac{5}{12}, 3\frac{3}{4}, 4\frac{3}{8}, 3\frac{1}{2} \qquad 4 > 3$$

   Then, use fraction bars to compare the fractional parts of the mixed numbers that have the same whole number.

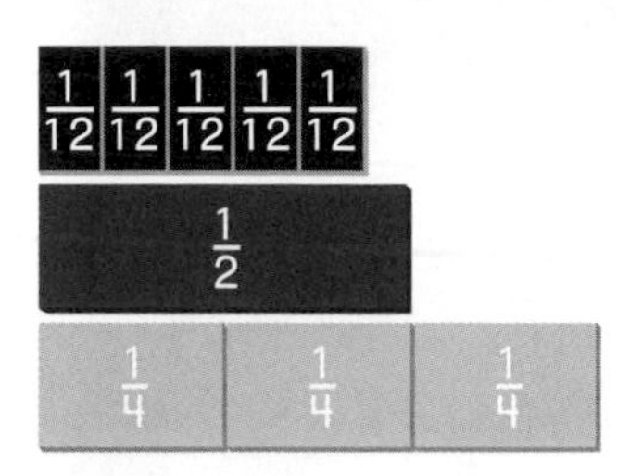

   Finally, find who jumped the longest distance and who jumped the shortest distance.

Length of Jump

Name	Length (in feet)
Amber	$3\frac{5}{12}$
Marcus	$3\frac{3}{4}$
Paul	$4\frac{3}{8}$
Shelly	$3\frac{1}{2}$

2. **What if** Shelly's jump was $3\frac{1}{6}$ feet long instead? Who would have made the longest and shortest jumps then? Explain.

3. Amber, Marcus, Paul, and Shelly line up to make their jumps. Shelly is not first. Amber has at least two people ahead of her. Paul was third. Give the order of the four.

Problem Solving Strategy Practice

Make a model to solve.

4. Mario bought 2 packs of invitations for a party. Each pack contains 10 invitations. Mario is inviting 7 classmates, 4 cousins, and 5 children from his neighborhood. What fraction of the invitations will Mario use?

5. Paul, Greg, and Hilda are meeting at Hilda's house before going to the park. Paul lives $8\frac{4}{5}$ miles from Hilda. Greg lives $8\frac{3}{4}$ miles from Hilda. Who lives closer to Hilda?

6. Tina's garden is 5 meters wide and 12 meters long. The flower section is the same width and twice as long as the vegetable section. How long is each section?

7. Steve bought 24 yellow balloons for a party. He returned 12 of the balloons and bought 9 red balloons. Then he decided to return 6 red balloons and buy 16 blue balloons. How many balloons does Steve have now?

8. WRITE Math **What's the Error?** Andy started out with 14 marbles. He gave 9 marbles to Claudia. Sue gave Andy 18 marbles. Then Andy gave Ryan 8 marbles. Andy says that he has 31 marbles now. Describe his error and use a model to show the solution.

Mixed Strategy Practice

Solve.

9. Hannah had a party and gave each of her friends some party favors. The favors included 7 yo-yos, 13 whistles, 6 kaleidoscopes, 9 maracas, and some marker sets. Altogether, Hannah handed out 41 favors. How many were marker sets?

10. Ryan sent 2 invitations to a party on Monday. On Tuesday, he sent 3 invitations, and on Wednesday, 5 invitations. On Thursday, he sent 8 invitations. If the pattern continued through Saturday, how many invitations will Ryan send in all?

Choose a STRATEGY

- Draw a Diagram or Picture
- Make a Model or Act It Out
- Make an Organized List
- Look for a Pattern
- Make a Table or Graph
- Guess and Check
- Work Backward
- Solve a Simpler Problem
- Write an Equation
- Use Logical Reasoning

USE DATA For 11–14, use the bar graph.

11. Santos, Alice, Otis, and Fred each voted for a different party theme. Alice voted for a Scavenger Hunt. Fred did not vote for a Hawaiian Luau or a Pirate Adventure. Otis did not vote for a Pirate Adventure. What theme did each student vote for?

12. The number of girls who voted for Fiesta Fun is three times as great as the number of boys who voted for it. How many boys voted for Fiesta Fun?

13. **Pose a Problem** Look back at Problem 12. Write a similar problem by changing the mathematical relationship between the numbers of girls and boys who voted for Fiesta Fun. Then solve the problem.

14. **Open-Ended** Use the data in the bar graph to write three different number sentences that use one or more operations.

CHALLENGE YOURSELF

A party supply store sells party favors for $0.75 each, hats for $0.45 each, and noisemakers for $0.60 each.

15. Trevor buys 12 party favors. He spends the same amount of money on hats as on party favors. He spends twice as much on noisemakers as on party favors. How many hats and noisemakers does he buy?

16. Heather paid $15.90 for party supplies. She spent $7.50 on party favors. She bought the same number of hats as noisemakers. How many hats and noisemakers did she buy?

LESSON 6 Relate Fractions and Decimals

OBJECTIVE: Relate fractions and decimals that name tenths, hundredths, and thousandths.

Quick Review

In a competition, Pat received a score of eight and seventy-five hundredths. Write Pat's score as a fraction and as a decimal.

Learn

On an average day, $\frac{1}{10}$ of radio listeners are tuned to a rock station and $\frac{15}{100}$ are tuned to a news station. What are the decimal equivalents for each fraction of the radio audience?

You can write a fraction as a decimal.

$$\frac{1}{10} = 0.1 \qquad \frac{15}{100} = 0.15$$

So, 0.1 of the radio audience are listening to a rock station, and 0.15 are listening to a news station.

HANDS ON Activity

You can use a model to find the decimal equivalent for $\frac{1}{5}$.

Step 1

Draw a model to show $\frac{1}{5}$.

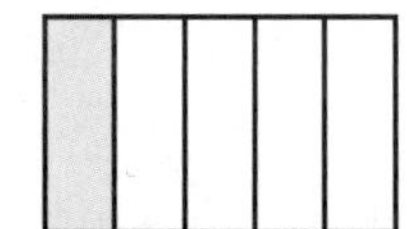

Step 2

Divide the model to show ten equal parts. Write an equivalent fraction for $\frac{1}{5}$.

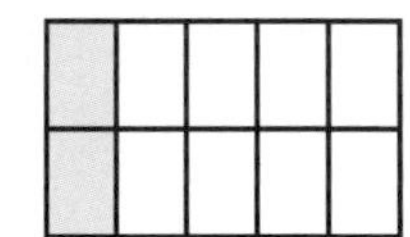

$\frac{1}{5} = \frac{2}{10}$

Step 3

Write a decimal equivalent.

So, $\frac{1}{5} = \frac{2}{10} = 0.2$.

Remember

You can write a number in word form, such as four tenths, to help you write a decimal or fraction, such as 0.4 or $\frac{4}{10}$.

Examples

On an average day, $\frac{1}{4}$ of the total radio audience listen to the radio at work. What is the decimal equivalent for $\frac{1}{4}$?

A Use a hundreths model. Shade $\frac{1}{4}$ of the model. Count the shaded squares.

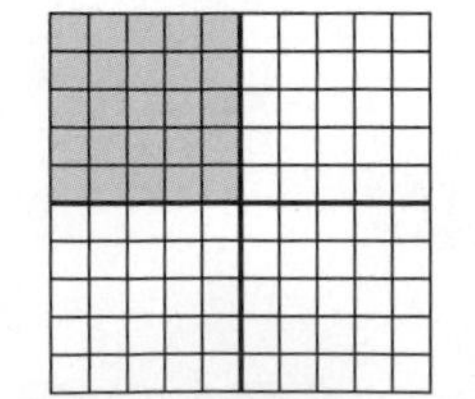

$\frac{1}{4} = 0.25$

B Write an equivalent fraction with a denominator of 100.

$$\frac{1 \times 25}{4 \times 25} = \frac{25}{100} = 0.25$$

So, 0.25 of the radio audience listen to the radio at work.

NS 1.2 Interpret percents as a part of a hundred; find decimal and percent equivalents for common fractions and explain why they represent the same value; compute a given percent of a whole number. *also* NS 1.0, MR 2.0, MR 2.3, MR 2.4, MR 3.2

Guided Practice

Write a decimal and a fraction for each model.

1. 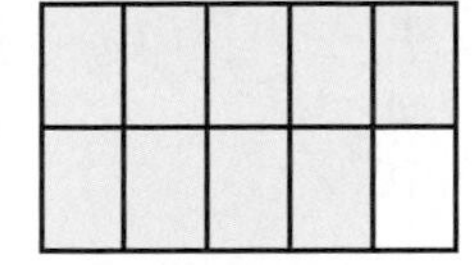

2. 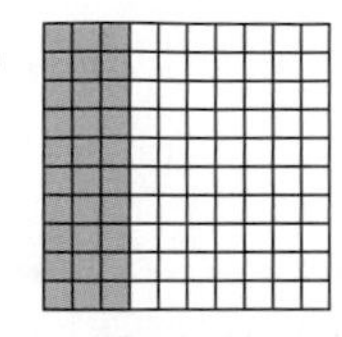

3. 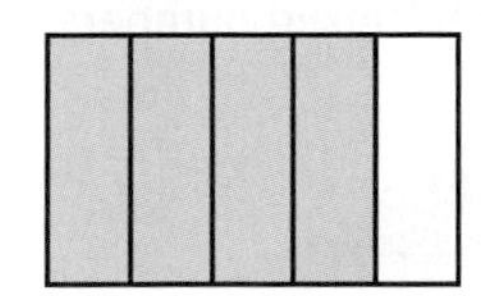

Write each fraction as a decimal. Write each decimal as a fraction in simplest form.

4. 0.7 **5.** $\frac{3}{5}$ **6.** 0.54 **7.** $\frac{24}{100}$ **8.** $\frac{35}{100}$ **9.** 0.22

10. TALK Math **Explain** how to change a decimal to a fraction and a fraction to a decimal.

Independent Practice and Problem Solving

Write each fraction as a decimal.

11. $\frac{1}{2}$ **12.** $\frac{3}{10}$ **13.** $\frac{4}{5}$ **14.** $\frac{10}{25}$ **15.** $\frac{21}{100}$ **16.** $\frac{33}{100}$

17. $\frac{24}{25}$ **18.** $\frac{26}{50}$ **19.** $\frac{3}{15}$ **20.** $\frac{2}{8}$ **21.** $\frac{58}{100}$ **22.** $\frac{18}{100}$

Write each decimal as a fraction in simplest form.

23. 0.8 **24.** 0.4 **25.** 0.50 **26.** 0.83 **27.** 0.78 **28.** 0.25

29. 0.42 **30.** 0.47 **31.** 0.1 **32.** 0.36 **33.** 0.95 **34.** 0.15

Use the design for 35–36.

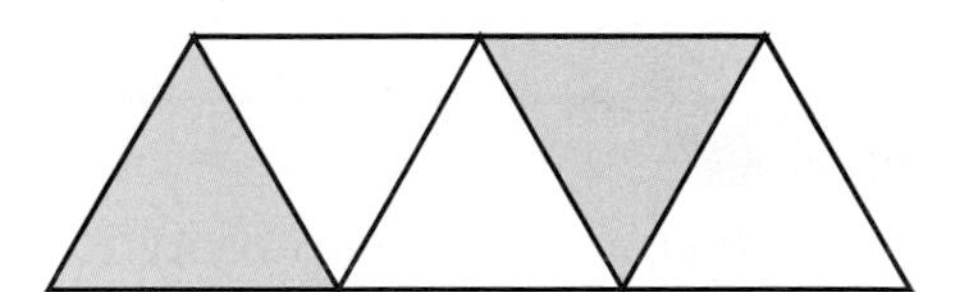

35. Write a decimal for the shaded part of the design.

36. WRITE Math **Explain** how you can change the design so that it shows tenths.

Achieving the Standards

37. The length of one side of a square is 4 inches. What is the square's perimeter? (Grade 4 MG 1.4)

38. Out of the total number of radio listeners, $\frac{40}{100}$ listen to the radio at home. Write the fraction in simplest form. (NS 2.3, p. 146)

39. What mixed number is the same as $\frac{14}{3}$? (NS 1.5, p. 150)

40. **Test Prep** Which fraction is equivalent to 0.33?

A $\frac{3}{10}$

B $\frac{33}{100}$

C $\frac{33}{1,000}$

D $\frac{1}{33}$

Extra Practice on page 165, Set E

Use a Number Line

OBJECTIVE: Identify, represent, and order decimals, fractions, and mixed numbers on a number line.

Quick Review

Write an equivalent fraction.

1. $\frac{2}{5}$
2. $\frac{3}{4}$
3. $\frac{5}{10}$
4. $\frac{25}{100}$
5. $\frac{4}{10}$

Vocabulary

benchmark fractions

Learn

PROBLEM The fifth-grade class is selling tickets to its first Track and Field Day. Marian sold $\frac{3}{5}$ of her tickets. Tawana sold $\frac{7}{10}$ of her tickets. Mannie sold 0.35 of his tickets. If they all started with the same number of tickets, who sold the most tickets?

Example 1

Step 1

Draw a number line. Label benchmark fractions.

Benchmark fractions are familiar fractions used for reference. The fractions $\frac{1}{4}$, $\frac{1}{2}$, and $\frac{3}{4}$ are often used as benchmarks on number lines.

Step 2

Use your benchmark fractions to help locate a point for each number.

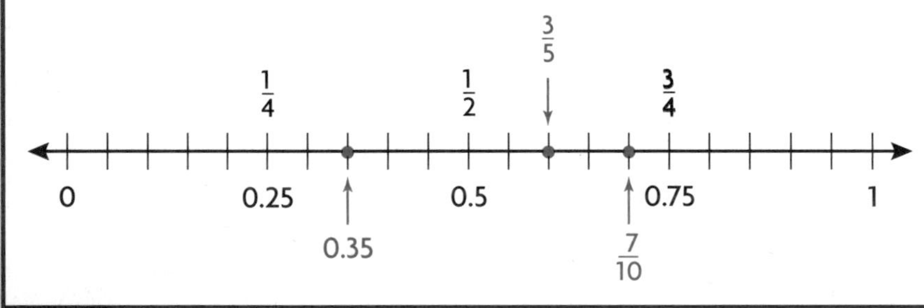

0.35 is between 0.25 and 0.5.

$\frac{3}{5}$ is between $\frac{1}{2}$ and $\frac{3}{4}$.

$\frac{7}{10}$ is a little less than $\frac{3}{4}$ and 0.75.

Step 3

Since you want to know who sold the most tickets, identify the point that is farthest to the right. So, Tawana sold the most tickets.

Example 2 Locate 1.35, $1\frac{3}{4}$, 1.98, and $1\frac{5}{8}$ on a number line. Then order the numbers from greatest to least.

Locate and graph a point for each number.

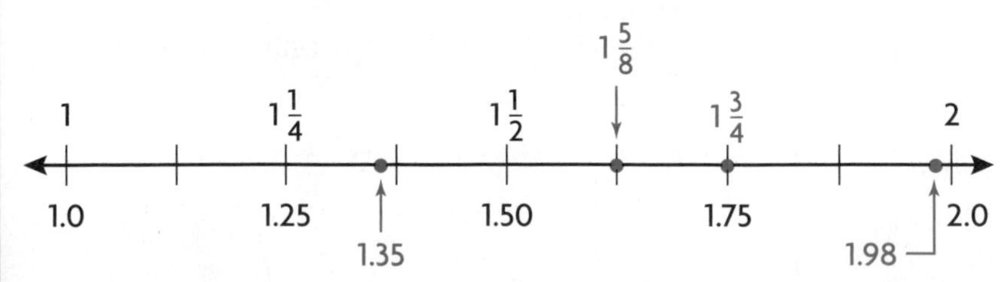

So, the numbers ordered from greatest to least are 1.98, $1\frac{3}{4}$, $1\frac{5}{8}$, 1.35.

NS 1.5 Identify and represent on a number line decimals, fractions, mixed numbers, and positive and negative integers. *also* **NS 1.0, MR 2.0, MR 2.3, MR 2.4, MR 3.2**

Guided Practice

Identify a decimal and a fraction for the point.

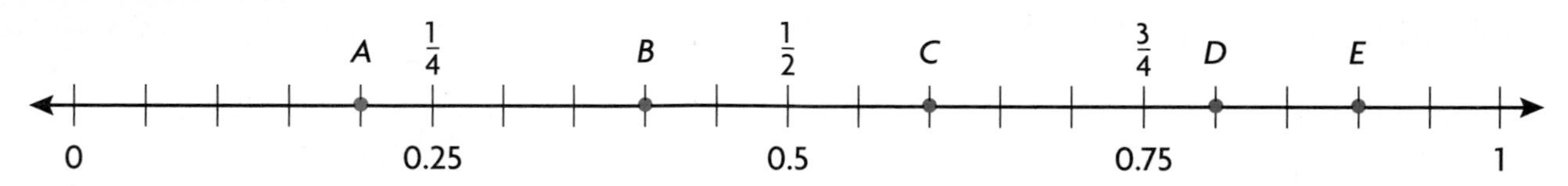

1. Point *C*
2. Point *A*
3. Point *E*
4. Point *B*
5. Point *D*

For 6–11, locate each mixed number or decimal on one number line. Then write the numbers in order from least to greatest.

6. 1.2
7. $1\frac{1}{4}$
8. 1.75
9. $1\frac{3}{8}$
10. 1.35
11. $1\frac{7}{8}$

12. TALK Math **Explain** how you would use a number line to represent 0.35 and $\frac{5}{12}$.

Independent Practice and Problem Solving

Locate each mixed number or decimal on one number line. Then write the numbers in order from least to greatest.

13. 1.4
14. $1\frac{5}{8}$
15. 1.55
16. $1\frac{1}{8}$
17. 1.8
18. $1\frac{1}{4}$

Use a number line to order each set of numbers from greatest to least.

19. $1\frac{3}{4}$, 1.50, $1\frac{3}{8}$
20. 1.25, 1.75, $1\frac{2}{5}$
21. 1.55, $1\frac{1}{10}$, $1\frac{3}{5}$
22. 0.65, $\frac{4}{5}$, 0.45,

23. Flo ran 0.84 of a mile. Connie ran $\frac{3}{4}$ of a mile. Tanya ran $\frac{5}{8}$ of a mile. Which person ran the farthest?

24. WRITE Math **What's the Error?** Mark and Tom started with the same number of tickets. Mark sold 0.7 of his tickets for Field and Track Day. Tom sold $\frac{3}{4}$ of his tickets. Mark says that they both sold the same number of tickets. Is Mark correct? Explain.

Achieving the Standards

25. Kris has $20. She would like to buy three T-shirts that cost $7.29 each. Does she have enough money? Explain. **(Grade 4 NS 2.0)**

26. A football field is 110 meters long and 49 meters wide. What is the area of a football field? **(Grade 4 MG 1.4)**

27. Write $2\frac{2}{5}$ as a fraction greater than one? **(NS 1.5 p. 150)**

28. **Test Prep** Which fraction is less than 0.55?

A $\frac{4}{5}$ B $\frac{9}{20}$ C $\frac{8}{9}$ D $\frac{24}{30}$

Extra Practice on page 165, Set F

Extra Practice

Set A Write an equivalent fraction. (pp. 144–145)

1. $\frac{3}{5}$ 2. $\frac{1}{8}$ 3. $\frac{4}{8}$ 4. $\frac{4}{5}$ 5. $\frac{3}{9}$ 6. $\frac{6}{12}$

7. $\frac{4}{6}$ 8. $\frac{2}{7}$ 9. $\frac{4}{10}$ 10. $\frac{3}{18}$ 11. $\frac{2}{5}$ 12. $\frac{3}{15}$

13. $\frac{1}{6}$ 14. $\frac{4}{12}$ 15. $\frac{1}{10}$ 16. $\frac{4}{16}$ 17. $\frac{5}{7}$ 18. $\frac{8}{9}$

19. Kenisha has 6 cans of fruit. Two of the cans contain peaches. Write two fractions that represent the cans containing peaches.

20. Jake and Evan are playing with 4 red cubes and 8 blue cubes. Jake says that $\frac{1}{2}$ of the cubes are red. Evan says that $\frac{1}{3}$ are red. Who is correct? **Explain.**

Set B Write each fraction in simplest form. (pp. 146–149)

1. $\frac{30}{40}$ 2. $\frac{4}{14}$ 3. $\frac{3}{3}$ 4. $\frac{4}{5}$ 5. $\frac{12}{24}$ 6. $\frac{40}{100}$

7. $\frac{5}{12}$ 8. $\frac{18}{20}$ 9. $\frac{8}{32}$ 10. $\frac{50}{75}$ 11. $\frac{18}{24}$ 12. $\frac{7}{49}$

13. $\frac{10}{80}$ 14. $\frac{9}{15}$ 15. $\frac{16}{16}$ 16. $\frac{25}{45}$ 17. $\frac{15}{16}$ 18. $\frac{75}{100}$

Set C Write each mixed number as a fraction. Write each fraction as a mixed number. (pp. 150–151)

1. $\frac{13}{4}$ 2. $2\frac{1}{5}$ 3. $\frac{5}{3}$ 4. $\frac{29}{4}$ 5. $1\frac{1}{2}$ 6. $4\frac{3}{8}$

7. $\frac{49}{12}$ 8. $\frac{7}{3}$ 9. $3\frac{4}{5}$ 10. $\frac{21}{20}$ 11. $5\frac{1}{3}$ 12. $\frac{20}{9}$

13. $\frac{4}{3}$ 14. $1\frac{5}{6}$ 15. $\frac{43}{10}$ 16. $\frac{19}{3}$ 17. $3\frac{2}{9}$ 18. $8\frac{1}{2}$

19. Mrs. Walters is making a chocolate cake. The recipe calls for $2\frac{1}{2}$ cups of sifted flour. How many $\frac{1}{2}$ cups of flour will she need? Write the mixed number as a fraction greater than 1.

20. Edmund ran nine fourths around a $\frac{1}{4}$ mile track. How many miles did Edmund run? Write the distance as a mixed number and a fraction greater than 1.

Technology
CD ROM Use Harcourt Mega Math, Fraction Action, *Fraction Flare Up*, Levels F, H, J.

Set D Compare. Write <, >, or = for each ●. (pp. 152–155)

1. $\frac{1}{3}$ ● $\frac{3}{5}$
2. $\frac{1}{2}$ ● $\frac{2}{4}$
3. $4\frac{5}{6}$ ● $4\frac{7}{12}$
4. $2\frac{2}{9}$ ● $1\frac{1}{2}$
5. $3\frac{3}{4}$ ● $3\frac{4}{5}$
6. $2\frac{1}{5}$ ● $2\frac{2}{3}$
7. $1\frac{3}{4}$ ● $2\frac{1}{16}$
8. $3\frac{2}{5}$ ● $3\frac{4}{10}$
9. $4\frac{5}{12}$ ● $4\frac{3}{8}$
10. $12\frac{3}{10}$ ● $12\frac{3}{5}$

Write in order from least to greatest.

11. $1\frac{5}{9}, 1\frac{2}{9}, 1\frac{7}{9}$
12. $\frac{4}{5}, \frac{3}{5}, \frac{7}{10}$
13. $\frac{1}{6}, \frac{1}{8}, \frac{1}{10}$
14. $1\frac{3}{4}, \frac{1}{3}, 1\frac{5}{12}$
15. $2\frac{1}{2}, 2\frac{5}{6}, \frac{3}{8}$

16. Toni has three cats: Lizzie, Kiki, and Lulu. Lizzie weighs $9\frac{1}{8}$ pounds, Kiki weighs $10\frac{1}{4}$ pounds, and Lulu weighs $9\frac{3}{4}$ pounds. Which cat weighs the least?

17. Ming gave his seedlings $\frac{3}{4}$ cup of water on Monday, $\frac{1}{2}$ cup of water on Tuesday, and $\frac{7}{8}$ cup of water on Wednesday. On which day did he give his seedlings the most water?

Set E Write each fraction as a decimal. (pp. 160–161)

1. $\frac{2}{5}$
2. $\frac{11}{20}$
3. $\frac{14}{100}$
4. $\frac{6}{8}$
5. $\frac{9}{10}$
6. $\frac{9}{20}$
7. $\frac{6}{10}$
8. $\frac{2}{5}$
9. $\frac{13}{50}$
10. $\frac{44}{100}$

Write each decimal as a fraction in simplest form.

11. 0.9
12. 0.03
13. 0.45
14. 0.75
15. 0.6
16. 0.14
17. 0.3
18. 0.52
19. 0.8
20. 0.99

Set F Use a number line to order each set of numbers from greatest to least. (pp. 162–163)

1. $0.65, \frac{2}{5}, 0.25$
2. $\frac{3}{10}, 0.5, \frac{1}{5}$
3. $1\frac{3}{4}, 1\frac{5}{8}, 0.75$
4. $1.80, 1.25, 1\frac{3}{5}$
5. $0.70, 0.85, \frac{4}{5}$
6. $0.35, \frac{1}{4}, \frac{1}{2}$
7. $1.20, \frac{1}{5}, 1.25$
8. $1\frac{4}{5}, 1.85, 1\frac{9}{10}$

Chapter 6 Review/Test

Check Vocabulary and Concepts

Choose the best term from the box.

VOCABULARY
common factor
common multiple
equivalent fraction
simplest form

1. _?_ are fractions that name the same amount. **(NS 1.0, p. 144)**
2. A number that is a multiple of two or more numbers is called a _?_. **(NS 1.0, p. 146)**
3. A fraction is in _?_ when the numerator and denominator have only 1 as their common factor. **(NS 1.0, p. 146)**

Check Skills

Wite an equivalent fraction. **(NS 1.0, pp. 144–145)**

4. $\frac{1}{6}$
5. $\frac{4}{12}$
6. $\frac{2}{10}$
7. $\frac{5}{8}$

Write each mixed number as a fraction. Write each fraction as a mixed number.
(NS 1.0, 🔑 NS 1.5, pp. 150–152)

8. $\frac{9}{2}$
9. $1\frac{1}{4}$
10. $5\frac{2}{3}$
11. $\frac{10}{3}$

Compare. Write $<$, $>$, or $=$ for each ●. **(NS 1.0, pp. 152–155)**

12. $\frac{2}{3}$ ● $\frac{5}{6}$
13. $1\frac{1}{2}$ ● $1\frac{5}{10}$
14. $3\frac{1}{5}$ ● $2\frac{3}{7}$
15. $1\frac{2}{3}$ ● $1\frac{4}{7}$

Write each fraction as a decimal. Write each decimal as a fraction in simplest form.
(🔑 NS 1.2, pp. 160–161)

16. 0.75
17. $\frac{19}{100}$
18. 0.48
19. $\frac{2}{8}$

Use a number line to order each set of numbers from greatest to least. **(🔑 NS 1.5, pp. 162–163)**

20. $\frac{3}{4}$, 0.45, $\frac{1}{2}$
21. 1.15, 1.25, $1\frac{3}{8}$
22. $\frac{3}{5}$, $\frac{1}{10}$, 0.5
23. $\frac{1}{4}$, 0.23, $\frac{1}{5}$

Check Problem Solving

Solve. **(NS 1.0, MR 1.1, pp. 156–159)**

24. Jen, Rick, and Katrina are making bead chains. Jen's chain is $4\frac{3}{8}$ feet long. Rick's chain is $4\frac{1}{2}$ feet long. Katrina's chain is $3\frac{3}{4}$ feet long. Whose chain is the longest?
25. **WRITE Math** Lin lives 0.9 mile from school. **Explain** how you could use a model to find the distance Lin travels to and from school during a 5-day week.

GO ONLINE **Technology** Use *Online Assessment.*

Enrich • Solve for Unknowns

Use the Clues

You can use what you know about equivalent fractions to solve.

Example 1

Find the unknown number. $\frac{6}{7} = \frac{■}{56}$

Clue 1: The unknown number is a two-digit even number greater than 40 but less than 60.

Clue 2: The sum of the digits is 12.

Step 1	**Step 2**
List all the even numbers greater than 40 but less than 60. 42, 44, 46, 48, 50, 52, 54, 56, 58	Find a number in the list whose digits have a sum of 12. $4 + 8 = 12$ So, the unknown number = 48.

Example 2

Find the unknown number. $\frac{2}{3} = \frac{■ - 8}{51}$.

Step 1	**Step 2**	**Step 3**
Find a fraction equivalent to $\frac{2}{3}$ that has 51 as a denominator. So, divide 51 by 3. $51 \div 3 = 17$	Since $3 \times 17 = 51$, multiply: 2×17. $\frac{2 \times 17}{3 \times 17} = \frac{34}{51}$	Solve for the unknown number. $■ - 8 = 34$ $42 - 8 = 34$ So, the unknown number is 42.

Try It

Solve.

1. $\frac{4}{5} = \frac{■}{60}$

Clue: The unknown number is an even number greater than 45 but less than 65.

2. $\frac{3}{4} = \frac{27}{■}$

Clue: The sum of the digits is 9.

3. $\frac{7}{13} = \frac{28}{■}$

Clue: The sum of the digits is 7.

WRITE Math **Explain** how you would find the unknown number in $\frac{■}{24} = \frac{2}{3}$.

Unit Review/Test
Chapters 5–6

Multiple Choice

1. $6^3 =$
(NS 1.3, p. 126)

A $6 + 6 + 6$

B $6 \times 6 \times 6$

C $3 + 3 + 3 + 3 + 3 + 3$

D $3 \times 3 \times 3 \times 3 \times 3 \times 3$

2. What is the value of 20^2? (NS 1.3, p. 128)

A 22

B 40

C 202

D 400

3. Which of the following is a prime number? (O-π NS 1.4, p. 120)

A 4

B 9

C 13

D 15

4. What is the prime factorization of 48? (O-π NS 1.4, p. 132)

A $2^3 \times 3^2$

B $2^3 \times 3^1$

C $2^3 \times 3^3$

D $2^4 \times 3^1$

5. Which of the following shows the fraction modeled in simplest form? (NS 1.0, p. 146)

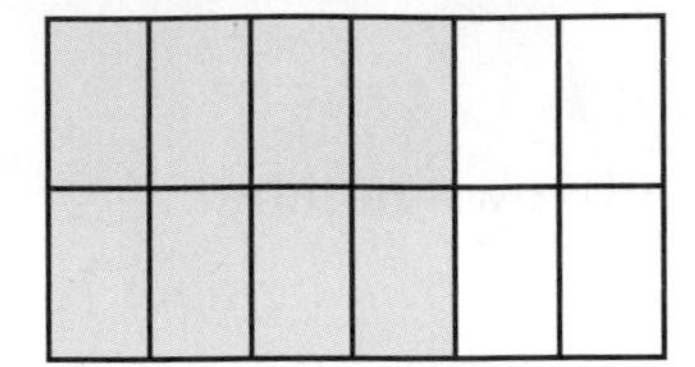

A $\frac{2}{3}$

B $\frac{1}{2}$

C $\frac{8}{11}$

D $\frac{3}{4}$

6. Which number line shows $2\frac{1}{4}$ represented by a point? (O-π NS 1.5, p. 150)

A
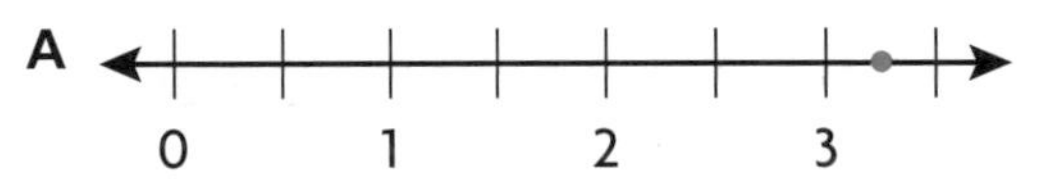

B
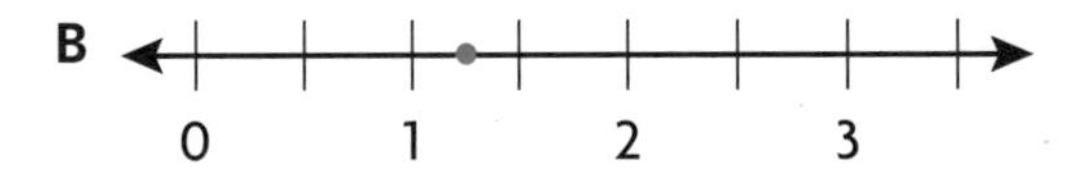

C
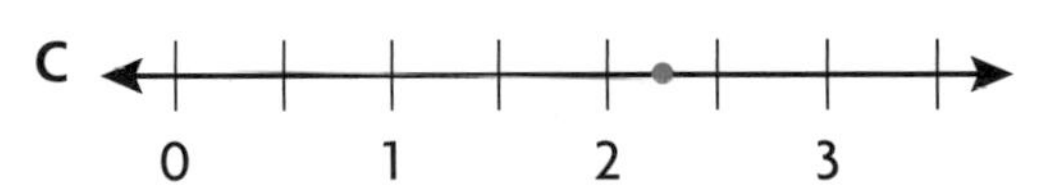

D
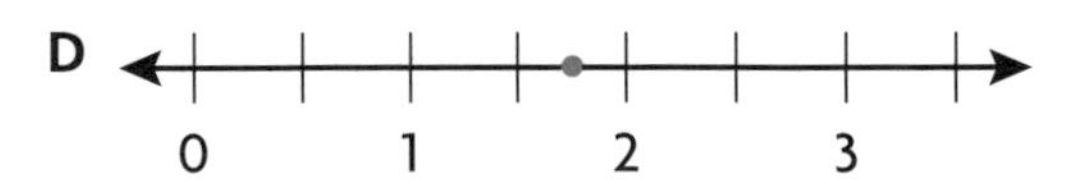

GO ONLINE **Technology** Use *Online Assessment.*

7. What is 0.5 written as a fraction?
(NS 1.2, p. 38)

A $\frac{1}{5}$

B $\frac{1}{2}$

C $\frac{2}{3}$

D $\frac{5}{6}$

8. 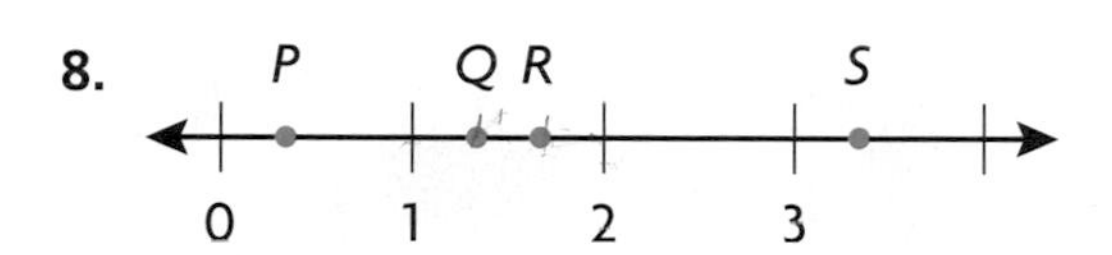

Which letter on the number line identifies the location of $1\frac{1}{3}$? (NS 1.5, p. 150)

A P

B Q

C R

D S

Short Response

9. 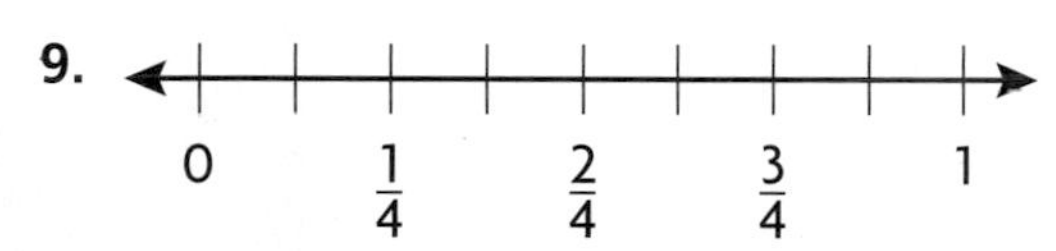

Use the number line to place the following fractions in order from least to greatest.
(NS 1.5, p. 152)

$$\frac{1}{2}, \frac{1}{4}, \frac{3}{8}$$

10. Which is greater: 3^4 or 4^3? (NS 1.3, p. 126)

11. Draw a number line from 0 to 4 as shown.

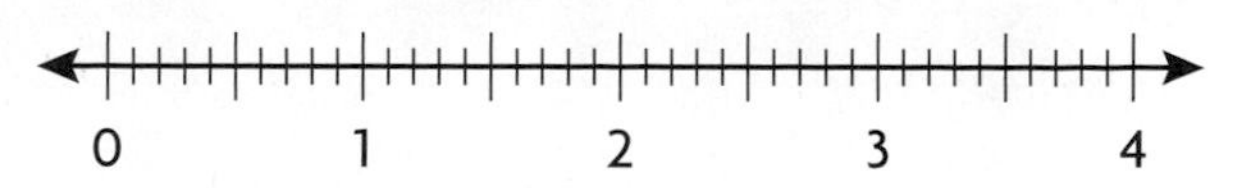

Place the following numbers on the number line: 1.4, 3.7, $2\frac{1}{5}$.
(NS 1.5, p. 44)

Extended Response WRITE Math

12. Use any of the digits 1, 2, 3, or 5 to find the prime factorization of a number that is greater than 40 but less than 50. **Explain** how you found your answer.
(NS 1.4, p. 132)

13. The basketball coach keeps score of the baskets and attempts made during each game. The table below shows the data for five players.

Player	Baskets made per attempt	Equivalent Decimal
Miles	$\frac{2}{4}$	■
Rona	$\frac{5}{10}$	■
Jerry	$\frac{7}{10}$	■
Erin	$\frac{3}{4}$	■
Dan	$\frac{3}{5}$	■

Copy the table and write an equivalent decimal for each fraction. Then place the players in order from most baskets made per attempt to fewest baskets made per attempt. You can use a number line or another model to solve. **Explain** how you found your answer. (NS 1.5, p. 144)

California

Problem Solving

from THE WORLD ALMANAC FOR KIDS

Music, Music, Music

I Hear a Symphony!

The Los Angeles Philharmonic is an orchestra known around the world for its beautiful music. It was founded in 1919. The orchestra usually plays classical music, by composers like Johann Sebastian Bach and Johannes Brahms.

▲ People sit outside to listen to the Philharmonic at SummerSounds.

Community involvement is important to The Los Angeles Philharmonic. Each summer they perform an outdoor concert for children called SummerSounds. There are also symphonies designed just for families, as well as programs for students from grades 3–12.

FACT·ACTIVITY

Composer Pieces Played in a Month

Composer	Number of Pieces Played
Bach	3
Brahms	3
Mozart	6
Schubert	2
Strauss	8
Telemann	2

Use the table to answer the questions.

1. What fraction of the pieces played were by Mozart?
2. What fraction of the pieces played were compositions by Brahms and Strauss?
3. Which two composers combined represent $\frac{1}{6}$ of the total pieces played by the symphony?
4. Write an inequality that compares the fraction of Bach pieces played and the fraction of Schubert pieces played.
5. WRITE Math ▸ **Explain** how you found your answer for Problem 4.

ALMANAC
Fact

The California Youth Orchestra was founded in 1952. It has taught over 15,000 children and has two full symphony orchestras.

Many Voices, One Orchestra

What do you call a large group of musicians? Both *orchestra* and *band* are correct, but the two musical groups are different. Orchestras have four sections: brasses, percussion, woodwinds, and strings. Marching bands do not have a string section.

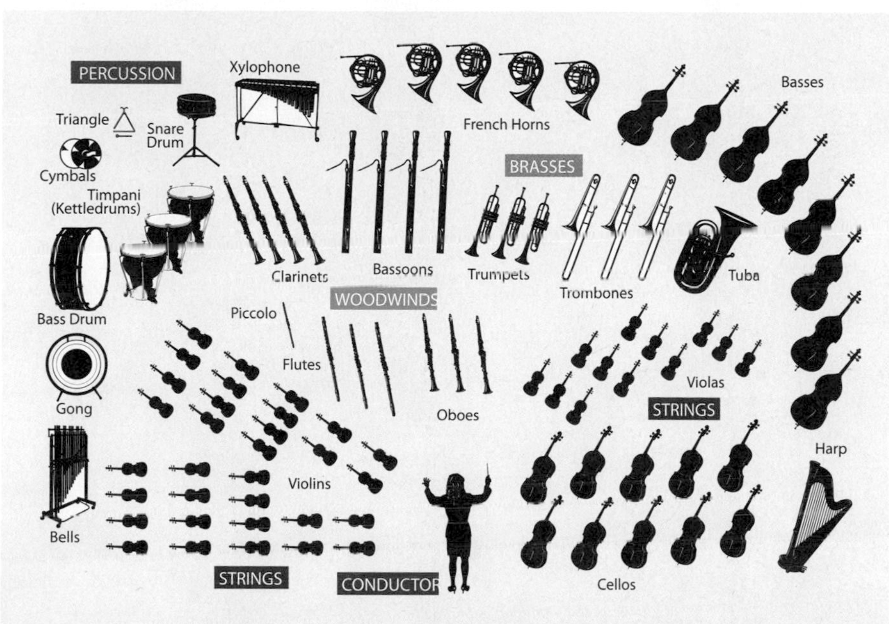

In an orchestra the strings include the violins, violas, cellos, basses, and a harp. The strings make up $\frac{63}{100}$ of the orchestra above.

FACT·ACTIVITY

1. Design your own group of musicians.
   - Decide the number of members that will be in your group.
   - Choose an instrument for each member. You may want to refer to the diagram above.
   - How many of each instrument will you need?
   - What fractions can you use to describe each part of your group?
2. Describe how the fractions will change if one member of your group is not able to perform.

UNIT 3 Fraction Operations

Math on Location

▲ The designer's idea sketches and drawings show measurements in fractions and mixed numbers.

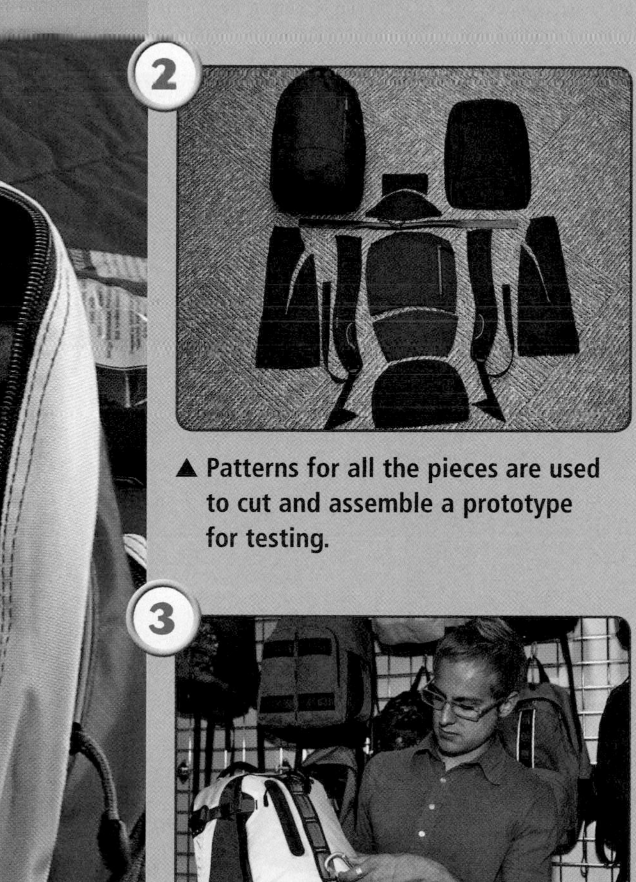

▲ Patterns for all the pieces are used to cut and assemble a prototype for testing.

▲ The designer looks at finished backpacks to be able to explain the benefits of his design.

VOCABULARY POWER

TALK Math

What math is used in the **Math on Location** photographs? What kinds of numbers do you need to use to measure and cut material in precise sizes?

READ Math

REVIEW VOCABULARY You learned the words below when you learned about operations with fractions and mixed numbers. How do these words relate to **Math on Location**?

equivalent fractions fractions that name the same amount

benchmark fraction a familiar fraction used as a point of reference

unit fraction a fraction that has a numerator of 1

WRITE Math

Copy and complete a word definition map like the one below. Use what you know about fractions.

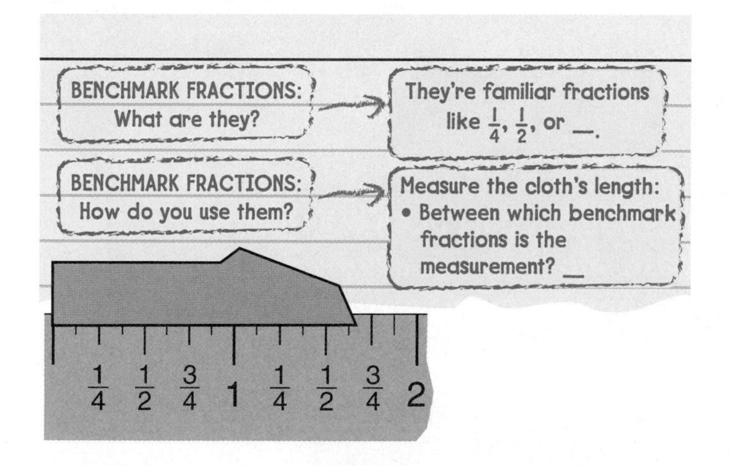

BENCHMARK FRACTIONS: What are they?
They're familiar fractions like $\frac{1}{4}$, $\frac{1}{2}$, or __.
BENCHMARK FRACTIONS: How do you use them?
Measure the cloth's length:
• Between which benchmark fractions is the measurement? __
$\frac{1}{4}$ $\frac{1}{2}$ $\frac{3}{4}$ 1 $\frac{1}{4}$ $\frac{1}{2}$ $\frac{3}{4}$ 2

Technology
Multimedia Math Glossary link at **www.harcourtschool.com/hspmath**

7 Add and Subtract Like Fractions

The Big Idea Addition and subtraction of like fractions are based on understanding equivalent fractions.

CALIFORNIA FAST FACT

The first two navel orange trees planted in the United States came from Brazil in 1873. Nearly all navel orange trees in the United States came from these two trees.

Investigate

Suppose you eat part of an orange for breakfast, and then you eat the rest for lunch. In how many ways could you eat the orange? Choose a number of sections, from 8 to 11, for your orange. Write the number of orange sections for both meals as a fraction. Write three pairs of fractions.

GO ONLINE **Technology** Student pages are available in the Student eBook.

Show What You Know

Check your understanding of important skills needed for success in Chapter 7.

▶ Equivalent Fractions

Write two equivalent fractions for each picture.

1. 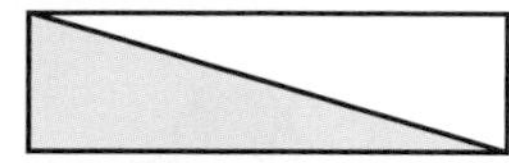

2. 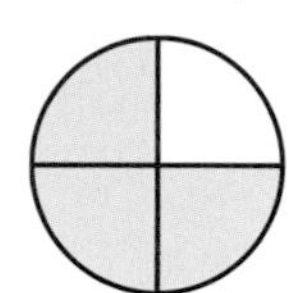

3. 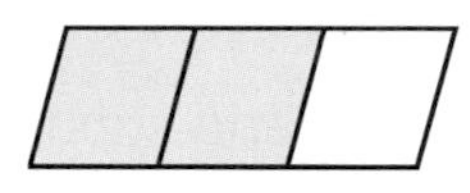

4. 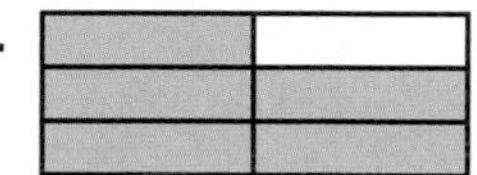

5. 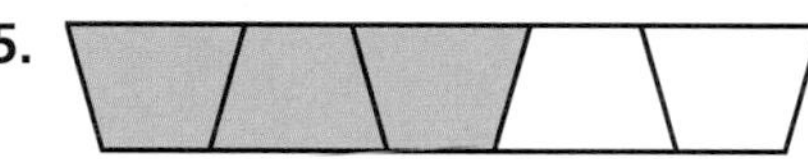

6. 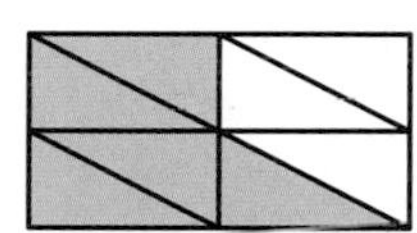

7. 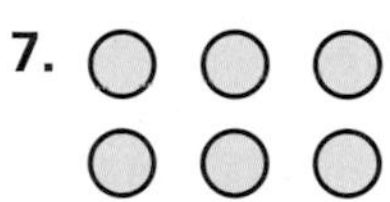

8. 

9. 

▶ Simplest Form

Write each fraction in simplest form.

10. $\frac{2}{4}$ **11.** $\frac{4}{6}$ **12.** $\frac{2}{8}$ **13.** $\frac{3}{9}$

14. $\frac{6}{10}$ **15.** $\frac{6}{12}$ **16.** $\frac{8}{10}$ **17.** $\frac{4}{20}$

18. $\frac{8}{12}$ **19.** $\frac{10}{30}$ **20.** $\frac{15}{25}$ **21.** $\frac{6}{18}$

VOCABULARY POWER

CHAPTER VOCABULARY

equivalent fractions
inverse operations
mixed number
rename
simplest form

WARM-UP WORDS

equivalent fractions fractions that name the same number or amount

simplest form A fraction is in simplest form when the numerator and denominator have only 1 as their common factor.

inverse operations operations that undo each other, like addition and subtraction or multiplication and division

LESSON 1 HANDS ON

Model Addition and Subtraction

OBJECTIVE: Model addition and subtraction of like fractions.

Quick Review

Write the fraction in simplest form.

1. $\frac{2}{4}$
2. $\frac{6}{8}$
3. $\frac{6}{6}$
4. $\frac{5}{10}$
5. $\frac{2}{8}$

Investigate

Materials ■ fraction bars

You can add and subtract fractions with like denominators using fraction bars.

Add. $\frac{1}{8} + \frac{5}{8}$

A Place one of the $\frac{1}{8}$ bars under a 1 whole bar.

1
$\frac{1}{8}$

B Place 5 more $\frac{1}{8}$ bars to show $\frac{5}{8}$. Count the fraction bars.

C Write the answer in simplest form.

D Use fraction bars to find $\frac{2}{6} + \frac{5}{6}$.

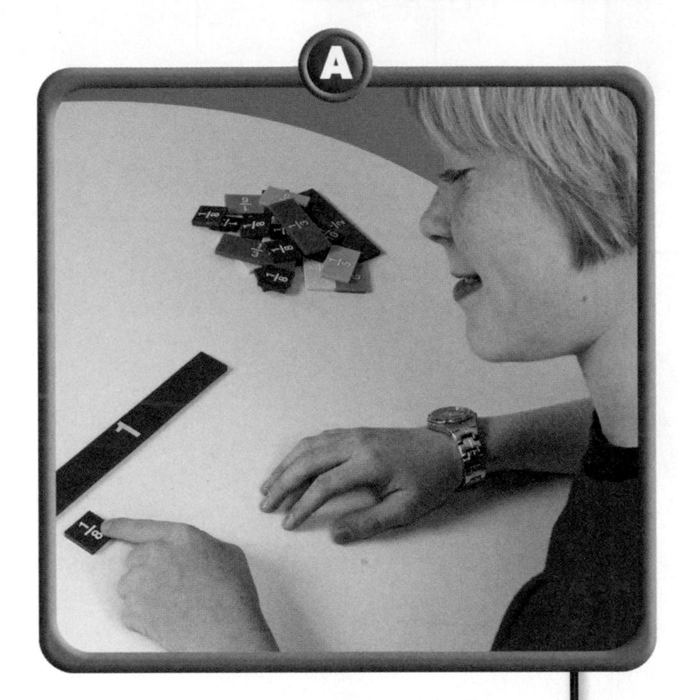

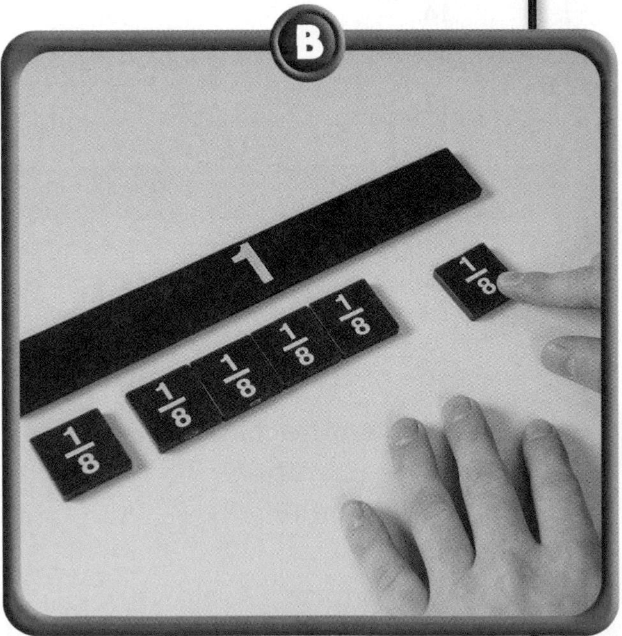

Draw Conclusions

1. In your model, how many $\frac{1}{8}$ bars equal $\frac{1}{2}$? What do you know about $\frac{4}{8}$ and $\frac{1}{2}$?
2. Look at your model for D. How do you know if the sum of two fractions is greater than 1?
3. **Application** Show how to apply the same method using fraction bars to find $\frac{3}{5} - \frac{1}{5}$.

NS 2.3 Solve simple problems, including ones arising in concrete situations, involving the addition and subtraction of fractions and mixed numbers, and express answers in the simplest form. *also* **MR 2.0, MR 2.3, MR 2.4, MR 3.2**

Connect

You can use fraction bars with like denominators to subtract fractions.

Subtract. $\frac{7}{10} - \frac{3}{10}$

Step 1

Place seven $\frac{1}{10}$ bars under the 1 whole bar.

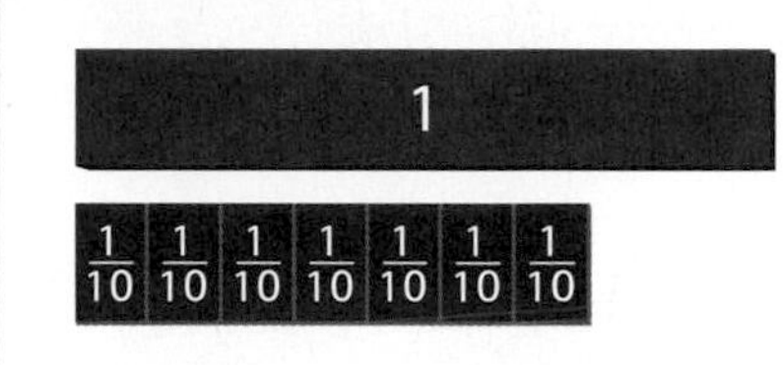

Step 2

Place three $\frac{1}{10}$ bars under the seven $\frac{1}{10}$ bars to show $\frac{3}{10}$.

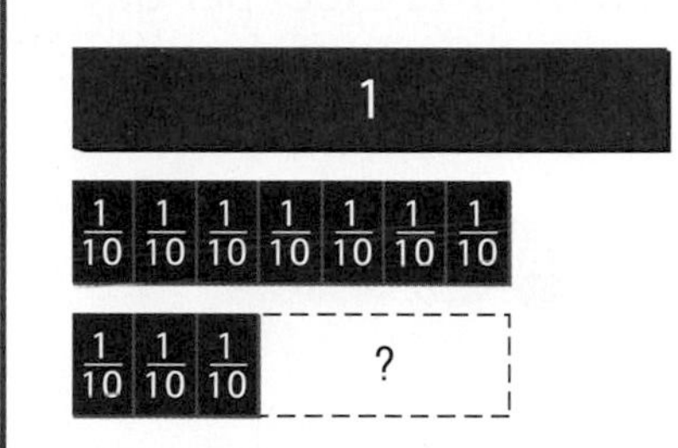

Step 3

Compare the rows of bars. Find the difference in simplest form.

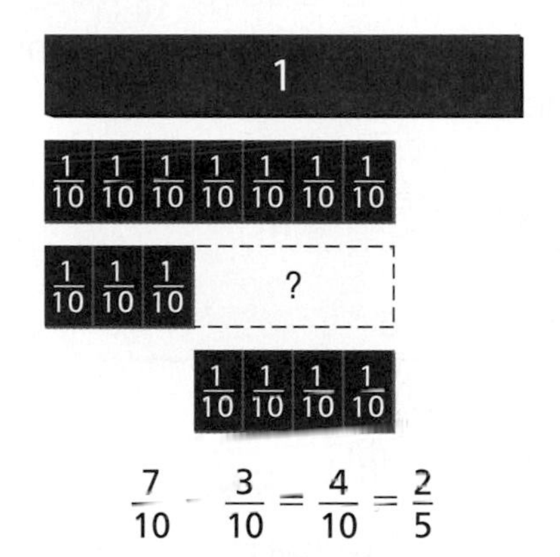

$\frac{7}{10} - \frac{3}{10} = \frac{4}{10} = \frac{2}{5}$

TALK Math

How would you find $\frac{5}{6} - \frac{2}{6}$?

Practice

Use fraction bars to find the sum or difference. Write the answer in simplest form.

1. 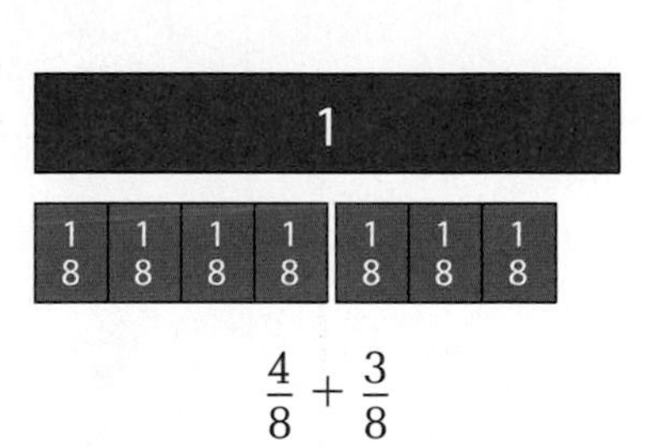

$\frac{4}{8} + \frac{3}{8}$

2. 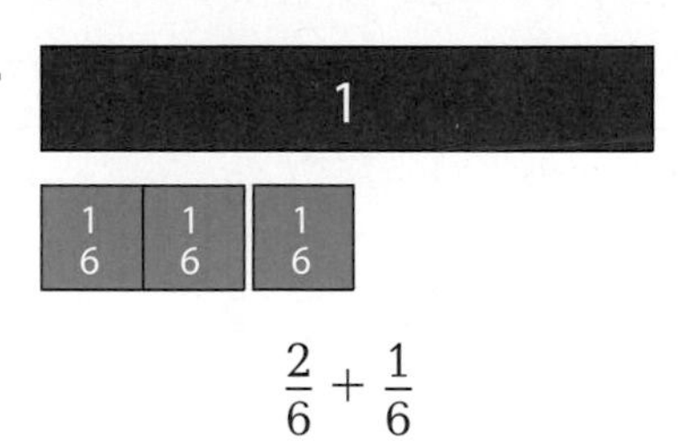

$\frac{2}{6} + \frac{1}{6}$

3. 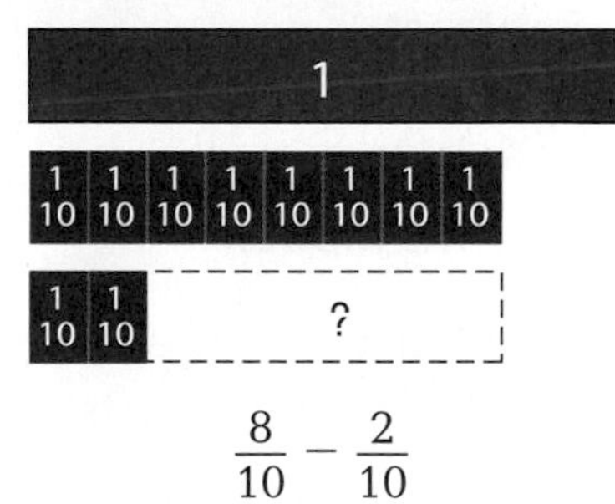

$\frac{8}{10} - \frac{2}{10}$

Find the sum or difference. Write it in simplest form.

4. $\frac{2}{10} + \frac{3}{10}$
5. $\frac{5}{12} + \frac{2}{12}$
6. ✓ $\frac{2}{3} - \frac{1}{3}$
7. ✓ $\frac{2}{9} + \frac{4}{9}$
8. $\frac{5}{6} - \frac{2}{6}$
9. $\frac{2}{4} + \frac{1}{4}$
10. $\frac{9}{12} - \frac{7}{12}$
11. $\frac{3}{7} + \frac{4}{7}$
12. **WRITE Math** Write a rule that you can use for adding or subtracting fractions with like denominators.

LESSON 2

Add and Subtract Like Fractions

OBJECTIVE: Add and subtract like fractions.

Quick Review

Write each fraction in simplest form.

1. $\frac{2}{10}$ **2.** $\frac{6}{8}$

3. $\frac{4}{8}$ **4.** $\frac{2}{6}$

5. $\frac{6}{9}$

Learn

PROBLEM Alaska's Columbia Glacier is one of North America's fastest moving glaciers. It moves at a rate of about 78 feet to 114 feet each day. Suppose the glacier moves 78 feet per day for two weeks. This is about $\frac{2}{10}$ mile. It then moves 114 feet per day for two weeks. This is about $\frac{3}{10}$ mile. How far in miles does the glacier move in four weeks?

ONE WAY **Use a model.**

Add. $\frac{2}{10} + \frac{3}{10}$

Shade 2 parts of a tenths model.

Shade 3 more parts.

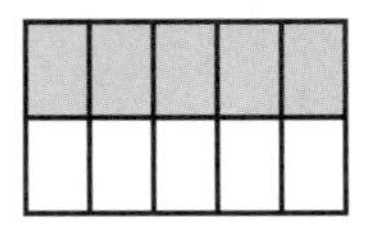

Write the fraction for the part that is shaded. $\frac{5}{10} = \frac{1}{2}$

ANOTHER WAY **Use paper and pencil.**

$$\frac{2}{10} + \frac{3}{10} = \frac{5}{10} = \frac{1}{2}$$

- Add the numerators.
- Write the sum over the denominator.
- Write the sum in simplest form.

So, the glacier moves $\frac{1}{2}$ mile every 4 weeks.

ONE WAY **Use a model.**

Subtract. $\frac{3}{10} - \frac{2}{10}$

Shade 3 parts of a tenths model.

Subtract $\frac{2}{10}$. Draw a line through 2 parts.

Write the fraction: $\frac{1}{10}$.

ANOTHER WAY **Use paper and pencil.**

$$\frac{3}{10} - \frac{2}{10} = \frac{1}{10}$$

- Subtract the numerators.
- Write the difference over the denominator.
- Check that the difference is in simplest form.

Guided Practice

1. Use the model to find $\frac{2}{8} + \frac{4}{8}$. Write the answer in simplest form.

NS 2.3 Solve simple problems, including ones arising in concrete situations, involving the addition and subtraction of fractions and mixed numbers (like and unlike denominators of 20 or less), and express answers in the simplest form. *also* **MR 2.3, MR 2.4, MR 3.2**

Find the sum or difference. Write it in simplest form.

2. $\frac{1}{4} + \frac{2}{4}$ 3. $\frac{3}{4} - \frac{1}{4}$ 4. $\frac{5}{8} + \frac{3}{8}$ ✓5. $\frac{2}{3} - \frac{1}{3}$ ✓6. $\frac{7}{10} + \frac{1}{10}$

7. **TALK Math** Explain how to find $\frac{2}{12} + \frac{4}{12}$.

Independent Practice and Problem Solving

Find the sum or difference. Write it in simplest form.

8. $\frac{1}{10} + \frac{3}{10}$ 9. $\frac{3}{6} - \frac{1}{6}$ 10. $\frac{4}{8} + \frac{3}{8}$ 11. $\frac{5}{7} - \frac{3}{7}$ 12. $\frac{7}{12} + \frac{5}{12}$

13. $\frac{4}{4} - \frac{1}{4}$ 14. $\frac{2}{7} + \frac{4}{7}$ 15. $\frac{5}{8} - \frac{3}{8}$ 16. $\frac{1}{3} + \frac{1}{3}$ 17. $\frac{3}{8} - \frac{1}{8}$

Algebra Find the missing number for each ■.

18. $■ + \frac{4}{9} = \frac{7}{9}$ 19. $\frac{3}{4} - ■ = \frac{1}{4}$ 20. $1 - ■ = \frac{2}{3}$ 21. $\frac{9}{12} + ■ = \frac{11}{12}$

USE DATA For 22–24, use the graph.

22. What fraction of students chose either spring or summer as their favorite season?

23. **Reasoning** Which two seasons were chosen by $\frac{2}{5}$ of the students?

24. **WRITE Math** **What's the Error?** To find the difference in the number of students who chose summer and those who chose winter, Cara found $\frac{5}{10} - \frac{2}{10}$ and got 3. What is her error?

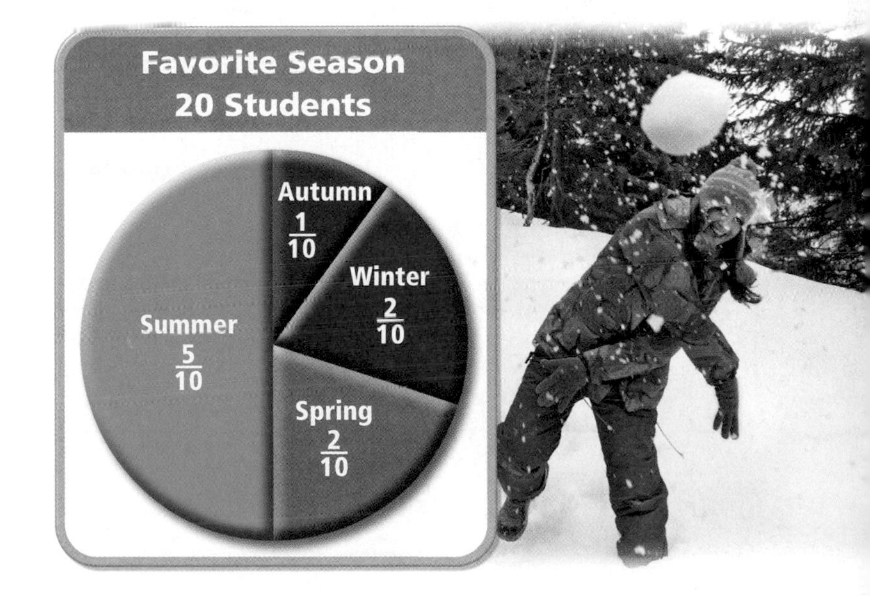

Achieving the Standards

25. Compare. Write <, >, or =. (NS 1.0, p. 8)

1,840,099 ● 1,840,215

26. Kenneth jogged $\frac{1}{4}$ mile. Write the distance he jogged as a decimal. (NS 1.2, p. 160)

27. Write the fraction $\frac{37}{8}$ as a mixed number. (NS 1.5, p. 150)

28. **Test Prep** Alex poured $\frac{1}{4}$ cup orange juice and $\frac{3}{4}$ cup pineapple juice into a glass. How many cups of juice are in the glass?

A $\frac{1}{4}$ cup
B $\frac{3}{8}$ cup
C $\frac{3}{4}$ cup
D 1 cup

LESSON 3

Add and Subtract Like Mixed Numbers

OBJECTIVE: Add and subtract like mixed numbers.

Quick Review

Add or subtract. Write the answer in simplest form.

1. $\frac{3}{7} + \frac{1}{7}$
2. $\frac{3}{5} - \frac{2}{5}$
3. $\frac{3}{10} + \frac{7}{10}$
4. $\frac{5}{6} - \frac{3}{6}$
5. $\frac{1}{4} + \frac{2}{4}$

Learn

PROBLEM Every weekend, Sam works at a supermarket. He works $2\frac{1}{4}$ hours Saturday and $3\frac{1}{4}$ hours Sunday. How many hours does Sam work every weekend?

ONE WAY **Use a model.**

Add. $2\frac{1}{4} + 3\frac{1}{4}$

Step 1

Model the problem.

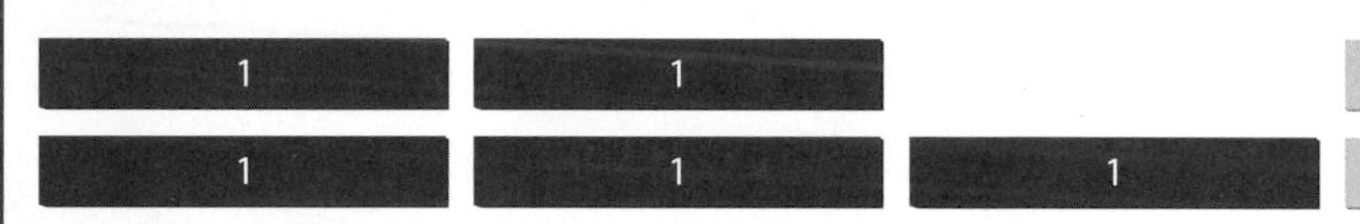

$2\frac{1}{4}$

$3\frac{1}{4}$

Step 2

Add the fractions first, and then add the whole numbers.

$2\frac{1}{4}$

$3\frac{1}{4}$

$2\frac{1}{4} + 3\frac{1}{4} = 5\frac{2}{4}$, or $5\frac{1}{2}$ Write the sum in simplest form.

ANOTHER WAY **Use paper and pencil.**

$$\begin{array}{r} 2\frac{1}{4} \\ +3\frac{1}{4} \\ \hline 5\frac{2}{4} = 5\frac{1}{2} \end{array}$$

- Add the fractions.
- Add the whole numbers.
- Write the sum in simplest form if needed.

So, Sam works $5\frac{1}{2}$ hours every weekend.

Math Idea

Add or subtract the fraction parts of mixed numbers just as you would two or more fractions.

NS 2.3 Solve simple problems, including ones arising in concrete situations, involving the addition and subtraction of fractions and mixed numbers (like and unlike denominators of 20 or less), and express answers in the simplest form. *also* **MR 1.0, MR 2.1, MR 2.2, MR 2.3, MR 2.4, MR 3.0, MR 3.2, MR 3.3**

Subtract Mixed Numbers

One weekend, Sam worked $3\frac{5}{6}$ hours at the supermarket on Saturday, and on Sunday he worked $2\frac{1}{6}$ hours. How much more time did Sam work on Saturday than on Sunday?

Subtract. $3\frac{5}{6} - 2\frac{1}{6}$

Use a model.

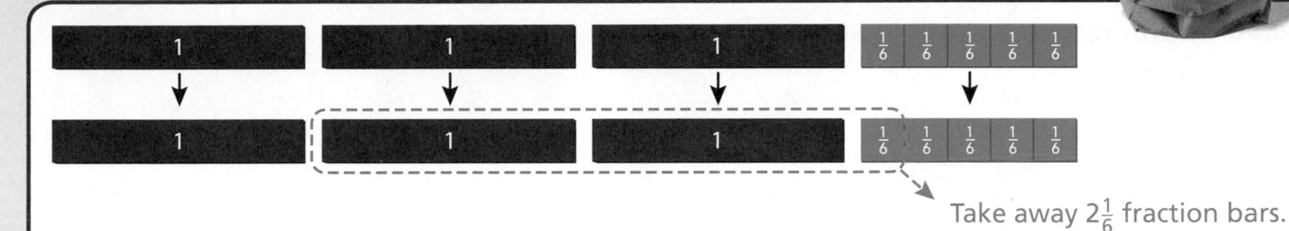

Take away $2\frac{1}{6}$ fraction bars.

$3\frac{5}{6} - 2\frac{1}{6} = 1\frac{4}{6}$, or $1\frac{2}{3}$ Write the difference in simplest form.

ANOTHER WAY **Use paper and pencil.**

$$\begin{array}{r} 3\frac{5}{6} \\ -2\frac{1}{6} \\ \hline 1\frac{4}{6} = 1\frac{2}{3} \end{array}$$

- Subtract the numerators of the fraction parts. Write the difference over the denominator.
- Subtract the whole numbers.
- Write the difference in simplest form.

So, Sam worked $1\frac{2}{3}$ hours more on Saturday than he did on Sunday.

- How would you estimate to check the difference?

More Examples

A

$$\begin{array}{r} 5\frac{4}{5} \\ +2\frac{2}{5} \\ \hline 7\frac{6}{5} \end{array} = 7 + 1\frac{1}{5} = 8\frac{1}{5}$$

B

$$\begin{array}{r} 1\frac{7}{12} \\ +3\frac{11}{12} \\ \hline 4\frac{18}{12} \end{array} = 4 + 1\frac{6}{12} = 5\frac{6}{12} = 5\frac{1}{2}$$

C

$$\begin{array}{r} 7\frac{7}{8} \\ -4\frac{1}{8} \\ \hline 3\frac{6}{8} \end{array} = 3\frac{3}{4}$$

Guided Practice

Use fraction bars to find the sum or difference. Write it in simplest form.

1. $2\frac{1}{5} + 4\frac{3}{5}$ Add the fractions. $\frac{1}{5} + \frac{3}{5} = \frac{■}{5}$

   Add the whole numbers. $2 + 4 = ■$

   Combine the whole number and the fraction to form a mixed number. $■ + \frac{■}{5} = ■\frac{■}{5}$

Find the sum or difference. Write it in simplest form.

2. $1\frac{1}{6} + 3\frac{3}{6}$
3. $7\frac{7}{8} - 5\frac{3}{8}$
4. $3\frac{10}{12} + 2\frac{5}{12}$
5. $6\frac{9}{10} - 3\frac{7}{10}$
6. $2\frac{1}{2} + 8\frac{1}{2}$
7. $1\frac{1}{4} + 8\frac{3}{4}$
8. $10\frac{2}{3} - 4\frac{1}{3}$
9. $4\frac{7}{9} + 6\frac{5}{9}$
10. $8\frac{3}{4} - 5\frac{1}{4}$
11. **TALK Math** **Explain** how to find $3\frac{7}{10} + 1\frac{9}{10}$.

Independent Practice and Problem Solving

Find the sum or difference. Write it in simplest form.

12. $10\frac{6}{7} - 5\frac{3}{7}$
13. $5\frac{5}{8} + 2\frac{2}{8}$
14. $6\frac{9}{14} - 3\frac{5}{14}$
15. $4\frac{3}{4} + 1\frac{3}{4}$
16. $8\frac{7}{10} - 2\frac{7}{10}$
17. $7\frac{4}{6} + 4\frac{3}{6}$
18. $10\frac{11}{12} - 5\frac{7}{12}$
19. $7\frac{1}{3} + 1\frac{2}{3}$
20. $2\frac{9}{10} - 2\frac{3}{10}$

USE DATA For 21–23, use the fruit punch recipe.

21. How many quarts of fruit punch does the recipe make?
22. How many more quarts of orange juice than pineapple juice does the recipe call for?
23. **Reasoning** Sandy wants to double the recipe. How much orange juice will she need?
24. **WRITE Math** **What's the Error?** Isaac added $2\frac{5}{8}$ to $6\frac{7}{8}$. His answer was $8\frac{1}{4}$. Describe Isaac's error and find the correct answer.

- $2\frac{3}{4}$ quarts orange juice
- $1\frac{2}{4}$ quarts pineapple juice
- 2 quarts lemon-lime soda
- Sliced fruit such as lemons, limes, strawberries, and oranges

CD ROM Technology Use Harcourt Mega Math, Fraction Action, *Fraction Flare Up*, Level H.

 Extra Practice on page 190, Set B

Achieving the Standards

25. Find the value of ■.

$$\frac{3}{7} + ■ = \frac{5}{7}$$

(NS 2.3, p. 176)

26. $\frac{4}{10} + \frac{2}{10} =$

(NS 2.3, p. 178)

27. Complete to write equivalent fractions.
(NS 1.0, p. 144)

$$\frac{1}{3} = \frac{2}{■}$$

28. Test Prep $9\frac{3}{4} - 2\frac{1}{4} =$

A $7\frac{1}{4}$ **C** $11\frac{1}{2}$

B $7\frac{1}{2}$ **D** 12

29. Test Prep Ken mixes together $4\frac{1}{2}$ cups of cornmeal and $2\frac{1}{2}$ cups of flour. What size container will hold the mixture?

A 1 cup **C** 6 cup

B 2 cup **D** 8 cup

Problem Solving and Reasoning

NUMBER SENSE You can estimate with mixed numbers just as you can with whole numbers.

- If the fraction part of the mixed number is less than $\frac{1}{2}$, round down to the nearest whole number.
- If the fraction part of the mixed number is equal to or greater than $\frac{1}{2}$, round up to the nearest whole number.

$1\frac{1}{4}$ rounds down to 1. 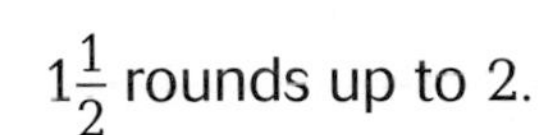 $1\frac{1}{2}$ rounds up to 2.

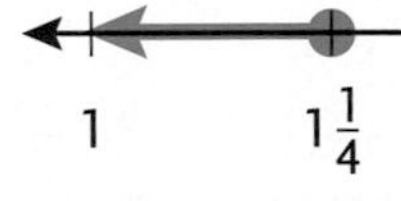 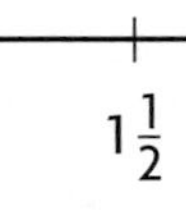 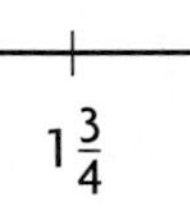  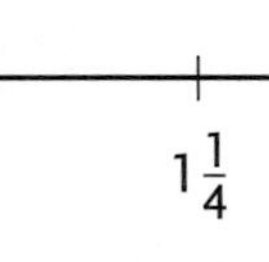 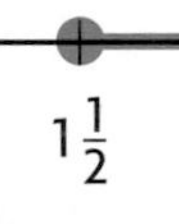 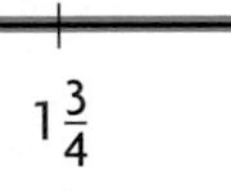 

1 $1\frac{1}{4}$ $1\frac{1}{2}$ $1\frac{3}{4}$ 2 1 $1\frac{1}{4}$ $1\frac{1}{2}$ $1\frac{3}{4}$ 2

After rounding, add or subtract to make your estimate.

$1\frac{1}{4} + 1\frac{1}{2}$? $1 + 2 = 3$. So, 3 is a reasonable estimate for the sum.

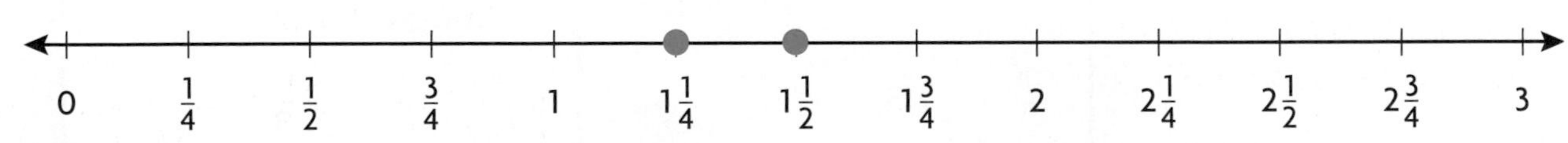

Estimate each sum or difference. For 1–4, use the number line to help you.

1. $1\frac{1}{4} + 2\frac{3}{4}$ **2.** $2\frac{1}{4} - 1\frac{1}{4}$ **3.** $1\frac{1}{6} + 2\frac{5}{6}$ **4.** $2\frac{1}{4} - \frac{3}{4}$

5. $3\frac{1}{5} + 4\frac{4}{5}$ **6.** $2\frac{2}{3} - 2$ **7.** $4\frac{6}{10} + 5\frac{9}{10}$ **8.** $5\frac{1}{8} - 3\frac{5}{8}$

Subtraction with Renaming

OBJECTIVE: Subtract mixed numbers with renaming.

Quick Review

Subtract. Write the answer in simplest form.

1. $\frac{3}{4} - \frac{1}{4}$
2. $\frac{2}{3} - \frac{1}{3}$
3. $1\frac{1}{2} - \frac{1}{2}$
4. $\frac{7}{8} - \frac{3}{8}$
5. $2\frac{5}{6} - \frac{1}{6}$

Learn

PROBLEM Gia is building scenery for a play. She cuts $1\frac{1}{6}$ feet from a 2-foot board. What is the length of the board that is left?

Sometimes you need to rename the whole number to subtract with mixed numbers. You can use fraction bars to help you.

Activity

Subtract. $2 - 1\frac{1}{6}$ **Materials** ■ fraction bars

Step 1

Model 2 by using two whole bars.

2

Step 2

To subtract $1\frac{1}{6}$, replace one of the 1 whole bars with six $\frac{1}{6}$ bars.

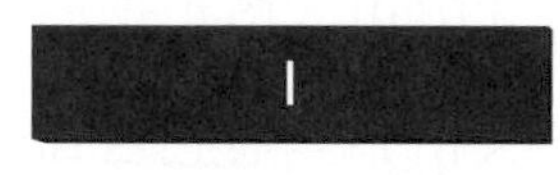
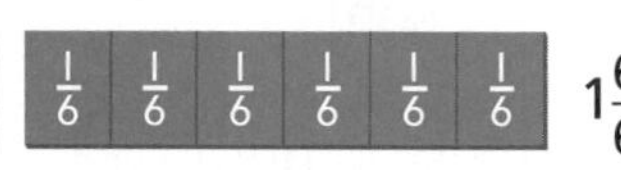

$1\frac{6}{6}$

Step 3

Subtract $1\frac{1}{6}$. Write the answer in simplest form.

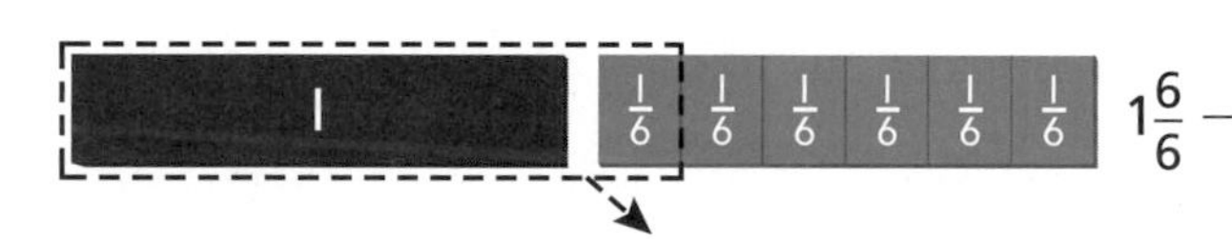

$1\frac{6}{6} - 1\frac{1}{6}$

So, the length of board left is $\frac{5}{6}$ foot.

Example Subtract. $3\frac{3}{8} - 1\frac{5}{8}$

Step 1

Rename the mixed number.

Think: Since $\frac{5}{8} > \frac{3}{8}$, rename $3\frac{3}{8}$.

$$3\frac{3}{8} = 2\frac{11}{8}$$
$$-1\frac{5}{8} = -1\frac{5}{8}$$

$3\frac{3}{8} = 2 + \frac{8}{8} + \frac{3}{8} = 2\frac{11}{8}$

Step 2

Subtract the fractions.

$$3\frac{3}{8} = 2\frac{11}{8}$$
$$-1\frac{5}{8} = -1\frac{5}{8}$$
$$\frac{6}{8}$$

Step 3

Subtract the whole numbers. Write the answer in simplest form.

$$3\frac{3}{8} = 2\frac{11}{8}$$
$$-1\frac{5}{8} = -1\frac{5}{8}$$
$$1\frac{6}{8} = 1\frac{3}{4}$$

So, $3\frac{3}{8} - 1\frac{5}{8} = 1\frac{3}{4}$.

NS 2.3 Solve simple problems, including ones arising in concrete situations, involving the addition and subtraction of fractions and mixed numbers, and express answers in the simplest form. *also* **MR 1.0, MR 1.1, MR 2.1, MR 2.3, MR 2.4, MR 3.2, MR 3.3**

Guided Practice

1. Copy the problem at the right. Find the difference using renaming.

$$\begin{array}{rcr} 2\frac{3}{6} & = & 1\frac{\blacksquare}{6} \\ -1\frac{4}{6} & = & -1\frac{4}{6} \\ \hline & & \blacksquare \end{array}$$

Use fraction bars to find the difference. Write it in simplest form.

2. $2\frac{1}{4} - 1\frac{3}{4}$
3. $1\frac{1}{3} - \frac{2}{3}$
4. $5\frac{2}{5} - 2\frac{4}{5}$
5. $4\frac{7}{10} - \frac{9}{10}$
6. $3\frac{5}{12} - 1\frac{8}{12}$
7. **TALK Math** **Explain** how to find $3 - 1\frac{2}{3}$.

Independent Practice and Problem Solving

Find the difference. Write it in simplest form.

8. $5\frac{2}{9} - 3\frac{5}{9}$
9. $2\frac{3}{15} - 1\frac{7}{15}$
10. $8\frac{3}{5} - 2\frac{4}{5}$
11. $2 - 1\frac{1}{4}$
12. $3\frac{1}{10} - 2\frac{9}{10}$
13. $3\frac{3}{7} - 1\frac{6}{7}$
14. $4\frac{3}{6} - 2\frac{5}{6}$
15. $6\frac{9}{12} - 3\frac{10}{12}$
16. $4\frac{6}{20} - 1\frac{11}{20}$
17. $8 - 5\frac{4}{9}$
18. Monique's father drives $20\frac{1}{4}$ miles each day. Her mother drives 25 miles each day. How much farther does Monique's mother drive than her father?
19. Joe wants to run 18 miles this week. He ran 3 miles, $2\frac{3}{4}$ miles, and $3\frac{2}{4}$ miles. How many more miles does Joe need to run to make his goal?
20. **WRITE Math** **What's the Question?** Rodrigo's piece of cloth that is $3\frac{5}{8}$ yards, is $1\frac{7}{8}$ yards longer than Kat's cloth. The answer is $1\frac{3}{4}$ yards.

Achieving the Standards

21. Dillon spent $\frac{1}{3}$ hour on math homework and $\frac{2}{3}$ hour on science homework. How much time did Dillon spend doing homework? (NS 2.3, p. 198)
22. A 9-inch cake pan holds $5\frac{1}{4}$ cups of batter. Karena's cake recipe makes 11 cups of batter. Will she need to use 2 pans or 3 pans? (NS 2.3, p. 184)
23. What kind of a quadrilateral always has 4 right angles and 4 equal sides? (Grade 4, MG 3.7)
24. **Test Prep** Lamont and Neil bought 2 pizzas and ate $\frac{2}{3}$ of one pizza as shown. What fraction of the 2 pizzas was left?

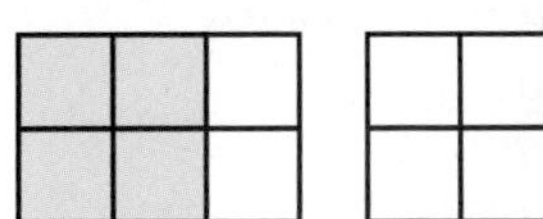

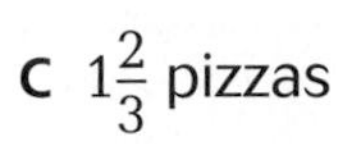

A $1\frac{1}{6}$ pizzas

B $1\frac{1}{3}$ pizzas

C $1\frac{2}{3}$ pizzas

D 2 pizzas

Extra Practice on page 190, Set C

Problem Solving Workshop
Strategy: Work Backward

OBJECTIVE: Solve problems by using the strategy *work backward.*

Learn the Strategy

Working backward can help you solve a problem. You can use this strategy when you know how a situation ends but do not know how it begins.

Work backward on a number line.

Sol made a dragon kite. He used a total of 3 yards of red, gold, and green ribbon for the kite's tail. First he used $1\frac{3}{8}$ yards of gold ribbon and $\frac{5}{8}$ yard of green ribbon. If the remainder of the ribbon was red, how many yards of red ribbon did Sol use?

Starting at 3 on the number line, move $1\frac{3}{8}$, or 11 eighths to the left. Then move another 5 eighths to the left.

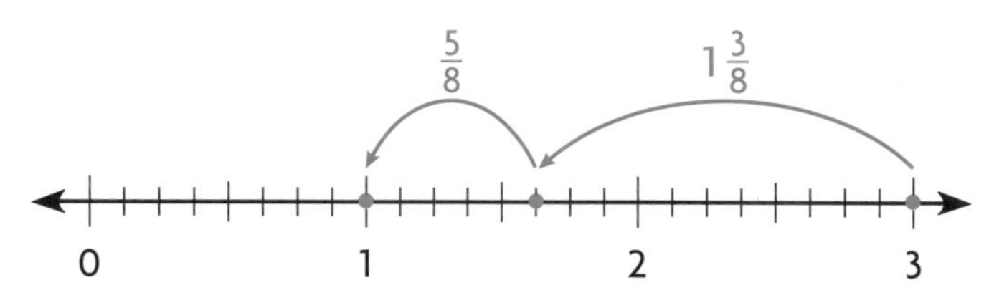

So, Sol used 1 yard of red ribbon.

Work backward by using an equation.

Elizabeth paid $32.00 for 3 fast-pitch softballs and 1 softball glove. The glove cost $20.00. She does not remember the exact price for the softballs. Can you find how much Elizabeth paid for each softball? Yes, you can. Work backward!

Write the equation.

($■ × 3 softballs) + glove = total $ paid

$(s \times 3) + \$20 = \$32$

Work backward by using inverse operations.

$s = (32 - 20) \div 3$

$s = 12 \div 3$

$s = 4$

So, Elizabeth paid $4 for each softball.

Check your answer.

$(\$4 \times 3) + \$20 = \$32$

$\$12 + \$20 = \$32$

$\$32 = \$32$ ✓

TALK Math

Why is it important to check your answer when you use the *work backward* strategy? **Explain** how you can check your answer.

NS 2.3 Solve simple problems, including ones arising in concrete situations, involving the addition and subtraction of fractions and mixed numbers, and express answers in the simplest form. *also* **AF 1.2, MR 1.0, MR 2.0, MR 2.1, MR 2.3, MR 2.4, MR 2.6, MR 3.0, MR 3.1, MR 3.2, MR 3.3**

Use the Strategy

PROBLEM Mr. Yin's fifth-grade class is presenting a puppet show about safety for the first and second grade. To make their own puppets, the fifth-grade students bought $1\frac{7}{8}$ yards of felt for three different-sized puppets. They cut $\frac{3}{8}$ yard for the smallest puppet and $\frac{7}{8}$ yard for the largest puppet. How many yards of felt did the students use for the medium-sized puppet?

Read to Understand

- **Identify the steps of the problem.**
- **What part of the problem is unknown?**

Plan

- **What strategy can you use to solve the problem?**

  You can work backward to solve the problem.

Solve

- **How can you use the strategy to solve the problem?**

  Draw a number line that shows eighths.

  Work backward. Starting at $1\frac{7}{8}$, move 7 eighths to the left.

  Then move another 3 eighths to the left.

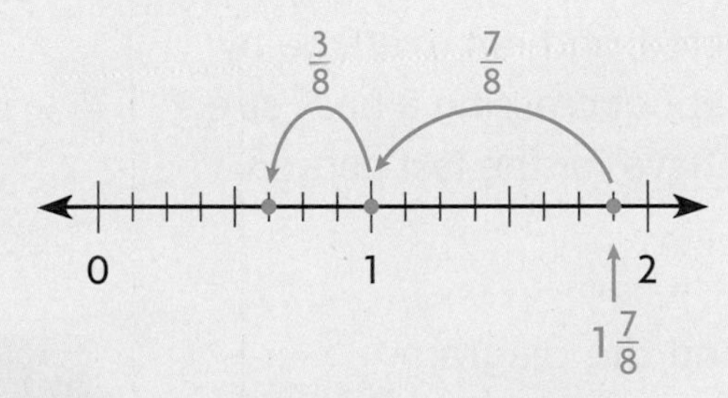

  Only 5 more eighths remain before 0 on the number line.

  So, they used $\frac{5}{8}$ yard of felt for the medium-sized puppet.

Check

- **How do you know the answer is correct?**
- **What other ways could you solve this problem?**

Guided Problem Solving

Read to Understand
Plan
Solve
Check

1. To build the puppet stage for their show, students used a total of $9\frac{5}{6}$ yards of felt to make the curtain, roof, and skirt for the stage. If they used $3\frac{1}{6}$ yards for the curtain and $3\frac{5}{6}$ yards for the skirt, how many yards of felt did they use for the roof?

   First, make a number line that shows 0 to 10. Divide each section into sixths.

   Then, work backward from the end to the beginning on the number line.

   Finally, check your answer.

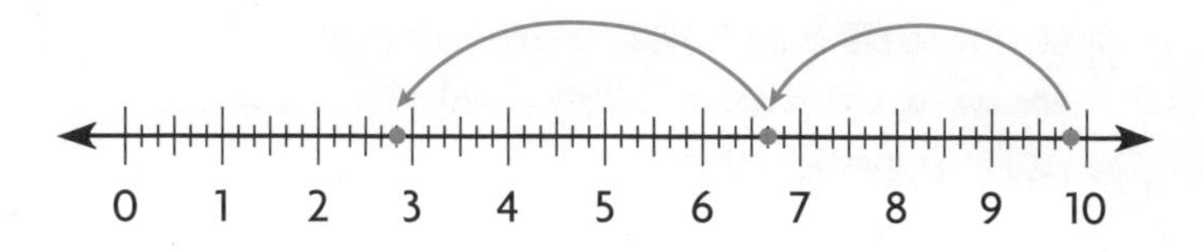

2. What if the students had $2\frac{5}{6}$ yards for the curtain? How much felt would be used for the roof?

3. Twenty minutes before the show's starting time, students were still working on the stage. Molly spent 12.5 minutes stapling the skirt and then passed the stapler to Jordan, who spent 6.75 minutes stapling the roof. By the time they were finished, how many minutes were there until show time?

Problem Solving Strategy Practice

Work backward to solve.

4. The students had $\frac{11}{12}$ hour to watch a puppet show about safety. The first $\frac{5}{12}$ hour was about playground safety, and the next $\frac{2}{12}$ hour was about safety in the cafeteria. The first two parts of the show got more laughs than expected, and ran overtime by $\frac{1}{12}$ hour. The remaining time was about crossing a busy street. How much time did the students have for the last part on crossing a busy street?

USE DATA For 5–7, use the chart and the diagram.

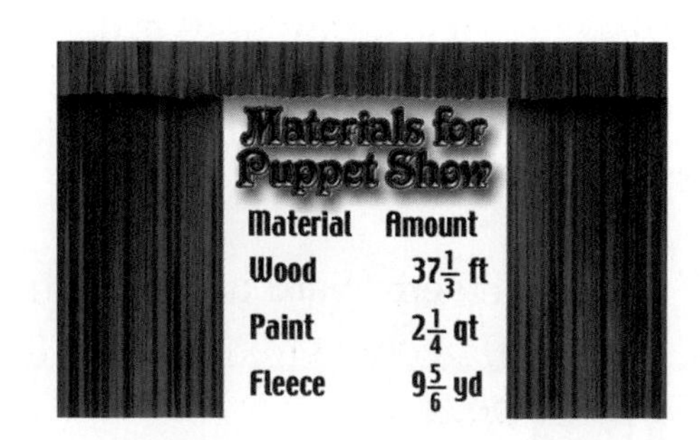

Materials for Puppet Show

Material	Amount
Wood	$37\frac{1}{3}$ ft
Paint	$2\frac{1}{4}$ qt
Fleece	$9\frac{5}{6}$ yd

5. Students used $\frac{2}{4}$ quart of paint for posters and $\frac{3}{4}$ quart of paint for props. How many quarts of paint were left to paint background scenery?

6. To build the puppet stage, students used 2 U-shaped frames supported by 4 legs. Each U-shaped frame used $11\frac{1}{3}$ feet of wood. How much wood did the students use for the 4 legs?

7. WRITE Math **Explain** how you would use a number line to find the length of each leg used to support the puppet stage. Show your work.

Mixed Strategy Practice

USE DATA For 8–11, use the table.

8. At the Shipshewana Indiana theater, the box office opened at noon to sell tickets. By 12:10, 20 tickets had been sold. By 12:20, 40 tickets had been sold. By the end of the first half hour, 60 tickets had been sold. If the pattern continues, by what time will all of the tickets be sold?

9. The Tucson puppet theater has 3 shows on Saturday afternoon, while the Seattle puppet theater has 1 show. If both theaters have a full house, which theater will sell the most tickets that day? How many more tickets will that theater sell?

10. **Pose a Problem** Look back at Problem 9. Write a similar problem by changing the theater and the pattern.

11. **Open-Ended** Suppose there is a 25-minute break between shows at the New York theater. If the theater is open from 1:00 P.M. to 4:30 P.M., how many tickets can it sell? How could the theater change the length of the show or the break between shows so that it can sell more tickets?

Choose a STRATEGY

- Draw a Diagram or Picture
- Make a Model or Act It Out
- Make an Organized List
- Find a Pattern
- Make a Table or Graph
- Predict and Test
- Work Backward
- Solve a Simpler Problem
- Write an Equation
- Use Logical Reasoning

Puppet Theaters

City, State	Number of Seats	Stage Size length × width (in ft)	Length of Show (in min)
New York City, NY	300	18 × 14	55
Shipshewana, IN	150	12 × 12	40
Seattle, WA	100–500	20 × 8	45
Tucson, AZ	100	6 × 7	30

CHALLENGE YOURSELF

UNICEF, an international organization for children, uses puppets to educate and entertain. In the African country of Namibia, teens use puppets to teach about safety. In a village square, 2,000 people watch the 1-hour puppet show.

12. In Vietnam, a similar puppet show attracts 1,200 people on average. If there are six puppet shows a month in Vietnam, about how many people can watch the UNICEF puppet show each month?

13. In Namibia, $\frac{2}{5}$ of the puppeteers are 12 to 14 years old. Of the rest of the puppeteers, one out of three is 10 to 11 years old. How many fifths of the total number of puppeteers are 10 to 11 years old?

Extra Practice

Set A Find the sum or difference. Write it in simplest form. (pp. 178–179)

1. $\frac{2}{5} + \frac{3}{5}$
2. $\frac{11}{12} - \frac{2}{12}$
3. $\frac{3}{10} + \frac{4}{10}$
4. $\frac{7}{8} - \frac{5}{8}$
5. $\frac{1}{6} + \frac{3}{6}$
6. $\frac{5}{7} - \frac{3}{7}$
7. $\frac{4}{9} + \frac{3}{9}$
8. $\frac{10}{11} - \frac{4}{11}$
9. $\frac{4}{10} - \frac{2}{10}$
10. $\frac{1}{5} + \frac{1}{5}$
11. $\frac{3}{3} - \frac{2}{3}$
12. $\frac{4}{6} + \frac{2}{6}$
13. $\frac{6}{8} - \frac{1}{8}$
14. $\frac{2}{4} + \frac{1}{4}$
15. $\frac{1}{2} - \frac{1}{2}$

Set B Find the sum or difference. Write it in simplest form. (pp. 180–183)

1. $2\frac{1}{6} + 1\frac{5}{6}$
2. $5\frac{1}{2} - 3\frac{1}{2}$
3. $7\frac{3}{10} + 2\frac{1}{10}$
4. $4\frac{4}{7} - 1\frac{3}{7}$
5. $6\frac{2}{3} + 1\frac{1}{3}$
6. $5\frac{3}{4} - 4\frac{1}{4}$
7. $7\frac{5}{9} + 3\frac{2}{9}$
8. $3\frac{5}{6} - 1\frac{1}{6}$
9. $4\frac{3}{5} - 2\frac{2}{5}$
10. $3\frac{1}{8} + 4\frac{3}{8}$
11. $3\frac{2}{3} - 2\frac{1}{3}$
12. $5\frac{4}{10} + 3\frac{4}{10}$
13. Sally uses $1\frac{3}{4}$ cups of flour to make a pie. How many cups of flour does she need to make two pies?
14. Ramona bought $5\frac{5}{8}$ pounds of fruit. She bought $3\frac{1}{8}$ pounds of apples. The rest were oranges. How many pounds of oranges did she buy?

Set C Find the difference. Write it in simplest form. (pp. 184–185)

1. $3\frac{5}{12} - 1\frac{7}{12}$
2. $4\frac{3}{8} - 3\frac{7}{8}$
3. $1 - \frac{3}{4}$
4. $5 - \frac{2}{7}$
5. $2\frac{4}{7} - 1\frac{5}{7}$
6. $5 - 2\frac{7}{8}$
7. $7\frac{3}{5} - 5\frac{4}{5}$
8. $3\frac{7}{10} - 2\frac{9}{10}$
9. $9 - 7\frac{8}{9}$
10. $4\frac{2}{9} - 1\frac{5}{9}$
11. $4\frac{1}{6} - 2\frac{3}{6}$
12. $6 - 1\frac{6}{10}$
13. $5\frac{3}{9} - 2\frac{4}{9}$
14. $8 - 7\frac{7}{8}$
15. $7\frac{2}{6} - 5\frac{5}{6}$
16. Will had 4 yards of string. He used $2\frac{3}{8}$ yards for a project. How much string does Will have left?
17. Nan read for $1\frac{3}{4}$ hours on Monday and $2\frac{1}{4}$ hours on Tuesday. How much longer did she read on Tuesday?

CD ROM **Technology**
Use Harcourt Mega Math, Fraction Action, *Fraction Flare Up*, Levels G, H.

PRACTICE GAME

PICK A PAIR

Who?
4 students

What?
- 32 index cards

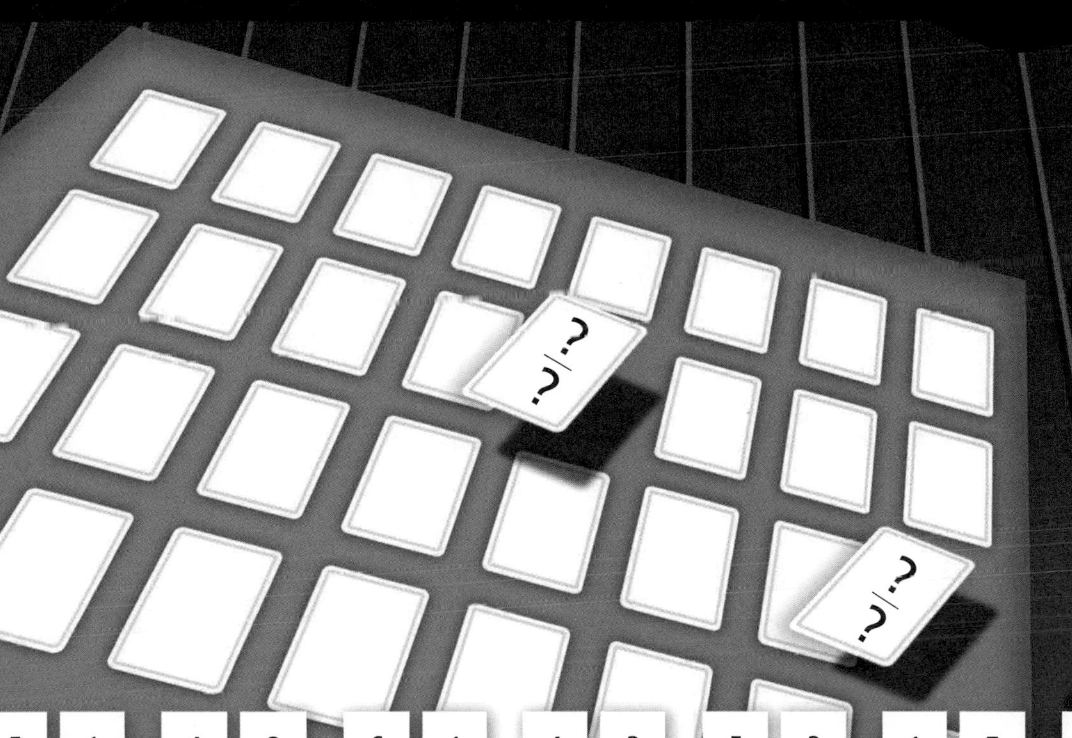

$\frac{5}{6}$	$\frac{1}{6}$	$\frac{4}{6}$	$\frac{2}{6}$	$\frac{6}{7}$	$\frac{1}{7}$	$\frac{4}{7}$	$\frac{3}{7}$	$\frac{5}{8}$	$\frac{3}{8}$	$\frac{1}{8}$	$\frac{7}{8}$	$\frac{7}{9}$	$\frac{2}{9}$	$\frac{4}{9}$	$\frac{5}{9}$
$\frac{2}{5}$	$\frac{3}{5}$	$\frac{4}{5}$	$\frac{1}{5}$	$\frac{1}{10}$	$\frac{9}{10}$	$\frac{3}{10}$	$\frac{7}{10}$	$\frac{1}{3}$	$\frac{2}{3}$	$\frac{1}{4}$	$\frac{3}{4}$	$\frac{1}{5}$	$\frac{4}{5}$	$\frac{1}{2}$	$\frac{1}{2}$

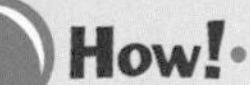

How!

- Label the index cards as shown. Shuffle them and place them facedown on a flat surface in a 8-by-4 array.
- The first player turns over two cards. If the fractions displayed have a sum of 1, the player keeps the cards and takes another turn.
- If the fractions do not have a sum of 1, they are returned facedown to their original positions.
- The next player repeats the process. Play continues until all cards have been picked up.
- The player with the greatest number of cards is the winner.

 Chapter 7 Review/Test

Check Concepts

1. Explain how you can add $\frac{2}{5} + \frac{1}{5}$ using fractions bars. (NS 2.3, p. 176)
2. Explain a rule you can use for subtracting fractions with like denominators. (NS 2.3, p. 178)

Check Skills

Find the sum or difference. Write it in simplest form. (NS 2.3, pp. 176–177, 178–179, 180–183)

3. $\frac{3}{5} + \frac{1}{5}$
4. $\frac{5}{6} - \frac{2}{6}$
5. $\frac{4}{9} + \frac{2}{9}$
6. $\frac{9}{10} - \frac{7}{10}$
7. $\frac{3}{7} + \frac{2}{7}$
8. $\frac{10}{11} - \frac{8}{11}$
9. $\frac{6}{10} + \frac{3}{10}$
10. $\frac{5}{6} - \frac{3}{6}$
11. $\frac{3}{7} + \frac{4}{7}$
12. $\frac{7}{8} - \frac{3}{8}$
13. $2\frac{1}{3} + 3\frac{2}{3}$
14. $4\frac{4}{5} - 1\frac{2}{5}$
15. $3\frac{5}{6} + 5\frac{4}{6}$
16. $7\frac{3}{8} - 2\frac{1}{8}$
17. $1\frac{9}{10} + 3\frac{3}{10}$

Find the difference. Write it in simplest form. (NS 2.3, pp. 186–187)

18. $3\frac{2}{5} - 1\frac{4}{5}$
19. $6\frac{1}{6} - 4\frac{5}{6}$
20. $8\frac{3}{5} - 4\frac{4}{5}$
21. $7\frac{1}{2} - 4\frac{1}{2}$
22. $6\frac{1}{8} - 5\frac{7}{8}$

Check Problem Solving

Solve. (NS 2.3, MR 2.3, pp. 186–189)

23. Gina used $4\frac{3}{8}$ yards of fabric to make a costume. She used $1\frac{5}{8}$ yards for the shirt and $2\frac{1}{8}$ yards for the pants. How many yards of fabric did she use to make the other parts of her costume?

24. Zack used $3\frac{1}{4}$ quarts of paint to decorate some furniture. He used $\frac{3}{4}$ quart on a desk and $1\frac{1}{4}$ quarts on a dresser. How much paint did Zack use on the other furniture?

25. **WRITE Math** Tara used $17\frac{1}{3}$ yards of fabric to make four flower costumes. **Explain** how you could use a number line to find the amount of fabric she used for one costume.

GO ONLINE **Technology** Use *Online Assessment.*

Enrich • Fraction Patterns

What's the Rule?

Rico is training for a race. During the first week, he runs $\frac{1}{3}$ mile each day. During the second week, he runs $\frac{2}{3}$ mile each day, and during the third week, he runs 1 mile each day. If he continues this pattern, during what week will Rico run 3 miles each day?

Step 1 Write all the distances as fractions with a common denominator. $\frac{1}{3}, \frac{2}{3}, \frac{3}{3}$	**Step 2** Look for a pattern. $\frac{1}{3}, \frac{2}{3}, \frac{3}{3}$ Find a rule. Rule: Add $\frac{1}{3}$.

Step 3
Continue the pattern. $\frac{1}{3}, \frac{2}{3}, \frac{3}{3}, \frac{4}{3}, \frac{5}{3}, \frac{6}{3}, \frac{7}{3}, \frac{8}{3}, \frac{9}{3}$

Stop at $\frac{9}{3}$ because it is equivalent to 3.

So, $\frac{9}{3}$ is the ninth fraction in the pattern. Rico runs 3 miles per day during his ninth week of training.

Example

Find the next three fractions in this pattern: $\frac{1}{4}, \frac{3}{8}, \frac{1}{2}, \frac{5}{8}$.

Step 1	**Step 2**	**Step 3**
Write the fractions with a common denominator. $\frac{2}{8}, \frac{3}{8}, \frac{4}{8}, \frac{5}{8}$	Find the rule. Rule: Add $\frac{1}{8}$. Continue the pattern. $\frac{2}{8}, \frac{3}{8}, \frac{4}{8}, \frac{5}{8}, \frac{6}{8}, \frac{7}{8}, \frac{8}{8}$	Write the next three fractions in simplest form. $\frac{6}{8} = \frac{3}{4}$ $\frac{7}{8} = \frac{7}{8}$ $\frac{8}{8} = 1$

So, the next three fractions are $\frac{3}{4}$, $\frac{7}{8}$, and $\frac{8}{8}$, or 1.

Try It

Find a rule. Use your rule to write the next three fractions in simplest form.

1. $\frac{1}{12}, \frac{1}{6}, \frac{1}{4}, \frac{1}{3}$
2. $\frac{3}{10}, \frac{2}{5}, \frac{1}{2}, \frac{3}{5}$
3. $\frac{11}{12}, \frac{5}{6}, \frac{3}{4}$
4. $3, 2\frac{3}{5}, 2\frac{1}{5}$

WRITE Math Make a fraction pattern that has $\frac{3}{4}$ as its third fraction.

Achieving the Standards

Chapters 1–7

Number Sense

Test Tip **Understand the problem.**

See item 1. The problem asks you to find the fastest time. The fastest time is the least amount of time it takes to win the race.

1. The table shows the time it took for each runner to complete the 200-yard dash.

200-Yard Dash Results	
Runner	**Time (in seconds)**
Ashley	33.5
Brooke	35.1
Cameron	33.2
Dennis	34.7

Which runner had the fastest time? (NS 1.0)

A Ashley
B Brooke
C Cameron
D Dennis

2. In a pie-eating contest, Fran ate $\frac{5}{12}$ of a pie. Lee ate $\frac{11}{12}$ of a pie. How much pie did they eat altogether? (O-n NS 2.3)

A $\frac{1}{2}$
B $\frac{2}{3}$
C $1\frac{1}{4}$
D $1\frac{1}{3}$

3. WRITE Math Emily says the values of 2^3 and 3^2 are the same. Do you agree? **Explain** why or why not. (NS 1.3)

Algebra and Functions

4. What is the value of the expression below if $b = 3$? (Grade 4 O-n AF 1.2)

$$17 - (b + 10)$$

A 4
B 13
C 14
D 30

5. Which property can be used to find the value of n? (AF 1.3)

$$7 \times (6 + 9) = (7 \times 6) + (7 \times n)$$

A Commutative Property of Addition
B Associative Property of Addition
C Distributive Property
D Identity Property

6. Jessica is 3 inches shorter than Tom. Jessica is 62 inches tall. Which equation can be used to find Tom's height, t? (Grade 4 AF 1.1)

A $t + 3 = 62$
B $t - 3 = 62$
C $62 - 3 = t$
D $62 - t = 3$

7. WRITE Math **Explain** how to use the Distributive Property to find the product of 5×39. (AF 1.3)

Measurement and Geometry

8. Which figure is formed when the pattern is folded on the dotted lines without overlapping? **(Grade 4 MG 3.6)**

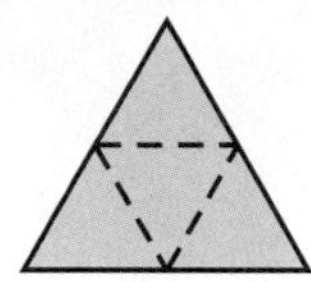

A triangular pyramid

B triangular prism

C cube

D square pyramid

9. What kind of a triangle always has 3 sides the same length? **(O‑π MG 2.1)**

A isosceles

B scalene

C acute

D equilateral

10. What kind of quadrilateral has only one pair of parallel sides? **(Grade 4 MG 3.8)**

A rectangle

B parallelogram

C trapezoid

D rhombus

11. **WRITE Math** The area of a square is 36 square feet. **Explain** how you can find its perimeter. **(Grade 4 MG 1.4)**

Statistics, Data Analysis, and Probability

12. Chandler got the following scores on her spelling tests.

89, 100, 95, 93, 96

What is Chandler's median test score? **(SDAP 1.1)**

A 89 **C** 95

B 93 **D** 96

13. The line plot shows the heights of the students, in inches, in a class.

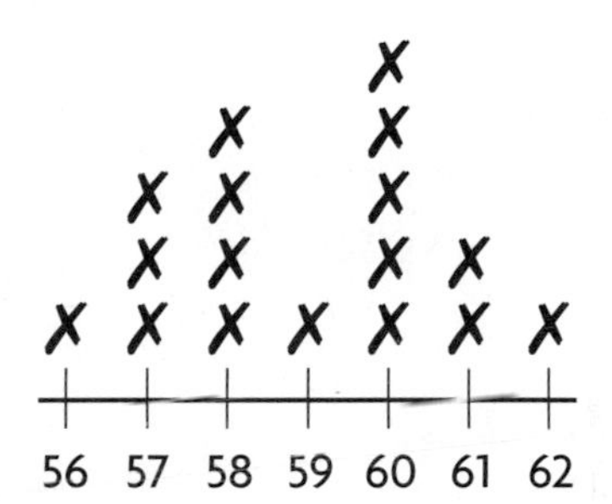

How many students are more than 59 inches tall? **(Grade 4 SDAP 1.0)**

A 1 **C** 8

B 3 **D** 9

14. **WRITE Math** In a survey of 100 students, $\frac{2}{5}$ of the students watched television when they got home from school, and $\frac{1}{4}$ of the students did their homework. Did more students watch television or do their homework after school? **Explain.** **(SDAP 1.0)**

8 Add and Subtract Unlike Fractions

The Big Idea Addition and subtraction of unlike fractions are based on understanding equivalent fractions.

Investigate

The table shows what part of the total trail each rider in a group of mountain bikers traveled on Mount Tamalpais. Choose 2 mountain bikers. Show how to find how much more of the trail one biker traveled than the other.

Mt. Tamalpais Mountain Bikers

Mountain Biker	Part of the Trail Traveled
Allison	$\frac{7}{10}$
Carl	$\frac{3}{4}$
Karen	$\frac{1}{2}$
Silvia	$\frac{4}{5}$

In the 1970s, a group in Marin County began racing old bicycles down Mt. Tamalpais. They played a vital role in the birth of the modern-day sport of mountain biking.

Technology
Student pages are available in the Student eBook.

Show What You Know

Check your understanding of important skills needed for success in Chapter 8.

▶ Equivalent Fractions

Write two equivalent fractions for each picture.

1.

2.

3.

4.

5.

6.

7.

8.

9.

▶ Simplest Form

Write each fraction in simplest form.

10. $\frac{3}{6}$

11. $\frac{6}{8}$

12. $\frac{2}{6}$

13. $\frac{6}{9}$

14. $\frac{3}{12}$

15. $\frac{4}{10}$

16. $\frac{12}{15}$

17. $\frac{15}{20}$

18. $\frac{8}{16}$

19. $\frac{14}{21}$

20. $\frac{18}{24}$

21. $\frac{5}{30}$

22. $\frac{4}{20}$

23. $\frac{6}{12}$

24. $\frac{8}{32}$

25. $\frac{6}{18}$

VOCABULARY POWER

CHAPTER VOCABULARY

benchmark fraction
common multiple
equivalent fractions
least common denominator (LCD)
multiples

WARM-UP WORDS

equivalent fractions fractions that name the same number or amount

least common denominator (LCD) the least common multiple of two or more denominators

common multiple a number that is a multiple of two or more numbers

LESSON 1 HANDS ON

Model Addition of Unlike Fractions

OBJECTIVE: Model addition of unlike fractions.

Quick Review

Find the sum or difference. Write it in simplest form.

1. $\frac{1}{4} + \frac{1}{4}$
2. $\frac{3}{8} - \frac{1}{8}$
3. $\frac{4}{8} + \frac{3}{8}$
4. $\frac{5}{10} - \frac{2}{10}$
5. $\frac{1}{5} + \frac{4}{5}$

Investigate

Materials ■ fraction bars

You can use fraction bars to add fractions with unlike denominators.

A Find $\frac{1}{2} + \frac{1}{4}$. Place a $\frac{1}{2}$ bar and a $\frac{1}{4}$ bar under a 1 whole bar.

1	
$\frac{1}{2}$	$\frac{1}{4}$

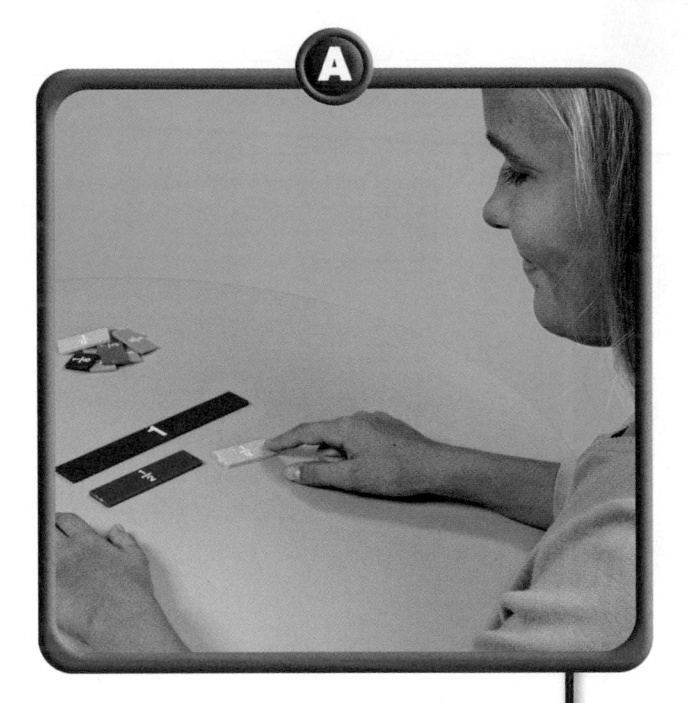

B Find like fraction bars that fit exactly under the sum $\frac{1}{2} + \frac{1}{4}$.

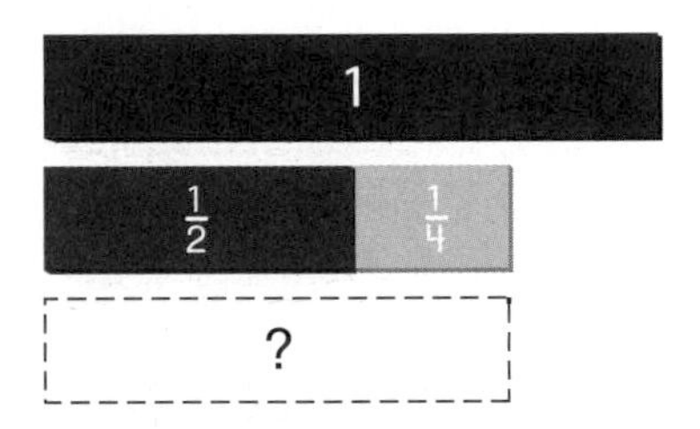

C Record the sum in simplest form.

D Use fraction bars to find $\frac{3}{5} + \frac{1}{2}$. Record the sum.

Draw Conclusions

1. What like fraction bars did you use to fit exactly under $\frac{1}{2} + \frac{1}{4}$? Could you have used any other like fraction bars? If so, which ones?
2. What like fraction bars did you use to find $\frac{3}{5} + \frac{1}{2}$? Is the sum greater than or less than 1?
3. **Analysis** In your model of $\frac{3}{5} + \frac{1}{2}$, how many $\frac{1}{10}$ bars equal $\frac{3}{5}$? How many equal $\frac{1}{2}$? What do you know about $\frac{3}{5}$ and $\frac{6}{10}$? about $\frac{1}{2}$ and $\frac{5}{10}$?

NS 2.3 Solve simple problems, including ones arising in concrete situations, involving the addition and subtraction of fractions and mixed numbers (like and unlike denominators of 20 or less), and express answers in the simplest form. *also* **MR 2.0, MR 2.3, MR 2.4, MR 3.2**

Connect

When you find the fraction bars that fit exactly under a sum, you are finding equivalent fractions.

Find: $\frac{2}{3} + \frac{1}{6}$.

Step 1

Place two $\frac{1}{3}$ fraction bars under a bar for 1. Then place one $\frac{1}{6}$ fraction bar beside the two $\frac{1}{3}$ bars.

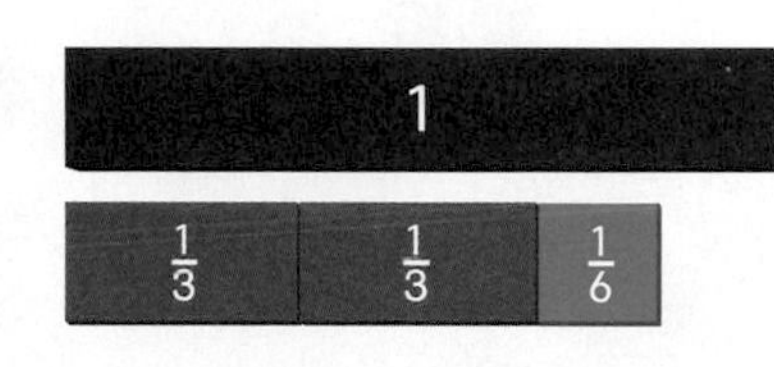

Step 2

Find like fraction bars that are equivalent to $\frac{2}{3}$ and $\frac{1}{6}$.

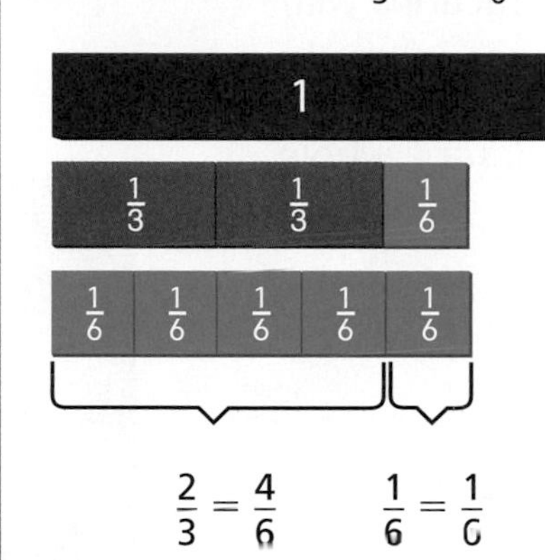

Step 3

Add the like fractions.

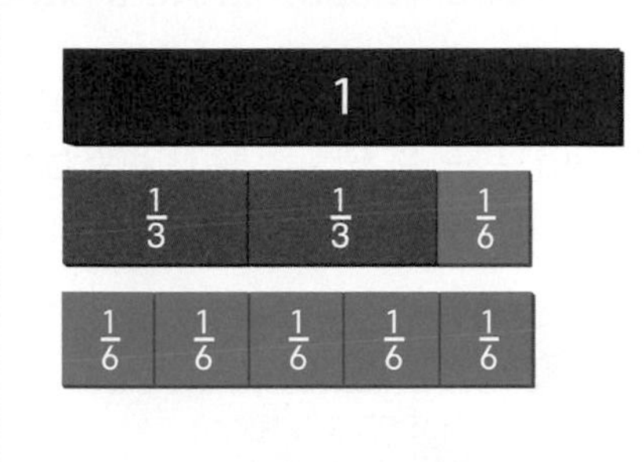

So, $\frac{4}{6} + \frac{1}{6} = \frac{5}{6}$.

TALK Math

Which equivalent fractions would you use to find $\frac{1}{2} + \frac{3}{4}$?

Practice

Find the sum. Write the answer in simplest form.

1. $\frac{1}{2} + \frac{3}{8}$

2. $\frac{3}{8} + \frac{1}{4}$

3. 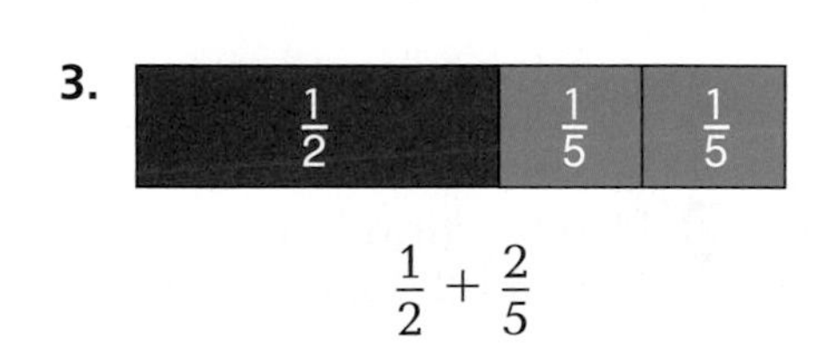

$\frac{1}{2} + \frac{2}{5}$

Find the sum using fraction bars. Write it in simplest form.

4. $\frac{2}{5} + \frac{3}{10}$
5. $\frac{1}{4} + \frac{2}{12}$
6. $\frac{1}{2} + \frac{3}{10}$
7. $\frac{1}{2} + \frac{1}{3}$
8. $\frac{1}{4} + \frac{4}{12}$
9. $\frac{1}{3} + \frac{3}{6}$
10. $\frac{1}{5} + \frac{1}{10}$
11. $\frac{3}{4} + \frac{1}{3}$
12. $\frac{3}{4} + \frac{1}{6}$
13. $\frac{2}{5} + \frac{1}{2}$
14. $\frac{2}{3} + \frac{1}{4}$
15. $\frac{3}{4} + \frac{5}{6}$
16. **WRITE Math** **Explain** how to add $\frac{2}{8}$ and $\frac{3}{4}$ by using fraction bars.

LESSON HANDS ON

2 Model Subtraction of Unlike Fractions

OBJECTIVE: Subtract unlike fractions using fraction bars.

Quick Review

Find the difference. Write it in simplest form.

1. $\frac{3}{4} - \frac{1}{4}$
2. $\frac{5}{8} - \frac{2}{8}$
3. $\frac{2}{3} - \frac{1}{3}$
4. $\frac{4}{5} - \frac{2}{5}$
5. $\frac{10}{10} - \frac{8}{10}$

Investigate

Materials ■ fraction bars

You can use fraction bars to subtract fractions with unlike denominators.

A Find $\frac{3}{4} - \frac{1}{8}$. Place three $\frac{1}{4}$ bars under a 1 whole bar. Then place one $\frac{1}{8}$ bar under the $\frac{1}{4}$ bars.

1

$\frac{1}{4}$ $\frac{1}{4}$ $\frac{1}{4}$

$\frac{1}{8}$

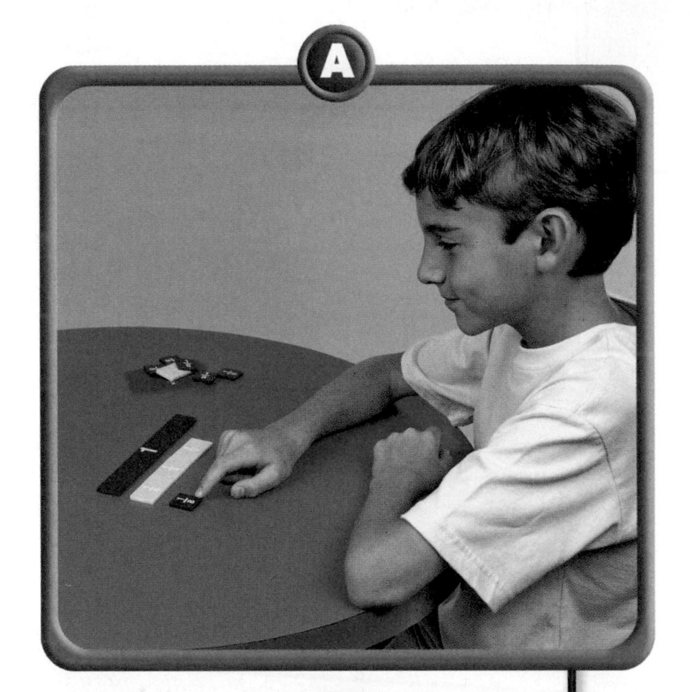

B Compare the bars. Find like fraction bars that fit exactly under the difference $\frac{3}{4} - \frac{1}{8}$.

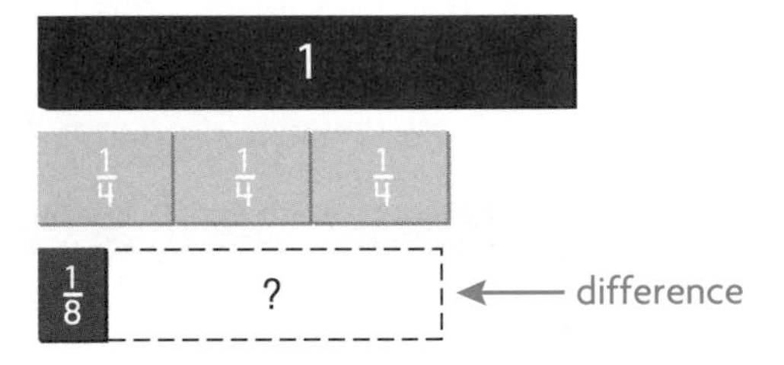

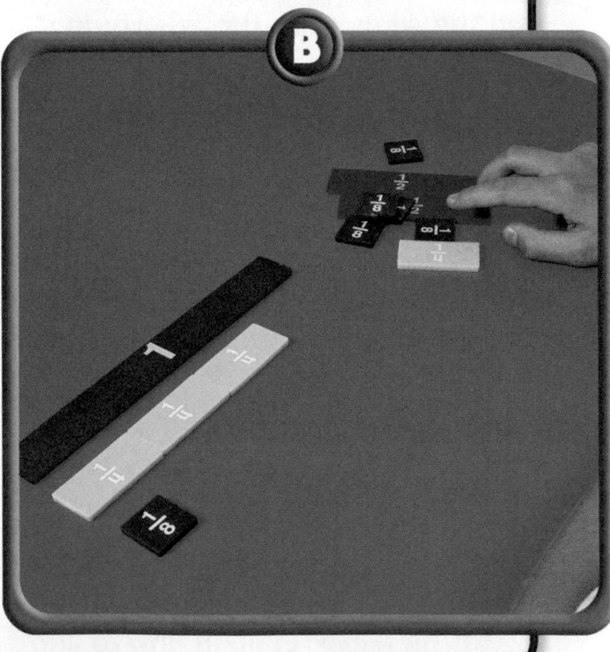

C Record the difference.

D Use fraction bars to find $\frac{1}{3} - \frac{1}{4}$.

Draw Conclusions

1. What like fraction bars did you use to fit exactly under $\frac{3}{4} - \frac{1}{8}$?
2. What like fraction bars did you use to find $\frac{1}{3} - \frac{1}{4}$?
3. **Analysis** In your model of $\frac{1}{3} - \frac{1}{4}$, how many $\frac{1}{12}$ bars equal $\frac{1}{3}$? How many equal $\frac{1}{4}$? What do you know about $\frac{1}{3}$ and $\frac{4}{12}$? $\frac{1}{4}$ and $\frac{3}{12}$?

NS 2.3 Solve simple problems, including ones arising in concrete situations, involving the addition and subtraction of fractions and mixed numbers (like and unlike denominators of 20 or less), and express answers in the simplest form. *also* **MR 2.0, MR 2.3, MR 2.4, MR 3.2**

Connect

You can use fraction bars with like denominators to subtract fractions with unlike denominators.

Subtract. $\frac{2}{3} - \frac{1}{4}$

Step 1

Place two $\frac{1}{3}$ bars under a 1 whole bar. Then place one $\frac{1}{4}$ bar under the two $\frac{1}{3}$ bars.

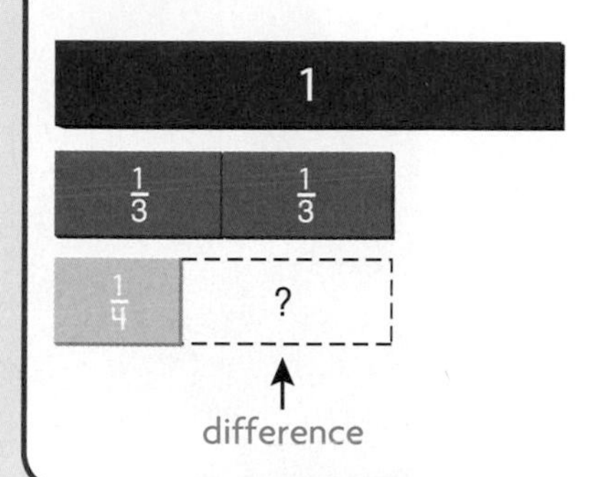

Step 2

Find like fraction bars that fit exactly under the difference $\frac{2}{3} - \frac{1}{4}$.

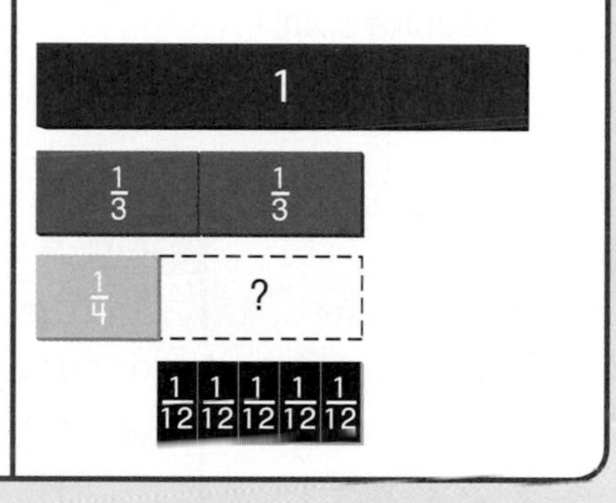

So, $\frac{2}{3} - \frac{1}{4} = \frac{5}{12}$.

TALK Math Which like fractions would you use to find $\frac{5}{6} - \frac{1}{2}$?

Practice

Use fraction bars to find the difference. Write the answer in simplest form.

1. $\frac{7}{10} - \frac{2}{5}$

1/10 1/10 1/10 1/10 1/10 1/10 1/10
1/5 1/5 ?

2. $\frac{2}{3} - \frac{1}{6}$

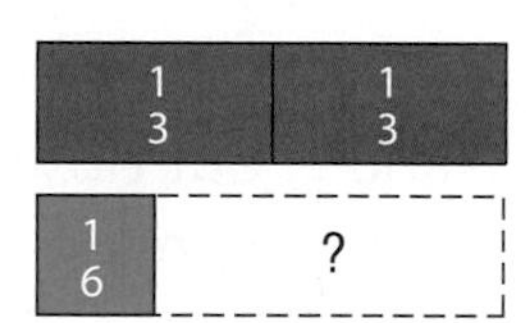

3. $\frac{1}{2} - \frac{3}{10}$

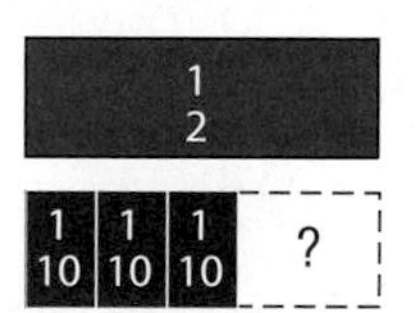

Find the difference using fraction bars. Write it in simplest form.

4. $\frac{3}{5} - \frac{3}{10}$
5. $\frac{5}{12} - \frac{1}{3}$
6. $\frac{1}{2} - \frac{1}{10}$
7. $\frac{3}{5} - \frac{1}{2}$
8. $\frac{7}{8} - \frac{1}{4}$
9. $\frac{2}{3} - \frac{3}{6}$
10. $\frac{3}{4} - \frac{1}{3}$
11. $\frac{5}{6} - \frac{1}{2}$
12. **WRITE Math** **Explain** how to use fraction bars to find $\frac{3}{4} - \frac{5}{8}$.

LESSON 3

Estimate Sums and Differences

OBJECTIVE: Estimate the sums and differences of fractions.

Quick Review

1. $\frac{3}{4} + \frac{1}{4}$
2. $\frac{2}{2} - \frac{1}{2}$
3. $\frac{2}{8} + \frac{3}{8}$
4. $\frac{5}{8} - \frac{1}{8}$
5. $\frac{2}{5} + \frac{3}{5}$

Learn

PROBLEM Kimberly is using different toppings for her banana split. First she pours $\frac{1}{6}$ cup fruit sauce on the ice cream. Then she drops $\frac{3}{8}$ cup of walnuts over the fruit sauce. Estimate the total amount of toppings Kimberly puts on her banana split.

Example 1 Estimate. $\frac{1}{6} + \frac{3}{8}$

Step 1

The fraction $\frac{1}{6}$ is close to 0. Round to 0.

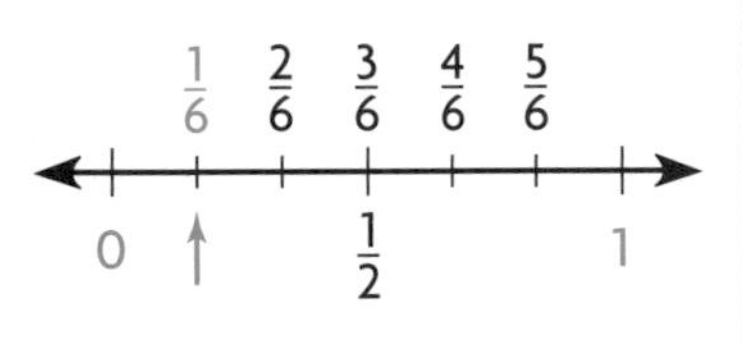

Step 2

The fraction $\frac{3}{8}$ is close to $\frac{1}{2}$. Round to $\frac{1}{2}$.

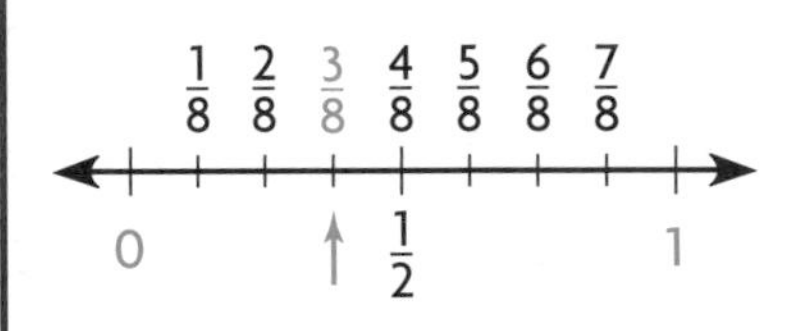

Step 3

Add the rounded fractions.

$$\frac{1}{6} \rightarrow 0$$
$$+\frac{3}{8} \rightarrow +\frac{1}{2}$$
$$\frac{1}{2}$$

So, Kimberly puts about $\frac{1}{2}$ cup of toppings on her banana split.

Example 2 Estimate. $\frac{7}{8} - \frac{2}{5}$

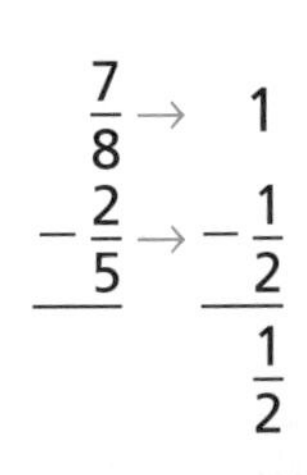

$$\frac{7}{8} \rightarrow 1$$
$$-\frac{2}{5} \rightarrow -\frac{1}{2}$$
$$\frac{1}{2}$$

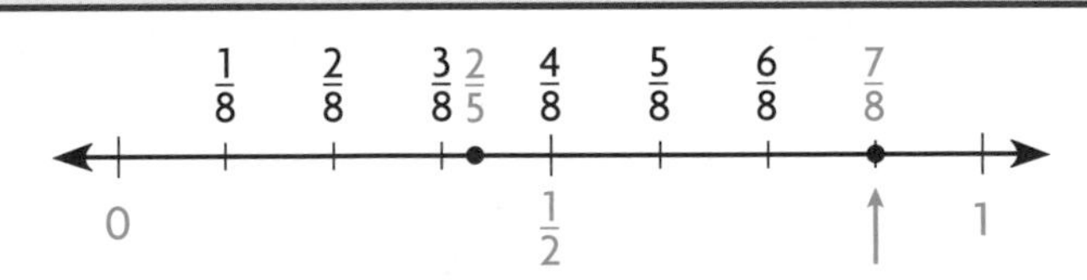

$\frac{2}{5}$ is between 0 and $\frac{1}{2}$, but close to $\frac{1}{2}$. The difference is greater than 0, but less than $\frac{1}{2}$.

- How can you estimate $\frac{4}{5} + \frac{2}{5}$?

Math Idea
You can estimate sums and differences by rounding fractions to benchmark fractions such as 0, $\frac{1}{2}$, or 1.

Guided Practice

1. Look at the number lines to complete.

   $\frac{3}{8}$ is between ■ and ■, but closer to ■.

   $\frac{2}{3}$ is between ■ and ■, but closer to ■.

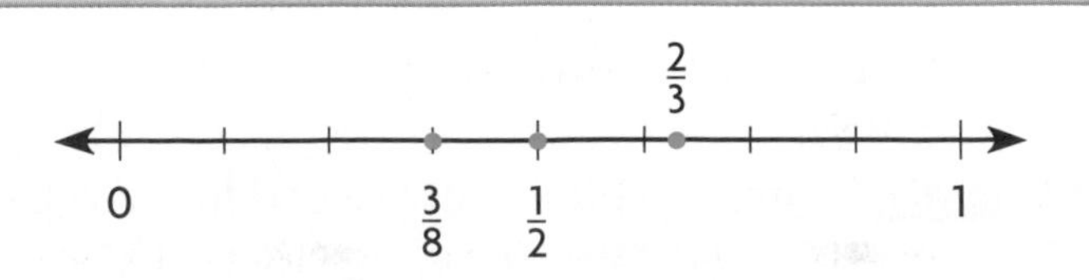

NS 1.1 Estimate, round, and manipulate very large (e.g., millions) and very small (e.g., thousandths) numbers. *also* NS 1.0, NS 2.3, MR 2.1, MR 2.3, MR 2.4, MR 2.5, MR 3.2

Estimate each sum or difference.

2. $\frac{4}{6} - \frac{1}{8}$ 3. $\frac{7}{10} + \frac{1}{3}$ 4. $\frac{5}{6} + \frac{2}{5}$ 5. $\frac{9}{10} - \frac{2}{9}$ 6. $\frac{4}{6} + \frac{1}{9}$ 7. $\frac{4}{10} - \frac{1}{9}$

8. **TALK Math** **Explain** how you know that $\frac{1}{8} + \frac{6}{10}$ is greater than $\frac{1}{2}$ but less than 1.

Independent Practice and Problem Solving

Estimate each sum or difference.

9. $\frac{5}{8} - \frac{1}{5}$ 10. $\frac{2}{6} + \frac{3}{8}$ 11. $\frac{6}{7} - \frac{3}{5}$ 12. $\frac{11}{12} + \frac{6}{10}$ 13. $\frac{9}{10} - \frac{1}{2}$

14. $\frac{3}{6} + \frac{4}{5}$ 15. $\frac{5}{6} - \frac{3}{8}$ 16. $\frac{1}{7} + \frac{8}{9}$ 17. $\frac{5}{12} - \frac{1}{10}$ 18. $\frac{3}{8} + \frac{3}{5}$

19. $\frac{1}{5} + \frac{5}{6}$ 20. $\frac{7}{12} - \frac{4}{10}$ 21. $\frac{3}{7} + \frac{8}{9}$ 22. $\frac{7}{8} - \frac{3}{5}$ 23. $\frac{10}{12} - \frac{1}{10}$

Estimate to compare. Write < or > for each ●.

24. $\frac{2}{3} + \frac{1}{9}$ ● 1 25. $\frac{3}{4} - \frac{1}{8}$ ● $\frac{1}{2}$ 26. $\frac{5}{12} + \frac{3}{5}$ ● 1 27. $\frac{7}{12} - \frac{1}{5}$ ● 0

28. Lisa and Valerie are picnicking in Roosevelt State Park in Mississippi. Lisa is using $\frac{3}{4}$ cup of strawberries and $\frac{2}{3}$ cup of peaches to make fruit salad. About how many cups does this make?

29. **WRITE Math** **What's the Error?** Nick estimated that $\frac{5}{8} + \frac{4}{7}$ is about 2. What is his error?

30. **FAST FACT** At Trace State Park in Mississippi, there is a 25-mile mountain bike trail. If Tommy rode his bike $\frac{1}{3}$ of the trail on Saturday and $\frac{1}{5}$ of the trail on Sunday, about what fraction of the trail did he ride?

Achieving the Standards

31. Find the value of b in the equation $5a - 7 = b$ if $a = 3$. (Grade 4 AF 1.5)

32. Estimate the sum of 178,021 and 146,973. (NS 1.1, p. 14)

33. Write the fraction $\frac{27}{45}$ in simplest form. (NS 1.0, p. 146)

34. **Test Prep** Tim caught a fish weighing $\frac{1}{4}$ pound and a fish weighing $\frac{1}{3}$ pound. About how much do the fish weigh together?

A $\frac{1}{2}$ pound
B 1 pound
C $1\frac{1}{2}$ pounds
D 2 pounds

Extra Practice on page 212, Set A

CD ROM **Technology** Use Harcourt Mega Math, Fraction Action *Number Line Mine*, Level K.

LESSON 4

Use Common Denominators

OBJECTIVE: Use a common denominator to add and subtract unlike fractions.

Quick Review

Find a common multiple of each pair.

1. 2 and 4
2. 5 and 10
3. 4 and 6
4. 3 and 9
5. 6 and 10

Vocabulary

least common denominator (LCD)

Learn

PROBLEM The Pomo tribes who lived in California during the 1800's, were highly skilled at weaving baskets. Suppose $\frac{1}{2}$ of a basket is woven in one month and $\frac{1}{4}$ of it is woven in the next two weeks. How much of the basket has been woven?

To add or subtract unlike fractions, rename them as like fractions with a common denominator.

Math Idea
Estimate the answer first. Then compare to the exact answer to see if it is reasonable.

Example 1 Add. $\frac{1}{2} + \frac{1}{4}$

Step 1

Multiply the denominators to find a common denominator.

$2 \times 4 = 8$ common denominator

Step 2

Use the common denominator to write equivalent fractions. Then add.

$$\frac{1}{2} = \frac{4}{8}$$
$$+\frac{1}{4} = +\frac{2}{8}$$
$$\frac{6}{8} = \frac{3}{4} \leftarrow \text{simplest form}$$

So, $\frac{3}{4}$ of the basket has been finished.

- Hillary estimated the sum to be close to $\frac{1}{2}$. Is her estimate reasonable?

Suppose a Pomo basket weaver had a grass reed that was $\frac{5}{6}$ yard long. He needed only $\frac{3}{4}$ yard to complete a basket. How much of the reed was left when the basket was completed?

Example 2 Subtract. $\frac{5}{6} - \frac{3}{4}$

Step 1

Multiply the denominators to find a common denominator.

$6 \times 4 = 24$ common denominator

Step 2

Use the common denominator to write equivalent fractions. Then subtract.

$$\frac{5}{6} = \frac{20}{24}$$
$$-\frac{3}{4} = -\frac{18}{24}$$
$$\frac{2}{24} = \frac{1}{12} \leftarrow \text{simplest form}$$

So, the basket weaver had $\frac{1}{12}$ yard of grass reed left.

NS 2.3 Solve simple problems, including ones arising in concrete situations, involving the addition and subtraction of fractions and mixed numbers, and express answers in the simplest form. *also* MR 2.3, MR 2.4, MR 3.2

The Least Common Denominator

To add or subtract unlike fractions, you can also write equivalent fractions with the least common denominator. The **least common denominator (LCD)** is the least common multiple of two or more denominators.

Remember

To find the least common denominator, first find the least common multiple of the denominators.

Example 3 Add. $\frac{1}{4} + \frac{3}{8}$

A basket weaver bought shell beads and glass beads to weave into designs in her baskets. She bought $\frac{1}{4}$ pound of shell beads and $\frac{3}{8}$ pound of glass beads. How many pounds of beads did she buy?

ONE WAY **Use a common denominator.**

Multiply the denominators to find a common denominator.

$4 \times 8 = 32$ ← common denominator

Use a common denominator to write equivalent fractions. Then add.

$$\frac{1}{4} = \frac{8}{32}$$
$$+\frac{3}{8} = +\frac{12}{32}$$
$$\frac{20}{32} = \frac{5}{8} \leftarrow \text{simplest form}$$

ANOTHER WAY **Use the least common denominator (LCD).**

List multiples of each denominator.

Multiples of 4: 4, 8, 12, 16, 20, 24

Multiples of 8: 8, 16, 24, 32, 40, 48

The least common multiple is 8. So, the LCD of $\frac{1}{4}$ and $\frac{3}{8}$ is 8. Write equivalent fractions. Then add.

$$\frac{1}{4} = \frac{1 \times 2}{4 \times 2} = \frac{2}{8}$$
$$+\frac{3}{8} \qquad +\frac{3}{8}$$
$$\frac{5}{8} \leftarrow \text{simplest form}$$

So, the basket weaver bought $\frac{5}{8}$ pound of beads.

More Examples

A **Add.** $\frac{1}{6} + \frac{1}{2}$

Use a common denominator to write equivalent fractions. Then add.

$$\frac{1}{6} \qquad \frac{1}{6}$$
$$+\frac{1}{2} = +\frac{3}{6}$$
$$\frac{4}{6} = \frac{2}{3}$$

So, $\frac{1}{6} + \frac{1}{2} = \frac{2}{3}$.

B **Subtract.** $\frac{11}{12} - \frac{5}{8}$

Find the least common denominator. Then write equivalent fractions to subtract.

$$\frac{11}{12} = \frac{11 \times 2}{12 \times 2} = \frac{22}{24}$$
$$-\frac{5}{8} = -\frac{5 \times 3}{8 \times 3} = -\frac{15}{24}$$
$$\frac{7}{24}$$

So, $\frac{11}{12} - \frac{5}{8} = \frac{7}{24}$.

Guided Practice

1. Copy the problem to the right. Show how to subtract unlike fractions by writing equivalent fractions. Write the answer in simplest form.

$$\frac{4}{5} = \frac{■}{30}$$
$$-\frac{2}{6} = -\frac{■}{30}$$

Find the sum or difference. Write the answer in simplest form.

2. $\frac{3}{4} - \frac{1}{8}$
3. $\frac{2}{5} + \frac{3}{10}$
4. $\frac{1}{4} - \frac{1}{7}$
5. $\frac{5}{12} + \frac{1}{3}$
6. $\frac{9}{10} - \frac{1}{2}$

7. **TALK Math** **Explain** how you can use common multiples to add $\frac{7}{8}$ and $\frac{1}{3}$.

Independent Practice and Problem Solving

Find the sum or difference. Write the answer in simplest form.

8. $\frac{3}{5} + \frac{1}{4}$
9. $\frac{5}{8} + \frac{1}{5}$
10. $\frac{1}{12} + \frac{1}{2}$
11. $\frac{7}{10} + \frac{1}{5}$
12. $\frac{2}{7} + \frac{3}{10}$
13. $\frac{5}{6} - \frac{3}{8}$
14. $\frac{3}{4} - \frac{1}{2}$
15. $\frac{7}{8} - \frac{1}{6}$
16. $\frac{3}{7} - \frac{3}{14}$
17. $\frac{5}{12} - \frac{1}{4}$

Algebra **Find the missing number for each ■. Write the answer in simplest form.**

18. $\frac{5}{8} - ■ = \frac{3}{8}$
19. $\frac{1}{6} + ■ = 1$
20. $\frac{9}{10} - ■ = \frac{1}{5}$
21. $\frac{5}{12} + ■ = \frac{1}{2}$

USE DATA For 22–24, use the picture.

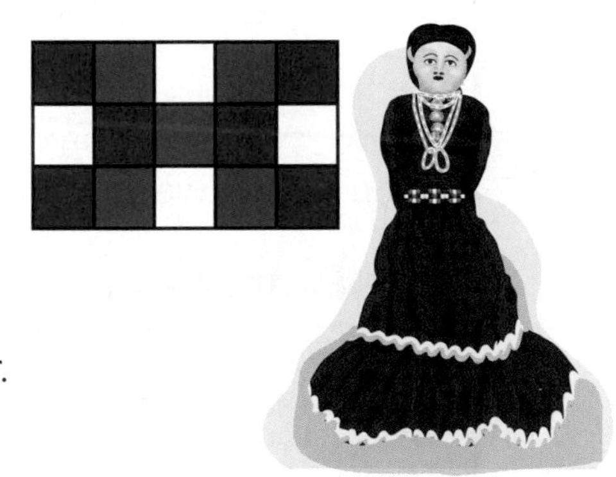

22. Sara is making a belt for a doll using the bead design shown. What fraction of the beads in her design are blue or red?
23. **WRITE Math** **What's the Question?** The answer is $\frac{2}{15}$ of the pattern.
24. In making the belt, Sara wants to repeat the pattern of beads 3 times. She has a total of 21 red beads, 18 blue beads, and 19 white beads. Write a fraction that shows the number of beads she will have left over.

Achieving the Standards

25. Erin has 4 red straws, 2 blue straws, and 6 yellow straws. If she chooses one without looking, what is the probability she will choose red? (Grade 4, SDAP 2.2)
26. $420 \div 15 =$ (O‑π NS 2.2, p. 96)
27. Write two equivalent fractions for $\frac{24}{32}$ using denominators less than 32. (NS 1.0, p. 144)
28. **Test Prep** Chad planted $\frac{2}{3}$ of the garden with marigolds and $\frac{1}{6}$ of the garden with petunias. How much of the garden did he plant with flowers?

    A $\frac{1}{6}$
    B $\frac{1}{2}$
    C $\frac{5}{6}$
    D 1

Presenting Patterns

Graphic Aids

One of the oldest known American Indian crafts is basket-weaving. Different tribes used different materials, such as wood, grass, pine needles, or willow, depending on what was available in their environment. The patterns and materials in the baskets could be used to identify which of the tribes had woven them.

These patterns, just like patterns in mathematics, often followed a rule, such as: *multiply by 5* or *add* $\frac{1}{4}$.

Look for the pattern in this list of fractions.

$$\frac{1}{4}, \frac{2}{4}, \frac{3}{4}, \frac{4}{4}, \frac{5}{4}$$

How do the values of these fractions change as the numerators increase? What is the pattern's rule?

You can use **graphic aids** to help you solve the problem. Choose a graphic aid that can help you show the problem or its solution. For example, you can use a number line to model the fractions.

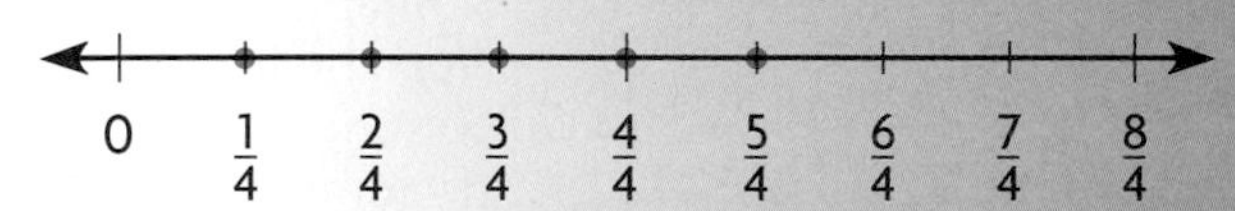

Think: To solve the problem, you might also use graphic aids such as fraction strips or fraction models.

These baskets show the different types of patterns used by American Indian craftsworkers.

Problem Solving Use a graphic aid to solve the problem.

1. Solve the problem above.
2. a. How do the values of these fractions change as the denominators increase?

   $$\frac{1}{2}, \frac{1}{3}, \frac{1}{4}, \frac{1}{5}, \frac{1}{6}, \frac{1}{n}$$

   b. What is the next fraction in the pattern?

LESSON 5

Add and Subtract Fractions

OBJECTIVE: Use the least common denominator to add and subtract fractions.

Quick Review

Estimate the sum or difference.

1. $\frac{1}{2}+\frac{1}{7}$
2. $\frac{3}{5}-\frac{1}{8}$
3. $\frac{1}{6}+\frac{7}{8}$
4. $\frac{3}{4}-\frac{3}{5}$
5. $\frac{7}{12}+\frac{2}{5}$

Learn

PROBLEM The length of a green sea turtle's shell was measured for two years. The first year the shell grew $\frac{2}{5}$ inch. The next year the shell grew $\frac{3}{10}$ inch. How much did the shell grow over the two-year period?

Example 1 Add. $\frac{2}{5}+\frac{3}{10}$

Step 1

The least common multiple of 5 and 10 is 10. So, the LCD of $\frac{2}{5}$ and $\frac{3}{10}$ is 10. Use the LCD to write like fractions.

$$\frac{2\times 2}{5\times 2}=\frac{4}{10}$$
$$+\frac{3}{10}=+\frac{3}{10}$$

Step 2

Add the fractions. Write the answer in simplest form.

$$\frac{2\times 2}{5\times 2}=\frac{4}{10}$$
$$+\frac{3}{10}=+\frac{3}{10}$$
$$\frac{7}{10}$$

So, the sea turtle's shell grew $\frac{7}{10}$ inch in two years.

Example 2

An adult hawksbill sea turtle's shell length measures $\frac{3}{4}$ yard. A tiny hatchling's shell measures $\frac{1}{5}$ yard. What is the difference in the lengths of their shells?

Subtract. $\frac{3}{4}-\frac{1}{5}$

Step 1

The least common multiple of 4 and 5 is 20. So, the LCD of $\frac{3}{4}$ and $\frac{1}{5}$ is 20. Use the LCD to change the fractions to like fractions.

$$\frac{3}{4}=\frac{3\times 5}{4\times 5}=\frac{15}{20}$$
$$-\frac{1}{5}=-\frac{1\times 4}{5\times 4}=-\frac{4}{20}$$

Step 2

Subtract the fractions. Write the answer in simplest form if needed.

$$\frac{3}{4}=\frac{3\times 5}{4\times 5}=\frac{15}{20}$$
$$-\frac{1}{5}=-\frac{1\times 4}{5\times 4}=-\frac{4}{20}$$
$$\frac{11}{20} \leftarrow \text{simplest form}$$

So, the difference in lengths is $\frac{11}{20}$ yard.

Math Idea
To add or subtract unlike fractions, find the least common denominator (LCD) to write equivalent fractions. Then add or subtract the numerators.

NS 2.3 Solve simple problems, including ones arising in concrete situations, involving the addition and subtraction of fractions and mixed numbers, and express answers in the simplest form. *also* **MR 2.3, MR 2.4, MR 3.2, MR 3.3**

Guided Practice

1. Look at the problem at the right. Find the sum of the fractions by writing like fractions. Write the answer in simplest form.

$$\begin{array}{r} \frac{1}{2} = \frac{■}{4} \\ +\frac{3}{4} = +\frac{■}{4} \\ \hline ■ \end{array}$$

Find the sum or difference. Write it in simplest form.

2. $\frac{3}{4} + \frac{1}{8}$
3. $\frac{7}{10} - \frac{2}{5}$
4. $\frac{1}{5} + \frac{1}{6}$
5. $\frac{2}{3} - \frac{1}{4}$
6. $\frac{5}{8} + \frac{1}{3}$

7. **TALK Math** **Explain** how you know that $\frac{11}{20}$ is in simplest form.

Independent Practice and Problem Solving

Find the sum or difference. Write it in simplest form.

8. $\frac{3}{7} + \frac{1}{8}$
9. $\frac{3}{4} - \frac{1}{2}$
10. $\frac{2}{3} + \frac{1}{4}$
11. $\frac{5}{6} - \frac{2}{3}$
12. $\frac{7}{8} + \frac{1}{4}$
13. $\frac{4}{9} - \frac{1}{6}$
14. $\frac{1}{3} + \frac{1}{5}$
15. $1 - \frac{3}{10}$
16. $\frac{3}{10} + \frac{3}{4}$
17. $\frac{6}{7} - \frac{2}{14}$

Algebra **Compare. Write < or > for each ●.**

18. $\frac{1}{3} + \frac{1}{8}$ ● $\frac{2}{3} + \frac{1}{7}$
19. $\frac{5}{6} - \frac{1}{4}$ ● $\frac{9}{10} - \frac{1}{2}$
20. $\frac{1}{4} + \frac{3}{8}$ ● $\frac{2}{3} - \frac{1}{2}$

USE DATA **Use the pictures for 21–23.**

21. How much longer is Turtle A than Turtle B?
22. What is the difference in lengths between the largest and the smallest hawksbill sea turtle?
23. **WRITE Math** **What's the Error?** Shane said that if Turtle C grew another $\frac{1}{3}$ yard, it would be $\frac{3}{5}$ yard in length. Describe his error. Write the correct answer.

A. $\frac{3}{4}$ yard

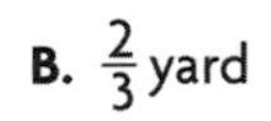

B. $\frac{2}{3}$ yard

C. $\frac{2}{5}$ yard

Achieving the Standards

24. $\frac{6}{10} + \frac{7}{10} =$ (NS 2.3, p. 178)
25. What is the decimal 0.45 written as a fraction? (NS 1.2, p. 160)
26. What is the LCD for $\frac{3}{4}$ and $\frac{1}{3}$? (NS 2.3, p. 204)
27. **Test Prep** It took Roxie $\frac{1}{3}$ hour to walk to the library and then $\frac{1}{4}$ hour to walk to Amy's house. How much time did it take Roxie in all to walk to both places?
    - **A** $\frac{1}{6}$ hour
    - **B** $\frac{1}{2}$ hour
    - **C** $\frac{7}{12}$ hour
    - **D** $\frac{3}{4}$ hour

Extra Practice on page 212, Set C

Problem Solving Workshop
Strategy: Compare Strategies

OBJECTIVE: Compare different strategies to solve problems.

Use the Strategy

PROBLEM In Natalie's science class, the students are observing the total monthly rainfall. At the end of each week, they record the amount of rain that fell. By the end of Week 3, there was a total of $\frac{5}{6}$ inch of rain. This was $\frac{2}{5}$ inch more than the amount recorded at the end of Week 2. During Week 2, $\frac{1}{3}$ inch more rain fell than the week before. What was the rainfall in Week 1?

- **Summarize what you are asked to find.**
- **What information is given?**
- **Is there information you will not use? If so, what?**

Plan

- **What strategy can you use to solve the problem?**
  Often you can use more than one strategy to solve a problem. Use *make a model* and *work backward.*

Solve

- **How can you use the strategy to solve the problem?**

Make a Model

You can use fraction bars to find the missing data.

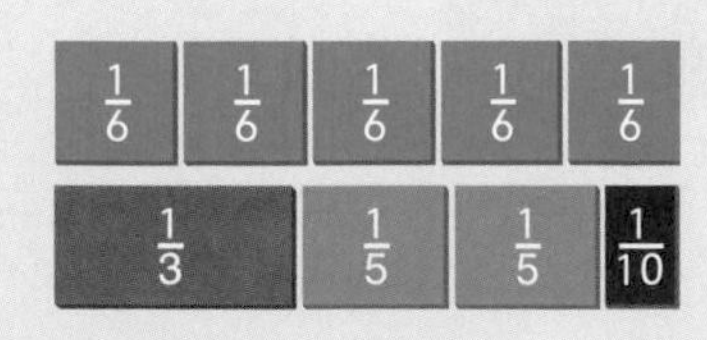

$$\frac{5}{6} = \frac{1}{3} + \frac{2}{5} + \frac{1}{10}$$

So, $\frac{1}{10}$ inch of rain fell in Week 1.

Work Backward

You can write an equation for the total rainfall.

Week 1 + Week 2 + Week 3 = Total

$$n + \frac{1}{3} + \frac{2}{5} = \frac{5}{6}$$

$$n = \frac{5}{6} - \frac{2}{5} - \frac{1}{3}$$ Find a common denominator.

$$n = \frac{25}{30} - \frac{12}{30} - \frac{10}{30}$$

$$n = \frac{3}{30}, \text{ or } \frac{1}{10}$$

Check

- **What other strategy could you use to solve the problem?**

NS 2.3 Solve simple problems, including ones arising in concrete situations, involving the addition and subtraction of fractions and mixed numbers, and express answers in the simplest form. *also* **MR 1.0, MR 2.0, MR 2.2, MR 2.3, MR 2.4, MR 2.6, MR 3.0, MR 3.1, MR 3.2, MR 3.3**

Guided Problem Solving

1. David worked on his science project for $7\frac{1}{2}$ hours. He spent $1\frac{1}{2}$ hours reading his science journal and $2\frac{4}{5}$ hours building a model. He then spent the rest of his time making posters for the project. How many hours did David spend making posters?

   First, use the *make a model* strategy.

   Then, use the *work backward* strategy.

   Finally, compare the answers.

2. **What if** David had worked on his science project for $6\frac{4}{5}$ hours? How many hours did he spend making posters?

3. David bought some supplies for the science project. He spent $3.99 for poster board, $1.24 for a glue stick, and $4.55 for color pencils. If David had $1.57 when he left the store, how much money did he have before his purchases?

Choose a STRATEGY

- Draw a Diagram or Picture
- Make a Model or Act It Out
- Make an Organized List
- Find a Pattern
- Make a Table or Graph
- Predict and Test
- Work Backward
- Solve a Simpler Problem
- Write an Equation
- Use Logical Reasoning

Mixed Strategy Practice

4. In Ms. Grant's science class, $\frac{1}{3}$ of the projects were about climate, $\frac{1}{6}$ were on earthquakes, and $\frac{1}{4}$ were on water and ecosystems. The rest of the projects were about hurricanes. What fraction of the science projects were about hurricanes?

5. Julia is building a rectangular base for the school's weather station. The perimeter is $3\frac{2}{3}$ feet. If the width is $\frac{1}{3}$ foot, what is the length?

USE DATA **For 6–9, use the table.**

6. Using Monday's rainfall, list the four towns in order from least to greatest rainfall.

7. On what day did two cities have the same amounts of rainfall greater than zero? What were the two cities and what were the amounts of rainfall?

8. On what day did the sum of the rainfall for two cities equal the amount of rainfall for a third city? What were the cities and what were the amounts of rainfall?

9. WRITE Math **Explain** how you could use the work backward strategy to solve one of the problems above.

Kansas Rainfall During a Week in August

Day	City Rainfall (inches)			
	Hays	Hesston	Hutchinson	St. John
Monday	$\frac{2}{5}$	$\frac{3}{10}$	$\frac{9}{10}$	$\frac{7}{10}$
Tuesday	0	0	0	$\frac{1}{100}$
Wednesday	0	0	0	0
Thursday	$\frac{1}{5}$	0	$\frac{1}{2}$	$\frac{3}{10}$
Friday	$\frac{3}{20}$	$\frac{1}{10}$	$\frac{1}{20}$	0
Saturday	$\frac{1}{10}$	$\frac{1}{25}$	$\frac{1}{10}$	0
Sunday	0	$\frac{4}{5}$	$\frac{1}{100}$	$\frac{3}{10}$

Extra Practice

Set A Estimate each sum or difference. (pp. 202–203)

1. $\frac{5}{6} + \frac{3}{5}$
2. $\frac{11}{12} - \frac{4}{7}$
3. $\frac{8}{10} + \frac{1}{9}$
4. $\frac{10}{12} - \frac{2}{7}$
5. $\frac{13}{14} + \frac{3}{5}$
6. $\frac{3}{4} - \frac{1}{3}$
7. $\frac{7}{11} + \frac{2}{9}$
8. $\frac{4}{5} - \frac{1}{8}$
9. $\frac{3}{4} + \frac{2}{3}$
10. $\frac{6}{7} - \frac{1}{5}$
11. $\frac{1}{12} + \frac{5}{6}$
12. $\frac{7}{8} - \frac{3}{4}$
13. $\frac{11}{12} + \frac{1}{4}$
14. $\frac{2}{5} - \frac{1}{9}$
15. $\frac{7}{9} + \frac{2}{7}$

Set B Find the sum or difference. Write the answer in simplest form. (pp. 204–207)

1. $\frac{4}{5} + \frac{1}{10}$
2. $\frac{7}{9} - \frac{1}{3}$
3. $\frac{3}{8} + \frac{1}{2}$
4. $\frac{11}{12} - \frac{5}{6}$
5. $\frac{2}{7} + \frac{1}{2}$
6. $\frac{8}{9} - \frac{2}{3}$
7. $\frac{3}{5} + \frac{2}{10}$
8. $\frac{5}{8} - \frac{1}{4}$
9. $\frac{3}{5} - \frac{4}{7}$
10. $\frac{9}{12} - \frac{2}{3}$
11. Russ mowed $\frac{1}{3}$ of the lawn in the morning and $\frac{1}{5}$ of the lawn in the afternoon. How much of the lawn has he mowed?
12. Sue read $\frac{5}{12}$ of a book last week and $\frac{1}{4}$ of the book this week. How much more of the book did she read last week?

Algebra Find the missing number for each ■. Write the answer in simplest form.

13. $\frac{3}{8} + ■ = \frac{7}{8}$
14. $\frac{7}{12} - ■ = \frac{1}{2}$
15. $■ - \frac{1}{4} = \frac{5}{8}$
16. $\frac{5}{6} - ■ = \frac{1}{3}$

Set C Find the sum or difference. Write it in simplest form. (pp. 208–209)

1. $\frac{7}{12} + \frac{1}{6}$
2. $\frac{7}{8} - \frac{1}{2}$
3. $\frac{1}{4} + \frac{3}{6}$
4. $\frac{7}{8} - \frac{1}{4}$
5. $\frac{5}{7} - \frac{1}{3}$
6. $\frac{6}{11} + \frac{1}{3}$
7. $\frac{5}{6} - \frac{1}{2}$
8. $\frac{3}{4} + \frac{2}{5}$
9. $\frac{4}{5} - \frac{1}{6}$
10. $\frac{11}{12} + \frac{1}{5}$
11. It took Mac $\frac{2}{3}$ hour to walk to school and $\frac{1}{6}$ hour to walk from school to the library. How much time did it take Mac to walk to school and then to the library?
12. Nancy studied for $\frac{10}{12}$ hour. Les studied for $\frac{3}{4}$ hour. How much longer did Nancy study than Les?

Algebra Compare. Write < or > for each ●.

13. $\frac{2}{3} - \frac{1}{4}$ ● $\frac{5}{6} - \frac{1}{5}$
14. $\frac{3}{8} + \frac{1}{3}$ ● $\frac{3}{4} + \frac{1}{6}$
15. $\frac{7}{8} - \frac{2}{3}$ ● $\frac{3}{10} + \frac{1}{4}$

CD ROM

Technology

Use Harcourt Mega Math, Fraction Action, *Fraction Flare Up,* Levels H, I.

PRACTICE GAME

What's the Difference?

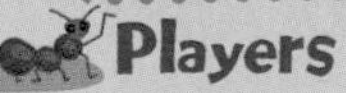

Players

4 students

Materials

4 sets of number cards (1–8)

$$\frac{5}{6} - \frac{1}{2} = ?$$

Start Playing!

- Each player draws a problem outline on a sheet of paper.
- The first player shuffles the number cards and hands out 4 cards to each player.
- Players use their cards to form two fractions that will have the least possible difference. Players display their subtraction problems by placing the cards on their problem outlines.
- Players solve one another's problems to determine which yields the least difference.
- The player who makes the problem with the least difference gets 1 point and reshuffles the cards for the next round.
- The first player to score 5 points wins the game.

Chapter 8 Review/Test

Check Vocabulary and Concepts

For 1, choose the better term from the box.

VOCABULARY
equivalent fraction
least common denominator (LCD)

1. The __?__ is the least common multiple of two or more denominators. (O-π NS 2.3, p. 206)

2. Explain how you can use fraction bars to add and subtract fractions with unlike denominators. (O-π NS 2.3, p. 198, 200)

Check Skills

Estimate each sum or difference. (NS 1.1, pp. 202–203)

3. $\frac{7}{9} - \frac{2}{5}$ **4.** $\frac{7}{8} + \frac{2}{3}$ **5.** $\frac{7}{11} + \frac{1}{3}$ **6.** $\frac{4}{7} + \frac{1}{2}$ **7.** $\frac{5}{6} - \frac{1}{8}$

Find the sum or difference. Write the answer in simplest form. (O-π NS 2.3, pp. 204–207)

8. $\frac{7}{8} - \frac{3}{4}$ **9.** $\frac{4}{9} + \frac{1}{3}$ **10.** $\frac{8}{10} - \frac{3}{5}$ **11.** $\frac{2}{3} + \frac{1}{12}$ **12.** $\frac{5}{6} - \frac{1}{4}$

Find the sum or difference. Write it in simplest form. (O-π NS 2.3, pp. 208–209)

13. $\frac{3}{8} - \frac{1}{6}$ **14.** $\frac{1}{3} + \frac{1}{4}$ **15.** $1 - \frac{7}{10}$ **16.** $\frac{9}{10} + \frac{1}{4}$ **17.** $\frac{5}{8} - \frac{3}{16}$

Check Problem Solving

Solve. (O-π NS 2.3, MR 2.3, pp. 210–211)

18. Annie used $\frac{7}{8}$ cup of blueberries to make muffins. She used $\frac{1}{4}$ cup fewer blueberries to make a blueberry tart. She used $\frac{1}{2}$ cup less blueberries to make a smoothie than to make a tart. What amount of blueberries did Annie use to make a smoothie?

19. The distance from the mall to the library is $\frac{9}{10}$ mile. The distance from the library to the post office is $\frac{1}{5}$ mile greater than this distance. The distance from the post office to Town Hall is $\frac{1}{2}$ mile less than the distance from the library to the post office. What is the distance from the post office to Town Hall?

20. WRITE Math **Explain** how you could use the strategy *work backward* to solve Problem 18.

GO ONLINE **Technology** Use *Online Assessment.*

Enrich • Adding and Subtracting Fractions

Egyptian Unit Fractions

A **unit fraction** is a fraction with a numerator of 1. Ancient Egyptians represented values less than 1 as the sum of different unit fractions.

$\frac{2}{5} = \frac{1}{3} + \frac{1}{15}$ $\frac{7}{8} = \frac{1}{2} + \frac{1}{4} + \frac{1}{8}$ $\frac{13}{20} = \frac{1}{2} + \frac{1}{10} + \frac{1}{20}$

To express a fraction as an Egyptian fraction, you continually subtract the largest unit fraction possible from the orginal fraction.

Example 1

Express $\frac{7}{12}$ as an Egyptian fraction.

The largest unit fraction less than $\frac{7}{12}$ is $\frac{1}{2}$.	Subtract the unit fraction. $\frac{7}{12} - \frac{1}{2} = \frac{7}{12} - \frac{6}{12} = \frac{1}{12}$	Stop subtracting when the difference is a unit fraction. Express the Egyptian fraction as a sum of unit fractions. $\frac{1}{2} + \frac{1}{12}$

So, $\frac{7}{12} = \frac{1}{2} + \frac{1}{12}$.

Example 2

Express $\frac{7}{8}$ as an Egyptian fraction.

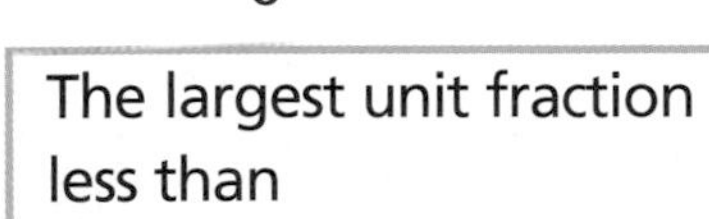

The largest unit fraction less than $\frac{7}{8}$ is $\frac{1}{2}$.	Subtract. $\frac{7}{8} - \frac{1}{2} = \frac{7}{8} - \frac{4}{8} = \frac{3}{8}$ The largest unit fraction less than $\frac{3}{8}$ is $\frac{1}{4}$.	Subtract this fraction. $\frac{3}{8} - \frac{1}{4} = \frac{3}{8} - \frac{2}{8} = \frac{1}{8}$

So, $\frac{7}{8} = \frac{1}{2} + \frac{1}{4} + \frac{1}{8}$.

Try It

Express each fraction as an Egyptian fraction.

1. $\frac{3}{4}$ **2.** $\frac{2}{3}$ **3.** $\frac{2}{5}$ **4.** $\frac{5}{6}$ **5.** $\frac{4}{5}$ **6.** $\frac{5}{9}$

Think About It

WRITE Math **Explain** how to express the Egyptian fraction $\frac{1}{2} + \frac{1}{3} + \frac{1}{12}$ as a single fraction.

Achieving the Standards
Chapters 1–8

Measurement and Geometry

1. Which best describes the pair of lines below? (Grade 4 MG 3.1)

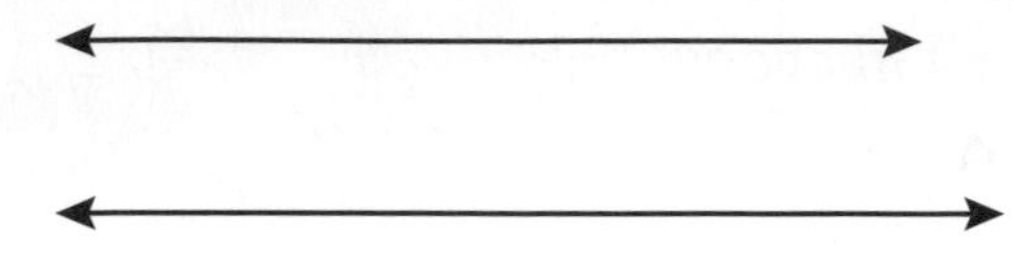

A parallel lines

B intersecting lines

C perpendicular lines

D obtuse lines

2. James made the grid below to show the locations of some vegetables in his garden.

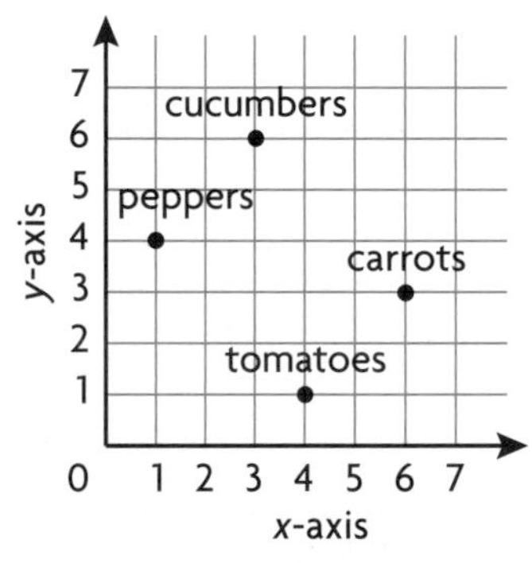

Which ordered pair *best* represents the location of the tomatoes? (Grade 4 MG 2.0)

A (1,4) C (4,1)

B (3,6) D (6,3)

3. WRITE Math **Explain** how you can tell if a figure has rotational symmetry. (Grade 4 MG 3.4)

Number Sense

4. The table shows the land areas of some counties in California.

County Sizes	
County	**Land Area (in square miles)**
Calaveras	1,020
Inyo	10,203
Kern	8,141
San Francisco	47
Alameda	738

Which county has a land area that is about 20 times as large as San Francisco County? (NS 1.0)

A Calaveras C Kern

B Inyo D Alameda

5. $\frac{4}{5} - \frac{1}{2} =$ (NS 2.3)

A $\frac{3}{10}$ C 1

B $\frac{1}{3}$ D $1\frac{3}{10}$

6. $2\frac{7}{8} + 4\frac{3}{8} =$ (NS 2.3)

A $6\frac{1}{8}$ C $6\frac{5}{8}$

B $6\frac{1}{4}$ D $7\frac{1}{4}$

7. WRITE Math **Explain** how to find the sum of $\frac{1}{6}$ and $\frac{4}{9}$. (NS 2.3)

Statistics, Data Analysis, and Probability

Understand the problem.

See item 8. You need to find the median. The median is the middle number when data are ordered from least to greatest.

8. The table shows the number of minutes that Carl practiced the piano each day.

Piano Practice	
Day	**Number of Minutes**
Monday	20
Tuesday	30
Wednesday	40
Thursday	35
Friday	25

Which day represents the median number of minutes that Carl practiced? (SDAP 1.1)

A Tuesday
B Wednesday
C Thursday
D Friday

9. Which type of graph would be *best* to display a baby's growth in height from birth to one year of age? (SDAP 1.2)

A circle graph
B line graph
C bar graph
D pictograph

10. **WRITE Math** Josh had the following scores in a bowling competition. (Grade 4 SDAP 2.2)

92, 89, 72, 101, 99

What is Josh's median score? **Explain** how you can find his median score.

Algebra and Functions

11. $(15 + 9) \div (4 - 3) =$
(Grade 4 AF 1.2)

A 24
B 23
C 21
D 3

12. Which equation below represents the area (A) of the rectangle in square inches? (Grade 4 AF 1.4)

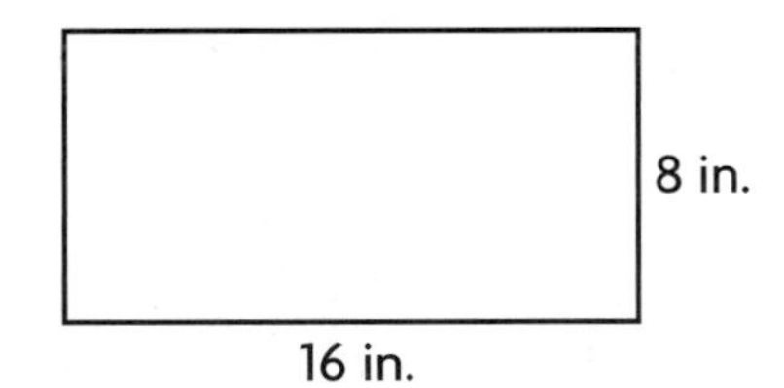

A $A = (2 \times 16) + (2 \times 8)$
B $A = 16 \times 8$
C $16 = A \times 8$
D $16 = (2 \times A) + (2 \times 8)$

13. The sum of p and q equals 25. If $p = 18$, which equation can be used to find the value of q? (Grade 4 AF 1.5)

A $p + 18 = 25$
B $p + q = 18 + 25$
C $18 + q = 25$
D $q - 18 = 25$

14. **WRITE Math** Which expression has the greater value: $16 - (19 - 15)$ or $15 - (19 - 16)$? **Explain.** (Grade 4 AF 1.2)

9 Add and Subtract Mixed Numbers

The Big Idea Addition and subtraction of mixed numbers are based on understanding equivalent fractions.

In 1889, San Francisco had a total of 53 miles of cable car lines within a 25-square-mile area.

Investigate

Both the Powell-Hyde and the Powell-Mason lines begin at Market Station. They end about $\frac{3}{10}$ mile apart. The east end of the California line is about $\frac{9}{10}$ mile from Market Station. Describe how you might travel, both walking and riding cable car lines, from the east end of the California line to the north end of the Powell-Hyde line. How far would you travel?

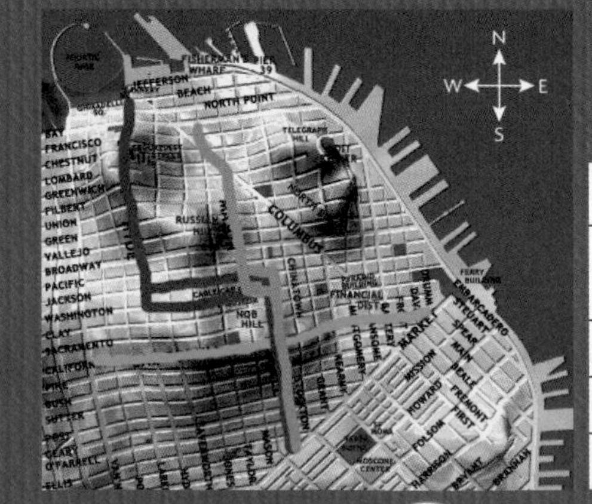

Key

Line	Approximate Length (mi)
Powell–Hyde	$2\frac{1}{10}$
Powell–Mason	$1\frac{11}{20}$
California	$1\frac{9}{20}$

Technology
Student pages are available in the Student eBook.

Show What You Know

Check your understanding of important skills needed for success in Chapter 9.

▶ Understand Mixed Numbers

Write a mixed number for each picture.

1. 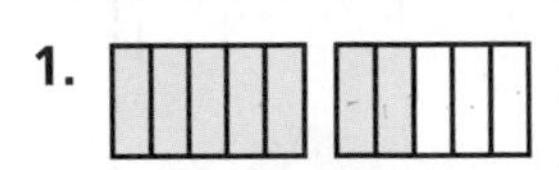

2.

3.

4. 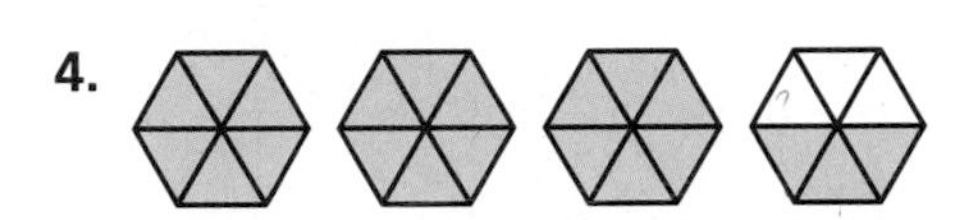

5. 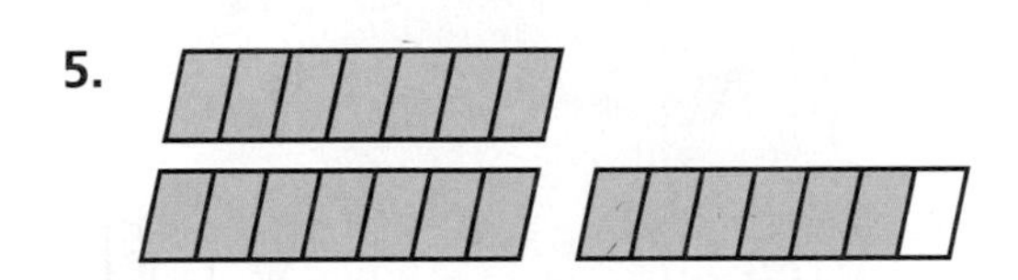

6. 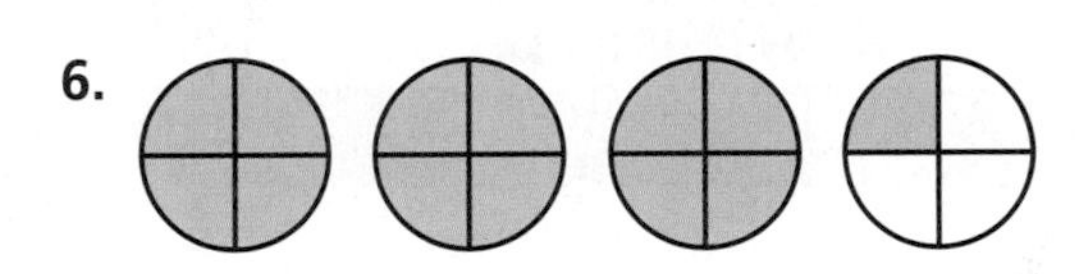

▶ Add and Subtract Fractions

Write the sum or difference in simplest form.

7. $\frac{1}{5} + \frac{2}{5}$

8. $\frac{3}{8} + \frac{1}{8}$

9. $\frac{5}{6} - \frac{1}{6}$

10. $\frac{11}{12} - \frac{5}{12}$

11. $\frac{1}{3} + \frac{1}{6}$

12. $\frac{7}{10} - \frac{2}{5}$

13. $\frac{2}{3} - \frac{4}{9}$

14. $\frac{1}{6} + \frac{3}{4}$

15. $\frac{3}{10} + \frac{7}{15}$

16. $\frac{5}{7} - \frac{3}{5}$

VOCABULARY POWER

CHAPTER VOCABULARY

equivalent fractions
least common denominator (LCD)
mixed number
multiples
renaming

WARM-UP WORDS

mixed number a number that is made up of a whole number and a fraction

least common denominator (LCD) the least common multiple of two or more denominators

equivalent fractions fractions that name the same number or amount

LESSON 1 HANDS ON

Model Addition of Mixed Numbers

OBJECTIVE: Add mixed numbers with models.

Quick Review

1. $\frac{1}{3} + \frac{1}{3}$
2. $\frac{1}{5} + \frac{3}{5}$
3. $\frac{3}{8} + \frac{4}{8}$
4. $\frac{2}{4} + \frac{1}{4}$
5. $\frac{3}{6} + \frac{2}{6}$

Investigate

Materials ■ fraction bars

You can use fraction bars to model the addition of mixed numbers.

A Use fraction bars to model $1\frac{3}{4} + 2\frac{1}{8}$.

1 | $\frac{1}{4}$ $\frac{1}{4}$ $\frac{1}{4}$ | $1\frac{3}{4}$

1 | 1 | $\frac{1}{8}$ | $2\frac{1}{8}$

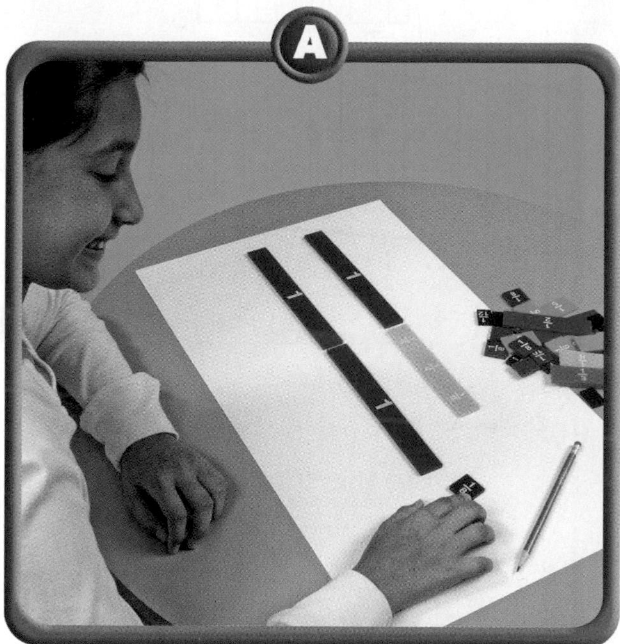

B Find like fraction bars for $\frac{3}{4}$ and $\frac{1}{8}$.

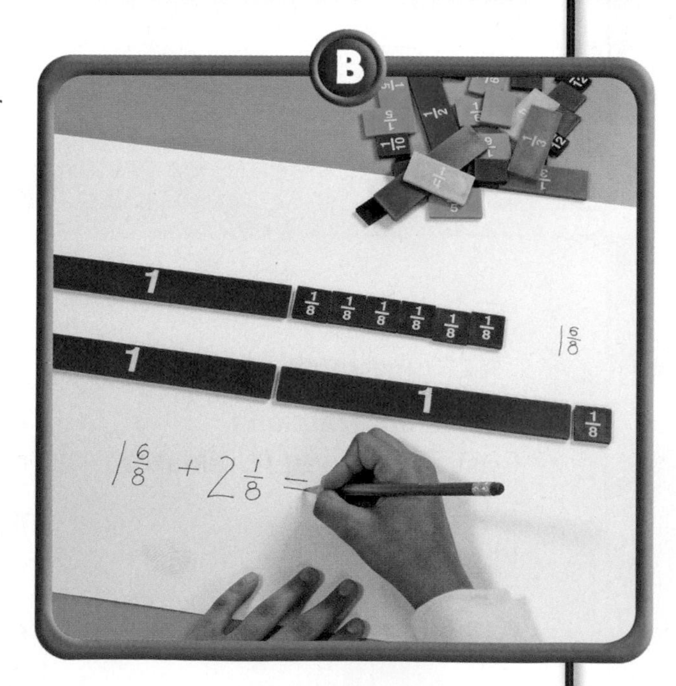

C Add the fractions, and add the whole numbers. Record your answer in simplest form.

D Use fraction bars to find $1\frac{2}{5} + 1\frac{3}{10}$. Write the answer in simplest form.

Draw Conclusions

1. In Part B, explain why you replaced the $\frac{1}{4}$ fraction bars.
2. When adding mixed numbers, explain how you know whether your answer is in simplest form.
3. **Analysis** Explain why $\frac{1}{8}$ fraction bars were used for like fraction bars in Part B.

NS 2.3 Solve simple problems, including ones arising in concrete situations, involving the addition and subtraction of fractions and mixed numbers (like and unlike denominators of 20 or less), and express answers in the simplest form. *also* **NS 2.0, MR 2.0, MR 2.3, MR 2.4, MR 3.2**

Connect

Sometimes, you need to rename the sum when you add mixed numbers.

Add. $2\frac{2}{3} + 2\frac{1}{2}$

Step 1

Model $2\frac{2}{3}$ and $2\frac{1}{2}$.

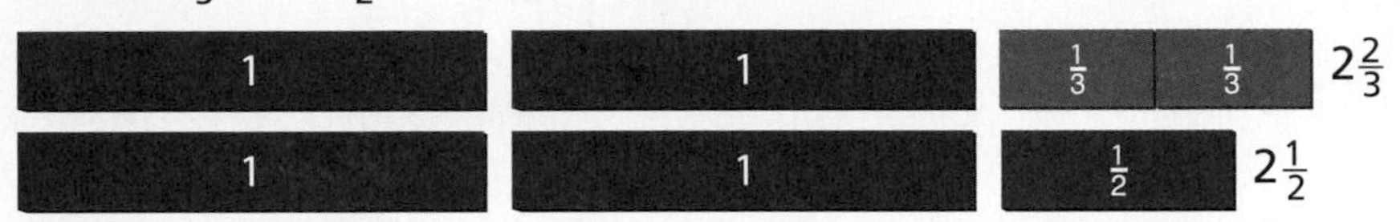

Step 2

Use like fraction bars.

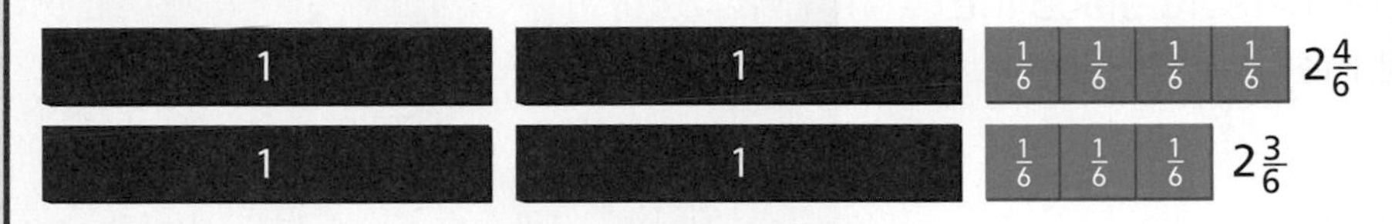

Step 3

Find the sum.

$2\frac{4}{6} + 2\frac{3}{6} = 4\frac{7}{6}$

$4\frac{7}{6} = 4 + 1 + \frac{1}{6} = 5\frac{1}{6}$ Rename $4\frac{7}{6}$.

$5\frac{1}{6}$

So, $2\frac{2}{3} + 2\frac{1}{2} = 5\frac{1}{6}$.

TALK Math

Explain how you could use twelfth bars to find $2\frac{2}{3} + 2\frac{1}{2}$.

Practice

Use fraction bars to find the sum. Write it in simplest form.

1. $4\frac{5}{12} + 1\frac{1}{6}$
2. $1\frac{3}{6} + 2\frac{1}{6}$
3. $2\frac{2}{5} + 1\frac{1}{2}$
4. $1\frac{1}{4} + 1\frac{1}{3}$
5. $3\frac{2}{6} + 2\frac{5}{6}$
6. $2\frac{5}{8} + 2\frac{3}{4}$
7. $5\frac{3}{4} + 2\frac{2}{3}$
8. $2\frac{3}{10} + 3\frac{4}{5}$
9. $3\frac{3}{4} + 1\frac{1}{2}$
10. **WRITE Math** **Explain** how fraction bars help you add mixed numbers.

LESSON 2 HANDS ON

Model Subtraction of Mixed Numbers

OBJECTIVE: Subtract mixed numbers with models.

Quick Review

Subtract. Write the answer in simplest form.

1. $\frac{3}{8} - \frac{1}{8}$
2. $\frac{5}{7} - \frac{2}{7}$
3. $\frac{7}{12} - \frac{1}{12}$
4. $\frac{4}{3} - \frac{1}{3}$
5. $\frac{7}{9} - \frac{1}{9}$

Investigate

Materials ■ fraction bars

You can use fraction bars to model the subtraction of mixed numbers.

A Use fraction bars to model $3\frac{3}{4} - 1\frac{5}{8}$.

B To subtract $1\frac{5}{8}$ find like fraction bars. Replace the three $\frac{1}{4}$ bars with $\frac{1}{8}$ bars until they are the same length.

$\frac{1}{4}$		$\frac{1}{4}$		$\frac{1}{4}$	
$\frac{1}{8}$	$\frac{1}{8}$	$\frac{1}{8}$	$\frac{1}{8}$	$\frac{1}{8}$	$\frac{1}{8}$

$\frac{3}{4} = \frac{6}{8}$

C Subtract the fractions, and subtract the whole numbers. Record your answer in simplest form.

D Use fraction bars to find $7\frac{5}{8} - 2\frac{3}{8}$. Write the answer in simplest form.

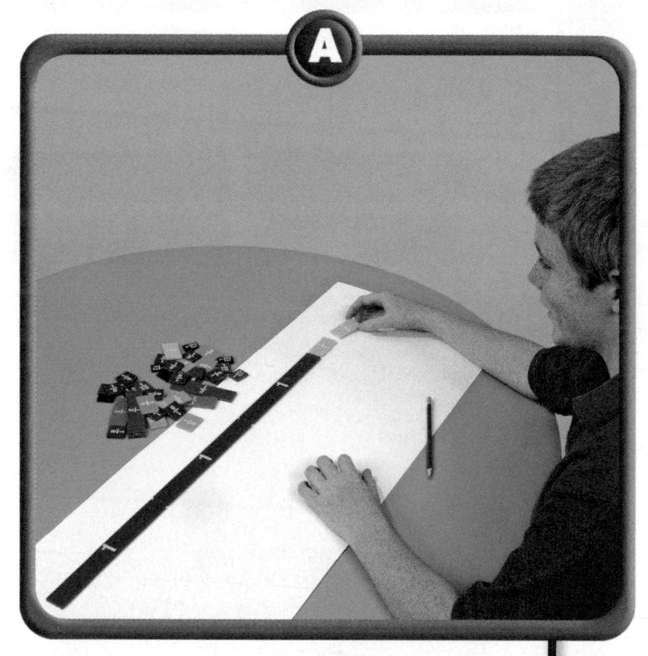

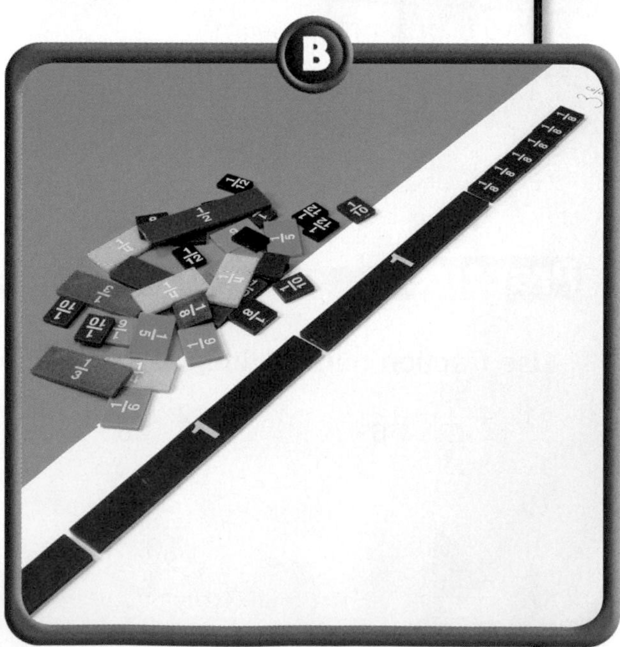

Draw Conclusions

1. Explain how you know which like fraction bars to use to model $\frac{3}{4}$ and $\frac{5}{8}$.
2. When subtracting mixed numbers, how do you know if your answer is in simplest form?
3. **Evaluation** How can equivalent fractions help you subtract?

NS 2.3 Solve simple problems, including ones arising in concrete situations, involving the addition and subtraction of fractions and mixed numbers (like and unlike denominators of 20 or less), and express answers in the simplest form. *also* **NS 2.0, MR 2.0, MR 2.3, MR 2.4, MR 3.2**

Connect

When you add or subtract mixed numbers that have unlike denominators, you can think of equivalent fractions that have like denominators.

Subtract. $2\frac{7}{8} - 1\frac{1}{2}$

Step 1

Draw a picture. Show $2\frac{7}{8}$.

Step 2

Subtract $1\frac{1}{2}$.

Think: $\frac{1}{2}$ is equivalent to $\frac{4}{8}$.

So, $2\frac{7}{8} - 1\frac{1}{2} = 1\frac{3}{8}$.

- Draw a picture to find $3\frac{1}{2} - 1\frac{1}{3}$.

TALK Math

To find $3\frac{1}{2} - 1\frac{1}{3}$, what equivalent fractions would you use?

Practice

Use fraction bars, or draw a picture to find the difference. Write it in simplest form.

1. $2\frac{3}{5} - 1\frac{1}{5}$
2. $3\frac{7}{10} - 1\frac{5}{10}$
3. $4\frac{5}{6} - 2\frac{2}{3}$
4. $2\frac{1}{2} - 1\frac{3}{8}$
5. $2\frac{2}{3} - \frac{1}{6}$
6. $3\frac{5}{8} - 1\frac{1}{4}$
7. $2\frac{5}{6} - 2\frac{1}{3}$
8. $1\frac{7}{8} - \frac{1}{4}$
9. $6\frac{3}{4} - 2\frac{3}{12}$
10. $5\frac{3}{4} - 2\frac{1}{8}$
11. $3\frac{1}{2} - 1\frac{3}{10}$
12. $4\frac{1}{3} - 2\frac{1}{4}$
13. $3\frac{1}{2} - 1\frac{1}{4}$
14. $2\frac{3}{4} - 1\frac{3}{8}$
15. $5\frac{3}{4} - 2\frac{3}{6}$
16. $3\frac{4}{6} - 1\frac{1}{6}$
17. **WRITE Math** **Explain** how you find the difference between $3\frac{7}{8}$ and $1\frac{1}{2}$.

LESSON 3

Record Addition and Subtraction

OBJECTIVE: Find the sums and differences of mixed numbers.

Quick Review

Write a common multiple for each pair.

1. 4 and 6
2. 3 and 5
3. 8 and 10
4. 12 and 9
5. 15 and 20

Learn

PROBLEM Denise mixed $1\frac{4}{5}$ ounces of blue paint with $2\frac{3}{10}$ ounces of yellow paint. How many ounces of paint did Denise mix in all?

To find the sum of mixed numbers with unlike denominators, you can use a common denominator.

Example 1 Add. $1\frac{4}{5} + 2\frac{3}{10}$

Step 1

Find a common denominator. Write equivalent fractions.

$$\begin{aligned} 1\frac{4}{5} &= 1\frac{8}{10} \\ +2\frac{3}{10} &= +2\frac{3}{10} \end{aligned}$$

Step 2

Add the fractions.

$$\begin{aligned} 1\frac{4}{5} &= 1\frac{8}{10} \\ +2\frac{3}{10} &= +2\frac{3}{10} \\ & \frac{11}{10} \end{aligned}$$

Step 3

Add the whole numbers. Write the answer in simplest form.

$$\begin{aligned} 1\frac{4}{5} &= 1\frac{8}{10} \\ +2\frac{3}{10} &= +2\frac{3}{10} \\ & 3\frac{11}{10} = 4\frac{1}{10} \end{aligned}$$

Simplest form

So, Denise mixed $4\frac{1}{10}$ ounces of paint in all.

- What other common denominator could you have used in Example 1?

Math Idea

When adding or subtracting mixed numbers, you can write equivalent fractions, using a common denominator.

Example 2

Subtract. $4\frac{2}{3} - 2\frac{1}{4}$

Step 1

Find the LCD. Write equivalent fractions.

$$\begin{aligned} 4\frac{2}{3} &= 4\frac{8}{12} \\ -2\frac{1}{4} &= -2\frac{3}{12} \end{aligned}$$

Step 2

Subtract the fractions.

$$\begin{aligned} 4\frac{2}{3} &= 4\frac{8}{12} \\ -2\frac{1}{4} &= -2\frac{3}{12} \\ & \frac{5}{12} \end{aligned}$$

Step 3

Subtract the whole numbers. Write the answer in simplest form.

$$\begin{aligned} 4\frac{2}{3} &= 4\frac{8}{12} \\ -2\frac{1}{4} &= -2\frac{3}{12} \\ & 2\frac{5}{12} \end{aligned}$$

So, $4\frac{2}{3} - 2\frac{1}{4} = 2\frac{5}{12}$.

NS 2.3 Solve simple problems, including ones arising in concrete situations, involving the addition and subtraction of fractions and mixed numbers (like and unlike denominators of 20 or less), and express answers in the simplest form. *also* **NS 2.0, MR 2.0, MR 2.3, MR 2.4, MR 3.2**

Guided Practice

1. Copy the problem. Write the equivalent fractions. Find the sum, and write it in simplest form if needed. $7\frac{2}{5} + 4\frac{3}{4} = 7\frac{■}{20} + 4\frac{■}{20}$

Find the sum or difference. Write it in simplest form.

2. $2\frac{3}{4} + 3\frac{3}{10}$
3. $9\frac{5}{6} - 2\frac{1}{3}$
4. $5\frac{3}{4} + 1\frac{1}{3}$
5. $10\frac{5}{9} - 9\frac{1}{6}$
6. $7\frac{2}{3} - 3\frac{1}{6}$
7. **TALK Math** **Explain** why you need to find equivalent fractions to add $4\frac{3}{6}$ and $1\frac{1}{8}$.

Independent Practice and Problem Solving

Find the sum or difference. Write it in simplest form.

8. $8\frac{1}{2} + 6\frac{3}{8}$
9. $9\frac{2}{3} - 4\frac{4}{9}$
10. $8\frac{1}{6} + 7\frac{3}{8}$
11. $10\frac{1}{2} - 2\frac{1}{5}$
12. $5\frac{1}{4} + 9\frac{1}{3}$
13. $5\frac{6}{7} - 1\frac{2}{3}$
14. $2\frac{1}{3} + 4\frac{5}{6}$
15. $14\frac{7}{12} - 5\frac{1}{4}$
16. $3\frac{4}{9} + 3\frac{1}{2}$
17. $12\frac{3}{4} - 6\frac{1}{6}$

USE DATA For 18–20, use the table.

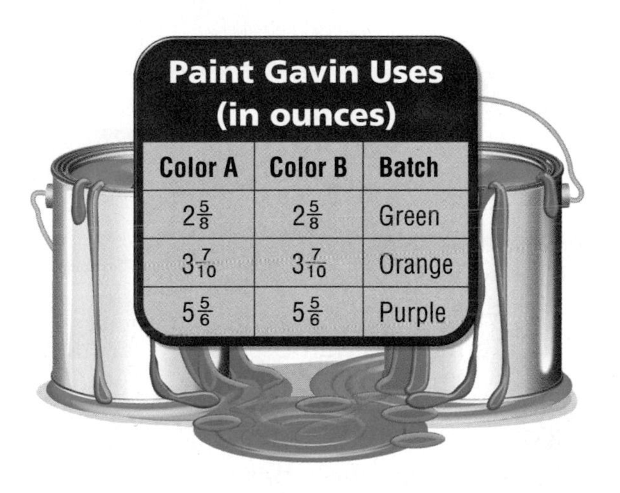

Paint Gavin Uses (in ounces)

Color A	Color B	Batch
$2\frac{5}{8}$	$2\frac{5}{8}$	Green
$3\frac{7}{10}$	$3\frac{7}{10}$	Orange
$5\frac{5}{6}$	$5\frac{5}{6}$	Purple

18. Gavin is mixing a batch of green paint for an art project. How much green paint did Gavin mix?
19. Gavin mixed $4\frac{3}{10}$ ounces of green paint with $3\frac{3}{8}$ ounces of blue to make turquoise. How much turquoise paint did he mix?
20. **WRITE Math** Gavin made 2 batches of purple paint and plans to store it in 10-ounce jars. **Explain** how to find the number of jars Gavin will need to hold the 2 batches of purple paint.

Achieving the Standards

21. What is the value of $(9 \times 3) + (14 - 9)$? (Grade 4 AF 1.2)
22. Write $4 \times 4 \times 4 \times 4 \times 4$ by using an exponent. (NS 1.4, p. 126)
23. Write a fraction and a mixed number for the shaded part below. (Grade 4 NS 1.7)
24. **Test Prep** A football game lasted $3\frac{1}{4}$ hours. The game clock was stopped for $1\frac{1}{12}$ hours. How much time did the actual game last?

A $2\frac{1}{6}$ hours

B $2\frac{2}{3}$ hours

C $2\frac{1}{3}$ hours

D $4\frac{1}{3}$ hours

Extra Practice on page 230, Set A

LESSON 4

Subtraction with Renaming

OBJECTIVE: Model subtraction of mixed numbers by using renaming.

Quick Review

Write each fraction as a mixed number in simplest form.

1. $\frac{5}{4}$ **2.** $\frac{7}{3}$ **3.** $\frac{9}{2}$

4. $\frac{13}{3}$ **5.** $\frac{20}{7}$

Learn

PROBLEM Dean and Faith are using colorful streamers to decorate a table before a party. They have $2\frac{1}{3}$ yards of streamers. They use $1\frac{7}{12}$ yards. How many yards of streamers do Dean and Faith have left?

Sometimes, you need to rename whole numbers to subtract mixed numbers.

Activity

Subtract. $2\frac{1}{3} - 1\frac{7}{12}$

Materials ■ fraction bars

Step 1

Model $2\frac{1}{3}$ using two whole bars and one $\frac{1}{3}$ bar.

Step 2

To subtract, think of the LCD for $\frac{1}{3}$ and $\frac{7}{12}$. Rename $\frac{1}{3}$ as $\frac{4}{12}$.

Step 3

Rename one whole bar as $\frac{12}{12}$.

$2\frac{1}{3} = 1\frac{16}{12}$

Step 4

Subtract $1\frac{7}{12}$. Write the answer in simplest form.

$1\frac{16}{12} - 1\frac{7}{12} = \frac{9}{12} = \frac{3}{4}$

So, $\frac{3}{4}$ yard is left.

- In Step 3, why do you rename one whole bar as $\frac{12}{12}$?

NS 2.3 Solve simple problems, including ones arising in concrete situations, involving the addition and subtraction of fractions and mixed numbers (like and unlike denominators of 20 or less), and express answers in the simplest form. *also* **NS 2.0, MR 2.0, MR 2.3, MR 2.4, MR 3.2**

Guided Practice

1. Use the model for $2\frac{1}{3} - 1\frac{5}{6}$ to find the difference. Write it in simplest form.

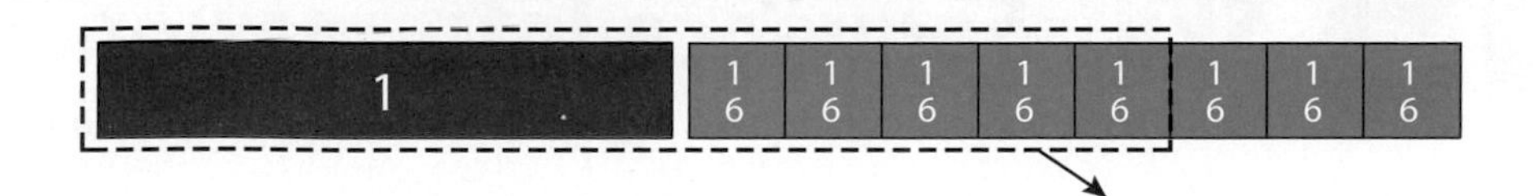

Use fraction bars to find the difference. Write it in simplest form.

2. $3\frac{1}{4} - 1\frac{3}{4}$
3. $2\frac{1}{5} - 1\frac{4}{5}$
4. $4\frac{1}{2} - 2\frac{5}{6}$
5. $2\frac{1}{2} - 1\frac{3}{4}$
6. TALK Math **Explain** how to find $1\frac{1}{5} - \frac{3}{10}$.

Independent Practice and Problem Solving

Use fraction bars to find the difference. Write it in simplest form.

7. $4\frac{2}{9} - 1\frac{6}{9}$
8. $5 - 3\frac{1}{2}$
9. $3\frac{1}{3} - \frac{5}{9}$
10. $6\frac{1}{3} - 4\frac{5}{6}$
11. $4\frac{7}{10} - 2\frac{4}{5}$
12. $5\frac{3}{8} - 2\frac{5}{8}$
13. $5\frac{2}{3} - 1\frac{11}{12}$
14. $4\frac{1}{2} - 3\frac{2}{3}$

USE DATA For 15–18, use the recipe.

Fruit Punch
$2\frac{1}{4}$ qt orange juice
$\frac{3}{4}$ qt pineapple juice
$1\frac{2}{3}$ qt cranberry juice
$\frac{1}{3}$ qt apple juice

15. For the party, Faith decided to reduce the amount of orange juice by $\frac{3}{4}$ quart. How much orange juice did Faith use?
16. Faith's recipe makes 5 quarts of fruit punch. If the cranberry juice is not included, how much punch is made?
17. Faith decided to reduce the amount of cranberry juice by $\frac{3}{4}$ quart from the original recipe. How much cranberry juice did she use? How much punch did Faith make in all?
18. WRITE Math **Explain** how to find how much more cranberry juice is needed than pineapple juice.

Achieving the Standards

19. What integer represents 8 meters below the ocean's surface? (Grade 4 NS 1.8)
20. Is a 180° angle the same as a $\frac{1}{4}$, $\frac{1}{2}$, $\frac{3}{4}$, or full turn? (Grade 4 MG 3.5)
21. $7\frac{3}{8} + 4\frac{1}{4} =$ (NS 2.3, p. 224)
22. **Test Prep** A small banana smoothie has $5\frac{1}{2}$ ounces of banana in it. A large smoothie has $8\frac{1}{4}$ ounces of banana. How many more ounces of banana does the large smoothie have?

   A $2\frac{3}{4}$ ounces
   B $2\frac{1}{4}$ ounces
   C $3\frac{3}{4}$ ounces
   D $3\frac{1}{4}$ ounces

Extra Practice on page 230, Set B

Problem Solving Workshop
Skill: Sequence Information

OBJECTIVE: Solve problems by using the skill *sequence information*.

Read to Understand
Plan
Solve
Check

Use the Skill

PROBLEM The Ross family drove from San Francisco to Los Angeles to visit their relatives. Jason remembered that they left home at 10:00 A.M. and arrived at their relatives' house at 6:00 P.M. When they were $\frac{1}{2}$ hour from their relatives' house, they phoned to say they would be arriving soon. They stopped for lunch for $1\frac{1}{6}$ hours. After lunch, they drove $3\frac{2}{3}$ hours before they phoned their relatives. How long after leaving home did the Rosses drive before lunch?

▲ **This California highway map shows different routes between cities. Interstate 5 goes from northern California to southern California.**

Sometimes, to solve a problem, you need to put events in order of time—you need to *sequence information.*

Make a list or table to sequence the information. First, break up the day into a series of events for which you know the times. Then write and solve an equation using the total amount of travel time.

Ross Family Trip

Event	Time (in hr)	Total Time (in hr)
• The Rosses drove until lunch.	■	■
• The Rosses had lunch.	$1\frac{1}{6}$	■ $+ 1\frac{1}{6}$
• The Rosses drove until they phoned their relatives.	$3\frac{2}{3}$	■ $+ 1\frac{1}{6} + 3\frac{2}{3}$
• The Rosses drove after having called their relatives.	$\frac{1}{2}$	■ $+ 1\frac{1}{6} + 3\frac{2}{3} + \frac{1}{2} = 8$

Look at the number sentence for the last event. ■ $+ 1\frac{1}{6} + 3\frac{2}{3} + \frac{1}{2} = 8$

So, the Ross family drove for $2\frac{2}{3}$ hours before stopping for lunch.

Think and Discuss

Sequence information to solve.

a. How many hours passed between the time the Ross family stopped for lunch and the time they arrived at their relatives' house?

b. If the Rosses stopped for gas 1 hour after they finished lunch, how much longer did they travel before calling their relatives?

NS 2.3 Solve simple problems, including ones arising in concrete situations, involving the addition and subtraction of fractions and mixed numbers (like and unlike denominators of 20 or less), and express answers in the simplest form. *also* **MR 1.1, MR 2.0, MR 2.3, MR 2.4, MR 3.2**

Guided Problem Solving

1. Mr. James walks 5 miles in his daily routine. At the end of his work day, he walks $1\frac{1}{2}$ miles from his office to the grocery store to buy food for dinner. Then Mr. James walks home $\frac{3}{4}$ mile from the grocery store. The distance from his home to his office is $1\frac{4}{5}$ miles. At lunchtime he takes a short walk around the park. How many miles is Mr. James' lunchtime walk?

Mr. James' Daily Routine

Event	Distance (in mi)	Miles Walked So Far
1. Mr. James walks from home to his office.	$1\frac{4}{5}$	$1\frac{4}{5}$
2. Mr. James takes a lunchtime walk around park.	$\blacksquare$	$1\frac{4}{5} + \blacksquare$
3. Mr. James walks from his office to the store.	$1\frac{1}{2}$	$1\frac{4}{5} + 1\frac{1}{2} + \blacksquare$
4. Mr. James walks home from the store.	$\frac{3}{4}$	$1\frac{4}{5} + 1\frac{1}{2} + \frac{3}{4} + \blacksquare = 5$

Look at the number sentence for the fourth event.

$$1\frac{4}{5} + 1\frac{1}{2} + \frac{3}{4} + \blacksquare = 5$$

2. **What if** Mr. James walked $1\frac{1}{3}$ miles, instead of $\frac{3}{4}$ mile, home from the grocery store? How many miles would he have walked after leaving the office?

3. Allison walked 4 miles around town. She walked $1\frac{1}{2}$ miles from home to the park and then walked to Jessie's house before going home. Allison lives $1\frac{1}{2}$ miles from Jessie. How far does Jessie live from the park?

Mixed Applications

USE DATA For 4–5, use the table.

Shasta Lake Elevation, 2006

Date	Elevation (in ft)
January 1	$1,040\frac{5}{6}$
April 1	$1,043\frac{1}{4}$
July 1	$1,056\frac{1}{6}$

4. Shasta Lake's level decreased by $6\frac{1}{6}$ feet from January 1 to February 1. The level increased by $\frac{1}{4}$ foot from March 1 to April 1. How much did the lake's level change between February 1 and March 1?

5. From June 1 to July 1, Shasta Lake's level decreased by $7\frac{5}{6}$ feet. Between May 1 and June 1, the level increased by $13\frac{1}{4}$ feet. How much did the lake's level change from April 1 to May 1?

6. WRITE Math Tami chose a mixed number. Then she subtracted $6\frac{1}{5}$ from it, added $1\frac{1}{10}$, and then subtracted $2\frac{1}{2}$. After she added $4\frac{3}{10}$ to the difference, she got $9\frac{3}{5}$. **Explain** how to find the number Tami chose.

Extra Practice

Set A Find the sum or difference. Write it in simplest form. (pp. 224–225)

1. $3\frac{1}{2} + 6\frac{5}{8}$
2. $9\frac{5}{6} - 2\frac{1}{2}$
3. $4\frac{1}{5} + 1\frac{2}{3}$
4. $7\frac{7}{9} - 3\frac{1}{3}$
5. $5\frac{3}{4} - 2\frac{1}{8}$
6. $2\frac{3}{4} + 5\frac{1}{3}$
7. $10\frac{4}{5} - 5\frac{3}{10}$
8. $8\frac{1}{2} + 6\frac{2}{3}$
9. $1\frac{3}{4} + 3\frac{3}{8}$
10. $6\frac{5}{6} - 3\frac{3}{5}$
11. $8\frac{4}{5} + 2\frac{4}{9}$
12. $6\frac{5}{14} - 3\frac{2}{7}$
13. $1\frac{11}{12} - 1\frac{2}{3}$
14. $5\frac{8}{15} + 7\frac{2}{5}$
15. $8\frac{5}{6} - 5\frac{3}{8}$
16. $7\frac{9}{10} + 4\frac{1}{4}$
17. $3\frac{4}{5} + 3\frac{1}{2}$
18. $15\frac{3}{4} - 14\frac{1}{2}$
19. $7\frac{5}{6} + 4\frac{3}{8}$
20. $12\frac{2}{3} - 4\frac{1}{6}$
21. Clarice bought $1\frac{1}{2}$ pounds of grapes and $1\frac{1}{4}$ pounds of cherries. How many pounds of fruit did she buy in all?
22. Mr. Grant weighed $5\frac{3}{4}$ pounds of apples and $3\frac{2}{3}$ pounds of pears. How many more pounds of apples did he have than pears?

Set B Use fraction bars to find the difference. Write it in simplest form. (pp. 226–227)

1. $4\frac{1}{3} - 2\frac{2}{3}$
2. $6\frac{2}{5} - 3\frac{4}{5}$
3. $4 - 1\frac{1}{2}$
4. $5\frac{1}{2} - 1\frac{3}{4}$
5. $7\frac{2}{3} - 2\frac{5}{6}$
6. $5\frac{1}{2} - 1\frac{2}{3}$
7. $5\frac{3}{4} - 4\frac{9}{10}$
8. $8\frac{1}{4} - 3\frac{3}{4}$
9. $5\frac{1}{2} - 2\frac{4}{5}$
10. $6\frac{1}{3} - 5\frac{1}{2}$
11. $6\frac{1}{3} - 1\frac{2}{3}$
12. $9 - 4\frac{2}{5}$
13. $3\frac{1}{3} - 1\frac{2}{3}$
14. $4\frac{1}{4} - 2\frac{2}{5}$
15. $5\frac{1}{2} - 3\frac{7}{10}$
16. The length of a piece of ribbon is $9\frac{1}{8}$ inches. How many inches need to be cut off in order for the length to be $5\frac{3}{4}$ inches?
17. On Tuesday, there were 6 rolls of wrapping paper. By Wednesday, $4\frac{1}{2}$ rolls had been used. How much wrapping paper is left?

PRACTICE GAME Picture Problems

Artists
4 students

Supplies
- 16 index cards
- Crayons or markers
- Drawing paper

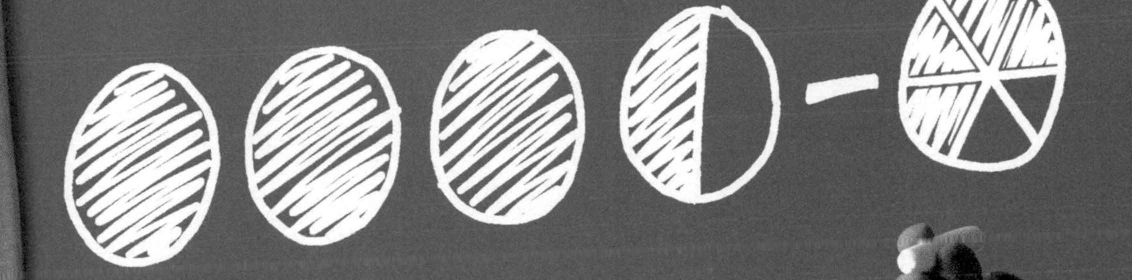

$3\frac{1}{2}$ − $\frac{4}{6}$

$\frac{7}{8}$ $1\frac{1}{4}$ $\frac{1}{2}$ $4\frac{3}{4}$ $\frac{4}{6}$ $1\frac{3}{8}$ $\frac{3}{4}$ $2\frac{1}{4}$ $\frac{5}{6}$ $3\frac{2}{8}$ $\frac{5}{8}$ $3\frac{1}{2}$ $\frac{1}{4}$ $4\frac{1}{2}$ $\frac{1}{8}$ $4\frac{1}{16}$

Start!

- Players write the fractions and mixed numbers shown above on index cards.
- A player shuffles the cards and places them facedown in a stack.
- The first player selects two cards. The player draws a picture that represents a subtraction problem using the two fractions. The pictures use completely shaded circles for whole numbers and partially shaded circles for fractions.
- The other three players use the picture to solve the subtraction problem. Each player with the correct answer earns one point.
- The next player then selects two cards, and play continues.
- The player with the most points after all the fraction cards have been used wins the game. If there is a tie, shuffle and continue play until a winner is determined.

Chapter 9 Review/Test

Check Concepts

1. Explain what you need to do first when adding $2\frac{1}{8}$ and $4\frac{1}{4}$. (NS 2.3, p. 220)
2. How can modeling problems with fraction bars help you add mixed numbers? (NS 2.3, p. 220)
3. Explain how you can subtract a mixed number from a whole number. (NS 2.3, p. 226)

Check Skills

Estimate. Then find the sum or difference. Write it in simplest form. (NS 2.3, pp. 224–225)

4. $1\frac{1}{4} + 2\frac{3}{8}$
5. $6\frac{3}{4} - 3\frac{1}{2}$
6. $2\frac{3}{4} + 2\frac{2}{3}$
7. $10\frac{7}{10} - 5\frac{3}{5}$
8. $8\frac{3}{8} - 8\frac{1}{4}$
9. $4\frac{2}{3} + 7\frac{5}{6}$
10. $11\frac{3}{5} - 9\frac{1}{4}$
11. $4\frac{1}{6} + 3\frac{7}{8}$
12. $9\frac{11}{20} - 4\frac{1}{4}$
13. $4\frac{7}{12} + 3\frac{1}{4}$
14. $6\frac{1}{3} - 2\frac{3}{4}$
15. $7\frac{7}{10} + 4\frac{3}{4}$

Use fraction bars to find the difference. Write it in simplest form. (NS 2.3, pp. 226–227)

16. $5\frac{2}{11} - 3\frac{7}{11}$
17. $6 - 3\frac{3}{4}$
18. $3\frac{3}{4} - 2\frac{7}{8}$
19. $6\frac{1}{4} - 3\frac{4}{5}$
20. $10 - 7\frac{1}{3}$
21. $5\frac{1}{15} - 4\frac{9}{15}$
22. $12\frac{1}{3} - 4\frac{5}{9}$
23. $6\frac{1}{4} - 5\frac{7}{12}$

Check Problem Solving

Solve. (NS 2.3, MR 2.3, pp. 228–229)

24. Roxanne has a pitcher that holds $5\frac{1}{4}$ cups of lemonade. To make the lemonade, she put lemonade concentrate in the pitcher. Then she added $3\frac{1}{2}$ cups of water. She drank $\frac{1}{2}$ cup of the lemonade, then added $1\frac{1}{2}$ cups more water so that the pitcher was full. How much lemonade concentrate did Roxanne use?

25. WRITE Math Allie walked $3\frac{1}{8}$ miles to get to Roxanne's house for a sleepover. First, she walked $\frac{1}{2}$ mile from her school to the library. Then she walked home from the library to change before going to the sleepover. Allie lives $1\frac{3}{8}$ miles from Roxanne. **Explain** how you could use the series of events to find how far Allie lives from the library.

GO ONLINE **Technology** Use *Online Assessment.*

Enrich • Mixed Numbers and Time

Part of an HOUR

At 1 P.M., a clerk told Risha that the train to New York City would leave in about $2\frac{1}{2}$ hours. To find the departure time, Risha thought:

- There are 60 minutes in 1 hour.
- $\frac{1}{2}$ of 60 is 30. So, my train leaves in 2 hours 30 minutes.
- If I add 2 hours 30 minutes to 1 P.M., the time will be 3:30 P.M.
- So, my train leaves at about 3:30 P.M.

Examples

A Write 3 hr 12 min as a mixed number.

12 min $= \frac{12}{60}$ hr $= \frac{1}{5}$ hr

So, 3 hr 12 min as a mixed number is $3\frac{1}{5}$ hr.

Think:
60 min = 1 hr
1 minute $= \frac{1}{60}$ hr

You can also add or subtract times and write the answer as a mixed number.

B

$$\begin{array}{r} 5 \text{ hr } 15 \text{ min} \\ +\ 2 \text{ hr } 50 \text{ min} \\ \hline 7 \text{ hr } 65 \text{ min} \end{array}$$

↓ ↓

7 hr (60 + 5) min

↓ ↓

7 hr + 1 hr + $\frac{5}{60}$ hr

↓

$8\frac{1}{12}$ hr

C Regroup one hour into minutes to subtract.

$$\begin{array}{r} 4 \text{ hr } 22 \text{ min} \\ -\ 1 \text{ hr } 40 \text{ min} \\ \hline \end{array} \longrightarrow \begin{array}{r} 3 \text{ hr } (60 + 22) \text{ min} \\ -\ 1 \text{ hr } 40 \text{ min} \\ \hline \end{array}$$

$$\begin{array}{r} 3 \text{ hr } 82 \text{ min} \\ -\ 1 \text{ hr } 40 \text{ min} \\ \hline 2 \text{ hr } 42 \text{ min} \end{array} = 2\frac{42}{60} = 2\frac{7}{10} \text{ hr}$$

Try It

Write as a mixed number.

1. 2 hr 25 min
2. 1 hr 24 min
3. 6 hr 30 min
4. 3 hr 50 min

Solve. Write the answer as a mixed number.

5. 6 hr 10 min − 3 hr 55 min
6. 3 hr 42 min + 2 hr 38 min

WRITE Math **Explain** how to write 5 hr 48 min as a mixed number.

Achieving the Standards

Chapters 1–9

Statistics, Data Analysis, and Probability

1. The circle graph below shows how Troy spent his day.

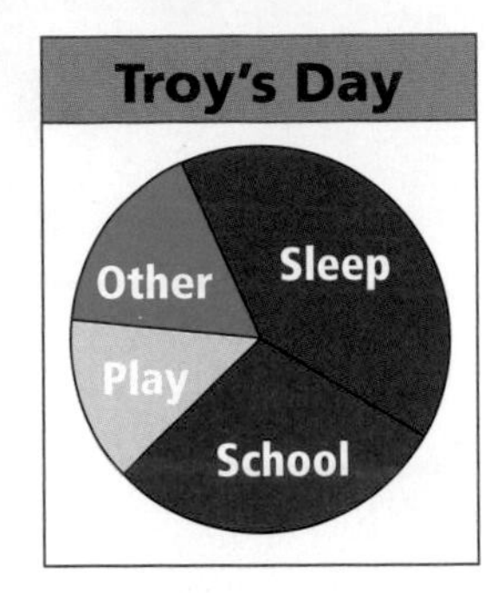

Which statement is true? (Grade 4 SDAP 1.3)

A Troy slept for half the day.

B Troy spent the most hours at school.

C Troy played for more hours than he slept.

D Troy spent the most hours sleeping.

2. The heights of five professional basketball players are 85, 82, 77, 77, and 79 inches. What is the mode of the height of these players? (SDAP 1.1)

A 77 inches

B 78 inches

C 79 inches

D 80 inches

3. **WRITE Math** The table shows the number of members of each club.

Club	Girls	Boys
Culture	10	6
Art	7	8
Math	6	9

What type of graph would you make to display the data? **Explain** your choice. (SDAP 1.2)

Number Sense

Eliminate choices.

See item 4. Think about the meaning of prime factorization. You can eliminate the choices in which all the factors are not prime numbers.

4. What is the prime factorization of 30? (NS 1.4)

A 3×10

B 5×6

C $2 \times 3 \times 5$

D $2^2 \times 5$

5. Tanya rode her bike $2\frac{3}{4}$ miles to school. After school, she rode her bike $1\frac{1}{2}$ miles to the library. Then she rode $1\frac{1}{4}$ miles home. How far did she ride in all? (NS 2.3)

A $6\frac{1}{2}$ miles

B $5\frac{1}{2}$ miles

C $5\frac{1}{4}$ miles

D $4\frac{1}{2}$ miles

6. **WRITE Math** Pamela solved the division problem as shown below. Do you agree? **Explain** why or why not. (NS 2.2)

$$12\overline{)540} = 46$$

Algebra and Functions

7. Look at the table below.

x	2	4	6	8
y	9	17	25	33

Which equation could have been used for the table? (Grade 4 O‑π AF 1.5)

A $y = x + 7$

B $y = 2x + 5$

C $y = 4x + 1$

D $y = 5x - 1$

8. Which of the following shows the Distributive Property? (AF 1.3)

A $6 + (20 + 4) = (6 + 20) + 4$

B $6 + (20 \times 4) = (6 + 20) \times (6 + 4)$

C $6 \times (20 \times 4) = (6 \times 20) \times 4$

D $6 \times (20 + 4) = (6 \times 20) + (6 \times 4)$

9. What is the value of the expression below if $p = 12$? (Grade 4 O‑π AF 1.2)

$$(p + 8) - 1$$

A 3

B 19

C 20

D 95

10. WRITE Math What number goes in the box to make this number sentence true?

$$(10 - 6) \times 7 = 4 \times \blacksquare$$

Explain how you know. (Grade 4 O‑π AF 2.2)

Measurement and Geometry

11. Look at the line segment below.

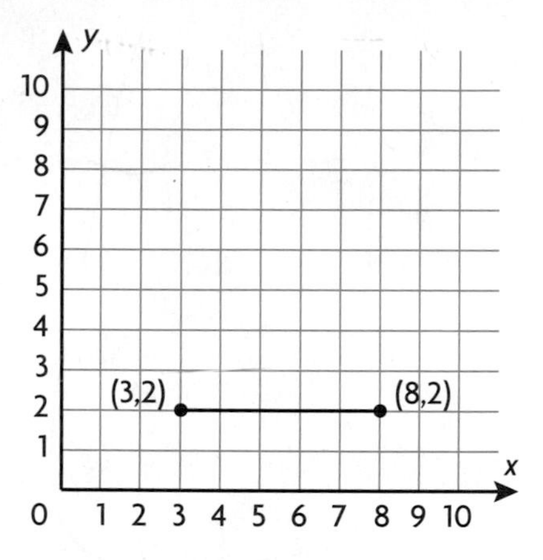

What is the length of the line segment? (Grade 4 O‑π MG 2.2)

A 8 units

B 5 units

C 3 units

D 2 units

12. Which of the following capital letters does NOT have line symmetry? (Grade 4 MG 3.4)

A W

B X

C T

D Z

13. The area of a square is 36 square feet. What is the perimeter of the square? (Grade 4 MG 1.4)

A 13 feet

B 24 feet

C 36 feet

D 64 feet

14. WRITE Math Cam used the equation $y = x$ to plot 3 points on a graph. He put the points at (1,2), (2,3), and (3,4). Do you agree? **Explain.** (Grade 4 O‑π MG 2.1)

CHAPTER

10 Multiply and Divide Fractions

The Big Idea Multiplication of fractions involves finding part of a part of the whole; division of fractions is related to repeated subtraction and can be shown with models.

Investigate

You are a scientist studying the travel habits of bobcats. Use the table of your findings to show how far one bobcat might travel in a week. Then show how far it might travel in half a day.

Bobcat Traveling Habits

Animal ID	Average Daily Travel (in miles)
Bobcat A	$\frac{1}{3}$
Bobcat B	$\frac{2}{5}$
Bobcat C	$\frac{3}{8}$

CALIFORNIA FAST FACT

Felis rufus, better known as the bobcat, is the only species of bobcat in California and the southwestern deserts. An average bobcat weighs between 15 and 20 pounds.

GO ONLINE **Technology**
Student pages are available in the Student eBook.

Show What You Know

Check your understanding of important skills needed for success in Chapter 10.

▶ Write Common Factors

Write the common factors for each pair of numbers.

1. 8 and 12 **2.** 10 and 20 **3.** 16 and 24 **4.** 21 and 42 **5.** 24 and 40

6. 30 and 45 **7.** 48 and 60 **8.** 40 and 100 **9.** 28 and 56 **10.** 75 and 125

▶ Rename Fractions and Mixed Numbers

Rename each fraction as a mixed number or each mixed number as a fraction.

11. $\frac{4}{3}$ **12.** $1\frac{1}{2}$ **13.** $\frac{5}{2}$ **14.** $3\frac{1}{4}$ **15.** $\frac{10}{3}$

16. $2\frac{4}{5}$ **17.** $\frac{18}{7}$ **18.** $4\frac{3}{5}$ **19.** $6\frac{5}{6}$ **20.** $5\frac{4}{9}$

▶ Parts of a Whole

Write a fraction to represent the group shown in red.

21. 

22. 

23. 

24. 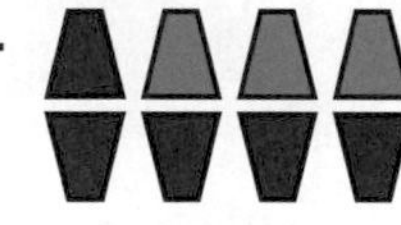

25. 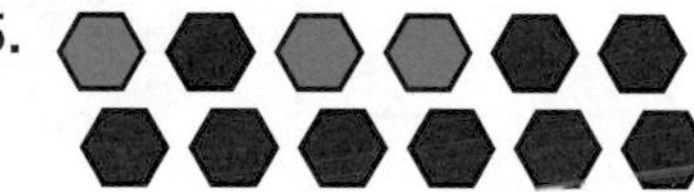

26. 

VOCABULARY POWER

CHAPTER VOCABULARY

fraction
mixed number
reciprocal

WARM-UP WORDS

reciprocal one of two numbers whose product is 1

fraction a number that names a part of a whole or a part of a group

mixed number a number that is made up of a whole number and a fraction

LESSON 1 HANDS ON

Model Multiplication of Fractions

OBJECTIVE: Use models to multiply fractions.

Quick Review

What fraction of the model is shaded?

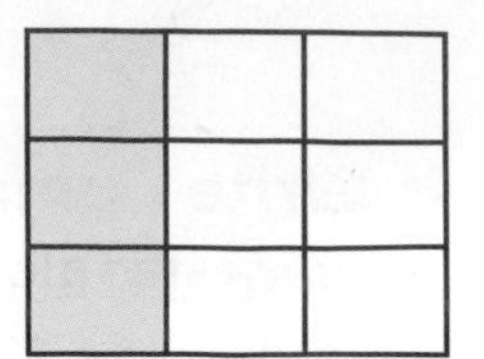

Investigate

Materials ■ yellow and blue crayons ■ paper

You can make a model to find $\frac{1}{3} \times \frac{1}{2}$.

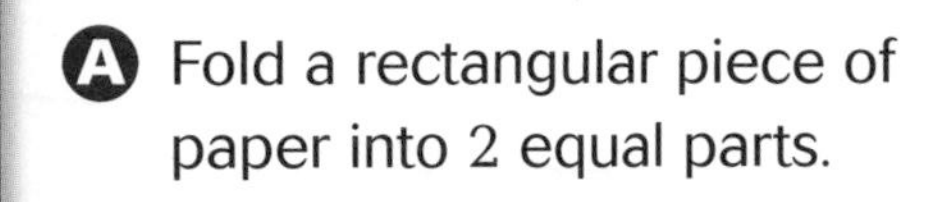

A Fold a rectangular piece of paper into 2 equal parts.

Shade $\frac{1}{2}$ yellow.

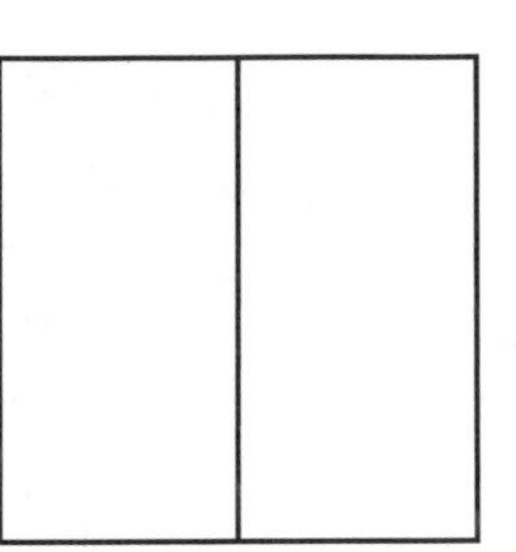

B Now fold the paper the other way into 3 equal parts.

To find $\frac{1}{3}$ of $\frac{1}{2}$, shade $\frac{1}{3}$ of the yellow section blue.

What fraction of the whole model is shaded twice? What is $\frac{1}{3} \times \frac{1}{2}$?

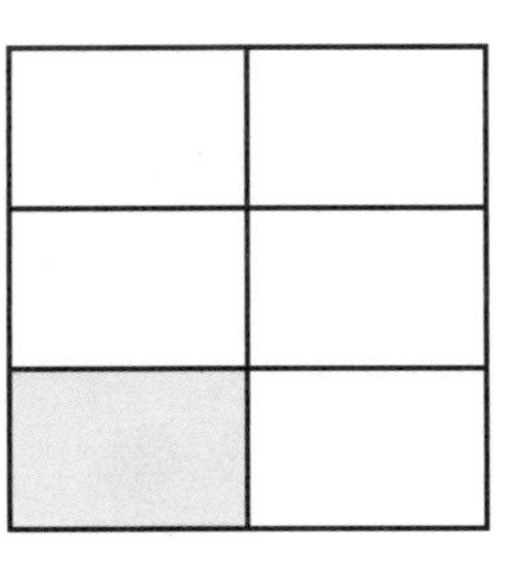

C Make a model to find $\frac{1}{2} \times \frac{1}{4}$.

Draw Conclusions

1. How many parts is your model folded into for $\frac{1}{2} \times \frac{1}{4}$? What is $\frac{1}{2} \times \frac{1}{4}$?
2. If you modeled $\frac{1}{3} \times \frac{2}{4}$, how many parts do you think your model would have? Explain your reasoning.
3. **Analysis** Look at the numerators and denominators of the factors and the product for $\frac{1}{3} \times \frac{2}{4}$. What relationships do you see?

NS 2.4 Understand the concept of multiplication and division of fractions. *also* **NS 2.5, MR 2.0, MR 2.3, MR 2.4, MR 3.2**

Connect

You can also draw a picture to multiply fractions.

Example **Multiply.** $\frac{2}{5} \times \frac{1}{2}$

Step 1

Draw a rectangle.
Divide it into 2 equal parts.

Shade $\frac{1}{2}$.

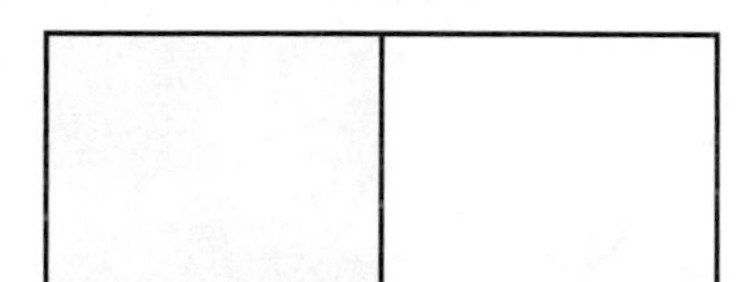

Step 2

Divide the rectangle the other way into 5 equal parts. Use a different color to shade $\frac{2}{5}$ of the parts that are already shaded.

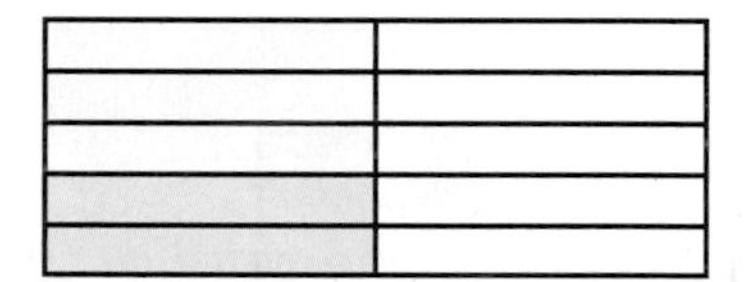

Step 3

Two-tenths of the model is shaded twice.

$\frac{2}{5} \times \frac{1}{2} = \frac{2}{10}$, or $\frac{1}{5}$.

TALK Math

Look at page 238. Is $\frac{1}{3} \times \frac{1}{2}$ greater than or less than $\frac{1}{2}$? Explain why. Look at the Example above. Is $\frac{2}{5} \times \frac{1}{2}$ greater than or less than $\frac{1}{2}$? Explain why.

Practice

Write the product each model represents.

1.

2.

3.

4. 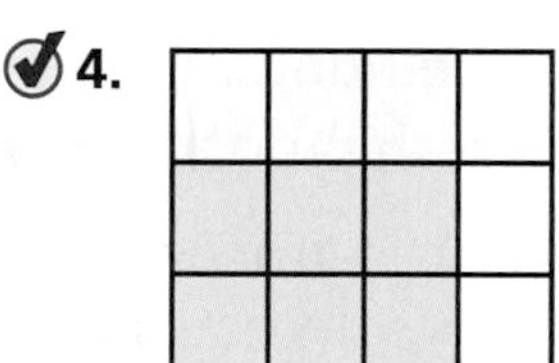

Find the product.

5. $\frac{1}{3} \times \frac{1}{4}$
6. $\frac{1}{4} \times \frac{2}{3}$
7. $\frac{1}{8} \times \frac{1}{2}$
8. $\frac{2}{3} \times \frac{1}{3}$
9. $\frac{1}{2} \times \frac{1}{2}$
10. $\frac{1}{4} \times \frac{3}{4}$
11. $\frac{2}{5} \times \frac{1}{4}$
12. $\frac{1}{2} \times \frac{4}{5}$
13. $\frac{1}{6} \times \frac{2}{3}$
14. $\frac{3}{4} \times \frac{1}{2}$
15. **WRITE Math** **Explain** why the product of two fractions that are less than 1 is always less than 1.

LESSON 2

Record Multiplication of Fractions

OBJECTIVE: Solve problems by multiplying fractions.

Quick Review

Write in simplest form.

1. $\frac{15}{20}$
2. $\frac{12}{18}$
3. $\frac{9}{15}$
4. $\frac{8}{16}$
5. $\frac{14}{20}$

Learn

PROBLEM In Maria's backyard, $\frac{2}{3}$ of the land is used for a garden. She grows vegetables in $\frac{1}{2}$ of the garden. What fraction of Maria's backyard is used for growing vegetables?

ONE WAY **Draw a picture.**

Multiply. $\frac{1}{2} \times \frac{2}{3}$

Step 1

Draw a rectangle. Divide it into 3 equal parts. Shade $\frac{2}{3}$.

Step 2

Divide the rectangle into 2 equal parts. Use a different color to shade $\frac{1}{2}$ of the parts that are already shaded.

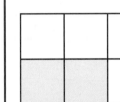

Step 3

One-third of the model is shaded twice.

$\frac{1}{2} \times \frac{2}{3} = \frac{2}{6}$, or $\frac{1}{3}$

So, $\frac{2}{6}$, or $\frac{1}{3}$, of Maria's backyard is used for growing vegetables.

- Compare the numerator and denominator of the product with the numerators and denominators of the factors. What relationship do you see?

To multiply a fraction by a fraction, you can multiply the numerators and then multiply the denominators.

ANOTHER WAY **Use paper and pencil.**

Multiply. $\frac{2}{5} \times \frac{3}{4}$

Step 1

Multiply the numerators.
Then multiply the denominators.

$\frac{2}{5} \times \frac{3}{4} = \frac{2 \times 3}{5 \times 4} = \frac{6}{20}$

Step 2

Write the product in simplest form.

$\frac{6}{20} = \frac{6 \div 2}{20 \div 2} = \frac{3}{10}$

NS 2.4 Understand the concept of multiplication and division of fractions. *also* **NS 2.5, MR 1.0, MR 2.1, MR 2.3, MR 2.4, MR 3.0, MR 3.2**

Guided Practice

1. Look at the model. How many parts are there? How many parts are shaded twice? What is $\frac{3}{5} \times \frac{3}{4}$?

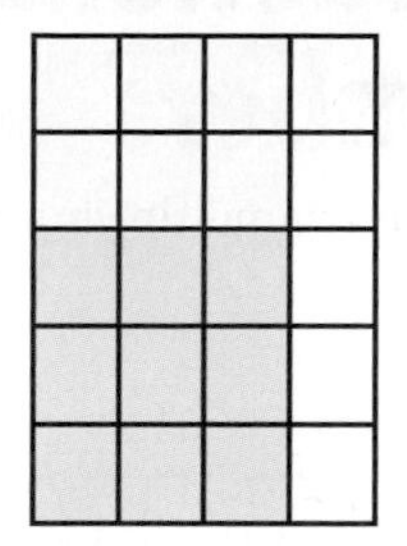

Find the product. Write it in simplest form.

2. $\frac{2}{5} \times \frac{1}{3}$
3. $\frac{5}{6} \times \frac{1}{10}$
4. $\frac{1}{8} \times \frac{1}{4}$
5. $\frac{3}{10} \times \frac{5}{6}$
6. $\frac{2}{3} \times \frac{3}{4}$
7. **TALK Math** **Explain** how to find $\frac{3}{4} \times \frac{2}{3}$.

Independent Practice and Problem Solving

Find the product. Write it in simplest form.

8. $\frac{1}{4} \times \frac{3}{4}$
9. $\frac{5}{8} \times \frac{7}{10}$
10. $\frac{1}{2} \times \frac{5}{12}$
11. $\frac{4}{9} \times \frac{2}{3}$
12. $\frac{2}{3} \times \frac{1}{6}$
13. $\frac{4}{5} \times \frac{3}{8}$

Algebra **Evaluate each expression. Then write <, >, or = for each ●.**

14. $\frac{1}{2} \times \frac{3}{4}$ ● $\frac{1}{4} \times \frac{3}{4}$
15. $\frac{2}{3} \times \frac{2}{5}$ ● $\frac{2}{5} \times \frac{6}{9}$
16. $\frac{7}{8} \times \frac{1}{3}$ ● $\frac{5}{6} \times \frac{1}{2}$
17. Pat used $\frac{2}{3}$ of a raisin package to make 2 loaves of bread. Her family ate $\frac{1}{2}$ of the bread. What fraction of the raisin package did her family eat?

18. **Reasoning** Lisa ate $\frac{1}{3}$ of a bag of pretzels, then half of what was left. Sam ate $\frac{1}{2}$ a bag of pretzels, then $\frac{1}{3}$ of what was left. If both bags were the same size, who ate more pretzels?
19. **WRITE Math** **What's the Question** Maria uses $\frac{3}{8}$ of her garden to grow greens. She plants lettuce in $\frac{2}{9}$ of the greens garden. The answer is $\frac{1}{12}$.

Achieving the Standards

20. Colin is making a rug with a perimeter of 14 feet. Find the whole numbers for the length and width of the rug with the greatest area. (Grade 4 MG 1.3)
21. Liza cuts $4\frac{1}{3}$ feet of rope from a roll $6\frac{1}{2}$ feet long. How many feet of rope are left on the roll? (NS 2.3, p. 226)
22. Write the whole number 8 as a fraction. (Grade 4 NS 1.5)
23. **Test Prep** Bryan ate $\frac{3}{8}$ of a pizza. Matt ate $\frac{2}{3}$ of what was left. What fraction of pizza did Matt eat?

    A $\frac{5}{24}$

    B $\frac{1}{12}$

    C $\frac{1}{8}$

    D $\frac{5}{12}$

Extra Practice on page 260, Set A

LESSON 3

Multiply Fractions and Whole Numbers

OBJECTIVE: Solve problems by multiplying fractions and whole numbers.

Quick Review

Write each product in simplest form.

1. $\frac{1}{2} \times \frac{1}{5}$
2. $\frac{3}{4} \times \frac{2}{3}$
3. $\frac{5}{6} \times \frac{1}{3}$
4. $\frac{1}{4} \times \frac{3}{8}$
5. $\frac{1}{4} \times \frac{3}{5}$

Learn

PROBLEM Simon, the candle maker, uses $\frac{5}{6}$ cup of wax for each white candle he makes. How many cups of wax does Simon need to make 5 candles?

Multiply. $5 \times \frac{5}{6}$

ONE WAY **Draw a picture.**

Step 1

Use circles to show 5 groups of $\frac{5}{6}$.

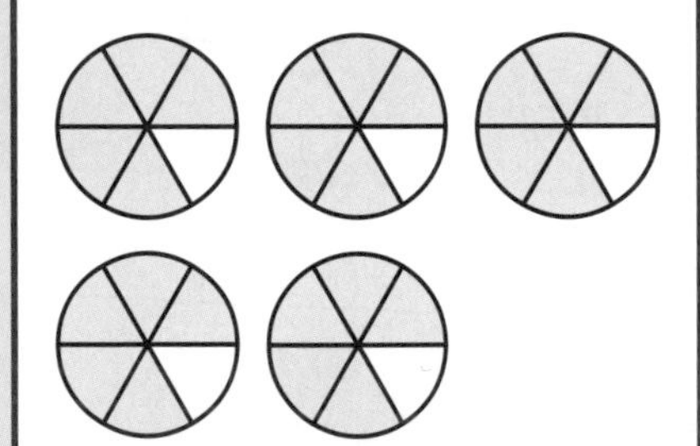

Step 2

Count the shaded sixths or use repeated addition to find the total amount.

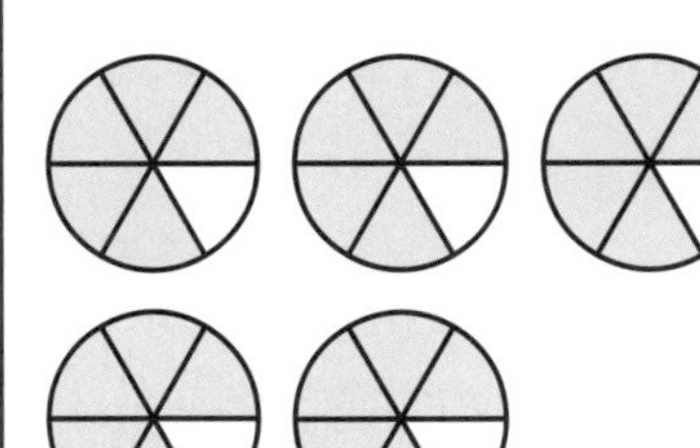

$\frac{5}{6} + \frac{5}{6} + \frac{5}{6} + \frac{5}{6} + \frac{5}{6} = \frac{25}{6}$

Step 3

Write the answer as a mixed number.

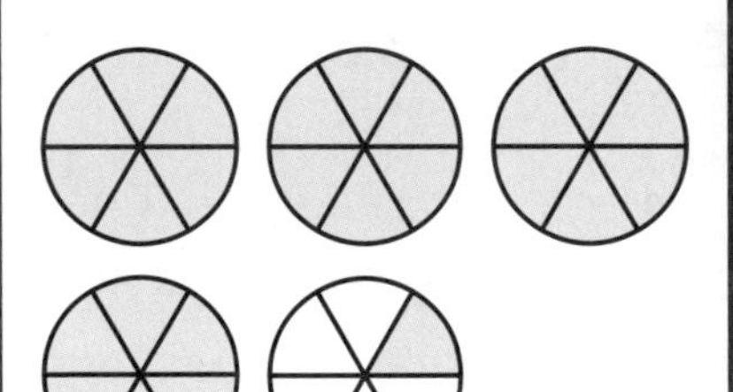

$\frac{25}{6} = 4\frac{1}{6}$

ANOTHER WAY **Use paper and pencil.**

Step 1

Write the whole number as a fraction.

$5 \times \frac{5}{6} = \frac{5}{1} \times \frac{5}{6}$

Step 2

Multiply the numerators. Then multiply the denominators.

$\frac{5}{1} \times \frac{5}{6} = \frac{5 \times 5}{1 \times 6} = \frac{25}{6}$

Step 3

Write the answer as a mixed number.

$\frac{25}{6} = 4\frac{1}{6}$

So, Simon needs $4\frac{1}{6}$ cups of wax.

- What picture could you draw to find $\frac{4}{5} \times 5$?

NS 2.4 Understand the concept of multiplication and division of fractions.
also **NS 2.5, MR 1.0, MR 2.1, MR 2.3, MR 2.4, MR 3.1, MR 3.2**

Guided Practice

1. Use the picture to find the product $6 \times \frac{1}{3}$.

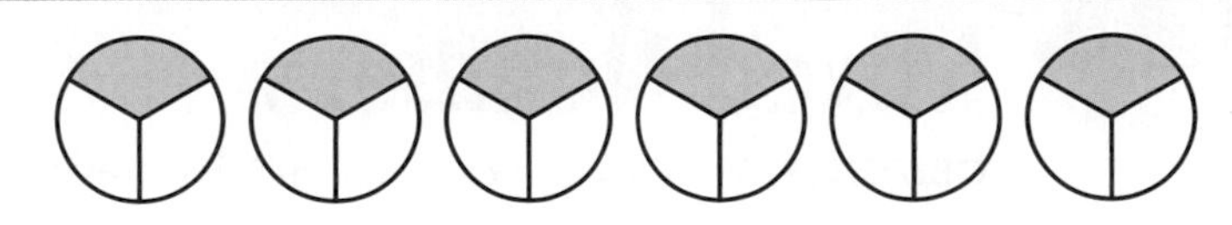

Find the product.

2. $\frac{1}{4} \times 2$
3. $9 \times \frac{1}{6}$
4. $\frac{2}{3} \times 4$
5. $\frac{3}{8} \times 8$
6. $\frac{2}{9} \times 5$
7. $10 \times \frac{4}{5}$
8. TALK Math **Explain** how to find $3 \times \frac{3}{5}$.

Independent Practice and Problem Solving

Find the product.

9. $\frac{5}{12} \times 4$
10. $7 \times \frac{3}{5}$
11. $\frac{1}{6} \times 15$
12. $4 \times \frac{2}{3}$
13. $7 \times \frac{4}{5}$
14. $5 \times \frac{1}{2}$
15. $6 \times \frac{1}{5}$
16. $5 \times \frac{3}{8}$
17. $8 \times \frac{3}{4}$
18. $7 \times \frac{5}{6}$
19. $5 \times \frac{1}{4}$
20. $12 \times \frac{3}{5}$

USE DATA For 21–22, use the table.

21. How many cups of wax does Simon need to make 10 blue candles?
22. How many more cups of wax does it take to make 6 orange candles than it takes to make 6 red candles?
23. WRITE Math **Explain** how you could use the product of $\frac{1}{2} \times 60$ to find the product $\frac{1}{4} \times 60$.

Simon's Candles

Color	Wax per Candle (in cups)
Purple	$\frac{1}{2}$
Red	$\frac{3}{8}$
Blue	$\frac{7}{8}$
Orange	$\frac{2}{3}$

Achieving the Standards

24. Roy bought 2 cans of tennis balls for $4.79 each. How much did 2 cans of tennis balls cost? (NS 2.1, p. 208)
25. Tori ate $\frac{1}{4}$ of the remaining $\frac{3}{4}$ of fruit salad. How much fruit salad did Tori eat? (NS 2.4, p. 240)
26. Carmen walked $2\frac{3}{4}$ miles to the park, $1\frac{1}{2}$ miles to the library, and $3\frac{1}{3}$ miles home. How many miles did Carmen walk in all? (NS 2.3, p. 220)
27. **Test Prep** Cassidy used $\frac{3}{4}$ of 3 gallons of paint for her room. How many gallons of paint did she use?

    A $1\frac{1}{4}$ gallons

    B $1\frac{3}{4}$ gallons

    C $2\frac{1}{4}$ gallons

    D $3\frac{3}{4}$ gallons

Extra Practice on page 260, Set B

LESSON 4 Multiply with Mixed Numbers

OBJECTIVE: Multiply two mixed numbers.

Quick Review

Rename each mixed number as a fraction.

1. $3\frac{1}{2}$ **2.** $1\frac{2}{3}$

3. $2\frac{5}{6}$ **4.** $5\frac{1}{4}$

5. $4\frac{3}{5}$

Learn

PROBLEM A neighborhood park is on $1\frac{1}{2}$ acres of land. Dogs are allowed in $\frac{3}{4}$ of the park. How many acres of the park are dogs allowed in?

ONE WAY **Use a model.**

Multiply. $\frac{3}{4} \times 1\frac{1}{2}$

Step 1

Use 2 whole squares. Divide each square in half. Shade $1\frac{1}{2}$, or $\frac{3}{2}$ of the parts.

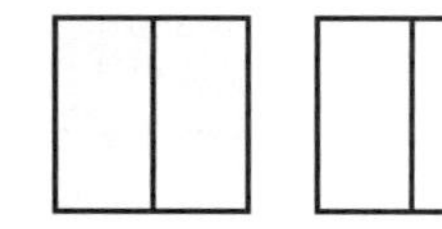

Step 2

Divide the squares into fourths the other way.

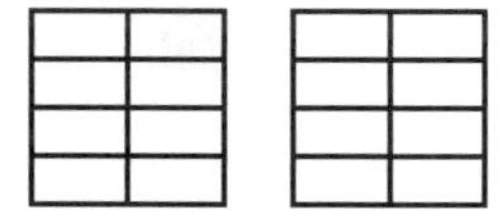

Step 3

Use another color to shade $\frac{3}{4}$ of the parts already shaded. Nine-eighths are shaded both colors.

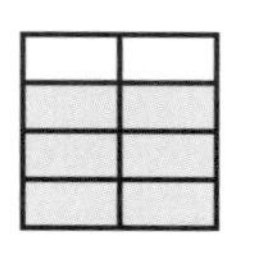

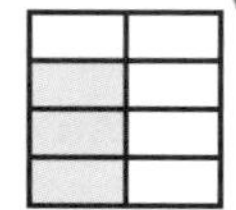

$\frac{3}{4} \times 1\frac{1}{2} = \frac{9}{8}$, or $1\frac{1}{8}$

ANOTHER WAY **Use paper and pencil.**

Multiply. $\frac{3}{4} \times 1\frac{1}{2}$

Step 1

Rename the mixed number as a fraction greater than 1.

Think: $1\frac{1}{2} = \frac{3}{2}$

$\frac{3}{4} \times 1\frac{1}{2} = \frac{3}{4} \times \frac{3}{2}$

Step 2

Multiply the numerators and the denominators.

$\frac{3}{4} \times \frac{3}{2} = \frac{3 \times 3}{4 \times 2} = \frac{9}{8}$

Step 3

Write the product as a mixed number in simplest form.

$\frac{9}{8} = 1\frac{1}{8}$

Remember

A mixed number can be written as a fraction.

$2\frac{3}{4} = 2 + \frac{3}{4}$

$= \frac{8}{4} + \frac{3}{4} = \frac{11}{4}$

So, dogs are allowed in $1\frac{1}{8}$ acres of the park.

- In Step 1, why do you rename the mixed number as a fraction greater than 1?

NS 2.4 Understand the concept of multiplication and division of fractions.
also NS 2.5, MR 1.0, MR 2.3, MR 2.4, MR 3.0, MR 3.1, MR 3.2

Multiply Two Mixed Numbers

To multiply two mixed numbers, follow the same steps you use to multiply a fraction and a mixed number.

ERROR ALERT

Remember to rename both mixed numbers as fractions when multiplying mixed numbers.

Example 1 **Multiply.** $2\frac{3}{4} \times 1\frac{2}{3}$

$2\frac{3}{4} \times 1\frac{2}{3} = \frac{11}{4} \times \frac{5}{3}$	Rename each mixed number as a fraction greater than 1.
$\frac{11}{4} \times \frac{5}{3} = \frac{11 \times 5}{4 \times 3} = \frac{55}{12}$	Multiply.
$= \frac{55}{12}$, or $4\frac{7}{12}$	Write the product as a mixed number in simplest form.

You can also simplify factors by dividing by a common factor of a numerator and a denominator.

Example 2 **Multiply.** $2\frac{4}{7} \times 1\frac{1}{6}$

$2\frac{4}{7} \times 1\frac{1}{6} = \frac{\overset{3}{\cancel{18}} \times \overset{1}{\cancel{7}}}{\underset{1}{\cancel{7}} \times \underset{1}{\cancel{6}}}$	Look for a numerator and denominator with common factors.
$= \frac{3}{1}$, or 3	Divide 18 and 6 by their greatest common factor, 6. Divide 7 and 7 by their greatest common factor, 7.

- How is multiplying two mixed numbers different from multiplying two fractions? How is it similar?

Guided Practice

1. What does one column of Figure 1 represent?

   Use Figures 1 and 2 to find the product $\frac{1}{3} \times 1\frac{1}{5}$.

Figure 1

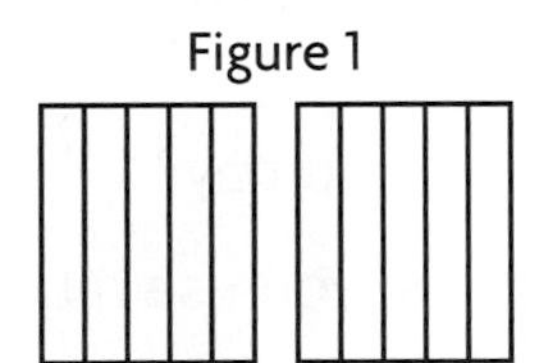

Figure 2

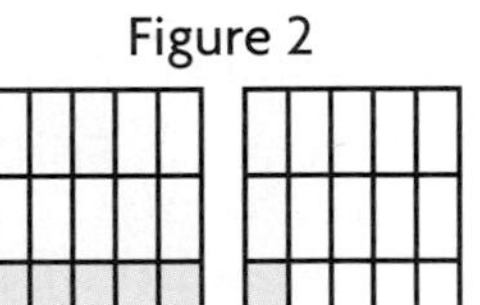

Find the product.

2. $\frac{2}{3} \times 1\frac{3}{8}$
3. $\frac{3}{5} \times 2\frac{1}{2}$
4. $1\frac{1}{3} \times 1\frac{1}{2}$
5. $1\frac{1}{2} \times 2\frac{1}{4}$
6. $2\frac{1}{3} \times 6$
7. $1\frac{2}{9} \times \frac{1}{3}$
8. $1\frac{2}{3} \times 2\frac{1}{3}$
9. $1\frac{1}{7} \times 1\frac{1}{6}$
10. $2\frac{1}{5} \times 1\frac{1}{3}$
11. $3\frac{3}{4} \times 2$
12. **TALK Math** **Explain** how you would find $3 \times 2\frac{3}{4}$.

Independent Practice and Problem Solving

Find the product.

13. $3 \times 1\frac{1}{4}$ **14.** $1\frac{2}{5} \times \frac{1}{3}$ **15.** $2\frac{3}{5} \times 1\frac{1}{4}$ **16.** $\frac{5}{6} \times 1\frac{3}{4}$ **17.** $\frac{5}{12} \times 2\frac{1}{3}$

18. $1\frac{1}{4} \times 1\frac{3}{5}$ **19.** $4\frac{1}{2} \times 1\frac{1}{9}$ **20.** $2\frac{7}{8} \times 4$ **21.** $3\frac{1}{5} \times 1\frac{3}{8}$ **22.** $4\frac{3}{4} \times \frac{2}{3}$

23. $1\frac{2}{3} \times 6$ **24.** $3 \times 2\frac{1}{2}$ **25.** $\frac{7}{8} \times 1\frac{1}{2}$ **26.** $2\frac{1}{4} \times \frac{5}{6}$ **27.** $3\frac{1}{2} \times 1\frac{1}{4}$

28. $\frac{1}{2} \times 1\frac{1}{3} \times 1\frac{2}{3}$ **29.** $2\frac{1}{4} \times \frac{3}{10} \times 1\frac{2}{3}$ **30.** $2\frac{1}{3} \times 1\frac{1}{2} \times 1\frac{3}{4}$

Algebra Find the missing number.

31. Find c if ▲ = 2.
◆ = 4 × ▲
w = ▲ × 6
$\frac{◆}{w} = \frac{▲}{c}$

32. Find s if ▲ = 4.
◆ = 3 × ▲
w = 4 + ▲
$\frac{w}{s} = \frac{▲}{◆}$

33. Find b if ▲ = 6.
◆ = 2 × ▲
w = ▲ − 2
$\frac{b}{◆} = \frac{w}{▲}$

34. A beach is $3\frac{3}{4}$ miles long. Pets on a leash are allowed on $\frac{1}{2}$ of the beach. On how many miles of beach are leashed pets allowed?

35. Sheri has a large dog and one small dog. She feeds the smaller dog $3\frac{3}{4}$ pounds of food each week. She feeds the large dog $1\frac{1}{2}$ times more food each week. How many pounds of food does Sheri feed the larger dog each week?

36. Andy took his dog to the park for $1\frac{1}{4}$ hours on Friday. On Saturday, they were at the park $\frac{2}{3}$ of the time they were there on Friday. How many total hours did Andy and his dog spend at the park on Friday and Saturday?

37. Reasoning How can you use multiplication to find $2\frac{3}{8} + 2\frac{3}{8} + 2\frac{3}{8}$?

38. What's the Error? Kelly says that $1\frac{2}{3} \times 3\frac{1}{3}$ is $3\frac{2}{9}$. Describe the error Kelly might have made. What is the correct answer?

39. WRITE Math **Explain** how multiplying mixed numbers is different than adding mixed numbers.

Extra Practice on page 260, Set C

Achieving the Standards

40. How many students read at least three books?
(Grade 4 SDAP 1.0)

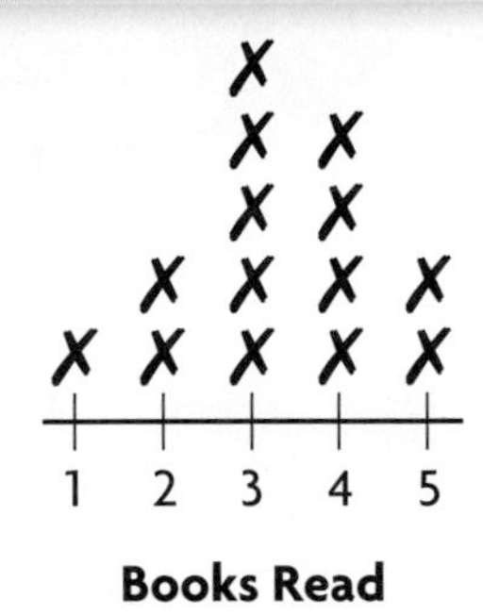

41. Bev makes 2 loaves of banana bread. She uses $\frac{2}{5}$ cup of mashed bananas for each loaf. How much mashed banana will Bev use? (NS 2.4, p. 242)

42. Write the product $\frac{1}{2} \times \frac{4}{5}$ in simplest form.
(NS 2.4, p. 240)

43. Test Prep Dejan has $2\frac{1}{2}$ pounds of clay. He uses $\frac{3}{4}$ of the clay to make a model. How much clay does he use for the model?

A $\frac{3}{8}$ pound
B $\frac{3}{10}$ pound
C $1\frac{1}{2}$ pounds
D $1\frac{7}{8}$ pounds

44. Test Prep Cierra worked for $1\frac{1}{3}$ hours on Tuesday. On Thursday she worked $\frac{3}{4}$ as long. How many hours did Cierra work on Thursday?

A $2\frac{1}{2}$ hours
B 1 hour
C $\frac{7}{12}$ hour
D $3\frac{5}{6}$ hours

Problem Solving connects to Social Studies

The California Trail led many pioneers westward from its starting point in Missouri. Today, parts of the trail are preserved as the California National Historic Trail. The trail passes through 10 states from Missouri to California. Pioneers traveling along the California trail could cover from 14 to 45 miles each day depending on the type of transportation they used.

Example

A pioneer family traveled $3\frac{1}{2}$ miles per hour using a team of horses. They traveled $6\frac{2}{3}$ hours each day for a week. How many miles did they travel in a week?

$$3\frac{1}{2} \times 6\frac{2}{3} \times 7 = \frac{7}{2} \times \frac{20}{3} \times \frac{7}{1} = \frac{980}{6} = \frac{490}{3} = 163\frac{1}{3}$$ Multiply to solve.

So, the pioneer family traveled $163\frac{1}{3}$ miles in a week.

1. A family traveled $2\frac{1}{4}$ miles per hour using a team of oxen. They traveled 8 hours each day for a week. How many miles did they travel in a week?

2. Sean walked $1\frac{3}{5}$ miles per hour. He walked $5\frac{1}{2}$ hours each day for 1 week. How many miles did he travel in 1 week?

LESSON 5 HANDS ON

Model Fraction Division

OBJECTIVE: Model fraction division.

Quick Review

Write the product in simplest form.

1. $\frac{1}{2} \times \frac{1}{3}$
2. $\frac{2}{3} \times \frac{3}{8}$
3. $\frac{5}{6} \times \frac{1}{5}$
4. $10 \times \frac{3}{5}$
5. $\frac{3}{4} \times \frac{4}{5}$

Investigate

Materials ■ fraction bars

You can use a model to find $2 \div \frac{1}{5}$.

A Use two whole bars to model 2.

Place a $\frac{1}{5}$ bar under the whole bars.

1	1

$\frac{1}{5}$

B See how many $\frac{1}{5}$ bars are equal to 2 wholes.

1					1				
$\frac{1}{5}$	$\frac{1}{5}$	$\frac{1}{5}$	$\frac{1}{5}$	$\frac{1}{5}$	$\frac{1}{5}$	$\frac{1}{5}$	$\frac{1}{5}$	$\frac{1}{5}$	$\frac{1}{5}$

C Write a number sentence to express what the model shows.

D Make a model to find $3 \div \frac{1}{4}$. Record the quotient.

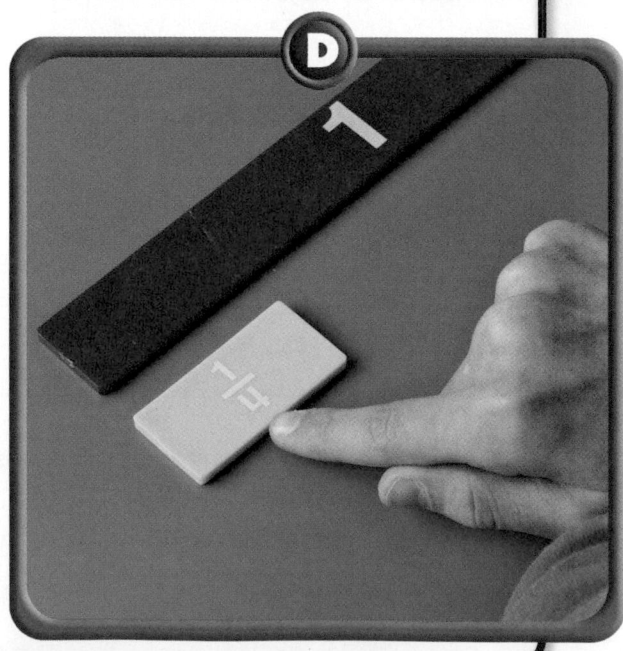

Draw Conclusions

1. How is dividing fractions like dividing whole numbers?
2. How do the fraction bars help you understand dividing fractions?
3. **Analyze** How can you use the quotient for $2 \div \frac{1}{5}$ to find the quotient for $6 \div \frac{1}{5}$?

NS 2.4 Understand the concept of multiplication and division of fractions. *also* NS 2.5, MR 2.0, MR 2.3, MR 2.4, MR 3.2

Connect

You can also use fraction bars to divide a fraction by a fraction.

Example **Divide.** $\frac{1}{2} \div \frac{1}{10}$

Step 1

Model $\frac{1}{2}$ and $\frac{1}{10}$ with fraction bars.

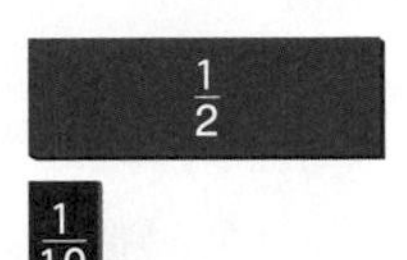

Step 2

See how many $\frac{1}{10}$ bars are equal to the $\frac{1}{2}$ bar.

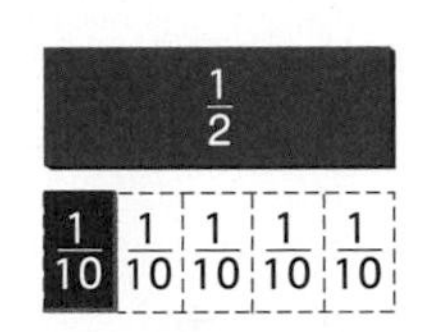

Five $\frac{1}{10}$ bars are equal to a $\frac{1}{2}$ bar.

Step 3

Write a number sentence to express what the model shows.

$$\frac{1}{2} \div \frac{1}{10} = 5$$

TALK Math

Find the product $\frac{1}{2} \times 4$ and the quotient $\frac{1}{2} \div \frac{1}{4}$. What do you notice?

Practice

Write a division number sentence for each model.

1.

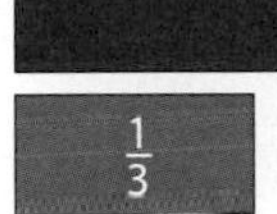

2.

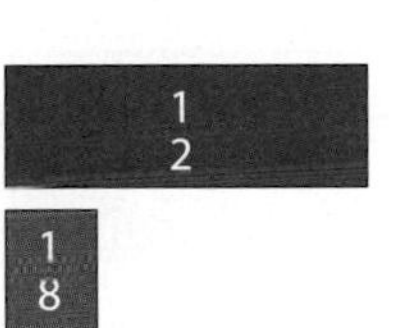

3.

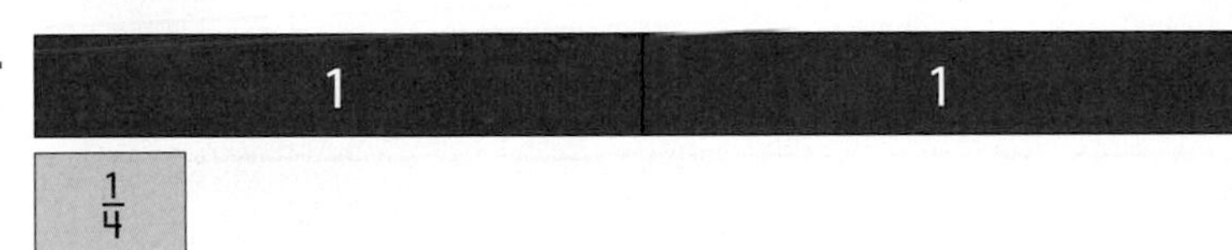

Use fraction bars to find the quotient.

4. $1 \div \frac{1}{6}$
5. $\frac{1}{3} \div \frac{1}{12}$
6. $\frac{1}{5} \div \frac{1}{10}$
7. $2 \div \frac{1}{8}$
8. $\frac{1}{6} \div \frac{1}{12}$
9. $\frac{1}{2} \div \frac{1}{6}$
10. $4 \div \frac{1}{5}$
11. $6 \div \frac{1}{3}$
12. $3 \div \frac{1}{4}$
13. $\frac{1}{3} \div \frac{1}{6}$
14. $6 \div \frac{1}{5}$
15. $2 \div \frac{1}{3}$
16. $\frac{1}{2} \div \frac{1}{8}$
17. $3 \div \frac{1}{6}$
18. $6 \div \frac{1}{4}$
19. $\frac{1}{4} \div \frac{1}{8}$

20. **WRITE Math** **Explain** how to use a model to find $3 \div \frac{1}{3}$.

LESSON 6

Divide Whole Numbers by Fractions

OBJECTIVE: Divide whole numbers by fractions.

Quick Review

1. $\frac{1}{2} \times 8$
2. $9 \times \frac{2}{3}$
3. $\frac{5}{6} \times 4$
4. $6 \times \frac{3}{8}$
5. $5 \times \frac{3}{10}$

Vocabulary

reciprocal

Learn

PROBLEM Students are painting a mural on a wall that is divided into three sections. It takes the students 4 hours to paint $\frac{2}{3}$ of the mural. If they spend the same amount of time painting each section, how many hours will it take the students to paint the mural?

Example 1 Use a common denominator to find $4 \div \frac{2}{3}$.

Step 1

Rename 4 with a denominator of 3.

Think: $4 = \frac{12}{3}$

$4 \div \frac{2}{3} = \frac{12}{3} \div \frac{2}{3}$

Step 2

Divide the numerators.
Divide the denominators.

$4 \div \frac{2}{3} = \frac{12}{3} \div \frac{2}{3}$

$= \frac{12 \div 2}{3 \div 3}$

$= \frac{6}{1}$

Step 3

Write the quotient in simplest form.

$\frac{6}{1} = 6$

So, it will take the students 6 hours to paint the mural.

- Why is 3 used as the common denominator?
- Why do you use a common denominator to divide?

Example 2 Use multiplication to find $6 \div \frac{1}{3}$.

Step 1

Write an equivalent multiplication problem with a missing factor.

Think: $6 \div \frac{1}{3} = \blacksquare$ is equivalent to

$\frac{1}{3} \times \blacksquare = 6$

Step 2

Find the missing factor.

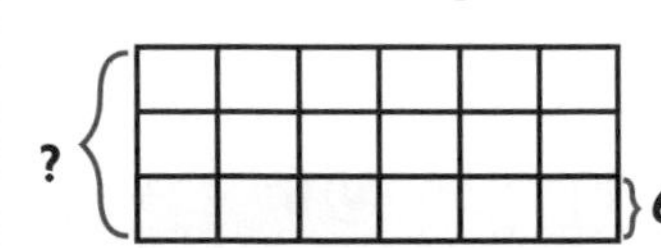

The model shows that $\frac{1}{3}$ of the missing number is 6. Since $\frac{1}{3} \times 18 = 6$, $6 \div \frac{1}{3} = 18$.

So, $6 \div \frac{1}{3} = 18$.

- How would you write an equivalent multiplication problem to find $6 \div \frac{2}{3}$?

NS 2.4 Understand the concept of multiplication and division of fractions.
also **NS 2.5, MR 2.3, MR 2.4, MR 3.0, MR 3.2, MR 3.3**

Use Reciprocals to Divide

You can also divide using the reciprocal of the divisor.

The product of a number and its **reciprocal** is 1.

Reciprocals

The reciprocal of $\frac{1}{8}$ is $\frac{8}{1}$, or 8.

$$\frac{1}{8} \times \frac{8}{1} = \frac{8}{8} = 1$$

The reciprocal of $\frac{5}{6}$ is $\frac{6}{5}$.

$$\frac{5}{6} \times \frac{6}{5} = \frac{30}{30} = 1$$

The reciprocal of 3, or $\frac{3}{1}$, is $\frac{1}{3}$.

$$\frac{3}{1} \times \frac{1}{3} = \frac{3}{3} = 1$$

You can write a related number sentence using the reciprocal and the inverse operation.

$\frac{1}{2} \times 2 = 1$ — $\frac{1}{2}$ and 2 are reciprocals.

$1 \div \frac{1}{2} = 2$ — Write a related division number sentence.

Example 3 Use the reciprocal of the divisor to find $8 \div \frac{1}{2}$.

$8 \div \frac{1}{2}$

$\frac{1}{2} \times \frac{2}{1} = 1$ — Find the reciprocal of the divisor.

$8 \times \frac{2}{1} = \frac{8}{1} \times \frac{2}{1}$ — Multiply the dividend by the reciprocal.

$\frac{8}{1} \times \frac{2}{1} = \frac{16}{1} = 16$ — Write the answer in simplest form.

So, $8 \div \frac{1}{2} = 16$.

- Why are the expressions $8 \div \frac{1}{2}$ and 8×2 equivalent?
- If you divide 1 by any number, what is the quotient?

Math Idea

To divide a whole number by a fraction, write the whole number as a fraction and then multiply it by the reciprocal of the divisor.

Example 4 Use the reciprocal to find $4 \div \frac{3}{5}$.

Step 1

Write the whole number as a fraction.

$$4 \div \frac{3}{5} = \frac{4}{1} \div \frac{3}{5}$$

Step 2

Use the reciprocal of the divisor to write a multiplication problem.

$$\frac{4}{1} \div \frac{3}{5} = \frac{4}{1} \times \frac{5}{3}$$

reciprocals

Step 3

Multiply. Write the answer in simplest form.

$$\frac{4}{1} \times \frac{5}{3} = \frac{20}{3}, \text{ or } 6\frac{2}{3}$$

So, $4 \div \frac{3}{5} = 6\frac{2}{3}$.

Guided Practice

1. Use the reciprocal of $\frac{7}{8}$ to write a multiplication problem to find $2 \div \frac{7}{8}$.

Find the quotient. Write it in simplest form.

2. $8 \div \frac{2}{3}$
3. $5 \div \frac{1}{10}$
4. $6 \div \frac{3}{5}$
5. $4 \div \frac{7}{8}$
6. $2 \div \frac{3}{4}$
7. **TALK Math** **Explain** two ways you can find $3 \div \frac{1}{4}$.

Independent Practice and Problem Solving

Find the quotient. Write it in simplest form.

8. $6 \div \frac{5}{12}$
9. $7 \div \frac{1}{2}$
10. $6 \div \frac{1}{4}$
11. $3 \div \frac{3}{10}$
12. $9 \div \frac{3}{4}$
13. $1 \div \frac{5}{9}$
14. $2 \div \frac{4}{5}$
15. $10 \div \frac{5}{6}$
16. $6 \div \frac{2}{3}$
17. $4 \div \frac{2}{5}$

Algebra **Find the missing number for each ■.**

18. $\frac{1}{4} \times \frac{■}{1} = 1$
19. $9 \times \frac{1}{■} = 1$
20. $\frac{7}{10} \times \frac{■}{7} = 1$
21. $5 \div \frac{1}{■} = 20$
22. $9 \div \frac{■}{3} = 27$
23. The fifth grade is painting scenery. It takes them 9 hours to paint $\frac{3}{4}$ of the scenery. At this rate, how long will it take them to complete the scenery?
24. **Pose a Problem** Write an equation that has a whole number dividend, a divisor that is a fraction, and a quotient of 8.
25. **WRITE Math** **Explain** how to use multiplication to find $3 \div \frac{5}{8}$.

Achieving the Standards

26. Cara spent \$2.29 on a can of tennis balls and \$3.99 on grip for her racket. How much did Cara spend? (Grade 4 NS 2.1)
27. Find the value of the expression $(270 \div 9) \times (12 - 8)$. (Grade 4 AF 1.2)
28. $2\frac{1}{2} \div \frac{4}{7} =$ (NS 2.4, p. 244)
29. **Test Prep** Ty has 6 cups of milk to make pancakes. Each batch uses $\frac{3}{4}$ cup of milk. How many batches can he make?

   A $\frac{1}{2}$
   B $4\frac{1}{2}$
   C 8
   D 24

Technology
CD ROM Use Harcourt Mega Math, Fraction Action, *Fraction Flare Up*, Level P.

 Extra Practice on page 260, Set D

Painting Plans

WRITE Math WORKSHOP

Write to Prove or Disprove

When you are given an equation, you may have to decide whether it is true or false. You must understand the reasoning used to create the equation to be able to decide its validity.

It took students 1 hour to paint $\frac{1}{10}$ of a mural at the playground. The students will paint another mural that is three times as large as the playground mural. Glen estimates it will take $3 \div \frac{1}{10}$, or 30 hours to complete the mural. Raven estimates it will take $3 \div \frac{3}{10}$, or 10 hours. Read about how the students proved whose statement was true and whose statement was false.

First, we checked their computations:

$$3 \div \frac{1}{10} = 3 \times \frac{10}{1} = \frac{30}{1} = 30$$

$$3 \div \frac{3}{10} = 3 \times \frac{10}{3} = \frac{30}{3} = 10$$

Both quotients are correct.

Next, we looked for an error in reasoning.

Looking back at the time it takes to paint the playground mural, we wrote the following equation: $1 \div \frac{1}{10} = 10$.

It takes 10 hours to complete the playground mural. Raven's equation must be false since the larger mural will take more time.

We think Glen correctly recognized that he could multiply the time for the smaller mural by 3 to estimate the time for the larger mural.

Tips

Tips for Writing to Prove or Disprove

- Decide whether an equation is true.
- Demonstrate why an equation is true or false.
- Compare statements for errors in reasoning.
- Explain why an error in reasoning may have occurred.

Problem Solving **Write to prove or disprove.**

1. It takes Dennis 4 hours to complete $\frac{2}{5}$ of a painting. He estimates it will take 15 hours to complete a painting that is 5 times as large.

2. It takes Sasha 8 hours to complete $\frac{2}{3}$ of a sculpture. She estimates it will take 4 hours to complete a sculpture that is half the size.

Divide Fractions

OBJECTIVE: Divide with fractions.

Quick Review

1. $\frac{1}{2} \times \frac{1}{6}$
2. $\frac{1}{4} \times \frac{2}{3}$
3. $\frac{5}{6} \times \frac{2}{5}$
4. $\frac{3}{4} \times \frac{3}{8}$
5. $\frac{1}{2} \times \frac{7}{10}$

Learn

PROBLEM For the school play, the drama teacher has $\frac{3}{4}$ yard of ribbon for costumes. Each costume needs $\frac{1}{12}$ yard of ribbon for trim. How many costumes can the teacher trim using $\frac{3}{4}$ yard?

Example 1 Divide. $\frac{3}{4} \div \frac{1}{12}$

ONE WAY Use fraction bars to divide fractions by fractions.

See how many $\frac{1}{12}$ bars are equal to three $\frac{1}{4}$ bars.

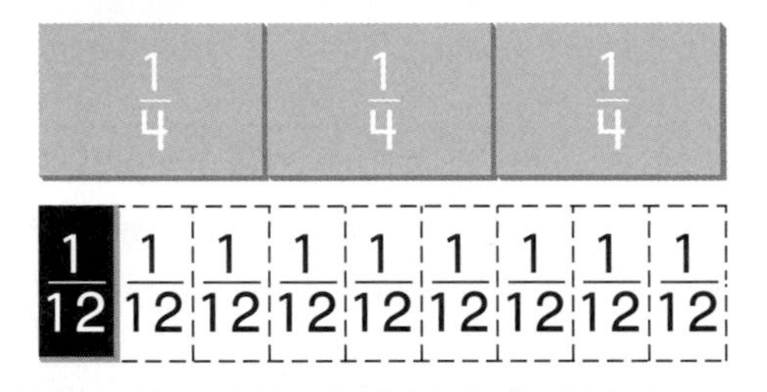

ANOTHER WAY Use reciprocals to divide fractions by fractions.

Step 1

Use the reciprocal of the divisor to write a multiplication problem.

$$\frac{3}{4} \div \frac{1}{12} = \frac{3}{4} \times \frac{12}{1}$$

reciprocals

Step 2

Multiply. Write the answer in simplest form.

$$\frac{3}{4} \times \frac{12}{1} = \frac{36}{4}, \text{ or } 9$$

$$\frac{3}{4} \div \frac{1}{12} = 9$$

So, $\frac{3}{4}$ yard of ribbon can make trim for 9 costumes.

- How can you find the number of pieces of trim the teacher would have if each piece of trim were $\frac{1}{8}$ yard long?

NS 2.4 Understand the concept of multiplication and division of fractions.
also **NS 2.5, MR 1.1, MR 2.1, MR 2.2, MR 2.3, MR 2.4, MR 3.0, MR 3.2, MR 3.3**

Reciprocals and Mixed Numbers

You can use reciprocals to divide mixed numbers by fractions or by other mixed numbers. You can also use reciprocals to divide whole numbers by mixed numbers.

Example 2 **Divide.** $2\frac{1}{3} \div \frac{4}{9}$

Step 1

Write the mixed number as a fraction.

$2\frac{1}{3} \div \frac{4}{9} = \frac{7}{3} \div \frac{4}{9}$

Step 2

Use the reciprocal of the divisor to write a multiplication problem.

$\frac{7}{3} \div \frac{4}{9} = \frac{7}{3} \times \frac{9}{4}$

reciprocals

Step 3

Multiply. Write the answer in simplest form.

$\frac{7}{3} \times \frac{9}{4} = \frac{63}{12} = \frac{21}{4}$, or $5\frac{1}{4}$

$2\frac{1}{3} \div \frac{4}{9} = 5\frac{1}{4}$

Example 3

Divide. $2\frac{3}{4} \div 1\frac{1}{3}$

$2\frac{3}{4} \div 1\frac{1}{3} = \frac{11}{4} \div \frac{4}{3}$ Rename each mixed number as a fraction.

$\frac{11}{4} \div \frac{4}{3} = \frac{11}{4} \times \frac{3}{4}$ Write a multiplication problem using the reciprocal of the divisor.

$= \frac{33}{16}$, or $2\frac{1}{16}$ Multiply. Write the answer in simplest form.

- How is dividing by fractions different than multiplying by fractions? How is it similar?

Guided Practice

1. Use the model at the right to find $\frac{4}{6} \div \frac{1}{3}$.

   How many $\frac{1}{3}$ fraction bars fit into four $\frac{1}{6}$ fraction bars?

   What is $\frac{4}{6} \div \frac{1}{3}$?

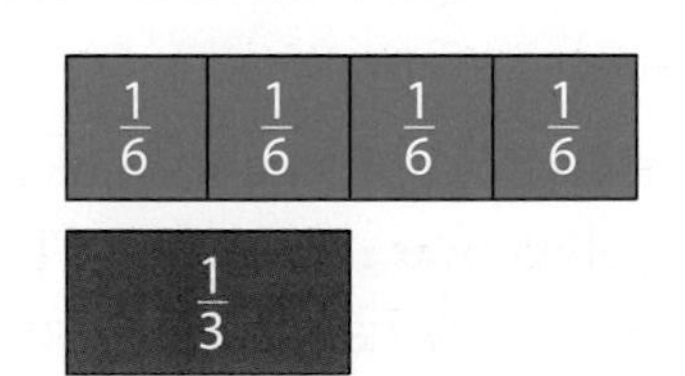

Write a division sentence for each model.

2. 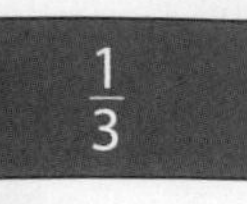

$\frac{1}{12}$

3. 

$\frac{1}{8}$

Divide. Write the answer in simplest form.

4. $\frac{3}{8} \div \frac{2}{3}$ **5.** $1\frac{1}{4} \div \frac{5}{6}$ **6.** $2\frac{1}{2} \div 1\frac{1}{3}$ **7.** $5 \div 2\frac{1}{8}$ **8.** $3\frac{1}{3} \div \frac{3}{8}$

9. TALK Math **Explain** how to use the reciprocal to find the quotient $2\frac{3}{4} \div 1\frac{1}{2}$.

Independent Practice and Problem Solving

Write a division sentence for each model.

10. 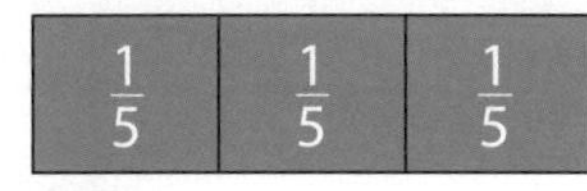

11. 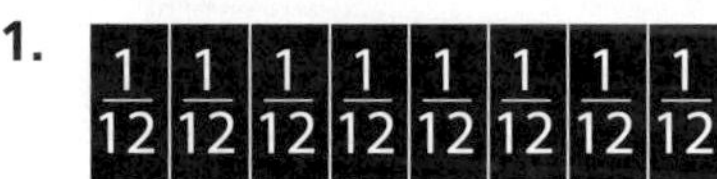

Divide. Write the answer in simplest form.

12. $1\frac{3}{4} \div 2$ **13.** $\frac{5}{8} \div 4$ **14.** $1\frac{1}{2} \div \frac{3}{5}$ **15.** $\frac{5}{12} \div \frac{1}{3}$ **16.** $4\frac{1}{5} \div 3$

17. $3\frac{2}{3} \div 1\frac{1}{4}$ **18.** $1\frac{7}{8} \div \frac{1}{2}$ **19.** $2\frac{1}{6} \div 1\frac{2}{3}$ **20.** $6 \div 1\frac{1}{4}$ **21.** $1\frac{1}{2} \div 1\frac{3}{4}$

Algebra Copy and complete the function table.

22.

y	$\frac{1}{2}$	$\frac{5}{6}$	3
$y \div \frac{1}{8}$	■	■	■

23.

n	$\frac{3}{10}$	$\frac{4}{5}$	2
$n \div \frac{1}{5}$	■	■	■

24.

w	$\frac{1}{6}$	$\frac{2}{3}$	$1\frac{1}{6}$
$w \div \frac{1}{3}$	■	■	■

25. Kate has $7\frac{1}{2}$ yards of material to make capes for the school play. She uses $\frac{3}{4}$ yard to make each cape. How many capes can Kate make?

26. Simone has 12 yards of material to make costumes. She uses $4\frac{1}{2}$ yards for a dress. She uses the rest to make shirts. She needs $1\frac{1}{2}$ yards for each shirt. How many shirts can Simone make?

27. WRITE Math **Explain** how to find n if $\frac{5}{8} \div \frac{n}{3} = \frac{5}{8} \times \frac{n}{3}$. Then use that value for n to find the value of the expression $\frac{5}{8} \div \frac{n}{3}$.

 Extra Practice on page 260, Set E

Achieving the Standards

28. Write the prime factorization for 36.
(NS 1.4, p. 132)

29. Round 237,925 to the nearest ten thousand.
(NS 1.1, p. 12)

30. **Test Prep** An art teacher has $3\frac{1}{2}$ cups of paint powder. It takes $\frac{1}{3}$ cup to make 1 jar of liquid paint. How many jars of liquid paint can he make?

A $\frac{6}{7}$ jar
B $1\frac{1}{6}$ jars
C $1\frac{1}{2}$ jars
D $10\frac{1}{2}$ jars

31. $8 \times \frac{2}{3} =$
(NS 2.4, p. 242)

32. **Test Prep** Mona can ride a bike $8\frac{1}{2}$ miles in $\frac{3}{4}$ hour. How far can she ride in 1 hour?

A $2\frac{5}{8}$ miles
B $9\frac{1}{4}$ miles
C $9\frac{2}{3}$ miles
D $11\frac{1}{3}$ miles

Problem Solving and Reasoning

ALGEBRA Multiplication and division are related operations.

If $a \times b = c$, then $c \div b = a$. This relationship is true for fractions as well as for whole numbers. You can draw a picture to show that $6 \times \frac{1}{3} = 2$ is the same as $2 \div \frac{1}{3} = 6$.

Draw 6 squares. Make thirds.

Think: Each third has 2 squares.

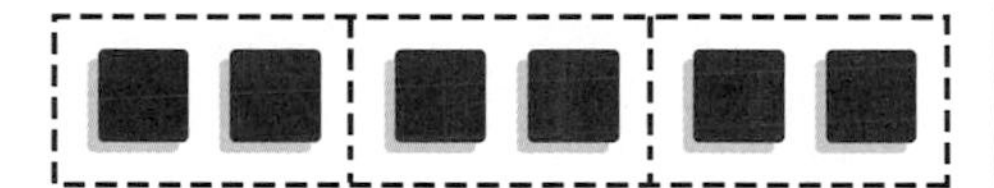

So, $\frac{1}{3}$ of $6 = 2$.

Draw one group of one third, which has 2 squares.

Think: 2 is one third of the total.

Draw the groups of one third with 2 squares three times there are 6 total squares.

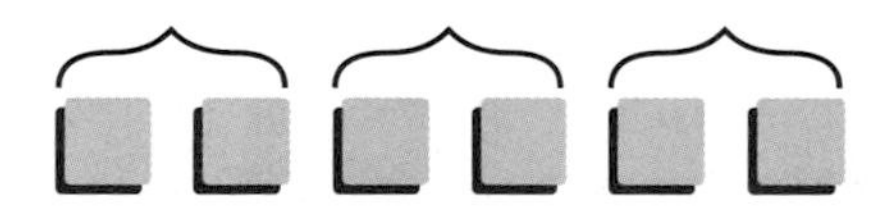

So, $2 \div \frac{1}{3} = 6$.

1. Draw pictures to model $8 \times \frac{1}{2} = 4$ is the same as $4 \div \frac{1}{2} = 8$.

2. Draw pictures to model $12 \times \frac{1}{4} = 3$ is the same as $3 \div \frac{1}{4} = 12$.

LESSON 8

Problem Solving Workshop
Skill: Multistep Problems

OBJECTIVE: Solve problems by using the skill *multistep problems.*

Read to Understand
Plan
Solve
Check

Use the Skill

PROBLEM Jasmine has 27 yards of fabric to make costumes for a play. She will use $\frac{1}{3}$ of the fabric for skirts, and will cut the skirt fabric into pieces that are each $\frac{3}{4}$ yard long. She will make $\frac{1}{2}$ of the skirts today. How many skirts will Jasmine make today?

Step 1

Find how much fabric will be used for the skirts.

fabric available		fraction for skirts		fabric for skirts
↓		↓		↓
27 yards	×	$\frac{1}{3}$	=	9 yards

Step 2

Find how many skirts will be made in all.

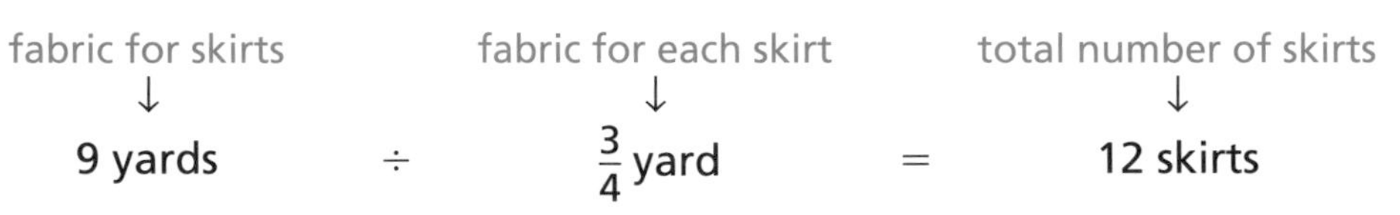

fabric for skirts		fabric for each skirt		total number of skirts
↓		↓		↓
9 yards	÷	$\frac{3}{4}$ yard	=	12 skirts

Step 3

Find how many skirts Jasmine will make today.

fraction made today		total number of skirts		skirts made today
↓		↓		↓
$\frac{1}{2}$	×	12	=	6 skirts

So, Jasmine will make 6 skirts today.

Think and Discuss

Describe the steps required to solve the problem. Then solve.

a. Brett used $\frac{5}{8}$ yard of wire to make key rings. Each key ring uses $\frac{1}{8}$ yard of wire. Brett sold $\frac{2}{5}$ of the key rings. How many key rings did he sell?

b. There are 90 students in the orchestra. Of the students, $\frac{1}{3}$ play a stringed instrument, $\frac{1}{2}$ of whom are girls. How many girls play a stringed instrument?

NS 2.4 Understand the concept of multiplication and division of fractions. *also* **NS 2.5, MR 1.0, MR 1.2, MR 2.0, MR 2.2, MR 2.3, MR 2.4, MR 2.5, MR 3.0, MR 3.1, MR 3.2, MR 3.3**

Guided Problem Solving

Describe the steps required to solve the problem. Then solve.

1. Next month there will be 36 concerts at the Pasadena Jazz Institute. Of the concerts, $\frac{3}{4}$ will be held on Friday nights, and $\frac{1}{6}$ will be held on Saturday nights. Of the concerts held on Friday and Saturday nights, $\frac{2}{3}$ of them are sold out. How many Friday and Saturday night concerts are sold out?

Find the number of concerts on Friday nights.	Find the number of concerts on Saturday nights.	Find how many concerts are held on Friday and Saturday nights.	Find how many concerts are sold out.
$\frac{3}{4} \times 36 = 27$	$\frac{1}{6} \times 36 = 6$	$27 + 6 = ■$	$\frac{2}{3} \times ■ = ■$

2. **What if** there were $\frac{1}{3}$ of the Friday and Saturday night concerts sold out? How many of the Friday and Saturday night concerts would be sold out?

3. Ellie has $\frac{2}{3}$ yard of ribbon to make hair bows. She used $\frac{1}{6}$ yard of ribbon for each bow. She gave $\frac{1}{2}$ of the bows to her friends. How many bows did Ellie give to her friends?

Mixed Applications

USE DATA For 4–7, use the circle graph.

4. Mark spent $\frac{1}{3}$ of his research time on the Internet. He spent $\frac{1}{2}$ of the time on the Internet researching hotels in San Diego. How long did Mark spend researching hotels in San Diego?

5. Mark completed $\frac{1}{4}$ of his paperwork before lunch and he completed the rest of it after lunch. How long did Mark work on his paperwork after lunch?

6. **WRITE Math** Tomorrow, Mark needs to spend $\frac{1}{2}$ of his workday in meetings. **Explain** how you can use the circle graph to find how long Mark will spend in meetings if he works the same number of hours each day.

7. **Pose a Problem** Write a problem about Mark's workday that requires more than one step to solve. Then solve.

Extra Practice

Set A **Find the product. Write it in simplest form.** (pp. 240–241)

1. $\frac{1}{2} \times \frac{2}{5}$
2. $\frac{3}{4} \times \frac{1}{2}$
3. $\frac{2}{9} \times \frac{3}{4}$
4. $\frac{2}{5} \times \frac{5}{8}$
5. $\frac{1}{4} \times \frac{2}{3}$
6. $\frac{3}{5} \times \frac{4}{5}$
7. Julia ate $\frac{1}{2}$ of $\frac{3}{4}$ of a bag of peaches. What fraction of the bag of peaches did Julia eat?
8. Charlotte spent $\frac{1}{4}$ of $\frac{1}{3}$ of her budget on baby food. What fraction of her budget did Charlotte spend on baby food?

Set B **Find the product.** (pp. 242–243)

1. $5 \times \frac{3}{4}$
2. $\frac{1}{2} \times 3$
3. $3 \times \frac{2}{3}$
4. $8 \times \frac{5}{6}$
5. $\frac{3}{5} \times 10$
6. $\frac{7}{10} \times 15$
7. $3 \times \frac{1}{4}$
8. $\frac{1}{6} \times 6$
9. $\frac{2}{5} \times 15$
10. $7 \times \frac{3}{5}$
11. $11 \times \frac{4}{7}$
12. $\frac{5}{7} \times 14$

Set C **Find the product.** (pp. 244–247)

1. $4 \times 1\frac{1}{2}$
2. $1\frac{2}{3} \times \frac{3}{5}$
3. $1\frac{1}{3} \times 1\frac{1}{4}$
4. $2\frac{2}{5} \times 1\frac{2}{3}$
5. $4\frac{1}{4} \times 2\frac{2}{5}$
6. $\frac{1}{4} \times 2\frac{1}{2} \times 1\frac{2}{5}$
7. $2\frac{1}{3} \times \frac{3}{8} \times 1\frac{1}{6}$
8. $1\frac{2}{3} \times 1\frac{3}{5} \times 1\frac{3}{4}$
9. $3\frac{3}{5} \times 4\frac{1}{6}$
10. $10\frac{1}{5} \times 8\frac{1}{3}$

Set D **Find the quotient. Write it in simplest form.** (pp. 250–253)

1. $9 \div \frac{3}{5}$
2. $3 \div \frac{3}{4}$
3. $8 \div \frac{2}{5}$
4. $6 \div \frac{3}{8}$
5. $5 \div \frac{5}{6}$
6. Wanda is making bracelets. It takes her 2 hours to string the beads for $\frac{4}{5}$ of the bracelets. How long will it take her to string the beads for all of the bracelets?
7. Juan cut 9 feet of wire into pieces that were each $\frac{3}{4}$ foot long. How many pieces did he cut?

Set E **Use a reciprocal to write a multiplication expression for the division problem.** (pp. 254–257)

1. $\frac{3}{5} \div \frac{3}{10}$
2. $1\frac{2}{3} \div \frac{4}{5}$
3. $2\frac{1}{4} \div 3$
4. $3\frac{1}{3} \div 2\frac{1}{2}$
5. $8 \div 1\frac{5}{6}$
6. $4 \div \frac{3}{8}$
7. $2\frac{1}{3} \div 6$
8. $1\frac{3}{4} \div 1\frac{1}{2}$
9. $5\frac{1}{6} \div 2$
10. $2 \div \frac{2}{3}$

CD ROM **Technology**
Use Harcourt Mega Math, Fraction Action, *Number Line Mine*, Level L.

Fraction Factors

On Your Mark!
2 players

Get Set!
- Gameboards
- Four sets of number cards (1–9)
- Score chart

	Player 1	Player 2
Round 1 Product		
Round 2 Product		
Round 3 Product		
Round 4 Product		
Round 5 Product		

Go!

- Players make their own gameboards to display expressions involving the products of two fractions.
- Players shuffle the number cards and place them facedown in a stack.
- Player 1 draws four cards and uses them to make two fraction factors on his or her gameboard. The factors should produce the greatest possible product.
- Player 2 solves Player 1's multiplication expression and records the product in the score chart. Reshuffle the cards after each round.
- Player 2 draws four new cards from the stack and repeats the process.
- At the end of each round, players compare products. The player who made the greater product earns 1 point. The first player to earn 5 points wins the game.

Chapter 10 Review/Test

Check Concepts

1. Explain why the product of two fractions that are each less than 1 will always be less than 1. (NS 2.4, p. 238)
2. Explain how you can use a model to find $\frac{1}{4} \times \frac{1}{3}$. (NS 2.5, p. 238)
3. Explain how to use a picture to find $2 \div \frac{1}{2}$. (NS 2.5, p. 248)

Check Skills

Find the product. Write it in simplest form. (NS 2.5, pp. 240–241, 242–243, 244–247)

4. $\frac{1}{3} \times \frac{3}{4}$
5. $9 \times 1\frac{1}{3}$
6. $6 \times \frac{1}{2}$
7. $\frac{3}{10} \times \frac{5}{9}$
8. $4\frac{1}{2} \times \frac{5}{6}$
9. $2\frac{1}{4} \times 1\frac{1}{3}$
10. $3\frac{2}{3} \times \frac{3}{5} \times 1\frac{1}{4}$
11. $1\frac{3}{4} \times 2\frac{2}{3} \times \frac{1}{12}$
12. $4\frac{1}{5} \times 15$
13. $\frac{7}{8} \times \frac{4}{5}$

Use a reciprocal to write a multiplication problem for the division problem. (NS 2.4, pp. 254–257)

14. $\frac{4}{7} \div 2$
15. $2\frac{1}{2} \div \frac{5}{6}$
16. $6 \div 1\frac{1}{5}$
17. $2\frac{1}{4} \div 2\frac{5}{8}$
18. $\frac{3}{4} \div 1\frac{1}{2}$

Find the quotient. Write it in simplest form. (NS 2.5, pp. 254–257)

19. $4 \div \frac{4}{7}$
20. $6 \div \frac{8}{9}$
21. $10 \div \frac{1}{3}$
22. $5 \div \frac{5}{8}$
23. $2 \div \frac{2}{5}$

Check Problem Solving

Solve. (NS 2.5, MR 2.6, pp. 258–259)

24. A summer camp director surveyed 24 campers to find their favorite activity. Of the campers surveyed, $\frac{5}{8}$ chose arts and crafts. Of the campers who chose arts and crafts, $\frac{1}{3}$ were boys. How many boys chose arts and crafts?

25. **WRITE Math** A camper is working on a project. She has a piece of wood that is $2\frac{2}{3}$ feet long. She uses $\frac{3}{4}$ of the wood for picture frames. She cuts the wood for the frames into $\frac{1}{4}$-foot pieces. **Explain** how to find the number of $\frac{1}{4}$-foot pieces she will have.

GO ONLINE **Technology** Use *Online Assessment.*

Enrich • Use Mental Math

MIND OVER MATH

You can use what you know about reciprocals and properties to solve problems using mental math. The product of 1 and any number except 0 is that number. So, when you divide any number except 0 by itself the quotient is 1.

$$3 \times 1 = 3 \quad \rightarrow \quad 3 \div 3 = 1$$

$$\frac{3}{2} \times 1 = \frac{3}{2} \quad \rightarrow \quad \frac{3}{2} \div \frac{3}{2} = 1$$

Understanding these problems will help you solve similar problems with greater numbers.

▲ Babylonian Clay Tablet

Example

Solve. Use mental math.

$\left(\frac{1{,}743}{3{,}820} \div \frac{1{,}743}{3{,}820}\right) \times \frac{22}{30} =$ The quotient of any number except 0 divided by itself is 1.

$1 \times \frac{22}{30} = \frac{22}{30}$, or $\frac{11}{15}$ The product of any number and 1 is that number.

Try It

Solve. Write the answer in simplest form.

1. $\left(\frac{2{,}972}{6{,}457} \div \frac{2{,}972}{6{,}457}\right) \times \frac{45}{50}$
2. $\frac{15}{30} \times \left(\frac{2{,}750}{4{,}200} \div \frac{2{,}750}{4{,}200}\right)$
3. $\left(\frac{1{,}080}{2{,}160} \times \frac{2{,}160}{1{,}080}\right) \div \frac{72}{88}$
4. $3\frac{45}{60} \times \left(\frac{550}{750} \div \frac{550}{750}\right)$
5. $\frac{112}{120} \div \left(\frac{2{,}834}{3{,}920} \times \frac{3{,}920}{2{,}834}\right)$
6. $\left(\frac{3{,}520}{7{,}180} \div \frac{3{,}520}{7{,}180}\right) \times \frac{24}{96}$
7. $\frac{1{,}080}{2{,}160} \times \frac{500}{1{,}000} \times \frac{2{,}160}{1{,}080}$
8. $\left(\frac{2{,}448}{7{,}344} \times \frac{7{,}344}{2{,}448}\right) \times \frac{2{,}400}{600}$

Think About It

9. WRITE Math **Explain** why using mental math makes finding the solution to the problems above easier.

Unit Review/Test
Chapters 7–10

Multiple Choice

1. $\frac{3}{8} + \frac{4}{8} =$
(NS 2.3, p. 176)

A $\frac{12}{8}$

B $\frac{7}{8}$

C $\frac{7}{16}$

D $\frac{7}{64}$

2. It took the Chow family $4\frac{3}{4}$ hours to drive to San Francisco. If they stopped at a park for $1\frac{1}{4}$ hours, how long were they actually driving? (NS 2.3, p. 180)

A $1\frac{1}{4}$ hours

B $1\frac{3}{4}$ hours

C $2\frac{1}{4}$ hours

D $3\frac{1}{2}$ hours

3. $\frac{3}{5} - \frac{1}{10} =$
(NS 2.3, p. 200)

A $\frac{3}{10}$

B $\frac{2}{5}$

C $\frac{1}{2}$

D $\frac{7}{10}$

4. It takes Ricardo $\frac{1}{4}$ hour to ride his bicycle to John's house and $\frac{1}{3}$ hour to ride his bicycle from John's house to the playground. How much time does it take Ricardo to ride his bicycle to John's house and then to the playground? (NS 2.3, p. 204)

A $\frac{1}{12}$ hour

B $\frac{1}{7}$ hour

C $\frac{2}{7}$ hour

D $\frac{7}{12}$ hour

5. $1\frac{1}{3} + 2\frac{1}{6} =$
(NS 2.3, p. 220)

A $3\frac{2}{9}$

B $3\frac{1}{2}$

C $3\frac{3}{4}$

D $4\frac{1}{2}$

6. Liza is keeping track of her fruit intake for a health project. On Monday she ate $2\frac{1}{4}$ cups of fruit. On Tuesday she ate $1\frac{3}{4}$ cups of fruit. How much more fruit did Liza eat on Monday than Tuesday? (NS 2.3, p. 184)

A $\frac{1}{4}$ cup

B $\frac{1}{2}$ cup

C $\frac{3}{4}$ cup

D 1 cup

GO ONLINE **Technology** Use *Online Assessment.*

7. $9\frac{5}{12} - 4\frac{7}{12} =$
(O-π NS 2.3, p. 184)

A $4\frac{5}{6}$

B $4\frac{11}{12}$

C $5\frac{1}{12}$

D $5\frac{5}{6}$

8. $\frac{2}{3} \times \frac{1}{2} =$
(NS 2.4, p. 240)

A $\frac{1}{3}$

B $\frac{2}{5}$

C $\frac{1}{2}$

D $\frac{3}{5}$

9. Melanie has 2 yards of ribbon to use for a craft project. She needs to cut the ribbon into pieces that are $\frac{1}{4}$ yard long. How many pieces of ribbon will Melanie have?
(O-π NS 2.3, p. 248)

A 4

B 6

C 8

D 10

Short Response

10. Mrs. Banek's class went on a field trip to a park. Before lunch they hiked $\frac{3}{4}$ mile. After lunch they hiked another $\frac{1}{3}$ mile. About how many miles did the class hike in all? Show your work. (NS 1.1, p. 202)

11. A restaurant cook prepared $2\frac{1}{2}$ gallons of spaghetti sauce. After serving dinner, he had $\frac{3}{4}$ gallon of sauce left. How many gallons of spaghetti sauce did he serve for dinner? Show your work. (O-π NS 2.3, p. 226)

12. A pitcher holds the amount of punch shown.

Dante pours $\frac{3}{4}$ cup of punch in each glass. How many glasses can he fill? How much punch will he have left over? (NS 2.5, p. 248)

Extended Response WRITE Math

13. On Friday, a tomato plant was $\frac{2}{3}$ foot tall. It had grown $\frac{1}{6}$ foot from Wednesday to Friday. It had grown $\frac{1}{12}$ foot from Monday to Wednesday. How tall was the plant on Monday? **Explain** your answer.
(O-π NS 2.3, p. 200)

14. Mr. Morgan put $\frac{1}{10}$ of his paycheck in savings. Then he paid bills with half of what was left. His paycheck was $500. How much money does he have left? **Explain** your answer. (NS 2.5, p. 242)

California

Problem Solving

from THE WORLD ALMANAC FOR KIDS

The Planets

Palomar Observatory

Palomar Observatory

The Palomar Observatory is located in San Diego County, California. It is home to many telescopes that help astronomers learn more about space. The largest of the telescopes, the Hale telescope, has a 200-inch reflecting mirror that is used to take pictures. The first picture by the Hale telescope was taken in 1949 by a young astronomer named Edwin Hubble.

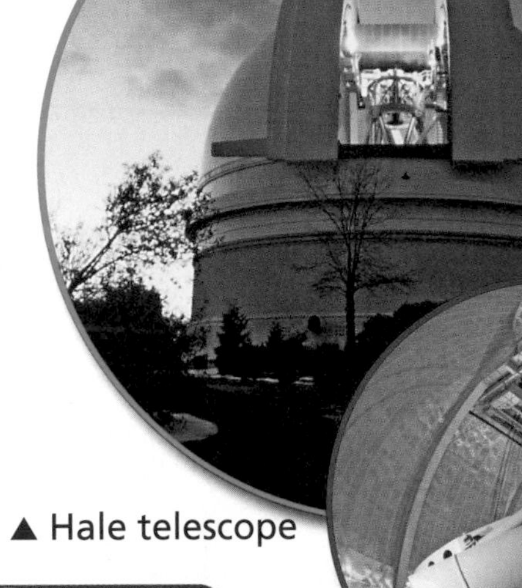

▲ Hale telescope

FACT · ACTIVITY

Use the table to answer the questions.

Amount of Time to Orbit the Sun

Planet	Earth	Jupiter	Mars	Mercury	Neptune	Pluto*	Saturn	Uranus	Venus
Time (in Earth years)	1	$11\frac{9}{10}$	$1\frac{9}{10}$	$\frac{1}{4}$	$164\frac{4}{5}$	$247\frac{9}{10}$	$29\frac{2}{5}$	84	$\frac{4}{5}$

*In 2006, scientists classified Pluto as a "dwarf planet."

1. Which planet takes the least amount of time to orbit the sun?
2. How much longer does it take for Mars to orbit the sun than it takes Earth?
3. Which planet takes longer to orbit the sun, Jupiter or Mars? How much longer?
4. Which planet takes about 7 times as long as Jupiter to orbit the sun?
5. **Pose a Problem** Write a problem similar to Problem 2, but change the planets. Ask a classmate to solve the problem.

SPACE ADVENTURE!

When you jump into the air, why don't you fly off into space? A force called *surface gravity* is what keeps you grounded. Every planet has surface gravity. A planet's surface gravity depends on the planet's size and mass. The surface gravity of a planet determines an object's weight on that planet.

ALMANAC Fact

Half of the space shuttle landings take place at either Edwards Air Force Base or Dryden Air Force Base in California.

FACT • ACTIVITY

The table at the right compares each planet's surface gravity to Earth's surface gravity. Suppose you are a space traveler. Your task is to design a space mission and then write a magazine article about the mission.

- Design a spaceship and draw a picture of it.
- Estimate the total weight of the spaceship on Earth. Include the weight of equipment, food, and passengers.
- Choose three planets to visit. Make a table like the one below, and determine how much the total weight of a spaceship will be on each planet.
- Write a story about your mission. Be sure to include changes in the weight of your spaceship.

Surface Gravity of Planets Compared to Earth's Surface Gravity

Planet	Number of Times Earth's Surface Gravity
Earth	1
Jupiter	$2\frac{1}{10}$
Mars	$\frac{2}{5}$
Mercury	$\frac{2}{5}$
Neptune	$1\frac{1}{10}$
Pluto*	$\frac{1}{10}$
Saturn	$\frac{3}{4}$
Uranus	$\frac{4}{5}$
Venus	$\frac{9}{10}$

*In 2006, scientists classified Pluto as a "dwarf planet."

Weight of Spaceship

Planet You Plan to Visit	Total Weight of Spaceship on Earth	Surface Gravity of Planet	Total Weight of Spaceship on Planet

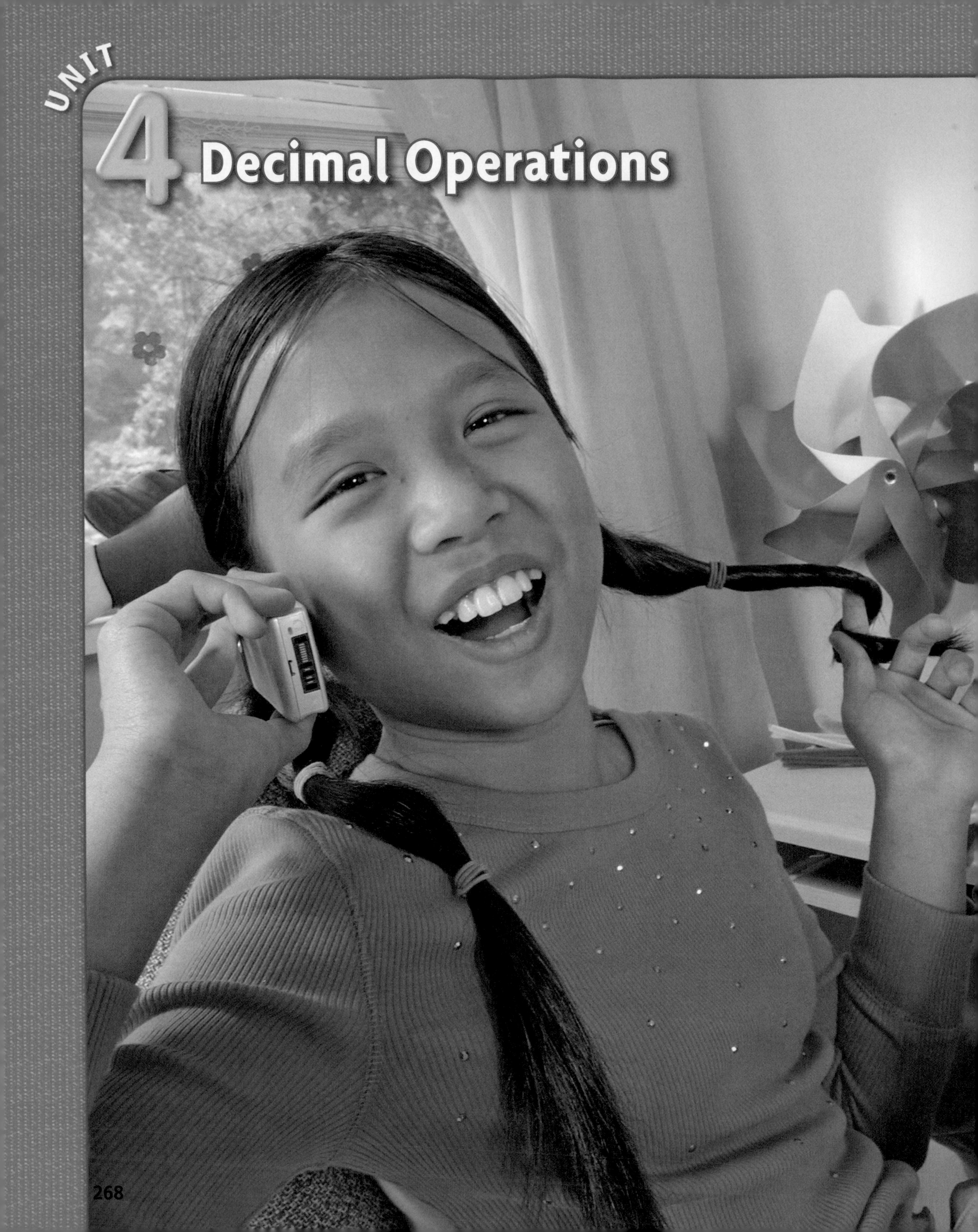

UNIT

4 Decimal Operations

Math on Location

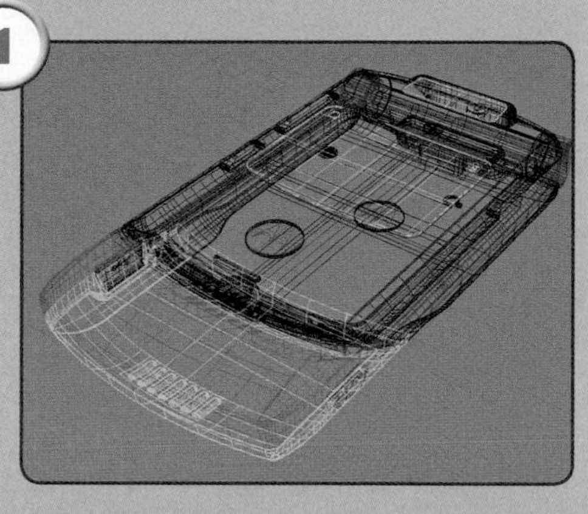

▲ A new cell phone design begins with a drawing that shows how the pieces fit together so it is easy to use and hold.

▲ Cell phones are much smaller than before even though many additional functions have been added.

▲ Decimal units are needed to measure the buttons on the key pad or the thinness of the metal case.

VOCABULARY POWER

TALK Math

What math is used in the **Math on Location**? How can you find a precise measurement of the width of the cell phones shown?

READ Math

REVIEW VOCABULARY You learned the words below when you learned about decimals and place value. How do these words relate to **Math on Location**?

equivalent decimals decimals that name the same number or amount

round to replace a number with another number that is simpler and is approximately the same size as the original number

thousandth one of one thousand equal parts

WRITE Math

Copy and continue the category map below. Use what you know about decimals.

	Whole numbers	Fractions	Decimals
Can represent counting numbers	YES	YES	YES
Can represent parts of numbers less than 1	NO	YES	YES
Can make precise measurements			

Technology
Multimedia Math Glossary link at
www.harcourtschool.com/hspmath

11 Add and Subtract Decimals

The Big Idea Addition and subtraction of decimals are based on place value and addition and subtraction with whole numbers.

CALIFORNIA FAST FACT

Royal Gorge Cross Country Ski Resort, in Soda Springs, California, has the largest groomed ski trail system in North America. The ski resort grooms 205 miles of ski trails that make up its 90 different ski runs.

Investigate

While on vacation at Lake Tahoe, you decide to ski on two different ski runs in the area. Write three equations that show the combined lengths of 2 different ski runs that you could choose to ski.

Lake Tahoe Ski Runs

Ski Resort	Longest Ski Run (in miles)
Bear Valley	3.0
Heavenly Mountain	2.4
Northstar at Tahoe	2.9
Sierra–at–Tahoe	2.5
Squaw Valley	3.2

Technology
Student pages are available in the Student eBook.

Show What You Know

Check your understanding of important skills needed for success in Chapter 11.

▶ Rounding

Round each number to the nearest hundred.

1. 562 **2.** 407 **3.** 638 **4.** 153

5. 4,709 **6.** 8,371 **7.** 6,881 **8.** 7,349

9. 16,535 **10.** 38,271 **11.** 42,764 **12.** 54,098

▶ Model Decimals

Write the decimal for the shaded part.

13. 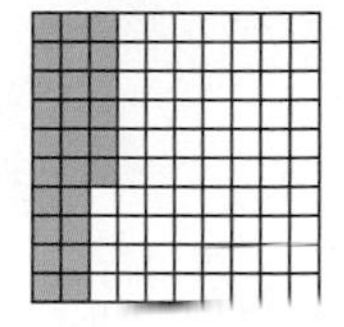

14. 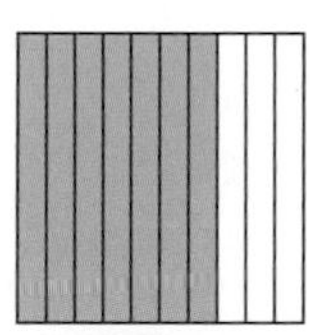

15. 

16. 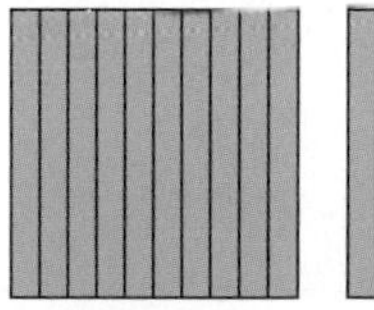

17. 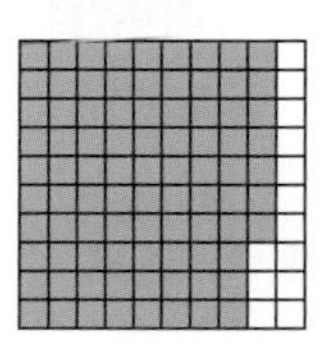

18. 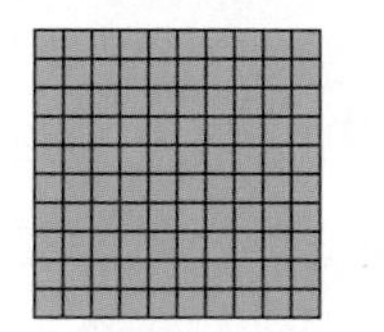

19. 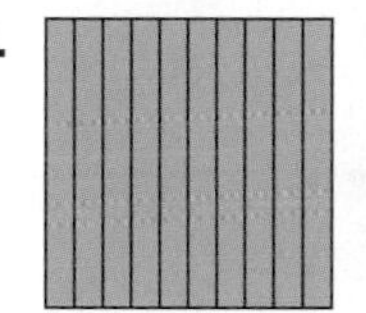 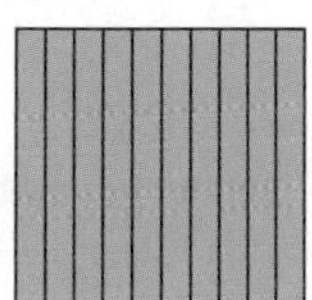 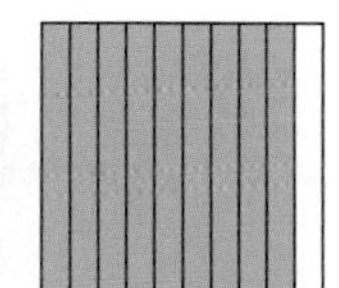

20. 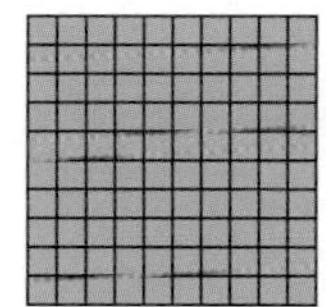

VOCABULARY POWER

CHAPTER VOCABULARY

decimal
decimal point
hundredth
tenth
thousandth

WARM-UP WORDS

tenth one of ten equal parts

hundredth one of one hundred equal parts

decimal a number with one or more digits to the right of the decimal point

Round Decimals

OBJECTIVE: Round decimals to a given place value.

Quick Review

Round each number to the place of the underlined digit.

1. $3\underline{9}1$
2. $5{,}0\underline{4}5$
3. $\underline{2}8{,}036$
4. $3\underline{4}{,}578$
5. $\underline{1}69{,}822$

Learn

PROBLEM In science, Ms. Cosa's class found that one cup of grated carrots has an average of 0.039 gram of salt. What is the salt content of one cup of grated carrots rounded to the nearest hundredth of a gram?

ONE WAY **Use a number line.**

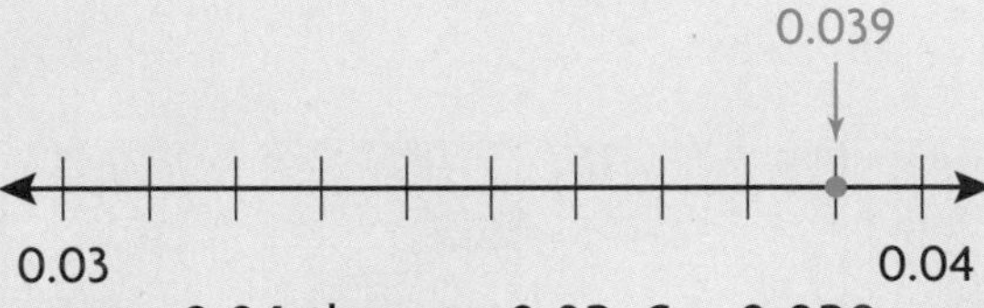

0.039 is closer to 0.04 than to 0.03. So, 0.039 rounded to the nearest hundredth of a gram is 0.04 gram.

ANOTHER WAY **Use the rounding rules.**

Round to the place of the underlined digit. Use the rounding rules.

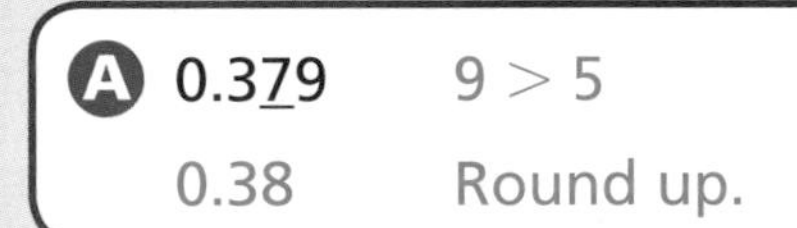

B $1.\underline{6}43$ $4 < 5$
1.6 Round down.

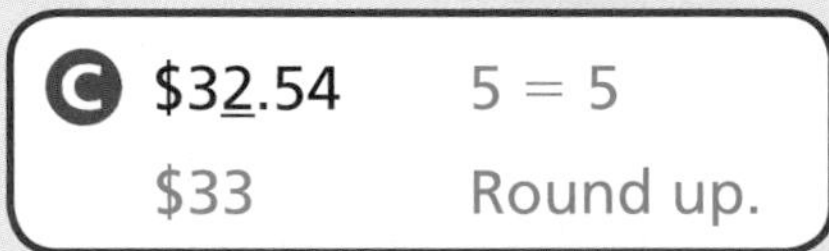

Guided Practice

1. Use the number line to round 0.486 to the nearest hundredth.

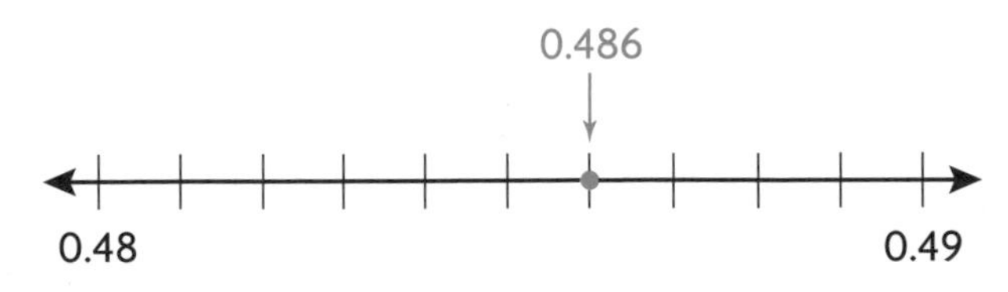

Round each number to the place of the underlined digit.

2. $0.3\underline{5}5$
3. $0.\underline{6}72$
4. $0.\underline{8}07$
5. $0.1\underline{3}4$

Round 0.859 to the place named.

6. tenths
7. hundredths
8. ones
9. TALK Math **Explain** how to round 7.86 to the nearest tenth.

Remember

Rounding rules:
- Find the place to which you want to round.
- If the digit to the right is < 5, round down.
- If the digit to the right is ≥ 5, round up.

NS 1.1 Estimate, round, and manipulate very large (e.g., millions) and very small (e.g., thousandths) numbers. *also* MR 2.3, MR 2.4, MR 3.2

Independent Practice and Problem Solving

Round each number to the place of the underlined digit.

10. $0.9\underline{3}4$ **11.** $23.\underline{1}73$ **12.** $\underline{0}.481$ **13.** $137.5\underline{4}5$ **14.** $42.\underline{8}57$

Round 2.306 to the place named.

15. tenths **16.** hundredths **17.** ones

Name the place to which each number was rounded.

18. 0.625 to 0.63 **19.** 7.846 to 7.85 **20.** 12.87 to 12.9

Round to the nearest tenth of a dollar and to the nearest dollar.

21. \$10.35 **22.** \$0.49 **23.** \$0.98 **24.** \$3.22 **25.** \$13.28

Round each number to the nearest hundredth.

26. seven hundred twenty-six thousandths

27. $10 + 4 + 0.5 + 0.009$

28. five and three hundred twenty-four thousandths

29. $3 + 0.4 + 0.06 + 0.008$

USE DATA For 30–32, use the graph.

30. Round the salt content of the blueberry muffin to the nearest hundredth of a gram.

31. Which muffin has a salt content of 0.30 gram when rounded to the nearest hundredth of a gram?

32. WRITE Math **Explain** how to round the salt content of a bran muffin to the nearest tenth of a gram.

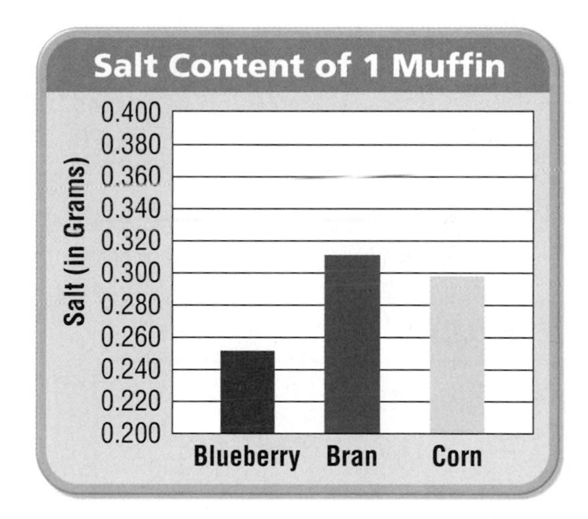

Achieving the Standards

33. A line segment connects the points (2,3) and (2,7). What is the length of the line segment? (Gr. 4 MG 2.3)

34. $2\frac{1}{2} \times 1\frac{1}{4} =$ (NS 2.5, p. 244)

35. A kitten weighs 1.6 kilograms. Its sister weighs 2.2 kilograms. What is the difference in their weights? (Grade 4 NS 2.1)

36. **Test Prep** Darrin rounded 5.849 pounds to 5.8 pounds. To which place did he round?

A ones **C** hundredths

B tenths **D** thousandths

Extra Practice on page 284, Set A

LESSON 2

Add and Subtract Decimals

OBJECTIVE: Find the sums and differences of decimals.

Quick Review

Write an equivalent decimal for each number.

1. 0.34
2. 1.8
3. 8.09
4. 0.01
5. 19.4

Learn

PROBLEM In his first luge run at the 2006 Winter Olympics, Armin Zoeggeler reached the first interval in 23.835 seconds. Zoeggeler reached the third interval 20.336 seconds later. What was Armin Zoeggeler's total race time when he reached the third interval?

You can add and subtract decimals the same way you add and subtract whole numbers if you line up the decimal points first.

Example 1 Add. 23.835 + 20.366

Step 1

Line up the decimal points to align place-value positions. Add the thousandths.

```
      1
  23.835
 +20.336
       1
```

Step 2

Add the hundredths. Add the tenths. Regroup as needed.

```
   1  1
  23.835
 +20.336
     171
```

Step 3

Add the ones and tens. Place the decimal point in the sum.

```
   1
  23.835
 +20.336
  44.171
```

So, Zoeggeler's time at the third interval was 44.171 seconds.

More Examples

A $12.48 + $3.93

```
  1 1
  12.48     ← Line up decimal points.
+  3.93
  16.41     ← Place the decimal point in the sum.
```

B 2.5 + 4.72 + 8.091

```
  1 1
  2.500    Place zeros to
  4.720    show equivalent
+ 8.091    decimals.
 15.311
```

- Why do you use equivalent decimals in Example B?

▲ A luge sledder can reach speeds of 86 miles per hour.

NS 2.1 Add, subtract, multiply, and divide with decimals; add with negative integers; subtract positive integers from negative integers; and verify the reasonableness of the results. *also* NS 1.0, NS 2.0, MR 1.0, MR 2.0, MR 2.3, MR 2.4, MR 3.2, MR 3.3

Subtraction

Zoeggeler's total time for his first run was 51.718 seconds. How many seconds did it take Zoeggeler to sled from the third interval to the finish line?

Example 2 Subtract. 51.718 − 44.171

Step 1

Line up the decimal points to align place-value positions. Subtract the thousandths.

$$\begin{array}{r} 51.718 \\ -44.171 \\ \hline 7 \end{array}$$

Step 2

Subtract the hundredths. Subtract the tenths. Regroup if needed.

$$\begin{array}{r} {\scriptstyle 6\,11} \\ 51.\not{7}\not{1}8 \\ -44.171 \\ \hline 547 \end{array}$$

Step 3

Subtract the ones and tens. Place the decimal point in the difference.

$$\begin{array}{r} {\scriptstyle 4\,11\;\;6\,11} \\ \not{5}\not{1}.\not{7}\not{1}8 \\ -44.171 \\ \hline 7.547 \end{array}$$

Place the decimal point.

So, it took Zoeggeler 7.547 seconds to sled from the third interval to the finish line.

More Examples

C 8 − 5.63

$$\begin{array}{r} {\scriptstyle 9} \\ {\scriptstyle 7\;\,10\,10} \\ \not{8}.\not{0}0 \\ -5.63 \\ \hline 2.37 \end{array}$$

Place 2 zeros to show an equivalent decimal.

D 0.78 − 0.471

$$\begin{array}{r} {\scriptstyle 7\;10} \\ 0.7\not{8}\not{0} \\ -0.471 \\ \hline 0.309 \end{array}$$

E 1.5 − 0.259

$$\begin{array}{r} {\scriptstyle 9} \\ {\scriptstyle 4\,10\,10} \\ 1.\not{5}\not{0}\not{0} \\ -0.259 \\ \hline 1.241 \end{array}$$

Guided Practice

1. Copy each of the steps at the right. Then tell what is happening in each step.

$$\begin{array}{r} 0.327 \\ +0.950 \\ \hline 7 \end{array} \quad \Bigg| \quad \begin{array}{r} 0.327 \\ +0.950 \\ \hline 77 \end{array} \quad \Bigg| \quad \begin{array}{r} {\scriptstyle 1} \\ 0.327 \\ +0.950 \\ \hline 1.277 \end{array}$$

Find the sum or difference.

2. $\begin{array}{r} 7 \\ +0.8 \\ \hline \end{array}$

3. $\begin{array}{r} 16.3 \\ -\;\;4.05 \\ \hline \end{array}$

4. $\begin{array}{r} 21.87 \\ +16.34 \\ \hline \end{array}$

✓5. $\begin{array}{r} \$13.04 \\ -\$\;\;0.95 \\ \hline \end{array}$

✓6. $\begin{array}{r} 2.5 \\ 6.88 \\ +0.19 \\ \hline \end{array}$

7. **TALK Math** **Explain** how to find 6.4 + 3.29 + 2.107.

Technology
Use Harcourt Mega Math, The Number Games, *Buggy Bargains,* Levels E, F, G, H, I.

Independent Practice and Problem Solving

Find the sum or difference.

8. $\begin{array}{r} 0.991 \\ -0.45 \\ \hline \end{array}$

9. $\begin{array}{r} 14.467 \\ +12.312 \\ \hline \end{array}$

10. $\begin{array}{r} 16 \\ -10.1 \\ \hline \end{array}$

11. $\begin{array}{r} \$32.98 \\ +\$18.25 \\ \hline \end{array}$

12. $\begin{array}{r} 5.86 \\ -2.391 \\ \hline \end{array}$

13. $\begin{array}{r} 1.18 \\ +2.039 \\ \hline \end{array}$

14. $\begin{array}{r} 3.704 \\ -1.325 \\ \hline \end{array}$

15. $\begin{array}{r} 0.75 \\ 0.359 \\ +1.4 \\ \hline \end{array}$

16. $\begin{array}{r} 23.002 \\ -\ 1.74 \\ \hline \end{array}$

17. $\begin{array}{r} 9.94 \\ 0.318 \\ +1.283 \\ \hline \end{array}$

Algebra Find a rule for the pattern. Use your rule to find the missing numbers in the pattern.

18. 2.1, 3.3, 4.5, 5.7, ■, 8.1, ■

19. 3.5, 4.6, 4.4, 5.5, 5.3, ■, 6.2, 7.3, ■

20. 4.10, 4.05, 4.00, 3.95, ■, 3.85, ■

21. 0.75, 1.00, 1.25, 1.50, 1.75, 2.00, ■, ■

Solve.

22. Martins Rubenis finished in fifth place in the first luge run at the 2006 Olympics. Rubenis' time was 0.195 second slower than Zoeggeler's time of 51.718 seconds. What was Rubenis' time for the first luge run?

24. When adding 0.3 and 0.15, why do you add 0.3 to 0.1?

23. WRITE Math **What's the Question?** At the 2006 Winter Olympics, one event combined ski jumping and cross-country skiing. After competing in the ski jump, Georg Hettich was in first place with 262.5 points. Magnus Moan was in ninth place with 237.5 points. The answer is 25.0.

Achieving the Standards

25. What is the prime factorization of 24 using exponents? (O━ NS 1.4, p. 132)

26. What number times 90 equals 45,000? (NS 1.0, p. 60)

27. Which two months had the greatest sneaker sales? (Grade 4 SDAP 1.3)

28. **Test Prep** Mark buys a notebook and a pen at the school store. If he pays with a $5.00 bill, how much change should Mark receive?

School Store	
1 notebook	$3.55
12 pencils	$1.59
1 pen	$0.89

A $0.56

B $1.45

C $1.55

D $4.44

 Extra Practice on page 284, Set B

Speedy Skates

Identify the Details

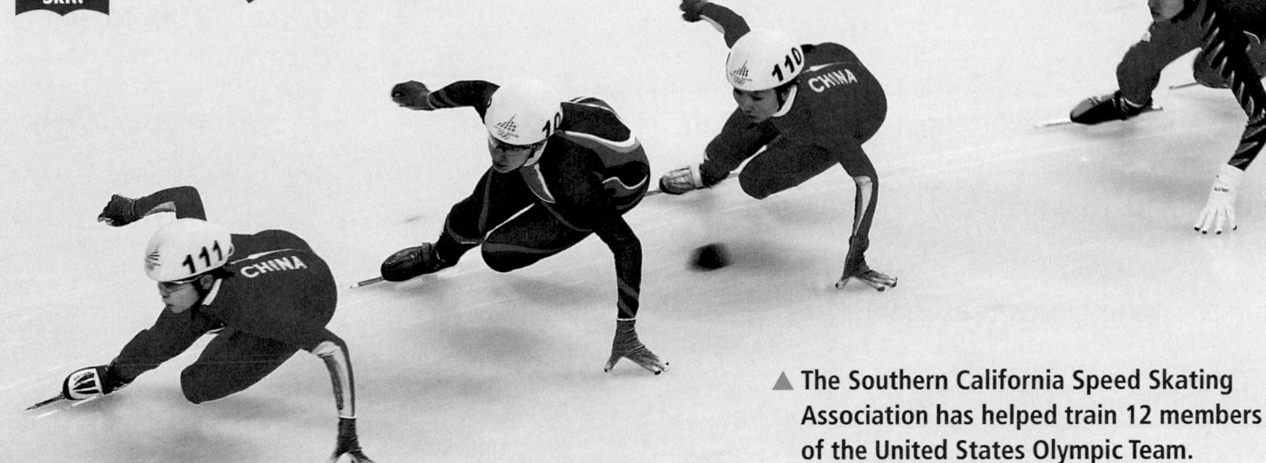

▲ The Southern California Speed Skating Association has helped train 12 members of the United States Olympic Team.

Speed skating is a popular event in the Winter Olympics. Athletes race on ice skates around a frozen track. In the 2006 Winter Olympics, there were three skaters in Race 9 of the ladies' 500-meter heats: K. Novotna, C. Tanaka, and E. Radanova. Their times were, respectively, 46.279, 46.387, and 45.703. How much faster was the first-place time than the third-place time?

Race 9 of Ladies' 500-meter Speed Skating Heats

Skater	Time (in sec)
K. Novotna	46.279
C.Tanaka	46.387
E. Radanova	45.703

Sometimes a problem has more information than you need. To solve the problem correctly, identify the details to answer the problem question. Begin by reading the question carefully. Then ask yourself what details you need to solve the problem. For example:

- Which column contains the skaters' times?
- What is the first-place time—look for the *least* time?
- What is the third-place time—look for the *greatest* time?

Problem Solving Identify the details you need to solve the problem.

1. Solve the problem above.
2. Only the skaters with the top two times in each heat will advance to the next race. Which two skaters will advance to the next race? **Explain** how you know.

LESSON

3 Estimate Sums and Differences

OBJECTIVE: Estimate the sums and differences of decimals to check reasonableness.

Quick Review

Round each number to the nearest tenth.

1. 0.45
2. 3.16
3. 0.284
4. 10.349
5. 6.727

Learn

PROBLEM A singer is recording a CD. He says the recording time is 10.37 minutes. The lengths of the three songs are 3.4 minutes, 2.78 minutes, and 4.19 minutes. How can you tell if his statement is reasonable?

You can estimate to check reasonableness.

Example Estimate. $3.4 + 2.78 + 4.19$

Round to the nearest whole number. Then add.

$$\begin{array}{rcr} 3.4 & \rightarrow & 3 \\ 2.78 & \rightarrow & 3 \\ +4.19 & \rightarrow & +\ 4 \\ \hline & & 10 \end{array}$$

So, the total recording time is about 10 minutes.

- Is the estimate greater than or less than the exact sum? Explain.

Math Idea
When estimating the total cost, it sometimes makes more sense to round up to the next whole dollar.

More Examples

A Nearest tenth

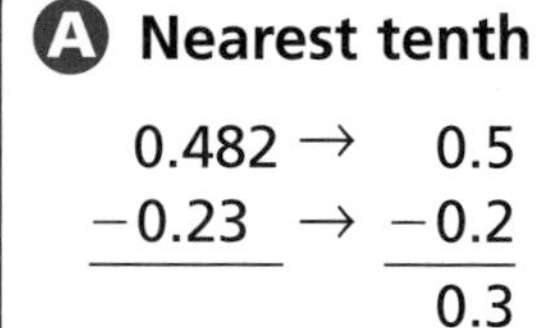

$$\begin{array}{rcr} 0.482 & \rightarrow & 0.5 \\ -0.23 & \rightarrow & -0.2 \\ \hline & & 0.3 \end{array}$$

B Nearest hundredth

$$\begin{array}{rcr} 4.039 & \rightarrow & 4.04 \\ +1.265 & \rightarrow & +1.27 \\ \hline & & 5.31 \end{array}$$

C Next whole dollar

$$\begin{array}{rcr} \$12.45 & \rightarrow & \$13 \\ +\$\ 9.72 & \rightarrow & +\$10 \\ \hline & & \$23 \end{array}$$

Guided Practice

1. Copy and complete the problems at the right to estimate the difference and the sum.

Round to the nearest whole number. Then subtract.

$$\begin{array}{r} 78.7 \\ -\ 2.58 \\ \hline \end{array}$$

Round up to the next whole dollar. Then add.

$$\begin{array}{r} \$42.35 \\ +\$18.79 \\ \hline \end{array}$$

NS 2.1 Add, subtract, multiply, and divide with decimals; add with negative integers; subtract positive integers from negative integers, and verify the reasonableness of the results. *also* **NS 1.1, NS 2.0, MR 2.1, MR 2.3, MR 2.4, MR 2.5, MR 3.1, MR 3.2**

Guided Problem Solving Practice

Tell whether you need an estimate or an exact answer. Then solve the problem.

1. In a baseball-throwing contest, the distances of a person's three throws are added to determine his or her final score. A score of 50 or more is needed to advance to the final round. Carson had throws of 16.35 meters, 18.44 meters, and 17.97 meters. Will Carson advance to the final round?

   First, decide if you need an estimate or an exact answer. You need to determine if Carson's score is greater than or less than 50. So, find an estimate. Then, compare it to 50.

$$\begin{array}{ccccccc} 16.35 & + & 18.44 & + & 17.97 & & \\ \downarrow & & \downarrow & & \downarrow & & \\ 16 & + & 18 & + & \blacksquare & = & \blacksquare \end{array}$$

2. **What if** Carson's second throw had been 16.44 meters instead of 18.44 meters? Would finding an estimate be a good way to determine if Carson should advance to the final round? **Explain.**

3. Jenna's first two throws were 16.64 meters and 15.33 meters. How long does her last throw need to be for her to advance to the final round?

Mixed Applications

For 4 and 5, use the table.

Tip-Toe Ballet Shop	
Item	**Cost**
Tights	\$11.98
Leotard	\$36.50
Ballet Shoes	\$23.48

4. Olivia is buying a pair of ballet shoes and tights. She has a discount coupon for \$10.00 off her total purchase. How much will Olivia pay for the tights and shoes?

5. Jackie has \$60 to spend on clothing for ballet class. She has to buy a leotard and wants to buy either 2 pairs of tights or a pair of shoes. Which items can Jackie buy?

6. Joe's backpack weighs 6.5 kilograms. Tino's backpack is 2.4 kilograms heavier than Joe's. Rod's backpack is 1.7 kilograms lighter than Joe's. About how much do the three backpacks weigh in all?

7. **WRITE Math** Wayne is buying wood trim that goes all around his room. The wood trim comes in pieces that are 12, 14, or 16 feet long. **Explain** how to find the number of feet of trim Wayne should buy if the room's size is 10 feet by 14 feet.

Extra Practice

Set A Round each number to the place of the underlined digit. (pp. 272–273)

1. $0.4\underline{6}3$ **2.** $7.\underline{2}58$ **3.** $\underline{0}.812$ **4.** $52.\underline{9}46$ **5.** $16.30\underline{2}$

6. $\underline{2}.055$ **7.** $137.\underline{9}91$ **8.** $0.1\underline{7}6$ **9.** $59.2\underline{0}9$ **10.** $8.\underline{6}57$

Name the place to which each number was rounded.

11. 0.738 to 0.74 **12.** 16.49 to 16.5 **13.** 29.516 to 29.52

Set B Estimate. Then find the sum or difference. (pp. 274–275)

1. $\begin{array}{r} 0.27 \\ +1.43 \\ \hline \end{array}$ **2.** $\begin{array}{r} 15.86 \\ -\ \ 9.72 \\ \hline \end{array}$ **3.** $\begin{array}{r} \$23.98 \\ +\$\ \ 2.45 \\ \hline \end{array}$ **4.** $\begin{array}{r} 0.92 \\ -0.437 \\ \hline \end{array}$ **5.** $\begin{array}{r} \$32.09 \\ +\$15.78 \\ \hline \end{array}$

6. $0.539 - 0.268$ **7.** $41.63 + 9.801$ **8.** $\$60.75 - \$10.09$

Set C Estimate by rounding. (pp. 278–279)

1. $\begin{array}{r} 0.863 \\ +0.27\ \ \\ \hline \end{array}$ **2.** $\begin{array}{r} 0.93 \\ -0.184 \\ \hline \end{array}$ **3.** $\begin{array}{r} 7 \\ +2.506 \\ \hline \end{array}$ **4.** $\begin{array}{r} 21.32 \\ -\ \ 4.19 \\ \hline \end{array}$ **5.** $\begin{array}{r} 1.94 \\ +2.63 \\ \hline \end{array}$

6. $\begin{array}{r} \$26.72 \\ +\$\ \ 9.45 \\ \hline \end{array}$ **7.** $\begin{array}{r} 0.397 \\ +0.265 \\ \hline \end{array}$ **8.** $\begin{array}{r} \$40.05 \\ -\$12.25 \\ \hline \end{array}$ **9.** $\begin{array}{r} 0.508 \\ -0.126 \\ \hline \end{array}$ **10.** $\begin{array}{r} 1.72 \\ -1.064 \\ \hline \end{array}$

11. $2.93 + 0.8 + 1.76$ **12.** $17.1 - 6.289$ **13.** $9.362 + 0.745$

14. Angie's total grocery bill is \$36.29. She pays for the groceries with a \$50-bill. How much change should she receive?

15. Simon scored 7.23, 6.94, and 8.32 points for his three dives at the competition. What was his total score for the three dives?

Set D Use mental math to find the sum or difference. (pp. 280–281)

1. $\begin{array}{r} 3.34 \\ +5.20 \\ \hline \end{array}$ **2.** $\begin{array}{r} 5.6 \\ -1.2 \\ \hline \end{array}$ **3.** $\begin{array}{r} 2.3 \\ 0.1 \\ +1.6 \\ \hline \end{array}$ **4.** $\begin{array}{r} 17.50 \\ -\ \ 6.25 \\ \hline \end{array}$ **5.** $\begin{array}{r} 18 \\ +\ \ 4.93 \\ \hline \end{array}$

6. $\begin{array}{r} 9.3 \\ +0.7 \\ \hline \end{array}$ **7.** $\begin{array}{r} 8.75 \\ +2.50 \\ \hline \end{array}$ **8.** $\begin{array}{r} \$148.19 \\ -\$\ \ 38.00 \\ \hline \end{array}$ **9.** $\begin{array}{r} \$16.79 \\ +\$\ \ 0.21 \\ \hline \end{array}$ **10.** $\begin{array}{r} 8.00 \\ -5.99 \\ \hline \end{array}$

11. Colleen spent \$3.20 for a magazine and \$5.80 for a book at the bookstore. How much more did the book cost than the magazine?

12. In March, 4.32 inches of rain fell in the city. In May, 1.5 more inches of rain fell than in March. How many inches of rain fell in the city in May?

CD ROM **Technology**
Use Harcourt Mega Math, Fraction Action, *Number Line Mine*, Level R.

PRACTICE GAME

RIDE THE COURSE

Racers
2 players

Equipment
- Addition and subtraction cards
- 3-section spinner labeled 1–3
- 2 different game pieces

START

FINISH

Food Station

FLAT TIRE
Lose a turn.

FIRST OVER THE MOUNTAIN
Take an extra turn.

ENERGY BOOST!
Take an extra turn.

CRASH
Lose a turn.

Go!

- Players shuffle the game cards and place them facedown in a stack.
- Each player selects a game piece and places it behind *START*.
- The first player selects a card and performs the addition or subtraction indicated. The second player checks the result.
- If the result is correct, the first player spins the spinner and moves the indicated number of spaces.
- Players reverse roles. Play continues as players take turns selecting a card.
- The first player to reach *FINISH* wins!

 Chapter 11 Review/Test

Check Concepts

1. Explain how to round to the nearest tenth to estimate $3.72 - 1.58$. (NS 1.1, p. 272)
2. Explain how to use mental math to find $4.25 + 2.5 + 1.25$. (NS 2.0, p. 280)

Check Skills

Round each number to the place of the underlined digit. (NS 1.1, pp. 272–273)

3. $0.2\underline{7}6$ **4.** $3.\underline{0}15$ **5.** $26.\underline{8}47$ **6.** $\underline{0}.521$ **7.** $6.2\underline{2}3$

Find the sum or difference. (NS 2.1, pp. 274–277)

7. $\begin{array}{r} 0.382 \\ +0.199 \\ \hline \end{array}$ **8.** $\begin{array}{r} 6.92 \\ -3.254 \\ \hline \end{array}$ **9.** $\begin{array}{r} 9.33 \\ +4.082 \\ \hline \end{array}$ **10.** $\begin{array}{r} 25.36 \\ -\ 7.28 \\ \hline \end{array}$

11. $\begin{array}{r} 0.83 \\ +0.264 \\ \hline \end{array}$ **12.** $\begin{array}{r} 5.21 \\ -1.74 \\ \hline \end{array}$ **13.** $\begin{array}{r} 18.93 \\ +17.68 \\ \hline \end{array}$ **14.** $\begin{array}{r} 6.3 \\ -2.59 \\ \hline \end{array}$

Estimate. Then find the sum or difference. (NS 1.1, pp. 278–279)

15. $\begin{array}{r} 2.93 \\ +5.48 \\ \hline \end{array}$ **16.** $\begin{array}{r} 11.78 \\ -\ 5.62 \\ \hline \end{array}$ **17.** $\begin{array}{r} \$35.49 \\ +\$\ 4.82 \\ \hline \end{array}$ **18.** $\begin{array}{r} 1.87 \\ -0.624 \\ \hline \end{array}$

Find the sum or difference. Use mental math. (NS 2.1, pp. 280–281)

19. $\begin{array}{r} 8.75 \\ +3.50 \\ \hline \end{array}$ **20.** $\begin{array}{r} 0.23 \\ +2.77 \\ \hline \end{array}$ **21.** $\begin{array}{r} 3.560 \\ +4.103 \\ \hline \end{array}$ **22.** $\begin{array}{r} 4.50 \\ -2.25 \\ \hline \end{array}$

Check Problem Solving

Solve. (NS 2.1, MR 2.5, pp. 282–283)

23. Tom wants to buy a sandwich for \$3.75 and some milk for \$1.85. He has \$6.00. Does he have enough money?

24. Rita scored 6.38 points and 5.29 points in an essay competition. She needs a total of 15 points to advance to the next round. How many more points does she need?

25. WRITE Math **Explain** why writing an equivalent decimal helps you find the difference of $4 - 1.83$. What is the difference?

GO ONLINE Technology Use *Online Assessment.*

Enrich • Addition Properties and Decimals

What's the Total?

You can find a decimal sum mentally by using the Commutative Property or Associative Property of Addition.

Example

Mr. Anderson stops at the grocery store after work. He has $15. He wants to buy chicken for $6.25, cheese for $5.15, and lettuce for $2.75. Does he have enough money to pay for the groceries?

Find the total cost of the groceries.

Use the Commutative Property.

Think: $0.25 + $0.75 = $1.	$6.25 + $5.15 + $2.75
Use the Commutative Property.	$6.25 + $2.75 + $5.15
Add. Use mental math.	$9 + $5.15 = $14.15

The total cost of the groceries is $14.15.

Compare $14.15 to $15. So, Mr. Anderson has enough money.

Remember:
The Commutative Property states that if the order of addends is changed, the sum stays the same.

The Associative Property states that addends can be grouped in different ways, and the sum does not change.

Another Example

Use the Associative Property.

	15.4 + (0.6 + 10.8)
Think: 0.4 + 0.6 = 1.	(15.4 + 0.6) + 10.8
Add. Use mental math.	16 + 10.8 = 26.8

Try It

Use the Commutative or Associative Property to find the sum.

1. $12.50 + $4.29 + $5.50
2. 36.3 + (12.7 + 12.1)
3. (56.3 + 8.9) + 121.1
4. 0.91 + 1.15 + 2.09
5. $5.65 + $5.18 + $4.35
6. 5.3 + (1.25 + 12.7)
7. 5.55 + 4.32 + 5.45
8. (3.25 + 6.2) + 1.75
9. 10.2 + 10.5 + 9.8
10. **Challenge** Find 1.15 + 11.8 + 3.85 + 9.2.

Think About It

WRITE Math **Explain** how you can use the properties to find decimal sums mentally.

 Achieving the Standards

Chapters 1–11

Algebra and Functions

1. What is the value of y? (Grade 4 O—π AF 1.2)

$$(24 \div 2) \times (6 - 2) = y$$

A 3

B 8

C 16

D 48

2. Karyn is reading a book for a report due in 4 weeks. To finish her book, she needs to read 87 pages each week. Which equation uses the Distributive Property to show the number of pages Karyn has left to read? (AF 1.3)

A $4 \times 87 = (4 + 80) \times (4 + 7)$

B $4 + 87 = (4 \times 80) + (4 \times 7)$

C $4 \times 87 = (4 \times 80) + (4 \times 7)$

D $4 + 87 = (4 \times 80) + 7$

3. Look at the equation below.

$$■ = ▲ - 7$$

If ▲ $= 21$, what is ■? (Grade 4 O—π AF 1.5)

A 3

B 14

C 28

D 142

4. WRITE Math The letters A and B stand for numbers and $A = B$.

Does $A + 20 = B + 20$?

Explain why or why not. (Grade 4 O—π AF 2.1)

Statistics, Data Analysis, and Probability

Test Tip **Get the information you need.**

See item 5. Find the height of the plant each week. Then find the difference from one week to the next. Identify which two weeks in which the plant grew the most.

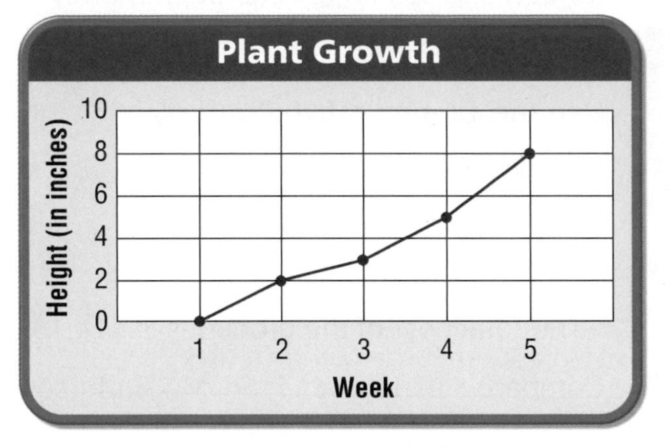

5. Between which two weeks did the plant grow the most? (Grade 4 SDAP 1.3)

A Weeks 1 and 2 **C** Weeks 3 and 4

B Weeks 2 and 3 **D** Weeks 4 and 5

6. Which type of graph would be best to show the number of votes for each person in an election? (SDAP 1.2)

A circle graph **C** pictograph

B bar graph **D** line graph

7. WRITE Math How do the medians for the two data sets shown below compare? **Explain** how you can use median to compare two sets of data. (SDAP 1.1)

Data set 1: 72, 89, 94, 81, 97
Data set 2: 86, 87, 92, 87, 86

Number Sense

8. What is the prime factorization of 40? (O-n NS 1.4)

   A $2^2 \times 4$
   B $2^3 \times 5$
   C $3^2 \times 5$
   D $5^2 \times 2$

9. The table below shows how far from school each student lives.

Distance to School	
Student	**Miles**
Randi	$1\frac{3}{4}$
Matthew	$2\frac{2}{3}$
Lindsay	$1\frac{7}{8}$
Jordan	$3\frac{1}{2}$

How much closer to school does Lindsay live than Jordan? (O-n NS 2.3)

   A $2\frac{5}{8}$ miles
   B $2\frac{3}{8}$ miles
   C $1\frac{5}{8}$ miles
   D $1\frac{3}{8}$ miles

10. Which letter on the number line best identifies the location of 0.6? (O-n NS 1.5)

   A L
   B M
   C N
   D O

11. WRITE Math **Explain** how to find the number represented by the prime factorization shown below. (O-n NS 1.4)

$$2^2 \times 3$$

Measurement and Geometry

12. Which figure below has 6 vertices? (Grade 4 MG 3.6)

A 
C 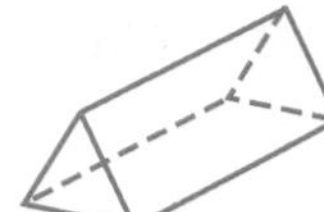
B 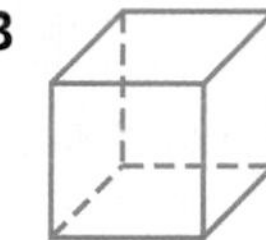
D 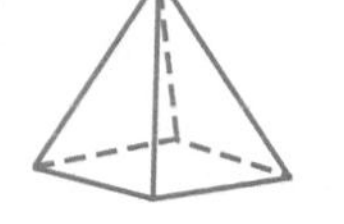

13. A line segment has point at (4,2) and (9,2). What is the length of the line segment? (Grade 4 O-n MG 2.2)

   A 4 units
   B 5 units
   C 6 units
   D 7 units

14. WRITE Math Look at the circle with center *O*. Name a diameter of the circle.

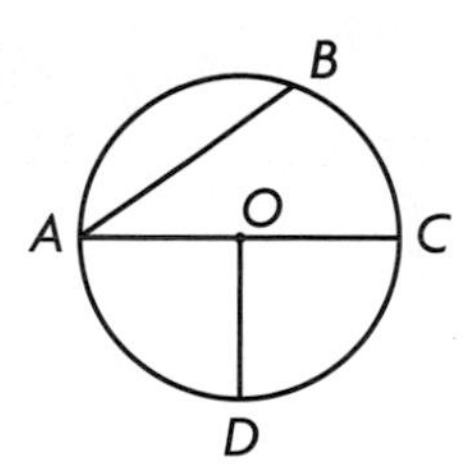

Explain how you know that the segment you named is a diameter. (Grade 4 MG 3.2)

12 Multiply Decimals

The Big Idea Multiplication of decimals is based on place value and multiplication with whole numbers.

Investigate

Some 5th-grade classes will be visiting Yosemite National Park. While at the park, each class will participate in an educational program on the park's natural history. Choose two classes and show how to find the total cost to participate in the program.

Students Attending the Yosemite Field Trip

Teacher	Class Size
Mr. Thompson	29
Ms. Jenkins	27
Mrs. Sawyer	32
Mr. Abrams	25
Ms. Morton	27
Cost per Student = $2.86	

CALIFORNIA FAST FACT

Yosemite Falls is the 3rd-highest measured waterfall in North America. The distance from the top of the upper falls to the base of the lower falls is 2,425 feet.

GO ONLINE Technology
Student pages are available in the Student eBook.

Show What You Know

Check your understanding of important skills needed for success in Chapter 12.

▶ Estimate Products

Estimate the product.

1. $\begin{array}{r} 57 \\ \times\ 4 \\ \hline \end{array}$ **2.** $\begin{array}{r} 32 \\ \times\ 8 \\ \hline \end{array}$ **3.** $\begin{array}{r} 74 \\ \times\ 5 \\ \hline \end{array}$ **4.** $\begin{array}{r} 426 \\ \times\ 7 \\ \hline \end{array}$

5. 926×2 **6.** 268×9 **7.** 97×3 **8.** 629×8

9. 83×5 **10.** 317×3 **11.** 692×6 **12.** 207×4

▶ Multiply by 2-Digit Numbers

Find the product.

13. $\begin{array}{r} 94 \\ \times\ 3 \\ \hline \end{array}$ **14.** $\begin{array}{r} \$47 \\ \times\ 5 \\ \hline \end{array}$ **15.** $\begin{array}{r} 83 \\ \times\ 7 \\ \hline \end{array}$ **16.** $\begin{array}{r} 32 \\ \times 29 \\ \hline \end{array}$

17. $\begin{array}{r} 18 \\ \times 64 \\ \hline \end{array}$ **18.** $\begin{array}{r} 92 \\ \times 23 \\ \hline \end{array}$ **19.** $\begin{array}{r} 76 \\ \times\ 8 \\ \hline \end{array}$ **20.** $\begin{array}{r} \$67 \\ \times\ 54 \\ \hline \end{array}$

21. 72×9 **22.** $\$78 \times 27$ **23.** 56×43 **24.** 25×81

▶ Multiply Money

Multiply.

25. $\begin{array}{r} \$0.25 \\ \times\ \ 6 \\ \hline \end{array}$ **26.** $\begin{array}{r} \$0.05 \\ \times\ \ 4 \\ \hline \end{array}$ **27.** $\begin{array}{r} \$0.10 \\ \times\ \ 5 \\ \hline \end{array}$ **28.** $\begin{array}{r} \$0.50 \\ \times\ \ 9 \\ \hline \end{array}$

29. $\$0.10 \times 3$ **30.** $\$0.01 \times 8$ **31.** $\$0.25 \times 7$ **32.** $\$0.05 \times 9$

VOCABULARY POWER

CHAPTER VOCABULARY

decimal
decimal point
factor
hundredth
tenth

WARM-UP WORDS

factor a number multiplied by another number to find a product

tenth one of ten equal parts

hundredth one of one hundred equal parts

LESSON 1 HANDS ON

Model Multiplication by a Whole Number

OBJECTIVE: Use models to multiply whole numbers and decimals.

Quick Review

1. 15×5
2. 22×8
3. 86×3
4. 64×6
5. 71×9

Investigate

Materials ■ hundredths model ■ color pencils

You can use models to help you multiply decimals by whole numbers.

A Find 3×0.61. Use the hundredths model. Shade 0.61 three times. Use a different color each time.

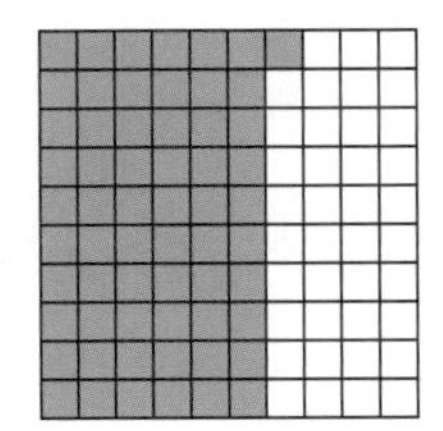

B Count the number of shaded hundredths. How many hundredths are there?

C Write 3×0.61 as repeated addition. Find the sum. How does the sum compare to your answer in B?

D Write the multiplication equation and the addition equation that represent your model.

Draw Conclusions

1. What is the value of one square in the hundredths model? What is the value of one column or one row?
2. How is multiplying 3×0.61 like multiplying 3×61?
3. Is the product 3×0.61 greater than or less than 3? Explain why.
4. **Synthesis** In what other ways can you express the product 3×0.61?

NS 2.1 Add, subtract, multiply, and divide with decimals; add with negative integers; subtract positive integers from negative integers; and verify the reasonableness of the results. *also* **NS 1.0, MR 2.0, MR 2.3, MR 2.4, MR 3.2**

Connect

You can write an equation for your model.

Step 1

Find 4 × 0.27.

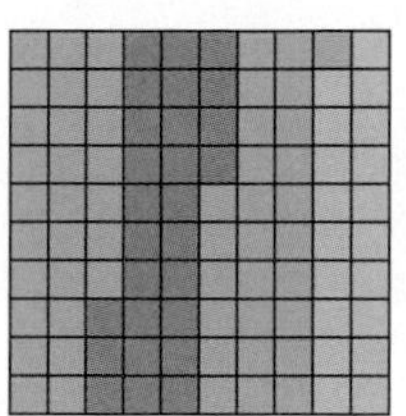
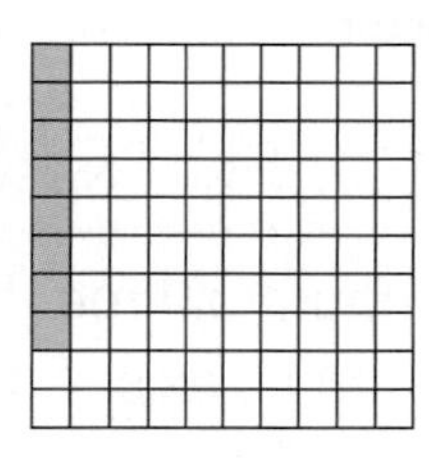

Use hundredths models. Shade 0.27 four times, using a different color each time. Count the shaded number of colored squares. There are 108 hundredths, or 1 whole and 8 hundredths.

Step 2

Record.

$$\begin{array}{r} \overset{2}{0.2}7 \\ \times \quad 4 \\ \hline 1.08 \end{array}$$

Use the model to place the decimal point. 4 × 0.27 is 1 whole and 8 hundredths, so place the decimal point after 1.

Practice

Copy and complete the multiplication expression for each model. Find the product.

1. 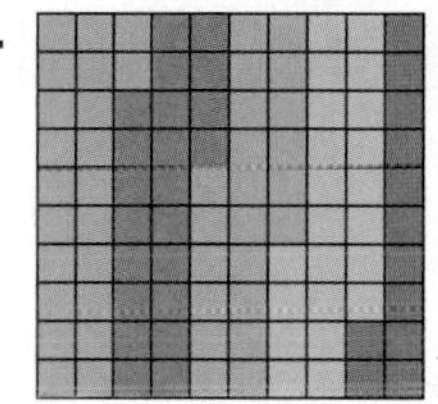 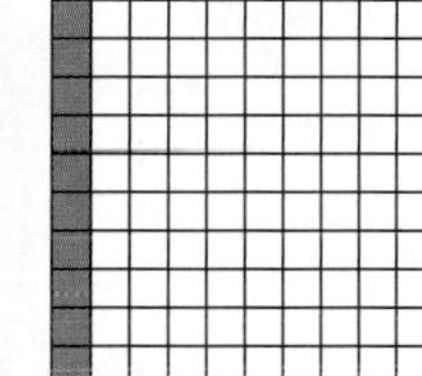

 × 0.22

2. 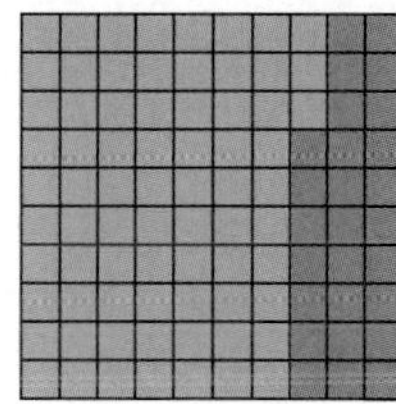 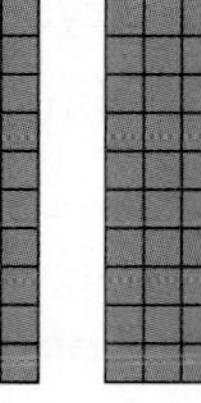 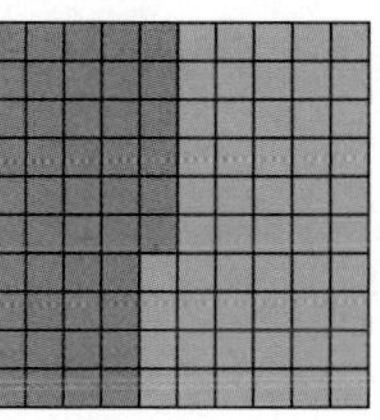 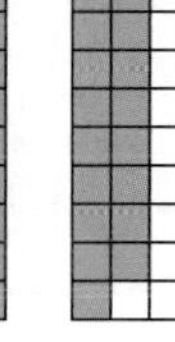

3 × ■

Use hundredths models to find the product.

3. 4 × 0.42 **4.** 0.13 × 5 **5.** 3 × 0.36 **6.** 0.33 × 6

7. 2 × 0.28 **8.** 0.48 × 5 **9.** 5 × 0.92 **10.** 8 × 0.04

Find the product.

11. 0.44 × 3 **12.** 0.67 × 4 **13.** 6 × 0.45 **14.** 2 × 0.96

15. 0.64 × 2 **16.** 0.51 × 3 **17.** 0.39 × 4 **18.** 7 × 0.61

19. 6 × 0.19 **20.** 0.92 × 3 **21.** 4 × 0.73 **22.** 5 × 0.17

23. WRITE Math **Explain** why the product of a decimal between 0 and 1 and a whole number greater than 1 is a number that is between both factors.

LESSON 2

ALGEBRA

Patterns in Decimal Factors and Products

OBJECTIVE: Use patterns in decimal factors to find products.

Quick Review

1. 8×1
2. 8×10
3. 8×100
4. $8 \times 1{,}000$
5. $8 \times 10{,}000$

Learn

PROBLEM The length of a day is the amount of time that it takes for a planet to make a complete rotation on its axis. A true Earth day is about 23.93 hours. A day on Mars is about 24.62 hours on Earth. How many hours are in 1,000 days on Earth? How many hours are in 1,000 days on Mars?

You can use basic facts and place-value patterns to find products.

Example

Earth		Mars
$23.93 \times 1 = 23.93$	1 day	$24.62 \times 1 = 24.62$
$23.93 \times 10 = 239.3$	10 days	$24.62 \times 10 = 246.2$
$23.93 \times 100 = 2{,}393.$	100 days	$24.62 \times 100 = 2{,}462.$
$23.93 \times 1{,}000 = 23{,}930.$	1,000 days	$24.62 \times 1{,}000 = 24{,}620.$

So, on Earth, there are about 23,930 hours in 1,000 days. On Mars, there are about 24,620 Earth hours in 1,000 days.

Math Idea
The decimal point moves one place to the right when you multiply by 10, two places to the right when you multiply by 100, and three places to the right when you multiply by 1,000.

More Examples

A

$6.75 × 1 = $6.75
$6.75 × 10 = $67.50
$6.75 × 100 = $675.00
$6.75 × 1,000 = $6,750.00
$6.75 × 10,000 = $67,500.00

B

$0.769 \times 1 = 0.769$
$0.769 \times 10 = 7.69$
$0.769 \times 100 = 76.9$
$0.769 \times 1{,}000 = 769$
$0.769 \times 10{,}000 = 7{,}690$

C

$0.004 \times 1 = 0.004$
$0.004 \times 10 = 0.04$
$0.004 \times 100 = 0.4$
$0.004 \times 1{,}000 = 4$
$0.004 \times 10{,}000 = 40$

Guided Practice

Copy and complete to find the missing products.

1. $1 \times 0.4 = 0.4$
   $10 \times 0.4 = 4$
   $100 \times 0.4 = 40$
   $1{,}000 \times 0.4 = ■$

2. $1 \times 9.81 = 9.81$
   $10 \times 9.81 = ■$
   $100 \times 9.81 = 981$
   $1{,}000 \times 9.81 = ■$

3. 1 × $0.07 = $0.07
   10 × $0.07 = ■
   100 × $0.07 = $7.00
   1,000 × $0.07 = ■

NS 2.1 Add, subtract, multiply, and divide with decimals; add with negative integers; subtract positive integers from negative integers; and verify reasonableness of the results. *also* **NS 1.0, NS 2.0, MR 2.3, MR 2.4, MR 3.2**

Use patterns to find the product.

4. 3.19×1; 3.19×10; 3.19×100; $3.19 \times 1{,}000$ (dollars: $\$3.19$)

5. 0.298×1; 0.298×10; 0.298×100; $0.298 \times 1{,}000$

6. 0.005×1; 0.005×10; 0.005×100; $0.005 \times 1{,}000$

7. 1.017×1; 1.017×10; 1.017×100; $1.017 \times 1{,}000$

8. TALK Math **Explain** why the product 2.78×10 is the same as the product 0.278×100.

Independent Practice and Problem Solving

Use patterns to find the products.

9. 9.35×10; 9.35×100; $9.35 \times 1{,}000$

10. 0.002×10; 0.002×100; $0.002 \times 1{,}000$

11. 3.105×10; 3.105×100; $3.105 \times 1{,}000$

12. $\$12.65 \times 100$; $\$12.65 \times 1{,}000$; $\$12.65 \times 10{,}000$

Multiply each number by 10, 100, 1,000, and 10,000.

13. 1.146
14. \$6.32
15. 33.52
16. 0.009
17. 0.78
18. 0.1
19. \$0.50
20. 483.2
21. 2.14
22. \$81.75

Find the value of n.

23. $10 \times 16.49 = n$
24. $\$3.24 \times n = \$324.00$
25. $1.41 \times n = 14{,}100$
26. $n \times 0.095 = 95$

USE DATA For 27–29, use the table.

27. How many hours are in 10 days on Neptune?

28. How many hours are in 1,000 days on Saturn?

29. **Reasoning** How many more hours are in 100 days on Uranus than in 100 days on Jupiter?

30. WRITE Math **Explain** how you know where to place the decimal point in 75.95×10.

Lengths of Planet Days

Planet	Length of Day (in Earth hours)
Jupiter	9.8
Saturn	10.2
Uranus	15.5
Neptune	15.8

Achieving the Standards

31. Kai drew two lines that intersected and formed right angles. What kind of lines did he draw? (Grade 4 MG 3.1)

32. If a cherry pie has about 250 cherries, about how many cherries are in 16 pies? (NS 1.0, p. 70)

33. The width of a field is 80 feet. Its perimeter is 480 feet. What is the length of the field? (Hint: perimeter $= 2 \times$ length $+ 2 \times$ width). (Grade 4 MG 1.4)

34. A car gets 22.8 miles per gallon of gas. How many miles can it go on 100 gallons of gas?

A 2.28 miles
B 22.8 miles
C 228 miles
D 2,280 miles

Extra Practice on page 308, Set A

LESSON 3 HANDS ON

Model Multiplication by a Decimal

OBJECTIVE: Model multiplication by decimals.

Quick Review

1. 4×0.3
2. 1.2×7
3. 6×21.5
4. 0.08×10
5. 100×75.1

Investigate

Materials ■ grid paper ■ color pencils

You can use a model to multiply decimals.

Find 0.7×0.4.

A Draw a square on grid paper. Divide the square into 10 equal columns.

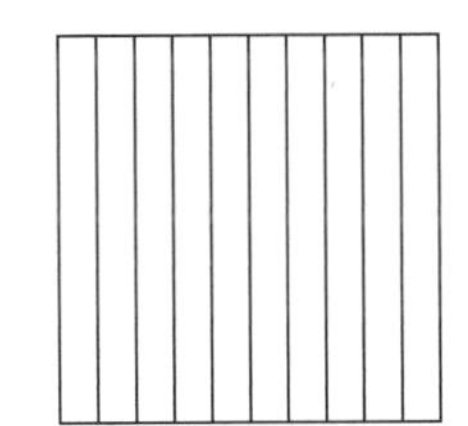

B Use a color pencil to shade 7 columns to represent the first factor.

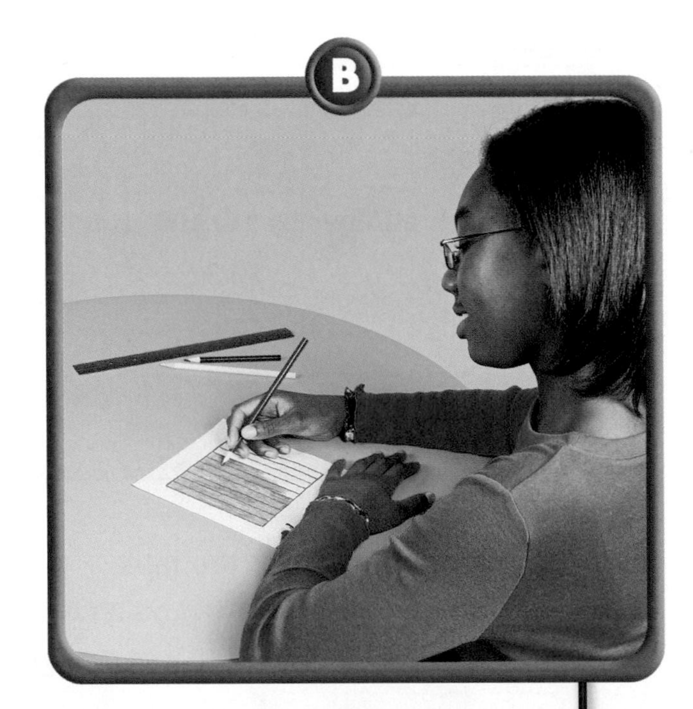

C Divide the square into 10 equal rows to make 100 equal parts. Use a different color to shade 4 parts of 7 columns to show the second factor.

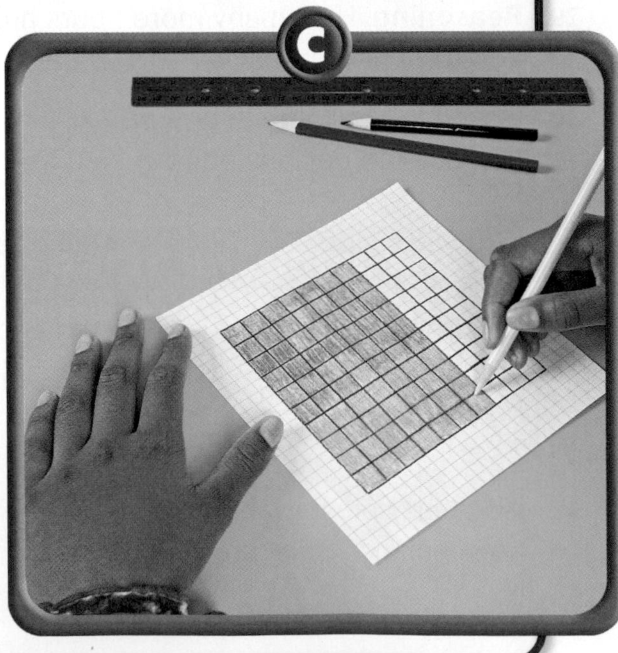

D Count the squares in the area in which the color shading overlaps. Record your answer. Write the equation that represents the model.

Draw Conclusions

1. Which product will be greater: 0.8×0.9 or 0.8×0.10? Explain your reasoning.
2. If the model represents one whole, how much does one column or one row represent? How much does each square represent?
3. How does using a model to multiply two decimals help to show the area of a rectangle?
4. **Comprehension** Why is the part of the model representing the product less than either factor?

NS 2.1 Add, subtract, multiply, and divide with decimals; add with negative integers; subtract positive integers from negative integers; and verify the reasonableness of the results. *also* **NS 1.0, MR 2.0, MR 2.3, MR 2.4, MR 3.2**

Connect

You can model multiplication for decimals greater than 1.

A **Find 1.3 × 0.3.**

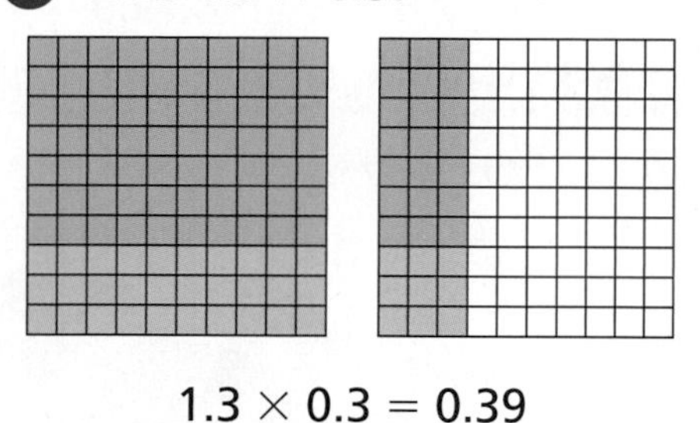

$1.3 \times 0.3 = 0.39$

B **Find 1.9 × 0.6.**

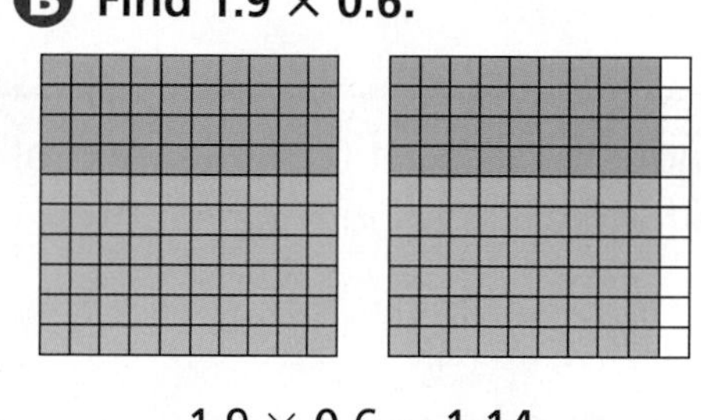

$1.9 \times 0.6 = 1.14$

Count the squares in the area in which the color shading overlaps to find the product.

TALK Math

How many digits do you think will follow the decimal for the product 1.2×1.1? Explain your thinking.

Practice

Use the model to find the product.

1. 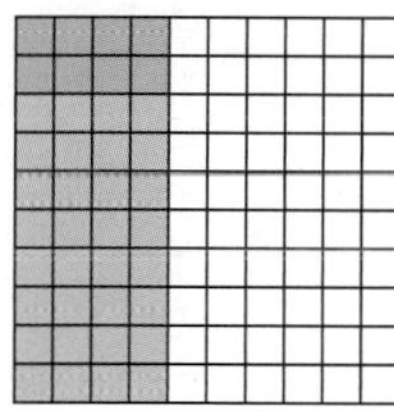

0.4×0.8

2. 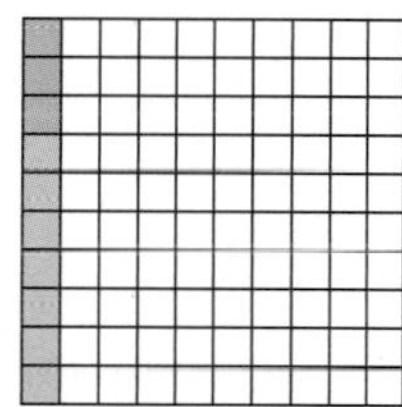

0.1×0.7

3. 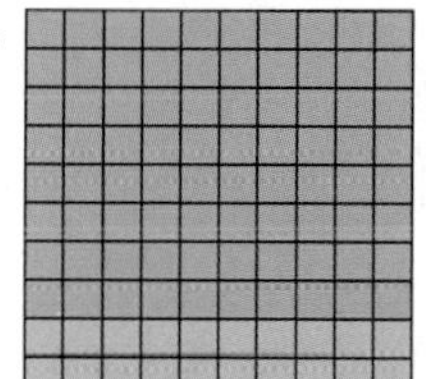

1.4×0.2

Make a model to find the product.

4. 0.3×0.2
5. 0.2×0.4
6. 0.6×0.9
7. 0.6×0.8
8. 0.9×0.1
9. 0.5×0.9
10. 1.5×0.3
11. 1.1×0.6
12. 1.2×0.4
13. 1.6×0.5

Algebra **Find the value of *n*.**

14. $0.5 \times 0.6 = n$
15. $0.7 \times n = 0.49$
16. $0.6 \times 0.6 = n$
17. $n \times 0.1 = 0.02$

Find the product.

18. 0.8×0.3
19. 0.2×0.7
20. 0.9×0.5
21. 0.3×0.6
22. 0.9×0.9
23. 0.9×0.8
24. 1.7×0.3
25. 1.5×0.5
26. 1.4×0.7
27. 1.3×0.8

28. **WRITE Math** **Explain** why you need a zero between the decimal point and the 1 in the product of the equation $0.1 \times 0.1 = 0.01$.

LESSON 4

Estimate Products

OBJECTIVE: Estimate products of decimals.

Quick Review

Round to the nearest whole number.

1. 2.3
2. 5.7
3. 7.8
4. 9.9
5. 11.4

Learn

PROBLEM A California condor eats about 0.91 kilogram of food each day. About how much food will a condor eat in 4 weeks, or 28 days?

▲ The head of a California condor is bald and pink. When the condor is scared or excited, its head turns bright red.

Example 1 Use compatible numbers. Estimate. 0.91×28

Step 1

Use compatible numbers.

0.91×28
↓ ↓
0.9×30

Step 2

Multiply as with whole numbers.

$$\begin{array}{r} 30 \\ \times\ 0.9 \\ \hline 270 \end{array}$$

Step 3

Use whole numbers to place the decimal point.

$$\begin{array}{r} 30 \\ \times\ 1 \\ \hline 30 \end{array} \rightarrow \begin{array}{r} 30 \\ \times\ 0.9 \\ \hline 27.0 \end{array}$$

Use the product 30×1 to place the decimal point in the estimate.

So, a condor eats about 27 kilograms of food in 4 weeks.

One kilogram is equal to about 2.205 pounds. About how many pounds of food does a condor eat in 4 weeks?

Example 2 Round to the nearest whole number. Estimate. 27×2.205

Step 1

Round to the nearest whole numbers.

27×2.205
↓ ↓
27×2

Step 2

Multiply.

$$\begin{array}{r} 27 \\ \times\ 2 \\ \hline 54 \end{array}$$

So, a condor eats about 54 pounds of food in 4 weeks.

Remember

Overestimate cost by rounding money amounts up to the next whole dollar amount.

More Examples Estimate.

A Rounding

3.65×2.34
↓ ↓
$4 \times 2 = 8$

B Compatible numbers

7.2×4.8
↓ ↓
$7 \times 5 = 35$

C Rounding money

$46 \times \$3.41$
↓ ↓
$50 \times \$4 = \$200$

NS 1.1 Estimate, round, and manipulate very large and very small numbers. *also* **MR 2.0, MR 2.2, MR 2.3, MR 2.4, MR 3.0, MR 3.2**

Guided Practice

Find the missing number or numbers in the estimate.

1. 2.6×1.8 Estimate: $3 \times ■ = 6$
2. 8.9×8.7 Estimate: $■ \times ■ = 81$
3. 2.39×3.1 Estimate: $2.4 \times ■ = 7.2$
4. $\$6.61 \times 52$ Estimate: $■ \times 50 = \$350$

Estimate the product.

5. 7.9×2.2
6. 13.1×6.5
7. $6 \times \$4.25$
8. 2.15×3.92
9. $\$89.73 \times 12$
10. TALK Math **Explain** how you know that 27 is an overestimate for 8.78×2.7.

Independent Practice and Problem Solving

Estimate the product.

11. 4.2×6.8
12. 5.3×7.4
13. $\$7.85 \times 5$
14. $\$2.98 \times 6$
15. 2.9×6.6
16. 21.13×9
17. $8 \times \$14.10$
18. 3.66×8.12
19. 3.7×19.5
20. $\$13.74 \times 19$

USE DATA For 21–24, use the table.

21. A condor has a wingspan that is about 2.6 times as great as the greatest wingspan of a peregrine falcon. Estimate the wingspan of the condor.

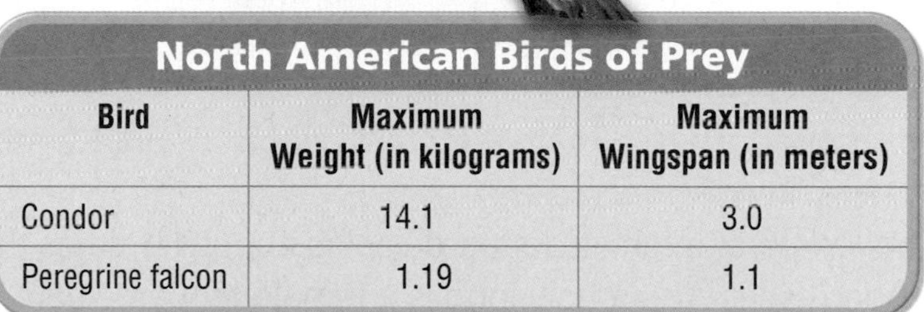

22. The female peregrine falcon is heavier than the male. The average male peregrine falcon has a weight that is about 0.67 times as great as the maximum weight. What is the average weight of a male peregrine falcon?

North American Birds of Prey

Bird	Maximum Weight (in kilograms)	Maximum Wingspan (in meters)
Condor	14.1	3.0
Peregrine falcon	1.19	1.1

23. **Pose a Problem** Use the data in the table to write an estimation problem. Have a classmate solve the problem.

24. WRITE Math **Explain** whether the answer given is reasonable or unreasonable.

$$21.4 \times 6.71 = 114.265$$

Achieving the Standards

25. Lily made 7 stacks of paper with 125 sheets of paper in each stack. How many sheets of paper did Lily use? (NS 1.0, p. 66)

26. Jorie scored 94, 89, 85, 87, and 88 on her math tests. What was Jorie's median score? (Grade 4 SDAP 1.2)

27. $0.8 \times 500 =$ (Key NS 2.1, p. 294)

28. Dave sold 22 snow cones for $1.75 each. Which expression gives the closest estimate for the amount of money Dave made selling snow cones?

A $20 \times \$1.00$

B $22 \times \$1.00$

C $22 \times \$2.00$

D $30 \times \$2.00$

Extra Practice on page 308, Set B

LESSON 5

Place the Decimal Point

OBJECTIVE: Place the decimal point in decimal multiplication.

Quick Review

Round to the nearest whole number.

1. 7.4 **2.** 22.8
3. 0.63 **4.** 5.59
5. 3.398

Learn

PROBLEM Leopard seals and elephant seals live on island coasts between southern Australia and Antarctica. An average male leopard seal is about 2.8 meters in length. An average male elephant seal is about 1.5 times as long. About what length is a male elephant seal?

▲ Leopard seals prey upon penguins and young seals of other species. Elephant seals are fiercely territorial and protect their home and their young.

ONE WAY Use estimation.

Multiply. 1.5×2.8

Step 1

Round each factor to estimate.

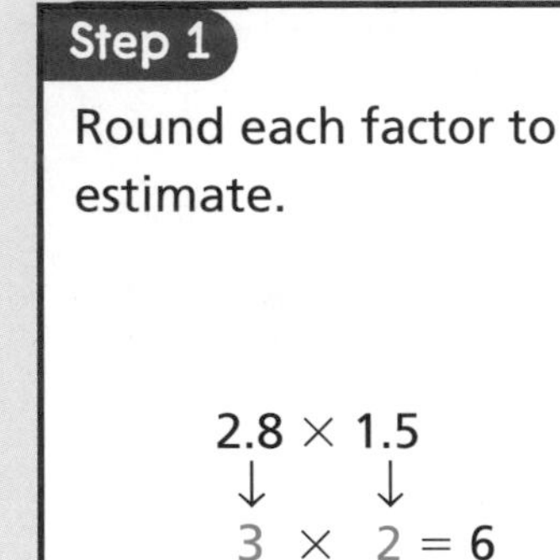

$$\begin{array}{ccc} 2.8 & \times & 1.5 \\ \downarrow & & \downarrow \\ 3 & \times & 2 = 6 \end{array}$$

Step 2

Multiply as with whole numbers.

$$\begin{array}{r} \overset{1}{\overset{4}{1.5}} \\ \times 2.8 \\ \hline 120 \\ +300 \\ \hline 420 \end{array}$$

Step 3

Use the estimate to place the decimal point.

$$\begin{array}{r} \overset{1}{\overset{4}{1.5}} \\ \times 2.8 \\ \hline 120 \\ +300 \\ \hline 4.20 \end{array}$$

Since the estimate is 6, the product should have one digit before the decimal point.

So, the length of a male elephant seal is about 4.2 meters.

The zeros at the end of a product should not be dropped until after you place the decimal point.

The length of a female leopard seal is about 1.1 times that of a male leopard seal. About how long is a female leopard seal?

ANOTHER WAY Count decimal places.

Multiply. 1.1×2.8 **Estimate.** $1 \times 3 = 3$

Step 1

Multiply as with whole numbers.

$$\begin{array}{r} 1.1 \\ \times 2.8 \\ \hline 88 \\ +220 \\ \hline 308 \end{array}$$

Step 2

Count the number of decimal places in both factors. Place the decimal point that number of places from the right in the product.

$$\begin{array}{rl} 1.1 & \leftarrow \text{1 decimal place in 1.1} \\ \times 2.8 & \leftarrow \text{1 decimal place in 2.8} \\ \hline 88 & \\ +220 & \\ \hline 3.08 & \leftarrow 1 + 1\text{, or 2 decimal places in the product} \end{array}$$

So, the length of a female leopard seal is about 3.08 meters.

- How many decimal places are in the product 2.38×1.77? Explain.

NS 2.1 Add, subtract, multiply, and divide with decimals; add with negative integers; subtract positive integers from negative integers; and verify the reasonableness of the results. *also* NS 1.0, NS 1.1, NS 2.0, MR 1.0, MR 1.1, MR 2.1, MR 2.3, MR 2.4, MR 3.2

Examples

A **Multiply.** $16 \times \$0.89$
Estimate. $16 \times \$1.00 = \$16.00$

$$\begin{array}{r} \$0.89 \\ \times \quad 16 \\ \hline 534 \\ +890 \\ \hline \$14.24 \end{array}$$

$0.89 ← 2 decimal places
16 ← 0 decimal places
$14.24 ← 2 + 0, or 2 decimal places in the product.

B **Multiply.** 0.16×0.565
Estimate. $0.2 \times 0.6 = 0.12$

$$\begin{array}{r} 0.565 \\ \times \; 0.16 \\ \hline 3390 \\ +5650 \\ \hline 0.09040 \end{array}$$

0.565 ← 3 decimal places
0.16 ← 2 decimal places
0.09040 ← 3 + 2, or 5 decimal places in the product.

C **Multiply.** 0.2×44.9
Estimate. $0.2 \times 40 = 8$

$$\begin{array}{r} 44.9 \\ \times \; 0.2 \\ \hline 8.98 \end{array}$$

D **Multiply.** 7.58×15
Estimate. $8 \times 15 = 120$

$$\begin{array}{r} 7.58 \\ \times \quad 15 \\ \hline 3790 \\ +7580 \\ \hline 113.70 \end{array}$$

E **Multiply.** 6.1×3.148
Estimate. $6 \times 3 = 18$

$$\begin{array}{r} 3.148 \\ \times \quad 6.1 \\ \hline 3148 \\ +188880 \\ \hline 19.2028 \end{array}$$

- In Example B, why do you need to add a zero between the decimal point and the 9?

Guided Practice

Estimate, then copy the exercise. Use the estimate to place the decimal point in the product.

1. 6.87×2.4
Estimate. ■ $\times 2 =$ ■

$$\begin{array}{r} 6.87 \\ \times \; 2.4 \\ \hline 16488 \end{array}$$

2. 48.1×2.9
Estimate. ■ $\times 3 = 144$

$$\begin{array}{r} 48.1 \\ \times \; 2.9 \\ \hline 13949 \end{array}$$

3. 0.773×0.05
Estimate. $1 \times$ ■ $= 0.05$

$$\begin{array}{r} 0.773 \\ \times \; 0.05 \\ \hline 003865 \end{array}$$

Estimate. Then find the product.

4. $\begin{array}{r} 32.3 \\ \times \; 0.4 \\ \hline \end{array}$ **5.** $\begin{array}{r} 0.07 \\ \times \; 62 \\ \hline \end{array}$ **6.** $\begin{array}{r} 8.5 \\ \times 0.3 \\ \hline \end{array}$ **7.** $\begin{array}{r} 1.09 \\ \times 0.02 \\ \hline \end{array}$ **8.** $\begin{array}{r} 0.41 \\ \times 0.56 \\ \hline \end{array}$

9. 7×2.8 **10.** 0.6×14 **11.** 0.5×0.9 **12.** 7.3×5.2 **13.** 0.08×2.2

14. TALK Math **Explain** how you know that 77.7 isn't a reasonable answer for 3.7×2.1

Independent Practice and Problem Solving

Estimate. Then find the product.

15. 0.2×26 **16.** 0.9×0.8 **17.** 3.7×0.4 **18.** 31.2×0.5 **19.** 6.06×7.3

20. $\$2.90 \times 0.8$ **21.** 442.4×0.8 **22.** 1.638×182 **23.** 97.5×7.13 **24.** $\$14.25 \times 1.8$

25. 34.7×5.29 **26.** 21×7.164 **27.** 0.331×1.2 **28.** 0.45×0.65 **29.** 282.6×0.403

◀ Ross seals are uncommon and are seldom seen by humans. They have a distinctive, warbling call that sounds like a siren.

USE SCIENCE DATA For 30–31, use the table.

Sizes of Seals

Type of Seal	Length (in meters)	Weight (in kilograms)
Leopard	up to 3.6 m	up to 450 kg
Harbor	from 1.2 m to 2.0 m	from 50 kg to 170 kg
Ross	up to 2.5 m	up to 200 kg
Monk	up to 2.8 m	from 240 to 400 kg

30. A monk seal at an aquarium has a weight 1.67 times as great as the heaviest Ross seal. What is the weight of the monk seal?

31. The length of one of the aquarium's leopard seals is 2.5 times as great as the length of a harbor seal of the smallest length. What is the length of the aquarium's leopard seal?

32. At a zoo, a gray seal eats about 7.75 pounds of fish every day. About how many pounds of fish will the seal eat in 31 days? About how many pounds of fish will it eat in 1 year? (Hint: 1 year = 365 days.)

33. ***FAST FACT*** A harbor seal can swim as fast as 19 kilometers per hour. If a harbor seal swims an average of 10.4 kilometers for 2.5 hours, how far will it swim?

34. Reasoning Why would you not use 4 decimal places in the product $\$2.98 \times 1.07$? How would you write your answer?

35. WRITE Math **What's the Error?** A pound of fish costs $7.50. Jon says 62.2 pounds of fish will cost $4,665.00. What is his error? What should Jon's answer have been?

Achieving the Standards

36. The thickness of a United States quarter is 0.955 inch. What is the thickness of a quarter rounded to the nearest hundredth? (NS 1.1, p. 272)

37. Find the product. $10 \times 0.6 =$ (O-n NS 2.1, p. 294)

38. Estimate the product. (NS 1.1, p. 298)

1.54×6.2

39. Test Prep Trisha put $1.25 in her bank each week for one year. How much money did she put in her bank?

A $65.00 **C** $6.50

B $62.50 **D** $6.25

 Extra Practice on page 308, Set C

Surf's Up

Sometimes you need to provide an explanation to justify an answer. If there are two possible ways to find an answer, explain both ways.

Tina's teacher asked her to solve the following problem and to justify the placement of the decimal point in her answer.

> In 2003, young people between the ages of 13 and 24 said they spent an average of 16.7 hours per week surfing the Internet. How many hours will a young person spend surfing the Internet in one year?

Read Tina's solution and justification of her answer.

Tips

To justify an answer:

- explain how you found the answer.
- explain each way you checked the answer.
- use correct math vocabulary.
- check all computations.
- write a conclusion to justify your answer in the last sentence.

How I Knew Where to Place the Decimal Point

Multiply the number of hours per week times the number of weeks in the year to find the number of hours a young person spends surfing the Internet in one year.

$16.7 \times 52 = 868.4$

One way is to use estimation to check placement of the decimal point. Round both factors to the nearest ten and then multiply: $50 \times 20 = 1{,}000$. The estimate shows that the product is close to 1,000. Since 868.4 is much closer to 1,000 than 8,684 is, 868.4 must be the product.

Another way to check placement of the decimal point is to count the number of decimal places in the factors. Since there is only one decimal place, the product will have only one decimal place.

Problem Solving **Solve. Then justify each answer.**

1. People between the ages of 13 and 24 spend an average of 12 hours a week listening to the radio. About how many hours does the average young person spend listening to the radio in 6.5 weeks?
2. In one week, young people between the ages of 13 and 24 watch TV for an average of 13.6 hours. About how many hours does an average young person spend watching TV in 52 weeks?

LESSON 6

Zeros in the Product

OBJECTIVE: Multiply decimals with zeros in the product.

Quick Review

1. 3×0.3
2. 5×0.2
3. 10×0.6
4. 20×0.5
5. 100×0.1

The thicker the string, the lower its pitch.

Learn

PROBLEM Guitar strings have different thicknesses, or gauges. The thickest string is about a 0.050-gauge string. The gauge of the next thickest string is about 0.84 times as thick. What is the gauge of that guitar string?

Example

Multiply. 0.05×0.84 **Estimate.** $0.05 \times 1 = 0.05$

Step 1

Multiply as with whole numbers.

$$\begin{array}{r} 0.84 \\ \times 0.05 \\ \hline 420 \end{array}$$

Step 2

Count the number of decimal places in both factors.

$$\begin{array}{rl} 0.84 & \leftarrow \quad 2 \text{ places} \\ \times 0.05 & \leftarrow + 2 \text{ places} \\ \hline 420 & \end{array}$$

Step 3

Write a zero to the left of the product to place the decimal point.

$$\begin{array}{rl} 0.84 & \\ \times 0.05 & \\ \hline 0.0420 & \leftarrow 4 \text{ places} \end{array}$$

So, the next thickest string on a guitar is about a 0.042-gauge string.

- If the lightest string is 0.24 times as thick as the 0.050 gauge string, what is its gauge?

Math Idea
When multiplying money amounts, round your answer to two decimal places.

More Examples

A Multiply.

7.3×0.004

$$\begin{array}{rl} 7.3 & \\ \times 0.004 & \\ \hline 0.0292 & \leftarrow 4 \text{ places} \end{array}$$

Write one zero to the left of the other digits.

B Multiply.

$\$16 \times 0.006$

$$\begin{array}{rl} \$16 & \\ \times 0.006 & \\ \hline \$0.096 & \leftarrow 3 \text{ places} \end{array}$$

Round the product to \$0.10.

Guided Practice

Find the number of decimal places in the product.

1. 0.09×3
2. 8×0.004
3. 0.02×0.6
4. 0.03×0.01
5. ✓ 0.07×0.006

Find the product.

6. $\begin{array}{r} 0.62 \\ \times 0.03 \\ \hline \end{array}$
7. $\begin{array}{r} \$12 \\ \times 0.007 \\ \hline \end{array}$
8. $\begin{array}{r} 0.05 \\ \times 0.09 \\ \hline \end{array}$
9. $\begin{array}{r} 4.1 \\ \times 0.06 \\ \hline \end{array}$
10. ✓ $\begin{array}{r} 0.007 \\ \times 12.2 \\ \hline \end{array}$

11. **TALK Math** **Explain** why 0.08×0.33 has the same product as 0.008×3.3.

NS 2.1 Add, subtract, multiply, and divide with decimals; add with negative integers; subtract positive integers from negative integers; and verify the reasonableness of the results. *also* **NS 1.0, NS 2.0, MR 2.0, MR 2.3, MR 2.4, MR 3.2, MR 3.3**

Independent Practice and Problem Solving

Find the product.

12. 0.36×0.06 **13.** 0.04×0.08 **14.** $\$23 \times 0.009$ **15.** 5.9×0.007 **16.** 1.06×0.014

17. 0.004×0.02 **18.** $\$6 \times 0.003$ **19.** 5.16×0.08 **20.** 0.04×0.07 **21.** 1.009×0.15

22. 0.9×0.11 **23.** 0.14×0.012 **24.** 0.13×0.007 **25.** 1.001×1.01 **26.** 2.92×0.207

Algebra Find the value of n.

27. $0.03 \times n = 0.0021$ **28.** $n \times 0.006 = \$0.09$ **29.** $0.001 \times 0.01 = n$ **30.** $1.2 \times n = 0.0132$

31. $n \times 0.8 = 0.96$ **32.** $0.6 \times 0.006 = n$ **33.** $\$1.23 \times 0.08 = n$ **34.** $0.04 \times n = 0.056$

Solve.

35. James has a stack of 15 guitar picks. If each pick is 0.008 inch thick, what is the height of the stack of picks?

36. Lyle has a guitar pick that is 0.029 inch thick. Liz has a pick that is 0.5 times as thick as Lyle's pick. How thick is Liz's pick?

37. Bonnie has 3 guitar picks that are 0.022 inch thick each and 5 guitar picks that are 0.014 inches thick each. What is the difference in height between the two stacks of picks?

38. **Reasoning** Joe has a stack of guitar picks that is 0.31 inch tall. If he paid $0.49 for each pick and $4.90 for the entire stack, what is the thickness of a single pick?

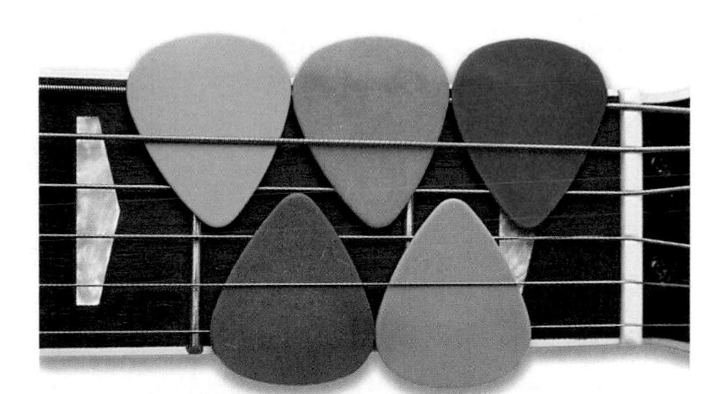

Guitar picks are usually between 0.014 inch and 0.060 inch thick. They are typically shaped like acute triangles with rounded corners.

39. WRITE Math **Explain** why 0.26×0.85 has only 3 decimal places in the product.

Achieving the Standards

40. Evaluate the expression $5x$ for $x = 8$.
(AF 1.2, p. 106)

41. $3.55 \times 1.5 =$ (NS 2.1, p. 300)

42. $8{,}100 \div 9 =$ (NS 2.2, p. 326)

43. The black truffle mushroom is one of the most expensive foods in the world. You can buy 0.078 ounce for $1. How many ounces can you buy for $5?

A 39 ounces **C** 0.39 ounce
B 3.9 ounces **D** 0.039 ounce

CD ROM **Technology**
Use Harcourt Mega Math, The Numbers Games, *Up, Up and Array,* Level P.

Extra Practice on page 308, Set D

Problem Solving Workshop
Skill: Choose the Operation

OBJECTIVE: Solve problems by using the skill *choose the operation.*

Use the Skill

PROBLEM The Science Club visited an aquarium. Club members 12 years old and under paid $11.95 for an admission ticket, members between the ages of 13 and 18 paid $18.95, and adults paid $19.95. If four adults, six 13-year-olds and twenty-two 12-year-olds went on the trip, how much did the Science Club pay for admission to the aquarium?

The way numbers are related can help you choose the operation needed to solve a problem.

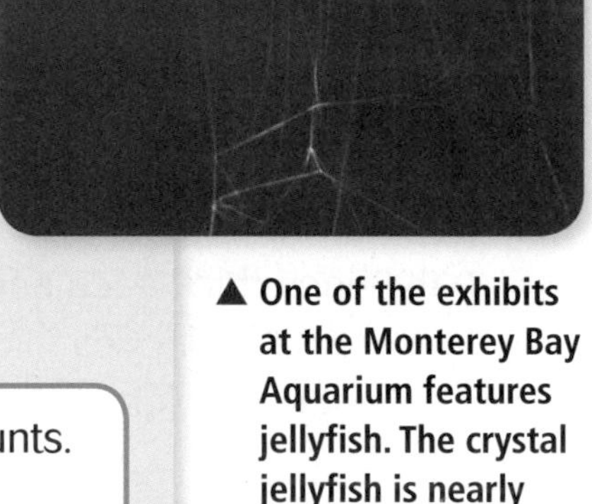

▲ One of the exhibits at the Monterey Bay Aquarium features jellyfish. The crystal jellyfish is nearly invisible in water.

This chart will help you decide which operation you can use.

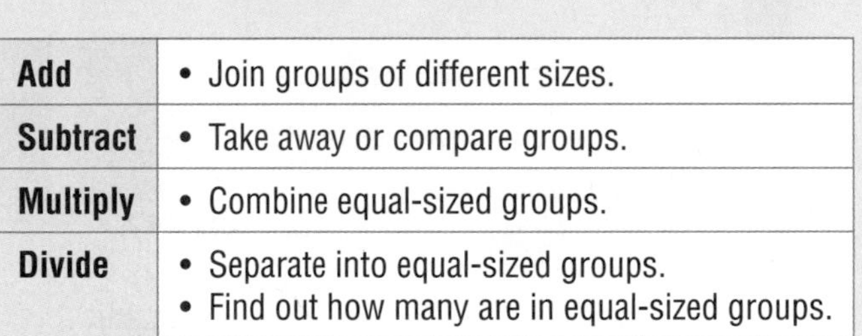

Add	• Join groups of different sizes.
Subtract	• Take away or compare groups.
Multiply	• Combine equal-sized groups.
Divide	• Separate into equal-sized groups. • Find out how many are in equal-sized groups.

There are 3 different groups of people and 3 different ticket price amounts. **Multiply** each amount by the number of tickets in each group.

Students 12 and under	Students 13 to 18	Adults
$\$11.95 \times 22 = \$262.90$	$\$18.95 \times 6 = \$113.70$	$\$19.95 \times 4 = \$79.80$

Add the ticket cost of each group to find the total amount that the Science Club paid for admission to the aquarium.

$$\$262.90 + \$113.70 + \$79.80 = \$456.40$$

Think and Discuss

Name the operation needed to solve the problem. Then solve.

a. Suppose the adults contribute $92.40 toward the cost of $456.40, and the 28 student members split the remaining cost equally among themselves. How much would each member pay?

b. Club members bought 18 large T-shirts at $29.95 each and 14 small T-shirts at $19.95 each. What was the total cost of the T-shirts?

NS 2.1 Add, subtract, multiply, and divide with decimals; add with negative integers; subtract positive integers from negative integers; and verify reasonableness of the results. *also* NS 1.0, NS 2.0, NS 2.2, MR 1.0, MR 2.0, MR 2.3, MR 2.4, MR 3.2

Guided Problem Solving

1. Kelly's class is planning a trip to see the aquarium exhibit called Jellies: Living Art. Each of the 21 students needs to buy a study packet for $1.65 and a sketchbook for $3.20. The PTA will pay $40 of the cost. How much will the class pay in all for the supplies?

Add to find how much the supplies will cost each student.	Multiply by the number of students.	Subtract the amount that the PTA will pay toward the cost.
$1.65 + $3.20 = $4.85	$4.85 × ■ = ■	$■ − $40 = $■

2. Suppose the total cost of the trip including transportation and lunch is $278.00. Kelly's teacher collects $7.50 from each of the 21 student for the trip. He will pay for the rest of the trip from a class trip fund. How much money will he need from that fund?

3. **What if** each of the 21 student bought lunch at the aquarium for $3.75? How much extra would it cost the class?

Mixed Applications

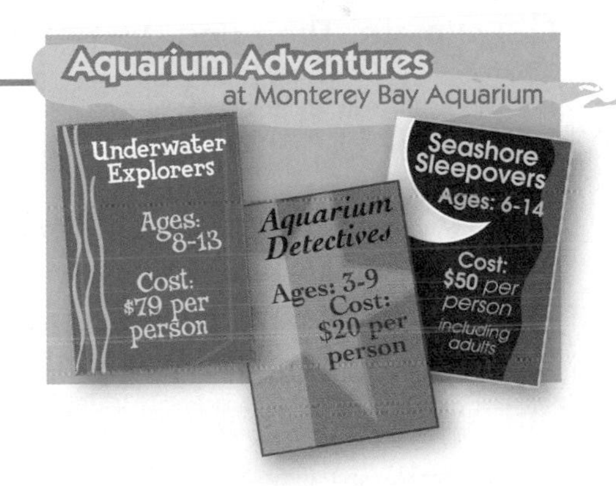

Aquarium Adventures
at Monterey Bay Aquarium
Underwater Explorers
Ages: 8-13
Cost: $79 per person
Aquarium Detectives
Ages: 3-9
Cost: $20 per person
Seashore Sleepovers
Ages: 6-14
Cost: $50 per person
including adults

USE DATA **For 4–7, use the flyer.**

4. A camp group of 11 children participated in Aquarium Adventures of the Monterey Bay Aquarium. Five children in the group attended *Underwater Explorers* and 6 attended *Aquarium Detectives.* How much did it cost the camp group to participate?

5. It will cost $237 for the 3 Linden children to attend the same program in Aquarium Adventures. In which program will the Linden children participate?

6. John wants to attend all three programs at the aquarium. He has saved $58 so far. How much more does John need to save before he has enough money?

7. The Madera Youth Club is going to the Seashore Sleepovers program. There are 31 club members and 6 chaperones. What will it cost the entire club to attend?

8. The Kelp Forest at the Monterey Bay Aquarium is one of the tallest aquarium exhibits in the world. In the ocean, kelp grows about 4 inches each day. How many inches could it grow in one year?

9. **WRITE Math** The Monterey Bay Aquarium has a giant octopus exhibit. A healthy, female giant Pacific octopus with 8 arms has about 2,240 suckers. Find the number of suckers the octopus has on each arm. If each arm has about the same number of suckers, **Explain** which operation you used and why.

Extra Practice

Set A Multiply each number by 10, 100, 1,000, and 10,000. (pp. 294–295)

1. 1.09
2. 548.1
3. 9.1
4. $1.25
5. 0.7
6. 0.245
7. 2.016
8. 0.003
9. $0.05
10. 38.62

Set B Estimate the product. (pp. 298–299)

1. 5.4×4.3
2. 2.4×2.5
3. $2 \times \$1.31$
4. 5.15×3.07
5. 1.68×5.1
6. 7.4×6.8
7. $48 \times \$2.26$
8. 3.52×2.5
9. 4.26×9.2
10. $30 \times \$4.38$

11. Alicia knitted 5.5 inches of a scarf on Monday. On Tuesday she knitted 1.75 times that amount. About how many inches did she knit on Tuesday?

12. Concert tickets are $10.85 each. About how much do 6 tickets cost?

Set C Estimate. Then find the product. (pp. 300–303)

1. 41.2×0.6
2. 3.2×0.7
3. 0.19×0.63
4. 2.01×43
5. $\$12.45 \times 3.2$
6. 0.455×2.4
7. 126.3×18.3
8. 1.24×9.56
9. 0.24×0.657
10. $125 \times \$3.50$

11. Eli's cat is 19.25 inches long. Katrina's cat is 1.2 times as long as Eli's cat. How long is Katrina's cat?

12. A museum charges a $6.50 entrance fee. A science center charges 1.5 times as much as the museum. How much does the science center charge?

Set D Find the product. (pp. 304–305)

1. 0.021×0.3
2. 0.2×0.3
3. 0.005×1.5
4. 0.16×0.04
5. 13.75×2.3
6. 3.83×0.6
7. $\$314.7 \times 0.4$
8. 1.307×413
9. 36.8×9.17
10. 56.85×8.43
11. 0.27×0.03
12. 6.1×0.009
13. 0.01×0.03
14. $\$8 \times 0.005$
15. 0.005×10.1

16. A container of cinnamon weighs 0.05 ounces. A container of nutmeg weighs 0.02 times as much as the container of cinnamon. What does the container of nutmeg weigh?

17. One teaspoon is equivalent to about 0.005 liters. How many liters are equivalent to 3.5 teaspoons?

Technology
Use Harcourt Mega Math, The Number Games, *Tiny's Think Tank*, Level R.

Powerful Products

Ready!
2 players

Set!
- Number cards (0–9)
- Decimal Product Outline
- Two-column chart
- Paper bag

Player 1			Player 2		
Product	Correct?	Points	Product	Correct?	Points

Play!

- Player 1 puts the number cards in the paper bag, shakes it, and then draws four cards. Player 1 uses the cards to make two decimal factors that will make the greatest product possible.
- Player 1 puts the cards on the decimal product outline to display the factors and finds the product. Player 1 records the product in the chart.
- Player 2 checks Player 1's product and writes yes or no after the product in the chart. If incorrect, a zero is placed in the chart.
- The cards are returned to the bag. Player 2 then draws four cards and repeats the process.
- At the end of each round, players compare chart entries. A player who has greater correct entry gets 1 point. The first player to earn 5 points wins the game.

Chapter 12 Review/Test

Check Concepts

Complete.

1. Explain how you can use a model to find the product of 4×0.37. (NS 2.1, p. 292)
2. Why do you need to add a zero after the decimal point to correctly place the decimal point in the product of 0.2×0.3? Explain. (NS 2.1, p. 300)

Check Skills

Multiply each number by 10, 100, 1,000, and 10,000. (NS 2.0, pp. 294–295)

3. 7.653
4. $8.59
5. 0.8
6. 4.025
7. 265.45

Estimate the product. (NS 1.1, pp. 298–299)

8. 2.6×9.4
9. $16 \times \$8.79$
10. $7 \times \$3.45$
11. 4.59×4.16

Find the product. (NS 2.1, pp. 300–303, 304–305)

12. 2.7×0.5
13. 4.07×5.2
14. 93.7×0.3
15. $\$9.15 \times 7.4$
16. 0.4×0.2
17. 0.09×0.023
18. 0.91×0.02
19. $\$12 \times 0.005$
20. 12×6.17
21. 3.6×18.7
22. 0.05×0.084
23. $0.08 \times \$1.59$

Check Problem Solving

Solve. (NS 2.1, pp. 306–307)

24. Jane and two of her friends are shopping for birthday presents. They buy 5 bracelets that cost $4.19 each and 3 shirts that cost $14.49 each. They buy a belt that costs $13.58. If Jane and her friends share the cost equally, how much will each of them spend?

25. WRITE Math At a roadside stand, Grace bought 2 pounds of peaches at $1.49 a pound, 2 pounds of cherries at $2.99 a pound, and a 3-pound piece of watermelon at $0.79 a pound. She gave the farmer $15. How much change did she receive? Tell which operations you used to find your answer and **explain** why.

GO ONLINE **Technology** Use *Online Assessment.*

Enrich • Expressions

Balancing Act

An expression is a mathematical phrase that combines numbers, operation signs, and sometimes variables.

$1.4 \times 4 = 5.6$

Warm Up

0.7×8 is an expression. 1.4×4 is an expression. Are the expressions equal?

Find the value of each expression.

$0.7 \times 8 = 5.6$ $\qquad$ $1.4 \times 4 - 5.6$

$5.6 = 5.6$, so $0.7 \times 8 = 1.4 \times 4$.

Try It

Choose one expression from Box A and an equivalent expression from Box B to balance each scale. Use each expression only once.

Box A	Box B
0.15×5	0.7×0.8
9×1.2	0.25×3
7×0.6	2×0.15
0.3×8	6×0.4
0.05×6	1.4×3
4×0.14	2.7×4

1.  

2. 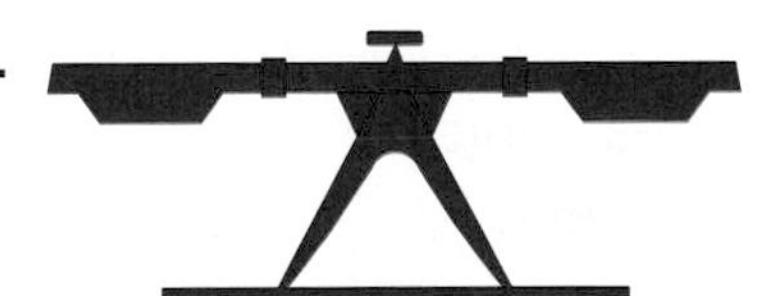

3. 

4. 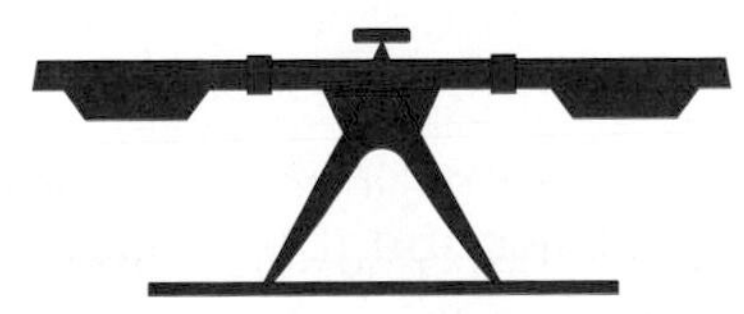

5. 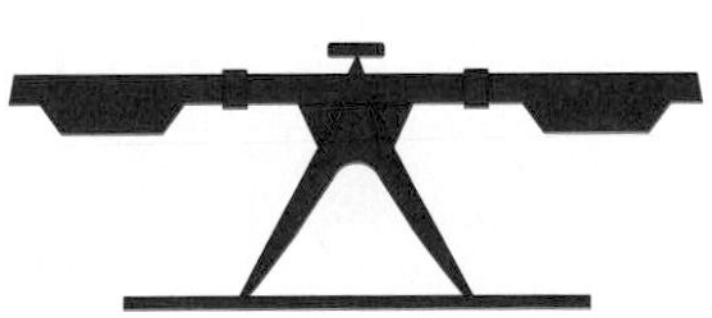

6. 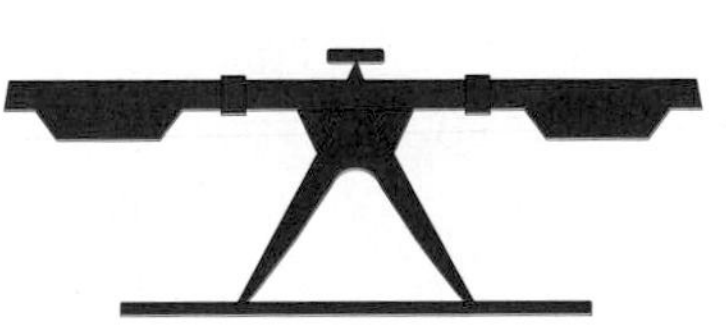

Think About It

WRITE Math **Explain** how to find the number of decimal places in a product.

Achieving the Standards
Chapters 1–12

Number Sense

1. The table below shows the dry ingredients needed to make two kinds of cakes.

Cake Ingredients		
Type of Cake	Flour	Sugar
Pineapple Chiffon Cake	$2\frac{1}{4}$ cups	$1\frac{1}{2}$ cups
Coffee Cake	$1\frac{1}{2}$ cups	$\frac{3}{4}$ cups

How many cups of sugar are needed to make one pineapple chiffon cake and one coffee cake? (Key NS 2.3)

A $2\frac{1}{4}$ cups

B $2\frac{2}{3}$ cups

C $3\frac{3}{4}$ cups

D 6 cups

2. Paul rolled 4 number cubes.

Paul made different 4-digit numbers with the numbers shown on the cubes. Which of the numbers can be divided evenly by 24? (Key NS 2.2)

A 1236

B 1632

C 3162

D 6132

3. WRITE Math **Explain** how to place the decimal point in the product 0.06×0.23. (Key NS 2.1)

Algebra and Functions

4. Which of the following shows the Distributive Property? (AF 1.3)

A $8 \times (30 + 2) = (8 \times 30) + (8 \times 2)$

B $(8 \times 30) \times 2 = 8 \times (30 \times 2)$

C $8 + (30 + 2) = (8 + 30) + 2$

D $(8 \times 30) + 2 = 8 \times (30 + 2)$

Understand the problem.

See item 5. The equation states that $n - 7$ equals $9 + 12$, which is 21. Since 7 is subtracted from n, you need to find a number that is 7 more than 21.

5. Which number is represented by n? (Grade 4 AF 1.1)

$$n - 7 = 9 + 12$$

A 14

B 21

C 28

D 35

6. $40 + 8 = 40 + \blacksquare$ (Grade 4 Key AF 2.1)

A 6×8

B 2×4

C 2×3

D 4×12

7. WRITE Math **Describe** the relationship between x and y in this table. (Grade 4 Key AF 1.5)

Input	x	18	30	48	72
Output	y	3	5	8	12

Statistics, Data Analysis, and Probability

8. The table below shows the numbers of points scored in 5 basketball games by 4 players.

Points Scored					
Name	**Game 1**	**Game 2**	**Game 3**	**Game 4**	**Game 5**
Emily	14	8	11	9	10
Abigail	12	12	8	11	13
Isabella	7	15	13	11	15
Olivia	10	9	12	14	11

Who had a median score of 11 points? (SDAP 1.1)

A Emily **C** Isabella

B Abigail **D** Olivia

9. How many students were absent more than 2 days and fewer than 6 days? (SDAP 1.0)

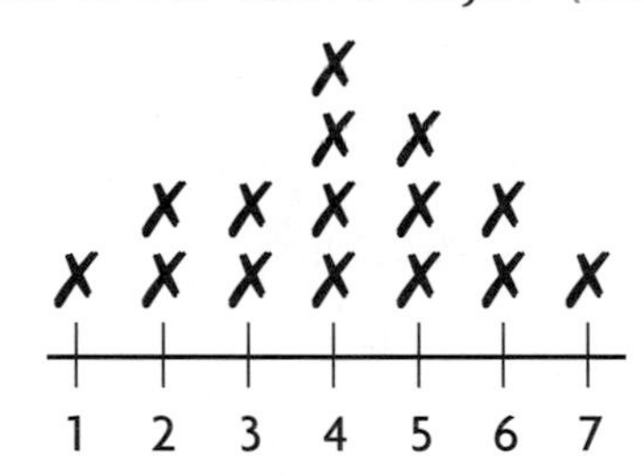

Number of Absences

A 14 students **C** 9 students

B 13 students **D** 8 students

10. WRITE Math Suppose you want to make a bar graph for the following data.

Recycled Cans					
Week	1	2	3	4	5
Number of Cans	16	25	12	19	27

Explain how you would choose the scale for the graph. What interval would you use? (SDAP 1.0)

Measurement and Geometry

11. Which figures below show pairs of lines that appear to be parallel? (Grade 4 MG 3.1)

A

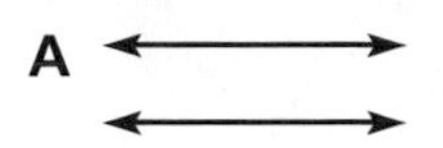

B

C

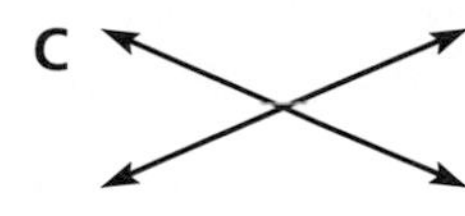

D

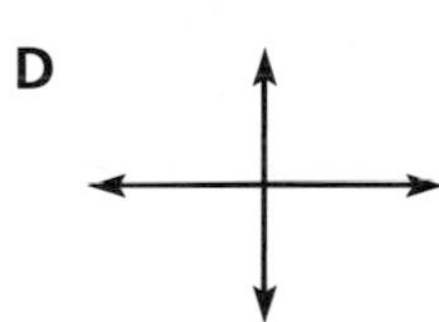

12. What is the length of a vertical line segment with endpoints at $(4,5)$ and $(4,^-2)$? (Grade 4 MG 2.3)

A 3 units

B 5 units

C 7 units

D 10 units

13. WRITE Math Look at the figure below. (Grade 4 MG 1.1)

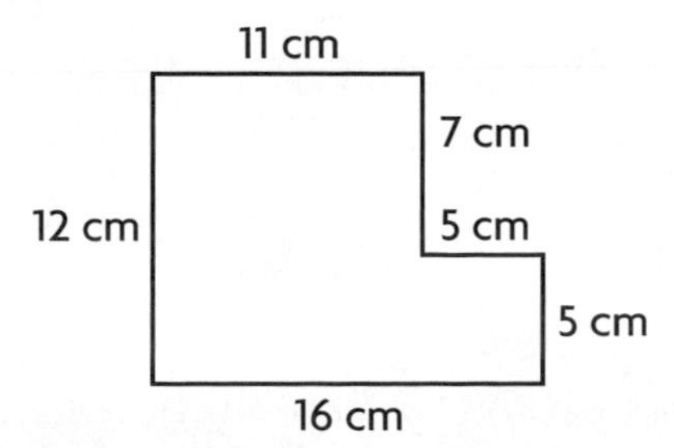

Explain how to find the area of the figure.

13 Divide Decimals

The Big Idea Division of decimals by whole numbers and by decimals is based on place value and division and multiplication with whole numbers.

CALIFORNIA FAST FACT

Black bears can be found throughout North America, from northern Alaska, through all of California, and in parts of central Mexico.

Investigate

The black bear cubs are light compared with the adult bears. Choose a weight, to a tenth of a kilogram, within the ranges shown in the table for a newborn cub and an adult female. How many times as great is the mass of the adult compared to the mass of the cub?

Black Bear Weights

Age	Weight Range (in kilograms)
Newborn cub	0.20–0.45
5 months	2–5
17 months	7–49
Adult male	47–409
Adult female	39–236

Technology
Student pages are available in the Student eBook.

Show What You Know

Check your understanding of important skills needed for success in Chapter 13.

▶ Division Patterns

Complete the pattern.

1. $24 \div 6 = 4$
$240 \div 6 = 40$
$2{,}400 \div 6 = n$

2. $21 \div 7 = 3$
$210 \div 7 = n$
$2{,}100 \div 7 = 300$

3. $32 \div 4 = n$
$320 \div 4 = 80$
$3{,}200 \div 4 = 800$

4. $30 \div 5 = 6$
$300 \div n = 60$
$3{,}000 \div 5 = 600$

5. $54 \div 9 = 6$
$n \div 9 = 60$
$5{,}400 \div 9 = 600$

6. $40 \div 8 = 5$
$400 \div n = 50$
$4{,}000 \div 8 = 500$

▶ Estimate Quotients

Estimate the quotient.

7. $8\overline{)316}$ **8.** $3\overline{)88}$ **9.** $5\overline{)437}$ **10.** $6\overline{)402}$

11. $956 \div 3$ **12.** $96 \div 4$ **13.** $479 \div 8$ **14.** $312 \div 6$

▶ Divide 3-Digit Dividends by 1-Digit

Divide.

15. $3\overline{)258}$ **16.** $5\overline{)210}$ **17.** $8\overline{)912}$ **18.** $4\overline{)276}$

19. $6\overline{)882}$ **20.** $9\overline{)342}$ **21.** $7\overline{)448}$ **22.** $3\overline{)651}$

23. $630 \div 5$ **24.** $924 \div 4$ **25.** $354 \div 6$ **26.** $584 \div 8$

VOCABULARY POWER

CHAPTER VOCABULARY

decimal
estimate
hundredth
quotient
tenth

WARM-UP WORDS

estimate to find a number that is close to an exact amount

hundredth one of one hundred equal parts

tenth one of ten equal parts

LESSON 1 HANDS ON

Divide Decimals by Whole Numbers

OBJECTIVE: Use models to divide decimals by whole numbers.

Quick Review

1. 329 ÷ 7
2. 475 ÷ 5
3. 804 ÷ 6
4. 756 ÷ 4
5. 891 ÷ 9

Investigate

Materials ■ decimal models ■ color pencils ■ scissors ■ play bills and coins

Make a model to divide a decimal by a whole number.

Find 2.4 ÷ 3.

A Shade the decimal model to show 2.4.

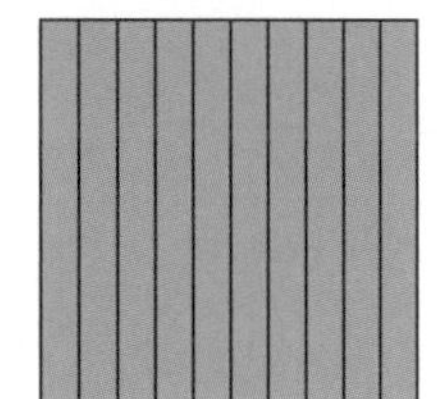
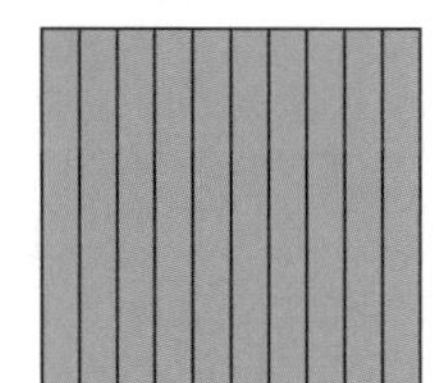
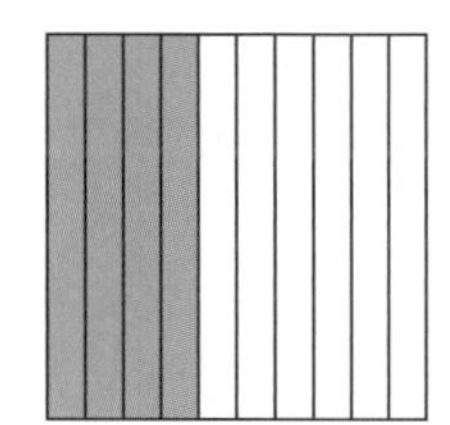

B Cut your model apart to show the number of tenths.

C Divide the tenths into 3 groups of the same size.

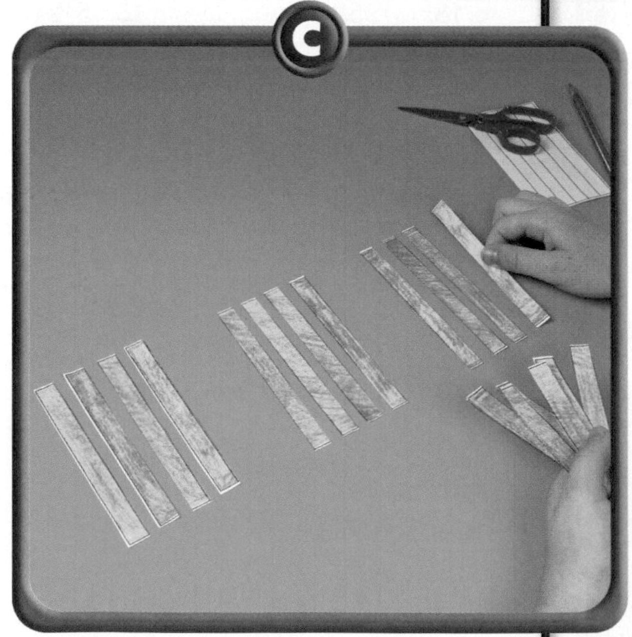

D Use your model to complete the division sentence.

2.4 ÷ 3 = ■

Draw Conclusions

1. Why did you cut the model into tenths?
2. How can you use your materials to find 1.4 ÷ 2?
3. **Synthesis** Explain how your model would be different for the problem 0.24 ÷ 3.

NS 2.2 Demonstrate proficiency with division, includiing division with positive decimals and long division with multidigit divisors. *also* **NS 2.1, MR 2.0, MR 2.3, MR 2.4, MR 3.2**

Connect

You can also use money to model division of a decimal by a whole number.

Find $7.32 \div 6$.

Step 1

Use $1 bills, dimes, and pennies to show $7.32.

Step 2

Divide the $1 bills into 6 equal groups. Exchange the remaining $1 bill for dimes.

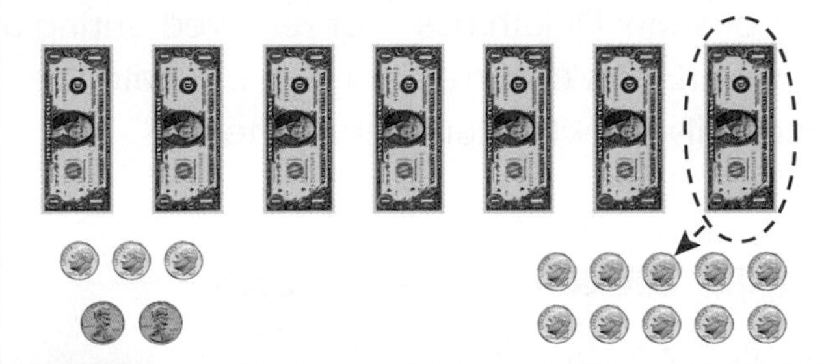

Step 3

Divide the dimes into 6 equal groups. Exchange the remaining dime for pennies.

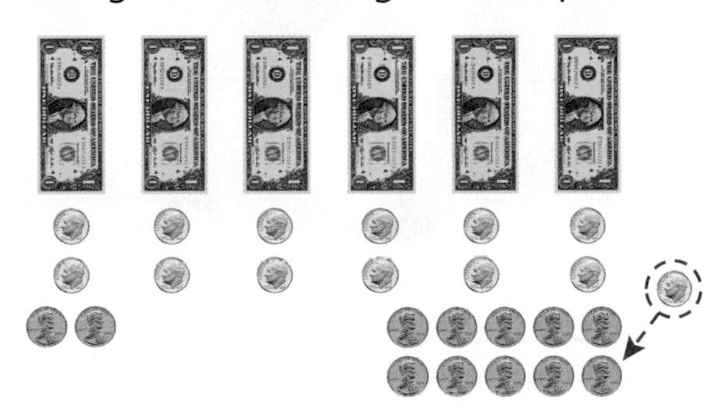

Step 4

Divide the pennies into 6 equal groups.

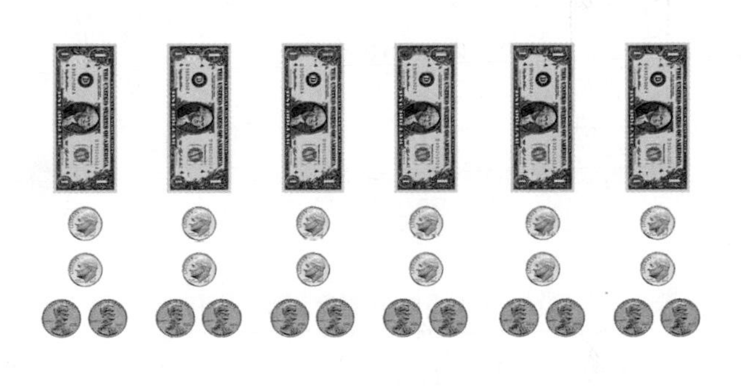

$7.32 ÷ 6 = $1.22, so $7.32 \div 6 = 1.22$.

TALK Math

Why wouldn't you use quarters or nickels to model division of decimals?

Practice

Use decimal models or play money to model the quotient. Record your answer.

1. $1.5 \div 3$ **2.** $3.2 \div 4$ **3.** $0.18 \div 9$ ✓**4.** $0.28 \div 4$

5. $6.96 ÷ 6 **6.** $6.45 ÷ 5 **7.** $4.68 \div 3$ ✓**8.** $5.11 \div 7$

9. **WRITE Math** Describe how you can use a model to find $0.39 \div 3$.

LESSON 2

Estimate Quotients

OBJECTIVE: Estimate decimal quotients.

Quick Review

Estimate.

1. 195 ÷ 7
2. 362 ÷ 5
3. 276 ÷ 39
4. 743 ÷ 84
5. 451 ÷ 63

Learn

PROBLEM Diana lives in Duluth, Minnesota. She likes to ski. She found that 3.3 feet was the greatest amount of snow Duluth has ever received during a 7-day period. This occurred in 1991. Estimate the average daily snowfall during this time.

The most snowfall for one year in the United States was recorded on Mount Rainier in Washington. From August 1973 through July 1974, it snowed 1,069.8 inches.

Example Use compatible numbers.

Estimate. 3.3 ÷ 7.

Think: 3.3 is 33 tenths.
28 and 7 are compatible numbers.
28 tenths divided by 7 is 4 tenths or 0.4.
35 and 7 are compatible numbers.
35 tenths divided by 7 is 5 tenths or 0.5.

So, the average daily snowfall was between 0.4 and 0.5 foot.

More Examples Estimate the quotients.

A Use two estimates.

Estimate 263.51 ÷ 62.

263.51 ÷ 62
240 ÷ 60 = 4
300 ÷ 60 = 5

So, 263.51 ÷ 62 is between 4 and 5.

B Use one estimate.

Estimate 70.61 ÷ 9.

70.61 ÷ 9 ≈ 72 ÷ 9

So, 70.61 ÷ 9 ≈ 8.

READ Math

The symbol ≈ is read "is approximately equal to." Use it when your solution to a problem is an estimate and not an exact answer.

- Explain the compatible numbers used in Examples A and B.

Guided Practice

Find two estimates for the quotient.

1. 52 ÷ 8
   64 ÷ 8 = ■
   56 ÷ 8 = ■
2. 26 ÷ 3 = ■
   27 ÷ 3 = ■
   24 ÷ 3 = ■
3. 122.6 ÷ 34
4. 4.812 ÷ 7

NS 1.1 Estimate, round, and manipulate very large and very small numbers. *also* MR 2.1, MR 2.3, MR 2.4, MR 3.2

Estimate the quotient.

5. $44.7 \div 6$
6. $68.32 \div 9$
7. $22.6 \div 42$
8. $3.409 \div 83$

9. TALK Math **Explain** how you could use compatible numbers to estimate $4 \div 5$.

Find two estimates for the quotient.

10. $2.36 \div 5$
11. $502.9 \div 8$
12. $13.1 \div 27$
13. $5.621 \div 6$

Use compatible numbers to estimate the quotient.

14. $39.6 \div 9$
15. $0.218 \div 4$
16. $336.4 \div 7$
17. $20.72 \div 3$
18. $4.37 \div 52$
19. $67.9 \div 84$
20. $32.51 \div 46$
21. $154.9 \div 19$

Independent Practice and Problem Solving

USE DATA For 22–24, use the table.

22. Estimate the average daily snowfall for the greatest 5-day snowfall, recorded in December, 1955.
23. How does the 6-day snowfall of February 1964 compare to the average daily snowfall for all of February 1964? Use estimation.
24. **Reasoning** Why are the two averages you found in Problem 23 different?
25. **What's the Error?** During a 6-hour storm, it snowed 3.8 inches. Maggie said that it snowed an average of 0.06 inch each hour.
26. WRITE Math How does estimation help you when you divide a decimal by a whole number?

Snowfalls Recorded at Thompson Pass, Alaska

Event	Amount (in inches)	Date Recorded
Greatest 5-Day Snowfall	175.4	Dec. 27–Dec. 31 1955
Greatest 6-Day Snowfall	174.3	Feb. 1–Feb. 6 1964
February Snowfall	346.1	1964

Achieving the Standards

27. Mr. Keller divided 2,700 pencils between the 30 classes in his school. How many pencils did each class receive?
(NS 2.2, p. 92)
28. What is the perimeter of a rectangular garden with a length of 12 meters and a width of 7 meters? (Grade 4 MG 1.4)
29. $203 \div 7 = \blacksquare$
(NS 2.2, p. 90)
30. **Test Prep** Nadia paid \$8.61 for 3 new bracelets. Which is the best estimate for how much each bracelet cost?

A \$2.00 **B** \$3.00 **C** \$4.00 **D** \$5.00

Extra Practice on page 334, Set A

LESSON 3

Divide Decimals by Whole Numbers

OBJECTIVE: Divide decimals by whole numbers.

Quick Review

1. 827 ÷ 7
2. 946 ÷ 23
3. 2,851 ÷ 9
4. 5,225 ÷ 4
5. 3,216 ÷ 57

Learn

PROBLEM In a swimming relay, each swimmer swims an equal part of the total distance. Donita and 3 other swimmers won a relay in 5.24 minutes. What is the average time each girl swam?

ONE WAY Use fractions.

Find 5.24 ÷ 4. **Estimate.** 4 ÷ 4 = 1

Step 1

Rewrite the dividend and divisor as fractions.

$$\frac{524}{100} \div \frac{4}{1}$$

Step 2

Divide.

$$\frac{524}{100} \div \frac{4}{1} = \frac{524}{100} \times \frac{1}{4} = \frac{524}{400} = \frac{131}{100} = 1.31$$

ANOTHER WAY Use long division.

Step 1

Write the decimal point of the quotient above the decimal point of the dividend.

$$4\overline{)5.24}$$ (with the decimal point written above in the quotient)

Step 2

Divide as you would with whole numbers.

```
   1.31
4)5.24
 -4
  12
 -12
   04
  - 4
    0
```

So, each girl swam an average of 1.31 minutes.

- Is this answer reasonable? Explain.

NS 2.2 Demonstrate proficiency with division, including division with positive decimals and long division with multidigit divisors. *also* NS 1.2, NS 2.1, MR 2.1, MR 2.3, MR 2.4, MR 2.5, MR 3.2

More Examples

A Divide money

Find \$22.95 ÷ 15.

$$\begin{array}{r} \$1.53 \\ 15\overline{)\$22.95} \\ -15 \\ \hline 79 \\ -75 \\ \hline 45 \\ -45 \\ \hline 0 \end{array}$$

Check.

$$\begin{array}{r} \$1.53 \\ \times15 \\ \hline 765 \\ +1530 \\ \hline \$22.95 \end{array}$$

B Greater divisor than dividend

Find 2.61 ÷ 3.

$$\begin{array}{r} 0.87 \\ 3\overline{)2.61} \\ -24 \\ \hline 21 \\ -21 \\ \hline 0 \end{array}$$

Check.

$$\begin{array}{r} 0.87 \\ \times3 \\ \hline 2.61 \end{array}$$

C Add zeros to the dividend

Find 9.08 ÷ 8.

$$\begin{array}{r} 1.135 \\ 8\overline{)9.080} \\ -8 \\ \hline 10 \\ -8 \\ \hline 28 \\ -24 \\ \hline 40 \\ -40 \\ \hline 0 \end{array}$$

Check.

$$\begin{array}{r} 1.135 \\ \times8 \\ \hline 9.080 \end{array}$$

- In Example B, why do you place a zero in the ones place of the dividend?
- In Example C, why is a zero placed to the right of 9.08?

TALK Math

Placing a zero to the right of the last digit after the decimal point does not change the value.

Guided Practice

Use fractions to find the quotient.

1. 4.11 ÷ 3

   $\frac{411}{100} \div \frac{3}{1}$

   $= \frac{411}{100} \times \frac{1}{3}$

   $= \frac{\blacksquare}{300} = \blacksquare$

2. 7.32 ÷ 4

   $\frac{732}{\blacksquare} \div \frac{4}{\blacksquare}$

   $= \frac{732}{\blacksquare} \times \frac{\blacksquare}{4}$

   $= \frac{\blacksquare}{400} = \blacksquare$

3. 3.78 ÷ 7

   $\frac{\blacksquare}{100} \div \frac{\blacksquare}{1}$

   $= \frac{\blacksquare}{100} \times \frac{1}{\blacksquare}$

   $= \frac{\blacksquare}{700} = \blacksquare$

4. 4.72 ÷ 8

   $\frac{\blacksquare}{100} \div \frac{8}{\blacksquare}$

   $= \frac{\blacksquare}{100} \times \frac{\blacksquare}{8}$

   $= \frac{\blacksquare}{800} = \blacksquare$

Write the quotient correctly.

5. $\begin{array}{r} 173 \\ 5\overline{)8.65} \end{array}$
6. $\begin{array}{r} 046 \\ 9\overline{)4.14} \end{array}$
7. $\begin{array}{r} 0008 \\ 7\overline{)0.056} \end{array}$
8. $\begin{array}{r} 135 \\ 38\overline{)\$51.30} \end{array}$

Find the quotient.

9. $3\overline{)224.7}$
10. $8\overline{)\$38.88}$
11. ✓ $5\overline{)3.15}$
12. ✓ $9\overline{)0.072}$
13. $27\overline{)97.2}$
14. $72\overline{)64.08}$
15. $54\overline{)\$93.42}$
16. $36\overline{)8.820}$
17. **TALK Math** **Explain** how you can check that the decimal point is correctly placed in the quotient.

Independent Practice and Problem Solving

Write the quotient correctly.

18. $\begin{array}{r} 237 \\ 4\overline{)94.8} \end{array}$

19. $\begin{array}{r} 0084 \\ 6\overline{)0.504} \end{array}$

20. $\begin{array}{r} 046 \\ 8\overline{)3.68} \end{array}$

21. $\begin{array}{r} 145 \\ 52\overline{)\$75.40} \end{array}$

Find the quotient.

22. $5\overline{)68.5}$
23. $3\overline{)7.92}$
24. $46\overline{)58.88}$
25. $61\overline{)\$83.57}$
26. $8.46 \div 9$
27. $8.12 \div 4$
28. $7.52 \div 16$
29. $10.20 \div 85$

Estimate the quotient. Then divide.

30. $8\overline{)0.032}$
31. $4\overline{)\$8.24}$
32. $59\overline{)2.006}$
33. $22\overline{)53.9}$
34. $6.24 \div 6$
35. $1.253 \div 7$
36. $\$65.28 \div 32$
37. $281.2 \div 74$

For 38–40, use the diagram and the table.

38. Eight lanes are usually marked in a pool. How much width is allowed for each lane division?

39. Suppose 10 lanes are marked in a pool. If the total width of the pool is 25 meters, how wide is the space on each side of the pool outside of the lanes used?

40. **Pose a Problem** Look at Problem 38. Use the table to change the number and write a new problem. Trade problems with a classmate and solve.

Competition Pool Dimensions

Number of Lanes Marked	Combined Width of all Lanes Marked (in meters)
8	21.92
9	21.96
10	21.30

41. **FAST FACT** A fin whale is the second largest whale. It is known for being the fastest moving whale. It can travel almost 24 miles per hour for short amounts of time. About how far can it travel in one minute at this speed? Hint: $24 = 24.0$.

42. **What's the Question?** Tickets for a state swim meet are \$8.00 for adults and \$4.50 for children. Mr. and Mrs. Bulabi spent \$29.50 for tickets. The answer is 3.

43. **Reasoning** Would you expect $72.43 \div 25$ to be greater than or less than 3? Explain.

44. **WRITE Math** How is dividing a decimal by a whole number the same as dividing a whole number by a whole number? How is it different?

CD ROM Technology
Use Harcourt Mega Math, The Number Games, *Buggy Bargains*, Level M.

 Extra Practice on page 334, Set B

Achieving the Standards

45. Which two class pets together received 10 votes? (Grade 4 SDAP 1.3)

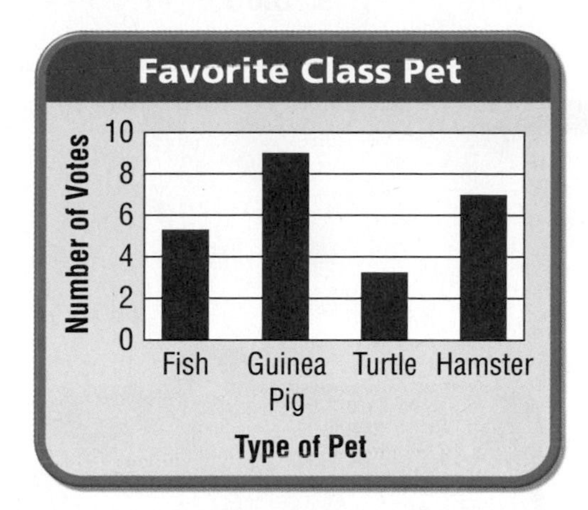

46. Nick ran 8.45 miles. Round this distance to the nearest tenth of a mile. (NS 1.1, p. 272)

47. Estimate the quotient $319 \div 8$. (NS 1.1, p. 86)

48. **Test Prep** $570.9 \div 33$.

   A 0.0173 **C** 17.3

   B 1.73 **D** 173

49. **Test Prep** Dan paid $40.00 for a monthly swimming pass. He swam 16 times that month. Which amount represents the cost of each swim?

   A $0.25 **C** $25

   B $2.50 **D** $250

Problem Solving and Reasoning

ALGEBRA You can use division to solve multiplication equations. Natalie bought 9 kickboards for her swimming class. She paid $71.55 altogether. What was the cost of one kickboard?

Let c = the cost of a kickboard.

$9 \times c = \$71.55$ Solve this equation.

Because multiplication and division are inverse operations, if $9 \times c = \$71.55$ then $\$71.55 \div 9 = c$.

$\$71.55 \div 9 = c$
$\$7.95 = c$

So, the cost of one kickboard is $7.95.

Use division to solve each equation.

1. $5 \times c = \$18.40$
2. $7 \times n = 16.8$
3. $3 \times a = 74.34$

LESSON 4 HANDS ON

Divide Decimals by Decimals

OBJECTIVE: Use models to divide decimals by decimals.

Quick Review

1. 5.6 ÷ 8
2. 4.5 ÷ 9
3. 0.36 ÷ 4
4. 2.8 ÷ 7
5. 0.66 ÷ 11

Investigate

Materials ■ decimal models ■ color pencils ■ scissors

Make a model to find the quotient of a decimal divided by a decimal.

Find 3.6 ÷ 0.3.

A Shade the decimal model to show 3.6.

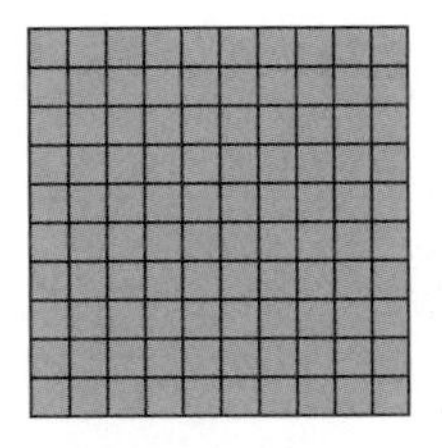
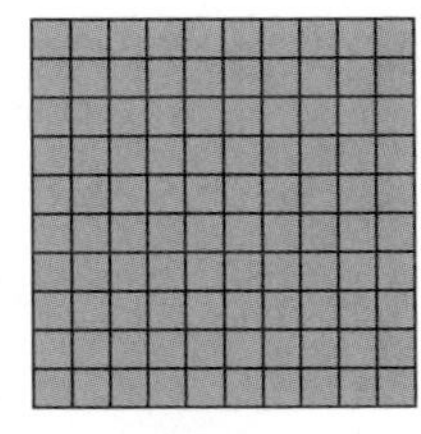
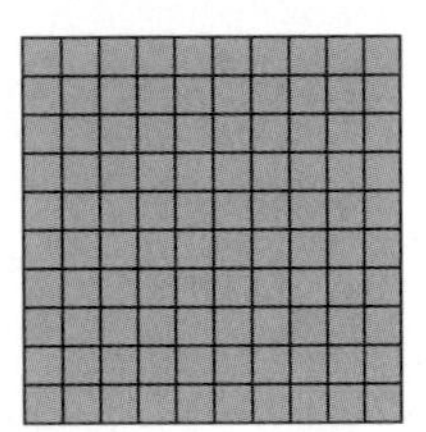
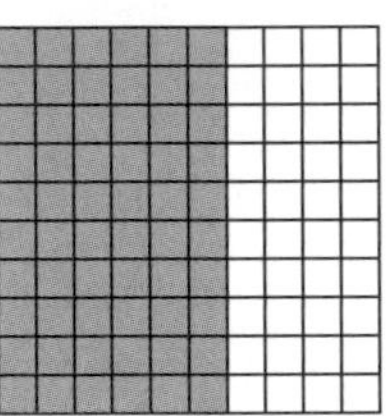

B Cut your model apart to make an equal number of groups of 0.3.

C Use your model to complete the division sentence.

3.6 ÷ 0.3 = ■

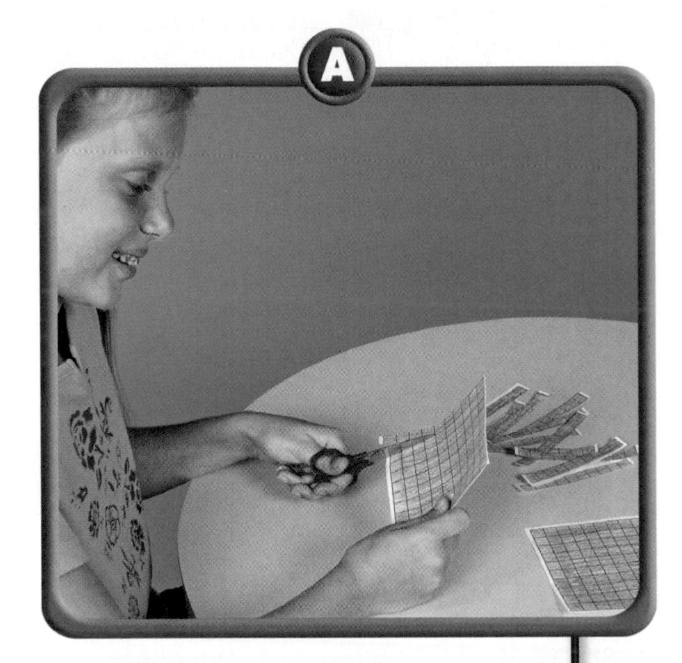

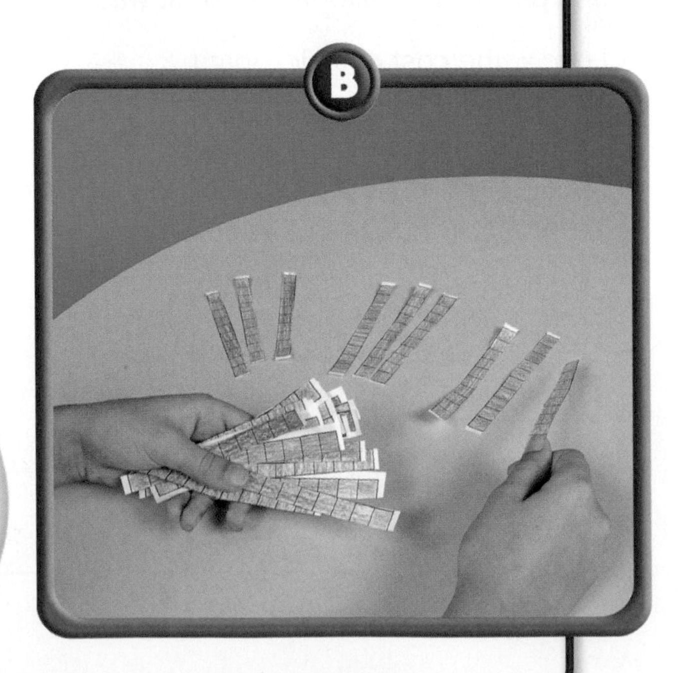

Draw Conclusions

1. Why do you make each group equal to the divisor?
2. How can you use a decimal model to find 2.1 ÷ 0.7?
3. **Evaluation** How does your model relate to the basic fact 36 ÷ 3 = 12?

Remember
The divisor can tell the number of same-size groups, or it can tell the number in each group.

NS 2.1 Add, subtract, multiply, and divide with decimals; add with negative integers; subtract positive integers from negative integers; and verify the reasonableness of the results. *also* **NS 2.0, NS 2.2, MR 2.0, MR 2.3, MR 2.4, MR 3.2**

Connect

You can also use fractions to divide a decimal by a decimal.

Find 0.36 ÷ 0.03.

$$\frac{36}{100} \div \frac{3}{100} = \frac{36}{100} \times \frac{100}{3} = \frac{36 \times 100}{100 \times 3} = \frac{3{,}600}{300} = \frac{36}{3} = 12$$

TALK Math
When the divisor is greater than zero but less than 1, how does the quotient compare with the dividend?

Practice

Make a model. Copy and complete the equation.

1. 1.2 ÷ 0.3 = ■

2.
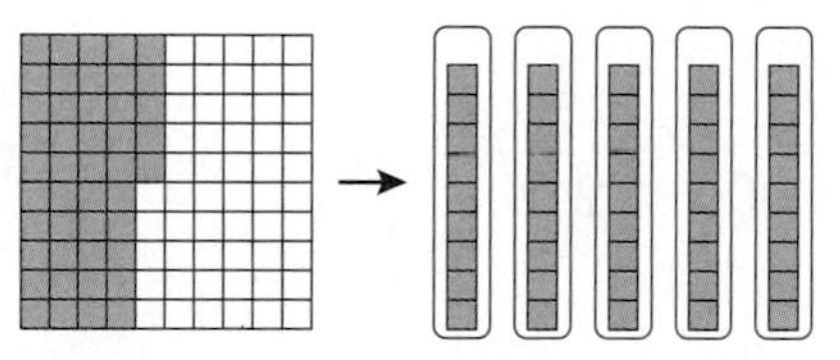
0.45 ÷ 0.09 = ■

3. 0.96 ÷ 0.24 = ■

4.

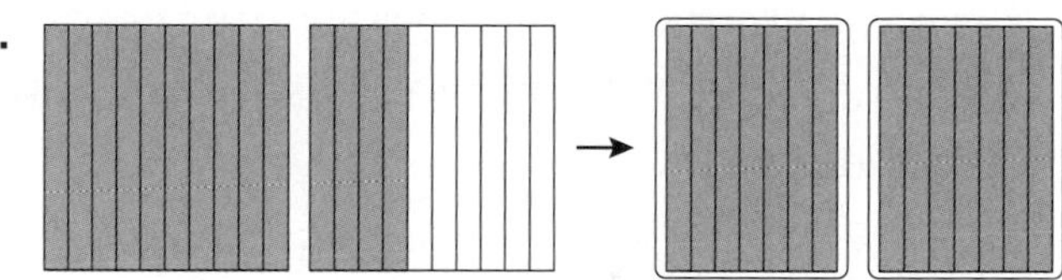
1.4 ÷ 0.7 = ■

Use a model to find the quotient.

5. 3.2 ÷ 0.8
6. 1.5 ÷ 0.5
7. 0.24 ÷ 0.03
8. 0.72 ÷ 0.9
9. 3.5 ÷ 0.7
10. 0.05 ÷ 0.01
11. 1.8 ÷ 0.9
12. 0.3 ÷ 0.05
13. 0.39 ÷ 0.13
14. 0.09 ÷ 0.03
15. 0.68 ÷ 0.17
16. 0.48 ÷ 0.16

Use fractions to find the quotient.

17. 1.6 ÷ 0.4
18. 4.2 ÷ 0.7
19. 0.18 ÷ 0.02
20. 0.48 ÷ 0.06
21. 0.52 ÷ 0.04
22. 0.64 ÷ 0.08
23. 0.57 ÷ 0.19
24. 0.7 ÷ 0.05

25. **WRITE Math** Describe how you can use pennies to find 1.04 ÷ 0.08.

LESSON 5

Decimal Patterns with Powers of 10

OBJECTIVE: Find patterns in division of decimals.

Quick Review

Estimate.

1. 0.43 ÷ 9
2. 0.34 ÷ 8
3. 0.29 ÷ 7
4. 0.137 ÷ 2
5. 0.35 ÷ 4

Learn

When you multiply both the divisor and the dividend by a power of 10, the quotient stays the same.

Whole numbers	Fractions
6 ÷ 3 = 2	$\frac{3}{9} = \frac{1}{3}$
60 ÷ 30 = 2	$\frac{30}{90} = \frac{1}{3}$
600 ÷ 300 = 2	$\frac{300}{900} = \frac{1}{3}$
6,000 ÷ 3,000 = 2	$\frac{3,000}{9,000} = \frac{1}{3}$

Example Find 0.36 ÷ 0.04.

It is easier to divide by a whole number than a decimal. Multiply both the dividend and the divisor by a power of 10 until the divisor is a whole number.

0.36 ÷ 0.04
3.6 ÷ 0.4
36 ÷ 4 = 9

So, 0.36 ÷ 0.04 = 9.

Remember
In any whole number, a decimal point can be placed to the right of the ones place.
50 = 50.0

More Examples

A Quotients of whole numbers divided by a decimal

6 ÷ 0.03
60 ÷ 0.3
600 ÷ 3 = 200

So, 6 ÷ 0.03 = 200.

B Quotients of decimals divided by a decimal

0.35 ÷ 0.5
3.5 ÷ 5 = 0.7

So, 0.35 ÷ 0.5 = 0.7.

Guided Practice

Copy and complete the pattern.

1. 42 ÷ 6 = ■
   4.2 ÷ 0.6 = ■
2. 800 ÷ 2 = ■
   8 ÷ ■ = 400
3. 8,100 ÷ 9 = ■
   ■ ÷ 0.09 = 900

NS 2.1 Add, subtract, multiply, and divide with decimals; add with negative integers; subtract positive integers from negative integers; and verify reasonableness of the results. *also* **NS 2.0, MR 1.1, MR 2.3, MR 2.4, MR 3.2**

Divide.

4. $0.12 \div 0.03$

5. $2 \div 0.4$

✓6. $0.72 \div 0.9$

✓7. $0.54 \div 0.6$

8. TALK Math **Explain** why the quotient of $0.2 \div 0.05$ is the same as the quotient of $200 \div 50$.

Independent Practice and Problem Solving

Copy and complete the pattern.

9. $0.45 \div 0.09 = ■$
$4.5 \div ■ = 5$
$■ \div 9 = 5$

10. $4 \div 0.05 = ■$
$40 \div ■ = 80$
$■ \div 5 = 80$

11. $0.18 \div 0.2 = ■$
$1.8 \div ■ = 0.9$
$■ \div 200 = 0.9$

Divide.

12. $6 \div 0.03$

13. $0.32 \div 0.08$

14. $0.27 \div 0.9$

15. $0.15 \div 0.03$

16. $0.28 \div 0.04$

17. $8 \div 0.02$

18. $0.49 \div 0.7$

19. $0.63 \div 0.9$

20. **Reasoning** At the school fair, Jay bought 7 bags of popcorn for $4.00. Did he pay more or less than $0.50 for each bag? **Explain.**

21. WRITE Math **What's the Error?** Shanti says that $0.56 \div 0.08$ is 0.7. Why is Shanti's answer incorrect? What is the correct answer?

Achieving the Standards

22. Copy and complete the pattern. (NS 2.1, p. 294)

$1 \times 2.385 = 2.385$
$10 \times 2.385 = ■$
$100 \times 2.385 = ■$
$1000 \times 2.385 = ■$

23. Gabriella drove from Sacramento to San Diego, a distance of 504.4 miles. If the drive took 8 hours, what was her average speed in miles per hour? (NS 2.2, p. 320)

24. **Test Prep** Copy and complete the table. Divide by 0.8.

Input	Output
40	■
4	■
0.4	■
0.04	■

25. **Test Prep** What is the quotient for $0.14 \div 0.7$?

A 2

B 0.2

C 0.02

D 0.002

Extra Practice on page 334, Set C

Division of Decimals by Decimals

OBJECTIVE: Divide decimals by decimals.

Quick Review

Find the missing numbers.

1. 4,200 ÷ 600 = ■
2. 420 ÷ 60 = ■
3. 42 ÷ ■ = 7
4. 4.2 ÷ ■ = 7
5. ■ ÷ 0.06 = 7

Learn

PROBLEM Sherri hikes on the Pacific Coast Trail. She plans to hike 3.72 miles. If she hikes at an average speed of 1.2 miles per hour, how long will she hike?

Divide 3.72 ÷ 1.2.

The Pacific Coast Trail is 2,650 miles long and runs from Mexico to Canada. It passes through California, Oregon, and Washington.

ONE WAY Use fractions.

Step 1

Write the decimals as fractions.

$3.72 \div 1.2$

$3\frac{72}{100} \div 1\frac{2}{10}$

$\frac{372}{100} \div \frac{12}{10}$

Step 2

Divide the fractions.

$\frac{372}{100} \div \frac{12}{10}$

$\frac{372}{100} \times \frac{10}{12} = \frac{3,720}{1,200} = \frac{372}{120} = 3\frac{12}{120} = 3\frac{1}{10}$

Step 3

Write the fraction as a decimal.

$3\frac{1}{10} = 3.1$

So, Sherri will hike 3.1 hours.

ANOTHER WAY Use a whole-number divisor.

Step 1

Move the decimal point one place to the right in both the dividend and the divisor.

$1.2\overline{)3.72}$

Multiply both the dividend and the divisor by 10.

Step 2

Write the decimal point in the quotient above the decimal point in the dividend.

$12\overline{)37.2}$

Step 3

Divide by the whole number.

$$\begin{array}{r} 3.1 \\ 12\overline{)37.2} \\ -36 \\ \hline 12 \\ -12 \\ \hline 0 \end{array}$$

- What power of 10 was used in Step 1 to rewrite the problem?
- How can you check your answer?

Math Idea

Multiply both the dividend and the divisor by the same power of 10 so that you have an expression that is equivalent to your original division equation.

NS 2.1 Add, subtract, multiply, and divide with decimals; add with negative integers; subtract positive integers from negative integers; and verify reasonableness of the results, *also* **NS 2.0, NS 2.2, MR 1.1, MR 2.3, MR 2.4, MR 3.2**

Other Examples

A Find 0.192 ÷ 2.4.

When the divisor is greater than the dividend, you may need to write zeros to the left of the first nonzero digit in the quotient.

```
                     0.08
2.4)0.192 → 24)1.92
                 −192
                 ----
                    0
```

B Find 72.6 ÷ 0.44.

When the dividend is greater than the divisor, you may need to write a zero to the right of the dividend so that you can move the decimal point.

```
                    165.
0.44)72.6 → 44)7260.
               −44
               ---
                286
               −264
               ----
                 220
                −220
                ----
                   0
```

C Find 15 ÷ 25.

To divide a whole number by a decimal, place the decimal point to the right of the whole number.

```
                                60.
0.25)15 → 0.25)15. → 25)1500.
                        −150
                        ----
                           0
```

D Find $11.52 ÷ 0.6.

When you divide a money amount, you may need to write a zero to the right of the dividend to provide two digits for the cents.

```
                     $19.20
0.6)$11.52 → 6)$115.20
                −6
                --
                 55
                −54
                ---
                  12
                 −12
                 ---
                   0
```

Guided Practice

Rewrite the problem so that it has a whole-number divisor.

1. 0.56)4.648 → 56)■
2. 2.1)53.34 → 21)■
3. 0.04)12.1 → 4)■

Write the quotient correctly.

4. 28)5.88 (quotient shown: 21)
5. 0.08)32.4 (quotient shown: 405)
6. 0.63)0.252 (quotient shown: 4)
7. 0.5)9 (quotient shown: 18)

Divide. Use multiplication to check your answer.

8. 0.09)1.341
9. 0.7)$2.45
10. 2.6)8.84
11. 0.65)1.56

12. TALK Math **Explain** where you need to write zeros to find the quotient of 0.7 ÷ 0.04.

Independent Practice and Problem Solving

Rewrite the problem so that it has a whole number divisor.

13. $0.17\overline{)3.978} \rightarrow 17\overline{)■}$ **14.** $3.4\overline{)78.88}$ **15.** $0.06\overline{)7.23}$

Write the quotient correctly.

16. $\overset{584}{0.9\overline{)5.256}}$ **17.** $\overset{27}{3.3\overline{)8.91}}$ **18.** $\overset{\$3555}{0.8\overline{)\$28.44}}$ **19.** $\overset{75}{0.38\overline{)28.5}}$

20. $0.153 \div 1.7 = 9$ **21.** $\$41.82 \div 3.4 = \$123$ **22.** $54 \div 0.24 = 225$ **23.** $91.76 \div 0.62 = 148$

Divide. Use multiplication to check your answer.

24. $4.2\overline{)9.66}$ **25.** $17\overline{)397.8}$ **26.** $0.48\overline{)84}$ **27.** $2.7\overline{)0.216}$

28. $\$38.60 \div 0.4$ **29.** $91.98 \div 0.73$ **30.** $77.5 \div 0.62$ **31.** $\$97.18 \div 4.3$

Algebra Solve for n.

32. $n \div 0.13 = 1.3$ **33.** $n \div 1.4 = 0.14$ **34.** $6.3 \div n = 0.21$ **35.** $96 \div n = 0.32$

USE DATA For 36–39, use the table.

36. Hikers make trail mix to carry on hikes. Jerry's trail mix recipe calls for 0.25 pound of apricots. How many batches of trail mix can he make with 1 package of apricots?

37. Which type of nut costs the most per pound? What is its cost per pound?

38. During a sale, customers can buy 1 pound of nuts and get 1 pound of a less expensive nut for half price. Sophie wants some almonds and some peanuts. How much will she pay?

39. Adam uses 1 pound each of cashews and peanuts in his trail mix. What is the cost of the nuts for one batch of Adam's trail mix?

40. WRITE Math **Sense or Nonsense?** Sara says that when you divide by a whole number greater than 0, the quotient is less than or equal to the dividend. But, she says, when you divide by a decimal, the quotient is greater than the dividend. Do Sara's statements make sense? **Explain.**

The Chewy House Price List
Packaged Fruits and Nuts

Item	Weight (Pounds)	Price
Raisins	1	$2.25
Apricots	1.5	$4.59
Almonds	0.75	$4.74
Peanuts	3	$7.32
Cashews	2.5	$12.60

Achieving the Standards

41. Shaun hikes an average of 20 miles a day for 2 weeks. Write an expression that represents the total distance he hikes.
(Grade 4 AF 1.0)

42. ***FAST FACT*** The deepest lake in the world is Lake Baikal in Siberia, Russia. Its greatest depth is 5,369 feet. Crater Lake in Oregon is the deepest lake in the United States. It is about 0.4 times as deep as Lake Baikal. About how deep is Crater Lake?
(NS 2.1, p. 298)

43. Estimate $2.281 \div 0.27$. (NS 2.1, p. 318)

44. **Test Prep** Which problem has the same quotient as $1.596 \div 0.42$?

A $1{,}596 \div 42$
B $159.6 \div 42$
C $15.96 \div 42$
D $0.1596 \div 4.2$

45. **Test Prep** During an experiment, Julia's plant grew 19.2 centimeters. She reported that it grew an average of 1.6 centimeters per day. How many days did the experiment last?

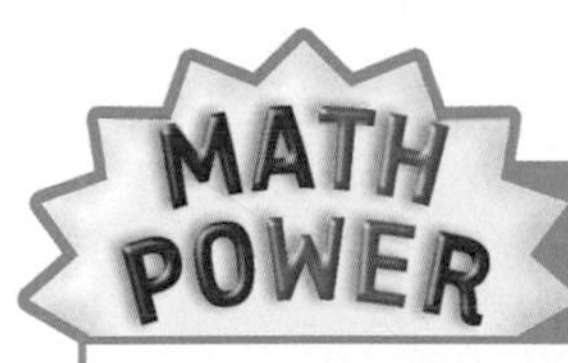

Problem Solving and Reasoning

NUMBER SENSE The exchange rate is the value of one country's currency in relation to another country's currency. The table shows the exchange rates in relation to the U.S. dollar for some countries on one day.

Ron traveled to Japan. The table shows the exchange rate for the Japanese yen is 120. This means that 120 Japanese yen have the same value as 1 U.S. dollar. How many yen did Ron receive in exchange for 200 U.S. dollars?

When Ron left Japan, he exchanged 3,600 yen for U.S. dollars at the same exchange rate. How many U.S. dollars did he receive?

Currency Exchange Rates

Country	Currency	Exchange Rate
United States	dollar	1.00
Canada	dollar	1.10
France	franc	5.40
Japan	yen	120.00
Mexico	peso	10.00
South Africa	rand	6.10
United Kingdom	pound	0.56

U.S. dollars × exchange rate = Japanese yen

$200 \times 120 = 24{,}000$

So, Ron received 24,000 Japanese yen.

Japanese yen ÷ exchange rate = U.S. dollars

$3{,}600 \div 120 = 30$

Ron received 30 U.S. dollars.

Use the table to find the value of each amount.

1. 40 U.S. dollars in French francs
2. 80 U.S. dollars in South African rands
3. 20.35 Canadian dollars in U.S. dollars
4. 168 British (United Kingdom) pounds in U.S. dollars
5. 26.50 U.S. dollars in Mexican pesos
6. 4,500 Mexican pesos in U.S. dollars

Problem Solving Workshop
Skill: Evaluate Answers for Reasonableness

OBJECTIVE: Solve problems by using the skill evaluate answers for reasonableness.

Use the Skill

PROBLEM Jennifer's family is going to London, England. Before going, the family members exchange U.S. dollars for British pounds. They get 1.725 British pounds for every 3 U.S. dollars. Jennifer says the exchange rate is 1 U.S. dollar = 0.575 British pound. Her brother Jack says the exchange rate is 1 U.S. dollar = 0.0575 British pound. Whose answer is reasonable?

Jennifer	Jack
0.575	0.0575
3)1.725	3)1.725
-15	-15
22	22
-21	-21
15	15
-15	-15
0	0

Many web sites offer a Foreign Exchange currency converter like the one shown here, which can convert U.S. dollars to more than 100 different foreign currencies.

Estimate $1.725 \div 3$.

Use compatible numbers to estimate. $1.8 \div 3 = 0.6$

Compare Jennifer's and Jack's answers with the estimate. Jennifer's answer of 0.575 is close to the estimate of 0.6. Jack's answer of 0.0575 is not close to the estimate of 0.6. So, Jennifer's answer is reasonable.

Think and Discuss

Answer without doing the computation.
Explain your reasoning.

a. Bob bought five identical books for \$14.75. He said the cost of one book was \$2.95. Is his statement reasonable?

b. Stella bought 3 bags of potting soil. Each bag weighs 0.79 kilogram. Stella said the total mass of the potting soil is 23.7 kilograms. Is her statement reasonable?

NS 2.1 Add, subtract, multiply, and divide with decimals; add with negative integers; subtract positive integers from negative integers; and very the reasonableness of the results. *also* **NS 1.1, NS 2.0, NS 2.2, MR 2.0, MR 2.1, MR 2.2, MR 2.3, MR 2.4, MR 2.5, MR 3.0, MR 3.1, MR 3.2**

Guided Problem Solving Practice

1. Alan's family is going to Cancun, Mexico. Before going, the family members exchange U.S. dollars for Mexican pesos. They get 86.88 Mexican pesos for every 8 U.S. dollars. Alan says the exchange rate is 1 U.S. dollar = 1.086 Mexican pesos. His sister Ellen says the exchange rate is 1 U.S. dollar = 10.86 Mexican pesos. Whose answer is reasonable?

Alan

```
    1.086
8)86.88
  -8
   6
  -0
   68
  -64
    48
   -48
     0
```

Ellen

```
   10.86
8)86.88
  -8
   6
  -0
   68
  -64
    48
   -48
     0
```

Divide using compatible numbers to estimate. What equation can you use to estimate the solution?

Compare Alan's answer with Ellen's answer. Whose answer is closer to the estimate? Which answer is more reasonable?

2. **What if** Alan says the exchange rate is 1 U.S. dollar = 10.9 Mexican pesos and Ellen's answer stays the same. Whose answer is reasonable then?

3. Britney bought 0.97 kilogram of apples, 1.05 kilograms of bananas, and 0.57 kilogram of oranges. Britney says she bought 25.9 kilograms of fruit. Brad says that Britney bought 2.59 kilograms of fruit. Use estimation to find whose answer is reasonable? **Explain.**

Mixed Applications

USE DATA For 4–6, use the table.

4. Tanesha says 1 U.S. dollar = 77.596 Hong Kong dollars. Andrew says 1 U.S. dollar = 7.759 Hong Kong dollars. Whose answer is reasonable? **Explain.**

5. **Pose a Problem** Write a problem like Problem 4, using different numbers from the table.

6. **WRITE Math** George exchanged 5 U.S. dollars for some Japanese yen. **Explain** how you can find the number of yen George received.

Currency Exchange Rates (September 2006)

U.S. Dollars	Currency
2	2.691 Australian dollars
5	3.928 European euros
8	943.320 Japanese yen
12	321.281 Russian rubles
15	116.868 Hong Kong dollars

Extra Practice

Set A Use compatible numbers to estimate the quotient. (pp. 318–319)

1. $37.2 \div 4$
2. $2.2 \div 7$
3. $87.3 \div 29$
4. $3.301 \div 51$
5. $49.03 \div 8$
6. $0.295 \div 7$
7. $118.6 \div 19$
8. $82.6 \div 9$
9. $5.63 \div 6$
10. $17.91 \div 62$
11. $4.063 \div 21$
12. $238.1 \div 4$
13. Zach spent \$11.97 on 3 packs of trading cards. About how much did each pack cost?
14. Nina ran 26.25 miles over 5 days. She ran the same route each day. About how many miles is her route?

Set B Find the quotient. (pp. 320–323)

1. $3\overline{)3.75}$
2. $4\overline{)3.84}$
3. $5\overline{)10.68}$
4. $12\overline{)\$13.80}$
5. $7\overline{)0.035}$
6. $45\overline{)148.5}$
7. $6\overline{)67.8}$
8. $2\overline{)0.038}$
9. $9\overline{)1.08}$
10. $8\overline{)24.84}$
11. $29\overline{)\$2.32}$
12. $96\overline{)364.8}$
13. $7.92 \div 4$
14. $254.8 \div 7$
15. $39.78 \div 13$
16. $\$284.05 \div 5$
17. $6.3 \div 21$
18. $468.72 \div 93$
19. $\$571.52 \div 47$
20. $32.65 \div 5$
21. Jake used 13.5 cups of flour to make 9 batches of pancakes. How many cups of flour did he use in each batch?
22. Silvia is cutting a length of twine that measures 73.5 inches into 14 same-sized pieces. How long is each piece of twine in inches?

Set C Divide. (pp. 326–327)

1. $8 \div 0.04$
2. $0.15 \div 0.05$
3. $0.48 \div 0.8$
4. $9 \div 0.3$
5. $0.14 \div 0.07$
6. $15 \div 0.05$
7. $0.54 \div 0.09$
8. $4 \div 0.2$
9. $0.56 \div 0.8$
10. $0.42 \div 0.07$
11. $2.1 \div 0.7$
12. $32 \div 0.04$
13. $24 \div 0.8$
14. $0.24 \div 0.3$
15. $3.5 \div 0.7$
16. $0.44 \div 1.1$

Set D Divide. Use multiplication to check your answer. (pp. 328–331)

1. $1.5\overline{)3.45}$
2. $5.6\overline{)0.168}$
3. $0.75\overline{)12}$
4. $0.22\overline{)27.5}$
5. $\$8.61 \div 0.7$
6. $24 \div 0.8$
7. $1.92 \div 1.2$
8. $7.5 \div 0.15$
9. $7.65 \div 1.7$
10. $59.5 \div 0.25$
11. $6 \div 0.6$
12. $\$57.02 \div 0.2$

Technology
Use Harcourt Mega Math, The Number Games, *Tiny's Think Tank*, Level S.

Ready!

2 players

Set!

- Division cards
- Compatible numbers cards
- Estimate cards

Play!

- Players shuffle the division cards and place them facedown in a 3-by-4 array.
- Players shuffle the compatible numbers cards and place them facedown in a separate 3-by-4 array.
- Players shuffle the estimate cards and place them facedown in a separate 3-by-4 array.
- Players take turns turning cards over in each array and determining whether all three cards match.
- If the cards match, the player keeps all three cards and takes another turn. If the cards do not match, they are returned facedown to their original positions.
- Play continues until no cards are left.
- The player who has more cards wins!

Chapter 13 Review/Test

Check Concepts

Complete.

1. Explain how to use a model to find $0.52 \div 4$. (O-π NS 2.1, pp. 316–317)
2. Explain where to place the decimal point of the quotient when you divide a decimal by a whole number. (O-π NS 2.1, pp. 320–323)
3. You can use fractions to divide a decimal by a decimal. Explain how to find $0.21 \div 0.07$ using fractions. (O-π NS 2.1, pp. 324–325)

Check Skills

Estimate the quotient. (O-π NS 2.1, pp. 318–319)

4. $1.9 \div 6$
5. $63.72 \div 8$
6. $18.5 \div 61$
7. $2.106 \div 43$
8. $251.43 \div 52$
9. $178.5 \div 19$
10. $0.364 \div 5$
11. $57.6 \div 9$

Find the quotient. (O-π NS 2.2, pp. 320–323)

12. $5\overline{)5.65}$
13. $8\overline{)15.6}$
14. $13\overline{)\$33.15}$
15. $5\overline{)1.25}$
16. $106.2 \div 45$
17. $6.36 \div 2$
18. $0.45 \div 9$
19. $\$29.76 \div 16$

Divide. (O-π NS 2.1, pp. 326–327, 328–331)

20. $18 \div 0.03$
21. $0.16 \div 0.4$
22. $0.72 \div 0.06$
23. $6 \div 0.2$
24. $1.3\overline{)6.24}$
25. $2.7\overline{)0.108}$
26. $0.75\overline{)9}$
27. $0.51\overline{)43.86}$
28. $\$2.10 \div 0.2$
29. $15 \div 1.5$
30. $409.6 \div 3.2$
31. $8 \div 0.4$

Check Problem Solving

Solve. (O-π NS 2.1, MR 2.0, MR 2.1, MR 3.1, pp. 332–333)

32. Alana bought a dozen identical pens for \$7.98. She says each pen cost about \$0.07. Is her statement reasonable?

33. WRITE Math Each time Chantal rides the bus, she buys a ticket for \$2.10. Jason buys a book of 6 tickets for \$11.50 in order to save money on each trip. **Explain** how to tell if Jason is saving money.

Technology Use *Online Assessment.*

Enrich • Fractions and Decimals

Different Names

Runner	Distance (in miles)
Andy	$\frac{5}{8}$
Carla	0.4
Dan	0.65

During a training session, three runners started with a 5-minute warm-up. From least to greatest, in what order of distance jogged did each runner finish?

The distance Andy jogged is shown as a fraction. You can divide 5 by 8 to rename $\frac{5}{8}$ as a decimal.

Step 1	**Step 2**
Divide as with whole numbers.	Compare the decimals.
$\begin{array}{r} 0.625 \\ 8\overline{)5.000} \\ -4\,8 \\ \hline 20 \\ -16 \\ \hline 40 \\ -40 \\ \hline \end{array}$	0.6 ⟶ Pat 0.4 ⟶ Carla 0.65 ⟶ Dan

So, listed from least to greatest distances, the runners are: Carla, Pat, Dan.

Warm Up

Use division to write $\frac{6}{8}$ as a decimal.

Think: Divide the numerator by the denominator.

Since 6 ÷ 8 is less than 1, place a 0 in the ones place.
Place the decimal point.
Divide as with whole numbers.

So, $\frac{6}{8} = 0.75$.

$$\begin{array}{r} 0.75 \\ 8\overline{)6.00} \\ -5\,6 \\ \hline 40 \\ -40 \\ \hline 0 \end{array}$$

Workout

Express each fraction as a decimal.

1. $\frac{2}{5}$
2. $\frac{1}{4}$
3. $\frac{7}{20}$
4. $\frac{3}{6}$
5. $\frac{11}{25}$
6. $\frac{1}{8}$
7. $\frac{6}{25}$
8. $\frac{6}{30}$
9. $\frac{13}{50}$
10. $\frac{9}{15}$

Cool Down

WRITE Math A fruit salad recipe calls for $\frac{7}{8}$ pound of apples, 0.75 pound of grapes, and 0.35 pound of cherries. **Explain** the steps you would take to write the weights of the fruits from least to greatest. Then follow your steps and solve.

Unit Review/Test
Chapters 11–13

Multiple Choice

1. What is 38.452 rounded to the nearest tenth? (NS 1.1, p. 272)

   A 40

   B 38.45

   C 38.5

   D 38.4

2. For lunch, Jesse bought a sandwich for \$3.25 and a fruit juice for \$0.95. How much did he spend? (🔑 NS 2.1, p. 274)

   A \$3.10

   B \$3.20

   C \$4.10

   D \$4.20

3. Carlotta is hiking a trail that is 3.2 miles long. She already has hiked 2.7 miles. How much farther does Carlotta have to hike? (🔑 NS 2.1, p. 274)

   A 0.5 miles

   B 0.7 miles

   C 1.9 miles

   D 5.9 miles

4. $17.3 \times 4.1 =$ (🔑 NS 2.1, p. 300)

   A 8.55

   B 49.93

   C 60.93

   D 70.93

5. $$\begin{array}{r} 43.13 \\ \times \quad 0.5 \\ \hline \end{array}$$
   (🔑 NS 2.1, p. 300)

   A 20.555

   B 20.565

   C 21.565

   D 215.65

6. Which of the following is the *best* estimate for 5.24×0.82? (NS 1.1, p. 298)

   A 0.4

   B 4

   C 40

   D 400

7. Neil can type 50 words a minute. At that rate, how many words can he type in 7.5 minutes? (🔑 NS 2.1, p. 294)

   A 370

   B 372

   C 375

   D 380

8. $342.6 \div 5 =$ (🔑 NS 2.1, p. 320)

   A 68.52

   B 68.5

   C 60.5

   D 58.52

GO ONLINE Technology Use *Online Assessment.*

Show What You Know

Check your understanding of important skills needed for success in Chapter 14.

▶ Multiplication Properties

Write the letter of the multiplication property used in each equation.

A. Commutative Property **C.** Identity Property
B. Associative Property **D.** Zero Property

1. $43 \times 1 = 43$ **2.** $6 \times 9 = 9 \times 6$ **3.** $(8 \times 2) \times 4 = 8 \times (2 \times 4)$

4. $7 \times 12 = 12 \times 7$ **5.** $3 \times (9 \times 5) = (3 \times 9) \times 5$ **6.** $62 \times 0 = 0$

▶ Addition Properties

Write the letter of the addition property used in each equation.

A. Commutative Property **B.** Associative Property **C.** Identity Property

7. $8 + 5 = 5 + 8$ **8.** $25 + 0 = 25$ **9.** $(6 + 7) + 2 = 6 + (7 + 2)$

10. $0 + 37 = 37$ **11.** $9 + (3 + 5) = (9 + 3) + 5$ **12.** $15 + 29 = 29 + 15$

▶ Expressions

Find each value.

13. $(6 + 9) - 3$ **14.** $4 + (16 - 5)$ **15.** $12 + (25 - 3)$

16. $(32 + 8) - 10$ **17.** $(9 + 8) - 7$ **18.** $20 - (3 + 4)$

19. $15 + (22 - 3)$ **20.** $36 - (9 + 3)$ **21.** $41 - (20 - 5)$

VOCABULARY POWER

CHAPTER VOCABULARY

algebraic expression
Distributive Property
equation
evaluate
expression
numerical expression
solution
variable

WARM-UP WORDS

order of operations a special set of rules which gives the order in which calculations are done in an expression

evaluate to find the value of an numerical or algebraic expression

equation an algebraic or numerical sentence that shows that two quantities are equal

LESSON 1

Write Expressions

OBJECTIVE: Write numerical and algebraic expressions for word expressions.

Quick Review

Write the expression.

The orchestra had 24 members last year. This year 7 new members joined.

Learn

PROBLEM Rufus, the German Shepherd dog, doubled his puppy weight when he was 1 week old. Then he put on 38 more pounds. Write an expression to represent the dog's adult weight.

Example Write an algebraic expression.

First, choose a variable to represent the dog's weight as a puppy.
Let p = the dog's weight as a puppy.

Then identify the operations.

twice	puppy weight	more than	38 pounds
↓	↓		↓
$2\times$	p	$+$	38

So, $2 \times p + 38$, or $2p + 38$ represents the dog's adult weight.

More Examples Write an algebraic or a numerical expression.

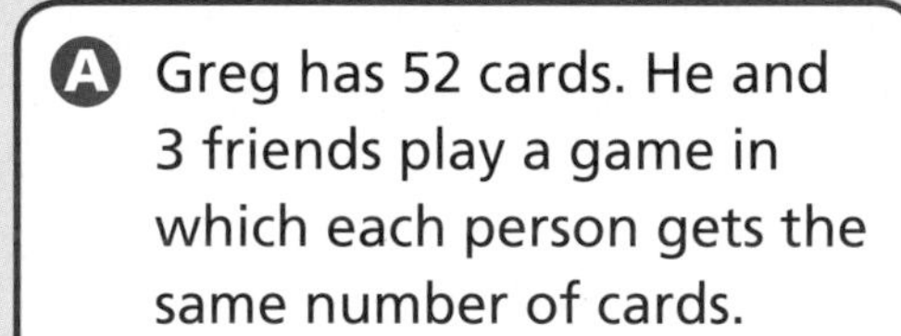

A Greg has 52 cards. He and 3 friends play a game in which each person gets the same number of cards.

$52 \div 4$

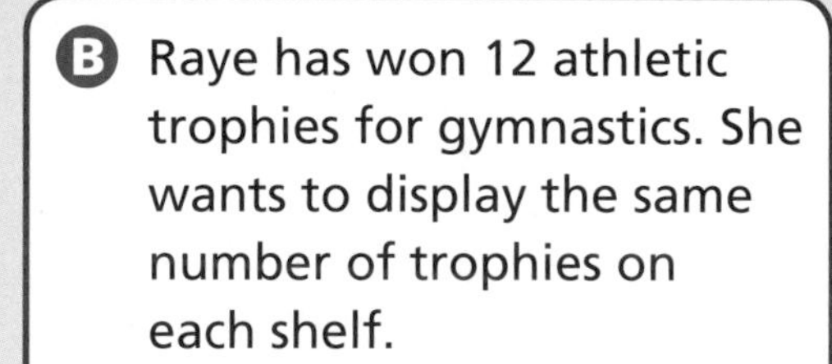

B Raye has won 12 athletic trophies for gymnastics. She wants to display the same number of trophies on each shelf.

$12 \div s$

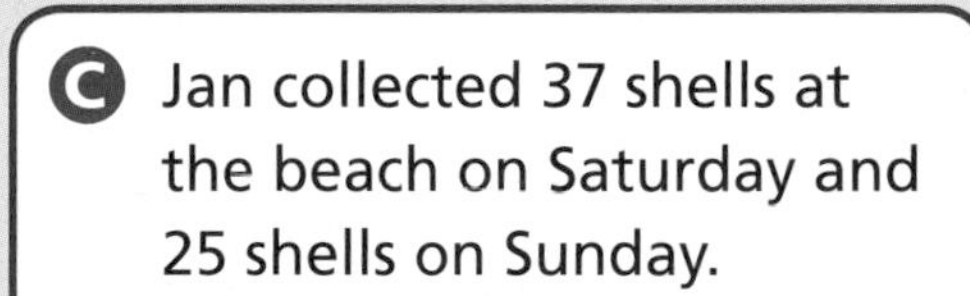

C Jan collected 37 shells at the beach on Saturday and 25 shells on Sunday.

$37 + 25$

D Les bought some melons. He gave 20 away and sold the rest for $2 each.

$(p - 20) \times 2$

Guided Practice

1. Copy and complete the expression for this situation. A restaurant had 75 tables. Five tables were added, and then 2 were removed.

tables in restaurant	plus	5 tables	minus	2 tables
↓		↓		↓
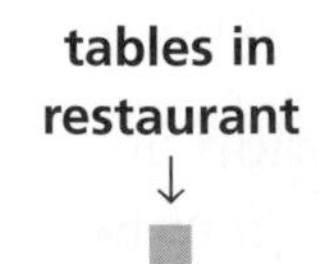	$+$	5	$-$	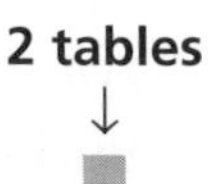

O━ AF 1.2 Use a letter to represent an unknown number; write and evaluate simple algebraic expressions in one variable by substitution. *also* AF 1.1, MR 2.2, MR 2.3, MR 2.4, MR 3.1, MR 3.2, MR 3.3

Write an expression for each situation. If you use a variable, explain what the variable represents.

2. Kim bought a length of ribbon and then cut off $12\frac{3}{8}$ feet of ribbon.

3. Twenty-nine people were at the party. Then 17 more arrived.

4. Jared has $19. He spends $7.48 on school supplies.

5. TALK Math **Explain** how to write an algebraic expression for this situation. Write what the variable represents. Rebecca bought 18 dog treats. Her dog ate some, and Rebecca bought 9 more.

Independent Practice and Problem Solving

Write an expression for each situation. If you use a variable, explain what the variable represents.

6. Lila has 5 fewer than 3 times the number of stickers Eve has.

7. Drake's family traveled 404 miles the first day and 350 miles the second day.

8. The distance to the waterfall is $1\frac{2}{3}$ miles farther than the distance in miles to the river.

9. Patrick had 45 baseball cards. He gave 18 cards to Sean and got back 13.

10. Tim hired a pet sitter for his dog, Rex. Tim left a note for the pet sitter that said to feed Rex $2\frac{1}{2}$ cups of food each day. Write an algebraic expression for the amount of food Rex eats in d days.

11. Rex ate the same number of cups of food every day except Sunday. On Sunday he ate $\frac{1}{2}$ cup less than usual. What expression shows how much Rex ate on Sunday?

12. WRITE Math The pet sitter took Rex for a 1.6-mile walk twice a day for d days. **Explain** how to write an algebraic expression for the total number of miles Rex walked.

Achieving the Standards

13. What is the value of $15 - 9 + 7$? (Grade 4 AF 1.0)

14. What is another way of writing 6^4? (NS 1.3, p. 126)

15. $19.52 \div 6.1 =$ (NS 2.2, p. 326)

16. **Test Prep** The height of a plant this month is 3.5 times as great as its height last month, h. Which expression represents this month's height?

A $3.5 + h$

B $3.5 - h$

C $3.5h$

D $3.5 \div h$

Extra Practice on page 368, Set A

LESSON 2

Evaluate Expressions

OBJECTIVE: Evaluate numerical and algebraic expressions.

Quick Review

Find the value.

1. 12 + 5 − 8
2. 10 − (8 − 4)
3. 18 − 7 + 4
4. 16 + (7 − 2)
5. 21 + 9 − 25

Vocabulary

order of operations

Learn

Some expressions may have more than one operation.

PROBLEM Simone went to the Natural History Museum of Los Angeles. To remember the butterfly exhibit, she bought 3 postcards at 25¢ each and 2 postcards at 45¢ each. How much did Simone spend on postcards?

$$(3 \times 25) + (2 \times 45)$$

When you evaluate an expression that has more than one operation, you need to use rules called the **order of operations**.

1. First, operate inside parentheses.
2. Next, multiply and divide from left to right.
3. Then, add and subtract from left to right.

▲ Butterfly wings show many different shapes and colors.

Example 1 Evaluate. (3 × 25) + (2 × 45)

(3 × 25) + (2 × 45) Operate inside parentheses.
75 + 90 Add.
165

So, Simone spent 165¢, or $1.65, for postcards.

More Examples

A Evaluate. 70 − 4 × (12 + 4)

70 − 4 × (12 + 4)
70 − 4 × 16
70 − 64
6

B Evaluate. 27 ÷ 9 × 4 + 7

27 ÷ 9 × 4 + 7
3 × 4 + 7
12 + 7
19

- **What if** the expression in Example A were 70 − 4 × 12 + 4? What is the new value?
- In Example B, why would the answer be the same if parentheses enclosed 27 ÷ 9?

🔑 **AF 1.2** Use a letter to represent an unknown number; write and evaluate simple algebraic expressions in one variable by substitution. *also* **AF 1.1, MR 2.2, MR 2.3, MR 2.4, MR 3.1, MR 3.2, MR 3.3**

Expressions with Variables

To evaluate an algebraic expression with a variable, replace the variable with a number. Then follow the order of operations to find the value of the expression.

Example 2 **Evaluate $(18 + n) \times 6 - 4$ if $n = 12$.**

$(18 + n) \times 6 - 4$	Replace n with 12.
$(18 + 12) \times 6 - 4$	Operate inside the parentheses.
$30 \times 6 - 4$	Multiply.
$180 - 4$	Subtract.
176	

More Examples

A **Evaluate $7 \times (n - 3.2)$ if $n = 6$.**

$7 \times (n - 3.2)$
$7 \times (6 - 3.2)$
7×2.8
19.6

B **Evaluate $3c + 5$ if $c = \frac{1}{3}$.**

$3c + 5$
$(3 \times \frac{1}{3}) + 5$
$1 + 5$
6

C **Evaluate $12 - (6 + c)$ if $c = 2\frac{1}{2}$.**

$12 - (6 + c)$
$12 - (6 + 2\frac{1}{2})$
$12 - 8\frac{1}{2}$
$3\frac{1}{2}$

D **Evaluate $\frac{x}{5} + 12 \times 2$ if $x = 20$.**

$\frac{x}{5} + 12 \times 2$
$\frac{20}{5} + 12 \times 2$
$4 + 24$
28

- Find the value of the expression in Example D if $x = 10$.

Guided Practice

1. Tell which operation you would do first, second, and third to evaluate the expression. $49 - 45 \div 5 \times 3$

Evaluate each expression.

2. $30 \div (8 + 7)$
3. $32 - (7 \times 3)$
4. $20 \times 4 - 2$
5. $(6 \div 3) \times 4 + 8$

Evaluate the algebraic expression for the given value of the variable.

6. $n + 2\frac{3}{8} - 3$ if $n = \frac{5}{8}$
7. $9 - (n + 2)$ if $n = 3$
8. $(n \times 6.2) - 12$ if $n = 4$
9. $8 \times (28 \div n)$ if $n = 4$

10. TALK Math **Explain** how to evaluate the expression $9m + (50 \div m)$ if $m = 10$.

Independent Practice and Problem Solving

Evaluate each expression.

11. $27 - (12 + 9)$ **12.** $41 - (42 \div 14)$ **13.** $13 \times 3 - 7$ **14.** $(56 \div 4) - 9$

Evaluate the algebraic expression for the given value of the variable.

15. $4 + (n + 3)$ if $n = 6$

16. $17 + d - 5$ if $d = 3$

17. $2c - 4$ if $c = 4.8$

18. $8 + \frac{24}{n}$ if $n = 3$

19. $3k - 1$ if $k = 5$

20. $7 + 5d$ if $d = 1.2$

21. $12\frac{1}{4} - n \times 3$ if $n = 2$

22. $5t + 2$ if $t = 4$

23. $6 + (q - 4\frac{3}{8})$ if $q = 10\frac{7}{8}$

24. $15\frac{1}{3} - b + 7$ if $b = 5\frac{1}{3}$

25. $3h - (2 + 0.3)$ if $h = 2.3$

26. $5 \times (r - 4.2)$ if $r = 12.6$

27. $37 - 3.4m$ if $m = 6$

28. $(3\frac{1}{2} + n) - 1\frac{1}{2}$ if $n = 7$

Write an algebraic expression using a variable. Then find the value.

29. Darius saw 5 monarch butterflies and some painted lady butterflies. Then 3 of the butterflies flew away. How many butterflies were left if Darius saw 4 painted lady butterflies?

30. Josie's camera can take 36 pictures. She took some pictures in the butterfly exhibit. Then she took 16 more pictures in the African Mammal Hall. If Josie took 13 pictures in the butterfly exhibit, how many pictures does she have left to take?

31. Cynthia bought bottles of water at the museum. Each bottle of water cost $2.75. She had $10.00 to start with. How much money did Cynthia have left if she bought 3 bottles of water?

32. **WRITE Math** A class of 24 students will be divided into equal groups at the museum. Each group will have 2 guides. The total number of people in each group must be less than 10. **Explain** whether the students should be divided into 2, 3, or 4 groups.

 Extra Practice on page 368, Set B

Achieving the Standards

33. What is the median of these driving speeds: 55 mph, 65 mph, 75 mph, 60 mph, 55 mph, 65 mph, 55 mph? **(Grade 4 SDAP 1.2)**

34. What value for ■ makes this number sentence true?

$33 - ■ = 24 + 6$ **(Grade 4 AF 1.0)**

35. **Test Prep** The expression $6m$ shows the cost of lunch for 6 people. If $m = \$3.50$, what was the total cost of the lunch?

A \$2.50 **C** \$18.50

B \$9.50 **D** \$21.00

36. Ten cards are numbered 1 to 10. The cards are mixed and then placed in a bag. What is the probability that Bill will pull an odd number out of the bag? **(Grade 4 SDAP 2.0)**

37. **Test Prep** If $d = 7$, what is the value of $5d + 2$?

A 35 **C** 39

B 37 **D** 41

Problem Solving and Reasoning

ALGEBRA An expression can contain more than one operation and more than one variable. To evaluate an expression with more than one variable, replace the given values for each variable in the expression. Then follow the order of operations to evaluate.

Evaluate the expression $4x + y - 6$ if $x = 5$ and $y = 2\frac{1}{2}$.

$4x + y - 6$

$(4 \times 5) + 2\frac{1}{2} - 6$ Replace each variable with its given value. Then operate inside parentheses.

$20 + 2\frac{1}{2} - 6$ Add.

$22\frac{1}{2} - 6$ Subtract.

$16\frac{1}{2}$

So, the value of the expression is $16\frac{1}{2}$.

Evaluate the algebraic expression for the given values of the variables.

1. $v + w - 7$ if $v = 3$ and $w = 8.6$

2. $r - 2 \times s$ if $r = 10$ and $s = 4$

3. $a + 2b + 3$ if $a = 14$ and $b = 4$

4. $3m + n$ if $m = 9$ and $n = 12$

5. $s + t - 9$ if $s = 4\frac{3}{5}$ and $t = 7\frac{2}{5}$

6. $c - 2d$ if $c = 15.4$ and $d = 6$

LESSON 3

Write Equations

OBJECTIVE: Write equations for words and word problems for equations.

Quick Review

Write an expression.

A baker divides some cookies evenly among 4 trays.

Vocabulary

equation

Learn

PROBLEM Ben has \$150 in his checking account. After making a deposit, he will have a total of \$220 in the account. How much money will Ben deposit in his checking account? Write an equation with a variable to represent the problem.

An **equation** is a number sentence that shows that two quantities are equal. Use the variable d for the amount of the deposit.

amount in account		deposit		total in account
↓		↓		↓
\$150	+	d	=	\$220

So, the equation is $150 + d = 220$.

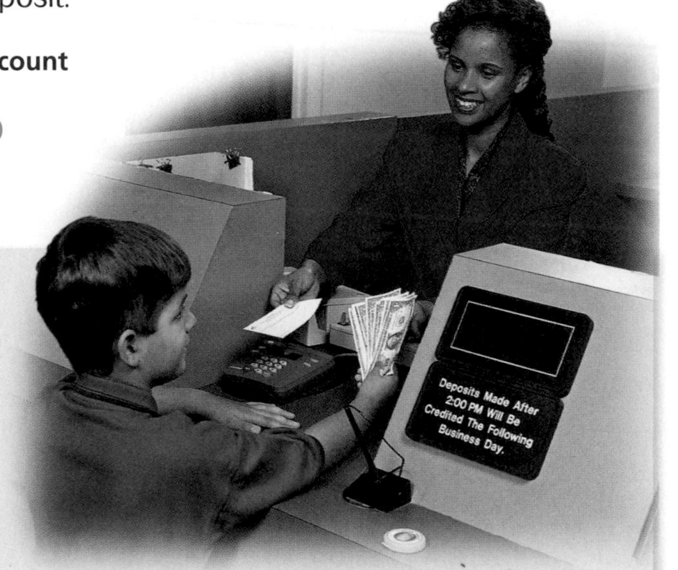

Example **Write an equation for this sentence: a number decreased by twenty-six is four.**

Choose a variable. Let n represent the number.

a number		twenty-six		four
↓		↓		↓
n	−	26	=	4

More Examples

A Write an equation for the problem.

When hatched, an emu is about 10 inches tall. How many inches will the emu grow to reach adult height of 60 inches?

height at birth		inches of growth		height as adult
↓		↓		↓
10	+	m	=	60

B Write a problem for the equation.

y	÷	12	=	18
↓		↓		↓
berries to start with		number of boxes		berries in each box

Ken divides berries into 12 boxes. Each box has 18 berries. How many berries did he start with?

Guided Practice

1. A bike tour is 35 miles. There is a break after 15 miles. Which equation shows d, the distance left after the break?

   a. $d - 15 = 35$
   b. $d \times 15 = 35$
   c. $35 \div d = 15$
   d. $15 + d = 35$

AF 1.2 Use a letter to represent an unknown number; write and evaluate simple algebraic exressions in one variable by substitution. *also* **AF 1.1, MR 1.1, MR 2.2, MR 2.3, MR 2.4, MR 3.2**

Write an equation for each. Tell what the variable represents.

2. Tia has 5 fewer keys than Omar. If Tia has 7 keys, how many does Omar have?

3. The cafeteria has 156 plates. It has 3 times as many plates as trays. How many trays are there?

4. TALK Math **Explain** how to write an equation for this word problem. Dylan has 520 books. He packs 20 books in each carton. How many cartons will he pack?

Independent Practice and Problem Solving

Write an equation for each. Tell what the variable represents.

5. Hunter had 16 CDs. He received more CDs for his birthday. Now he has 23 CDs. How many CDs did Hunter get for his birthday?

6. Hilary paid \$4 for breakfast and \$6 for lunch. Then she bought dinner. Hilary spent a total of \$25. How much did dinner cost?

Write a problem for each equation. Tell what the variable represents.

7. $5 + n = 16$
8. $x - 4 = 7$
9. $3y = 24$
10. $2a + 1 = 7$

For 11–12, use the information in the picture to write an equation with a variable. Tell what the variable represents.

11. Tim spent \$89 on a bicycle seat and another item from Bruce's Bike Shop.

12. Whitney had \$53 and bought two of the same item. She had \$19 left. How much did one of the items cost?

13. WRITE Math Hoshi has saved some money. After he buys a new bicycle seat he has \$26 left. **Explain** how to write an equation with a variable to show the amount of money Hoshi started with.

Achieving the Standards

14. What is 0.086 rounded to the nearest hundredth? (NS 1.1, p. 272)

15. What triangle has exactly two congruent sides? (Grade 4 MG 3.7)

16. Which number is represented by ■? (Grade 4 AF 1.1)

    24 + ■ = 32

17. **Test Prep** Jessica has 4 times as many crayons as markers. She has 20 crayons. Which equation shows the number of markers, *m*, Jessica has?

    A $4 + m = 20$
    B $m - 4 = 20$
    C $4 \times m = 20$
    D $m \div 4 = 20$

Extra Practice on page 369, Set C

LESSON 4 Solve Equations

OBJECTIVE: Write and solve equations.

Quick Review

What value for ■ makes the number sentence true?

1. ■ + 4 = 13
2. 24 ÷ ■ = 6
3. ■ − 5 = 12
4. 3 × ■ = 24
5. ■ ÷ 9 = 7

Vocabulary

solution

Learn

PROBLEM The American black bear is active for 7 months of the year. It usually hibernates the rest of the year. How many months does the bear hibernate?

Write an equation to represent the problem.

months active	+	months in hibernation	=	months in year
↓		↓		↓
7	+	m	=	12

To solve an equation, you find a value for the variable to make the equation true. That value is called the **solution**.

▲ The American black bear is found only in North America.

HANDS ON Activity **Materials** ■ balance, weights

You can use a balance to show which of the numbers 4, 5, or 6 is the solution of the equation $7 + m = 12$.

Step 1

Show 7 on the left and 12 on the right.

Step 2

Replace m with 4.	Place 4 on the left side.
$7 + 4 \stackrel{?}{=} 11$	$11 = 12$ false
Replace m with 5.	Place 5 on the left side.
$7 + 5 \stackrel{?}{=} 12$	$12 = 12$ true
Replace m with 6	Place 6 on the left side.
$7 + 6 \stackrel{?}{=} 13$	$13 = 12$ false

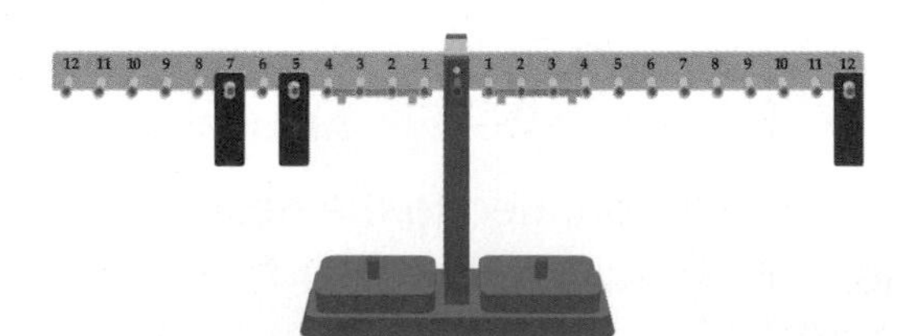

The solution is 5. The values on both sides of the balance are equal. So, the black bear usually hibernates 5 months of the year.

Example Is 3, 5, or 9 the solution of $23 - x = 14$?

$23 - 3 \stackrel{?}{=} 14$ Replace x with 3.	$23 - 5 \stackrel{?}{=} 14$ Replace x with 5.	$23 - 9 \stackrel{?}{=} 14$ Replace x with 9.
$20 = 14$ false	$18 = 14$ false	$14 = 14$ true

AF 1.2 Use a letter to represent an unknown number; write and evaluate simple algebraic expressions in one variable by substitution. *also* **AF 1.1, MR 2.1, MR 2.2, MR 2.3, MR 2.4, MR 3.2**

Mental Math

A 2-year-old female black bear weighs about 4 times as much as it weighed as a 6-month-old cub. If the bear weighs 120 pounds, how much did it weigh as a cub?

Write an equation to solve the problem.

6-month weight	**multiplied by**	**4**	**=**	**2-year weight**
↓	↓	↓		↓
w	$\times$	4	=	120

Solve the equation using mental math.

$4w = 120$ **Think:** 4 times what number equals 120?
$w = 30$

Check: $4 \times 30 = 120$ Replace w with 30.

$120 = 120$ The equation checks.

So, the bear weighed 30 pounds as a 6-month cub.

More Examples **Use mental math to solve each equation.**

A $h \times 0.6 = 5.4$ **Think:** What number times 0.6 equals 5.4?
$h = 9$

Check: $9 \times 0.6 = 5.4$
$5.4 = 5.4$ ✓

B $n - \$10.00 = \$5.25$ **Think:** How much minus \$10.00 equals \$5.25?
$n = \$15.25$

Check: $\$15.25 - \$10.00 = \$5.25$
$\$5.25 = \$5.25$ ✓

C $a + 4\frac{1}{3} = 6\frac{2}{3}$ **Think:** What number plus $4\frac{1}{3}$ equals $6\frac{2}{3}$?
$a = 2\frac{1}{3}$

Check: $2\frac{1}{3} + 4\frac{1}{3} = 6\frac{2}{3}$
$6\frac{2}{3} = 6\frac{2}{3}$ ✓

D $36 \div x = 3$ **Think:** 36 divided by what number equals 3?
$x = 12$

Check: $36 \div 3 = 12$
$12 = 12$ ✓

- Why do you check the solution after solving the equation using mental math?

Guided Practice

1. Which of the numbers 2, 6, or 7 is the solution of the equation $8 - n = 2$?

$8 - n = 2$	$8 - n = 2$	$8 - n = 2$
$8 - 2 \stackrel{?}{=} 2$	$8 - 6 \stackrel{?}{=} 2$	$8 - 7 \stackrel{?}{=} 2$

Which of the numbers 5, 8, or 10 is the solution of the equation?

2. $11 + n = 19$
3. $8 \times a = 40$
4. $y - 1\frac{1}{4} = 6\frac{3}{4}$
5. $s \div 5 = 2$

Use mental math to solve each equation. Check your solution.

6. $m + 6 = 17$
7. $31 - x = 15$
8. $4 \times n = 48$
9. $15 \div r = 5$

10. TALK Math **Explain** why $y = 80$ is the solution to the equation $y \div 8 = 10$.

Independent Practice and Problem Solving

Which of the numbers 3, 6, or 16 is the solution of the equation?

11. $n \times 0.7 = 4.2$
12. $42 - w = 39$
13. $25\frac{1}{3} + q = 41\frac{1}{3}$
14. $27 \div x = 9$

Use mental math to solve each equation. Check your solution.

15. $32 = 11 + r$
16. $4 \times n = 28$
17. $9 = h \div 2$
18. $x - 4 = 4.6$
19. $3.6 \div t = 0.6$
20. $1.9 = c + 0.7$
21. $57 = 68 - a$
22. $\$24.25 + s = \$29.50$
23. $k - 9\frac{1}{5} = 3\frac{2}{5}$
24. $n + 100.6 = 142.8$
25. $\$8 \times y = \$64$
26. $50 \div x = 25$

For 27–30, each variable represents one number. Find the value of each variable.

27. $x + 4 = 9$
    $3 + y = x$
28. $a + 5 = 11$
    $a - b = 2$
29. $3 \times c = 12$
    $c \div d = 4$
30. $6 + s = 14$
    $s \div t = 4$

USE DATA For 31–33, use the table to write the equation. Then solve.

31. The average one-year old male bear weighs 20 pounds more than the average one-year old female. What is the average weight of the one-year old female bear?

32. When an adult male bear came out of hibernation, it weighed n pounds less than the average weight. In 6 months, it gained 85 pounds and weighed 295 pounds. Find the number of pounds the bear lost during hibernation.

33. The sum of the weights of the average adult male and female bears is 400 pounds. What is the average weight of the adult female bear?

34. WRITE Math A black bear cub usually stays with its mother for about 17 months. If a cub has been with its mother for 11 months, about how much longer will the cub stay with its mother? **Explain** how to use an equation to solve the problem.

Black Bears

	Average Weight Male (lb)	Average Weight Female (lb)
One-year old	70	f
Adult	250	a

CD ROM
Technology
Use Harcourt Mega Math, Ice Station Exploration, *Arctic Algebra*, Levels S, T.

Extra Practice on page 369, Set D

Achieving the Standards

35. $\begin{array}{r} 3.8 \\ \times\ 6 \\ \hline \end{array}$ (NS 2.1, p. 298)

36. If $b = 15$, what is the value of $b \div 3 + 9$?
(AF 1.2, p. 348)

37. Maddie skated twice as long as Roy. Maddie skated for 6 hours. How long did Roy skate? Write an equation to represent the problem.
(AF 1.2, p. 352)

38. **Test Prep** The equation $6 \times c = \$48$ shows the total cost of 6 movie tickets. How much does each movie ticket cost?

A $8   **C** $42

B $12   **D** $54

39. **Test Prep** What value for x makes this equation true?

$$6x + 3 = 33?$$

A 3   **C** 5

B 4   **D** 6

Problem Solving and Reasoning

ALGEBRA The parts of algebraic expressions and equations that are separated by addition or subtraction signs are called terms. Before you solve equations, you can simplify them by adding or subtracting like terms.

Equation	Like Terms	Simplified
$4x + 2x = 24$	$4x$ and $2x$	$6x = 24$
$7y - 3y = 32$	$7y$ and $3y$	$4y = 32$

Simplify $8x - 2x = 18$ by combining like terms. Then solve.

$8x - 2x = 18$ Simplify. **Think:** $8x - 2x = 6x$

$6x = 18$ Solve.

$x = 3$

$9h - 2h = 42$

$7h = 42$

$h = 6$

Simplify. Use mental math to solve the equation.

1. $5y + 2y = 63$

2. $9n - 4n = 75$

3. $6x + 3x = 81$

LESSON 5

Use the Distributive Property

OBJECTIVE: Use the Distributive Property in equations and expressions with variables.

Quick Review

Use the Distributive Property to find the value.

1. 8×24 **2.** 3×17
3. 5×47 **4.** 9×29
5. 7×52

Learn

You have used the Distributive Property to find products. You can also use the Distributive Property with variables in equations and expressions.

Example 1 Use the Distributive Property in an expression.

Find the value of $6 \times (n + 8)$ if $n = 40$.

$6 \times (n + 8) = (6 \times n) + (6 \times 8)$ Use the Distributive Property.
$= (6 \times 40) + (6 \times 8)$ Replace n with 40.
$= 240 + 48$ Add.
$= 288$

So, $6 \times (n + 8) = 288$ if $n = 40$.

Example 2 What value for d makes the equation true?

$9 \times 38 = (9 \times 30) + (9 \times d)$ **Think:** $38 = 30 + 8$
$= (9 \times 30) + (9 \times 8)$

So, $d = 8$ makes the equation true.

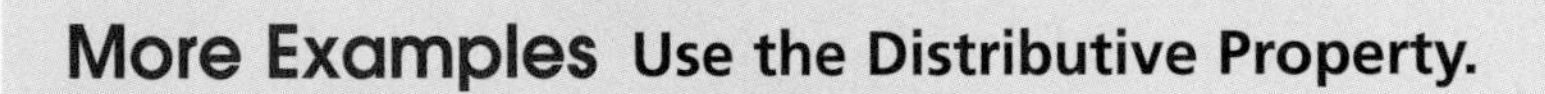

More Examples Use the Distributive Property.

A Find the value of $8 \times (n - 9)$ if $n = 30$.

$8 \times (n - 9) = (8 \times n) - (8 \times 9)$ Use the Distributive Property.
$= (8 \times 30) - (8 \times 9)$ Replace n with 30.
$= 240 - 72$ Subtract.
$= 168$

B What value of w makes the equation true?

$3 \times 84 = (3 \times 80) + (3 \times w)$
$= (3 \times 80) + (3 \times 4)$

So, $w = 4$ makes the equation true.

Guided Practice

Copy. Then use the Distributive Property to find the value of the expression.

1. $7 \times (8 + n)$ if $n = 30$
$= (7 \times 8) + (7 \times ■)$
$= ■ + ■$
$= ■$

2. $3 \times (10 - n)$ if $n = 10$
$= (3 \times 10) - (3 \times n)$
$= ■ - ■$
$= ■$

✓ **3.** $4 \times (n + 6)$ if $n = 20$

AF 1.3 Know and use the distributive property in equations and expressions with variables. *also* **AF 1.0, AF 1.2, MR 1.2, MR 2.3, MR 2.4, MR 3.2**

What value for the variable makes the equation true?

4. $4 \times 27 = (4 \times 20) + (4 \times m)$

5. $5 \times 89 = (5 \times 80) + (5 \times t)$

6. TALK Math **Explain** how you can use the Distributive Property to find the value of $8 \times (n + 6)$ if $n = 10$.

Independent Practice and Problem Solving

Use the Distributive Property to find the value of the expression.

7. $8 \times (m + 6)$ if $m = 10$
8. $9 \times (5 + n)$ if $n = 20$
9. $3 \times (a + 7)$ if $a = 30$
10. $6 \times (4 + h)$ if $h = 60$
11. $2 \times (75 - c)$ if $c = 10$
12. $4 \times (s + 3)$ if $s = 90$
13. $5 \times (45 - g)$ if $g = 20$
14. $7 \times (2 + c)$ if $c = 50$
15. $8 \times (60 - h)$ if $h = 30$

What value makes the equation true?

16. $5 \times 19 = (5 \times 10) + (5 \times t)$
17. $9 \times 89 = (9 \times 90) - (9 \times v)$
18. $8 \times 26 = (8 \times 20) + (8 \times s)$
19. $6 \times 71 = (6 \times 70) + (6 \times r)$
20. $4 \times 58 = (4 \times 50) + (4 \times s)$
21. $4 \times 58 = (4 \times 60) - (4 \times j)$
22. Use the Distributive Property to check whether the equation $4 \times (n + 3) = 172$ is true if $n = 40$.
23. Each day, the zoo takes groups of 24 students and some chaperones on 5 tours through the reptile exhibit. How many students and chaperones visit the reptile exhibit each day if each tour group has 3 chaperones?

24. WRITE Math **What's the Error?** Tommy says the value of $7 \times (n - 4)$ is 66 if n is 10. Rachel says the value is 42. Who is correct? **Explain.**
25. A Galapagos tortoise in the reptile exhibit eats about 36 pounds of fruit each month. Write a number sentence using the Distributive Property to show how much fruit the tortoise eats in 6 months.

Achieving the Standards

26. Which property of multiplication shows that $4 \times 18 \times 25 = 4 \times 25 \times 18$? (Grade 4 AF 1.3)
27. If $w = 8$, what is the value of $7w + 4$? (AF 1.2, p. 348)
28. What is the prime factorization of 36? (NS 1.4, p. 132)
29. What value for t makes this equation true?

$$4 \times 78 = (4 \times 70) + (4 \times t)$$

A 4
B 8
C 10
D 12

Extra Practice on page 369, Set E

LESSON 6

MENTAL MATH

Use the Properties

OBJECTIVE: Use the properties and mental math to solve problems.

Quick Review

Identify the property used.

1. $(6 + 4) + 7 = 6 + (4 + 7)$
2. $15 \times 9 = 9 \times 15$
3. $1 \times 34 = 34$
4. $0 + 302 = 302$
5. $4 \times 37 = (4 \times 30) + (4 \times 7)$

Learn

PROBLEM At the Point Defiance Zoo and Aquarium in Tacoma, Washington, Bruce and Tani saw 4 sea otters in one of the exhibit pools. Then they saw 6 tufted puffins and 3 walruses.

Use mental math to find the total number of sea animals they saw.

You can find the sum mentally by using the Associative Property.

Example 1 Use the Associative Property to solve mentally.

$4 + (6 + 3) = (4 + 6) + 3$ Associative Property of Addition
$= 10 + 3$ Use mental math.
$= 13$

So, Bruce and Tani saw 13 sea animals.

- Why does grouping the numbers differently make it easier to find the value mentally?

You can use other properties to help you mentally solve problems.

More Examples Use the Commutative and Associative Properties.

A $(13 + 2) + 7 = (2 + 13) + 7$ Commutative Property of Addition
$= 2 + (13 + 7)$ Associative Property of Addition
$= 2 + 20$ Use mental math.
$= 22$

B $5 \times (2 \times 75) = (5 \times 2) \times 75$ Associative Property of Multiplication
$= 10 \times 75$ Use mental math.
$= 750$

- Does the Commutative Property work for subtraction? Explain.

A sea otter's fur is the thickest and finest of any mammal. Sea otters have 850,000 to 1,000,000 hairs per square inch and two coats of hairs. ▼

NS 1.0 Students compute wth very large and very small numbers, positive integers, decimals, and fractions and understand the relationship between decimals, fractions, and percents. They understand the relative magnitudes of numbers. *also* **MR 1.2, MR 2.1, MR 2.2, MR 2.3, MR 2.4, MR 3.2**

Use the Distributive Property

You can also use the Distributive Property to mentally solve a problem.

Find 4×29.

Example 2 Use the Distributive Property.

4×29

$4 \times 29 = 4 \times (25 + 4)$ Break 29 into parts.

$= (4 \times 25) + (4 \times 4)$ Use the Distributive Property.

$= 100 + 16$ Use mental math.

$= 116$

So, $4 \times 29 = 116$.

- In Example 2, why might it be easier to break 29 into 25 and 4 than into 20 and 9 when doing mental math?

You can also use the Distributive Property with subtraction.

Example 3 Use the Distributive Property.

6×17

$6 \times 17 = 6 \times (20 - 3)$ Use $20 - 3$.

$= (6 \times 20) - (6 \times 3)$ Use the Distributive Property. Multiply mentally.

$= 120 - 18$ Subtract.

$= 102$

More Examples

A 8×38

$8 \times 38 = 8 \times (40 - 2)$

$= (8 \times 40) - (8 \times 2)$

$= 320 - 16$

$= 304$

B 4×275

$4 \times 275 = 4 \times (300 - 25)$

$= (4 \times 300) - (4 \times 25)$

$= 1{,}200 - 100$

$= 1{,}100$

Guided Practice

Copy and complete. Name the property used.

1. $(29 + 8) + 24 = 29 + (8 + 24)$
$= 29 + ■$
$= ■$

2. $2 \times 8 \times 5 = 2 \times 5 \times 8$
$= ■ \times 8$
$= ■$

Use properties and mental math to find the value.

3. $4 \times 17 \times 50$
4. $7 + 63 + 25$
5. 5×29
6. 108×6

7. **TALK Math** **Explain** how to use the Commutative Property to find the value of $4 \times 7 \times 5$. How does this property make this problem easier to solve mentally?

Independent Practice and Problem Solving

Use properties and mental math to find the value.

8. $19 + (28 + 21)$
9. 3×270
10. $(86 + 27) + 3$
11. $(10 \times 8) \times 3$
12. $8 \times (3 \times 5)$
13. $(36 + 42) + 24$
14. $4 \times (9 \times 5)$
15. 4×23
16. $78 + (64 + 2)$
17. 9×510
18. $(47 + 58) + 13$
19. $50 \times (7 \times 2)$
20. $25 \times (3 \times 4)$
21. 28×8
22. $29 + (18 + 32)$
23. 19×6
24. 24×9
25. 6×18
26. $7 \times 8 \times 6$
27. 17×9

USE DATA For 28–31, use the table.

28. An aquarium has 6 sea lions in one tank. How many pounds of food do the sea lions eat in one day?

29. A harbor seal made 2 dives that lasted the greatest amount of time it can stay underwater. It also made a 14-minute dive and an 11-minute dive. How much time was the harbor seal underwater?

30. A California sea lion's exhibit time is 24 minutes, 3 times per day. How many minutes is the sea lion's total exhibit time in a 7-day week?

31. A bottlenose dolphin made 3 dives in an hour. On the first dive, it swam to a depth of 58 feet. The second dive was to 32 feet and the third dive was to the dolphin's maximum depth. What is the total distance for all 3 dives?

Sea Mammal Facts

Sea Mammal	Maximum Dive Depth (in ft)	Average Daily Food Intake (in lb)	Greatest Time Underwater (in min)
California sea lion	899	27	10
Bottlenose dolphin	150	23	8
Harbor seal	1,450	14	28

32. ***FAST FACT*** Dolphins travel in social groups called pods with as many as 15 dolphins. Pods work together to catch food. About how many pounds of food would a pod of 14 dolphins eat in one day?

33. Tell which property you would use to mentally find the value of 35×12. Then find the value.

34. **WRITE Math** To multiply 4×97 Trevor wrote $4 \times (99 - 2)$. Will writing it this way allow him to use mental math? **Explain** how Trevor can solve the problem mentally.

 Extra Practice on page 369, Set F

Achieving the Standards

35. There are 4 blue pens and 5 black pens in a drawer. What is the probability of choosing a blue pen without looking? (Grade 4 SDAP 2.2)

36. The temperature was 32°F yesterday. Today it is 29°F. Write an equation using the variable *c*, to describe the change in temperature. (AF 1.2, p. 350)

37. Draw a number line. Locate $^{-}5$ on your number line. (Grade 4 NS 1.8)

38. **Test Prep** Which value of *n* makes this equation true?

    $(23 + 15) + 7 = n + (15 + 7)$

    A 7 **C** 23

    B 15 **D** 38

39. **Test Prep** There are 5 cartons. Each has 3 sections that hold 8 doorknobs. Which expression shows the total number of doorknobs?

    A 24×3 **C** 15×40

    B 15×3 **D** 5×24

Problem Solving connects to Science

Male California sea lions weigh about 390 kilograms and grow to a length of about 2.1 meters. Females weigh about 110 kilograms and are about 1.8 meters long.

Sea lions are quite social and float together in "rafts" or rest together in large groups. Baby sea lions, or pups, are born early in the summer. Mothers and pups recognize each other by the sounds they make called barking. The male lions patrol the group's territories to protect the newborn pups from predators such as killer whales and great white sharks.

Use mental math to solve.

1. A group of 7 male seal lions and 7 female sea lions are floating together. About how much does the group weigh in all?

2. A line of 27 male sea lions is patrolling around the island where their group lives. If they were lined up nose to tail, about what would the total length of the 27 males be?

3. An aquarium had 16 adult sea lions and 13 pups. Then 14 sea lions arrived. What is the total number of sea lions at the aquarium?

4. Sea lions eat about 27 pounds of food each day. How much food does a sea lion eat in 30 days?

Problem Solving Workshop
Strategy: Write an Equation

OBJECTIVE: Solve problems by using the strategy *write an equation.*

Learn the Strategy

You can solve problems by writing and solving an equation.

An equation changes when the unknown quantity changes.

Notice how the equations change.

Noah has 4 jars of marbles with 35 marbles in each jar. How many marbles does Noah have?

number of jars	×	number of marbles in each jar	=	total number of marbles
↓		↓		↓
4	×	35	=	t

Noah has 140 marbles. He puts an equal number of marbles into 4 jars. How many marbles are in each jar?

number of jars	×	number of marbles in each jar	=	total number of marbles
↓		↓		↓
4	×	c	=	140

Noah has 140 marbles in some jars. Each jar has 35 marbles. How many jars does Noah have?

number of jars	×	number of marbles in each jar	=	total number of marbles
↓		↓		↓
s	×	35	=	140

TALK Math

Explain how the equations above are similar and how they are different.

AF 1.2 Use a letter to represent an unknown number; write and evaluate simple algebraic expressions in one variable by substitution. *also* **AF 1.0, AF 1.1, MR 1.0, MR 2.0, MR 2.3, MR 2.4, MR 2.6, MR 3.0, 3.1, MR 3.2, MR 3.3**

Use the Strategy

PROBLEM When U.S. astronaut Shannon Lucid spent more than 180 days aboard the space station *Mir*, she set the women's record for a single space flight. A new astronaut just found out how long her first space flight will be. She realized that Lucid's record flight was 6 times as long as her flight will be. How long will the new astronaut's first space flight be?

Astronaut Shannon Lucid aboard a space shuttle.

Read to Understand

- **Identify the details. What are you asked to find?**
- **What information is given?**

Plan

- **What strategy can you use to solve the problem?**
  You can write an equation to solve the problem.

Solve

- **How can you use the strategy to solve the problem?**

Choose a variable, and write an equation.

Let d represent the number of days of space flight for the new astronaut.

new astronaut's days in space	multiplied by	6	=	Lucid's days in space
↓		↓		↓
d	$\times$	6	=	180

$$d \times 6 = 180$$
$$d = 30$$

Use mental math to solve. **Think:** What number multiplied by 6 equals 180?

So, the new astronaut's first space flight will be 30 days long.

Check

- **How can you check your answer?**
- **What other ways could you solve the problem?**

Guided Problem Solving

Read to Understand
Plan
Solve
Check

1. The average person in the United States uses 68 L of water for one shower. This is 17 times as great as the amount that an astronaut on the ISS (International Space Station) uses for one shower. How many liters of water does an astronaut on the ISS use for one shower?

First, choose a variable to represent the unknown information.

Let s = the number of liters of water for one shower on the ISS.

Then, write an equation.

17	**multiplied by**	**one shower amount**	**=**	**68**
↓		↓		↓
17	×	s	=	68

Finally, solve the equation.

2. **What if** the average person used 72 L of water for one shower? What if that amount of water was 18 times the amount used by an astronaut on the ISS? How would the equation change? Would the answer change?

3. In 1987, Yuri Romanenko set a record for the longest space flight. In 1995, Valery Polyakov beat that record by 113 days. If Polyakov spent 439 days in space, how many days did Romanenko spend in space?

Problem Solving Strategy Practice

Write and solve an equation.

4. The *Mir* space station had a living area that was 13 m long and 4.3 m wide. The living area on the ISS is 4 times as long. What is the length in meters of the ISS living area?

5. The guide to space camp explained that each camper could pack items that weighed no more than 35 pounds. Nathan packed sneakers, sandals, and hiking boots which weighed a total of 10.2 pounds. How many more pounds may he pack?

USE DATA For 6–7, use the table.

6. Before his ISS mission, Pavel Vinogradov had spent 16.5 times as much time in space as the U.S. astronaut Mark Kelly. How many days had Vinogradov spent in space?

7. Sergei Avdeyev holds the record for time spent in space. He has spent 32 days more than 4 times the number of days that Thomas Reiter has spent in space. How much time has Avdeyev spent in space?

International Space Station Crew

Astronaut	Country	Space Time (in days)
Steven Lindsey	USA	37.3
Mark Kelly	USA	12
Michael Fossum	USA	0
Thomas Reiter	Germany	179

Mixed Strategy Practice

8. Stephanie used the satellite phone to talk to mission control for $\frac{2}{3}$ hour and for $\frac{1}{12}$ hour. How many minutes did Stephanie spend on the telephone?

9. Lisa has a piece of computer cable 30.42 meters. She cuts off a section which is 8.12 meters. How long is the piece of cable that is left?

USE DATA **For 10–12, use the table.**

10. How much more time did Solovyov spend walking in space than Ross?

11. **Pose a Problem** Look at Problem 10. Write and solve a similar problem by using different astronauts or cosmonauts in the table.

12. **Open-Ended** Suppose you wanted to compare the number of EVAs of the astronauts and cosmonauts in the table. What type of table or graph could you use to compare the data? Explain or draw your answer.

13. **WRITE Math** Mark can type 30 words per minute. He has to type a 150-word report and e-mail it back to base, but his computer has just 6 minutes of energy left. Can Mark do the report in time?

Choose a STRATEGY

- Draw a Diagram or Picture
- Make a Model or Act It Out
- Make an Organized List
- Find a Pattern
- Make a Table or Graph
- Predict and Test
- Work Backward
- Solve a Simpler Problem
- Write an Equation
- Use Logical Reasoning

Top 5 Space Walk (EVAs) Records for Total Time

Astronaut/Cosmonaut	EVAs	Hours	Minutes
Anatoly Solovyov	16	77	41
Jerry Ross	9	58	18
Steven Smith	7	49	48
Nikolai Budarin	9	46	14
James Newman	6	43	13

CHALLENGE YOURSELF

An astronaut planned a space walk of 1 hour 20 minutes. Unexpected problems caused the space walk to take longer.

14. The astronaut started with a 4-hour supply of oxygen. When the astronaut returned to the space station, there were 15 minutes of oxygen left in the tank. How much longer did the space walk take than expected?

15. A full oxygen tank lasts about 7 hours. Five astronauts plan to go on space walks, each lasting 1 hour 20 minutes. If they go one after another, can all five use the same tank?

Space walks are more like space hauls. Astronauts pull themselves along by using their arms, hand over hand. The term for a space walk is EVA, extravehicular.

Extra Practice

Set A Write an expression for each situation.

If you use a variable, explain what the variable represents. (pp. 346–347)

1. Jeff has 48 sports cards. He places the same number of cards on each of 4 pages in an album.
2. David strings 10 beads. He takes some off and then adds 4 more.
3. Four friends paid $6.50 each to see a movie.
4. Yoko is 5 years older than her sister.
5. Olivia read 85 pages of her book on Saturday and 55 pages on Sunday.
6. Branden picks some apples. He separates the apples equally into 2 baskets.
7. Maya had $15.75. She bought a pair of socks for $5.25. Then she earned $12 raking leaves.
8. Nina puts $3\frac{1}{4}$ cups of milk in a stew. Then she adds more milk just before serving.
9. There were 98 fans at the game. Before the game was over, 15 fans left.
10. Kara goes on a 3-day field trip. She hikes the same number of miles each day.
11. Malik had 75 stickers. He gave away 12 stickers to his brother and 15 stickers to his sister.
12. Ossie ran some miles at a park after school. His friend Jack ran $2\frac{1}{2}$ fewer miles.

Set B Evaluate each expression. (pp. 348–351)

1. $6 \times (8 - 3)$
2. $8 - (5 + 1)$
3. $12 \times 6 \div 6$
4. $63 \div (5 + 4)$
5. $8 \times 15 \div 5$
6. $48 - (4 + 5) \times 4$
7. $100 - 7 \times 6$
8. $49 + 12 \div (4 + 2)$
9. $35 \div 7 + 5 \times 3$
10. $18 \div (6 - 4) + 5$
11. $23 + (12 \times 6) - 2$
12. $13 + 5 - 3 \times 6$

Evaluate the algebraic expression for the given value of the variable.

13. $g - 7$ for $g = 9$
14. $h + 4.5$ for $h = 1$
15. $7 - (b + 4)$ for $b = 0$
16. $20.5 - p$ for $p = 10$
17. $4s + 2$ for $s = 8$
18. $2 + \frac{18}{c}$ for $c = 3$
19. $2 \times r - 4$ for $r = 5\frac{1}{2}$
20. $8 \div (1 + w)$ for $w = 3$
21. $9 \div (y \times 3)$ for $y = 1$
22. $9 + e + 16$ for $e = 4$
23. $5 - (t + 2)$ for $t = 3$
24. $9 - 2d$ for $d = 3$

CD ROM
Technology
Use Harcourt Mega Math, Ice Station Exploration, *Arctic Algebra*, Levels F, G, H, I.

Set C Write an equation for each. Tell what the variable represents. (pp. 352–353)

1. Rosita has 6 times as many crayons as markers. She has 108 crayons. How many markers does she have?
2. Twenty-five times a number is 125. What is the number?
3. Haley is looking for 35 shells to complete her collection. She has 12 shells so far. How many more shells does Haley need?
4. A florist had 9 lily plants. At noon, he had 4 left. How many plants did he sell that morning?
5. Kevin paid $6 for a game ticket, $3 for a sandwich, and he bought a drink. He spent a total of $10. How much money did Kevin spend on the drink?
6. A librarian arranges some books on 3 shelves. He places 12 books on each shelf. How many books did he arrange?

Set D Use mental math to solve each equation. Check your solution. (pp. 354–357)

1. $5c = 25$
2. $\$9.75 \div p = \$3.25$
3. $r - 5 = 20$
4. $t + 4\frac{1}{2} = 20$
5. $10 - d = 8$
6. $v \times 6 = 54$
7. $1.2 \div t = 0.2$
8. $1 = x + 1$
9. $50.5 = z + 10.5$
10. $12 = f \div 4$
11. $q - \frac{1}{4} = 7\frac{3}{4}$
12. $d \times 10 = 100$
13. $39 = 71 - a$
14. $\$36.85 + p = \$50.00$
15. $r + 20.8 = 136.9$
16. $120 \div x = 6$

Set E Use the Distributive Property to find the value of the expression. (pp. 358–359)

1. $7 \times (m + 3)$ if $m = 30$
2. $4 \times (9 + n)$ if $n = 10$
3. $6 \times (a + 7)$ if $a = 40$
4. $3 \times (4 + h)$ if $h = 50$
5. $2 \times (75 - g)$ if $g = 50$
6. $4 \times (p + 3)$ if $p = 90$
7. $5 \times (35 - n)$ if $n = 20$
8. $9 \times (2 + r)$ if $r = 10$
9. $8 \times (60 - t)$ if $t = 30$
10. $6 \times (c - 5)$ if $c = 40$
11. $3 \times (m + 7)$ if $m = 20$
12. $5 \times (f - 9)$ if $f = 60$

Set F Use properties and mental math to find the value. (pp. 360–363)

1. $(2 + 4) + 6$
2. $18 + 6 + 2$
3. $4 \times (5 \times 8)$
4. $5 \times 9 \times 2$
5. 3×32
6. $(5 \times 3) \times 4$
7. 4×509
8. 7×18
9. 4×125
10. $3 + 25 + 2$
11. $3 + (7 + 4)$
12. $4 \times 7 \times 5$
13. 14×6
14. $56 + 12 + 44$
15. $4 \times 7 \times 25$
16. 23×8

Chapter 14 Review/Test

Check Vocabulary and Concepts

Choose the best term from the box.

VOCABULARY
equation
evaluate
solution

1. The ___?___ is the value that makes the equation true. (AF 1.2, p. 354)
2. A number sentence that shows two quantities equal is a(n) ___?___. (AF 1.2, p. 352)

Check Skills

Write an expression for each situation. If you use a variable, explain what the variable represents. (AF 1.2, pp. 346–347)

3. Tom puts 48 oranges equally into 8 crates.
4. Stella is 30 years younger than her dad.

Evaluate each expression. (AF 1.2, pp. 348–351)

5. $18 - 2 \times 5.5 + 1$
6. $\left(1\frac{1}{2} + n\right) \times 3$ if $n = 4\frac{1}{2}$

Write an equation for each. Tell what the variable represents. (AF 1.2, pp. 352–353)

7. Lea played 14 sets of tennis in two days. She played 5 sets the first day. How many sets did she play the next day?
8. Stephanie is 3 years younger than her brother. If Stephanie is 8 years old, how old is her brother?

Use mental math to solve each equation. Check your solution. (AF 1.2, pp. 354–357)

9. $42 \div x = 6$
10. $48 = 6y$
11. $60 = c - 12.5$
12. $p + 5\frac{1}{4} = 20$

What value makes the equation true? (AF 1.3, pp. 358–359)

13. $3 \times 85 = (3 \times 80) + (3 \times m)$
14. $9 \times 48 = (9 \times 50) - (9 \times c)$

Use mental math to find the value. (AF 1.3, pp. 360–363)

15. $(6 \times 2) \times 5$
16. $5 + 4 + 5$
17. 5×22
18. 7×19

Check Problem Solving

Solve. (AF 1.2, MR 2.4, MR 2.6, pp. 364–367)

19. Tanya baked four times the number of corn muffins as Jin. Tanya baked 60 muffins. How many muffins did Jin bake?
20. WRITE Math Alan lives 3 miles farther from school than Kara. Alan lives 15 miles from school. **Explain** how you could use an equation to find how far Kara lives from school.

GO ONLINE **Technology** Use *Online Assessment.*

Enrich • Fahrenheit & Celsius

Swim Meet

The manager at the Santa José Swim Club must keep the temperature of the pool water at least 76°F so that a competition can be held. When the teams arrive, the pool temperature is 25°C. Is the pool water warm enough?

Remember
°F = degrees Fahrenheit
°C = degrees Celsius

You can use the expression $\left(\frac{9}{5} \times C\right) + 32$ to convert from degrees Celsius to degrees Fahrenheit. Then compare the temperatures in degrees Fahrenheit.

Dive In

Evaluate $\left(\frac{9}{5} \times C\right) + 32$ if $C = 25$.

Replace *C* with 25.	
Operate inside parentheses.	$\left(\frac{9}{5} \times C\right) + 32 = \left(\frac{9}{5} \times 25\right) + 32$
Add.	$= 45 + 32$
So, 25°C = 77°F.	$= 77$
Since 77°F > 76°F, the temperature of the water is warm enough.	

You also can convert from 76°F to °C and compare the temperatures in degrees Celsius. Use the expression $\frac{5}{9} \times (F - 32)$ to convert from degrees Fahrenheit to degrees Celsius.

Evaluate $\frac{5}{9} \times (F - 32)$ if $F = 76$.

Replace *F* with 76.	
Operate inside parentheses.	$\frac{5}{9} \times (F - 32) = \frac{5}{9} \times (76 - 32)$
Multiply. Round.	$= \frac{5}{9} \times 44$
So, 76°F ≈ 24°C.	
Since 25°C > 24°C, the temperature of the water is warm enough.	$= 24\frac{4}{9} \approx 24$

≈ means "is approximately equal to."

Race!

Convert to degrees Fahrenheit or degrees Celsius. Round to the nearest degree.

1. 30°C = ■ °F
2. 85°F = ■ °C
3. 0°C = ■ °F
4. 113°F = ■ °C
5. 48°F = ■ °C
6. 10°C = ■ °F
7. 100°F = ■ °C
8. 90°C = ■ °F

WRITE Math **Explain** how to convert 32°F to degrees Celsius.

Achieving the Standards
Chapters 1–14

Algebra and Functions

1. If $n = 2$, what is the value of $3n - 1$? (AF 1.2)

A 7 **C** 5

B 6 **D** 4

2. What value for x makes this equation true? (AF 1.2)

$$2x + 5 = 27$$

A 16 **C** 9

B 11 **D** 2

Eliminate choices.

See item 3. Another way of stating that Rachel scored 15 fewer points than James is that James scored 15 more points than Rachel. You can eliminate answer choices that do not involve addition or subtraction.

3. James and Rachel are playing a game. In the first round, Rachel scored 15 fewer points than James. Let r represent the points that Rachel scored in the first round. Which expression shows how many points James scored? (AF 1.2)

A $r + 15$ **C** $r - 15$

B $15 \div r$ **D** $15r$

4. WRITE Math **Explain** how to evaluate the expression $8 \times (n + 9)$ if $n = 10$. (AF 1.2)

Number Sense

5. $4 \div \frac{1}{8} =$ (NS 2.4)

A $\frac{1}{2}$ **C** 12

B 2 **D** 32

6. $47.25 \div 3.5 =$ (NS 2.2)

A 1.35 **C** 43.75

B 13.5 **D** 135

7. The table shows the typing speeds of four students.

Typing Speeds	
Name	**Words per Minute**
Archie	40
Brooke	45
Calista	48
Damian	52

Which student can type 408 words in 8.5 minutes? (NS 2.1)

A Archie

B Brooke

C Calista

D Damian

8. WRITE Math Find the prime factorization of 72 using exponents. **Explain** how you found the prime factorization. (NS 1.4)

Statistics, Data Analysis, and Probability

9. The circle graph shows the results of a survey in which dog owners were asked where their dogs sleep.

Where did most owners say their dog sleeps? (SDAP 1.0)

A dog bed
B doghouse
C owner's bed
D floor

10. The table shows the number of votes that each person received in the election for class president.

Election Results	
Candidate	**Number of Votes**
Jamal	68
Nicholas	47
Keisha	53

What type of graph would best display this data? (SDAP 1.2)

A line plot
B line graph
C pictograph
D bar graph

11. WRITE Math Julia says the mode of the scores 94, 86, 84, 99, 78, 84, and 86 is 84. Do you agree? **Explain** why or why not? (Grade 4 SDAP 1.2)

Measurement and Geometry

12. Armando drew the following line segment on the coordinate grid.

The endpoints were located at (3,5) and (3,0). What is the length of this line segment? (Grade 4 O-n MG 2.3)

A 0 units
B 3 units
C 5 units
D 8 units

13. Lou made this quilt.

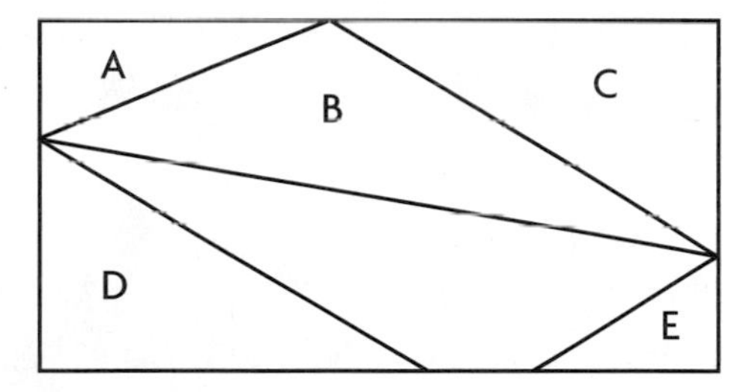

Which pieces of the quilt appear to be congruent? (Grade 4 MG 3.3)

A triangles A and D
B triangles A and E
C triangles C and D
D triangles B and D

14. WRITE Math Zach says he can place a point at (2,3) when graphing the equation $y = 2x$. Do you agree? **Explain** your answer. (Grade 4 O-n MG 2.1)

15 Algebra: Integers

The Big Idea The number line can be extended to show negative numbers and to model addition and subtraction of integers.

Investigate

Suppose you are measuring the growth of a young kelp plant over 7 weeks. Write two different expressions to show a change in height of the kelp. Use a negative integer in at least one of your expressions. Find the value of each expression.

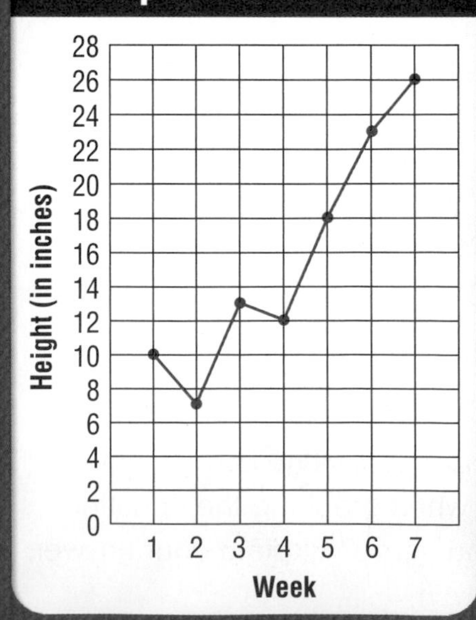

CALIFORNIA FAST FACT

A kelp forest is home to a variety of animals. It provides food for sea urchins, sea stars, and snails. A kelp frond can grow more than 12 inches in one day and reach a length of more than 100 feet!

GO ONLINE **Technology** Student pages are available in the Student eBook.

Show What You Know

Check your understanding of important skills needed for success in Chapter 15.

▶ Compare and Order Whole Numbers

Compare. Use <, >, or = for each ●.

1. 15 ● 20	**2.** 132 ● 133	**3.** 95 ● 92	**4.** 78 ● 87	**5.** 121 ● 121
6. 211 ● 201	**7.** 415 ● 415	**8.** 59 ● 65	**9.** 11 ● 10	**10.** 475 ● 75

▶ Temperature

Write the Fahrenheit temperature reading for each.

11.
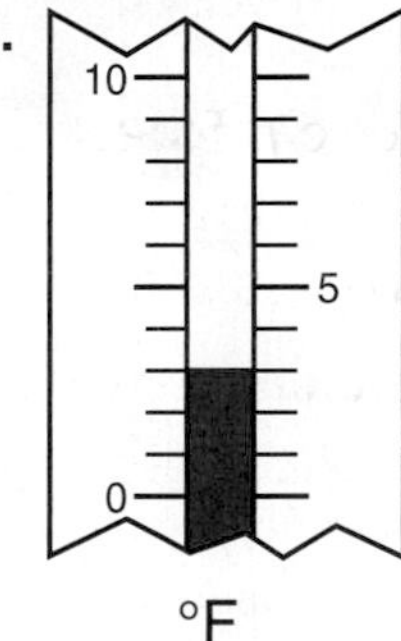

°F

12.
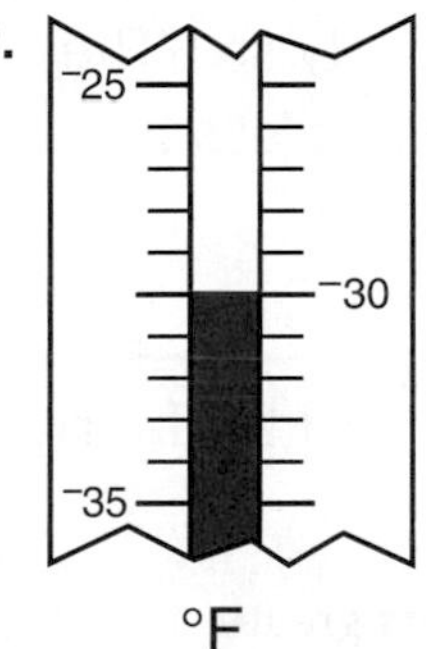

°F

13.
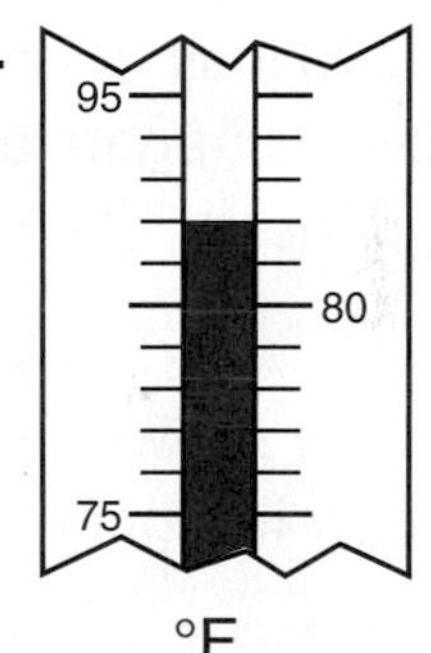

°F

14.
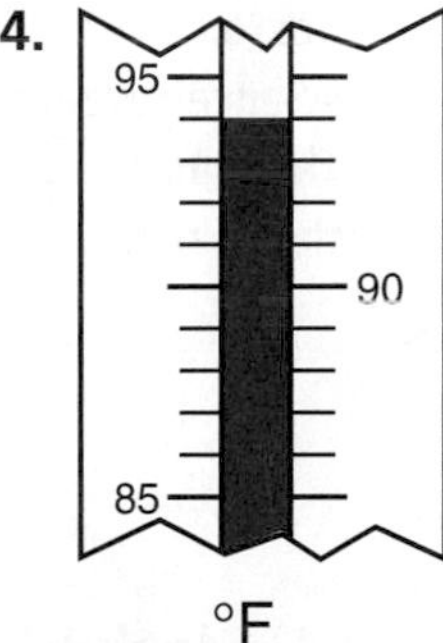

°F

15.
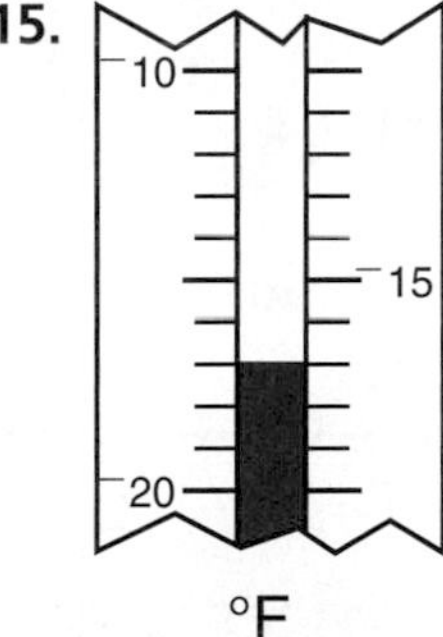

°F

16.
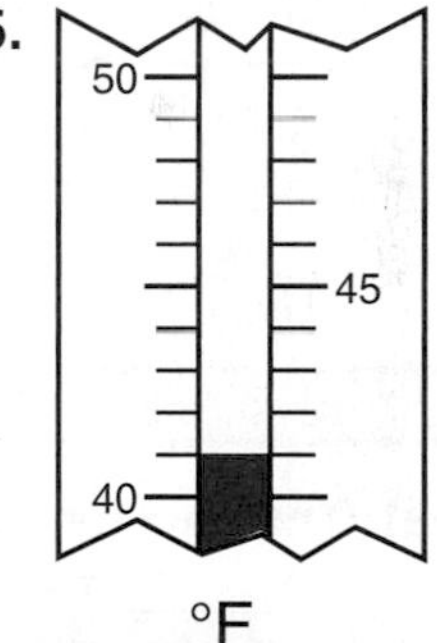

°F

VOCABULARY POWER

CHAPTER VOCABULARY

absolute value
integers
negative integers
positive integers

WARM-UP WORDS

integers the set of whole numbers and their opposites

positive integers any integer greater than zero

negative integers any integer less than zero

LESSON
1

Understand Integers

OBJECTIVE: Identify and represent integers, their opposites, and their absolute value.

Quick Review

Identify the points on the number line.

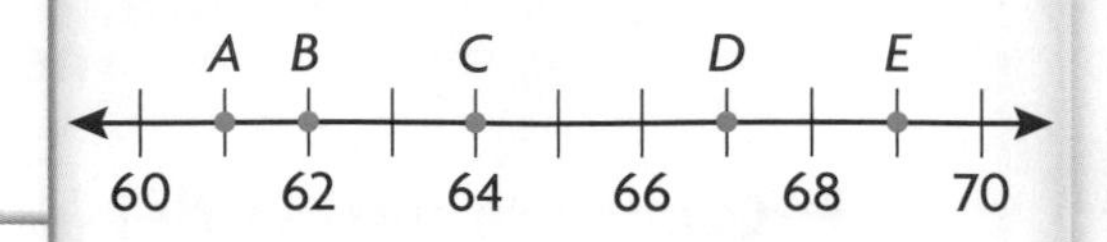
A B C D E
60 62 64 66 68 70

Vocabulary

integers
positive integer
negative integer
absolute value

Learn

PROBLEM The world's highest temperature, recorded in El Azizia, Libya, in 1922, was $^{+}136$°F. The lowest temperature, recorded in Vostok, Antarctica, in 1974, was $^{-}129$°F.

The numbers $^{+}136$ and $^{-}129$ are integers. **Integers** are the set of whole numbers and their opposites. Opposite integers are the same distance from 0 on a number line in opposite directions. The number $^{+}136$ is a **positive integer** because it is greater than 0. You read it as "positive one hundred thirty-six." The number $^{-}129$ is a **negative integer** because it is less than 0. You read it as "negative one hundred twenty-nine."

▲ The Amundsen-Scott South Pole Station near Vostok, Antarctica, is a science research facility. The average temperature there in July is $^{-}76$°F.

A number line shows numbers to the left and to the right of 0. You can show integers on a number line.

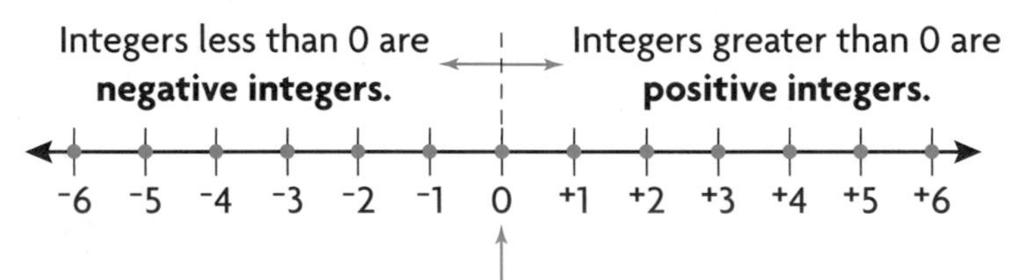
Integers less than 0 are **negative integers.**
Integers greater than 0 are **positive integers.**
−6 −5 −4 −3 −2 −1 0 +1 +2 +3 +4 +5 +6
The integer 0 is neither positive nor negative.

Many situations can be represented as integers.

Situation	Integer
Death Valley, California, the lowest point in the United States, is 282 feet below sea level.	$^{-}282$
Larry deposits $25 in his bank account.	$^{+}25$
Sea level	0
The Bruins gained 5 yards for a first down.	$^{+}5$
Larry withdraws $30 from his bank account.	$^{-}30$
Mt. McKinley, Alaska, the highest peak in the United States, is 20,320 feet above sea level.	$^{+}20,320$

- Represent the integers $^{+}4$, $^{-}4$, 0, $^{-}1$, and $^{+}8$ on a number line.

Math Idea
You can write integers in several ways. For instance, positive three can be written as $^{+}3$, $+3$, or 3. Negative three can be written as $^{-}3$ or -3.

NS 1.5 Students Identify and represent on a number line decimals, fractions, mixed numbers, and positive and negative integers. *also* NS 1.0, MR 1.1, MR 2.0, MR 2.3, MR 2.4, MR 3.2

Opposite Numbers and Absolute Value

If you walk forward 2 steps, you are 2 steps away from where you started. If you walk backward 2 steps, you are also 2 steps from where you started. In both cases, the same distance, 2 steps, is traveled.

Integers that are opposites are the same distance from 0 on the number line, but in opposite directions. The integer $^{+}2$ is the same distance from 0 as the integer $^{-}2$. For every positive integer, there is an opposite, negative integer.

The number line shows pairs of opposites. These opposites are graphed below:

$^{-}5$ and $^{+}5$ $^{-}3$ and $^{+}3$ $^{-}1$ and $^{+}1$

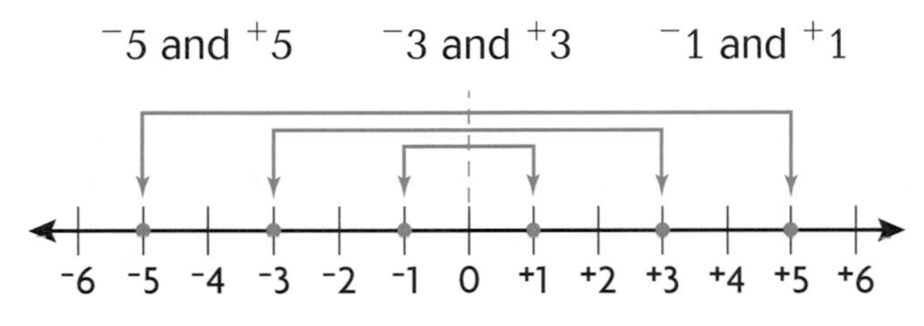

The integers in each pair shown above have the same absolute value. The **absolute value** of an integer is its distance from 0 on a number line.

Write: $|^{-}5| = 5$. **Read:** The absolute value of negative five is five.
Write: $|^{+}5| = 5$. **Read:** The absolute value of positive five is five.

Examples

A Opposite

Name the opposite of $^{-}13$.

$^{-}13 \longrightarrow {}^{+}13$

B Absolute Value

Use the number line to find $|^{+}6|$.

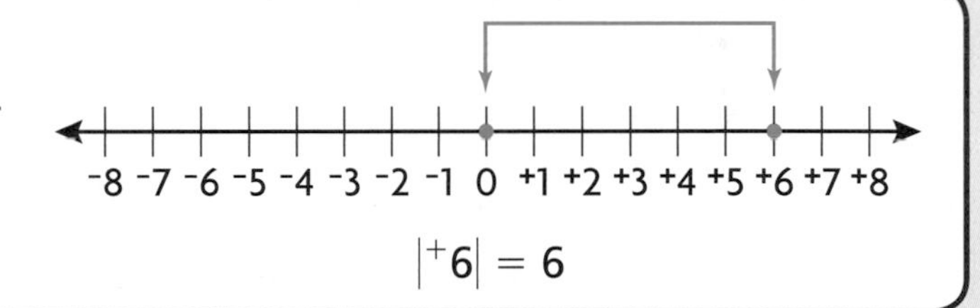

$|^{+}6| = 6$

C Opposite

Name the opposite of 6.

$6 \longrightarrow {}^{-}6$

D Absolute Value

Use the number line to find $|^{-}7|$.

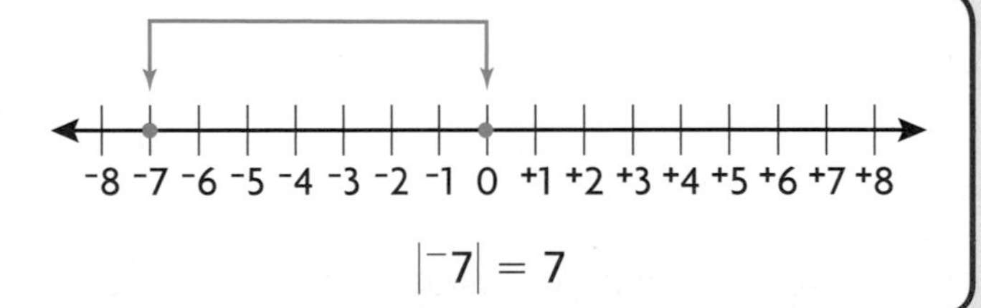

$|^{-}7| = 7$

Guided Practice

1. The number line shows the integer $^{+}2$. What is the opposite of $^{+}2$?

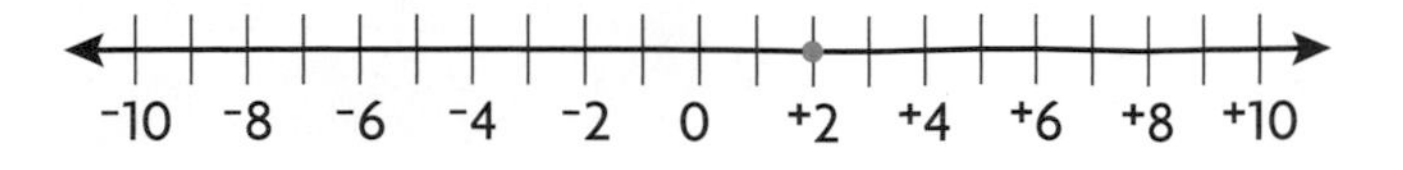

2. The number line shows the integer $^{-}8$. What is the opposite of $^{-}8$?

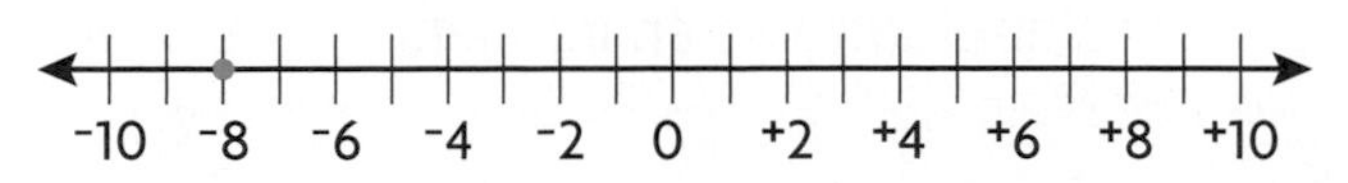

Identify the integers graphed on the number line.

3. **✓4.**

Write an integer to represent each situation.

5. 30 feet above sea level

6. a deposit of \$18

✓7. 79 degrees below 0

8. TALK Math **Explain** how to locate the integer $^{-}27$ and its opposite on a number line.

Independent Practice and Problem Solving

Identify the integers graphed on the number line.

9.

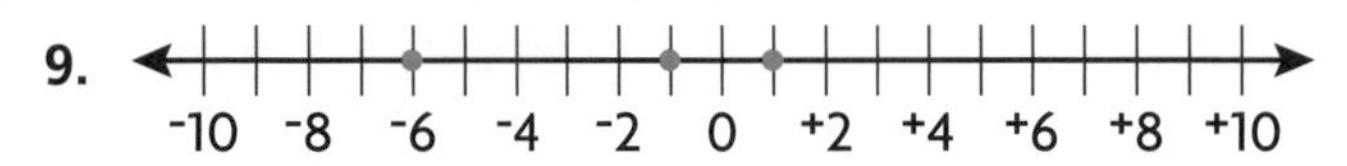

10.

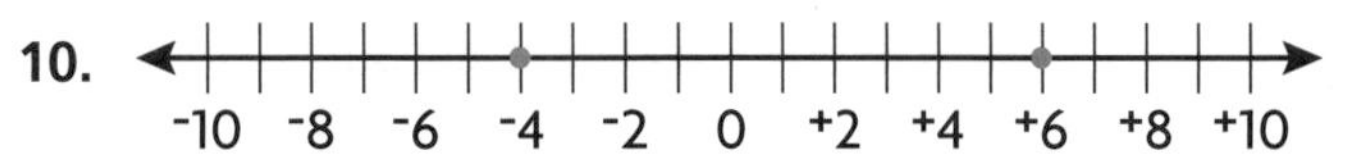

Write an integer to represent each situation.

11. a gain of 10 yards

12. 39 degrees above zero

13. 8 feet below sea level

14. no change in earnings

15. a loss of 23 yards

16. a profit of \$100

Write the opposite of each integer.

17. $^{+}6$ **18.** $^{-}9$ **19.** $^{-}14$ **20.** $^{+}10$ **21.** $^{+}51$

22. $^{+}100$ **23.** $^{-}365$ **24.** $^{-}33$ **25.** $^{+}430$ **26.** $^{-}5{,}280$

Write the integer's absolute value.

27. $|^{-}100|$ **28.** $|^{+}25|$ **29.** $|^{-}36|$ **30.** $|0|$ **31.** $|^{-}10{,}000|$

A B C D E F G H I J K

-5 0 +5

For 32–34, use the number line.

32. Write the letter for each integer.

a. $^{-}4$ **b.** $^{+}3$ **c.** 0 **d.** $^{+}1$

33. Write the letter for the opposite of each integer.

a. $^{-}3$ **b.** $^{+}2$ **c.** $^{-}2$ **d.** $^{+}5$

34. Write the absolute value of the integer at each letter.

a. B **b.** D **c.** F **d.** K

35. **Reasoning** Neil earns \$17. He owes his brother \$23. What integers represent the amount Neil has earned and the amount he owes?

36. ***FAST FACT*** The lowest temperature in Maryland was 40°F below zero, recorded in Oakland on January 13, 1912. Write the temperature as an integer.

37. WRITE Math **Explain** three situations that the integer $^{-}13$ might represent.

 Extra Practice on page 396, Set A

Achieving the Standards

38. $87 \times 4{,}092 =$ (NS 1.0, p. 70)

39. What is the value of the expression $2 \times n \times 5$ for $n = 9$? (AF 1.2, p. 348)

40. Order the numbers from least to greatest. 15, 10, 18, 16 (NS 1.2, Grade 4)

41. Test Prep What integer does the letter *A* represent?

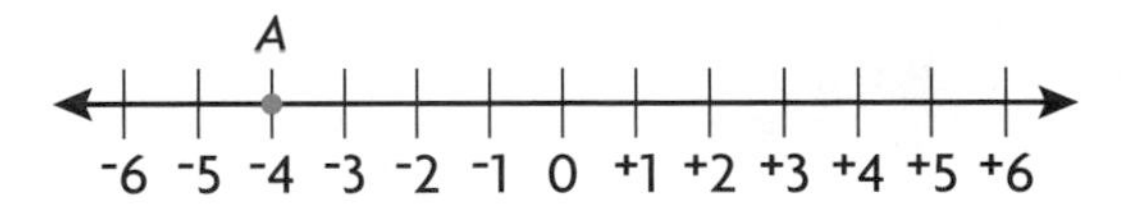

A $^{-}4$

B $^{-}1$

C $^{+}1$

D $^{+}4$

Problem Solving connects to Science

The Kelvin temperature scale is another way to measure temperature besides Celsius or Fahrenheit. The Kelvin scale does not use negative integers. Its units are the same size as the units on the Celsius scale. The temperature in kelvins can be found by adding 273 to the Celsius temperature.

When you write a temperature using the Kelvin scale, you do not use the degree symbol. Water freezes at 273 kelvins, not at 273 degrees kelvin.

The lowest temperature on the Kelvin scale is 0 K, or "absolute zero." At absolute zero, all particles are completely at rest. They have zero heat energy. In theory, it is not possible for a system to have zero energy. The closest scientists have come to absolute zero in a laboratory is about $\frac{1}{2}$ of a billionth of 1 K. This is nearly zero.

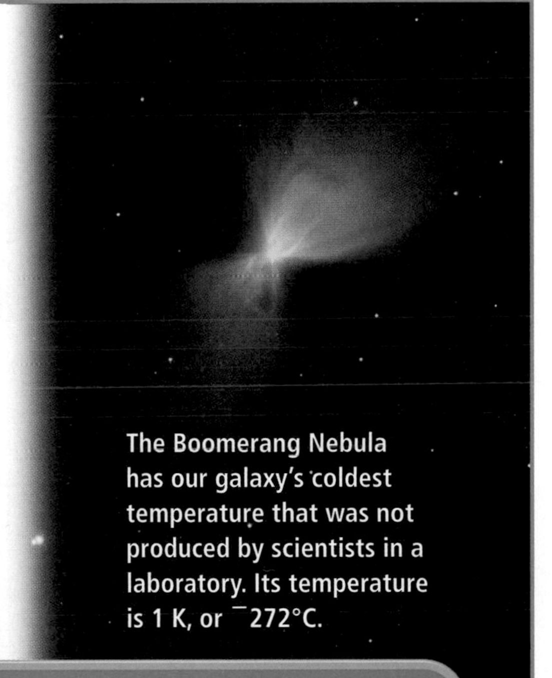

The Boomerang Nebula has our galaxy's coldest temperature that was not produced by scientists in a laboratory. Its temperature is 1 K, or $^{-}272$°C.

For 1–3, use the table.

1. Find the average Kelvin temperature for Mercury, Venus, and Earth.
2. Using the Celsius scale, write the absolute value of the temperature of each planet.
3. Using the Fahrenheit scale, write the integer that describes the temperature of each planet. Then write the absolute value of each integer.

Average Planet Temperatures

Planet	Celsius	Kelvin	Fahrenheit
Mercury	160°C	■	320°F
Venus	452°C	■	846°F
Earth	15°C	■	59°F
Mars	$^{-}63$°C	210 K	$^{-}81$°F
Jupiter	$^{-}153$°C	120 K	$^{-}243$°F
Saturn	$^{-}185$°C	88 K	$^{-}301$°F
Uranus	$^{-}214$°C	59 K	$^{-}353$°F
Neptune	$^{-}225$°C	48 K	$^{-}373$°F

LESSON 2

Compare and Order Integers

OBJECTIVE: Identify, compare, and order integers.

Quick Review

Write the opposite of each integer.

1. $^{-}50$ **2.** 15
3. $^{-}3$ **4.** $^{-}67$
5. 22

Learn

PROBLEM The black-vented shearwater plunges from the sky into the water below the ocean's surface to feed on small fish. Suppose two shearwaters are diving for fish. The first shearwater dives to a depth of 20 meters below the surface of the ocean, and the second shearwater dives to a depth of 10 meters below the surface of the ocean. Which shearwater's dive is closer to the ocean's surface?

▲ **Black-vented shearwaters are seabirds that live off the coast of southern California.**

Example 1

Step 1

Name the integer that represents each situation.

the ocean's surface: 0
a dive of 10 meters below the surface of the ocean: $^{-}10$
a dive of 20 meters below the surface of the ocean: $^{-}20$

Step 2

Show the integers $^{-}10$, $^{-}20$, and 0 on a number line.

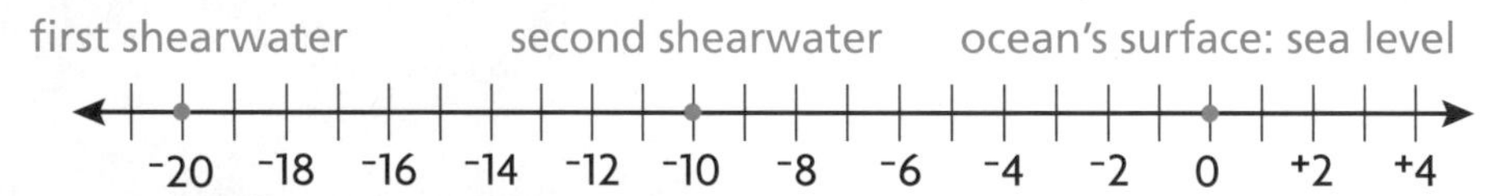

On the number line, $^{-}10$ is closer to 0 than $^{-}20$.

So, since $^{-}10 > {}^{-}20$, the second shearwater's dive is closer to the ocean's surface.

Example 2

Use a number line to order the integers $^{-}2$, $^{-}4$, $^{-}7$, $^{+}8$, $^{+}6$, and $^{+}4$ from least to greatest.

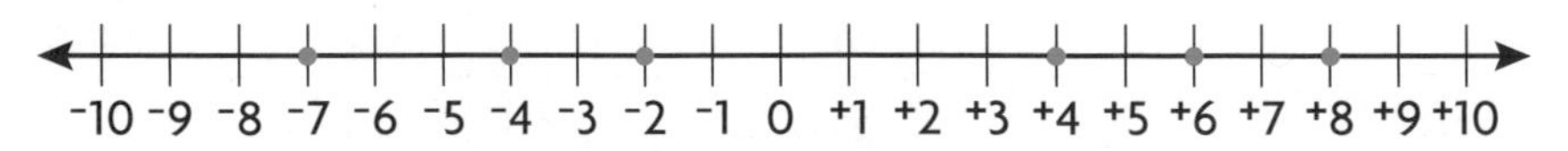

So, the order from least to greatest is $^{-}7$, $^{-}4$, $^{-}2$, $^{+}4$, $^{+}6$, and $^{+}8$.

Remember

On a number line, a number to the right is always greater than a number to the left.

NS 1.5 Identify and represent on a number line decimals, fractions, mixed numbers, and positive and negative integers. *also* **NS 1.0, MR 1.0, MR 2.0, MR 2.3, MR 2.4, MR 3.0, MR 3.2, MR 3.3**

Compare Integers

Lone Pine, California, is in the Sierra Nevada mountain range. The lowest recorded temperature there for any December was $^-2$°F in 1990. For any January, the lowest recorded temperature was $^-5$°F in 1937, and for a February, the lowest recorded temperature was $^+3$°F, also in 1937. What is the order of the temperatures from least to greatest?

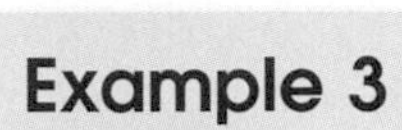

Example 3

Step 1

Find the temperatures on a thermometer.

Step 2

Write the temperatures as integers.

$^-2$, $^-5$, $^+3$

Step 3

Compare the integers on a number line

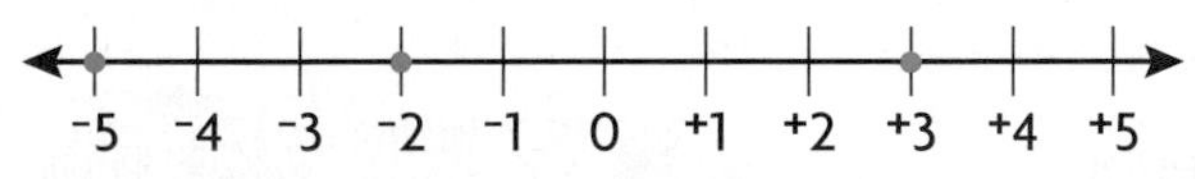

The order of the integers from least to greatest is $^-5$, $^-2$, and $^+3$. So, the order of the temperatures from least to greatest is $^-5$°F, $^-2$°F, $^+3$°F.

More Examples

A Gabe has money in a savings account. He withdraws \$8. Then he deposits \$3.

Write the amounts as integers.

Withdrawing \$8: $^-8$ Depositing \$3: $^+3$

Compare the integers on the number line.

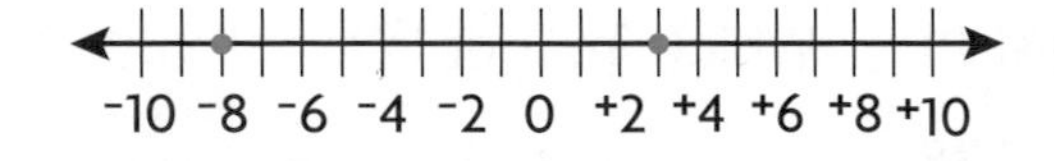

B In band practice, a drummer marched 6 steps forward and a trombone player took 5 steps backward.

Write the amounts as integers.

6 steps forward: $^+6$ 5 steps backward: $^-5$

Compare the integers on the number line.

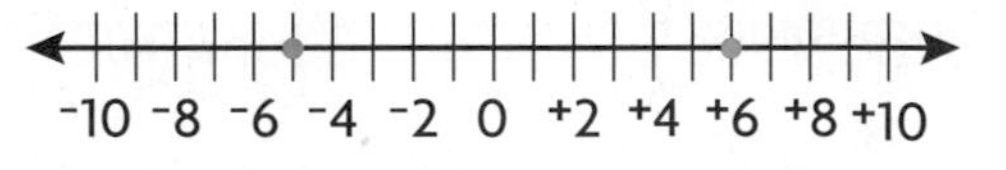

Guided Practice

1. Which integer is greater than $^{-}7$?

   a. $^{+}75$ b. $^{-}7$ c. $^{-}10$

2. Which integer is less than $^{-}7$?

   a. $^{+}10$ b. $^{+}7$ c. $^{-}8$

Compare. Write $<$, $>$, or $=$ for each ●.

3. $^{+}6$ ● 0
4. $^{-}3$ ● $^{+}2$
5. ✓ $^{-}5$ ● $^{-}9$
6. ✓ $^{+}4$ ● $^{-}8$
7. TALK Math **Explain** how you would order 0, $^{-}2$, and $^{+}2$ from greatest to least.

Independent Practice and Problem Solving

Compare. Write $<$, $>$, or $=$ for each ●.

8. $^{-}10$ ● $^{+}2$
9. $^{-}10$ ● $^{+}10$
10. $^{-}6$ ● $^{-}6$
11. $^{+}17$ ● $^{+}27$
12. $^{-}3$ ● $^{-}12$
13. 0 ● $^{+}7$
14. $^{-}20$ ● $^{-}2$
15. $^{+}112$ ● $^{-}113$
16. $^{-}14$ ● $^{+}15$
17. $^{-}322$ ● $^{-}323$

Order each set of integers from greatest to least.

18. $^{+}2$, $^{-}6$, $^{-}8$
19. $^{+}4$, $^{-}4$, $^{-}9$
20. $^{-}10$, 0, $^{-}5$, $^{+}7$
21. 0, $^{+}1$, $^{-}1$, $^{-}3$
22. $^{-}3$, $^{-}2$, 1, 0

For 23–24, use the table.

23. Write each depth in the table as an integer. Order the integers from greatest to least.
24. WRITE Math The record for the greatest depth achieved by a freediver is 223 meters, held by Tom Sietas of Germany. Write the amount as an integer. **Explain** whether the integer is a greater or less than the integers in Problem 23.

Freediving Results

Name	Depth Below Surface
Audrey Mestre	115 meters
Angela Bandini	52 meters
Tanya Streeter	113 meters

Achieving the Standards

25. CeCe made necklaces with 223 beads each. If she made 36 necklaces, how many beads did she use in all? (NS 1.0, p. 70)
26. What is the value of $4 \times n + 3$ for $n = 8$? (AF 1.2, p. 348)
27. One beehive produced 22.8 kg of honey. Another hive produced 19.9 kg of honey. How much honey did both hives produce? (O-π NS 2.1, p. 274)
28. **Test Prep** At 7:00 A.M., the temperature was $^{-}3$°F, then rose to 2°F. By how many degrees did the temperature rise?
29. **Test Prep** Which integer is less than $^{-}38$?

   A $^{+}38$
   B 0
   C $^{-}36$
   D $^{-}39$

READ Math WORKSHOP

High and Low

Visualize

What are some of the highs and lows in California? At 6,468 feet above sea level, the town of Bridgeport is the highest county seat in California. Calipatria, California is known as "the lowest-down city in the western hemisphere" because it is 184 feet below sea level.

Compare the elevations of Bridgeport and Calipatria.

You can visualize the information given in the problem to help you understand the situation. When you visualize, you picture something in your mind.

▲ **Bridgeport is the county seat of Mono County. The courthouse was built in 1880. It is the second-oldest courthouse in California that is still in use today.**

Think: 6,468 feet can be represented with the positive integer $^{+}6,468$, and 184 feet below sea level can be represented with the negative integer $^{-}184$. Visualize a number line. Is 6,468 to the left or to the right of $^{-}184$?

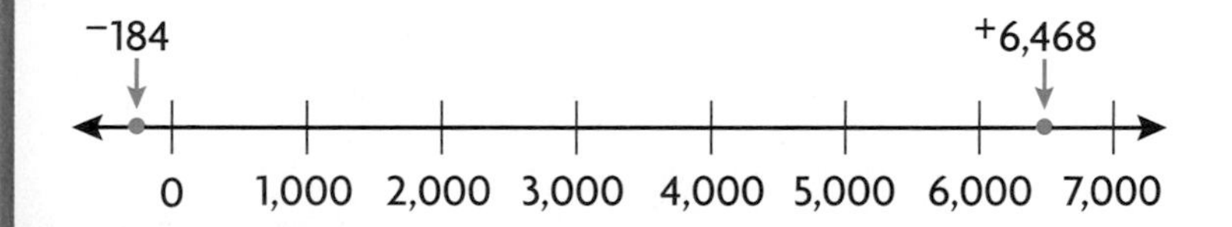

Problem Solving Visualize to understand the problem.

1. Solve the problem above.
2. The highest place in California is Mt. Whitney. Its elevation is 14,494 feet above sea level. The lowest place in California is Badwater in Death Valley, with an elevation of 282 feet below sea level. Order the integers that represent the elevations of Mt. Whitney, Badwater, Bridgeport, and Calipatria from least to greatest.

LESSON 3 HANDS ON

Model Integer Addition

OBJECTIVE: Use counters and number lines to model the addition of integers.

Quick Review

1. 2 + 4
2. 9 − 3
3. 5 − 5
4. 1 + 10
5. 7 − 6

Investigate

Materials ■ two-color counters

You can use two-color counters to model the addition of integers.

Find $^{+}3 + {}^{-}4$.

A Use yellow counters to represent the positive integer. Make a horizontal row to show $^{+}3$.

B Use red counters to represent the negative integer. Make a horizontal row of red counters beneath the yellow counters.

C Make as many opposite pairs of one yellow counter and one red counter as possible. The sum of each opposite pair is 0.

D The number and color of the unpaired counters represent the sum.

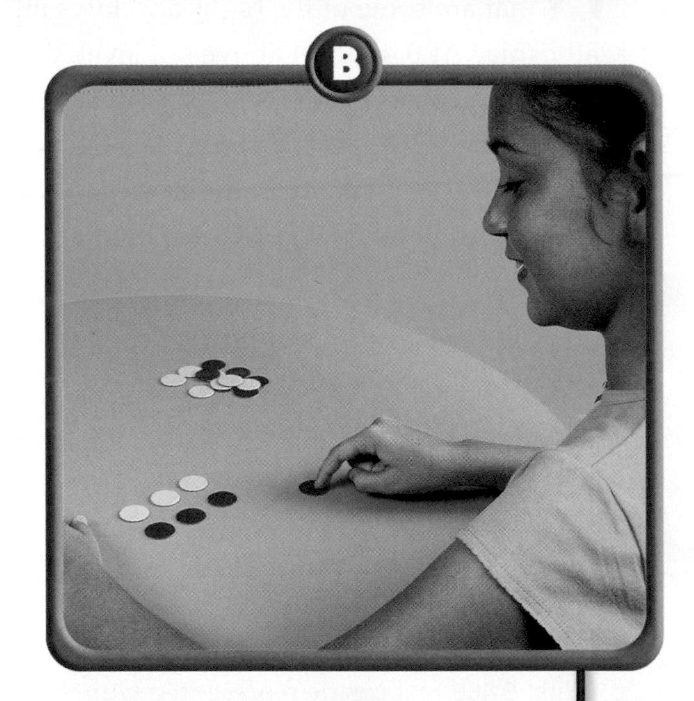

Draw Conclusions

1. How many yellow counters did you use? How many red counters did you use?
2. How many pairs of one yellow and one red counter did you make?
3. How many unpaired counters were left? What color were they?
4. Why do you think you can take away each pair of opposite counters?
5. **Application** Show how to use two-color counters to model $^{-}5 + {}^{+}7$.

NS 2.1 Add, subtract, multiply, and divide with decimals; add with negative integers; subtract positive integers from negative integers; and verify the reasonableness of the results **NS 1.5** Identify and represent on a number line decimals, fractions, mixed numbers, and positive and negative integers. *also* **MR 1.0, MR 2.0, MR 2.3, MR 2.4, MR 3.2**

Connect

Another way to model the addition of integers is to use a number line.

Find $^{+}8 + {}^{-}5$.

TALK Math

How could you use a number line to find $^{-}7 + {}^{+}4$?

Step 1

Draw a number line. Begin at zero.

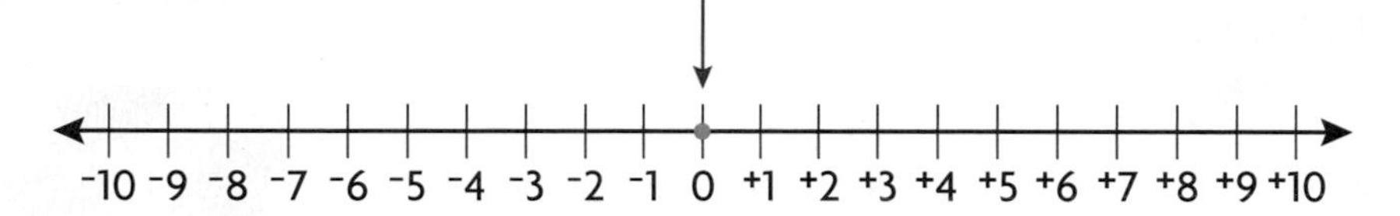

Step 2

From zero, move the same number of units to the left or to the right as the first integer in the expression. Move to the left if the integer is negative. Move to the right if the integer is positive.

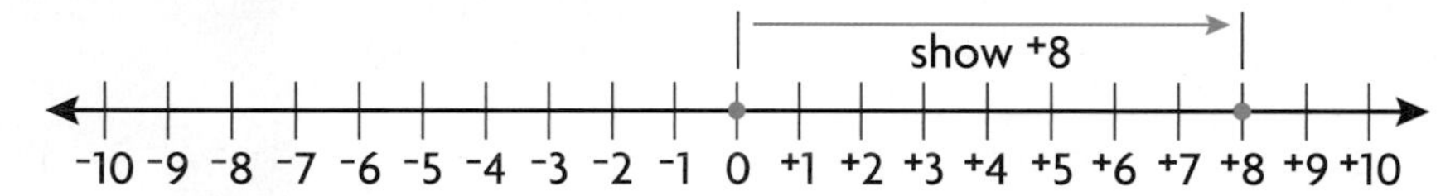

Step 3

Add the next integer. Move to the left if the integer is negative. Move right if the integer is positive.

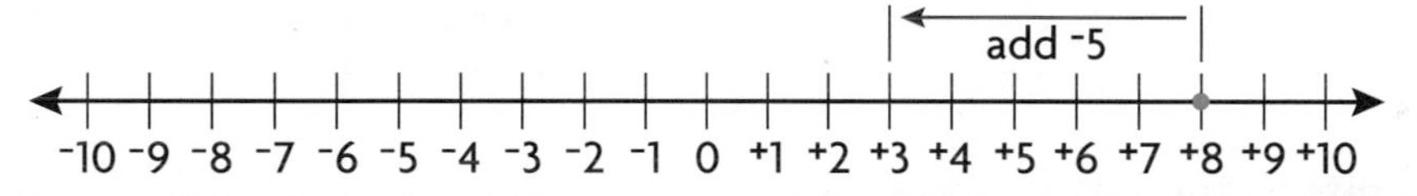

So, $^{+}8 + {}^{-}5 = {}^{+}3$.

Practice

Use counters to find the sum.

1. $^{+}6 + {}^{-}2$

2. $^{-}7 + {}^{+}3$

3. $^{-}5 + {}^{+}2$ **4.** $^{+}3 + {}^{-}8$ **5.** $^{-}1 + {}^{-}8$ **6.** $0 + {}^{-}4$

7. $^{+}9 + {}^{-}5$ **8.** $^{-}7 + {}^{+}7$ **9.** $^{-}2 + {}^{-}10$ ✓**10.** $^{-}13 + 0$

Use a number line to find the sum.

11. $^{+}1 + {}^{-}6$ **12.** $^{-}2 + {}^{+}5$ **13.** $^{-}6 + 0$ ✓**14.** $^{-}4 + {}^{+}4$

15. $0 + {}^{-}8$ **16.** $^{-}7 + {}^{+}10$ **17.** $^{+}9 + {}^{-}12$ **18.** $^{-}2 + {}^{-}11$

19. WRITE Math **Explain** how you would use either two-color counters or a number line to find $^{-}9 + {}^{+}2$. List the steps you would take to find the sum.

LESSON 4

Record Integer Addition

OBJECTIVE: Find and record the sum of integers.

Quick Review

Write the opposite of each integer.

1. $^{+}6$ **2.** $^{-}2$
3. $^{-}9$ **4.** $^{+}1$
5. $^{+}11$

Learn

PROBLEM Space travel may one day be possible by a space elevator. People and cargo could travel to space in an elevator instead of a shuttle or rocket.

Suppose the elevator stops at a space station. It travels 4 levels into the space station to deliver cargo. Then it travels back 2 levels to pick up people. How many levels away is the space elevator from where it entered the space station?

Example 1 Add. $^{+}4 + ^{-}2$

Step 1

Draw a number line. Begin at 0.
Move 4 units to the right to show $^{+}4$.

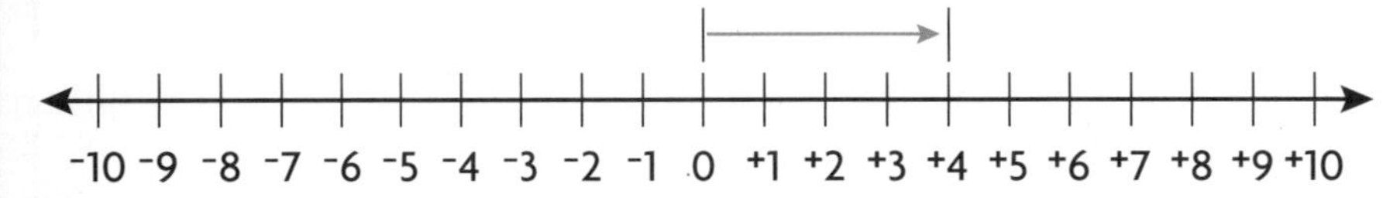

Step 2

From $^{+}4$, move 2 units to the left to show $^{-}2$.
This takes you to $^{+}2$.

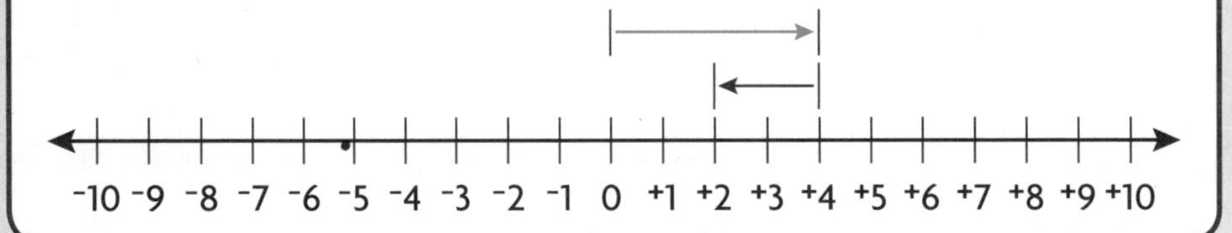

So, the space elevator would be 2 levels from where it entered the space station.

Math Idea
The sum of two negative integers will always be negative.

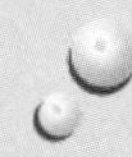

More Examples

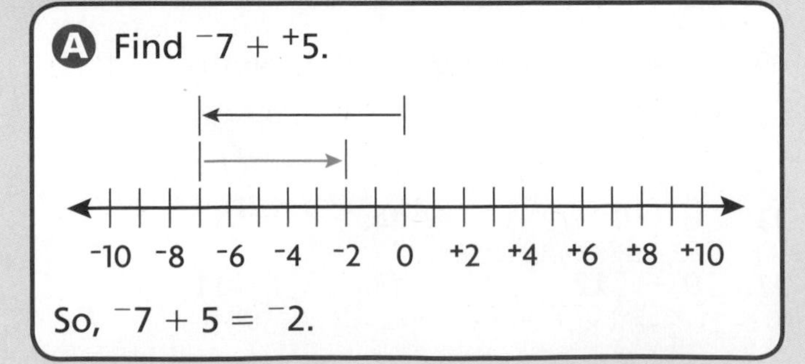

A Find $^{-}7 + ^{+}5$.

So, $^{-}7 + 5 = ^{-}2$.

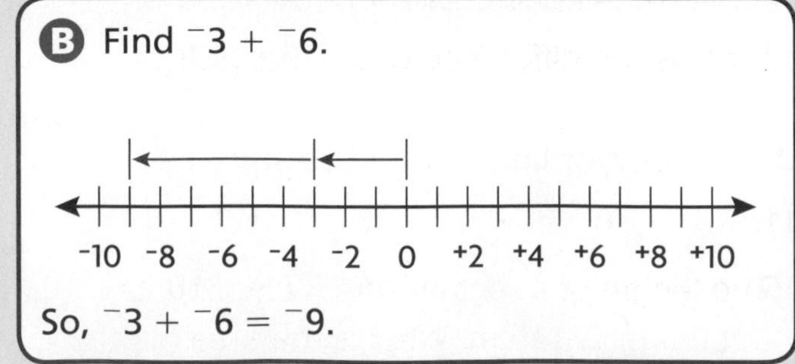

B Find $^{-}3 + ^{-}6$.

So, $^{-}3 + ^{-}6 = ^{-}9$.

NS 2.1 Add, subtract, multiply, and divide with decimals; add with negative integers; subtract positive integers from negative integers; and verify the reasonableness of the results *also* **NS 1.0, MR 1.0, MR 1.1, MR 2.0, MR 2.3, MR 2.4, MR 3.0**

Guided Practice

Use the number line to find the sum.

1. 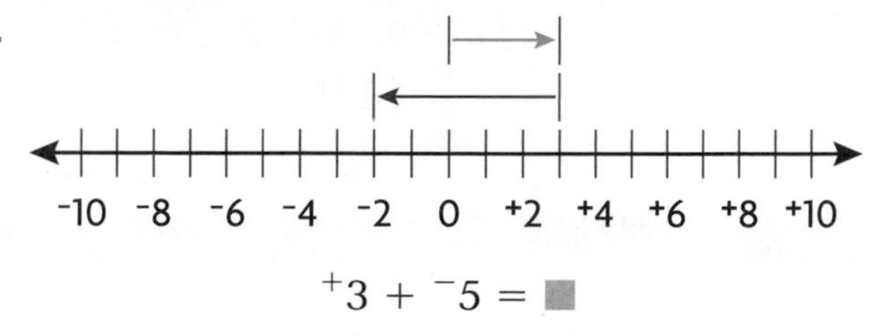

$^{+}3 + ^{-}5 = \blacksquare$

2. 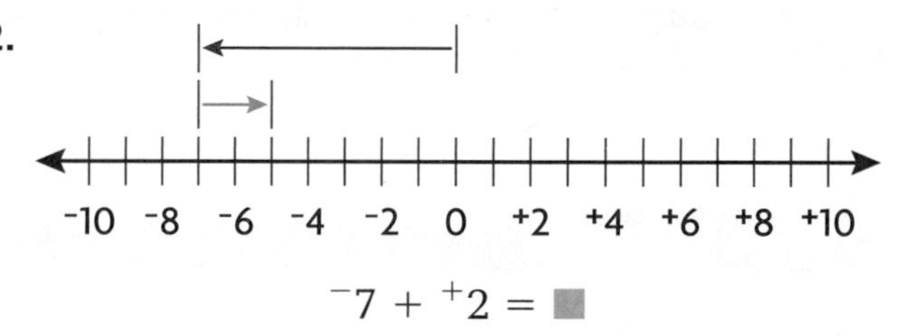

$^{-}7 + ^{+}2 = \blacksquare$

Find the sum.

3. $^{+}2 + ^{-}1$
4. $^{-}6 + ^{+}5$
5. $^{-}8 + ^{+}7$
6. $^{+}9 + ^{-}9$
7. $^{+}6 + ^{-}4$
8. **TALK Math** **Explain** how to use a number line to solve $^{-}1 + ^{+}6$.

Independent Practice and Problem Solving

Find the sum.

9. $^{+}1 + ^{-}6$
10. $^{-}5 + 0$
11. $^{-}1 + ^{+}10$
12. $^{+}8 + ^{+}9$
13. $^{+}6 + ^{-}5$
14. $^{-}4 + ^{-}4$
15. $^{-}3 + ^{-}2 + ^{-}1$
16. $0 + ^{+}12$
17. $^{-}7 + ^{-}4 + 0$
18. $^{-}5 + 5 + ^{-}5$

For 19–20, use an addition equation to solve.

19. An elevator at the Transamerica Pyramid is on the 12th floor. It drops 5 floors. What floor is the elevator on now?
20. The elevator is on the 16th floor. It goes up 5 floors and then goes down 15 floors. What floor is the elevator on now?
21. **WRITE Math** How do you know without adding whether the sum of one positive and one negative integer will be a positive or negative integer? **Explain** how you know.

◀ **The Transamerica Pyramid in San Francisco is 853 feet high and has 48 floors. It takes an entire month to wash the building's 3,678 windows.**

Achieving the Standards

22. What is the difference of 63 and 19.8? (**NS 2.0, p. 274**)
23. Show the integer $^{-}7$ on a number line. (**NS 1.5, p. 374**)
24. The length of a rectangle is 5 cm, and its perimeter is 14 cm. What is the area of the rectangle in square inches? (**Grade 4 MG 1.4**)
25. A fish is swimming 2 feet below the surface of a lake. Then it swims to a depth 9 feet lower than where it was first swimming. Which equation describes the depth where the fish is swimming?

A $^{+}2 + ^{+}7 = ^{+}9$
B $^{-}2 + ^{+}9 = ^{+}7$
C $^{+}2 + ^{-}9 = ^{-}7$
D $^{-}2 + ^{-}9 = ^{-}11$

Extra Practice on page 396, Set C

LESSON 5 HANDS ON

Model Integer Subtraction

OBJECTIVE: Use counters and number lines to model the subtraction of integers.

Quick Review

1. 4 − 4
2. 6 − 1
3. 8 − 2
4. 9 − 7
5. 10 − 3

Investigate

Materials ■ two-color counters

You can use two-color counters to model subtraction of integers.

Find $^-5 - {}^+2$.

A Use red counters to represent the negative integer.

B Use yellow counters to represent the positive integers. Remember that the value of an opposite pair is 0. In order to subtract $^+2$, you need 2 yellow counters to take away, so add 2 opposite pairs.

C Now, take away the two yellow counters to subtract $^+2$.

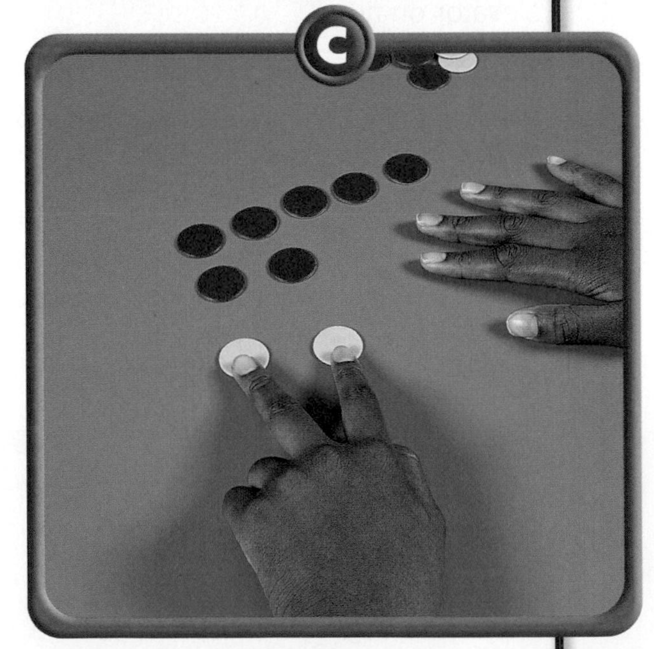

D Count the red counters remaining. The number and color of the unpaired counters represent the difference.

Draw Conclusions

1. How many red counters in all did you use? How many yellow counters in all did you use?
2. How many counters remained? What color were they?
3. Why do you think you had to add the opposite pairs?
4. **Application** Describe how to use two-color counters to model $^-3 - {}^+6$.

NS 1.5 Identify and represent on a number line decimals, fractions, mixed numbers, and positive and negative integers. *also* **NS 2.1, MR 1.0, MR 2.0, MR 2.3, MR 2.4, MR 3.2**

Connect

You can also use a number line to model the subtraction of integers.

Step 1

Find $^{-}1 - {}^{+}8$. Draw a number line. Begin at 0.

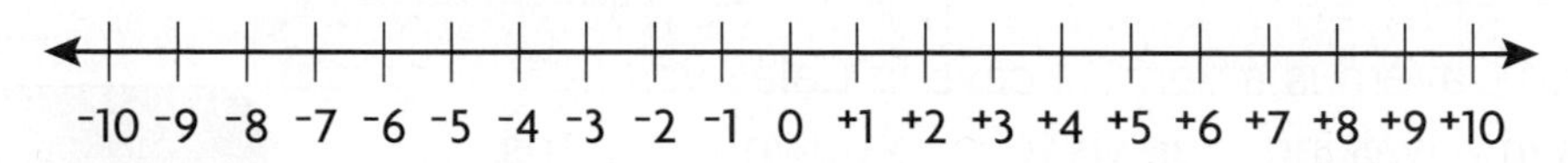

Step 2

Move 1 unit to the left to show $^{-}1$.

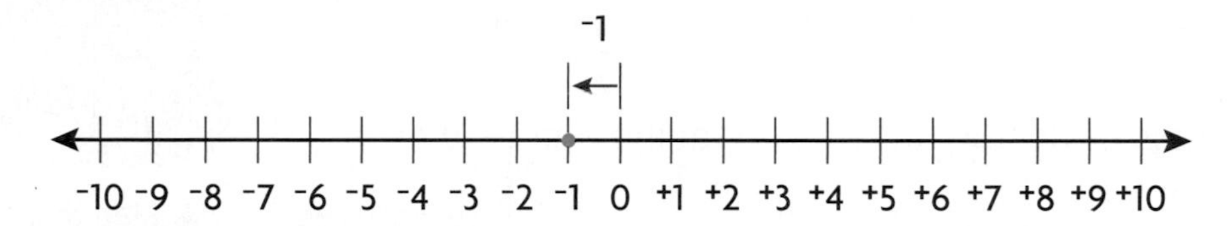

Step 3

Move 8 units to the left to subtract $^{+}8$.

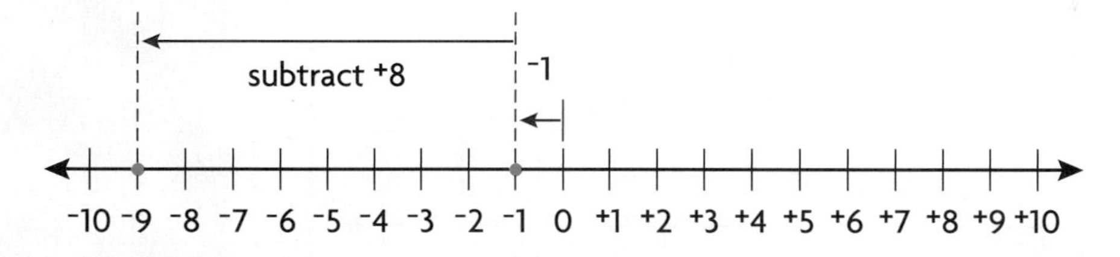

So, $^{-}1 - {}^{+}8$ is $^{-}9$.

TALK Math

How could you use a number line to find $^{-}2 - {}^{+}4$?

Practice

Use counters to find the difference.

1. $^{-}2 - {}^{+}2$
2. $^{-}8 - {}^{+}6$
3. $^{-}3 - {}^{+}6$
4. $0 - {}^{+}5$
5. $^{-}1 - {}^{+}6$
6. $^{-}9 - {}^{+}3$
7. $^{-}5 - {}^{+}3$
8. $^{-}11 - 0$
9. $^{-}4 - {}^{+}4$
10. $^{-}9 - {}^{+}4$

Use a number line to find the difference.

11. $^{-}5 - 0$
12. $^{-}7 - {}^{+}3$
13. $^{-}4 - {}^{+}1$
14. $^{-}11 - {}^{+}5$
15. $^{-}2 - {}^{+}12$
16. $0 - {}^{+}8$
17. $^{-}10 - {}^{+}4$
18. $^{-}1 - {}^{+}9$
19. $^{-}5 - {}^{+}7$
20. $^{-}3 - {}^{+}11$

21. **WRITE Math** **What's the Error? Explain** why this model cannot be used to find $^{-}2 - {}^{+}2$. How would you change the model to find $^{-}2 - {}^{+}2$?

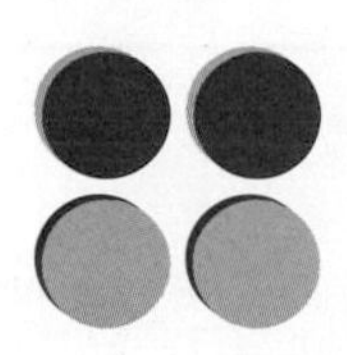

LESSON 6

Record Integer Subtraction

OBJECTIVE: Find and record the difference of integers.

Quick Review

Find the sum.

1. $^{+}4 + ^{-}3$
2. $^{-}2 + ^{+}7$
3. $^{-}5 + ^{-}8$
4. $0 + ^{-}1$
5. $^{+}6 + ^{-}6$

Learn

PROBLEM Moaning Cavern is a vertical cave in Calaveras County, California. On a walking tour, visitors go down 234 steps to a depth of 165 feet. The cave extends at least 410 feet below the surface.

Suppose Carlos starts the tour at a point that is 4 feet below the cave's entrance. Then he climbs down another 10 feet into the cave. How many feet is Carlos below the floor at the entrance of the cave?

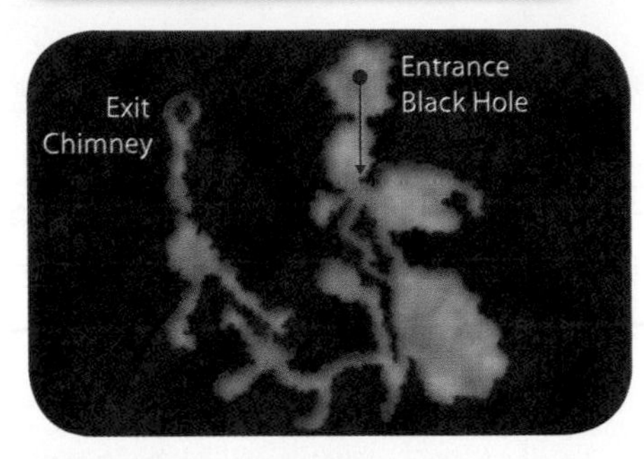

▲ Map of Moaning Cavern

Example 1 Subtract. $^{-}4 - ^{+}10$.

Step 1

Draw and label a number line. Start at 0 and move 4 spaces to the left to show $^{-}4$.

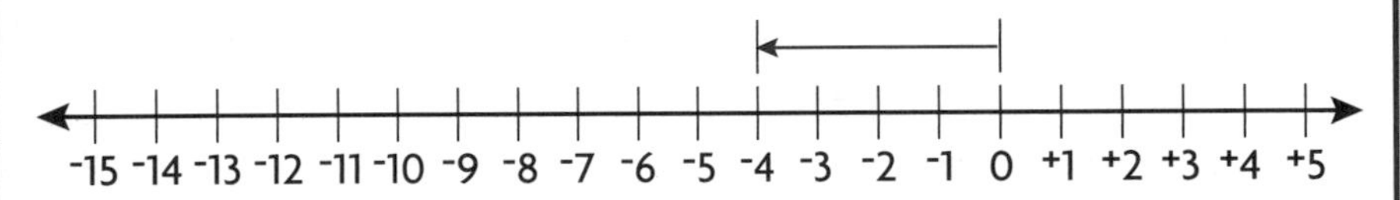

Step 2

To subtract $^{+}10$, move 10 spaces to the left from $^{-}4$. This takes you to $^{-}14$.

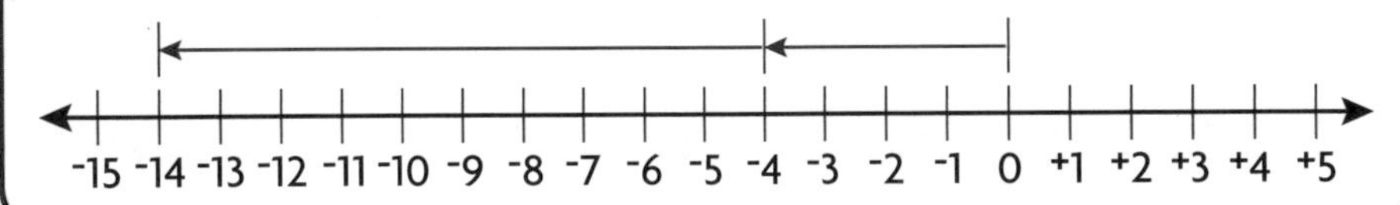

So, Carlos is $^{-}14$ feet from, or 14 feet below, the floor at the entrance of the cave.

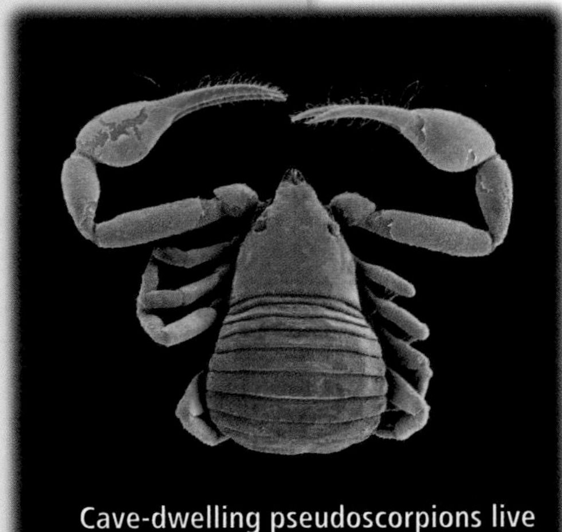

Cave-dwelling pseudoscorpions live in many of the caves of California. They are closely related to spiders, not to scorpions.

More Examples

A Find $^{-}1 - ^{+}4$.

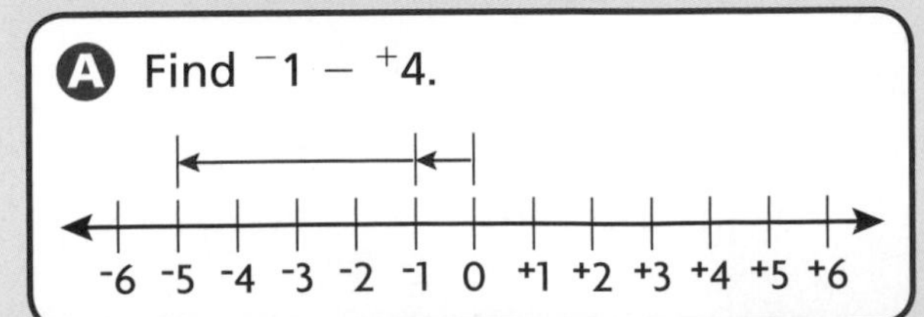

B Find $^{-}4 - ^{+}3$.

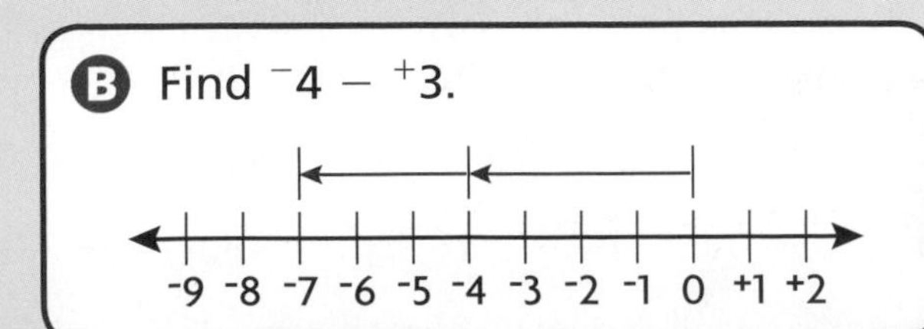

NS 2.1 Add, subtract, multiply, and divide with decimals; add with negative integers; subtract positive integers from negative integers; and verify the reasonableness of the results. *also* **NS 1.0, MR 1.0, MR 1.1, MR 2.0, MR 2.3, MR 2.4, MR 3.0, MR 3.2**

Relating Addition and Subtraction

Suppose a bat is perched in a vertical cave at a depth that is 5 feet below the cave's floor entrance. Then it flies deeper into the cave to a depth 2 feet lower than its original perch. How far is the bat below the floor at the entrance to the cave?

The California myotis is a fluffy, orange bat with mouselike ears. *Myotis* means "mouse ears" in Latin.

You can use a number line to show how the addition and subtraction of integers are related. Compare $^{-}5 - {}^{+}2$ and $^{-}5 + {}^{-}2$. Look at the number lines below.

Example

Subtraction

Find $^{-}5 - {}^{+}2$.

$^{-}9$ $^{-}8$ $^{-}7$ $^{-}6$ $^{-}5$ $^{-}4$ $^{-}3$ $^{-}2$ $^{-}1$ 0 $^{+}1$ $^{+}2$

Addition

Find $^{-}5 + {}^{-}2$.

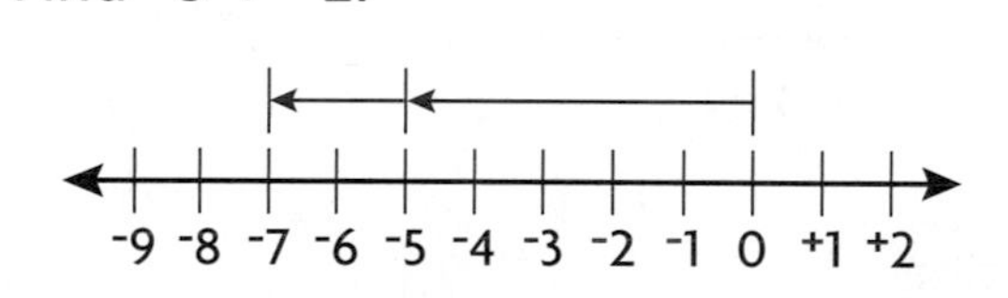

You started at zero. You moved the same number of spaces the same distance in the same direction and ended up at the same number. So, $^{-}5 - {}^{+}2 = {}^{-}5 + {}^{-}2$.

The answer to the problem is $^{-}7$. Although negative numbers can be used to find distances, distances are usually stated in positive numbers. So, the bat is perched 7 feet below the floor at the cave's entrance.

More Examples

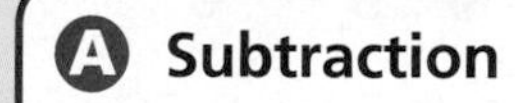

A Subtraction

Find $^{-}1 - 8$.

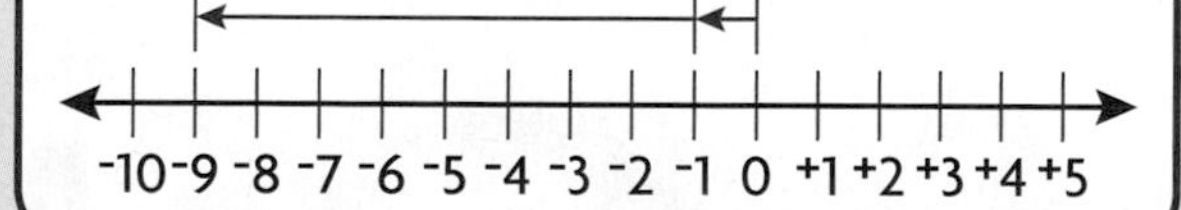

B Addition

Find $^{-}1 + {}^{-}8$.

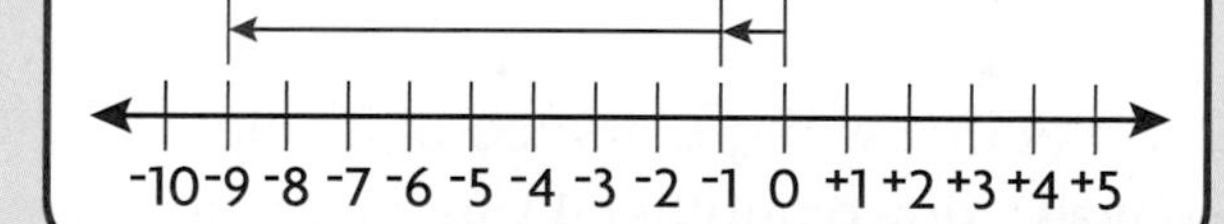

Guided Practice

Use the number line to find the difference.

1. $^{-}3 - {}^{+}1$

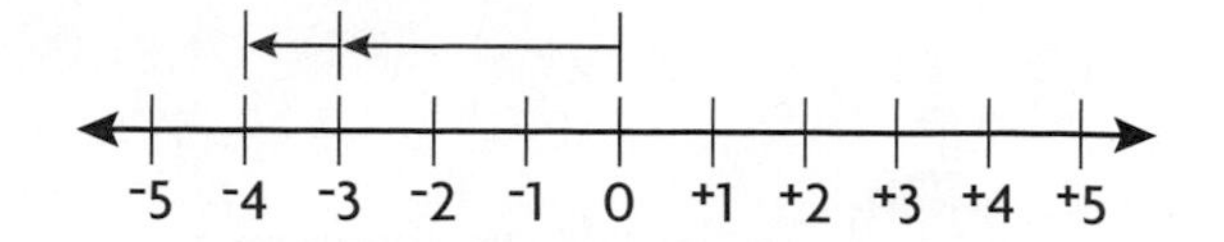

2. $^{-}2 - {}^{+}3$

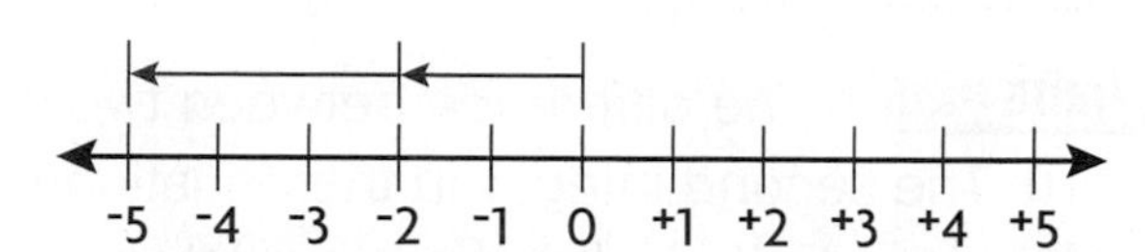

Draw a number line to find the difference.

3. $^{-}3 - {}^{+}2$ 4. $^{-}5 - {}^{+}6$ ✓5. $^{-}8 - {}^{+}1$ ✓6. $^{-}2 - {}^{+}2$

7. **TALK Math** **Explain** whether subtracting a positive integer from a negative integer will result in a difference that is a positive or a negative integer.

Independent Practice and Problem Solving

Draw a number line to find the difference.

8. $^{-}4 - {}^{+}3$ 9. $^{-}1 - {}^{+}5$ 10. $^{-}2 - {}^{+}6$ 11. $^{-}7 - {}^{+}2$

Write the subtraction equation that each number line models.

12.

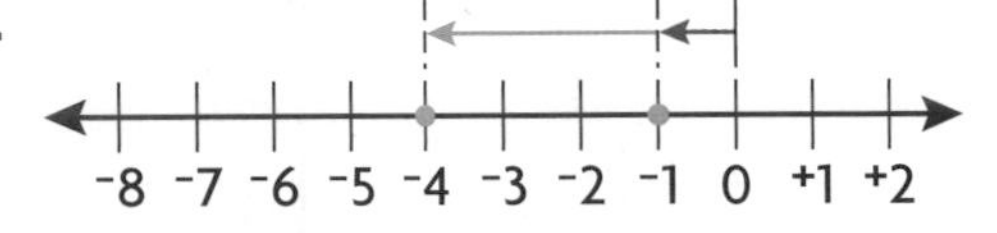

13.

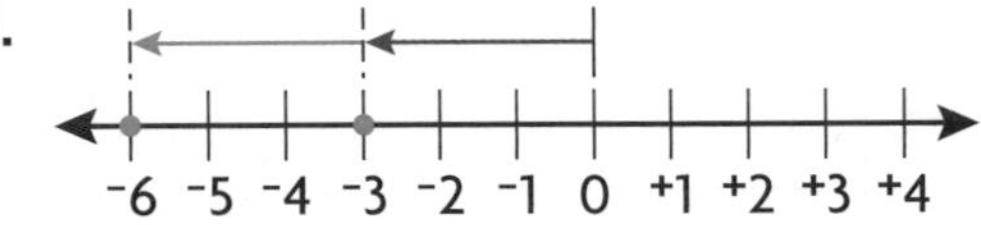

Find the difference.

14. $^{-}4 - {}^{+}5$ 15. $^{-}8 - {}^{+}8$ 16. $^{-}12 - {}^{+}11$ 17. $^{+}9 - {}^{+}16$

18. $^{-}1 - {}^{+}9$ 19. $^{-}6 - {}^{+}3$ 20. $^{-}15 - 0$ 21. $^{-}2 - {}^{+}13$

Algebra Complete the addition sentence.

22. $^{-}12 - {}^{+}11 = {}^{-}12 + ■$ 23. $^{-}8 - {}^{+}8 = {}^{-}8 + ■$ 24. $^{-}2 - {}^{+}13 = {}^{-}2 + ■$

Compare. Write <, >, or = for each ●.

25. $^{-}4 - {}^{+}5$ ● $^{-}4 + {}^{+}5$ 26. $^{-}3 - {}^{+}15$ ● $^{-}3 + {}^{+}15$ 27. $^{-}6 + {}^{+}3$ ● $^{-}3 - {}^{+}6$

28. $^{-}7 - {}^{+}8$ ● $^{-}15 - 0$ 29. $^{-}9 - {}^{+}1$ ● $^{+}10 + 0$ 30. $^{-}20 - {}^{+}4$ ● $^{-}18 + {}^{-}6$

Solve.

31. Ari starts 11 feet below the entrance of Boyden Cavern. He walks down another 11 feet into the cavern. Then Ari walks down another 3 feet. How many feet below the entrance to the cavern is Ari?

32. The lowest temperature on record in Modesto, California is $^{-}8$°C, set on December 13, 1932. Suppose the high temperature that day was $^{-}4$°C. What would the change from high to low temperature have been?

33. **WRITE Math** The difference between two integers is $^{-}10$. The second integer in the equation is $^{+}9$. **Explain** how to find what the other integer is.

CD ROM Technology Use Harcourt Mega Math, Fraction Action, *Number Line Mine,* Level W.

 Extra Practice on page 396, Set D

Achieving the Standards

34. Reese ate $\frac{1}{4}$ of a quesadilla. Write two equivalent fractions to show how much of the quesadilla she ate. **(NS 1.6, p. 144.)**

35. Make a bar graph for the following data on how students get to school: bus, 10; bike, 6; walk, 9; car, 11. **(Grade 4, SDAP 1.1)**

36. J.W. bought 3 pieces of cheese weighing 0.60 pound, 0.65 pound, and 0.6 pound. Which weights are equivalent? **(NS 1.0, p. 136)**

37. **Test Prep** The temperature at 6:00 A.M. was $^{-}9$°C. At noon, the temperature was $^{-}4$°C. By how much had the temperature risen?

    A $^{-}13$°C **C** 5°C
    B $^{-}5$°C **D** 13°C

38. **Test Prep** An ant travels in an anthill from 2 inches below the ground to 6 inches below the ground. What integer represents how far the ant traveled in inches?

    A $^{+}8$ **B** $^{-}8$ **C** $^{+}4$ **D** $^{-}4$

Problem Solving and Reasoning

NUMBER SENSE To find $^{-}1{,}386 - ^{+}931$ using counters or a number line would take a lot of counters or a long number line. Another way to add and subtract integers is to use their absolute values.

To add integers with the same sign, or to subtract a positive integer from a negative integer:

Find $^{-}85 - ^{+}103$. ← Use an addition equation. If you are subtracting, use the equivalent addition equation. $^{-}85 - ^{+}103 = ^{-}85 + ^{-}103$

$|^{-}85| + |^{-}103| = 85 + 103 = 188$ ← Add the absolute values of the integers.

$^{-}85 + ^{-}103 = ^{-}188$ ← In your answer, use the same sign as the integers had.

So, $^{-}85 - ^{+}103 = ^{-}188$.

To add integers with different signs:

Find $^{+}65 + ^{-}83$.

$|^{-}83| - |^{+}65| = 83 - 65 = 18$ ← **Think:** $|65| < |^{-}83|$. Subtract the lesser absolute value from the greater absolute value.

$^{+}65 + ^{-}83 = ^{-}18$ ← In your answer, use the sign of the integer with greater absolute value.

So, $^{+}65 + ^{-}83 = ^{-}18$.

Find the sum or difference using absolute values.

1. $^{+}14 + ^{-}93$
2. $^{-}236 - ^{+}771$
3. $^{-}303 - ^{+}199$
4. $^{+}495 - ^{+}814$
5. $^{-}1{,}374 + ^{-}3{,}257$

Problem Solving Workshop
Strategy: Compare Strategies

OBJECTIVE: Solve problems by comparing strategies.

Laguna Beach

Use the Strategy

PROBLEM At 3:33 P.M. in Laguna Beach, the water level at low tide was 6 feet below sea level. At 9:44 A.M., the water level at high tide had risen by 5 feet. What was the water level in Laguna Beach at high tide?

Read to Understand

- **What do you visualize when you read the problem?**
- **What information is given?**

Plan

- **What strategies can you use to solve the problem?**

  You can use *draw a diagram* or *make a model.*

Solve

- **How can you use the strategies to solve the problem?**

Draw a Diagram

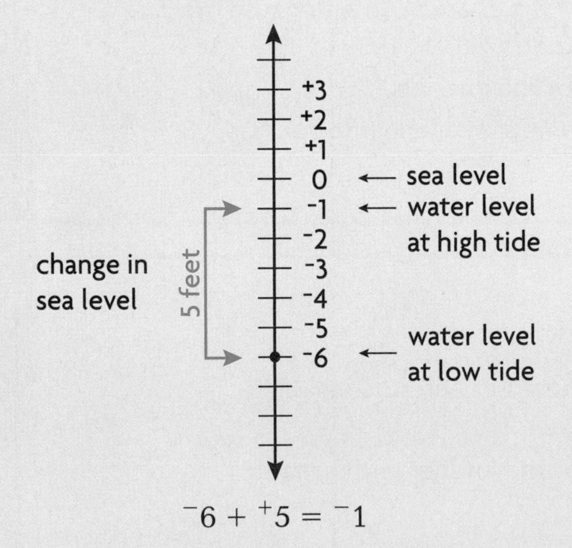

$^{-}6 + {}^{+}5 = {}^{-}1$

Make a Model

Use counters to make a model.

water level at low tide

rise in sea level

$^{-}6 + {}^{+}5 = {}^{-}1$

Remember that opposite pairs equal zero. The number and color of counters that remain provide the answer.

So, the water level at high tide was 1 foot below sea level.

Check

- **How do you know your answer is correct?**

NS 1.5 Identify and represent on a number line decimals, fractions, mixed numbers, and positive and negative integers. *also* **NS 2.1, MR 1.0, MR 2.0, MR 2.3, MR 2.4, MR 3.2**

Guided Problem Solving

1. Ethan is making a tide chart, but is missing a water level. He knows that the water level in San Clemente was 2 feet below sea level at low tide. At high tide, the water level was 4 feet higher. How can Ethan find the water level at high tide?

   First, choose a strategy. You can use counters to make a model.

   Then, use the strategy. Ethan used counters to represent the positive and negative integers in the problem.

   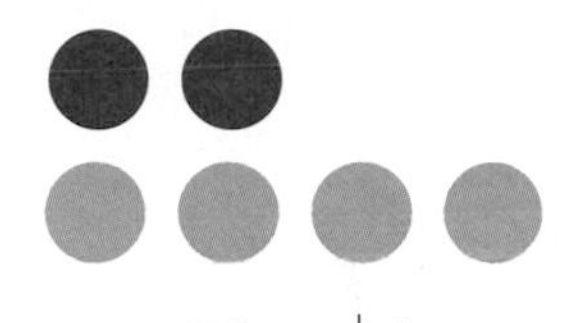

   $^{-}2 + {}^{+}4$

   Finally, solve the problem. Check your answer by using a different strategy.

2. **What if** the water level was 5 feet below sea level at low tide and rose 6 feet by high tide? What would the water level at high tide be?

3. The lowest recorded temperature in Laguna Beach is $^{-}6$°C. The highest recorded temperature is 48°C higher. What is the highest recorded temperature in Laguna Beach?

Choose a STRATEGY

- Draw a Diagram or Picture
- Make a Model or Act It Out
- Make an Organized List
- Find a Pattern
- Make a Table or Graph
- Predict and Test
- Work Backward
- Solve a Simpler Problem
- Write an Equation
- Use Logical Reasoning

Cow balloon at the Sonoma County Hot Air Balloon Classic

Mixed Strategy Practice

4. A hot air balloon was traveling at a height 121 feet above the ground. It traveled to a height of 66 feet, then climbed another 18 feet. What was the new height of the hot air balloon? What was the change in the balloon's height?

5. **WRITE Math** The temperature in San Diego was 22°C in the afternoon. That was an increase of 8°C over the morning temperature. What was the temperature in the morning? **Explain** how you know your answer is correct.

USE DATA For 6, use the picture on the right.

6. The picture shows the mileage on Tim's car after he drove to Santa Cruz. The mileage on his car was 5,645 miles before his trip. How many miles did Tim drive to get to Santa Cruz?

Extra Practice

Set A **Identify the integers graphed on the number line.** (pp. 376–379)

1. 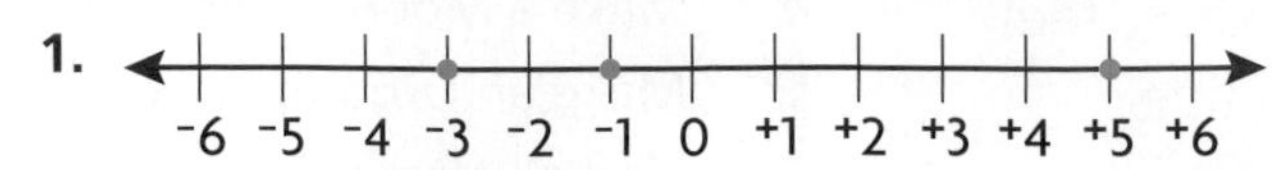

2. 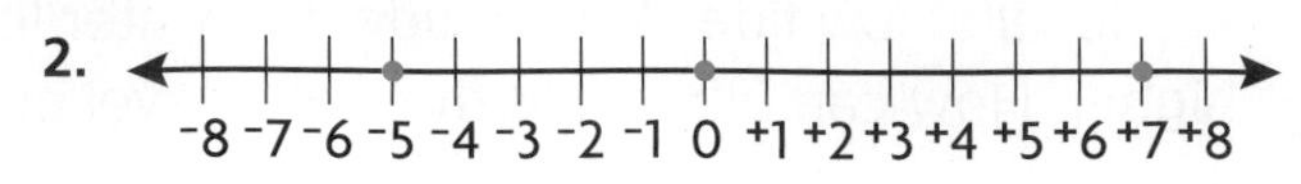

Write an integer to represent each situation.

3. a loss of 4 pounds
4. a profit of $29
5. 12 degrees below zero
6. a gain of 8 yards
7. 18 feet below sea level
8. no change in temperature

Write the opposite of each integer.

9. $^{-}11$
10. $^{+}35$
11. $^{+}47$
12. $^{-}54$
13. $^{+}315$
14. $^{-}457$
15. $^{-}1{,}365$
16. $^{+}3{,}817$

Set B **Compare. Write <, >, or = for each ●.** (pp. 380–383)

1. $^{-}6$ ● $^{+}3$
2. $^{+}5$ ● $^{-}10$
3. $^{-}1$ ● $^{+}4$
4. $^{-}2$ ● $^{-}9$

Order each set of integers from greatest to least.

5. $^{-}6, {}^{+}2, {}^{-}3, {}^{+}5$
6. $^{-}10°, 0°, {}^{-}1°, 10°$
7. $^{+}4, {}^{-}4, {}^{-}3, {}^{+}2$
8. $^{-}9°, {}^{-}7°, {}^{-}12°, 11°$

Set C **Find the sum.** (pp. 386–387)

1. $^{-}6 + {}^{-}4$
2. $^{+}9 + {}^{-}5$
3. $^{-}5 + {}^{-}5$
4. $^{+}9 + {}^{-}3$
5. $^{-}7 + {}^{-}3$
6. $^{+}11 + {}^{-}9$
7. $^{-}2 + {}^{+}3$
8. $^{-}6 + {}^{-}7$
9. The elevator is on the 12th floor. It goes up 6 floors and then down 14 floors. What floor is the elevator on now?
10. A fish is 3 feet below the lake's surface. Then it swims to a depth 8 feet lower. How many feet below the lake's surface is the fish now?

Set D **Find each difference.** (pp. 390–393)

1. $^{-}8 - {}^{+}5$
2. $^{+}12 - {}^{+}7$
3. $^{+}9 - {}^{+}6$
4. $^{-}7 - {}^{+}4$
5. $^{+}2 - {}^{+}10$
6. $^{-}3 - {}^{+}15$
7. $^{+}7 - {}^{+}8$
8. $^{+}9 - {}^{+}16$
9. A hiker is 8 feet above the entrance to a cavern. She walks down 8 feet into the cavern and then down another 5 feet. What is the change in feet of the hiker's position?

CD ROM **Technology**
Use Harcourt Mega Math, Fraction Action, *Number Line Mine,* Levels S, T, X.

Think Positively!

Divers
2 players

Equipment
- 33 index cards
- 2 counters, 1 red, 1 yellow

START

FINISH

Begin!

- Players write the numbers 0 to 10 on index cards so that there are three of each integer in the set. Players shuffle the cards and place them facedown in a stack. Each player chooses a counter and places it on *START*.
- Players take turns drawing three cards from the stack. The player uses the cards to make an addition equation with 3 terms. The player can choose to make each integer negative or positive, then solves the equation to find the sum.
- If the sum equals zero, the player moves ahead four spaces.
- If the sum is a number between $^{-}2$ and $^{+}2$ besides 0, the player moves ahead two spaces.
- If the sum is between $^{-}5$ and $^{-}3$, or $^{+}3$ and $^{+}5$, the player moves ahead one space. If the sum is less than $^{-}5$ or greater than $^{+}5$, the player moves back one space.
- If the sum is negative, the player moves ahead 1 bonus space.
- The first player to reach *FINISH* wins.

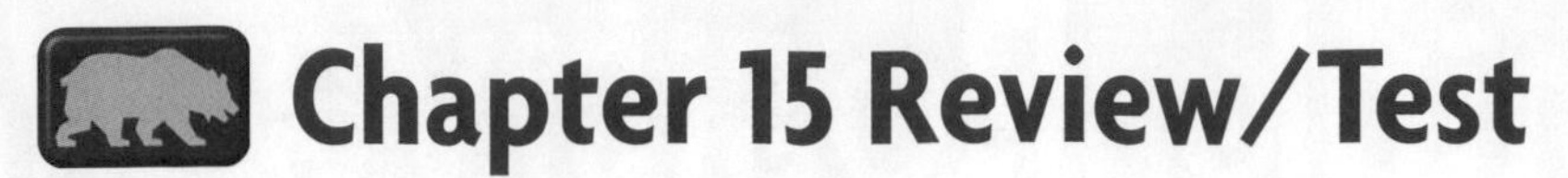

Chapter 15 Review/Test

Check Vocabulary and Concepts

For 1–2, choose the best term from the box.

VOCABULARY
integers
negative integers
positive integers

1. Integers greater than zero are called __?__. (NS 1.5, p. 376)
2. Integers less than zero are called __?__. (NS 1.5, p. 376)
3. Explain how you can use two-color counters to solve $^{-}4 + ^{+}3$. (NS 2.1, pp. 384–385)
4. Explain how you can use a number line to find $^{-}2 - ^{+}1$. (NS 2.1, pp. 388–389)

Check Skills

Write an integer to represent each situation. (NS 1.5, pp. 376–379)

5. 42 degrees below 0
6. a deposit of $9
7. a loss of 15 yards

Write the opposite of each integer. (NS 1.5, pp. 376–379)

8. $^{-}29$
9. $^{+}17$
10. $^{+}38$
11. $^{-}55$

Compare. Write <, >, or = for each ●. (NS 1.5, pp. 380–383)

12. $^{-}15$ ● $^{+}13$
13. $^{+}11$ ● $^{-}2$
14. $^{-}5$ ● $^{-}3$
15. $^{+}8$ ● $^{-}6$

Find the sum. (NS 2.1, pp. 386–387)

16. $^{-}12 + ^{+}5$
17. $^{+}8 + ^{-}6$
18. $^{+}11 + ^{-}11$
19. $^{-}20 + ^{+}15$

Find the difference. (NS 2.1, pp. 390–393)

20. $^{-}10 - ^{+}4$
21. $^{+}13 - ^{+}8$
22. $^{-}9 - ^{+}15$
23. $^{+}21 - ^{+}14$

Check Problem Solving

Solve. (NS 2.1, pp. 394–395, MR 2.2, MR 2.3)

24. At the start of an experiment, the temperature of a water sample was 6°F. By the end, the temperature had dropped 8°F. What was the water's temperature at the end of the experiment?
25. **WRITE Math** The temperature in Palo Alto was 28°C at noon. That was 14°C warmer than the morning temperature. What was the temperature in the morning? **Explain** how you know your answer is correct.

GO ONLINE **Technology** Use *Online Assessment.*

Enrich • Integer Sums

Complete the SQUARE

You can use magic squares to practice finding integer sums. Integers are placed in the squares to form addition sentences. Each row, column, and diagonal of the magic square must have the same sum.

Example Complete the magic square for a sum of 0.

−1	■	■
■	0	■
■	■	1

−1	3	−2
−1	0	1
2	−3	1

−1	−1	2
3	0	−3
−2	1	1

Two possible solutions.

Try It!

Complete each magic square so that each row, column, and diagonal have the given sum. Integers can be used more than once.

1. Sum of 0

−3		
		−1
	−5	

2. Sum of 3

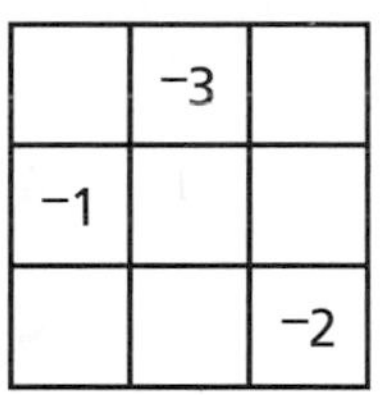

	−3	
−1		
		−2

3. Sum of −6

		−1
−4		
	2	

4. Sum of 0

	−10	
2		
		−4

5. Sum of 9

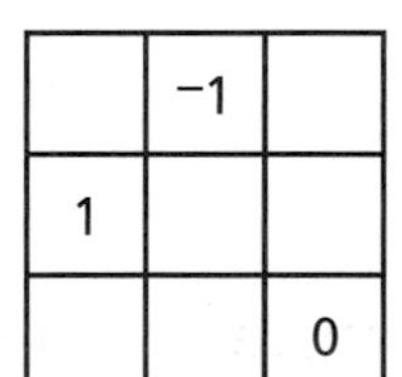

	−1	
1		
		0

6. Sum of 6

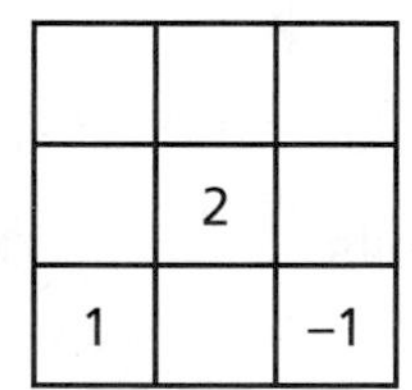

	2	
1		−1

Think About It

WRITE Math Is it possible to complete a magic square containing twice as many −1s as +1s, and have a magic sum of 0? **Explain.**

Achieving the Standards

Chapters 1–15

Measurement and Geometry

1. In the figure below, which two lines appear to be perpendicular? (MG 2.1)

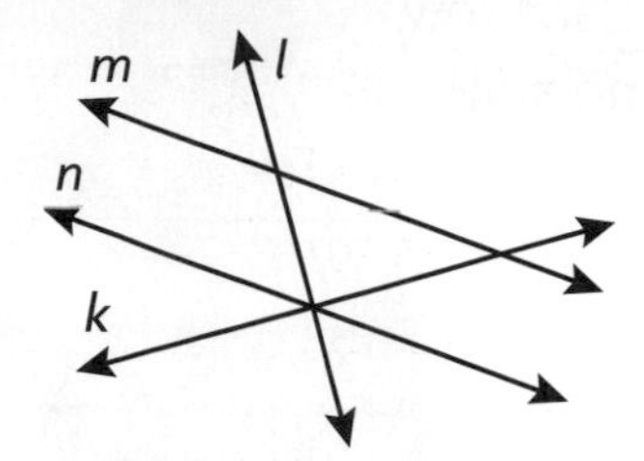

A lines k and l

B lines m and n

C lines k and n

D lines l and m

2. What is the length of the line segment shown on the grid? (Grade 4 MG 2.3)

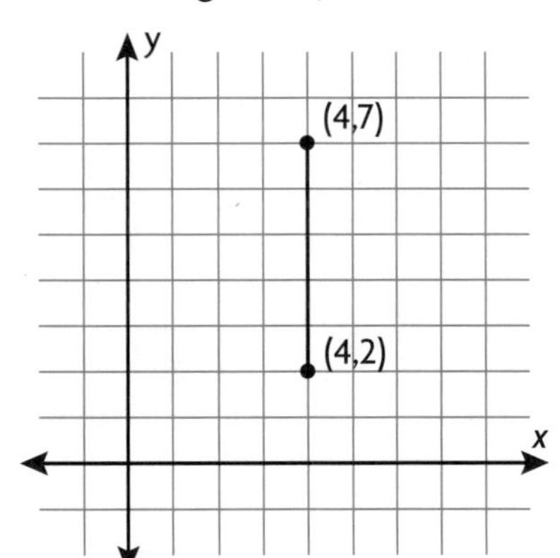

A 4 units

B 5 units

C 6 units

D 7 units

3. WRITE Math A rectangle has a width of 4 inches and a length of 6 inches. What is the area of a square with the same perimeter as the rectangle? How does the area of the rectangle compare to the area of the square? **Explain** how you found your answers. (Grade 4 MG 1.3)

Number Sense

4. $63.09 \div 0.3$. (NS 2.2)

A 2103

B 210.3

C 21.03

D 2.103

5. Lucas is adding 4.892 and 63.71. After he aligns the decimal points, to which digit in 4.892 will he add the 1 in 63.71? (NS 2.1)

A 2

B 4

C 8

D 9

6. Which of the following has the greatest value? (NS 1.4)

A 8^2

B 4^3

C 3^4

D 2^5

7. $\frac{6}{7} \cdot \frac{7}{15}$ (NS 2.4)

A $\frac{4}{15}$

B $\frac{2}{5}$

C $\frac{3}{5}$

D $\frac{4}{5}$

8. WRITE Math **Explain** how to find the difference $^{-}16 - {}^{+}13$. (NS 2.1)

Statistics, Data Analysis, and Probability

9. Which point represents (2,3) on this graph? (O‑key SDAP 1.5)

A *A** **C** *C*

B *B* **D** *D*

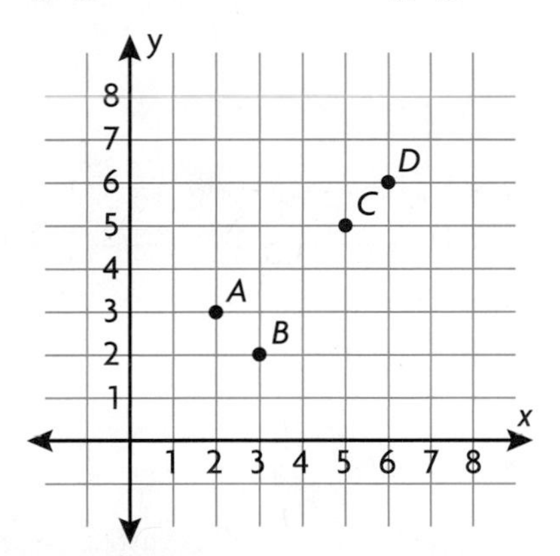

Test Tip **Get the information you need.**

See item 10. Find the median, mode, range, and any outliers of the data. Decide which statement is not true.

10. Which statement is NOT true about the data? (SDAP 1.1)

20, 31, 15, 27, 59, 15, 26, 13, 12

A The outlier is 12.

B The range is 47.

C The median is 20.

D The mode is 15.

11. WRITE Math The table shows the number of students with each type of pet.

Class Pets					
Pet	Dog	Cat	Bird	Fish	Other
Number	12	6	3	2	4

What kind of graph would you make to show the data? **Explain** your choice. (SDAP 1.2)

Algebra and Functions

12. Which situation could be described by the expression $h + 3$? (O‑key AF 1.2)

A Nan worked *h* hours yesterday, and 3 hours less today.

B Nan worked *h* hours yesterday and 3 hours more today.

C Nan worked 3 hours yesterday, and *h* hours less today.

D Nan worked 3 hours yesterday, and *h* times as many hours today.

13. If $b = 15$, what is the value of $^{-}9 - b$? (O‑key AF 1.2)

A 24

B 6

C -6

D -24

14. If $w = 9$, what is the value of $7 \times w - 37$? (O‑key AF 1.2)

A 100 **C** 36

B 42 **D** 26

15. What value for *a* makes this equation true? (AF 1.3)

$$4 \times 78 = (4 \times a) + (4 \times 8)$$

A 4 **C** 70

B 8 **D** 78

16. WRITE Math **Explain** how to evaluate the expression $8x$ for $x = 4$. (O‑key AF 1.2)

16 Percent

The Big Idea Percents can be expressed as fractions and decimals.

Investigate

Each person in California uses approximately 20 kilowatt-hours of electricity each day. Choose a source of electricity from the graph. Out of 20 kilowatt-hours of electricity, how many kilowatt-hours come from that source in a day? How many in a week?

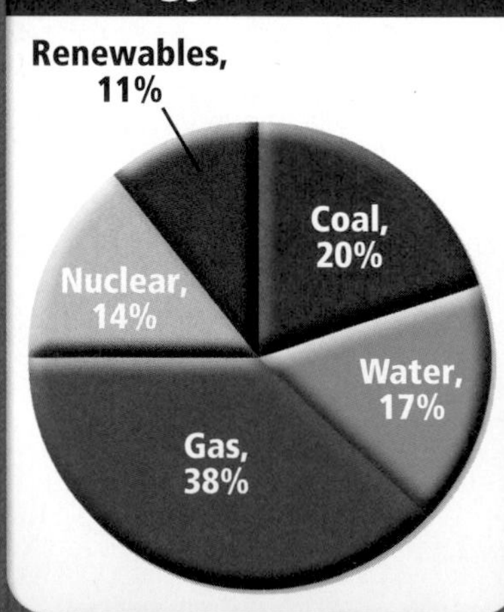

CALIFORNIA FAST FACT

Energy from wind turbines in California produced 4,446 million kilowatt-hours of electricity in 2005. Renewable wind energy represents 1.5% of California's total energy sources.

GO ONLINE **Technology** Student pages are available in the Student eBook.

Show What You Know

Check your understanding of important skills needed for success in Chapter 16.

▶ Relate Fractions and Decimals

Write a decimal and a fraction for the shaded part.

1. 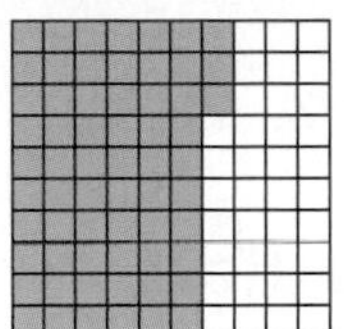

2. 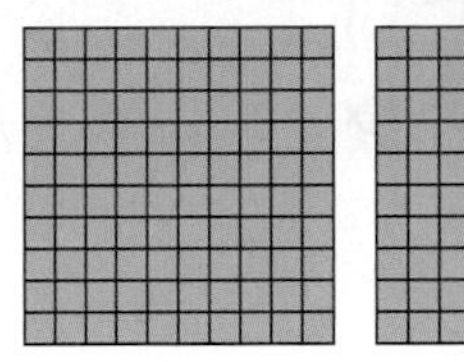

3. 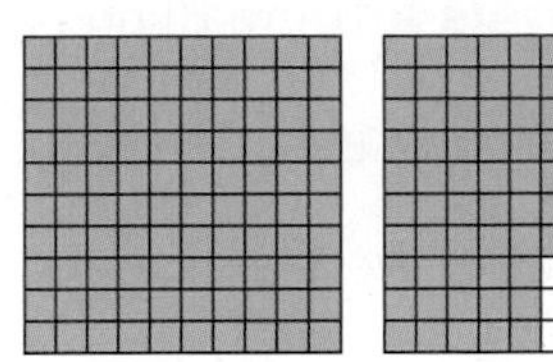

Write as a decimal.

4. $\frac{7}{10}$ **5.** $1\frac{13}{100}$ **6.** $\frac{3}{4}$ **7.** $3\frac{2}{5}$ **8.** $4\frac{8}{100}$

Write as a fraction.

9. 1.5 **10.** 0.6 **11.** 7.44 **12.** 1.023 **13.** 18.001

▶ Multiply Decimals by Whole Numbers

Find the product.

14. 0.25×4 **15.** 0.42×3 **16.** 0.76×5 **17.** 0.38×6 **18.** 0.84×9

19. 0.56×7 **20.** 0.19×8 **21.** 0.62×3 **22.** 0.47×9 **23.** 0.73×5

VOCABULARY POWER

CHAPTER VOCABULARY

decimal
fraction
percent

WARM-UP WORDS

percent a fractional part of a number to 100

fraction a number that names a part of a whole or a part of a group

decimal a number with one or more digits to the right of the decimal point

LESSON 1 HANDS ON

Understand Percent

OBJECTIVE: Model, read, and write percents.

Quick Review

Write an equivalent fraction with a denominator of 100.

1. $\frac{1}{4}$
2. $\frac{3}{10}$
3. $\frac{4}{5}$
4. $\frac{8}{25}$
5. $\frac{25}{50}$

Vocabulary

percent

Investigate

Materials ■ 10-by-10 grids ■ colored pencils

You can use a 10-by-10 grid to explore percent.

Percent is the fractional part of a number to 100.

A On five different 10-by-10 grids, show 5 squares shaded, 10 squares shaded, 25 squares shaded, 50 squares shaded, and 75 squares shaded.

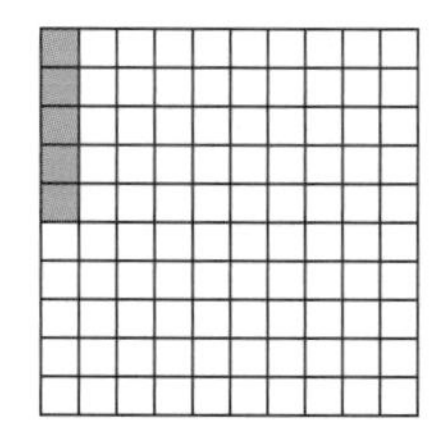

5 out of 100 or $\frac{5}{100}$; 0.05

B Write a fraction and a decimal below each model to show the part of shaded squares to total squares.

C Review the definition for percent. Write a percent below each of your models.

D Now use a 10-by-10 grid to show 30%.

Draw Conclusions

1. Explain how you determined the percent for each model.
2. How would you use a 10-by-10 grid to show $\frac{1}{2}$?
3. How does one model show $\frac{50}{100}$, 0.50 and 50%?
4. **Application** How would you show 200% using 10-by-10 grids?

NS 1.2 Interpret percents as a part of a hundred; find decimal and percent equivalents for common fractions and explain why they represent the same value; compute a given percent of a whole number. *also* **NS 1.0, MR 2.0, MR 2.3, MR 2.4, MR 3.2**

Connect

The table shows the results of a survey that asked 100 students which technology was the most important to them. You can use a fraction, a decimal, and a percent to represent each survey result.

Remember that *percent* means "per hundred." So, for notebook computers, 26 out of 100, 0.26, or 26% of students chose this technology.

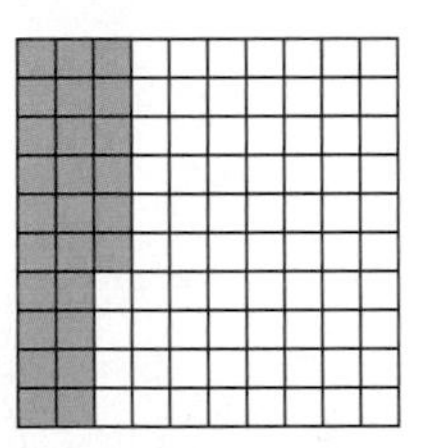

26 out of 100 or $\frac{26}{100}$
0.26
26%

Technology Survey

Technology	Number of Students
Notebook Computers	26
Portable MP3 Players	12
Personal Digital Assistants	5
Digital Cameras	4
Cell Phones	53

- Make a model for each type of technology and then label your model with a fraction, a decimal, and a percent.

TALK Math
Explain how you could model all of the data on one grid. How many squares would you shade?

Practice

Write a fraction and a percent to represent the shaded part.

1. 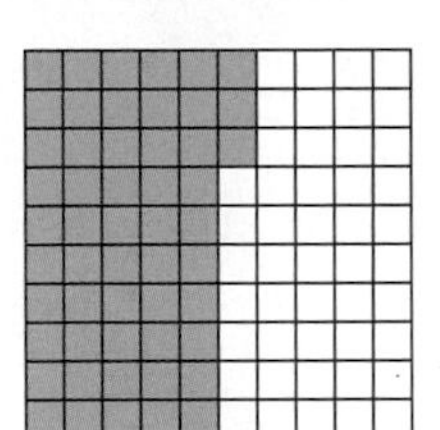

2. 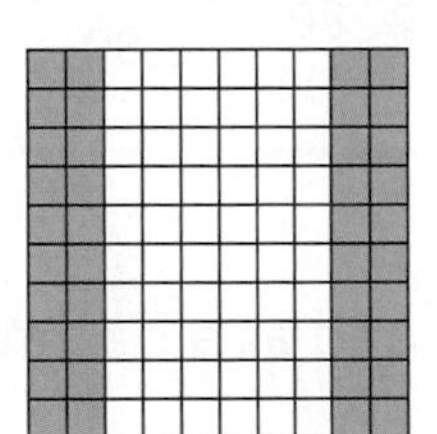

3. 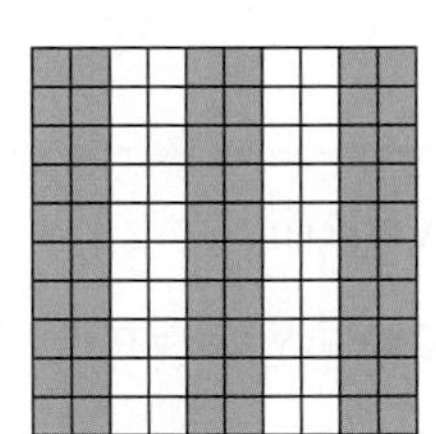

Write a decimal and a percent to represent the shaded part.

4. 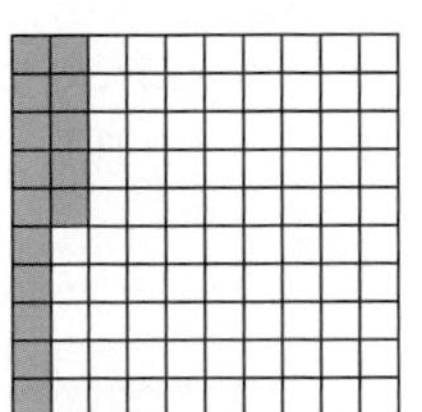

5. 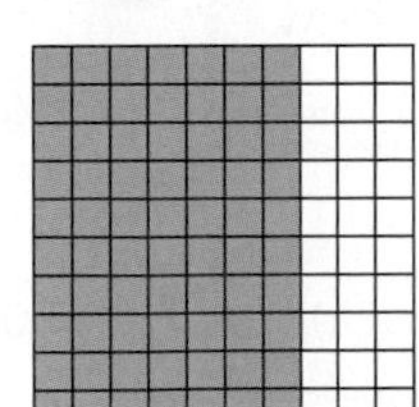

6. 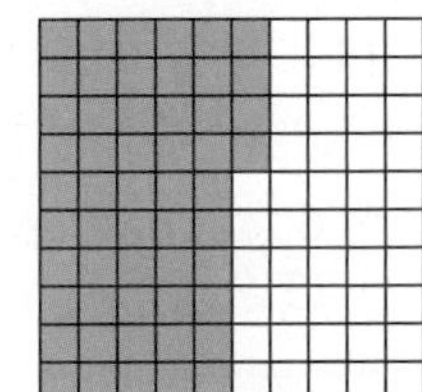

7. WRITE Math **Explain** why $\frac{1}{4}$, 0.25, and 25% are equivalent.

LESSON 2

Fractions, Decimals, and Percents

OBJECTIVE: Write equivalent forms of fractions, decimals, and percents.

Quick Review

Write each fraction in simplest form.

1. $\frac{2}{4}$ **2.** $\frac{4}{6}$ **3.** $\frac{6}{8}$

4. $\frac{2}{10}$ **5.** $\frac{35}{50}$

Learn

PROBLEM Asparagus is grown in every state in the United States. About 80% of all the asparagus grown in the United States is grown in California. What fraction of the asparagus grown in the United States is grown in California?

Example 1 Write the percent as a fraction in simplest form.

Step 1	Step 2
Write the percent as a fraction with a denominator of 100.	Write the fraction in simplest form.
$80\% = \frac{80}{100}$	$\frac{80 \div 20}{100 \div 20} = \frac{4}{5}$

So, $\frac{4}{5}$ of the asparagus in the United States is grown in California.

You can write a percent as a decimal.

Example 2 Write 80% as a decimal.

Step 1	Step 2
Write the percent as a fraction with a denominator of 100.	Write the fraction as a decimal.
$80\% = \frac{80}{100}$	$\frac{80}{100} = 0.80$

So, 80% written as a decimal is 0.80.

- How would you write 95% as a fraction and as a decimal?

More Examples

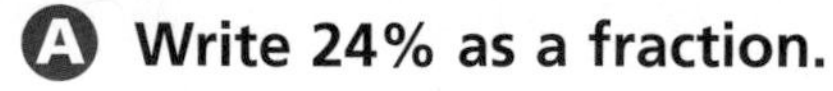

A Write 24% as a fraction.

$24\% = \frac{24}{100}$ Write the percent as a fraction with a denominator of 100.

$\frac{24 \div 4}{100 \div 4} = \frac{6}{25}$ Write the fraction in simplest form.

B Write 7% as a decimal.

$7\% = \frac{7}{100}$ Write the percent as a fraction with a denominator of 100.

$\frac{7}{100} = 0.07$ Write the fraction as a decimal.

NS 1.2 Interpret percents as a part of a hundred; find decimal and percent equivalents for common fractions and explain why they represent the same value; compute a given percent of a whole number. *also* **NS 1.0, MR 2.3, MR 2.4, MR 3.2**

Write Decimals and Fractions as Percents

You can use place value or multiplication to write a decimal as a percent.

Example 3

ONE WAY **Use place value.**

Write 0.75 as a percent.

Step 1

Use place value to express the decimal as a fraction.

$$0.75 \rightarrow \frac{75}{100}$$

Step 2

Since percent means "out of one hundred", write the fraction as a percent.

$$\frac{75}{100} = 75\%$$

ANOTHER WAY **Use multiplication.**

Write 0.04 as a percent.

Step 1

Multiply the decimal by 100.

$$0.04 \times 100 = 4$$

Step 2

Write the product as a percent.

$$0.04 \times 100 = 4\%$$

You can use equivalent fractions or division to write a fraction as a percent. Use equivalent fractions when the denominator of a fraction is a factor of 100. Use division when the denominator of a fraction is *not* a factor of 100.

Example 4

ONE WAY **Use equivalent fractions.**

Write $\frac{1}{4}$ as a percent.

Step 1

Write an equivalent fraction in fraction form with a denominator of 100.

$$\frac{1 \times 25}{4 \times 25} = \frac{25}{100}$$

Step 2

Since percent is a fraction that has a number over 100, write the fraction as a percent.

$$\frac{25}{100} = 25\%$$

ANOTHER WAY **Use division.**

Write $\frac{3}{8}$ as a percent.

Step 1

Divide the numerator by the denominator.

$$\frac{3}{8} = 8\overline{)3} \qquad \begin{array}{r} 0.375 \\ 8\overline{)3.000} \end{array}$$

Step 2

Multiply 0.375 by 100. Write the product as a percent.

$$0.375 \times 100 = 37.5\%$$

- Write 0.05 as a fraction and as a percent.

Guided Practice

1. Write $\frac{1}{2}$ as a percent. $\frac{1 \times \blacksquare}{2 \times \blacksquare} = \frac{50}{100} = \blacksquare\%$

Write each percent as a decimal and as a fraction in simplest form.

2. 20% 3. 65% 4. 70% ✓5. 98% 6. 43%

Write each fraction or decimal as a percent.

7. $\frac{1}{5}$ 8. 0.15 9. $\frac{3}{10}$ ✓10. 0.80 11. 0.64

12. **TALK Math** **Explain** whether 0.04 is equivalent to 40%.

Independent Practice and Problem Solving

Write each percent as a decimal and as a fraction in simplest form.

13. 14% 14. 30% 15. 49% 16. 85% 17. 2%

18. 23% 19. 64% 20. 71% 21. 96% 22. 54%

Write each fraction or decimal as a percent.

23. $\frac{7}{10}$ 24. 0.28 25. $\frac{2}{5}$ 26. 0.03 27. $\frac{1}{8}$

28. 0.325 29. $\frac{5}{8}$ 30. 0.011 31. $\frac{6}{20}$ 32. 0.09

USE DATA For 33–37, use the table.

33. Write as a decimal the percent of American households that eat strawberries.

34. What fraction of strawberries in the United States does Hillsborough County produce?

35. **Reasoning** If you eat 8 medium strawberries one day, what fraction of vitamin C for that day do you still need?

36. Write a fraction that shows the 7- to 9-year-olds who *do not choose* strawberries as their favorite fruit.

37. **WRITE Math** **What's the Question?** The answer is 6%.

Facts About Strawberries
• If you eat 8 medium strawberries, you'll get 93% of the vitamin C you should have every day.
• 94% of households in the United States eat strawberries.
• 53% of 7- to 9-year-olds choose strawberries as their favorite fruit.
• Hillsborough County, Florida, produces about 15% of the strawberries in the United States.

CD ROM Technology
Use Harcourt Mega Math, Fraction Action, *Fraction Flare Up*, Level N.

 Extra Practice on page 424, Set A

Achieving the Standards

38. A chef spent 45 minutes preparing a meal. What fraction of an hour is this? (Grade 4 NS 1.5)

39. Evaluate the expression $24b + 17$ for $b = 8$. (AF 1.2, p. 348)

40. Write 75% as a fraction. (NS 1.2, p. 402)

41. **Test Prep** Sam correctly answered 93% of the questions on his math test. What is that percent written as a decimal?

A 0.93 **B** 9.3 **C** 93 **D** 930

42. **Test Prep** At the Rocking R Ranch, $\frac{17}{20}$ of the stalls have horses in them. What percent of the stalls are filled?

A 8.5% **C** 85%

B 17% **D** 850%

Problem Solving and Reasoning

NUMBER SENSE If you write a percent that is less than 1% as a decimal, the decimal will be less than 0.01. If you write a percent that is greater than 100% as a decimal, the decimal will be greater than 1.

Examples

A Write 0.5% as a decimal.

Write the percent as a fraction with a denominator of 100.

$\frac{0.5}{100} = 100\overline{)0.5}$

Divide.

$100\overline{)0.5} = 100\overline{)0.500}$, quotient 0.005

So, 0.5% = 0.005.

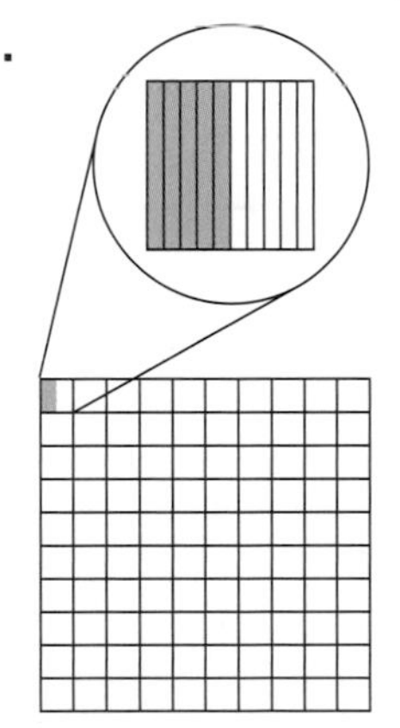

B Write 150% as a decimal.

Write the percent as a fraction with a denominator of 100.

$\frac{150}{100} = 100\overline{)150}$

Divide.

$100\overline{)150} = 100\overline{)150.0}$, quotient 1.5

So, 150% = 1.5.

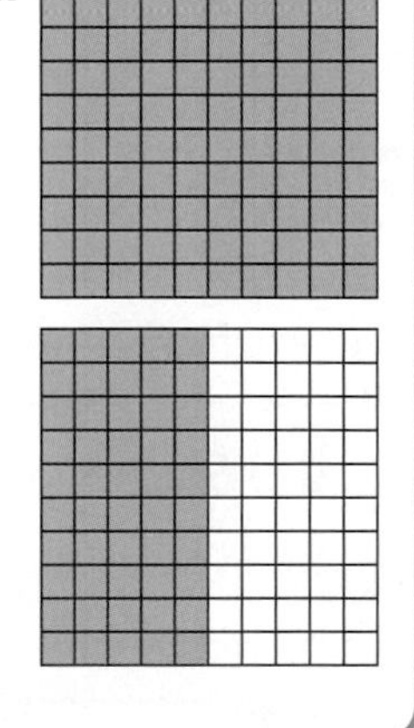

Write each percent as a decimal and as a fraction in simplest form.

1. 0.25% **2.** 0.80% **3.** 200% **4.** 175%

5. 130% **6.** 0.1% **7.** 105% **8.** 0.9%

LESSON 3

Use a Number Line

OBJECTIVE: Identify, represent, and order fractions, decimals, and percents on a number line.

Quick Review

Compare. Use <, >, or =.

1. 0.6 ● 0.06
2. 0.53 ● 0.48
3. 0.12 ● 0.79
4. $\frac{1}{4}$ ● $\frac{3}{4}$
5. $\frac{4}{5}$ ● $\frac{2}{5}$

Learn

You can use a number line to represent fractions, decimals, and percents.

PROBLEM Three baseball teams played the same number of games, and recorded their win-loss record for the season. The Bears won 60% of their games, the Sliders won 0.75 of their games, and the Foxes won $\frac{3}{10}$ of their games. Which team won the most games?

Example 1

Step 1

Draw a number line and label the benchmarks 0, $\frac{1}{2}$, and 1.

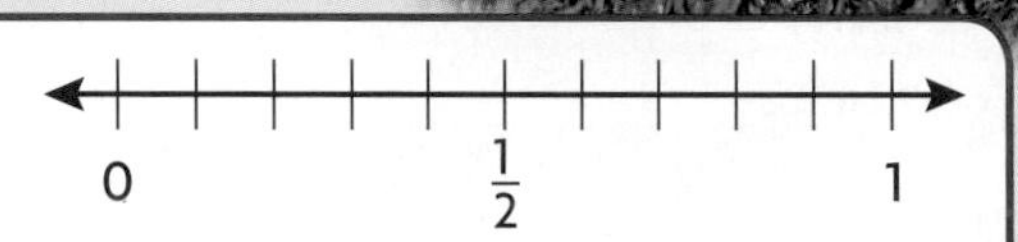

Step 2

Locate and graph a point for each quantity.

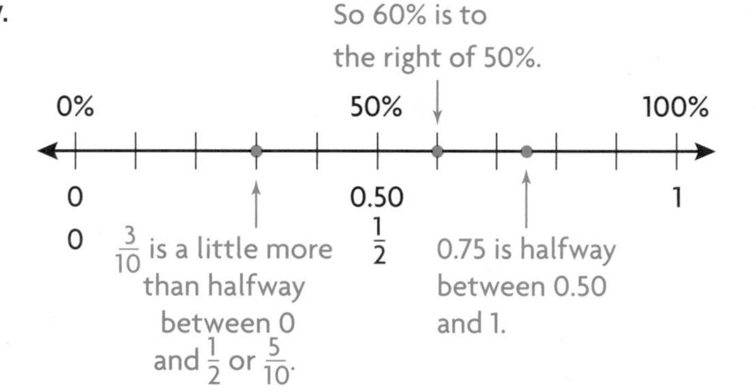

Step 3

Since you want to find the team that won the most games, identify the point that is farthest to the right.

So, the Sliders won the most games.

Example 2 Locate $1\frac{3}{8}$, 1.75, and 96% on a number line. Then, order the numbers from least to greatest.

Step 1

Draw a number line.

Step 2

Locate and graph a point for each quantity.

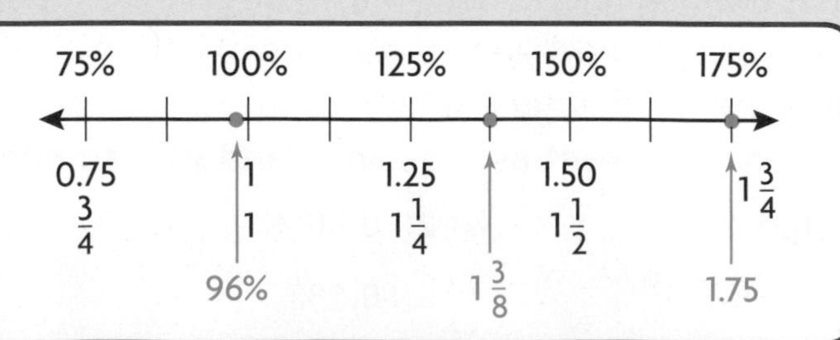

So, the numbers ordered from least to greatest are 96%, $1\frac{3}{8}$, and 1.75.

NS 1.5 Identify and represent on a number line decimals, fractions, mixed numbers, and positive and negative integers. *also* **NS 1.0, NS 1.2, MR 2.3, MR 2.4, MR 3.2.**

Guided Practice

1. For 0.8, 90%, and $\frac{3}{5}$, write the letter that represents each amount on the number line.

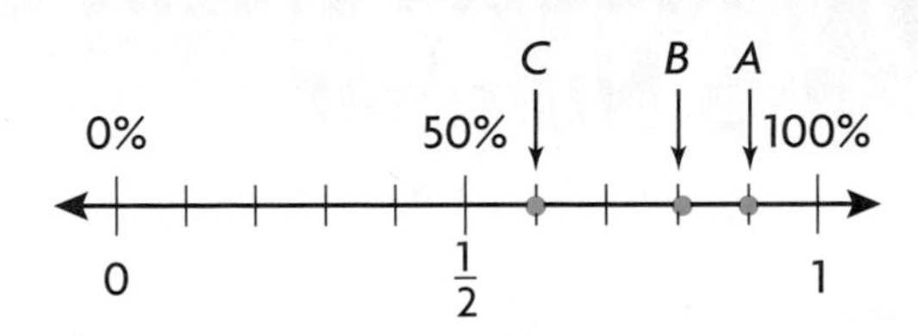

For 2–6, make a number line. Then, locate each quantity on the number line.

2. $\frac{3}{4}$
3. 0.10
4. 0.35
5. 25%
6. $\frac{9}{10}$
7. **TALK Math** **Explain** how you would use a number line to represent 0.55, 63%, and $\frac{9}{12}$.

Independent Practice and Problem Solving

For 8–12, make a number line. Then, locate each quantity on the number line.

8. $\frac{1}{10}$
9. 0.85
10. 15%
11. $1\frac{1}{4}$
12. 0.40

13. Sandy has a batting average of .284 for the season. Marcus has a batting average of 25%. Which player has the greater batting average?
14. **WRITE Math** **What's the Error?** 50% of the 12 baseball players on the Sliders team and $\frac{3}{8}$ of the 16 players on the Bears team played at every game. Sean says the number of players who played at every game is greater for the Sliders than the Bears since 50% is greater than $\frac{3}{8}$.

Achieving the Standards

15. Joel has 8 ounces of soup. Ben has 0.75 of that amount. How many ounces of soup does Ben have? (NS 2.1, p. 300)
16. The temperature at noon was 8 degrees. By 2 P.M., it had fallen 10 degrees. What was the temperature at 2 P.M.? (NS 2.1, p. 384)
17. What value for n makes this equation true? $9 \times 45 = (9 \times 40) + (9 \times n)$ (AF 1.3, p. 64)
18. **Test Prep** Which of the following numbers is the least?

    0.63, 7%, 0.09, $\frac{3}{10}$

    A 0.63 **C** 0.09

    B 7% **D** $\frac{3}{10}$

Extra Practice on page 424, Set B

LESSON 4 HANDS ON

Model Percent of a Number

OBJECTIVE: Use a model to find the percent of a number.

Quick Review

1. 0.6×12
2. 0.9×9
3. 1.3×4
4. 0.25×22
5. 0.48×317

Investigate

Materials ■ two-color counters

You can use two-color counters to model a percent of a number.

Monica likes to shop for bargains. She finds a $40 backpack marked "30% off." How can she find the amount she would save, 30% of 40?

A Let each counter represent 10%. Put down 10 red counters to represent 100%. Each 10% represents 4 since $10 \times 4 = 40$.

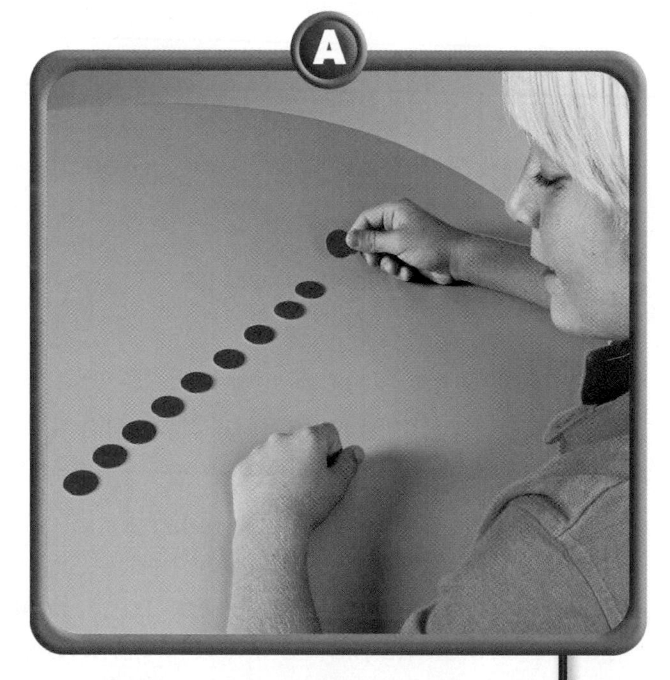

B Now flip over three of the counters. The three yellow counters show $3 \times 10\%$, or 30%.

C Since each counter represents 4, what is 30% of 40? How much would Monica save?

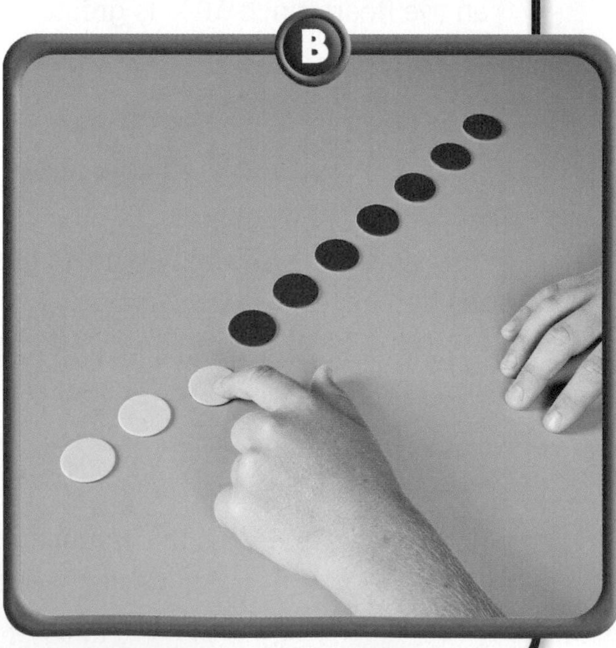

Draw Conclusions

1. What percent do the 3 yellow counters represent in your model?
2. What decimal could you write to represent the 3 yellow counters?
3. What fraction could you write to represent the 3 yellow counters?
4. **Comprehension** Explain how you would change the model to find 40% of 40.

NS 1.2 Interpret percents as a part of a hundred; find decimal and percent equivalents for common fractions and explain why they represent the same value; compute a given percent of a whole number.
also **NS 1.0, MR 2.0, MR 2.3, MR 2.4, MR 3.2**

Connect

You can write a percent as a fraction and then make a model to solve a problem.

Find 75% of 20.

Show 20 red counters.

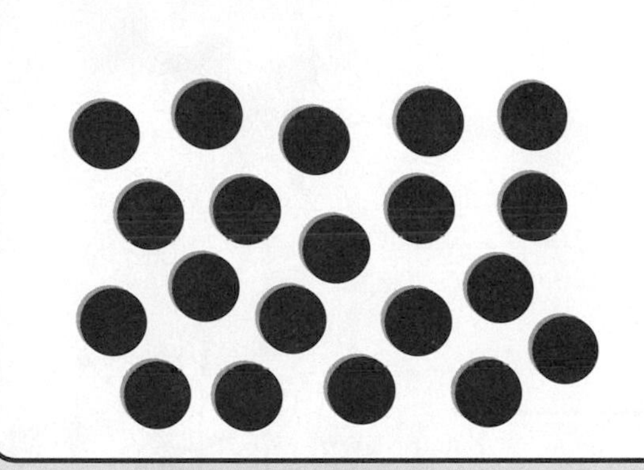

Step 2

Since 75% equals $\frac{3}{4}$, separate the counters into four equal groups. Change the color of three groups to yellow. What is $\frac{3}{4}$ of 20?

So, 75% of 20 is 15.

TALK Math

How does a model make finding the percent of some numbers easier?

Practice

Complete the sentence. Then, use each model to find the percent of each number.

1. 60% of 50

10 counters represent 100%, or 50.
So, each counter represents 10%, or ■.

2. $20\% \text{ of } 15 = \frac{\blacksquare}{\blacksquare}$ of 15

Find the percent of each number. Use counters to solve.

3. 30% of 30 **4.** 50% of 8 **5.** 75% of 24 ✓**6.** 90% of 10

Write each percent as a fraction. Then, use counters to find the percent of each number.

7. 20% of 25 **8.** 50% of 80 **9.** 25% of 16 ✓**10.** 25% of 24

11. WRITE Math **Explain** how you would use counters to find 20% of 30.

LESSON 5

Percent Problems

OBJECTIVE: Solve three types of percent problems.

Quick Review

1. $\frac{1}{2} \times 40$
2. $\frac{2}{5} \times 25$
3. 0.5×90
4. 0.70×60
5. 0.95×30

Learn

PROBLEM The Roll-In Skate Store is having a sale on skateboards. Danica wants to buy a skateboard that is on sale for 25% off the original price of $60. How much will Danica save if she buys the skateboard during the sale?

About 82% of skateboarders are 18 years old or younger.

You can find a percent of a number by changing the percent to a fraction and multiplying.

Find 25% of 60.

ONE WAY **Use a fraction.**

Step 1	Step 2	Step 3
Write 25% as a fraction. $25\% = \frac{25}{100}$	Write the fraction in simplest form. $\frac{25 \div 25}{100 \div 25} = \frac{1}{4}$	Multiply. $\frac{1}{4} \times \frac{60}{1} = \frac{60}{4} = 15$

So, Danica will save $15 if she buys the skateboard during the sale.

You can also change the percent to a decimal and then multiply.

ANOTHER WAY **Use a decimal.**

Step 1	Step 2
Write 25% as a decimal. $25\% = 0.25$	Multiply. $0.25 \times 60 = 15$

More Examples

A **Find 8% of 120.**

$8\% = \frac{8}{100} = \frac{2}{25}$ Write the percent as a fraction.

$\frac{2}{25} \times \frac{120}{1} = \frac{240}{25} = 9\frac{3}{5}$ Multiply.

B **Find 45% of 58.**

$45\% = 0.45$ Write the percent as a decimal.

$0.45 \times 58 = 26.1$ Multiply.

- Would you change 20% to a fraction or a decimal to find 20% of 100? **Explain.**

NS 1.2 Interpret percents as a part of a hundred; find decimal and percent equivalents for common fractions and explain why they represent the same value; compute a given percent of a whole number. *also* NS 1.0, MR 2.3, MR 2.4, MR 3.2

Other Percent Problems

You can use fractions to find what percent one number is of another number.

Example 1

Paul practices different types of skateboard jumps for 60 minutes. He spends 15 minutes doing ollies, a type of jump. What percent of his practice time does Paul spend doing ollies?

$\frac{15}{60}$	Write a fraction.
$\frac{15}{60} = \frac{1}{4} = \frac{25}{100}$	Use equivalent fractions to write the fraction with a denominator of 100.
$\frac{25}{100} = 25\%$	Write a percent.

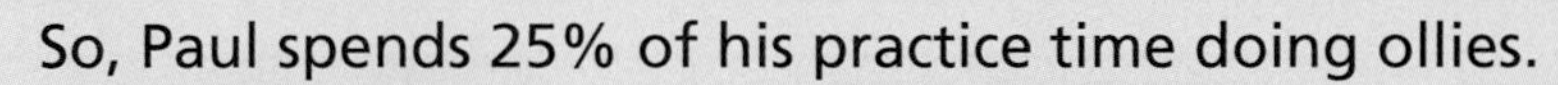

So, Paul spends 25% of his practice time doing ollies.

You can use a model to find a number when a percent of the number is known.

Example 2

Thirty members of the skateboard club are between the ages of 10 and 13. This is 20% of the club members. How many members does the club have?

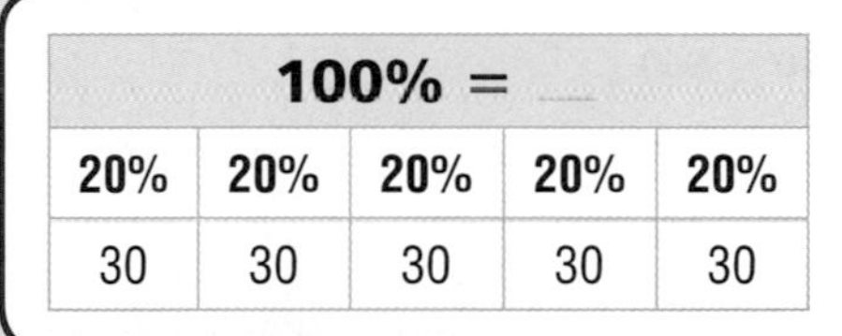

100% = ___				
20%	20%	20%	20%	20%
30	30	30	30	30

Think: 100 ÷ 20 = ■
100 ÷ 20 = 5 and each 20% = 30 people.
Multiply 30 × 5 to find the total or 100%.
30 × 5 = 150. So, 30 is 20% of 150.

So, the skateboard club has 150 members.

More Examples

A What percent of 36 is 27?

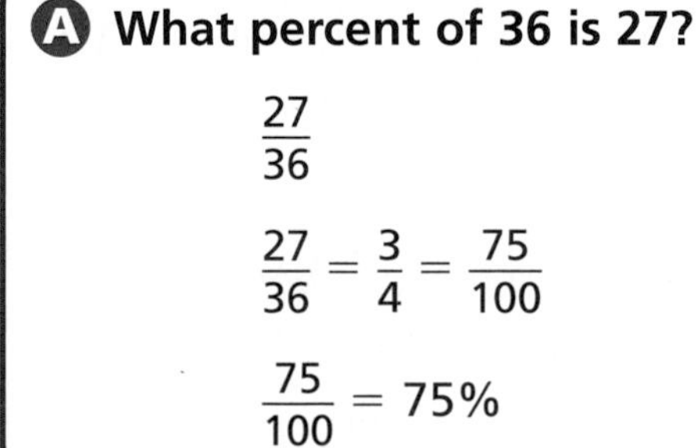

$\frac{27}{36}$

$\frac{27}{36} = \frac{3}{4} = \frac{75}{100}$

$\frac{75}{100} = 75\%$

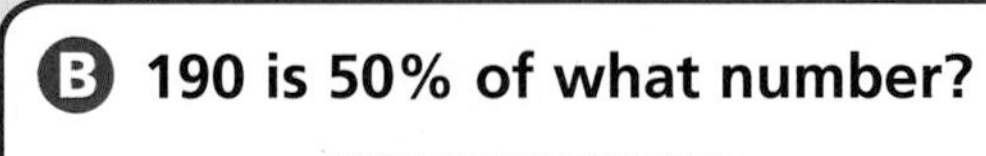

B 190 is 50% of what number?

100% = ___	
50%	50%
190	190

190 is 50% of 380.

Guided Practice

1. What is 20% of 80? Think: $20\% = \frac{1}{5}$
   So, $\frac{1}{5} \times 80 =$ ■.

Solve each percent problem.

2. What is 25% of 16?
3. What is 2% of 80?
4. What percent of 10 is 2?
5. What percent of 55 is 33?
6. 14 is 50% of what number?
7. 8 is 80% of what number?
8. TALK Math **Explain** how a diagram helps you solve percent problems.

Independent Practice and Problem Solving

Solve each percent problem.

9. What is 90% of 300?
10. What is 50% of 68?
11. What is 30% of 119?
12. What percent of 36 is 18?
13. What is 20% of 18?
14. What percent of 160 is 40?
15. 19 is 20% of what number?
16. 28 is 40% of what number?
17. What is 45% of 32?

For 18–20, use the sign at the right.

18. If you bought the $40 deck with the black wheels, how much would you save with a 15% discount?
19. The Skateboard Shop has 210 of the $29 decks in stock. If these decks represent 25% of their stock, how many decks do they have in stock? Is the sign correct? **Explain.**
20. If the Skateboard Shop has a 2-hour sale, what percent of the daily store hours does the sale represent?

SKATEBOARD SHOP – HOURS: 9 A.M. TO 5 P.M.
OVER 1,000 SKATEBOARD DECKS IN STOCK!
CRASHRIDE
SKID SKATEBOARDS
CARBS
CARBS
$29
$40
$60
$60
$25
$20

21. WRITE Math **Explain** how to find 25% of 24 in two different ways.

Achieving the Standards

22. Order the following numbers from least to greatest: 11%, $\frac{9}{10}$, 0.8. (NS 1.0, p. 410)
23. Which is greater, 0.75 or $\frac{4}{5}$? (NS 1.0, p. 160)
24. **Test Prep** Of the 32 students in class, 8 have perfect attendance. What percent of the students have perfect attendance?

    A 8%
    B 25%
    C 32%
    D 75%

25. Explain whether the following statement is true: All rectangles are squares. (Grade 4 MG 3.8)
26. **Test Prep** Scott correctly answered 96% of the 200 questions on a test. How many questions did he answer correctly?

    A 8
    B 96
    C 192
    D 200

 Extra Practice on page 424, Set C

WRITE Math WORKSHOP

Describe an Error

You must understand a math concept before you can identify an error. It is important to describe the error and explain how to correct it.

The Skateboard Sizzlers are planning to buy new skateboards for their team. Kirsten said that the 20% savings on the $80 skateboard will be $20.

Read how Cole described Kirsten's error.

SKID SKATEBOARDS $29
CARBS $40
$80 CARBS
$33 20% OFF
$22 30% OFF
$40 10% OFF
$50 25% OFF
$62 25% OFF
$20
$25

First, I need to solve the problem to find out what error Kirsten made.

To find the amount of savings on the $80 skateboard, I can write 20% as a fraction in simplest form and multiply it by $80.

$20\% = \frac{20}{100}$

$\frac{20}{100} \div \frac{20}{20} = \frac{1}{5}$

$\frac{1}{5} \times \$80 = \$16.$

So, a 20% discount on the $80 skateboard is a savings of $16.

Kirsten said that the savings on the $80 skateboard is $20. Her error is that she did not correctly write 20% as a fraction. She used the fraction $\frac{1}{4}$ instead of $\frac{1}{5}$ to find the amount of savings.

Tips

Tips for Describing an Error

- Identify what the problem is about.
- Solve the problem.
- Recheck all computations.
- Describe the steps you took to evaluate the incorrect answer.
- State the correct solution to the problem.
- In the last paragraph of your description, state the reason for the error.

Problem Solving Identify and describe each error.

1. Cole compared the amounts of savings on the gray and black helmets. He said the savings on the gray helmet is greater than the savings on the black helmet.
2. Phillip plans to buy the gray kneepads. He figures that the amount of savings is $12.40.

Problem Solving Workshop
Strategy: Make a Graph

OBJECTIVE: Solve problems by using the strategy *make a graph*.

Learn the Strategy

Making a graph can help you understand a problem and see its solution more easily. You can use different types of graphs for different problems.

Make a line graph to show change over time.

Which year had the greatest difference between the number of acres planted and the number of acres harvested?

Acres of Corn in the U.S. (rounded to the nearest million)		
Year	**Planted**	**Harvested**
2001	76	69
2002	79	69
2003	79	71
2004	81	74
2005	82	75

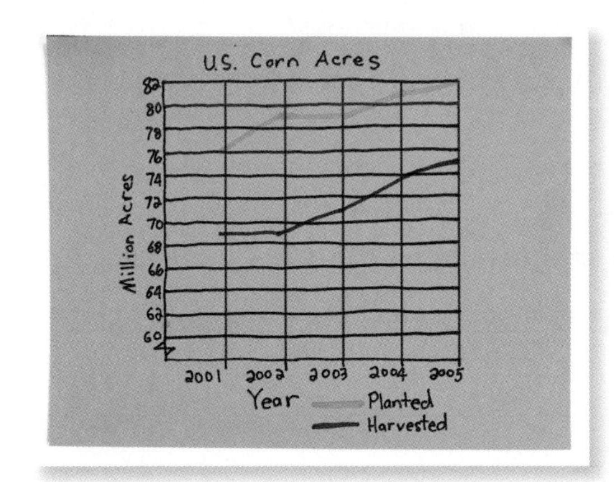

Make a circle graph to compare parts to the whole and to each other.

How does the amount of cheddar cheese compare to the other types of cheeses?

Cheese Produced in California	
Type of Cheese	**Percent**
Mozzarella	45
Cheddar	24
Monterey Jack	16
Other	15

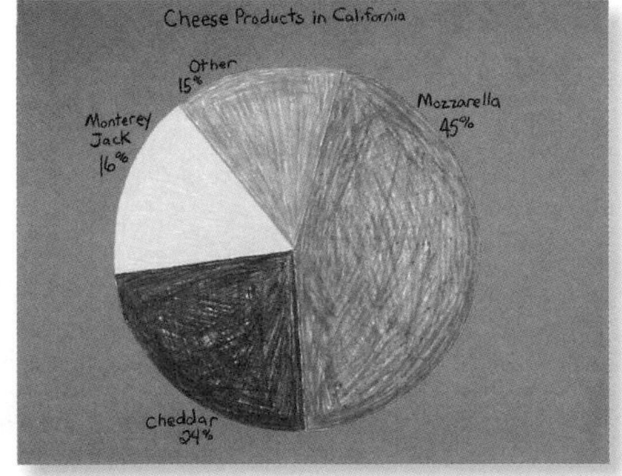

TALK Math

Explain why the type of graph is important when choosing how to represent data.

SDAP 1.2 Organize and display single-variable data in appropriate graphs and representations (e.g., histogram, circle graphs) and explain which types of graphs are appropriate for various data sets. *also* **NS 1.0, SDAP 1.3, MR 1.0, MR 2.0, MR 2.3, MR 2.4, MR 3.0, MR 3.1, MR 3.2, MR 3.3**

Read to Understand
Plan
Solve
Check

Use the Strategy

PROBLEM Noel surveyed 200 members of his 4-H Club. How does the number of 4-H members who are raising each type of livestock compare to the total number of 4-H members who are raising livestock?

4-H Livestock				
Type of Livestock	Swine	Cattle	Goats or Sheep	Poultry
Number of Members	80	40	50	30

Read to Understand

- What are you asked to find?
- What information is given?

Plan

- **What strategy can you use to solve the problem?**
  Since you want to show how the parts relate to the whole, make a circle graph.

Solve

- **How can you use the strategy to find a solution?**
  A **circle graph** shows how parts of the data are related to the whole and to each other.

  First, divide a circle into ten equal sections. Each section represents 10% of the 200 4-H members.

  Then, find the percent of 4-H members for each type of livestock.

Swine	Cattle	Goats or Sheep	Poultry
$\frac{80}{200} = 40\%$	$\frac{40}{200} = 20\%$	$\frac{50}{200} = 25\%$	$\frac{30}{200} = 15\%$

  Shade the sections to represent each percent. Label and title the graph.

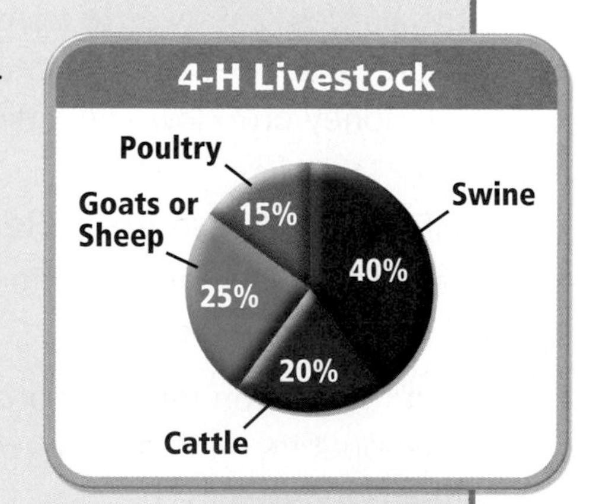

  So, the graph shows how the number of members raising each type of livestock compares to the total number of members raising livestock.

Check

- **Is the graph you made appropriate for the set of data? Explain.**

Read to Understand
Plan
Solve
Check

Guided Problem Solving

1. Leona surveyed the members of her 4-H Club to see how old they were. She organized her data in a table. How does the number of members in each age group compare to the number of members in the whole club?

Ages of 4-H Club Members

Group	Number	Age (years)
Cloverbud	45	5–8
Junior	90	9–11
Intermediate	18	12–13
Teen	27	14–19

Decide what type of graph would best display the data.

Make the graph. Label and title the graph.

Use the graph to answer the question.

2. What if there were 36 members in the Teen group and 81 members in the Junior group? How would that change your data? How would your graph change?

3. Of the top 10 prizes awarded at a state fair, 3 out of 10 went to Intermediates. How does the number of winners in the Intermediate group compare to the other groups?

Problem Solving Strategy Practice

Make a graph to solve.

4. Out of $100 that Leona spent at the state fair, $\frac{1}{10}$ was for the carnival rides, 20% was to transport her prize lamb, 30% was for bus fare, and $\frac{2}{5}$ was for the hotel room. What did Leona spend the most money on? How much did she spend?

USE DATA For 5–6, use the table. Make a graph to solve.

California 4-H Prizes Awarded by Region

Region	Prizes
North	12
North Central	20
South	16
South Central	32

5. What percent of prizes went to 4-H members from the North and North Central regions?

6. Which region won the most prizes? How many times greater is that amount than the amount won by the region with the least number of prizes?

7. WRITE Math Look back at problems 5 and 6. For each, which type of graph is most helpful? **Explain** why.

Mixed Strategy Practice

8. The 4-H Club has set up a special pen for a llama. The fence surrounding the pen is 50 ft in perimeter. The pen is a rectangle 1.5 times as long as it is wide. What are the length and width of the llama's pen?

9. The 4-H competition is from 10:30 A.M. to 2:30 P.M. It will take Penny's family 45 minutes to drive to the fairgrounds and another 1 hour 45 minutes to unload her animal and prepare for the competition. What time should Penny leave her house for the fairgrounds?

Choose a STRATEGY

- Draw a Diagram or Picture
- Make a Model or Act It Out
- Make an Organized List
- Look for a Pattern
- Make a Table or Graph
- Guess and Check
- Work Backward
- Solve a Simpler Problem
- Write an Equation
- Use Logical Reasoning

USE DATA For 10–12, use the circle graph. At California's 4-H Project Competition, there were 5 categories and 100 prizes awarded.

10. How many prizes were awarded in *Technology & Education* and *Art & Fashion?* Was this number greater than or less than the number of prizes for *Livestock & Pets?* How do you know?

11. **Pose a Problem** Look back at Problem 10. Write a similar problem by changing one of the categories and the total number of prizes awarded.

12. **Open-Ended** Use <, >, and = to make three comparisons about the different sections in the circle graph.

CHALLENGE YOURSELF

At another 4-H Club Competition, 50 of the top prizes went to Agriculture and Nutrition projects. The group for dairy cattle received 10% of the 50 prizes and the group for horses received 20%. The group for nutrition received 6 prizes. The groups for rabbits, sheep, and swine combined received 29 top prizes.

13. The groups for rabbits and horses combined received 26% of the 50 prizes. How many prizes went to the group for rabbits?

14. The groups for cattle, nutrition, and horses received 21 of the 50 prizes. How many prizes was each group awarded?

LESSON 7

Compare Data Sets

OBJECTIVE: Compare data sets of different sizes using percents.

Quick Review

1. Find 10% of 30.
2. Find 25% of 44.
3. Find 30% of 60.
4. Find 50% of 82.
5. Find 92% of 300.

Learn

PROBLEM Two fifth-grade classes voted on where they wanted to go for a field trip. The two circle graphs compare the sets of data from the two classes. In which class did the Exploratorium get more votes?

Class 5A Survey: 20 students

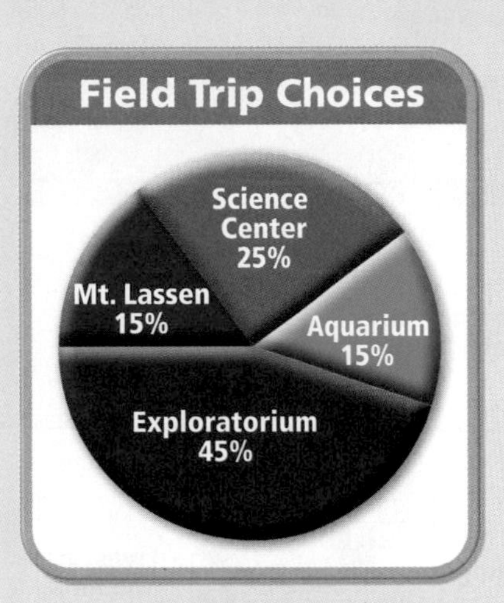

Find 45% of 20.

Step 1

Write the percent as a fraction in simplest form.

$45\% = \frac{45}{100} = \frac{9}{20}$

Step 2

Multiply to find 45% of 20.

$\frac{9}{20} \times \frac{20}{1} = 9$

So, 9 students in Class 5A voted for the Exploratorium.

Class 5B Survey: 40 students

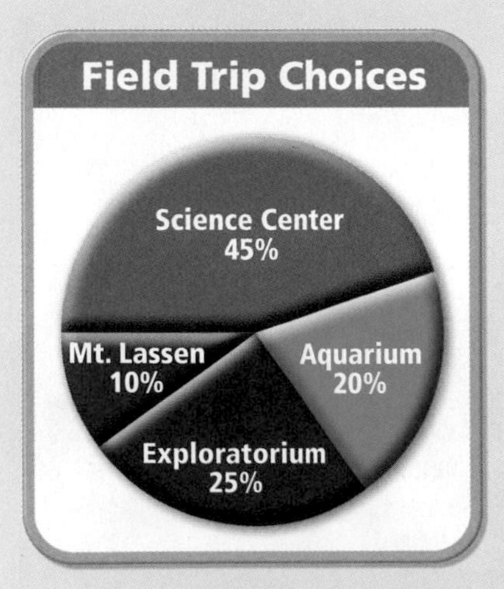

Find 25% of 40.

Step 1

Write the percent as a decimal.

$25\% = 0.25$

Step 2

Multiply to find 25% of 40.

$0.25 \times 40 = 10$

So, 10 students in Class 5B voted for the Exploratorium.

So, since $10 > 9$, the Exploratorium received more votes in class 5B.

SDAP 1.3 Use fractions and percentages to compare data sets of different sizes. *also* **NS 1.0, MR 2.3, MR 2.4, MR 3.2**

Guided Practice

1. Copy and complete the steps shown at the right. Which class had more students vote for Mt. Lassen?

Class 5A: $\frac{15}{100} = \frac{3}{20}$; $\frac{3}{20} \times 20 = ■$

Class 5B: $\frac{10}{100} = \frac{1}{10}$; $\frac{1}{10} \times 40 = ■$

2. TALK Math **Explain** how you can compare two circle graphs with different sized data sets.

Independent Practice and Problem Solving

For 3–6, use the table.

3. Which class spent less time at the electricity exhibit? How many fewer minutes did this class spend at this exhibit?
4. Altogether, how many minutes did both classes spend at the dinosaur exhibit?
5. Which class spent more time at the weather exhibit? How many more minutes did this class spend at this exhibit?
6. WRITE Math **Sense or Nonsense?** The number of minutes that class 5B spent at the weather exhibit was greater than the amount class 5A spent there since 50% is greater and the number of minutes at the Science Center is greater. Explain.

Science Center		
Exhibits	Time Spent (in percent)	
	Class 5A 200 min	Class 5B 220 min
Electricity	15%	25%
Dinosaur	35%	10%
Weather	20%	50%
Human Body	30%	15%

Achieving the Standards

7. Margo answered 95% of 20 questions correctly. How many questions did Margo answer correctly? (NS 1.2, p. 412)
8. What is the median of the following data: 38, 42, 36, 36, 40? (Grade 4 SDAP 1.2)
9. Which letter on the number line best identifies 50%? (NS 1.2, p. 410)

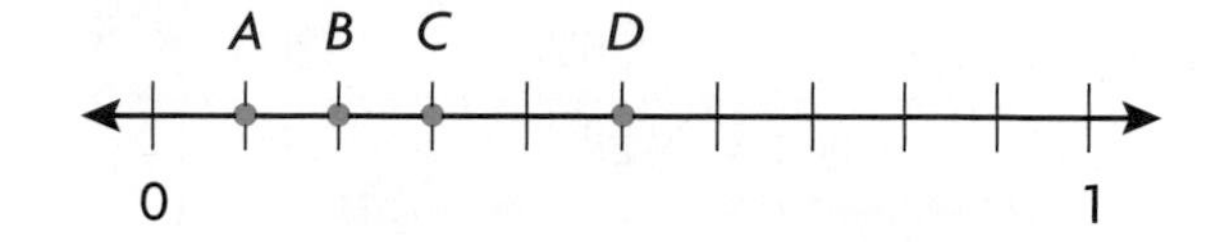

10. **Test Prep** Compare the number of red markers for each student. How many more does Tom have than Maggie?

Number of Markers		
Student	Total Number of Markers	Red markers (%)
Maggie	20	30%
Tom	30	40%

A 0
B 6
C 10
D 60

Extra Practice on page 424, Set D

Extra Practice

Set A Write each percent as a decimal and as a fraction in simplest form. (pp. 406–409)

1. 18%
2. 37%
3. 60%
4. 72%
5. 29%
6. 66%
7. 53%
8. 48%

Write each fraction or decimal as a percent.

9. 0.125
10. $\frac{3}{8}$
11. $\frac{9}{20}$
12. 0.07
13. $\frac{7}{8}$
14. $\frac{6}{25}$
15. 0.14
16. 0.092
17. Tom answered 18 out of 20 questions on his science test correctly. What percent did he answer correctly?
18. Four-fifths of the members of the swim team swim every Saturday. What percent of team members swim every Saturday?

Set B Make a number line. Then, locate each quantity on a number line. (pp. 410–411)

1. $\frac{1}{4}$
2. 0.80
3. 0.45
4. 10%
5. $\frac{7}{10}$
6. $\frac{3}{5}$
7. 0.95
8. 0.55
9. 30%
10. $\frac{9}{10}$

Set C Solve each percent problem. (pp. 414–417)

1. What is 40% of 500?
2. What is 75% of 72?
3. What percent of 45 is 36?
4. What percent of 240 is 72?
5. 19 is 20% of what number?
6. 18 is 60% of what number?
7. In a survey of 80 students, 30% take music lessons. How many of those surveyed take music lessons?
8. Twelve of the students in the class play soccer. If 60% of the class plays soccer, how many students are in the class?

Set D For 1–3, use the table. (pp. 422–423)

1. Which class had more votes for adventure books? How many more?
2. Which class had more votes for mystery books? How many more?
3. How many students in each class voted for science fiction books?

Book Report Votes

Type of Book	Class 5A 24 students	Class 5B 30 students
Mystery	25%	50%
Adventure	50%	30%
Science Fiction	25%	20%

Technology
Use Harcourt Mega Math, The Number Games, *Buggy Bargains*, Levels Q, R, S, T.

SAVINGS ACCOUNT

Savers
2 players

Materials
- 10 index cards
- 2 number cubes labeled 1–6
- Paper and pencil

10%	25%	30%	40%	50%
60%	70%	75%	80%	90%

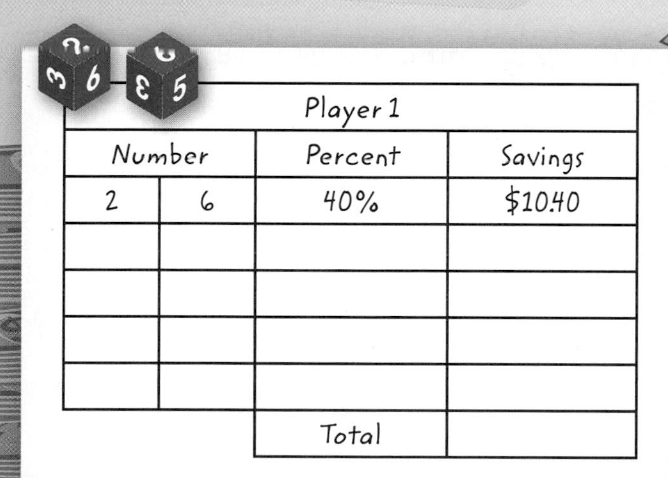

Player 1			
Number		Percent	Savings
2	6	40%	$10.40
		Total	

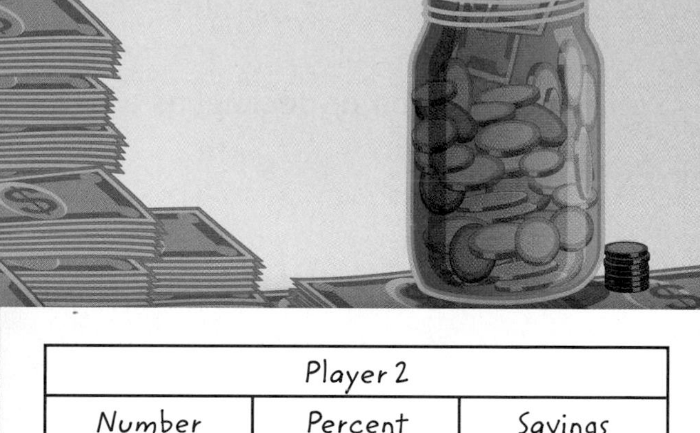

Player 2			
Number		Percent	Savings
5	4	25%	$13.50
		Total	

Start Saving!

- Players make one set of percent cards and two score cards as shown above.
- Players shuffle the percent cards and place them in a stack facedown on the table.
- Player 1 rolls each number cube one at a time to form a 2-digit number. The first number cube is used as the tens digit. The second number cube is used as the ones digit.
- Player 1 draws a percent card from the stack. Player 1 then calculates that percent of the number that was rolled and writes the percent as dollars and cents.
- Player 2 repeats the process. Play continues in this manner until all the percent cards have been used.
- Each player finds the total amount in his or her savings account. The player with the greater total amount of savings wins the game!

Chapter 16 Review/Test

Check Vocabulary and Concepts

Choose the best term from the box.

VOCABULARY
graph
decimal
percent

1. The fractional part of a number to 100 is the ? . (NS 1.2, p. 404)
2. You can find a percent of a number by changing the percent to a ? and multiplying. (NS 1.2, p. 414)

Check Skills

Write each percent as a decimal and as a fraction in simplest form. (NS 1.2, pp. 406–409)

3. 35%
4. 80%
5. 24%
6. 50%

Write each fraction or decimal as a percent. (NS 1.2, pp. 406–409)

7. 0.09
8. $\frac{18}{25}$
9. 0.61
10. $\frac{1}{4}$

Locate each fraction, decimal, and percent on a number line. (NS 1.5, pp. 410–411)

11. $\frac{2}{3}$
12. 0.30
13. 40%
14. $\frac{9}{10}$
15. 0.75

Solve each percent problem. (NS 1.2, pp. 414–417)

16. What is 30% of 50?
17. What is 75% of 900?
18. What percent of 45 is 27?
19. What percent of 80 is 20?
20. 48 is 80% of what number?
21. What is 25% of 360?

For 22–23, use the table. (SDAP 1.3, pp. 422–423)

22. Which grade had more votes for ham and cheese? How many more?
23. Which grade had more votes for veggie burgers? How many more?

Favorite Sandwich Votes

Sandwich	Grade 5 120 students	Grade 6 150 students
Ham and Cheese	55%	50%
Hamburger	25%	40%
Veggie Burger	20%	10%

Check Problem Solving

Solve. (SDAP 1.3, MR 2.3, MR 2.4, pp. 418–421)

24. At practice the tennis team spends 40% of the time on drills, 10% on warm up and cool down, and 50% on game play. If practice lasts 90 minutes, how much more time do they spend on game play than on drills?

25. WRITE Math Grady put $60 of his birthday money in the bank. If Grady had $80 in birthday money, what percent of the money did he put in the bank? **Explain** how to use equivalent fractions to find what percent $60 is of $80.

GO ONLINE Technology Use *Online Assessment.*

Enrich • Simple Interest

When you keep money in a bank account, the bank adds a certain amount to the account over time. This added money is called **interest**. The amount of interest you receive is based on the bank's interest rate.

Example 1

Melba put $2,000 in a bank account. The bank's interest rate is 4% per year. How much interest will Melba earn after one year? How much money will be in her account after 1 year?

Amount of Money in the Account	×	Interest Rate	=	Interest Earned for 1 Year

Write the interest rate as a decimal. $4\% = 0.04$

- Multiply the amount of money in the account by the interest rate. $\$2{,}000 \times 0.04 = \$80.00$
- Add the interest earned to the amount of money in the account. $\$2{,}000 + \$80 = \$2{,}080$

So, Melba will earn $80.00 in interest and have $2,080 in her account after one year.

Try It

Find the interest earned in 1 year.

1. $5,000 at 6%
2. $2,500 at 4%
3. $1,500 at 7%
4. $800 at 10%
5. $4,000 at 5%
6. $2,800 at 6%
7. $3,500 at 4%
8. $6,000 at 8%
9. $9,000 at 3%

Think About It

WRITE Math Jack opened a bank account with $900. The account earns 6% interest a year, which is added at the end of each year. **Explain** how to find the amount of money Jack will have in his account at the end of 2 years.

Unit Review/Test
Chapters 14–16

Multiple Choice

1. What situation could be described by the expression $2.5c$? (AF 1.2, p. 346)

   A The cost of a computer, c, times 2.5.

   B The cost of a computer, c, decreased by 2.5.

   C The cost of a computer, c, increased by 2.5 dollars.

   D The cost of a computer, c, decreased by 2.5 dollars.

2. If $y = 4$, what is the value of $3y - 7$? (AF 1.2, p. 348)

   A 0 **C** 5

   B 2 **D** 12

3. What situation could be described by the equation below? (AF 1.2, p. 352)
   $n \div 12 = 10$

   A The number of coins, n, less 12 students equals 10 coins per student.

   B The number of coins, n, plus 12 students equals 10 coins per student.

   C The number of coins, n, multiplied by 12 students equals 10 coins per student.

   D The number of coins, n, divided by 12 students equals 10 coins per student.

4. What value for k makes this equation true? (AF 1.2, p. 354)

   $$3 \times (k + 2) = 27$$

   A 6

   B 7

   C 9

   D 11

5. What value for z makes this equation true? (AF 1.3, p. 358)

   $$8 \times 7 = (8 \times 2) + (8 \times z)$$

   A 2

   B 5

   C 7

   D 10

6. Which letter on the number line best identifies the location of $^-5$? (NS 1.5, p. 376)

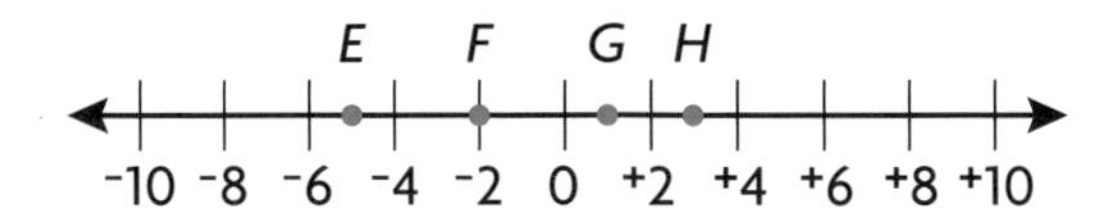

   A E

   B F

   C G

   D H

GO ONLINE Technology Use *Online Assessment.*

7. $^{-}5 + {^{-}3} + 0 =$
(NS 2.1, p. 384)

A 8

B $^{-}2$

C $^{-}7$

D $^{-}8$

8. What is 0.6 written as a percent?
(NS 1.5, p. 406)

A 6%

B 16%

C 30%

D 60%

9. A restaurant donated 500 pounds of food to a local food bank. If 200 pounds are breads, what percent of the donated food are breads? (NS 1.5, p. 414)

A 20%

B 40%

C 50%

D 75%

Short Response

10. Use the Distributive Property to restate the expression. Find the product. (AF 1.3, p. 358)

$$14 \times 9$$

11. Copy the numbers below. Next to each number, write the letter that represents the quantity on the number line.
(NS 1.5, p. 376)

$^{-}20$ 15 $^{-}12$ $^{-}4$

A B C D

-20 -10 0 +10 +20

12. The temperature at midnight was $^{-}3$°F. From midnight to 5:00 A.M. the temperature dropped 12°F. Write an expression to find the temperature at 5:00 A.M. Find the value of your expression. (NS 2.1, p. 376)

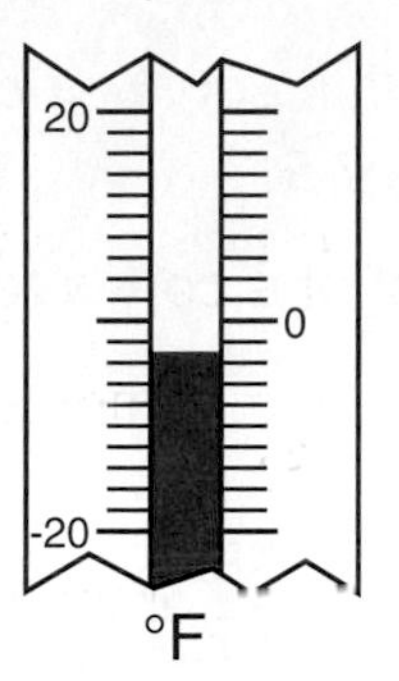

Extended Response WRITE Math

13. If r is a number that satisfies $3r + 11 = 20$, can r be equal to 5? **Explain.**
(AF 1.2, p. 354)

14. Results from two different surveys are shown below.

What is your favorite food?	
Food	**Number of Students**
Pizza	27
Hamburger	22
Chicken nuggets	10
Hot dog	16

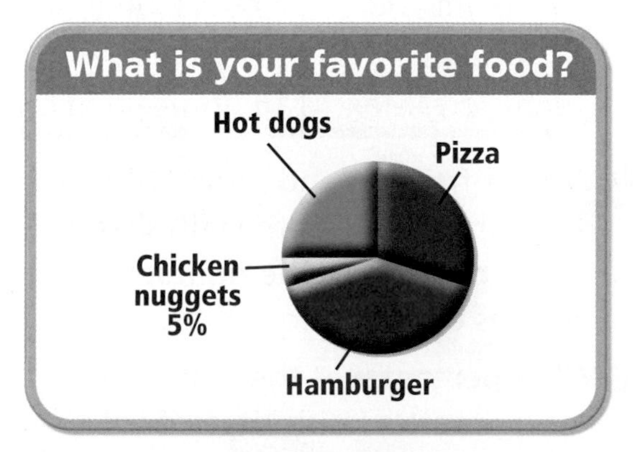

In which survey did the greatest percentage choose pizza as their favorite food? **Explain** your reasoning. (NS 1.2, p. 420)

California

Problem Solving

from THE WORLD ALMANAC FOR KIDS

Robots: A Way of the Future?

THE GRAND ROBOT RACE

The DARPA Grand Challenge is a 132-mile race across the Mojave Desert. The cars that compete in the race are piloted, not by people, but by robots made from computers. In 2005, "Stanley," a robot car designed by a Stanford University team, won the race. It was the first time a vehicle finished the entire course. Of the 23 finalists in the 2005 race, only 5 vehicles completed the race.

Stanford Scientist Sebastian Thrun and "Stanley."

FACT·ACTIVITY

Use the introduction and table to answer.

Teams of the DARPA Challenge

Team	Finish Time
Stanford Racing	6 hours 53 minutes
Red Team	7 hours 4 minutes
Red Team Too	7 hours 14 minutes
Gray Team	7 hours 30 minutes
Team TerraMax	10 hours 30 minutes

1. Write a fraction and percent for the number of vehicles that finished the race compared to the number of vehicles that started the race.
2. What percent of the vehicles that completed the race finished in less than 10 hours?
3. What percent was the Stanford Racing team's finish time of the Gray Team's finish time? (Hint: convert times to minutes.)
4. **Pose a Problem** Look back at Problem 3. Write a similar problem comparing the finish times of two teams.

On October 9, 2005, Stanley won The Grand Robot Race by traveling an average of 19 miles per hour over rugged terrain.

Underwater Robots

In August 2006 in Monterey, California, a group of underwater robots monitored the ocean without the help of humans. The robots measured ocean temperature, salt content, and currents. These robots were able to track endangered sea life, monitor oil spills, and collect data about the biomes where sea creatures live. The robots did this with less disturbance to the habitat than a human performing similar tasks might cause.

FACT · ACTIVITY

Underwater robot

Answer the questions.

1. An underwater robot is 5 feet above sea level before it is launched. Once launched, the robot is at a depth of 8 feet below sea level. How many feet has the robot traveled?
2. An underwater robot traveled 26 miles and then reversed direction. The robot traveled back along the same route for 15 miles. Does $^{+}26 + {}^{+}15$ or $^{+}26 + {}^{-}15$ tell how far the robot is from its starting point? **Explain.**
3. One underwater robot traveled 63 miles and another robot traveled 135 miles. Write an equation to show how many more miles the second robot traveled than the first robot.
4. Sketch a picture of a sloping shoreline and the ocean beside it. Draw a number line to represent feet above and below sea level. Write a word problem that can be solved by an integer equation.

UNIT 6

Geometry

Math on Location

1

▲ Precious and semi-precious gems are found on Earth as shapeless, dull stones.

2

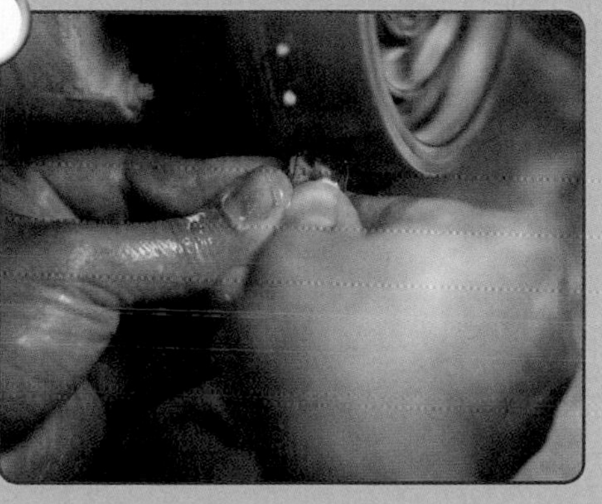

▲ Flat faces, called facets, are precisely cut to form the gems into 3-dimensional shapes.

3

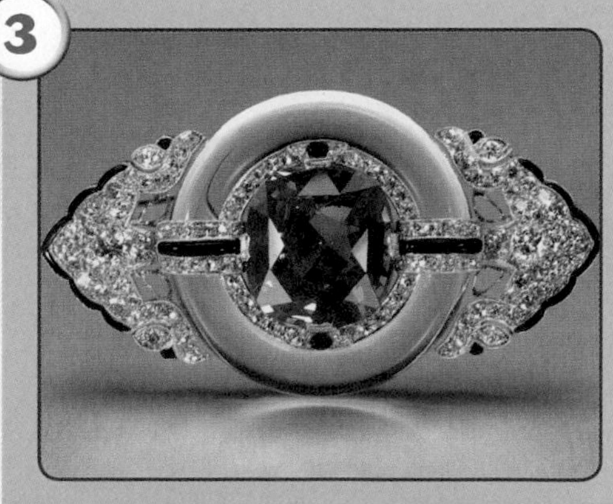

▲ Colorful gems are used in jewelry design that incorporates lines and angles in symmetry.

VOCABULARY POWER

TALK Math

What math do you see in the **Math on Location**? What kinds of angles and polygons can you identify in the jewelry shown?

READ Math

REVIEW VOCABULARY You learned the words below when you learned about lines, angles, and geometric figures. How do these words relate to **Math on Location**?

right angle an angle that has a measure of 90°

acute angle an angle that has a measure less than a right angle (less than 90°)

obtuse angle an angle whose measure is greater than 90° and less than 180°

WRITE Math

Copy and complete the chart below. Use what you know about triangles.

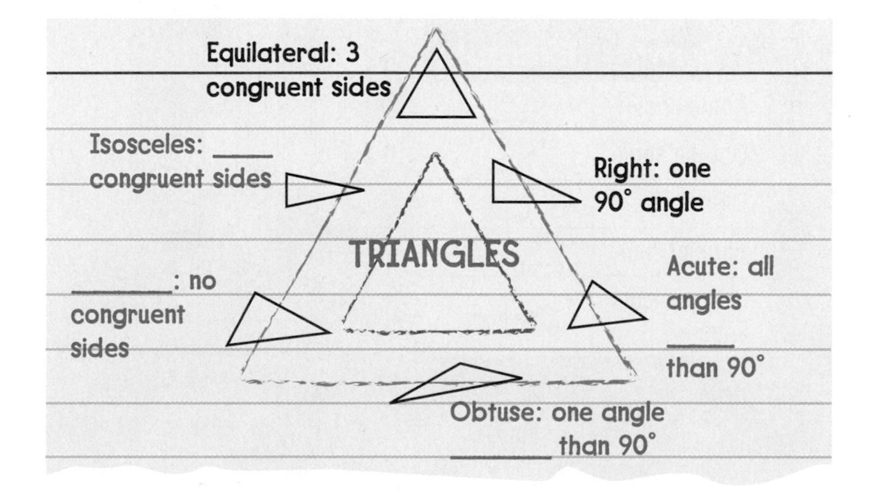

Technology
Mulitimedia Math Glossary link at www.harcourtschool.com/hspmath

17 Geometric Figures

The Big Idea Points, lines, planes, and their classifications and relationships are the building blocks of geometry; two-dimensional figures can be classified according to their geometric properties.

CALIFORNIA FAST FACT

The Golden Gate Bridge, spanning a distance of 1.7 miles, crosses the Golden Gate, the opening between San Francisco Bay and the Pacific Ocean.

Investigate

Look at the photo of the Golden Gate Bridge. Make a list of the different types of angles you see. Identify examples of acute, obtuse, and right angles. Then look for pairs of lines that have special relationships. Give examples of parallel and perpendicular lines.

Term	Example
Acute angle	
Obtuse angle	
Right angle	
Parallel lines	
Perpendicular lines	

GO ONLINE Technology Student pages are available in the Student eBook.

Show What You Know

Check your understanding of important skills needed for success in Chapter 17.

▶ Name Polygons

Name each polygon. Tell the number of sides and angles.

1. 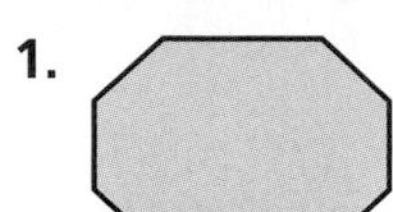
2. 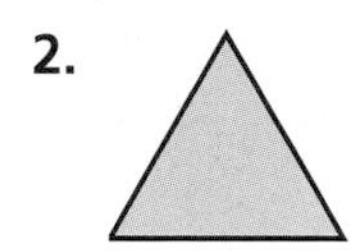
3. 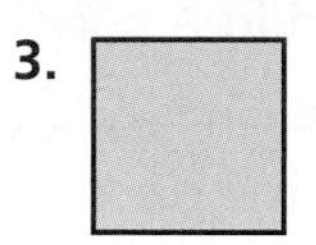
4. 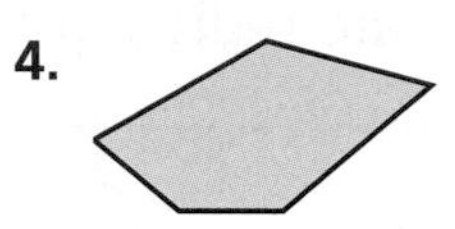
5. 
6. 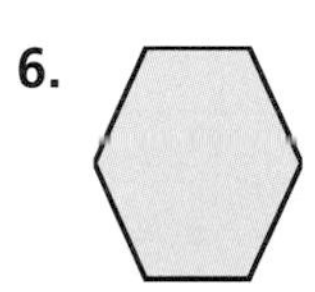
7. 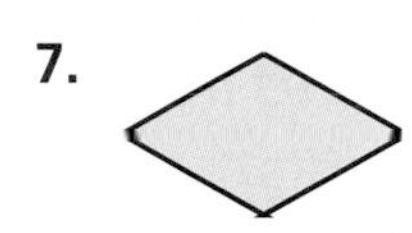
8. 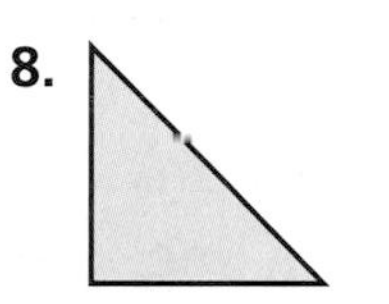

▶ Angles

Tell whether each angle is a *right angle, greater than a right angle,* or *less than a right angle.*

9.
10. 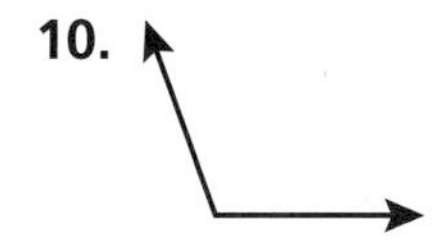
11. 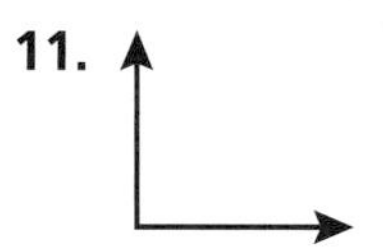
12. 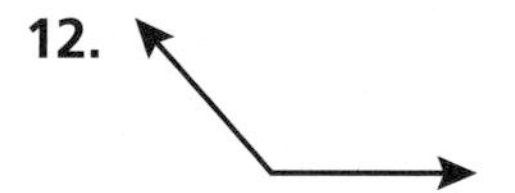

VOCABULARY POWER

CHAPTER VOCABULARY

acute angle
angle
arc
chord
circle
congruent
corresponding angles
corresponding sides
diameter
intersecting lines
line
line segment
obtuse angle
polygon
parallel lines
perpendicular lines
plane
point
protractor
radius
ray
regular polygon
right angle
similar
straight angle
vertex

WARM-UP WORDS

point an exact location in space, usually represented by a dot

line a straight path in a plane, extending in both directions with no endpoints

line segment a part of a line between two endpoints

Points, Lines, and Angles

OBJECTIVE: Identify and use the concepts of point, line, and angle and classify angles as acute, right, or obtuse.

Quick Review

Write the number of sides and angles for each figure.

1. 
2. 
3. △
4. 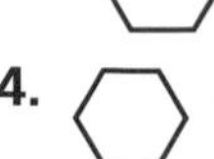
5. 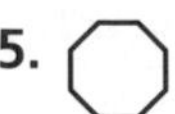

Vocabulary

point, line, line segment, ray, plane, right angle, acute angle, obtuse angle, straight angle, parallel lines, intersecting lines, perpendicular lines

Learn

The figures below are the building blocks of geometry. These figures are represented and named in a special way.

A **point** marks an exact location in space. Use a letter to name a point.	• *A* point *A*
A **line** is a straight path, extending in both directions with no endpoints. To name a line, use any two points that are on the line.	line *BC* or $\overleftrightarrow{BC}$ or line *CB* or $\overleftrightarrow{CB}$
A **line segment** is a part of a line between two endpoints. To name a line segment, use both endpoints.	line segment *DE* or $\overline{DE}$ or line segment *ED* or $\overline{ED}$
A **ray** is a part of a line with one endpoint. It extends without end in one direction. To name a ray, use the endpoint and any other point that is on the ray.	ray *FG* or $\overrightarrow{FG}$
A **plane** is an endless flat surface. To name a plane, name any three points that are on the plane, but not on the same line.	plane *HIJ*

Examples Name the labeled geometric figure in each picture.

A

The part labeled on the bicycle has two endpoints. So, the figure represented is line segment *MN*, or $\overline{MN}$.

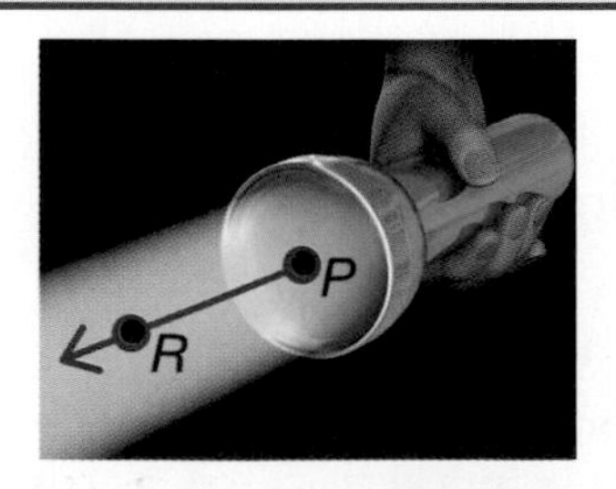

The beam from the flashlight has one endpoint. So, the figure represented is ray *PR* or $\overrightarrow{PR}$.

The wall is a flat surface. Three points are labeled on it. So, the figure represented is plane *STU*.

MG 2.1 Measure, identify, and draw angles, perpendicular and parallel lines, rectangles, and triangles by using appropriate tools (e.g., straightedge, ruler, compass, protractor, drawing software). *also* **MG 2.0, MR 2.3, MR 2.4, MR 3.2**

Other Geometric Figures

Two rays that have a common endpoint, or vertex, form an angle. To name an angle, use three points, with the vertex in the middle, or use only the point at the vertex.

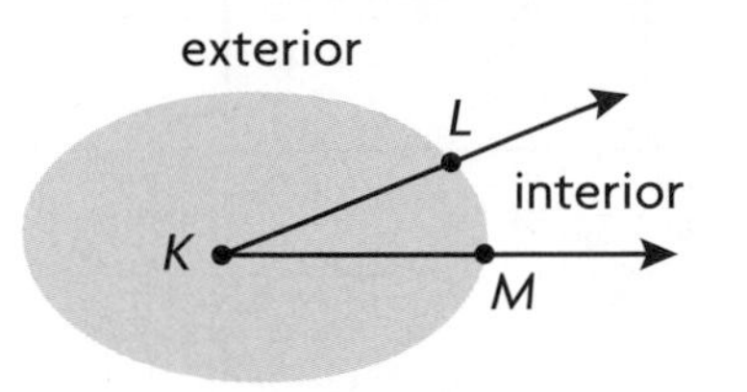

$\angle LKM$, $\angle MKL$, or $\angle K$

▼ The Seattle Public Library

You can classify angles by their size. The size of an angle is measured in degrees. The lengths of the drawings of the rays that form an angle do not affect the measure of an angle.

A **right angle** is an angle that measures 90°.

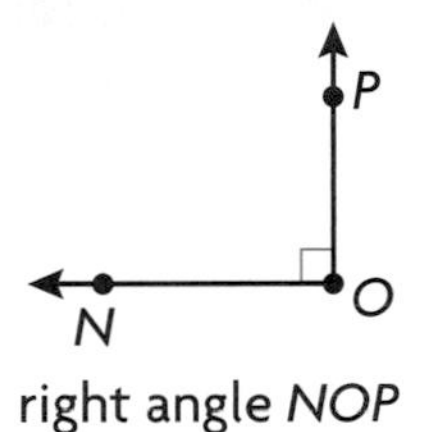

right angle *NOP*

An **acute angle** is an angle that measures less than 90°.

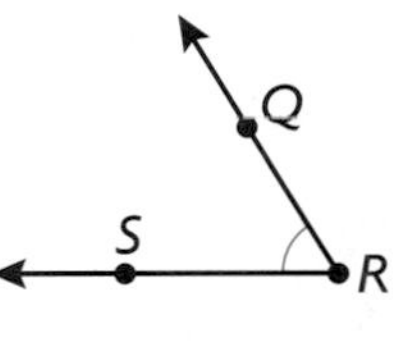

acute angle *QRS*

An **obtuse angle** is an angle that is greater than 90° and less than 180°.

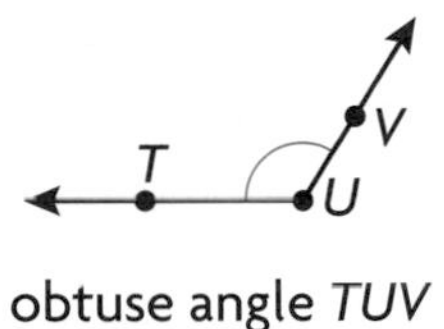

obtuse angle *TUV*

A **straight angle** is an angle that measures 180°.

W Y X

straight angle *WXY*

- On the photos of the Seattle Public Library, can you see examples of angles that appear to be right, acute, obtuse, or straight?

In a plane, lines can have different relationships with each other.

Parallel lines are lines in a plane that are always the same distance apart.

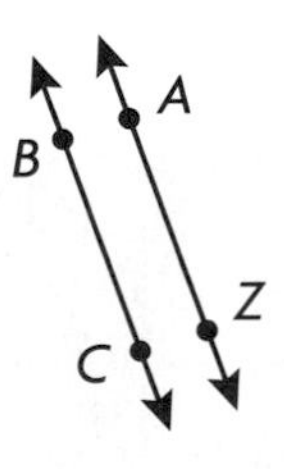

$\overleftrightarrow{BC} \parallel \overleftrightarrow{AZ}$

Intersecting lines are lines that cross at exactly one point.

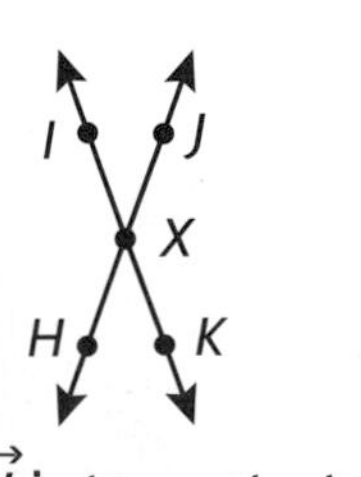

$\overleftrightarrow{IK}$ and $\overleftrightarrow{HJ}$ intersect at X.

Perpendicular lines are lines that intersect to form 4 right angles.

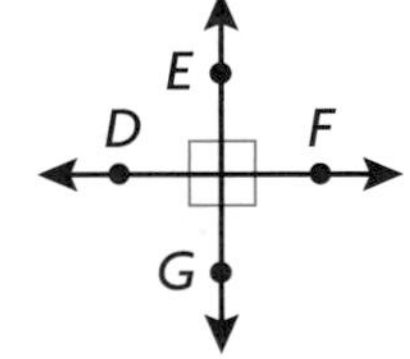

$\overleftrightarrow{DF} \perp \overleftrightarrow{EG}$

- Line segments can also be parallel, intersecting, or perpendicular. Draw and label line segments that are parallel, intersecting, and perpendicular.

Guided Practice

1. Name each angle, and identify it as right, acute, obtuse, or straight. Use grid paper to draw and label the kind of angle not shown.

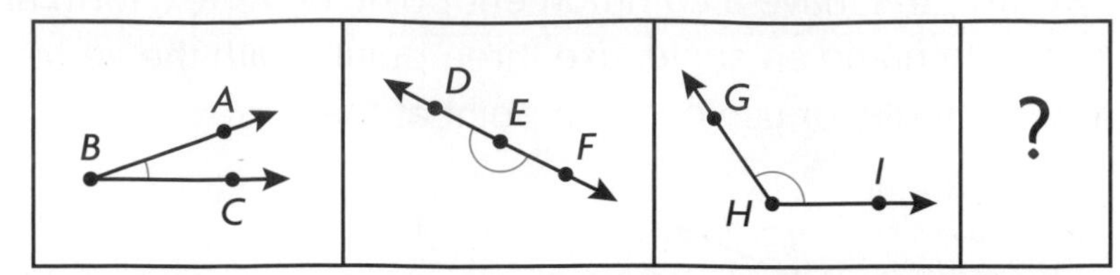

For 2–5, use the figure. Name an example of each.

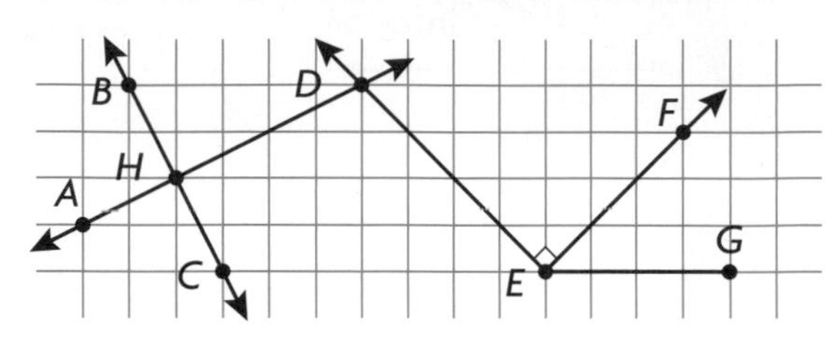

2. ray
3. point
4. line
5. intersecting lines

For 6–9, use the figure above. Classify each angle. Write *obtuse, acute, straight,* or *right*.

6. $\angle FED$
7. $\angle DEG$
8. $\angle FEG$
9. $\angle BHC$

10. TALK Math **Explain** how $\overleftrightarrow{BC}$ is different from $\overline{BC}$.

Independent Practice and Problem Solving

For 11–16, use the figure. Name an example of each.

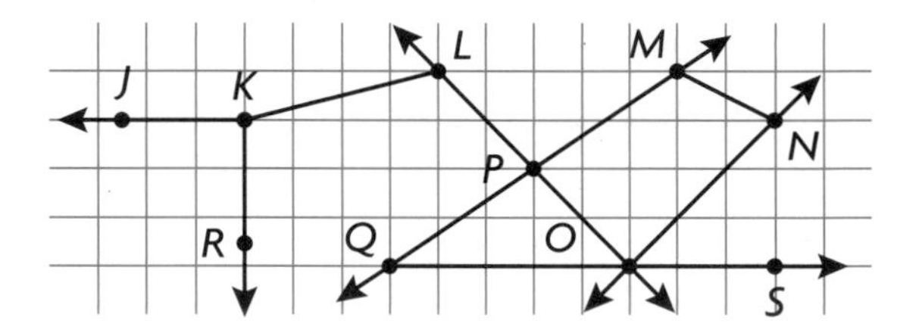

11. point
12. line segment
13. line
14. plane
15. vertex
16. angle

For 17–24, use the figure above. Classify each angle. Write *obtuse, acute, straight,* or *right*.

17. $\angle JKR$
18. $\angle LPQ$
19. $\angle NOS$
20. $\angle LOS$
21. $\angle QPM$
22. $\angle MPL$
23. $\angle SQM$
24. $\angle NOP$

USE DATA For 25–27, use the map.

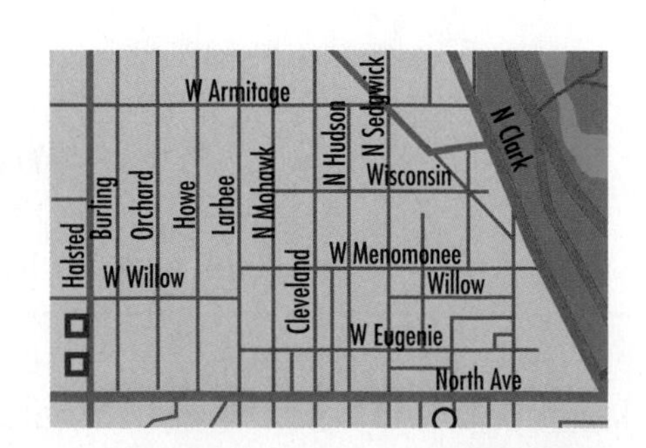

25. Name three streets that are parallel to Orchard.
26. Name three streets that are perpendicular to Halsted.
27. Find an acute angle that N. Clark forms with another street. What is the name of the other street?
28. WRITE Math Explain how intersecting and perpendicular lines are both similar and different.

CD ROM **Technology**
Use Harcourt Mega Math, Ice Station Exploration, *Polar Planes*, Levels A, B.

 Extra Practice on page 460, Set A

Achieving the Standards

29. Which number is greater, -3.25 or $3\frac{2}{5}$? (NS 1.2, p. 160)

30. What is 30% of 50? (NS 1.2, p. 412)

31. Classify the angle as *acute, obtuse,* or *right.* (Grade 4 MG 3.5)

32. **Test Prep** Which of the following best describes the figure?

    A intersecting lines

    B parallel lines

    C perpendicular lines

    D acute angles

33. **Test Prep** Which is the greatest whole number of degrees an acute angle can have?

    A $89°$ **C** $269°$

    B $179°$ **D** $359°$

Problem Solving and Reasoning

VISUAL THINKING Vertical angles are opposite each other and are equal.

Find the measures of ∠*AED*, ∠*CED*, and ∠*BEC*.

Step 1

Note that ∠*BEA* and ∠*AED* together make up a straight angle, ∠*DEB*.

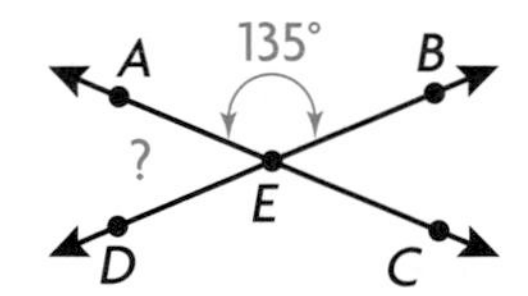

Step 2

Subtract the measure of ∠*BEA* from 180° to find the measure of ∠*AED*.

$180° - 135° = 45°$

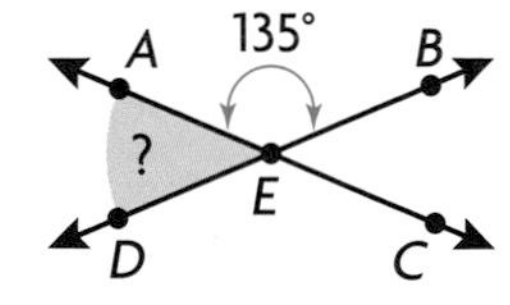

So, the measure of ∠*AED* is 45°.

Step 3

∠*AEB* and ∠*DEC* are vertical angles. ∠*AED* and ∠*BEC* are vertical angles. Vertical angles have equal measures.

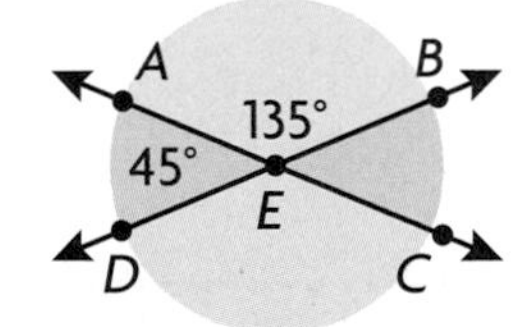

So, the measure of ∠*DEC* is equal to 135° and the measure of ∠*BEC* is equal to 45°.

Use the drawing to find the measure of each angle. Tell whether you used straight or vertical angles to find the measure of each angle.

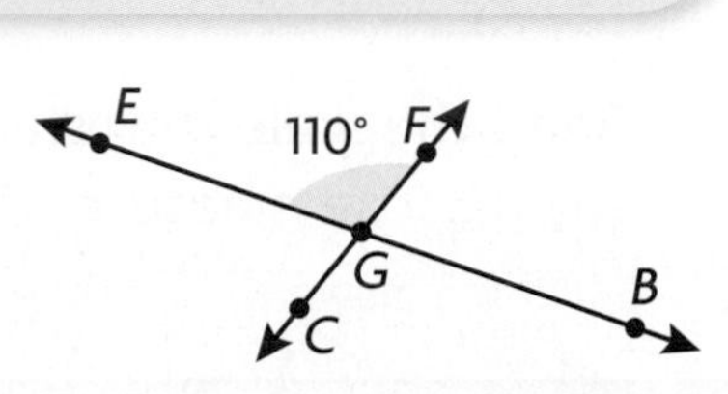

1. ∠*EGB* 2. ∠*FGB* 3. ∠*BGC*

LESSON 2

Measure and Draw Angles

OBJECTIVE: Estimate, measure, and draw angles.

Quick Review

Classify each angle as *acute, right,* or *obtuse.*

1. 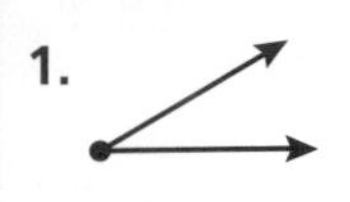
2. 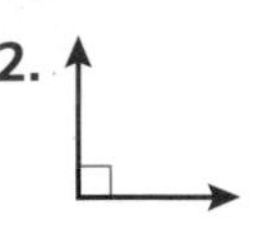
3. 
4. 
5. 

Vocabulary

protractor

Learn

To estimate the measure of an angle you can use benchmarks and what you know about acute, right, and obtuse angles.

Examples Estimate the measure of each angle.

A

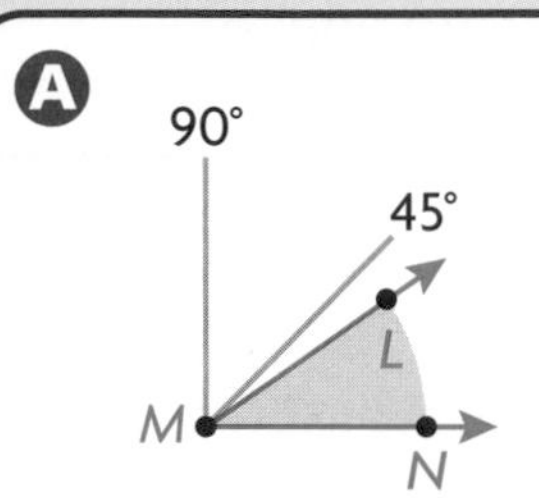

Angle *LMN* is an acute angle, so its measure is less than 90°.

A benchmark, 45°, is halfway between 0° and 90°.

So, the measure of ∠*LMN* is about 45° or a little less than 45°.

B

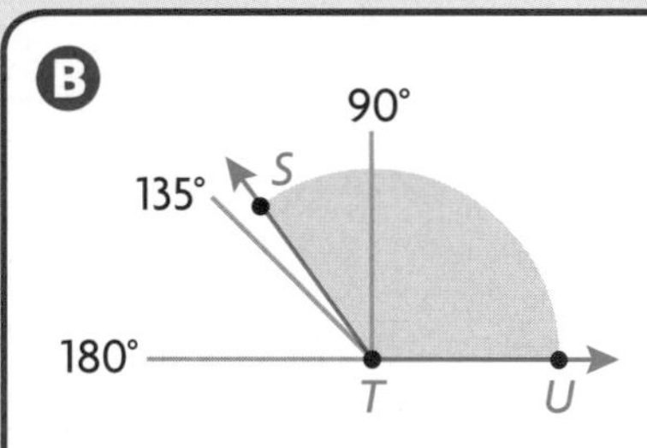

Angle *STU* is an obtuse angle, so its measure is greater than 90° and less than 180°.

A benchmark, 135°, is halfway between 90° and 180°.

So, the measure of ∠*STU* is about 135° or a little less than 135°.

You can use a protractor to measure angles. A **protractor** is a tool used for measuring or drawing angles.

Surveyors use a tool called a theodolite to measure angles.

HANDS ON

Activity Materials ■ protractor

Measure ∠*JKL*.

1. Place the center point of the protractor on the vertex of the angle.
2. Place the base of the protractor along ray *KL*.
3. Read the scale that starts with 0° at ray *KL*. The measure of ∠*JKL* is 60°.

Extend the rays if you need to.

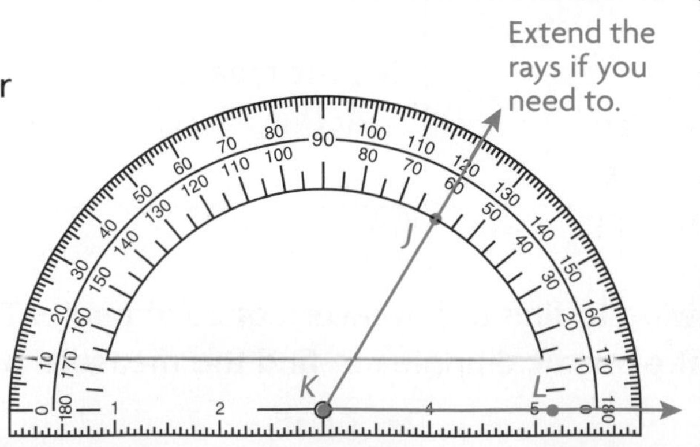

MG 2.1 Measure, identify, and draw angles, perpendicular and parallel lines, rectangles, and triangles by using appropriate tools (e.g., straightedge, ruler, compass, protractor, drawing software). *also* **MR 2.3, MR 2.4, MR 3.2**

Draw Angles

You can also use a protractor to draw angles of a given measure.

Activity **Materials** ■ protractor ■ straightedge

Use a protractor to draw $\angle FDE$ with a measure of 60°.

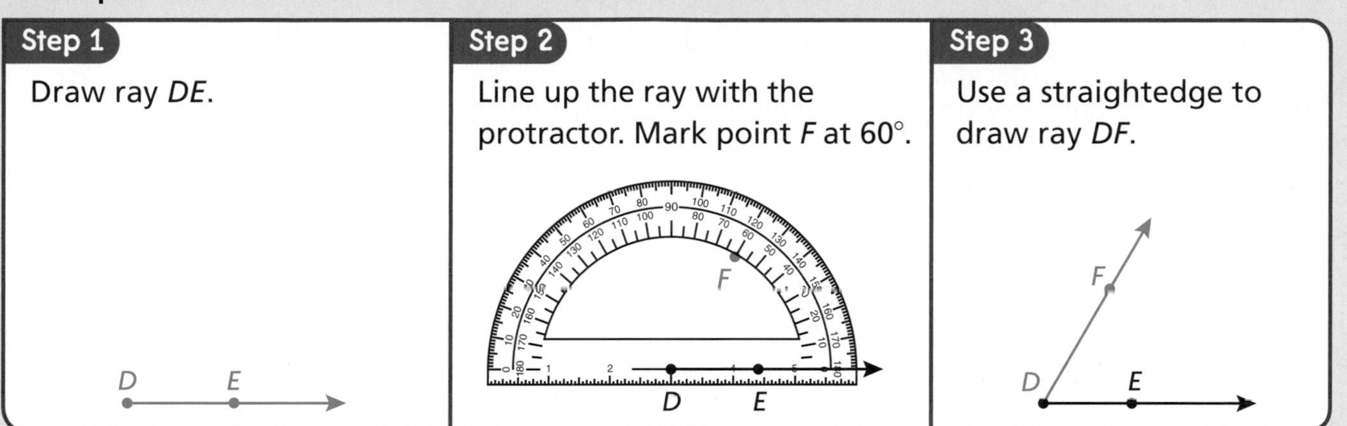

Step 1
Draw ray *DE*.
D
E
Step 2
Line up the ray with the protractor. Mark point *F* at 60°.
F
D
E
Step 3
Use a straightedge to draw ray *DF*.
F
D
E

When angles appear to be equal, measure them with a protractor and then compare.

More Examples **Find the measure of each angle. How do $\angle ABC$ and $\angle XYZ$ compare?**

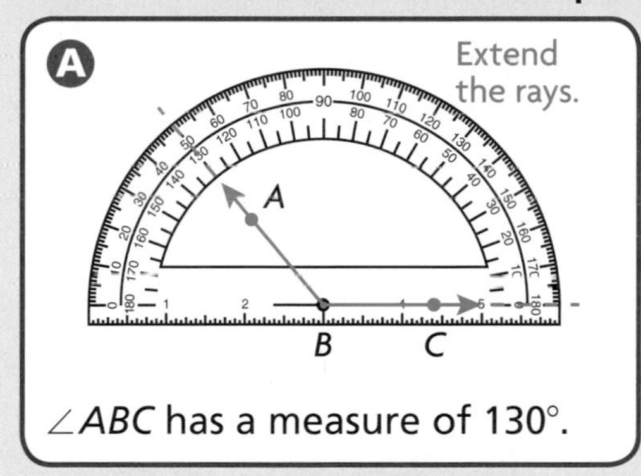

$\angle ABC$ has a measure of 130°.

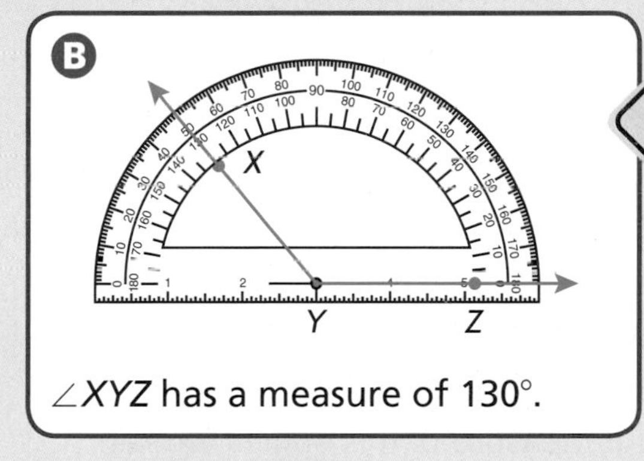

$\angle XYZ$ has a measure of 130°.

So, $\angle ABC$ and $\angle XYZ$ both have the same measure, 130°.

ERROR ALERT

Remember that the measure of an angle is determined by the degree of rotation of a ray and not the length that is drawn for a ray.

Guided Practice

1. Draw and label an angle with about the same measure as $\angle MOQ$, shown at the right.
   a. Is your angle acute, obtuse, or right? Estimate the measure of your angle.
   b. Use a protractor to find the measure of your angle. How does your estimate compare to the actual measure of the angle?

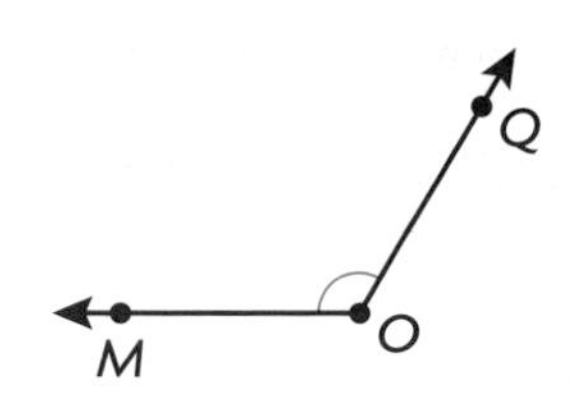

Estimate the measure of each angle. Then use a protractor to find the measure.

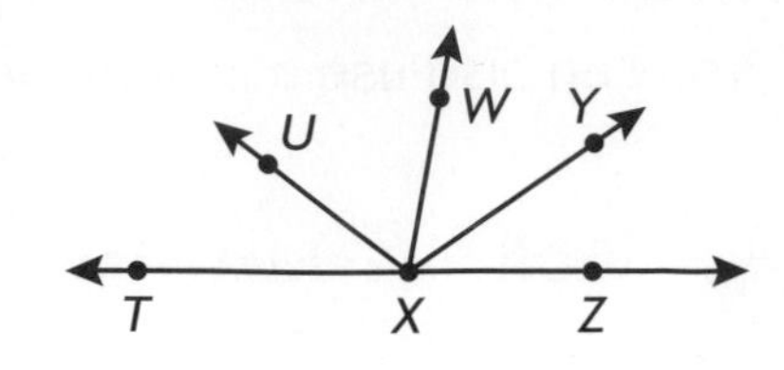

2. $\angle TXW$
3. $\angle WXY$
4. $\angle UXY$
5. $\angle YXZ$
6. $\angle TXU$
7. $\angle UXW$

Use a protractor to draw each angle. Classify each angle.

8. 45°
9. 60°
10. 125°
11. 14°

12. **TALK Math** **Explain** how you can estimate and find the measure of $\angle WXZ$ in the figure above.

Independent Practice and Problem Solving

Estimate the measure of each angle. Then use a protractor to find the measure.

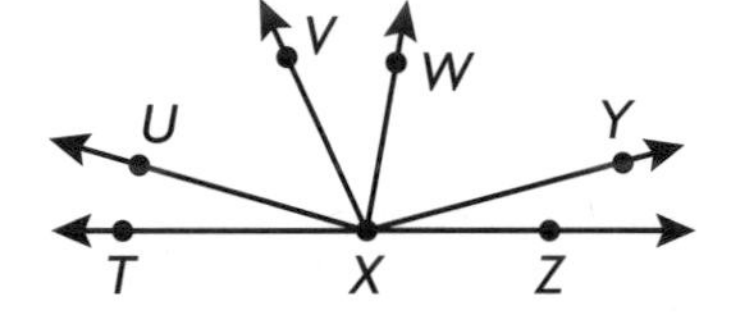

13. $\angle YXZ$
14. $\angle VXT$
15. $\angle WXZ$
16. $\angle VXU$
17. $\angle VXW$
18. $\angle UXT$
19. $\angle VXZ$
20. $\angle UXY$
21. $\angle TXZ$

Use a protractor to draw each angle. Classify each angle.

22. 35°
23. 159°
24. 16°
25. 95°
26. 120°
27. 44°
28. 180°
29. 135°
30. an angle whose measure is between 110° and 130°
31. an angle whose measure is less than 65°

USE DATA For 32–34, use the clocks.

32. Copy the angle made by the hands of the clock that shows 6:00. What is the measure of this angle? Explain how you know.
33. At what hours do the hands of a clock form a right angle?
34. Estimate the measure of the angle formed by the hands of the clock that shows 3:05. Then measure the angle.
35. **WRITE Math** **What's the Error?** Tracy measured an angle as 50° that was actually 130°. Describe her error.

 Extra Practice on page 460, Set B

Achieving the Standards

36. If $n = 6$, what is the value of $5n - 2$? (AF 1.2, p. 348)

37. What figure is a surface that extends without end in all directions? (MG 2.0, p. 436)

38. Classify the angle. (MG 2.1, p. 436)

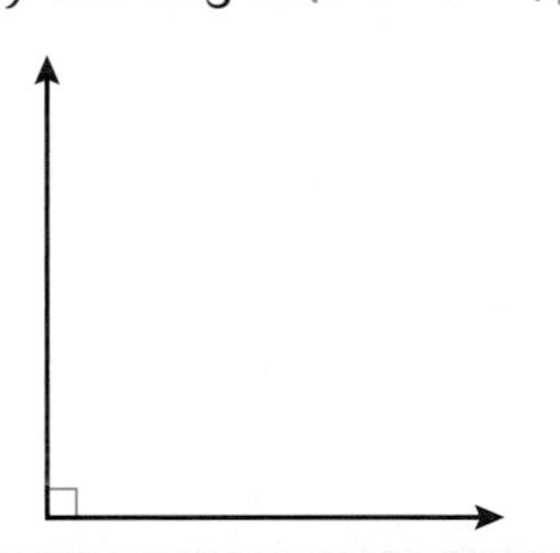

39. **Test Prep** Which is true about obtuse angles on a protractor?

 A They go from 0° to 89°.

 B They go from 45° to 135°.

 C They go from 0° to 180°.

 D They go from 91° to 180°.

40. **Test Prep** Which angle measures less than 90°?

 A straight angle C acute angle

 B right angle D obtuse angle

Problem Solving connects to Science

Why does Earth have seasons? The planet is tilted on its axis. To see how this causes the seasons, look at the diagrams, which show the sun's angle with Earth's axis.

Examples Northern Hemisphere

Winter
The axis is tilted away from the sun on the first day of winter, often on December 21.

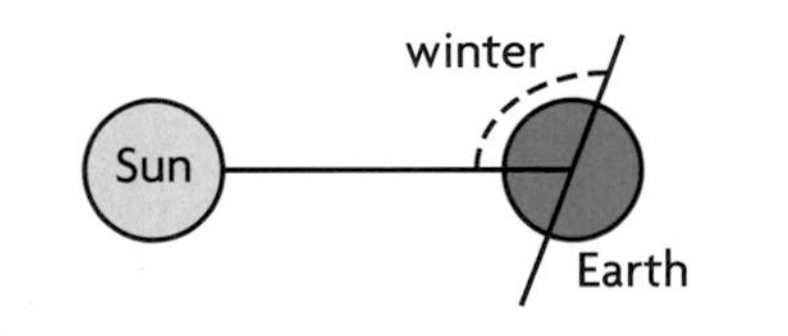

Spring and Fall
The axis is not tilted away from or toward the sun on the first day of spring and fall, often on March 20 and September 22.

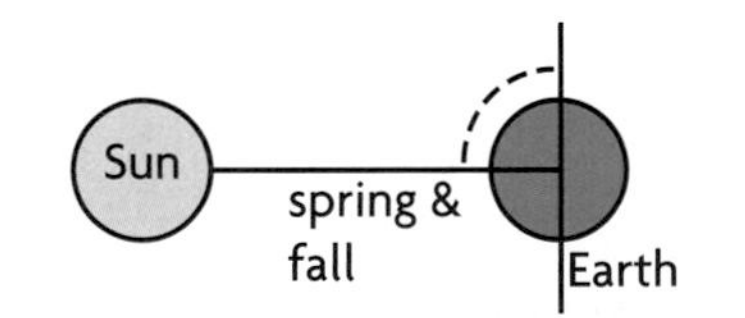

Summer
The axis is tilted toward the sun on the first day of summer, often on June 21.

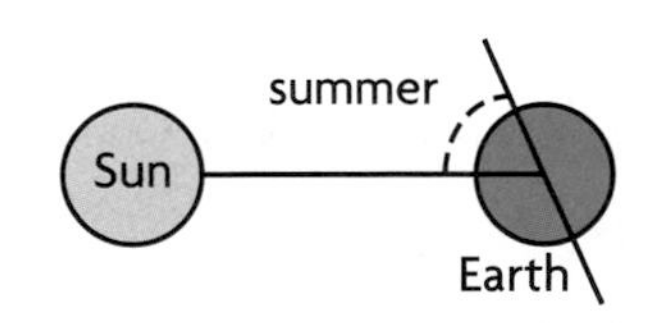

Use the diagrams to find the angle measures.

1. What is the marked angle on the shortest day of the year, the first day of winter?
2. What is the marked angle on the longest day of the year, the first day of summer?
3. What is the marked angle on the first day of spring and fall?

LESSON 3 HANDS ON

Construct Parallel and Perpendicular Lines

OBJECTIVE: Construct parallel and perpendicular lines.

Quick Review

Name the angle shown. Write *acute, right, obtuse,* or *straight*.

Investigate

Materials ■ compass ■ straightedge ■ protractor

You can use a compass and a straightedge to construct parallel lines.

A Use a straightedge to draw line *BC*. Draw point *A* above line *BC*. Draw a line through points *A* and *B*. Line *AB* intersects line *BC* at point *B*.

B Copy ∠*ABC*. Place the point of the compass on point *B,* and open the compass to the length of line segment *BC*. Then, draw an arc that passes through *C* and intersects line *AB* to locate point *D*. Now, place the point of the compass on point *A*. Without changing the compass setting, draw an arc to locate point *E* on line *AB*.

C Place the point of the compass on point *D,* and draw an arc that passes through *C*. Then, place the compass point on *E*. Without changing the compass setting, draw an arc to locate point *F*.

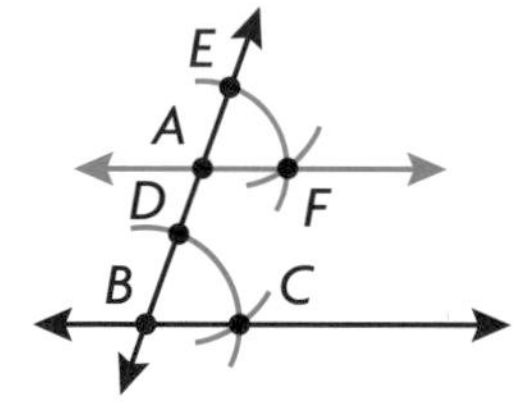

D Use a straightedge to draw line *AF*. Line *BC* and line *AF* are parallel.

Draw Conclusions

1. Measure ∠*ABC* and ∠*EAF*. How do their measures compare?
2. **Synthesize** Describe how copying an angle helps you draw parallel lines.

MG 2.1 Measure, identify, and draw angles, perpendicular and parallel lines, rectangles, and triangles by using appropriate tools (e.g., straightedge, ruler, compass, protractor, drawing software). *also* **MR 2.0, MR 2.3, MR 2.4, MR 3.2**

Connect

You can also use a compass and a straightedge to construct perpendicular lines. Remember that perpendicular lines intersect and form four right angles.

ERROR ALERT

Be careful not to change the compass setting when you move the compass from one point to another.

Step 1

Draw a line. Mark and label point *A* on the line. Then place the point of your compass on *A* and open the compass. Draw an arc on the line, above the line, and below the line. Mark and label point *B* where the arc intersects the line.

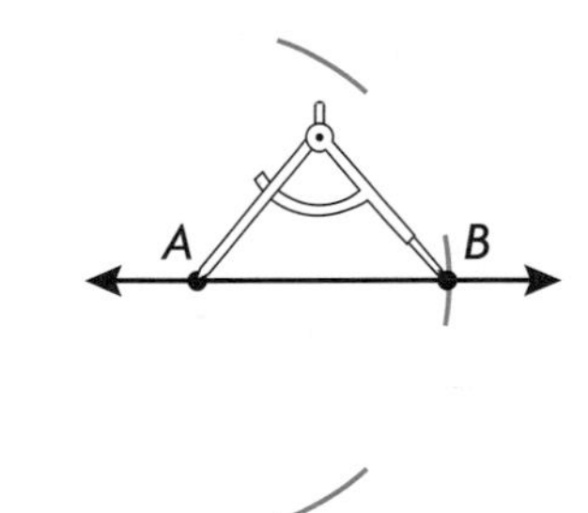

Without changing the compass setting, place the point of the compass on *B* and draw intersecting arcs above the line and below the line. Locate and label points *C* and *D* where the arcs intersect.

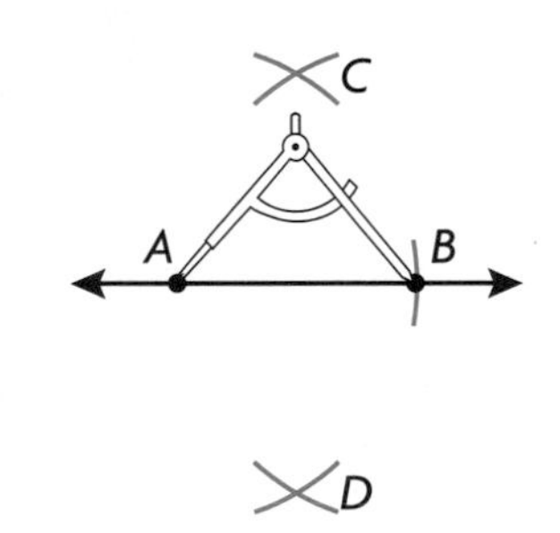

Use a straightedge to draw line *CD*. Line *AB* is perpendicular to line *CD*.

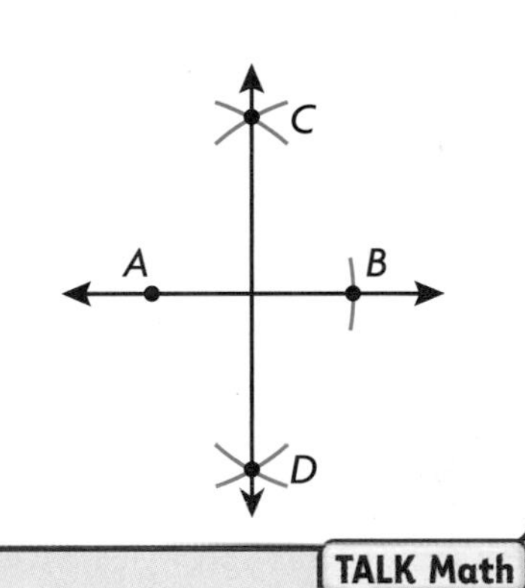

TALK Math

Explain how you can determine if the lines you constructed are perpendicular lines.

Practice

Trace each line. Use a compass and a straightedge to construct a line that is parallel to each line.

1.
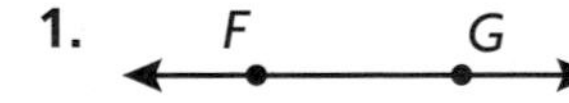

2.
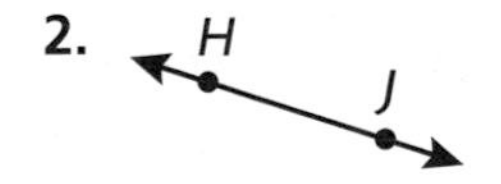

3.
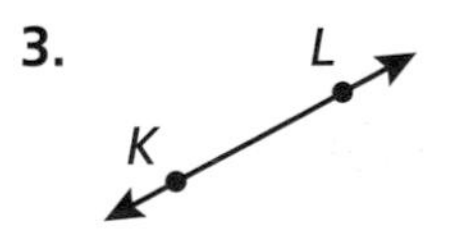

Trace each line. Use a compass and a straightedge to construct a line that is perpendicular to each line.

4. *M* *N*

5.
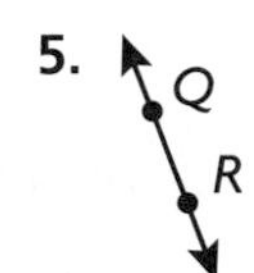

6. *O* *P*

7. **WRITE Math** **Explain** how to construct parallel lines by using a compass and a straightedge.

Polygons

OBJECTIVE: Identify, classify, and draw polygons.

Quick Review

Find the measure of $\angle ABC$.

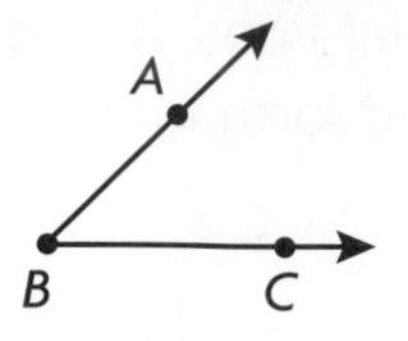

Vocabulary

polygon

regular polygon

Learn

PROBLEM The Castel del Monte in Apulia, Italy, was built sometime between A.D. 1240 and 1250. The main building and the center courtyard have 8 sides. Each of the 8 towers also has 8 sides. What polygon matches these features of Castel del Monte?

A **polygon** is a closed plane figure formed by three or more straight sides that are connected line segments. Polygons are named by the number of their sides and angles.

Polygon	Number of Sides and Angles
Triangle	3
Quadrilateral	4
Pentagon	5
Hexagon	6
Octagon	8
Decagon	10

Courtyard view of Castel del Monte looking up

So, an octagon matches the Castel del Monte's main structure, courtyard, and towers.

In a **regular polygon**, all sides have the same length and all angles have the same measure. A polygon that has sides and angles that are not the same measure are not regular polygons.

Examples Classify each figure.

	Polygon	Numbers of Sides and Angles	Name of Polygon	Types of Angles	Regular Polygon?
		6 sides and 6 angles	hexagon	6 obtuse angles	Yes; the hexagon appears to have sides of equal length and angles of equal measure.
		6 sides and 6 angles	hexagon	2 acute angles and 4 obtuse angles	No; the sides have different lengths, and the angles have different measures.
		5 sides and 5 angles	pentagon	5 obtuse angles	Yes; the pentagon appears to have sides of equal length and angles of equal measure.

MG 2.0 Students identify, describe, and classify the properties of, and the relationships between, plane and solid geometric figures. *also* **MR 2.3, MR 2.4, MR 3.2**

Guided Practice

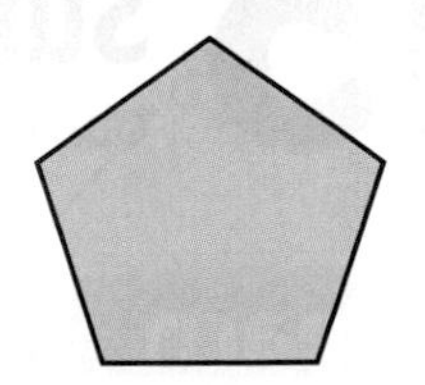

1. Classify the polygon at the right.
   a. How many sides and angles does this polygon have?
   b. Name the polygon.
   c. What types of angles does this polygon have?
   d. Is the polygon a regular polygon?

Name each polygon, and tell whether it is regular or not regular.

2. 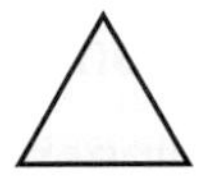

3. 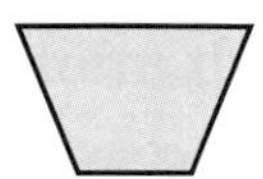

4. 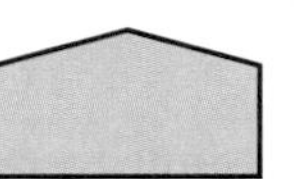

5. 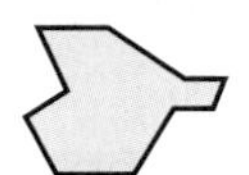

6. **TALK Math** **Explain** how you know how to classify a polygon.

Independent Practice and Problem Solving

Name each polygon, and tell whether it is regular or not regular.

7. 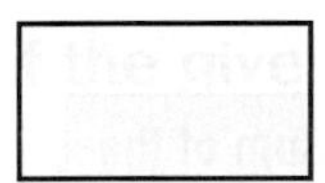

8. 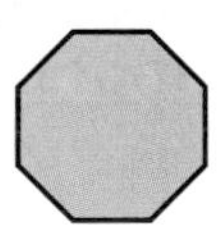

9. 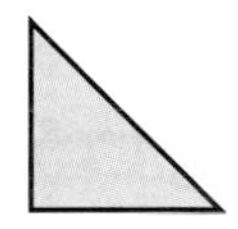

10. 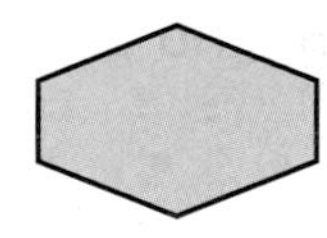

Complete each statement.

11. A regular quadrilateral has $\underline{\ ?\ }$ equal sides and $\underline{\ ?\ }$ equal angles.

12. A regular triangle has 3 $\underline{\ ?\ }$ angles.

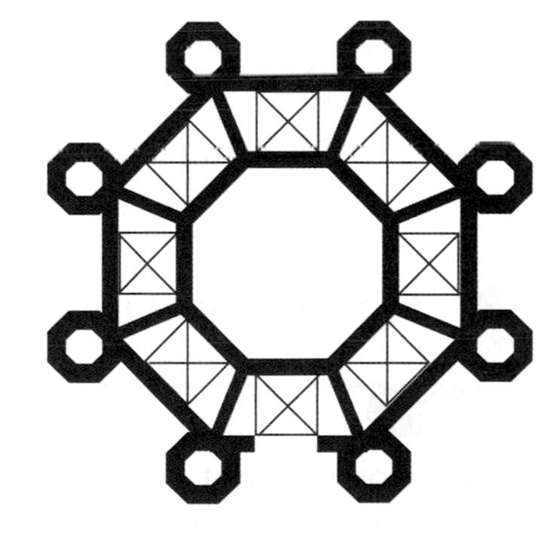

USE DATA For 13–14, use the Castel del Monte floor plan.

13. Which polygons in the drawings have 4 equal sides and 2 pairs of parallel sides? How many of these polygons are there?

14. What other regular polygons can you identify in the drawing? How many are there?

15. **WRITE Math** Explain how to determine if a polygon is a regular polygon.

Achieving the Standards

16. A rectangle has a length of 6 centimeters and a width of 4 centimeters. What is the area of the rectangle? (Grade 4 MG 1.4)

17. What percent is equivalent to $\frac{5}{8}$? (NS 1.2, p. 408)

18. Is $\angle ABC$ acute, right, or obtuse? (MG 2.0, p. 436)

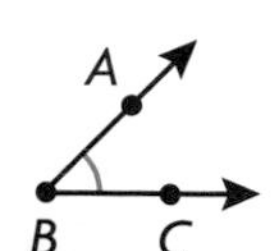

19. **Test Prep** Which best describes a polygon with 6 equal sides and 6 equal angles?
   A hexagon
   B quadrilateral
   C regular polygon
   D regular hexagon

Extra Practice on page 460, Set C

Circles

OBJECTIVE: Identify, describe, and draw a circle and its parts; relate the radius and the diameter.

Quick Review

Name and identify the figure.

Vocabulary

circle radius
diameter chord

Learn

A **circle** is a closed plane figure with all points the same distance from a point called the center of the circle. Circles are named by the center point.

Examples

A A line segment with one endpoint at the center of a circle and the other endpoint on the circle is called a **radius**. All radii in a given circle have the same length. So, $\overline{RE}$, $\overline{RC}$, and $\overline{RD}$ are radii.

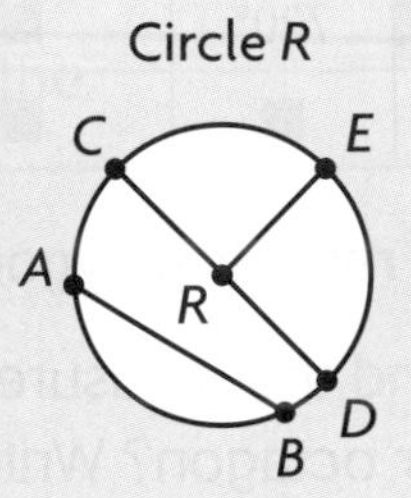

B A line segment that passes through the center of the circle and has both of its endpoints on the circle is called a **diameter**. So, $\overline{CD}$ is a diameter.

C A line segment with its endpoints on the circle is called a **chord**. So, $\overline{AB}$ and $\overline{CD}$ are chords. A diameter is also a chord.

▲ Capitol Records Building

Math Idea
In any given circle, the length of a diameter measures twice the length of a radius.

HANDS ON

Activity

Materials: ■ compass ■ straightedge

Step 1	Step 2	Step 3	Step 4
Draw and label point C. Place the point of the compass on point C.	Open the compass to 6 cm. This will be the radius of the circle.	Use the compass to draw the circle.	Draw and label a radius, a diameter, and a chord of circle C.
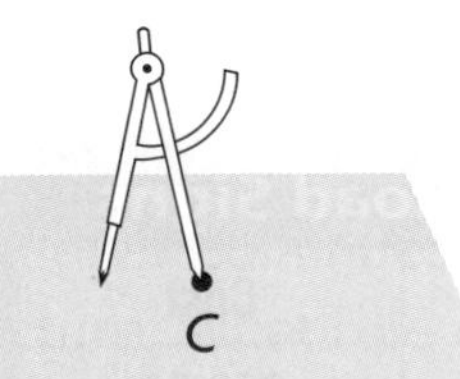	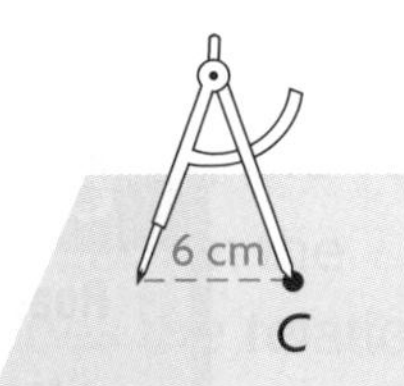	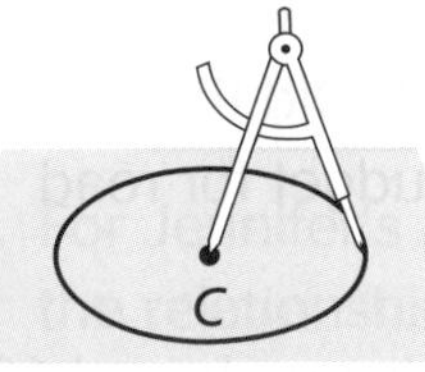	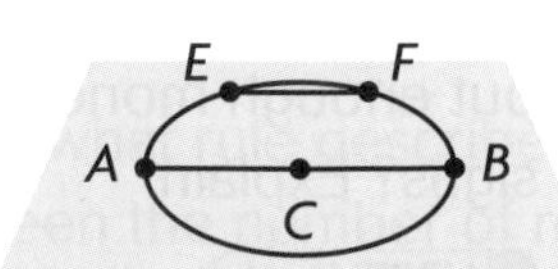

- In circle C, what is the length of the diameter?

MG 2.0 Students identify, describe, and classify the properties of, and the relationships between, plane and solid geometric figures. *also* MR 2.3, MR 2.4, MR 3.2

Guided Practice

For 1–4, use the circle at the right.

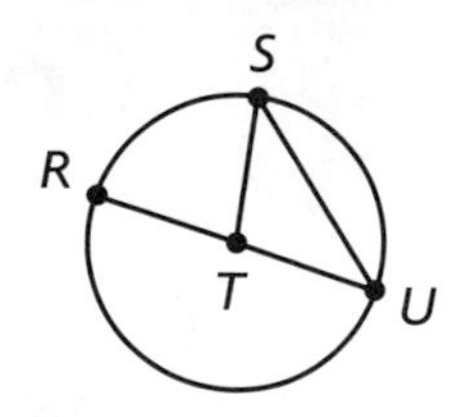

1. Name the circle.
2. Name a radius.
3. Name a chord.
4. Name a diameter.

Complete 5–8. Then use a compass to draw each circle. Draw a radius and a diameter, and label their measurements.

5. radius = 5 cm
   diameter = ■
6. radius = ■
   diameter = 8 in.
7. radius = 3.5 in.
   diameter = ■
8. radius = ■
   diameter = 16 cm

9. **TALK Math** **Explain** why every radius in a circle has the same length.

Independent Practice and Problem Solving

Complete 10–13. Then use a compass to draw each circle. Draw a radius and a diameter, and label their measurements.

10. radius = ■
    diameter = 9 cm
11. radius = 4.2 cm
    diameter = ■
12. radius = 2 in.
    diameter = ■
13. radius = ■
    diameter = 2 in.

14. A music CD has a radius of 60 millimeters. What is the diameter of the CD?

15. **FAST FACT** Before music CDs, music was produced on records. The diameter of a long-play record was 12 inches. The diameter of a single was $5\frac{1}{8}$ inches less than that of a long-play record. What was the radius of an album? What was the radius of a single?

16. **Reasoning** Can a circle's chord be greater in length than a circle's radius? than a circle's diameter? Explain.

17. **WRITE Math** **Explain** how knowing the radius of a circle tells you the diameter of the circle.

Achieving the Standards

18. What is the area of a rectangle that has a length of 5 inches and a width of 2.5 inches? (Grade 4 MG 1.4)

19. What is 20% of 30? (NS 1.2, p. 412)

20. What is the name of a polygon that has 5 equal sides and 5 angles that have the same measure? (MG 2.0, p. 446)

21. **Test Prep** The diameter of circle *O* is 27 centimeters. What is the length of a radius in circle *O*?

    A 27 centimeters
    B 14 centimeters
    C 13.5 centimeters
    D 13 centimeters

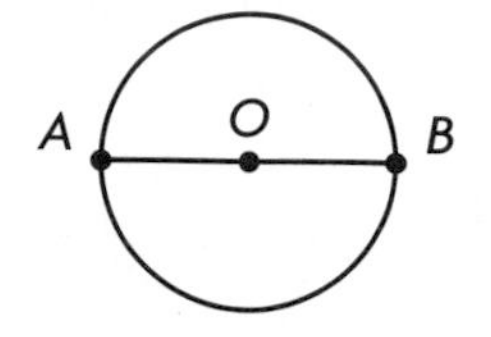

Extra Practice on page 461, Set E

LESSON 8 HANDS ON

Construct Polygons

OBJECTIVE: Construct regular polygons.

Quick Review

Name the number of sides and the number of angles for each polygon.

1. triangle
2. pentagon
3. hexagon
4. octagon
5. quadrilateral

Investigate

Materials ■ compass ■ straightedge ■ protractor

You can use a compass and a straightedge to construct regular polygons.

A Open the compass to 5 centimeters to draw circle *O*. Use a ruler to draw diameter *AB*. Keeping the same compass opening, place the compass point on point *B*.

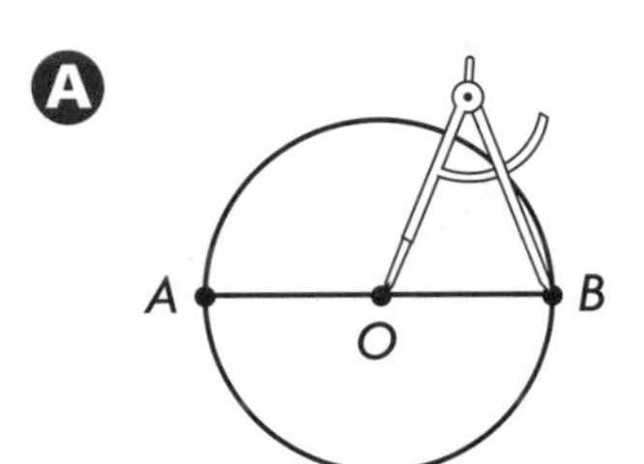

B From point *B*, draw an arc that passes through point *O* and intersects the circle at two points. Keeping the same compass opening, place the compass point on *A* and draw a second arc that passes through *O* and intersects the circle at two points.

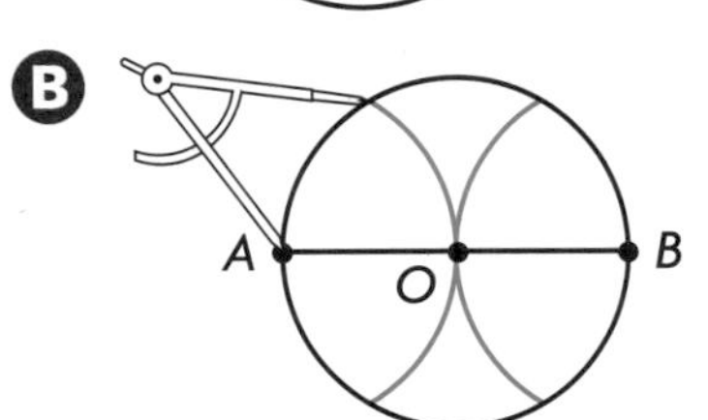

C Label points *C*, *D*, *E*, and *F* as shown. Use a straightedge to draw a chord that connects adjacent points *D* and *B*.

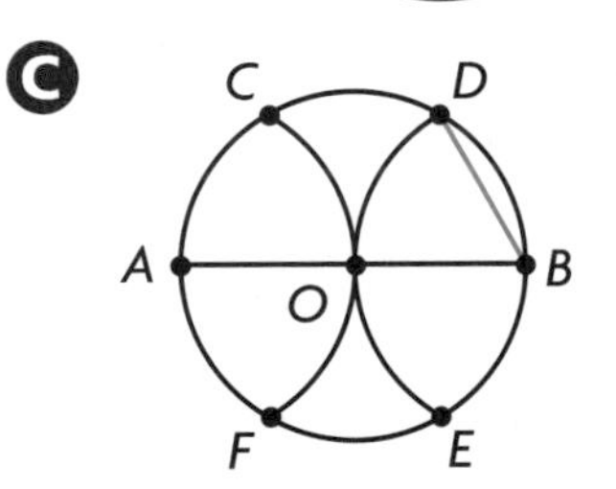

D Use a straightedge to draw chords *DC*, *CA*, *AF*, *FE*, and *EB* and construct hexagon *ACDBEF*.

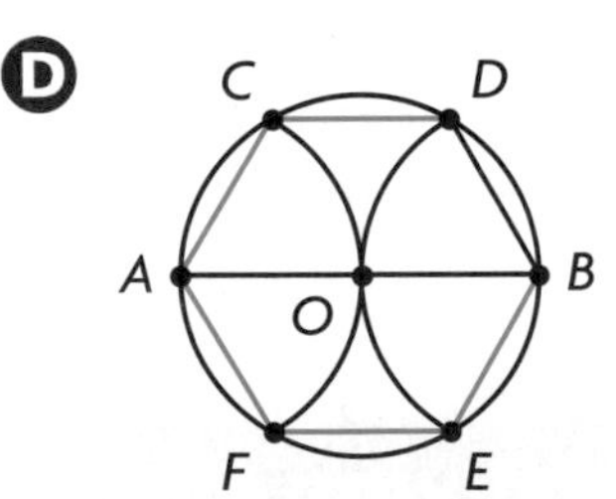

Draw Conclusions

1. How does the radius of the circle relate to the sides of the hexagon?
2. Use a straightedge to measure the length of each side of your hexagon. How do the lengths of the sides compare?
3. Use a protractor to measure the angles of your hexagon. How do the measures of the angles compare?
4. **Evaluation** Have you constructed a regular hexagon? **Explain** how you know.

MG 2.1 Measure, identify, and draw angles, perpendicular and parallel lines, rectangles, and triangles by using appropriate tools (e.g., straightedge, ruler, compass, protractor, drawing software). *also* **MR 2.0, MR 2.3, MR 2.4, MR 3.2**

Connect

You can use a compass and a straightedge to construct an equilateral triangle.

Step 1

Draw a line. Mark a point and label the point *S*. Open the compass to 7 centimeters and place the point on *S* to mark another point on your line. Label this point *T*.

Step 2

Keeping the same compass opening, place the compass point on *S* and then *T* to draw an arc above the line. Where the arcs intersect, mark the point and label the point *U*.

Step 3

Use a straightedge to draw $\overline{SU}$ and $\overline{TU}$.

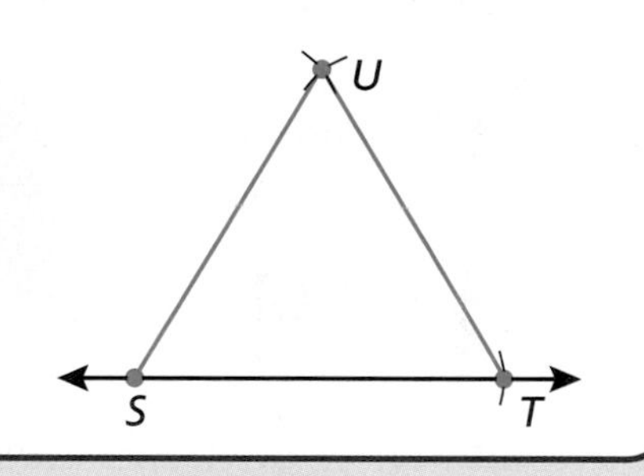

TALK Math

How is the length of each side of the triangle you constructed related to the compass opening?

Practice

Use a compass and a straightedge to construct each hexagon.

1. hexagon with sides that are 3 centimeters long
2. hexagon inside a circle with a radius of 4 inches

Use a compass and straightedge to construct each triangle.

3. equilateral triangle with sides that have a measure of 5 inches
4. equilateral triangle with sides that have a measure of 10.5 centimeters
5. **WRITE Math** **Explain** how you could change the steps above to construct an isosceles triangle.

LESSON 9

Congruent and Similar Figures

OBJECTIVE: Identify congruent and similar figures

Quick Review

Name the angle below.

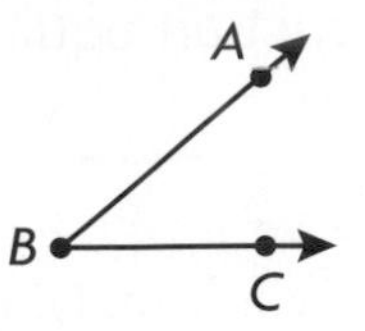

Vocabulary

congruent
similar
corresponding sides
corresponding angles

Learn

PROBLEM Susie's mother ordered a package of school pictures that included 4-inch × 6-inch photos and wallet-size photos. How do the wallet-size photos compare to each other? How do the wallet-size photos compare to the 4-inch × 6-inch photos?

Congruent figures have the same shape and size. The wallet-size photos are the same shape and size. So, these photos are congruent.

Similar figures have the same shape but may not have the same size. The wallet-size photos and the 4-inch × 6-inch photos are the same shape but are different sizes. So, these photos are similar.

Figures can be congruent, similar, or neither. All congruent figures are similar, but similar figures may not be congruent.

Math Idea
Congruent figures have the same area.

More Examples

A

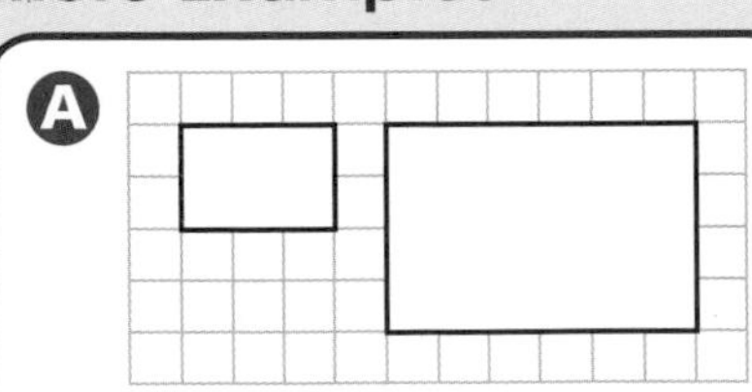

- Same shape
- Different sizes

The figures are similar but not congruent.

B

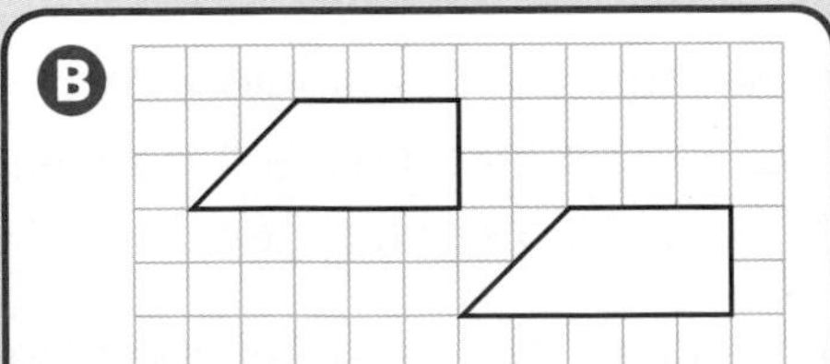

- Same shape
- Same size

The figures are congruent and similar.

C

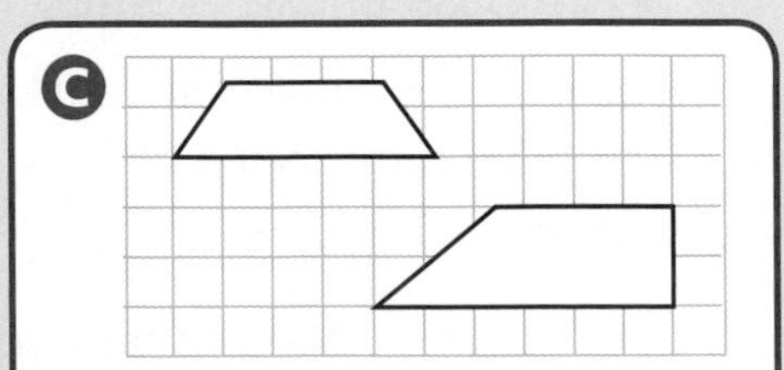

- Different shapes
- Different sizes

The figures are neither similar nor congruent.

MG 2.0 Students identify, describe, and classify the properties of, and the relationships between, plane and solid geometric figures. *also* MR 2.3, MR 2.4, MR 3.2

Corresponding Sides and Angles

Figures that are congruent or similar have corresponding sides and angles. **Corresponding sides** and **corresponding angles** are in the same related position in different figures.

Examples

A Triangles *ABC* and *DEF* are similar.

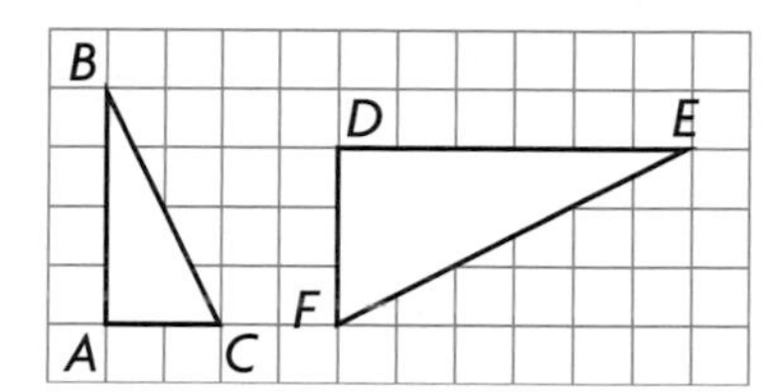

Corresponding Sides

$\overline{AB}$ corresponds to $\overline{DE}$.
$\overline{AC}$ corresponds to $\overline{DF}$.
$\overline{BC}$ corresponds to $\overline{EF}$.

Corresponding Angles

$\angle A$ corresponds to $\angle D$.
$\angle B$ corresponds to $\angle E$.
$\angle C$ corresponds to $\angle F$.

B Quadrilaterals *GHIJ* and *KLMN* are congruent.

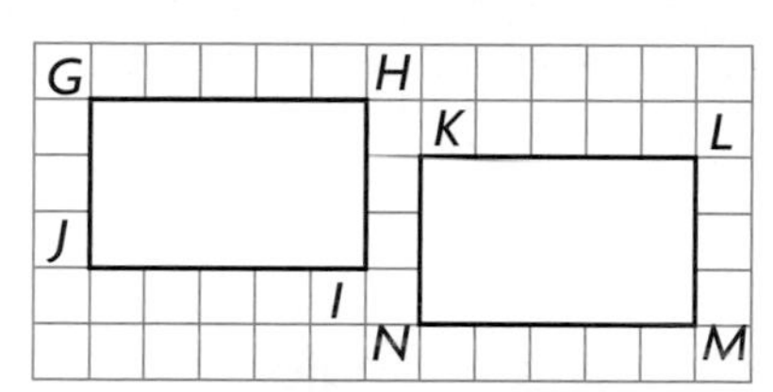

Corresponding Sides

$\overline{GH}$ corresponds to $\overline{KL}$.
$\overline{HI}$ corresponds to $\overline{LM}$.
$\overline{IJ}$ corresponds to $\overline{MN}$.
$\overline{JG}$ corresponds to $\overline{NK}$.

Corresponding Angles

$\angle G$ corresponds to $\angle K$.
$\angle H$ corresponds to $\angle L$.
$\angle I$ corresponds to $\angle M$.
$\angle J$ corresponds to $\angle N$.

You can measure corresponding sides and angles to determine whether two figures are congruent or similar. Corresponding sides and angles of congruent figures have the same measure. The triangles below are similar.

Activity

Materials ■ centimeter grid paper ■ ruler ■ protractor

Step 1

The symbol for *triangle* is $\triangle$. Copy $\triangle STU$ and $\triangle WXY$ on grid paper.

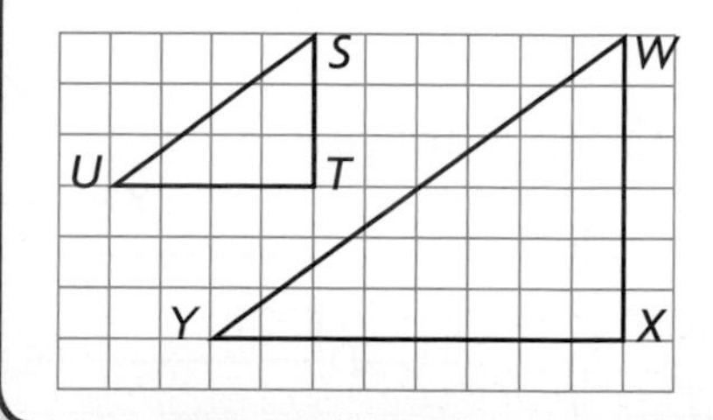

Step 2

Use a centimeter ruler to measure corresponding sides.

$\overline{ST} = 3$ cm $\overline{WX} = 6$ cm
$\overline{TU} = 4$ cm $\overline{XY} = 8$ cm
$\overline{SU} = 5$ cm $\overline{WY} = 10$ cm

Step 3

Use a protractor to measure corresponding angles.

$\angle S = 53°$ $\angle W = 53°$
$\angle T = 90°$ $\angle X = 90°$
$\angle U = 37°$ $\angle Y = 37°$

- What conclusion can you draw about corresponding sides and corresponding angles of similar triangles?

Guided Practice

1. Are the two figures at the right the same shape?
   Are the two figures the same size?
   Review the definitions for congruent and similar. Then, write whether the two figures appear to be *congruent, similar,* or *neither.*

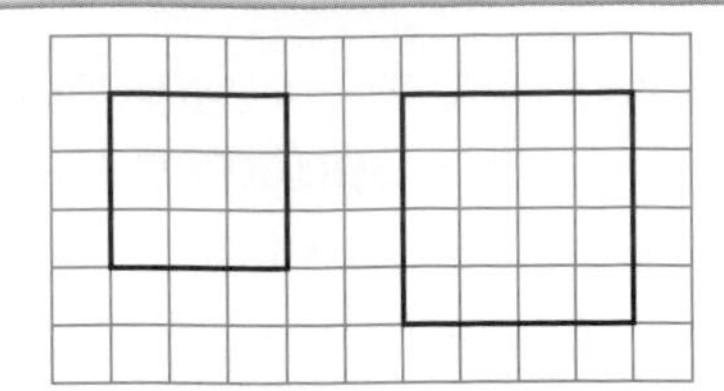

Write whether the two figures appear to be *congruent, similar,* or *neither.*

2.

3.

4.

5.

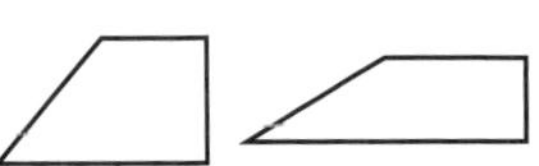

Identify the corresponding side or angle.

6. $\overline{ST}$
7. $\overline{RT}$
8. $\angle R$
9. $\angle T$

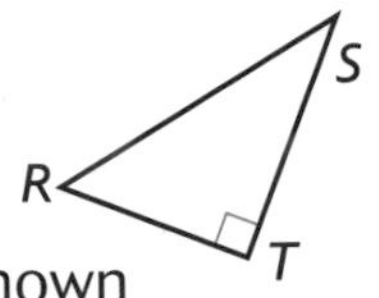

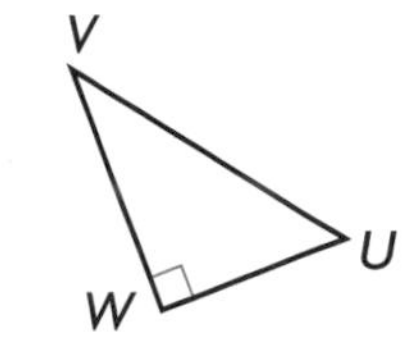

10. TALK Math **Explain** how you can decide whether the two figures shown are congruent or similar.

Independent Practice and Problem Solving

Write whether the two figures appear to be congruent, similar, or neither.

11.

12.

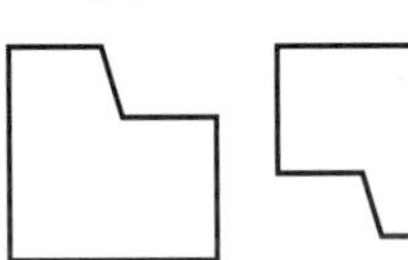

13.

14.

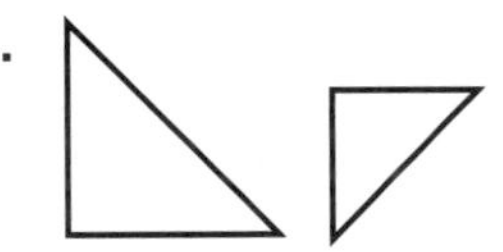

Identify the corresponding side or angle.

15. $\overline{ST}$
16. $\angle R$
17. $\overline{RU}$
18. $\angle U$
19. $\overline{SR}$
20. $\overline{TU}$
21. $\angle T$
22. $\angle S$

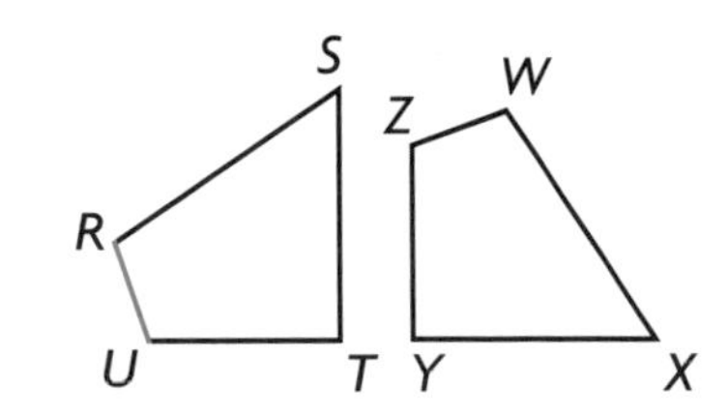

USE DATA For 23–25, use the figures shown.

23. Copy the figures on centimeter grid paper. Use a centimeter ruler and a protractor to measure the sides and angles of each figure.
24. Do any of the figures appear to be congruent? Which figures? Explain.
25. Do any of the figures appear to be similar? Which figures? Explain.
26. WRITE Math **Explain** how corresponding sides and corresponding angles of two congruent figures are related.

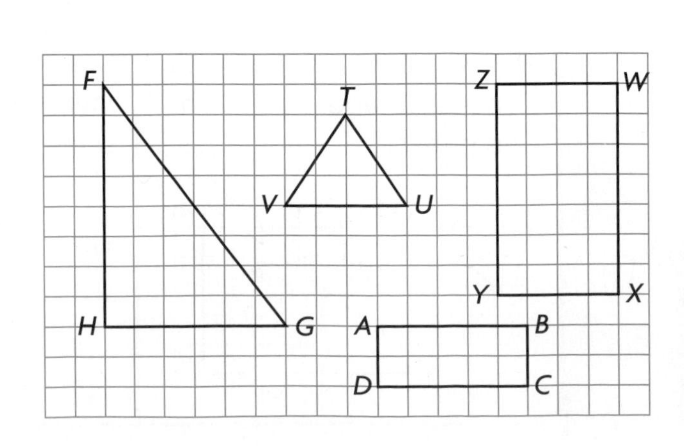

 Extra Practice on page 461, Set F

Achieving the Standards

27. At basketball practice, Samantha missed 6 out of 25 free throws. What percent of her shots did Samantha make?
(O─π NS 1.2, p. 414)

28. What is the sum of the angles in a circle?
(MG 2.0, p. 452)

29. How many sides and how many angles does a triangle have? (MG 2.0, p. 446)

30. Test Prep Which is always true about similar figures?

- **A** They are regular polygons.
- **B** They are congruent.
- **C** They are the same shape.
- **D** They are polygons.

31. Test Prep Which angle corresponds to $\angle B$?

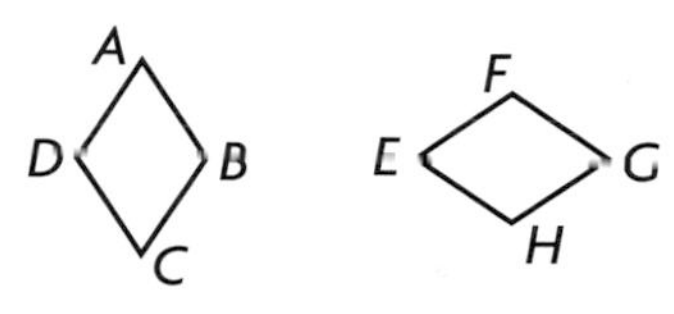

A $\angle E$ **B** $\angle F$ **C** $\angle G$ **D** $\angle H$

Problem Solving and Reasoning

GEOMETRY You can use a compass and a straightedge to copy any angle. Trace $\angle ABC$. Then construct $\angle DEF$ so that it is congruent to $\angle ABC$.

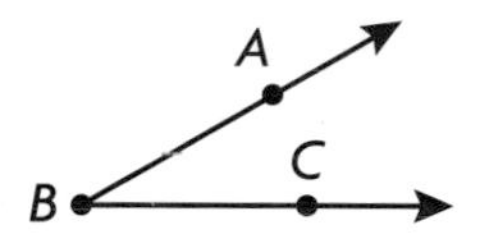

Step 1
Place the compass point on vertex *B*. Draw an arc through *A* and *C*.

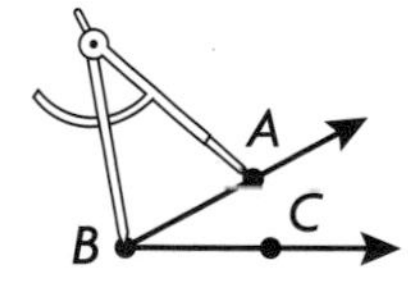

Step 2
Draw ray *EF*. Without changing the compass, draw an arc touching *F*.

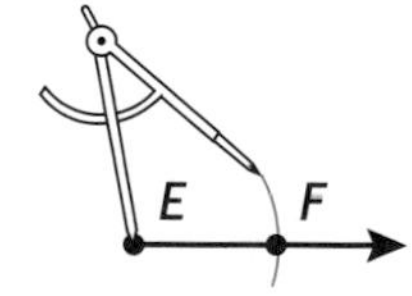

Step 3
Go back to $\angle ABC$. With the compass point on *C*, open the compass so it touches *A*.

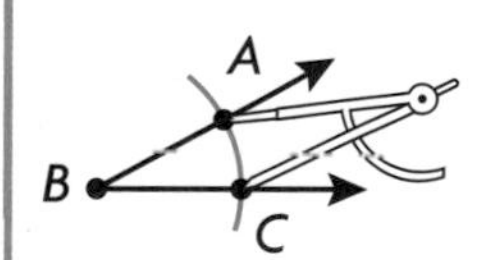

Step 4
Without changing the compass, draw an arc to make point *D*.

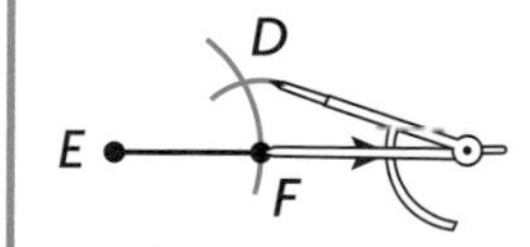

Step 5
Use a straightedge to draw ray *ED*.

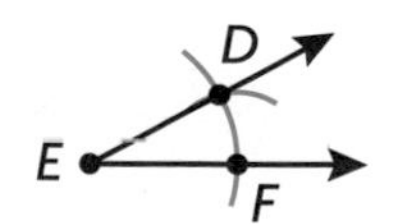

1. Draw $\angle ABC$ with a measure of 60°. Then use a compass and a straightedge to construct an angle that is congruent to the given angle.

2. Draw $\angle JKL$ with a measure of 110°. Then use a compass and a straightedge to construct an angle that is congruent to the given angle.

Extra Practice

Set A For 1–8, use the figure. Name an example of each. (pp. 436–439)

1. point
2. intersecting lines
3. ray
4. line segment
5. acute angle
6. vertex
7. obtuse angle
8. perpendicular lines

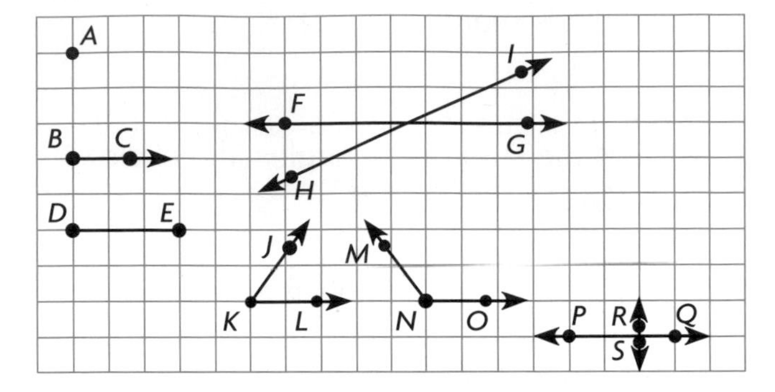

Set B Estimate the measure of each angle. Then use a protractor to find the exact measure. (pp. 440–443)

1. $\angle GBC$
2. $\angle EBG$
3. $\angle EBF$
4. $\angle EBC$
5. $\angle DBA$
6. $\angle FBA$

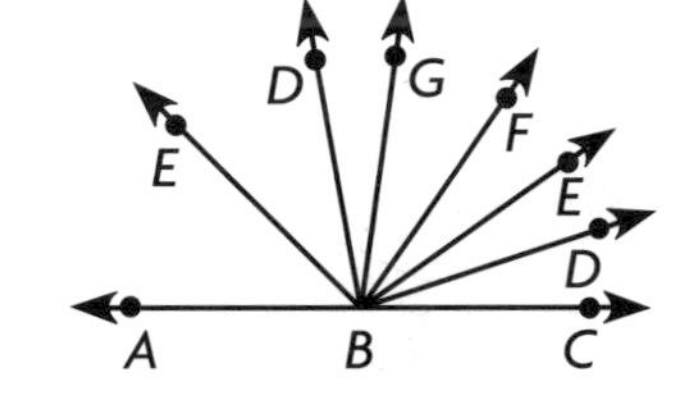

Use a protractor to draw each angle. Classify each angle.

7. 25°
8. 145°
9. 115°
10. 90°
11. an angle whose measure is between 50° and 85°
12. an angle whose measure is greater than 115° and less than 180°

Set C Name each polygon, and tell whether it is regular or not regular. (pp. 446–447)

1. 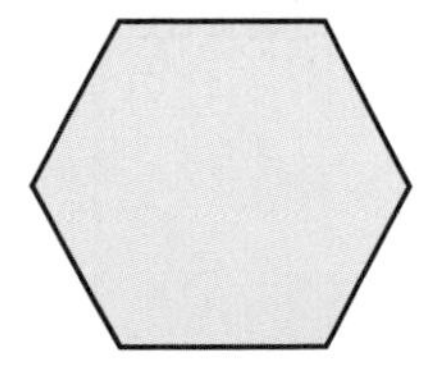
2. 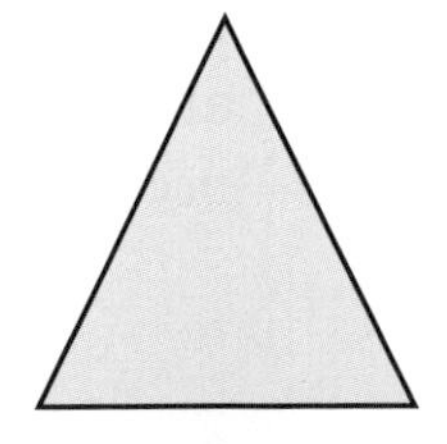
3. 
4. 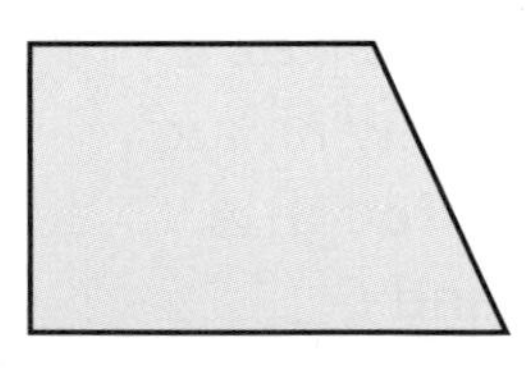
5. 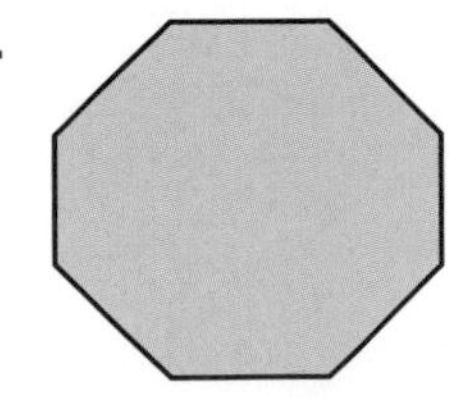
6. 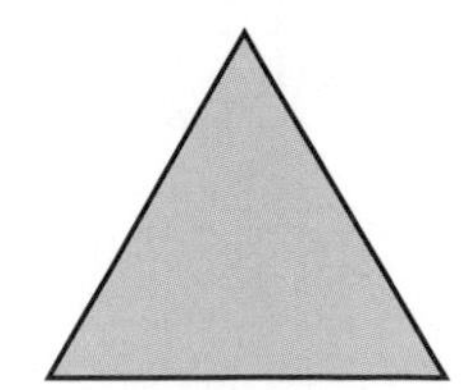
7. 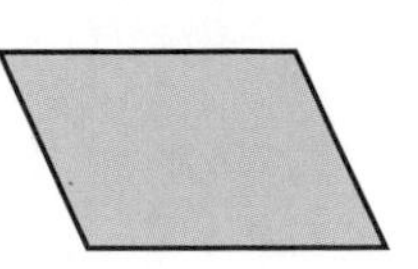
8. 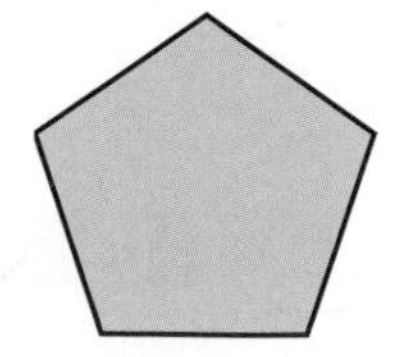

CD ROM Technology
Use Harcourt Mega Math, Ice Station Exploration, *Polar Planes*, Level D.

Set D Tell if the given angles could form a triangle. (pp. 448–449)

1. 25°, 68°, 87°
2. 45°, 45°, 70°
3. 60°, 30°, 90°
4. 20°, 116°, 39°

Tell if the given angles could form a quadrilateral.

5. 57°, 45°, 110°, 150°
6. 88°, 91°, 89°, 92°
7. 23°, 79°, 150°, 98°
8. 100°, 37°, 16°, 80°

9. Rachel drew an obtuse triangle. None of the angles have the same measure. What could be the measures of the angles?

10. Joe made cutouts for a collage. Two angle measures of a triangle-shaped cutout are 60°. What is the measure of the third angle?

Set E Complete 1–8. Then use a compass to draw each circle. Draw a radius and a diameter, and label their measurements. (pp. 452–453)

1. radius = 2 in.
   diameter = ■
2. radius = ■
   diameter = 3 cm
3. radius = ■
   diameter = $1\frac{1}{2}$ in.
4. radius = 5 in.
   diameter = ■
5. radius = ■
   diameter = 4.2 cm
6. radius = $3\frac{1}{4}$ in.
   diameter = ■
7. radius = 4.6 cm
   diameter = ■
8. radius = ■
   diameter = 7 in.

Set F Write whether the two figures appear to be *congruent*, *similar*, or *neither*. (pp. 456–459)

1. 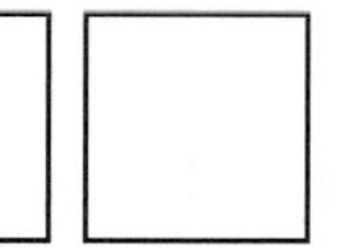

2. 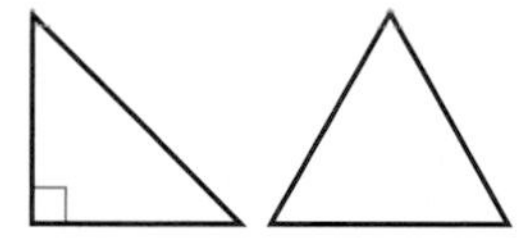

3. 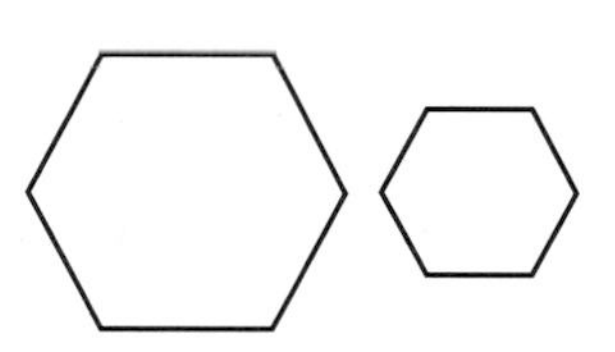

4. 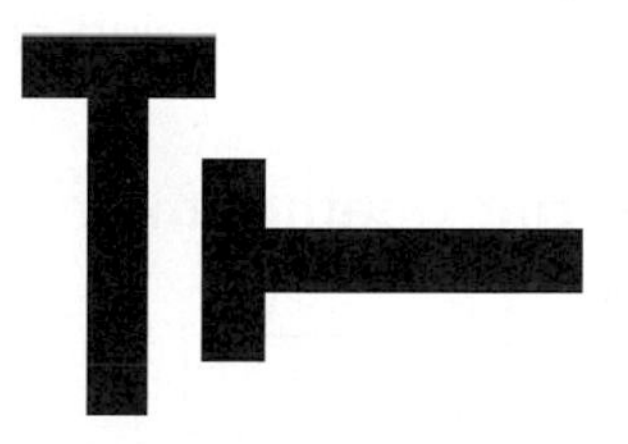

Name the angle or side that corresponds to the angle or side that is marked in blue.

5. 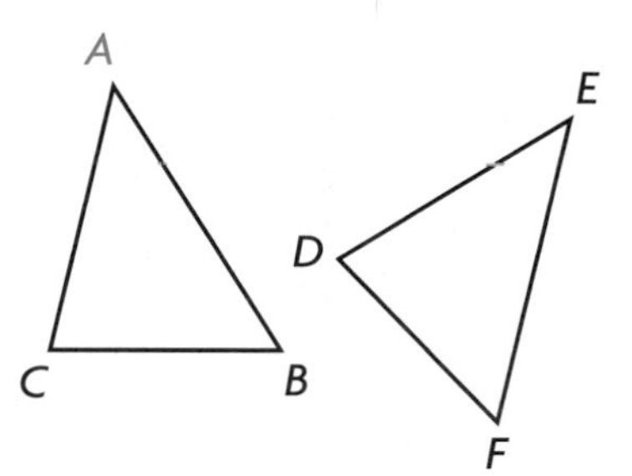

6. 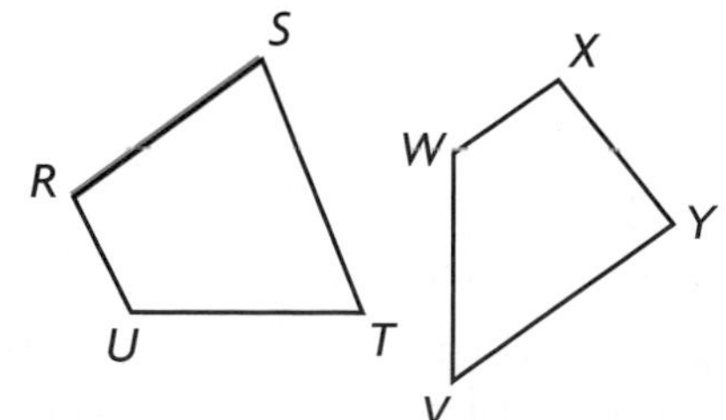

7. 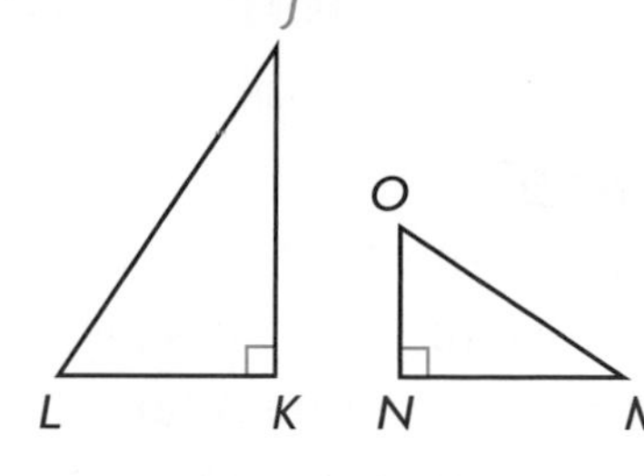

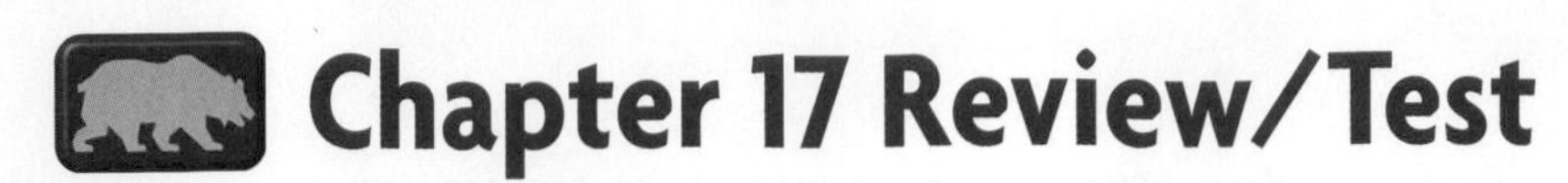

Chapter 17 Review/Test

Check Vocabulary and Concepts

For 1–2, choose the best term from the box.

VOCABULARY
acute angle
congruent
obtuse angle

1. Figures that have the same size and shape are __?__. **(MG 2.0, p. 456)**
2. A(n) __?__ is an angle that is greater than 90° and less than 180°. **(O–π MG 2.1, p. 437)**

Check Skills

Use a protractor to draw each angle. **(O–π MG 2.1, pp. 440–443)**

3. 55°
4. 140°
5. 31°
6. 128°

Name each polygon and tell if it is regular or not regular. **(MG 2.0, pp. 446–447)**

7. 
8. 
9.
10. 

Tell if the given angles could form a quadrilateral. **(O–π MG 2.2, pp. 448–449)**

11. 115°, 150°, 65°, 30°
12. 85°, 72°, 113°, 90°
13. 90°, 110°, 90°, 75°

Draw and label the following. **(MG 2.0, pp. 452–453)**

14. Circle *K* with radius 12 centimeters and chord *LM*
15. Circle *T* with diameter *SU* measuring 3 meters
16. Circle *F* with intersecting diameters *EG* and *CD*

Write whether the two figures appear to be *congruent, similar,* or *neither*. **(MG 2.0, pp. 456–459)**

17. 
18. 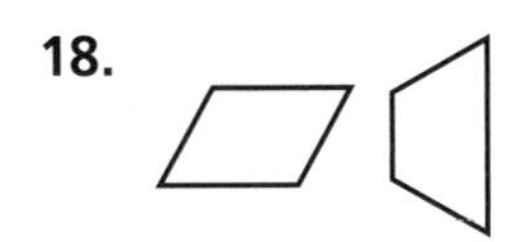
19. 

Check Problem Solving

Solve. **(O–π MG 2.2, MR 1.1, MR 3.2, pp. 450–451)**

20. **WRITE Math** Chris is constructing a wooden puzzle. He cuts a piece shaped like a regular hexagon. What is the sum of the angle measures in Chris's piece? Suppose Chris cuts the hexagon into triangles. **Explain** how that a rule describes the relationship between the number of triangles and the number of sides in the hexagon can help solve this problem.

GO ONLINE **Technology** Use *Online Assessment.*

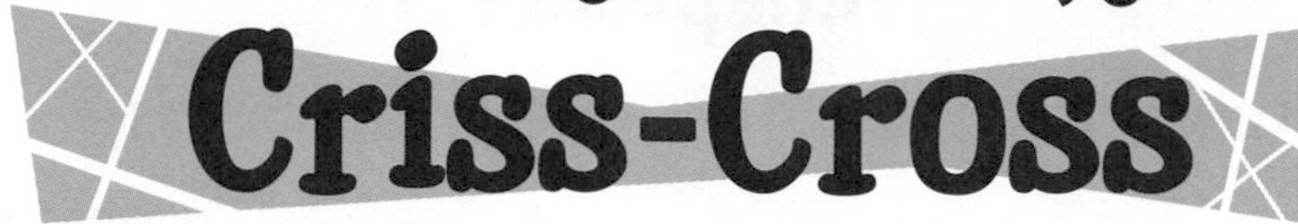

A point where two sides of a polygon meet is called a vertex. A **diagonal** is a line segment that connects two vertices.

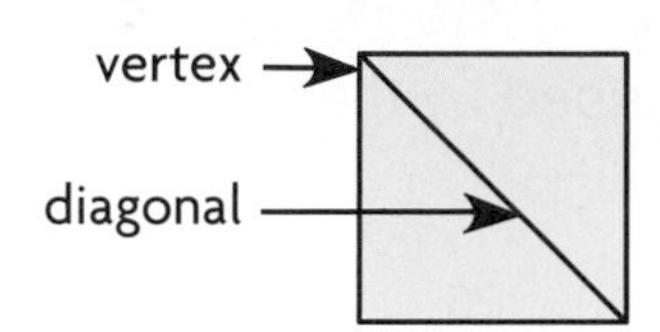

Example 1

Find the number of diagonals in an octagon by using a model.

Step 1	Choose a vertex. Draw line segments connecting it to every other vertex in the octagon.	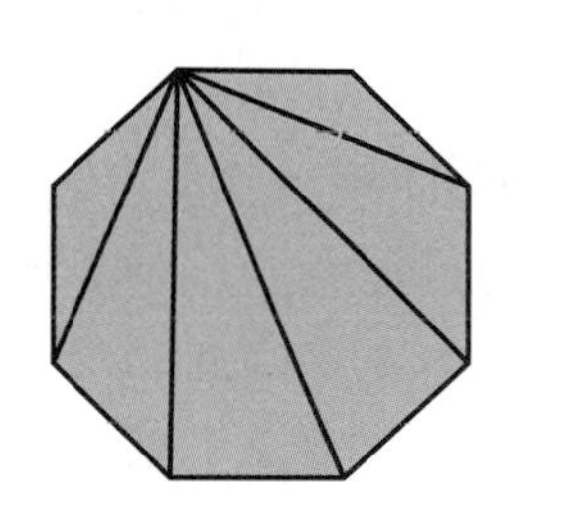
Step 2	Choose a new vertex. Repeat Step 1. Continue in this manner until you have connected all the vertices with line segments.	
Step 3	Count the line segments.	

So, an octagon has 20 diagonals.

Example 2

Use a formula to find the number of diagonals in a hexagon.

Use the formula $\frac{n(n-3)}{2}$ for n = the number of sides in a polygon. $\frac{n(n-3)}{2} = \frac{6(6-3)}{2} = \frac{6 \times 3}{2} = \frac{18}{2} = 9$	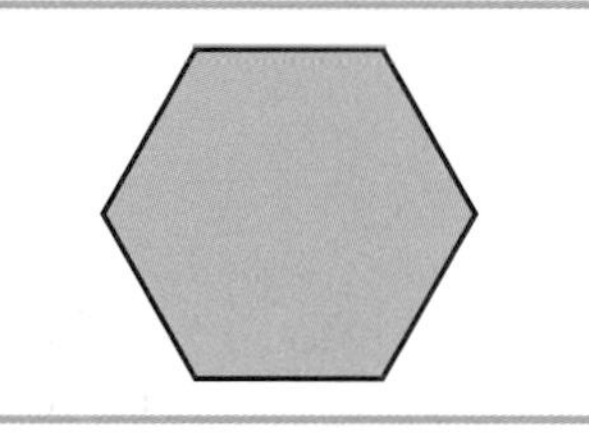

So, a hexagon has 9 diagonals.

Try It

Use the formula to find the number of diagonals in each polygon.

1. triangle
2. decagon
3. quadrilateral
4. pentagon

Think About It

WRITE Math **Explain** why a rhombus, trapezoid, and parallelogram each have two diagonals.

Achieving the Standards
Chapters 1–17

Algebra and Functions

1. $84 \div p = 7.$

Which situation could be described by the equation above? (AF 1.1)

A John has a board that is 84 inches long. He cuts it into p equal pieces. The length of each piece is 7 inches.

B John has a board that is 84 inches long. He cuts off p inches. The board is now 7 inches long.

C John has a board that is 84 inches long. Before he cut off 7 inches, the board was p inches long.

D John has 7 boards that are each 84 inches long. The total length in inches of all 7 boards is p.

2. If $a = 24$, what is the value of $(^-8) + a$? (AF 1.2)

A 32 **C** $^-16$

B 16 **D** $^-32$

3. Which one of the following equations does not have a solution of $n = 6$? (AF 1.2)

A $9n + 6 = 60$

B $14n - 6 = 84$

C $16n + 6 = 102$

D $19n - 6 = 108$

4. WRITE Math **Explain** how to find the value of t in the equation

$7 \times t = (7 \times 50) + (7 \times 3)$. (AF 1.3)

Number Sense

5. There are 20 fish in Mindy's fish tank. If 40% of Mindy's fish are mollies, what number of the fish in Mindy's tank are mollies? (NS 1.2)

A 4 **C** 12

B 8 **D** 40

Test Tip **Decide on a plan.**

See item 6. The number line is divided into tenths. Write the fractional part of the mixed number with a denominator of 10. Find the whole number on the number line. Then count up by tenths to find the fractional part of the mixed number.

6. Which letter on the number line *best* identifies the location of $1\frac{4}{5}$? (NS 1.5)

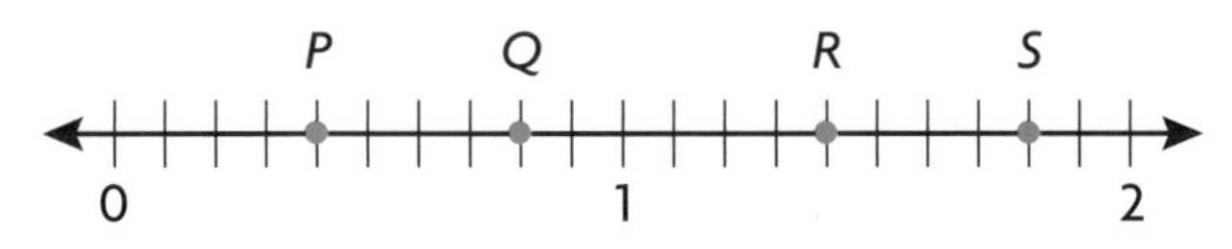

A P **C** R

B Q **D** S

7. WRITE Math **Explain** how to find the difference $5\frac{1}{3} - 2\frac{1}{2}$. (NS 2.3)

Statistics, Data Analysis, and Probability

8. The table below shows the number of books donated to the library by two donors.

Books Donated			
	Fiction	**Non-Fiction**	**Total**
Richard	130	70	200
Evan	45	105	150

Who donated 70% of one type of book, and which type of book was it? (SDAP 1.3)

A Richard, fiction **C** Evan, fiction

B Richard, non-fiction **D** Evan, non-fiction

9. Four students disagree about the mode for the following data.

17, 19, 20, 15, 23, 20, 15

Name	Mode
Pedro	15
Rosa	19
Sean	20
Tara	15 and 20

Which student is correct? (SDAP 1.1)

A Pedro **C** Sean

B Rosa **D** Tara

10. WRITE Math The median and mode of the data set 5, 11, 13, 9, 7, and n is the same number. What is n? **Explain** how you know. (SDAP 1.1)

Measurement and Geometry

11. In the figure below, which two angles appear to be obtuse? (MG 2.1)

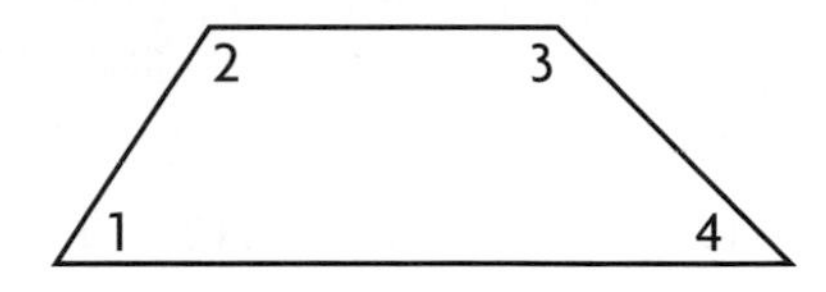

A angles 1 and 2

B angles 2 and 3

C angles 1 and 3

D angles 1 and 4

12. Which is *closest* to the measure of the angle shown below? (MG 2.1)

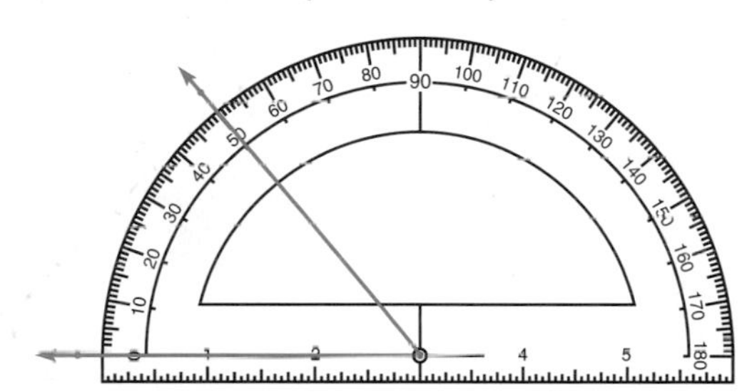

A 50°

B 60°

C 120°

D 130°

13. WRITE Math **Explain** how to use a protractor to draw a pair of perpendicular lines. (MG 2.1)

18 Plane and Solid Figures

The Big Idea Two- and three-dimensional figures can be classified according to their geometric properties.

CALIFORNIA FAST FACT

The city of San Diego is the seventh largest city in the United States. Its recent population was 1,294,032 people. San Diego is the second largest city in California, after Los Angeles.

Investigate

Look for examples of plane and solid figures in the San Diego Skyline. Then, on a sheet of paper, draw your own city skyline. Include different plane and solid figures. Describe the properties of your figures.

Plane Figures	Solid Figures
triangles	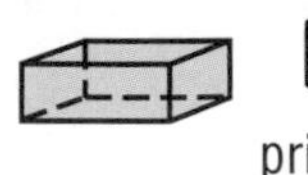 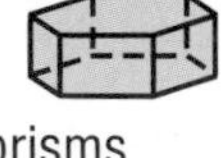 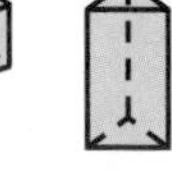 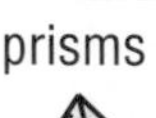 prisms
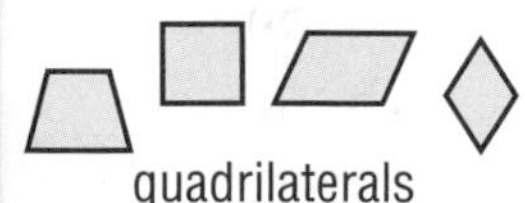 quadrilaterals	  pyramids
 other plane figures	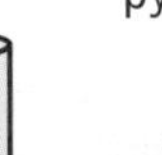    other solid figures

Technology
Student pages are available in the Student eBook.

Show What You Know

Check your understanding of important skills needed for success in Chapter 18.

▶ Measure and Classify Angles

Classify the angle. Write *acute, right,* or *obtuse*.

1. 

2. 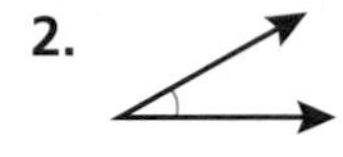

3. 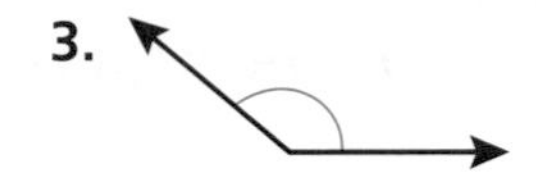

4. 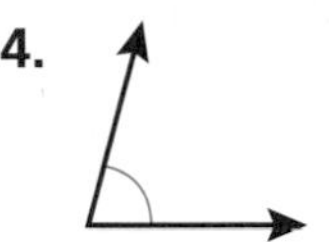

▶ Faces of Solid Figures

Name the plane figure that is the shaded face of the solid figure.

5. 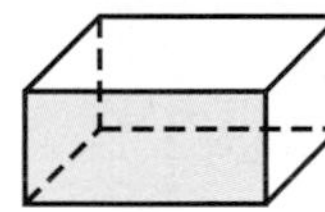

6. 

7. 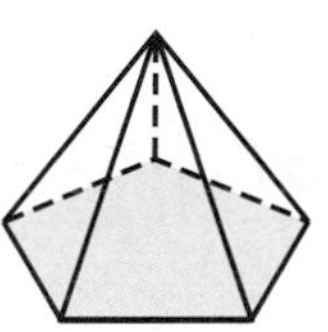

8. 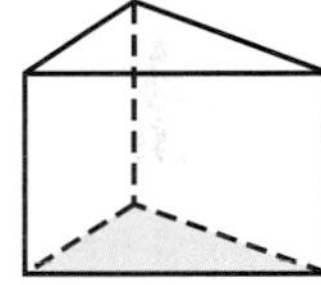

9. 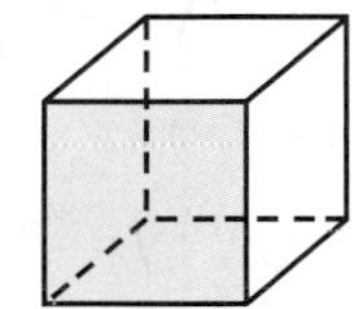

10. 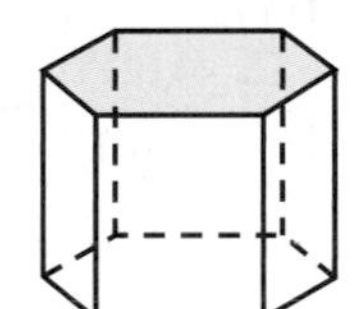

11. 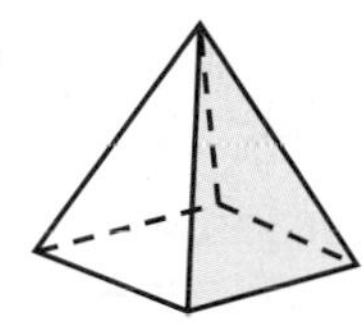

12. 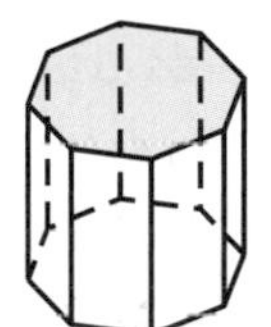

VOCABULARY POWER

CHAPTER VOCABULARY

acute triangle	polyhedron
base	prism
equilateral triangle	pyramid
isosceles triangle	rhombus
net	right triangle
obtuse triangle	scalene triangle
parallelogram	trapezoid

WARM-UP WORDS

isosceles triangle a triangle with exactly two congruent sides

scalene triangle a triangle with no congruent sides

equilateral triangle a triangle with three congruent sides

LESSON 1

Triangles

OBJECTIVE: Identify, describe, and classify types of triangles; find an unknown angle in a triangle.

Quick Review

Classify each angle as right, acute, or obtuse.

1.

2.

3.

4.

5.

Vocabulary

isosceles triangle
scalene triangle
equilateral triangle
right triangle
acute triangle
obtuse triangle

Learn

PROBLEM The *Santa Maria* is one of the ships Christopher Columbus sailed to North America. The sail in the back of the ship was a triangle that had a right angle but whose sides were all different lengths. What type of triangle was the sail?

You can classify triangles by the lengths of their sides. In the examples below, the slashes indicate congruent sides.

Examples

A

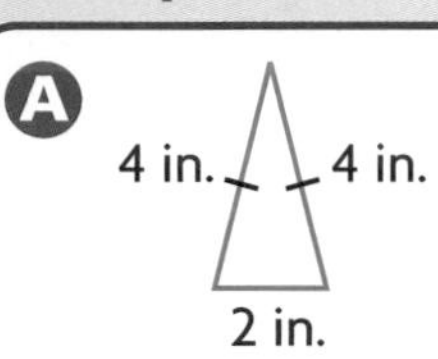

An **isosceles triangle** has exactly two congruent sides.

B

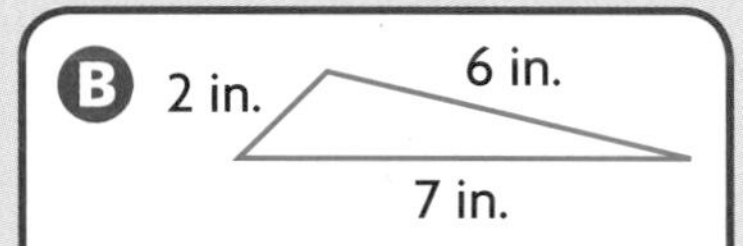

A **scalene triangle** has no congruent sides.

C

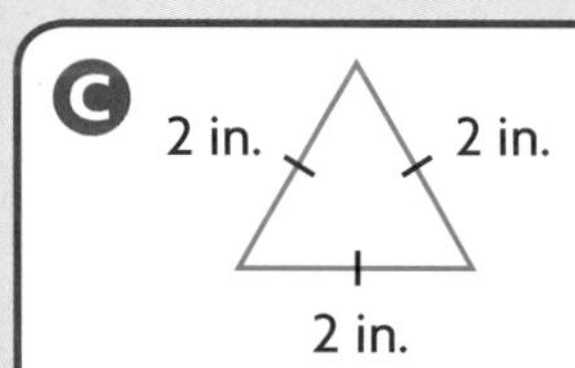

All of the sides of an **equilateral triangle** are congruent.

You can also classify triangles by the measures of their angles.

Examples

D

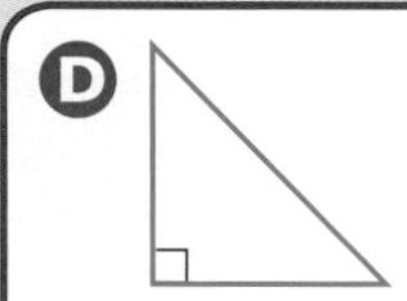

A **right triangle** has a right angle.

E

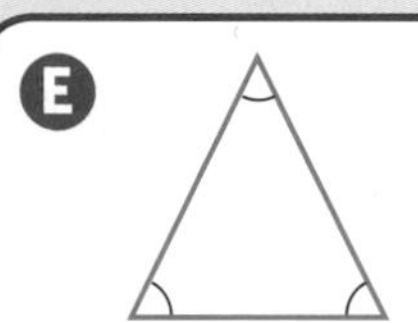

An **acute triangle** has three acute angles.

F

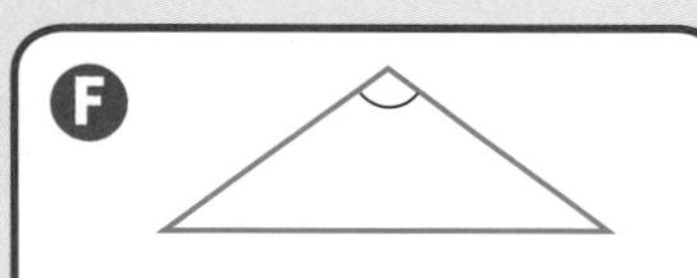

An **obtuse triangle** has one obtuse angle.

So, the sail was a scalene triangle and a right triangle.

- Without actually measuring the angles, how can you determine whether a triangle has an obtuse angle?

▲ This is a model of the *Santa Maria*.

Math Idea
An equilateral triangle has 3 congruent angles. An isosceles triangle has 2 congruent angles. A scalene triangle has no congruent angles.

MG 2.2 Know that the sum of the angles of any triangle is 180° and the sum of the angles of any quadrilateral is 360° and use this information to solve problems. *also* **MG 2.0, MR 2.3, MR 2.4, MR 3.2**

Finding an Unknown Angle

In a triangle, you can find the measure of an unknown angle if you know the measures of the other two angles.

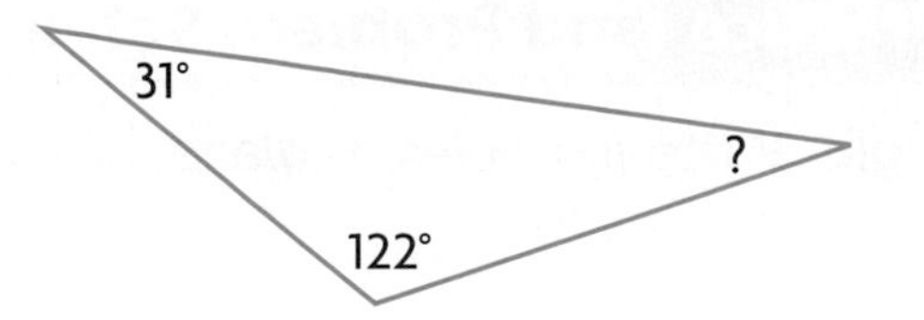

Example

What is the measure of the unknown angle in the triangle above?

Step 1	Step 2
Find the sum of the measures of the known angles. $31° + 122° = 153°$	Subtract the sum of the known angle measures from 180°. $180° - 153° = 27°$

So, the measure of the unknown angle is 27°.

Remember
The sum of the measures of the interior angles of a triangle is always 180°.

Guided Practice

1. Copy triangle *ABC* at the right.

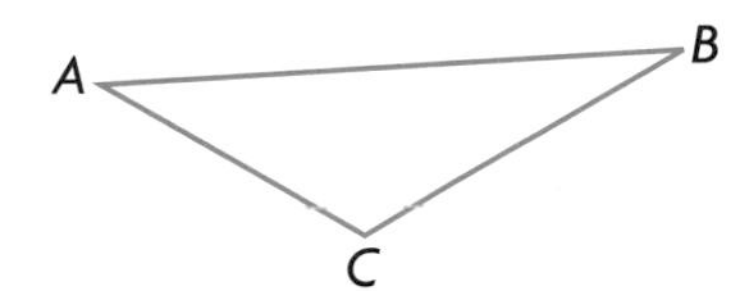

   a. Are any of the sides congruent? Mark the congruent sides with slashes. Classify the triangle by the lengths of its sides.

   b. The triangle has 2 acute angles. Is the third angle a right angle, an acute angle, or an obtuse angle? Classify the triangle by the measures of its angles.

Classify each triangle. Write *isosceles, scalene,* or *equilateral*.

2. 3 cm, 3 cm, 3 cm

3. 6 in., 2 in., 6 in.

✓4. 2 cm, 7 cm, 8 cm

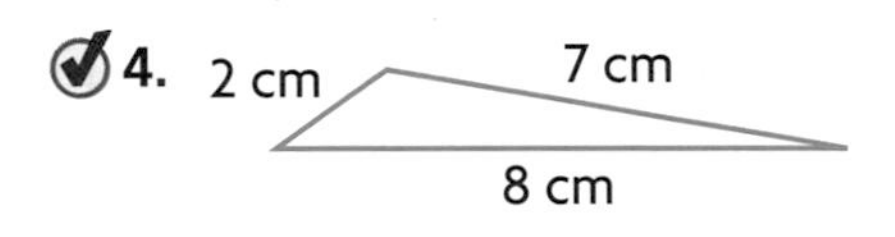

Classify each triangle. Write *acute, right,* or *obtuse*.

5.

6.

✓7.

8. TALK Math **Explain** the difference between an obtuse triangle and an acute triangle.

Independent Practice and Problem Solving

Classify each triangle. Write *isosceles*, *scalene*, or *equilateral*.

9. 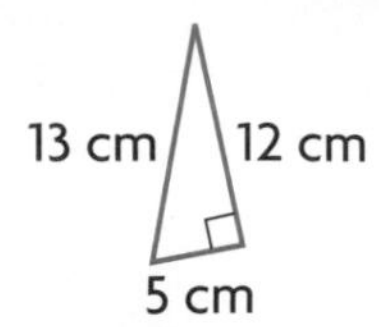

10. 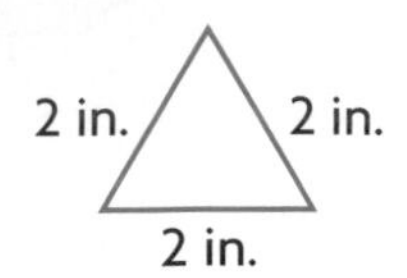

11. 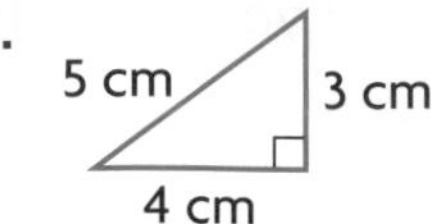

12. 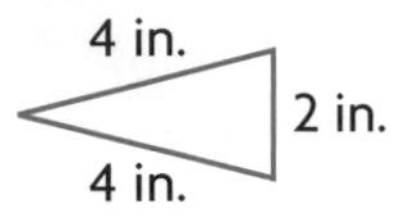

13. 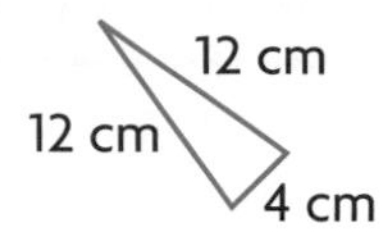

14. 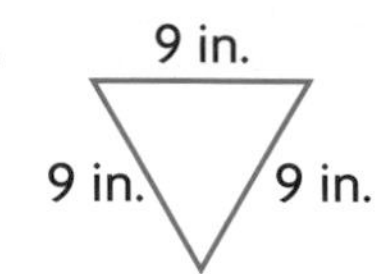

Classify each triangle. Write *acute, right,* or *obtuse*.

15. 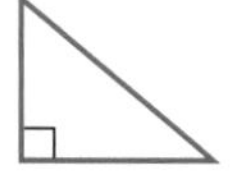

16. 

17. 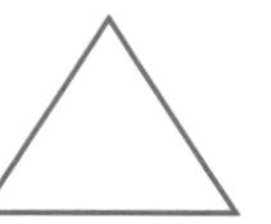

18. 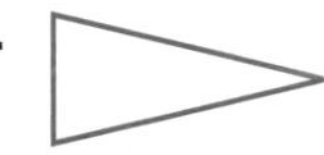

19. 

20. 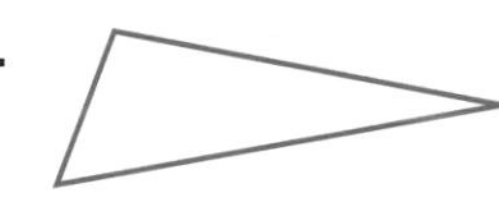

Algebra **Find the unknown angle measure for each triangle.**

21. 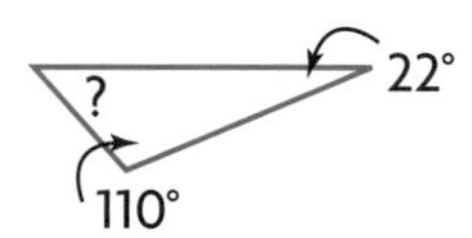

22. 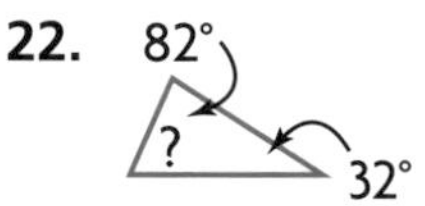

23. 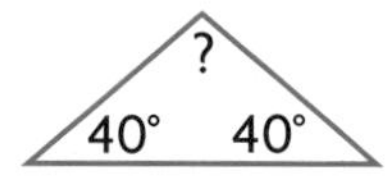

USE DATA **For 24–25, use the models of the sails.**

24. What type of triangle was the *Mayflower* sail?

25. What type of triangle was the *El Toro* sail?

26. Two of the angles in the *El Toro* lateen sail measure 83° and 64°. What is the measure of the third angle?

27. **Reasoning** Jade wants to draw a right triangle. She begins by drawing an angle that measures 70°. What are the measures of the other two angles Jade should draw?

28. **FAST FACT** The sides of a sail are 15 ft, 12 ft, and 9 ft. One of the angles of the sail is a right angle. Classify the triangular sail by the lengths of its sides and also by the measures of its angles.

29. **WRITE Math** **Explain** how an isosceles triangle can also be an acute triangle or an obtuse triangle.

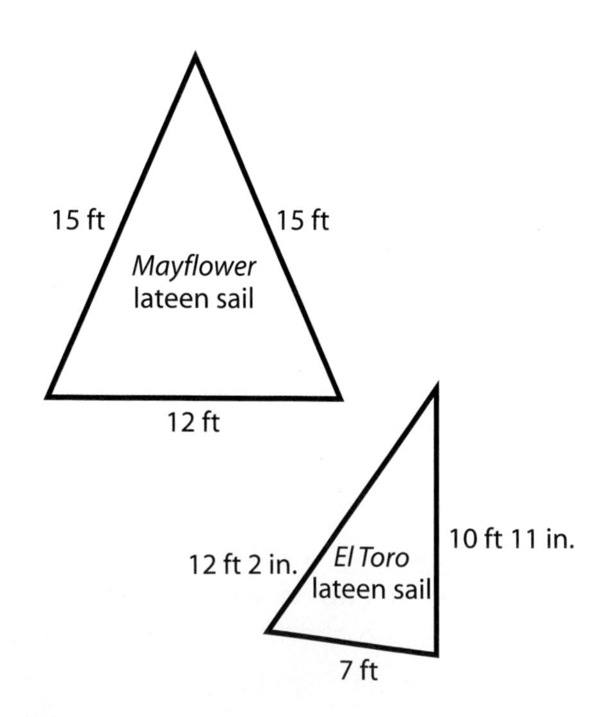

CD ROM **Technology**
Use Harcourt Mega Math, Ice Station Exploration, *Polar Planes*, Levels E, F.

 Extra Practice on page 490, Set A

Achieving the Standards

30. Estimate the difference between 39,346 and 26,844. (NS 1.1, p. 16)

31. Nellie drew a triangle with three equal sides. What kind of triangle did Nellie draw? (Grade 4 MG 3.7)

32. **Test Prep** The measure of two angles in a triangle is 150°. What is the measure of the third angle?

A 30°
B 35°
C 90°
D 210°

33. Find 70% of 480. (NS 1.2, p. 414)

34. **Test Prep** A picture frame has no congruent sides and 1 right angle. What type of triangle is the picture frame?

A rectangle
B acute and equilateral
C right and scalene
D obtuse and isosceles

Problem Solving and Reasoning

GEOMETRY You have learned how a triangle can be named by the lengths of its sides and by the measures of its angles. But can you have a triangle that is obtuse and isosceles? How about a triangle that is acute and isosceles? How about a triangle that is right and equilateral?

Examples

Use a geoboard to try to make the triangles in the questions above. If it is not possible to make the triangle, explain why.

A

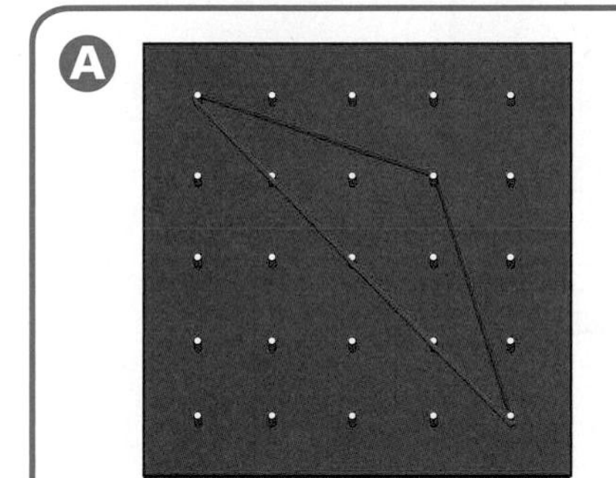

So, an obtuse isosceles triangle is possible.

B

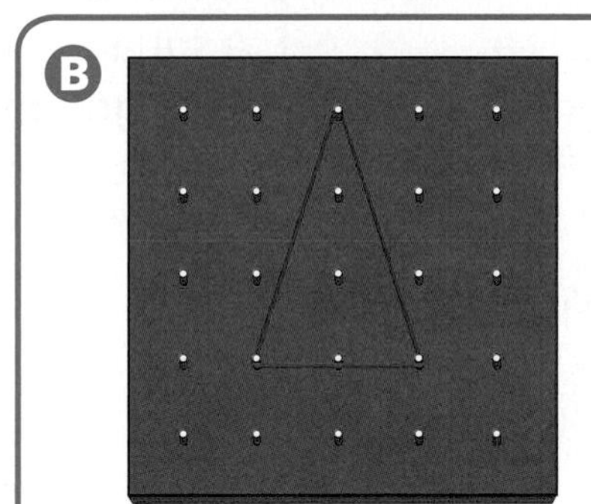

So, an acute isosceles triangle is possible.

An equilateral triangle has 3 congruent angles, and a right triangle has 1 angle that is 90°. It is not possible to have a triangle with three 90° angles.

So, a right equilateral triangle is not possible.

Use a geoboard to try to make each type of triangle. If it is not possible to make the triangle, explain why.

1. right scalene triangle
2. right isosceles triangle
3. obtuse scalene triangle
4. obtuse equilateral triangle

LESSON 2

Quadrilaterals

OBJECTIVE: Identify, describe, and classify quadrilaterals; find an unknown angle in a quadrilateral.

Quick Review

Sunny draws a pentagon. How many sides does the polygon have?

Vocabulary

trapezoid **parallelogram** **rhombus**

Learn

In a recent year, Amish quilts were featured in United States stamps. Quilts use many shapes, such as quadrilaterals, in their designs.

This quilt was made by an Amish quilt maker in Pennsylvania.

There are five special types of quadrilaterals. On the quadrilaterals below, the sides with the same number of slashes are congruent.

general quadrilateral	**trapezoid**	**parallelogram**
 A quadrilateral has 4 sides and 4 angles.	 A **trapezoid** has exactly 1 pair of parallel sides.	 A **parallelogram** has opposite sides parallel and congruent.
rectangle	**rhombus**	**square**
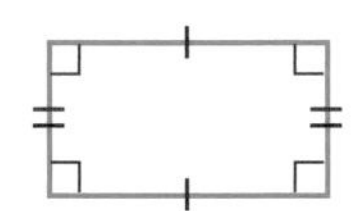 A rectangle has 4 right angles with opposite sides parallel and congruent.	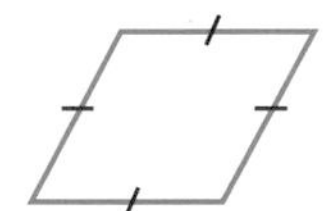 A **rhombus** is a parallelogram with 4 congruent sides. The plural of *rhombus* is *rhombi*.	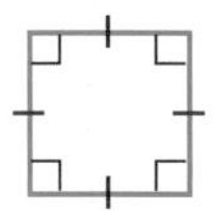 A square has 4 congruent sides and 4 right angles.

Example

Name the parallel and congruent sides. Then use the diagram to name the quadrilateral in as many ways as possible.

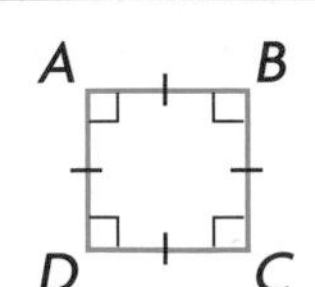

$\overline{AB}$ and $\overline{CD}$ are parallel; so are $\overline{AD}$ and $\overline{BC}$.
All angles are right angles.
Sides $\overline{AB}$, $\overline{BC}$, $\overline{CD}$, and $\overline{AD}$ are congruent.

Possible names: square, rectangle, rhombus, parallelogram, and quadrilateral

Quadrilaterals
Parallelogram
Trapezoid
Rectangle
Rhombus
Square

MG 2.2 Know that the sum of the angles of any triangle is 180° and the sum of the angles of any quadrilateral is 360° and use this information to solve problems *also* **MG 2.0, MR 2.3, MR 2.4, MR 3.2**

Find the Unknown Angle

In a quadrilateral, you can find the measure of an unknown angle if you know the measures of the other three angles.

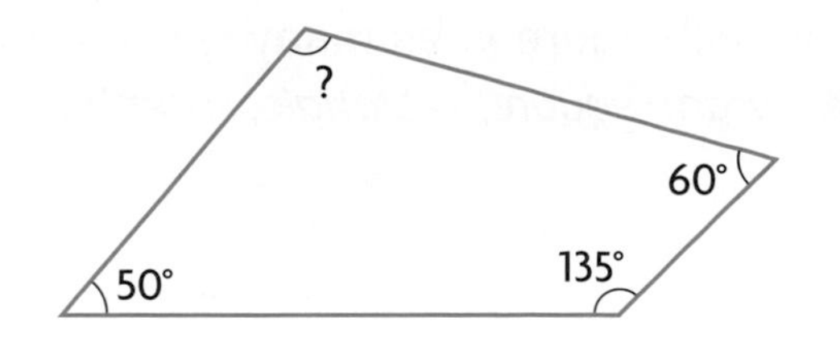

Example **What is the measure of the unknown angle in the quadrilateral above?**

Step 1	Step 2
Find the sum of the measures of the known angles. $50^\circ + 135^\circ + 60^\circ = 245^\circ$	Subtract the sum of the known angle measures from 360°. $360^\circ - 245^\circ = 115^\circ$

So, the measure of the unknown angle is 115°.

For any type of quadrilateral, you can find the measure of an unknown angle by subtracting the sum of the known angles from 360°.

Remember
The sum of the angles in a quadrilateral is always 360°.

More Examples

A rectangle

$90^\circ + 90^\circ + 90^\circ = 270^\circ$

$360^\circ - 270^\circ = 90^\circ$

B parallelogram

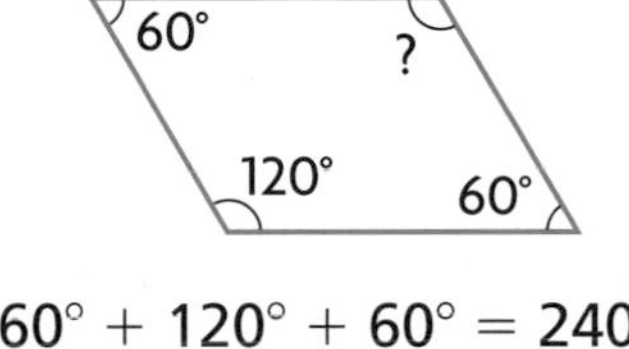

$60^\circ + 120^\circ + 60^\circ = 240^\circ$

$360^\circ - 240^\circ = 120^\circ$

C rhombus

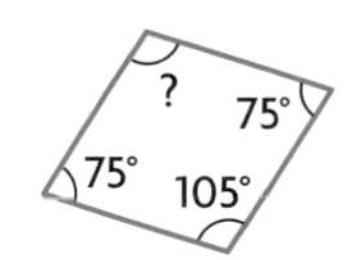

$75^\circ + 105^\circ + 75^\circ = 255^\circ$

$360^\circ - 255^\circ = 105^\circ$

- What is the measure of an unknown angle in a quadrilateral with angles that measure 105°, 75°, and 105°? What type of quadrilateral could it be? Draw a picture of each type.

Guided Practice

1. Copy the quadrilateral at the right.
   - Are any of the sides congruent? Mark the congruent sides. Then name them.
   - Does the quadrilateral have perpendicular sides? Name them.
   - Does the quadrilateral have parallel sides? Name them.
   - Which term best describes quadrilateral *STUV—trapezoid, parallelogram, rectangle, rhombus,* or *square*?

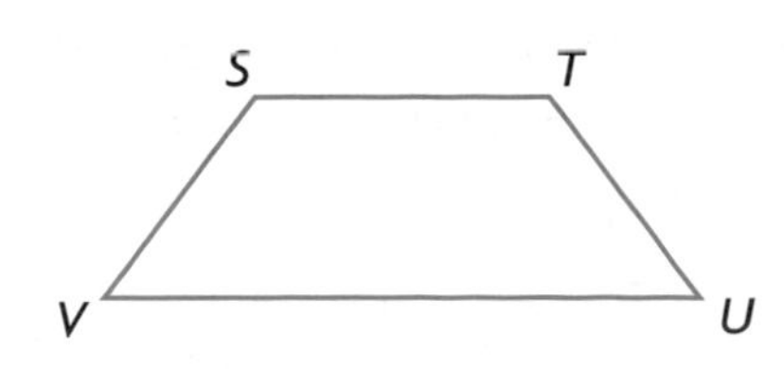

Classify each figure in as many ways as possible. Write *quadrilateral, parallelogram, square, rectangle, rhombus,* or *trapezoid*.

2. 

3. 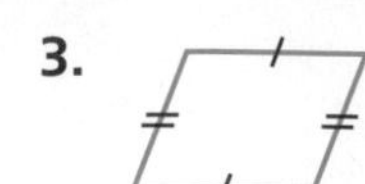

4. 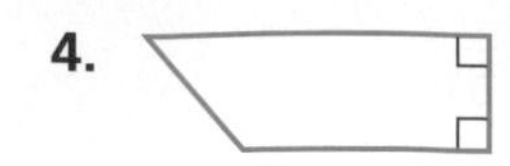

5. 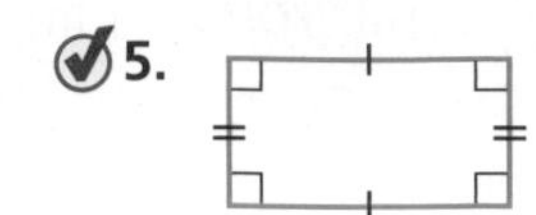

For each quadrilateral, name the parallel, perpendicular, and congruent sides.

6. 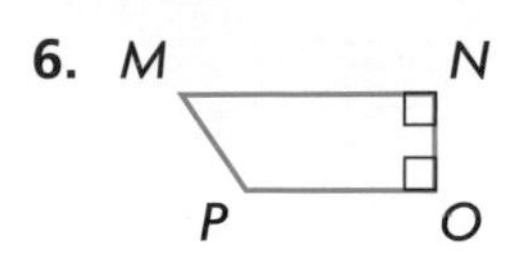

7. 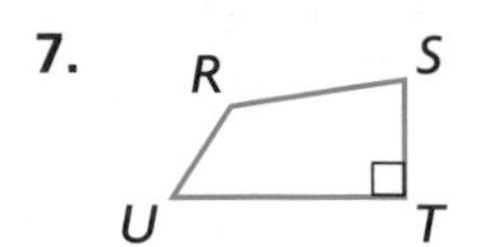

8. 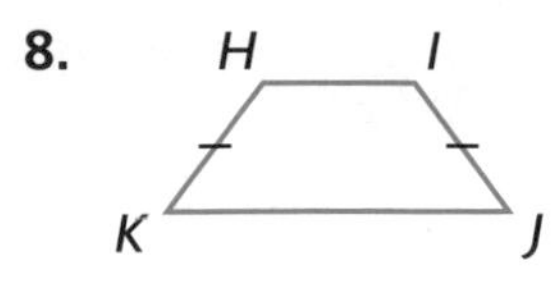

9. 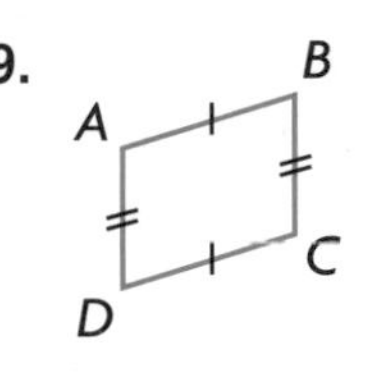

10. TALK Math **Explain** how a square and a rectangle are similar and how they are different.

Independent Practice and Problem Solving

Classify each figure in as many ways as possible. Write *quadrilateral, parallelogram, square, rectangle, rhombus,* or *trapezoid*.

11. 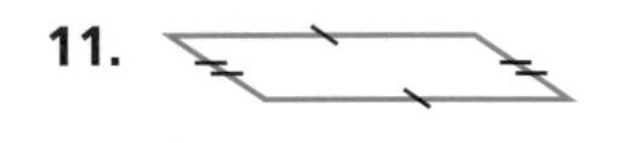

12. 

13. 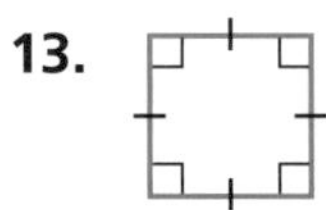

14. 

For each quadrilateral, name the *parallel, perpendicular,* and *congruent* sides.

15. 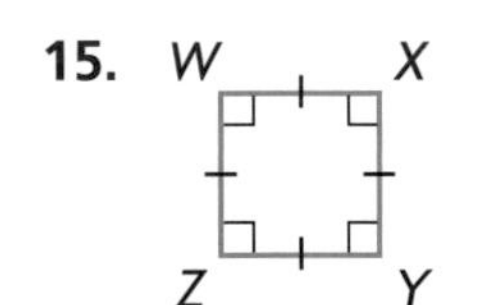

16. 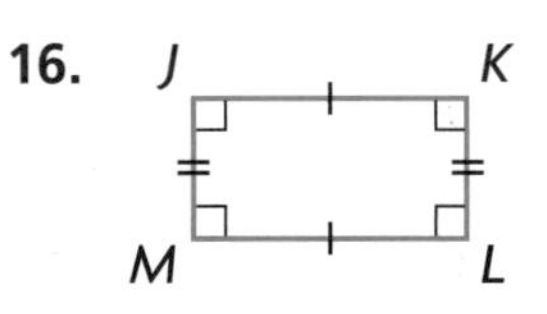

17. 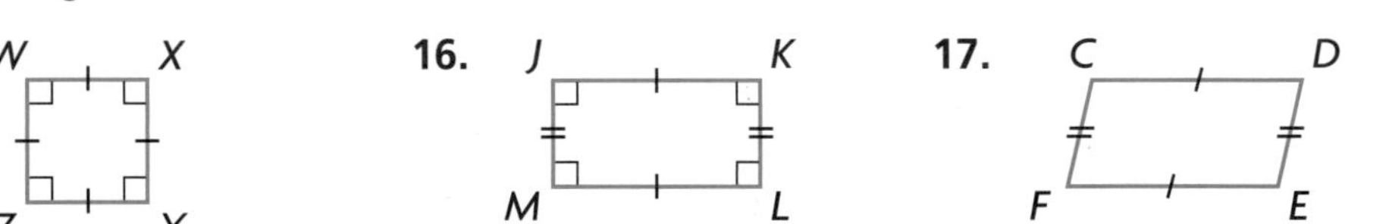

18. 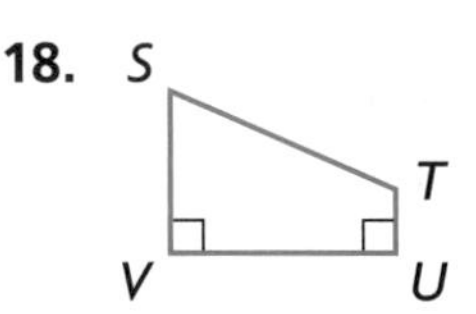

Algebra Find the unknown angle measure for each quadrilateral.

19. 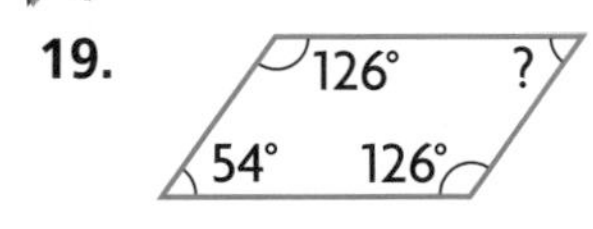

20. 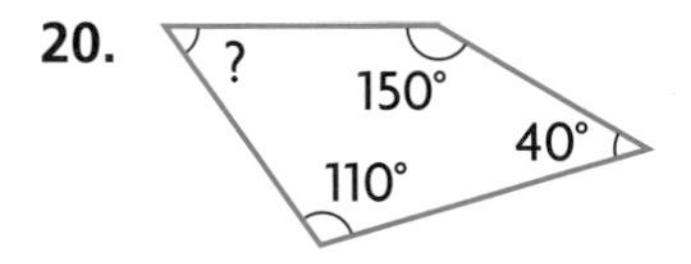

21. 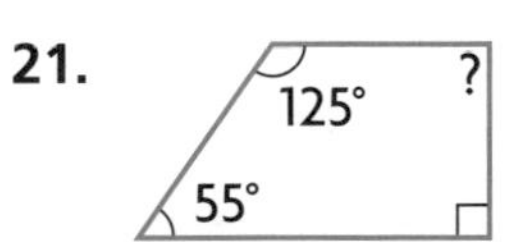

22. 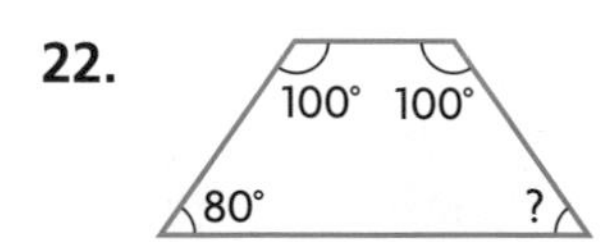

23. Draw and name a quadrilateral with 4 right angles and 2 pairs of congruent sides.

24. Reasoning Can you draw a quadrilateral that is both a rhombus and a rectangle? **Explain.**

25. Algebra All parallelograms have two pairs of congruent angles. If each angle in one pair is 48°, what is the measure of each of the unknown angles?

26. WRITE Math **Sense or Nonsense** The measure of an unknown angle in a quadrilateral always has to be equal to or less than 90°.

 Extra Practice on page 490, Set B

Achieving the Standards

27. Find the value of the expression $x \div 4$ for $x = 36$. (AF 1.2, p. 348)

28. Are the figures congruent, similar, or neither? (MG 2.0, p. 456)

29. How many faces does a rectangular prism have? (Grade 4 MG 3.6)

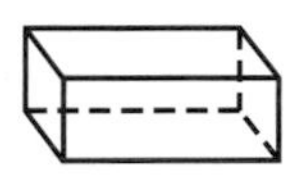

30. **Test Prep** A quadrilateral has 1 pair of parallel sides and no congruent sides. What type of quadrilateral is it?

A rectangle **C** parallelogram

B rhombus **D** trapezoid

31. **Test Prep** Cleo drew a quadrilateral with angles that measure 85°, 120°, and 70°. What is the measure of the third angle?

A 70° **C** 90°

D 85° **D** 120°

Problem Solving and Reasoning

LOGICAL REASONING The diagram on page 472 shows how quadrilaterals are related. The Venn diagram below is another way to show these relationships.

As you read the Venn diagram, think about how you could apply the words *always*, *sometimes*, and *never* to describe how the quadrilaterals are related to one another.

For example:

- A square is *always* a rectangle.
- A rectangle is *sometimes* a square.
- A rectangle is *never* a trapezoid.

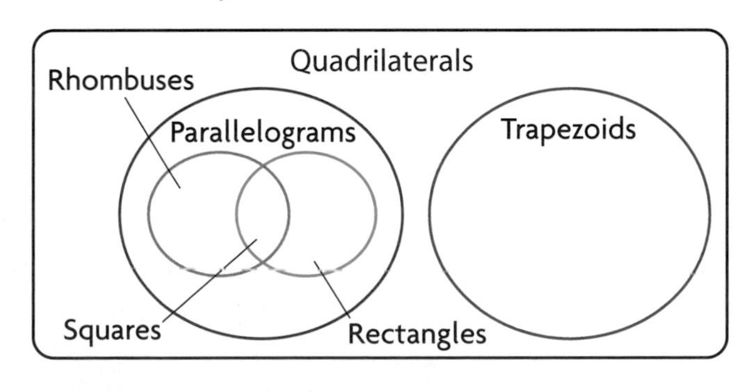

Complete. Write *always, sometimes,* or *never.*

1. A rhombus is ___?___ a square.
2. A trapezoid is ___?___ a parallelogram.
3. A parallelogram is ___?___ a rectangle.
4. A square is ___?___ a rhombus.
5. A rhombus is ___?___ a parallelogram.
6. A parallelogram is ___?___ a rectangle.

LESSON 3 HANDS ON

Draw Plane Figures

OBJECTIVE: Draw and identify triangles and quadrilaterals.

Quick Review

Classify each triangle or quadrilateral.

1. 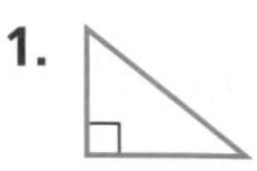

2. 

3. 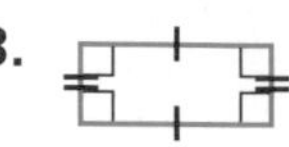

4. 

5. 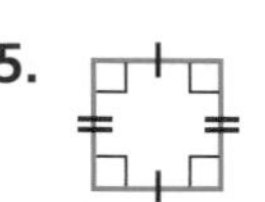

Investigate

Materials ■ straightedge ■ protractor

Draw triangle *ABC* so that it has two congruent sides and a right angle. Each congruent side should have a length of 2 inches.

A Use the protractor to draw a 90° angle. Mark a point at the vertex, and label the point *A*.

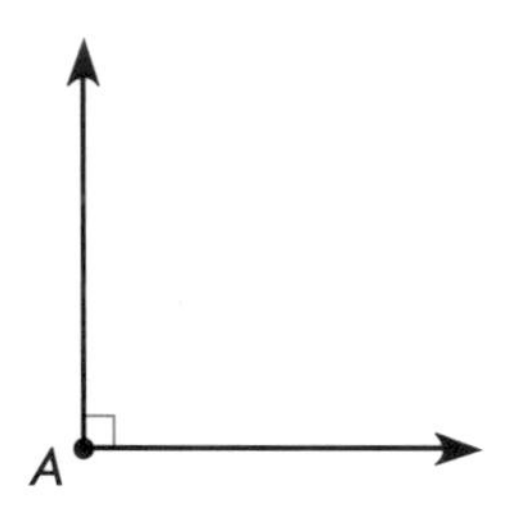

B Measure 2 inches from *A* along one of the rays, and mark a point. Label the point *B*.

C To draw the congruent side, measure 2 inches from *A* along the other ray, and mark a point. Label the point *C*.

D Draw a line to connect points *B* and *C*.

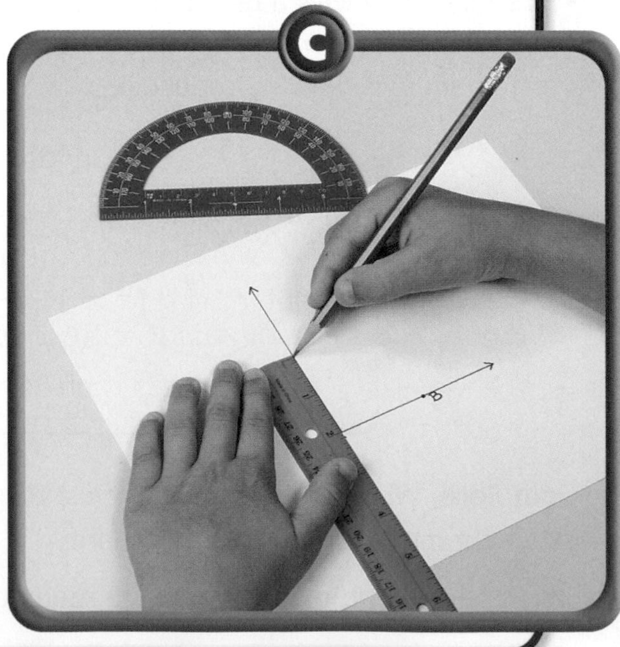

Draw Conclusions

1. What type of triangle is triangle *ABC*?
2. What is the measure of $\angle B$?
3. Without measuring, explain whether $\angle C$ is congruent to $\angle B$.
4. **Comprehension** Describe how you would draw a triangle with congruent angles and congruent sides.

MG 2.1 Measure, identify, and draw angles, perpendicular and parallel lines, rectangles, and triangles by using appropriate tools (e.g., straightedge, ruler, compass, protractor, drawing software) *also* **MG 2.0, MR 2.0, MR 2.3, MR 2.4**

Connect

You can use a ruler and a protractor to draw a quadrilateral.

Draw quadrilateral *ABCD* so that it has two pairs of parallel and congruent sides measuring 3 inches and 4 inches. One pair of congruent angles should measure 40°, and the other pair of congruent angles should measure 140°.

Step 1

Use a protractor to draw a 40° angle. Mark a point at the vertex, and label the point *A*. Measure 4 inches from *A* along one of the rays. Mark a point, and label the point *B*.

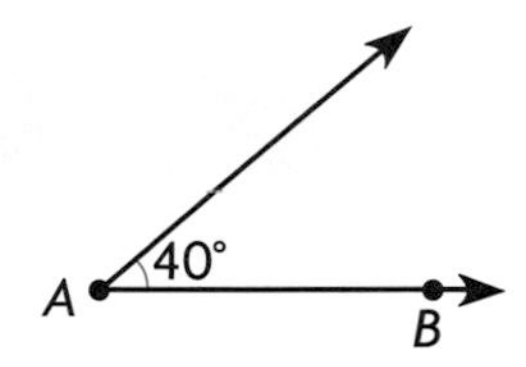

Step 2

Measure 3 inches from *A* along the other ray. Mark a point, and label the point *D*. At point *B*, measure a 140° angle and draw a ray.

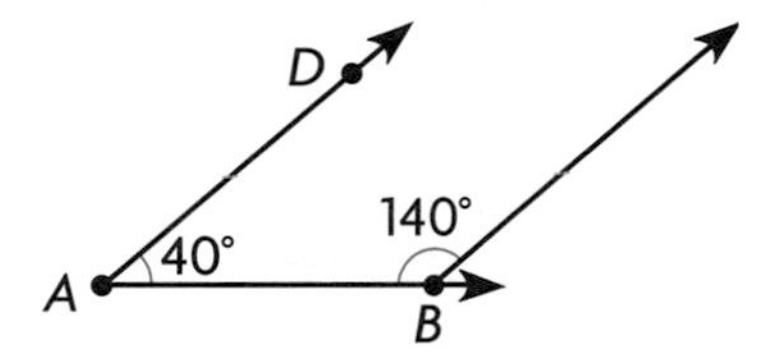

Step 3

Measure 3 inches along the ray from point *B*. Mark a point, and label the point *C*.

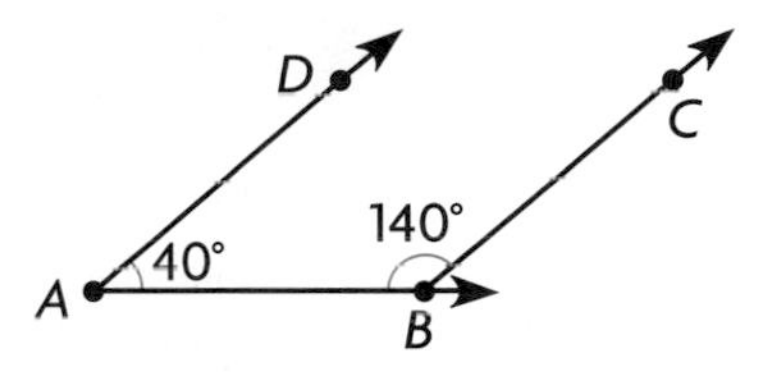

Step 4

Connect points *C* and *D*. Check the measure of angles *C* and *D*.

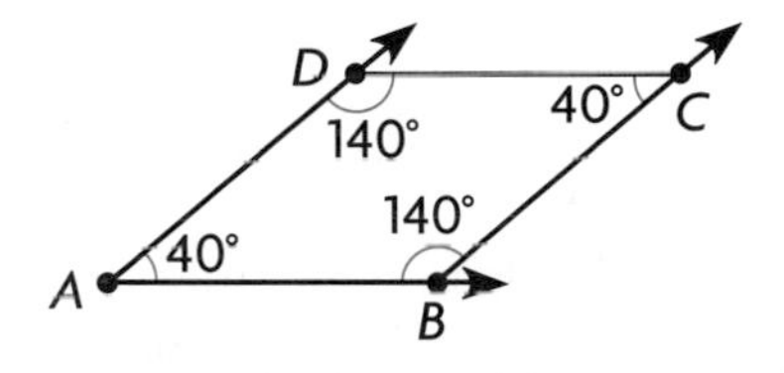

TALK Math

Classify the quadrilateral you drew. **Explain** how you identified it.

Practice

Use a protractor and a ruler to draw each figure. Classify each figure by writing the name that best describes it.

1. a triangle with angles measuring 20°, 110°, 50°; no congruent sides

2. a quadrilateral with 4 right angles; 4 congruent sides each measuring 1 inch

3. **WRITE Math** **Explain** how you would use a ruler and a protractor to draw a rectangle.

LESSON 4

Solid Figures

OBJECTIVE: Identify, describe, and classify solid figures.

Quick Review

Name each figure.

1. (triangle) 2. (pentagon) 3. (hexagon)
4. (rectangle) 5. (square)

Vocabulary

polyhedron prism
base pyramid

Learn

A **polyhedron** is a solid figure with flat faces that are polygons. Prisms and pyramids are polyhedrons.

A **prism** has two congruent and parallel polygons as **bases**. All the other faces in a prism are rectangles. A prism is named for the shape of its bases. A cube is a special rectangular prism.

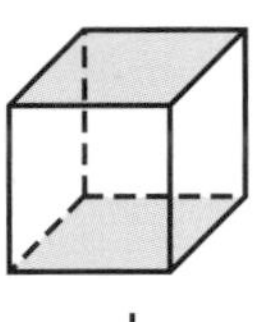
cube

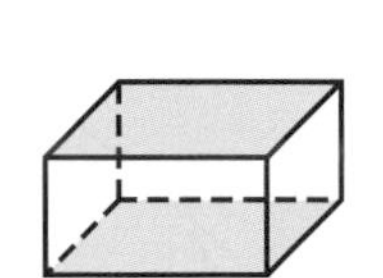
rectangular prism

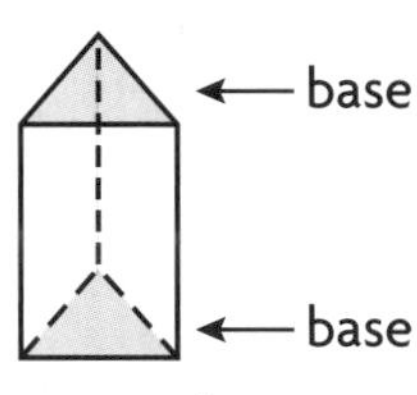

triangular prism

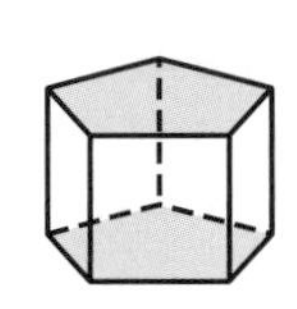
pentagonal prism

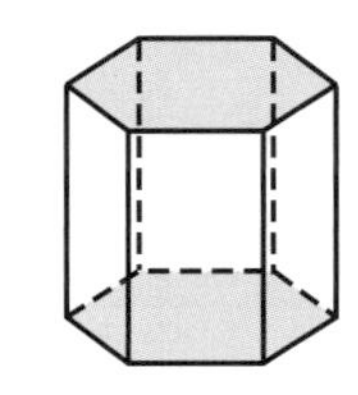
hexagonal prism

▲ The John F. Kennedy Library in Massachusetts suggests different solid figures in its design.

A **pyramid** is a polyhedron with only one base. All the other faces are triangles that meet at a common vertex. The shape of its base names the pyramid.

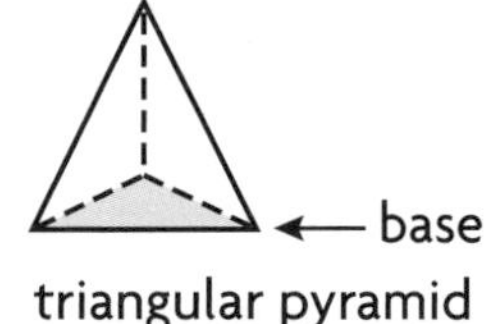

triangular pyramid

square pyramid

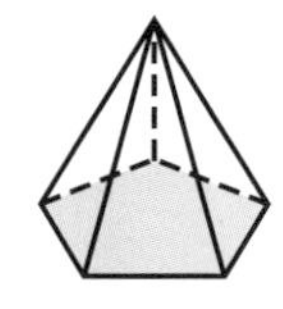
pentagonal pyramid

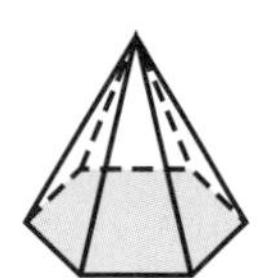
hexagonal pyramid

Some solid figures have curved surfaces. These solid figures are *not* polyhedrons.

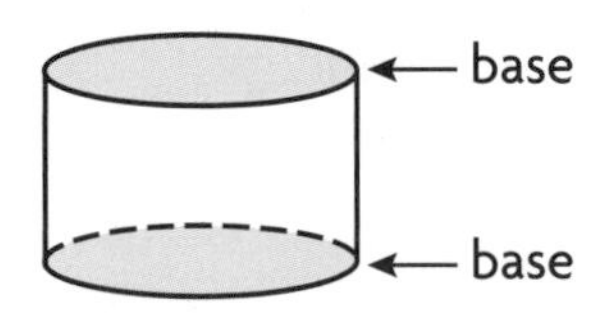

A **cylinder** has 2 congruent circular bases and 1 curved surface.

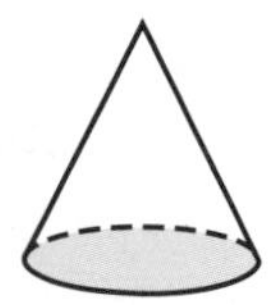

A **cone** has 1 circular base and 1 curved surface.

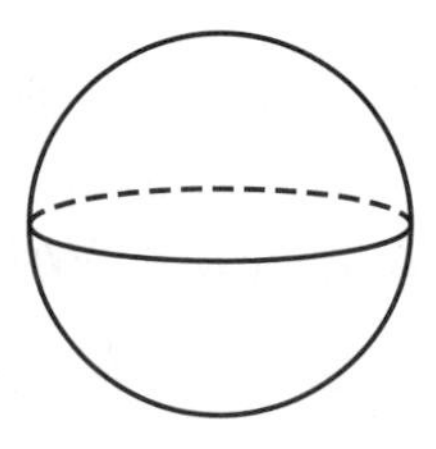

A **sphere** has no base and 1 curved surface.

MG 2.0 Students identify, describe, and classify the properties of, and the relationships between, plane and solid geometric figures. *also* **MR 2.3, MR 2.4, MR 3.2**

Faces, Edges, and Vertices

Solid figures can be classified by the shape and the number of their bases, faces, edges, and vertices.

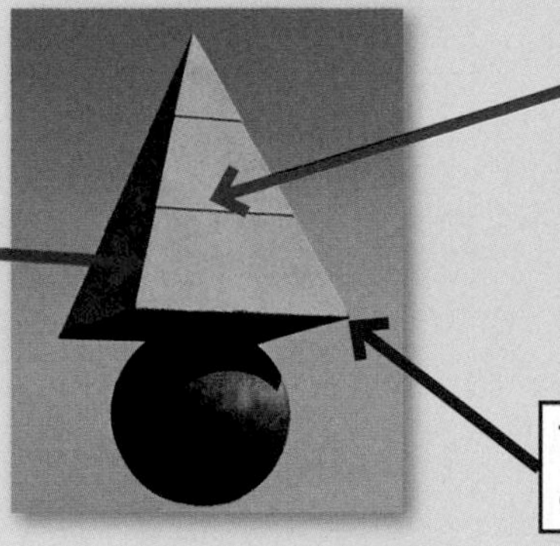

The line where two faces meet is an **edge**.

All the flat surfaces are called **faces**.

The point where several edges meet is a **vertex**.

Examples

If the figure is a polyhedron, identify the number of faces, vertices, and edges. Then classify each solid figure.

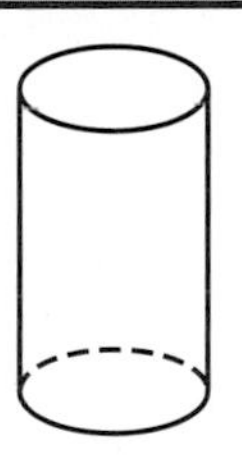

This figure has 2 circular bases. It is *not* a polyhedron.

Classify: cylinder

B

This figure has a triangular base.

Faces: 4 **Vertices:** 4
Edges: 6

Classify: triangular pyramid

C

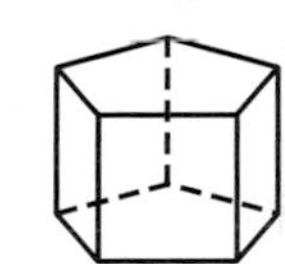

This figure has 2 pentagonal bases.

Faces: 7 **Vertices:** 10
Edges: 15

Classify: pentagonal prism

Guided Practice

Match each statement with the correct solid figure. Then, name each figure.

a 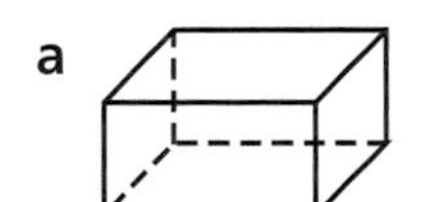 b  c 

1. A polyhedron that has 2 congruent polygons as bases
2. A polyhedron with only one base
3. A solid figure with 1 circular base and 1 curved surface

Classify each solid figure. Write *prism, pyramid, cone, cylinder,* or *sphere*.

4. 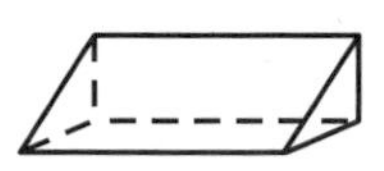
5. 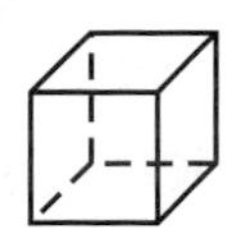
6. 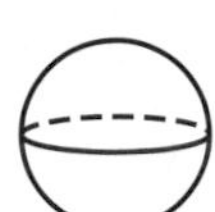
7. 

8. **TALK Math** **Compare** a prism and a pyramid. Tell how they are similar and how they are different.

Extra Practice on page 490, Set C

Independent Practice and Problem Solving

Classify each solid figure. Write *prism, pyramid, cone, cylinder,* or *sphere*.

9. 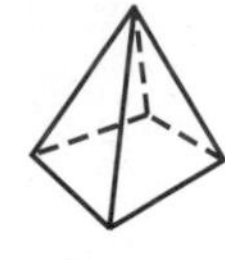

10. 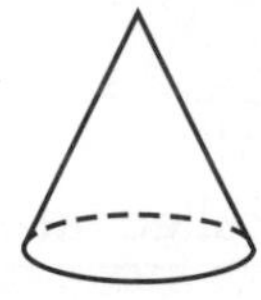

11. 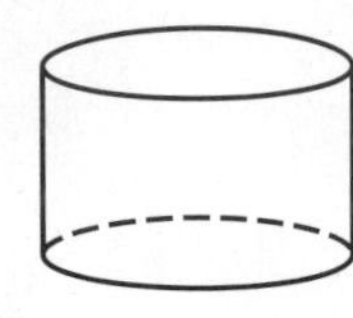

12. 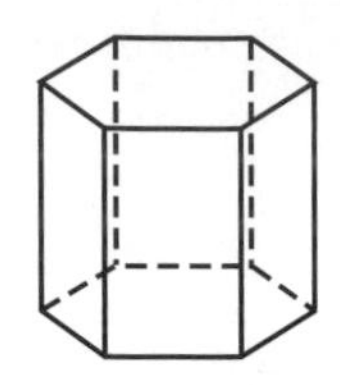

Write the number of faces, edges, and vertices. Then classify each solid figure.

13. 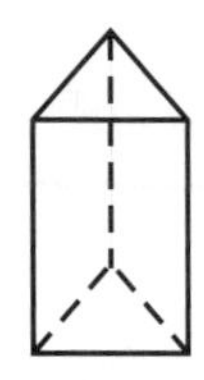

14. 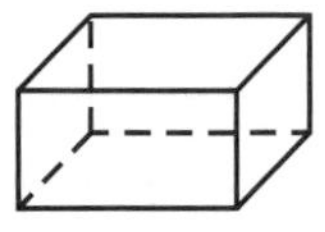

15. 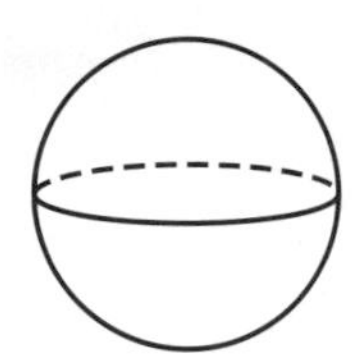

16. 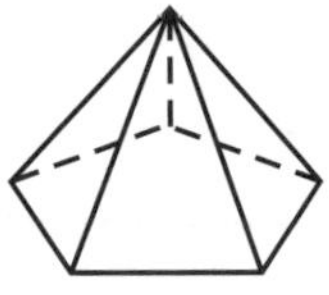

For 17–20, use the photo at the right.

17. What shape is suggested by the floor of the arena?
18. What shape is suggested by the outside walls of the arena?
19. How many faces, edges, and vertices does the arena have?
20. What kind of solid figure does the arena suggest?
21. ***FAST FACT*** The arena has congruent faces that are triangles. Each side of the base is 180 meters wide. The arena is 98 meters tall. What is the distance around the base of the arena?
22. **WRITE Math** **What's the Error?** Margo says that any polyhedron can be named if you know the number of faces it has. Describe Margo's error.

This arena in Memphis, Tennessee, has a square base.

Achieving the Standards

23. Marisol bought 6 postcards for $0.65 each. How much in all did Marisol spend on the postcards? (NS 2.1, p. 300)
24. $4\frac{2}{5} + 1\frac{3}{7} =$ (NS 2.3, p. 224)
25. What plane figures make up the faces of a square pyramid? (Grade 4 MG 3.6)
26. **Test Prep** Len has a block with 2 bases and 7 faces. Which solid figure is the block?
    - **A** rectangular prism
    - **B** cylinder
    - **C** hexagonal pyramid
    - **D** pentagonal prism

READ Math WORKSHOP

A City's Water

Classify and Categorize

In the late 1800s, the city of Boston built the Chestnut Hill Pumping Station. This is how the growing city got its drinking water. Large pumps inside the station pumped water from two nearby reservoirs. Reservoirs are places where water is stored.

How would you classify and categorize the solid figures you see in the Chestnut Hill Pumping Station building?

You can classify and categorize the information given in a problem to help you solve it. When you classify and categorize, you

- identify the items you want to classify.
- select an important item in the group.
- identify other items in the group that are like it and other items that are not like it.
- state a rule that describes the categories all the items belong in.

▲ The Chestnut Hill station also had a public park. People could ride around the reservoir in carriages.

Problem Solving **Classify and categorize to understand each problem.**

1. Answer the question above.

2. Use different types of solid figures to design and draw your own building.

LESSON 5

Nets for Solid Figures

OBJECTIVE: Identify and make nets for solid figures.

Quick Review

Name each polygon.

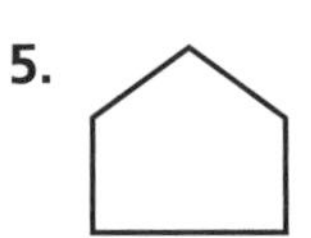

Vocabulary

net

Learn

The wooden crate is a cube. You can make a model of this crate by making and folding a net. A **net** is a two-dimensional pattern that can be folded into a three-dimensional polyhedron.

Activity

Materials ■ 1-inch grid paper ■ scissors ■ tape

A cube has 6 congruent square faces.

Step 1

Draw the net on grid paper. Cut it out.

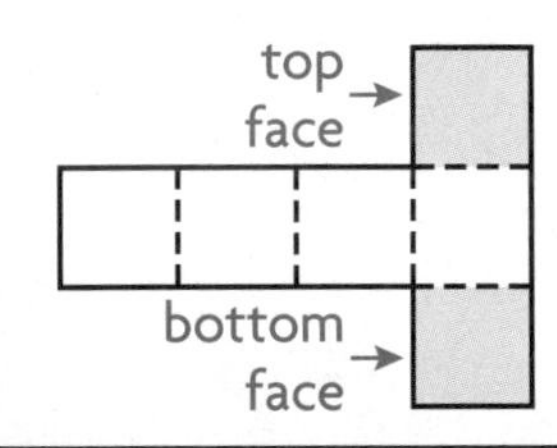

Step 2

Fold along the dashed lines.

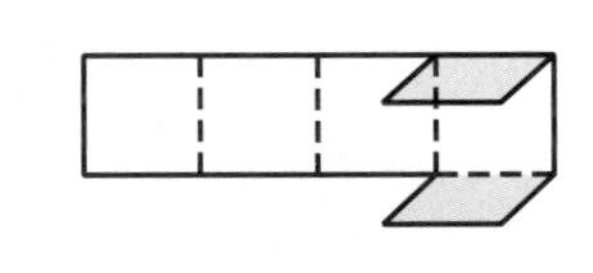

Step 3

Tape the edges together. Be sure there are no gaps and that none of the sides overlap.

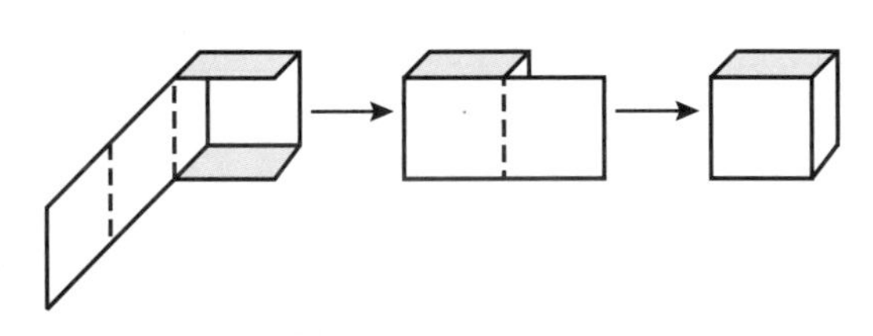

Examples

Name the solid figure that can be made by folding the net.

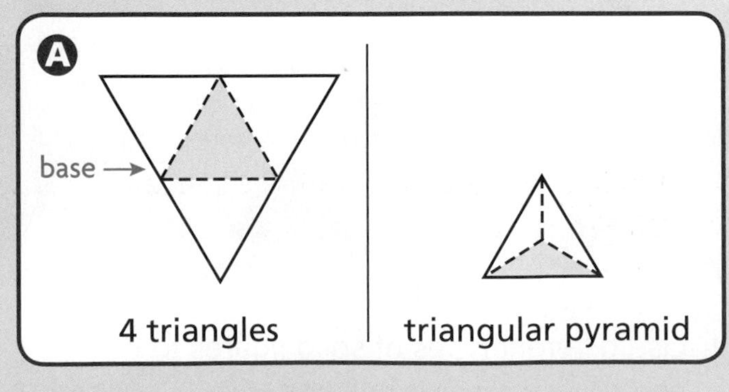

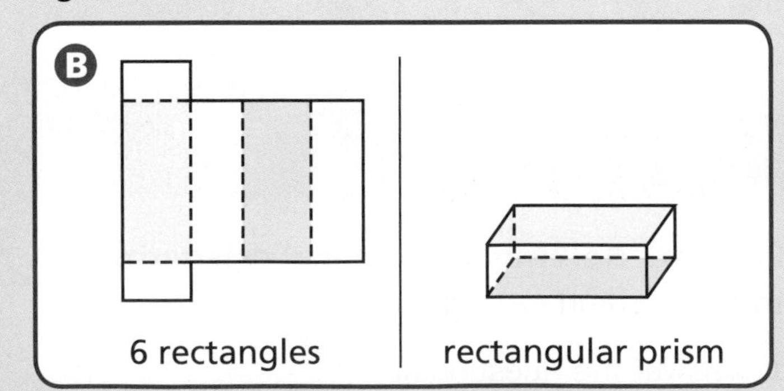

- **Explain** how identifying the shapes in a net can help you identify the solid figure that may be made by folding the net.

MG 1.2 Construct a cube and rectangular box from two-dimensional patterns and use these patterns to compute the surface area for these objects. *also* **MG 2.0, MR 2.0, MR 2.3, MR 2.4, MR 3.2**

Guided Practice

Match each solid figure with its net.

1. 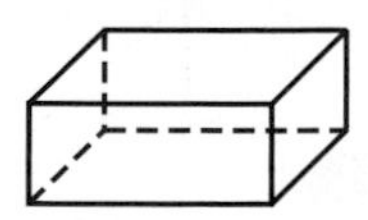

2. 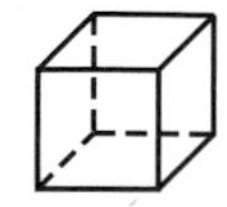

✓3. 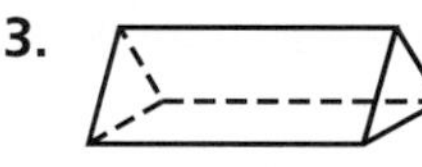

✓4. 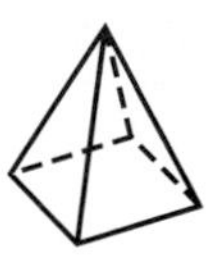

a 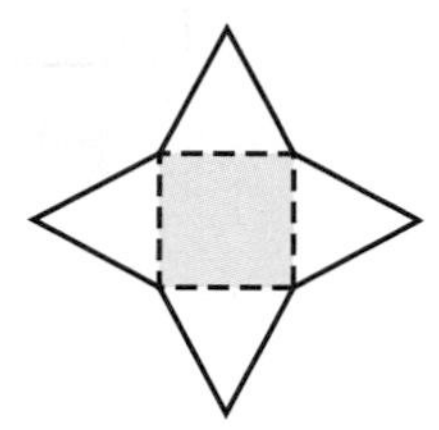

b 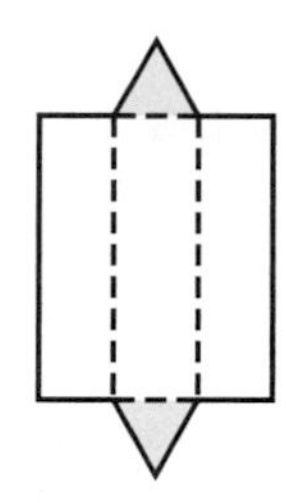

c 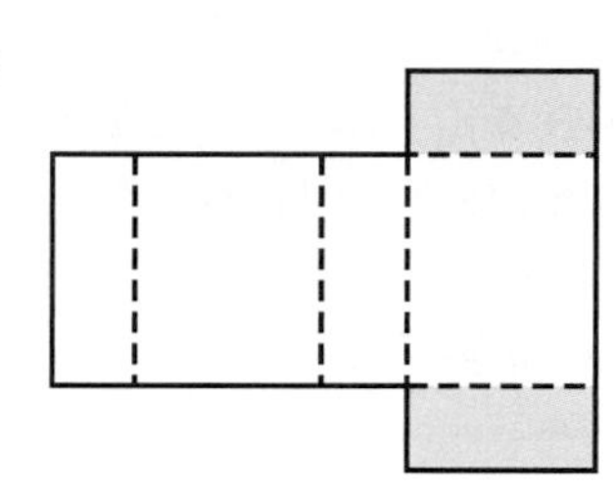

d 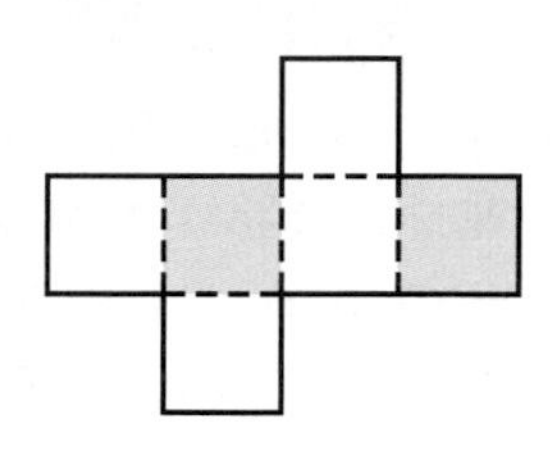

5. **TALK Math** What shapes will always appear in a net for a triangular prism? **Explain.**

Independent Practice and Problem Solving

Match each solid figure with its net.

6. 

7. 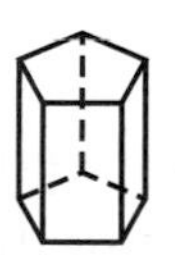

8. 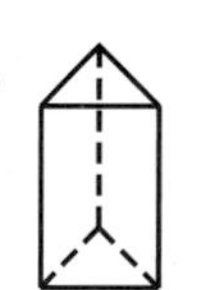

9. 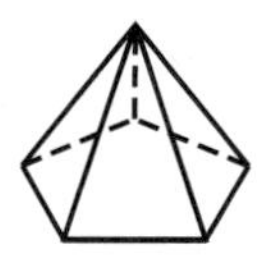

a 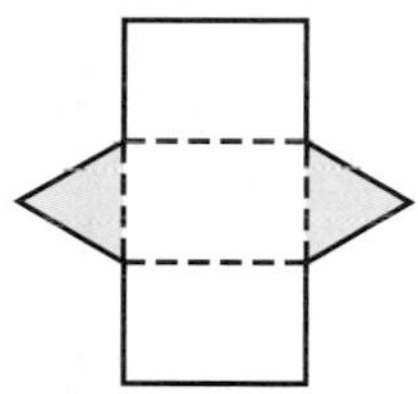

b 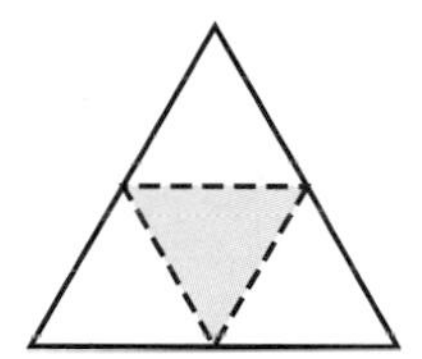

c 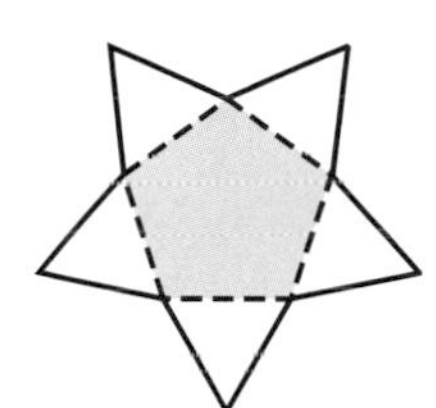

d 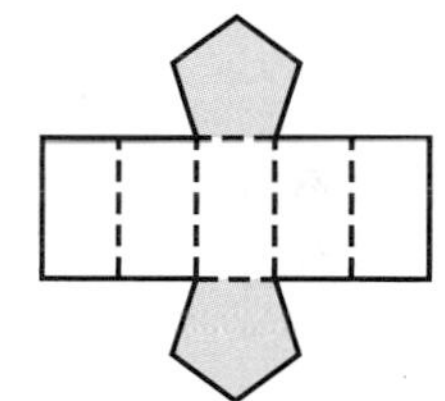

10. **WRITE Math** Copy the net at the right. Then cut it out and try to fold it to make a cube. **Explain** why the net cannot be folded to form a cube.

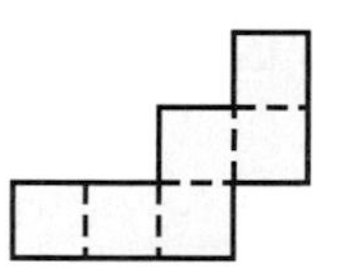

Achieving the Standards

11. What is the mode of the set of data? (Grade 4 SDAP 1.2)

    12, 10, 11, 12, 15, 9

12. $1\frac{1}{8} + 2\frac{3}{4} =$
    (O‑π NS 2.3, p. 224)

13. What is the value of h in the equation $27 \times h = 135$? (O‑π AF 1.2, p. 354)

14. **Test Prep** How many triangles does the net for a triangular pyramid contain?

    A 2 **B** 3 **C** 4 **D** 5

Extra Practice on page 490, Set D

Problem Solving Workshop
Strategy: Solve a Simpler Problem

OBJECTIVE: Solve problems by using the strategy *solve a simpler problem.*

Learn the Strategy

You can use the strategy *solve a simpler problem* to solve problems that might, at first, seem too difficult to solve. To solve a simpler problem, think about ways to use easier numbers, break a problem into simpler parts, or find a relationship.

To solve a simpler problem, use easier numbers for computing.

Some gardeners planted $\frac{3}{5}$ of 35,000 seeds on Tuesday. How many seeds did they plant?

A simpler problem is to find $\frac{3}{5}$ of 35. Then find the actual number of seeds planted by multiplying the answer by 1,000.

Break the problem into parts to solve a simpler problem.

Find the area of the figure below.

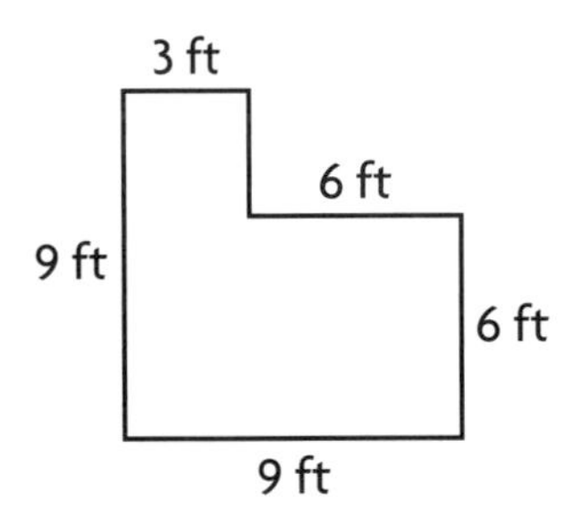

A simpler problem is to find the area of each of the parts and then add to find the total area.

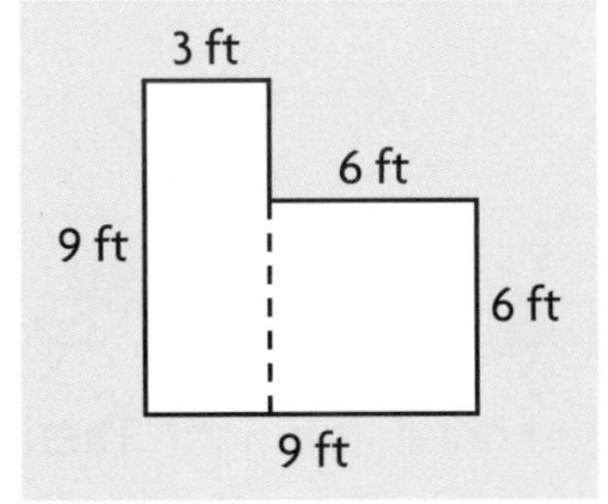

Find a relationship to solve a simpler problem.

How many edges and vertices are there in a prism with a 12-sided base?

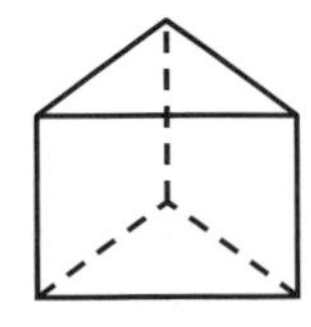

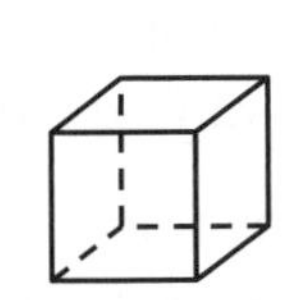

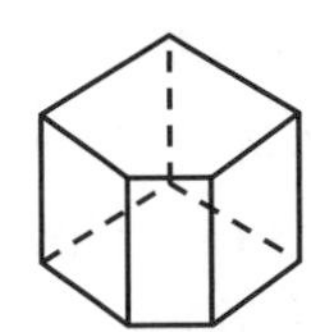

A simpler problem is to find a relationship of the numbers of vertices and edges of prisms whose bases have 3, 4, and 5 sides.

Sides on a Base	3	4	5
Vertices	6	8	10
Edges	9	12	15

TALK Math

How does solving a simpler problem help you solve a problem?

MG 2.0 Students identify, describe, and classify the properties of, and the relationships between, plane and solid geometric figures. *also* **MR 1.0, MR 1.1, MR 1.2, MR 2.0, MR 2.2, MR 2.3, MR 2.4, MR 3.0, MR 3.2, MR 3.3**

Use the Strategy

PROBLEM Randall wants to make a model of an octagonal pyramid. He already has models of a triangular, a square, and a pentagonal pyramid. If Randall uses balls of clay for the vertices and straws for the edges, how many balls of clay and straws will he need to make an octagonal pyramid?

Read to Understand

- Visualize what you are asked to find.
- What information is given?

Triangular pyramid	Square pyramid	Pentagonal pyramid
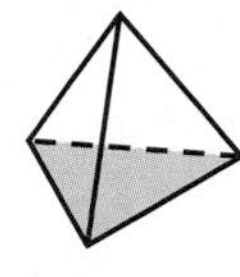	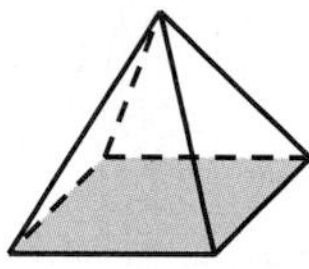	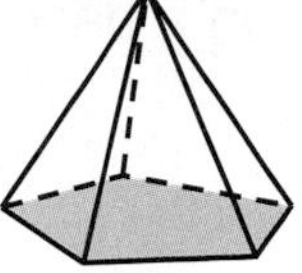

Plan

- **What strategy can you use to solve the problem?**
  You can use the strategy *solve a simpler problem*.

Solve

- **How can you use the strategy to solve the problem?**
  Find the number of vertices and edges in a triangular, a square, and a pentagonal pyramid.

Sides on a Base	3	4	5
Faces	$3 + 1 = 4$	$4 + 1 = 5$	$5 + 1 = 6$
Vertices	$4 + 1 = 4$	$4 + 1 = 5$	$5 + 1 = 6$
Edges	$3 + 3 = 6$	$4 + 4 = 8$	$5 + 5 = 10$

Then look for a relationship you can use to find the number of vertices and edges in an octagonal pyramid.

Sides on a Base	n	8
Faces	$n + 1$	$8 + 1 = 9$
Vertices	$n + 1$	$8 + 1 = 9$
Edges	$2n$	$2 \times 8 = 16$

The number of faces is 1 more than the number of sides on a base.
The number of vertices is 1 more than the number of sides on a base.
The number of edges is twice the number of sides on a base.

An octagonal pyramid has 9 faces, 9 vertices, and 16 edges. So, Randall will need 9 balls of clay and 16 straws.

Check

- **How can you check your answer?**

Guided Problem Solving

1. Angela is going to make a model of a building frame by using toothpicks for edges and small foam balls for the vertices. Before she makes the model, she needs to make sure she has enough foam balls. If she is going to build a hexagonal prism, how many foam balls and how many toothpicks does she need?

   First, organize the information.

   Next, look for a relationship by looking at prisms with fewer sides on a base.

Sides on a Base	3	4	5	n
Vertices	$3 + 3 = 6$	$4 + 4 = 8$	$5 + 5 = 10$	$2 \times n$
Edges	$3 + 3 + 3 = 9$	$4 + 4 + 4 = 12$	$5 + 5 + 5 = 15$	$3 \times n$
Faces	$3 + 2 = 5$	$4 + 2 = 6$	$5 + 2 = 7$	$n + 2$

   Last, find the total number of vertices and edges needed to make a hexagonal prism.

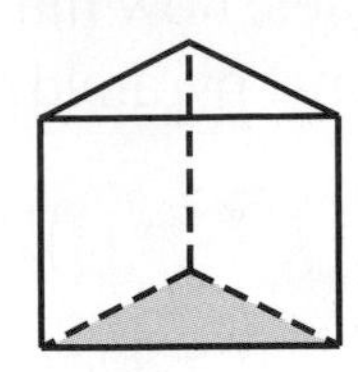
Triangular prism

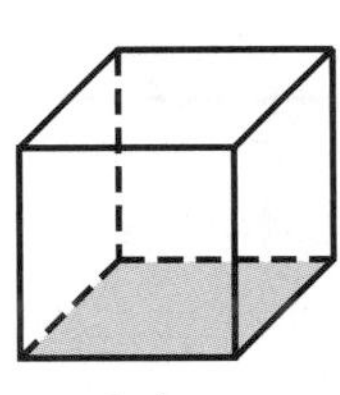
Cube

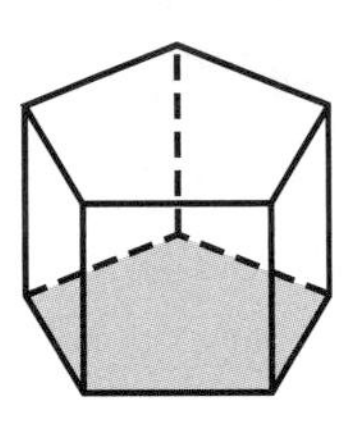
Pentagonal prism

2. **What if** Russell wanted to use paper to cover each of the faces of the hexagonal prism in Exercise 1? How many faces would he need to cover?

3. Sharon has measured a castle to be 250 feet high. If her apartment building is $\frac{3}{5}$ as tall, how tall is Sharon's apartment building?

Problem Solving Strategy Practice

Solve a simpler problem to solve.

4. Juan designed an office building in the shape of a hexagonal pyramid. How many triangular faces does this building have?

5. Fevi paints all of the inside and outside walls, except for one, of an octagonal prism barn. If each wall requires 38 gallons of paint, how many gallons of paint will Fevi need?

6. Stephanie and Penny both walk to work. Penny has to walk 6,000 feet to get to work. Stephanie lives $\frac{2}{3}$ as far away from the office as Penny does. How far does Stephanie have to walk to get to work?

7. WRITE Math There are three office buildings on Main Street. The first building is 12,000 feet from the second building. The distance between the second and third buildings is $\frac{5}{6}$ the distance between the first and the second buildings. **Explain** how to find the distance between the second and third buildings.

Mixed Strategy Practice

USE DATA For 8–10, use the data in the diagram.

8. Cathy is designing a new bridge. It will be as tall and as wide as the George Washington Bridge shown below, but it will be only $\frac{3}{5}$ as long. What is the length of the bridge Cathy is designing?

9. **Pose a Problem** Look back at problem 8. Write and solve a similar problem by changing the relationship of the dimensions of the new bridge to the George Washington Bridge.

10. Claire walked across the George Washington Bridge and back. Write and solve an equation that describes how far she walked.

11. A quadrilateral has angle measures of 120°, 60°, and 40°. What is the measure of the fourth angle?

12. Bob has planted flowers around the perimeter of a rectangular garden. On the short sides, he planted 19 flowers 1 foot apart. On the long sides, he planted 98 flowers 1 foot apart. How many flowers in all did Bob plant?

13. **Open Ended** Kathy made a cardboard model of a rectangular prism building with the following dimensions: 2 inches by 3 inches by 5 inches. Can you make more than one net for the same rectangular prism? Draw a sketch to **explain.**

Choose a STRATEGY

- Draw a Diagram
- Make a Model
- Make an Organized List
- Look for a Pattern
- Make a Table or Graph
- Guess and Check
- Work Backward
- Solve a Simpler Problem
- Write an Equation
- Use Logical Reasoning

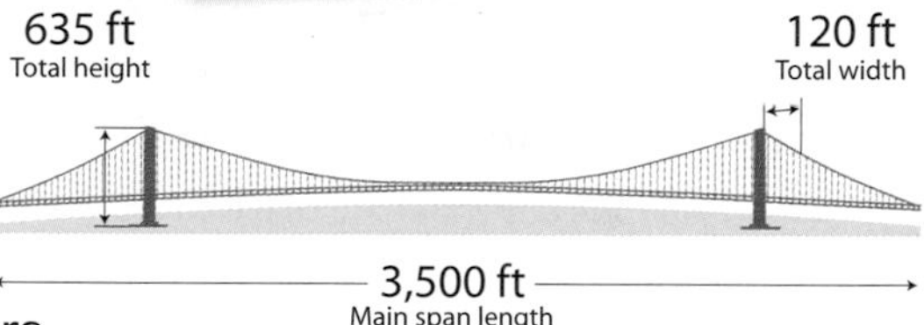

CHALLENGE YOURSELF

The Secrest Octagonal barn in Downey, Iowa, has stalls for 32 horses and 16 cows, and room for 200 tons of hay.

14. A farmer feeds hay to the cows and horses by opening the four hay chutes and unloading the hay from the loft to the stalls below. Assuming that hay from each chute feeds an equal number of horses and cows, how many horses and cows could receive hay from each chute?

15. Each of the eight walls of the barn is $28\frac{1}{4}$ feet wide and $27\frac{1}{2}$ feet high. What is the area of each wall? Assuming the barn is a regular octagon, what is the area of all eight walls?

LESSON HANDS ON

7 Draw Solid Figures from Different Views

OBJECTIVE: Visualize and draw two-dimensional views of three-dimensional objects.

Quick Review

Identify the solid figure that has the base or bases described.

1. 2 circles
2. 1 square
3. 1 circle
4. 2 squares
5. 2 rectangles

Investigate

Materials ■ grid paper ■ tape ■ connecting cubes

When you look at solid figures from the top, front, and side, you see different two-dimensional figures.

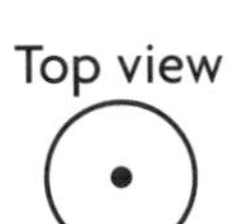

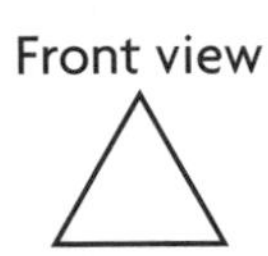

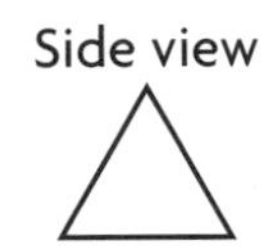

Copy the net shown below onto grid paper, and cut it out. Then fold the net, and tape the edges to make a rectangular prism.

A Look at the top of your rectangular prism, and draw the top view on grid paper.

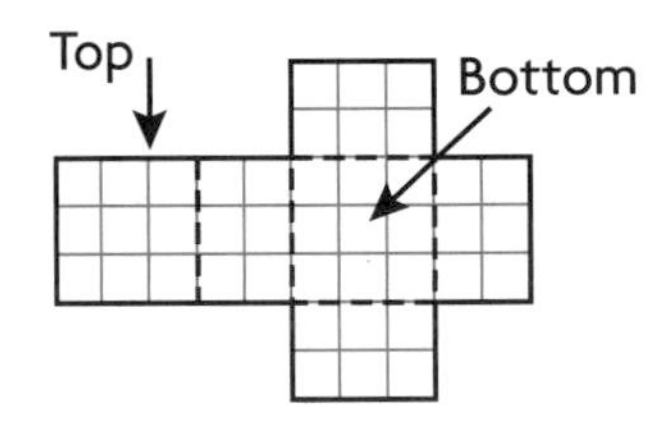

B Look at the front of your rectangular prism, and draw the front view.

C Look at the side of your rectangular prism, and draw the side view.

Draw Conclusions

1. How do the top, front, and side views of a rectangular prism compare?
2. How would the top view of a triangular prism compare to the top view of a rectangular prism?
3. **Application** Look at the top, front, and side views of the solid figure at the right. Identify the solid figure. **Explain** how the top, front, and side views helped you identify the solid figure.

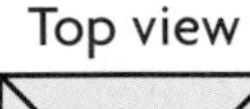
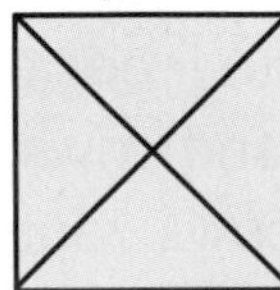

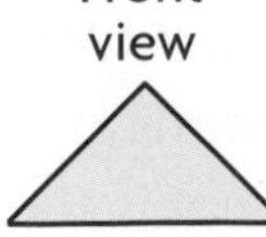

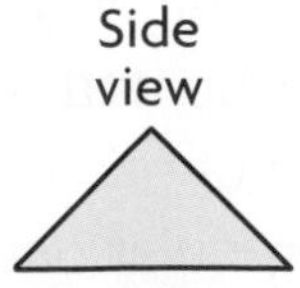

MG 2.3 Visualize and draw two-dimensional views of three-dimensional objects made from rectangular solids. *also* **MG 2.0, MR 2.0, MR 2.3, MR 2.4, MR 3.2**

Connect

How would the solid figure below look if you viewed it from the top, front, and side? Build a model to find out. Use connecting cubes to build the solid figure shown below. Then use grid paper to draw the top view, front view, and side view of the solid figure.

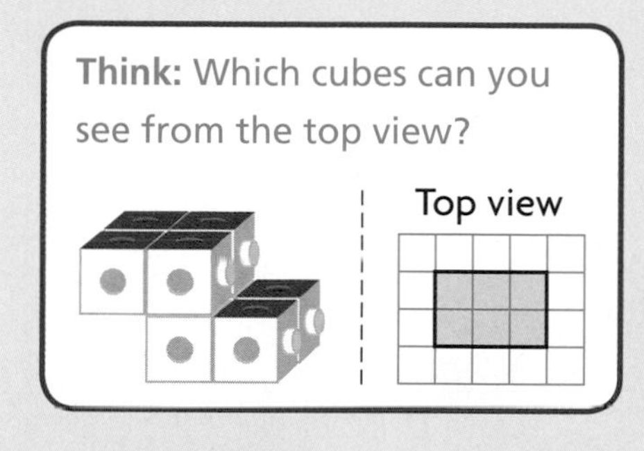

Think: Which cubes can you see from the top view?
Top view

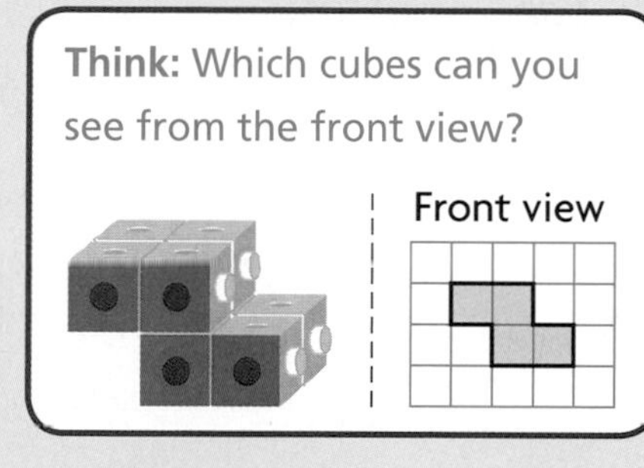

Think: Which cubes can you see from the front view?
Front view

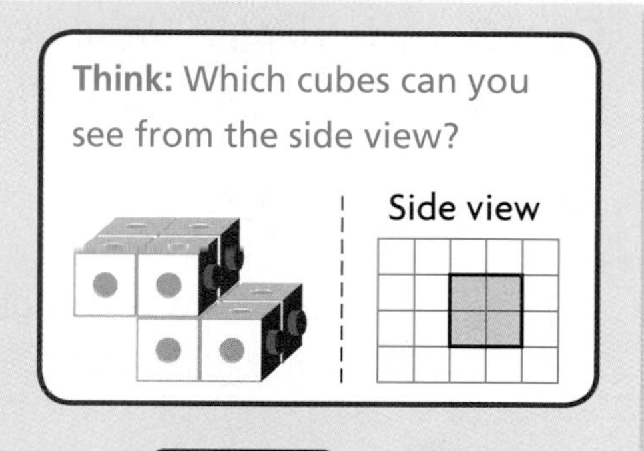

Think: Which cubes can you see from the side view?
Side view

TALK Math

How many cubes can you see from the left side view? How does this compare to the right side view?

Practice

Identify the solid figure that has the given views.

1.

top front side

2.

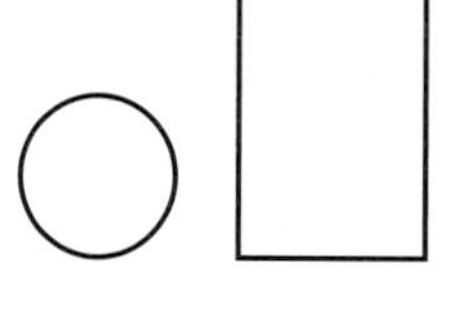

top front side

✓3.

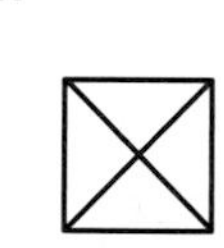

top front side

Use cubes to build the figure. On grid paper, draw the figure from the top, front, and side.

4.

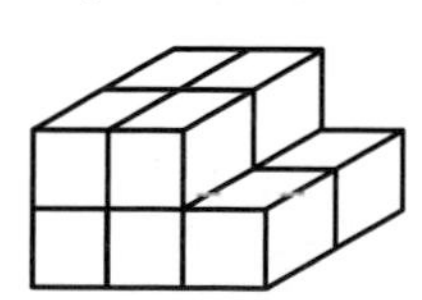

5.

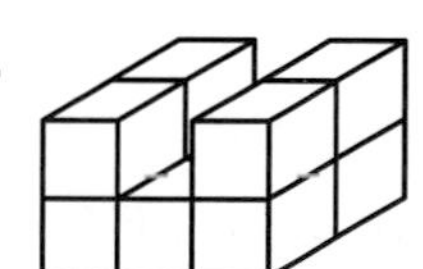

✓6.

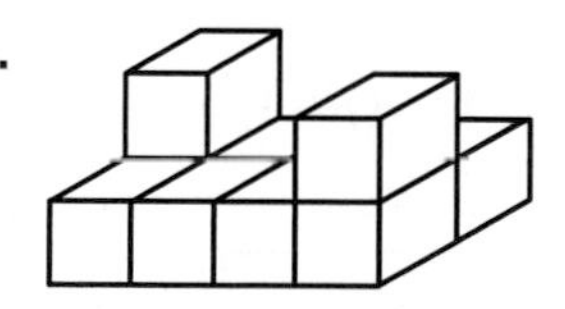

7. **WRITE Math** **Explain** which solid figures have a top view that is the same as the bottom view.

Extra Practice

Set A **Classify each triangle. Write *isosceles*, *scalene*, or *equilateral*.** (pp. 468–471)

1. 3 m 9 m 7 m

2. 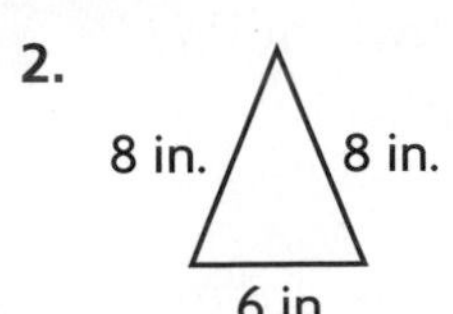

3. 6 cm 6 cm 6 cm

Classify each triangle. Write *acute*, *right*, or *obtuse*.

4. 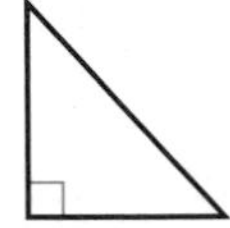

5.

6. 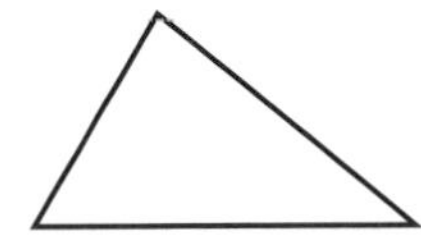

7. Two of the angles of a triangle measure 35° and 55°. What is the measure of the third angle?

Set B **Classify each figure in as many ways as possible. Write *quadrilateral*, *parallelogram*, *square*, *rectangle*, *rhombus*, or *trapezoid*.** (pp. 472–475)

1. 

2. 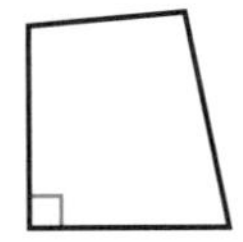

3. 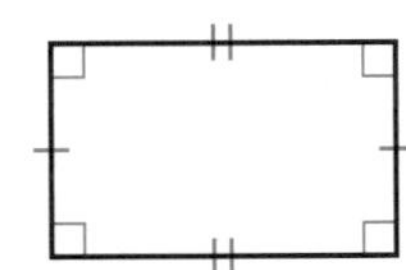

4. 

5. Three of the angles of a quadrilateral measure 90°, 60°, and 90°. What is the measure of the fourth angle?

Set C **Classify each solid figure. Write *prism*, *pyramid*, *cone*, *cylinder*, or *sphere*.** (pp. 478–481)

1. 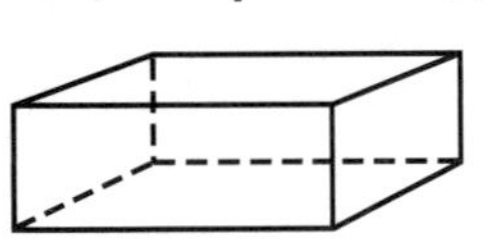

2. 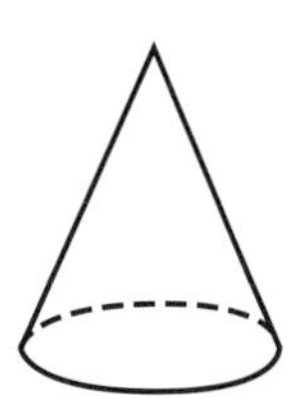

3. 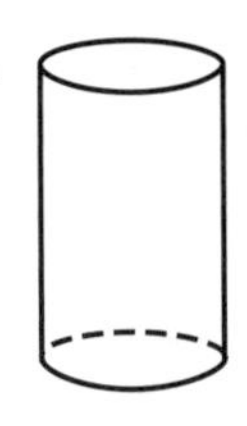

4. 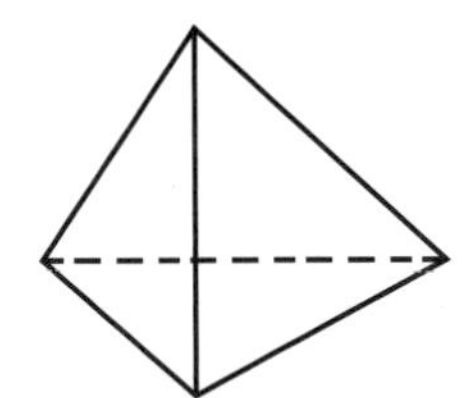

Set D **Match each solid figure with its net.** (pp. 482–483)

1. 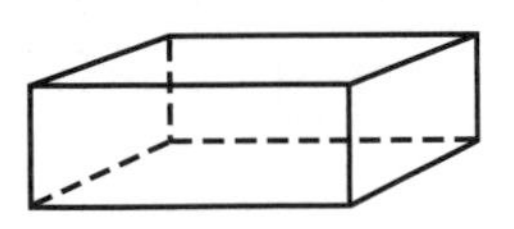

2. 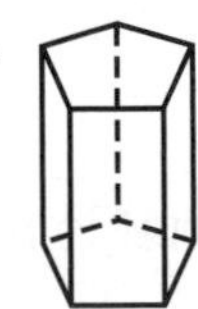

a. 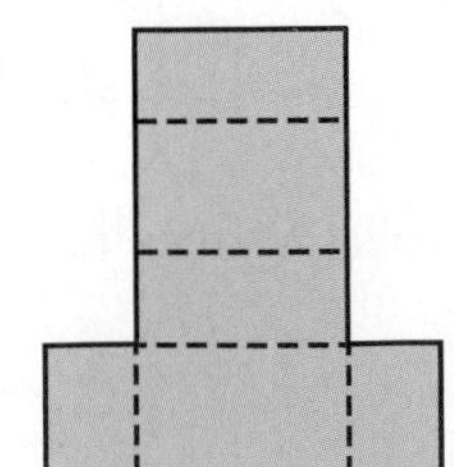

b. 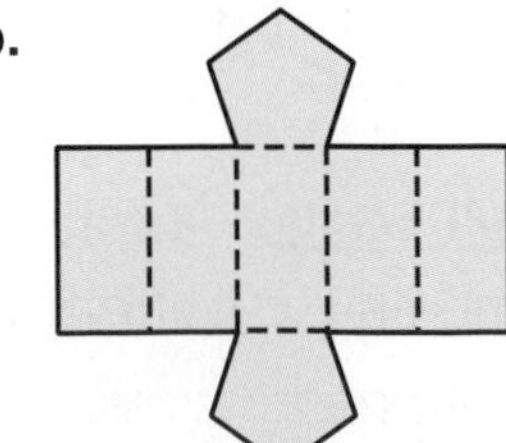

CD ROM **Technology**
Use Harcourt Mega Math, Ice Station Exploration, *Polar Planes*, Level G.

PRACTICE GAME

MODEL MAKERS

Get Ready!
4 players

Get Set!
- Toothpicks
- 24 slips of paper
- Container

I am a quadrilateral with exactly one pair of parallel sides.

I am

I am

I am

I am

Go!

- On a piece of paper, each player writes an "I am" clue about each of the following plane figures: quadrilateral, trapezoid, parallelogram, rectangle, rhombus, and square.
- The clues are placed in a container. Player 1 draws one clue and reads it aloud.
- Player 2 listens to the clue and makes a toothpick model of the plane figure described.
- If the model is correct, Player 2 earns a point. If the model is incorrect, Player 3 can try to earn a point by making the correct model.
- Player 2 draws the next "I am" clue and repeats the activity with Player 3 and Player 4. Play continues in this manner until all the clues have been drawn.
- The player with the most points after all the clues are drawn wins.

 Chapter 18 Review/Test

Check Vocabulary and Concepts

VOCABULARY
prism
pyramid
scalene triangle

For 1–2, choose the best term from the box.

1. A _?_ has no congruent sides. (O-π MG 2.1, p. 468)
2. A _?_ is a polyhedron with only one base. (MG 2.0, p. 478)
3. Explain how you can use a protractor to draw a right triangle. (O-π MG 2.1, pp. 476–477)

Check Skills

Classify each triangle. Write *isosceles*, *scalene*, or *equilateral*. (O-π MG 2.1, pp. 468–471)

4. 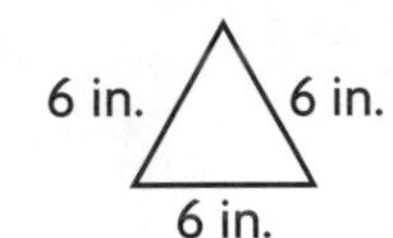

5. 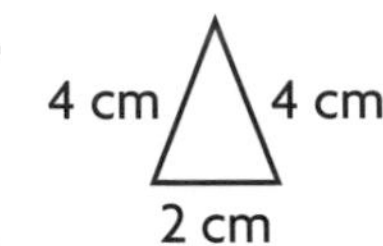

6. 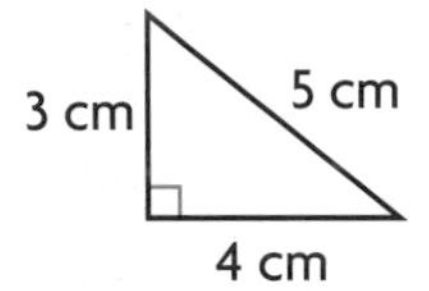

7. 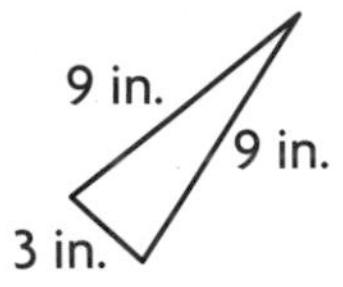

Classify each figure in as many ways as possible. Write *quadrilateral*, *parallelogram*, *square*, *rectangle*, *rhombus*, or *trapezoid*. (MG 2.0, pp. 472–475)

8. 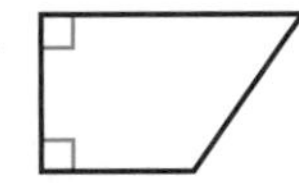

9. 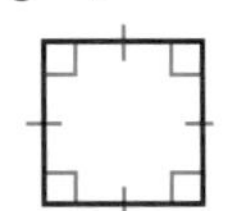

10. 

11. 

Classify each solid figure. Write *prism*, *pyramid*, *cone*, *cylinder*, or *sphere*. (MG 2.0, pp. 478–481)

12. 

13. 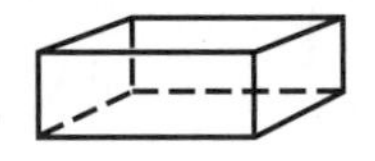

14. 

15. 

Match each solid figure with its net. (MG 2.3, pp. 482–483)

16. 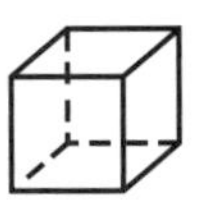

17. 

18. 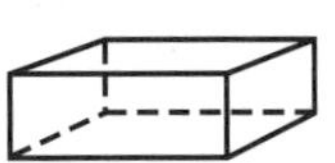

19. 

a. 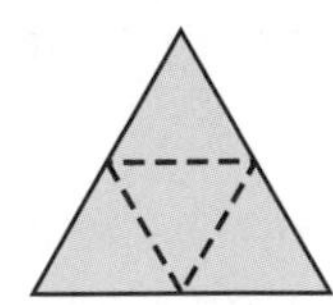

b. 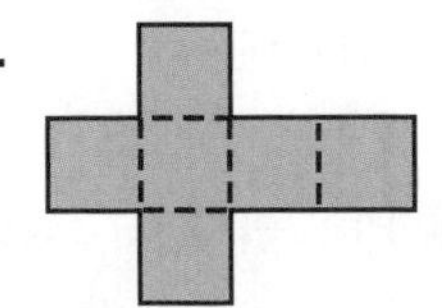

c. 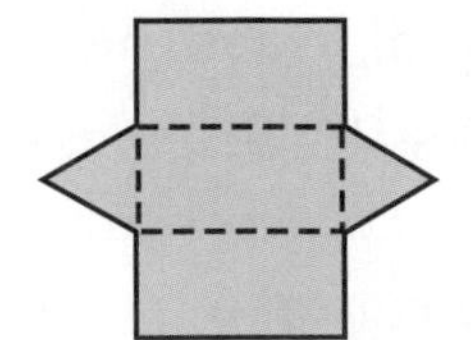

d. 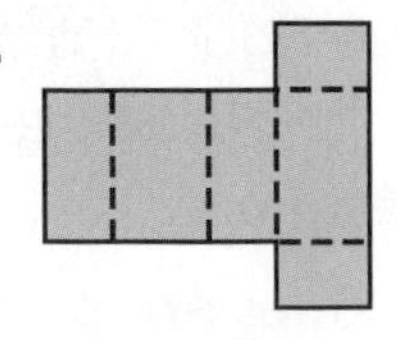

Check Problem Solving

Solve. (MG 2.0, MR 1.1, MR 2.3, pp. 477–481)

20. **WRITE Math** A tabletop terrarium is in the shape of a hexagonal prism. How many faces does it have? **Explain** how to solve.

GO ONLINE **Technology** Use *Online Assessment.*

Enrich • Quadrilaterals

What Could It Be?

A **quadrilateral** is a four-sided polygon. A square, rectangle, parallelogram, rhombus, and trapezoid are types of quadrilaterals.

Square

Rectangle

Parallelogram

Rhombus

Trapezoid

In each example below, part of a quadrilateral is hidden on the other side of the black line.

Example

Name some possible quadrilaterals this figure could be.

- The figure has a right angle.
  Only squares and rectangles are quadrilaterals with right angles.

So, the figure could be a square or a rectangle.

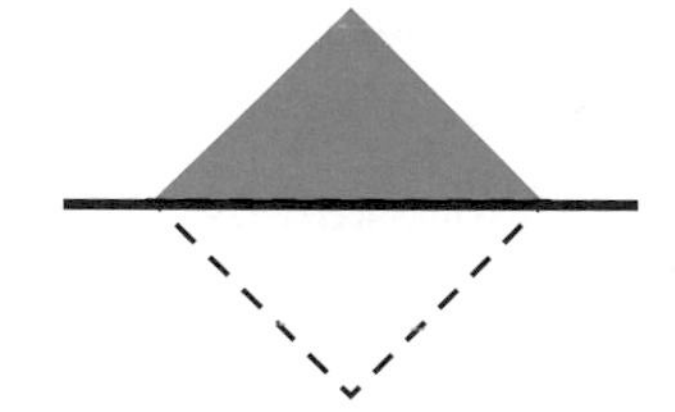

Try It

Name some possible quadrilaterals each figure could be. Give reasons for your answers.

1. 

2. 

3. 

4. 

WRITE Math Is a rhombus a parallelogram? Is a parallelogram a rhombus? **Explain** why or why not.

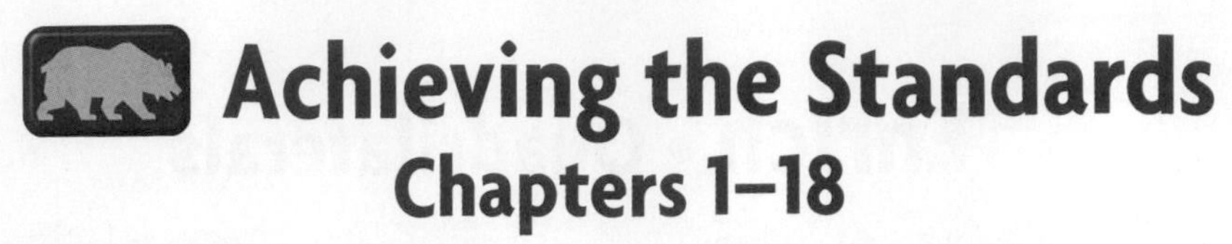

Achieving the Standards
Chapters 1–18

Measurement and Geometry

Decide on a plan.

See item 1. *Draw a diagram* to see what the triangles look like. Find the term that describes the triangles.

1. Alicia drew two triangles. Both triangles had identical angle measures, but different side lengths. Which term *best* describes the triangles? (O-π MG 2.0)

   A corresponding **C** similar

   B congruent **D** equilateral

2. What figure can be made from the pattern below? (MG 2.3)

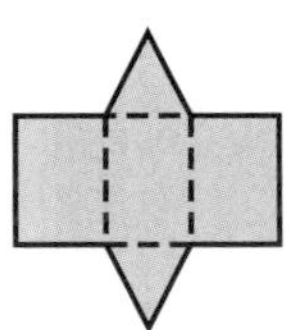

   A triangular pyramid **B** triangular prism

   C square pyramid **D** square prism

3. **WRITE Math** Annie made a triangle by cutting a corner from a sheet of paper. One angle is 60°. What is the measure of the third angle? **Explain** your answer. (O-π MG 2.2)

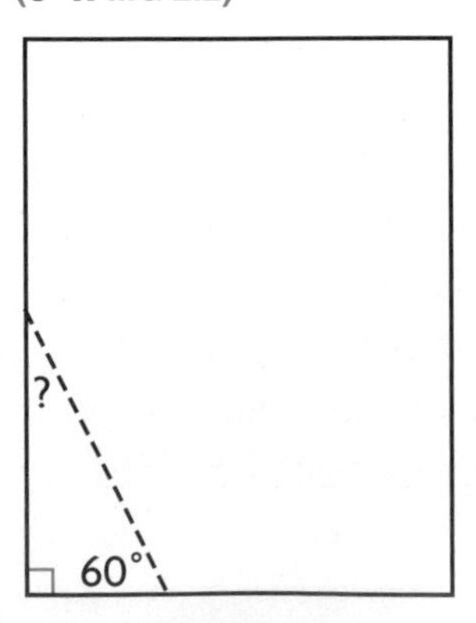

Statistics, Data Analysis, and Probability

4. Alana made this list of her math test scores: 87, 97, 93, 95, 91, 100, 82, 79, 95. What is Alana's median test score? (SDAP 1.1)

   A 91 **C** 94

   B 93 **D** 95

5. Sean wants to make a graph that shows the favorite movies for both girls and boys in his class. Which graph would Sean use that would best display this data? (SDAP 1.2)

   A bar graph **C** line graph

   B circle graph **D** double-bar graph

6. The table shows the number of books bought by each grade during a book fair.

Book Fair Sales

Grade	K	1	2	3	4	5
Number of Books	112	125	130	103	121	145

   Which is the most appropriate type of graph to display the data? (SDAP 1.2)

   A bar graph **C** line graph

   B circle graph **D** line plot

7. **WRITE Math** Find the outlier of the data set 6, 15, 22, 68, 23, 7. **Explain** how you got your answer. (SDAP 1.1)

Algebra and Functions

8. Andrew and Judy collect stamps. Andrew has half as many stamps as Judy. Let s represent the number of stamps that Andrew has. Which expression can be used to find the number of stamps that Judy has? (AF 1.2)

   A $\frac{s}{2}$

   B $2s$

   C $s + 2$

   D $s - 2$

9. If $k = {}^{-}7$, what is the value of $k + {}^{-}17$? (AF 1.2)

   A 24

   B 10

   C $^{-}10$

   D $^{-}24$

10. Jeremiah had 80 peanuts. He put the peanuts into 4 equal-sized groups to give to four friends. Let p represent the number of peanuts he gave each friend. Which equation can be used to find the number of peanuts each friend got? (AF 1.2)

    A $80 \div 4 = p$

    B $p \div 4 = 80$

    C $4 \times 80 = p$

    D $4 \div p = 80$

11. WRITE Math If x is a number that satisfies $2x - 3 = 17$, can x be equal to 9? **Explain** why or why not. (AF 1.2)

Number Sense

12. Look at the table.

Sports Balls	
Type	**Diameter (inches)**
Baseball	2.86
Golf ball	1.68
Handball	1.875
Tennis ball	2.5

Which shows the diameters of the balls listed in order from *least* to *greatest*? (NS 1.0)

   A 2.5, 1.68, 1.875, 2.86

   B 2.86, 2.5, 1.875, 1.68

   C 1.68, 1.875, 2.5, 2.86

   D 1.876, 1.68, 2.86, 2.5

13. A test had 30 problems. Ian got 24 problems correct. What percent were correct? (NS 1.2)

    A 8%

    B 80%

    C 88%

    D 94%

14. What is $\frac{3}{8}$ written as a decimal? (NS 1.2)

    A 0.267

    B 0.375

    C 0.38

    D 3.75

15. WRITE Math Sydney tries to practices the piano for at least 1 hour each day. On Monday, she practiced $\frac{1}{2}$ hour before dinner and $\frac{1}{3}$ hour after dinner. Did she practice for 1 hour? **Explain** your answer. (NS 2.3)

19 Geometry and the Coordinate Plane

The Big Idea The coordinate plane can be used to graph functions and equations.

CALIFORNIA FAST FACT

On August 9, 2005, the space shuttle *Discovery* landed at Edwards Air Force Base. The shuttle returned to Kennedy Space Center on August 21 atop the *Shuttle Carrier Aircraft*.

Investigate

Suppose you are aboard the space shuttle, and have recorded the data at the right. Graph the data on a coordinate grid. Describe the relationship between flight days and orbits, and tell how many orbits would be made in other numbers of flight days.

Space Shuttle Orbits

Flight days, x	3	4	5	6	7
Orbits, y	48	64	80	96	112

Technology
Student pages are available in the Student eBook.

Show What You Know

Check your understanding of important skills needed for success in Chapter 19.

Use a Coordinate Grid/Graph Coordinate Pairs

Use the ordered pairs to name each point of the grid.

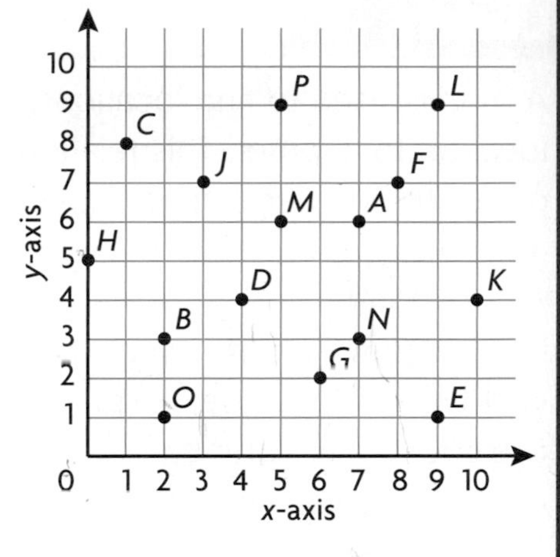

1. (9,9) **2.** (8,7) **3.** (7,6)

4. (2,3) **5.** (6,2) **6.** (5,6)

7. (7,3) **8.** (0,5) **9.** (1,8)

10. (4,4) **11.** (3,7) **12.** (2,1)

13. (5,9) **14.** (10,4) **15.** (9,1)

▶ Number Patterns and Functions

Find a rule. Use the rule to complete the function table.

16.

a	*b*
12	8
14	10
16	12
18	■

17.

h	*k*
20	22
15	17
10	12
5	■

18.

w	*x*
6	48
7	56
8	64
9	■

19.

m	*n*
33	11
27	9
21	7
15	■

VOCABULARY POWER

CHAPTER VOCABULARY

coordinate plane
function
function table
ordered pair
origin
***x*-axis**
***y*-axis**
***x*-coordinate**
***y*-coordinate**

WARM-UP WORDS

ordered pair a pair of numbers used to locate a point on a coordinate grid

***x*-axis** the horizontal number line on a coordinate plane

***y*-axis** the vertical number line on a coordinate plane

ALGEBRA

Graph Ordered Pairs

OBJECTIVE: Graph and identify points on a coordinate grid using ordered pairs.

Quick Review

Barry rides 16 blocks south, 17 blocks west, and 12 blocks south. How many blocks does Barry ride?

Vocabulary

ordered pair

x-axis | *x*-coordinate

y-axis | *y*-coordinate

Learn

A map is used to find locations, and the relationship of one location to another. This relationship, and the relationship of one object to another can be shown on a coordinate grid.

A coordinate grid is formed by two perpendicular number lines. The horizontal number line is called the **x-axis**. The vertical number lines is called the **y-axis**. Each point on the coordinate grid can be located by using an **ordered pair** of numbers, (*x*,*y*)

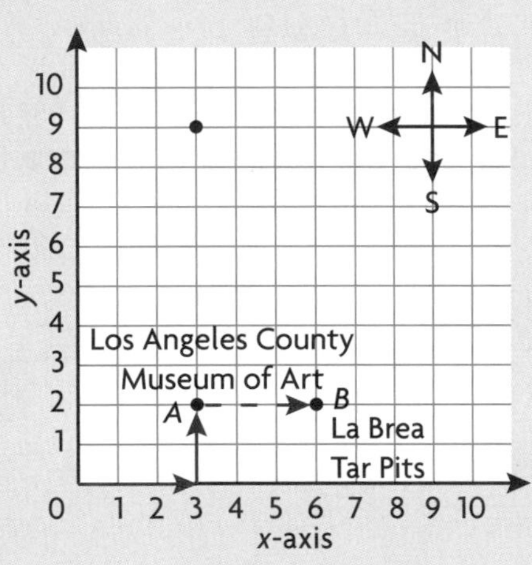

To get to point *A*, start where the number lines intersect, at (0,0). The first number in an ordered pair is the *x*-coordinate. The **x-coordinate** tells the distance to move in a horizontal direction from (0,0). The ordered pair at point *A* has an *x*-coordinate of 3.

The second number in an ordered pair, or **y-coordinate**, tells the distance to move vertically. Point *A* has a *y*-coordinate of 2. The ordered pair (3,2) gives the location of point *A*.

- What ordered pair gives the location of the La Brea Tar Pits?

Example Graph the ordered pair (5,7).

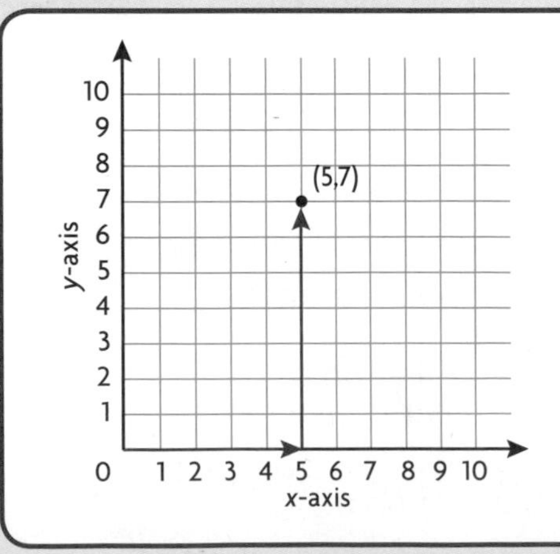

Start at (0,0).
Move 5 units to the right.
Move 7 units up.
Graph the point.

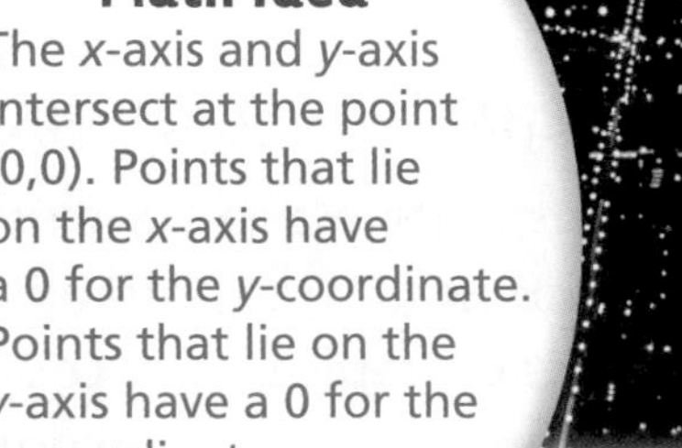

Math Idea

The *x*-axis and *y*-axis intersect at the point (0,0). Points that lie on the *x*-axis have a 0 for the *y*-coordinate. Points that lie on the *y*-axis have a 0 for the *x*-coordinate.

- The point (0,6) lies on one of the axes. Which axis?

SDAP 1.5 Know how to write ordered pairs correctly; for example, (*x*,*y*). *also* SDAP 1.4, AF 1.1, AF 1.5, SDAP 1.0, MR 1.1, MR 2.0, MR 2.3, MR 2.4, MR 3.2, MR 3.3

Guided Practice

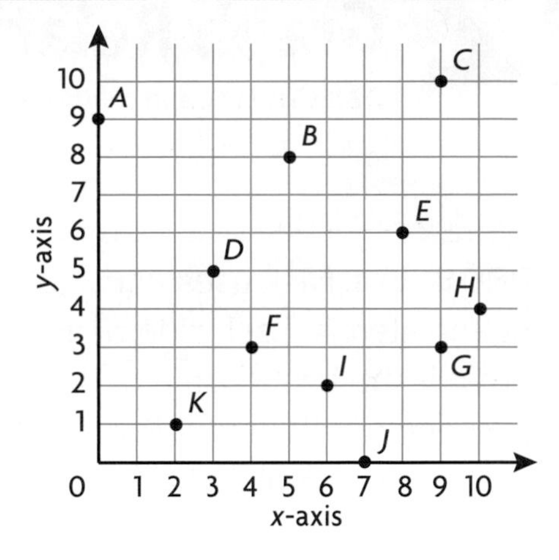

1. Use the coordinate grid. Start at (0,0). Move 6 units to the right and 2 units up. What point is at (6,2)?

Use the coordinate grid. Write an ordered pair for each point.

2. *D* 3. *G* 4. *C*

Graph and label the following points on a coordinate grid.

5. *X* (9,0) 6. *Y* (6,8) 7. *Z* (4,10)

8. **TALK Math** **Explain** how to write the ordered pair for point *K* on the coordinate grid.

Independent Practice and Problem Solving

Use the coordinate grid above. Write an ordered pair for each point.

9. *B* 10. *H* 11. *F* 12. *J* 13. *A* 14. *E*

Graph and label each the following points on a coordinate grid.

15. *J* (1,1) 16. *K* (0,4) 17. *L* (2,5) 18. *P* (5,2) 19. *S* (6,0)

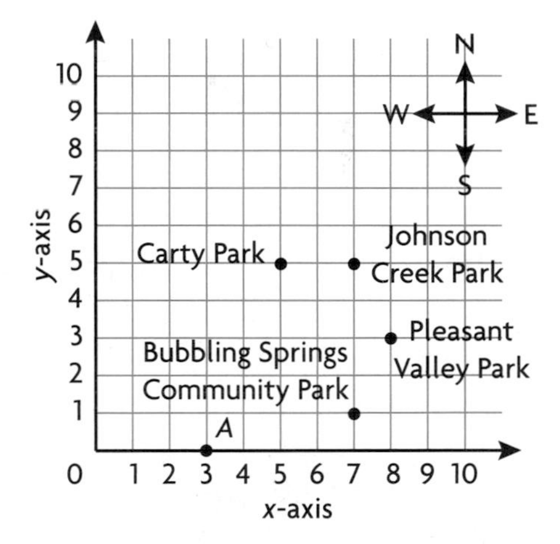

USE DATA **For 20–22, use the map.**

20. What ordered pair gives the location of Pleasant Valley Park?
21. Moranda Park is located at point *A* on the map grid. What ordered pair gives the location of Moranda Park?
22. **Reasoning** What location is 2 units west and 4 units north of Bubbling Springs Community Park?
23. **WRITE Math** **Explain** why order is important when graphing an ordered pair on a coordinate grid.

Achieving the Standards

24. What integer is graphed on the number line? (NS 1.5, p. 376)

$^{-}5$ $^{-}4$ $^{-}3$ $^{-}2$ $^{-}1$ 0 $^{+}1$ $^{+}2$ $^{+}3$ $^{+}4$ $^{+}5$

25. What is the length of a line segment joining the points $(5, ^{-}1)$ and $(10, ^{-}1)$? (Grade 4 AF 2.2)

26. How many faces will the net for a cube contain? (MG 1.2, p. 482)

27. **Test Prep** The point (5,0) is:

A not an ordered pair
B on the *x*-axis
C on the origin
D on the *y*-axis

Extra Practice on page 512, Set A

ALGEBRA

Graph Relationships

OBJECTIVE: Graph relationships from input-output tables.

Quick Review

Copy and complete the table.

Number of Squares	1	2	3	4	5	6	7
Number of Sides	4	8					

Learn

PROBLEM Nick uses equilateral triangles to make quadrilaterals. Each side of an equilateral triangle is 1 unit. What is the relationship of the number of triangles to the perimeter of the quadrilateral? What is the perimeter of a quadrilateral that is made of 6 equilateral triangles?

Example

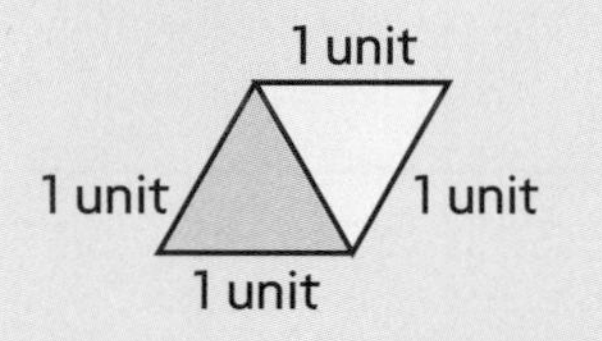

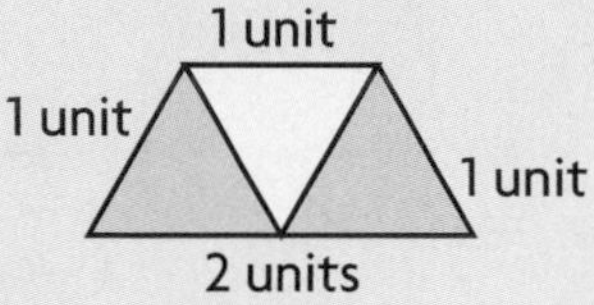

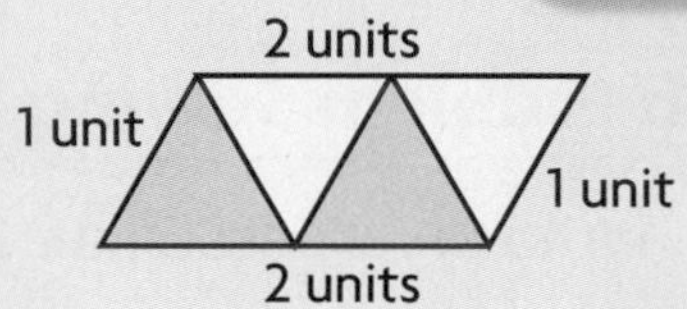

You can show the relationship in a table.

Number of Triangles, x	2	3	4	5	6
Perimeter, in Inches, y	4	5	6	7	?

An ordered pair represents the relationship in the table on a graph. The first number in the ordered pair represents the number of triangles in the quadrilateral. The second number in the ordered pair represents the perimeter.

The perimeter of each quadrilateral is 2 more than the number of equilateral triangles that make it up. For this relationship, the number on the y-axis is always 2 more than the number on the x-axis.

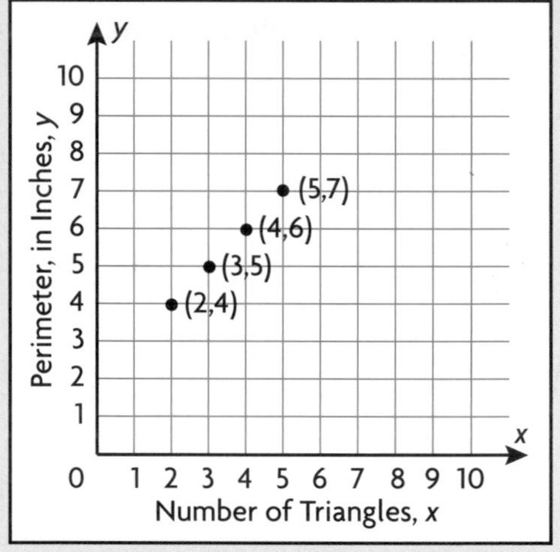

So, the perimeter of a quadrilateral made up of 6 equilateral triangles is 8 units.

Example

Graph the relationship shown in the table.

Number of Triangles, x	1	2	3	4
Number of Sides, y	3	6	9	12

Write the ordered pairs for the data. (1,3), (2,6), (3,4), (4,12)

Graph the ordered pairs.

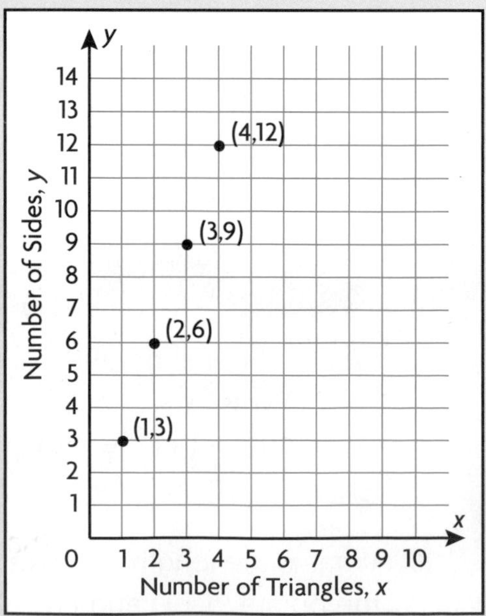

SDAP 1.5 Know how to write ordered pairs correctly; for example, (x,y). *also* SDAP 1.4, AF 1.1, AF 1.5, SDAP 1.0, MR 1.1, MR 2.0, MR 2.3, MR 2.4, MR 3.2, MR 3.3

Guided Practice

1. Use the table and the graph to complete the ordered pairs.

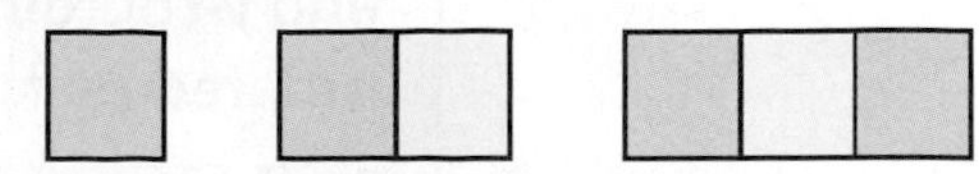

Number of Squares, x	1	2	3	4
Perimeter of Rectangle, in units, y	4	■	■	■

(1,4), (2,6), (3,■), (4,■)

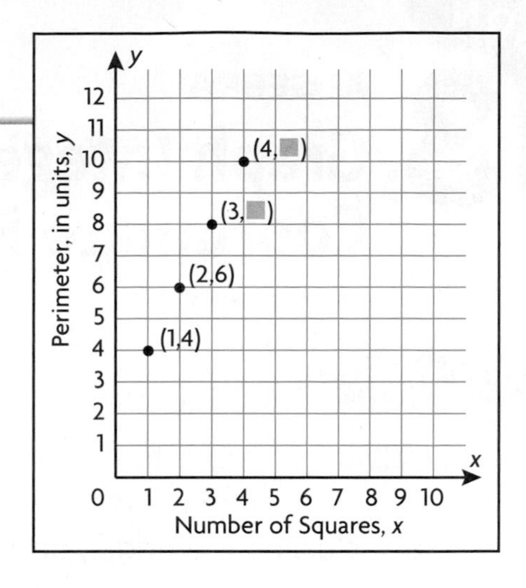

Write the ordered pairs. Then graph them.

2.

Number of Sides, x	3	6	9	12
Number of Triangles, y	1	2	3	4

3.

Number of Pentagons, x	1	2	3	4
Number of Sides, y	5	10	15	20

4. TALK Math **Explain** what each number of the ordered pair (6,8) means.

Independent Practice and Problem Solving

Write the ordered pairs. Then graph them.

5.

Number of Cones, x	1	4	6	8
Number of Vertices, y	1	4	6	8

6.

Number of Cylinders, x	2	3	4	5
Number of Flat Bases, y	4	6	8	10

For 7–9, use the table.

Number of Equilateral Triangles, x	1	2	3	4
Number of Interior Angles of 60°, y	3	6	9	12

7. Write the ordered pairs in the table. Then graph each ordered pair.

8. **Reasoning** What does (3,9) mean in the graph for the table?

9. WRITE Math **What's the Error?** Nikki wrote the ordered pair (18,6) for 6 equilateral triangles with 18 interior angles of 60°. What is her error? What should she have written?

Achieving the Standards

10. Find the value of n in the equation $5 \times 105 = (5 \times 100) + (5 \times n)$. (AF 1.3, p. 64)

11. Which number in the ordered pair (7,6) is the y-coordinate? (SDAP 1.5, p. 498)

12. What integer is one less than $^-3$? (NS 1.5, p. 380)

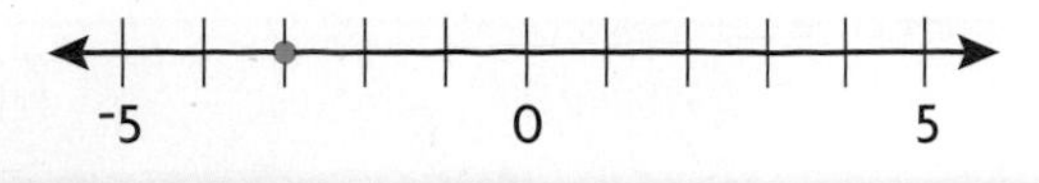

13. The x-coordinate in an ordered pair that shows the relationship of number of pentagons to number of sides is 3. What is the y-coordinate?

A 3
B 5
C 10
D 15

Extra Practice on page 512, Set B

LESSON 3

ALGEBRA

Graph Integers on the Coordinate Plane

OBJECTIVE: Identify and graph integers on the coordinate plane.

Quick Review

Identify the *x*-coordinate and *y*-coordinate in each ordered pair.

1. (1,6)
2. (2,0)
3. (10,8)
4. (9,9)
5. (7,12)

Vocabulary

coordinate plane origin

Learn

A **coordinate plane** is formed by two intersecting and perpendicular number lines. The point where the two lines intersect is called the **origin**, or (0,0).

The positive *x*-coordinate numbers are to the **right** of the *y*-axis and the negative *x*-coordinate numbers are to the **left.** The positive *y*-coordinate numbers are above the *x*-axis and the negative *y*-coordinate numbers are below.

Start at the origin. Move 3 units to the left on the *x*-axis and 4 units up on the *y*-axis. The coordinates are ($^-3$,4).

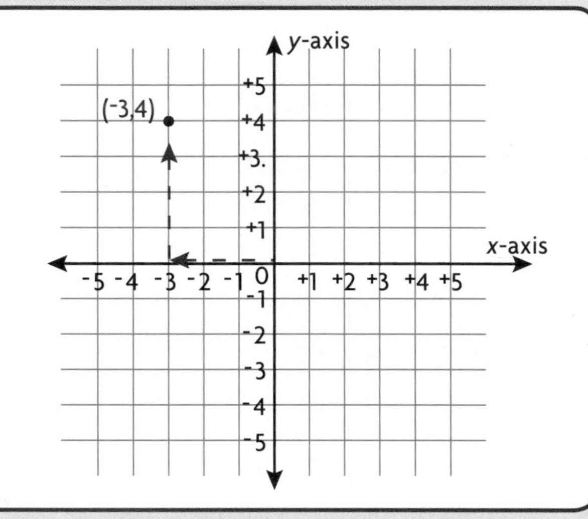

Examples

A Positive *x*-coordinate, negative *y*-coordinate

To graph (5,$^-2$), start at the origin.
Move 5 units to the ***right*** and 2 units ***down***.

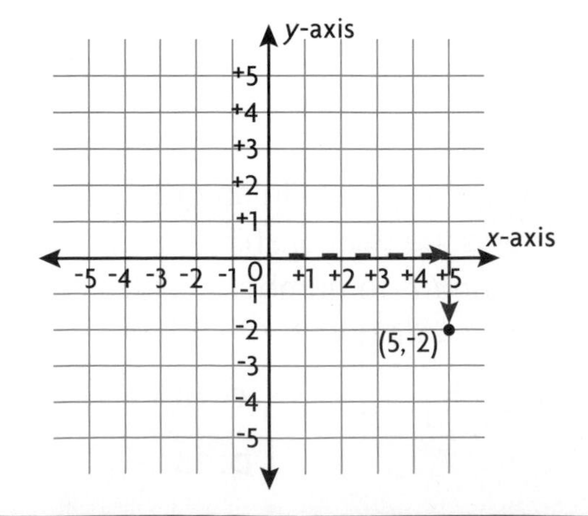

B Two negative coordinates

To graph ($^-3$,$^-3$), start at the origin.
Move 3 units to the ***left*** and 3 units ***down***.

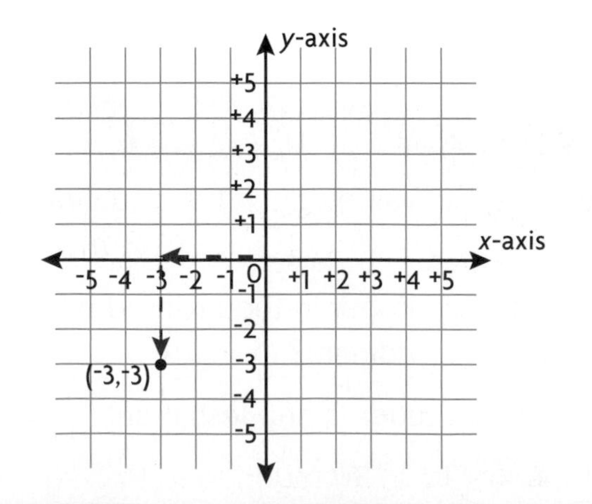

AF 1.4 Identify and graph ordered pairs in the four quadrants of the coordinate plane. *also* SDAP 1.4, SDAP 1.5, AF 1.1, AF 1.5, SDAP 1.0, MR 1.1, MR 2.0, MR 2.3, MR 2.4, MR 3.2

Guided Practice

Choose *right, left, up,* or *down* to fill in the blanks.

1. To graph $(^-1,^+1)$, you would start at (0,0) and then go __?__ to $^-1$ and __?__ to $^+1$.

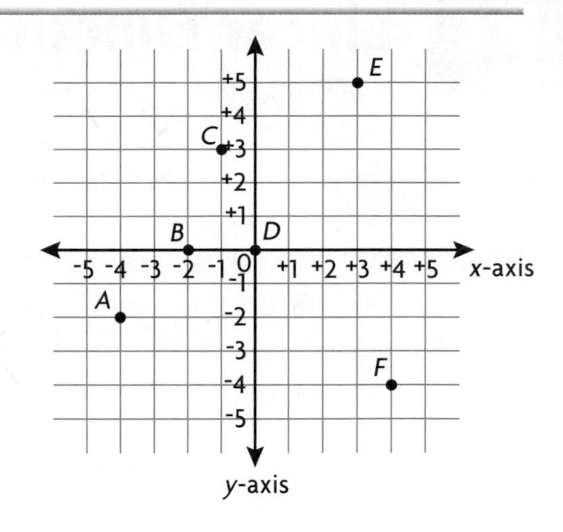

For 2–5, identify the ordered pair for each point.

2. point *A*
3. point *B*
4. point *C*
5. point *D*
6. point *E*
7. point *F*

8. **TALK Math** **Explain** how you would graph $(0,^-4)$ on a coordinate plane.

Independent Practice and Problem Solving

For 9–14, identify the ordered pair for each point.

9. point *A*
10. point *C*
11. point *E*
12. point *F*
13. point *B*
14. point *D*

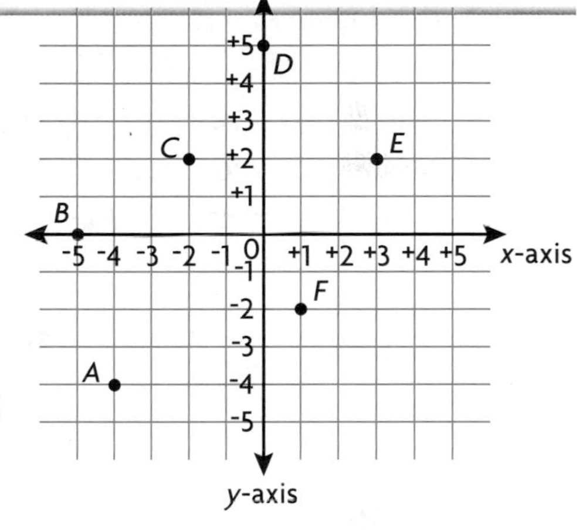

For 15–18, graph and label the ordered pairs on a coordinate plane.

15. *M* $(6,^-1)$
16. *N* $(^-2,2)$
17. *O* $(^-6,0)$
18. *T* $(^-4,^-4)$

Name the ordered pair that is described.

19. Start at the origin. Move 2 units to the right and 5 units down.

20. Start at the origin. Move 4 units to the left and 7 units up.

Solve.

21. **Sense or Nonsense?** An ordered pair can never contain integers that are both negative. Explain why you agree or disagree.

22. **WRITE Math** Why is a coordinate plane more useful than a grid that only uses positive integers? **Explain.**

Achieving the Standards

23. Identify the integers 0, $^-8$, 9, and $^-2$ on a number line. Then order them from greatest to least. (NS 1.5, p. 380)

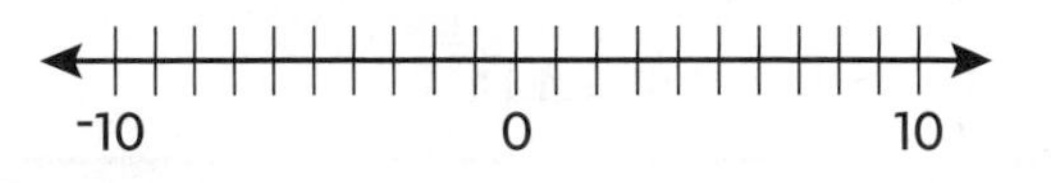

24. What is 1.136 rounded to the nearest tenth? (NS 1.1, p. 272)

25. What does y equal if $x = 6$ for the equation $y = 3x + 5$? (Grade 4 AF 1.5)

26. **Test Prep** Start at the origin. Go to the left 2 units. Go down 2 units. What is the ordered pair?

    A (2,2)
    B $(2,^-2)$
    C $(^-2,2)$
    D $(^-2,^-2)$

Extra Practice on page 512, Set C

LESSON 4

Linear Functions

OBJECTIVE: Solve linear functions with integer values.

Quick Review

Solve for $x = 2$.

1. $y = x + 7$
2. $y = x - 1$
3. $y = 5x$
4. $y = 8 \div x$
5. $y = 3x - 1$

Vocabulary

function **function table**

Learn

PROBLEM Larry takes care of pets while his neighbors are on vacation. He earns \$8 for each day he walks and feeds their dog, Milo. On 4 days, last week, he walked and fed Milo. How much money did Larry earn walking and feeding Milo last week?

A **function** is a relationship between two quantities in which one quantity depends on the other. A **function table** shows the function with a matching output value for each input value. A function can also be shown by an equation.

You can use a function table to show the amount of money Larry earns for walking and feeding Milo for different numbers of days. The table matches each input value of days, d, with an output value of dollars, m.

Number of Days, d	1	2	3	4
Amount of Dollars, m	8	16	24	32

Rule: Multiply the number of days, d, by 8.

You can use the table to find the rule for the function.

You can use the rule to write an equation for the relationship.

dollars earned **equals** **dollars earned per day** **times** **number of days**

↓ ↓ ↓ ↓ ↓

m $=$ 8 $\times$ d

Substitute 4 for d in the equation to find m. This is how much Larry earned in 4 days.

$$m = 8 \times d \rightarrow m = 8 \times 4 \rightarrow m = 32$$

So, Larry earned \$32 for walking and feeding Milo.

Example

Use an equation.

Larry took care of the Petersens' dog for 12 days. The Petersens paid him an extra \$15 to water their plants. How much did Larry earn?

Write the equation.

$m = 8 \times d + 15$

$m = 8 \times 12 + 15$ Replace d with 12.

$m = 96 + 15 = 111$

So, Larry earned \$111 from the Petersens.

AF 1.5 Solve problems involving linear functions with integer values; write the equation; and graph the resulting ordered pairs of integers on a grid. *also* **AF 1.0, AF1.1, MR 1.0, MR 1.1, MR 2.0, MR 2.3, MR 2.4, MR 3.2, MR 3.3**

Guided Practice

1. Find a rule. Then copy and complete the equation and the function table.

   Rule: Add ■. Equation: $y = x +$ ■

Input, x	1	2	3	■	5
Output, y	5	6	■	8	■

Find a rule to complete the function table. Then write the rule as an equation.

2.

Input, x	1	2	3	4	5	6
Output, y	3	6	9	12	■	■

3.

Input, x	12	■	8	6	4	2
Output, y	6	5	4	■	2	■

4. TALK Math **Explain** the rule that the equation $y = 7x - 6$ represents.

Independent Practice and Problem Solving

Find a rule to complete the function table. Then write the rule as an equation.

5.

Input, x	11	10	9	■	7
Output, y	4	3	2	1	■

6.

Input, x	1	2	3	■	5	6
Output, y	5	7	9	11	■	■

Algebra Use the function. Find the output, y, for each input, x.

7. $y = x + 8$, for $x = 2, 4, 6, 8$

8. $y = 3x + 50$, for $x = 3, 6, 9, 12$

Solve.

9. Anita requires a \$10 deposit for her dog-walking services, then \$5 daily for each day that she walks a dog. Write a function to show how much Anita earns for walking a dog.

10. WRITE Math **What's the Question?** The answer is the function at the right.

Input, x	1	2	3	4	5
Output, y	7	14	21	28	35

Achieving the Standards

11. Solve $y = 12 \div x$, for $x = 2, 3$, and 4. (AF 1.2, p. 348)

12. Find the median for the following data: 108, 93, 88, 80, and 46. (G4 SDAP 1.0)

13. Solve $y = 4x + 6$, for $x = 1, 5$, and, 6. (AF 1.2, p. 344)

14. Which equation represents this rule: Divide by 2 and subtract 4?

    A $y = (x \div 2) - 4$

    B $y = x \div (2 - 4)$

    C $y = (x - 2) \div 4$

    D $y = 2x - 4$

Extra Practice on page 513, Set D

LESSON 5

ALGEBRA

Write and Graph Equations

OBJECTIVE: Write and graph equations on a coordinate plane.

Quick Review

Graph the ordered pairs.

1. (3,5)
2. (0,6)
3. (8,2)
4. (7,7)
5. (1,0)

Learn

PROBLEM Erika is making a rectangle pattern for a quilt she is making with her grandmother. Each side of a square is 1 inch. What is the perimeter of a rectangle pattern that has 3 square pieces?

1 inch   2 inches   3 inches

1 inch

You can show the relationship between the number of squares and the perimeter in a function table. Then you can write ordered pairs and graph the equation on a coordinate plane.

Example 1

Step 1

Write an equation that shows the relationship.

Rule: Multiply by 2 and add 2.

perimeter = 2 × length + 2 × width

$y = 2x + 2$

The width does not change. It always equals 1.

Step 2

Use the equation to create a function table.

$y = 2x + 2$

Number of squares, x	1	2	3	4
Perimeter, in inches, y	4	6	8	10

Step 3

Use the function table to write the ordered pairs.

(1,4), (2,6), (3,8), (4,10)

Graph the ordered pairs.

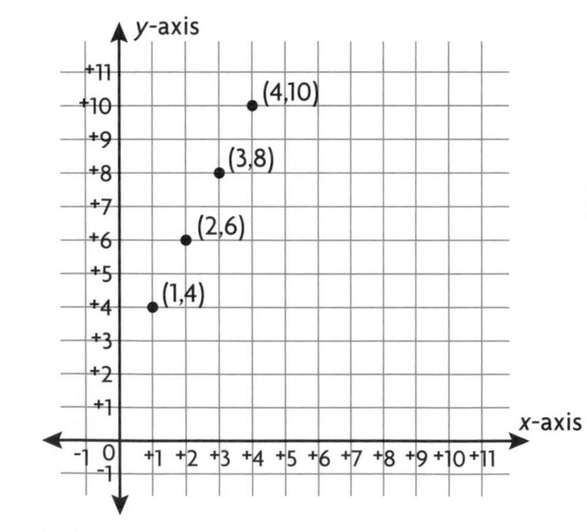

Math Idea

You can use an equation to find ordered pairs and then use the ordered pairs to graph the relationship.

So, the perimeter of a rectangle pattern with 3 square pieces is 8 inches.

AF 1.5 Solve problems involving linear functions with integer values; write the equation; and graph the resulting ordered pairs of integers on a grid. *also* **SDAP 1.5, AF 1.4, AF 1.0, AF 1.1, SDAP 1.0, MR 2.0, MR 2.3, MR 2.4, MR 3.3**

Example 2

Ella is 2 years older than her brother, Mike. Write an equation that shows how much older than her brother Ella is.

Step 1

Write an equation that shows the relationship.
Rule: Add 2.

Ella's age	equals	Mike's age	plus	years older
↓	↓	↓	↓	↓
y	$=$	x	$+$	2

Step 2

Use the equation to create a function table.

x	4	5	6	7
y	6	7	8	9

Step 3

Write the data in the table as ordered pairs.

(4,6), (5,7), (6,8), (7,9)

Graph the ordered pairs.

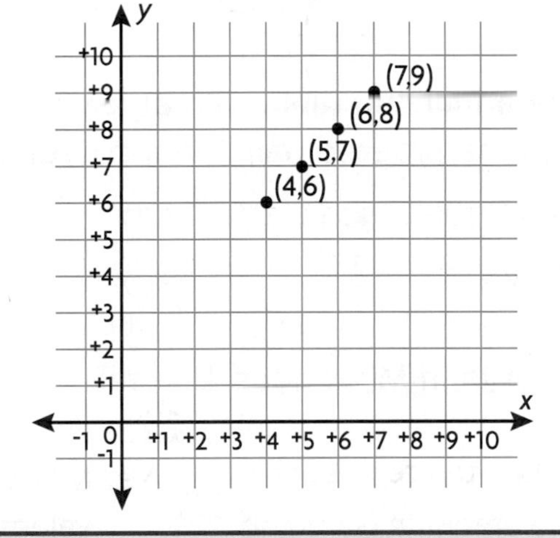

Example 3

Graph the equation $y = 2x - 4$.

x	0	1	2	3
y	$^-4$	$^-2$	0	2

(0,$^-$4), (1,$^-$2), (2,0), (3,2)

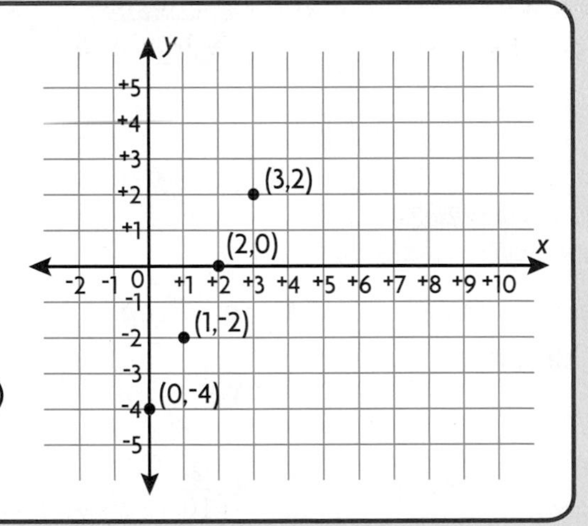

Guided Practice

1. Copy and complete the function table. Write the data in the table as ordered pairs.

Rule: Add 2.

Equation: $y = x + 2$

Input, x	1	2	3	4	■
Output, y	3	4	■	6	7

Find a rule to copy and complete the function table. Then write an equation.

2.

x	1	2	3	4	5
y	6	12	18	24	■

3.

x	0	1	2	3	4
y	■	4	8	12	16

4.

x	1	2	3	4	5
y	3	5	■	9	11

5. TALK Math **Explain** how you found the equation in Exercise 3.

Independent Practice and Problem Solving

Find a rule to copy and complete the function table. Then write an equation.

6.

x	4	3	2	1	0
y	0	$^{-}1$	$^{-}2$	$^{-}3$	■

7.

x	10	■	6	4	2
y	5	4	3	2	■

8.

x	4	3	2	1	0
y	20	■	10	5	■

Use each equation to make a function table with at least 4 ordered pairs. Then graph the ordered pairs on a coordinate plane.

9. $y = x - 8$

10. $y = 2x + 2$

11. $y = 3x$

12. $y = 2x - 3$

13. $y = x - 1$

14. $y = 2x - 5$

15. $y = 3x - 4$

16. $y = {}^{-}x + 2$

Gary makes $3 more an hour than Miles does. Use this information for 17–19.

17. Write an equation to show the relationship between the amounts Gary and Miles make.

18. Make a function table with at least four values. Show Gary's salary as an input value and Miles' salary as an output value.

19. Use a function table or an equation to make a graph that shows the relationship between Gary's salary and Miles' salary.

20. WRITE Math **Explain** why the equations $y = x + 4$ and $y = 4 + x$ are the same.

Achieving the Standards

21. What is the perimeter of a rectangle with an area of 18 square inches and a length of 9 inches? (Grade 4 MG 1.0)

22. The length of a rectangle is 7 cm. Its perimeter is 28 cm. What is its area? (Grade 4 MG 1.0)

23. Anna spent $13.47. Carson spent $9.87. How much did they spend in all? (NS 2.1, p. 276)

24. **Test Prep** $\frac{2}{5} \div \frac{1}{2}$.

A $\frac{1}{5}$

B $\frac{2}{10}$

C $\frac{2}{5}$

D $\frac{4}{5}$

25. **Test Prep** If you graph the equation $y = x - 7$, which of the following pairs would you graph?

A (3,4)

B (3,10)

C (4,3)

D (10,3)

Step by Step

How to Draw to Explain

To prove or disprove an answer, use logical reasoning and the math skills to solve the problem.

PROBLEM San Francisco is a city built on hills. So, there are stairways to climb. If you want to visit Coit Tower, you can climb the Filbert Steps. Suppose the height of each step is 7 inches. What is the height of the stairs at the top of seventh step?

Amy said that the height at the seventh step is 49 inches. Alexander's teacher asked him to prove or disprove Amy's answer. Alexander wrote this explanation.

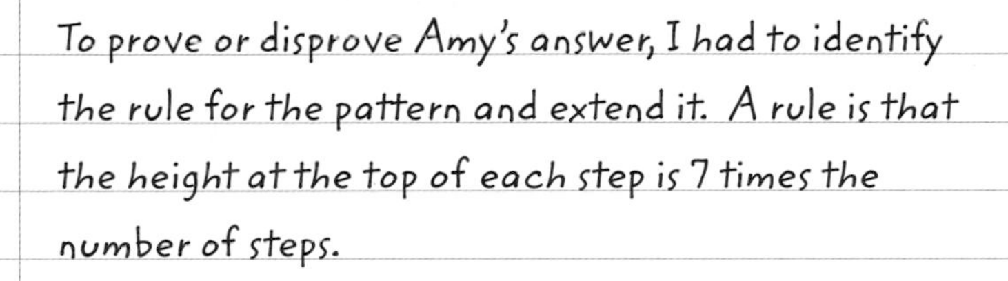

To prove or disprove Amy's answer, I had to identify the rule for the pattern and extend it. A rule is that the height at the top of each step is 7 times the number of steps.

Then, I made a function table to extend the pattern to the seventh step and wrote this equation to show the relationship in the table.

$$h = 7s$$

Step (s)	1	2	3	4	5	6	7
Height (inches) (h)	7	14	21	28	35	42	49

Next, I made a graph to show the data in the function table. The pattern in the function table shows a value of 49 inches for the height of the seventh step. The ordered pair for the seventh step is (7, 49). So, Amy's answer is proved to be correct.

Tips

To prove or disprove an answer:

- Solve the problem.
- Explain your solution.
- Show more than one way to solve the problem.
- Use logical reasoning to explain how your solution proves or disproves the answer.
- Use the words so or *therefore* to write a concluding statement to your proof.

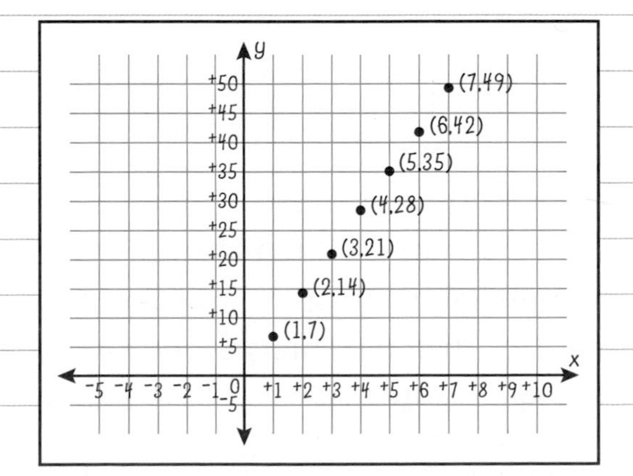

Problem Solving **Write an explanation to prove or disprove each statement.**

1. Pia can climb 5 steps in 1 second. She says that if she maintains that rate, she can climb 60 steps in less than 12 seconds.

2. Chris says that the ordered pair for the eleventh step of the Filbert Steps is (11,77).

Problem Solving Workshop
Skill: Relevant or Irrelevant Information

OBJECTIVE: Solve problems by using the skill *relevant or irrelevant information.*

Read to Understand
Plan
Solve
Check

Use the Skill

PROBLEM Marcus is making a map of his neighborhood on a coordinate plane for his new neighbors. They are looking for the school.

Marcus told them that the shoe store was located at the coordinates $(^-4, ^-1)$. The cinema is located 5 units to the right and 1 unit down from the shoe store. The library is located 7 units to the right and 5 units up from the shoe store. The school has the same *x*-coordinate as the shoe store and the same *y*-coordinate as the library. Where is the school?

Sometimes a problem contains information you need for one question and not for another. You must decide which information is relevant, or needed, to solve the problem.

Fact	Coordinates	Relevant or Irrelevant
The shoe store is located at $(^-4, ^-1)$.	$(^-4, ^-1)$	relevant
The cinema is located 5 units to the right and 1 unit down from the shoe store.	$(^+1, ^-2)$	irrelevant
The library is located 7 units to the right and 5 units up from the shoe store.	$(^+3, ^+4)$	relevant
The school has the same *x*-coordinate as the shoe store and the same *y*-coordinate as the library.	$(^-4, ^+4)$	relevant

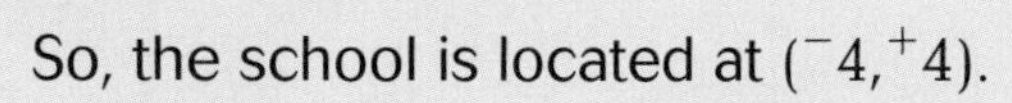

So, the school is located at $(^-4, ^+4)$.

Think and Discuss

For a and b, use the map above. Tell the relevant information and solve.

a. The *y*-coordinate of Marcus's house is 3 greater than the shoe store's, and it is less than the library's. The *x*-coordinate of his house is the opposite of the shoe store's. What are the coordinates of Marcus's house?

b. The pet store moved from its old location at $(^-2, ^+2)$. The new location has the same *x*-coordinate as the library, and is directly right of the cinema. Where is the pet store?

AF 1.4 Identify and graph ordered pairs in the four quadrants of the coordinate plane. *also* **MR 1.1, AF 1.1, AF 1.5, SDAP 1.5, MR 1.0, MR 2.0, MR 2.1, MR 2.3, MR 2.4, MR 3.2, MR 3.3**

Guided Problem Solving

For 1–3, use the map. Tell the relevant information and solve.

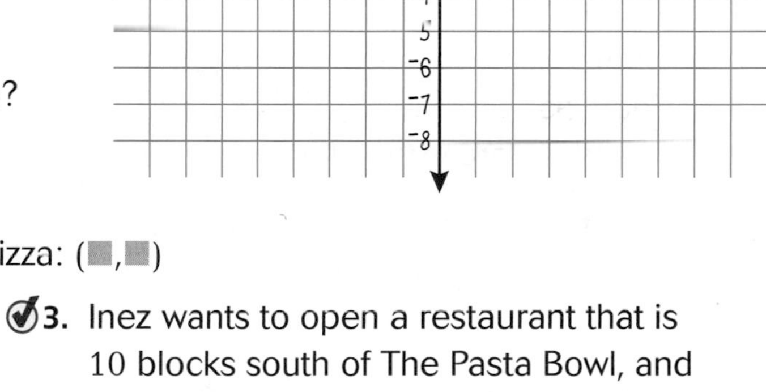

1. Pam mapped out her favorite restaurants in town. Burger Bistro is located at the coordinates (2,1). Sam's Deli is 5 blocks directly north of Burger Bistro. The Pasta Bowl is located 4 blocks west of Sam's Deli. Val's Pizza has a *y*-coordinate that is 2 blocks south of Sam's Deli and an *x*-coordinate that is 1 block east of Burger Bistro. What are the coordinates for Val's Pizza?

   Think: What do you need to find?
   the coordinates for Val's Pizza

   Which facts are relevant to solving the problem?
   the coordinates for Burger Bistro and the coordinates for Sam's Deli

   Burger Bistro: (2,1) Sam's Deli: (2,■) Val's Pizza: (■,■)

2. **What if** Val's Pizza was directly south of The Pasta Bowl and directly west of Burger Bistro? What would the coordinates of Val's Pizza be then?

3. Inez wants to open a restaurant that is 10 blocks south of The Pasta Bowl, and 4 blocks west of Burger Bistro. What will the coordinates of her restaurant be?

Mixed Applications

4. Cindy started walking at 11:00 A.M. She walked 2 blocks north, 3 blocks west, 2 blocks south, and 3 blocks east. She walked for $\frac{3}{4}$ hour. What shape did her route make?

5. Brad and Al are brothers. The sum of their ages is 22 years, and the difference in their ages is 2 years. Brad is older than Al. How old is each boy? Explain how you know your answer is correct.

6. The Garden Club needs 50 plants. If 15 plants cost $46.95, how much would the Garden Club pay for 50 plants?

7. **WRITE Math** Sue used a coordinate plane to plan her garden. She planted rose bushes in a square around her garden as a border. Each side of the square is 10 feet in length. If 1 unit on the coordinate plane equals 1 foot and the center of the square is at the point of (0,0), where are the 4 vertices of the square? **Explain** how you know.

Extra Practice

Set A Write an ordered pair for each point. Use the grid. (pp. 498–499)

1. point *J*
2. point *M*
3. point *T*
4. point *K*
5. point *F*
6. point *L*

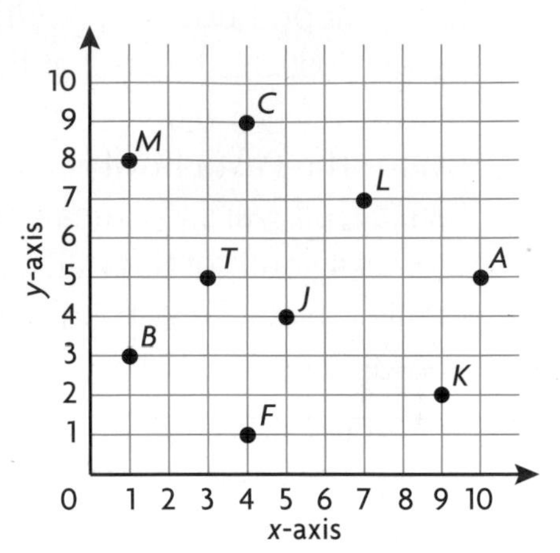

Copy the grid. Graph and label each of the following points.

7. (4,2)
8. (0,5)
9. (2,1)
10. (1,0)
11. (5,3)
12. (4,1)
13. (3,3)
14. (0,0)

Set B Write the ordered pairs. Then graph them. (pp. 500–501)

1.

Number of Triangles, *x*	1	2	3	4
Number of Angles, *y*	3	6	9	12

2.

Number of Hexagons, *x*	1	2	3	4
Number of Sides, *y*	6	12	18	24

Set C For 1–10, identify the ordered pair for each point. (pp. 502–503)

1. point *A*
2. point *F*
3. point *C*
4. point *E*
5. point *B*
6. point *D*
7. point *G*
8. point *H*
9. point *I*
10. point *J*

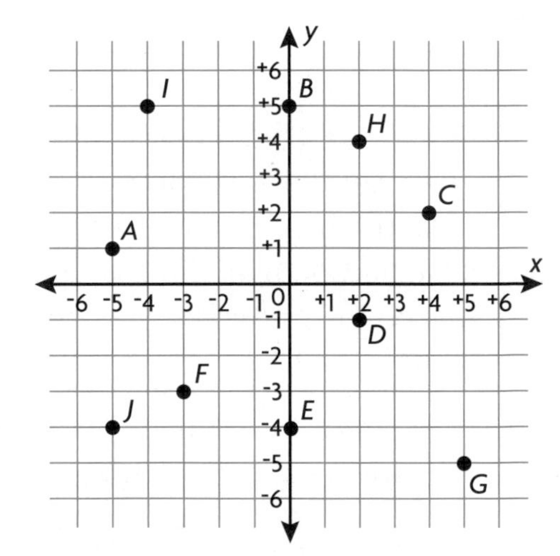

For 11–16, graph and label the ordered pairs on the coordinate plane.

11. *M* $(^{-}2,0)$
12. *N* $(4,^{-}5)$
13. *P* $(0,^{-}3)$
14. *R* $(^{-}1,6)$
15. *S* $(0,^{-}1)$
16. *T* $(2,^{-}2)$

Technology
CD ROM
Use Harcourt Mega Math, The Number Games, *Arachna Graph*, Levels G, H, L.

Set D

Find a rule to complete the function table. Then write the rule as an equation. (pp. 504–505)

1.

Input, x	19	17	15	■	11
Output, y	14	12	10	8	■

2.

Input, x	1	2	3	4	5
Output, y	4	7	10	■	■

3.

Input, x	4	8	16	24	■
Output, y	2	4	8	■	24

4.

Input, x	3	4	5	■	■
Output, y	4	5	6	7	8

Make a function table for each equation.

5. $y = x - 3$
6. $y = x + 1$
7. $y = 2x + 1$
8. $y = 3x - 2$

9. A miniature golf course charges \$8 per person for a round of golf plus a \$1 putter cleaning fee for the group. Write a function to show how much the course charges for a round of golf.

10. Russ charges \$12 for every lawn he mows. Write a rule and an equation to show how much Russ can earn mowing lawns.

Set E

Find the rule to complete the function table. Then write an equation. (pp. 506–509)

1.

x	5	4	3	■	1
y	0	−1	−2	−3	■

2.

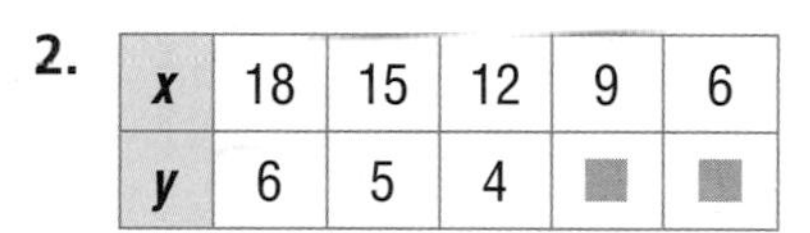

x	18	15	12	9	6
y	6	5	4	■	■

Use each equation to make a function table with at least 4 ordered pairs. Then graph the ordered pairs on a coordinate plane.

3. $y = 2x + 2$
4. $y = 5 + x$
5. $y = 3x + 1$
6. $y = 10 - x$

7. Maria earns \$4 less than Richard. Write an equation to show how much Maria and Richard make.

8. Choose five values for x in the equation you wrote for Exercise 7. Make a function table.

 Chapter 19 Review/Test

Check Vocabulary and Concepts

VOCABULARY
ordered pair
origin
x-axis

Choose the best term from the box.

1. A(n) __?__ is a set of two numbers that locates a single point on the coordinate grid. (AF 1.4, p. 498)
2. The point where the two lines intersect is called the __?__, or (0,0). (AF 1.4, p. 502)

Check Skills

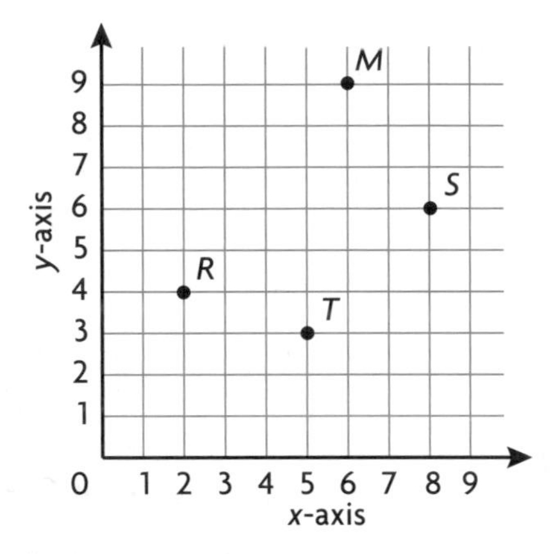

Write an ordered pair for each point. Use the figure.
(AF 1.4, pp. 498–499)

3. point S
4. point M
5. point T

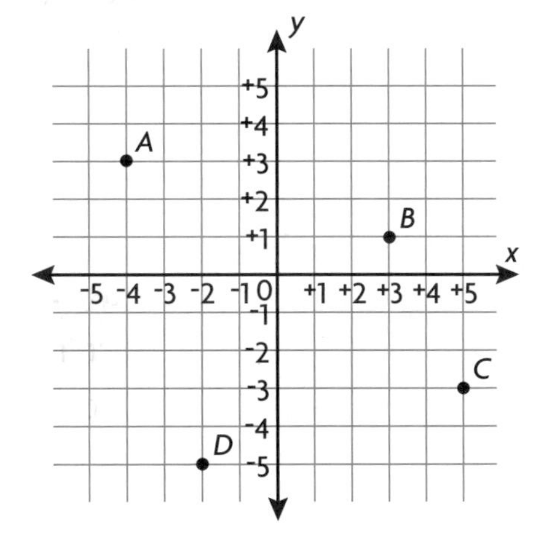

Write an ordered pair for each point. (AF 1.4, pp. 502–503)

6. point A
7. point B
8. point C

Find a rule to complete the function table. Then write the rule as an equation. (AF 1.5, pp. 504–505)

9.

x	4	3	2	1	0
y	12	9	■	■	0

10.

x	4	3	2	1	0
y	4	5	6	■	■

Make a function table for each equation. (AF 1.5, pp. 506–509)

11. $y = 3x - 2$
12. $y = x - 1$
13. $y = 2x + 3$

Check Problem Solving

Solve. (AF 1.4, MR 1.1, MR 2.3, pp. 510–511)

14. A neighborhood map shows the coordinates of the park as ($^-2$,4). The y-coordinate of Town Hall is the same as the park. The x-coordinate of Town Hall is the opposite of the park. Where is Town Hall?

15. **WRITE Math** Suppose there are plans to build a new park on the opposite side of town. What if the new park is built 5 units right and 8 units below the existing park in Exercise 14? **Explain** where the new park would be located.

Technology Use *Online Assessment.*

Enrich • Graphing Equations

A Point in Common

Some equations contain two variables. To find the value of each variable, replace the first variable with a value. Then solve the equation to find the value of the second variable.

Examples

A What values of x and y make the equation $4 - x = y$ true?

$4 - x = y$

Make a table. List 3 values for x.

x	y
0	
1	
2	

Solve the equation for y.

x	y
0	4
1	3
2	2

B What values of x and y make the equation $y = x + 2$ true?

$y = x + 2$

Make a table. List 3 values for x.

x	y
0	
2	
3	

Solve the equation for y.

x	y
0	2
1	3
2	4

Do the two equations have a common solution? Graph both equations on a coordinate plane to find out!

The point (1, 3) is a common point, so it is a solution to both equations.

Try It

Complete the tables for each pair of equations.
Then graph the equations to find a common solution.

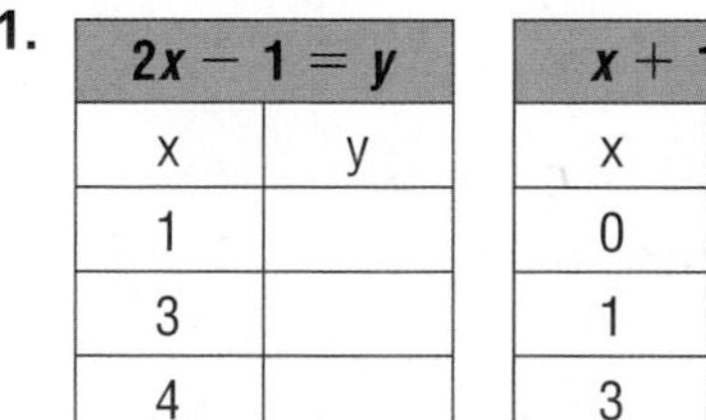

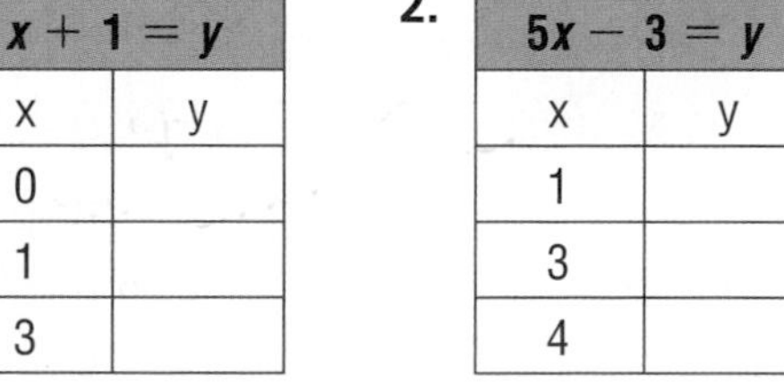

1.

$2x - 1 = y$	
x	y
1	
3	
4	

$x + 1 = y$	
x	y
0	
1	
3	

2.

$5x - 3 = y$	
x	y
1	
3	
4	

$3x + 1 = y$	
x	y
0	
1	
3	

Think About It

WRITE Math **Explain** how you could find a common solution of two equations by simply looking at a graph of the equations.

Unit Review/Test
Chapters 17–19

Multiple Choice

1. Which of the following *best* describes the figure below? (MG 2.1, p. 436)

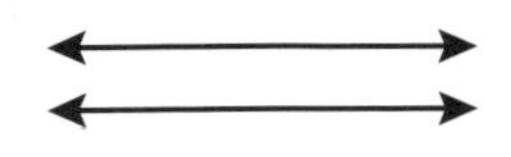

A acute angles

B right angles

C parallel lines

D perpendicular lines

2. What is the approximate measure of this angle in degrees? (MG 2.1, p. 440)

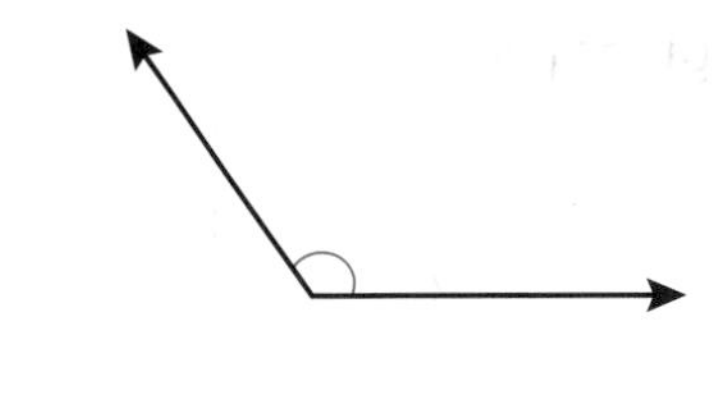

A 35° C 90°

B 70° D 115°

3. What is the total measure of the angles in this rectangle? (MG 2.2, p. 448)

A 180° C 360°

B 270° D 450°

4. What is the measure of angle *D*? (MG 2.2, p. 468)

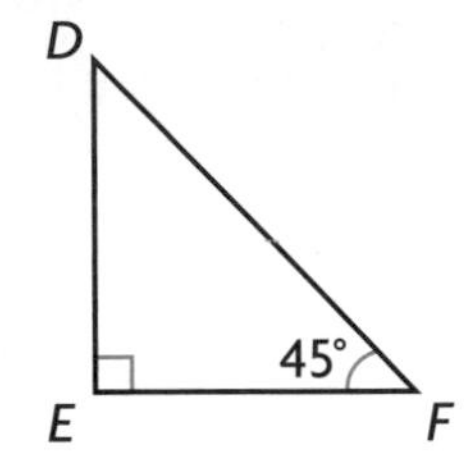

A 30°

B 45°

C 55°

D 60°

5. In the graph below, what ordered pair names point *P*? (SDAP 1.5, p. 498)

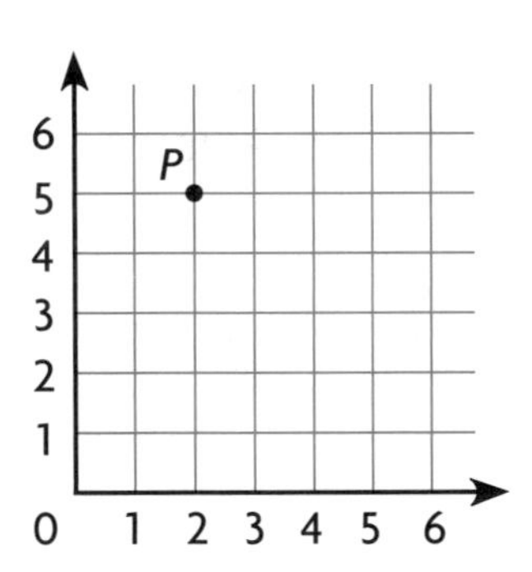

A (2,5)

B (2,4)

C (1,5)

D (5,2)

GO ONLINE Technology Use *Online Assessment.*

6. The map below shows the locations of 4 different stores. Which store is located at $(2, {}^{-}2)$? (AF 1.4, p. 502)

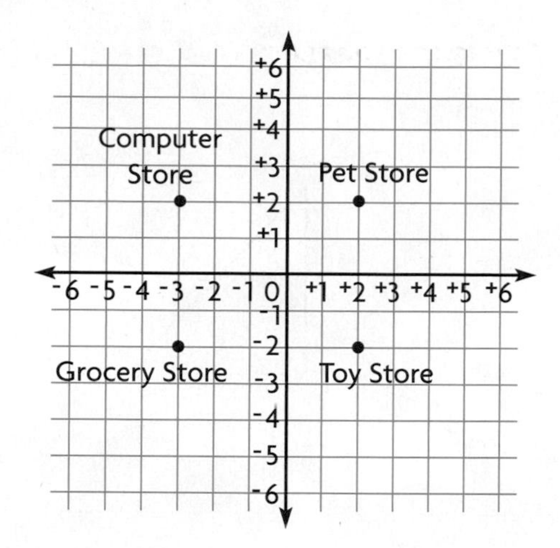

A Pet Store

B Computer Store

C Grocery Store

D Toy Store

7. Which equation shows the relationship of all the values in the table below? (AF 1.5, p. 504)

x	y
$^{-}2$	6
4	12
7	15
10	18

A $y = 3 - x$

B $y = x + 4$

C $y = x + 8$

D $y = x - 4$

Short Response

8. Draw an equilateral triangle. Use a protractor to measure and label its angles. (MG 2.1, p. 476)

9. Using a ruler, draw two rectangles that are similar but not congruent. (MG 2.1, p. 456)

10. Draw a base of the prism below. Then write the prism's name. (MG 2.3, p. 478)

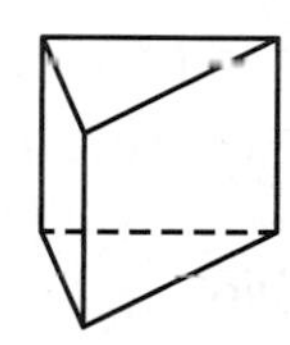

Extended Response WRITE Math

11. Using grid paper, draw a net for the rectangular prism below. How many of the faces are rectangles? How many are squares? **Explain** how you know. (MG 2.3, p. 482)

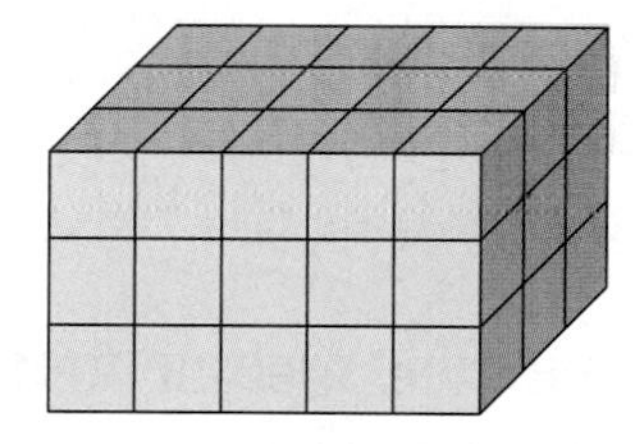

12. Write an equation for the relationship shown in the table. Graph the equation.

x	3	4	5	6	10
y	5	6	7	8	■

What is y when $x = 10$? **Explain.** (AF 1.5, p. 506)

California

Problem Solving

from THE WORLD ALMANAC FOR KIDS

California Rocks!

Crystal Geometry

Well-formed crystal shapes occur when minerals are allowed to grow freely. Crystals are solid shapes that form by a regular repeated pattern of molecules connecting together. Different minerals form different-shaped crystals. You can find a variety of crystals in California, such as neptunite, dolomite, benitoite, and gold.

Neptunite ▶ black prisms

FACT·ACTIVITY

Use the Shapes of Crystals chart to answer the questions.

1. How many faces, edges, and vertices does the gold crystal have? Name the solid shape.
2. What polygon do the faces of the sulphur crystal appear to be? **Explain.**
3. What solid figure describes the shape of the talc crystal?
4. Which crystal has a face with obtuse angles?
5. WRITE Math Silver is also found in California. Each silver crystal face has the same shape and size, and all the angles are right angles. What solid shape is the silver crystal? **Explain.**

Shapes of Crystals

Crystal	Geometric shape
Gold	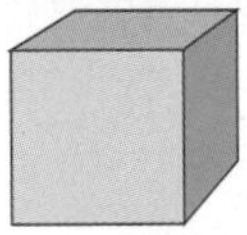
Dolomite	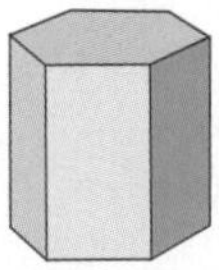
Sulphur	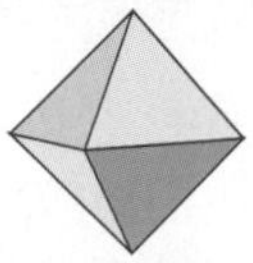
Talc	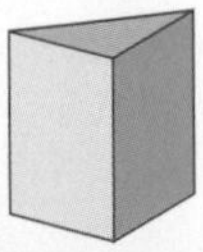

ALMANAC Fact

Benitoite is the state gem of California. This gem was discovered in 1907 in San Benito, California. Benitoite can only be found in San Benito.

CRYSTALS IN CALIFORNIA

Each October, many rock and mineral collectors travel to a mineral show at Searles Lake in Trona, California. Searles Lake is a dry lake bed where many rare minerals can be found.

Some collectors gather rare hanksite crystals in a popular "blow hole" field trip. A local mining company will drill a line of 6 to 8 holes 60 feet from each other. The miners use explosives and compressed air to loosen hanksite crystals and bring them up to the top of each "blow hole".

▲ Benitoite

FACT·ACTIVITY

Suppose you are laying out the drilling sites for the hanksite collecting field trip. The holes you blast will be in a line 60 feet apart from each other.

1. Copy the map and coordinate grid. Plot the location of the first hole at (1,1).
2. Use the scale to figure out where a point 60 feet from the first point should be. You can go in any direction. Hint: Each point should land on an intersection.
3. Plot 4 more points so the holes will be 60 feet apart in a straight line. Describe in words how far east or west and how far north or south each hole is from the other.
4. Draw a line connecting the points. Compare your line with a classmate's line. Are the two lines in the same place? Are the two lines going in the same direction? **Explain** how the lines are similar.

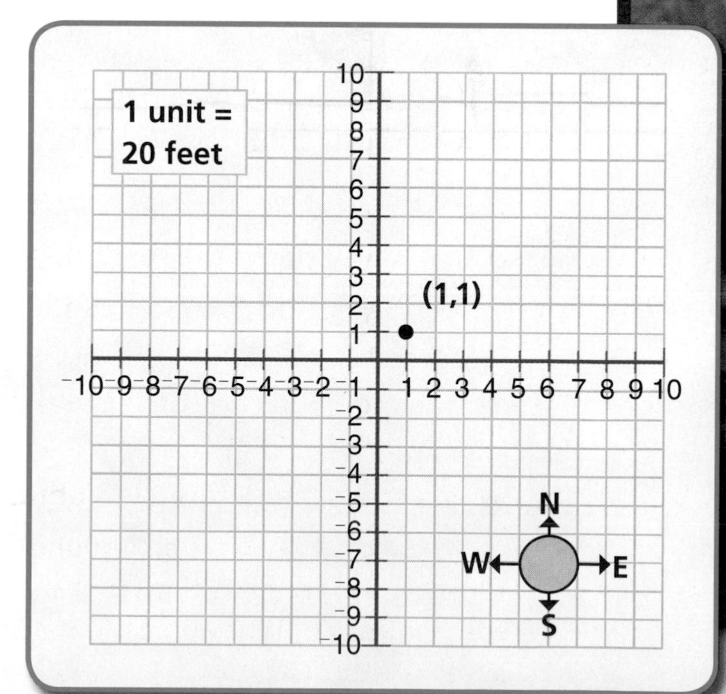

UNIT 7 Measurement

Math on Location

1

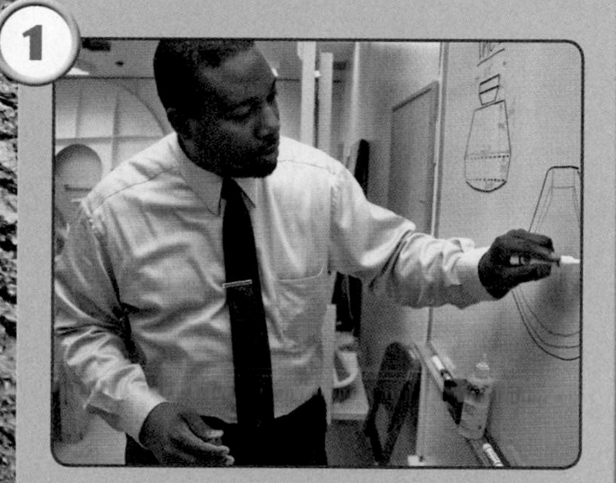

▲ Dimensions, weight, and capacity are critical for the design of a space capsule.

2

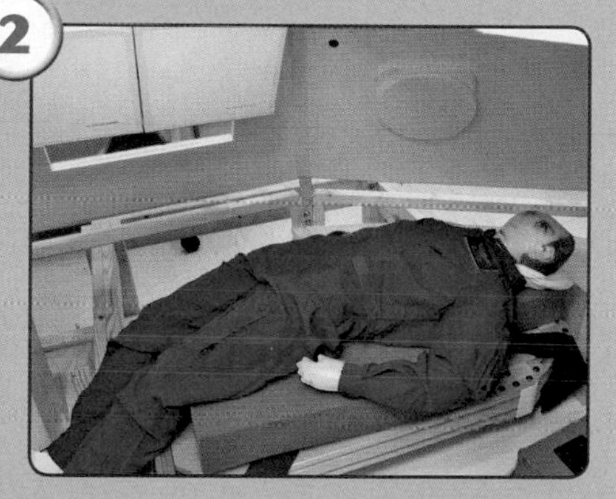

▲ A life-sized model of a human is placed in the model of the capsule to judge how much space is necessary.

3

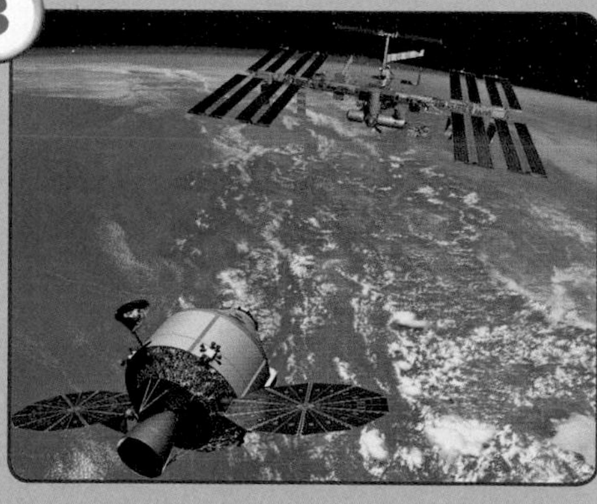

▲ This rendering shows both 2- and 3-dimensional shapes in one possible Orion Space Capsule design.

VOCABULARY POWER

TALK Math

What math is used in **Math on Location**? What types of measurements would you need to build a life-sized model of a space capsule?

READ Math

REVIEW VOCABULARY You learned the words below when you learned about measuring. How do these words relate to **Math on Location**?

volume the measure of the space a solid figure occupies

formula a set of symbols that expresses a mathematical rule

WRITE Math

Copy and complete word association trees like the ones below. Use what you know about measurement units and formulas to identify what type of measurement is described.

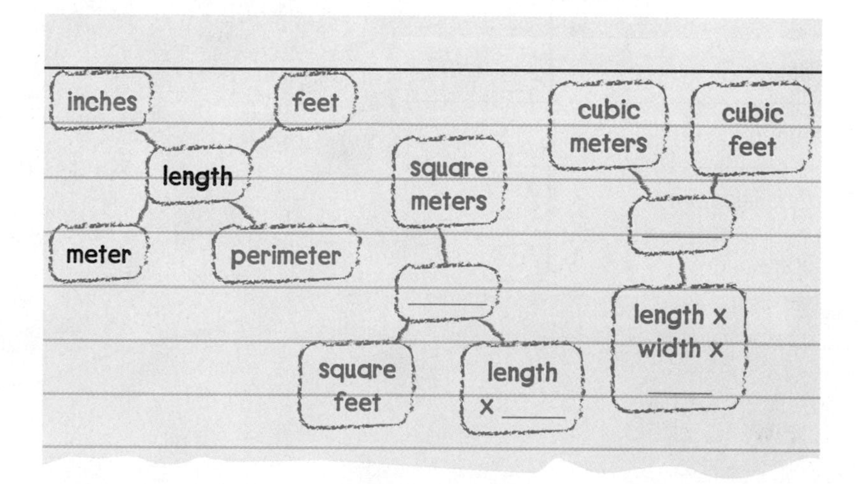

CHAPTER

20 Measurement and Perimeter

The Big Idea Attributes of two-dimensional figures can be measured using metric and customary units.

Investigate

Suppose you are an archaeologist working on a dig in Death Valley. You outline a rectangular area measuring 50 feet by 15 feet using string. Show and describe three other possible plane figures that you could make from the same amount of string.

Plane Figures	
Square	□
Triangle	△
Parallelogram	▱
Trapezoid	⏢

CALIFORNIA FAST FACT

The lowest point of elevation in the Western Hemisphere is in Death Valley. Temperatures in Death Valley can reach 130°F in the summer.

GO ONLINE **Technology** Student pages are available in the Student eBook.

Show What You Know

Check your understanding of important skills needed for success in Chapter 20.

▶ Perimeter—Count Units

Find the perimeter of each figure.

1.

2.

3.

4.

5.

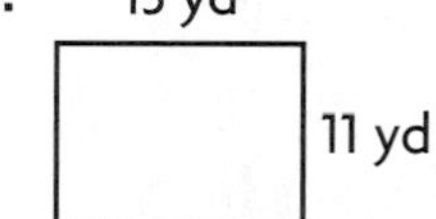

6.

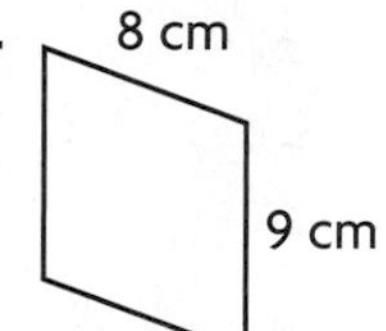

7.

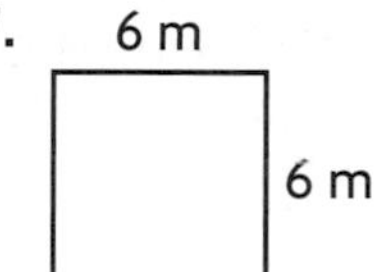

8.

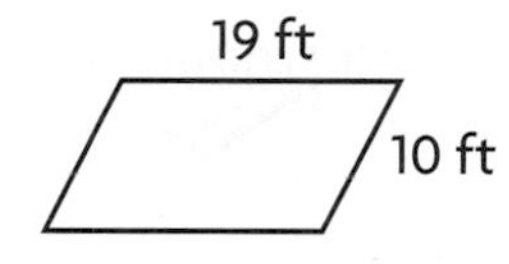

▶ Choose the Appropriate Unit

Choose the appropriate customary unit.

9. height of a room
inches or **feet**

10. length of your finger
inches or **feet**

11. width of a baseball field
yards or **miles**

Choose the appropriate metric unit.

12. length of your desk
centimeters or **meters**

13. distance biked in 1 hour
meters or **kilometers**

14. width of a room
centimeters or **meters**

VOCABULARY POWER

CHAPTER VOCABULARY

formula
perimeter
polygon
rectangular prism

WARM-UP WORDS

perimeter the distance around a closed plane figure

polygon a closed plane figure formed by three or more line segments

formula a set of symbols that expresses a mathematical rule

rectangular prism a solid figure in which all six faces are rectangles

LESSON 1

Length

OBJECTIVE: Identify and convert customary and metric units of length.

Quick Review

1. 15×3
2. $60 \div 12$
3. 8×12
4. $4 \times 5{,}280$
5. $15{,}840 \div 5{,}280$

Learn

PROBLEM Matt needs 36 feet of chain for his craft project. The chain is sold by the yard. How many yards of chain does he need?

Example 1 Change feet to yards.

Find the number of yards in 36 feet.

Think: 36 feet = ■ yards $36 \div 3 = y$

To change smaller units to larger units, divide.

number of feet	÷	number of feet in 1 yard	=	number of yards
↓		↓		↓
36	÷	3	=	12

So, Matt needs 12 yards of chain.

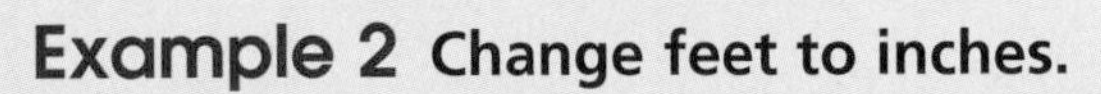

Example 2 Change feet to inches.

Terri needs 4 feet of fabric for her craft project. How many inches of fabric does she need?

Find the number of inches in 4 feet.

Think: 4 feet = ■ inches $4 \times 12 = x$

To change larger units to smaller units, multiply.

number of feet	×	number of inches in 1 foot	=	number of inches
↓		↓		↓
4	×	12	=	48

So, Terri needs 48 inches of fabric.

Customary Units of Length
12 inches (in.) = 1 foot (ft)
3 feet = 1 yard (yd)
36 inches = 1 yard
5,280 feet = 1 mile (mi)
1,760 yards = 1 mile

More Examples

A Change 132 inches to feet.

number of inches	÷	number of inches in 1 foot	=	number of feet
↓		↓		↓
132	÷	12	=	11

So, 132 inches is 11 feet.

B Change 3 miles to feet.

number of miles	×	number of feet in 1 mile	=	number of feet
↓		↓		↓
3	×	5,280	=	15,840

So, 3 miles is 15,840 feet.

AF 1.2 Use a letter to represent an unknown number; write and evaluate simple algebraic expressions in one variable by substitution. *also* **MR 2.2, MR 2.4, MR 3.2, MR 3.3**

Metric Length

You can use multiplication and division to change metric units of length.

Example 3 Change centimeters to meters.

Alberto measures a 125-centimeter piece of poster board. What is the length in meters?

Think: 125 centimeters = ■ meters $125 \div 100 = m$

To change smaller units to larger units, divide.

number of cm	÷	number of cm in 1 m	=	number of m
↓		↓		↓
125	÷	100	=	1.25

So, there are 1.25 meters in 125 centimeters.

Metric Units of Length
10 millimeters (mm) = 1 centimeter (cm)
100 centimeters = 1 meter (m)
1,000 meters = 1 kilometer (km)

Example 4 Change centimeters to millimeters.

Fran measures a 15-centimeter length of yarn. What is the length in millimeters?

Think: 15 centimeters = ■ millimeters $15 \times 10 = n$

To change larger units to smaller units, multiply.

number of cm	×	number of mm in 1 cm	=	number of mm
↓		↓		↓
15	×	10	=	150

So, there are 150 millimeters in 15 centimeters.

Math Idea
Since there are 10 mm in 1 cm, 1 mm is the same as $\frac{1}{10}$, or 0.1, cm.

Guided Practice

1. How many feet are in 168 inches?
   Think: Change to larger units, so divide.
   12 inches = 1 foot
   $168 \div 12 =$ ■ feet

2. How many millimeters are in 12 centimeters?
   Think: Change to smaller units, so multiply.
   1 centimeter = 10 millimeters
   $12 \times 10 =$ ■ millimeters

Change the given units.

3. 7 yd = ■ ft
4. 6 ft = ■ in.
5. 3,520 yd = ■ mi
6. 45 ft = ■ yd
7. 22 cm = ■ mm
8. 30 mm = ■ cm
9. 2 km = ■ m
10. 5 m = ■ cm
11. 108 in. = ■ ft
12. 12 km = ■ m
13. 42 ft = ■ yd
14. 0.5 mi = ■ ft
15. **TALK Math** **Explain** how to change 36 inches to feet.

Technology
Use Harcourt Mega Math, Ice Station Exploration, *Linear Lab*, Levels C–J.

Independent Practice and Problem Solving

Change the given units.

16. 48 in. = ■ ft
17. 12 yd = ■ ft
18. 4 mi = ■ ft
19. 42 ft = ■ yd
20. 6 mi = ■ yd
21. 9 ft = ■ in.
22. 3.5 m = ■ cm
23. 480 mm = ■ cm
24. 1.6 km ■ m
25. 6.4 cm = ■ mm
26. 2.5 m = ■ cm
27. 4,200 cm = ■ m
28. 2.5 km = ■ m
29. 110 mm = ■ cm
30. 15 yd = ■ ft
31. 192 in. = ■ ft

Complete.

32. 145 cm = ■ m 45 cm
33. 32 ft 12 in. = ■ yd
34. 3 ft = 1 ft ■ in.
35. 2 cm 35 mm = ■ mm
36. 12 yd 2 ft = 11 yd ■ ft
37. 12 m = 10 m ■ cm

USE DATA For 38–42, use the table.

38. How many 10–inch pieces can Les cut from one rail? How many inches of rail will be left over?
39. Rita cuts a 1-m 50-cm piece from a post to make it shorter. How long is the post now?
40. John cuts a plank into three equal lengths. How many centimeters long is each length?
41. Aaron cuts two equal-size pieces from one post. A piece measuring 2 ft 4 in. long is left. How long are the two pieces that Aaron cut?
42. WRITE Math **Explain** how you would subtract the length of a plank from the length of a post. Use the table above.

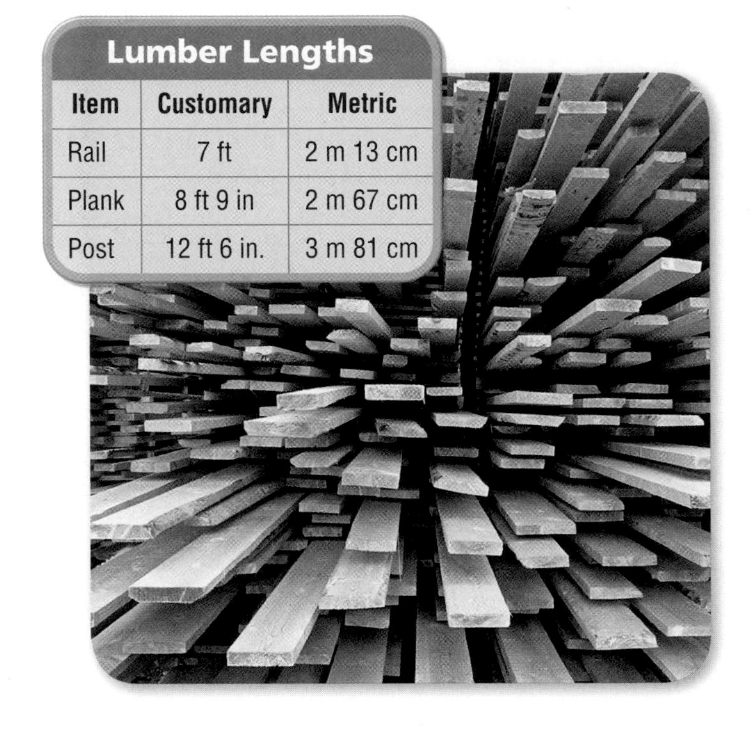

Lumber Lengths

Item	Customary	Metric
Rail	7 ft	2 m 13 cm
Plank	8 ft 9 in	2 m 67 cm
Post	12 ft 6 in.	3 m 81 cm

Achieving the Standards

43. The sum of two angles of a triangle is 60°. What is the measure of the third angle?
(MG 2.2, p. 468)

44. Tony spent 25% of his savings on a computer. What fraction of his savings are left? (NS 1.2, p. 404)

45. **Test Prep** A length of 3.28 meters is equal to which of the following?
    - A 32.8 cm
    - B 328 cm
    - C 0.328 km
    - D 328 km

46. **Test Prep** A length of 2 yd 2 ft is equal to which of the following?
    - A 4 ft
    - B 6 ft
    - C 10 ft 10 in.
    - D 96 in.

Extra Practice on page 538, Set A

WRITE Math WORKSHOP

Pose a Problem

Different problems can be posed using a given set of data. To do this, you may want to change the units in the data. Ms. Thomas asked her class to use the data in the table to write a problem that involved the lengths of the swing sets.

Swing Sets

Size	Length (ft)	Width (ft)
Large A	27	24
Large B	21	30
Medium A	21	25
Medium B	12	24
Small A	20	21
Small B	17	23

First, I converted the dimensions of the swing sets to yards so that I can better compare the given lengths to an exact space described in my problem.

Size	Length	Width
Large A	9 yd	8 yd
Large B	7 yd	10 yd
Medium A	7 yd	8 yd 1 ft
Medium B	4 yd	8 yd
Small A	6 yd 2 ft	7 yd
Small B	5 yd 2 ft	7 yd 2 ft

Finally, I wrote this problem about the data. "In his backyard Mr. Torres has a space that is 7 yd long and 8 yd wide. Which swing sets can fit in the space in his backyard?"

Solution: Mr. Torres can use the Medium B, the Small A, or the Small B swing set.

Tips

To pose a problem:

- Understand what your problem will be about.
- Study the data.
- Complete all the computations needed to solve the problem.
- Solve the problem to check that you have written it so that others can solve it.

Problem Solving **Pose a problem using the swing-set data in the following ways.**

1. Convert the length and width of one swing set from feet to inches.
2. Compare the lengths in inches of the two swing sets in the large, medium, or small group.

LESSON 2 HANDS ON

Estimate Perimeter

OBJECTIVE: Estimate perimeter.

Quick Review

Estimate by rounding to the nearest whole number.

1. 4.74
2. 5.2 + 6.8
3. 3.84 + 1.9
4. 5.8 + 7.1
5. 7.2 + 15.14

Vocabulary

perimeter

Investigate

Materials ■ metric ruler ■ string ■ paper

The **perimeter** is the distance around a figure. One way to estimate the perimeter of a figure is by using a string, a ruler, and a tracing of a figure.

A Trace the outline of your shoe on a sheet of paper. Make the outline as close to the shape and size of your shoe as you can.

B Lay a piece of string around the tracing of your shoe. Align the string carefully in order to get a good estimate of the perimeter. Mark the string where it meets itself.

C Now lay the string in a straight line, and use a ruler to measure the marked section in centimeters. Record your answer.

A

B

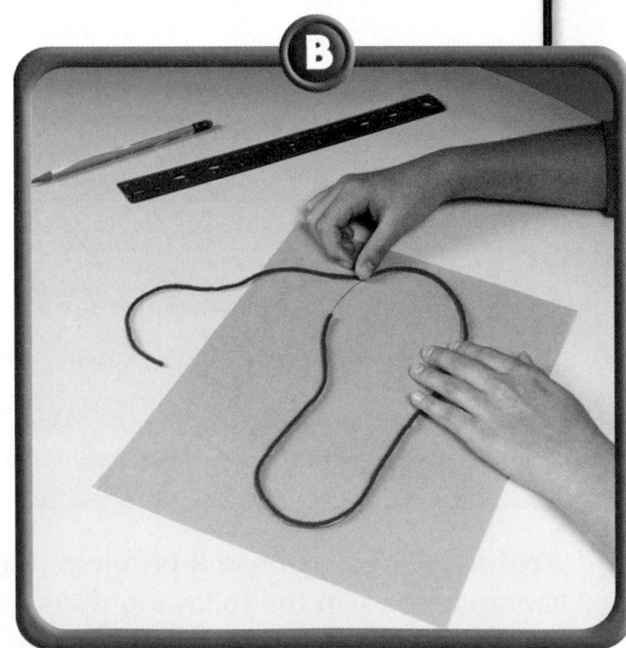

Draw Conclusions

1. Compare the estimated perimeter of your shoe with those of your classmates. How different are the measurements? Are any the same?
2. **Comprehension** What does it mean to estimate a measurement?

MG 1.4 Differentiate between, and use appropriate units of measures for, two- and three-dimensional objects (i.e., find the perimeter, area, volume). *also* **MR 2.0, MR 2.3, MR 2.4, MR 2.5, MR 3.2**

Connect

You can use a ruler to measure the perimeter of polygons.

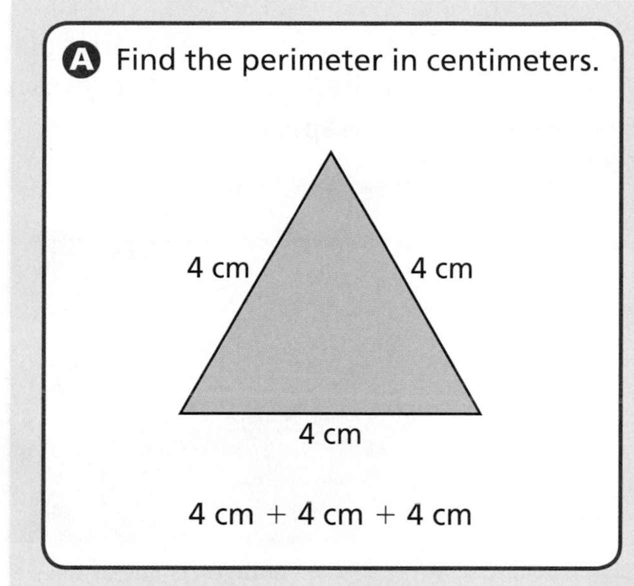

So, the perimeter is 12 cm.

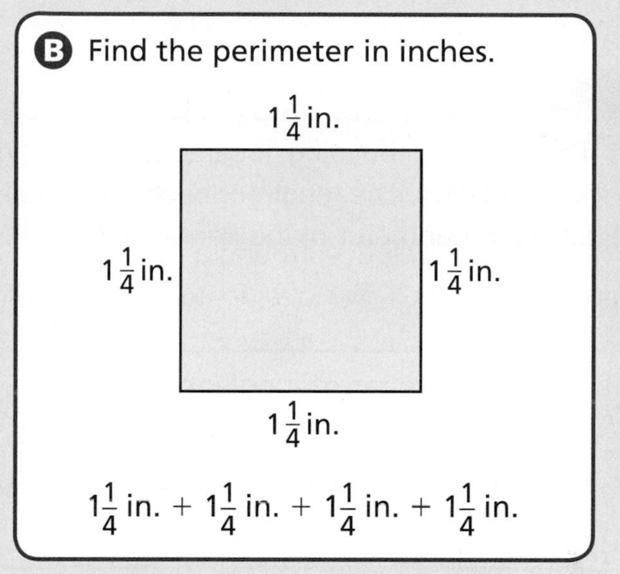

So, the perimeter is 5 in.

TALK Math

Explain how you can use a ruler to find the perimeter of any polygon.

Practice

1. On a sheet of paper, trace around the outline of your hand with your fingers closed. Draw a line to make a closed figure. Then use string and a ruler to estimate the perimeter in centimeters.

2. Using a string and a ruler, estimate the perimeter of your math book in centimeters.

Find the perimeter of each polygon in centimeters.

3. 4.

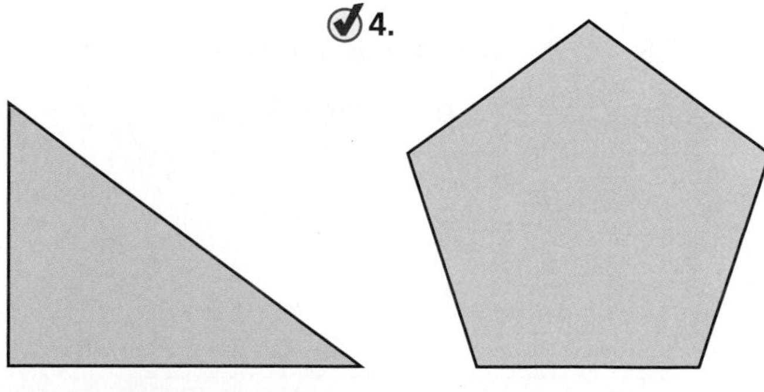

5.

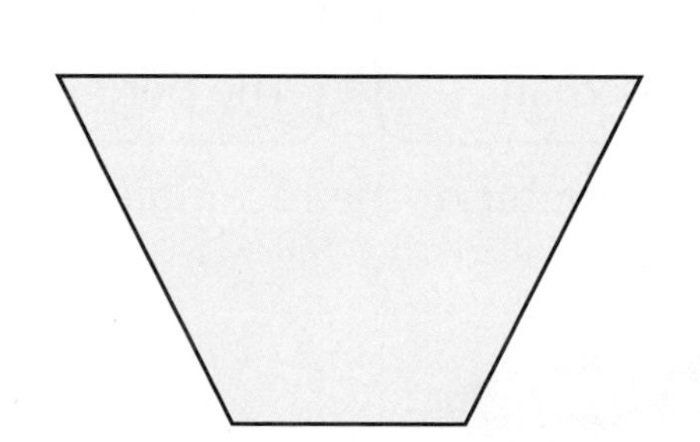

6.

7. **WRITE Math** **Explain** how you can estimate the perimeter of a regular polygon.

LESSON 3

Find Perimeter

OBJECTIVE: Find the perimeter of polygons.

Quick Review

Name the number of sides for each figure.

1. square
2. triangle
3. hexagon
4. octagon
5. trapezoid

Learn

PROBLEM The Pentagon building, located near Washington, D.C., is a regular polygon. The length of each outer wall is 922 feet. What is the perimeter of the Pentagon?

The Pentagon is one of the world's largest office buildings.

ONE WAY **Use addition.**

You can find the perimeter of a polygon by adding the lengths of its sides.

$922 + 922 + 922 + 922 + 922 = 4{,}610$

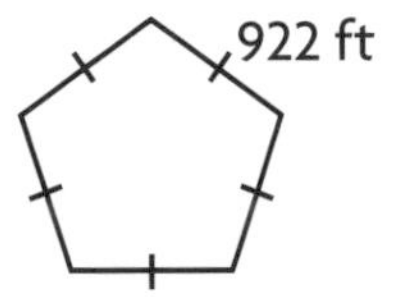

ANOTHER WAY **Use multiplication.**

Since the pentagon is a regular polygon, multiply the length of one side by the number of sides.

$922 \times 5 = 4{,}610$

So, the perimeter is 4,610 feet.

More Examples Find the perimeter of each figure.

A

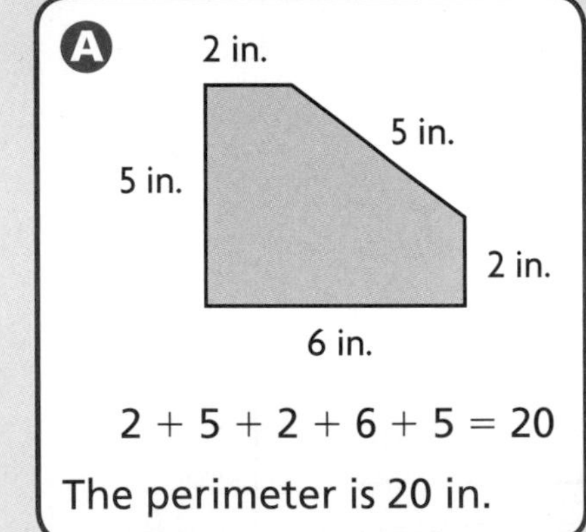

$2 + 5 + 2 + 6 + 5 = 20$

The perimeter is 20 in.

B

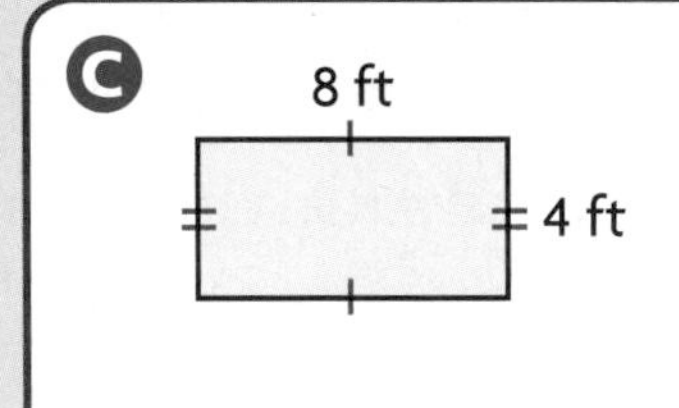

$5.4 + 2.7 + 5.4 = 13.5$

The perimeter is 13.5 cm.

C

8 ft

4 ft

$8 + 4 + 8 + 4 = 24$

The perimeter is 24 ft.

- What is the perimeter of the rectangle in Example C in yards?

Guided Practice

1. Find the perimeter of the square.

$10 + ■ + ■ + ■ = ■$ cm or $■ \times 10 = ■$ cm

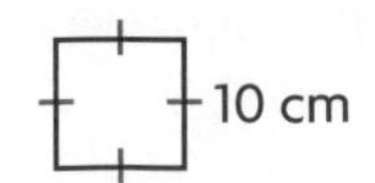

MG 1.4 Differentiate between, and use appropriate units of measures for, two- and three-dimensional objects (i.e., find the perimeter, area, volume). *also* **MR 2.3, MR 2.4, MR 3.2**

Find the perimeter of each polygon.

2.

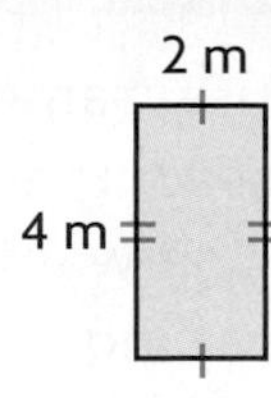

3.

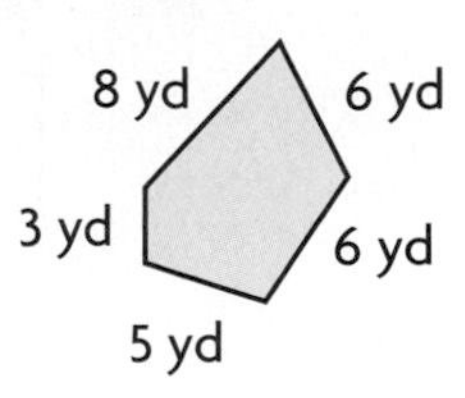

✓4.

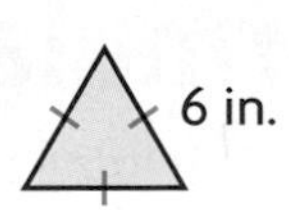

✓5.

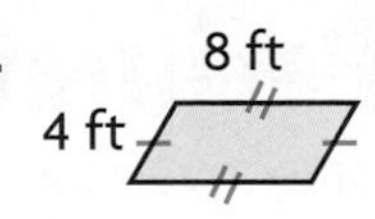

6. TALK Math **Explain** how to find the perimeter of a square.

Independent Practice and Problem Solving

Find the perimeter of each polygon.

7.

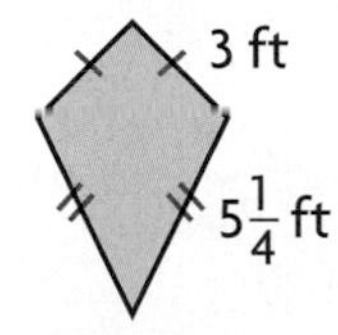

8.

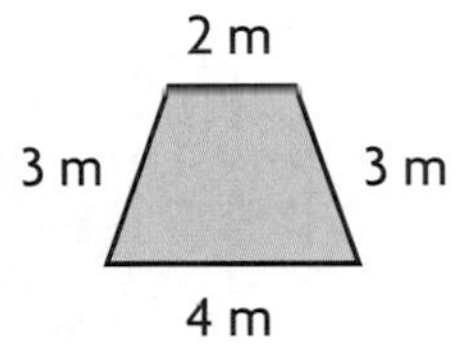

9.

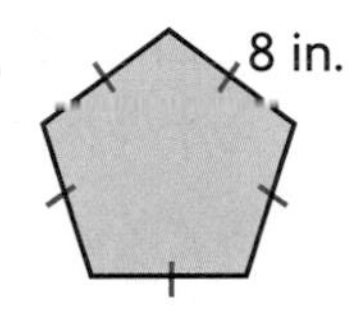

10.

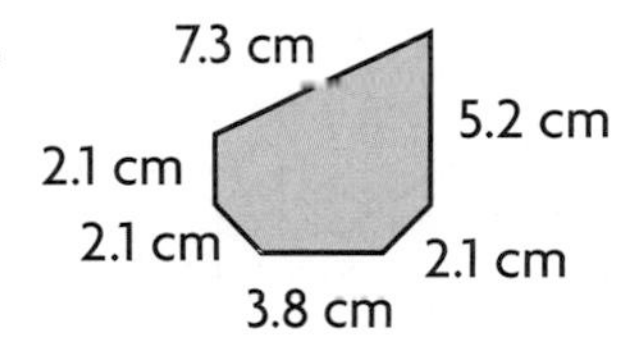

11.

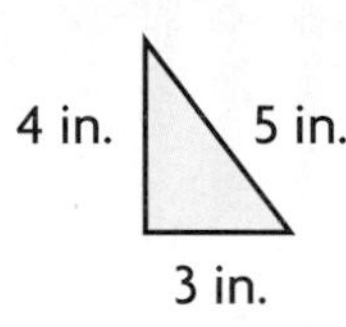

12.

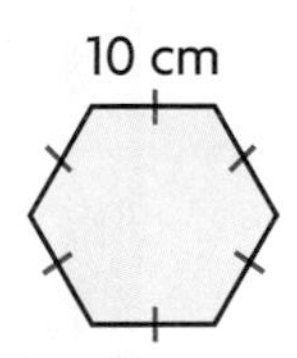

13.

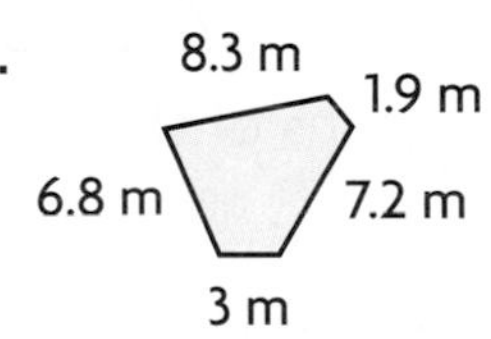

14.

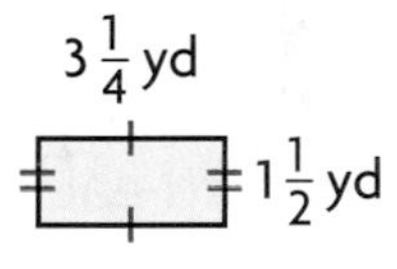

15. Dora made a scale model of the Pentagon building. The length of each side of the model is 9.2 centimeters. What is the perimeter of Dora's Pentagon model?

16. WRITE Math **What's the Error?** Denzel labeled one side of a rectangle 3 cm and another side 5 cm. Denzel said that the perimeter of his rectangle is 8 cm. What did he do wrong?

Achieving the Standards

17. Scott made a quadrilateral. Three of the angles of his quadrilateral have a measure of 112°, 98°, and 52°. What is the measure of the fourth angle? (MG 2.2, p. 472)

18. Sue scored the following numbers of points in 5 games: 20, 32, 16, 12, 40. What is the median score? (Grade 4 SDAP 1.2)

19. How many sides does a rectangle have? (MG 2.0, p. 472)

20. **Test Prep** The polygon below is regular hexagon.

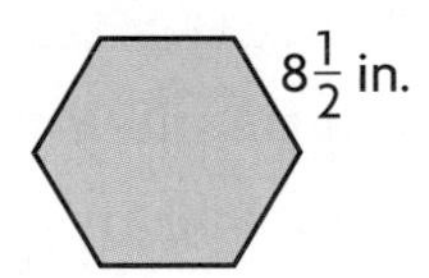

What is the perimeter?

A 40 in.

B 48 in.

C 51 in.

D 60 in.

Extra Practice on page 538, Set B

ALGEBRA

Perimeter Formulas

OBJECTIVE: Find the perimeter of polygons by using formulas.

Quick Review

Ann has a picture frame that is 15 inches long and 9 inches wide. She wants to put some beading around the edge. How many inches of beading does Ann need?

Learn

You can find the perimeter of a polygon by using a formula.

Activity **Materials** ■ metric ruler

- Draw a square, a rectangle, and a parallelogram. Make a table for your data.

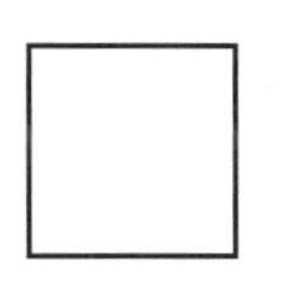
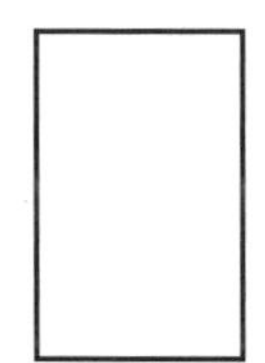
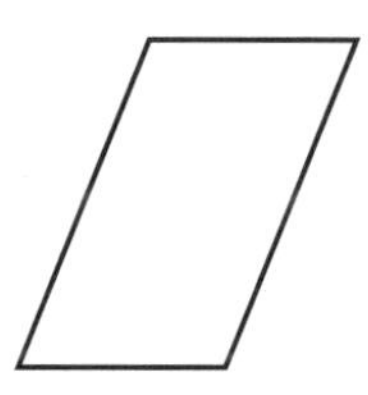

- Measure and record the lengths of the sides of each figure. Then record each perimeter.
- Look for a relationship between the lengths of the sides and the perimeter. Generate a formula for finding the perimeter of each figure, and record it.

The Lincoln Memorial was built between 1915 and 1922.

Example

The base of the Lincoln Memorial, in Washington, D.C., is 188 feet long and 118 feet wide. What is the perimeter of the Lincoln Memorial's base?

$P = l + l + w + w$, or $2l + 2w$ | P = perimeter
$P = (2 \times 188) + (2 \times 118)$ | l = length
$P = 376 + 236$ | w = width
$P = 612$

So, the perimeter of the Lincoln Memorial's base is 612 feet.

Remember

The opposite sides of a rectangle are equal in length.

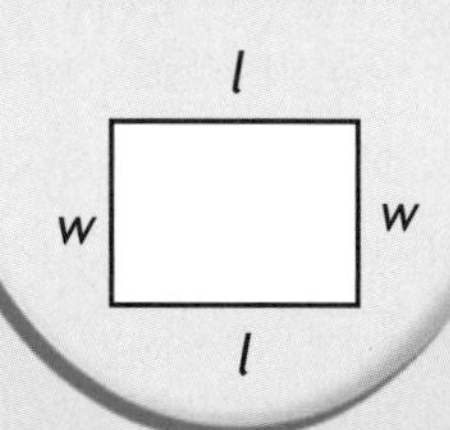

More Examples

A Perimeter of a parallelogram

a = length b = width

$P = 2a + 2b$

$P = (2 \times 5) + (2 \times 3)$

$P = 16$ cm

5 cm
3 cm

B Perimeter of a regular hexagon

s = length of side

$P = (\text{number of sides}) \times s$

$P = 6 \times 2$

$P = 12$ ft

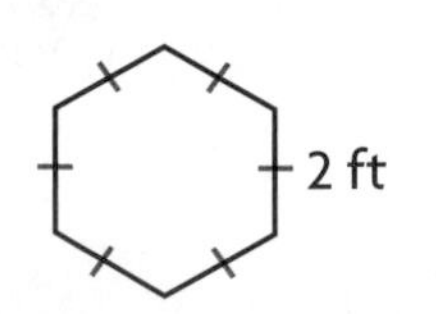

MG 1.4 Differentiate between, and use appropriate units of measures for, two- and three-dimensional objects (i.e., find the perimeter, area, volume). *also* AF 1.2, MR 2.2, MR 2.3, MR 2.4, MR 3.2

Guided Practice

Find the perimeter of each polygon by using a formula.

1. 6 m, 4 m

$P = 2a + 2b$

$P = (2 \times 6) + (2 \times ■)$

$P = ■$

2. 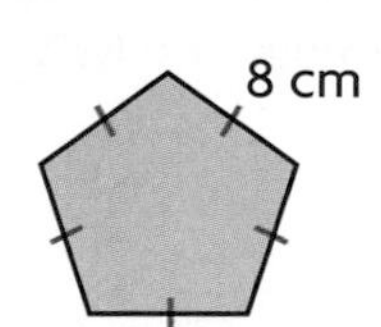

3. 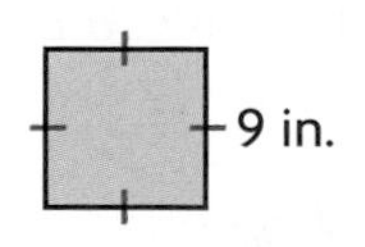

4. **TALK Math** **Explain** why you can use the same formula, $P = 2l + 2w$, for finding the perimeter of a rectangle and a square.

Independent Practice and Problem Solving

Find the perimeter of each polygon by using a formula.

5. 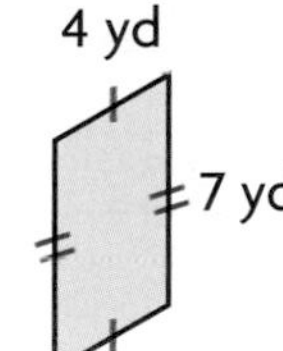

6. 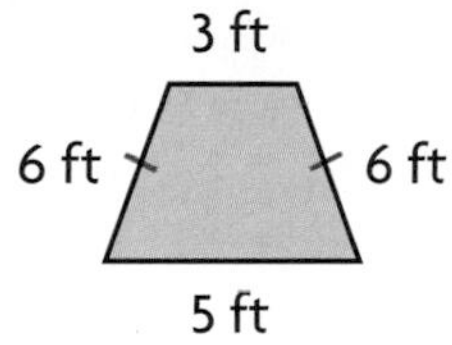

7. 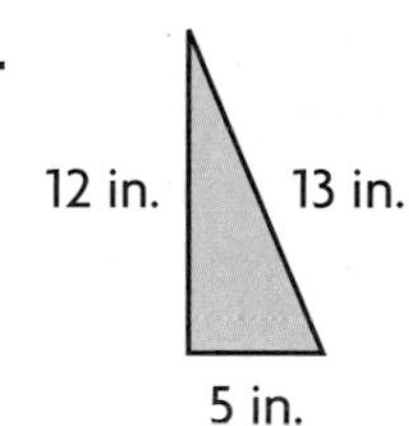

8. 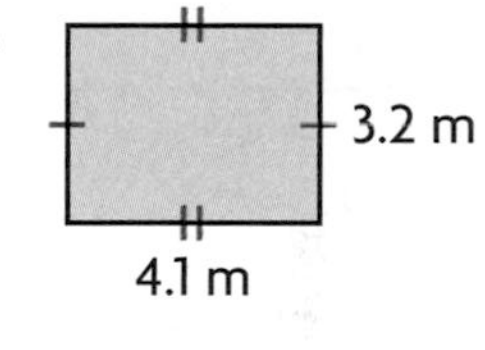

Find the perimeter of each regular polygon by using a formula.

9. 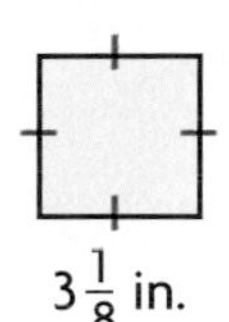

10. 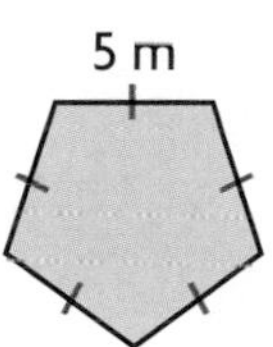

11. 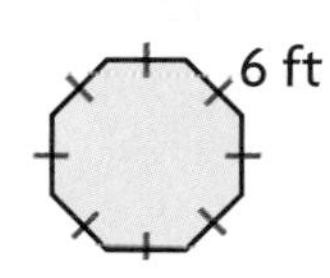

12. 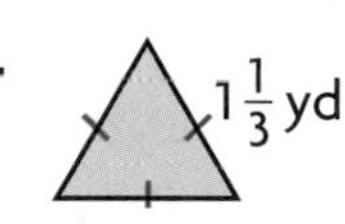

13. ***FAST FACT*** A sculpture of Abraham Lincoln is in the central chamber of the Lincoln Memorial. The central chamber is 74 feet long and 60 feet wide. What is the perimeter of the central chamber?

14. **WRITE Math** **Explain** how to find the length of each side of an equilateral triangle that has a perimeter of 84 m.

Achieving the Standards

15. Galen is doubling a pretzel recipe. The recipe calls for $2\frac{3}{4}$ cups bread flour. How much flour should Galen use? (NS 2.5, p. 242)

16. What is the perimeter of a regular pentagon with a side length of 4 cm? (MG 1.4, p. 530)

17. $64.12 \div 4 = ■$ (NS 2.1, p. 320)

18. **Test Prep** For which polygon could you use the formula $P = 2l + 2w$ to find its perimeter?

A hexagon
B rectangle
C pentagon
D octagon

Extra Practice on page 538, Set C

LESSON 5

ALGEBRA

Use Perimeter Formulas

OBJECTIVE: Use a perimeter formula to solve problems.

Quick Review

Solve the equation.

1. $a + 24 + 32 = 71$
2. $28 + x + 28 + 14 = 84$
3. $45 + 18 + m + 12 = 91$
4. $(2 \times r) + (2 \times 16) = 74$
5. $(2 \times 34) + (2 \times t) = 102$

Learn

PROBLEM Cindy is putting a border around her room. Her room has a perimeter of 52 feet. The floor plan at the right shows the lengths of the walls in her room. How much border paper will Cindy need for the side whose length is unknown?

You can use a formula to find the unknown length of a side when you know the perimeter and the lengths of the other sides.

Cindy's Bedroom

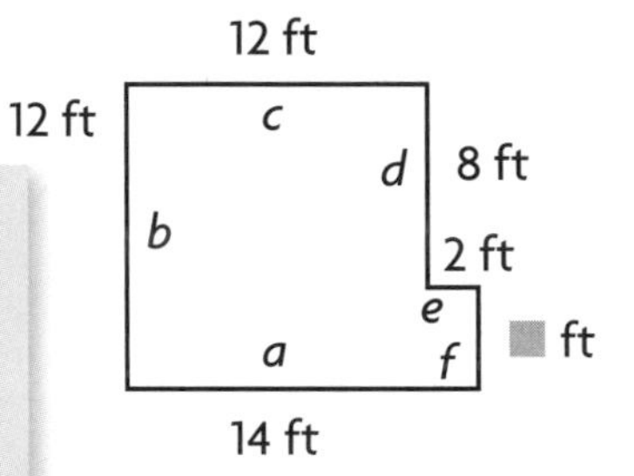

Example

$P =$ sum of the lengths of the sides	**Think:** Use a variable to represent the length of each side.
$52 = a + b + c + d + e + f$	
$52 = 14 + 12 + 12 + 8 + 2 + f$	
$52 = 48 + f$	Replace f with 4 to check your solution. $48 + 4 = 52$ ✓
$f = 4$	

So, Cindy will need 4 feet of border paper for the final side.

- Suppose you know that the perimeter of a regular hexagon is 48 meters. What formula would you use to find the length of each side?

Examples Find the unknown length.

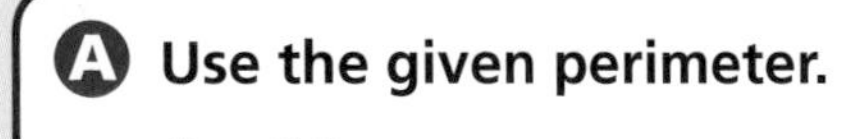

A Use the given perimeter.

$P = 29$ m

8.4 m, 7.5 m, 6.4 m, ■ m (sides b, a, c, d)

$P = a + b + c + d$

$29 = 7.5 + 8.4 + 6.4 + d$

$29 = 22.3 + d$

$d = 6.7$

So, the unknown length is 6.7 m.

B Compare equal sides.

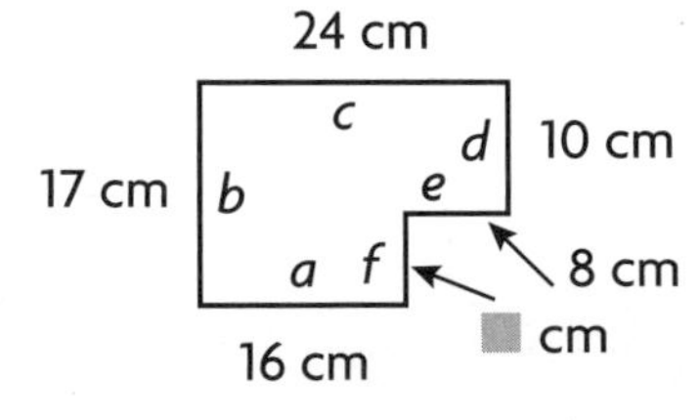

side d + side f = side b, or $d + f = b$

$d = 10$ and $b = 17$

$10 + f = 17$

$f = 7$

So, the unknown length is 7 cm.

MG 1.4 Differentiate between, and use appropriate units of measures for, two- and three-dimensional objects (i.e., find the perimeter, area, volume). *also* AF 1.2, MR 1.0, MR 2.2, MR 2.3, MR 2.4, MR 3.0, MR 3.2, MR 3.3

Guided Practice

1. Complete to find the unknown length.

$P = a + b + c + d + e$

$38 = 6 + \blacksquare + 10 + 5 + e$

$38 = \blacksquare + e$

$e = \blacksquare$

The perimeter is given. Find the unknown length.

2. $P = 36$ cm

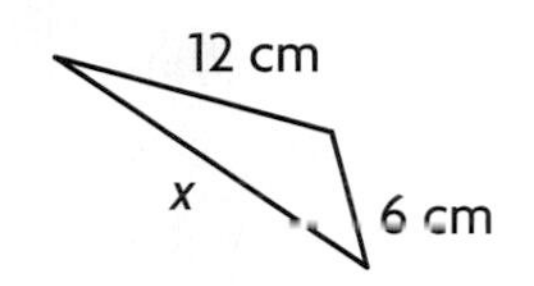

3. $P = 98$ in.

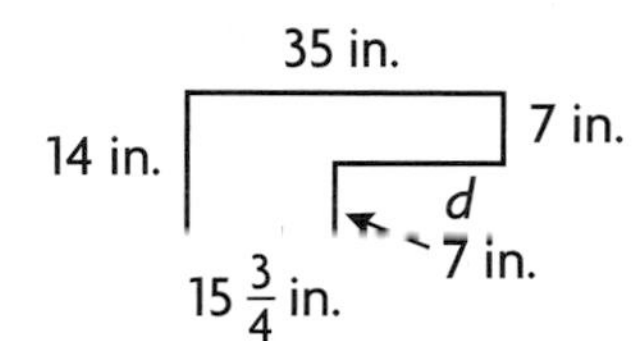

4. $P = 144.25$ m

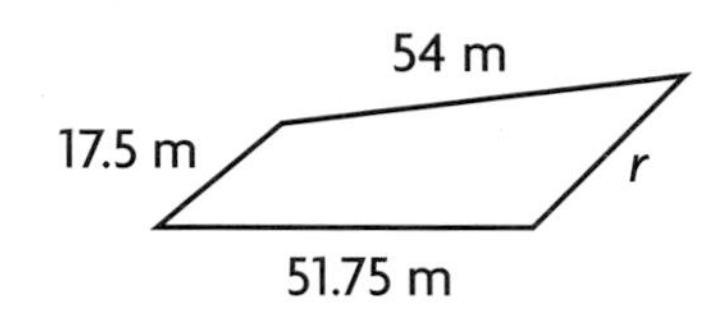

5. TALK Math **Explain** how you use a formula to find the unknown length of a side.

Independent Practice and Problem Solving

The perimeter is given. Find the unknown length.

6. $P = 51$ ft

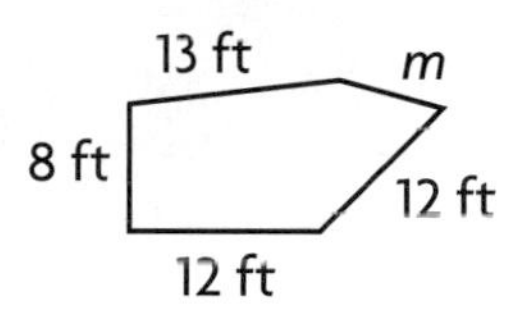

7. $P = 21.2$ cm

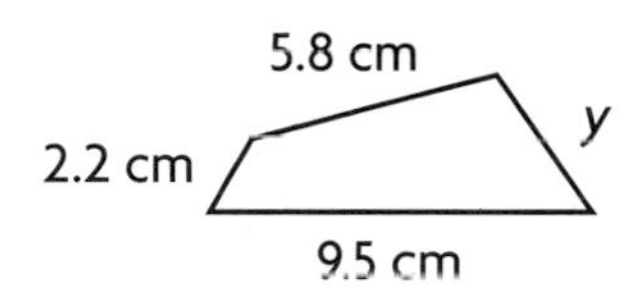

8. $P = 48$ in.

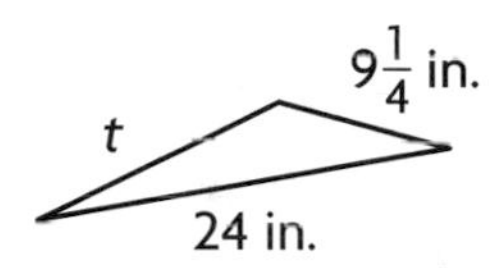

9. $P = 64.5$ m

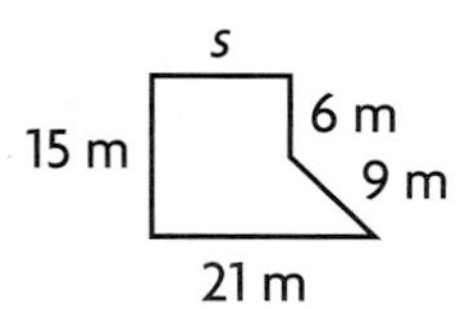

10. $P = 117$ in.

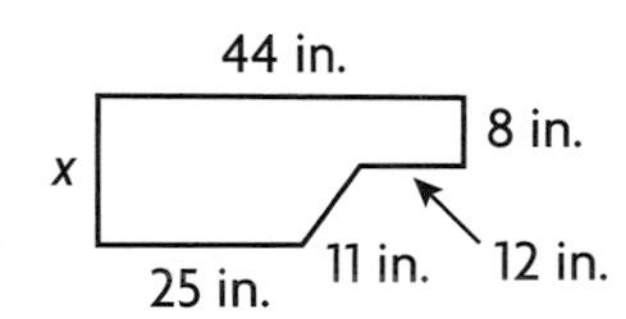

11. $P = 41.4$ cm

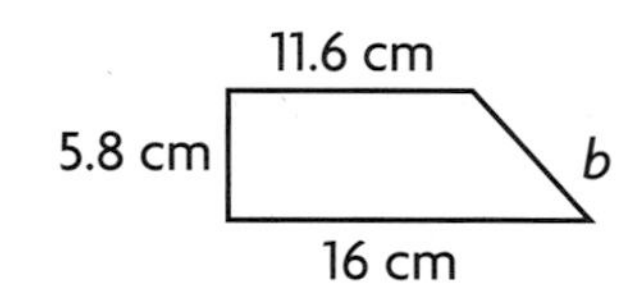

12. What is the perimeter of the square at the right?

13. WRITE Math **Explain** how you would find the length of side d in Exercise 3 if you were not given the perimeter.

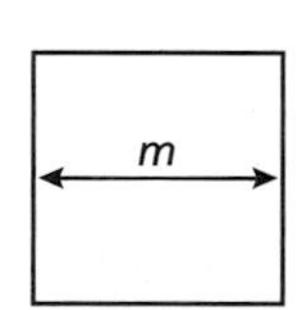

Achieving the Standards

14. $\frac{1}{3} \times \frac{2}{4} =$ (NS 2.4, p. 240)

15. What is the measure of angle C in the triangle? (MG 2.2, p. 468)

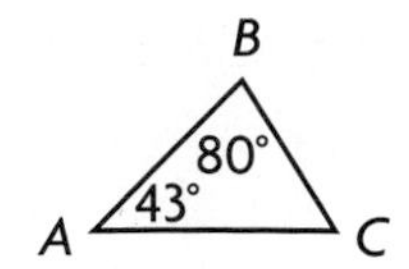

16. **Test Prep** A square has a perimeter of 16 in. What is the length of each side?

A 16 in.
B 8 in.
C 6 in.
D 4 in.

Extra Practice on page 538, Set D

Problem Solving Workshop
Make Generalizations

OBJECTIVE: Solve problems by using the skill make generalizations.

Read to Understand
Plan
Solve
Check

Use the Skill

PROBLEM Trump World Tower and Leighton House are both skyscrapers in New York City and are the same shape. Trump World Tower is a rectangular prism. Its base is 145 feet long and 78 feet wide. The perimeter of the base of the Leighton House is 112 feet less than the perimeter of the base of the Trump World Tower. What is the perimeter of the base of the Leighton House?

Trump World Tower

Sometimes you need to *make generalizations* to solve a problem. When you generalize, you make a statement that is true about a whole group of similar situations or objects.

What You Know	Generalization	Conclusion
Trump World Tower is a rectangular prism. Leighton House is the same shape.	Rectangular prisms have rectangular bases.	Leighton House has a rectangular base.
Trump World Tower is 145 ft long and 78 ft wide.	The perimeter of a rectangle is $(2 \times \text{length}) + (2 \times \text{width})$.	The perimeter of the base of Trump World Tower is $(2 \times 145 \text{ ft}) + (2 \times 78 \text{ ft})$, or 446 ft.
The perimeter of the base of Leighton House is 112 ft less than the perimeter of the base of Trump World Tower.	To find an amount less than a given amount, you subtract.	The perimeter of the base of Leighton House is 446 ft − 112 ft, or 334 ft.

So, the perimeter of the base of Leighton House is 334 ft.

Leighton House

Think and Discuss

Make a generalization. Then solve the problem.

a. A plane figure has 5 congruent sides. The perimeter of the figure is 90 ft. What is the length of each side?

b. A quadrilateral has a perimeter of 24 cm. Three of its sides each have a measure of 6 cm. What is the length of the fourth side?

MG 1.4 Differentiate between, and use appropriate units of measures for, two- and three-dimensional objects (i.e., find the perimeter, area, volume). *also* **AF 1.2, MR 1.0, MR 2.0, MR 2.3, MR 2.4, MR 3.0, MR 3.1, MR 3.2, MR 3.3**

Guided Problem Solving

Make generalizations to solve.

1. Donna bought two boxes of cereal that are the same shape. The cornflakes box is a rectangular prism. Its base is 12 in. long and 4 in. wide. The perimeter of the base of the oatmeal box is 4 in. more than the perimeter of the base of the cornflakes box. What is the perimeter of the base of the oatmeal box?

   Make a table similar to the one on page 536. Write what you know about the cereal boxes. Then make a generalization, and draw a conclusion.

   The perimeter of the base of the oatmeal box is ■ in.

2. **What if** the base of the cornflakes box was 10 in. long and 3 in. wide? What would the perimeter of the base of the oatmeal box be?

3. Two tissue boxes are congruent cubes. If the perimeter of the base of one tissue box is 16 in., what is the length of one side of the base of the other tissue box?

Mixed Applications

USE DATA For 4–7, use the pictures.

4. The Pyramid of Menkaure is a square pyramid. The Pyramid of Khafre is the same shape. What is the length of each side of the base of the Pyramid of Khafre?

5. The Pyramid of Khufu is also a square pyramid with an original height of about 481 ft. What is the length of each side of the base of the Pyramid of Khufu?

6. The Pyramid of Menkaure has three square pyramids standing along its south wall. The perimeter of the base of the largest of these three pyramids is 800 ft less than the perimeter of the base of the Pyramid of Menkaure. What is the length of each side of the base of the largest of these three pyramids?

7. **WRITE Math** Kim says the length of each side of the base of the Pyramid of Menkaure is greater than the length of each side of the base of the Pyramid of Khufu. Is Kim's statement reasonable? **Explain.**

Extra Practice

Set A Change the given unit. (pp. 524–527)

1. 18 ft = ■ yd
2. 60 in = ■ ft
3. 8 yd = ■ in
4. 7 mi = ■ ft
5. 12 cm = ■ mm
6. 4.3 km = ■ m
7. 3,400 mm = ■ cm
8. 900 cm = ■ m
9. Mike needs 40 yards of line for his sailboat. The line is sold by the foot. How many feet of line does Mike need?

Set B Find the perimeter of each polygon. (pp. 530–531)

1. 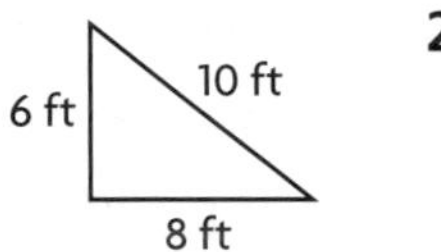

2. 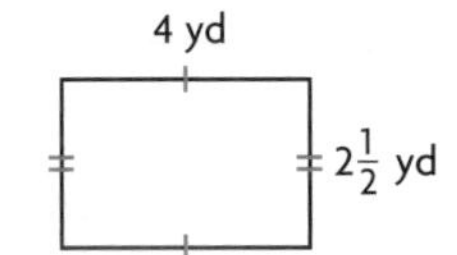

3. 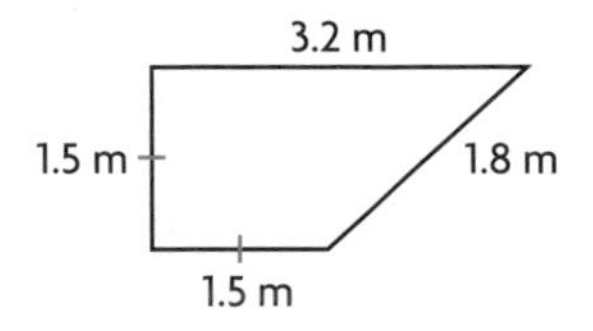

4. 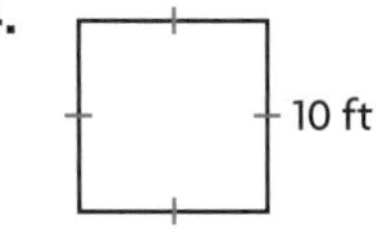

5. Pete is cutting string to mark the perimeter of his garden. How much string does he need to cut?

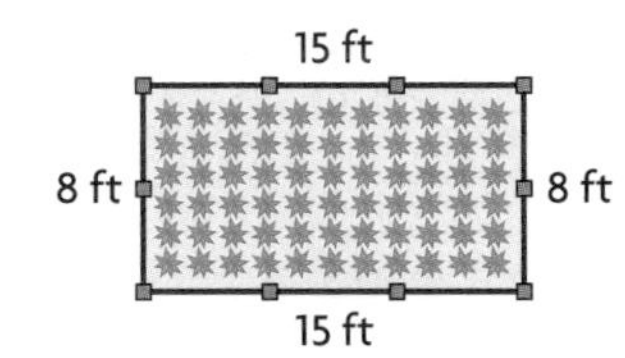

Set C Find the perimeter of each polygon by using a formula. (pp. 532–533)

1. 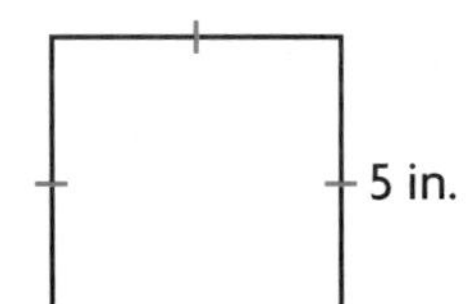

2. 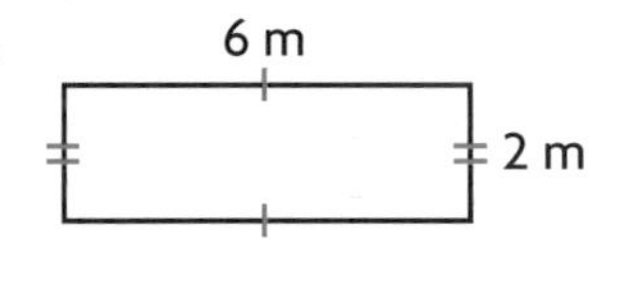

3. 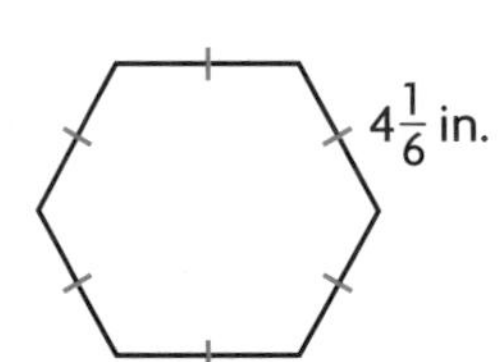

4. 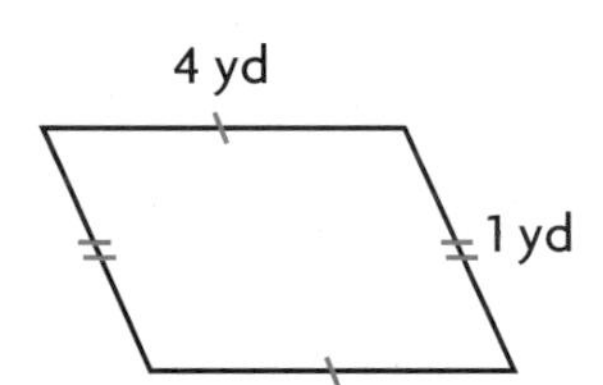

5. Maggie is cutting rickrack to use as the border for a square tablecloth. How much rickrack does she need to cut?

Set D The perimeter is given. Find the unknown length. (pp. 534–535)

1. $P = 19$ ft

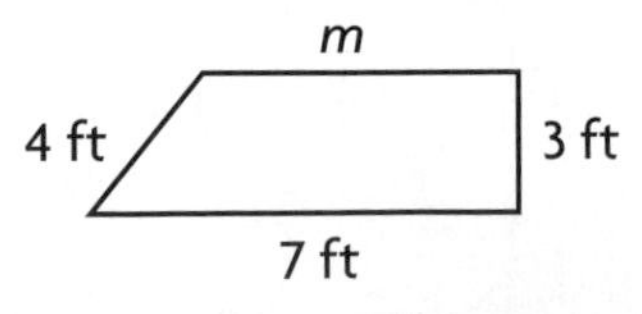

2. $P = 18$ m

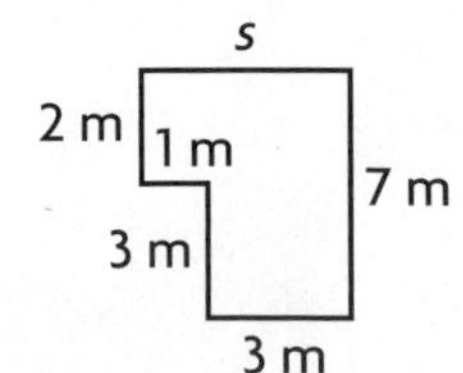

3. $P = 20$ in.

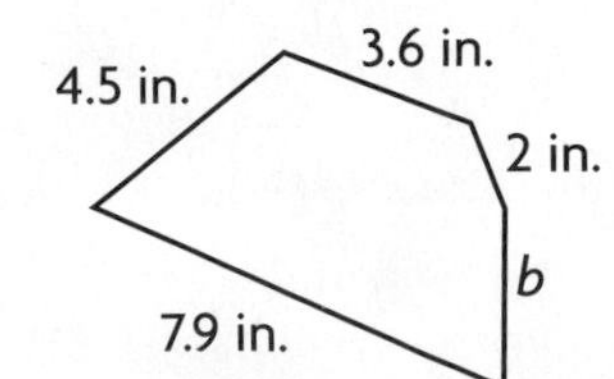

4. $P = 27$ cm

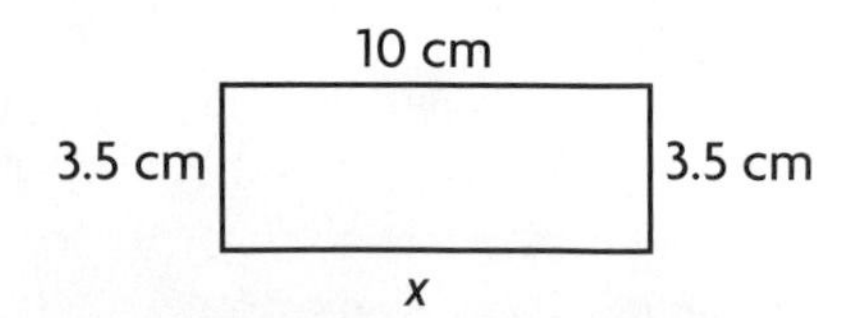

Technology
Use Harcourt Mega Math, Ice Station Exploration, *Polar Planes*, Level P.

PRACTICE GAME

Around the Block

Walkers!

2 players

Equipment!

- 2 different-colored counters
- 3-section spinner labeled 1–3
- grid paper

START

16	24	4	14	30	20
8					28
26					12
34	18	6	32	22	10

Start Walking!

- Each player chooses a different-colored counter and places it on START.
- Players spin the pointer on the spinner and move their counter the number of spaces indicated.
- Each square contains a perimeter. Player 1 draws on grid paper as many rectangles as possible with the perimeter. Lengths must be whole units.
- Player 1 scores a point for each rectangle drawn. Any congruent rectangles count as only 1 point. For example, a 3×4 rectangle and a 4×3 rectangle count only as 1 point.
- Player 2 spins, and play continues.
- After each player has made a trip around the block, the player with the greater number of points wins.

Check Concepts

For 1–2, choose the best term from the box.

1. Explain how you can estimate the perimeter of a regular polygon. (MG 1.4, p. 528)
2. Explain how to use tracing paper, pencil, a piece of string, and a ruler to estimate the perimeter of an object. (MG 1.4, p. 528)

Check Skills

Change the given unit. (O‑n AF 1.2 pp. 524–527)

3. 24 ft = ■ yd 4. 5.2 cm = ■ mm 5. 6 ft = ■ in. 6. 4 m = ■ cm 7. 4 km = ■ m

Find the perimeter of each polygon. (MG 1.4, pp. 530–531)

8. 5.5 cm; 3.5 cm

9. 8 yd

10. 7 in.; 7 in.; 4 in.

11. 5 m; 3 m; 3 m; 2 m

12. 5 m; 6 m; 2 m; 2 m

Find the perimeter of each polygon by using a formula. (MG 1.4, pp. 534–535)

13. 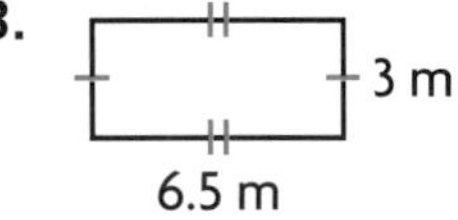

14. 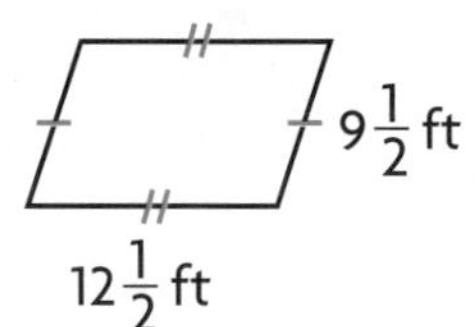

15. 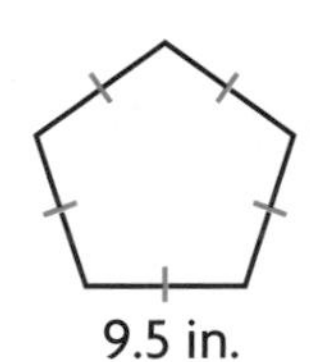

16. 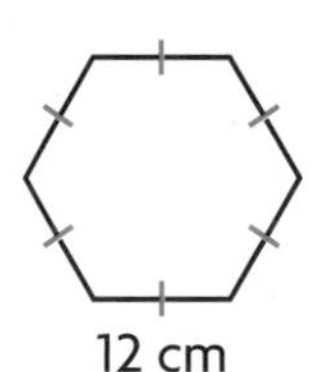

17. 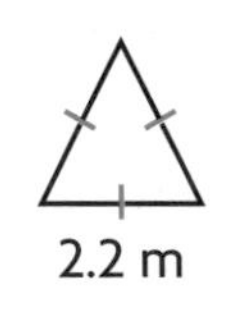

Check Problem Solving

Solve. (MG 1.4, MR 2.0, pp. 534–535, 536–537)

18. Two rectangles are congruent. If one rectangle has a length of 10 inches and a width of 2 inches, what is the perimeter of the other rectangle?

19. A triangle has a perimeter of 12 feet. One leg has a length of 3 feet, and another leg has a length of 5 feet. What is the length of the third leg?

20. A regular pentagon has a side with a length of 12 centimeters. What is its perimeter?

21. **WRITE Math** The base of Cube A and the base of Cube B have the same perimeter. Are the cubes congruent? **Explain** your answer.

GO ONLINE **Technology** Use *Online Assessment.*

Enrich • Networks

Find the Shortest Route

A **network** is a figure made up of vertices and edges. A network is sometimes used to represent distances between locations.

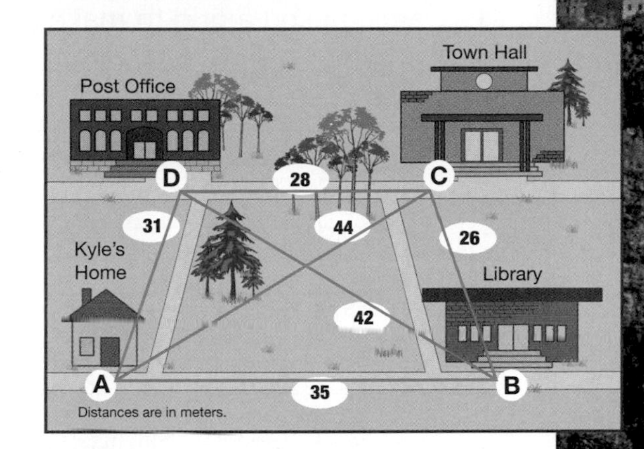

Kyle drew this network to show the distances from his home *(A)* to the library *(B)*, the post office *(C)*, and Town Hall *(D)*. Starting from *A*, find the shortest route that includes all four locations.

Example

Step 1 List the different routes. Find the total distance for each route.	$ABDC = 35 + 42 + 28 = 105$ $ABCD = 35 + 26 + 28 = 89$ $ADBC = 31 + 42 + 26 = 99$
Step 2 Compare the distances.	$ADCB = 31 + 28 + 26 = 85$ $ACBD = 44 + 26 + 42 = 112$ $ACDB = 44 + 28 + 42 = 114$

So, the shortest route in Kyle's network is *ADCB*.

Try It

Start at *A*. Find all the possible routes that include each vertex. Name the shortest route.

1. 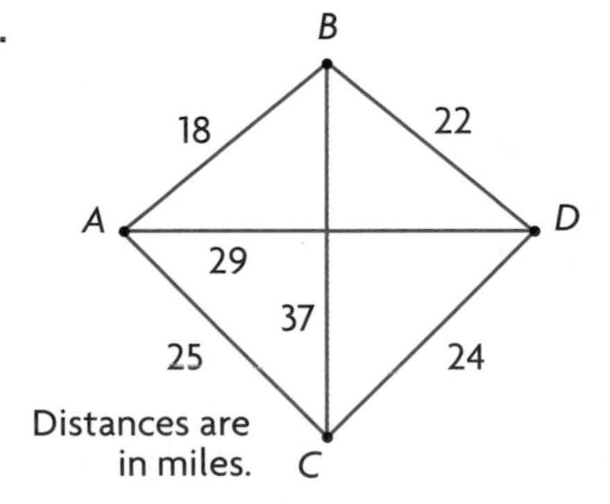

Distances are in miles.

2. 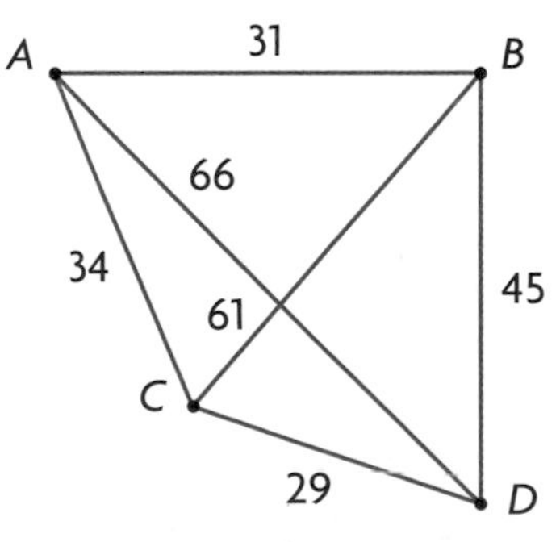

Distances are in miles.

Think About It

WRITE Math **Explain** how to use a network to find the shortest route.

Achieving the Standards
Chapters 1–20

Algebra and Functions

1. Damian used a grid to make a map of some buildings in his neighborhood.

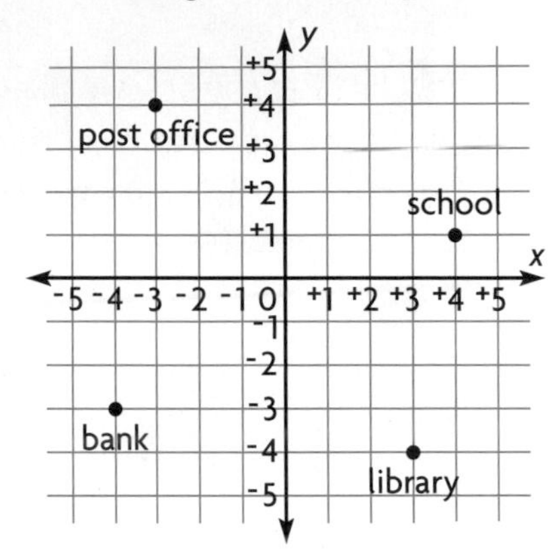

Which building is at $(^-4, ^-3)$? (AF 1.4)

A bank

B library

C post office

D school

2. Which equation shows the relationship of all the values in the table below? (AF 1.5)

x	−2	−1	0	1	2
y	−8	−7	−6	−5	−4

A $x = 6 - y$

B $x = y - 6$

C $y = x + {}^-6$

D $y = {}^-6 - x$

3. WRITE Math **Explain** how to graph the equation $y = 2x + 1$ on a coordinate plane. (AF 1.5)

Measurement and Geometry

4. What is the measure of angle x in the figure below? (MG 2.2)

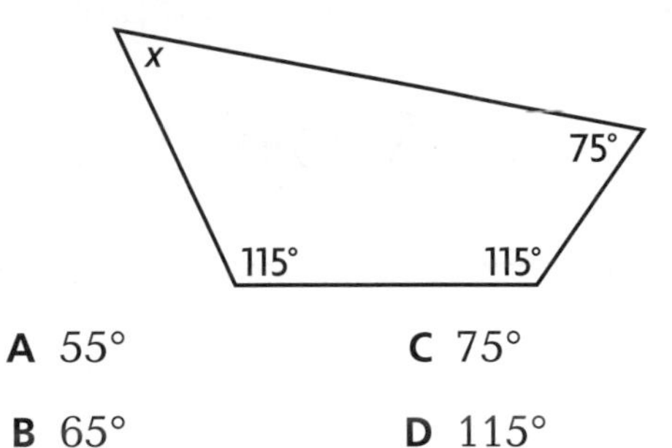

A 55°

B 65°

C 75°

D 115°

5. Triangle *ABC* is a right triangle. The measure of angle *A* is twice the measure of angle *B*. What is the measure of angle *A*? (MG 2.2)

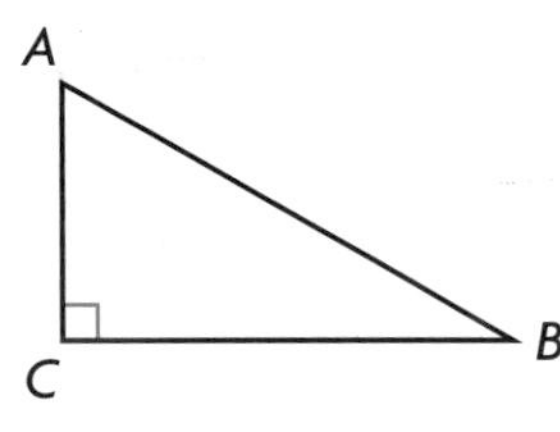

A 30°

B 45°

C 60°

D 90°

6. WRITE Math **Explain** how to determine how many cubes are in the solid figure with the views shown below. (MG 2.3)

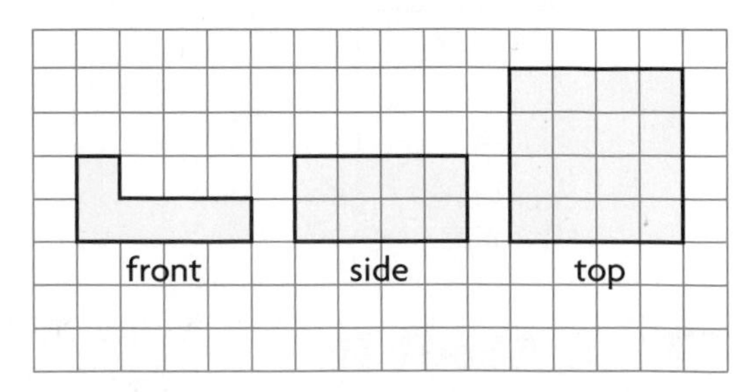

Statistics, Data Analysis, and Probability

7. The line graph shows the daily high temperatures for five days.

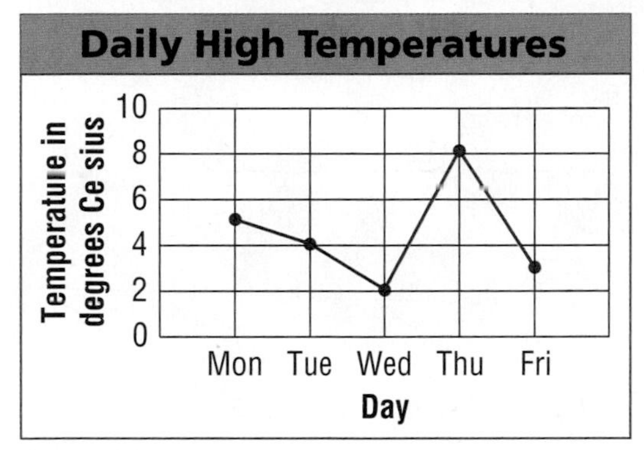

On which day was the high temperature 3°C lower than the high temperature on Monday? **(SDAP 1.0)**

A Tuesday
B Wednesday
C Thursday
D Friday

8. **WRITE Math** The circle graph below shows the percentage that the library spent in one month in each category.

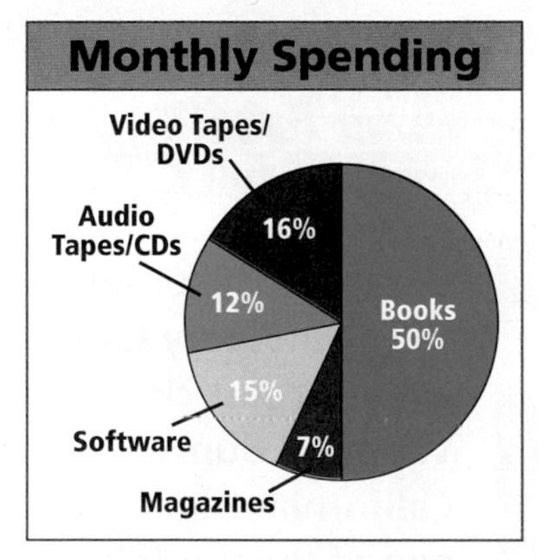

If the library spent $800 that month, how much more was spent on software than magazines? **Explain** how you got your answer. **(SDAP 1.3)**

Number Sense

Get the information you need.

See item 9. Find the fraction of the total number of students who play the flute. Then write the fraction as a percent.

9. Look at the table below.

Band Members

Instrument	Number of Students
Clarinet	12
Flute	9
Trombone	8
Trumpet	7

What percentage of the students in the band play the flute? **(NS 1.2)**

A 36%
B 33%
C 25%
D 9%

10. Which letter on the number line *best* identifies the location of $^{-}4$? **(NS 1.5)**

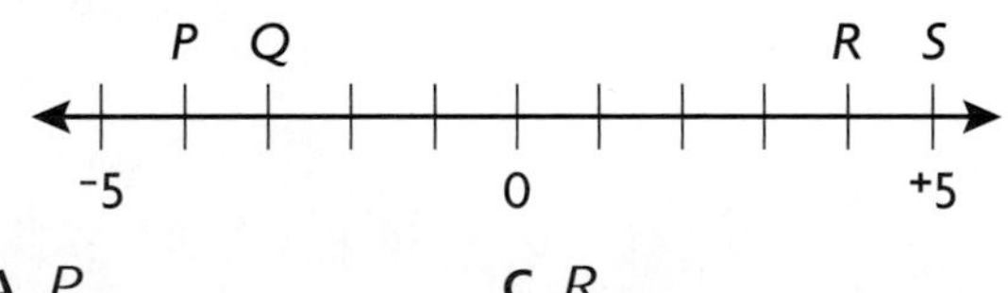

A *P*
B *Q*
C *R*
D *S*

11. **WRITE Math** Find the product $2\frac{2}{3} \times 2\frac{1}{4}$. **Explain** how you found the answer. **(NS 2.4)**

21 Area

The Big Idea Attributes of two-dimensional figures can be measured.

Investigate

You have a rectangular field where you want to plant strawberries. The field measures 75 yards by 50 yards. Suppose you want to divide the entire field into smaller sections. Describe a way to divide the field into two or more smaller sections, and give their areas.

75 yards

50 yards

CALIFORNIA FAST FACT

Oxnard, also known as the Strawberry Capital, is the largest city in Ventura County, California. Oxnard is one of the world's most important agricultural centers.

GO ONLINE **Technology**
Student pages are available in the Student eBook.

Show What You Know

Check your understanding of important skills needed for success in Chapter 21.

▶ Find Area using Grid Paper

Find the area of each figure in square units.

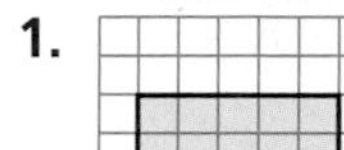

1. 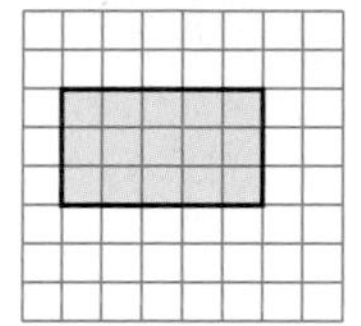

2. 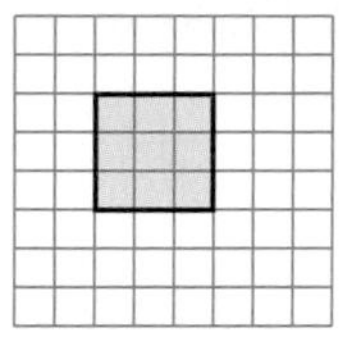

3. 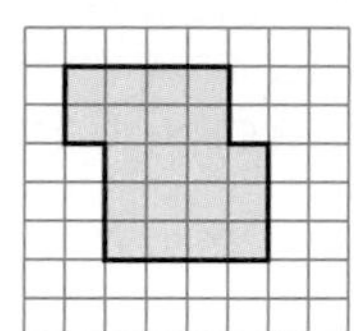

4. 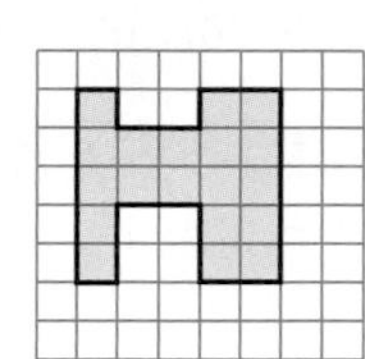

5. 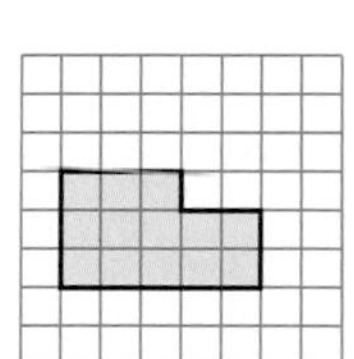

6. 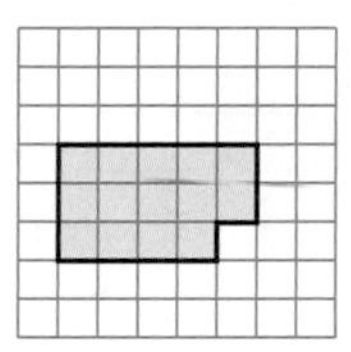

7. 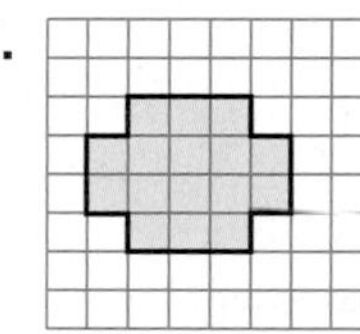

8. 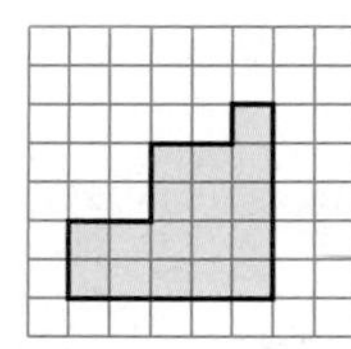

▶ Multiply 2-Digit by 1-Digit Numbers

Find the product.

9. 39×6

10. 45×3

11. 18×7

12. 70×4

13. 56×8

14. 27×5

15. 98×6

16. 32×2

17. 65×7

18. 44×5

VOCABULARY POWER

CHAPTER VOCABULARY

area
base
height
square unit

WARM-UP WORDS

area the number of square units needed to cover a surface

square unit a unit of area with dimensions 1 unit × 1 unit

base one side of a triangle or parallelogram which is used to help find the area

Estimate Area

OBJECTIVE: Estimate the area of regular and irregular figures.

Quick Review

Find the sum.

1. $11 + 12\frac{1}{4}$
2. $10\frac{1}{2} + 5\frac{1}{2}$
3. $3\frac{3}{4} + 6$
4. $15 + 18$
5. $9\frac{1}{4} + 10\frac{2}{4}$

Vocabulary

area square unit

Learn

PROBLEM Joseph and Bonnie are putting together a jigsaw puzzle. How can they estimate the area of one puzzle piece?

The **area** of a figure is the number of **square units** needed to cover it.

Activity

Materials: centimeter grid paper

Copy the diagram of the puzzle piece shown above. Each square on the grid is a one-centimeter square.

Step 1

Count the number of full squares. There are 14 full squares.

Step 2

Count the number of squares that are more than half full. There are 5. Do not count the squares that are less than half full.

Step 3

Add the numbers of squares you counted. $14 + 5 = 19$

So, the area of the puzzle piece is about 19 sq cm, or 19 cm^2.

READ Math

Area is measured in square units, such as square feet (ft^2), square centimeters (cm^2), square inches ($in.^2$), and square miles (mi^2).

Example

Joseph and Bonnie completed their puzzle. They drew a diagram of it on a grid so they could estimate its area. Each square of the grid is a one-centimeter square.

Count the squares. There are 52 full green squares and 8 almost-full orange squares.

There are 8 almost half-full yellow squares. Combine them to make 4 full squares.

Find the sum of the squares counted.

$52 + 8 + 4 = 64$

So, the area of the puzzle is about 64 cm^2.

MG 1.0 Students understand and compute the volumes and areas of simple objects. *also* MG 1.4, MR 2.0, MR 2.4, MR 2.5, MR 3.2

Guided Practice

Estimate the area of the shaded figure.

1. How many full squares are there?
2. How many squares are more than half full?
3. What is the estimated area?

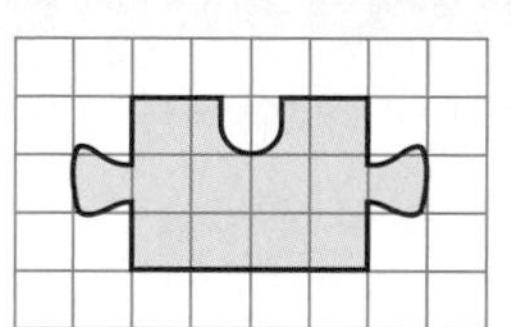

□ = 1 cm^2

Estimate the area of the shaded figure. Each square on the grid is 1 $in.^2$

4. 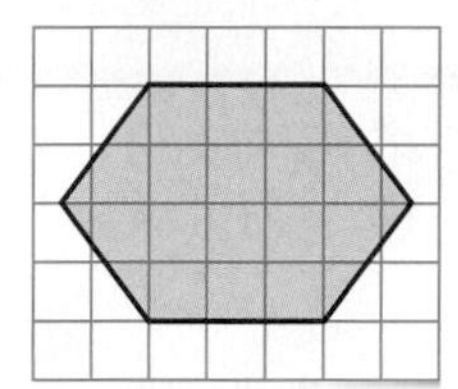

5. 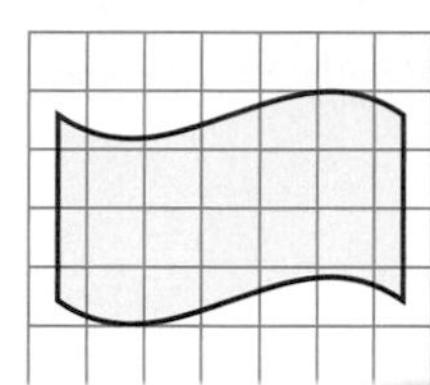

6. 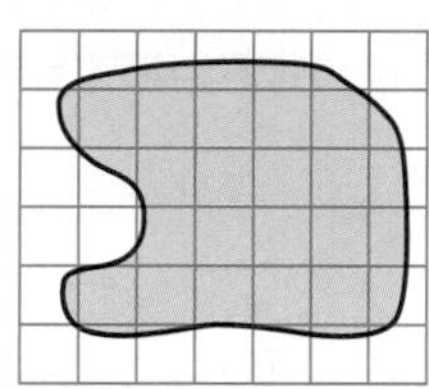

7. TALK Math **Explain** how to estimate the area of the figure in Problem 5.

Independent Practice and Problem Solving

Estimate the area of the shaded figure. Each square on the grid is 1 cm^2.

8. 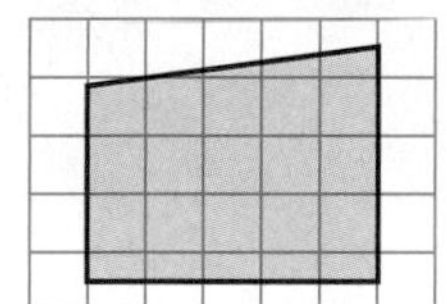

9. 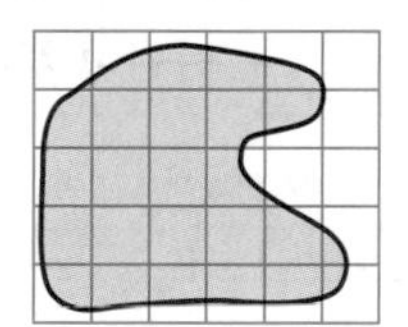

10. 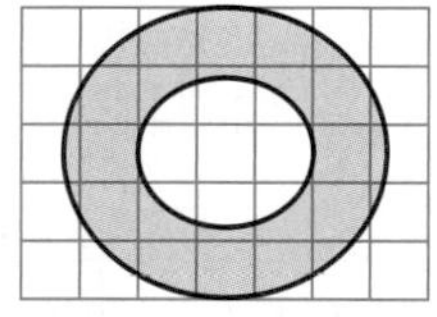

11. ***FAST FACT*** One of the world's largest jigsaw puzzles has more than 18,000 pieces. A model of the puzzle is shown on the grid. If each square on the grid represents 1 ft^2, estimate its actual area.

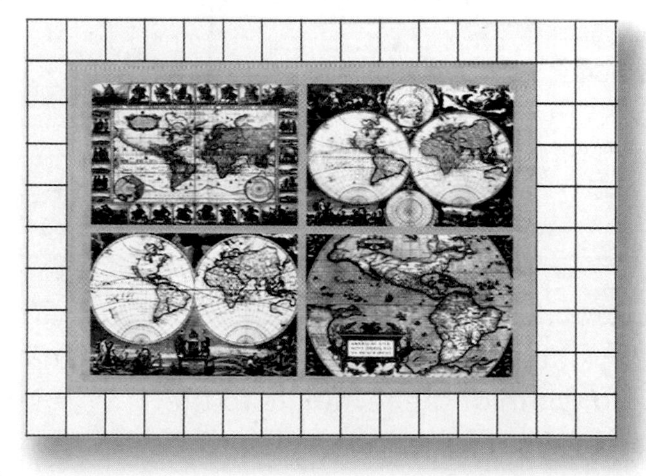

12. WRITE Math **Explain** how you can estimate the area of the center of the doughnut shape in Problem 10.

Achieving the Standards

13. What is the value of the expression $(6 + n) - 3$ for $n = 9$? (AF 1.2, p. 348)

14. A square has sides of 5.2 meters. Is its perimeter more than or less than 21 meters? (MG 1.4, p. 530)

15. $6.5 \times 9 =$ (NS 2.1, p. 292)

16. **Test Prep** Which of the following is a reasonable estimate of the area of the figure?

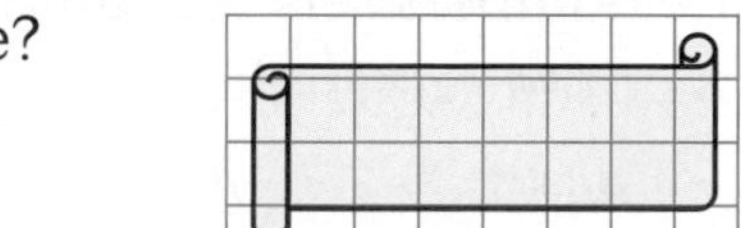

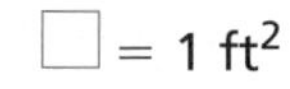

A about 6 ft^2

B about 9 ft^2

C about 11 ft^2

D about 16 ft^2

Extra Practice on page 566, Set A

LESSON 2

ALGEBRA

Area of Rectangles

OBJECTIVE: Find the area of squares and rectangles by using formulas.

Quick Review

Find the product.

1. 6×6
2. 10×8.5
3. 13×4
4. 0.7×0.8
5. 9×14

Learn

PROBLEM In art class, Mina is drawing plans for a flower garden. Mina's plans are for a garden that is 7 yards by 9 yards. What is the area of Mina's garden?

You can use square units to find the area.

Activity

Materials: grid paper

Step 1

Let each square in the grid represent 1 sq yd. Draw a rectangle 7 squares by 9 squares and shade it.

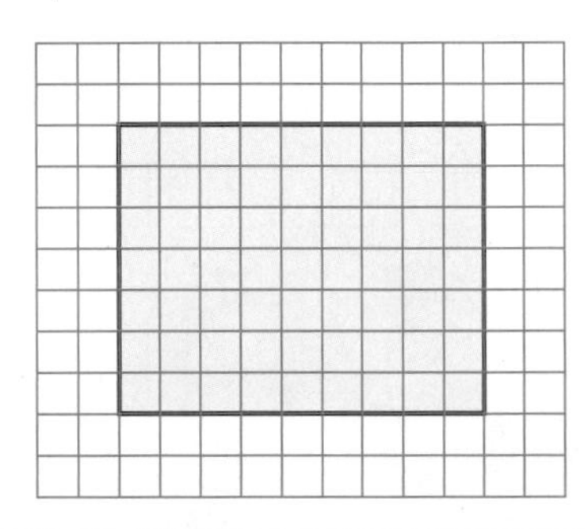

Step 2

Count the number of squares. Record your answer in square units.

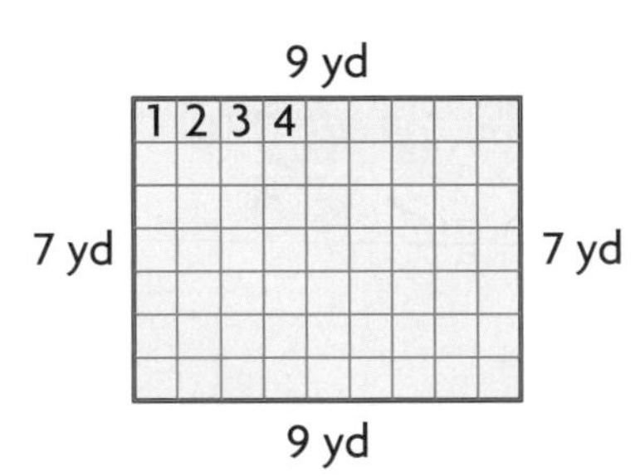

Area = 63 square yards, or 63 yd^2

So, the area of Mina's garden is 63 yd^2.

Look at the relationship of the length and width of the rectangle to the area. What equation can you write to find the area?

Area = 7 rows of 9, or 63

How are the numbers related to the dimensions of the rectangle?

length = 9   width = 7   Area = 63

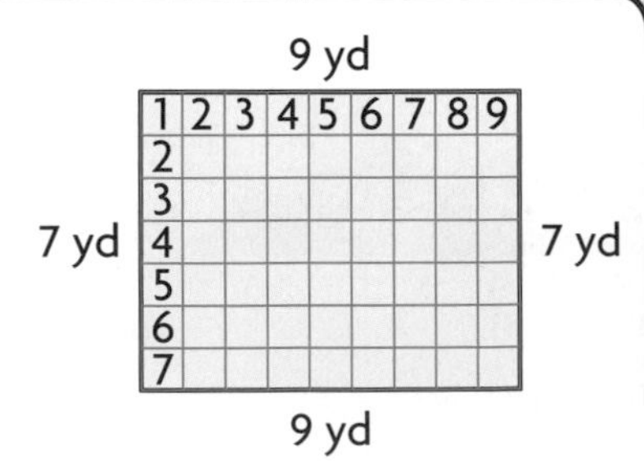

- What formula could you write for the area of a rectangle?
- How do the length and width of a rectangle relate to its area?

MG 1.4 Differentiate between, and use appropriate units of measures for two- and three-dimensional objects (i.e. find the perimeter, area, volume). *also* **MG 1.0, AF 1.2, MR 1.2, MR 2.0, MR 2.2, MR 2.3, MR 2.4, MR 3.2**

Use Formulas

To find the area of a rectangle or a square, you can use these formulas.

Example 1 **Area of a rectangle**

Example 2 **Area of a square**

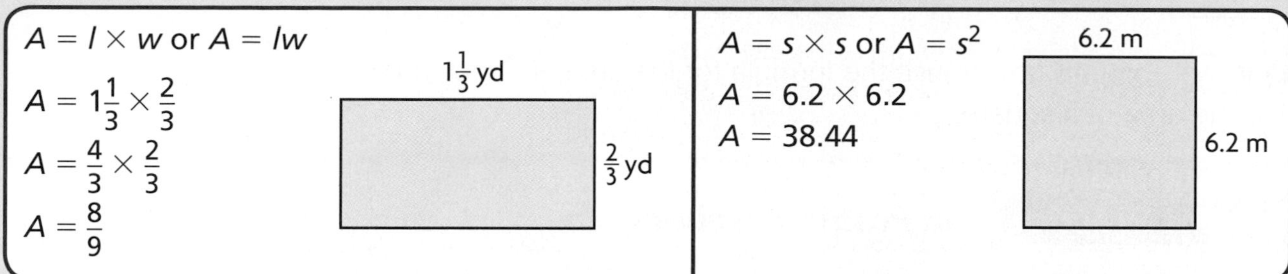

$A = l \times w$ or $A = lw$

$A = 1\frac{1}{3} \times \frac{2}{3}$

$A = \frac{4}{3} \times \frac{2}{3}$

$A = \frac{8}{9}$

So, the area of the rectangle is $\frac{8}{9}$ yd^2.

$A = s \times s$ or $A = s^2$

$A = 6.2 \times 6.2$

$A = 38.44$

So, the area of the square is 38.44 m^2.

Example 3 **Area of a polygon**

Find the area of a polygon by dividing it into two or more simpler polygons. Sophie's design for a garden is divided into a rectangle and a square. The area of the whole garden is equal to the sum of the areas of the parts.

5 m, 4.5 m, 3 m, 3 m

Parts of Garden		Whole Garden
Area of Rectangle	**Area of Square**	**Area of Whole Garden**
$A = (4.5 \times 5)$	$A = (3 \times 3)$	$A = (4.5 \times 5) + (3 \times 3)$
$A = 22.5$	$A = 9$	$A = 22.5 + 9 = 31.5$
The area is 22.5 m^2.	The area is 9 m^2.	The area is 31.5 m^2.

So, the area of the combined garden is 31.5 m^2.

Guided Practice

Find the area of each figure. Each square is 1 yd^2.

1. 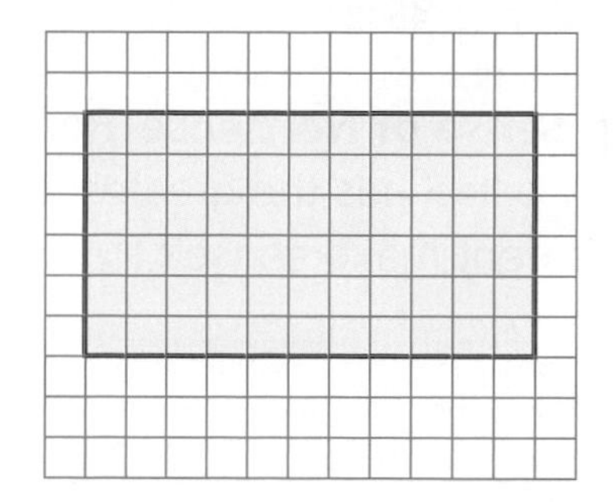

2. 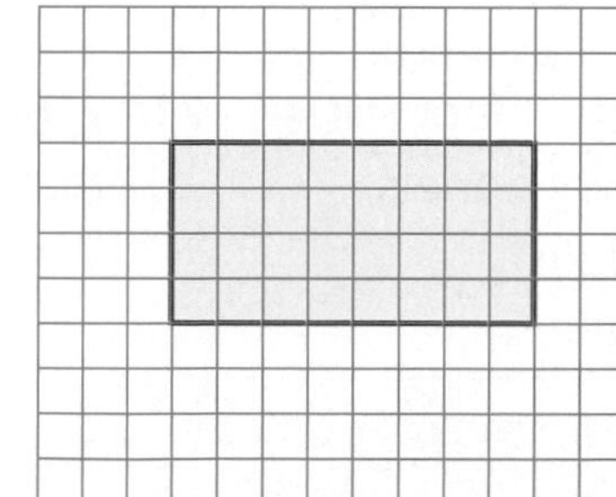

3. 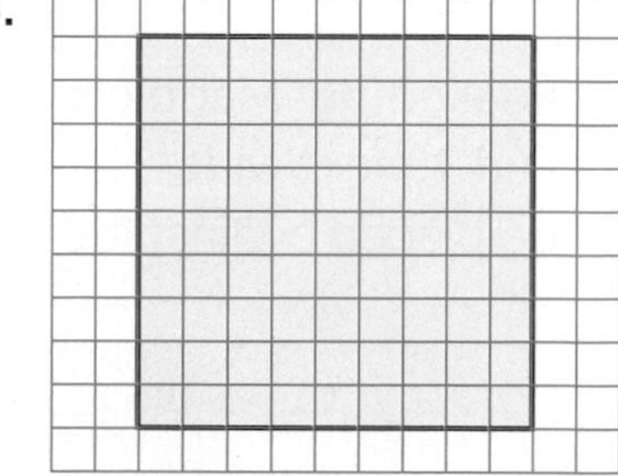

Find the area of each figure.

4. 3.3 m, 3.3 m

5.

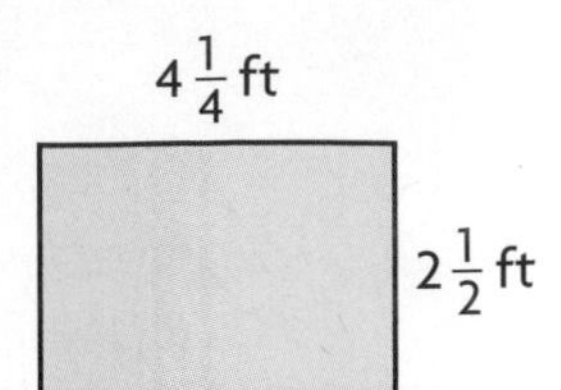

6. 12.4 km, 6 km, 9.6 km, 12.4 km

7. TALK Math **Explain** how to use the formula for the area of a rectangle to find the area of a square.

Independent Practice and Problem Solving

Find the area of each figure.

8.

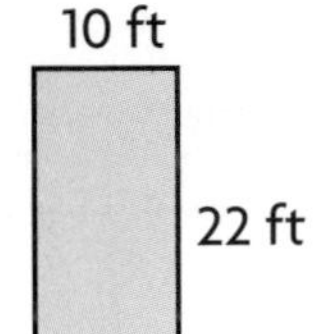

9.

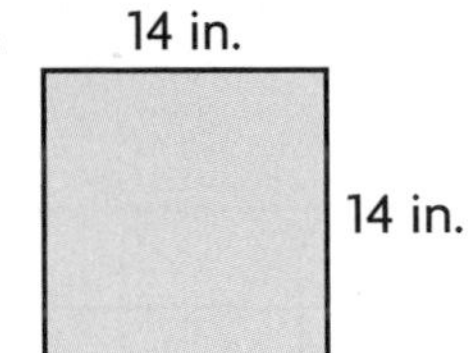

10.

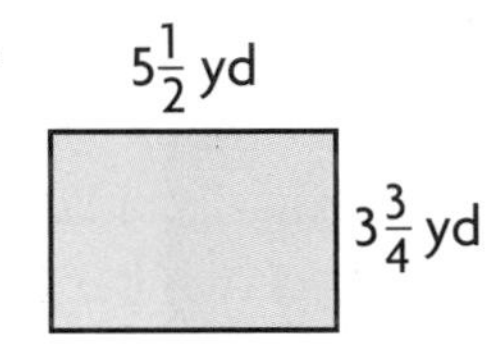

11.

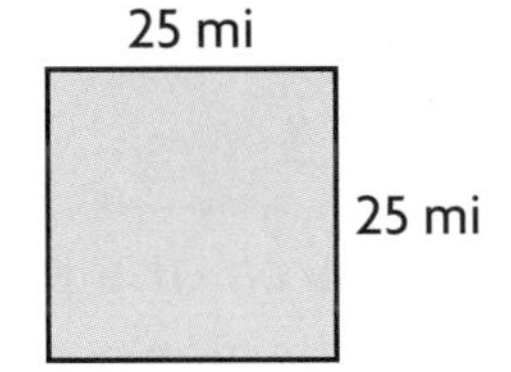

12.

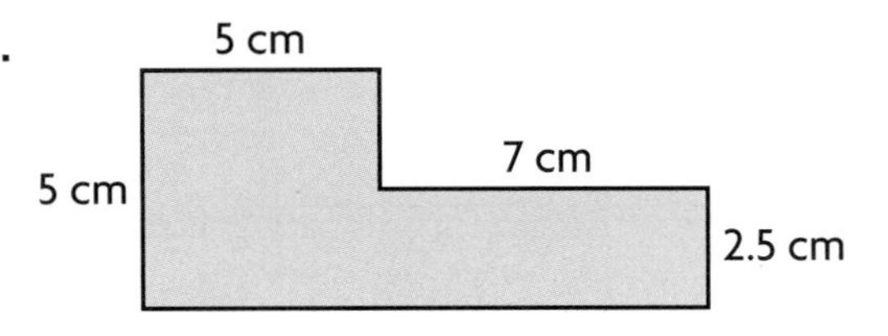

13.

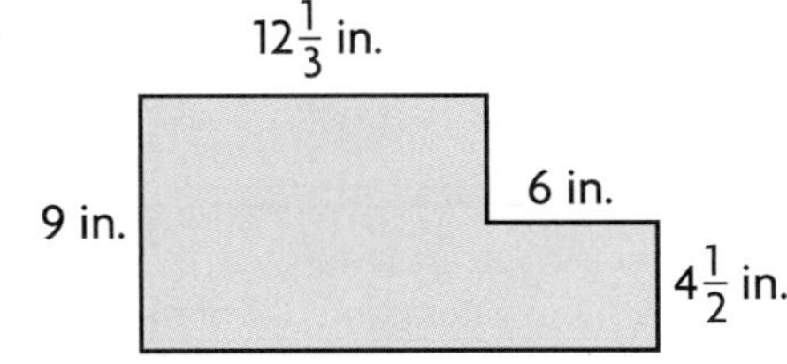

For each square or rectangle, find each missing measurement.

14. $s = 6.2$ m
$A = ■$

15. $s = 7$ in.
$A = ■$

16. $l = 3\frac{2}{5}$ ft
$w = 2$ ft
$A = ■$

17. $l = 4.3$ km
$w = 5.0$ km
$A = ■$

USE DATA Use the table for 18–21.

Wood Panel	Height	Width
Oak	60 in.	36 in.
Maple	68 in.	42 in.
Cherry	65 in.	48 in.

18. Brent plans to stain an oak panel. What is its area?

19. Which panel has an area of about 2,800 in.^{2}?

20. **Reasoning** Maddie's office wall is 8 feet tall and 10 feet wide. Can three cherry panels be placed against the wall? **Explain.**

21. WRITE Math **Sense or Nonsense** Ron says that the cherry panel has the greatest area. Does his statement make sense? **Explain.**

CD ROM **Technology**
Use Harcourt Mega Math, Ice Station Exploration, *Arctic Algebra*, Level CC; Ice Station Exploration *Polar Planes*, Level P.

 Extra Practice on page 566, Set B

Achieving the Standards

22. A triangle has a right angle and a 57° angle. What is the measure of the third angle? (MG 2.2, p. 448)

23. Ty trimmed $\frac{2}{4}$ of the bushes around his house in the morning. In the afternoon, he trimmed another $\frac{1}{4}$ of the bushes. What fraction of the bushes does Ty have left to trim? (NS 2.3, p. 208)

24. A square has sides measuring 4.3 meters. Is its perimeter greater than or less than 17 meters? (MG 1.4, p. 530)

25. **Test Prep** How many one-foot square tiles are needed to cover a patio that is 14 feet × 20 feet?

A 68 tiles
B 140 tiles
C 280 tiles
D 560 tiles

26. **Test Prep** What is the area of a sheet of paper that measures $8\frac{1}{2}$ inches wide by 11 inches long?

A 39 in.^{2}
B $93\frac{1}{2}$ in.^{2}
C 99 in.^{2}
D $100\frac{1}{2}$ in.^{2}

Problem Solving and Reasoning

VISUAL REASONING You can draw a diagram to find out how many smaller units of area make up a larger unit of area. For example, how can you show the number of square feet in a square yard?

Step 1

Draw a square with sides labeled 1 yard.

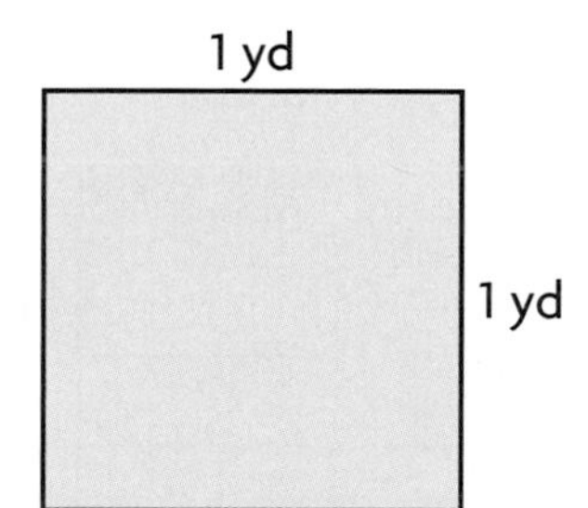

Step 2

Divide the square into feet by dividing it into three equal rows and columns.

Think: 1 yd = 3 ft

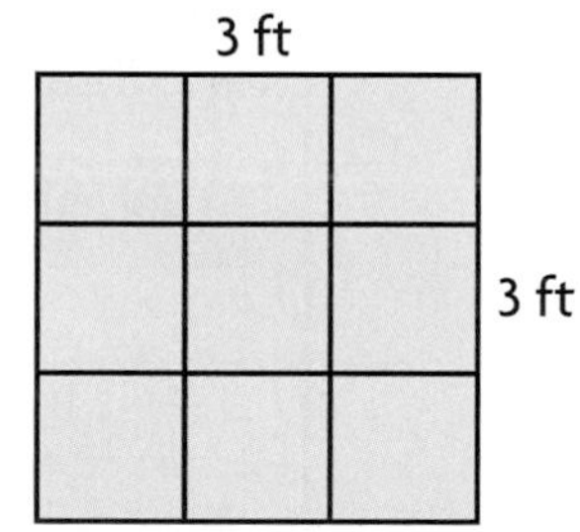

Step 3

Count the number of squares you made.

3 ft

1	2	3
4	5	6
7	8	9

3 ft

So, there are 9 square feet in 1 square yard.

Use visual reasoning to answer each question.

1. **Explain** how to draw a diagram to find the number of square inches in 1 square foot.

2. How many square decimeters are in 1 square meter?

3. You want to carpet a square room that has an area of 16 yd^2. How many square feet of carpeting will you need?

LESSON 3

ALGEBRA

Relate Perimeter and Area

OBJECTIVE: Identify how perimeter and area are related.

Quick Review

Find the missing measurement.

1. $l = 6$ ft
   $w = 12$ ft
   $A = ■$
2. $l = 8.2$ m
   $w = 5.5$ m
   $A = ■$

Learn

PROBLEM The students at Central Valley School are painting a rectangular panel for a class play. The panel has the greatest possible area for a perimeter of 16 ft. What are the length and width of the panel?

Activity

Materials: dot paper

You can use models to find the rectangle with the *greatest area.*

Step 1

On dot paper, draw rectangles with perimeters of 16 units.

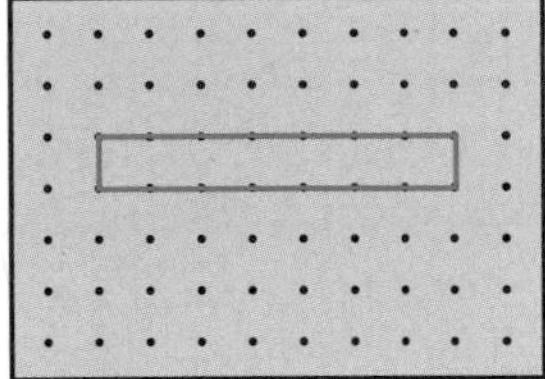

1×7

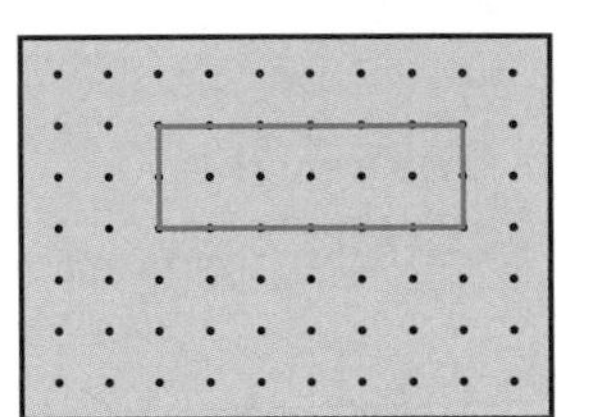

2×6

3×5

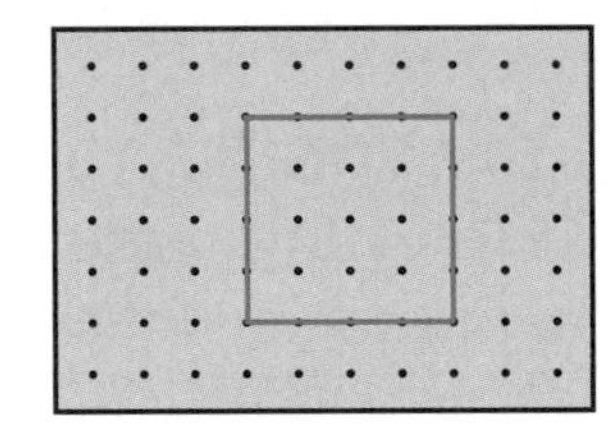

4×4

Step 2

Find and record the area of each rectangle. Each square unit represents 1 ft^2.

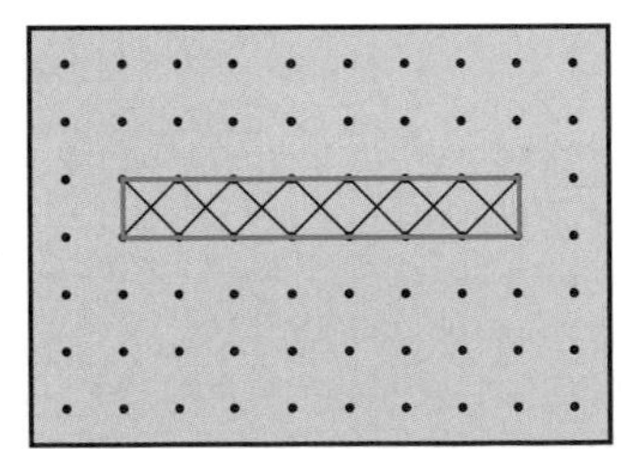

$A = 7$

Step 3

Make a table to record the length, width, perimeter, and area of each rectangle. Which length and width give the greatest area?

Length (ft)	Width (ft)	Perimeter (ft)	Area (ft^2)
7	1	16	7

So, to have the greatest area, the panel should be a square with 4-ft sides. The area is 4 ft $\times$ 4 ft, or 16 ft^2.

- If the panel had a perimeter of 12 ft, what would the length and width have to be for it to have the greatest area?
- What would the shape of the rectangle be?

Math Idea
For a given perimeter, a square has the greatest area of all possible rectangles.

MG 1.4 Differentiate between, and use appropriate units of measures for, two- and three-dimensional objects (i.e. find the perimeter, area, volume). *also* **AF 1.2, MG 1.0, MR 2.0, MR 2.3, MR 2.4, MR 3.2**

Anna's father wants to plant a garden and enclose it with bricks. He wants to use the least possible number of bricks. The area of the garden will be 36 m^2. Which rectangle with this area will have the least perimeter?

Activity

Materials: tiles, grid paper

You can use models to find the rectangle with the *least perimeter.*

Step 1

Use square tiles to make different rectangles with areas of 36 m^2. Let each tile be 1 m^2. You can use grid paper to record each rectangle.

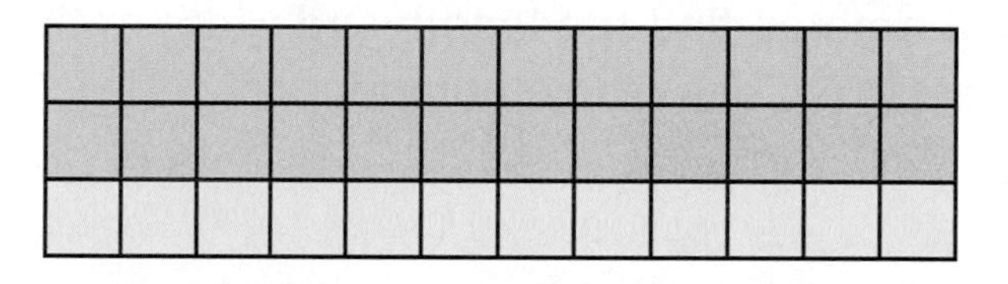

Step 2

Copy and complete the table to record your results. (HINT: To find all the possible whole number lengths and widths, find all the factors of 36.)

Length (m)	Width (m)	Perimeter (m)	Area (m^2)
36	1	■	36
■	2	■	36
■	3	■	36
■	■	■	36
■	■	■	36

So, the least perimeter is 24 meters. The garden should be a square with sides of 6 meters.

- As rectangles with the same areas get closer to being a square, what happens to their perimeters?

Math Idea

For a given area, a square has the least perimeter of all possible rectangles.

Example

Anna's father made another garden with an area of 20 m^2. Using whole numbers only, what rectangle has the least perimeter for this area?

Use tiles and make a table. Use factors of 20 as lengths and widths.

Length (m)	Width (m)	Perimeter (m)	Area (m^2)
20	1	42	20
10	2	24	20
5	4	18	20

So, the least perimeter is 18 meters. The length of the rectangle is 5 meters and the width is 4 meters.

- Why isn't this garden shaped like a square?

Guided Practice

For 1–3, use the rectangles at the right.

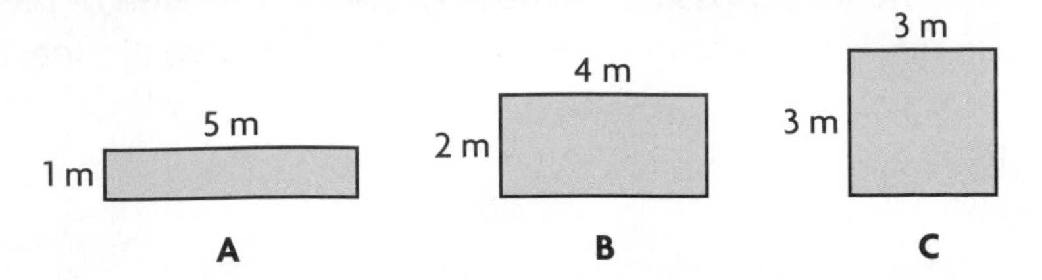

1. What is the perimeter of each rectangle?
2. Which rectangle has the greatest area?
3. What is the shape of the rectangle with the greatest area?

For the given perimeter, find the length and width of the rectangle with the greatest area. Use whole numbers only.

4. 8 in.
5. 28 m
6. 34 ft
7. 10 cm
8. 44 yd

For the given area, find the length and width of the rectangle with the least perimeter. Use whole numbers only.

9. 28 cm^2
10. 32 km^2
11. 64 $in.^2$
12. 54 ft^2
13. 49 mi^2
14. TALK Math **Explain** what happens to the area of a rectangle with a given perimeter as the difference between the length and width increases.

Independent Practice and Problem Solving

For the given perimeter, find the length and width of the rectangle with the greatest area. Use whole numbers only.

15. 60 yd
16. 54 cm
17. 4 mi
18. 100 ft
19. 46 mm

For the given area, find the length and width of the rectangle with the least perimeter. Use whole numbers only.

20. 40 $in.^2$
21. 9 km^2
22. 15 m^2
23. 45 ft^2
24. 100 cm^2
25. Copy and complete the table to find the areas of rectangles with a perimeter of 10 m. Describe the patterns you see.

Width (m)	0.5	1	1.5	2	2.5
Length (m)	■	■	■	■	■
Area (m^2)	■	■	■	■	■

26. **Pose a Problem** about a swimming pool with a length of 40 m and a width of 20 m.
27. Using 100 feet of fencing, what is the greatest area that can be fenced? the least area? Use whole numbers.
28. WRITE Math **What's the Error?** Jay says that with a given perimeter, the rectangle with the greatest width has the greatest area. What error did Jay make?

 Extra Practice on page 566, Set C

Achieving the Standards

29. Find the value of the expression $(5 \times m) + 21$ if $m = 12$. (AF 1.2, p. 348)

30. What is the area of the patio? (MG 1.4, p. 548)

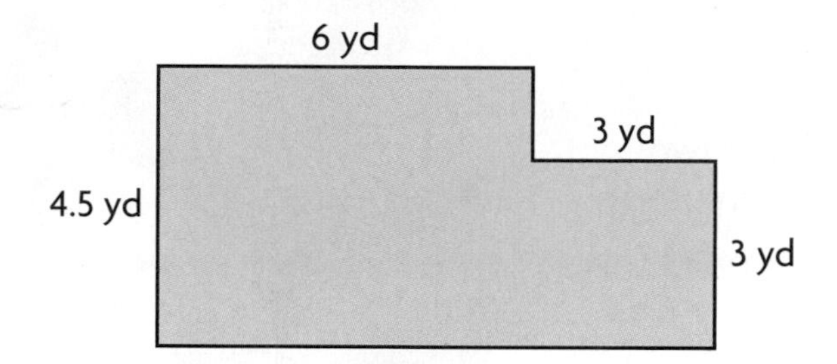

31. Carter used $\frac{2}{3}$ of a 5-gallon bucket of paint. How many gallons of paint did Carter use? (NS 2.5, p. 242)

32. **Test Prep** What is the greatest possible area of a rectangle with a perimeter of 24 meters?

 A 10 m^2 **C** 30 m^2

 B 24 m^2 **D** 36 m^2

33. **Test Prep** What is the least possible perimeter of a rectangle with an area of 144 square feet?

 A 12 feet **C** 48 feet

 B 24 feet **D** 148 feet

Problem Solving and Reasoning

LOGICAL REASONING A pentomino is a shape made from five squares. Each square must touch the entire side of another square. Two examples are shown at the right.

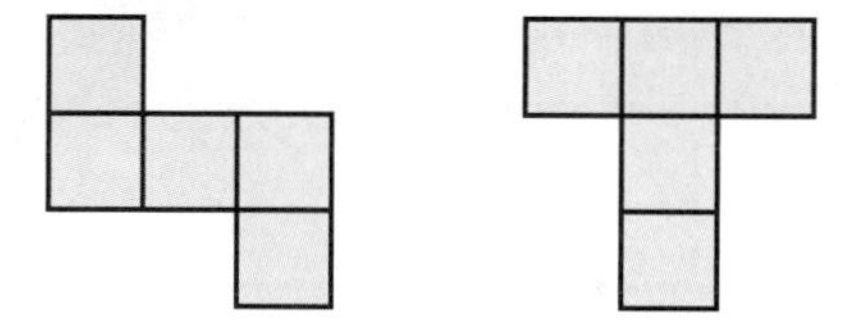

Do all pentominoes have the same perimeter?

Materials grid paper

Use grid paper to draw at least three more examples of different pentominoes. Then find their perimeters.

In the drawings at the right, two pentominoes have perimeters of 12 units, but one pentomino has a perimeter of 10 units.

$P = 12$ units $P = 10$ units $P = 12$ units

So, not all pentominoes have the same perimeter.

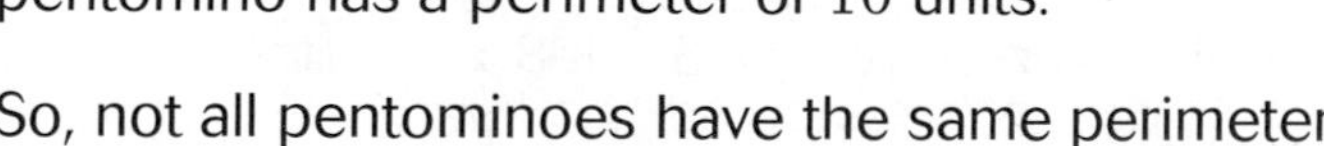

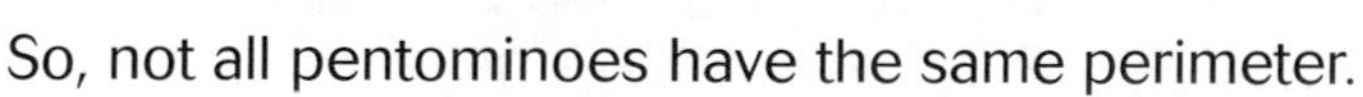

Use logical reasoning to answer the questions.

1. Do all pentominoes have the same area? **Explain.**

2. Draw as many different pentominoes as you can. Then share your pentominoes with a classmate. How many possible pentominoes are there?

Problem Solving Workshop
Strategy: Compare Strategies

OBJECTIVE: Compare different strategies for solving problems.

Use the Strategy

PROBLEM Jay's father is building a walkway with 5 rows of two-foot square pavers. He starts with one row of 3 pavers. Each additional row has 2 more pavers than the row before. What is the area of the fifth row of the walkway?

Read to Understand

- What do you visualize when you read the problem?
- What information is given?

Plan

- **What strategies can you use to solve the problem?**
  You can use more than one strategy to solve a problem. Use *draw a diagram* and *find a pattern*.

Solve

- **How can you use each strategy to solve the problem?**

Draw a Diagram

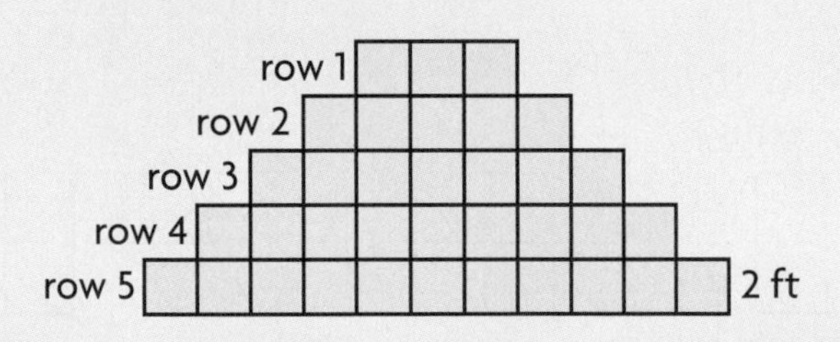

area of 1 paver: $2 \times 2 = 4 \text{ ft}^2$

area of 11 pavers in row 5: $4 \times 11 = 44 \text{ ft}^2$

Find a Pattern

Row	1	2	3	4	5
Number of Pavers	3	5	7	9	11
Area (ft^2)	12	20	28	36	?

+8 +8 +8 +8

area of pavers in row 5: $36 + 8 = 44 \text{ ft}^2$

So, the area of the fifth row of the walkway is 44 square feet.

Check

- **How do you know the answer is correct?**

MG 1.4 Differentiate between, and use appropriate units of measures for, two-and three-dimensional objects (i.e., find the perimeter, area, volume). *also* **MG 1.0, MR 1.0, MR 1.1, MR 2.0, MR 2.3, MR 2.4, MR 3.0, MR 3.1, MR 3.2, MR 3.3**

Guided Problem Solving

1. Rachel is building a wall with 6 rows of square blocks. The bottom row has 17 blocks. Each of the other rows has 3 fewer blocks than the row below. The side of each block is 10 inches. What is the area of the top row?

   First, *draw a diagram* to solve the problem. Draw the blocks in each row. Find the area of 1 block. Then multiply that area by the number of blocks in the top row.

   top row
   row 5
   row 4
   row 3
   row 2 — 10 in.
   bottom row — 10 in.

   Then, *find a pattern* to solve the problem. Make a table and record the number of blocks in each row. Find the area of each of the first 3 rows and look for a pattern.

Row	bottom	2	3	4	5	top
Number of Blocks	17	14	11	■	■	■
Area (in.^{2})	1,700	1,400	■	■	■	■

   Finally, compare the answers you found using both strategies.

2. **What if** each row had 2 fewer blocks than the row below? What would be the area of the top row?

3. A garden center has 5 rectangular flower boxes displayed in a row. The first flower box is 24 in. long and 4 in. wide. All the flower boxes have the same length, but each is 2 in. wider than the previous one. What is the perimeter of the fifth flower box?

Choose a STRATEGY

- Draw a Diagram or Picture
- Make a Model or Act It Out
- Make an Organized List
- Find a Pattern
- Make a Table or Graph
- Predict and Test
- Work Backward
- Solve a Simpler Problem
- Write an Equation
- Use Logical Reasoning

Mixed Strategy Practice

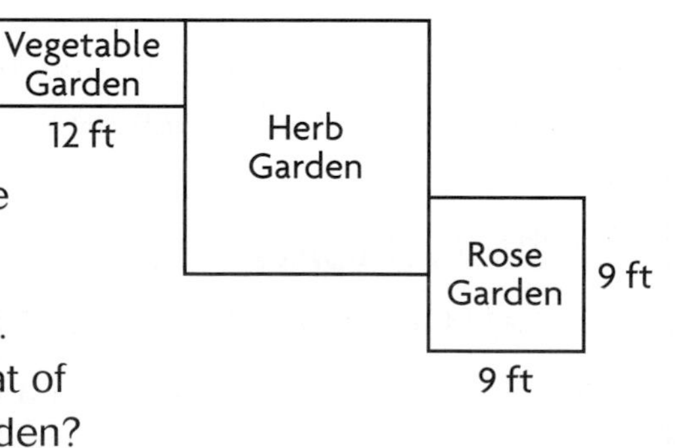

USE DATA For 4–5, use the diagram.

4. The total area of the gardens is 366 ft^2. What is the area of the square herb garden? What is the herb garden's perimeter?

5. Pam planted 6 more rose gardens like the one in the diagram. Each garden is a square with a side length 1 foot less than that of the previous garden. What is the area of the seventh rose garden?

6. **WRITE Math** Brian paid \$87 for a statue and a fountain. He paid \$15 more for the statue than the fountain. **Explain** how you can find the price of each item Brian purchased. How much did each item cost?

LESSON HANDS ON

5 Model Area of Triangles

OBJECTIVE: Model area of triangles.

Quick Review

1. $\frac{1}{2} \times 8$
2. $\frac{1}{2} \times 20$
3. $\frac{1}{2} \times 15$
4. $\frac{1}{2} \times 4.2$
5. $\frac{1}{2} \times (2 \times 5)$

Investigate

Materials ■ centimeter grid paper ■ ruler

You can use grid paper and what you know about the area of a rectangle to find the area of a triangle.

A Draw a 6×15 rectangle on the grid paper.

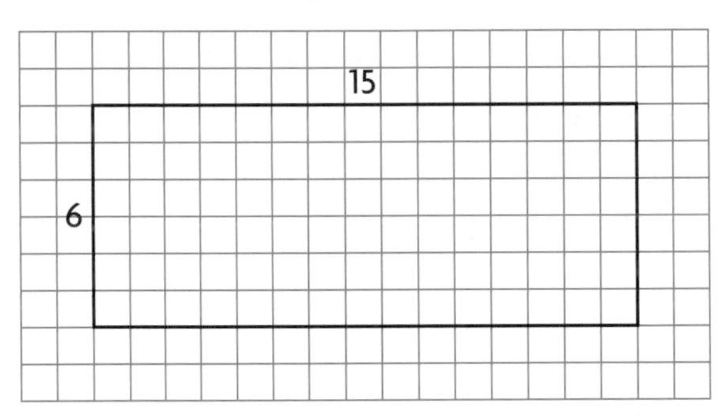

B Cut out the rectangle and find and record its area.

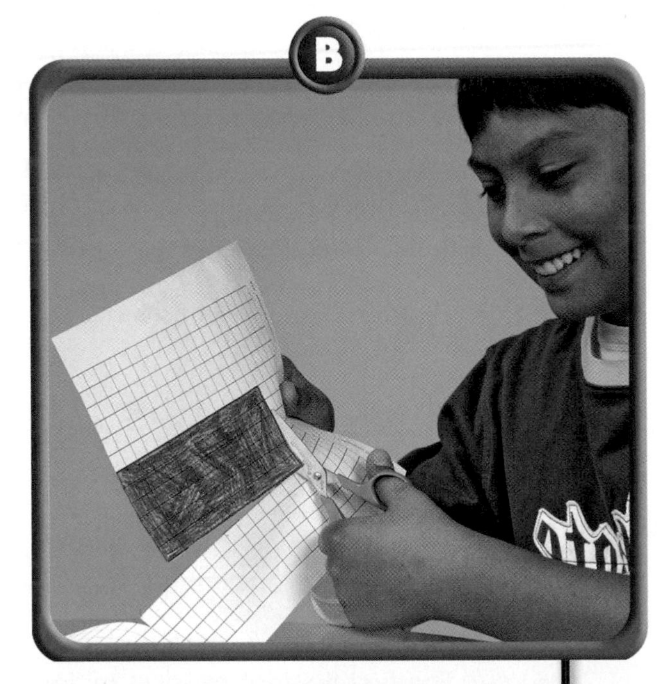

C Draw a diagonal line across the rectangle. Cut along the line to make two congruent triangles. What is the area of each triangle?

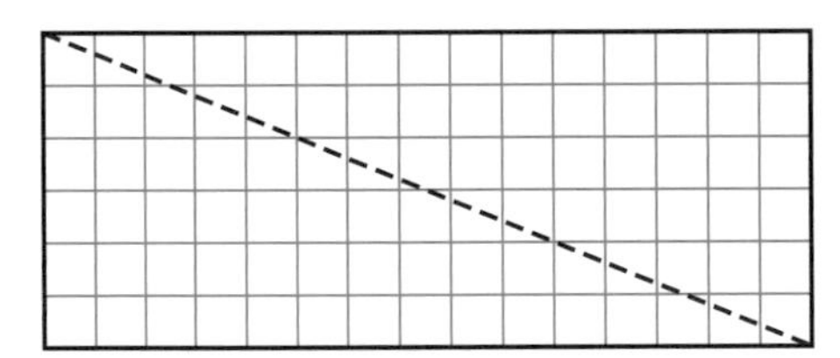

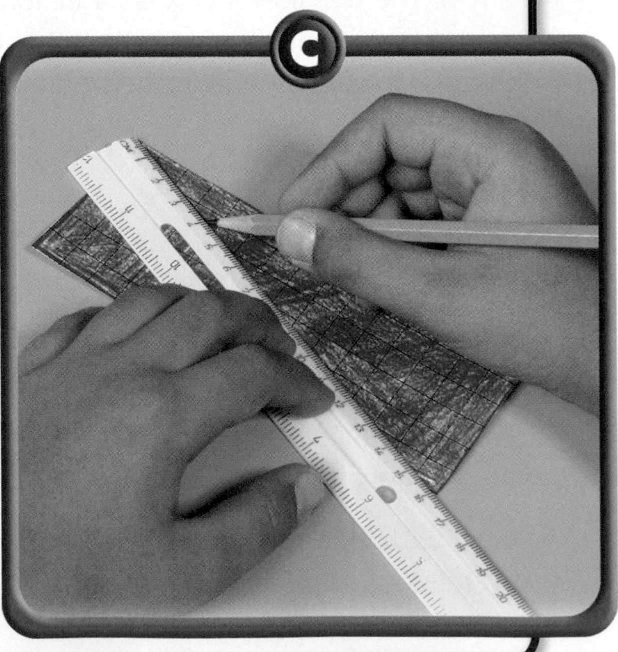

D Repeat Steps A through C with an 8×18 rectangle. What is each new triangle's area?

Draw Conclusions

1. Explain how you found the area of each triangle.
2. Does drawing a diagonal in a rectangle always make two congruent triangles? Explain.
3. **Application** How does the area of one of the triangles compare to the area of the rectangle?

MG 1.1 Derive and use the formula for the area of a triangle and of a parallelogram by comparing it with the formula for the area of a rectangle (i.e., two of the same triangles make a parallelogram with twice the area; a parallelogram is compared with a rectangle of the same area by pasting and cutting a right triangle on the parallelogram). *also* **MG 1.4, MR 2.0, MR 2.3, MR 2.4, MR 3.2**

Connect

You can use grid paper to find the area of any triangles.

Step 1

Draw and shade a model of a triangle inside a rectangle.

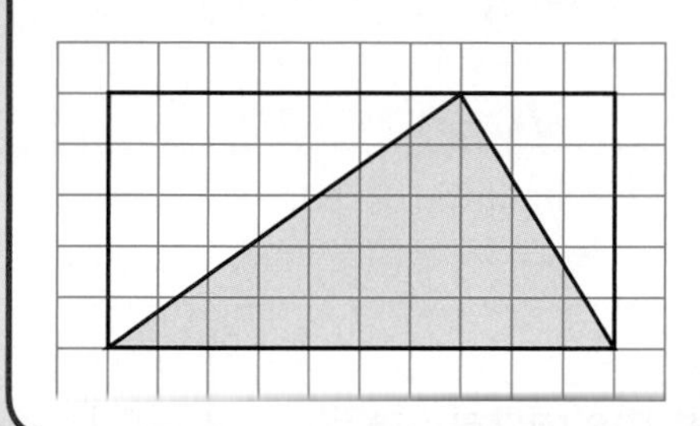

Step 2

Cut out the rectangle and then the shaded triangle.

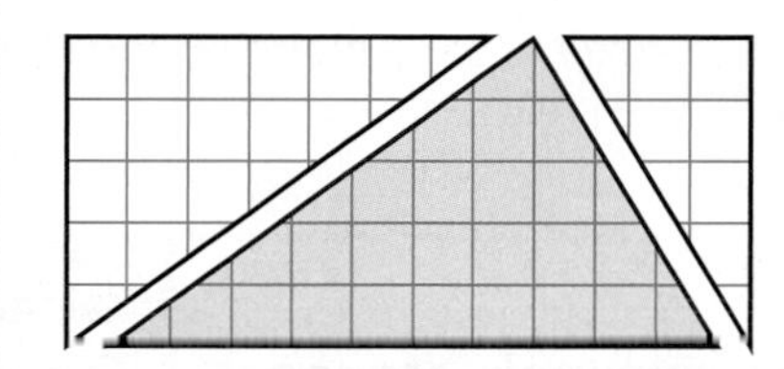

Step 3

Place the unshaded parts of the rectangle over the shaded triangle. What do you notice?

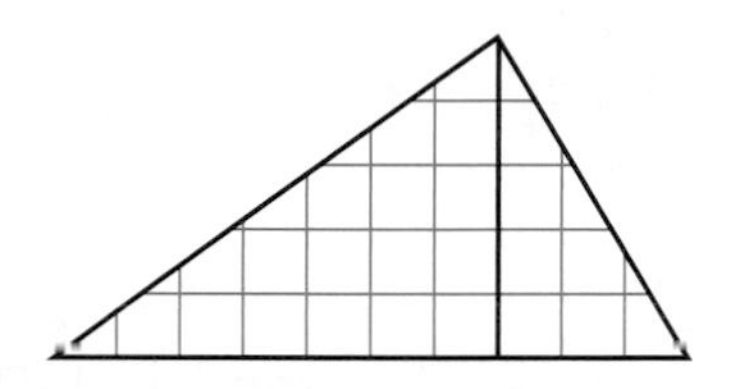

So, the area of the triangle is half the area of the rectangle.

TALK Math

The formula for the area of a rectangle is $A = l \times w$. What formula could you use for the area of a triangle?

Practice

Use the rectangle at the right to answer 1–3.

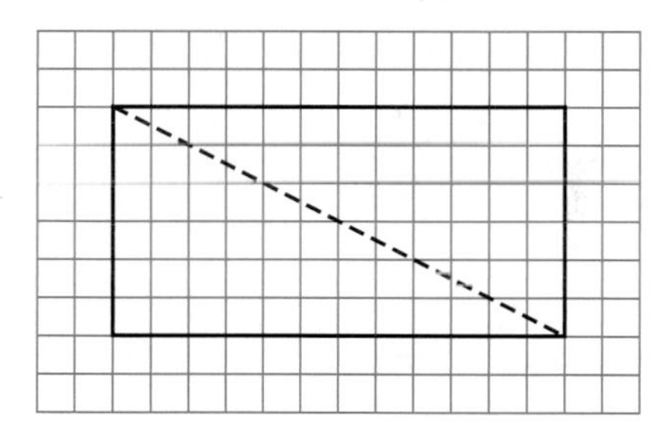

1. How many units long is the rectangle? How many units wide is it?
2. What is the area of the rectangle in square units?
3. What is the area of each triangle in square units?

Find the area in square centimeters of each shaded triangle.

4. 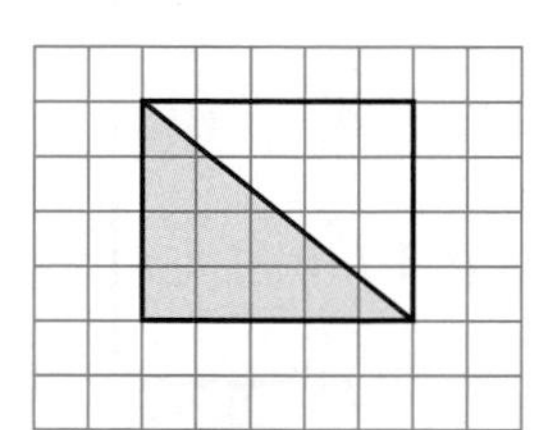

5. 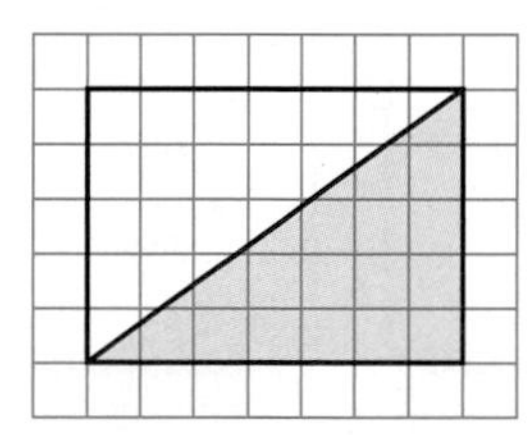

6. 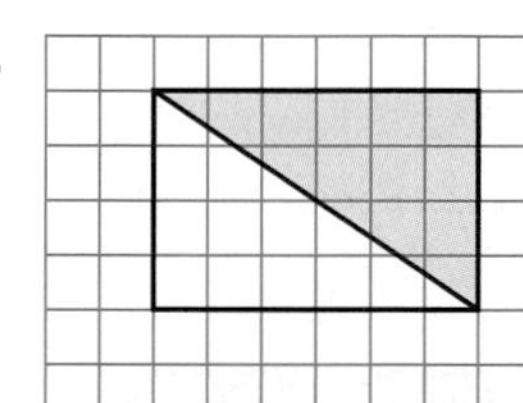

7. 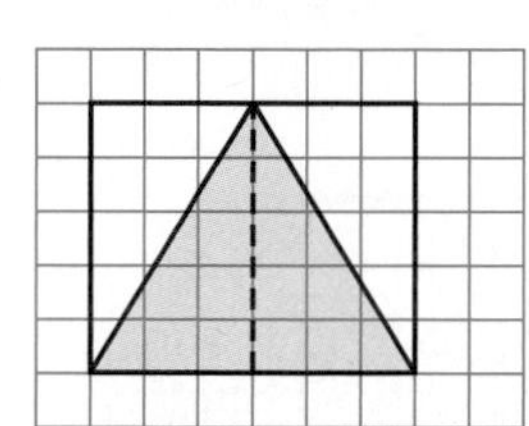

8. 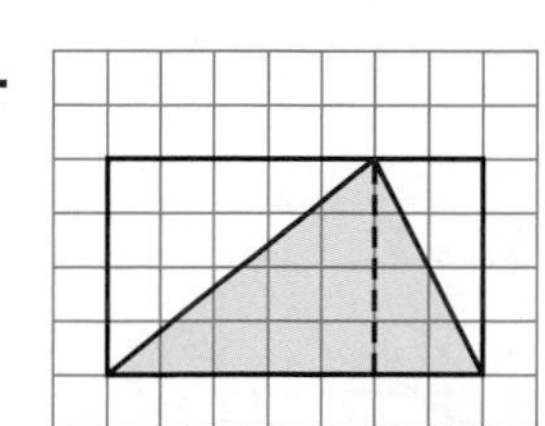

9. 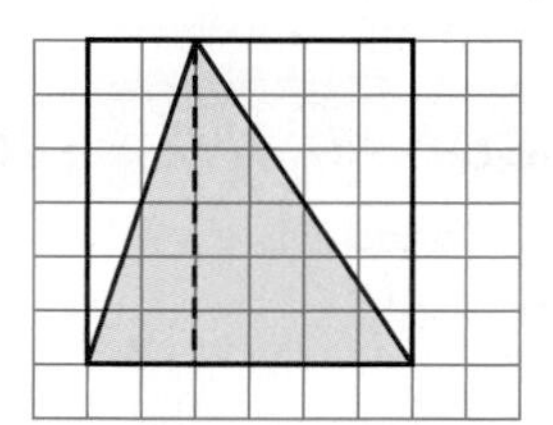

10. WRITE Math **Explain** how you use a rectangle to find the area of a triangle.

ALGEBRA

Area of Triangles

OBJECTIVE: Find the area of triangles by using a formula.

Quick Review

Find the sum.

1. $\frac{1}{2} \times 4$
2. $\frac{1}{2} \times 21$
3. $\frac{1}{2} \times 16$
4. $\frac{1}{2} \times 4 \times 2$
5. $\frac{1}{2} \times 3 \times 4$

Vocabulary

height base

Learn

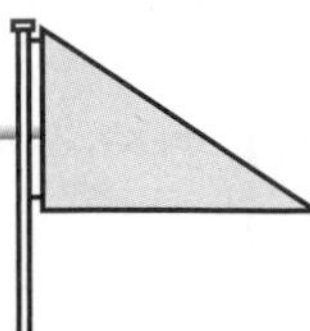

PROBLEM How much material is needed to make a triangular banner with a base of 6 ft and a height of 4 ft?

HANDS ON **Activity** **Materials:** ■ grid paper ■ scissors

Step 1

Draw and shade a model of the banner.

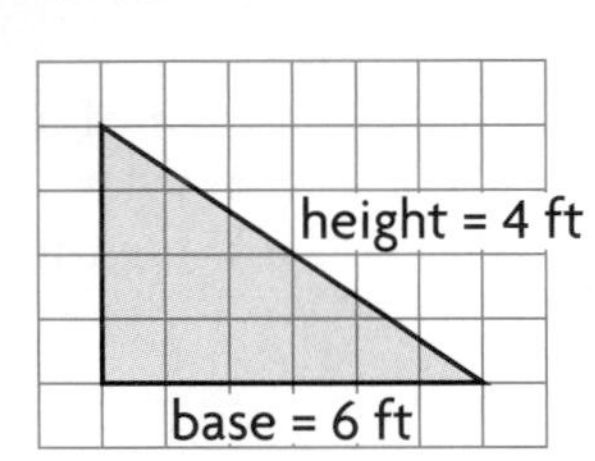

The **height** is the length of a line segment perpendicular to the **base** of the triangle.

Step 2

Draw a rectangle around the triangle as shown. Find the area of the rectangle.

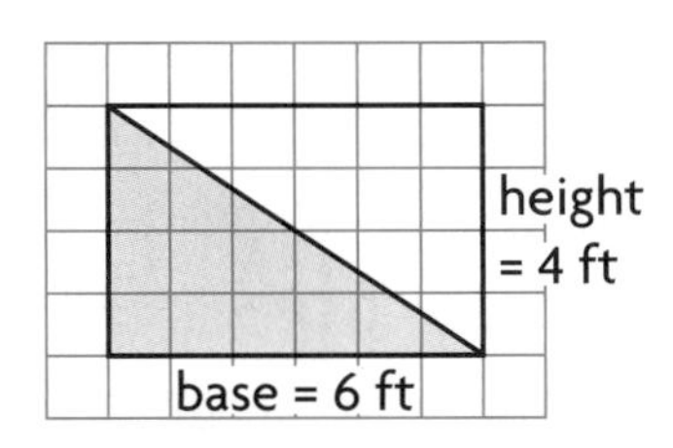

Rectangle:

$A = b \text{ (base)} \times h \text{ (height)}$

$A = 6 \times 4 = 24$

Step 3

Cut out the rectangle. Cut it in half to make two congruent triangles.

The area of each triangle is half the area of the rectangle.

Triangle:

$A = \frac{1}{2} \times (b \times h)$

$A = \frac{1}{2} \times 24 = 12$

So, the amount of material needed for the banner is 12 ft^2.

Math Idea

You can use the formula $A = \frac{1}{2} \times (b \times h)$ to find the area of any triangle.

More Examples Use the formula.

A Find the area.

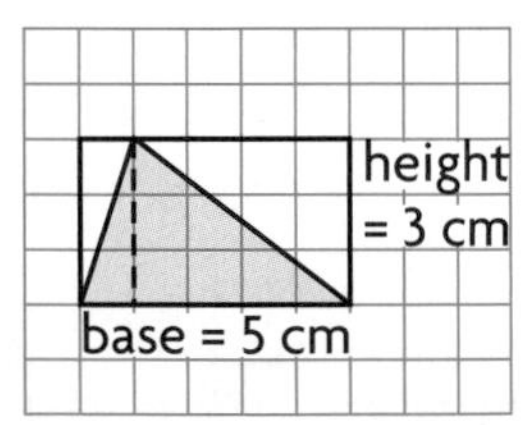

$A = \frac{1}{2} \times (b \times h)$

$A = \frac{1}{2} \times (5 \times 3) = 7.5$

The area is 7.5 cm^2.

B Find the area.

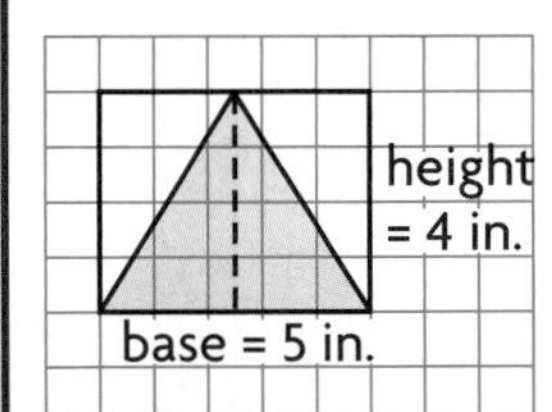

$A = \frac{1}{2} \times (b \times h)$

$A = \frac{1}{2} \times (5 \times 4) = 10$

The area is 10 $in.^2$

Guided Practice

Find the area of each triangle.

1. 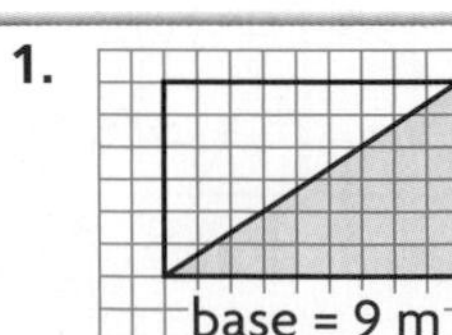

2. 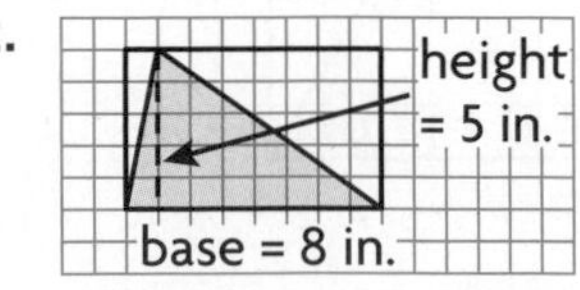

MG 1.1 Derive and use the formula for the area of a triangle and of a parallelogram by comparing it with the formula for the area of a rectangle (i.e., two of the same triangles make a parallelogram with twice the area; a parallelogram is compared with a rectangle of the same area by pasting and cutting a right triangle on the parallelogram). *also* **AF 1.2, MG 1.4, MR 2.2, MR 2.3, MR 2.4, MR 3.2**

Find the area of each triangle.

3.

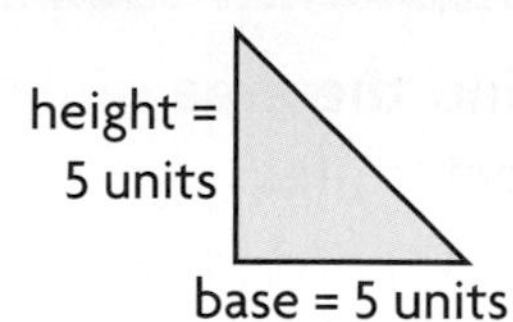

4.

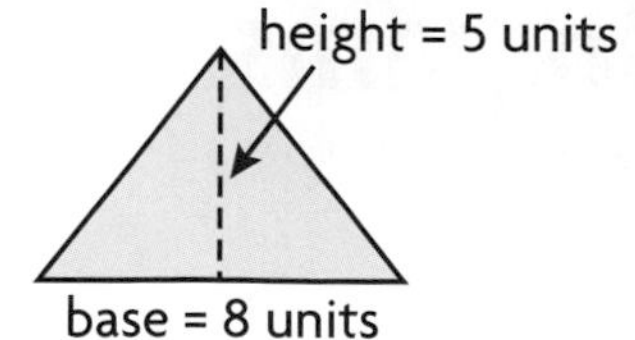

5.

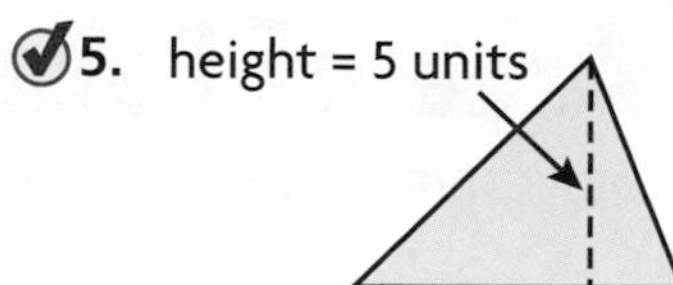

6. TALK Math **Explain** the relationship between the area of a rectangle and the area of a triangle.

Independent Practice and Problem Solving

Find the area of each triangle.

7.

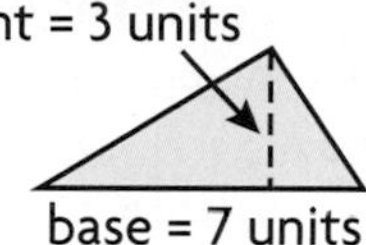

8.

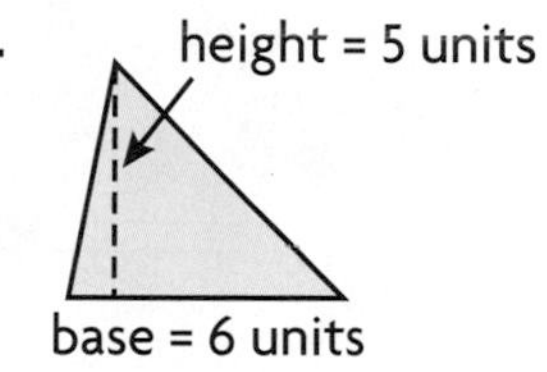

9.

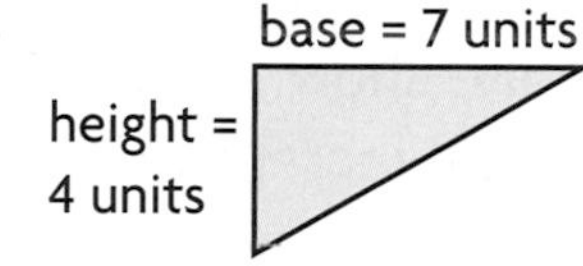

10. base (b) = 14 ft
height (h) = 8 ft
Area (A) = ■

11. base (b) = 7 in.
height (h) = 11 in.
Area (A) = ■

12. base (b) = 6 m
height (h) = 10 m
Area (A) = ■

For 13–14, use the diagram.

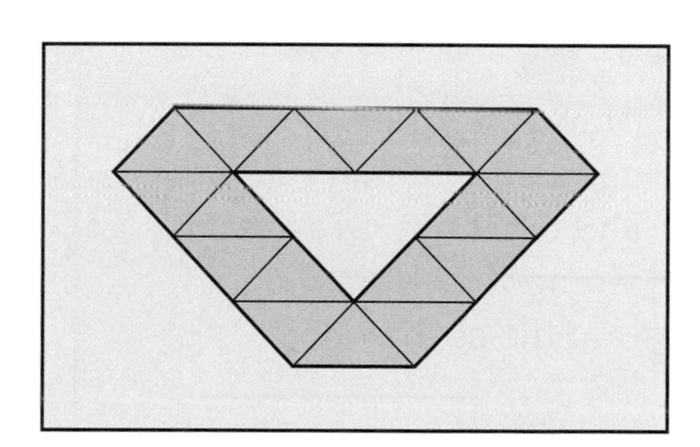

13. To fill the middle of the pattern, Natalie bought white tiles the same size and shape as the purple tiles. How many white tiles did she buy?

14. **Reasoning** The tiles in the pattern are right isosceles triangles. The two shorter sides of each triangle are each 1 inch long. Estimate the area of the purple part.

15. WRITE Math **What's the Error?** A triangle has a base of 4 m and a height of 8 m. Kara says its area is 32 m^2. Describe and correct her error.

Achieving the Standards

16. Tom is painting a 4 ft by 4 ft sign. What is its area? (MG 1.0, 1.4, p. 548)

17. What is the perimeter of a 12 ft by 15 ft room? (MG 1.0, MG 1.4, p. 530)

18. What is 5% of 60? (O—π NS 1.2, p. 414)

19. **Test Prep** A triangular flag has a base of 5 feet and an area of 25 ft^2. What is the flag's height?

A 5 ft
B 10 ft
C 15 ft
D 20 ft

Extra Practice on page 567, Set D

ALGEBRA

Area of Parallelograms

OBJECTIVE: Find the area of parallelograms.

Quick Review

Find the area of each rectangle.

1. 5 in. × 11 in.
2. 4 ft × 12 ft
3. 6.2 cm × 5.3 cm
4. 10.5 m × 13 m
5. 35 km × 40 km

Learn

PROBLEM Jeremy's dog goes to a dog run shaped like a parallelogram. The dog run is covered with sand. One bag of sand covers 1 square meter. How many bags of sand does it take to cover the dog run?

The lengths of the base and height of the dog run are shown below. Find the area of the parallelogram.

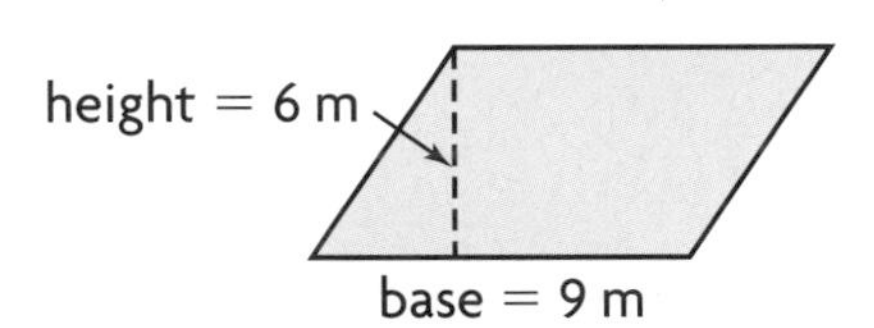

Remember

A *parallelogram* is a quadrilateral whose opposite sides are parallel and congruent.

ONE WAY **Use the area of a rectangle.**

You can use grid paper and what you know about the area of a rectangle to find the area of a parallelogram.

Step 1

Draw a diagram of the parallelogram on grid paper and cut it out. Draw a line segment to form a right triangle as shown.

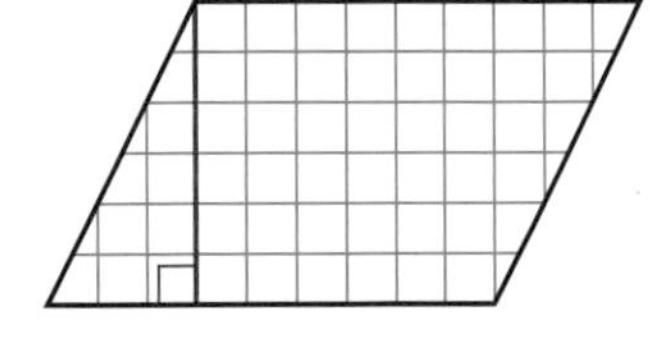

Step 2

Cut out the right triangle on the left, and move it to the right of the parallelogram to form a rectangle.

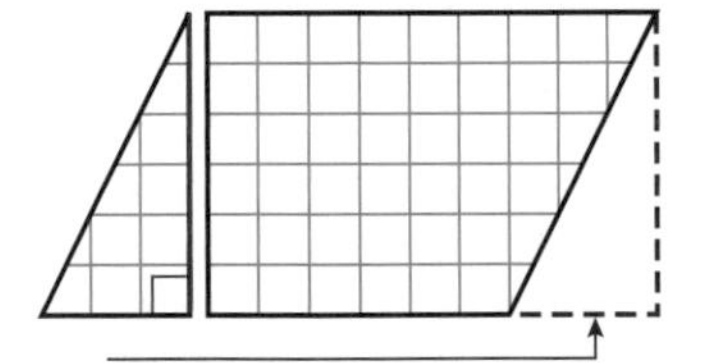

Step 3

Count the grid squares to find the area of the parallelogram.

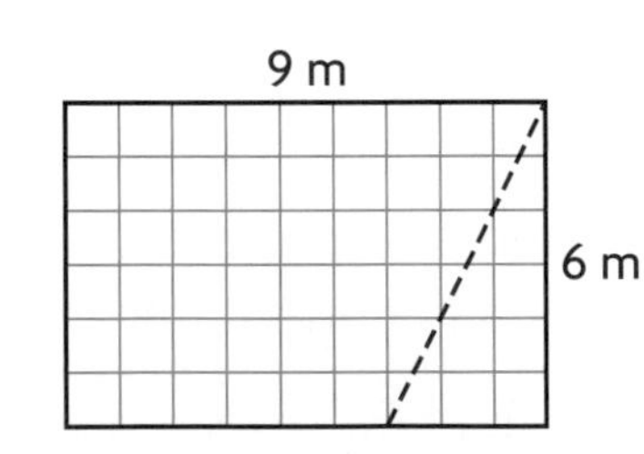

There are 6 rows of 9 squares, or 54 squares.

So, it takes 54 bags of sand to cover the dog run.

- How do the base and height of the parallelogram in Step 1 relate to the length and width of the rectangle in Step 3?

MG 1.1 Derive and use the formula for the area of a triangle and of a parallelogram by comparing it with the formula for the area of a rectangle (i.e., two of the same triangles make a parallelogram with twice the area; a parallelogram is compared with a rectangle of the same area by pasting and cutting a right triangle on the parallelogram). *also* **AF 1.2, MG 1.0, MG 1.4, MR 2.0, MR 2.2, MR 2.3, MR 2.4, MR 3.0, MR 3.2**

The area of a parallelogram is equal to the area of a rectangle with the same base (length) and height (width).

Area of a rectangle = length × width $A = l \cdot \times w$

Area of a parallelogram = base × height $A = b \times h$

ERROR ALERT

The slanted side of a parallelogram is *not* its height. The height must form a 90° angle with the base.

More Examples **Find the area.**

A

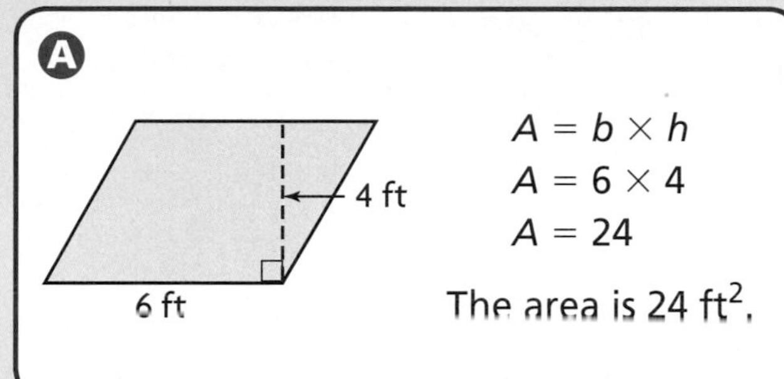

$A = b \times h$
$A = 6 \times 4$
$A = 24$

The area is 24 ft^2.

B

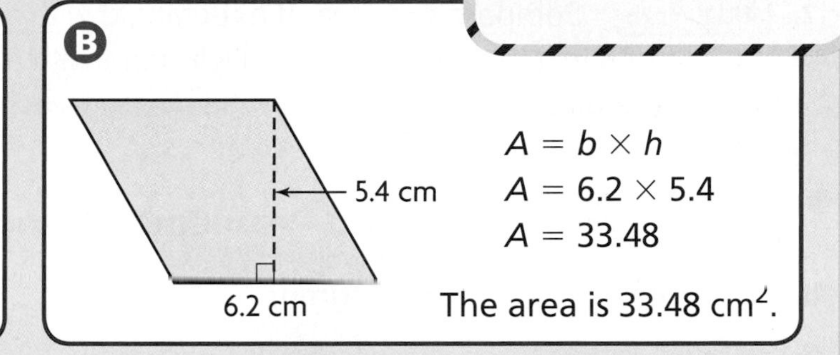

$A = b \times h$
$A = 6.2 \times 5.4$
$A = 33.48$

The area is 33.48 cm^2.

ANOTHER WAY **Use the area of a triangle.**

What would the area of the dog run be if the base were 11 meters and the height were 5 meters?

Step 1

Draw a 5 m × 11 m parallelogram on grid paper and cut it out.

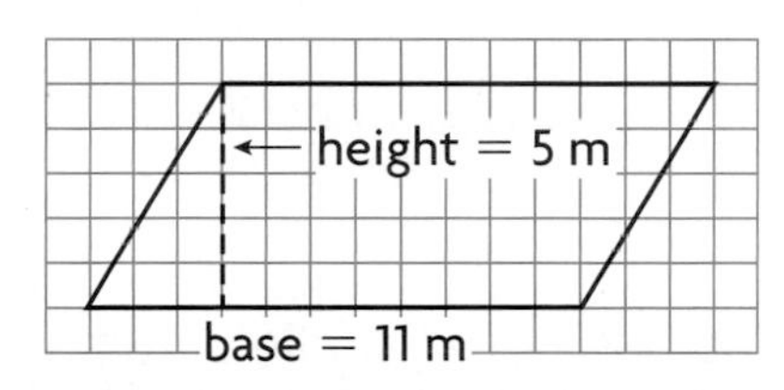

Step 2

Cut the parallelogram on a diagonal to form two congruent triangles.

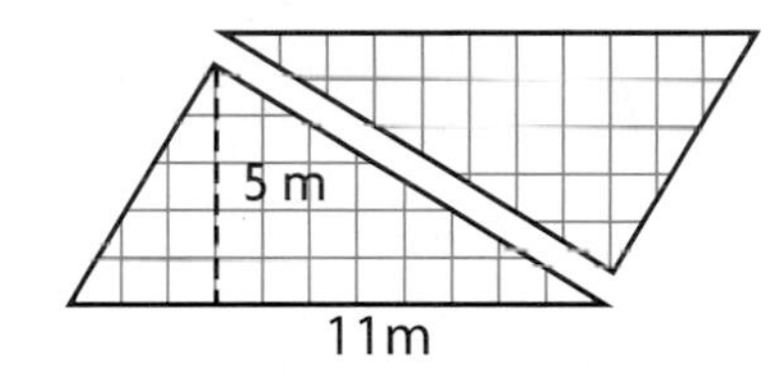

Step 3

Find the area of one triangle.

$A = \frac{1}{2} \times 11 \times 5$

$A = 27.5$

The area of two triangles is 2×27.5, or 55 m^2.

So, the area of the dog run would be 55 m^2.

- How is the area of the triangle related to the area of the parallelogram?

Guided Practice

Write the base and height of each parallelogram. Then find its area in square units.

1.

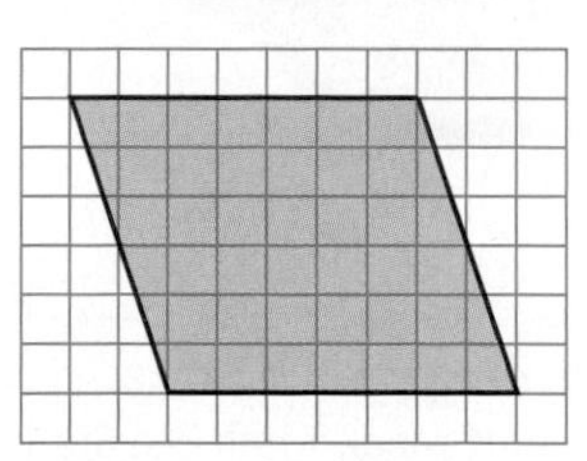

2.

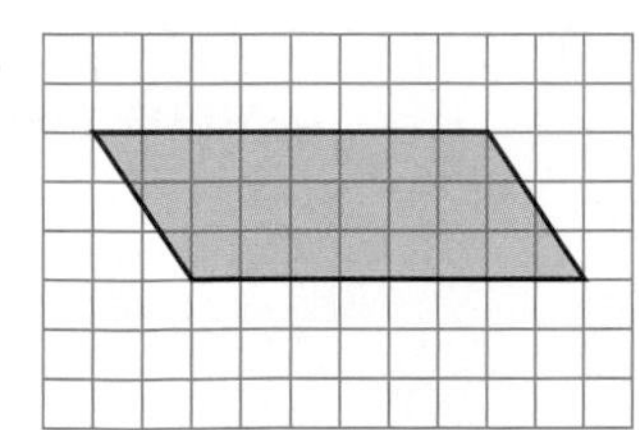

3.

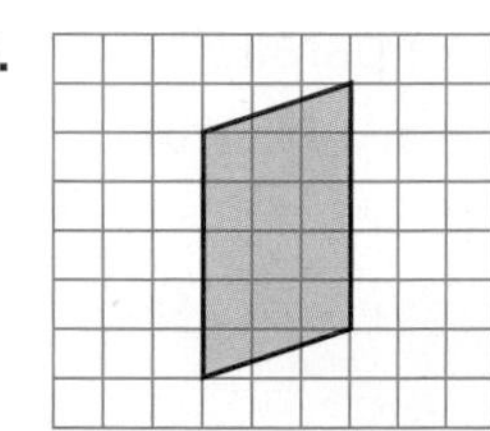

Find the area of each parallelogram.

4. 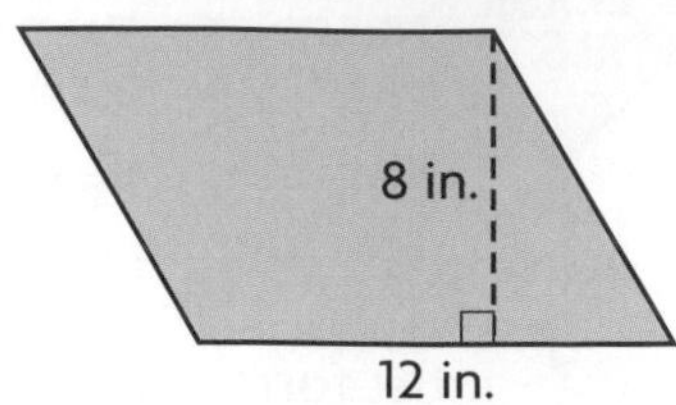

5. 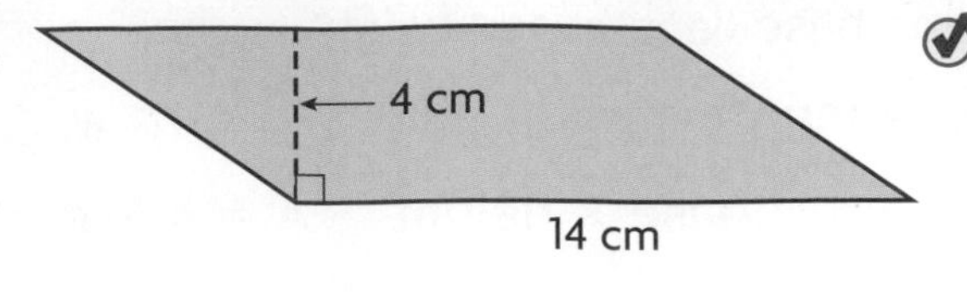

✓6. 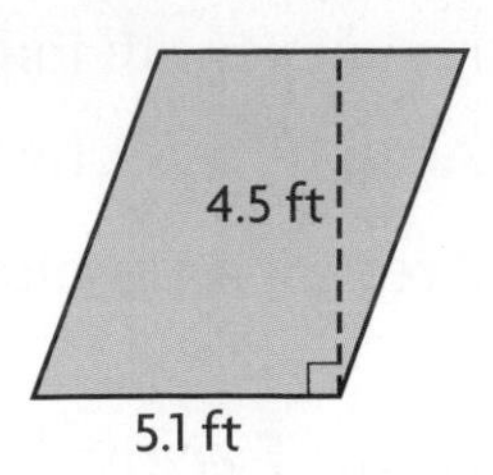

7. **TALK Math** Compare the area of a rectangle with a length of 5 in. and a width of 6 in. to the area of a parallelogram with a base of 5 in. and a height of 6 in.

Independent Practice and Problem Solving

Find the area of each parallelogram.

8. 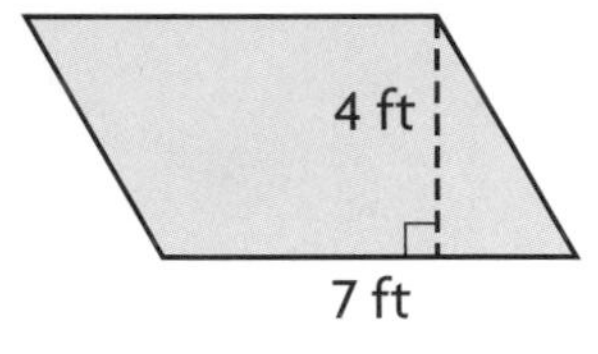

9. 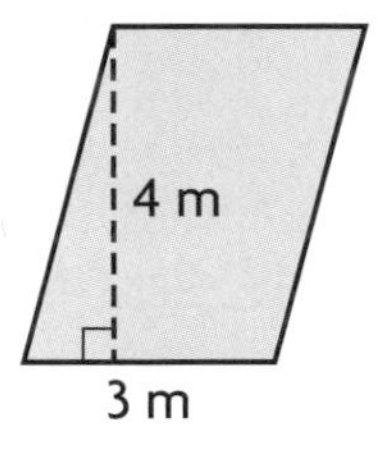

10. 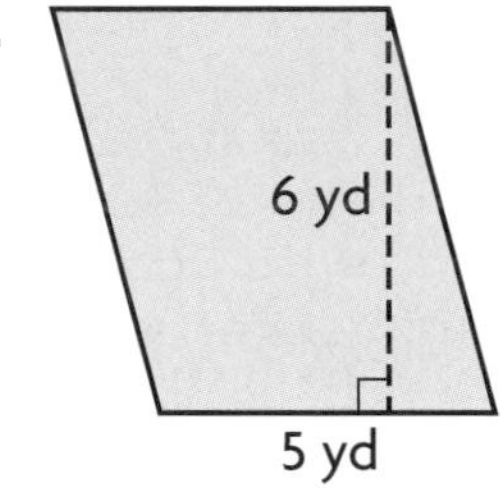

11. 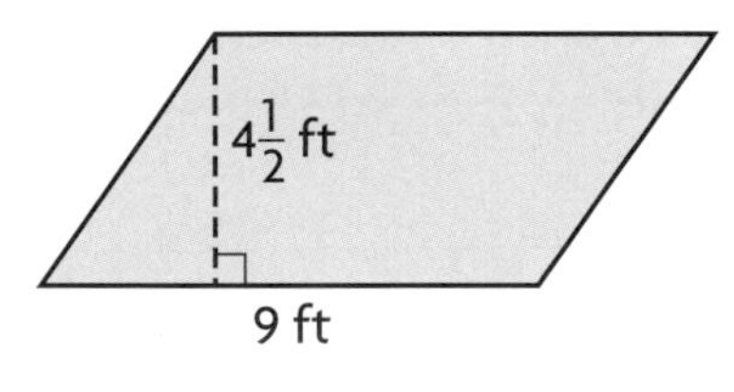

12. 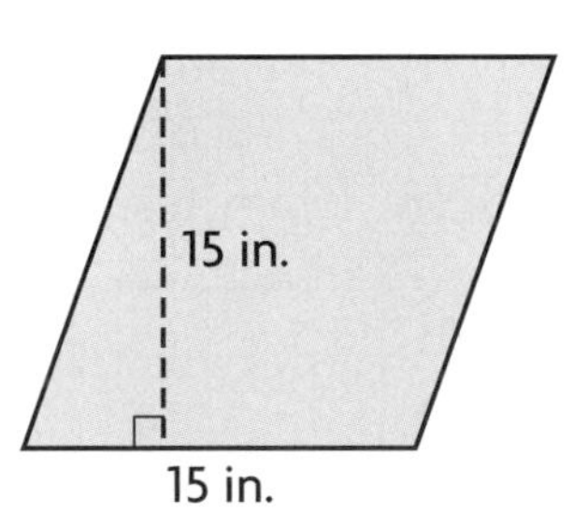

13. 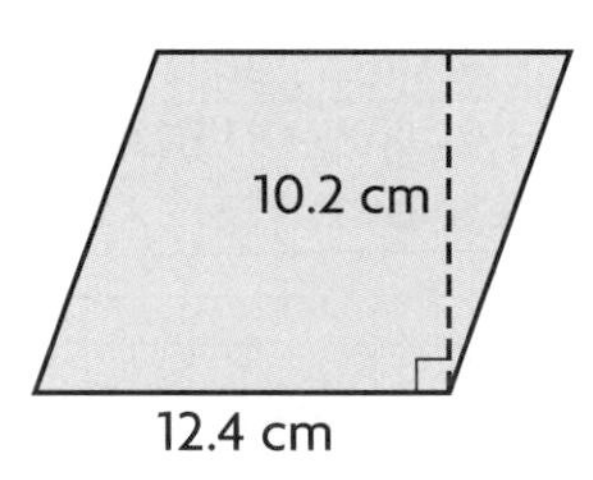

14. A playground is shaped like a parallelogram with a base of 34 m and a height of 20 m. The playground is divided into two congruent triangles. What is the area of each triangle?

15. **Reasoning** The base of a parallelogram is two times its height. If the base is 12 cm, what is its area?

16. ***FAST FACT*** The state of Tennessee is shaped roughly like a parallelogram. It is about 410 miles long and about 110 miles wide. Estimate the area of Tennessee.

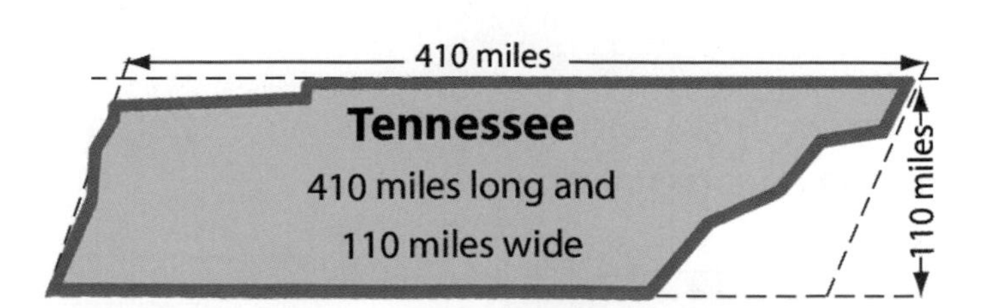

17. **WRITE Math** **What's the Question?** The base of a parallelogram is 7 yd. The area is 28 yd^2. The answer is 4 yd.

CD ROM Technology
Use Harcourt Mega Math, Ice Station Exploration, *Polar Planes*, Level Q; Ice Station Exploration, *Arctic Algebra*, Level CC.

 Extra Practice on page 567, Set E

Achieving the Standards

18. Start at the origin. Move right 3 units and then down 6 units. What ordered pair is described? (AF 1.4, p. 502)

19. A triangular sail has a base of 5 yards and a height of 6 yards. What is its area? (MG 1.1, p. 566)

20. Gina is making a hollow wooden cube. She has already cut 4 square pieces of wood for the faces of the cube. How many more pieces does she need? (Grade 4 MG 3.6)

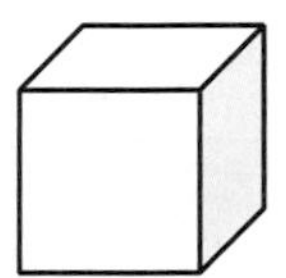

21. **Test Prep** The area of a parallelogram is 112 in^2. The height is 7 inches. What is the length of the base?

A 16 inches　　**C** 392 inches

B 56 inches　　**D** 784 inches

22. **Test Prep** What is the area of the entire figure if it is divided into two congruent parallelograms?

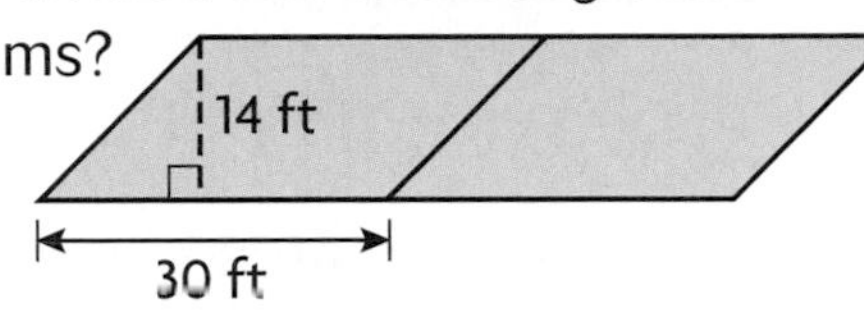

A 74 ft^2　　**C** 840 ft^2

B 420 ft^2　　**D** 1,680 ft^2

Problem Solving and Reasoning

ALGEBRA AND GEOMETRY You can use grid paper and what you know about the area of a parallelogram to find the area of a trapezoid.

Step 1

Draw these two identical trapezoids on grid paper. Label them and cut them out.

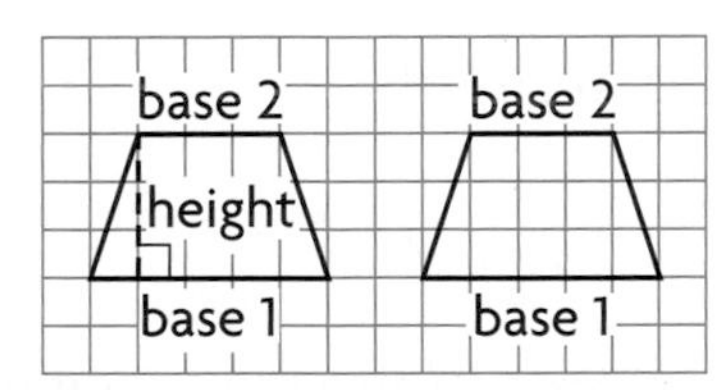

Step 2

Arrange the trapezoids to form a parallelogram.

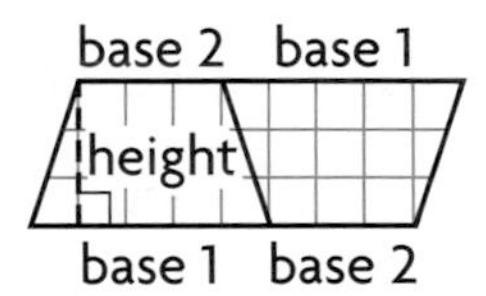

Use the trapezoids to answer the questions.

1. What is the base of the parallelogram?
2. What is the area of the parallelogram?
3. How do the areas of the trapezoids relate to the area of the parallelogram?
4. Find the area of one trapezoid. Explain how you found your answer.
5. The formula for the area of a trapezoid is Area $= \frac{1}{2} \times$ height $\times$ (base 1 + base 2). Use the formula to verify the area of either trapezoid.

Extra Practice

Set A Estimate the area of the shaded figure. Each square on the grid is 1 yd^2. (pp. 546–547)

1. 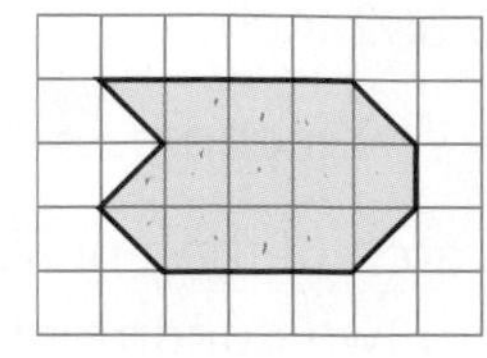

2. 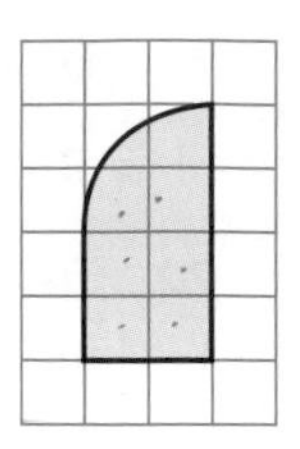

3. 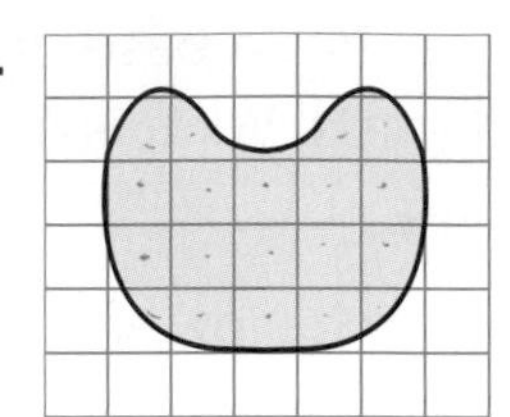

Set B Find the area of each figure. (pp. 548–551)

1. 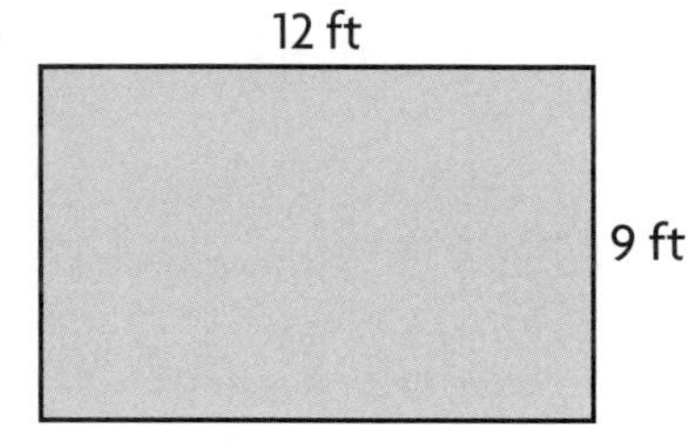

2. 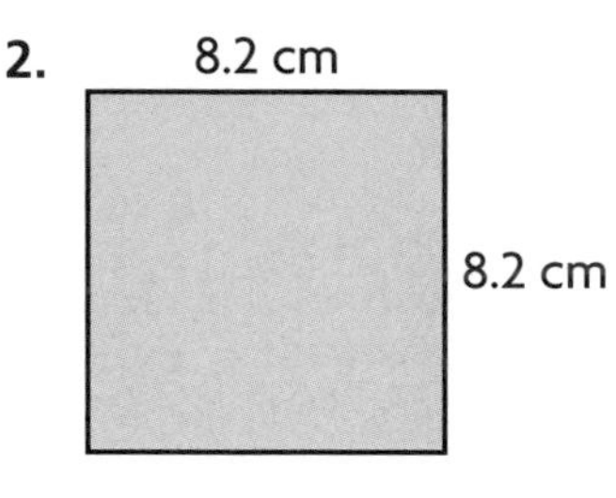

3. 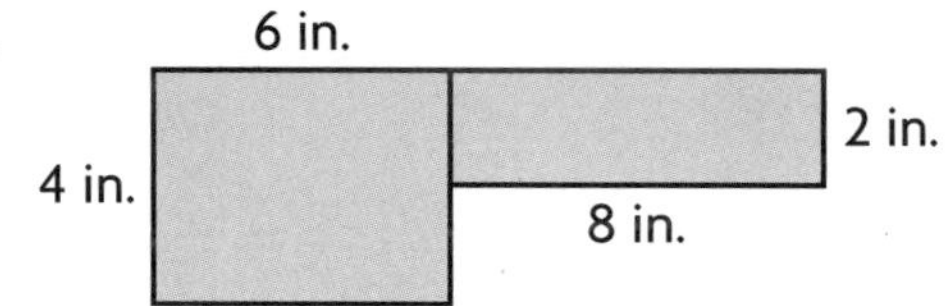

4. Owen is using a 4-foot by 8-foot piece of sheetrock for a project. What is the area of the sheetrock?

5. Owen's friend Alice cut a 3-foot by 10-foot piece of sheetrock. Whose piece has the greater area, Alice's or Owen's?

Set C For the given perimeter, find the length and width of the rectangle with the greatest area. Use whole numbers only. (pp. 552–555)

1. 20 in.
2. 18 cm
3. 32 yd
4. 40 km
5. 30 mi

For the given area, find the length and width of the rectangle with the least perimeter. Use whole numbers only.

6. 14 ft^2
7. 24 m^2
8. 18 cm^2
9. 42 in.^{2}
10. 36 ft^2

11. Kira has a 24-foot long strip of fringe which she plans to use as a border around a rectangular piece of fabric. What is the length and width of the rectangle with the greatest area?

12. What is the area of the playground?

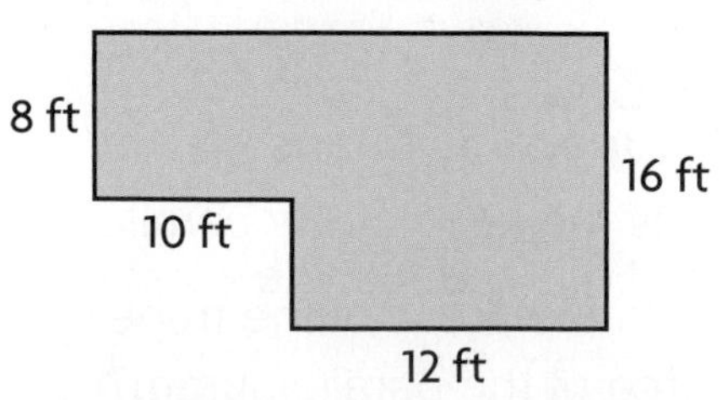

13. Maria is designing a rectangular wall hanging with an area of 38 in.^{2} She wants to use the least amount of gold braid as a border. Which rectangle will have the least perimeter?

Technology
CD ROM
Use Harcourt Mega Math, Ice Station Exploration, *Polar Planes*, Levels Q, R, S.

Set D Find the area of each triangle. (pp. 560–561)

1.
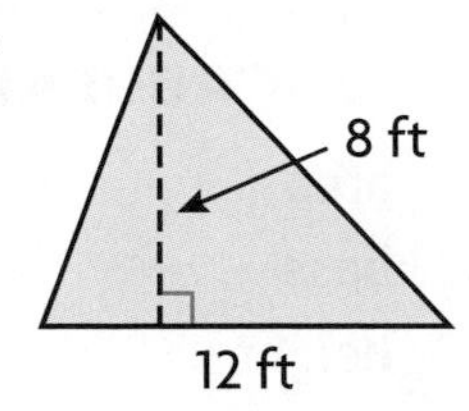

2.
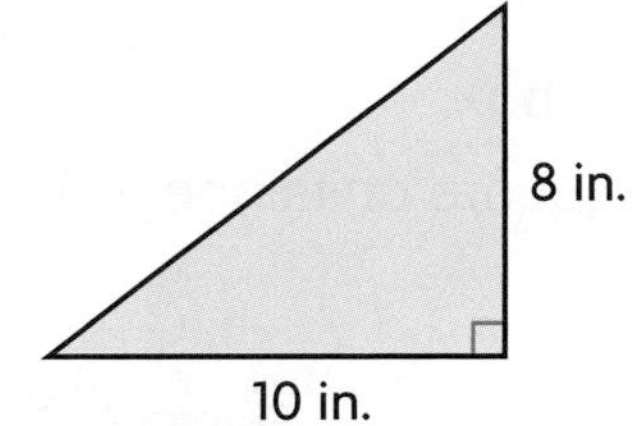

3.
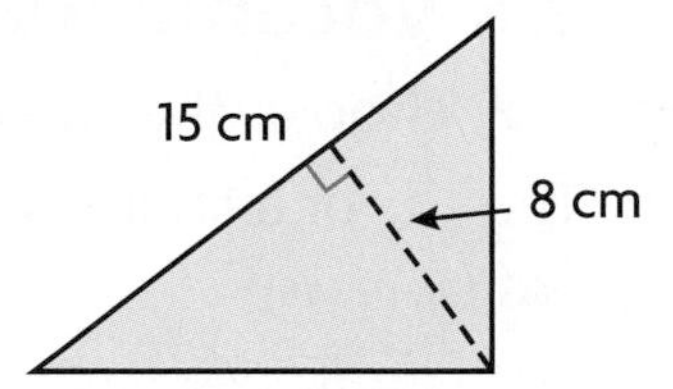

4.
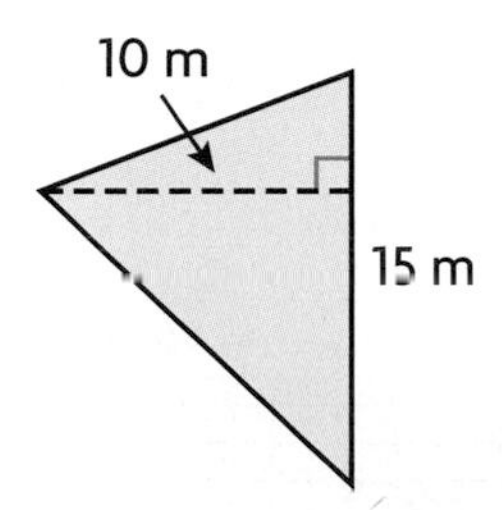

5.
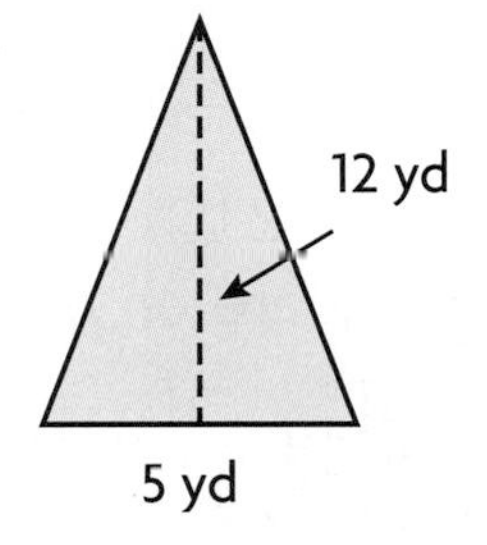

6.
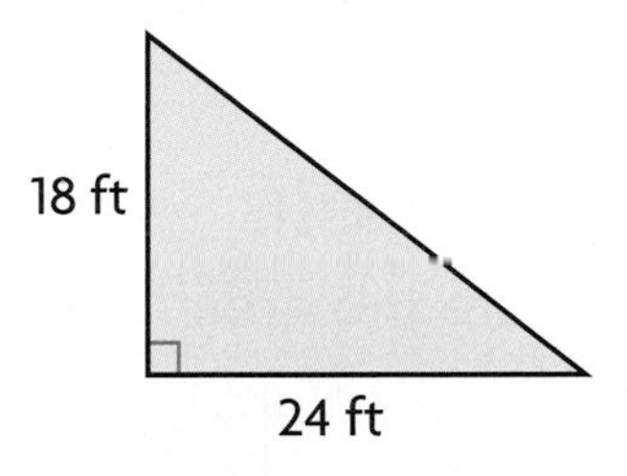

7. A triangular sail on a boat model has a base of 1 meter and a height of 3 meters. What is the area of the sail?

8. A boat model has a triangular flag at the top of its mast. The flag has a base of 30 centimeters and a height of 15 centimeters. What is the area of the flag?

Set E Find the area of each parallelogram. (pp. 562–565)

1.
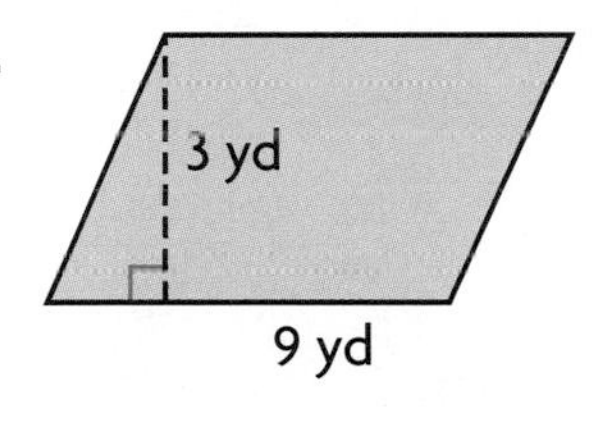

2.
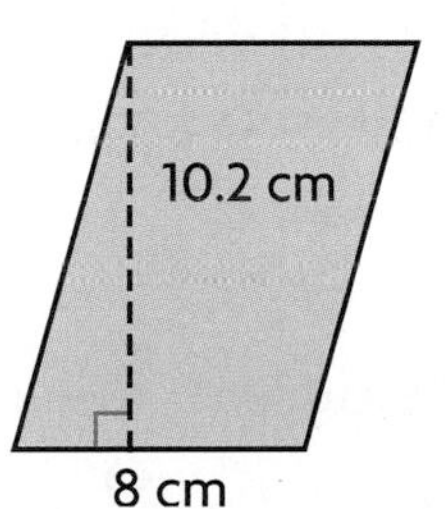

3.
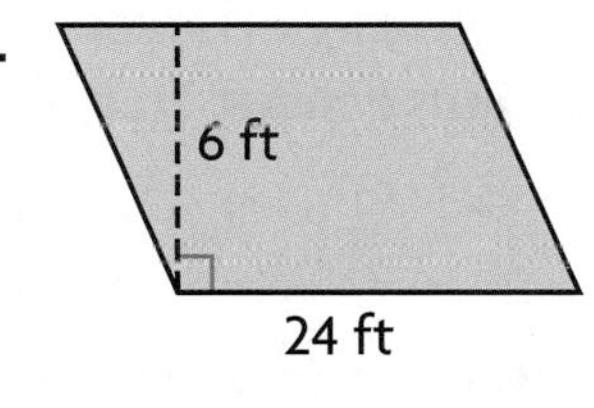

4.
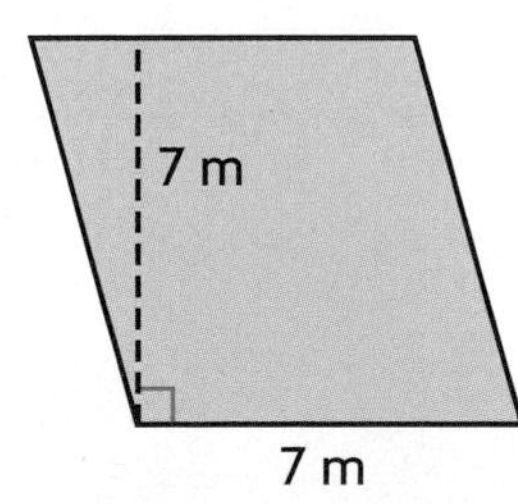

5.
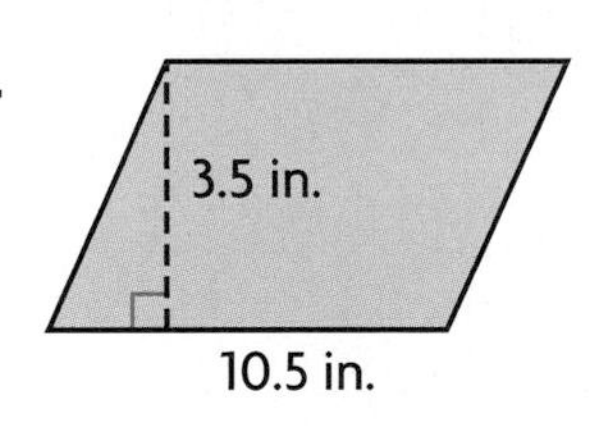

6.
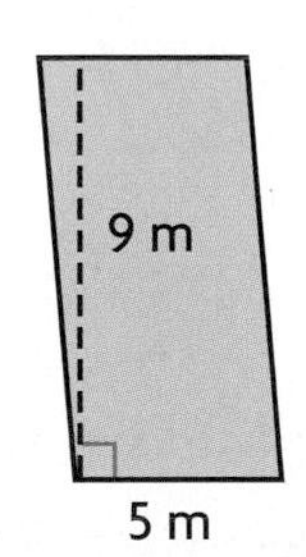

7. A patio is shaped like a parallelogram. It has a base of 7 yd and a height of 4 yd. What is the area of the patio?

Chapter 21 Review/Test

Check Vocabulary and Concepts

VOCABULARY
area
base
height

For 1–2, choose the best term from the box.

1. The _?_ of a figure is the number of square units needed to cover it. (MG 1.0, p. 546)
2. The length of a line segment perpendicular to the _?_ of a triangle is the height. (O-π MG 1.1, p. 560)

Check Skills

Estimate the area of the shaded figure. Each square on the grid is 1 cm^2. (MG 1.0, pp. 546–547)

3. 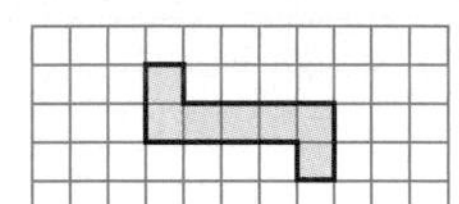
4. 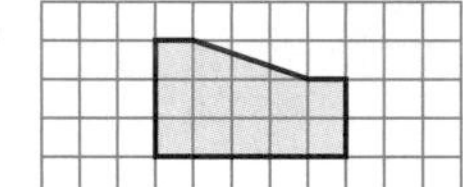
5. 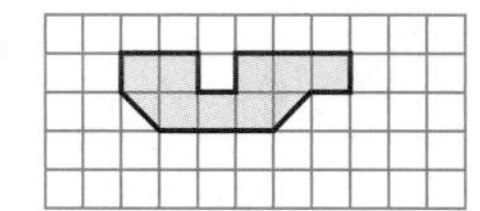

Find the area of each figure. (MG 1.4, pp. 548–551)

6. 8 yd, 13 yd
7. 5 cm, 4 cm, 3.5 cm, 4 cm
8. 15 mi, 15 mi
9. 6 in., 9 in., 7 in., 3.5 in.

For the given perimeter, find the length and width of the rectangle with the greatest area. Use whole numbers only. (MG 1.4, pp. 552–555)

10. 12 in.
11. 34 km
12. 14 ft
13. 20 cm
14. 24 m

Find the area of each triangle or parallelogram. (O-π MG 1.1, pp. 560–561, 562–565)

15. 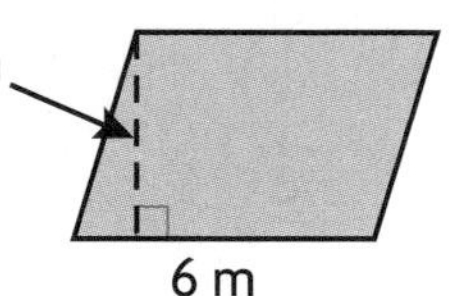

16. 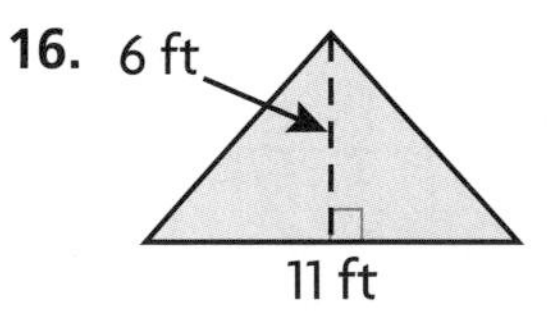

17. 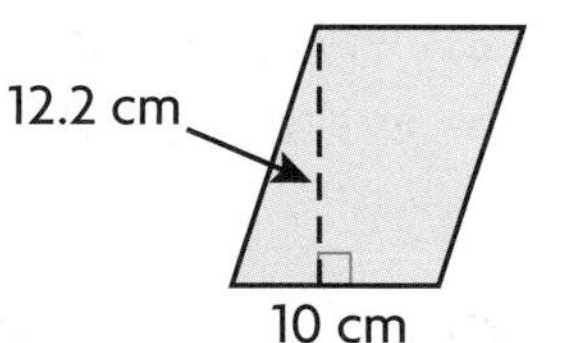

18. 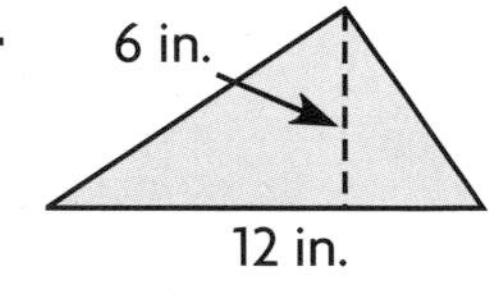

Check Problem Solving

Solve. (MG 1.4, MR 2.3, MR 3.0, pp. 556–557)

19. Julie used 3-inch square pieces of fabric to make a pattern. The first row contained 3 pieces. Each of the other rows had 3 more pieces than the one above it. What is the area of the fourth row of pieces?
20. **WRITE Math** Explain how you could find the area of the pieces in a pattern containing 6 rows in Exercise 19. What is the area?

GO ONLINE **Technology** Use *Online Assessment.*

Enrich • Finding Area

Complex Areas

Area is the number of square units needed to cover a surface. You find the area of a rectangle by multiplying length times width: $A = l \times w$. Sometimes, you need to find only a part of the total area.

Example

Ron is putting decorative tile on the outer edges of a floor. The shaded part of the diagram shows the area that will be covered with tile. How many square feet of decorative tile does Ron need?

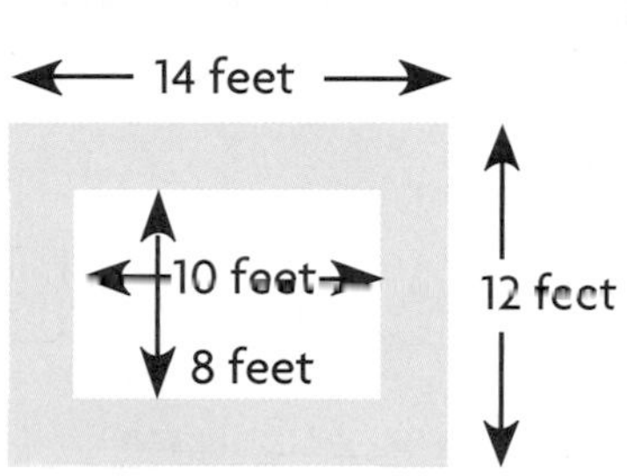

Step 1 Find the area of the entire floor.	$14 \times 12 = 168$
Step 2 Find the area of the floor that will not be covered with tile.	$10 \times 8 = 80$
Step 3 Subtract. The difference is the area of the shaded part of the diagram.	$168 - 80 = 88$

So, Ron needs 88 ft^2 of tile.

Try It

1. The diagram shows a wall that Anna wants to wallpaper. The white areas are windows that are 3 feet long and 2 feet wide. How much wallpaper will Anna need?

2. Don is painting scenery for a play. The shaded part of the diagram will be green. Each square is 2 feet by 2 feet. How much of the scenery will be green? How much will be yellow?

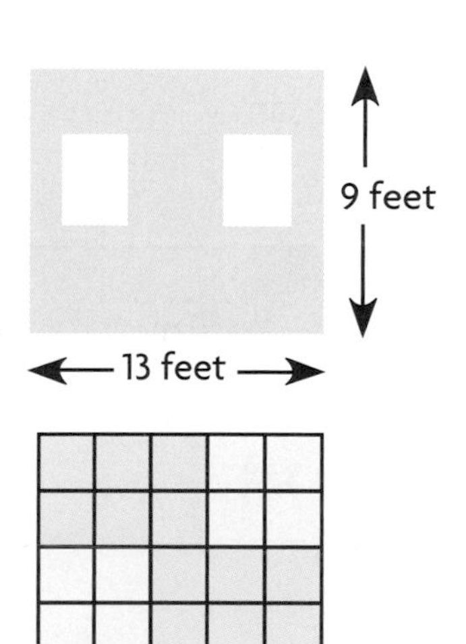

Think About It

WRITE Math Mica wants to wallpaper an 8-foot by 12-foot wall. The wall has one square window. One side of the window is 3 feet. How much wallpaper does he need? **Explain** how you found your answer.

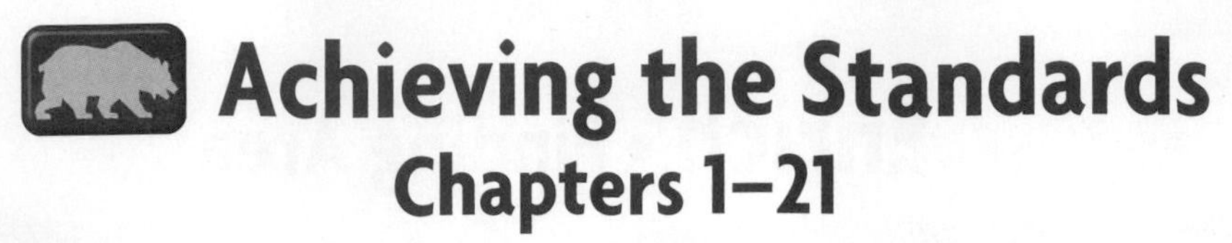

Achieving the Standards
Chapters 1–21

Measurement and Geometry

1. In the figure below, *PQRS* is a parallelogram.

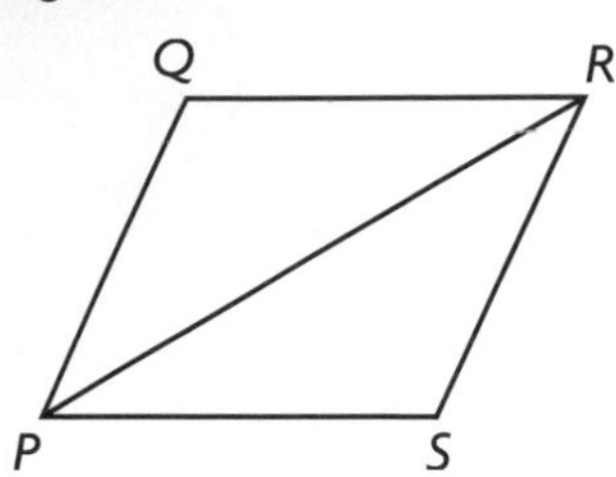

If the area of triangle *PQR* is 24 square inches, what is the area of parallelogram *PQRS*? **(O‑ᵗ MG 1.1)**

A 12 square inches

B 24 square inches

C 36 square inches

D 48 square inches

2. What is the approximate measure of this angle in degrees? **(O‑ᵗ MG 2.1)**

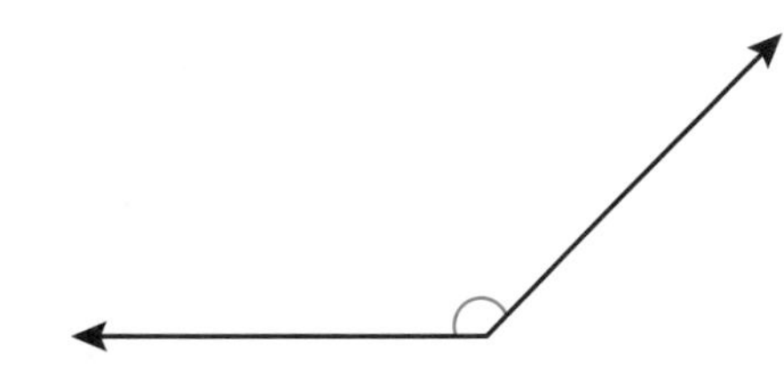

A 45°

B 55°

C 135°

D 175°

3. **WRITE Math** **Explain** how to find the area of the parallelogram below.
(O‑ᵗ MG 1.1)

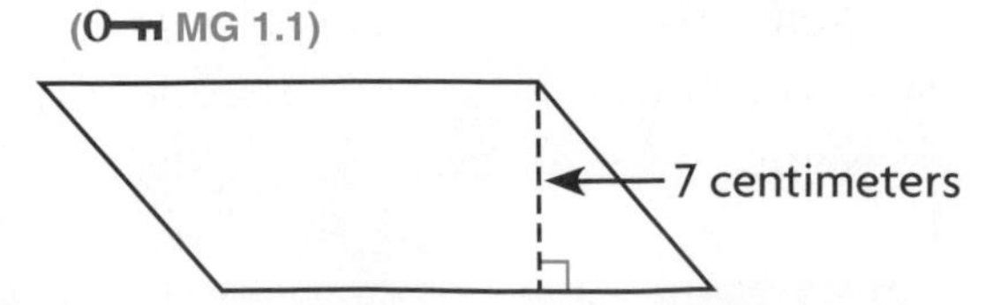

Statistics, Data Analysis, and Probability

4. Look at the table below.

Results of Marble Experiment		
Red	**Blue**	**Yellow**
卌 |||	卌 |	卌 卌

Based on the results in the table, what are the chances of pulling a red marble on the next pull? **(Grade 4 SDAP 2.2)**

A $\frac{1}{4}$ **C** $\frac{5}{12}$

B $\frac{1}{3}$ **D** $\frac{2}{3}$

5. The high temperatures for seven days are shown in the table.

Weekly High Temperatures	
Day	**Temperature**
Sunday	83°F
Monday	80°F
Tuesday	87°F
Wednesday	84°F
Thursday	84°F
Friday	75°F
Saturday	82°F

What is the median temperature for the seven days? **(SDAP 1.1)**

A 82°F **C** 84°F

B 83°F **D** 87°F

6. **WRITE Math** **Explain** how to graph the point (3, 7) on a coordinate grid.
(O‑ᵗ SDAP 1.4)

Number Sense

7. The table below shows the ages of four people in the Green family.

Green Family Ages	
Name	**Age (years)**
Steven	24
Jill	27
Wendy	48
Craig	51

Whose age is equivalent to $2^4 \times 3$? (NS 1.4)

A Steven
B Jill
C Wendy
D Craig

Check your work.

See item 8. Check your work by multiplying each monthly payment by 12, then adding \$60. The answer should be the cost of the dishwasher.

8. Mrs. Becker bought a new dishwasher that cost \$395.52 including tax. She made a down payment of \$60 then paid the remaining amount in 12 equal monthly payments. How much was each monthly payment? (NS 2.2)

A \$22.96
B \$27.96
C \$32.96
D \$37.96

9. **WRITE Math** A bottle of apple juice that holds 64 ounces is over $\frac{3}{4}$-full. Is there enough juice in the bottle to fill six 8-ounce glasses? **Explain** how you know. (NS 2.5)

Algebra and Functions

10. Which function table represents values of x and y such that $y = x + 3$? (AF 1.5)

A

x	y
2	6
3	0

B

x	y
$^-1$	$^-4$
0	$^-3$

C

x	y
$^-1$	2
0	3

D

x	y
1	$^-2$
2	$^-1$

11. Ashley is making a pattern with equilateral triangles.

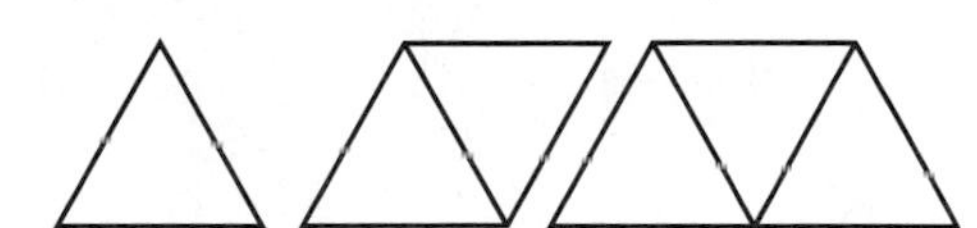

Which equation can be used to find the number of line segments, s, to form a figure with t triangles? (AF 1.5)

A $t = 3s$
B $s = 2t - 1$
C $s = 3t$
D $s = 2t + 1$

12. **WRITE Math** Write a problem that can be modeled with the equation $a - 10 = 6$. Tell what a represents. Solve the equation and **explain** how you solved it. (AF 1.1)

22 Surface Area and Volume

The Big Idea Attributes of three-dimensional figures can be measured.

Investigate

A new concrete dam uses rectangular beams measuring 300 feet high, 50 feet wide, and 50 feet long. What are some different dimensions for beams that would have the same volume?

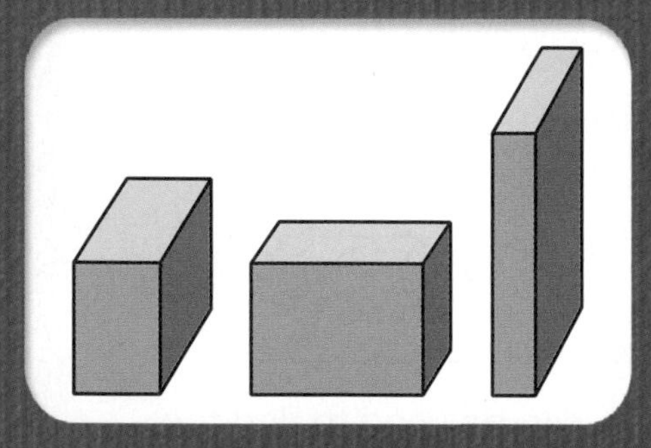

CALIFORNIA FAST FACT

Shasta Dam, on the Sacramento River, has a volume of concrete measuring 6,270,000 cubic yards. The dam stands taller than the Washington Monument.

GO ONLINE **Technology** Student pages are available in the Student eBook.

Show What You Know

Check your understanding of important skills needed for success in Chapter 22.

▶ Perimeter and Area

Find the perimeter and area of each figure.

1.
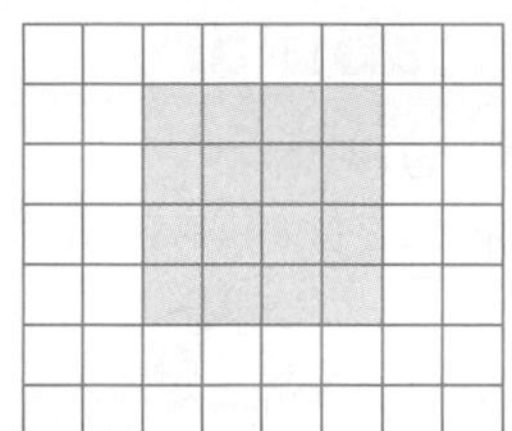

2.
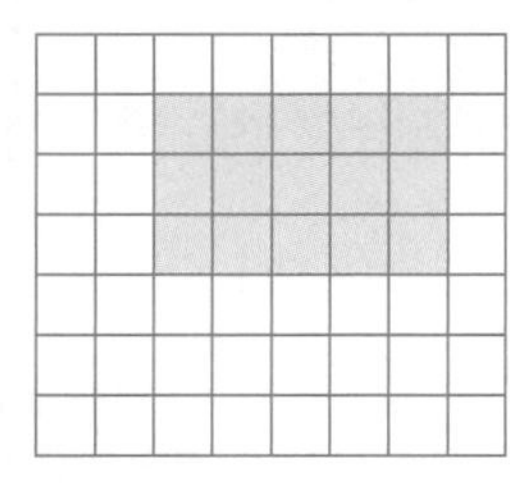

3.
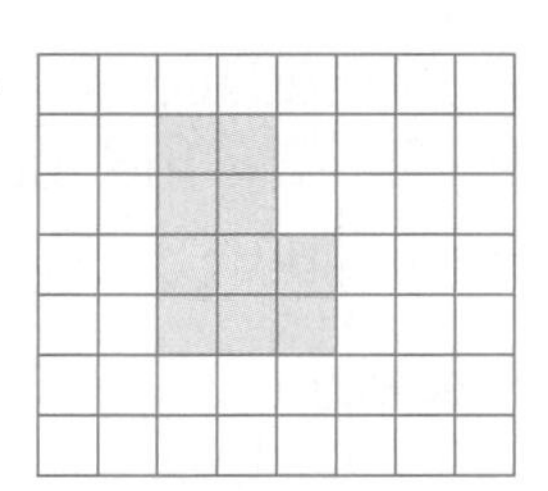

4.
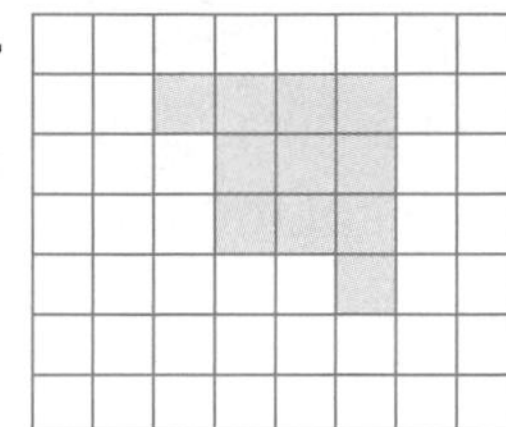

5.
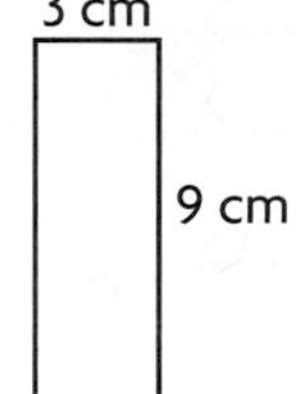

6.
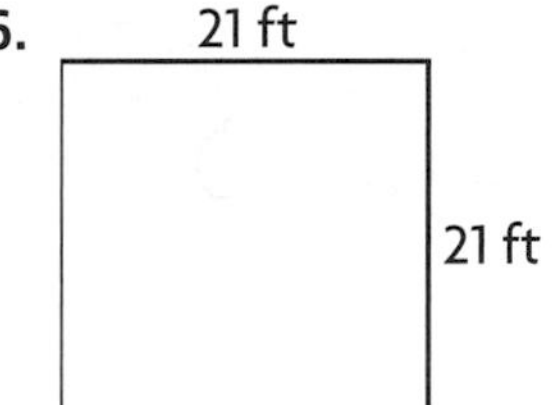

7.
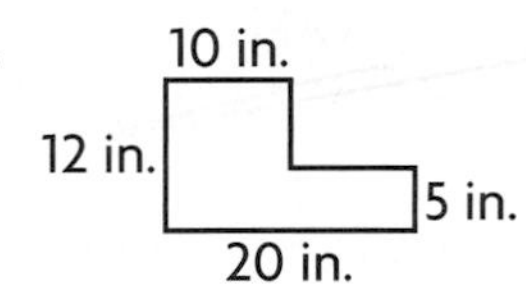

8. 16 m, 6 m

▶ Multiply with Three Factors

Find the product.

9. $4 \times (4 \times 15)$	**10.** $(2 \times 6) \times 4$	**11.** $3 \times (5 \times 5)$	**12.** $8 \times 8 \times 8$
13. $8.4 \times (2 \times 3)$	**14.** $3.6 \times (4 \times 10)$	**15.** $(7 \times 5.7) \times 1$	**16.** $3.3 \times (2 \times 6)$
17. $7 \times 4 \times 7$	**18.** $(1.9 \times 2) \times 5$	**19.** $5.5 \times (3 \times 8)$	**20.** $4 \times 11 \times 7$

VOCABULARY POWER

CHAPTER VOCABULARY

area
base
cubic unit
perimeter
surface area
volume

WARM-UP WORDS

surface area the sum of the areas of all the faces, or surfaces, of a solid figure

volume the measure of the space a solid figure occupies

cubic unit a unit of volume with dimensions 1 unit × 1 unit × 1 unit

LESSON 1 HANDS ON

Surface Area

OBJECTIVE: Find the surface areas of rectangular prisms and square pyramids.

Quick Review

Name each polygon.

1. (triangle)
2. (square)
3. (trapezoid)
4. 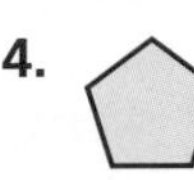
5. (rectangle)

Vocabulary

surface area

Investigate

Materials ■ centimeter grid paper ■ scissors

You can use a net to find the surface area of a rectangular prism. **Surface area** is the sum of all the areas of the faces of a solid figure.

A On centimeter grid paper, draw and label the net shown below.

B Cut out the net and fold it on the lines to make a rectangular prism.

C Unfold the prism and lay it flat. Find the area of each face, *A–F*. Record the length, width, and area of each face in a table.

D Find the surface area of the prism.

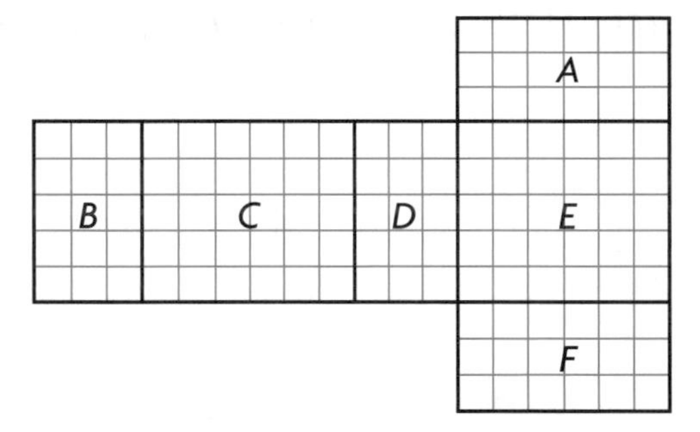

E Repeat the steps to find the surface area of a cube. Each face of the cube should be a 5×5 square.

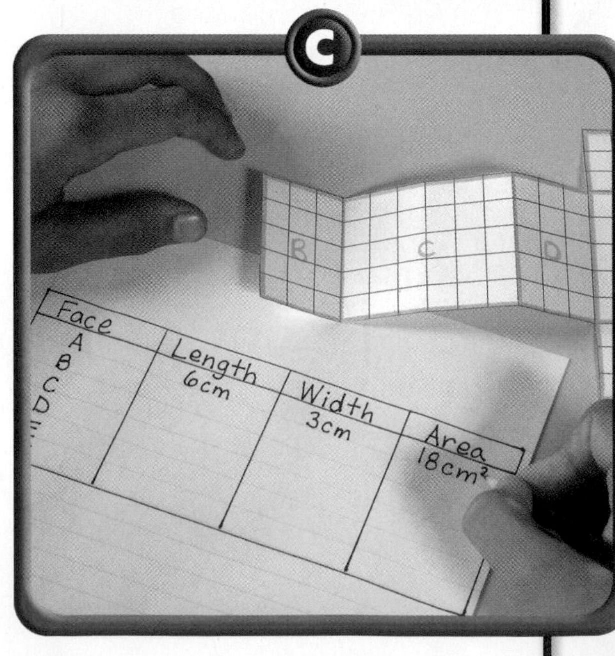

Draw Conclusions

1. Which faces of the rectangular prism are congruent? Do they have the same area?
2. Copy and complete the following expression for finding the surface area of a rectangular prism.

   ■ × (area of front) + ■ × (area of top) + ■ × (area of side)
3. **Synthesis** What expression could you write to find the surface area of a cube?

MG 1.2 Construct a cube and rectangular box from two-dimensional patterns and use these patterns to compute the surface area for these objects. *also* **MR 1.2, MR 2.0, MR 2.2, MR 2.3, MR 2.4, MR 3.2**

Connect

You can also use a net to find the surface area of a square pyramid.

Step 1

Copy the net on centimeter grid paper.

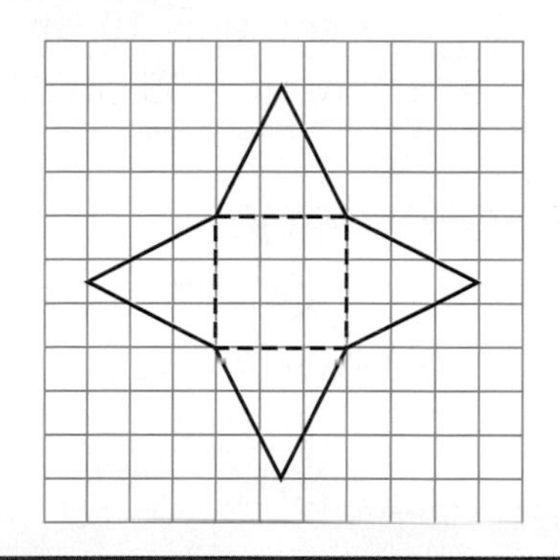

Step 2

Cut out the net and fold it on the lines to make a square pyramid.

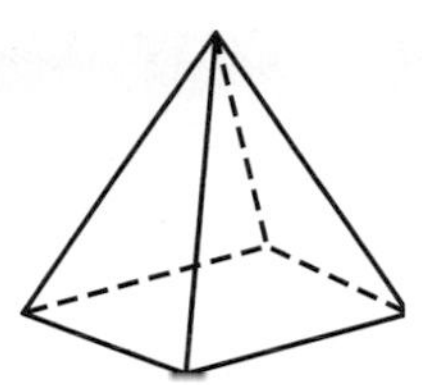

Step 3

Unfold the prism. Add the areas of the faces to find the surface area.

$9 + 4.5 + 4.5 + 4.5 + 4.5 = 27$

So, the surface area of the square pyramid is 27 cm^2.

TALK Math

Explain how to use a net to find the surface area of a square pyramid.

Practice

Use the net to find the surface area of each figure in square units.

1. Which faces are congruent?

   What is the area of each face?

   What is the surface area of the prism?

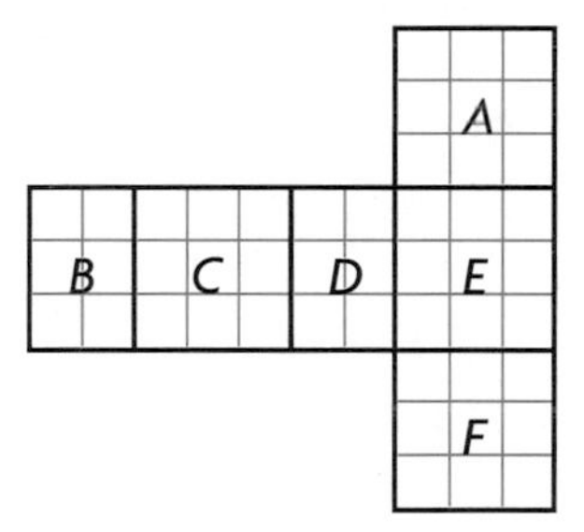

2.

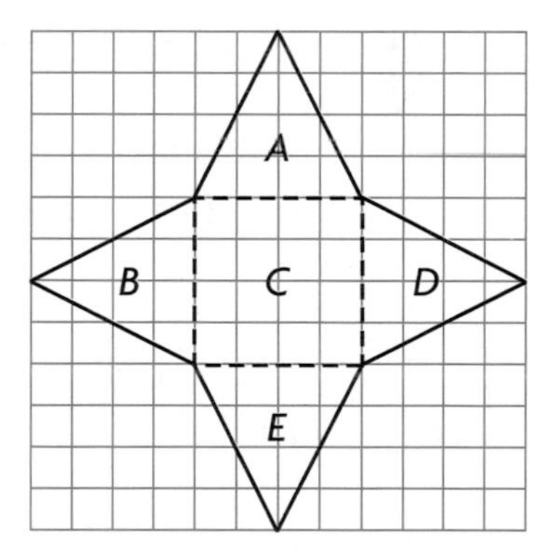

Find the surface area.

3.

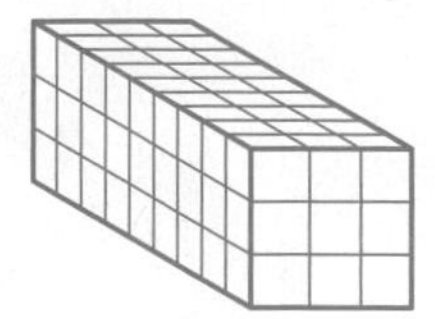

4.

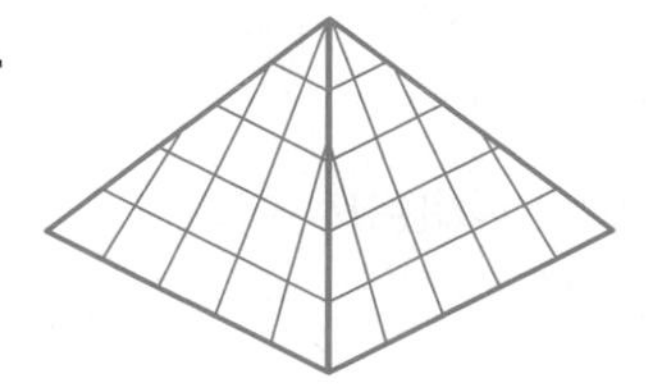

square pyramid

5.

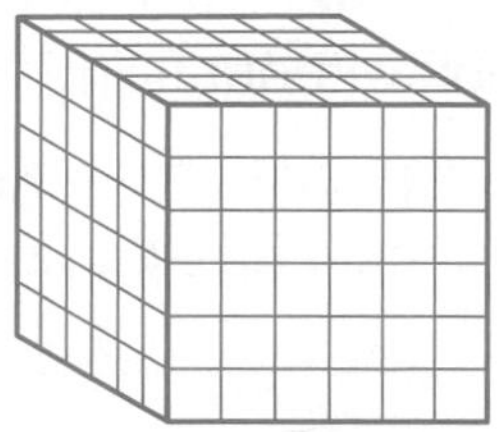

6. **WRITE Math** **Explain** the difference between *area* and *surface area*.

LESSON HANDS ON

2 Estimate Volume

OBJECTIVE: Estimate the volume of rectangular prisms.

Quick Review

Find the area of each rectangle in square centimeters.

1. $l = 3.5$ cm, $w = 4$ cm
2. $l = 2$ cm, $w = 2.4$ cm
3. $l = 9$ cm, $w = 18$ cm
4. $l = 12.7$ cm, $w = 10$ cm
5. $l = 15$ cm, $w = 35$ cm

Vocabulary

volume **cubic units**

Volume is the amount of space a solid figure occupies. Volume is measured in **cubic units**.

Investigate

Materials ■ centimeter cubes ■ small box in the shape of a rectangular prism

You can estimate the volume of a rectangular prism by visualizing how many cubes will fill it.

A Place a row of cubes along the inside length and width of the box. Stack a column of cubes along the inside height of the box.

B Estimate the volume of the box by visualizing how many cubes will fill it. Record your answer in cubic units.

C Fill the box with cubes. Count the cubes to estimate the volume. Record your result. Compare this estimate to your estimate in Step B.

D Count the number of cubes along the length, width, and height of the box. Record your results.

E Observe the relationship among the length, width, and height of the box and the number of cubes needed to fill the box.

Draw Conclusions

1. **Explain** how you estimated the volume of the box without filling it with cubes.
2. **Synthesis** What formula could you write to find the volume of a rectangular prism?

MG 1.3 Understand the concept of volume and use the appropriate units in common measuring systems (i.e., cubic centimeter [cm^3], cubic meter [m^3], cubic inch [$in.^3$], cubic yard [$yd.^3$]) to compute the volume of rectangular solids. *also* **MG 1.0, MR 2.0, MR 2.3, MR 2.4, MR 2.5, MR 3.2**

Connect

A formula that can be used to find the volume of a rectangular prism is Volume = length × width × height.

You can use this formula and estimate to compare the volumes of two different rectangular prisms.

Suppose you have two rectangular prisms.

Prism A measures 2.3 cm × 3.7 cm × 8.4 cm.

Prism B measures 7.5 cm × 2.4 cm × 3.1 cm.

Estimate which prism has the greater volume.

TALK Math

Which dimension used to measure the volume of a rectangular prism is **not** used to measure the area of a rectangle? **Explain.**

	Prism A	Prism B
Step 1 Round the measurements to the nearest centimeter.	**Prism A** $2.3 \times 3.7 \times 8.4 \rightarrow 2 \times 4 \times 8$	**Prism B** $7.5 \times 2.4 \times 3.1 \rightarrow 8 \times 2 \times 3$
Step 2 Multiply to estimate the volume.	$2 \times 4 \times 8 = 64$ A = about 64 cm^3	$8 \times 2 \times 3 = 48$ A = about 48 cm^3

Since $64 > 48$, Prism A has the greater volume.

Practice

Estimate the volume of each rectangular prism. Write your estimates in cubic units.

1. 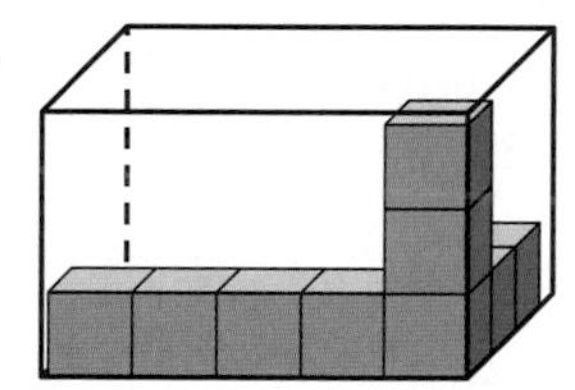

2. 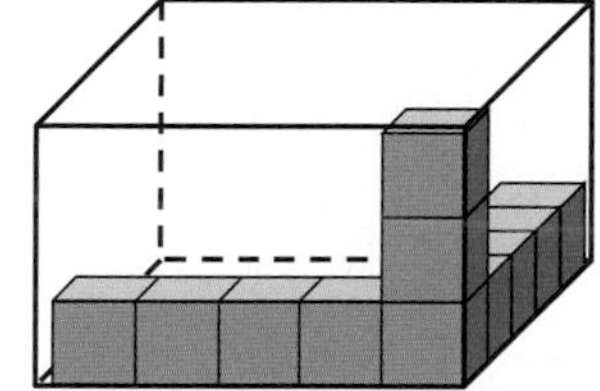

✓3. 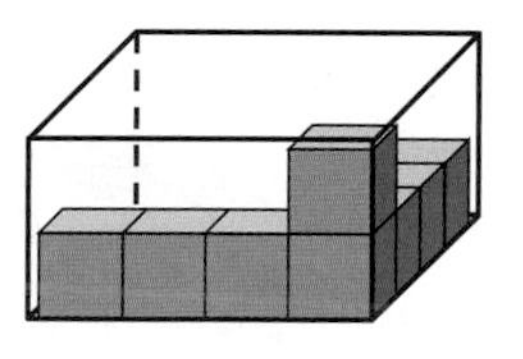

Estimate the volume of each rectangular prism with these measurements.

4. 5.2 cm × 3.3 cm × 4.7 cm
5. 2.4 cm × 2.4 cm × 2.7 cm
✓6. 8.1 m × 9.5 m × 10.3 m
7. 25 yd × 42 yd × 39 yd
8. 12 in. × 10 in. × 21 in.
9. 68 ft × 16 ft × 34 ft
10. Rectangular prism C measures 3.8 m × 4.5 m × 2.3 m. Rectangular prism D measures 4.6 m × 1.8 m × 3.4 m. Which rectangular prism has the greater volume?
11. **Reasoning** How could you estimate the volume of a cereal box?
12. **WRITE Math** **What's the Error?** Gordon estimated that the volume of a 2.3 cm × 4.6 cm × 6.5 cm box is 10 cm^2. Describe and correct his error.

LESSON 3

ALGEBRA

Find Volume

OBJECTIVE: Find the volume of rectangular prisms.

Quick Review

1. $4 \times 3 \times 2$
2. $5 \times 5 \times 3$
3. $7 \times 5 \times 6$
4. $8 \times 4 \times 6$
5. $3 \times 9 \times 10$

Learn

PROBLEM Tony's dad builds storage cabinets. Each cabinet is shaped like a rectangular prism. He built three cabinets for Tony's room. The following table shows the length, width, and height of the three cabinets, measured in feet. The volume is in cubic feet.

Tony's Storage Cabinets

	Length	Width	Height	Volume
CD	1	1	6	6
Clothes	3	4	8	96
Hobby	4	3	2	?

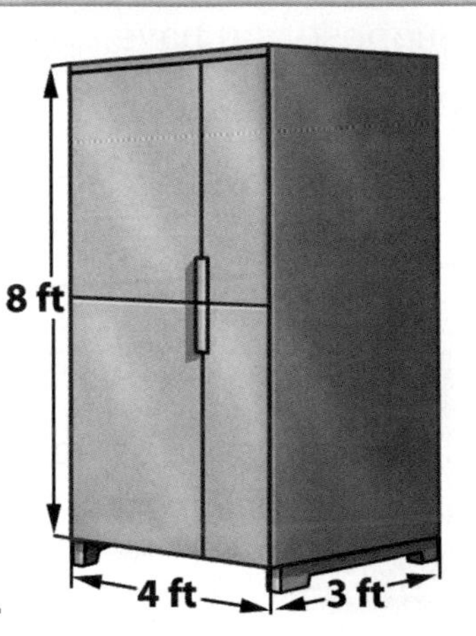

▶ Tony's clothes cabinet has a volume of 3 ft × 4 ft × 8 ft, or 96 ft^3 of storage space.

Example What is the volume of Tony's hobby cabinet?

ONE WAY **Make a model.**

Glenn used centimeter cubes to model the problem. Each centimeter cube represents 1 cubic foot.
Glenn counted 12 centimeter cubes in each layer, or 24 centimeter cubes in both layers.

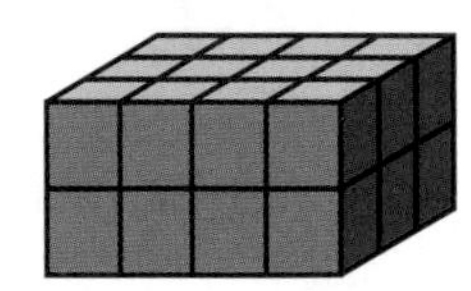

ANOTHER WAY **Use a formula.**

Emily found the volume of the hobby cabinet by using a formula.

Volume = length × width × height

$V = l \times w \times h$, or $V = lwh$

$V = 4 \times 3 \times 2$

$= 24$

So, the volume of Tony's hobby cabinet is 24 ft^3.

More Examples **Find the volume.**

A **Volume of a rectangular prism**

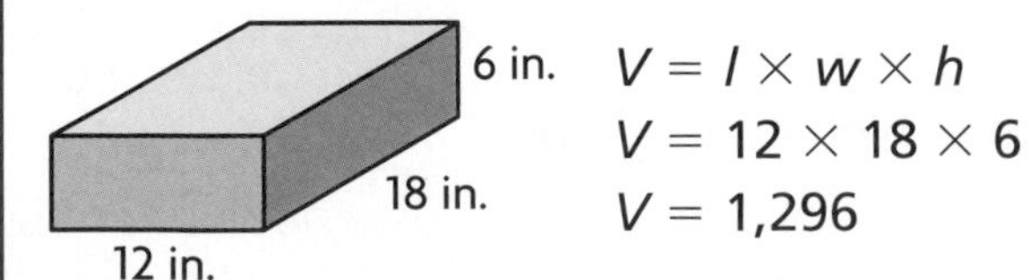

$V = l \times w \times h$

$V = 12 \times 18 \times 6$

$V = 1{,}296$

So, the volume is 1,296 $in.^3$

B **Volume of a cube**

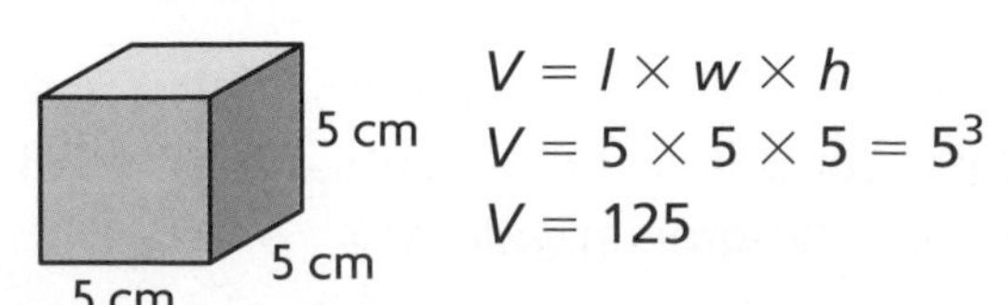

$V = l \times w \times h$

$V = 5 \times 5 \times 5 = 5^3$

$V = 125$

So, the volume is 125 cm^3.

MG 1.3 Understand the concept of volume and use the appropriate units in common measuring systems (i.e., cubic centimeter [cm^3], cubic meter [m^3], cubic inch [$in.^3$], cubic yard [$yd.^3$]) to compute the volume of rectangular solids. *also* **MG 1.0, MR 2.0, MR 2.3, MR 2.4, MR 3.2**

Guided Practice

For 1–4, use the rectangular prism at the right.

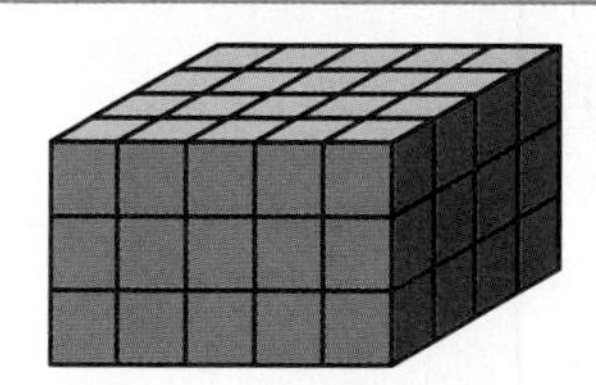

1. What is the length?
2. What is the width?
3. What is the height?
4. What is the volume?

Find the volume of each rectangular prism.

5. 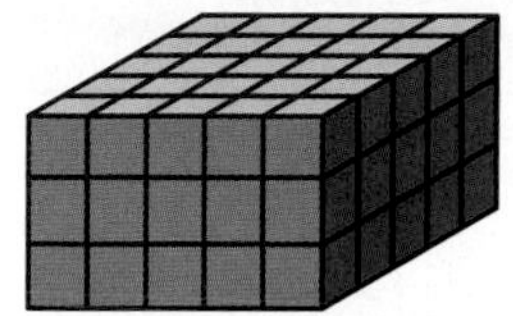

✓6. 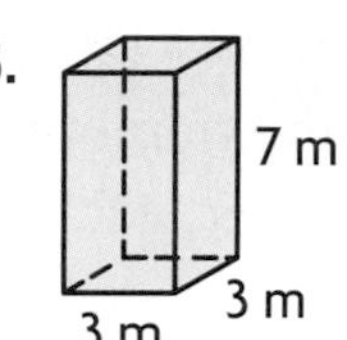

✓7. 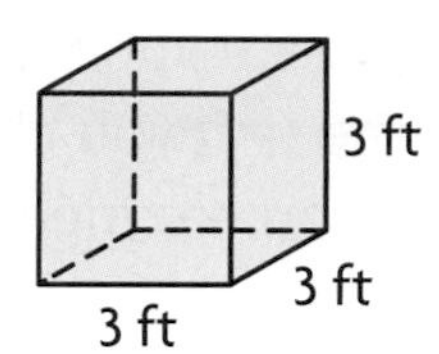

8. TALK Math When finding the volume of a rectangular prism, does the order in which you multiply the dimensions affect your answer? **Explain.**

Independent Practice and Problem Solving

Find the volume of each rectangular prism.

9. 

10. 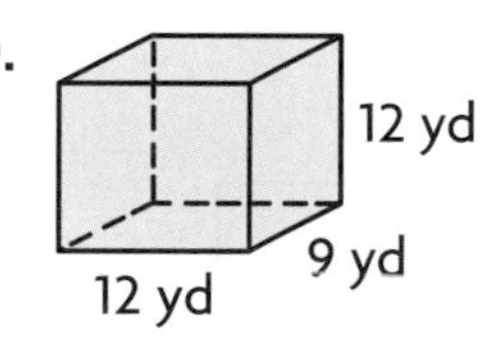

11. 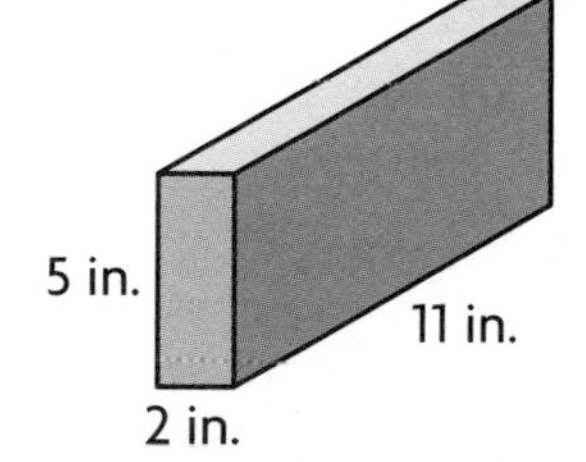

USE DATA For 12, use the table.

12. The swimming pools are in the shape of a rectangular prism. Which of the three pools has the greatest volume?
13. WRITE Math **Explain** the difference between an inch, a square inch, and a cubic inch.

Swimming Pool Dimensions (in meters)

Pool	Length	Width	Depth
Olympic Pool	50	25	2.0
Lap Pool	50	20	2.2
Pool for Young Swimmers	25	25	2.0

Achieving the Standards

14. What is the perimeter of Angie's yard?
(MG 1.4, p. 530)

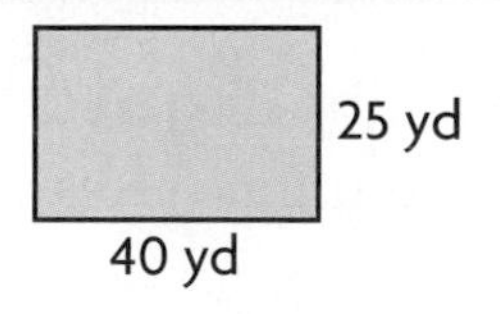

15. Find the surface area of the cube. Each square is 1 square centimeter.
(MG 1.2, p. 574)

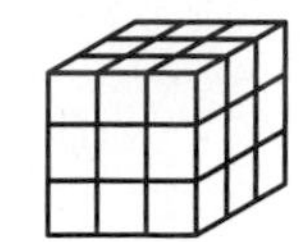

16. The area of a painting is 154 in.^{2}. Its length is 14 in. What is the width?
(AF 1.2, p. 548)

17. **Test Prep** Your lungs can hold about the same volume of air as a 10 in. × 6 in. × 5 in. rectangular prism. About how much air can your lungs hold?

A about 60 in.^{3}
B about 300 in.^{3}
C about 500 in.^{3}
D about 3,000 in.^{3}

Extra Practice on page 586, Set A

Relate Perimeter, Area, and Volume

OBJECTIVE: Identify the appropriate units of measure for perimeter, area, and volume.

Quick Review

1. 36 in. = ■ ft
2. 36 in. = ■ yd
3. 2 yd = ■ ft
4. 2 m = ■ cm
5. 75 cm = ■ m

Learn

Geometric figures can be measured in one, two, and three dimensions. The unit you choose depends on the number of dimensions you are measuring.

PROBLEM Mari and her dad want to build a dog bed with the dimensions shown. What units should they use to measure the perimeter of the bed? The area of the top surface of the bed? The volume of the bed?

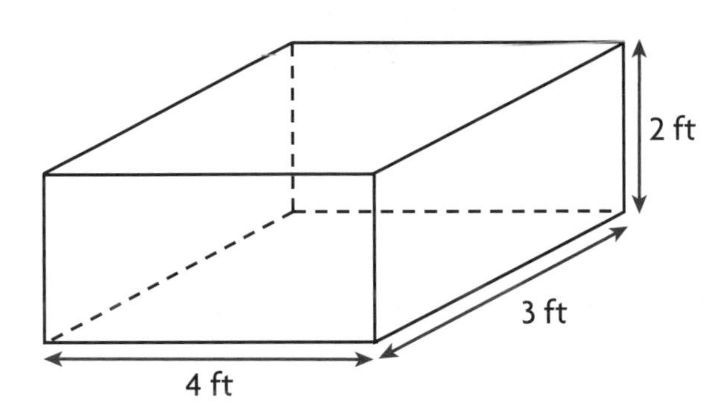

Perimeter is the distance around a figure.

Its measure is in one dimension, *length*. Use linear units such as in., ft, yd, mi, cm, m, or km.

Area is the measure of the flat surface of a figure.

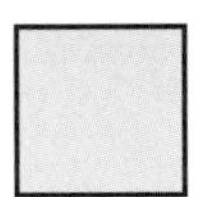

Its measure is in two dimensions, *length* and *width*. Use square units such as in.^{2}, ft^2, yd^2, mi^2, cm^2, m^2, or km^2.

Volume is the measure of the space a figure occupies.

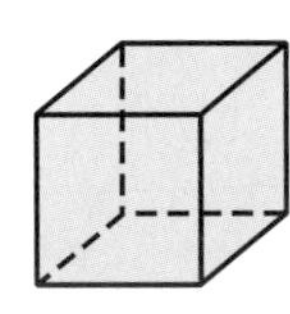

Its measure is in three dimensions, *length*, *width*, and *height*. Use cubic units such as in.^{3}, ft^3, yd^3, mi^3, cm^3, m^3, or km^3.

So, Mari and her father should use feet to measure the perimeter of the dog bed.

They should use square feet to measure the area of the top surface of the dog bed.

They should use cubic feet to measure the volume of the dog bed.

- How are the units used to measure perimeter, area, and volume different?

MG 1.4 Differentiate between, and use appropriate units of measures for, two- and three-dimensional objects (i.e., find the perimeter, area, volume). *also* **MG 1.0, MR 2.0, MR 2.3, MR 2.4, MR 3.2**

Activity **Materials:** centimeter grid paper, centimeter cubes

Mari and her father are ready to build the dog bed. What are the perimeter, area, and volume of the dog bed?

Let each ■ equal 1 square foot.

Step 1

Draw a 4 × 3 rectangle on grid paper. Count to find the perimeter of the rectangle.

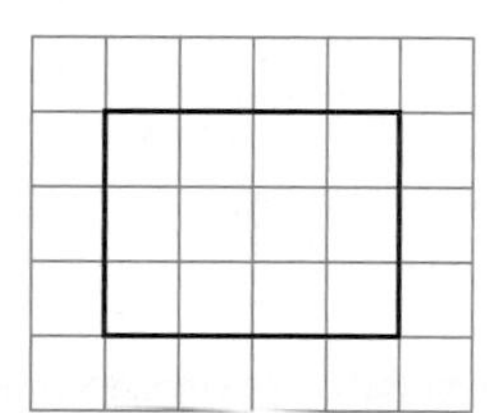

The perimeter of the dog bed, measured in linear units, is 14 ft.

Step 2

Shade the squares to show the area of the rectangle. Count the number of shaded squares to find the area.

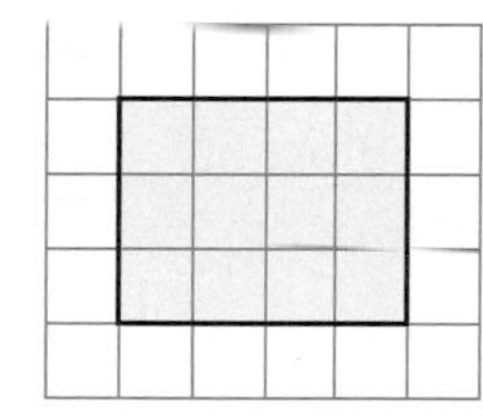

The area of the top surface of the dog bed, measured in square units, is 12 square feet.

Step 3

Use centimeter cubes to build a 2-layer prism on the rectangle. Count the number of cubes to find the volume of the prism.

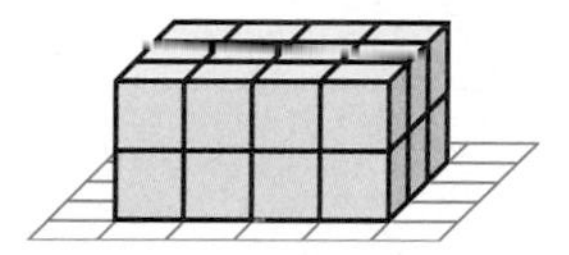

The volume of the dog bed, measured in cubic units, is 24 cubic feet.

Guided Practice

Tell the units you would use for measuring each. Write *linear*, *square*, or *cubic*.

1. volume
2. area
3. length
4. perimeter
5. fence to enclose a garden
6. matting for a picture frame
7. space inside a cabinet
8. size of a playground

Write the units you would use for measuring each.

9. volume of this prism

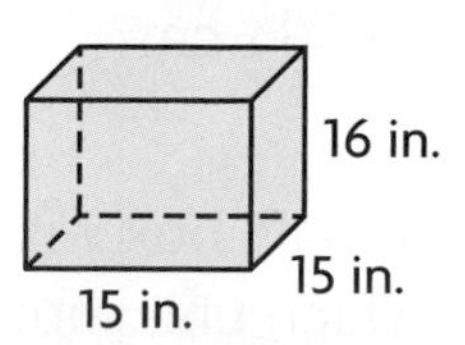

10. perimeter of this trapezoid

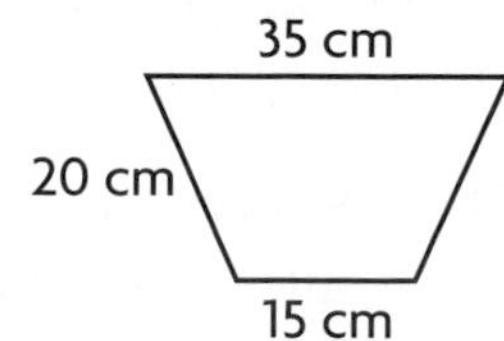

✓11. area of this triangle

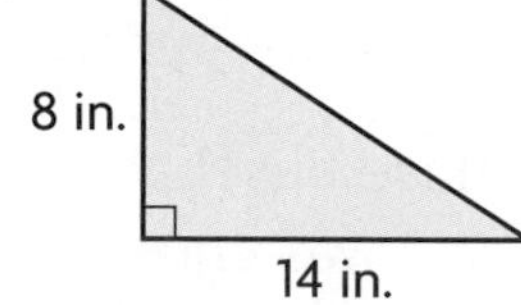

✓12. perimeter of this regular hexagon

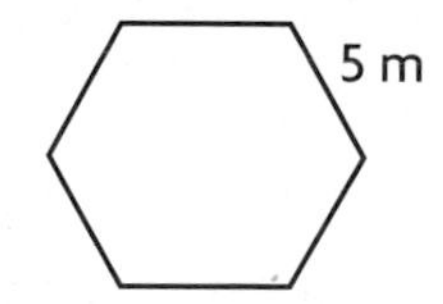

13. **TALK Math** Describe how you would use formulas to find the perimeter, area of the top surface of the dog bed and volume of the dog bed.

Independent Practice and Problem Solving

Tell the units you would use for measuring each. Write *linear, square,* or *cubic*.

14. carpet needed to cover a floor

15. amount of air in a room

16. picture frame

17. tile needed to cover a wall

Write the units you would use for measuring each.

18. perimeter of this triangle

2.5 cm 2.5 cm 2.5 cm

19. volume of this prism

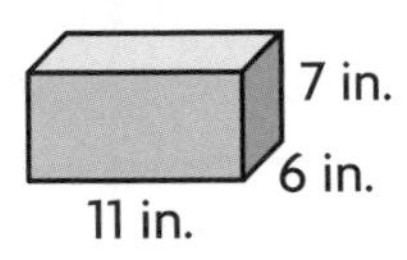

20. volume of this prism

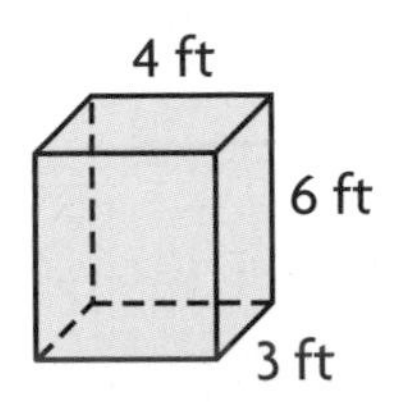

21. area of this parallelogram

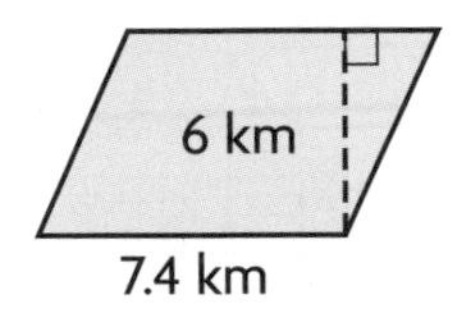

For 22–24, use the picture of the aquarium.

22. What is the aquarium's volume?

23. What is the area of the water that is exposed to the air?

24. ***FAST FACT*** An aquarium should have no more than 1 inch of fish for every 10 square inches of water exposed to the air. For example, an aquarium with a surface area of 120 square inches should have 120 ÷ 10, or 12 inches of fish. How many fish and of what length would you recommend for the aquarium shown?

25. WRITE Math **Explain** what units you would use to find the area of a wall that you planned to paint.

Achieving the Standards

26. Find the volume of a cube that measures 4.3 inches on each side. (MG 1.3, p. 578)

27. In a survey, 12 students chose baseball as their favorite sport. Tennis was chosen by 8 students and basketball was chosen by 15 students. How many students were surveyed in all? (Grade 4 SDAP 1.0)

28. What is the greatest possible area for a rectangle with a perimeter of 34 cm? (MG 1.0, p. 552)

29. **Test Prep** Suzanne bought a gift box with a surface area of 32 in.^{2}. Which unit should she use for the volume of the box?

A m^2

B in.^{2}

C m^3

D in.^{3}

 Extra Practice on page 586, Set B

READ Math WORKSHOP

Building Measurements

Generalize

Library Tower in Los Angeles is the tallest building in California. It is also the tallest building with a helipad on the roof. Its 73 floors rise to about 310 meters above ground level. The combined floor space is about 121,167 square meters. Library Tower, officially the U.S. Bank Tower, gets its nickname from its location. It stands across the street from the Los Angeles Central Library.

▲ The Library Tower is capped with a large glass "crown" that lights up at night.

You can generalize from what you know about length, area, and volume to complete these sentences. Use the data in the paragraph above.

a. The total height of the Library Tower is about ____.

b. The combined area of its floor space is ____.

Generalize:
Length is in units such as feet and meters.
Area is in units such as square feet and square meters.
Volume is in units such as cubic feet and cubic meters.
So, 310 meters completes the first sentence and 121,167 square meters completes the second sentence.

The Transamerica Pyramid in San Francisco stands 850 feet tall to the top of its spire. Its 48 floors have a combined floor space of about 530,000 square feet. The building rests on a base made of about 16,000 cubic yards of concrete. ▶

Problem Solving **Generalize to complete the sentences. Use the data at the right.**

1. The height of the Transamerica Pyramid is about ________.
2. The total area of the floor space of the Transamerica Pyramid is about _______.
3. The volume of the base the Transamerica Pyramid rests on is about _______.

Problem Solving Workshop
Strategy: Write an Equation

OBJECTIVE: Solve problems by using the strategy *write an equation.*

Use the Strategy

PROBLEM Nathan is putting a microwave oven in his kitchen. The microwave oven has a total volume of 1.8 cubic feet. To fit between the cabinets, the length needs to be 1.5 feet and the width needs to be 1.2 feet. What must the height of the microwave oven be?

Read to Understand

- **Write a general statement that describes what you are asked to find.**
- **What information is given?**

Plan

- **What strategy can you use to solve the problem?**
  You can *write an equation* to help you solve the problem.

Solve

- **How can you use the strategy to solve the problem?**
  The formula for the volume of a rectangular prism is an equation. So, use the formula to find the height of the microwave oven.

$V = l \times w \times h$	Write the equation.
$1.8 = 1.5 \times 1.2 \times h$	Substitute the known dimensions of the microwave oven for the variables in the equation.
$1.8 = 1.8 \times h$	
$1 = h$	Solve the problem.

So, the microwave oven must have a height of 1 foot.

Check

- **How do you know the answer is correct?**

MG 1.3 Understand the concept of volume and use the appropriate units in common measuring systems (i.e., cubic centimeter [cm^3], cubic meter [m^3], cubic inch [$in.^3$], cubic yard [yd^3] to compute the volume of rectangular solids. *also* **MG 1.0, MR 1.0, MR 2.0, MR 2.3, MR 2.4, MR 3.0, MR 3.1, MR 3.2, MR 3.3**

Guided Problem Solving

1. The air conditioner that fits in a window in Maria's house is 2 feet long and 1.3 feet high. It has a volume of 3.9 cubic feet. What is the width of the air conditioner?

   First, write an equation. $V = l \times w \times h$

   Then, substitute the known dimensions of the air conditioner for the variables in the equation.

   Finally, solve the equation.

2. **What if** the volume of the air conditioner were 3.12 cubic feet? What would the width be?

3. The area of a triangular table top is 108 square inches. The two sides are against a wall and meet at a right angle. One side that is against the wall is 12 inches long. What is the length of the other side that is against the wall?

Choose a STRATEGY

- Draw a Diagram or Picture
- Make a Model or Act It Out
- Make an Organized List
- Find a Pattern
- Make a Table or Graph
- Predict and Test
- Work Backward
- Solve a Simpler Problem
- Write an Equation
- Use Logical Reasoning

Mixed Strategy Practice

Write an equation to solve.

4. The stove top in Matt's kitchen has an area of 5.2 square feet. The length of the stovetop is 2.6 feet. What is the width?

5. The original price of a toaster oven was \$54.00. For a one-day sale, the price was \$49.95. By how much was the price reduced for the sale?

USE DATA For 6–7, use the advertisement.

6. Mr. Valdez, Mrs. Jones, Ms. Chan, and Mr. Kent each bought a different appliance. Mr. Kent did not buy the oven or the water dispenser. Ms. Chan did not buy the refrigerator or the oven. Mr. Valdez bought the dishwasher. Which appliance did each customer buy?

7. **WRITE Math** The price of the dishwasher is \$51 less than the amount Mr. Valdez paid for a dishwasher in 1998. **Explain** how to find the price of the dishwasher Mr. Valdez purchased in 1998. What was the price?

8. Customers at an appliance store were asked in a survey what types of ovens they liked. A total of 9 customers liked microwave ovens, 12 liked convection ovens, and 16 liked traditional ovens. Three chose microwave and convection, 5 chose convection and traditional, 3 chose microwave and traditional, and 2 chose all three types. How many customers were in the survey?

Extra Practice

Set A **Find the volume of each rectangular prism.** (pp. 578–579)

1. 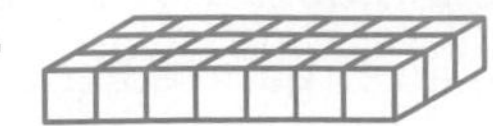

2. 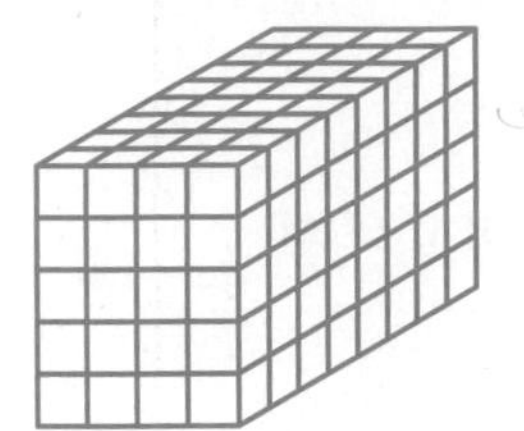

3. 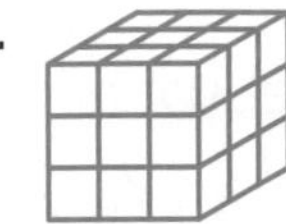

4. 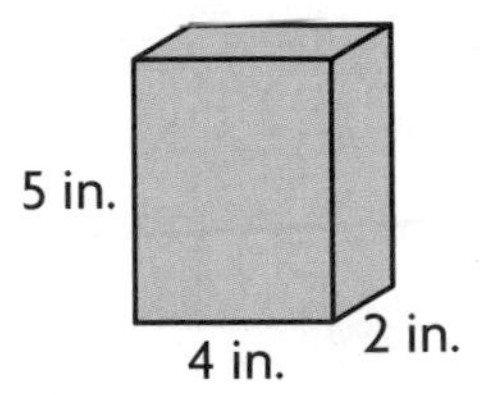

5. 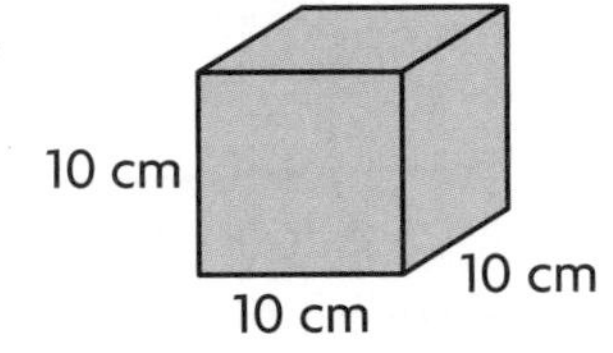

6. 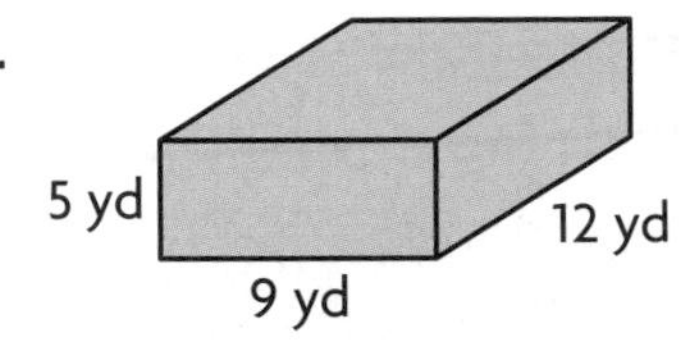

7. A garden shed is 12 feet long, 9 feet wide and 7 feet high. What is the volume of the garden shed?

8. A box in the shed is 18 inches long, 15 inches wide and 6 inches high. How much storage space does the box have?

Set B **Tell the units you would use for measuring each. Write *linear*, *square*, or *cubic*.** (pp. 580–583)

1. space in a refrigerator
2. window frame
3. amount of sod to cover a lawn
4. ceiling beam

Write the units you would use for measuring each.

5. perimeter of this parallelogram

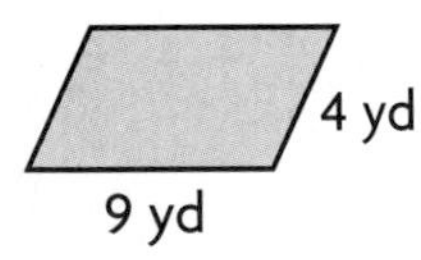

6. area of this rectangle

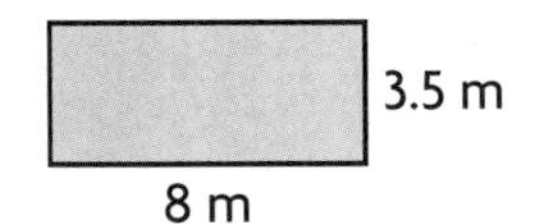

7. volume of this prism

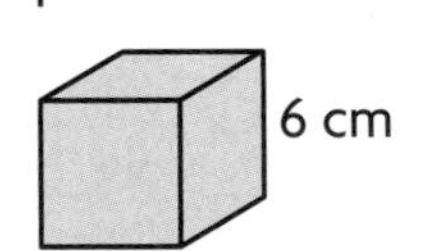

8. area of this square

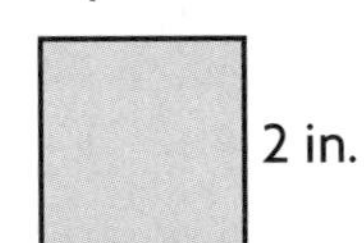

9. volume of this prism

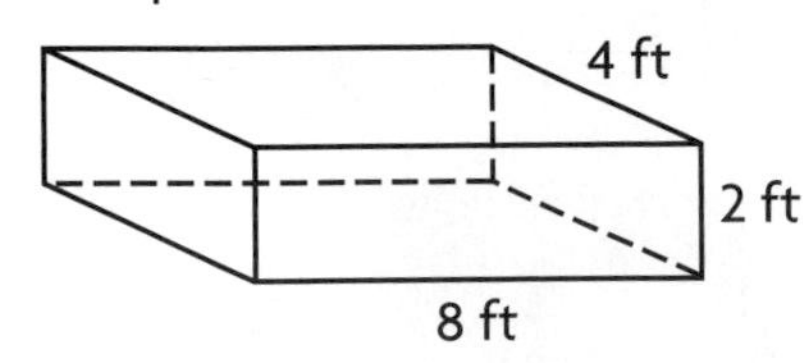

10. perimeter of this square

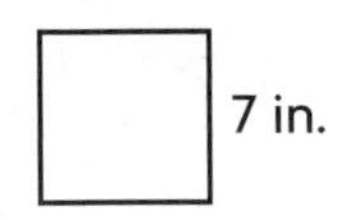

11. area of this parallelogram

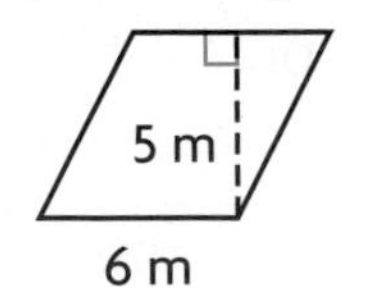

12. perimeter of this triangle

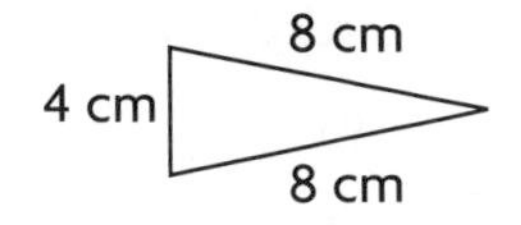

13. Stella is covering a craft box with paper. The box measures 12 inches × 9 inches × 6 inches. What units should she use to measure the paper?

14. At the chalkboard, Ken is outlining a triangle with 36 centimeter sides. What units should he use to measure the line?

CD ROM
Technology
Use Harcourt Mega Math, Ice Station Exploration, Arctic Algebra, Levels CC, DD.

PRACTICE GAME

Triple Play

Ready!

2 players

Set!

- 3 number cubes, each labeled 2, 2, 3, 3, 4, 4
- 2 charts like the one shown below
- 64 centimeter cubes

Toss 1 (length)	Toss 2 (width)	Toss 3 (height)	Volume
3 units	4 units	2 units	$3 \times 4 \times 2 = 24$ cubic units

Play!

- Player 1 tosses the three number cubes, representing length, width, and height, and records the results in the chart.
- Player 1 then finds the volume of a rectangular prism with sides of those measurements.
- Player 2 checks Player 1's work. If correct, Player 1 is awarded a point.
- If Player 1 is correct, he or she will then use centimeter cubes to construct a different prism with the same volume. Player 1 is awarded another point if successful.
- Player 2 repeats the process. Play continues until each player has tossed the number cubes 10 times.
- The player with more points after 10 rounds wins.

 Chapter 22 Review/Test

Check Concepts

Complete.

1. Explain the difference between the surface area of a figure and the area of a figure. (MG 1.2, pp. 574–575)
2. Explain how you could estimate the volume of a gift box in cubic inches. (MG 1.3, pp. 576–577)

Check Skills

Find the volume of each rectangular prism. (MG 1.3, pp. 578–579)

3. 

4. 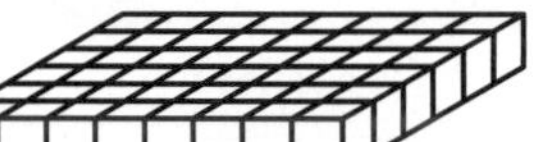

5. 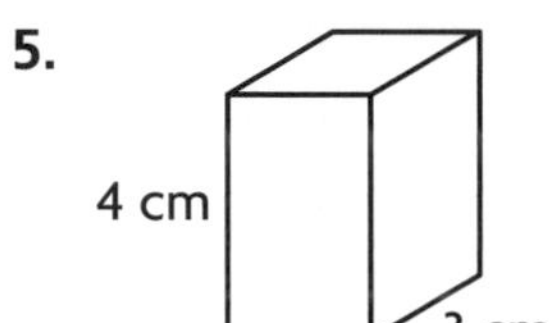

6. 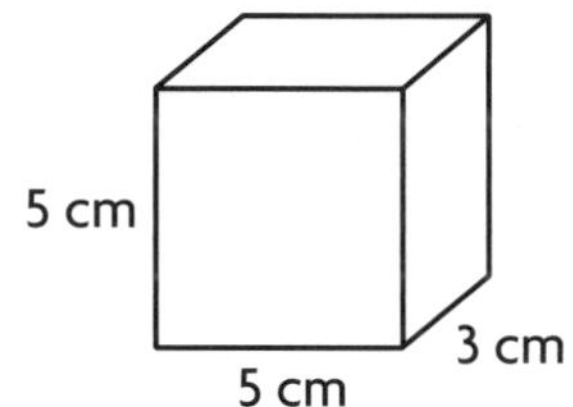

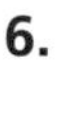

Tell the units you would use for measuring each. Write *linear*, *square*, or *cubic*. (MG 1.4, pp. 580–581)

7. the amount of space in a box
8. how much tile is needed to cover a floor
9. the amount of fence around a pool
10. space inside a refrigerator

Write the units you would use for measuring each. (MG 1.4, pp. 580–581)

11. perimeter of this rectangle

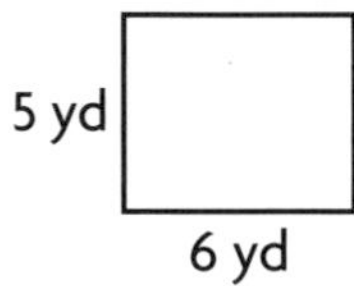

12. volume of this prism

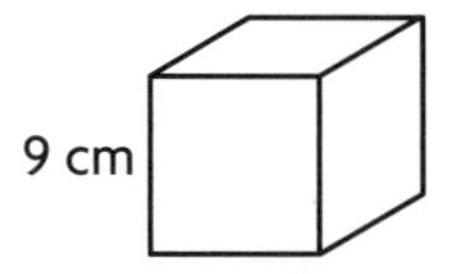

13. area of this triangle

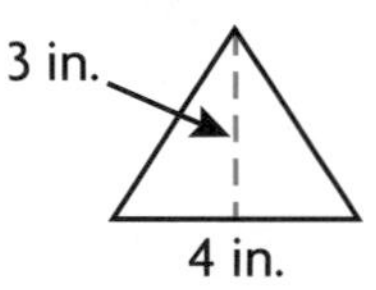

14. surface area of this prism

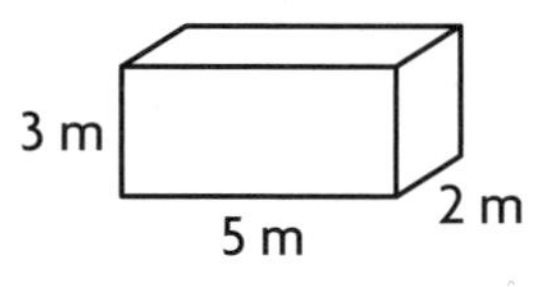

15. wood for a 6 in. by 8 in. picture frame
16. fabric covering a 2 ft by 3 ft by 4 ft trunk
17. perimeter of a 2 m by 2 m rug
18. space inside a 35 cm by 15 cm by 15 cm shoebox

Check Problem Solving

Solve. (MG 1.3, MG 1.4, MR 3.1, MR 3.2, pp. 584–585)

19. A wooden compost bin has a volume of 144 cubic feet. The compost bin is 6 feet long and 8 feet wide. What is the height of the wooden compost bin?
20. WRITE Math Suppose the area of a garden is 180 square feet and its length is 15 feet. **Explain** how to determine the garden's width. What is the width?

GO ONLINE **Technology** Use *Online Assessment.*

Enrich • Surface Area and Volume

Inside and Outside

A rectangular prism has 3 pairs of opposite faces that are congruent. You can find the surface area of a rectangular prism by finding the area of each unique face, multiplying each area by 2, and finding the sum of the products.

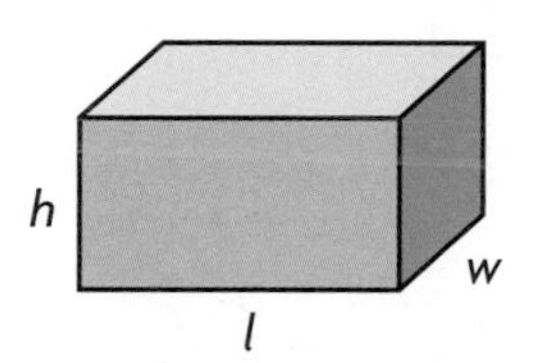

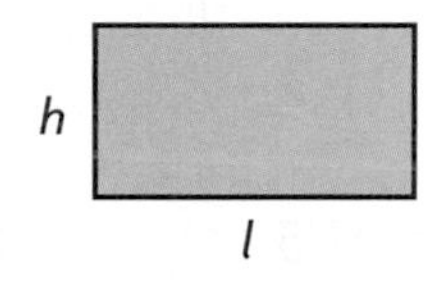

$A = h \times l$

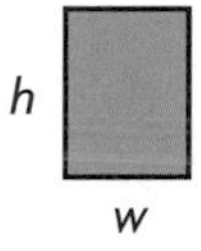

$A = h \times w$

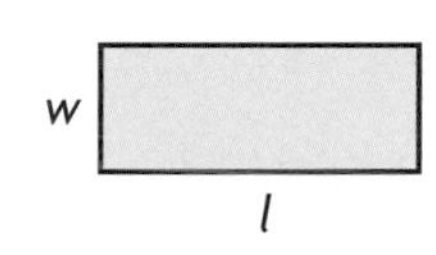

$A = w \times l$

To find the volume of a rectangular prism, use the formula $V = l \times w \times h$.

Warm Up

Find the surface area and volume of the rectangular prism.

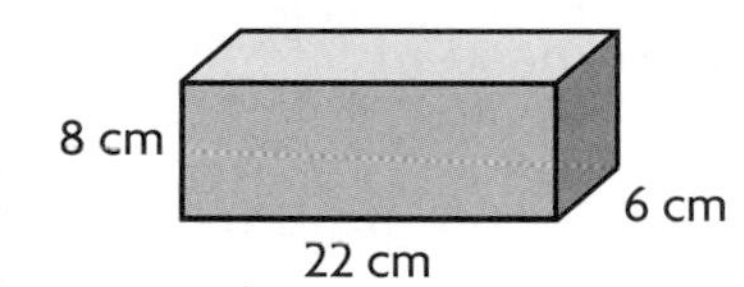

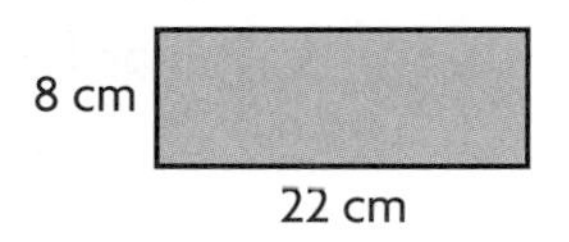

$8 \times 22 = 176$

8 cm
6 cm

$8 \times 6 = 48$

6 cm
22 cm

$6 \times 22 = 132$

Multiply the areas of each face by 2, and then add the products to find the surface area of the rectangular prism.

$2 \times 132 = 264$ $\quad 2 \times 48 = 96$ $\quad 2 \times 176 = 352$

$S = 264 + 96 + 352 = 712$

$V = l \times w \times h = 22 \times 8 \times 6 = 1{,}056$

So, the surface area of the rectangular prism is 712 cm^2 and the volume is $1{,}056 \text{ cm}^3$.

Work Out

Find the surface area and volume of each rectangular prism.

1.

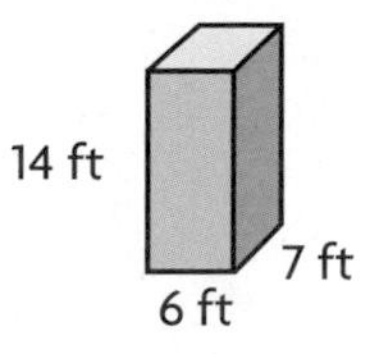

2.

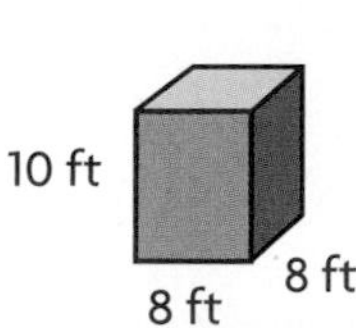

3.

55 ft
2 ft
2 ft

WRITE Math ▸ Look at the surface areas of the rectangular prisms in the problems above. What do you notice about the rectangular prism with the single greatest dimension? Find the dimensions of two rectangular prisms that each have a volume of 64 cm and compare the surface areas.

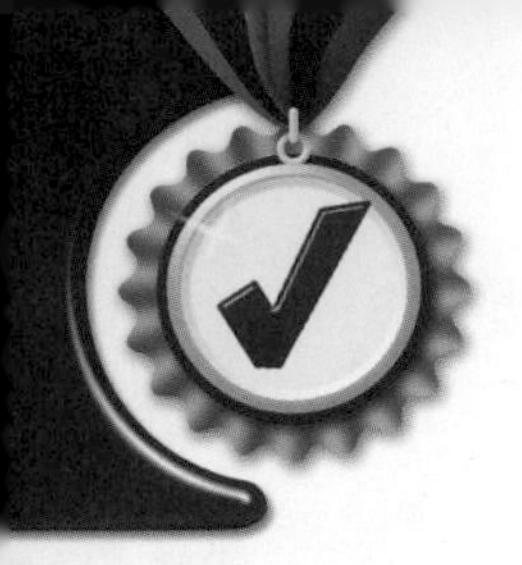

Unit Review/Test
Chapters 20–22

Multiple Choice

1. Which is the *best* estimate of the perimeter of the trapezoid? **(MG 1.4, p. 528)**

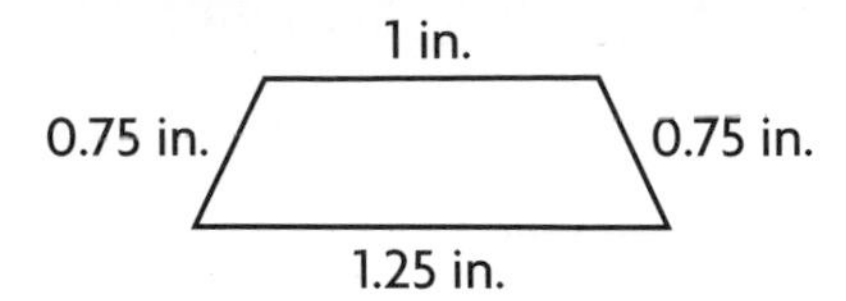

A 2 inches
B 4 inches
C 6 inches
D 8 inches

2. What is the perimeter of the rectangle below? **(MG 1.4, p. 530)**

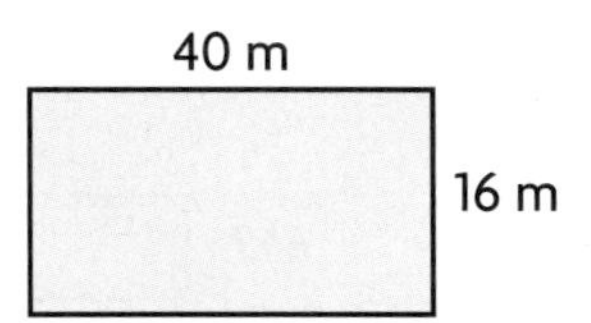

A 56 meters
B 96 meters
C 112 meters
D 640 meters

3. The perimeter of the figure shown below is 132 cm. What is the length of the unknown side? **(MG 1.4, p. 534)**

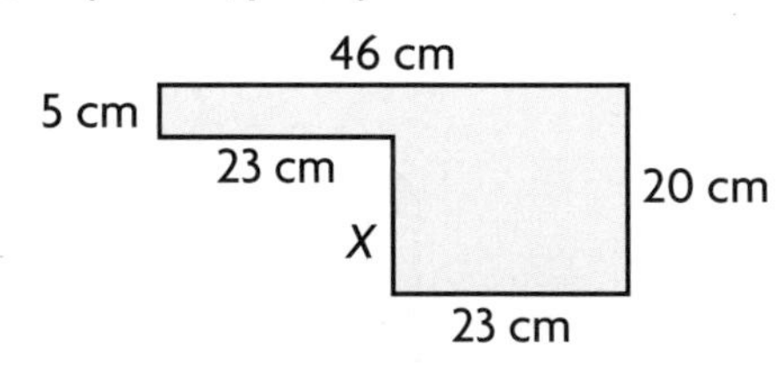

A 15 cm
B 18 cm
C 20 cm
D 22 cm

4. What is the area of the rectangle? **(MG 1.4, p. 548)**

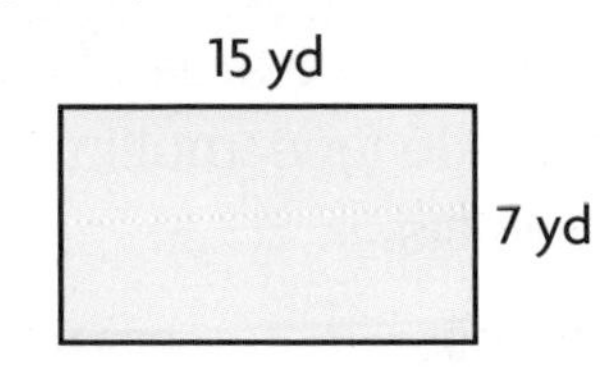

A 22 square yards
B 105 square yards
C 210 square yards
D 1,575 square yards

5. Jeanette is sewing a flag for a school team. How much material will she need to make a triangular flag with a base of 5 feet and a height of 7 feet? **(MG 1.1, p. 560)**

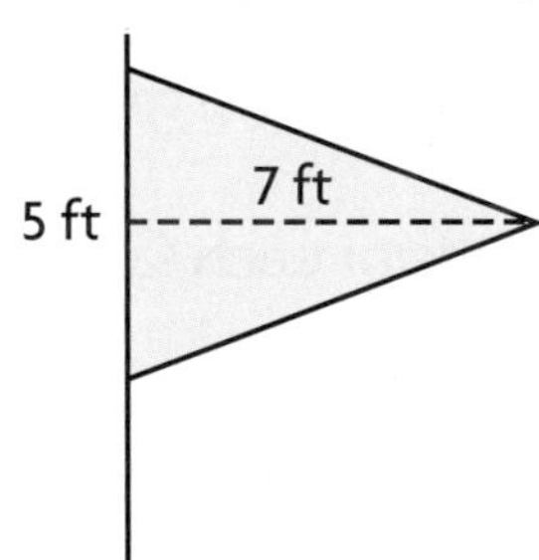

A 6 square feet
B 12 square feet
C 17.5 square feet
D 35 square feet

Technology Use *Online Assessment.*

6. What is the surface area of the box formed by the pattern below? (MG 1.2, p. 574)

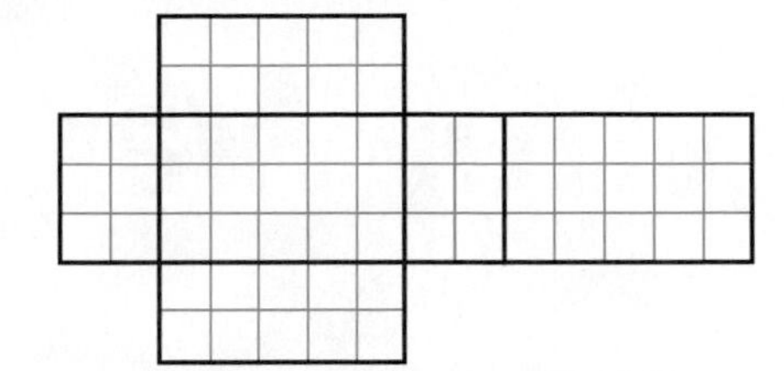

A 31 square units

B 50 square units

C 62 square units

D 75 square units

7. The rectangular prism below has a length of 10.4 centimeters, a height of 6.5 centimeters, and a width of 5 centimeters. What is its volume? (MG 1.3, p. 578)

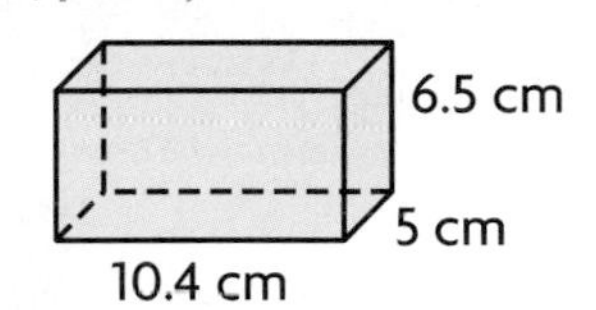

A 21.9 cubic centimeters

B 52 cubic centimeters

C 67.6 cubic centimeters

D 338 cubic centimeters

8. The volume of the box below is 84 cubic feet. What is its length? (MG 1.3, p. 578)

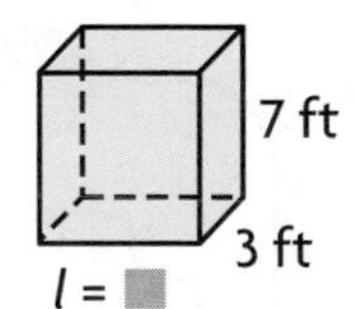

A 4 feet

B 8.4 feet

C 10 feet

D 252 feet

Short Response

9. Find the perimeter of the pentagon in centimeters. (MG 1.4, p. 530)

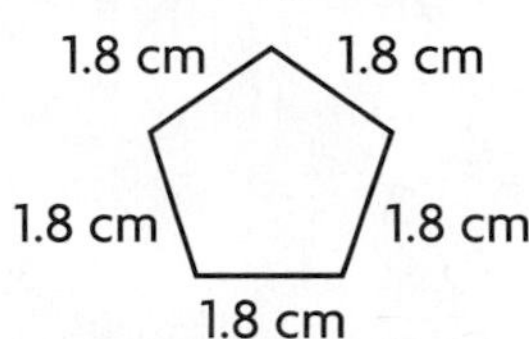

10. Renardo wants to gift wrap a box that measures 11 inches × 14 inches × 3 inches. What units should he use to decide how much wrapping paper he will need? How much wrapping paper does Renardo need? Show your work. (MG 1.3, p. 574)

Extended Response WRITE Math

11. Suppose you have a choice of the flat gold bars shown in the table. Each has the same perimeter and thickness. You want the largest gold bar—the one with the greatest area. Which gold bar should you choose? **Explain** your reasoning. (MG 1.4, p. 552)

Gold Bar	Length (inches)	Width (inches)	Perimeter (inches)	Area (square inches)
A	5	1	12	■
B	4	■	12	■
C	3	■	12	■

12. In the figure below, *EFGH* is a parallelogram. If the area of triangle *EFH* is 18 square inches, what is the area of *EFGH*? **Explain.** (MG 1.1, p. 556)

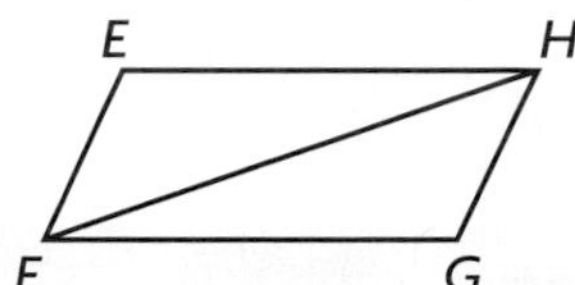

California

Problem Solving

from THE WORLD ALMANAC FOR KIDS

Playing in the Water

BUILT TO THRILL

Have you ever been to a water park? There are about 20 water parks in California. Raging Waters is located in San Dimas, California. The park attracts more than 700,000 visitors every year. It is the largest water park on the West Coast, with dozens of rides and other attractions.

▲ Raging Waters

FACT·ACTIVITY

1. Barracuda Blaster, at Raging Waters, has 500 feet of twists and turns going down the slide. How many inches long is the slide?
2. The same water park has a gigantic wave pool. It is 325 feet wide and 220 feet long. About how wide and how long is the wave pool in yards?
3. The ground space needed for a water slide to be built is called its footprint. Use the footprint shown at the right to estimate the perimeter and area.
4. WRITE Math **Explain** how the numbers would change if you estimated the area and perimeter in yards instead of feet.

Footprint

19 feet 4 inches

17 feet 9 inches

ALMANAC **Fact**

Located at Wild Water Adventure, the Blue Wave is the largest wave pool in California, with over one million gallons of water.

Make Waves!

Many water parks have wave pools, as well as water rides. The largest wave pools in the world range from 75,000 to 140,000 square feet. Hydraulic pumps can make waves that are 9 feet tall, allowing people to surf in a wave pool!

FACT·ACTIVITY

Design a splash area for a wave pool. One of the largest pools holds 350,000 gallons of water—equal to about 1,733 cubic yards. Your pool splash area should have a rectangular or triangular footprint. Make sure that it has the same depth throughout.

- Using any depth up to 2 yards and whole numbers for length and width, what dimensions give you a volume that is close to 1,733 cubic yards? What is that volume?
- What if your wave pool splash area were long and narrow, with the same depth throughout? How close could you come to having a wave pool with a volume of 1,733 cubic yards?
- What would the dimensions be if you kept a depth of 2 yards, but made your pool's splash area a square?

UNIT 8 Data and Graphs

Math on Location

▲ Meteorology is the study of weather and climate. Data on the number of strikes of lightning is recorded.

▲ Equipment used to collect data is moved by truck to locations where storms or tornadoes might occur.

▲ Data is collected from thousands of weather stations and represented in many graphical forms.

VOCABULARY POWER

TALK Math

What math ideas are used in **Math on Location**? What kind of data could you collect at a weather station? How would you display this data?

READ Math

REVIEW VOCABULARY You learned the words below when you learned about collecting and displaying data. How do these words relate to **Math on Location**?

circle graph a graph that shows how parts of the data are related to the whole and to each other

line graph a graph that uses line segments to show how data change over time

WRITE Math

Copy and complete a match graphic like the one below. Use what you know about graphs to match the name of a graph to the drawing that looks most like it.

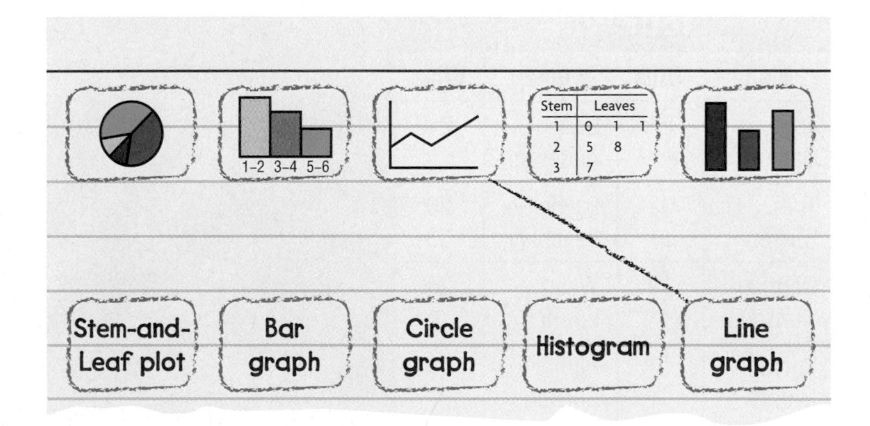

Technology
Multimedia Math Glossary link at
www.harcourtschool.com/hspmath

23 Analyze Data

The Big Idea Data can be collected and analyzed.

CALIFORNIA FAST FACT

In 1907, at Redondo Beach, George Freeth gave the first surfing demonstration. Redondo Beach is known as the birthplace of mainland surfing.

Investigate

There are 12 surfing events each year in the World Championship Tour. The table shows men and women who have won many tour events. Compare the data for men and for women by using two measures of central tendency.

World Championship Tour Wins

Men	Wins	Women	Wins
Tom Carroll	26	Lisa Anderson	21
Tom Curren	33	Layne Beachley	26
Damien Hardman	19	Wendy Botha	24
Barton Lynch	17	Pam Burridge	20
Mark Richards	17	Pauline Menczer	20
Kelly Slater	31	Freida Zamba	18

Technology
Student pages are available in the Student eBook.

Show What You Know

Check your understanding of important skills needed for success in Chapter 23.

▶ Read Bar Graphs

For 1–3, use the bar graph.

1. List the endangered species in order from greatest to least.
2. Estimate the total number of endangered species in 2006.
3. Which type of animal had more endangered species, birds or reptiles? About how many more endangered species did it have?

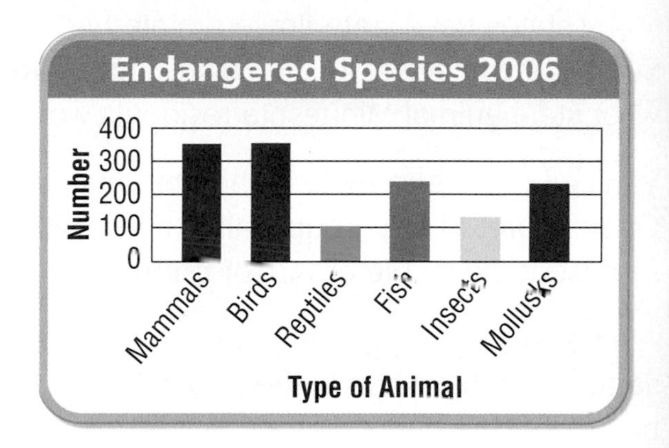

▶ Read Frequency Tables

For 4–6, use the frequency table.

4. Which bird has the greatest frequency?
5. What is the total number of birds shown in the data?
6. What is the difference between the number of Starlings and the number of Woodpeckers?

Bird Watching

Type of Bird	Frequency
Starling	18
Finch	9
Woodpecker	5
Warbler	13

VOCABULARY POWER

CHAPTER VOCABULARY

bar graph
circle graph
frequency table
line graph
mean
median
mode
outlier
pictograph
population
range
random sample
sample
survey
trend

WARM-UP WORDS

survey a method of gathering information about a group

sample a part of a population

population the entire group of objects or individuals considered for a survey

LESSON 1 Collect and Organize Data

OBJECTIVE: Collect data by using surveys and organize data in tables and line plots.

Quick Review

1. 18 + 9
2. 22 + 45
3. 350 + 120
4. 90 − 65
5. 275 − 150

Vocabulary

survey, sample, population, random sample, frequency table, range, outlier

Learn

Many states have state flowers, state birds, and state trees. Some states have state animals. Suppose you wanted to find what state animal Minnesota residents would choose.

You can use a **survey** to gather information about a group. Often, a part of the group, called a **sample**, is chosen to represent the whole group, or **population**.

A sample must represent the population fairly. In a **random sample**, each person in the population has an equal chance of being chosen.

Example 1

Suppose a marketing company is hired to find which animal is preferred among residents of Minnesota for a state animal. Which random sample best represents the population?

a 100 children	**b** 100 men
c 100 adults in southern Minnesota	**d** 100 Minnesota residents in different parts of the state

Choice **d** is the only one that represents the population fairly. Every Minnesota resident would have an equal chance of being selected.

▲ Minnesota's state flower is the pink-and-white showy lady's-slipper.

Activity

Write a survey and collect data.

A Choose a topic. Select one of the following topics: pets, homework, or games.

B Decide what population you want to survey. How can you choose a random sample that is fair?

C Write a survey question. The question should be clear, easy to understand, and require only a single response.

D Make a recording sheet. Be sure to include your survey question so that you ask each person the same question. Survey a random sample of at least 30 students.

Pet Survey

Number of Pets	Tally
0	𝍸 III
1	𝍸 I
2	𝍸 IIII
3	
4	
5	I

Shows that 8 people do not have any pets.

SDAP 1.0 Students display, analyze, compare, and interpret different data sets, including data sets of different sizes *also* MR 2.3, MR 2.4, MR 3.2

Organizing Data

A **frequency table** shows the total for each category or group.

Example 2 **Organize data in a frequency table.**

Count by 5s in the tally table at the right to find each frequency.

Survey Question: Which animal would you choose as Minnesota's state animal—badger, mink, red fox, or river otter?

Minnesota State Animal	
Badger	𝍸 𝍸 𝍸 𝍸 𝍸 𝍸 𝍸 𝍸 𝍸
Mink	𝍸 𝍸 𝍸 𝍸 𝍸 |
Red fox	𝍸 𝍸 𝍸 𝍸 𝍸 ||||
River otter	𝍸 𝍸 𝍸 𝍸 𝍸

Minnesota State Animal Survey

Animal	Frequency
Badger	45
Mink	26
Red fox	29
River otter	25

In the frequency table, the frequency shows the total for each type of animal.

A line plot gives you a visual picture of the data and can also be used to identify the range and any outliers. The **range** is the difference between the greatest number and the least number in a set of data. An **outlier** is a value that is separated from the rest of the data.

Example 3 **Organize the pet survey data in a line plot. Find the range.**

Step 1

Draw a number line from 0 to 5. Include a title. Graph an X for each response in the tally table.

Step 2

Find the range. The greatest number of pets is 5. The least number of pets is 0.

So, the range is $5 - 0$, or 5.

Pet Survey

Number of Pets	Frequency
0	6
1	5
2	7
3	0
4	0
5	1

5 is an outlier since it is separated from the rest of the data.

Guided Practice

1. Complete the table. Find the missing frequencies.

Favorite Flower

Type of Flower	Tally	Frequency
Rose	𝍸 𝍸 𝍸 𝍸 𝍸 𝍸 𝍸 |||	■
Tulip	𝍸 𝍸 𝍸 |	■

A fruit juice company wants to survey children ages 10–14. Tell whether each sample represents the population. If it does not, explain.

2. a random sample of 100 children

✓3. a random sample of 100 children, ages 10–14

✓4. a random sample of 100 children at one school

5. TALK Math **Explain** how you could collect and organize data about choosing a mascot for a new school.

Independent Practice and Problem Solving

A toy company wants to find out if children ages 8–12 like the company's new action figures. Tell whether each sample represents the population. If it does not, explain.

6. a random sample of 300 girls, ages 8–12

7. a random sample of 300 adults

8. a random sample of 300 children, ages 8–12

Make a line plot. Find the range of hours.

9.

Homework Survey	
Number of Hours	**Frequency**
1	8
2	16
3	4
4	2

10.

Weekly Activity Survey	
Number of Hours	**Frequency**
1	3
2	9
3	10
4	12

For 11–14, use the tally table.

11. Make a frequency table of the data.

12. Which state bird has the greatest frequency?

13. What is the range of the data?

14. WRITE Math **What's the Question?** Twenty-one states have either a cardinal, western meadowlark, mockingbird, or robin as their state bird.

Most Common State Birds	
Bird	**Number of States**
Cardinal	𝍸 II
Western Meadowlark	𝍸 I
Mockingbird	𝍸
Robin	III

Achieving the Standards

15. Kurt bought 3 cans of soup for $5.07. How much did each can cost? (NS 2.1, p. 320)

16. Find the quotient of 921 ÷ 3. (NS 1.0, p. 90)

17. **Test Prep** Karen swam 20, 25, 17, 32, and 15 laps. Which is the range of the data?

A 5 **B** 10 **C** 17 **D** 22

18. **Test Prep** What is the range of the data 6, 7, 5, 5, 6, 3, 2, 3, 3, and 4?

 Extra Practice on page 616, Set A

Most Common State Bird

Write a Conclusion

The northern cardinal is the most common choice of state bird. It can be spotted from Minnesota, South Dakota, and Maine southward through southern Florida. Barry used the data in the table to write a conclusion about the number of northern cardinals.

- First, I looked at the data in the table. The table shows the number of northern cardinals people counted in California, Minnesota, Ohio, Pennsylvania, and Texas.
- Next, I ordered the data in the table from least to greatest.

2 ← least
1,318
8,698
10,081
11,723 ← greatest

- Last, I wrote a conclusion.

My Conclusion: Of the states listed, I would be more likely to see a northern cardinal in either Texas or Ohio.

Northern Cardinals Counted

State	Frequency
California	2
Minnesota	1,318
Ohio	10,081
Pennsylvania	8,698
Texas	11,723

Tips

- Review the data and any other related information you know.
- Look for relationships in the data.
- Then write a conclusion.

Problem Solving For 1–2, use the data shown on the map.

1. Write a conclusion about the number of northern cardinals in western states compared to eastern states.
2. Write a conclusion about the states that have the least number of northern cardinals counted.

Northern Cardinal Bird Count

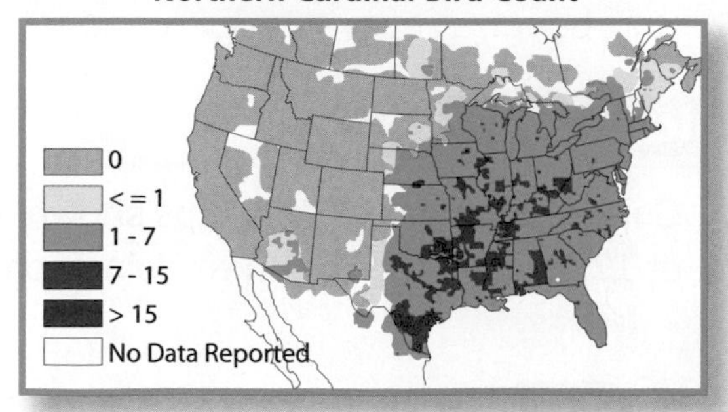

LESSON 2

Find the Mean

OBJECTIVE: Find the mean of a set of data.

Quick Review

1. $90 \div 3$
2. $100 \div 4$
3. $64 \div 8$
4. $84 \div 6$
5. $126 \div 7$

Vocabulary

mean

Learn

PROBLEM California has many lighthouses along its coast. What is the mean height of the lighthouses shown in the numbers?

The **mean** is the average of a set of numbers.

Example 1

Step 1

Add the heights to find the sum.

$20 + 30 + 35 + 35 = 120$

Step 2

Divide the sum by the number of addends.

$120 \div 4 = 30$

So, the mean height of these lighthouses is 30 feet.

California Lighthouses

Lighthouse	Height (in feet)
Lime Point	20
Point Montara	30
Table Bluff	35
Point Reyes	35

More Examples Find the mean for each set of data.

A 7.2, 8.3, 7.6, 9.1, 6.8

Find the sum.

$7.2 + 8.3 + 7.6 + 9.1 + 6.8 = 39$

Divide by the number of addends.

$39 \div 5 = 7.8$

B 120, 300, 260, 120, 800, 200

Find the sum.

$120 + 300 + 260 + 120 + 800 + 200 = 1{,}800$

Divide by the number of addends.

$1{,}800 \div 6 = 300$

You can find a missing value in a set of data if you know the mean.

Example 2 Use the given mean to help find the missing value in the following set of data. 10, 18, 14, ■, 10; mean: 15.

Step 1

Multiply the mean by the total number of values in the set of data.

$15 \times 5 = 75$

Step 2

Add the values in the set of data to find the sum without the missing value.

$10 + 18 + 14 + 10 = 52$

Step 3

Subtract the sum from the product.

$75 - 52 = 23$

So, the missing value in the set of data is 23.

Guided Practice

1. Copy and complete the steps shown to find the mean of 12, 8, 15, and 9. Then explain each step.

Step 1: $12 + 8 + 15 + 9 = 44$
Step 2: $44 \div 4 = ■$

SDAP 1.1 Know the concepts of mean, median, and mode; compute and compare simple examples to show that they may differ. *also* **MR 1.1, MR 2.3, MR 2.4, MR 3.2, MR 3.3**

Find the mean for each set of data.

2. 15, 32, 16
3. 2.1, 2.4, 3.1, 2.9, 3.2, 4.3
4. 13.5, 10.2, 14.9, 12.1, 12.8
5. \$50, \$65, \$80, \$65
6. 71, 88, 90, 71
7. \$118, \$207, \$125
8. TALK Math **Explain** what the mean represents for a set of data.

Independent Practice and Problem Solving

Find the mean for each set of data.

9. 11, 7, 10, 12, 15
10. \$62, \$78, \$53, \$87
11. 20.2, 16.8, 17.6
12. \$5, \$9, \$6, \$5, \$7, \$7
13. 5.1, 5.5, 5.8, 5.4, 5.2
14. 223, 189, 204, 204
15. 44, 38, 44
16. 100, 300, 200, 350
17. 9.8, 7.1, 9.8, 1.6, 6.2

Algebra **Use the given mean to find the missing value in each set of data.**

18. 16, 14, 20, ■; mean: 14
19. \$120, \$118, ■; mean: \$90
20. 25.9, 18.4, ■; mean: 20.6
21. 7.9, 8.6, 8.2, ■; mean: 8.5
22. 7, 9, 12, 4, ■; mean: 8
23. 84, 92, 99, ■; mean: 90

USE DATA For 24–26, use the lighthouse pictures.

24. What is the mean height of the lighthouses?
25. **Reasoning** How would the mean change if only the 4 tallest lighthouses were used to find the mean?
26. **Pose a Problem** Use the heights of the lighthouses to write a problem for a classmate to solve.
27. WRITE Math **What's the Error?** Jake says that 91 is the mean for the test scores 87, 98, 100, and 79. Then a test score of 74 is added. Jake now says the mean is 109.5. What is his error?

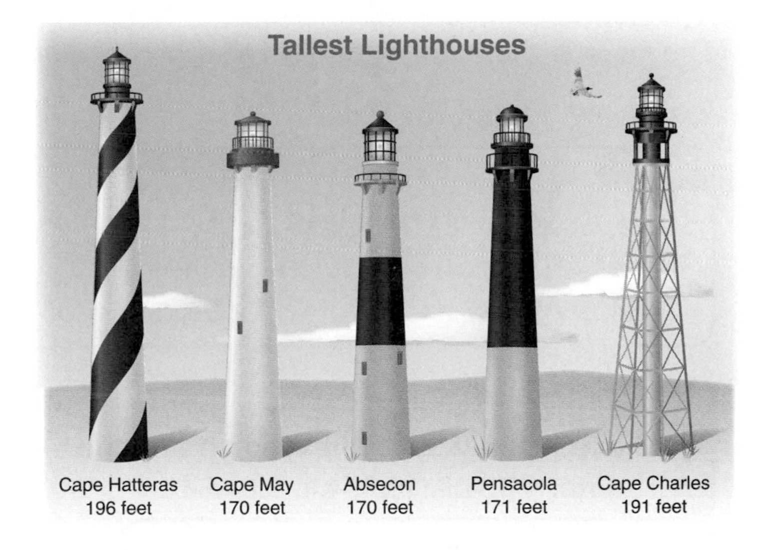

Achieving the Standards

28. A rectangular prism has a length of 10 inches, a height of 6 inches, and a width of 3 inches. What is the volume? (MG 1.3, p. 578)
29. Order 192, 186, 188, 194 from least to greatest. (NS 1.0, p. 8)
30. For $n = 12$, what is $12n$? (AF 1.2, p. 348)
31. **Test Prep** What is the mean for the following set of numbers? 63, 51, 34, 51, 32, 28, 46, 15, 17, 89, 146

    A 40 **C** 52
    B 50 **D** 139

Extra Practice on page 616, Set B

LESSON 3

Find the Median and Mode

OBJECTIVE: Find and compare the median and mode of a data set.

Quick Review

Order from least to greatest.

1. 16, 13, 26 **2.** 49, 67, 45
3. 58, 80, 59 **4.** 32, 31, 23
5. 126, 101, 138, 126

Vocabulary

median **mode**

Learn

PROBLEM The table shows the ages of five California governors when they took office. What are the median and the mode?

The **median** is the middle number of a data set arranged in order.

Ages of California Governors

Governor	Age
34th: Edmund "Jerry" Brown	36
35th: George Deukmejian	54
36th: Pete Wilson	57
37th: Gray Davis	56
38th: Arnold Schwarzenegger	56

Example 1 Find the median.

Step 1

Order the numbers from least to greatest.

36, 54, 56, 56, 57

Step 2

Find the middle number.

36, 54, 56, 56, 57

So, the median age is 56.

The **mode** is the number or item that occurs most often in a set of data.

Math Idea

For some data sets, the mode and the median are the same value. For other data sets, the mode and the median are different values.

Example 2 Find the mode.

Step 1

Order the numbers from least to greatest.

36, 54, 56, 56, 57

Step 2

Find the number that occurs most often.

36, 54, 56, 56, 57

So, the mode is 56.

More Examples Find the median and the mode for the following set of data. 4.8, 4.2, 10.3, 4.1, 9.6, 7.4

A Find the median.

Order the data from least to greatest.

4.1, 4.2, 4.8, 7.4, 9.6, 10.3

Add the two middle numbers, then divide by the number of addends, 2.

$4.8 + 7.4 = 12.2$

$12.2 \div 2 = 6.1$

The median is 6.1.

B Find the mode.

Data sets can have no mode, one mode, or more than one mode.

Order the data from least to greatest.

4.1, 4.2, 4.8, 7.4, 9.6, 10.3

No value occurs more than any other, so there is no mode.

SDAP 1.1 Know the concepts of mean, median, and mode; compute and compare simple examples to show that they may differ. *also* **MR 2.3, MR 2.4, MR 3.2**

Guided Practice

Order each set of data from least to greatest. Then find the median and the mode.

1. 12, 19, 21, 30, 18
2. 1.5, 3.2, 7.3, 5.8, 3.2
3. 120, 132, 117, 120

Find the median and the mode for each set of data.

4. 18, 12, 19, 15, 12
5. 37, 29, 62, 53, 29, 37
6. $98, $100, $56, $98, $100

7. TALK Math **Explain** how a set of data can have more than one mode.

Independent Practice and Problem Solving

Find the median and the mode for each set of data.

8. 7, 5, 11, 13, 5
9. $20, $50, $60, $30
10. 75, 125, 65, 125, 90, 75
11. 10.8, 12.9, 10.8, 9.6, 14.7
12. 482, 319, 608, 319, 319
13. 2,600; 3,500; 5,000

Find the median and the mode for each set of data. Tell how the median and the mode compare.

14. $45, $60, $10, $60, $85
15. 17, 13, 28, 16
16. 4.5, 8.5, 10.5, 4.5, 8.5

17. Find the median of 75, 90, 90, 99, and 65. Then find the median of 75, 90, 90, 99, and 95. How do the medians compare?
18. **Reasoning** The range of three numbers is 45. Both the mode and the median are 52. Name the three numbers.
19. Show examples of three data sets with one mode, more than one mode, and no mode at all.
20. WRITE Math **Explain** how a number can be both the median and the mode.

Achieving the Standards

21. James had the following bowling scores: 86, 105, 102, 97. What is the mean of these numbers? (SDAP 1.0, p. 602)
22. A rectangle has a length of 8 cm and a width of 5 cm. What is the area of the rectangle? (MG 1.0, p. 548)
23. A rectangular prism has a length of 10 inches, a width of 4 inches, and a height of 6 inches. What is its volume? (MG 1.3, p. 578)
24. **Test Prep** What is the median of this set of data: $28, $35, $17, $28?

    A $17 **B** $27 **C** $28 **D** $35

Extra Practice on page 616, Set C

LESSON 4

Compare Data

OBJECTIVE: Compare two or more sets of data.

Quick Review

Find the median for each set of data.

1. 12, 8, 15, 21, 17
2. 7.5, 9.2, 8.6, 7.9, 9.5
3. 5, 5, 5, 9, 3
4. 32, 41, 38, 45
5. 4.2, 6.9, 5.3, 4.8

Learn

PROBLEM The word used most often in English is *the*. Leah and Javier collected data on the number of times the word *the* occurs. Are Leah's and Javier's results similar?

To compare their data, you can calculate the mean.

Example 1

Leah's Survey

Leah asked 10 students to choose a sentence and to tell how many times the word *the* occurred.

Times *The* Occurred				
2	3	4	3	1
4	2	4	4	0

Mean: $27 \div 10 = 2.7$
The mean is 2.7 times.

Javier's Experiment

Javier asked 15 students to write a sentence. Then he counted the number of times *the* occurred.

Times *The* Occurred				
1	1	3	4	3
2	3	1	0	5
3	4	5	2	2

Mean: $39 \div 15 = 2.6$
The mean is 2.6 times.

The means for the two sets of data are similar.
So, Leah's and Javier's results are similar.

You can compare two sets of data by calculating the range and median.

Example 2 The line plots below show the results from two battery experiments. Are the results similar?

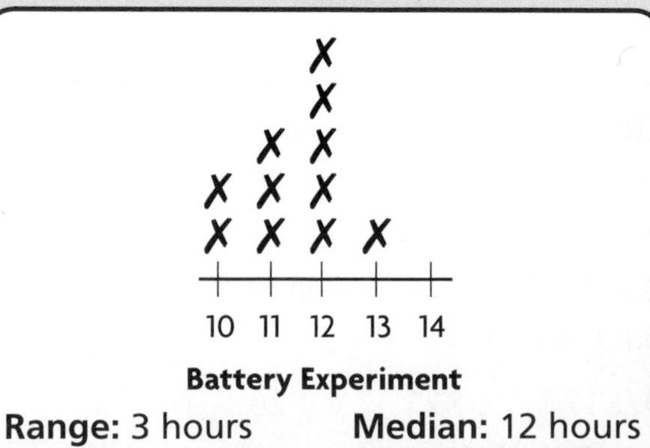

Range: 3 hours **Median:** 12 hours

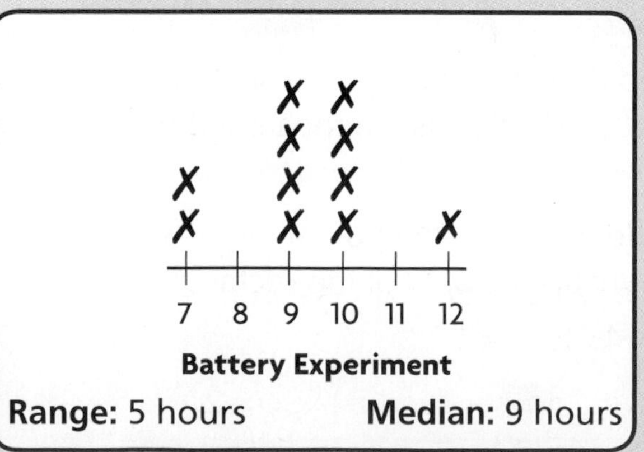

Range: 5 hours **Median:** 9 hours

The range and the median for the two sets of data are different.
So, the results from the battery experiments are not similar.

SDAP 1.1 Know the concepts of mean, median, and mode; compute and compare simple examples to show that they may differ. *also* **MR 1.1, MR 2.4, MR 3.2**

Guided Practice

1. Jane collected data about the number of minutes her classmates spent on homework. Mark collected the same type of data from his classmates. Explain how the medians from their results compare.

- Jane's data: Median is 2.5 hours.
- Mark's data: Median is 1.25 hours.

Tell how the data sets compare.

2.

A: Pages Students Read					
43	10	68	65	31	12
79	24	52	52	68	69

B: Pages Students Read					
32	53	68	12	52	37
15	72	60	52	22	68

3. TALK Math Explain how mean, median, and range help you compare two similar sets of data.

Independent Practice and Problem Solving

Tell how the data sets compare.

4.

A: Weights of Backpacks (pounds)							
0	3	1	8	3	2	8	1
5	4	3	2	3	4	0	0

B: Weights of Backpacks (pounds)						
2	9	8	10	9	4	5
10	2	8	10	6	10	6

For 5–7, use the double-bar graph.

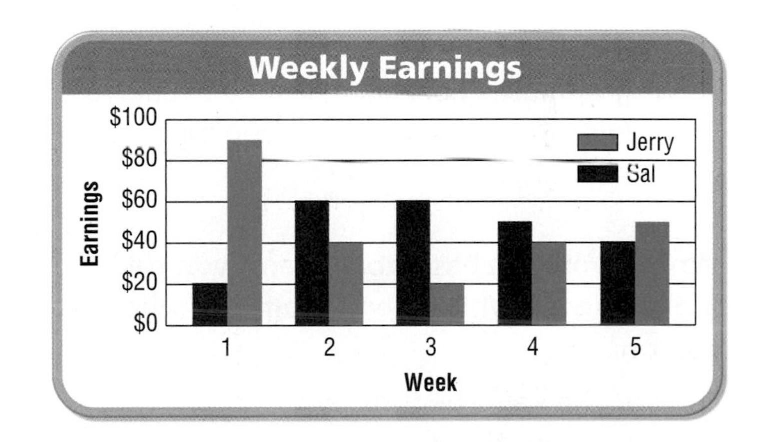

5. How do the ranges of the weekly earnings compare for Sal and Jerry?

6. **What if** Jerry got a bonus of \$30 in week 3? How would the median for these sets of data compare then?

7. WRITE Math Explain why using the mean, median, mode, or range makes it easier to compare two sets of data.

Achieving the Standards

8. $3.7 \times 8{,}920 =$ (NS 2.1, p. 300)

9. What is the value of the expression $(28 \div r) \times 16$ for $r = 7$? (AF 1.2, p. 348)

10. On 5 different days a boat took people on a trip. 14, 15, 11, 14, and 16

    What was the mean number of people on the boat? (SDAP 1.1, p. 602)

11. **Test Prep** Which shows how the median scores for each set of data compare?

Bowling Team 1 Scores			
110	250	98	136

Bowling Team 2 Scores			
103	99	158	146

A $101 < 123$

B $123 < 123.5$

C $124.5 > 123.5$

D $124.5 > 123$

Extra Practice on page 617, Set D

LESSON

5 Analyze Graphs

OBJECTIVE: Read, interpret, and analyze the data in graphs.

Quick Review

Write $<$ or $>$ for each ●.

1. 34 ● 48
2. 16 ● 19
3. 73 ● 71
4. 84 ● 121
5. 109 ● 98

Vocabulary

pictograph
bar graph
circle graph
line graph
trend

Learn

When you analyze graphs, you can answer questions, draw conclusions, and make predictions about the data.

A **pictograph** displays countable data with symbols or pictures. A key shows how many each symbol or picture represents.

2004–2005 Baseball Wins

UNC Wilmington	⚾⚾⚾⚾
UNLV	⚾⚾⚾◖
Georgia Tech	⚾⚾⚾⚾◖
George Mason	⚾⚾⚾◖

Key: ⚾ = 10 wins

How many games did Georgia Tech win?

This key shows that each symbol represents 10 wins. A half symbol represents 5 wins.

For Georgia Tech, it shows ⚾⚾⚾⚾◖:
$(4 \times 10) + 5 = 45$.

So, Georgia Tech had 45 wins.

A **bar graph** uses horizontal or vertical bars to display countable data. You can use bar graphs to compare data. The graph below is a double-bar graph.

Which women's basketball team won the most games? Which men's team won the most games?

Look at the key. The different-colored bars represent the men's and women's basketball teams.

For the women, the longest bar is above the label for Michigan State. It shows that this team won 33 games.

For the men, the longest bar is for Duke. It shows that this team won 27 games.

So, Michigan State won the most women's games and Duke won the most men's games in the 2004–2005 season.

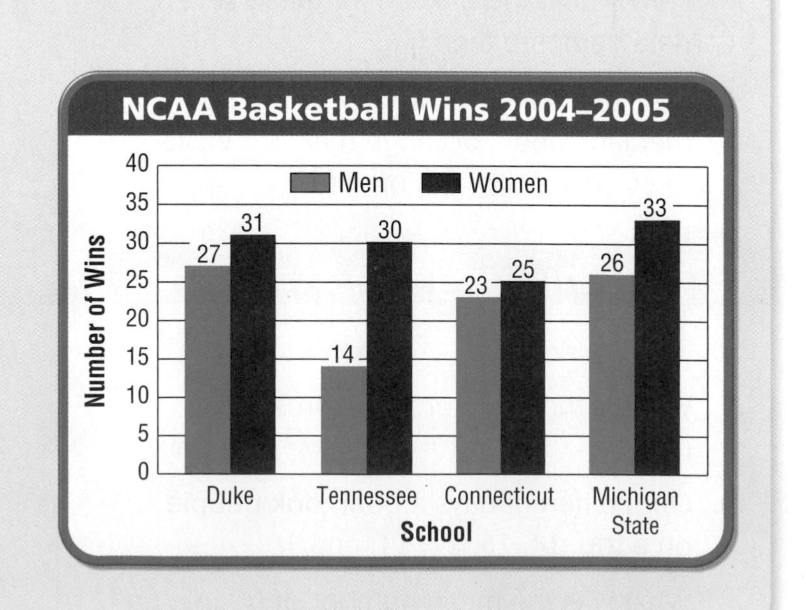

AF 1.1 Use information taken from a graph or equation to answer questions about a problem situation. *also* SDAP 1.0, MR 2.3, MR 2.4, MR 3.2

A **circle graph** shows how parts of the data are related to the whole and to each other.

How does the amount of time Eric spends swimming compare to the total time of his workout?

The circle graph represents the whole set of data. Each section in the circle graph represents a part of the whole.

Find the part of the circle graph that represents swimming. Eric swims for 1 hour.

The entire workout is 1 + 2 + 1 + 1, or 5 hours.

So, Eric spends 1 hour out of 5 hours, or $\frac{1}{5}$ of his workout swimming.

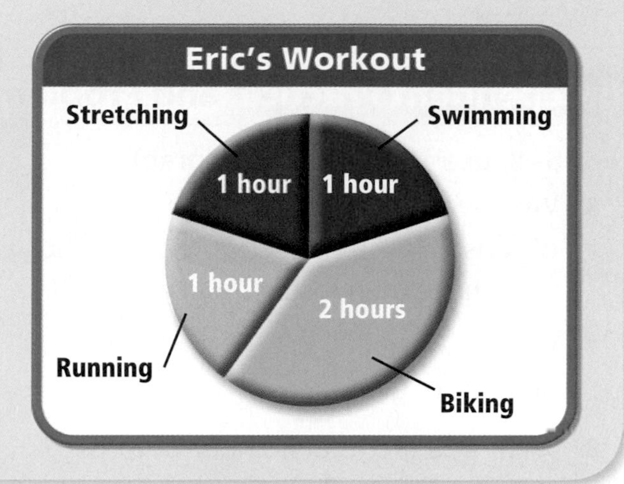

A **line graph** uses line segments to show how data change over time. A line graph may show a trend. A **trend** is a pattern over time, in all or part of a graph, in which the data increase, decrease, or stay the same.

In which week do you predict Sarah will run an 11-minute mile?

To identify a trend, look at the direction of the line from one point to the next.

- If the line is going up from one point to the next, the pattern is increasing.
- If the line is going down from one point to the next, the pattern is decreasing.

The general pattern shown by the graph is decreasing.

So, if the trend continues, Sarah will probably run an 11-minute mile in week 7.

Guided Practice

For 1–4, use the pictograph on page 608.

1. Thirty-five wins would be shown as ● ● ● ◖. Which teams had this number of wins?
2. What if a fifth team had 55 wins? How would this number of wins be shown on the pictograph?
3. How many wins did UNC Wilmington have?
4. Which team had the most wins?

5. TALK Math Suppose you have a pictograph with a key that shows each symbol represents 8. Explain how you would determine the number of symbols you would need to show 20.

Independent Practice and Problem Solving

For 6–8, use the double-bar graph.

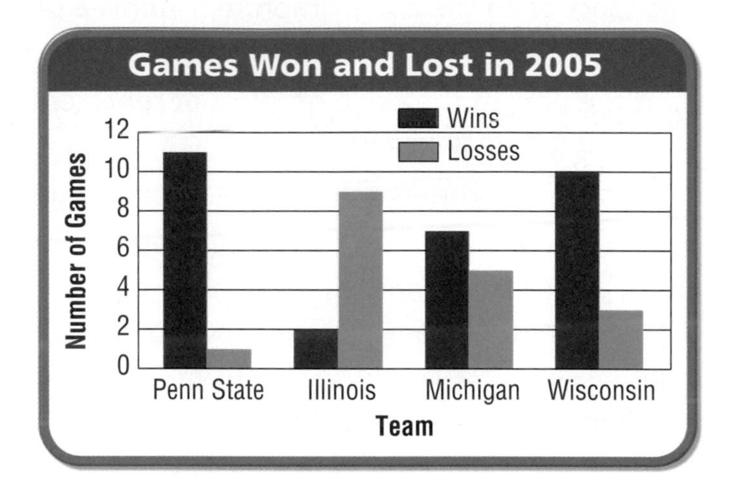

6. Which team had the greatest number of wins? How many more wins did the team have than losses?
7. Which two teams played the same number of games?
8. What was the total number of wins for all the teams?

For 9–12, use the circle graph.

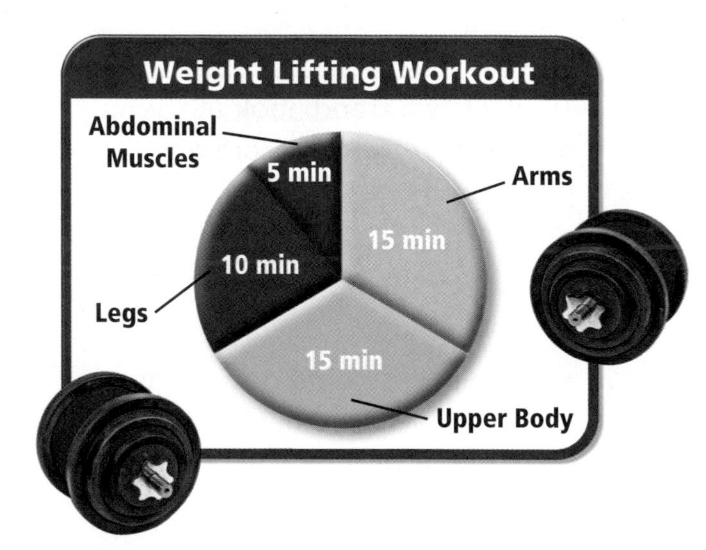

9. Which part of the workout takes the least time?
10. Which parts of the workout take the same amount of time?
11. Which part of the whole workout is leg exercises?
12. Which exercises take up $\frac{1}{9}$ of the workout?

For 13–15, use the line graph.

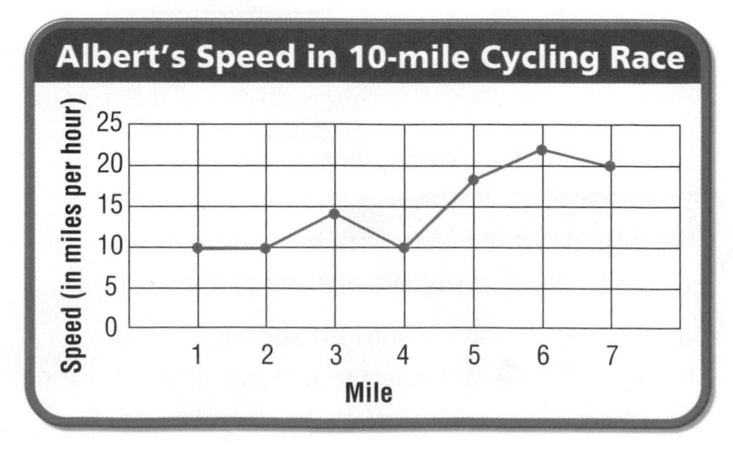

13. Which part of the graph shows the greatest increase from one mile to the next?
14. How would you describe the trend shown in the graph from mile 2 to mile 3?
15. **Reasoning** Suppose the course from mile 7 to mile 10 is uphill. What trend do you think the graph would show from mile 7 to mile 10?
16. ***FAST FACT*** Lance Armstrong retired from bicycle racing in 2005. His average speed during the 2005 season was 41.65 kilometers per hour. At this speed, how far could he travel in 3 hours? in *n* hours?
17. WRITE Math **Explain** how a line graph might show an increasing or decreasing pattern.

 Extra Practice on page 617, Set E

Achieving the Standards

18. Lost Pine Trail is 2.6 miles long. Mesa Trail is 4.3 miles long. How much longer is Mesa Trail? (NS 2.1, p. 274)

19. Lori has a basket 12 inches tall, 10 inches wide, and 18 inches long. What is the volume of the basket? (MG 1.3, p. 578)

20. Find the range of the data set: 10, 15, 8, 12, 14, 8, 20, and 16. (SDAP 1.0, p. 598)

21. **Test Prep** Look at the double-bar graph at the top of page 610. Which statement about the data shown on the graph is **NOT** true?

    A Penn State had the most wins.

    B The median number of wins is 7.

    C Wisconsin played the most games.

    D The median number of losses is 4.

Problem Solving and Reasoning

VISUAL THINKING You can use a double-line graph to compare two sets of data. A key shows what each line represents.

Example For the two cities, what is the difference in rainfall in March?

Look at the graph and the key.

- Yuma's average is 0.3 inch for March.
- Reno's average is 0.7 inch for March.

Find the difference.

$0.7 - 0.3 = 0.4$

So, the difference in rainfall amounts for the two cities is 0.4 inch.

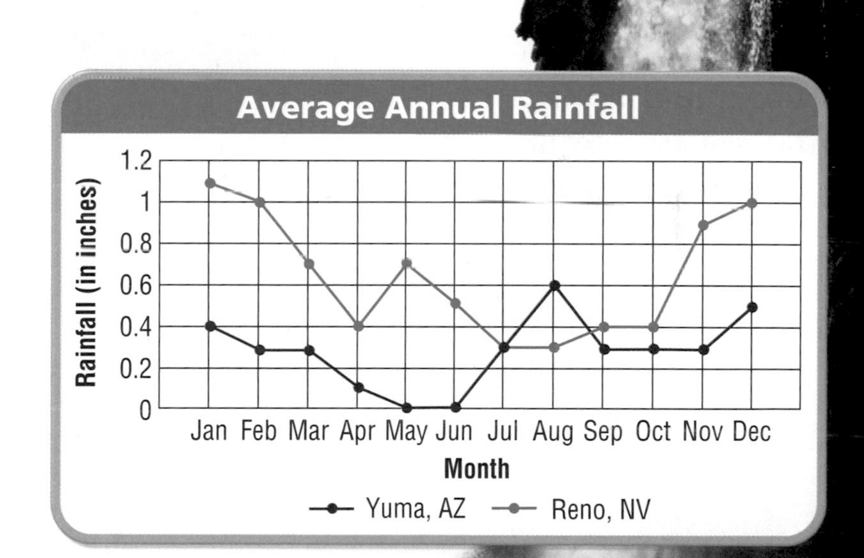

For 1–2, use the double-line graph.

1. **Reasoning** Without adding to find the total annual rainfall, describe how the annual rainfall amounts for the two cities compare.

2. In which month did Yuma receive a greater amount of rainfall than Reno?

Problem Solving Workshop
Strategy: Use Logical Reasoning

OBJECTIVE: Solve problems by using the strategy *use logical reasoning.*

Logical reasoning can help you solve problems based on what you know. You can use diagrams and tables to help you collect and organize information so that you are able to analyze all of the data you have.

A Venn diagram can show relationships.

Find all factors that 132 and 72 have in common.

Factors of 132 | Factors of 72

Factors of 132 only: 132, 66, 44, 33, 22, 11

Both: 1, 2, 3, 4, 12, 6

Factors of 72 only: 72, 24, 18, 8, 36, 9

A table can help you collect and organize.

Tim and Alex play baseball. They got at least one hit in each of their first five baseball games.

Tim's hits per game were 2, 2, 4, 3, 3.
Alex's hits per game were 3, 2, 2, 1, 1.

First 5 Baseball Games

	Game 1	Game 2	Game 3	Game 4	Game 5
Tim	2	2	4	3	3
Alex	3	2	2	1	1

TALK Math

What logical conclusions might you draw from the Venn diagram and the table?

AF 1.1 Use information taken from a graph or equation to answer questions about a problem situation. *also* **MR 1.0, MR 1.1, MR 2.0, MR 2.3, MR 2.4, MR 3.0, MR 3.1, MR 3.2, MR 3.3**

Use the Strategy

Read to Understand
Plan
Solve
Check

PROBLEM The students in a fifth-grade class were asked to write a report. For data sources, 12 students used the Internet, 8 used an encyclopedia, and 13 used other reference books. Four students used the Internet and an encyclopedia, 5 used an encyclopedia and other reference books, 7 used the Internet and other reference books, and 2 used all three. How many students wrote reports?

Read to Understand

- **Generalize what you are asked to find.**
- **Is there information you will not use? If so, what?**

Plan

- **What strategy can you use to solve the problem?**
  You can use logical reasoning to help you solve the problem.

Solve

- **How can you use the strategy to solve the problem?**

a. Draw a Venn diagram with three overlapping ovals. Two students used all three sources, so write 2 in the part common to all three ovals.

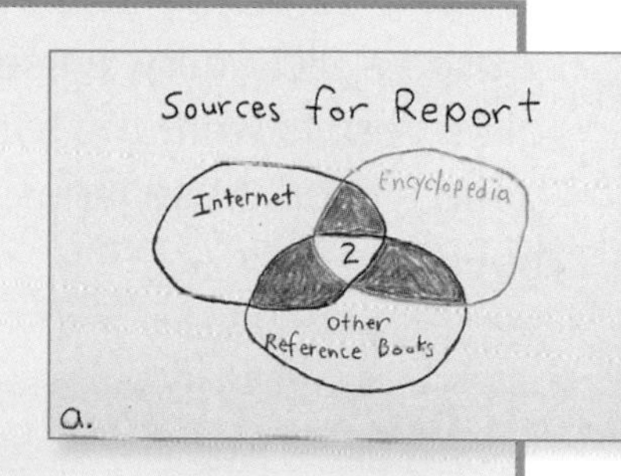

b. Four students used the Internet and an encyclopedia. Since 2 students used all three sources, subtract 2 from 4 to find the number of students who used an encyclopedia and the Internet: $4 - 2 = 2$. Write 2 in the part where only the Internet and encyclopedia ovals overlap. Use the same process to complete the other two middle parts.

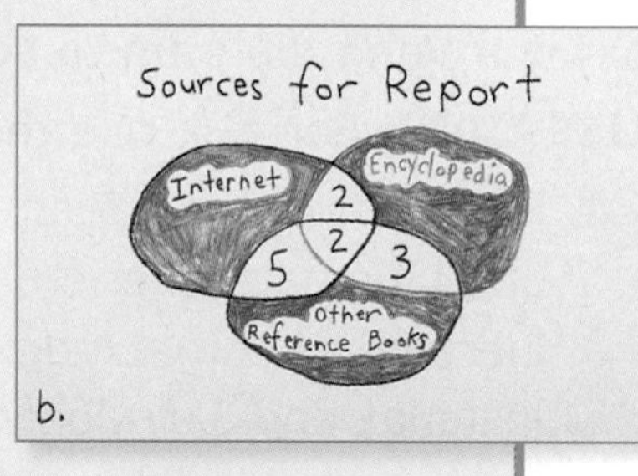

c. Look at the four parts of the oval labeled Internet. Since 12 students used the Internet, the sum of these parts must be 12. Since $12 - 9 = 3$, write 3 in the remaining part of the oval labeled Internet. Use the same process to complete the diagram. Then add all the numbers in the diagram to find how many students wrote reports: $3 + 2 + 1 + 5 + 2 + 3 + 3 = 19$.

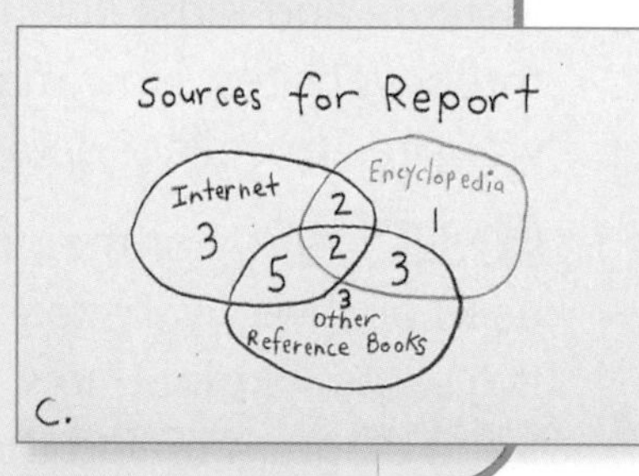

So, 19 students wrote reports.

Check

- **What other strategy could you use to solve the problem?**

Read to Understand
Plan
Solve
Check

Guided Problem Solving

1. During one hour in a library, 7 people used an encyclopedia, 8 used a dictionary, 7 used an atlas, 2 used an encyclopedia and a dictionary, 3 used an encyclopedia and an atlas, 4 used a dictionary and an atlas, and 1 used all three. How many people used an encyclopedia, a dictionary, or an atlas during this hour?

   First, draw and label three overlapping ovals. In the part common to all three ovals, write the number of people who used all three types of books.

   Next, fill in the overlapping parts for each pair of book types.

   Last, fill in the remaining parts. Add all the numbers in the diagram to find the number of people who used these library books.

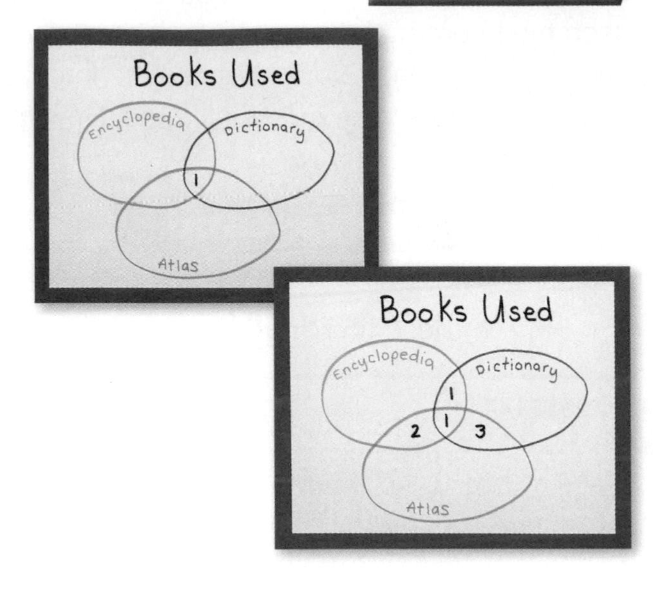

2. **What if** 12 people used an encyclopedia, 7 used a dictionary, 8 used an atlas, and all other results were the same? How many people used these types of books during this hour?

3. Five students wrote reports about U.S. Presidents, 8 wrote reports about U.S. first ladies, and 3 wrote reports about both U.S. Presidents and first ladies. How many students wrote reports?

Problem Solving Strategy Practice

Draw a Venn diagram to solve.

USE DATA For 4–5, use the picture.

4. For a book report, 7 students used KidsClick! and Librarians Internet Index, 5 students used Librarians Internet Index and Smithsonian Institute, and 5 students used Smithsonian Institute and KidsClick! Four students used all three websites. How many students used these websites to collect data?

5. WRITE Math For their next report, no student used all three websites, and all other results were the same. **Explain** how you could change your Venn diagram to find the number of students who used these websites.

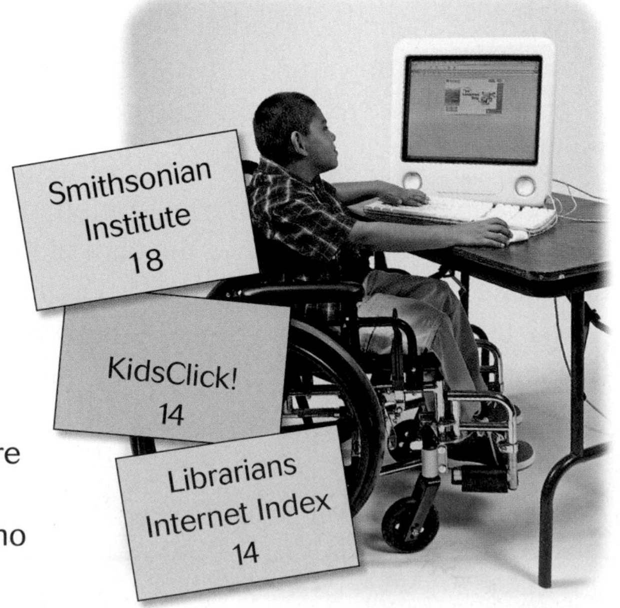

Mixed Strategy Practice

USE DATA For 6–10, use the information in the picture.

6. Samantha and Maria went to the book sale together. Samantha bought *Astronomy* and *Famous Women*. Maria bought *Insects* and *Almanac for Kids*. How much more did Maria spend on books than Samantha?

7. Ricardo spent $21.35 on two books. Which two books did he buy?

8. **Pose a Problem** Look back at Problem 7. Write a similar problem by changing the total cost and the number of books.

9. What is the median price of the books in the sale? What is the mode of the prices?

10. **Open-Ended** Write three number sentences that show different ways to buy three books for less than $35.00.

CHALLENGE YOURSELF

The owner of the store kept track of the number of books people bought so he could restock the books he sold.

11. During the sale, 8 people bought *Insects*, 8 bought *Astronomy*, 9 bought *World Geography*, 3 bought *Insects* and *Astronomy*, 5 bought *Insects* and *World Geography*, 6 bought *Astronomy* and *World Geography*, and 2 bought *Insects*, *Astronomy*, and *World Geography*. How many people bought these books?

12. At the end of the day, the store had the following sales. From 9 A.M. to 10:59 A.M., 12 books were sold; from 11 A.M. to 12:59 P.M., 30 books were sold; from 1 P.M. to 2:59 P.M., 18 books were sold; and from 3 P.M. to 4:59 P.M., 15 books were sold. Between what two time periods in a row did the sales decrease the most?

Extra Practice

Set A An after-school center wants to find out what games the children in its 8–10 age group like to play. Tell whether each sample represents the population. If it does not, explain. (pp. 598–601)

1. a random sample of 100 children, ages 8–10
2. a random sample of 100 children, ages 8–10, who attend the after-school center
3. a random sample of 100 children who attend the after-school center

Make a line plot. Find the range.

4.

Weekly Violin Practice	
Number of Hours	**Frequency**
1	8
2	6
3	9
4	11
5	3

5.

Sandwiches Sold	
Number of Sandwiches	**Frequency**
1	14
2	10
3	6
4	5

Set B Find the mean for each set of data. (pp. 602–603)

1. 26, 38, 17
2. 316, 156, 239, 621
3. $25, $15, $20, $30, $20
4. 5.1, 6.7, 4.9, 5.8, 2.6
5. 148, 152, 124, 200, 101
6. $12, $9, $15, $18
7. $30, $157, $64, $13
8. 37.4, 24.4, 1.3, 10.5, 16.9
9. 327, 802, 464

Set C Find the median and mode for each set of data. (pp. 604–605)

1. $12, $14, $16, $14, $24
2. 18, 16, 27, 10, 24, 10
3. 3.8, 4.4, 7.6, 4.6
4. 638, 525, 470, 505
5. 21, 22, 27, 21, 31, 21, 18
6. 3.02, 3, 3.1, 2.02
7. Janna made four phone calls to different members of her family. The lengths of the calls were 27 minutes, 34 minutes, 30 minutes, and 34 minutes. What is the median length of Janna's phone calls? What is the mode?
8. Darius runs 5 times each week. Last week, he ran 4.3 miles, 6.5 miles, 7.2 miles, 6.8 miles, and 4.3 miles. What is the median number of miles Darius ran last week? What is the mode?

Technology
Use Harcourt Mega Math, Fraction Action, *Fraction Flare Up*, Level N.

Set D Tell how the data sets compare. (pp. 606–607)

1.

A: Science Club Attendance						
6	12	9	6	10	7	13

B: Math Club Attendance						
8	15	16	7	9	6	9

2.

A: Play Ticket Sales (this year)		
\$510	\$480	\$600

B: Play Ticket Sales (last year)			
\$400	\$395	\$450	\$625

3.

A: July Plant Heights (inches)				
10	9	12	13	11
12	10	9	11	13

B: August Plant Heights (inches)				
9	8	7	10	6
8	10	5	8	9

4.

A: Kelly's Monthly Volunteer Hours					
4	6	7	5	1	8
3	5	12	6	11	10

B: Renita's Monthly Volunteer Hours					
5	4	2	3	8	6
7	8	7	10	9	12

Set E For 1–4, use the circle graph. (pp. 608–611)

1. On which item does Mike spend the most?
2. Which part of total expenses does Mike spend on clothing?
3. Which items are each $\frac{1}{10}$ of the total expenses?
4. How does the amount Mike spends on his clothing compare to the amount he spends on his shoes?

For 5–8, use the double-bar graph.

5. Whose team won the most races in Year 2?
6. In which year did Inez's team win fewer races, Year 1 or Year 2?
7. Whose team won the same number of races in both years?
8. Which team won the greatest number of races overall? How many races?

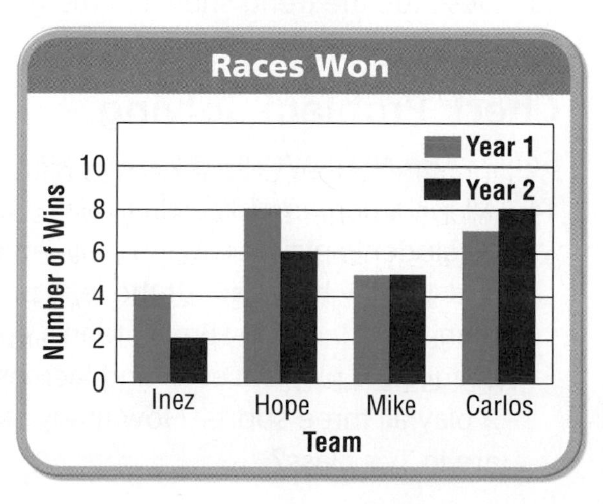

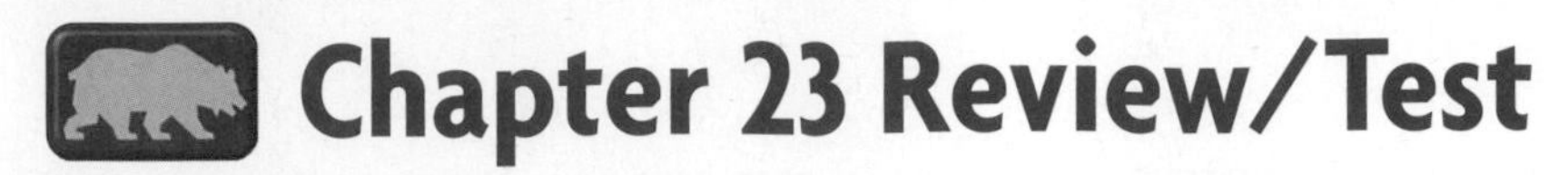

Chapter 23 Review/Test

Check Vocabulary and Concepts

Choose the best term from the box.

VOCABULARY
mean
median
trend

1. A _?_ is a pattern over time, in all or part of a graph. (AF 1.1, p. 608)
2. The average of a set of numbers is the _?_. (SDAP 1.1, p. 602)

Check Skills

A theater owner wants to find out what kinds of movies are popular with boys ages 8–12. Tell whether each sample represents the population. If it does not, explain. (SDAP 1.0, pp. 598–601)

3. a random sample of 150 boys, ages 8–12
4. a random sample of 150 boys
5. a random sample of 150 children, ages 8–12

Find the mean, median, and mode for each set of data. (SDAP 1.1; pp. 602–603, 604–605)

6. \$28, \$44, \$12, \$16
7. 201, 198, 211, 197, 201
8. 11.5, 13.4, 12, 10.6, 6.5

Tell how the data sets compare. (SDAP 1.1, pp. 606–607)

9.

1: Cans Collected		
435	619	428

2: Cans Collected		
594	435	375

10.

Nora's Math Test Scores				
85	90	94	78	95

Nora's Science Test Scores				
100	84	92	75	84

For 11–13, use the line graph. (AF 1.1, pp. 608–611)

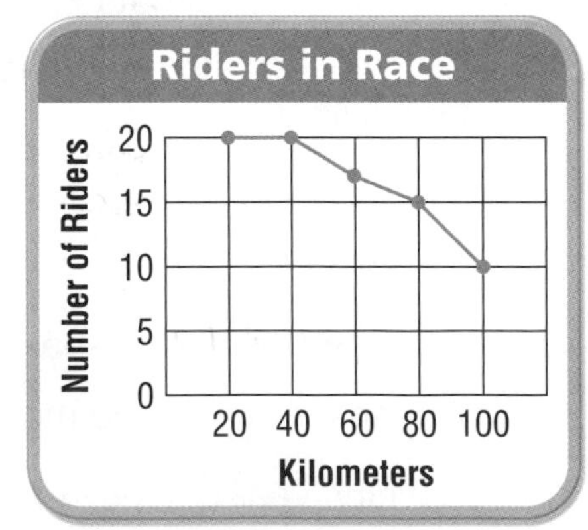

11. Where does the graph show the greatest decrease?
12. When does the first change in the number of riders occur?
13. Describe the trend shown in the graph.

Check Problem Solving

Solve. (AF 1.2, MR 2.0, MR 2.3, pp. 612–615)

14. All the students in Ty's class play sports: 12 students play tennis, 15 play lacrosse, and 18 play baseball. Of those, 5 play tennis and lacrosse, 6 play tennis and baseball, 8 play baseball and lacrosse, and 2 play all three sports. How many students are in Ty's class?

15. WRITE Math Suppose no student in Ty's class played all three sports. If all the other results were the same, how would you change your diagram to find the number of students in the class?

GO ONLINE Technology Use *Online Assessment.*

Enrich • Misleading Graphs

Read the Fine Print

A **misleading graph** gives a false impression of data. Some traits of a misleading graph include:

- a scale that begins with a number other than zero
- uneven spaces between the values on the scale
- bars that have different widths

Example

This graph compares the costs of two types of cars. At first glance, it seems that the Roadster costs twice as much as the Falcon. But if you read the scale carefully, you discover that the Roadster costs only $3,000 more than the Falcon. The scale begins with a number other than zero and it is not labeled correctly.

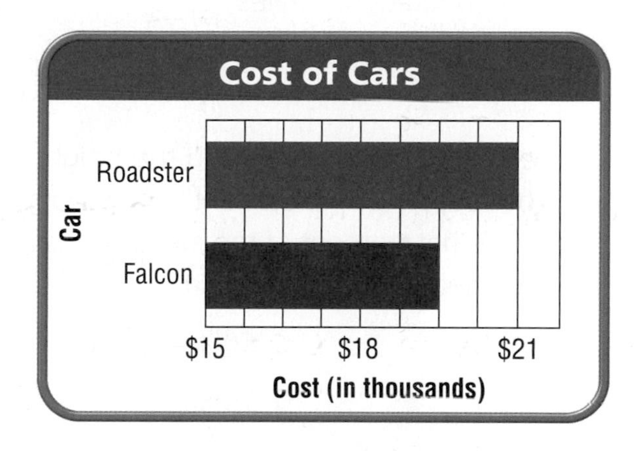

Try It

Read the graph. Then answer the questions.

1. About how many times taller does the fifth grade bar appear to be than the fourth grade bar?
2. How many more cans were actually collected by fifth-grade students than by fourth-grade students?
3. What false impression does the graph give?

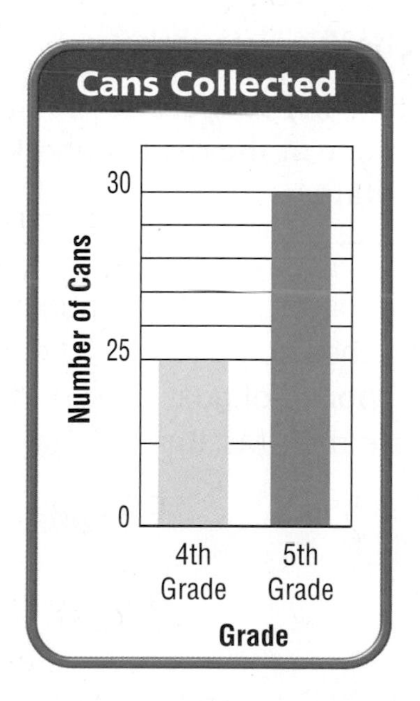

Think About It

WRITE Math **Explain** how you would correct the "Cans Collected" graph so that it is not misleading.

 Achieving the Standards

Chapters 1–23

Number Sense

1. The land area of California is 155,959 square miles. Which shows the area rounded to the nearest ten thousand? **(NS 1.1)**

   A 200,000 square miles

   B 160,000 square miles

   C 156,000 square miles

   D 155,960 square miles

2. The school nurse measured the height of three fourths of the students in Jacob's class. What percent of the students have been measured? **(NS 1.2)**

   A 10% **C** 50%

   B 25% **D** 75%

Check your work.

See item 3. If your answer doesn't match one of the choices, check your computation.

3. At the market, Ms. Ruiz bought $\frac{1}{3}$ pound of Swiss cheese, $\frac{1}{4}$ pound of cheddar cheese, and $\frac{1}{2}$ pound of goat cheese. How much cheese does Ms. Ruiz buy? **(NS 2.3)**

   A $\frac{1}{2}$ pound **C** $1\frac{7}{12}$ pounds

   B $1\frac{1}{12}$ pounds **D** $3\frac{1}{2}$ pounds

4. **WRITE Math** **Explain** how to use your answer to item 2 to find the number of students the nurse has measured in a class of 20 students. **(NS 1.2)**

Algebra and Functions

5. If $n = 12$, what is the value of the expression $n - 4$? **(AF 1.2)**

   A 3 **C** 16

   B 8 **D** 48

6. Ethan baked 4 more pretzels than twice the number that Reba baked. Which expression models the situation? **(AF 1.2)**

   A $4 - \frac{1}{2}p$

   B $4 + \frac{1}{2}p$

   C $4 - 2p$

   D $4 + 2p$

7. Which ordered pair represents point A? **(AF 1.4)**

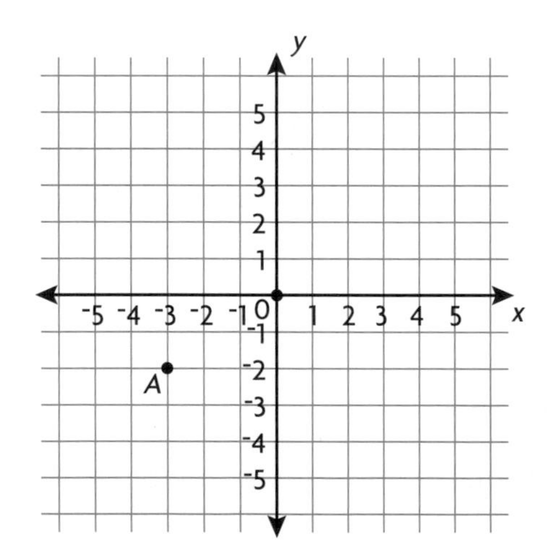

   A (3,2) **C** $(^-3,^-2)$

   B $(^-3,2)$ **D** $(^-2,3)$

8. **WRITE Math** **Explain** how you would use the Distributive Property to check if the equation $4 \times (n + 2) = 48$ is true for $n = 10$. **(AF 1.3)**

Measurement and Geometry

9. Which solid figure matches the net? (MG 1.2)

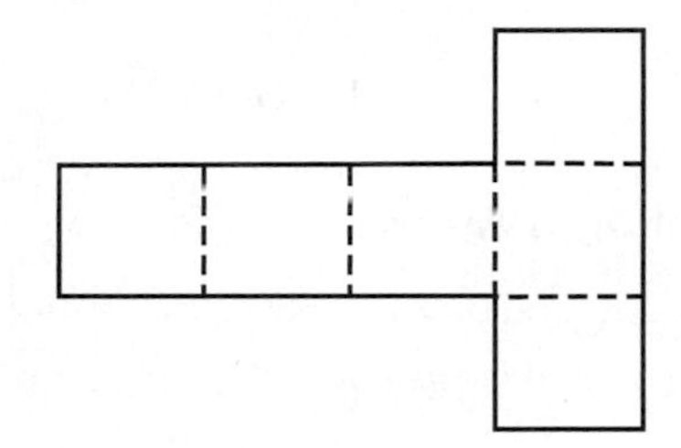

A square pyramid

B triangular prism

C cone

D rectangular prism

10. What is the unknown angle measure? (MG 2.2)

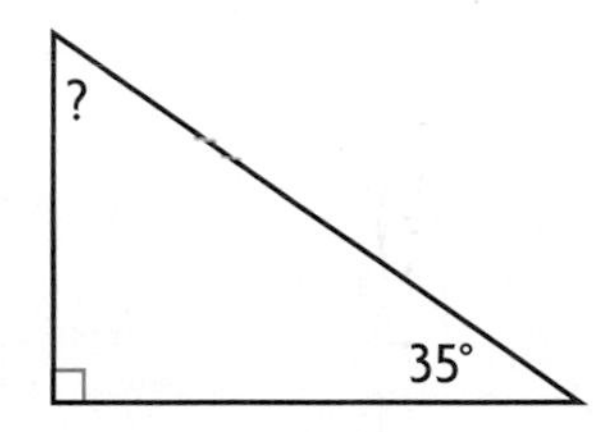

A 45°

B 55°

C 90°

D 180°

11. **WRITE Math** **Explain** how you could find the surface area of a cube with faces that each measure 3 centimeters by 3 centimeters. (MG 1.2)

Statistics, Data Analysis, and Probability

12. Josh surveyed his classmates to find the number of pets that each person had. The line plot shows the results.

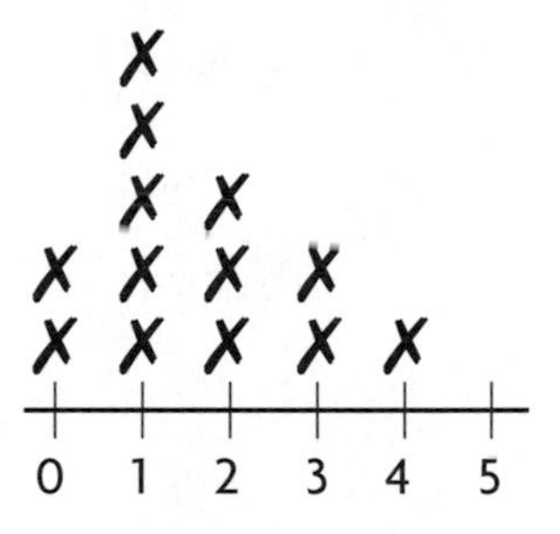

Number of Pets

How many classmates have more than 2 pets? (SDAP 1.0)

A 10

B 9

C 6

D 3

13. What is the probability that the pointer will land on a number greater than 15? (Grade 4 SDAP 2.2)

A $\frac{1}{6}$

B $\frac{2}{3}$

C $\frac{1}{2}$

D 1

14. **WRITE Math** **Explain** how to find the mode of the data in item 12. (NS 1.2)

24 Display and Interpret Data

The Big Idea Data can be analyzed and displayed in various graphical formats.

Investigate

The circle graph displays the types of cheeses produced in California in a recent year. What observations can you make about the data?

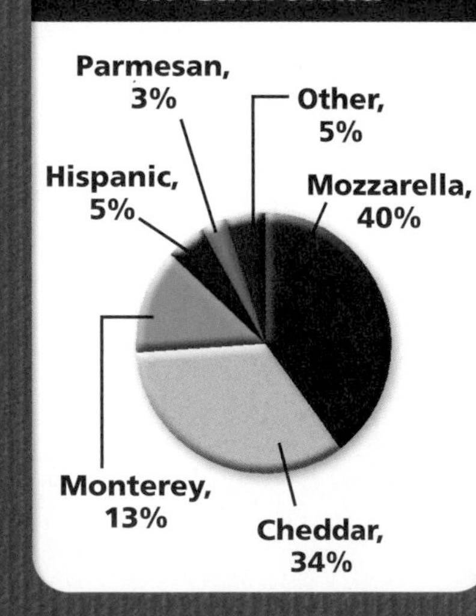

CALIFORNIA FAST FACT

California leads the United States in total milk production, producing nearly 19 percent of the country's milk supply, and ranks second in cheese production.

GO ONLINE Technology Student pages are available in the Student eBook.

Show What You Know

Check your understanding of important skills needed for success in Chapter 24.

▶ Extend Patterns

Write a rule for each pattern. Then find the missing numbers.

1. 0, 4, 8, 12, 16, ■, ■, ■
2. 0, 5, 10, 15, 20, ■, ■, ■
3. 90, 80, 70, 60, ■, ■, ■
4. 1, 3, 9, 27, ■, ■, ■
5. 3, 6, 12, 24, ■, ■, ■
6. 25, 50, 75, 100, ■, ■, ■
7. 48, 40, 32, 24, ■, ■, ■
8. 3, 7, 15, 31, ■, ■, ■

▶ Make a Bar Graph

Make a bar graph for the data set.

T-Shirts in Cleo's Store	
Purple	3
Yellow	18
Black	14
Red	23
Blue	16

9. The set of data shows the number of different colored T-shirts in Cleo's store. How many shirts are there in all?
10. Which bar in your T-shirt graph is the tallest? Which is the shortest?
11. How many more red shirts than yellow shirts are there in Cleo's store?
12. Suppose you used an interval of 2 to make your bar graph. How would the bars change if you used an interval of 5?

VOCABULARY POWER

CHAPTER VOCABULARY

categorical data
double-line graph
histogram
numerical data
stem-and-leaf plot

WARM-UP WORDS

histogram a bar graph that shows the number of times data occur within intervals

stem-and-leaf plot a table that shows groups of data arranged by place value

double-line graph line graph that represents two sets of data

Make Histograms

OBJECTIVE: Represent data by making a histogram.

Quick Review

Find the next number in the pattern.

1. 5, 10, 15, 20, ■
2. 6, 9, 12, 15, ■
3. 4, 9, 14, 19, ■
4. 1, 11, 21, 31, ■
5. 28, 32, 36, 40, ■

Vocabulary

histogram

Learn

PROBLEM The data shows the ages of runners who preregistered for a 5K race. Make a graph of the data.

Ages of Runners

32	17	26	24	35	13	19	23	27	41
38	9	16	28	8	37	18	59	40	43
52	29	12	10	25	28	32	39	46	24

Sometimes you want to show how often data occur. A **histogram** is a bar graph that shows the number of times data occur within intervals.

Activity

Follow the steps to make a histogram for the data above.

Step 1

Make a frequency table with intervals of 15. Start with 1. Record the number of times data occur for each interval, or age group.

Age Group	Frequency
1–15	5
16–30	13
31–45	9
46–60	3

Step 2

Make a histogram.

Choose an appropriate scale and interval for the vertical axis. Label the axis.

List the age groups, and label the horizontal axis.

Draw a bar for the number of runners in each age group. The bars should touch but not overlap.

Write a title for the graph.

SDAP 1.2 Organize and display single-variable data in appropriate graphs and representations (e.g., histogram, circle graphs) and explain which types of graphs are appropriate for various data sets. *also* **AF 1.1, SDAP 1.0, MR 1.1, MR 2.3, MR 2.4, MR 3.2**

Guided Practice

For 1–3, use the table.

1. Use 3 years for each interval. List the intervals.
2. Make a histogram of the data.
3. How many children ages 4–6 take swimming lessons?
4. TALK Math **Explain** how a histogram and a bar graph are similar and how they are different.

Swimming Lessons				
9	11	6	4	2
3	8	7	4	6
6	3	10	12	11
6	5	11	12	4

Independent Practice and Problem Solving

For 5–6, use the table.

5. What is a reasonable interval for the practice times?
6. Make a histogram of the data.

Practice Time (in minutes)					
25	32	20	35	37	33
28	42	36	32	23	41

For 7–8, decide whether a bar graph or a histogram would better represent the data. Then make the graph.

7.

Color of Car	Number of Cars
Black	35
White	25
Red	10

8.

Height (in inches)	Number of Students
48–51	2
52–55	4
56–59	12

USE DATA For 9–11, 13, and 15, use the graph.

9. How many more runners are in the age group 25–29 than in the age group 5–9?
10. How many people ran in the road race?
11. WRITE Math Can you tell from the histogram how many people are 15 years old? **Explain.**

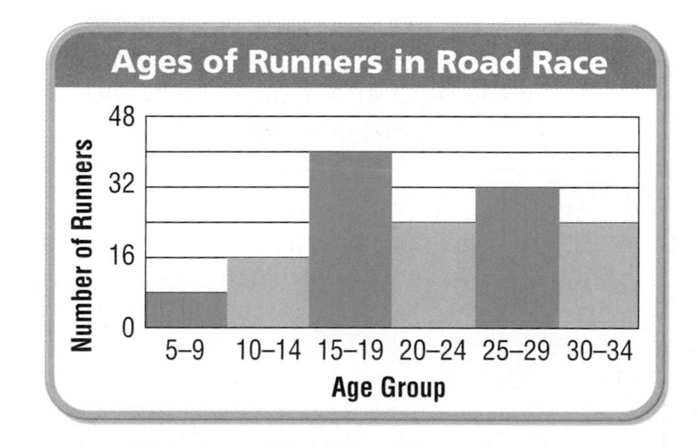

Achieving the Standards

12. Order from least to greatest: 0.6, 1.4, 0.09, and 1.37. (NS 1.1, p. 46)
13. In the graph above, which age group is the mode? How do you know? (SDAP 1.1, p. 612)
14. If y is a number that satisfies $4y - 2 = 18$, is y equal to 4 or to 5? (AF 1.2, p. 356)
15. **Test Prep** How many people in the road race are 5–14 years old?

A 16 **B** 24 **C** 32 **D** 48

Extra Practice on page 638, Set A

LESSON 2

Make Stem-and-Leaf Plots

OBJECTIVE: Represent data appropriately by making a stem-and-leaf plot.

Quick Review

Order from least to greatest.

1. 90, 67, 39, 58
2. 34, 27, 101, 243
3. 73, 82, 78, 85
4. 116, 122, 130, 109
5. 152, 160, 93, 129

Vocabulary

stem-and-leaf plot

Learn

PROBLEM How can you organize the data below to make it easier to interpret?

Numbers of Floors in San Francisco's High-Rise Buildings

31	37	26	48	52	33	34	43	38	38
27	30	30	32	40	45	38	39	48	27
29	30	48	33	32	28	34	45	43	43

A **stem-and-leaf plot** is a table that shows groups of data arranged by place value. It allows you to show each data value.

HANDS ON

Activity

Make a stem-and-leaf plot of the high-rise data.

Step 1

Order the data from least to greatest.

26, 27, 27, 28, 29, 30, 30, 30, 31, 32, 32, 33, 33, 34, 34, 37, 38, 38, 38, 39, 40, 43, 43, 43, 45, 45, 48, 48, 48, 52

Step 2

Separate the data into groups, each with the same stem. List the stems in order in one column.

Step 3

Write each set of leaves in order from least to greatest to the right of their stem. Add a title to your plot.

The tens digit of each number is its stem.

The ones digit of each number is its leaf.

San Francisco High-Rise Buildings

Stem	Leaves
2	6 7 7 8 9
3	0 0 0 1 2 2 3 3 4 4 7 8 8 8 9
4	0 3 3 3 5 5 8 8 8
5	2

5 | 2 represents 52.

SDAP 1.2 Organize and display single-variable data in appropriate graphs and representations (e.g., histogram, circle graphs) and explain which types of graphs are appropriate for various data sets. *also* **AF 1.1, SDAP 1.0, MR 2.3, MR 2.4, MR 3.2**

Guided Practice

1. Look back at the San Francisco High-Rise Buildings stem-and-leaf plot. How many buildings have 32 floors? How does the plot show this?

For 2–4, use the bowling scores.

2. Use the data to make a stem-and-leaf plot.
3. What was the team's lowest score? highest score?
4. TALK Math **Explain** the relationship between a leaf and a stem in the stem-and-leaf plot you made with the bowling score data.

Team Bowling Scores

76	92	85	73	94	98	61	74
79	73	81	85	92	86	86	75
69	67	82	86	93	89	76	80

Independent Practice and Problem Solving

For 5–8, use the April temperature data.

5. Use the data to make a stem-and-leaf plot.
6. What was the lowest temperature? the highest temperature?
7. Which temperature occurred most often?
8. Were more temperatures recorded in the 60's, 70's, or 80's?

April High Temperatures (in °F)

67	72	62	67	68	65
75	79	76	72	86	83
86	79	72	88	75	89
87	85	72	84	87	86

For 9–10 and 15, use the stem-and-leaf plot.

9. How many buildings have from 10 to 19 floors?
10. How many buildings have exactly 17 floors?
11. WRITE Math **Explain** What kinds of questions can you answer using a stem-and-leaf plot?

Number of Floors in Chicago Buildings

Stem	Leaves
1	2 2 5 7 7 7 7 9
2	5 6 7
3	4 6
4	1 4
5	
6	0 1
7	0 4

Achieving the Standards

12. What is the volume of a rectangular prism 3 inches tall, 6 inches wide, and 10 inches long? (MG 1.3, p. 586)

13. For the equation $y = x + 2$, what are the values of y in a function table if $x = {}^{-}2, 0,$ and 2? (AF 1.5, p. 508)

14. Graph the ordered pair (2,5) on a coordinate grid. (SDAP 1.5, p. 500)

15. **Test Prep** How many buildings are shown in the data in the stem-and-leaf plot above?

A 8 **B** 19 **C** 20 **D** 29

Extra Practice on page 638, Set B

LESSON 3

Make Line Graphs

OBJECTIVE: Represent data by making a line graph.

Quick Review

What scale would you use to graph the data?

1. 5, 9, 15, 6, 3
2. 28, 75, 36, 48, 31
3. 58, 69, 94, 86, 90
4. 12, 30, 25, 48, 41
5. 90, 120, 85, 125, 80

Vocabulary

double-line graph

Learn

A line graph is a good way to show data that changes over time.

Average Monthly Temperature in Philadelphia, PA

Month	Jan (1)	Feb (2)	Mar (3)	Apr (4)	May (5)	Jun (6)	Jul (7)	Aug (8)	Sep (9)
Temperature (in °F)	30	33	42	52	63	72	77	76	68

Activity

Step 1

Choose an appropriate scale and interval for the data. Since there are no temperatures between 0°F and 29°F, show a break in the scale.

Step 2

Write the months along the bottom of the graph. Label the horizontal and vertical axes. Write a title for the graph.

Step 3

Write related pairs from the data as ordered pairs. Graph the ordered pairs. Connect the points with straight line segments.

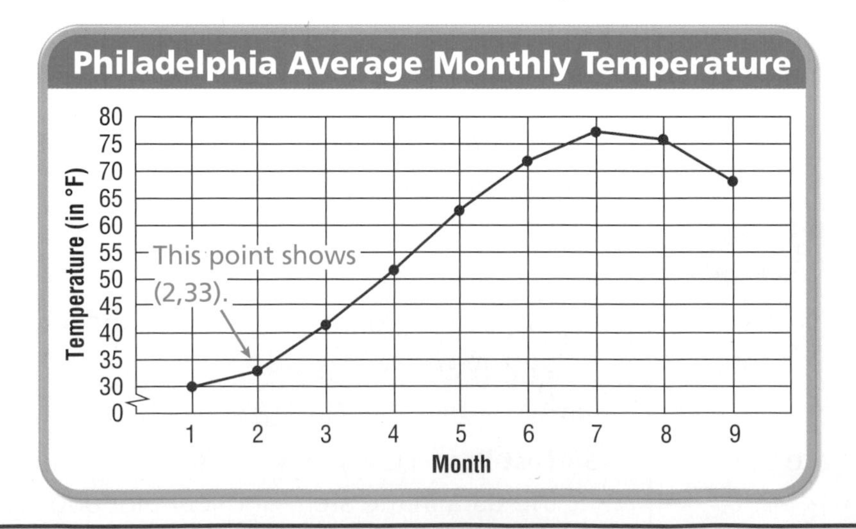

Math Idea

You can write related pairs of data as ordered pairs. In the set of data above, each month has a related temperature. You would write (1,30) for the first related pair.

SDAP 1.4 Identify ordered pairs of data from a graph and interpret the meaning of the data in terms of the situation depicted by the graph. *also* **AF 1.1, SDAP 1.0, SDAP 1.2, SDAP 1.5, MR 2.3, MR 2.4, MR 3.2**

Double-Line Graph

The table shows the average monthly temperatures for Long Beach, California. Make a graph to compare the data for Philadelphia from page 628 with the data for Long Beach.

Average Monthly Temperature in Long Beach									
Month	1	2	3	4	5	6	7	8	9
Temperature (in °F)	56	57	59	62	65	69	73	75	73

A **double-line graph** is one way to show two sets of related data for the same period of time.

Example Make a double-line graph.

Step 1

Choose an appropriate scale and interval.

Step 2

Write the months along the bottom of the graph. Label the horizontal and vertical axes. Write a title for the graph.

Step 3

Make a key. Use one color for Philadelphia and another color for Long Beach.

Step 4

Using the appropriate color, graph the ordered pairs for Philadelphia and connect the points with straight lines.

Use the other color to graph the ordered pairs for Long Beach and connect the points with straight lines.

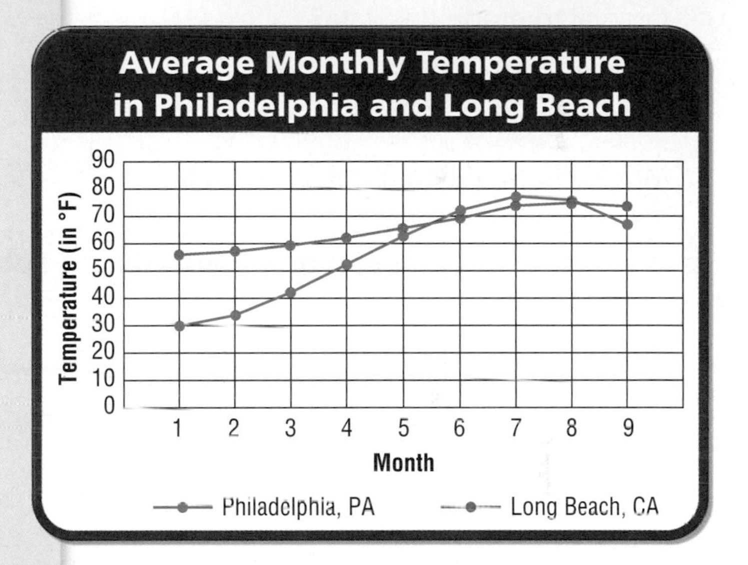

Guided Practice

1. Suppose you add the data at the right to the graph above. Would the lines go up or down for each city?

Average October Monthly Temperature	
City	Temperature (in °F)
Philadelphia	56
Long Beach	68

For 2–5, use the graph.

Average Monthly Temperature in Tupelo, MS					
Month	1	2	3	4	5
Temperature (in °F)	40	44	54	62	70

2. What would be an appropriate scale and interval to use in graphing the data?
3. Write the related pairs as ordered pairs.
4. Make a line graph of the data.
5. TALK Math **Explain** what types of data you need to make a line graph.

Independent Practice and Problem Solving

For 6–8, use the table.

Daily Temperatures					
Day	1	2	3	4	5
High	80°F	84°F	78°F	78°F	85°F
Low	68°F	70°F	65°F	70°F	73°F

6. What would be an appropriate scale and interval to graph the data?
7. Write the related pairs from the data as ordered pairs.
8. Make a double-line graph of the data.

For 9–10, make a line graph or a double-line graph for each set of data.

9.

Skating Rink Sales					
Week	1	2	3	4	5
East Rink	\$120	\$150	\$180	\$170	\$180
West Rink	\$110	\$130	\$160	\$170	\$150

10.

Stock X Price				
Month	1	2	3	4
Price	\$48	\$55	\$62	\$38

USE DATA For 11–13, use the graph.

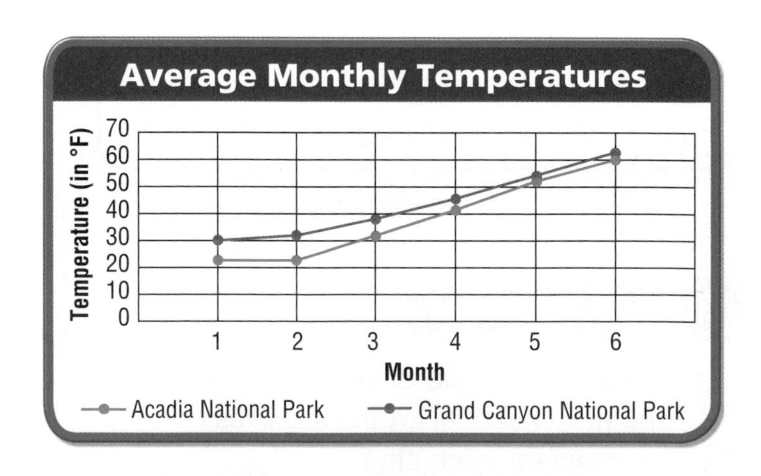

11. During which of the months shown is the temperature difference between the two national parks the greatest?
12. Which park has an average temperature represented by (4,45)?
13. WRITE Math **Explain** how graphing an ordered pair on a coordinate grid is similar to graphing an ordered pair on a line graph.

Technology
Use Harcourt Mega Math, The Number Games, *ArachnaGraph*, Levels I and J.

 Extra Practice on page 638, Set C

Achieving the Standards

For 16–18, use the Average Monthly Temperatures graph on page 630.

14. A rectangular prism has a length of 9 inches, a height of 4 inches, and a width of 3 inches. What is the volume? (MG 1.3, p. 578)

15. What is 20% of 40? (NS 1.2, p. 412)

16. Which park has the lowest average monthly temperature? (SDAP 1.0, p. 608)

17. Test Prep Which park has a point at (1,30)?

18. Test Prep Which ordered pair represents an average July temperature of 70° Fahrenheit?

A (6,70) **C** (7,70)

B (1,70) **D** (70,7)

Problem Solving connects to Science

The Water Cycle

Water changes to water vapor by evaporation and then condenses to form rain. This process is called the water cycle. The ocean is an important part of this cycle and has a strong effect on climate. The ocean absorbs heat from the sun and then loses heat by evaporation, often causing precipitation and even storms. The overlay graph at the right uses two vertical scales to show monthly average temperatures and precipitation for Redding, California.

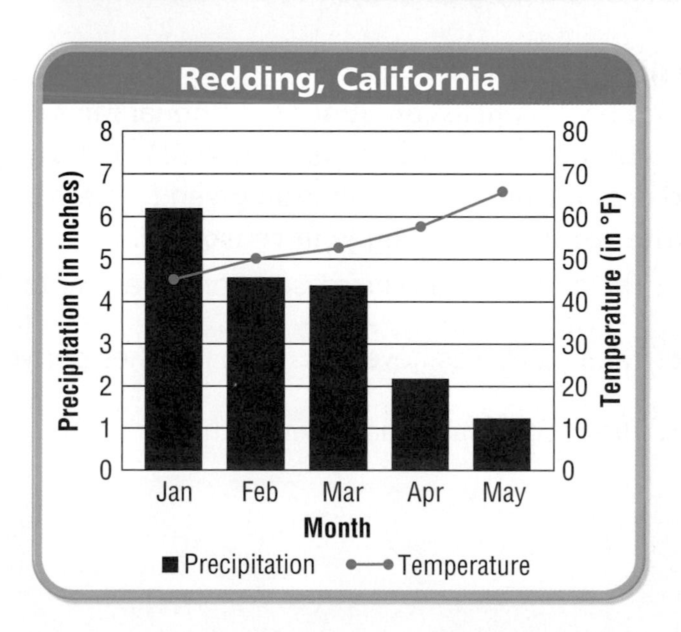

For 1–3, use the graph.

1. About how much precipitation falls in Redding, California, in February?
2. What is the average temperature for Redding, California, in February?
3. How does the overlay graph help you compare temperature and precipitation for each month?

Problem Solving Workshop
Skill: Draw Conclusions

OBJECTIVE: Solve problems by using the skill *draw conclusions.*

Read to Understand
Plan
Solve
Check

Use the Skill

PROBLEM The National Weather Service records the total rainfall for different cities and states each month. The bar graph shows the annual rainfall for San Diego, California for the years 2000–2005. Was the annual rainfall during this period usually greater than 10 inches?

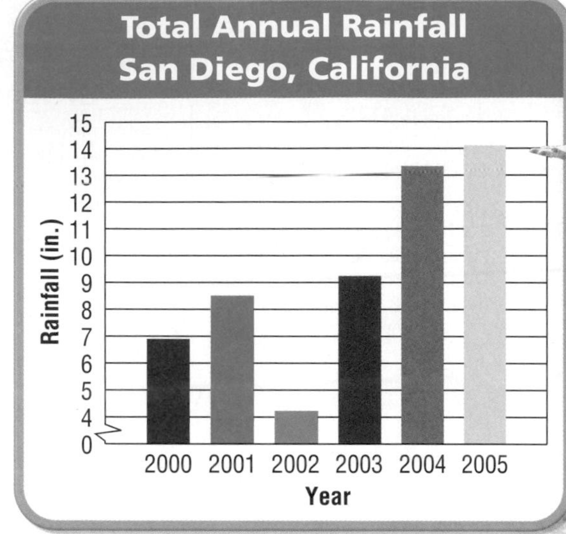

You can analyze the data to draw a conclusion.

Analyze	Conclusion
During which years was the annual rainfall greater than 10 inches?	The annual rainfall in 2004 was between 13 and 14 inches. The annual rainfall in 2005 was between 14 and 15 inches.
During which years was the annual rainfall less than 10 inches?	In 2000, 2001, 2002, and 2003 the annual rainfall was less than 10 inches.

So, the annual rainfall during this time period was not usually greater than 10 inches.

Think and Discuss

Read each conclusion about the annual rainfall in San Diego during the years 2000–2005. Tell whether it can be drawn from the information given in the bar graph. Write *yes* or *no*. Explain your reasoning.

a. The annual rainfall increased from one year to the next.

b. The rainfall was never less than 6 inches per year.

c. The rainfall was usually during the spring and summer.

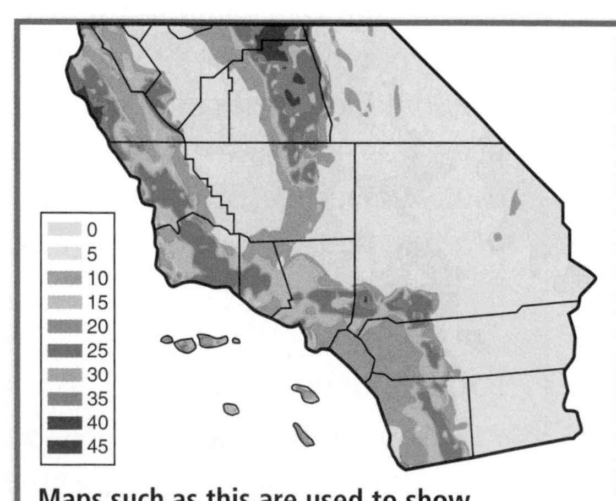

Maps such as this are used to show the annual average rainfall in Southern California.

SDAP 1.0 Students display, analyze, compare, and interpret different data sets, including data sets of different sizes. *also* **MR 2.3, MR 2.4, MR 3.2**

Guided Problem Solving

1. The bar graph shows the rainfall for San Diego for the months from January to June. Was the monthly rainfall during this time period usually less than 3 inches?

   Think: Which months had rainfall greater than 3 inches? Which months had rainfall less than 3 inches?

   Compare the number of months that had rainfall greater than 3 inches with the number of months that had rainfall less than 3 inches. Did more months have rainfall less than 3 inches?

   Draw a conclusion.

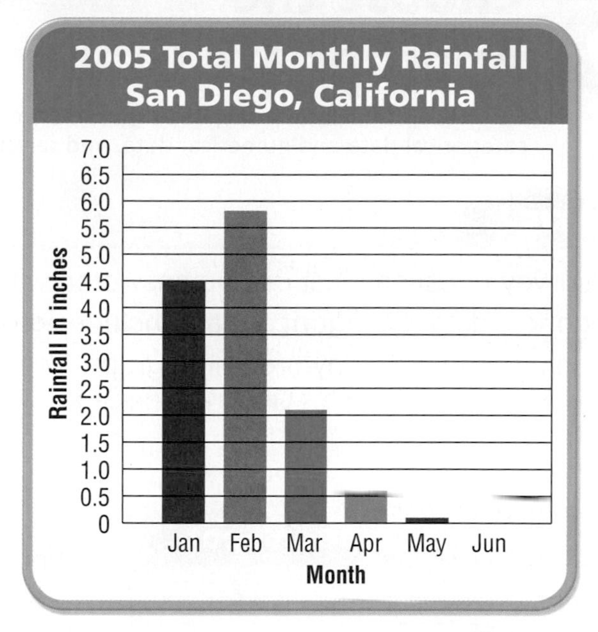

2. **What if** the bar graph included the rainfall data for July 2005? What conclusion could you make if the rainfall for July was 0.01 inch?

3. In 2005, the September rainfall was 0.10 inch. In October it was 0.46 inch, in November it was 0.12 inch, and in December it was 0.33 inch. What conclusion can you draw about the rainfall during this period?

Mixed Applications

Solve. For 7–8, use the stem-and-leaf plot.

4. Michael has 1,098 pennies. He plans to put the pennies into coin rolls with 50 pennies in each roll. How many coin rolls will Michael completely fill?

5. Grace charges $7.50 an hour for babysitting. Is it reasonable to say that Grace earns about $250 for 30 hours of babysitting? Explain.

6. Paul is having a party that starts in 2 hours 45 minutes. He needs $1\frac{3}{4}$ hours to clean, $\frac{1}{2}$ hour to decorate, and $\frac{3}{4}$ hour to make food. Will Paul be ready on time? Explain.

7. Tanesha wants to find out the total number of minutes she exercised over ten days. Did Tanesha exercise more than 5 hours? Explain.

Minutes Tanesha Exercised

Stem	Leaves
2	0 2 4 5 7
3	0 3
4	5
5	2 4

8. WRITE Math The median for the data is 5.5 minutes less than the range. Use this information to find the median number of minutes Tanesha exercised. **Explain** your answer.

5 Choose the Appropriate Graph

OBJECTIVE: Compare the types of graphs that can be used for categorical data and numerical data, and select an appropriate graph.

Quick Review

William wants to show the number of students in third, fourth, and fifth grade at his school. What type of graph could he use for this data?

Vocabulary

categorical data

numerical data

Learn

In a survey questions that can be answered with words are categorical data. **Categorical data** includes groups or choices. The data is shown in any order in a graph. You can use a bar graph or a circle graph to show data that is categorical.

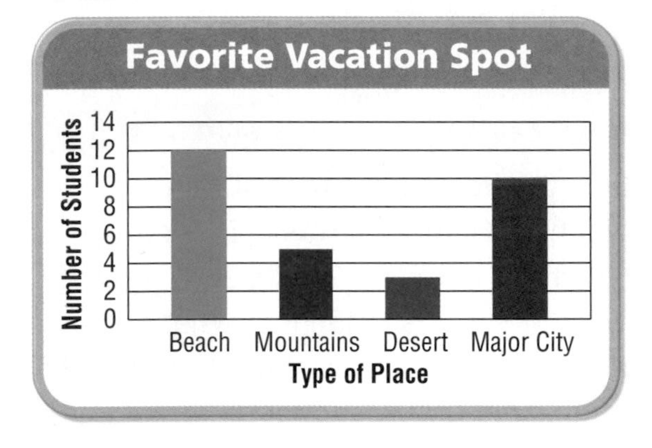

The horizontal axis on this bar graph shows different locations.

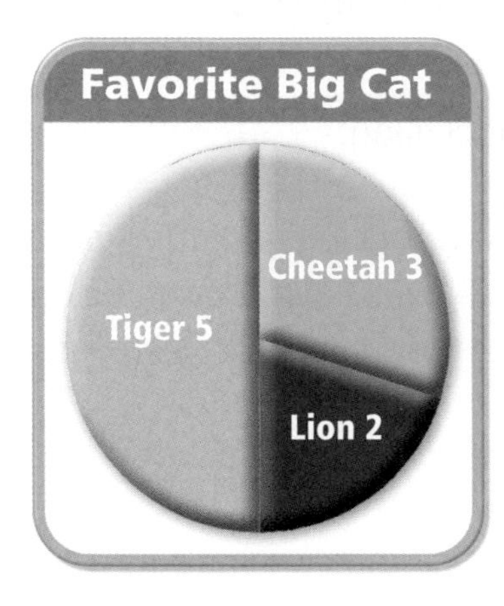

The parts on this circle graph show different types of big cats.

Numerical data includes numbers. The data is ordered numerically. You can use a line graph, a stem-and-leaf plot, a line plot, a bar graph, or a circle graph to show data that is numerical.

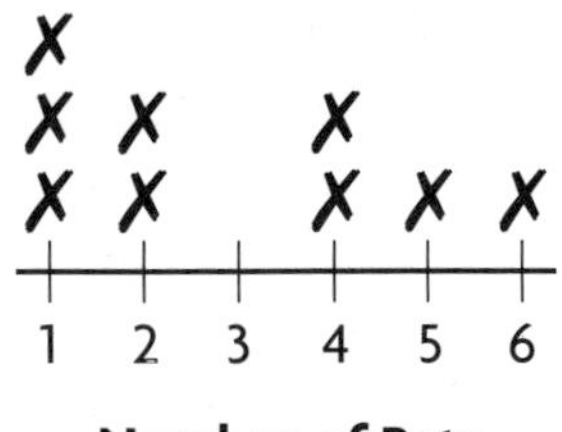

This line plot shows numbers of pets students have. For example, two students have 4 pets.

Student Heights (in inches)

Stem	Leaves
3	5 7 7 9
4	0 3 5 7 8
5	1 3 6

4 | 1 represents 41

A stem-and-leaf plot shows a number for each student's height.

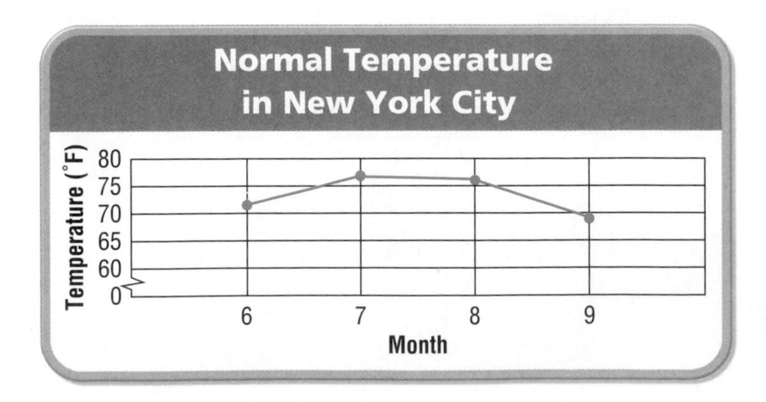

This line graph shows the numerical data for temperature and time.

SDAP 1.2 Organize and display single-variable data in appropriate graphs and representations (e.g., histogram, circle graphs) and explain which type of graphs are appropriate for various data sets. *also* **SDAP 1.0, MR 2.3, MR 2.4, MR 3.2**

What is the best graph for the data?

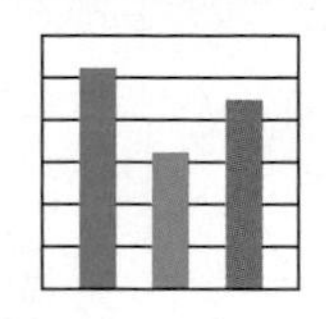

A bar graph or a double-bar graph compares data by category.

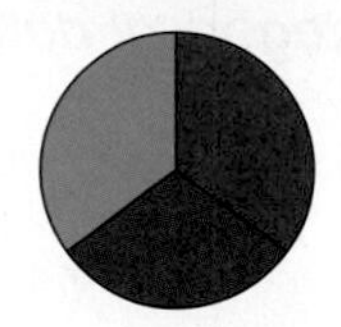

A circle graph compares parts of a group to the whole group.

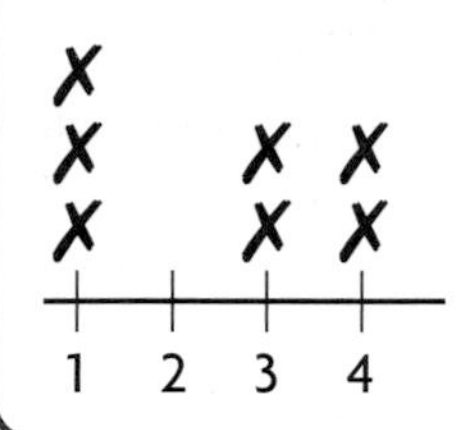

A line plot keeps count of data to show frequency.

A line graph shows how data changes over time.

Stem	Leaves
3	1 7
4	5

A stem-and-leaf plot organizes data by place value.

Neil, Moira, and Chuck each displayed the rainfall data in a graph. Who chose the best graph?

Average March Rainfall	
City	**Rainfall (in inches)**
San Diego, CA	1.8
El Paso, TX	0.3
Lansing, MI	2.4

Neil's Stem-and-Leaf Plot

Average March Rainfall

Stem	Leaves
0	3
1	8
2	4

1 | 8 represents 1.8

This graph does not include which city had a given rainfall. So, a stem-and-leaf plot is *not* the best way to display the data.

Moira's Bar Graph

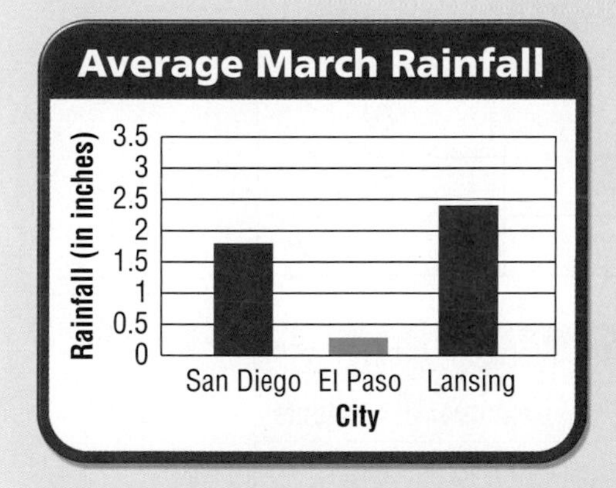

The bar graph compares the rainfall measured in different cities for the same month. So, a bar graph is a good choice to display the data.

Chuck's Line Graph

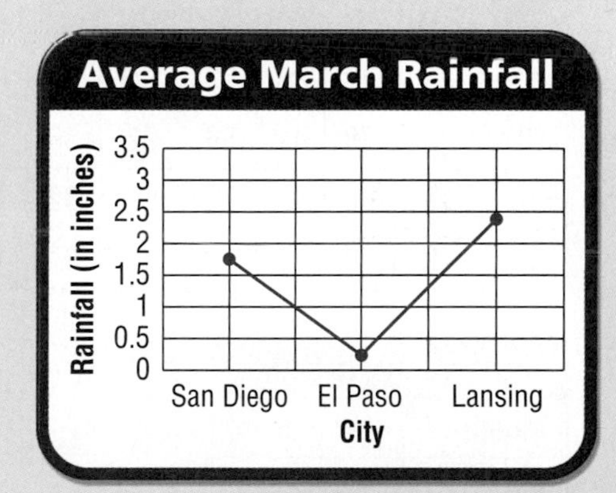

The data in the table does not change over time. The average amount of rainfall is given for different cities, not one city. So, a line graph is *not* the best way to display the data.

So, Moira's bar graph is the best choice to display the data.

Guided Practice

Tell whether each graph can show *categorical data, numerical data,* or *both.*

1. 

2. 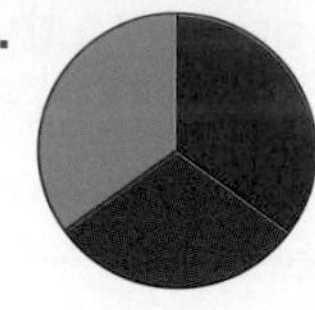

3. 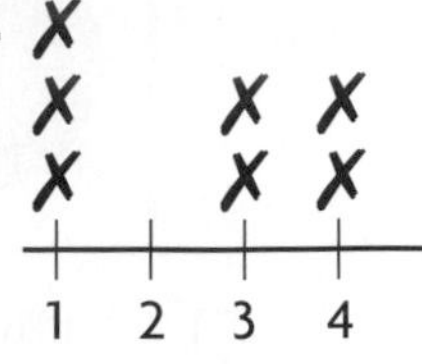

4.

Stem	Leaves
3	1
4	5

✓5. 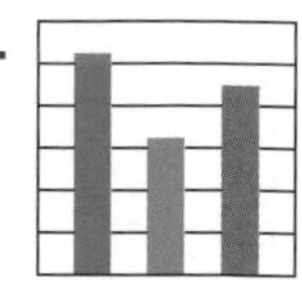

Choose the best type of graph or plot for the data. Explain your choice.

6. video game scores of 20 players
7. book sales each day for 5 days
✓8. how Jen spends the hours in one day
9. TALK Math **Explain** how you can determine if a graph shows numerical or categorical data.

Independent Practice and Problem Solving

Choose the best type of graph or plot for the data. Explain your choice.

10. numbers of students in six schools
11. minutes students spend practicing piano
12. high temperature each day for one week

Draw the graph or plot that best displays each set of data. Tell whether the data is *categorical* or *numerical.*

13.

Dog Weights (in pounds)							
35	32	48	89	93	125	12	17
132	116	78	41	56	92	36	87
10	15	38	45	76	99	82	105
56	72	39	14	23	83	97	112

14.

Henry's Allowance Budget	
Activity	**Amount**
Savings	$3
Entertainment	$5
Other	$2

15.

Skateboard Sales	
Month	**Sales**
April	$325
May	$450
June	$265

16.

Favorite Winter Activity	
Activity	**Number of Students**
Hockey	8
Skiing	17
Snowboarding	21

17. **Reasoning** Which graph would you make if you wanted to identify the median and mode from the graph?

18. WRITE Math **Explain** how you decide which type of graph is most appropriate for a set of data.

 Extra Practice on page 638, Set D

Achieving the Standards

19. Kyle ran m miles yesterday. Today he ran 5.25 miles. If $m = 6.5$, how many miles did Kyle run in all? (AF 1.2, p. 348)

20. **Test Prep** What type of graph would best display the data in the table? **Explain.**

Yearbook Sales				
Week	1	2	3	4
Amount	\$6	\$75	\$95	\$40

21. **Test Prep** Which set of data is categorical?

 A test scores of 30 students

 B amount of snowfall in five cities during January

 C alma's bowling scores in four consecutive games

 D low temperature each month for six months

Problem Solving and Reasoning

VISUAL THINKING A graph can show data that is discrete or continuous. A graph that shows **continuous data** can be read between points. A graph that shows **discrete data** can only be read at its points.

Example **Tell whether the graph shows *discrete* or *continuous* data.**

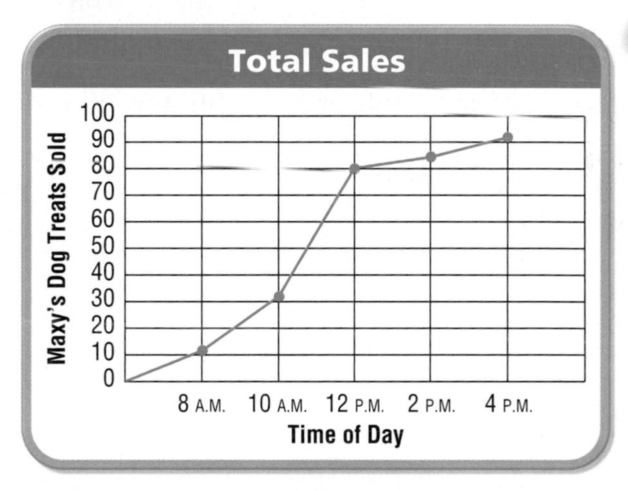

Maxy's dog treats are sold only in 8-ounce boxes. **Think:** Can I buy $1\frac{1}{2}$ boxes of Maxy's dog treats? Since the answer is no, this graph shows discrete data.

Time is continuous. **Think:** Were Maxy's dog treats sold between 8 A.M. and 10 A.M.? Since the answer is yes, this graph shows continuous data.

1. What question could you ask yourself to determine if a graph of a dog's weight over several months shows discrete or continuous data?

2. Tell whether a graph of a dog's weight shows continuous or discrete data. Explain.

Extra Practice

Set A Decide whether a bar graph or a histogram would better represent the data. Then make the graph. (pp. 624–625)

1.

Music Lessons	
Instrument	**Number of Lessons**
Piano	10
Guitar	28
Cello	12
Drum	16

2.

Number of Hours Worked			
11	8	12	14
16	17	6	4
10	5	15	9
3	20	6	15

Set B For 1–5, use the hiking data. (pp. 626–627)

1. Use the data to make a stem-and-leaf plot.
2. What is the greatest number of hikers? the least number of hikers?
3. What is the range of hikers?
4. How many days had more than 70 hikers?
5. Which number of hikers occurred most often?

Daily Number of Hikers				
68	71	54	62	85
80	79	85	73	67
86	92	70	64	92
59	90	85	87	71

Set C Make a line graph or a double-line graph for each set of data. (pp. 628–631)

1.

Amount of Rainfall	
Month	**Amount (in inches)**
Jan (1)	8
Feb (2)	12
March (3)	20
Apr (4)	16

2.

School Store Sales					
Day	1	2	3	4	5
Middle School	\$45	\$30	\$125	\$100	\$25
High School	\$105	\$90	\$80	\$95	\$50

Set D Choose the best type of graph or plot for the data. Explain your choice. (pp. 634–637)

1. population of an island over a 3-month period
2. how Juan spent his week of vacation
3. number of family members
4. math test scores for the students in a fifth-grade class
5. magazine sales each day for 7 days
6. ages of the children in an after-school program

CD ROM
Technology
Use Harcourt Mega Math, The Number Games, *Arachna-Graph*, Levels I, J.

IT'S A TOSS-UP

Get Ready!
2 players

Get Set!
- 10 beanbags
- large coordinate grid

Start Tossing!

- Player 1 stands about 10 feet from the grid and tries to toss 10 bean bags onto it.
- Player 2 graphs the results on a coordinate grid. For example, in Round 1, a result of 4 tosses on the grid would be graphed as the ordered pair (1,4) where the *x*-coordinate is the round number and the *y*-coordinate is the number of tosses that landed on the grid.
- Player 2 repeats the process.
- After 4 rounds, players connect the points marked.
- Players compare results and discuss how their results changed over time.
- Players decide how to choose a winner. Should the player who had the greater number of tosses that landed on the grid in any round win the game? Or, should the player who shows the greater increase between Round 1 and Round 4 win the game? Is there another way to determine the winner?

Check Vocabulary and Concepts

Choose the best term from the box.

VOCABULARY
categorical data
double-line graph
histogram
numerical data
stem-and-leaf plot

1. A table that shows groups of data arranged by place value is a _?_. (SDAP 1.2, p. 626)
2. A _?_ is a type of bar graph that shows frequency. (SDAP 1.2, p. 624)
3. When graphed, _?_ shows groups or choices in any order. (SDAP 1.2, p. 634)
4. When graphed, _?_ shows numbers in order on a numerical scale of the graph. (SDAP 1.2, p. 634)

Check Skills

Make the graph for each set of data. (SDAP 1.2, O-π SDAP 1.4; pp. 624–625, 626–627, 628–631)

5. histogram

Ages of Cyclists			
11	9	12	13
25	7	18	9
11	15	20	8
15	10	26	28

6. stem-and-leaf plot

Lunches Served			
45	39	49	53
45	47	38	45
51	39	51	38
45	37	46	44

7. line graph

Rainfall	
Month	Amount (in inches)
April	16
May	12
June	10
July	9

Choose the best type of graph or plot for the data. (SDAP 1.2, pp. 634–637)

8. ages of all the runners in a marathon by range
9. height of a plant over a one-month period
10. number of students in five clubs
11. heights of students in a fifth-grade class
12. frequency of library visits
13. how Janine spends her allowance money

Check Problem Solving

Solve. (SDAP 1.0, MR 2.3, MR 2.4, pp. 632–633)

14. Write *yes* or *no* to tell whether each conclusion can be drawn from the data in the line graph. **Explain.**
    a. Membership decreased from year 3 to year 4.
    b. Membership was never greater than 20.
15. WRITE Math **Explain** what conclusion you could make if the membership for year 6 was 43.

GO ONLINE **Technology** Use *Online Assessment.*

Enrich • Relationships in Graphs

Graphs are used to show relationships between different quantities. The graph below shows the relationship between the number of people attending a concert and the time period during which people arrive at the concert pavilion and then leave. The concert occurs from the second through the fourth hour, but people arrive and leave during a 5-hour span.

Example

- **From 0 to 1 hours:** People begin arriving at the pavilion for the concert.
- **From 1 to 2 hours:** Most people arrive. At the end of the interval, the concert begins.
- **Hour 2:** The concert starts.
- **From 2 to 4 hours:** It is a long concert.
- **Hour 4:** The concert ends. The audience members leave to go home.

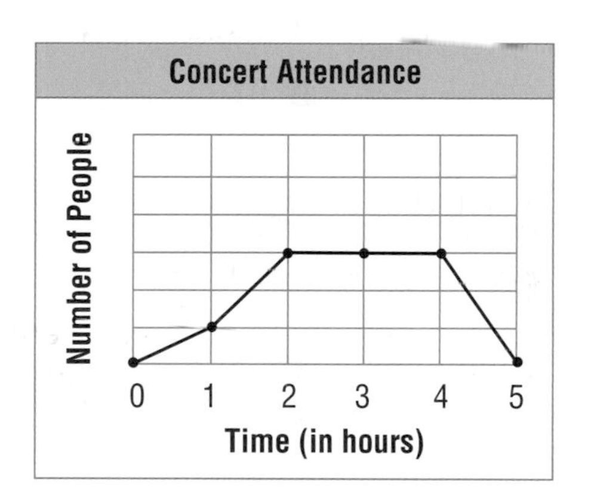

Try It

For each graph, choose the correct description.

1.

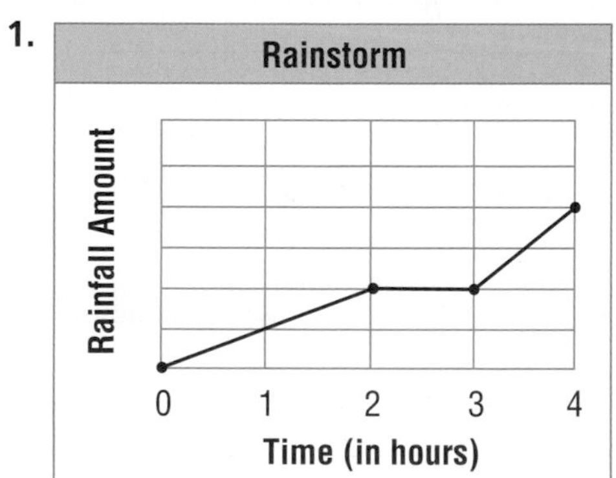

a. The amount of rainfall decreases or is steady.
b. It stops raining for 2 hours.
c. The amount of rainfall increases or is steady.

2.

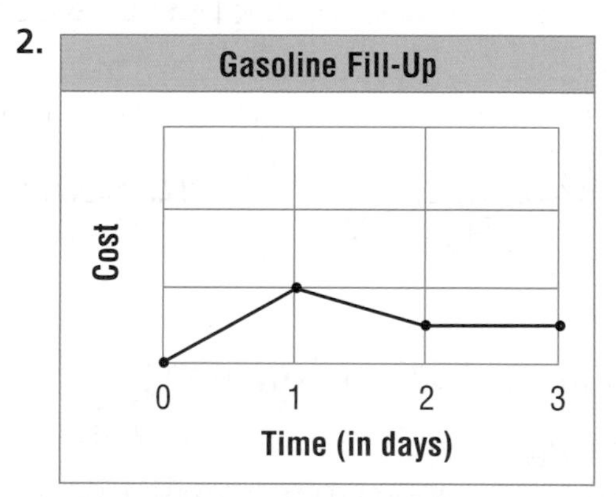

a. After 1 day, the cost rises.
b. After 2 days, the cost stabilizes.
c. The cost after 2 days is the lowest.

WRITE Math Graph the relationship of the distance traveled in a car and the amount of time it takes to travel that distance. **Explain** what might be taking place when your graph increases or decreases, or the graph is steady.

Unit Review/Test
Chapters 23–24

Multiple Choice

1.

Jonquil's Test Scores						
94	93	95	78	94	81	85

What is the median of Jonquil's test scores? **(SDAP 1.1, p. 604)**

A 85 **C** 93

B 87 **D** 94

2.

The Hawks' Game Scores				
42	50	45	43	42

What is the mean of the scores for the 5 games played? **(SDAP 1.1, p. 602)**

A 42 **C** 44

B 43.5 **D** 44.4

3. Which student had the highest mean test score? **(SDAP 1.1, p. 602)**

Name	Test 1	Test 2	Test 3	Test 4
Ally	87	93	99	95
Brad	95	90	91	91
Charles	87	92	88	90
Dill	74	100	92	98

A Ally

B Brad

C Charles

D Dill

4. What is the mode of the data? **(SDAP 1.1, p. 604)**

Number of Tickets Sold

Stem	Leaves
1	1 1 4
2	0 2 6 8
3	1 2 7 7 7
4	0 2 2 3 5

A 11 **C** 42

B 37 **D** 45

5. If the trend continues, about how long would it take Casey to walk 20 miles? **(O-π SDAP 1.4, p. 608)**

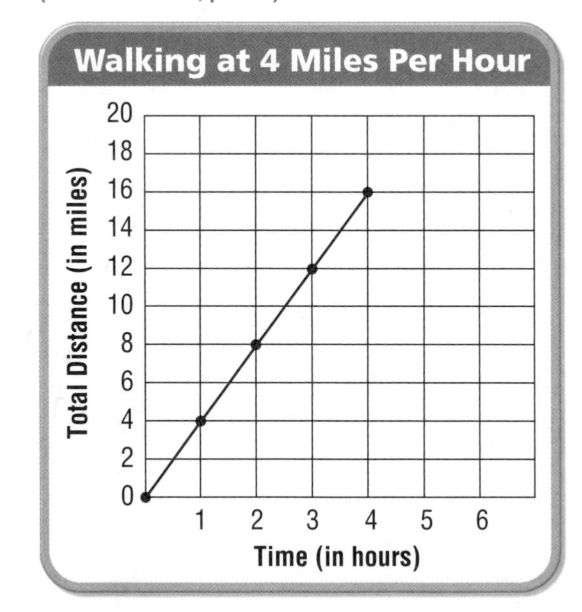

A 4 hours

B 5 hours

C 6 hours

D 20 hours

GO ONLINE **Technology** Use *Online Assessment.*

6. Which type of graph would *best* display the following data? **(SDAP 1.2, p. 634)**

Swim Team Size	
Grade	**Number of Swimmers**
Third Grade	18
Fourth Grade	20
Fifth Grade	26
Sixth Grade	24

A bar graph

B histogram

C line graph

D circle graph

Short Response

7. Of the students surveyed, what is the most popular type of exercise? What is the least popular? **(SDAP 1.2, p. 608)**

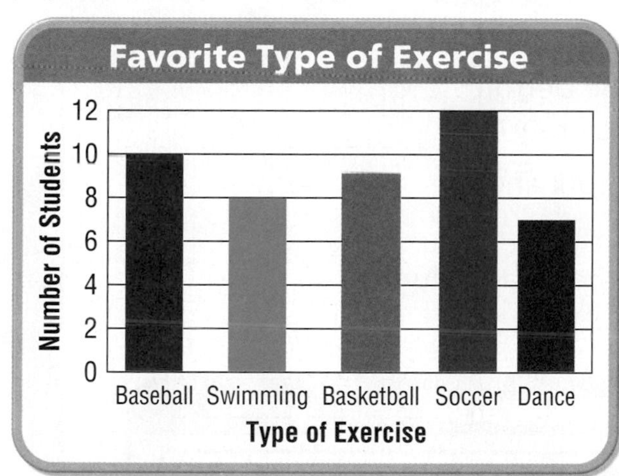

8. Sue has taken 4 tests in math class. She has a mean test score of 89. Her mode is 88 and her highest score is 99. What are her 4 test scores? Show your work. **(SDAP 1.1, p. 604)**

Extended Response WRITE Math

9.

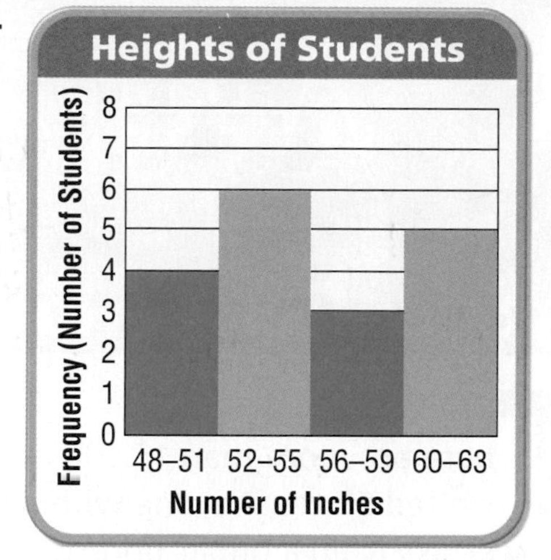

Look at the histogram. In which group do the heights of the most students fall? Where do the least fall? How would the histogram change if the following students' data were added? **Explain.** **(SDAP 1.2, p. 624)**

Jayne:	56 inches
Carol:	61 inches
Matt:	59 inches

10. Use grid paper to make a line graph of the clock radio data.

Cal's Clock Radio Prices	
Year	**Price (dollars)**
1990	\$35
1995	\$32
2000	\$29

Are the prices increasing or decreasing? If the trend continues, how much do you predict the radio will cost in 2010? **Explain.** **(O-π SDAP 1.4, p. 628)**

California

Problem Solving

from THE WORLD ALMANAC FOR KIDS

At the Library

Library Collections

There are more than 15,000 public libraries in the United States. Anyone with a current library card can borrow books from a public library. Many library systems have thousands of volumes. The Los Angeles Public Library has more than 6 million! Volumes include books and magazines. However, most libraries also have music, movies, or recorded books that can be checked out to enjoy. Some libraries have special programs like reading contests.

Use the graph to answer the questions.

1. How many more volumes in millions does the Detroit Public Library hold than the Chicago Public Library?
2. How many volumes in millions do the New York and Los Angeles Libraries have combined?
3. WRITE Math **Explain** how you could find the mean volumes of the libraries in the graph.

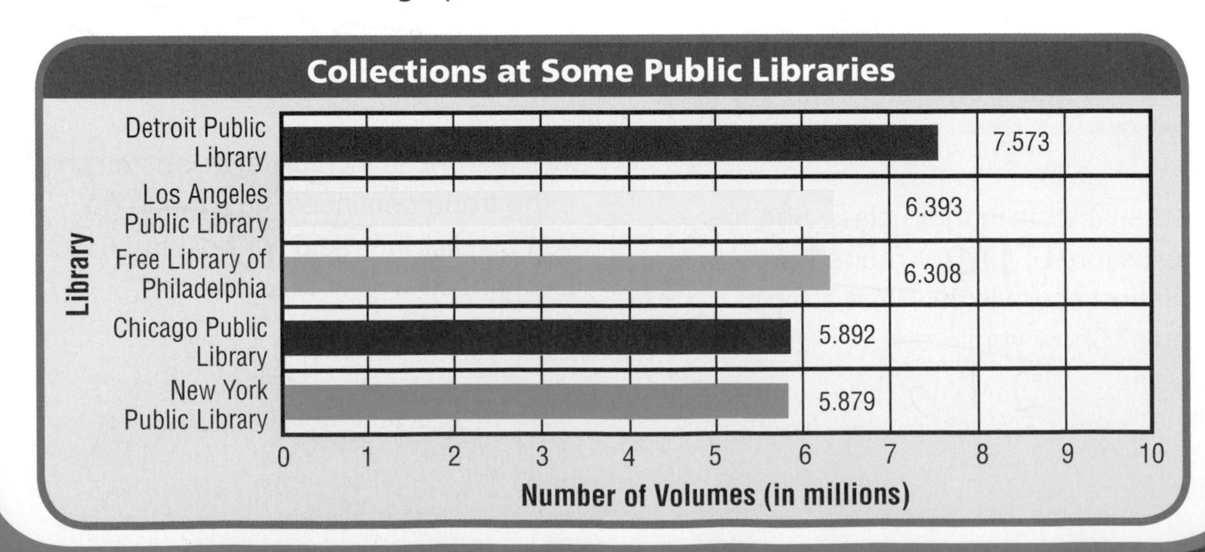

ALMANAC Fact

The San Francisco Public Library has a historical photograph collection that includes thousands of San Francisco and California photographs.

KEEP THEM CIRCULATING

In 1731, Benjamin Franklin helped launch the Library Company, which became the first public library that circulated books. A book "circulates" when someone borrows it and then returns it. Circulation statistics show how many library books are checked out during a specific amount of time.

FACT·ACTIVITY

Use the table to answer the questions.

1. Stack 10 books from your classroom in one pile. Measure the height of the stack with a yardstick. What is the mean height of one book?
2. If you could make one pile of all of the books in San Diego's circulation, estimate how high would the stack be.
3. Choose four of the circulation numbers. Round each to the nearest hundred thousand.
   - Decide what kind of graph would be best to compare the rounded amounts. Then make a scale for your graph. Draw your graph, but do not label the library names.
   - Switch graphs with a partner. Determine the four libraries on your partner's graph and finish the graph.

Circulation for a Year in Some California Libraries

Library	Circulation
Alameda County Library	5,072,419
Los Angeles Public Library	15,333,869
Orange County Public Library	6,875,502
San Diego Public Library	7,242,394
San Francisco Public Library	6,802,185
San Jose Public Library	14,170,776

Student Handbook

Review the Key Standards

Percent as Part of a Hundred

NS 1.2 Interpret percents as a part of a hundred; find decimal and percent equivalents for common fractions and explain why they represent the same value; compute a given percent of a whole number.

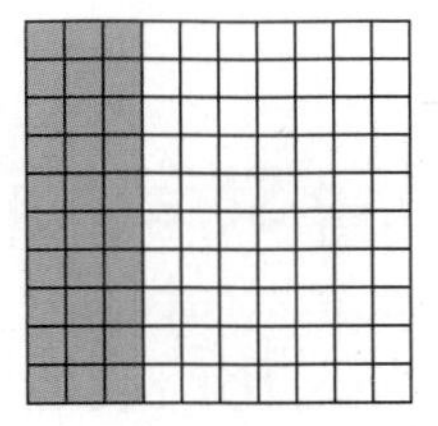

Percent is the fractional part of a number to 100. The symbol for percent is %. 1% means 1 out of 100. In the figure at the right, 30 out of 100 squares are shaded. Write: 30%

Examples

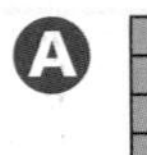

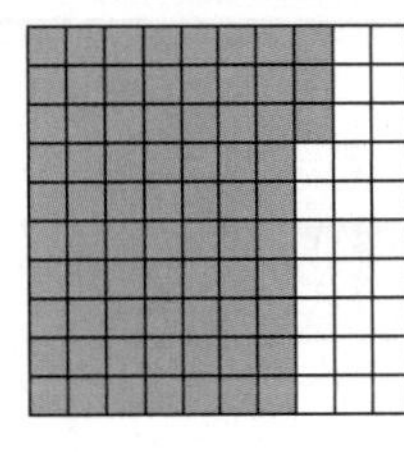

$\frac{73}{100} = 73\%$

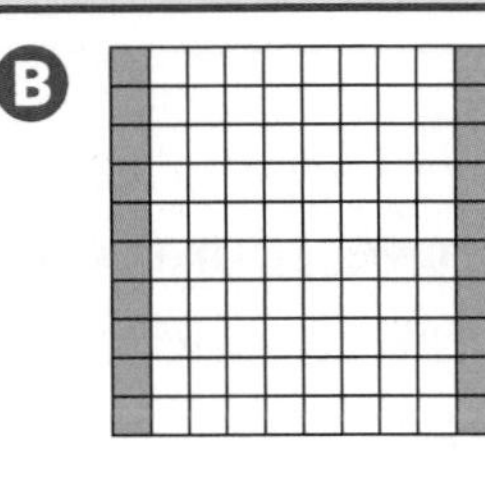

$\frac{20}{100} = 20\%$

ERROR ALERT

The total number of parts is 100. Then write the number of shaded parts with a % sign to describe the percent that is shaded.

Try It

Write a percent to represent the shaded part.

1. 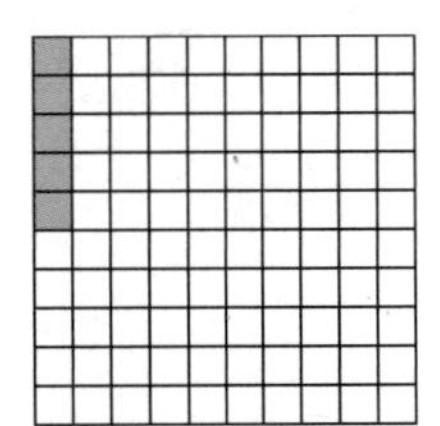

2. 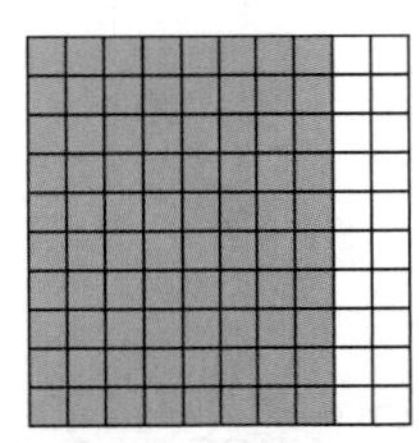

3. 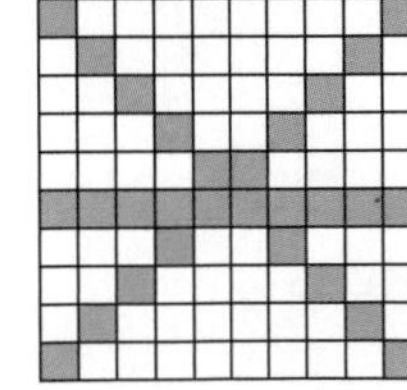

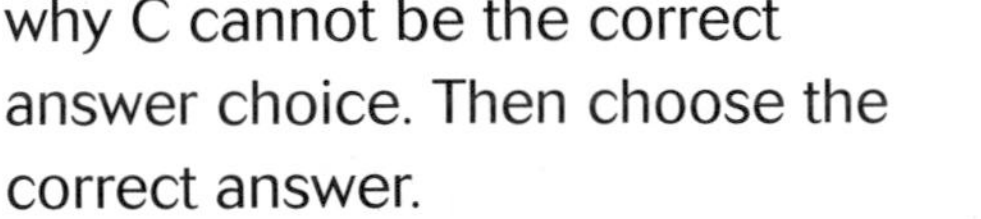

4. Read the problem below. **Explain** why C cannot be the correct answer choice. Then choose the correct answer.

COMMON ERROR

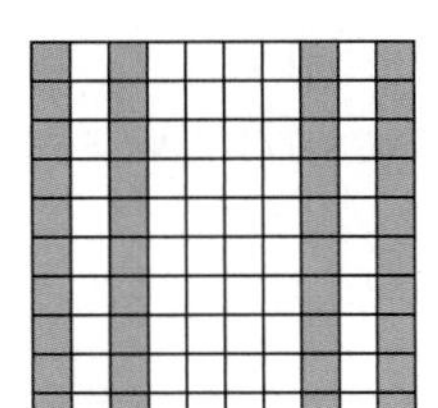

Which of the following best describes the shaded part of the whole?

A 4

B 4%

C 40

D 40%

Review the Key Standards

Fractions, Decimals, and Percents

NS 1.2 Interpret percents as a part of a hundred; find decimal and percent equivalents for common fractions and explain why they represent the same value; compute a given percent of a whole number.

A fraction can be written as a percent and as a decimal.

A Decimal

Use equivalent fractions.

$\frac{3}{4} = \frac{3 \times 25}{4 \times 25} = \frac{75}{100}$

$\frac{75}{100} = 75\%$

$\frac{75}{100} = 0.75$

B Percent

Use division.

$\frac{1}{8} = 8\overline{)1} \quad 8\overline{)1.000}$ = 0.125

$0.125 = 12.5\%$

More Examples

C $\frac{2}{5} = \frac{2 \times 20}{5 \times 20} = \frac{40}{100}$

$\frac{40}{100} = 40\%$

$\frac{40}{100} = 0.40$

D $\frac{7}{8} = 8\overline{)7}$

$8\overline{)7.000}$ = 0.875

$0.875 = 87.5\%$

ERROR ALERT

Be sure to write an equivalent fraction with a denominator of 100 to find the percent and decimal for a fraction.

Try It

Write a decimal and a percent for the fraction.

1. $\frac{1}{2}$
2. $\frac{3}{10}$
3. $\frac{11}{25}$
4. $\frac{5}{8}$
5. $\frac{4}{5}$
6. $\frac{7}{20}$
7. $\frac{3}{15}$
8. $\frac{1}{4}$
9. $\frac{3}{8}$
10. $\frac{9}{20}$

11. Read the problem below. **Explain** why B cannot be the correct answer choice. Then choose the correct answer.

What is the fraction $\frac{3}{5}$ written as a percent?

A 3.5%

B 6%

C 35%

D 60%

Review the Key Standards

Percent of a Number

NS 1.2 Interpret percents as a part of a hundred; find decimal and percent equivalents for common fractions and explain why they represent the same value; compute a given percent of a whole number.

To find the percent of a number, write the percent as a decimal and multiply.

$$\begin{array}{l} 75\% \text{ of } 48 \\ \downarrow \quad \downarrow \ \downarrow \\ 0.75 \times 48 = 36 \end{array}$$

You can also change the percent to a fraction and multiply.

$$75\% = \frac{75}{100} = \frac{75 \div 25}{100 \div 25} = \frac{3}{4} \qquad \frac{3}{4} \times \frac{48}{1} = \frac{144}{4} = 36$$

Examples

A What is 5% of 180?

$5\% = 0.05$

$0.05 \times 180 = 9$

So, 5% of 180 is 9.

B What is 60% of 25?

$60\% = \frac{60}{100} = \frac{60 \div 20}{100 \div 20} = \frac{3}{5}$

$\frac{3}{5} \times \frac{25}{1} = \frac{75}{5} = 15$

So, 60% of 25 is 15.

ERROR ALERT

Be sure to use hundredths when writing a percent as a decimal.

5% is 0.05, not 0.5.

Try It

Find the percent of the number.

1. 25% of 30
2. 70% of 120
3. 8% of 80
4. 20% of 225
5. 95% of 32
6. 3% of 45
7. 4% of 74
8. 31% of 98
9. 30% of 30
10. 85% of 42
11. 25% of 64
12. 60% of 60
13. 15% of 120
14. 85% of 34
15. 90% of 90
16. 75% of 300
17. 13% of 12
18. 1% of 100
19. 8% of 72
20. 19% of 60

21. Read the problem below. **Explain** why D cannot be the correct answer choice. Then choose the correct answer. **COMMON ERROR**

What is 9% of 180?

A 0.05

B 16.2

C 20

D 162

Review the Key Standards

Prime Factors

NS 1.4 Determine the prime factors of all numbers through 50 and write the numbers as the product of their prime factors by using exponents to show multiples of a factor. (e.g., $24 = 2 \times 2 \times 2 \times 3 = 2^3 \times 3$).

All composite numbers can be written as the product of prime factors. This is called the prime factorization of the number. When a prime factor is repeated in a factorization, an exponent is used to show the number of times the factor is repeated.

$$18 = 2 \times 3 \times 3 = 2 \times 3^2$$

Prime Numbers less than 25:

2, 3, 5, 7, 11, 13, 17, 19, 23

Examples

A factor tree is a diagram that shows the prime factorization of a composite number.

A Prime factorization of 30

30

5 × 6

5 × 2 × 3

So, $30 = 5 \times 2 \times 3$.

B Prime factorization of 36

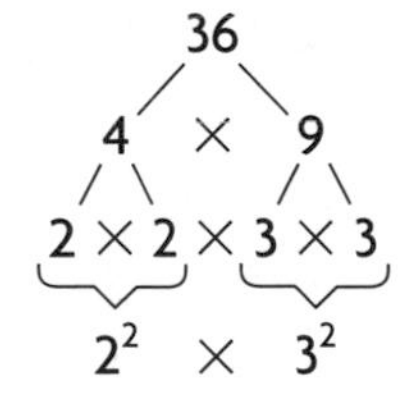

So, $36 = 2^2 \times 3^2$.

ERROR ALERT

Be sure that all the factors in a prime factorization are prime numbers.

Try It

Find the prime factorization.

1. 32
2. 27
3. 48
4. 42
5. 20
6. 28
7. 40
8. 12
9. 81
10. 24
11. 155
12. 630

Rewrite the prime factorization using exponents.

13. $3 \times 2 \times 2$
14. $2 \times 11 \times 2$
15. $2 \times 3 \times 2 \times 2$
16. $5 \times 2 \times 5$
17. $2 \times 3 \times 5 \times 5$
18. $7 \times 7 \times 11 \times 11$
19. $2 \times 13 \times 13$
20. $2 \times 5 \times 19 \times 5$

21. Read the problem below. **Explain** why D cannot be the correct answer choice. Then choose the correct answer.

What is the prime factorization of 45?

A 5×3^2

B 5×2^3

C 3×5^2

D 5×9

Review the Key Standards

Decimals, Fractions, and Mixed Numbers on a Number Line

NS 1.5 Identify and represent on a number line decimals, fractions, mixed numbers, and positive and negative integers.

A fraction or decimal can be shown on a number line.

Benchmark fractions are familiar fractions used for reference. The fractions $\frac{1}{4}$, $\frac{1}{2}$, and $\frac{3}{4}$ are often used as benchmarks on number lines. The decimals 0.25, 0.50, and 0.75 are equivalent to the benchmark fractions.

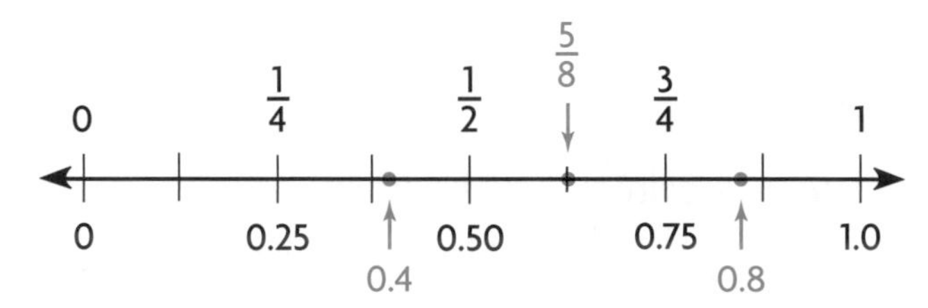

You can use the benchmarks to locate other decimals and fractions on the number line.

Example

Identify the numbers at points *A* and *B*.

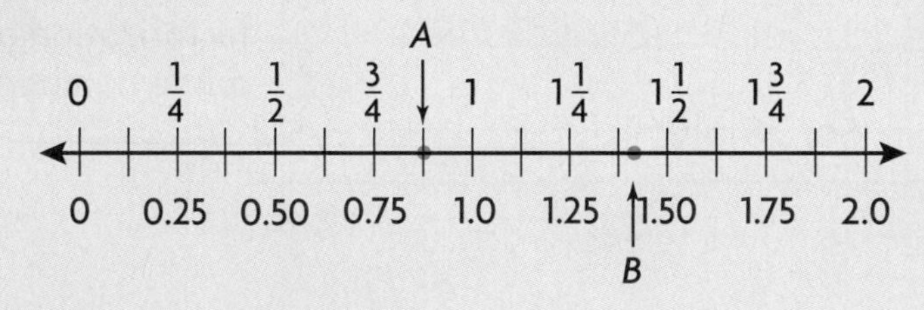

The fraction at point *A* is $\frac{7}{8}$.
The decimal at point *B* is 1.40.

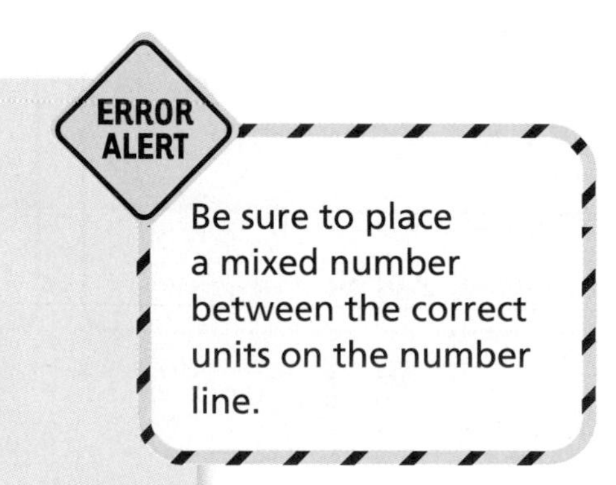

ERROR ALERT
Be sure to place a mixed number between the correct units on the number line.

Try It

Identify a fraction and a decimal for each point.

1. *A* **2.** *B* **3.** *C* **4.** *D*

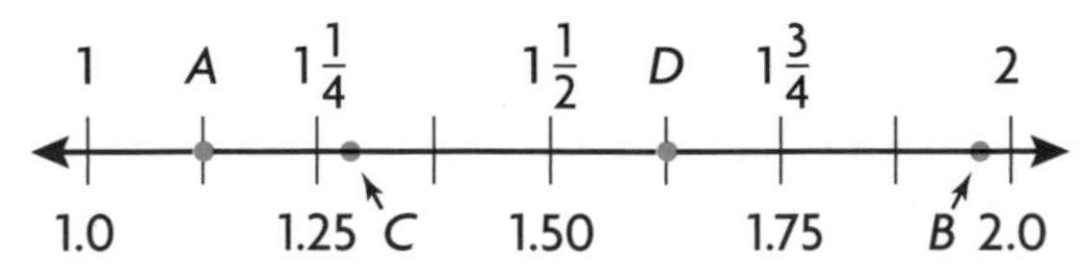

Locate each mixed number or decimal on a number line.

5. $1\frac{3}{4}$ **6.** $1\frac{2}{5}$ **7.** $\frac{3}{8}$

8. 1.9 **9.** 0.3 **10.** 1.2

11. Read the problem below. **Explain** why A cannot be the correct answer choice. Then choose the correct answer.

What is the decimal at point *P*?

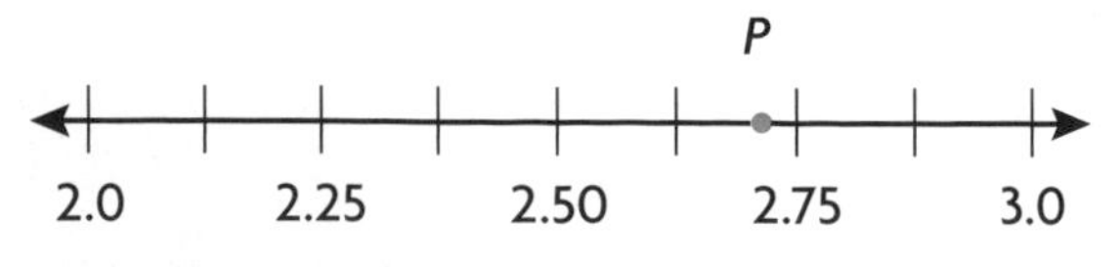

A 1.70 **C** 2.60

B 2.55 **D** 2.70

Review the Key Standards

Integers on a Number Line

NS 1.5 Identify and represent on a number line decimals, fractions, mixed numbers, and positive and negative integers.

Integers are the set of whole numbers and their opposites. You can show integers on a number line.

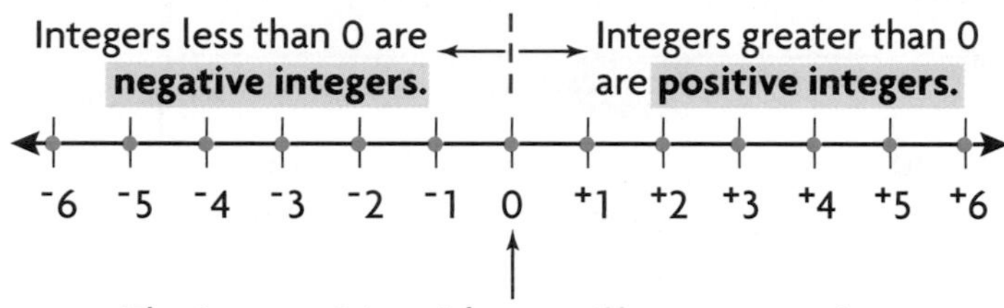

The integer 0 is neither positive nor negative.

Examples

A Identify the integer at point *P*.

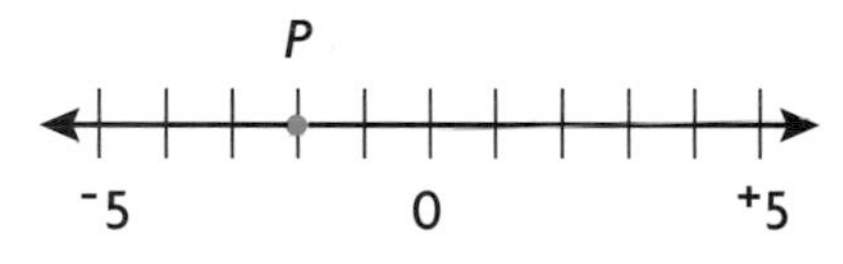

The integer at point *P* is $^{-}2$.

B Write an integer to represent the situation.

10 seconds before liftoff

$^{-}10$ is 10 seconds before liftoff.

ERROR ALERT

Use a negative sign for an integer to the left of zero and a positive sign for an integer to the right of zero.

Try It

Use the number line. Write the letter for each integer.

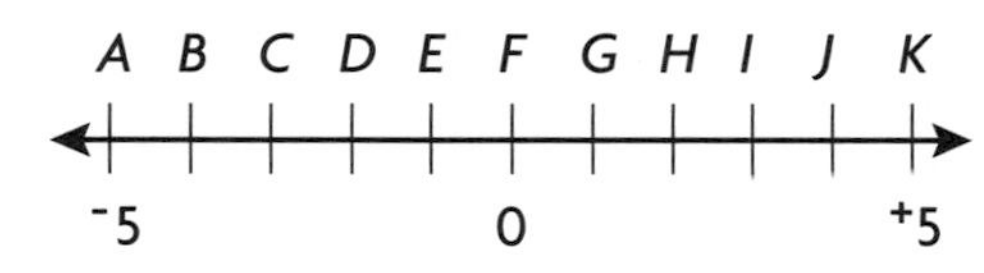

1. $^{-}1$ **2.** $^{+}4$ **3.** $^{-}3$ **4.** 0
5. $^{-}4$ **6.** $^{+}2$ **7.** $^{-}2$ **8.** $^{+}1$

Write an integer to represent each situation.

9. a profit of $200
10. 25 feet below sea level
11. 8 degrees above 0
12. 60 feet above the ground
13. a hole 6 feet deep
14. withdrawal of $130

15. Read the problem below. **Explain** why D cannot be the correct answer choice. Then choose the correct answer.

COMMON ERROR

What is the integer at point *T*?

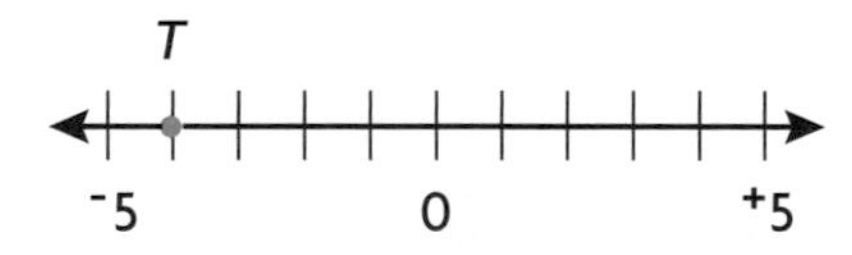

A $^{-}4$
B $^{-}2$
C $^{+}2$
D $^{+}4$

Review the Key Standards

Add and Subtract Decimals

NS 2.1 Add, subtract, multiply, and divide with decimals; add with negative integers; subtract positive integers from negative integers; and verify the reasonableness of the results.

Add. 38.924 + 15.457 Estimate. 38 + 15 = 53

Step 1

Line up the decimal points to align place-value positions. Add the thousandths.

$$\begin{array}{r} \scriptstyle 1 \\ 38.924 \\ +\,15.457 \\ \hline 1 \end{array}$$

Step 2

Add the hundredths. Add the tenths. Regroup as needed.

$$\begin{array}{r} \scriptstyle 1\ \ 1 \\ 38.924 \\ +\,15.457 \\ \hline 381 \end{array}$$

Step 3

Add the ones and tens. Place the decimal point in the sum.

$$\begin{array}{r} \scriptstyle 1 \\ 38.924 \\ +\,15.457 \\ \hline 54.381 \end{array}$$

Examples

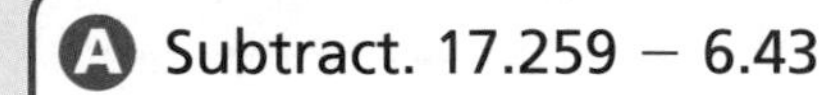

A Subtract. 17.259 − 6.43

$$\begin{array}{r} \scriptstyle 6\ 12 \\ 1\not{7}.\not{2}59 \\ -\ 6.430 \\ \hline 10.829 \end{array}$$

B Add. 7.1 + 5.96 + 2.805

$$\begin{array}{r} \scriptstyle 1 \\ 7.100 \\ 5.960 \\ +\ 2.805 \\ \hline 15.865 \end{array}$$

Place zeros to make equivalent decimals if the decimals do not have the same number of decimal places.

2.79 = 2.790

Try It

Estimate. Then find the sum or difference.

1. $4.79 + $2.25
2. 8.349 − 2.561
3. 32.087 + 59.63
4. 82.397 − 54.8
5. $\begin{array}{r} 23.09 \\ 15.471 \\ +\ 7.8 \\ \hline \end{array}$
6. $\begin{array}{r} 46.75 \\ -\ 5.369 \\ \hline \end{array}$

7. Read the problem below. **Explain** why D cannot be the correct answer choice. Then choose the correct answer. COMMON ERROR

Subtract. 56.78 − 39.013

A 17.65 **C** 17.767

B 17.695 **D** 17.773

Review the Key Standards

Multiply and Divide Decimals

NS 2.1 Add, subtract, multiply, and divide with decimals; add with negative integers; subtract positive integers from negative integers; and verify the reasonableness of the results.

Multiply. 5.3×2.47

Step 1

Multiply as with whole numbers.

$$\begin{array}{r} {}^{2\ 3}_{1\ 2} \\ 2.47 \\ \times\ \ 5.3 \\ \hline 741 \\ +\ 12350 \\ \hline 13091 \end{array}$$

Step 2

Count the decimal places in both factors. Place the decimal point that number of places from the right in the product.

$$\begin{array}{rl} {}^{2\ 3}_{1\ 2} & \\ 2.47 & \leftarrow \text{2 decimal places in 2.47} \\ \times\ \ 5.3 & \leftarrow \text{1 decimal place in 5.3} \\ \hline 741 & \\ +\ 12350 & \\ \hline 13.091 & \leftarrow \text{2 + 1, or 3 decimal places in the product} \end{array}$$

Examples

A Divide. $4.56 \div 1.2$

$$1.2\overline{)4.56} \rightarrow \begin{array}{r} 3.8 \\ 12\overline{)45.6} \\ -\ 36 \\ \hline 96 \\ -\ 96 \\ \hline 0 \end{array}$$

B Multiply. 0.24×0.318

$$\begin{array}{r} 0.318 \\ \times\ 0.24 \\ \hline 1272 \\ 6360 \\ \hline 0.07632 \end{array}$$

ERROR ALERT

Insert zeros at the left in the product to keep the same number of decimal places in the product as in the factors.

Try It

Estimate. Then find the product.

1. $18 \times \$0.79$
2. 9.23×3.7
3. 0.08×0.041
4. 0.35×51.2

Divide.

5. $85.3 \div 0.5$
6. $2.4\overline{)45.84}$
7. $3.28 \div 0.16$
8. $0.8\overline{)\$31.36}$

9. Read the problem below. **Explain** why D cannot be the correct answer choice. Then choose the correct answer.

Multiply. 0.094×0.86

A 0.08084

B 0.0804

C 0.80804

D 0.8084

Review the Key Standards

Add with Negative Integers

NS 2.1 Add, subtract, multiply, and divide with decimals; add with negative integers; subtract positive integers from negative integers; and verify the reasonableness of the results.

Use a number line to add integers.

Add. ${}^{-}6 + {}^{+}2$

Step 1

Draw a number line. Start at 0. Move 6 spaces to the left to represent ${}^{-}6$.

Step 2

From ${}^{-}6$, move 2 spaces to the right to represent ${}^{+}2$.

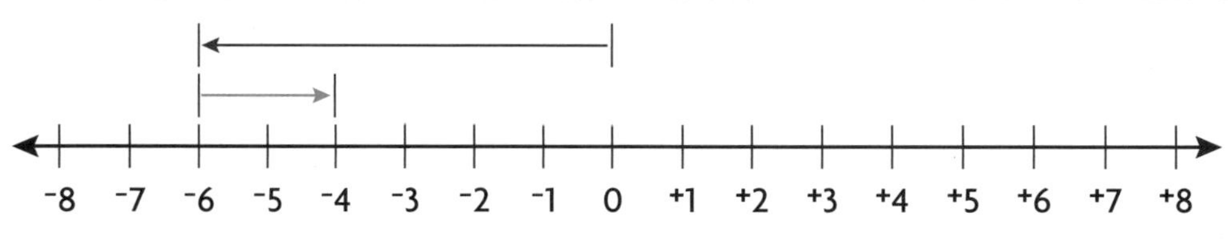

So, ${}^{-}6 + {}^{+}2 = {}^{-}4$.

Examples

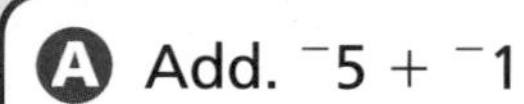

A Add. ${}^{-}5 + {}^{-}1$

Move 5 spaces to the left. Then move 1 space left. This takes you to ${}^{-}6$.

So, ${}^{-}5 + {}^{-}1 = {}^{-}6$.

B Add. ${}^{+}7 + {}^{-}2$

Move 7 spaces to the right. Then move 2 spaces left. This takes you to ${}^{+}5$.

So, ${}^{+}7 + {}^{-}2 = {}^{+}5$.

ERROR ALERT

The sum of two negative integers will always be a negative integer.

Try It

Find the sum.

1. ${}^{+}5 + {}^{-}7$
2. ${}^{-}2 + {}^{-}2$
3. ${}^{-}8 + {}^{+}3$
4. ${}^{+}6 + {}^{-}5$
5. ${}^{-}7 + {}^{+}10$
6. ${}^{+}1 + {}^{-}8$
7. ${}^{-}4 + {}^{-}1$
8. ${}^{+}2 + {}^{-}3$
9. ${}^{+}6 + {}^{-}6$
10. ${}^{-}1 + {}^{-}7$

11. Read the problem below. **Explain** why D cannot be the correct answer choice. Then choose the correct answer. **COMMON ERROR**

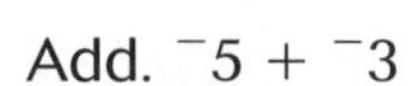

Add. ${}^{-}5 + {}^{-}3$

A ${}^{-}8$ **C** ${}^{+}2$

B ${}^{-}2$ **D** ${}^{+}8$

Review the Key Standards

Subtract Positive Integers from Negative Integers

NS 2.1 Add, subtract, multiply, and divide with decimals; add with negative integers; subtract positive integers from negative integers; and verify the reasonableness of the results.

Use a number line to subtract a positive integer from a negative integer.

Subtract. $^{-}3 - {}^{+}5$

Step 1

Draw a number line. Start at 0. Move 3 spaces to the left to represent $^{-}3$.

Step 2

To subtract $^{+}5$, move 5 spaces to the left from $^{-}3$.

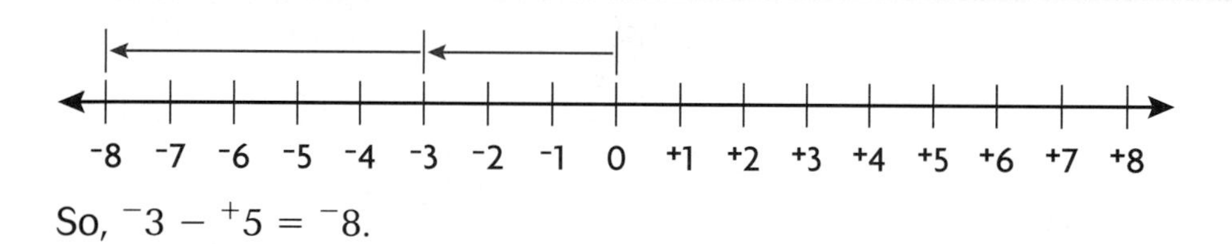

So, $^{-}3 - {}^{+}5 = {}^{-}8$.

Examples

 Subtract. $^{-}1 - {}^{+}4$

Move 1 space to the left. Then move 4 spaces left. This takes you to $^{-}5$.

So, $^{-}1 - {}^{+}4 = {}^{-}5$.

B Subtract. $^{-}2 - {}^{+}2$

Move 2 spaces to the left. Then move 2 spaces left. This takes you to $^{-}4$.

So, $^{-}2 - {}^{+}2 = {}^{-}4$.

ERROR ALERT

When subtracting a positive integer from a negative integer, the difference will be less than the integer you are subtracting from.

Try It

Find the difference.

1. $^{-}5 - {}^{+}1$
2. $^{-}3 - {}^{+}2$
3. $^{-}6 - {}^{+}3$
4. $^{-}7 - {}^{+}5$
5. $^{-}5 - {}^{+}10$
6. $^{-}9 - {}^{+}9$
7. $^{-}4 - {}^{+}6$
8. $^{-}2 - {}^{+}7$
9. $^{-}6 - {}^{+}1$
10. $^{-}8 - {}^{+}3$
11. $^{-}9 - {}^{+}4$
12. $^{-}2 - {}^{+}1$

13. Read the problem below. **Explain** why C cannot be the correct answer choice. Then choose the correct answer. **COMMON ERROR**

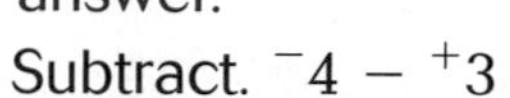

Subtract. $^{-}4 - {}^{+}3$

A $^{-}7$ **C** $^{+}1$

B $^{-}1$ **D** $^{+}7$

Review the Key Standards

Divide Decimals

NS 2.2 Demonstrate proficiency with division, including division with positive decimals and long division with multidigit divisors.

To divide by a decimal, move the decimal point the same number of places to the right in both the dividend and divisor.

Divide. $57.96 \div 4.2$

Step 1

Move the decimal point 1 place to the right in the divisor to get a whole-number divisor. Then move the decimal point in the dividend the same number of places. Write the decimal point in the quotient above the decimal point in the dividend.

$4.2\overline{)57.96} \rightarrow 42\overline{)579.6}$

Step 2

Divide by the whole number.

$$\begin{array}{r} 13.8 \\ 42\overline{)579.6} \\ -42 \\ \hline 159 \\ -126 \\ \hline 336 \\ -336 \\ \hline 0 \end{array}$$

Examples

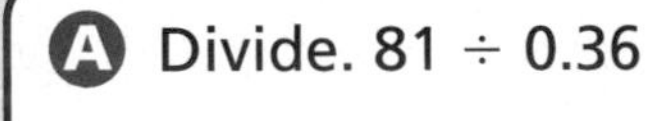

A Divide. $81 \div 0.36$

$$\begin{array}{r} 225 \\ 0.36\overline{)81} \rightarrow 36\overline{)8100} \\ -72 \\ \hline 90 \\ -72 \\ \hline 180 \\ -180 \\ \hline 0 \end{array}$$

B Divide. $14.76 ÷ 7.2

$$\begin{array}{r} \$2.05 \\ 7.2\overline{)\$14.76} \rightarrow 72\overline{)\$147.60} \\ -144 \\ \hline 360 \\ -360 \\ \hline 0 \end{array}$$

ERROR ALERT

Write extra zeros as placeholders after the last digit in the dividend, if necessary.

Try It

Divide.

1. $3.278 \div 1.1$
2. $24.12 \div 0.04$
3. $0.24\overline{)65.4}$
4. $1.8\overline{)0.576}$
5. $\$50.94 \div 0.9$
6. $7.812 \div 18$
7. $3.1\overline{)54.56}$
8. $0.35\overline{)14}$

9. Read the problem below. **Explain** why C cannot be the correct answer choice. Then choose the correct answer.

Divide. $7.5 \div 0.15$

A 0.02 **B** 0.5 **C** 5 **D** 50

Review the Key Standards

Divide with Multidigit Divisors

NS 2.2 Demonstrate proficiency with division, including division with positive decimals and long division with multidigit divisors.

To divide by a two-digit divisor, first estimate in order to place the first digit in the quotient.

Divide. $6,816 \div 32$

Step 1	Step 2	Step 3	Step 4
Estimate to place the first digit.	Divide the 68 hundreds. Bring down 1 ten.	Divide the 41 tens. Bring down 6 ones.	Divide the 96 ones.
$\begin{array}{r} 200 \\ 30\overline{)6,000} \end{array}$	$\begin{array}{r} 2 \\ 32\overline{)6,816} \\ \underline{-64} \\ 41 \end{array}$	$\begin{array}{r} 21 \\ 32\overline{)6,816} \\ \underline{-64} \\ 41 \\ \underline{-32} \\ 96 \end{array}$	$\begin{array}{r} 213 \\ 32\overline{)6,816} \\ \underline{-64} \\ 41 \\ \underline{-32} \\ 96 \\ \underline{-96} \\ 0 \end{array}$

The quotient is close to the estimate of 200. So, $6,816 \div 32 = 213$.

ERROR ALERT

Write a zero as a placeholder in the quotient, if necessary.

Try It

Divide.

1. $3,758 \div 13$
2. $5,016 \div 24$
3. $63\overline{)567}$
4. $18\overline{)5,765}$
5. $5,974 \div 90$
6. $7,824 \div 52$
7. $21\overline{)54,586}$
8. $35\overline{)215,846}$

9. Read the problem below. **Explain** why A cannot be the correct answer choice. Then choose the correct answer.

Divide. $15,219 \div 19$

A 81 **C** 810

B 801 **D** 8,010

Review the Key Standards

Addition and Subtraction of Fractions and Mixed Numbers

NS 2.3 Solve simple problems, including ones arising in concrete situations, involving the addition and subtraction of fractions and mixed numbers (like and unlike denominators of 20 or less), and express answers in the simplest form.

To add or subtract fractions or mixed numbers, they must have like denominators.

To add two fractions that have like denominators, add the numerators and write the sum over the denominator. To subtract two fractions that have like denominators, subtract the numerators and write the difference over the denominator. Write the answer in simplest form.

$$\begin{array}{r} \frac{5}{9} \\ +\frac{1}{9} \\ \hline \frac{6}{9} = \frac{2}{3} \end{array} \qquad \begin{array}{r} \frac{7}{10} \\ -\frac{3}{10} \\ \hline \frac{4}{10} = \frac{2}{5} \end{array}$$

To add or subtract unlike fractions, you need to rename them as fractions with like denominators.

$$\begin{array}{rcr} \frac{2}{3} & = & \frac{8}{12} \\ +\frac{1}{4} & = & +\frac{3}{12} \\ \hline & & \frac{11}{12} \end{array} \qquad \begin{array}{rcr} \frac{11}{15} & = & \frac{11}{15} \\ -\frac{1}{3} & = & -\frac{5}{15} \\ \hline & & \frac{6}{15} = \frac{2}{5} \end{array}$$

Examples

A **Add.** $2\frac{3}{5} + 3\frac{1}{2}$

Estimate. $3 + 4 = 7$

$$\begin{array}{rcr} 2\frac{3}{5} & = & 2\frac{6}{10} \\ +3\frac{1}{2} & = & +3\frac{5}{10} \\ \hline & & 5\frac{11}{10} = 5 + 1\frac{1}{10} = 6\frac{1}{10} \end{array}$$

So, $2\frac{3}{5} + 3\frac{1}{2} = 6\frac{1}{10}$.

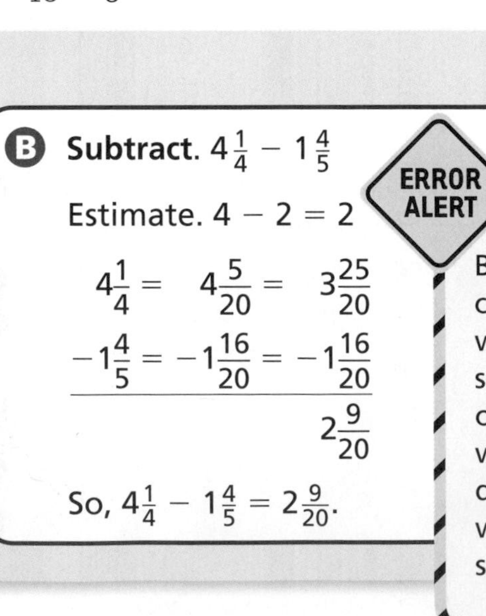

B **Subtract.** $4\frac{1}{4} - 1\frac{4}{5}$

Estimate. $4 - 2 = 2$

$$\begin{array}{rcrcr} 4\frac{1}{4} & = & 4\frac{5}{20} & = & 3\frac{25}{20} \\ -1\frac{4}{5} & = & -1\frac{16}{20} & = & -1\frac{16}{20} \\ \hline & & & & 2\frac{9}{20} \end{array}$$

So, $4\frac{1}{4} - 1\frac{4}{5} = 2\frac{9}{20}$.

ERROR ALERT

Be sure to find a common denominator when adding or subtracting fractions or mixed numbers with unlike denominators. Then write the answer in simplest form.

Try It

Find the sum or difference. Write the answer in simplest form.

1. $\frac{1}{8} + \frac{3}{8}$ **2.** $\frac{5}{6} - \frac{1}{6}$ **3.** $\frac{4}{5} + \frac{3}{5}$ **4.** $\frac{11}{12} - \frac{1}{12}$ **5.** $\frac{7}{10} + \frac{3}{10}$

6. $10\frac{7}{9} - 5\frac{5}{9}$ **7.** $4\frac{7}{8} + 3\frac{1}{8}$ **8.** $8\frac{13}{15} - 5\frac{8}{15}$ **9.** $2\frac{5}{6} + 5\frac{5}{6}$ **10.** $9\frac{7}{10} - 2\frac{1}{10}$

11. $6\frac{3}{5} - 1\frac{4}{5}$ **12.** $9\frac{3}{8} - 3\frac{7}{8}$ **13.** $6\frac{7}{12} + 3\frac{11}{12}$ **14.** $4\frac{9}{20} + 1\frac{7}{20}$ **15.** $7 - 5\frac{2}{3}$

16. $\frac{3}{4} + \frac{1}{8}$ **17.** $\frac{9}{10} - \frac{1}{2}$ **18.** $\frac{1}{3} + \frac{3}{4}$ **19.** $\frac{19}{20} - \frac{4}{5}$ **20.** $\frac{5}{6} + \frac{4}{9}$

21. $1\frac{3}{4} + 6\frac{1}{6}$ **22.** $12\frac{9}{10} - 8\frac{1}{2}$ **23.** $7\frac{5}{8} + 5\frac{2}{3}$ **24.** $9\frac{4}{5} - 3\frac{1}{6}$ **25.** $8\frac{7}{12} - 2\frac{1}{3}$

26. $6\frac{3}{8} - 5\frac{3}{4}$ **27.** $9 - 2\frac{1}{2}$ **28.** $4\frac{2}{9} - 2\frac{1}{6}$ **29.** $8\frac{13}{20} + 2\frac{2}{5}$ **30.** $5\frac{11}{12} + 4\frac{3}{8}$

Solve.

31. Matt bought $\frac{1}{2}$ pound of Swiss cheese and $\frac{3}{4}$ pound of American cheese. How much cheese did Matt buy in all?

32. Mindy bought $3\frac{2}{3}$ yards of ribbon. She used $2\frac{7}{8}$ yards of it. How much ribbon does Mindy have left?

33. Read the problem below. **Explain** why D cannot be the correct answer choice. Then choose the correct answer.

Find the sum in simplest form.

$$5\frac{1}{3} + 2\frac{5}{12}$$

A $7\frac{9}{12}$

B $7\frac{3}{4}$

C $7\frac{6}{15}$

D $7\frac{2}{5}$

34. Read the problem below. **Explain** why B cannot be the correct answer choice. Then choose the correct answer.

Find the difference in simplest form.

$$6\frac{9}{10} - 2\frac{2}{5}$$

A $3\frac{1}{2}$

B $4\frac{5}{10}$

C $4\frac{1}{2}$

D $4\frac{7}{10}$

Review the Key Standards

Algebraic Expressions

AF 1.2 Use a letter to represent an unknown number; write and evaluate simple algebraic expressions in one variable by substitution.

Find the value of an expression by replacing the variable with a number. Then follow the **order of operations** to find the value of the expression.

Evaluate $(14 - p) \times 4 \div 6$ if $p = 5$.

$(14 - p) \times 4 \div 6$	Replace p with 5.
$(14 - 5) \times 4 \div 6$	Operate inside the parentheses. Subtract.
$9 \times 4 \div 6$	Multiply.
$36 \div 6$	Divide.
6	

So, $(14 - p) \times 4 \div 6 = 6$ if $p = 5$.

ERROR ALERT
Follow the order of operations to find the value of an expression.

Examples

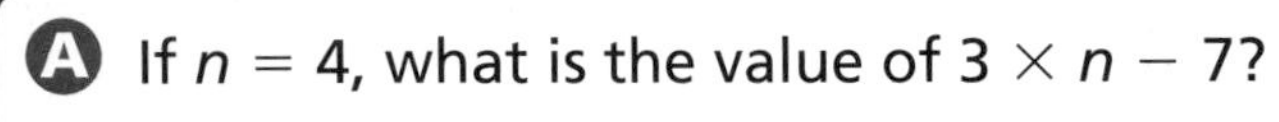

A If $n = 4$, what is the value of $3 \times n - 7$?

$3 \times n - 7$
$3 \times 4 - 7$
$12 - 7$
5

So, if $n = 4$, $3 \times n - 7 = 5$.

B Evaluate $7 \times (54 \div b)$ if $b = 6$.

$7 \times (54 \div b)$
$7 \times (54 \div 6)$
7×9
63

So, $7 \times (54 \div b) = 63$ if $b = 6$.

Try It

Evaluate the algebraic expression for the given value of the variable.

1. $5n - 2$ if $n = 3.2$
2. $(14 + d) \div 7$ if $d = 35$
3. $\frac{x}{4} + 7 \times 3$ if $x = 20$
4. $8b + 2$ if $b = \frac{1}{8}$

5. Read the problem below. **Explain** why B cannot be the correct answer choice. Then choose the correct answer.

COMMON ERROR

If $a = 5$, what is the value of $(9 + a) \times 2$?

A 8
B 19
C 28
D 190

Review the Key Standards

Ordered Pairs in the Coordinate Plane

AF 1.4 Identify and graph ordered pairs in the four quadrants of the coordinate plane.

A coordinate plane is formed by two intersecting and perpendicular number lines called axes. The point where the two lines intersect is called the origin, or (0,0). The numbers to the left of the origin on the *x*-axis and below the origin on the *y*-axis are negative. The numbers to the right of the origin on the *x*-axis and above the origin on the *y*-axis are positive.

To get to point *A*, move 2 units left and 3 units down. Point *A* has coordinates $(^-2,^-3)$.

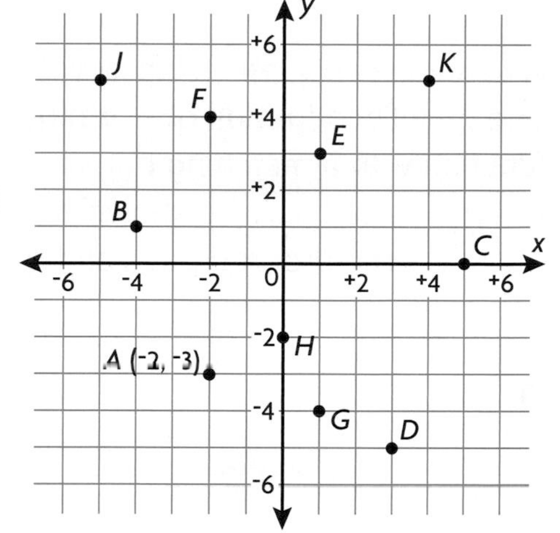

Examples

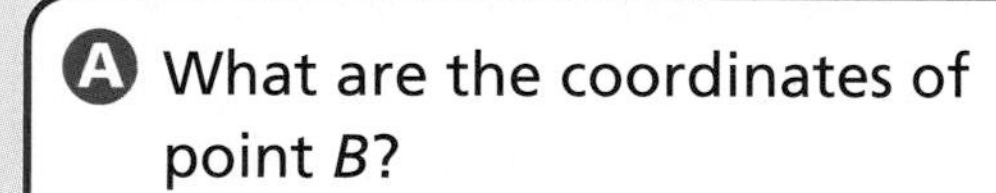

A What are the coordinates of point *B*?

To get to point *B*, move 4 units left and 1 unit up. Point *B* has coordinates $(^-4,1)$.

B Which point has coordinates $(3,^-5)$?

To get to $(3,^-5)$, move 3 units right and 5 units down. Point *D* has coordinates $(3,^-5)$.

ERROR ALERT

Be sure to move right or left first, then up or down.

Try It

For 1–6 and 13, use the coordinate plane above. Identify the ordered pair for each point.

1. *G*
2. *H*
3. *J*
4. *K*
5. *C*
6. *E*

Graph and label the ordered pairs on a coordinate plane.

7. *P* (0,1)
8. *Q* $(^-4,^-2)$
9. *R* $(3,^-3)$
10. *S* (4,2)
11. *T* $(^-2,0)$
12. *U* $(^-1,5)$

13. Read the problem below. **Explain** why B cannot be the correct answer choice. Then choose the correct answer.

Use the coordinate plane above. What are the coordinates of point *F*?

A $(^-2,4)$

B $(4,^-2)$

C $(^-2,^-4)$

D $(^-4,^-2)$

Review the Key Standards

Linear Functions

AF 1.5 Solve problems involving linear functions with integer values; write the equation; and graph the resulting ordered pairs of integers on a grid.

A function is a relationship between two quantities in which one quantity depends on the other. A function table shows the function with a matching output value for each input value. A function can also be shown by an equation. Use the function table to write ordered pairs and graph them.

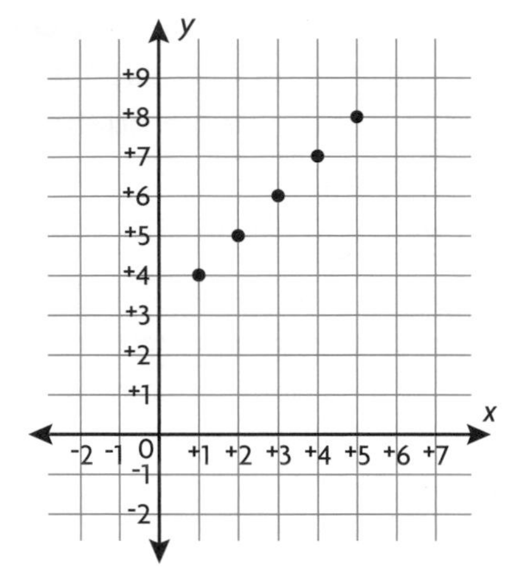

Input, x	1	2	3	4	5
Output, y	4	5	6	7	8

Rule: Add 3. Equation: $y = x + 3$

Ordered pairs: (1,4), (2,5), (3,6), (4,7), (5,8)

Examples

A Write an equation that could be used to make the function table.

Input, x	Output, y
$^{-}1$	$^{-}4$
0	$^{-}3$
1	$^{-}2$
2	$^{-}1$
3	0

Rule: Subtract 3.

Equation: $y = x - 3$

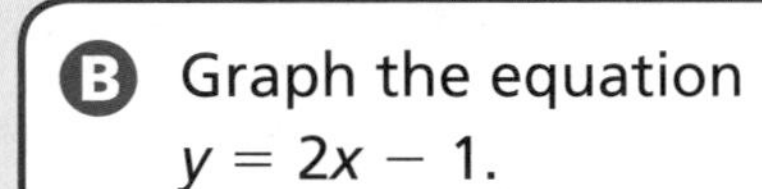

B Graph the equation $y = 2x - 1$.

Use the equation to make a function table.

Input, x	0	1	2	3	4
Output, y	$^{-}1$	1	3	5	7

Write the data in the table as ordered pairs: (0,$^{-}$1), (1,1), (2,3), (3,5), (4,7). Then graph the ordered pairs.

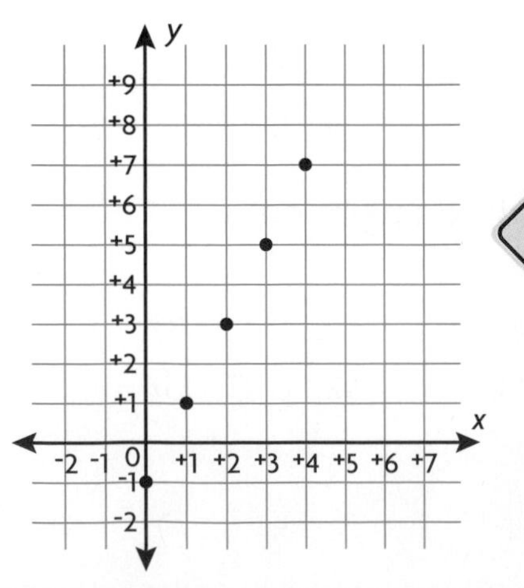

ERROR ALERT

Check that each ordered pair in a function table satisfies the equation.

Try It

Find a rule for the function table. Then write the rule as an equation.

1.

x	12	10	8	6	4
y	6	4	2	0	$^{-}2$

2.

x	4	3	2	1	0
y	8	6	4	2	0

3.

x	0	1	2	3	4
y	$^{-}5$	$^{-}4$	$^{-}3$	$^{-}2$	$^{-}1$

4.

x	0	3	6	9	12
y	0	1	2	3	4

5.

x	$^{-}2$	$^{-}1$	0	1	2
y	$^{-}8$	$^{-}4$	0	4	8

6.

x	$^{-}7$	$^{-}3$	1	5	9
y	$^{-}3$	1	5	9	13

Use each equation to make a function table with at least 4 ordered pairs. Then graph.

7. $y = x + 2$

8. $y = x - 4$

9. $y = 2x$

10. $y = 3x + 1$

11. $y = 2x - 3$

12. $y = {}^{-}x + 1$

Solve.

13. Read the problem below. **Explain** why D cannot be the correct answer choice. Then choose the correct answer.

Which equation could have been used to create the function table?

x	y
$^{-}2$	$^{-}4$
0	$^{-}2$
2	0
4	2

A $y = \frac{x}{2}$

B $y = x - 2$

C $y = x + 2$

D $y = 2x$

14. Read the problem below. **Explain** why C cannot be the correct answer choice. Then choose the correct answer.

Which table represents the values of x and y such that $y = x + 7$?

A

x	y
$^{-}1$	6
0	7

B

x	y
$^{-}1$	$^{-}8$
0	$^{-}7$

C

x	y
2	5
5	$^{-}2$

D

x	y
3	4
4	0

Review the Key Standards

Area of Triangles and Parallelograms

MG 1.1 Derive and use the formula for the area of a triangle and of a parallelogram by comparing it with the formula for the area of a rectangle (i.e., two of the same triangles make a parallelogram with twice the area; a parallelogram is compared with a rectangle of the same area by pasting and cutting a right triangle on the parallelogram).

The area of a parallelogram is equal to the area of a rectangle with the same base (length) and height (width).

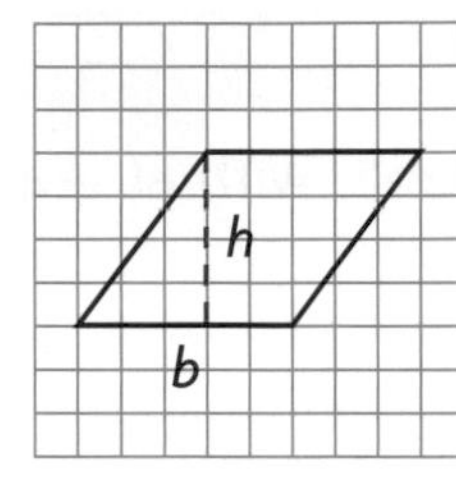

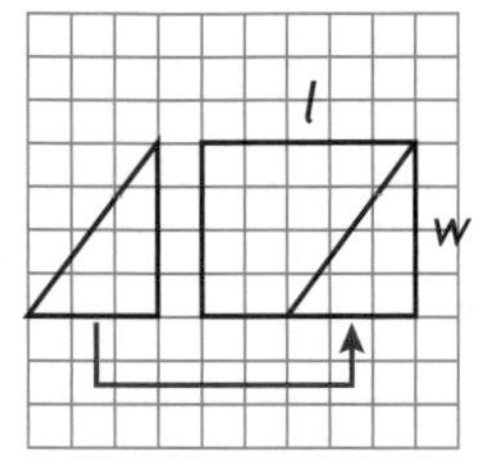

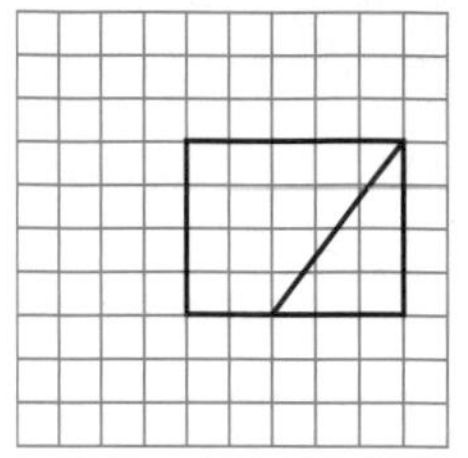

Area of a rectangle = length × width

$A = l \times w$

Area of a parallelogram = base × height

$A = b \times h$

The area of a triangle is half the area of the rectangle or parallelogram with the same base and height.

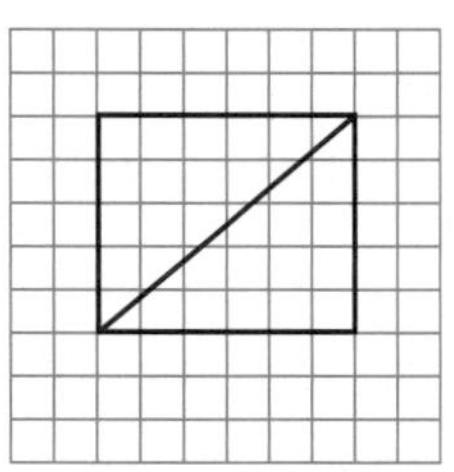

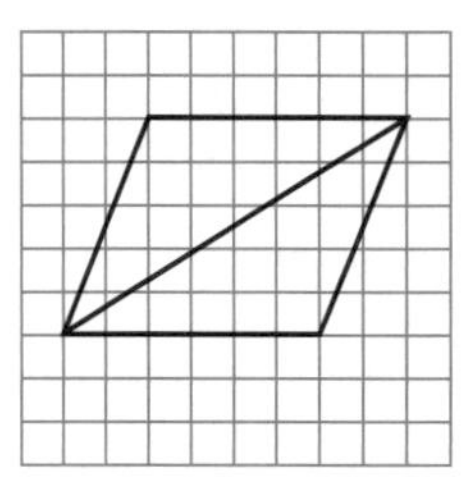

Area of a triangle = $\frac{1}{2}$ × base × height

$A = \frac{1}{2} \times (b \times h)$

Examples

A In the figure below, *ABCD* is a parallelogram.

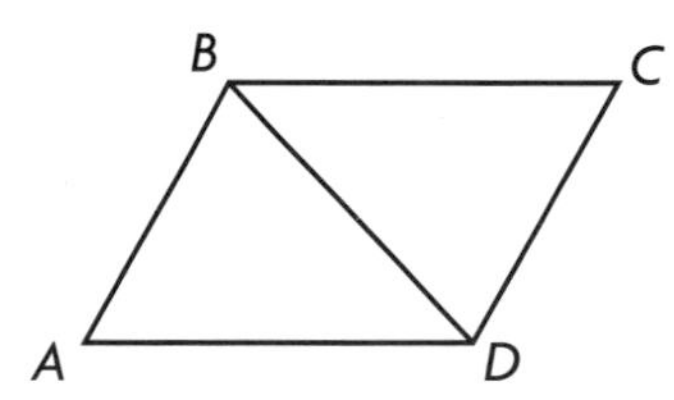

If the area of parallelogram *ABCD* is 28 square inches, what is the area of triangle *ABD?*

The area of a triangle is $\frac{1}{2}$ the area of a parallelogram with the same base and height.

$A = \frac{1}{2} \times 28 = 14$

So, the area of the triangle is 14 square inches.

B Find the area.

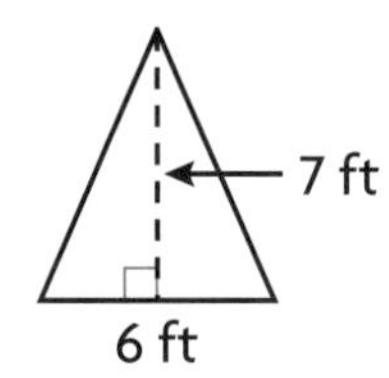

$A = \frac{1}{2} \times b \times h$

$A = \frac{1}{2} \times 6 \times 7$

$A = 21$

The area is 21 ft^2.

ERROR ALERT

Multiply the base × height by $\frac{1}{2}$ when finding the area of a triangle.

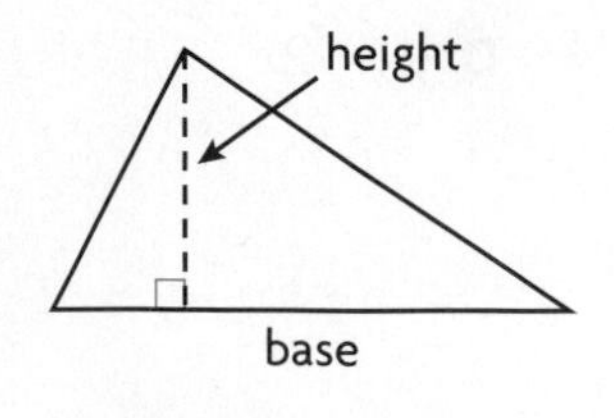

$A = \frac{1}{2} \times (b \times h)$

Try It

Find the area of each parallelogram.

1.

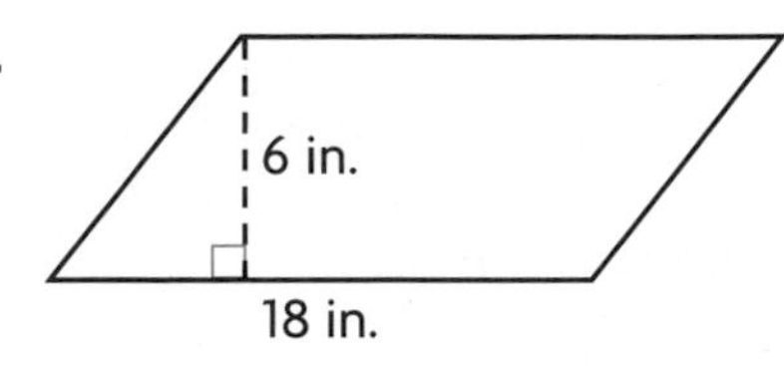

2.

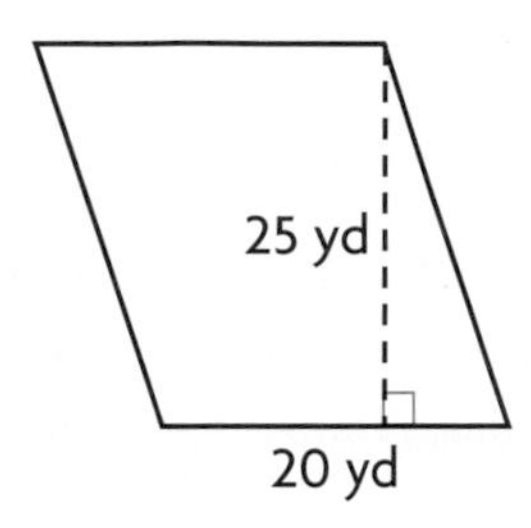

3.

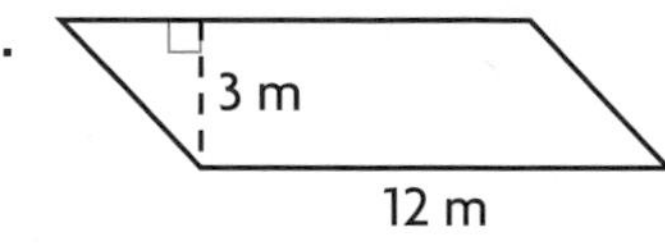

Find the area of each triangle.

4.

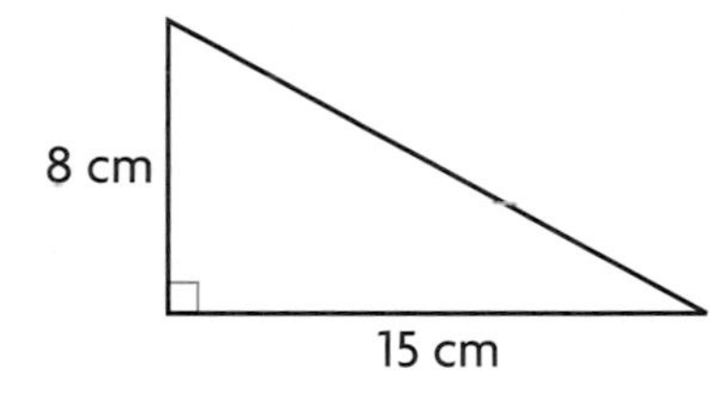

5.

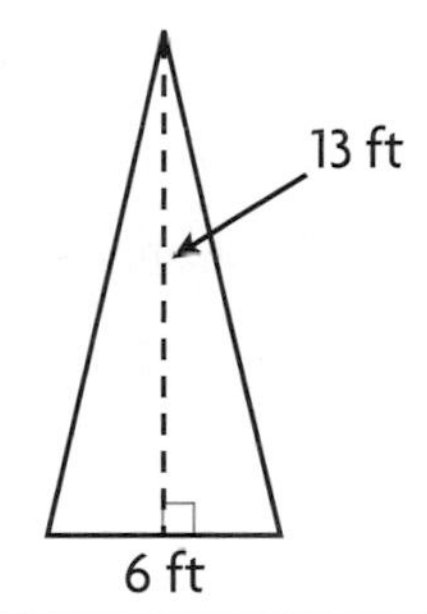

6.

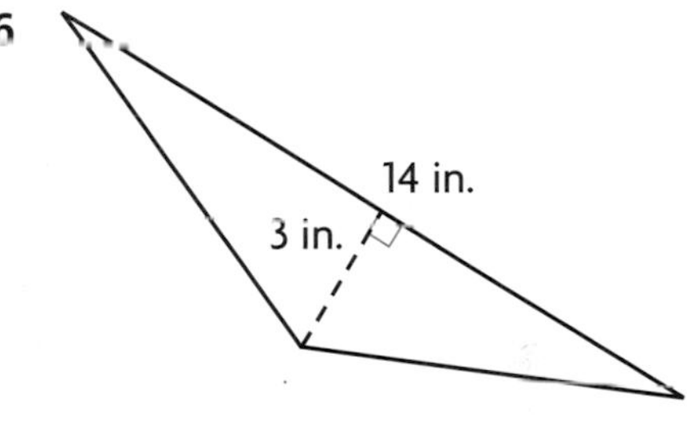

Solve.

7. Read the problem below. **Explain** why C cannot be the correct answer choice. Then choose the correct answer.

What is the area of the triangle below?

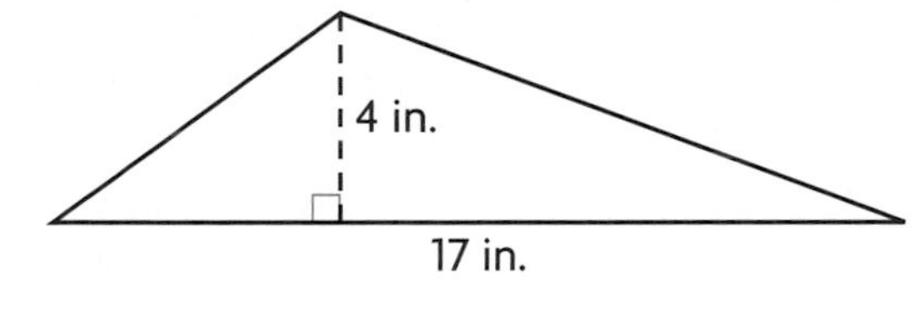

A 21 in.^{2}

B 34 in.^{2}

C 68 in.^{2}

D 136 in.^{2}

8. Read the problem below. **Explain** why B cannot be the correct answer choice. Then choose the correct answer.

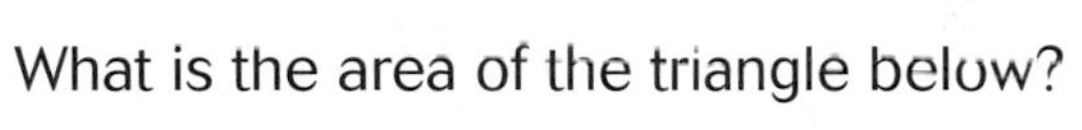

What is the area of the triangle below?

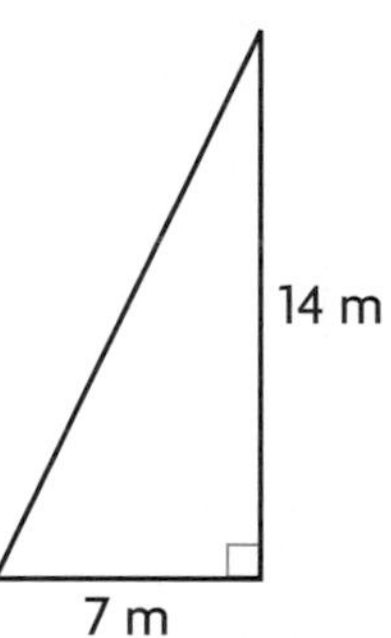

A 196 m^2

B 98 m^2

C 49 m^2

D 24.5 m^2

Review the Key Standards

Surface Area of Cubes and Rectangular Boxes

MG 1.2 Construct a cube and a rectangular box from two-dimensional patterns and use these patterns to compute the surface area for these objects.

Surface area is the sum of all the areas of the faces of a solid figure. The surface area of a three-dimensional figure can be found by using a two-dimensional pattern.

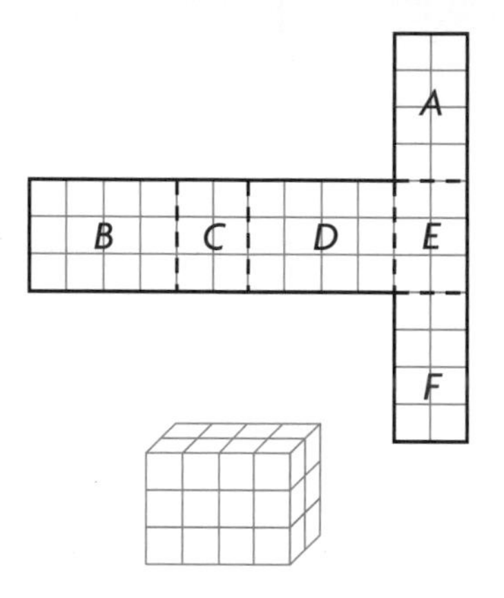

Face	Area
Top *(A)*	$2 \times 4 = 8$ square units
Bottom *(F)*	$2 \times 4 = 8$ square units
Front *(D)*	$4 \times 3 = 12$ square units
Back *(B)*	$4 \times 3 = 12$ square units
Left *(C)*	$2 \times 3 = 6$ square units
Right *(E)*	$2 \times 3 = 6$ square units

Add the areas of the faces to find the surface area.
$8 + 8 + 12 + 12 + 6 + 6 = 52$ square units

Examples

A Find the surface area of the cube formed by the pattern below.

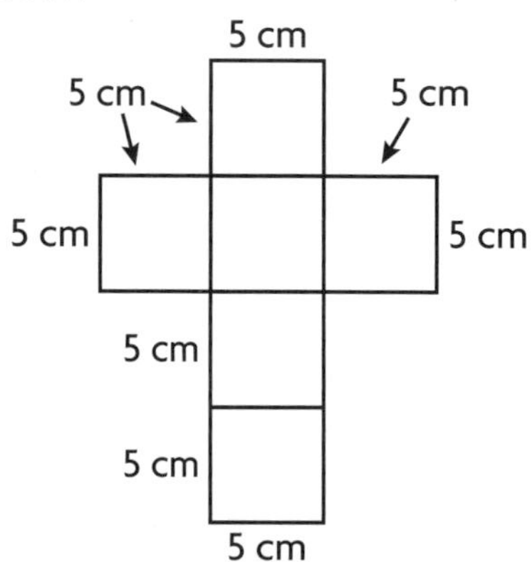

The area of each face is 5×5, or 25 cm^2. The surface area of the cube is 6×25, or 150 cm^2.

B Find the surface area of the box formed by the pattern below.

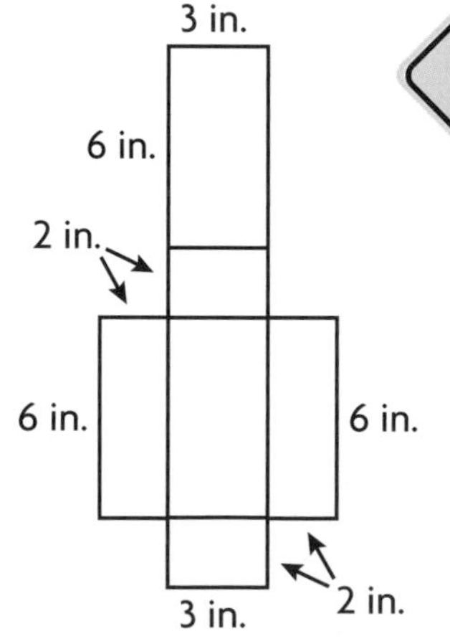

$6 \times 3 = 18$, $2 \times 3 = 6$,

$2 \times 6 = 12$, $6 \times 3 = 18$,

$2 \times 3 = 6$, $2 \times 6 = 12$

$18 + 6 + 12 + 18 + 6 + 12 = 72$

The surface area is 72 $in.^2$

ERROR ALERT

Be sure to find the area of each of the six faces of a cube or rectangular box when finding the surface area of a three-dimensional figure.

Try It

Use the pattern to find the surface area of each prism in square units.

1.

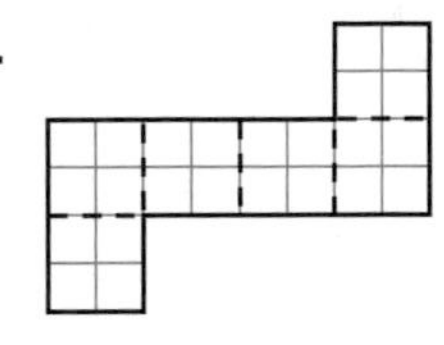

2.

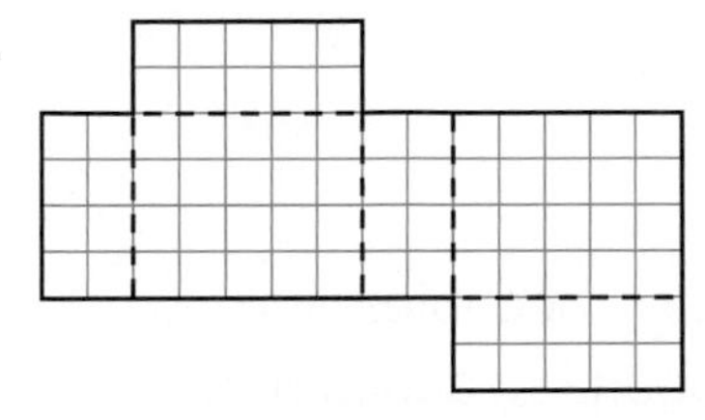

3.

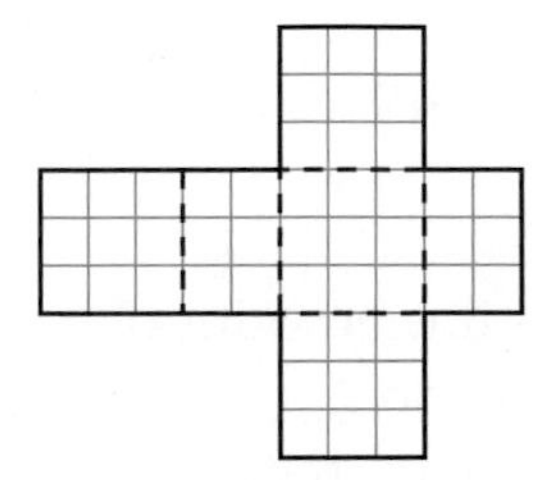

Find the surface area.

4.

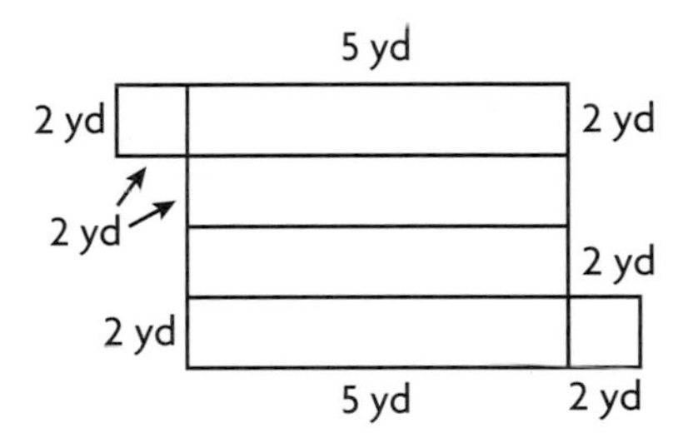

5.

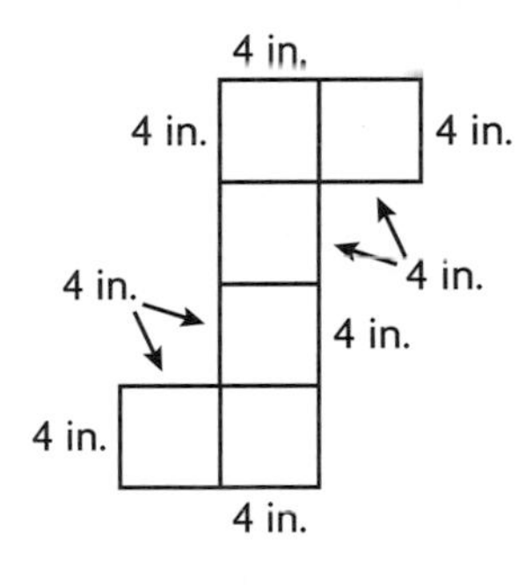

6.

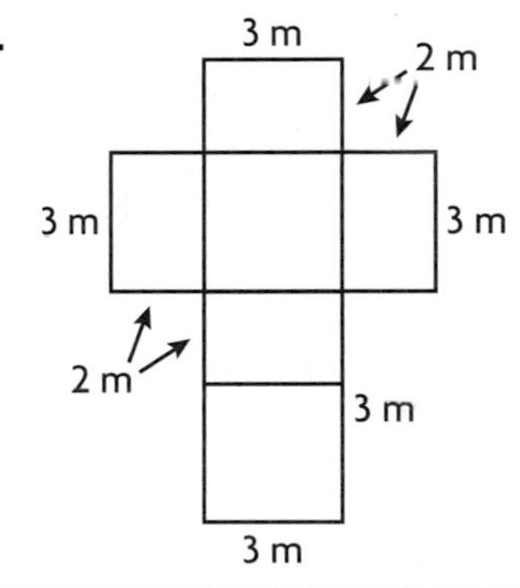

Solve.

7. Read the problem below. **Explain** why A cannot be the correct answer choice. Then choose the correct answer.

What is the surface area of the box formed by the pattern?

3 cm, 3 cm, 1 cm, 4 cm, 4 cm, 1 cm, 1 cm, 3 cm

A 19 cm^2

B 28 cm^2

C 38 cm^2

D 48 cm^2

8. Read the problem below. **Explain** why D cannot be the correct answer choice. Then choose the correct answer.

What is the surface area of the cube formed by the pattern?

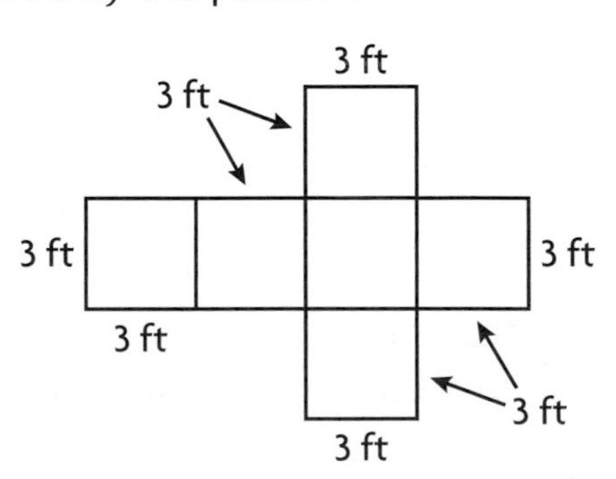

A 54 ft^2

B 42 ft^2

C 18 ft^2

D 9 ft^2

Review the Key Standards

Volume

MG 1.3 Understand the concept of volume and use the appropriate units in common measuring systems (i.e. cubic centimeter [cm^3], cubic meter [m^3], cubic inch [$in.^3$],cubic yard [yd^3]) to compute the volume of rectangular solids.

Volume is the amount of space a solid figure occupies. Volume is measured in cubic units. You can use counting cubes or a formula to find the volume of a rectangular prism.

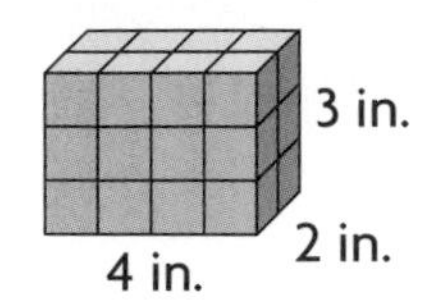

Volume = length × width × height

$V = l \times w \times h$

$V = 4 \times 2 \times 3 = 24$ cubic inches, or 24 $in.^3$

Examples

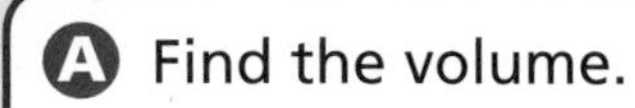

A Find the volume.

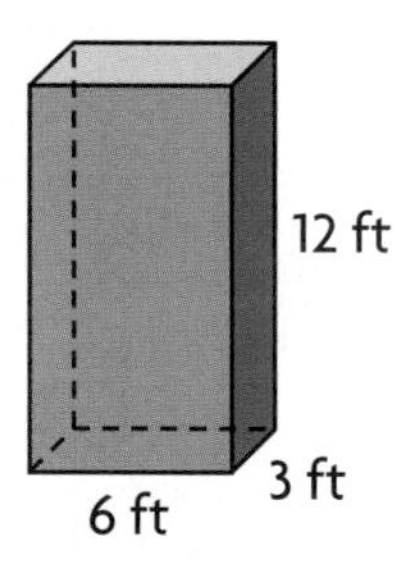

$V = l \times w \times h$

$V = 6 \times 3 \times 12 = 216$

The volume is 216 ft^3.

B Find the volume.

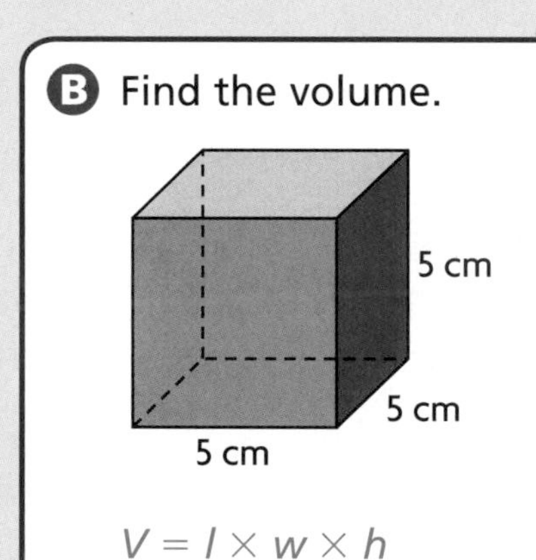

$V = l \times w \times h$

$V = 5 \times 5 \times 5 = 125$

The volume is 125 cm^3.

ERROR ALERT

Write the volume of a figure in cubic units.

If you know the volume of a rectangular prism and two of its dimensions, you can use the formula to find the unknown dimension.

Volume = 120 $in.^3$ length = 5 in. width = 4 in. height = ?

$V = l \times w \times h$

$120 = 5 \times 4 \times h$

$120 = 20 \times h$ **Think:** What multiplied by 20 equals 120?

$h = 6$

So, the height of the rectangular prism is 6 in.

Try It

Find the volume.

1. 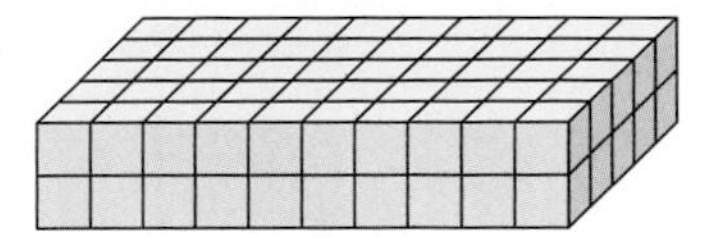

2. 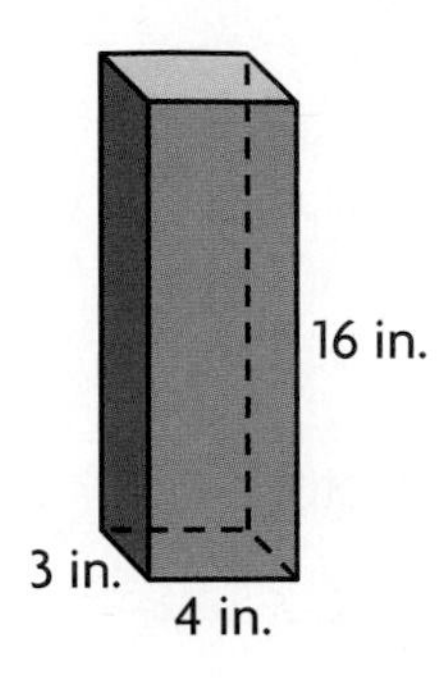

3. 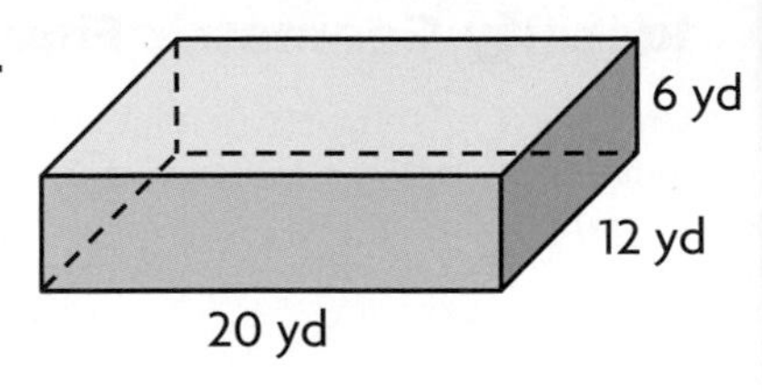

4. 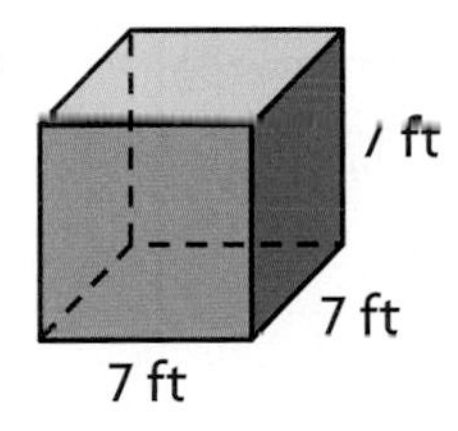

5. 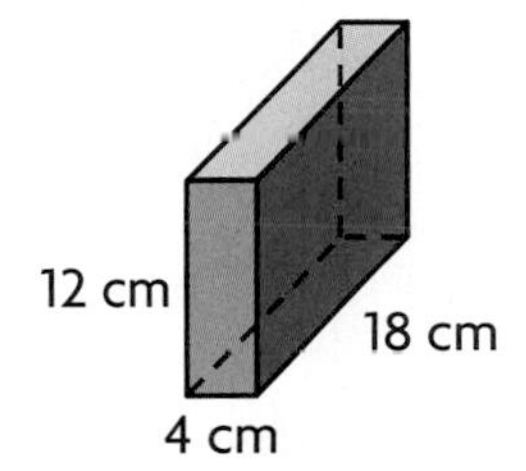

6. 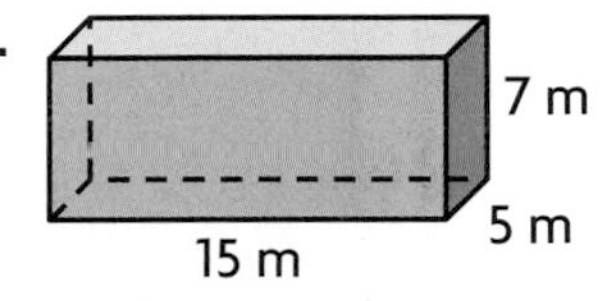

Solve.

7. Read the problem below. **Explain** why A cannot be the correct answer choice. Then choose the correct answer.

This rectangular prism has a length of 11 inches, a height of 6 inches, and a width of 4 inches. What is the volume?

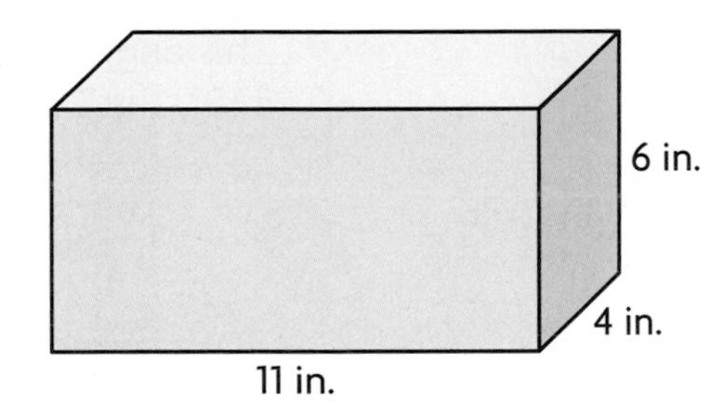

A 264 $in.^2$

B 264 $in.^3$

C 268 $in.^2$

D 268 $in.^3$

8. Read the problem below. **Explain** why B cannot be the correct answer choice. Then choose the correct answer.

This cube has a length, width, and height of 9 meters. What is the volume?

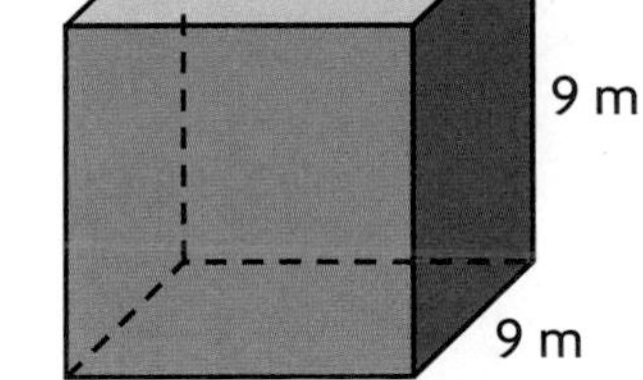

A 486 m^3

B 729 m

C 729 m^2

D 729 m^3

Review the Key Standards

Identify Geometric Figures

MG 2.1 Measure, identify, and draw angles, perpendicular and parallel lines, rectangles, and triangles, using appropriate tools (e.g. straightedge, ruler, compass, protractor, drawing software).

An angle can be measured by using a protractor. This angle has a measure of $50°$.

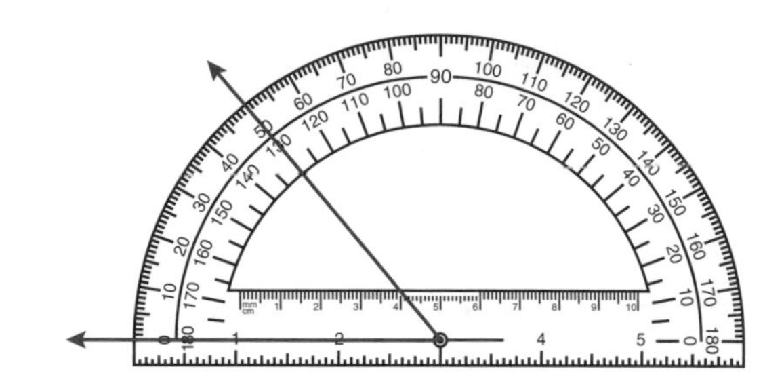

A **right angle** is an angle that measures $90°$.

An **acute angle** is an angle that measures less than $90°$.

An **obtuse angle** is an angle that measures greater than $90°$ and less than $180°$.

A **straight angle** is an angle that measures $180°$.

Examples

A Which two lines are parallel?

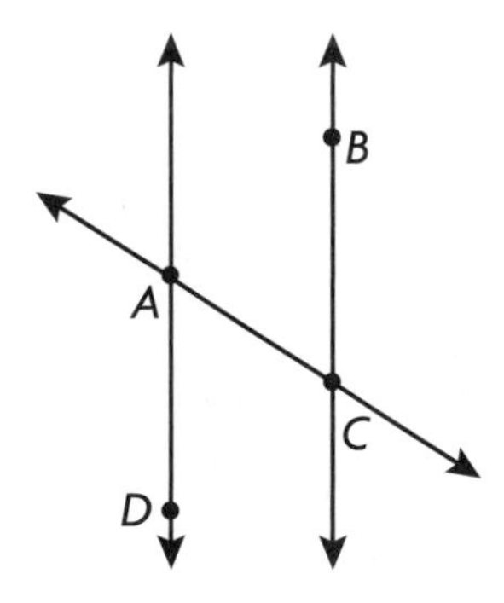

Parallel lines are lines in a plane that never intersect and are the same distance apart at every point.

So, $\overleftrightarrow{AD} \parallel \overleftrightarrow{BC}$.

B Which two lines are perpendicular?

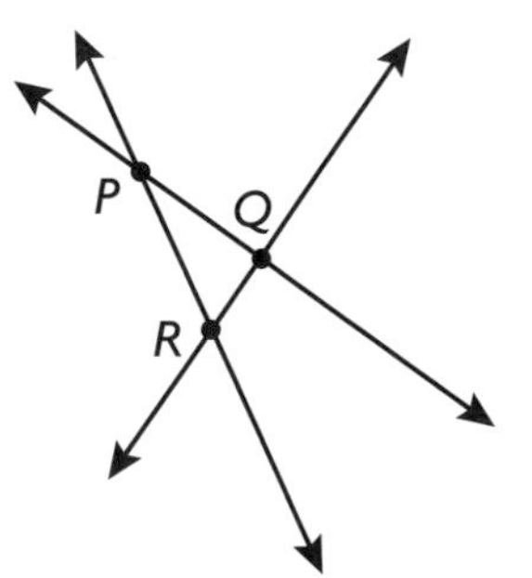

Perpendicular lines are two lines that intersect to form four right angles.

So, $\overleftrightarrow{PQ} \perp \overleftrightarrow{QR}$.

ERROR ALERT

Use the correct scale on a protractor when measuring angles.

This angle measures 110°, not 70°.

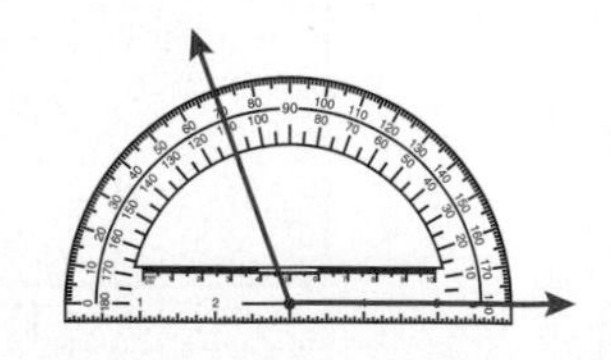

Try It

Use a protractor to find the measure of each angle.

1.

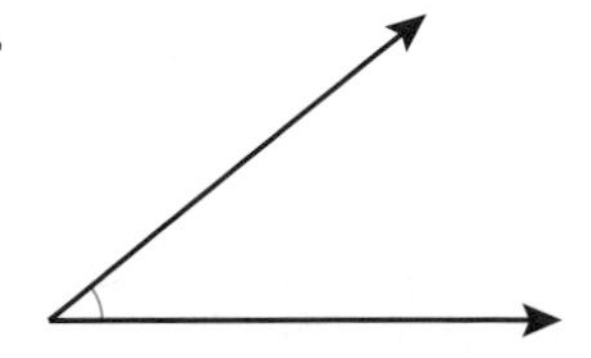

2.

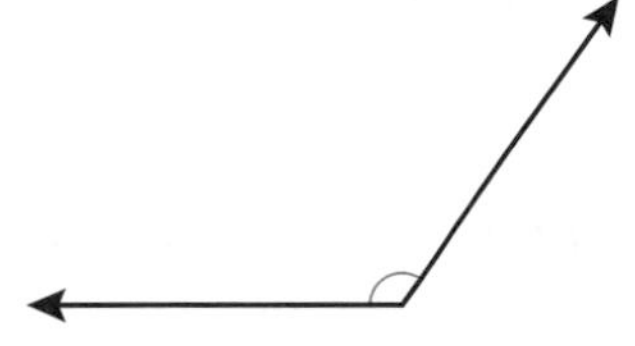

3.

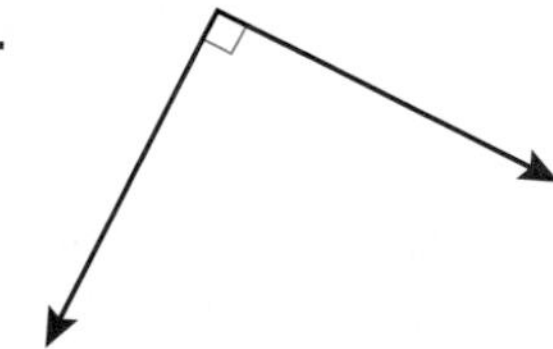

Use the figure at the right.

4. Identify a pair of perpendicular lines.
5. Identify a pair of parallel lines.
6. Identify a right angle.
7. Identify an obtuse angle.
8. Identify an acute angle.

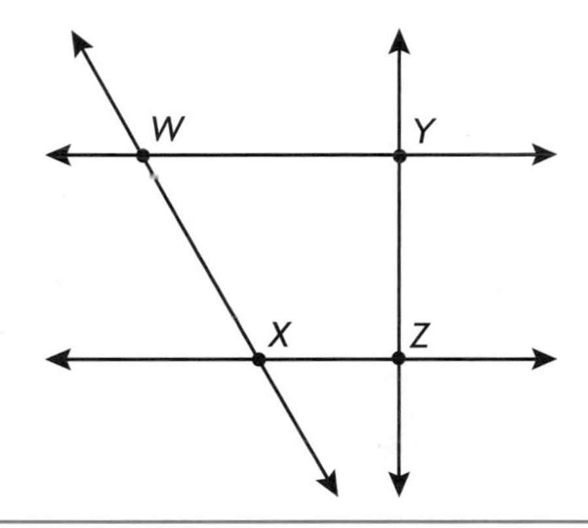

Solve.

9. Read the problem below. **Explain** why B cannot be the correct answer choice. Then choose the correct answer.

Which is closest to the measure of the angle shown below?

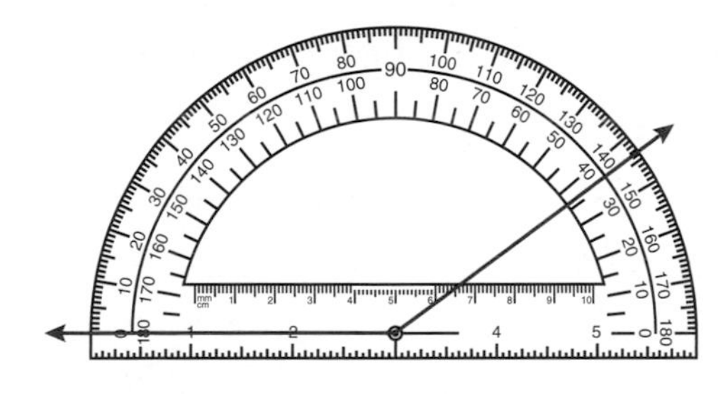

A 35°

B 45°

C 135°

D 145°

10. Read the problem below. **Explain** why C cannot be the correct answer choice. Then choose the correct answer.

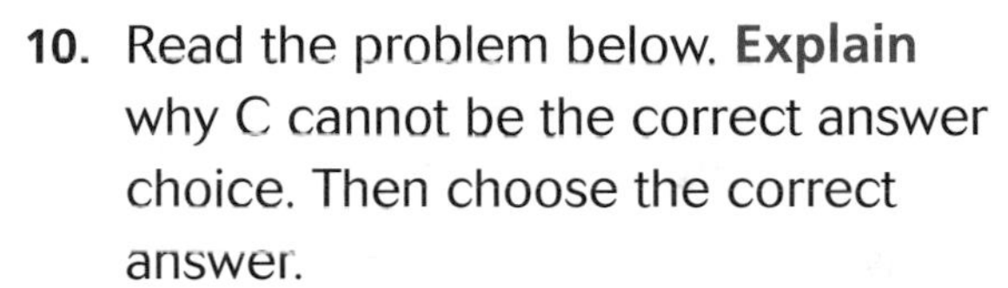

What is the approximate measure of this angle in degrees?

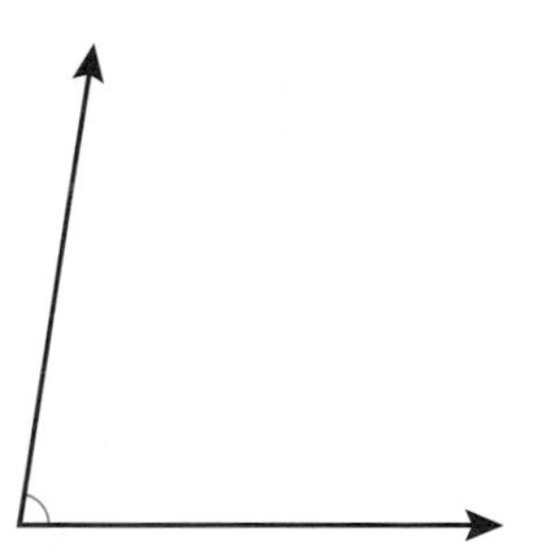

A 80°

B 90°

C 100°

D 180°

Review the Key Standards

Sum of the Angles of a Triangle

MG 2.2 Know that the sum of the angles of any triangle is 180° and the sum of the angles of any quadrilateral is 360° and use this information to solve problems.

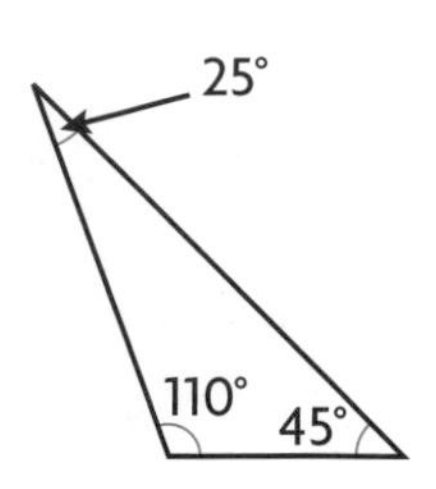

The sum of the angle measures of any triangle is 180°. Look at the triangle at the right. Find the sum of its angle measures.

$$45° + 110° + 25° = 180°$$

Examples

A Do the angle measures 43°, 117°, and 30° form a triangle?

$43° + 117° + 30° = 190°$

190° does not equal 180°.

So, the angle measures 43°, 117°, and 30° do not form a triangle.

B Two angles of a triangle each measure 65°. What is the measure of the third angle of the triangle?

$65° + 65° = 130°$

$180° - 130° = 50°$

So, the measure of the third angle is 50°.

ERROR ALERT

Subtract the sum of the measures of the other two angles of a triangle from 180° in order to find the measure of the third angle.

Try It

Tell if the given angle measures would form a triangle.

1. 52°, 105°, 23°
2. 90°, 60°, 30°
3. 35°, 35°, 70°
4. 114°, 10°, 66°
5. 157°, 11°, 12°
6. 32°, 47°, 79°

Find the unknown angle measure.

7.

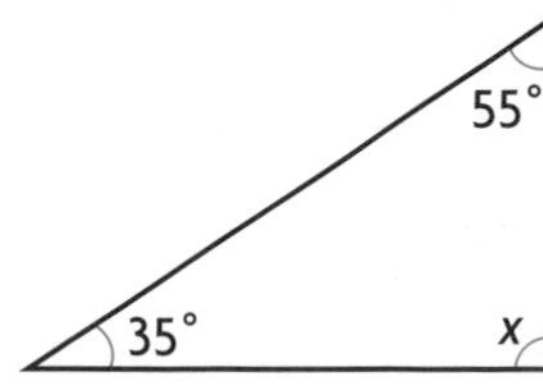

8.

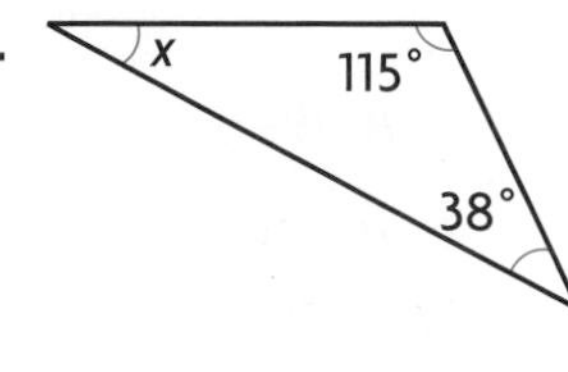

9. Read the problem below. **Explain** why B cannot be the correct answer choice. Then choose the correct answer.

What is the measure of angle p in the figure?

120°
45°
p

A $p = 15°$

B $p = 60°$

C $p = 135°$

D $p = 165°$

Review the Key Standards

Sum of the Angles of a Quadrilateral

MG 2.2 Know that the sum of the angles of any triangle is 180° and the sum of the angles of any quadrilateral is 360° and use this information to solve problems.

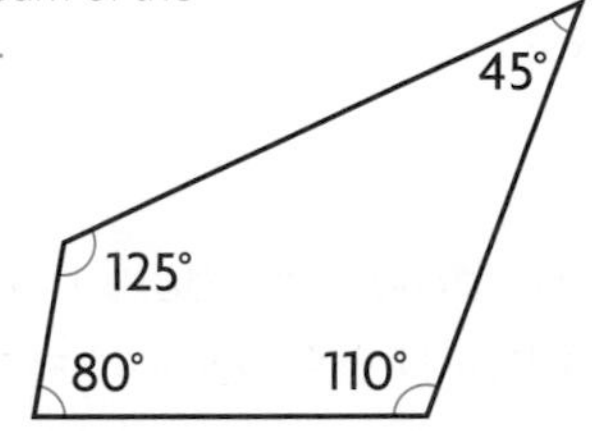

The sum of the angle measures of any quadrilateral is 360°. Look at the quadrilateral at the right. Find the sum of its angle measures.

$$45° + 110° + 80° + 125° = 360°$$

Examples

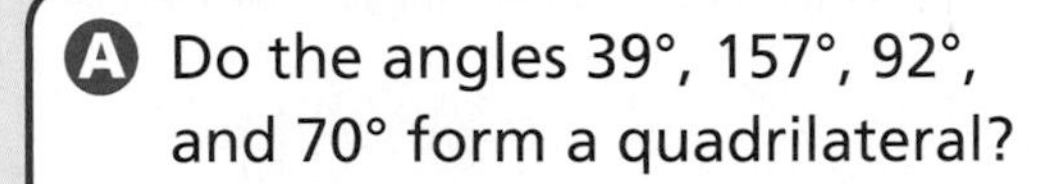

A Do the angles 39°, 157°, 92°, and 70° form a quadrilateral?

39° + 157° + 92° + 70° = 358°

358° does not equal 360°.

So, the angles 39°, 157°, 92°, and 70° do not form a quadrilateral.

B Three angles of a quadrilateral measure 70°, 95°, and 150°. What is the measure of the fourth angle of the quadrilateral?

70° + 95° + 150° = 315°

360° − 315° = 45°

So, the measure of the fourth angle is 45°.

ERROR ALERT

Subtract the sum of the measures of the other three angles of a quadrilateral from 360° in order to find the measure of the fourth angle.

Try It

Tell if the given angle measures would form a quadrilateral.

1. 102°, 118°, 55°, 95°
2. 90°, 160°, 30°, 80°
3. 57°, 135°, 70°, 98°
4. 124°, 110°, 66°, 60°
5. 75°, 65°, 120°, 100°
6. 110°, 90°, 110°, 90°

Find the unknown angle measure.

7.

8.

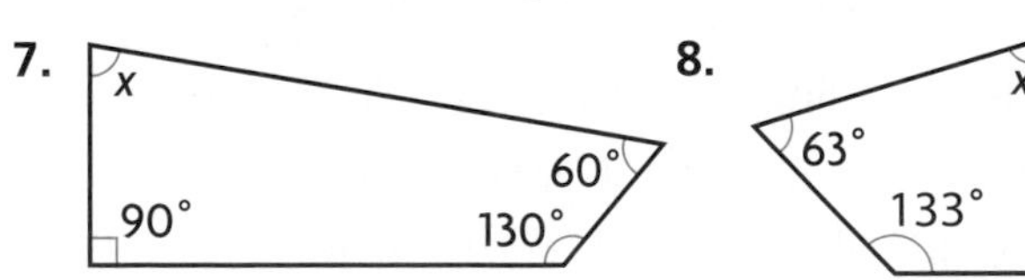

9. Read the problem below. **Explain** why D cannot be the correct answer choice. Then choose the correct answer.

What is the measure of angle *r* in the figure?

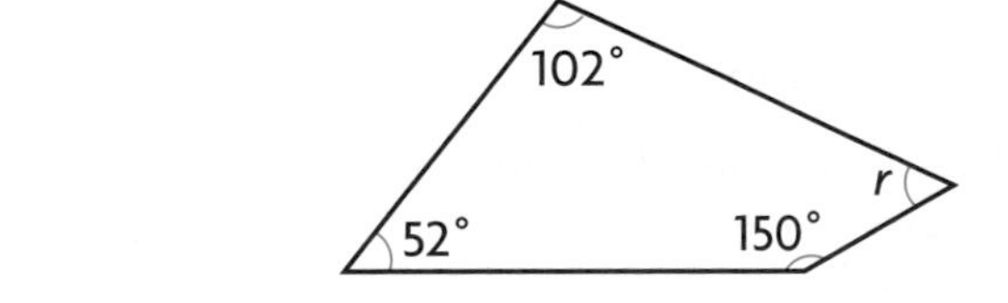

A 35°

B 56°

C 155°

D 304°

Review the Key Standards

Identify Ordered Pairs

SDAP 1.4 Identify ordered pairs of data from a graph and interpret the meaning of the data in terms of the situation depicted by the graph.

A line graph is used to show how data change over time. This line graph shows the height of a plant at the end of each week.

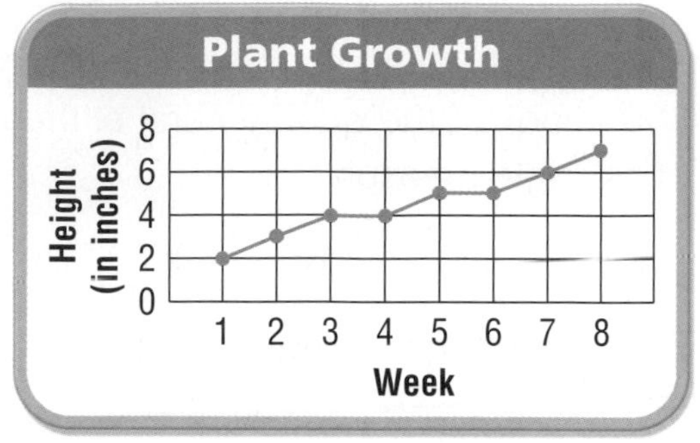

Examples

A Look at the graph above. At week 2 how tall was the plant?

Move in a vertical direction above week 2. The value is 3.

So, at week 2, the plant was 3 inches tall.

B Look at the graph above. Between which two weeks, did the plant show no growth?

The line is flat between weeks 3 and 4 and between weeks 5 and 6.

So, there was no growth between weeks 3 and 4 and between weeks 5 and 6.

ERROR ALERT

Be sure to understand and read the scale of a graph correctly.

Try It

Solve. Use the graph above.

1. How tall was the plant at the end of week 6?
2. What does the ordered pair (1,2) represent on the graph?
3. How much did the plant grow between weeks 1 and 7?
4. How much did the plant grow between the ends of weeks 2 and 5?
5. Read the problem below. **Explain** why D cannot be the correct answer choice. Then choose the correct answer.

Use the line graph above. At the end of Week 10, the plant had reached its final height of 12 inches. At the end of which week had the plant reached half its height?

A Week 5

B Week 6

C Week 7

D Week 8

Review the Key Standards

Write Ordered Pairs

SDAP 1.5 Know how to write ordered pairs correctly; for example, (x,y).

Each point on a coordinate grid can be located by using an ordered pair of numbers.

The first number in an ordered pair is the x-coordinate. It tells the distance to move in a horizontal direction from (0,0).

The second number in an ordered pair is the y-coordinate. It tells the distance to move vertically.

Point A is 4 spaces to the right of (0,0) so its x-coordinate is 4. It is 6 spaces above the x-axis, so its y-coordinate is 6. The ordered pair for point A is (4,6).

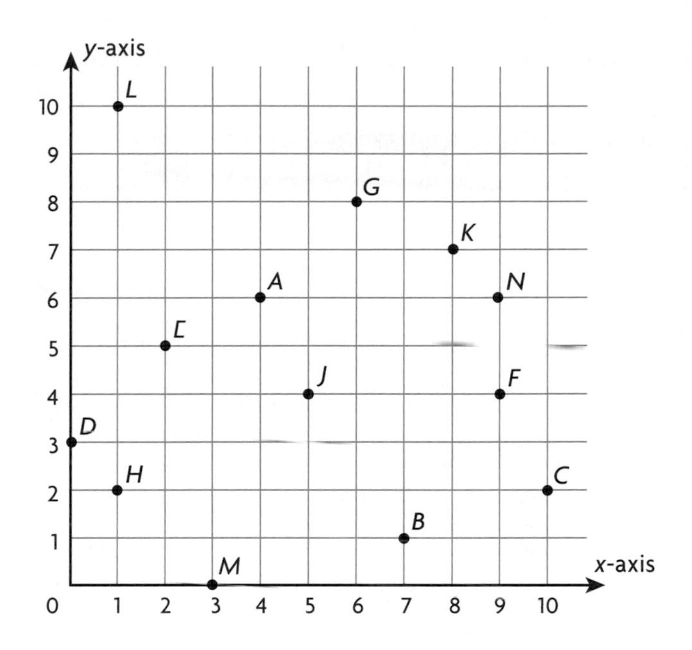

Examples

A What is the ordered pair for point B?

To get to point B, move 7 units right and 1 unit up. The ordered pair for point B is (7,1).

B Which point has coordinates (3,0)?

To get to (3,0), move 3 units right. Since the y-coordinate is 0, do not move up. Point M has coordinates (3,0).

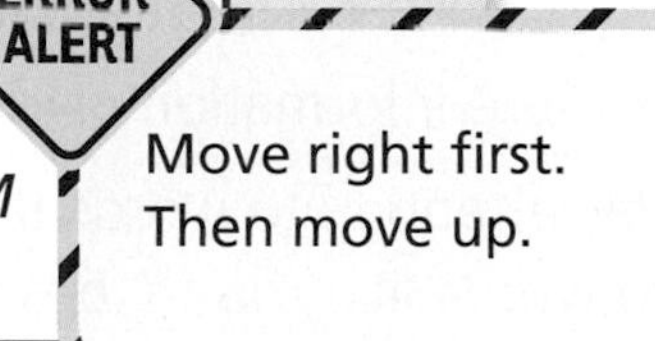

Move right first. Then move up.

Try It

Use the coordinate grid above. Write an ordered pair for each point.

1. F
2. G
3. H
4. J
5. K
6. L

Use the coordinate grid above. Identify the point with the given coordinates.

7. (0,3)
8. (9,6)
9. (10,2)

10. Read the problem below. **Explain** why C cannot be the correct answer choice. Then choose the correct answer.

What are the coordinates of point E?

A (0,5)

B (2,5)

C (5,2)

D (2,0)

Test-Taking Strategies

Tips for Taking Math Tests

Being a good test-taker is like being a good problem-solver. When you answer test questions, you are solving problems. Remember to **UNDERSTAND**, **PLAN**, **SOLVE**, and **CHECK**.

Read to Understand

Read the problem.

- Look for math terms and recall their meanings.
- Reread the problem and think about the question.
- Use the details in the problem and the question.

1. There are 460 campers and counselors at Summit Camp. Each table in the dining hall can seat 12 people. How many tables are needed?

A 40 **C** 38

B 39 **D** 4

Test Tip **Understand the problem.**

The critical information is that there are 460 campers and counselors. List all the given relationships and express them as equations. Use this information to begin solving the problem. Be sure to answer the question asked. The answer is **B**.

- Each word is important. Missing a word or reading it incorrectly could cause you to get the wrong answer.
- Is there information given that you do not need?
- Pay attention to words that are in all CAPITAL letters or *italics* and to words like *round*, *best*, *about* and *least to greatest*.

2. In 1995, Mariko ran the 100-yard dash in 12.40 seconds. In 1996, she ran it in 12.343 seconds. In 1997, she ran it in 12.6 seconds. In 1998, she ran it in 12.502 seconds. In what year was Mariko's fastest time?

A 1995 **C** 1997

B 1996 **D** 1998

Test Tip **Look for important words.**

The word *fastest* is important. The fastest runner takes the *least* amount of time. So, the least number of seconds is her fastest time. The answer is **B**.

Plan

Think about how you can solve the problem.

- Can you solve the problem with the information given?
- Pictures, charts, tables, and graphs may have the information you need.

3. Lisa made a line graph showing how much her plant grew each week.

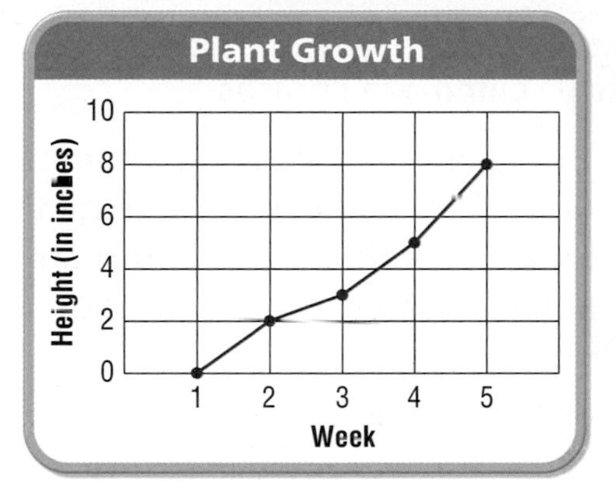

Between which two weeks did the plant grow the most?

A Weeks 1 and 2 **C** Weeks 3 and 4

B Weeks 2 and 3 **D** Weeks 4 and 5

Test Tip **Get the information you need.**

You need to find the two weeks between which the height of the plant increased the most. Find the difference from one week to the next and identify the two consecutive weeks with the greatest difference in height. The answer is **D**.

- You may need to write and solve an equation.
- Some problems have two steps or more.
- In some problems you need to look at relationships instead of computing an answer.
- If the path to the solution isn't clear, choose a problem solving strategy and use it to solve the problem.

4. A gravel path surrounds a rectangular grass field. The field is 60 feet long and 40 feet wide. The path is 3 feet wide. What is the area covered by the path?

A 300 ft^2 **C** 600 ft^2

B 309 ft^2 **D** 636 ft^2

Decide on a plan.

Using the strategy *draw a diagram* will help you find the dimensions of the larger rectangle so you can find the area. Match the description in the problem and label the diagram. First find the area of the field and the path. Then subtract the area of the field. The answer is **D**.

Solve

Follow your plan, working logically and carefully.

- Estimate your answer. Are any answer choices unreasonable?
- Use reasoning to find the most likely choices.
- Make sure you solved all steps needed to answer the problem.
- If your answer does not match any of the answer choices, check the numbers you used. Then check your computation.

5. What is the prime factorization of 30?

A 3×10 **C** $2 \times 3 \times 5$

B 5×6 **D** $2^2 \times 5$

Test Tip **Eliminate choices.**

Think about the meaning of *prime factorization*. You can eliminate the choices in which all the factors are not prime numbers. The answer is **C**.

- If your answer still does not match any of the choices, look for another form of the number, such as a decimal instead of a fraction.
- If answer choices are given as pictures, look at each one by itself while you cover the other three.
- If answer choices are statements, relate each one to the problem.
- Change your plan if it isn't working. Try a different strategy.

6. Andrew and Judy collect stamps. Andrew has half as many stamps as Judy. Let s represent the number of stamps that Andrew has. Which expression can be used to find the number of stamps that Judy has?

A $\frac{s}{2}$ **C** $s + 2$

B $2s$ **D** $s - 2$

Test Tip **Choose the answer.**

You need to determine how the number of stamps Andrew has is related to the number of stamps Judy has. The problem states, "Andrew has half as many stamps as Judy." So, Judy has two times the number of stamps Andrew has. Look at the answer choices and choose the answer that describes Judy's stamps in relation to Andrew's. The answer is **B**.

Check

Take time to catch your mistakes.

- Be sure you answered the question asked.
- Check that your answer fits the information in the problem.
- Check for important words you might have missed.
- Be sure you used all the information you needed.
- Check your computation by using a different method.
- Draw a picture when you are unsure of your answer.

7. At the market, Ms. Ruiz bought $\frac{1}{3}$ pound of Swiss cheese, $\frac{1}{4}$ pound of cheddar cheese, and $\frac{1}{2}$ pound of goat cheese. How much cheese did Ms. Ruiz buy?

A $\frac{1}{2}$ pound

B $1\frac{1}{12}$ pounds

C $1\frac{7}{12}$ pounds

D $3\frac{1}{2}$ pounds

Test Tip **Check your work.**

If your answer does not match any of the choices, check your computation. The answer is **B**.

Don't Forget!

Before the test

- Listen to the teacher's directions and read the instructions.
- Write down the ending time if the test is timed.
- Know where and how to mark your answers.
- Know whether you should write on the test page or use scratch paper.
- Ask any questions you may have before the test begins.

During the test

- Work quickly but carefully. If you are unsure how to answer a question, leave it blank and return to it later.
- If you cannot finish on time, look over the questions that are left. Answer the easiest ones first. Then, go back to answer the others.
- Fill in each answer space carefully. Erase completely if you change an answer. Erase any stray marks.
- Check that the answer number matches the question number, especially if you skip a question.

Addition Facts

	K	L	M	N	O	P	Q	R
A	6 + 7	9 + 6	3 + 5	8 + 9	0 + 7	2 + 8	6 + 4	7 + 7
B	1 + 6	8 + 4	5 + 1	2 + 7	3 + 3	8 + 2	4 + 5	2 + 6
C	6 + 6	3 + 7	7 + 8	4 + 6	9 + 0	4 + 2	10 + 4	3 + 8
D	6 + 1	5 + 9	10 + 6	5 + 7	3 + 9	9 + 8	8 + 7	8 + 1
E	7 + 6	7 + 1	6 + 9	4 + 3	5 + 5	8 + 0	9 + 5	2 + 9
F	9 + 1	8 + 5	7 + 0	8 + 3	7 + 2	4 + 7	10 + 5	4 + 8
G	5 + 3	9 + 9	3 + 6	7 + 4	0 + 8	4 + 4	7 + 10	6 + 8
H	8 + 6	10 + 7	0 + 9	7 + 9	5 + 6	8 + 10	6 + 5	9 + 4
I	9 + 7	8 + 8	1 + 9	5 + 8	10 + 9	6 + 3	6 + 2	9 + 10
J	9 + 2	7 + 5	6 + 0	10 + 8	5 + 4	4 + 9	9 + 3	10 + 10

Subtraction Facts

	K	L	M	N	O	P	Q	R
A	13 − 4	7 − 1	9 − 7	9 − 9	11 − 5	6 − 3	12 − 7	8 − 5
B	8 − 8	16 − 8	15 − 6	10 − 2	6 − 5	8 − 7	14 − 4	11 − 9
C	9 − 5	12 − 8	15 − 8	11 − 7	14 − 8	18 − 9	15 − 5	8 − 1
D	10 − 4	16 − 10	13 − 9	9 − 1	7 − 2	7 − 0	13 − 8	6 − 4
E	10 − 9	9 − 6	17 − 9	7 − 3	6 − 0	11 − 8	8 − 6	9 − 4
F	8 − 4	13 − 6	11 − 2	15 − 7	19 − 10	12 − 3	17 − 8	7 − 5
G	9 − 8	13 − 7	7 − 4	15 − 9	8 − 2	10 6	14 − 7	12 − 5
H	10 − 7	6 − 6	8 − 0	12 − 4	14 − 6	11 − 4	6 − 2	17 − 7
I	13 − 5	12 − 9	16 − 7	7 − 6	10 − 5	11 − 3	12 − 6	14 − 9
J	10 − 8	11 − 6	14 − 5	16 − 9	9 − 3	5 − 4	18 − 10	20 − 10

Multiplication Facts

	K	L	M	N	O	P	Q	R
A	5×6	5×9	7×7	9×10	7×5	12×2	10×6	6×7
B	6×6	0×6	2×7	12×8	9×2	3×5	5×8	8×3
C	7×0	5×1	4×5	9×9	6×8	8×11	11×7	10×5
D	1×7	9×4	0×7	2×5	9×7	10×9	3×3	12×7
E	5×7	1×9	4×3	7×6	11×3	3×8	4×2	10×10
F	10×12	5×5	6×4	9×8	0×8	9×6	11×2	12×6
G	5×3	4×6	6×3	7×9	12×5	0×9	5×4	12×11
H	7×1	6×9	1×6	4×4	3×7	11×11	4×8	12×9
I	7×4	2×4	8×6	3×4	11×5	2×9	8×9	7×8
J	8×0	3×9	12×12	8×5	4×7	6×2	9×5	8×8

Division Facts

	K	L	M	N	O	P	Q	R
A	$7\overline{)56}$	$5\overline{)40}$	$6\overline{)24}$	$6\overline{)30}$	$6\overline{)18}$	$7\overline{)42}$	$8\overline{)16}$	$9\overline{)45}$
B	$3\overline{)9}$	$10\overline{)90}$	$1\overline{)1}$	$1\overline{)6}$	$10\overline{)100}$	$3\overline{)12}$	$10\overline{)70}$	$8\overline{)56}$
C	$6\overline{)48}$	$12\overline{)60}$	$4\overline{)32}$	$6\overline{)54}$	$7\overline{)0}$	$3\overline{)18}$	$9\overline{)90}$	$11\overline{)55}$
D	$2\overline{)16}$	$3\overline{)21}$	$5\overline{)30}$	$3\overline{)15}$	$11\overline{)110}$	$9\overline{)9}$	$8\overline{)64}$	$9\overline{)63}$
E	$4\overline{)28}$	$2\overline{)10}$	$9\overline{)18}$	$1\overline{)5}$	$7\overline{)63}$	$8\overline{)32}$	$2\overline{)8}$	$9\overline{)108}$
F	$8\overline{)24}$	$4\overline{)4}$	$2\overline{)14}$	$11\overline{)66}$	$8\overline{)72}$	$4\overline{)12}$	$7\overline{)21}$	$6\overline{)36}$
G	$12\overline{)36}$	$5\overline{)20}$	$7\overline{)28}$	$7\overline{)14}$	$4\overline{)24}$	$11\overline{)121}$	$9\overline{)36}$	$11\overline{)132}$
H	$9\overline{)27}$	$3\overline{)27}$	$7\overline{)49}$	$4\overline{)20}$	$9\overline{)72}$	$5\overline{)60}$	$8\overline{)88}$	$10\overline{)80}$
I	$4\overline{)44}$	$8\overline{)48}$	$5\overline{)35}$	$8\overline{)40}$	$5\overline{)10}$	$2\overline{)12}$	$10\overline{)60}$	$9\overline{)54}$
J	$10\overline{)120}$	$12\overline{)72}$	$9\overline{)81}$	$4\overline{)16}$	$1\overline{)7}$	$12\overline{)60}$	$12\overline{)96}$	$12\overline{)144}$

Table of Measures

METRIC	CUSTOMARY
Length	
1 centimeter (cm) = 10 millimeters (mm)	1 foot (ft) = 12 inches (in.)
1 meter (m) = 1,000 millimeters	1 yard (yd) = 3 feet, or 36 inches
1 meter = 100 centimeters (cm)	1 mile (mi) = 1,760 yards, or 5,280 feet
1 meter = 10 decimeters (dm)	
1 kilometer (km) = 1,000 meters	
Capacity	
1 liter (L) = 1,000 milliliters (mL)	1 tablespoon (tbsp) = 3 teaspoons (tsp)
1 metric cup = 250 milliliters	1 cup (c) = 8 fluid ounces (fl oz)
1 liter = 4 metric cups	1 pint (pt) = 2 cups
1 kiloliter (kL) = 1,000 liters	1 quart (qt) = 2 pints, or 4 cups
	1 gallon (gal) = 4 quarts
Mass/Weight	
1 gram (g) = 1,000 milligrams (mg)	1 pound (lb) = 16 ounces (oz)
1 kilogram (kg) = 1,000 grams	1 ton (T) = 2,000 pounds

TIME
1 minute (min) = 60 seconds (sec)
1 hour (hr) = 60 minutes
1 day = 24 hours
1 week (wk) = 7 days
1 year (yr) = 12 months (mo) or about 52 weeks
1 year = 365 days
1 leap year = 366 days
1 decade = 10 years
1 century = 100 years
1 millennium = 1,000 years

SYMBOLS

$=$	is equal to	$\perp$	is perpendicular to
$\neq$	is not equal to	$\parallel$	is parallel to
$>$	is greater than	$\overleftrightarrow{AB}$	line AB
$<$	is less than	$\overrightarrow{AB}$	ray AB
$\geq$	is greater than or equal to	$\overline{AB}$	line segment AB
$\leq$	is less than or equal to	$\angle ABC$	angle ABC
2^3	the third power of 2	$\triangle ABC$	triangle ABC
10^2	ten squared	$^{+}8$	positive 8
10^3	ten cubed	$^{-}8$	negative 8
10^4	the fourth power of 10	$^\circ$	degree
(2,3)	ordered pair (x,y)	°C	degrees Celsius
%	percent	°F	degrees Fahrenheit
$\approx$	is approximately equal to		

FORMULAS

Perimeter		Area	
Polygon	$P =$ sum of the lengths of the sides	Rectangle	$A = l \times w$, $A = lw$
		Square	$A = s^2$
Rectangle	$P = (2 \times l) + (2 \times w)$ or $2l + 2w$	Parallelogram	$A = b \times h$, or $A = bh$
Square	$P = 4 \times s$, $P = 4s$	Triangle	$A = \frac{1}{2} \times b \times h$, or $A = \frac{1}{2}bh$

Volume	
Rectangular prism	$V = l \times w \times h$

Grade Five California Mathematics Content Standards

By the end of grade five, students increase their facility with the four basic arithmetic operations applied to fractions and decimals and learn to add and subtract positive and negative numbers. They know and use common measuring units to determine length and area and know and use formulas to determine the volume of simple geometric figures. Students know the concept of angle measurement and use a protractor and compass to solve problems. They use grids, tables, graphs, and charts to record and analyze data.

Number Sense

1.0 Students compute with very large and very small numbers, positive integers, decimals, and fractions and understand the relationship between decimals, fractions, and percents. They understand the relative magnitudes of numbers:

1.1 Estimate, round, and manipulate very large (e.g., millions) and very small (e.g., thousandths) numbers.

0⅂ 1.2 Interpret percents as a part of a hundred; find decimal and percent equivalents for common fractions and explain why they represent the same value; compute a given percent of a whole number.

What is 40% of 250? (CST released test question, 2004)

A test had 48 problems. Joe got 42 correct.

1. What percent were correct?
2. What percent were wrong?
3. If Moe got 93.75% correct, how many problems did he get correct?

1.3 Understand and compute positive integer powers of nonnegative integers; compute examples as repeated multiplication.

Which is bigger: 3^5 or 5^3?

0⅂ 1.4 Determine the prime factors of all numbers through 50 and write the numbers as the product of their prime factors by using exponents to show multiples of a factor (e.g., $24 = 2 \times 2 \times 2 \times 3 = 2^3 \times 3$).

Find the prime factorization of 48 and use exponents where appropriate.

0⅂ 1.5 Identify and represent on a number line decimals, fractions, mixed numbers, and positive and negative integers.

Next to each number, write the letter that represents the quantity on the number line.

2.2 ______ 0.3 ______ $^{-}0.5$ ______

$2\frac{6}{10}$ ______ $\frac{75}{100}$ ______ 1.5 ______

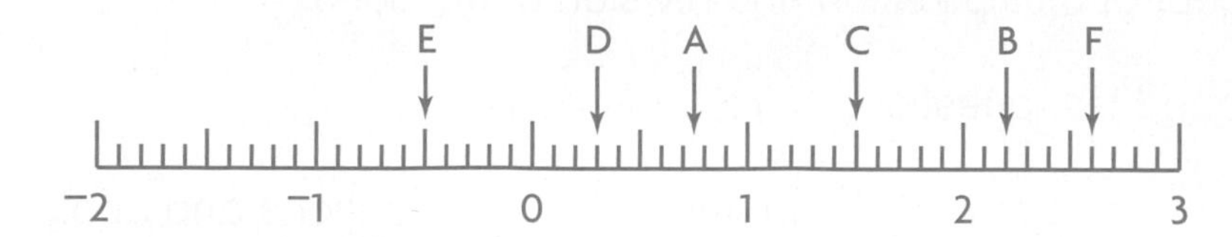

Place the following numbers, in approximate positions, on the number line: $1\frac{3}{7}$, 1.43, $\frac{23}{14}$.

2.0 Students perform calculations and solve problems involving addition, subtraction, and simple multiplication and division of fractions and decimals:

2.1 Add, subtract, multiply, and divide with decimals; add with negative integers; subtract positive integers from negative integers; and verify the reasonableness of the results.

Determine the following numbers:

1. $11 + (^{-}23)$
2. $(^{-}15) - 128$
3. $51 - 24.7$
4. 8.2×24.7
5. $68.13 \div 3$

2.2 Demonstrate proficiency with division, including division with positive decimals and long division with multidigit divisors.

Find the quotient: 6 divided by 0.025.

15. $12 \div 2.4 = ?$ (CST released test question, 2004)

2.3 Solve simple problems, including ones arising in concrete situations, involving the addition and subtraction of fractions and mixed numbers (like and unlike denominators of 20 or less), and express answers in the simplest form.

Suppose a galleon is a type of money worth 17 sickles. If Ludo borrows $2\frac{3}{17}$ galleons from Harry, then gives him back 12 sickles, how many galleons and sickles does Ludo still owe?

Sally is training to walk in a marathon. In her second week of training, she walked $5\frac{3}{4}$ miles on Tuesday, $5\frac{1}{16}$ miles on Thursday, and $16\frac{3}{8}$ miles on Sunday. How many miles altogether did Sally walk on those three days?

Jerry and Larry both ordered personal-sized pizzas for lunch. Jerry ate $\frac{3}{4}$ of his pizza, and Larry ate $\frac{2}{3}$ of his pizza. Who ate more pizza and how much more did he eat?

Given the following three pairs of fractions: $\frac{3}{8}$ and $\frac{1}{16}$, $5\frac{1}{4}$ and $1\frac{3}{4}$, 16 and $3\frac{1}{5}$, find for each pair its:

1. Sum
2. Difference

2.4 Understand the concept of multiplication and division of fractions.

$\frac{3}{4} \div \frac{3}{5} = \frac{?}{-}$ (CST released test question, 2004)

2.5 Compute and perform simple multiplication and division of fractions and apply these procedures to solving problems.

Given the following three pairs of fractions: $\frac{3}{8}$ and $\frac{1}{16}$, $5\frac{1}{4}$ and $1\frac{3}{4}$, 16 and $3\frac{1}{5}$), find for each pair its:

1. Product
2. Quotient in simplest terms

Ericka has $3\frac{1}{2}$ yards of cloth to make shirts. Each shirt requires $\frac{7}{8}$ yard. How many shirts can she make? How much cloth will she have left over?

Algebra and Functions

1.0 Students use variables in simple expressions, compute the value of the expression for specific values of the variable, and plot and interpret the results:

1.1 Use information taken from a graph or equation to answer questions about a problem situation.

1.2 Use a letter to represent an unknown number; write and evaluate simple algebraic expressions in one variable by substitution.

If x is a number that satisfies $3x + 2 = 14$, can x be equal to 3?
If $N = 4$, what is the value of $6 \times N - 3$?
(CST released test question, 2004)

1.3 Know and use the distributive property in equations and expressions with variables.

What value for z makes this equation true?

$8 \times 37 = (8 \times 30) + (8 \times z)$ (CST released test question, 2004)

1.4 Identify and graph ordered pairs in the four quadrants of the coordinate plane.

Plot these points on a coordinate plane:
(1,2), ($^-4$,$^-3$), (12,$^-1$), (0,4), ($^-4$,0)

0→ **1.5** Solve problems involving linear functions with integer values; write the equation; and graph the resulting ordered pairs of integers on a grid.

Which equation could have been used to create this function table? (CST released test question, 2004)

x	y
$^{-}9$	$^{-}5$
$^{-}2$	2
4	8
11	15

$y = \frac{x}{2}$ $\qquad y = 2x$ $\qquad y = x - 4$ $\qquad y = x + 4$

One can build rows of squares with toothpicks, as shown below for the case of 1, 2, 3, and 6 squares, respectively:

Explain why the following formula

$y = 3n + 1$

for the number of toothpicks y needed to form a row of n squares is correct. Graph this equation on a grid and remember that n takes on only whole number values 1, 2, 3, 4, . . .

Measurement and Geometry

1.0 Students understand and compute the volumes and areas of simple objects:

0→ **1.1** Derive and use the formula for the area of a triangle and of a parallelogram by comparing each with the formula for the area of a rectangle (i.e., two of the same triangles make a parallelogram with twice the area; a parallelogram is compared with a rectangle of the same area by pasting and cutting a right triangle on the parallelogram).

In the figure below, $WXYZ$ is a parallelogram.

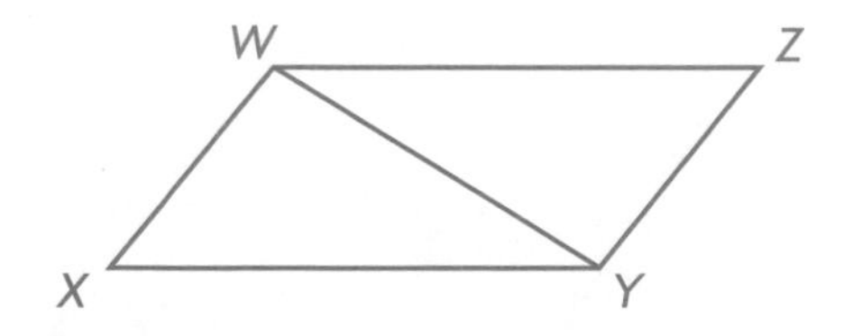

If the area of triangle *WXY* is 22 square inches, what is the area of *WXYZ*? (CST released test question, 2004)

1.2 Construct a cube and rectangular box from two-dimensional patterns and use these patterns to compute the surface area for these objects.

1.3 Understand the concept of volume and use the appropriate units in common measuring systems (i.e., cubic centimeter [cm^3], cubic meter [m^3], cubic inch [$in.^3$], cubic yard [$yd.^3$]) to compute the volume of rectangular solids.

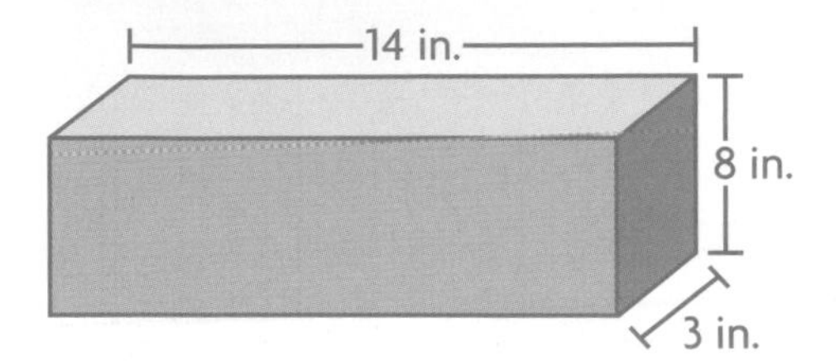

This rectangular prism has a length of 14 inches, a height of 8 inches, and a width of 3 inches. What is the volume? (CST released test question, 2004)

1.4 Differentiate between, and use appropriate units of measures for, two- and three-dimensional objects (i.e., find the perimeter, area, volume).

2.0 Students identify, describe, and classify the properties of, and the relationships between, plane and solid geometric figures:

2.1 Measure, identify, and draw angles, perpendicular and parallel lines, rectangles, and triangles by using appropriate tools (e.g., straightedge, ruler, compass, protractor, drawing software).

2.2 Know that the sum of the angles of any triangle is 180° and the sum of the angles of any quadrilateral is 360° and use this information to solve problems.

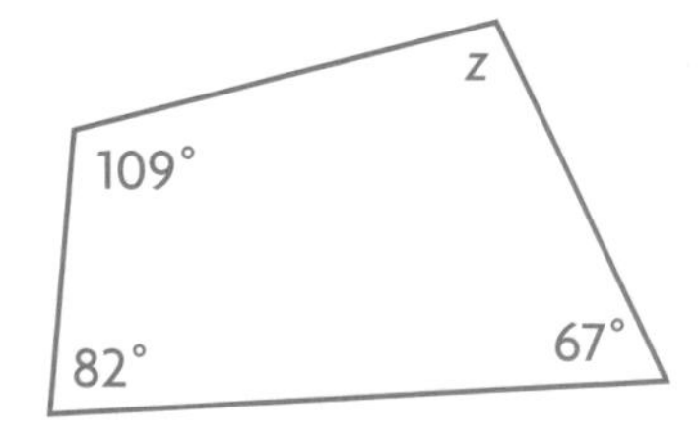

What is the measure of angle *z* in the figure above? (CST released test question, 2004)

2.3 Visualize and draw two-dimensional views of three-dimensional objects made from rectangular solids.

Statistics, Data Analysis, and Probability

1.0 Students display, analyze, compare, and interpret different data sets, including data sets of different sizes:

1.1 Know the concepts of mean, median, and mode; compute and compare simple examples to show that they may differ.

Compute the mean, median, and mode of the following collection of 27 numbers:

$\underbrace{1,1,\ldots,1}_{23}, 2, 3, 26, 135$

1.2 Organize and display single-variable data in appropriate graphs and representations (e.g., histogram, circle graphs) and explain which types of graphs are appropriate for various data sets.

1.3 Use fractions and percentages to compare data sets of different sizes.

🔑 1.4 Identify ordered pairs of data from a graph and interpret the meaning of the data in terms of the situation depicted by the graph.

🔑 1.5 Know how to write ordered pairs correctly; for example, (x,y).

Mathematical Reasoning

1.0 Students make decisions about how to approach problems:

1.1 Analyze problems by identifying relationships, distinguishing relevant from irrelevant information, sequencing and prioritizing information, and observing patterns.

1.2 Determine when and how to break a problem into simpler parts.

2.0 Students use strategies, skills, and concepts in finding solutions:

2.1 Use estimation to verify the reasonableness of calculated results.

2.2 Apply strategies and results from simpler problems to more complex problems.

2.3 Use a variety of methods, such as words, numbers, symbols, charts, graphs, tables, diagrams, and models, to explain mathematical reasoning.

2.4 Express the solution clearly and logically by using the appropriate mathematical notation and terms and clear language; support solutions with evidence in both verbal and symbolic work.

2.5 Indicate the relative advantages of exact and approximate solutions to problems and give answers to a specified degree of accuracy.

2.6 Make precise calculations and check the validity of the results from the context of the problem.

3.0 Students move beyond a particular problem by generalizing to other situations:

3.1 Evaluate the reasonableness of the solution in the context of the original situation.

3.2 Note the method of deriving the solution and demonstrate a conceptual understanding of the derivation by solving similar problems.

3.3 Develop generalizations of the results obtained and apply them in other circumstances.

Glossary

Pronunciation Key

a	add, map	ē	equal, tree	m	move, seem	o͞o	pool, food	û(r)	burn, term
ā	ace, rate	f	fit, half	n	nice, tin	p	pit, stop	yo͞o	fuse, few
â(r)	care, air	g	go, log	ng	ring, song	r	run, poor	v	vain, eve
ä	palm,	h	hope, hate	o	odd, hot	s	see, pass	w	win, away
	father	i	it, give	ō	open, so	sh	sure, rush	y	yet, yearn
b	bat, rub	ī	ice, write	ô	order, jaw	t	talk, sit	z	zest, muse
ch	check, catch	j	joy, ledge	oi	oil, boy	th	thin, both	zh	vision,
d	dog, rod	k	cool, take	ou	pout, now	t̶h̶	this, bathe		pleasure
e	end, pet	l	look, rule	o͝o	took, full	u	up, done		

ə the schwa, an unstressed vowel representing the sound spelled *a* in above, *e* in sicken, *i* in possible, *o* in melon, *u* in circus

Other symbols:
- • separates words into syllables
- ʹ indicates stress on a syllable

absolute value [ab•sə•lo͞otʹ valʹyo͞o] **valor absoluto** The distance of an integer from zero on a number line (p. 377)

acute angle [ə•kyo͞otʹ angʹgəl] **ángulo agudo** An angle that has a measure less than a right angle (less than 90°) (p. 437)
Example:

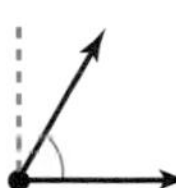

Word History

The Latin word for needle is *acus*. This means "pointed" or "sharp." You will recognize the root in the words acid (sharp taste), acumen (mentally sharp), and *acute*, which describes a sharp or pointed angle.

acute triangle [ə•kyo͞otʹ trīʹang•gəl] **triángulo acutángulo** A triangle that has three acute angles (p. 468)

addends [adʹendz] **sumandos** Numbers that are added in an addition problem (p. 20)

addition [ə•dishʹen] **suma** The process of finding the total number of items when two or more groups of items are joined; the opposite of subtraction (p. 16)

algebraic expression [al•jə•brāʹik ik•spreʹshən] **expresión algebraica** An expression that includes at least one variable (p. 23)
Examples: $x + 5$, $3a - 4$

angle [angʹgəl] **ángulo** A figure formed by two rays that meet at a common endpoint (p. 437)
Example:

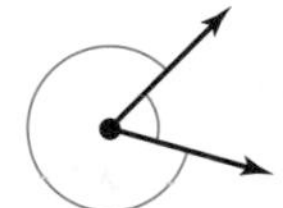

arc [ärk] **arco** Part of a circle between two points (p. 444)
Example:

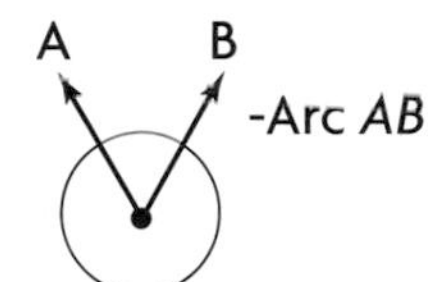

area [ârʹē•ə] **área** The number of square units needed to cover a surface (p. 546)

array [ə•rāʹ] **matriz** An arrangement of objects in rows and columns (p. 64)
Example:

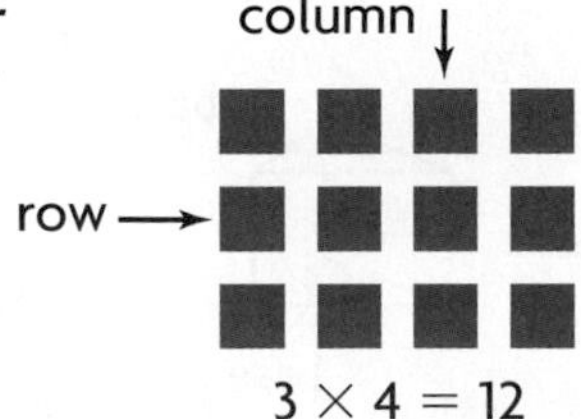

Associative Property of Addition [ə•sōʹshē•ə•tiv präʹ pər•tē əv ə•diʹshən] **propiedad asociativa de la suma** The property that states that when the grouping of addends is changed, the sum is the same (p. 20) *Example:* $(5 + 8) + 4 = 5 + (8 + 4)$

Associative Property of Multiplication [ə•sō′shē•ə•tiv prä′pər•tē əv mul•tə•plə•kā′shən] **propiedad asociativa de la multiplicación** The property that states that the way factors are grouped does not change the product (p. 360)
Example: $(2 \times 3) \times 4 = 2 \times (3 \times 4)$

average [av′rij] **promedio** See *mean.* (p. 600)

axis [ak′səs] **eje** The horizontal or vertical number line used in a graph or coordinate plane (p. 500)

bar graph [bär graf] **gráfica de barras** A graph that uses horizontal or vertical bars to display countable data (p. 608)
Example:

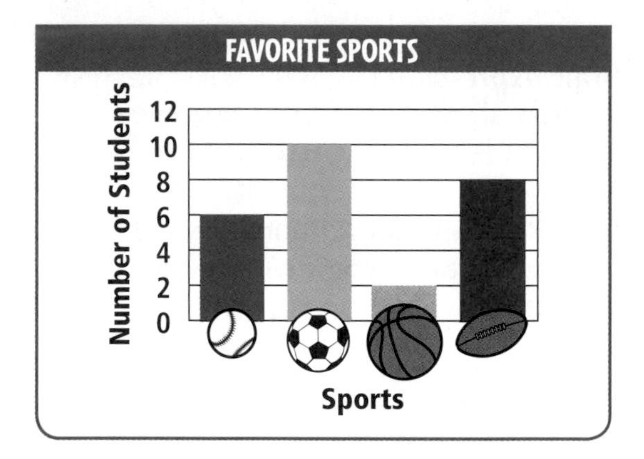

base [bās] (arithmetic) **base** A number used as a repeated factor (p. 126)
Example: $8^3 = 8 \times 8 \times 8$. The base is 8.

base [bās] (geometry) **base** In two dimensions, one side of a triangle or parallelogram which is used to help find the area. In three dimensions, a plane figure, usually a polygon or circle, which is used to partially describe a solid figure and is used to help find the volume of some solid figures. See *height* (p. 478)
Examples:

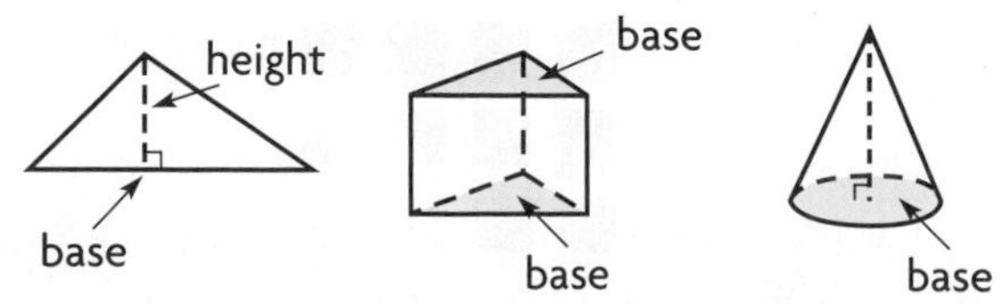

benchmark [bench′märk] **punto de referencia** A familiar number used as a point of reference (p. 162)

benchmark fraction [bench′märk frak′shən] **fracción de referencia** Familiar fractions used as a point of reference (p. 162)

billion [bil′yən] **millardo** 1000 millions; written as 1,000,000,000 (p. 4)

categorical data [ka•tə•gor′i•kəl dā′tə] **datos categóricos** When graphed, data that shows groups or choices in any order (p. 634)

centimeter (cm) [sen′tə•mē•tər] **centímetro (cm)** A metric unit for measuring length or distance; 0.01 meter = 1 centimeter (p. 524)

chord [kôrd] **cuerda** A line segment with endpoints on a circle (p. 452)
Example:

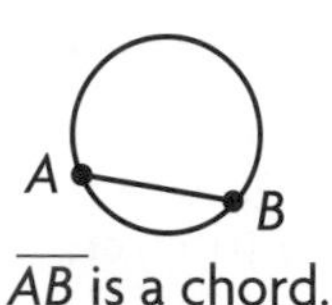

$\overline{AB}$ is a chord.

circle [sər′kəl] **círculo** A closed figure with all points on the figure the same distance from the center point (p. 452)
Example:

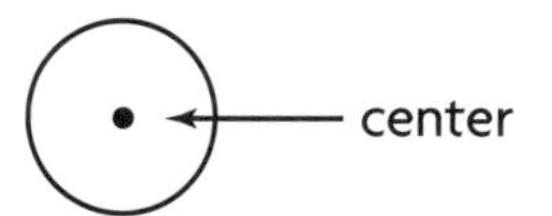

circle graph [sər′kəl graf] **gráfica circular** A graph that shows how parts of the data are related to the whole and to each other (p. 418)
Example:

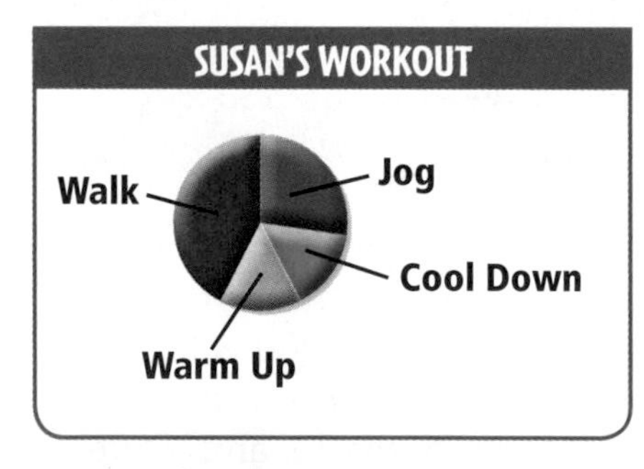

common factor [kä′mən fak′tər] **factor común** A number that is a factor of two or more numbers (p. 147)

common multiple [kä′mən mul′tə•pəl] **múltiplo común** A number that is a multiple of two or more numbers (p. 152)

Commutative Property of Addition [kə•myo͞o′tə•tiv prä′pər•tē əv ə•di′shən] **propiedad conmutativa de la suma** The property that states that when the order of two addends is changed, the sum is the same (p. 20) *Example:* $4 + 5 = 5 + 4$

Commutative Property of Multiplication [kə•myo͞o′tə•tiv prä′pər•tē əv mul•tə•plə•kā′shən] **propiedad conmutativa de la multiplicación** The property that states that when the order of two factors is changed, the product is the same *Example:* 4 × 5 = 5 × 4 (p. 360)

compass [kum′pəs] **compás** A tool used to construct circles and arcs (p. 444)

compatible numbers [kəm•pa′tə•bəl num′bərz] **números compatibles** Numbers that are easy to compute mentally (p. 86)

compensation [kam•pən•sa′shən] **compensación** An estimation strategy in which you change one addend to a multiple of ten and then adjust the other addend to keep the balance (p. 20)

composite number [käm•pä′zət num′bər] **número compuesto** A number having more than two factors (p. 120)
Example: 6 is a composite number, since its factors are 1, 2, 3, and 6.

cone [kōn] **cono** A solid figure that has a flat, circular base and one vertex (p. 478)
Example:

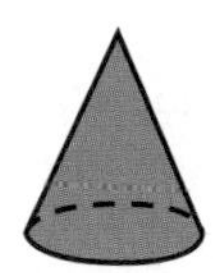

congruent [kən•gro͞o′ənt] **congruente** Having the same size and shape (p. 456)

coordinate plane [kō•ôr′də•nət plān] **plano de coordenadas** A plane formed by two intersecting and perpendicular number lines called axes (p. 502)
Example:

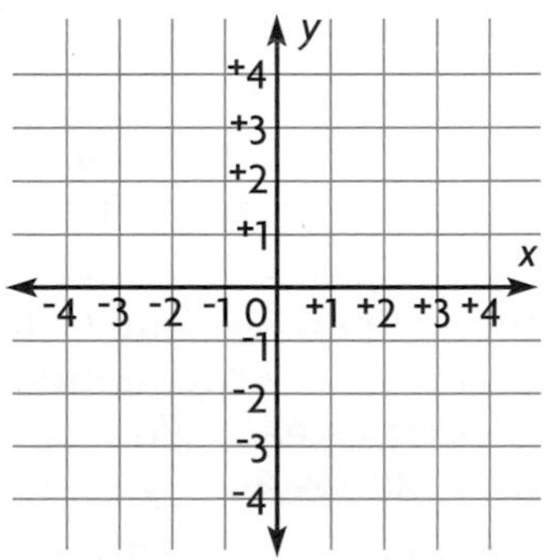

corresponding angles [kôr•ə•span′ding ang′gəlz] **ángulos correspondientes** Angles that are in the same position in similar figures (p. 457)
Example:

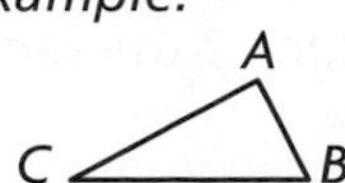

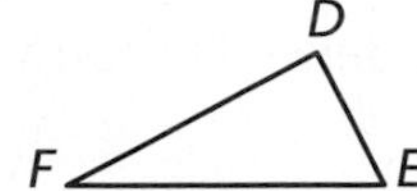

∠A and ∠D are corresponding angles.

corresponding sides [kôr•ə•span′ding sīdz] **lados correspondientes** Sides that are in the same position in similar figures (p. 457)
Example:

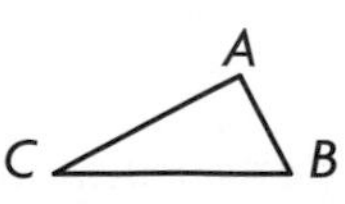

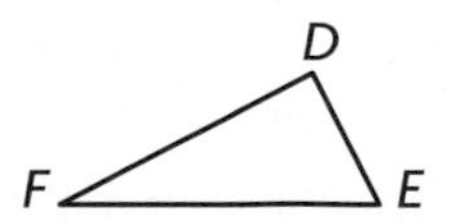

$\overline{CA}$ and $\overline{FD}$ are corresponding sides.

cube [kyo͞ob] **cubo** A solid figure with six congruent square faces (p. 478)
Example:

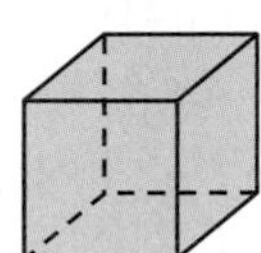

cubic unit [kyo͞o′bik yo͞o′nət] **unidad cúbica** A unit of volume with dimensions 1 unit × 1 unit × 1 unit (p. 576)

cylinder [si′lən•dər] **cilindro** A solid figure that has two parallel bases that are congruent circles (p. 478)
Example:

D

data [dā′tə] **datos** Information collected about people or things, often to draw conclusions about them (p. 596)

decagon [dek′ə•gän] **decágono** A polygon with 10 sides (p. 446)
Examples:

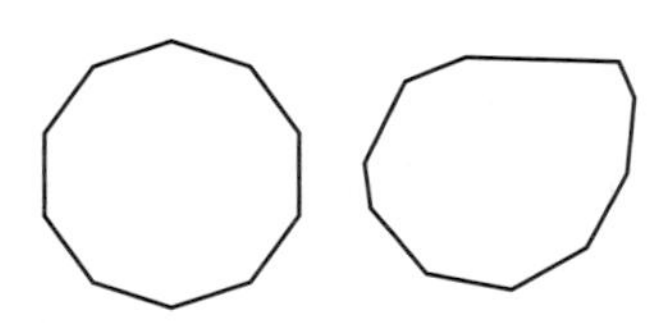

decimal [de′sə•məl] **decimal** A number with one or more digits to the right of the decimal point (p. 38)

decimal point [de′sə•məl point] **punto decimal** A symbol used to separate dollars from cents in money, and the ones place from the tenths place in decimal numbers (p. 38)

decimal system [de′sə•məl sis′təm] **sistema decimal** A system of computation based on the number 10

decimeter (dm) [de′sə•mē•tər] **decímetro (dm)** A unit of length in the metric system; 10 decimeters = 1 meter (p. 524)

degree (°) [di•grē′] **grado (°)** A unit for measuring angles or for measuring temperature (p. 437)

denominator [di•nä′mə•nā•tər] **denominador** The number below the bar in a fraction that tells how many equal parts are in the whole (p. 144)

Example: $\frac{3}{4}$ ←denominator

diameter [dī•am′ə•tər] **diámetro** A line segment that passes through the center of a circle and has its endpoints on the circle (p. 452)
Example:

difference [dif′ər•əns] **diferencia** The answer to a subtraction problem (p. 17)

digit [di′jit] **dígito** Any one of the ten symbols 0, 1, 2, 3, 4, 5, 6, 7, 8, 9 used to write numbers (p. 4)

Distributive Property [di•strib′yə•tiv prä′pər•tē] **propiedad distributiva** The property that states that multiplying a sum by a number is the same as multiplying each addend in the sum by the number and then adding the products (p. 64)
Example: $3 \times (4 + 2) = (3 \times 4) + (3 \times 2)$
$3 \times 6 = 12 + 6$
$18 = 18$

dividend [di′və•dend] **dividendo** The number that is to be divided in a division problem (p. 86)
Example: $36 \div 6$; $6\overline{)36}$ The dividend is 36.

division [də•vi′zhən] **división** The process of sharing a number of items to find how many groups can be made or how many items will be in a group; the operation that is the opposite of multiplication (p. 88)

divisor [də•vī′zər] **divisor** The number that divides the dividend (p. 86)
Example: $15 \div 3$; $3\overline{)15}$ The divisor is 3.

double-line graph [du′ bəl līn graf] **gráfica de doble línea** A line graph that represents two sets of data. (p. 629)

edge [ej] **arista** The line made where two or more faces of a solid figure meet (p. 479)
Example:

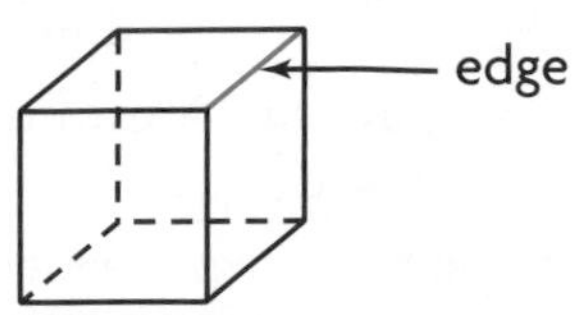

equation [i•kwā′zhən] **ecuación** An algebraic or numerical sentence that shows that two quantities are equal (p. 352)

equilateral triangle [ē•kwə•la′tə•rəl trī′ang•gəl] **triángulo equilátero** A triangle with three congruent sides (p. 468)
Example:

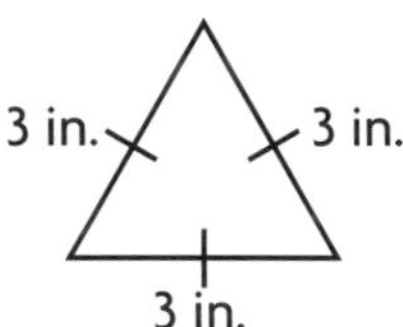

equivalent [ē •kwiv′ə•lənt] **equivalente** Having the same value (p. 46)

equivalent decimals [ē•kwiv′ə•lənt de′sə•məlz] **decimales equivalentes** Decimals that name the same number or amount (p. 42)
Example: 0.4 = 0.40 = 0.400

equivalent fractions [ē•kwiv′ə•lənt frak′shənz] **fracciones equivalentes** Fractions that name the same amount or part (p. 144)
Example: $\frac{3}{4} = \frac{6}{8}$

estimate [es′tə•māt] *noun* **estimación (s)** A number close to an exact amount (p. 14)

estimate [es′tə•mət] *verb* **estimar (v)** To find a number that is close to an exact amount (p. 14)

evaluate [ē•val′yo͞o•wāt] **evaluar** To find the value of a numerical or algebraic expression (p. 106)

expanded form [ek•spand′id fôrm] **forma desarrollada** A way to write numbers by showing the value of each digit (p. 4)
Example: 832 = 800 + 30 + 2

exponent [ek′spō•nənt] **exponente** A number that shows how many times the base is used as a factor (p. 126)
Example: $10^3 = 10 \times 10 \times 10$;
3 is the exponent.

Word History

Exponent is the combination of the Latin roots *exo* (out of) + *ponere* (place). In the 17th century, mathematicians began to use complicated quantities. The idea of positioning a number by raising it "out of place" is traced to Descartes.

expression [ek•spre′shən] **expresión** A mathematical phrase or the part of a number sentence that combines numbers, operation signs, and sometimes variables, but does not have an equal sign (p. 22)

face [fās] **cara** A polygon that is a flat surface of a solid figure (p. 479)
Example:

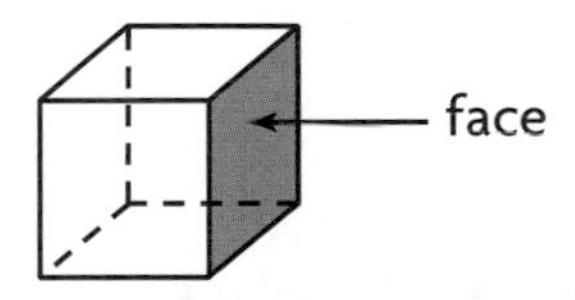

factor [fak′tər] **factor** A number multiplied by another number to find a product (p. 120)

factor tree [fak′tər trē] **árbol de factores** A diagram that shows the prime factors of a number (p. 132)

foot (ft) [fo͝ot] **pie** A unit of length in the customary system; 1 foot = 12 inches (p. 524)

formula [fôr′myə•lə] **fórmula** A set of symbols that expresses a mathematical rule (p. 532)
Example: $A = l \times w$

fraction [frak′shən] **fracción** A number that names a part of a whole or a part of a group (p. 144)

frequency table [frē′kwen•sē tā′bəl] **tabla de frecuencia** A table that uses numbers to record data about how often something happens (p. 599)

function [funk′shən] **función** A relationship between two quantities in which one quantity depends on the other (p. 504)

function table [funk′shən tā′bəl] **tabla de funciones** A table that matches each input value with an output value. The output values are determined by the function. (p. 504)

greater than (>) [grā′tər thàn] **mayor que (>)** A symbol used to compare two numbers, with the greater number given first (p. 8)
Example: $6 > 4$

greatest common factor (GCF) [grā′təst kä′mən fak′tər] **máximo común divisor (MCD)** The greatest factor that two or more numbers have in common (p. 146)
Example: 6 is the GCF of 18 and 30.

height [hīt] **altura** The length of a perpendicular from the base to the top of a plane figure or solid figure (p. 560)
Example:

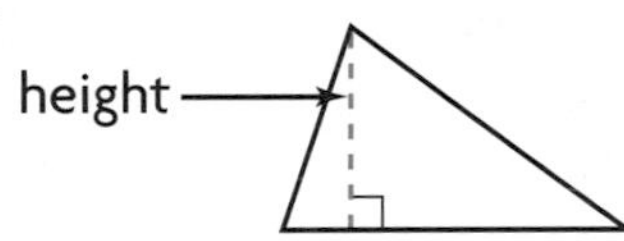

hexagon [hek′sə•gän] **hexágono** A polygon with six sides and six angles (p. 446)
Examples:

histogram [his′tə•gram] **histograma** A bar graph that shows the number of times data occurs within intervals (p. 624)

hundredth [hun′drədth] **centésimo** One of one hundred equal parts (p. 38)
Examples: 0.56 fifty-six hundredths
$\frac{45}{100}$ forty-five hundredths

Identity Property of Addition [ī•den′tə•tē prä′pər•tē əv ə•di′shən] **propiedad de identidad de la suma** The property that states that when you add zero to a number, the result is that number

Identity Property of Multiplication [ī•den′tə•tē prä′pər•tē əv mul•tə•plə•kā′shən] **propiedad de identidad de la multiplicación** The property that states that the product of any number and 1 is that number

inch (in.) [inch] **pulgada (pulg)** A customary unit for measuring length or distance; 12 inches = 1 foot (p. 524)

inequality [in•i•kwä′lə•tē] **desigualdad** A number sentence that contains the symbols (p. 9) $<$, $>$, $\leq$, $\geq$, or $\neq$

integers [in′ti•jərz] **enteros** The set of whole numbers and their opposites (p. 376)

intersecting lines [in•tər•sek′ting līnz] **líneas secantes** Lines that cross each other at exactly one point (p. 437)
Example:

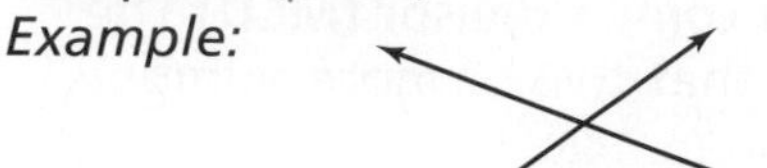

interval [in′tər•vəl] **intervalo** The difference between one number and the next on the scale of a graph (p. 624)

inverse operations [in′vərs ä•pə•rā′shənz] **operaciones inversas** Operations that undo each other, like addition and subtraction or multiplication and division (p. 17)

isosceles triangle [ī•sä′sə•lēz trī′ang•gəl] **triángulo isósceles** A triangle with exactly two congruent sides (p. 468)
Example:

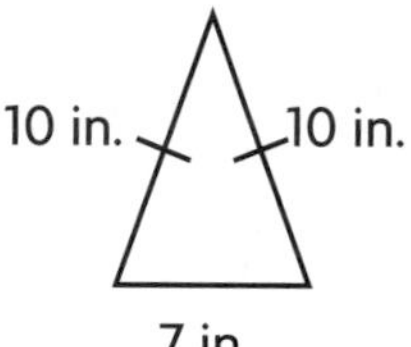

kilometer (km) [kə•lä′mə•tər] **kilómetro (km)** A metric unit that is used to measure length or distance; 1,000 meters = 1 kilometer (p. 524)

leaf [lēf] **hoja** A ones digit in a stem-and-leaf plot (p. 626)

least common denominator (LCD) [lēst kä′mən di•nä′mə•nā•tər] **mínimo común denominador (m.c.d.)** The least common multiple of two or more denominators (p. 205)
Example: The LCD for $\frac{1}{4}$ and $\frac{5}{6}$ is 12.

least common multiple (LCM) [lēst kä′mən mul′tə•pəl] **mínimo común múltiplo (m.c.m.)** The least number, other than zero, that is a common multiple of two or more numbers (p. 205)

less than (<) [les *th*an] **menor que (<)** A symbol used to compare two numbers, with the lesser number given first (p. 8)
Example: $4 < 6$

like fractions [līk frak′shənz] **fracciones semejantes** Fractions that have the same denominator (p. 176)
Example: $\frac{2}{5}$ and $\frac{4}{5}$ are like fractions.

line [līn] **línea** A straight path in a plane, extending in both directions with no endpoints (p. 436) *Example:*

linear unit [li′nē•ər yōō′nət] **unidad lineal** A measure of length, width, height, or distance

line graph [līn graf] **gráfica lineal** A graph that uses line segments to show how data change over time (p. 607)

line plot [līn plät] **diagrama de puntos** A graph that shows frequency of data along a number line (p. 598)
Example:

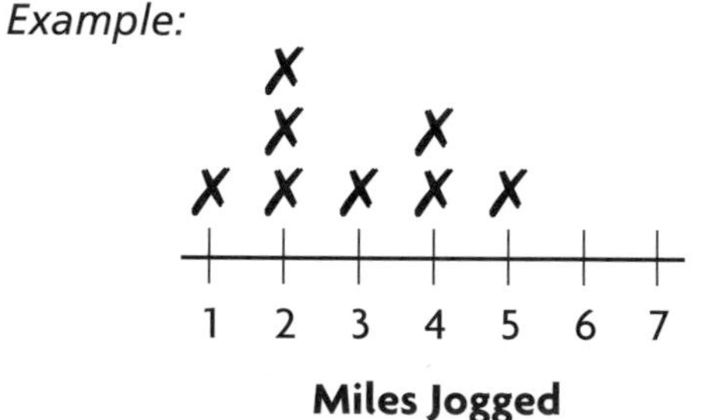

line segment [līn seg′mənt] **segmento** A part of a line between two endpoints (p. 436)

mean [mēn] **media** The average of a set of numbers, found by dividing the sum of the set by the number of addends (p. 600)

median [mē′dē•ən] **mediana** The middle number in a set of data that are arranged in order (p. 602)

meter (m) [mē′tər] **metro (m)** A metric unit for measuring length or distance; 1 meter = 100 centimeters (p. 13)

mile (mi) [mīl] **milla (mi)** A customary unit for measuring length or distance; 5,280 feet = 1 mile (p. 11)

millimeter (mm) [mi′lə•mē•tər] **milímetro (mm)** A metric unit for measuring length or distance; 1 millimeter = 0.001 meter (p. 524)

million [mil′yən] **millón** 1,000 thousands; written as 1,000,000 (p. 4)

mixed number [mikst num′bər] **número mixto** A number that is made up of a whole number and a fraction (p. 150) *Example:* $1\frac{5}{8}$

mode [mōd] **moda** The number or item that occurs most often in a set of data (p. 602)

multiple [mul′tə•pəl] **múltiplo** The product of a given whole number and another whole number (p. 60)

multiplication [mul•tə•plə•kā′shən] **multiplicación** A process to find the total number of items made up of equal-sized groups, or to find the total number of items in a given number of groups. It is the opposite operation of division (p. 60)

negative integer [ne′gə•tiv in′ti•jər] **entero negativo** Any integer less than zero (p. 376)
Examples: ⁻4, ⁻5, and ⁻6 are negative integers.

net [net] **plantilla** A two-dimensional pattern that can be folded into a three-dimensional polyhedron (p. 482)
Example:

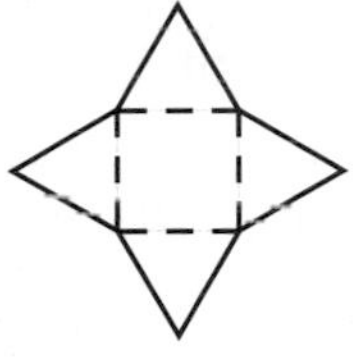

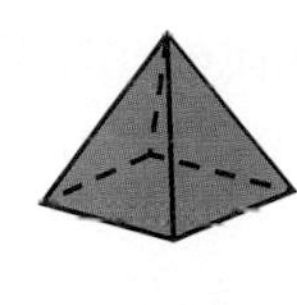

number line [num′bər līn] **recta numérica** A line on which numbers can be located. (p. 8)
Example:

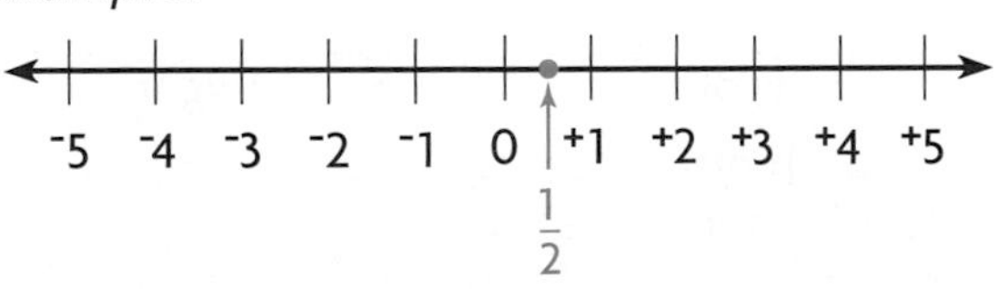

numerator [nōō′mə•rā•tər] **numerador** The number above the bar in a fraction that tells how many equal parts of the whole are being considered (p. 144)

Example: $\frac{3}{4}$ ←numerator

numerical data [nōō•mer′i•kəl dā′tə] **datos numéricos** When graphed, data that shows numbers in order on some numerical scale of the graph (p. 634)

numerical expression [nōō•mer′i•kəl ek•spre′shən] **expresión numérica** A mathematical phrase that uses only numbers and operation symbols (p. 22)

obtuse angle [äb•tōōs′ ang′gəl] **ángulo obtuso** An angle whose measure is greater than 90° and less than 180° (p. 437)
Example:

obtuse triangle [äb•tōōs′ trī′ang•gəl] **triángulo obtusángulo** A triangle that has one obtuse angle (p. 468)

octagon [äk′tə•gän] **octágono** A polygon with eight sides and eight angles (p. 446)
Examples:

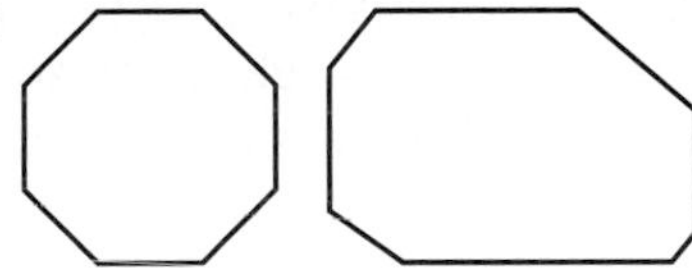

opposites [ä′pə•zəts] **opuestos** Two numbers that are the same distance, but in opposite directions, from zero on a number line (p. 376)

ordered pair [ôr′dərd pâr] **par ordenado** A pair of numbers used to locate a point on a grid. The first number tells the left-right position and the second number tells the up-down position. (p. 498)

order of operations [ôr′dər əv ä•pə•rā′shənz] **orden de las operaciones** A special set of rules which gives the order in which calculations are done in an expression (p. 348)

origin [ôr′ə•jən] **origen** The point where the two axes of a coordinate plane intersect, (0,0) (p. 502)

outlier [out′lī•ər] **valor atípico** A value separated from the rest of the data (p. 599)

overestimate [ō•vər•es′tə•mət] **sobrestimar** An estimate that is greater than the exact answer (p. 14)

P

parallel lines [par′ə•lel līnz] **líneas paralelas** Lines in a plane that are always the same distance apart (p. 437)
Example:

parallelogram [pâ•rə•lel′ə•gram] **paralelogramo** A quadrilateral whose opposite sides are parallel and have the same length, or are congruent (p. 472)
Example:

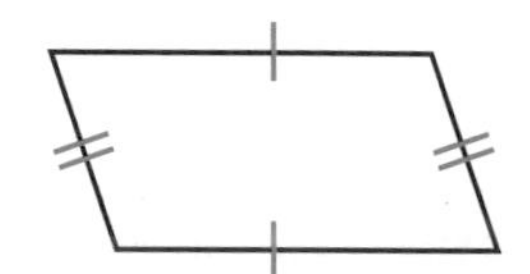

parentheses [pə•ren′thə•sēz] **paréntesis** The symbols used to show which operation or operations in an expression should be done first (p. 348)

partial product [pär′shəl prä′dəkt] **producto parcial** A method of multiplying in which the ones, tens, hundreds, and so on are multiplied separately and then the products are added together (p. 70)

pentagon [pen′tə•gän] **pentágono** A polygon with five sides and five angles (p. 446)
Examples:

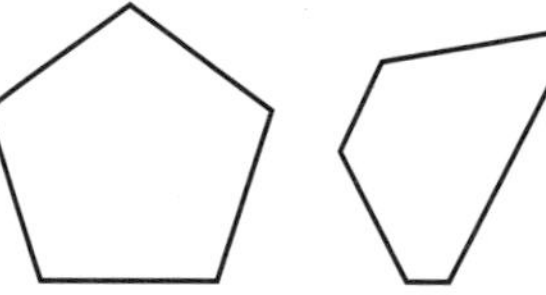

percent [pər•sent′] **porcentaje** A fractional part of a number to 100 (p. 404)

perfect square [pər′-fikt skwâr] **cuadrado perfecto** The product of a number and itself (p. 129)

perimeter [pə•rim′ə•tər] **perímetro** The distance around a closed plane figure (p. 528)

perpendicular lines [pər•pen•dik′yə•lər līnz] **líneas perpendiculares** Two lines that intersect to form right angles (p. 437)
Example:

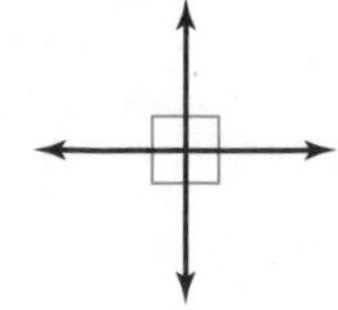

pictograph [pik′tə•graf] **pictografía** A graph that displays countable data with symbols or pictures (p. 608)
Example:

HOW WE GET TO SCHOOL

Walk	✳ ✳ ✳
Ride a Bike	✳ ✳ ✳ ✳
Ride a Bus	✳ ✳ ✳ ✳ ✳ ✳
Ride in a Car	✳ ✳

Key: Each ✳ = 10 students

place value [plās val′yōō] **valor posicional** The value of a place, such as ones or tens, in a number (p. 4)

plane [plān] **plano** A flat surface that extends without end in all directions (p. 436)
Example:

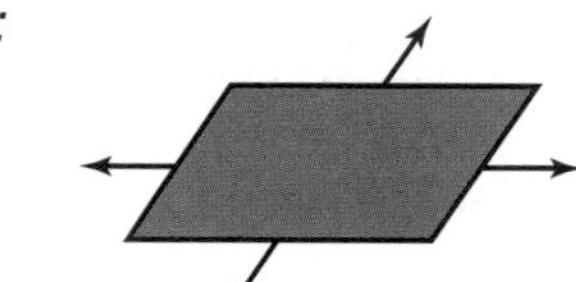

plane figure [plān fig′yər] **figura plana** A figure that lies in a plane (p. 476)

point [point] **punto** An exact location in space, usually represented by a dot (p. 436)

polygon [pol′•i•gon] **polígono** A closed plane figure formed by three or more line segments (p. 446)
Examples:

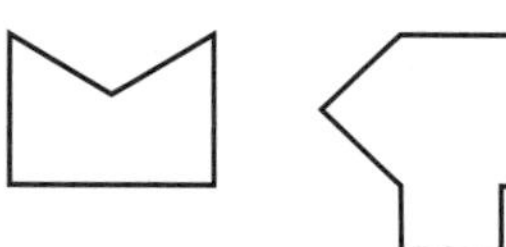

Polygons

Not Polygons

polyhedron [pol•i•hē′drən] **poliedro** A solid figure with faces that are polygons (p. 478)
Examples:

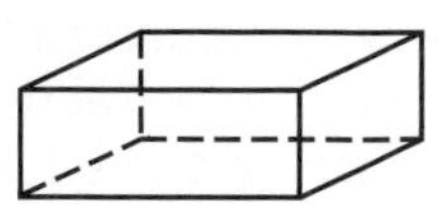

population [pä•pyə•lā′shən] **población** The entire group of objects or individuals considered for a survey (p. 596)

positive integer [pä′zə•tiv in′ti•jər] **entero positivo** Any integer greater than zero (p. 376)

prime factorization [prīm fak•tə•ri•zā′shən] **descomposición en factores primos** A number written as the product of all its prime factors (p. 132)

prime number [prīm num′bər] **número primo** A number that has exactly two factors: 1 and itself (p. 120)
Examples: 2, 3, 5, 7, 11, 13, 17, and 19 are prime numbers. 1 is not a prime number.

prioritize [prī•or′ə•tīz] **priorizar** To put events in order of importance (p. 228)

prism [priz′əm] **prisma** A solid figure that has two congruent, polygon-shaped bases, and other faces that are all rectangles (p. 478)
Examples:

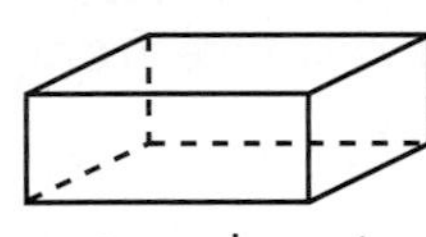

rectangular prism

triangular prism

product [prä′dəkt] **producto** The answer to a multiplication problem (p. 60)

protractor [prō′trak•tər] **transportador** A tool used for measuring or drawing angles (p. 440)

pyramid [pir′ə•mid] **pirámide** A solid figure with a polygon base and all other faces triangles that meet at a common vertex (p. 478)
Example:

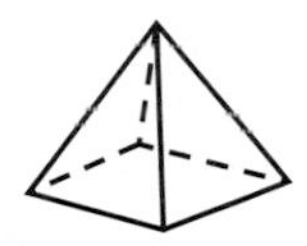

Word History

A fire is sometimes in the shape of a pyramid, with a point at the top and a wider base. This may be how *pyramid* got its name. The Greek word for fire was *pura,* which may have been combined with the Egyptian word *mer.*

quadrilateral [kwäd•rə•lat′ə•rəl] **cuadrilátero** A polygon with four sides and four angles (p. 446)
Example:

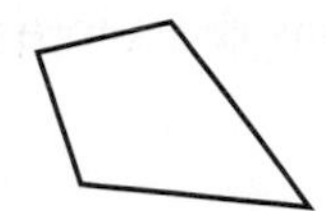

quotient [kwō′shənt] **cociente** The number, not including the remainder, that results from dividing (p. 86)
Example: $8 \div 4 = 2$. The quotient is 2.

radius [rā′dē•əs] **radio** A line segment with one endpoint at the center of a circle and the other endpoint on the circle (p. 452)
Example:

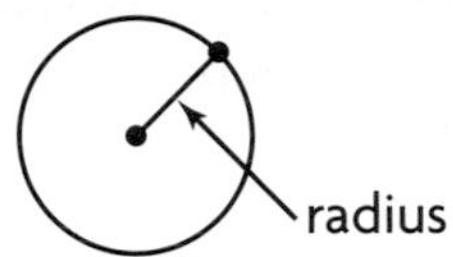

random sample [ran′dəm sam′pəl] **muestra al azar** A sample in which each subject in the population has an equal chance of being chosen (p. 596)

range [rānj] **rango** The difference between the greatest number and the least number in a set of data (p. 598)
Example: 2, 2, 3, 5, 7, 7, 8, 9
The range is $9 - 2 = 7$.

ray [rā] **rayo** A part of a line; it begins at one endpoint and extends forever in one direction. (p. 436)
Example:

reciprocal [ri•sip′rə•kəl] **recíproco** One of two numbers whose product is 1 (p. 251)
Example: 8 and $\frac{1}{8}$ are reciprocals since $8 \times \frac{1}{8} = 1$.

rectangle [rek′tang•gəl] **rectángulo** A parallelogram with four right angles (p. 472)
Example:

rectangular prism [rek•tang′gyə•lər pri′zəm] **prisma rectangular** A solid figure in which all six faces are rectangles (p. 478)
Example:

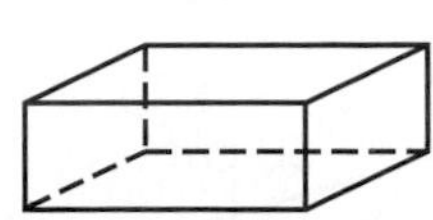

regular polygon [re′gyə•lər pä′lē•gän] **polígono regular** A polygon in which all sides are congruent and all angles are congruent (p. 446)

remainder [ri•mān′dər] **residuo** The amount left over when a number cannot be divided equally (p. 88)

rhombus [räm′bəs] **rombo** A parallelogram with four equal, or congruent, sides (p. 472)
Example:

Word History

Rhombus is almost identical to its Greek origin, *rhombos.* The original meaning was "spinning top" or "magic wheel," which is easy to imagine when you look at a rhombus, an equilateral parallelogram.

right angle [rīt ang′gəl] **ángulo recto** An angle which is half of a straight angle with its measurement being 90° (p. 437)
Example:

90°

right triangle [rīt trī′ang•gəl] **triángulo rectángulo** A triangle that has a right angle (p. 468) *Example:*

round [round] **redondear** To replace a number with one that is simpler and is approximately the same size as the original number (p. 12)
Example: 114.6 rounded to the nearest ten is 110 and to the nearest unit is 115

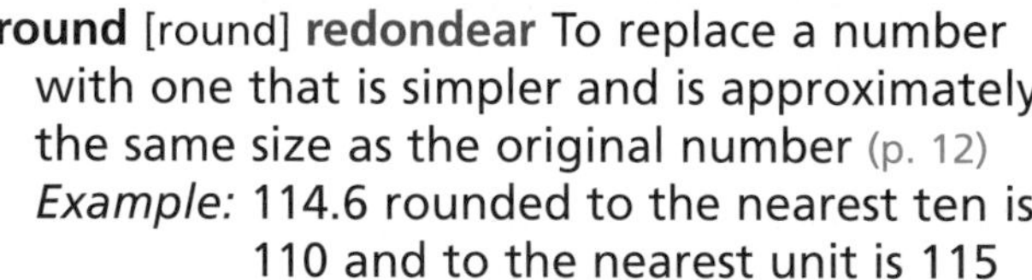

sample [sam′pəl] **muestra** A part of a population (p. 596)

scalene triangle [skā′lēn trī′ang•gəl] **triángulo escaleno** A triangle with no congruent sides (p. 468)
Example:

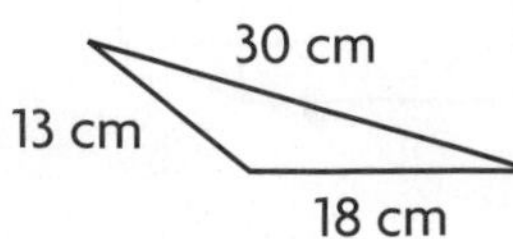

similar [si′mə•lər] **semejante** Having the same shape, but not necessarily the same size (p. 456)
Example:

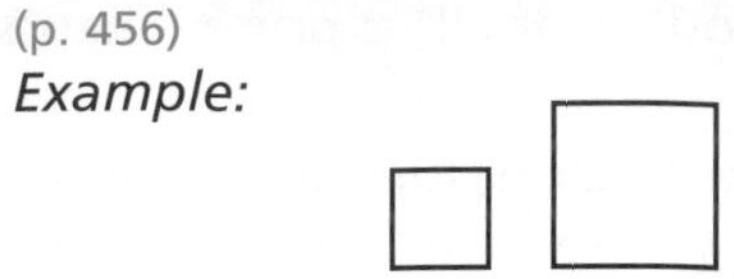

simplest form [sim′pləst fôrm] **mínima expresión** A fraction is in simplest form when the numerator and denominator have only 1 as their common factor. (p. 146)

solid figure [sä′ləd fig′yər] **cuerpo geométrico** A three-dimensional figure (p. 478)

solution [sə•lo͞o′shən] **solución** A value that, when substituted for the variable, makes an equation true (p. 354)

sphere [sfir] **esfera** A round object whose curved surface is the same distance from the center to all its points (p. 478)
Example:

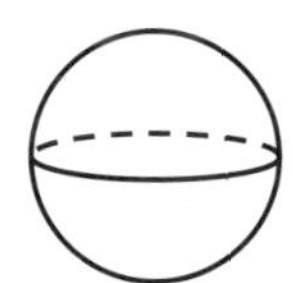

square [skwâr] **cuadrado** A polygon with four equal, or congruent, sides and four right angles (p. 472)

square number [skwâr num′bər] **número cuadrado** The product of a number and itself (p. 129) *Example:* $4^2 = 16$; 16 is a square number.

square pyramid [skwâr pir′ə•mid] **pirámide cuadrada** A solid figure with a square base and with four triangular faces that have a common vertex (p. 478)
Example:

square root [skwâr ro͞ot] **raíz cuadrada** One of two equal factors of a number (p. 131)

square unit [skwâr yo͞o′nət] **unidad cuadrada** A unit of area with dimensions 1 unit × 1 unit (p. 546)

standard form [stan′dərd fôrm] **forma normal** A way to write numbers by using the digits 0–9, with each digit having a place value (p. 4)
Example: 456 ←standard form

stem [stem] **tallo** A tens digit in a stem-and-leaf plot (p. 626)

stem-and-leaf plot [stem and lēf plot] **diagrama de tallo y hojas** A table that shows groups of data arranged by place value (p. 626)
Example:

Stem	Leaves
1	1 2 4
2	0 3 4 5
3	4 5 7
4	0 0 1 2

Number of Tickets Sold

straight angle [strāt ang′gəl] **ángulo llano** An angle whose measure is 180° (p. 437)
Example:

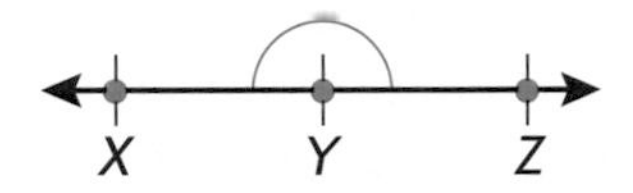

subtraction [səb•trak′shən] **resta** The process of finding how many are left when a number of items are taken away from a group of items; the process of finding the difference when two groups are compared; the opposite of addition (p. 16)

sum [sum] **suma o total** The answer to an addition problem (p. 17)

surface area [sûr′fəs âr′ē•ə] **área total** The sum of the areas of all the faces, or surfaces, of a solid figure (p. 574)

survey [sûr′vā] **encuesta** A method of gathering information about a group (p. 596)

tenth [tenth] **décimo** One of ten equal parts (p. 38) *Example:* 0.7 = seven tenths

thousandth [thou′zəndth] **milésimo** One of one thousand equal parts (p. 40)
Example: 0.006 = six thousandths

trapezoid [tra′pə•zoid] **trapecio** A quadrilateral with exactly one pair of parallel sides (p. 472)
Examples:

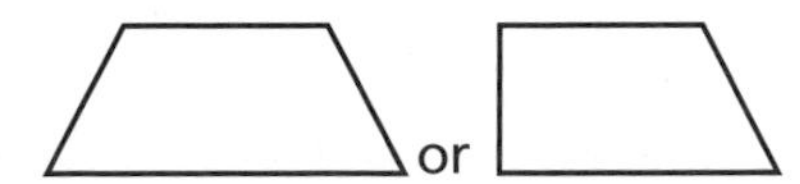

tree diagram [trē dī′ə•gram] **diagrama de árbol** An organized list that shows all possible outcomes for an event (p. 122)

trend [trend] **tendencia** A pattern over time, in all or part of a graph, where the data increase, decrease, or stay the same (p. 607)

triangle [trī′ang•gəl] **triángulo** A polygon with three sides (p. 446)
Examples:

underestimate [un•dər•es′tə•mət] **subestimar** An estimate that is less than the exact answer (p. 14)

unit fraction [yo͞o′-nət frak′shən] **fracción unitaria** A fraction that has 1 as a numerator (p. 148)

unlike fractions [un•līk′ frak′shənz] **fracciones no semejantes** Fractions that have different denominators (p. 198)

Example: $\frac{3}{4}$ and $\frac{2}{5}$ are unlike fractions.

variable [vâr′ē•ə•bəl] **variable** A letter or symbol that stands for one or more numbers (p. 23)

Venn diagram [ven dī′ə•gram] **diagrama de Venn** A diagram that shows relationships among sets of things (p. 611)
Example:

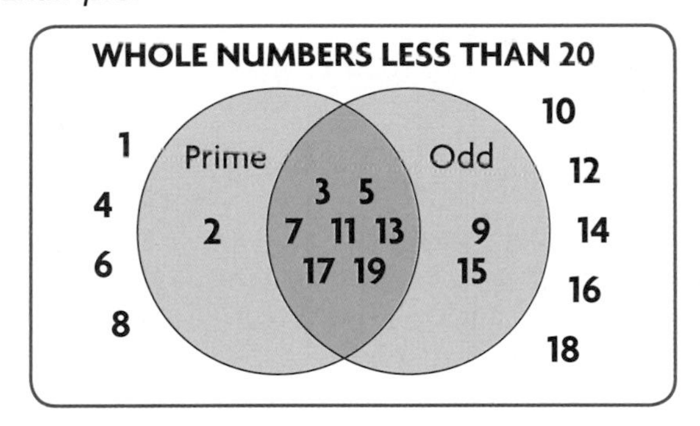

vertex [vûr′teks] **vértice** The point where two or more rays meet; the point of intersection of two sides of a polygon; the point of intersection of three (or more) edges of a solid figure; the top point of a cone; the plural of vertex is vertices (pp. 437, 479)
Examples:

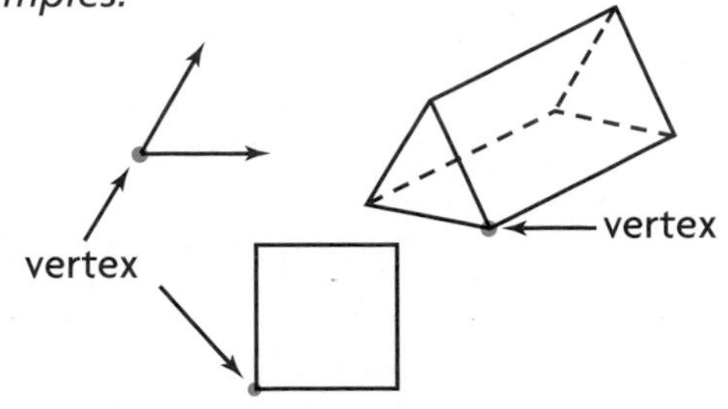

Word History

The Latin word *vertere* means to turn and also relates to highest. You can turn a figure around a point or *vertex*.

volume [väl′yəm] **volumen** The measure of the space a solid figure occupies (p. 576)

whole number [hōl num′bər] **número entero** One of the numbers 0, 1, 2, 3, 4, ... The set of whole numbers goes on without end.

word form [wurd fôrm] **en palabras** A way to write numbers in standard English (p. 4)
Example: 4,829 = four thousand, eight hundred twenty-nine

x*-axis** [eks•ak′səs] **eje de la *x The horizontal number line on a coordinate plane (p. 498)

x*-coordinate** [eks•kō•ôr′də•nət] **coordenada *x The first number in an ordered pair, which tells the distance to move right or left from (0,0) (p. 498)

y*-axis** [wī•ak′səs] **eje de la *y The vertical number line on a coordinate plane (p. 498)

y*-coordinate** [wī•kō•ôr′də•nət] **coordenada *y The second number in an ordered pair, which tells the distance to move up or down from (0,0) (p. 498)

Zero Property of Multiplication [zē′rō prä′pər•tē əv mul•tə•plə•kā′shən] **propiedad del cero de la multiplicación** The property that states that when you multiply by zero, the product is zero

Index

B

C

E

F

G

M

N

O

Q

R

S

T

U

Photo Credits

KEY: (t) top, (b) bottom, (l) left, (r) right, (c) center, (bg) background, (fg) foreground.

Front Cover: (l) Photo Network/Alamy; Front cover (r) Larry Mulvehill/Corbis.

Back Cover: (r) Philip James Corwin/CORBIS; Back cover (l) Larry Mulvehill/Corbis.

Front Endsheets: Page 1 & 2, Digital Vision/Veer; Page 3, Craig Aurness/Corbis.

Back Endsheets: Page 1, Charles C. Place/Photographer's Choice RF/Getty Images; Page 2 & 3, Digital Vision/ Getty Images.

Title Page: (l) Photo Network/Alamy; (r) Larry Mulvehill/Corbis.

Copyright Page: Charles C. Place/Photographer's Choice RF/Getty Images.

Table of Contents: iv Alanie/Life File/Getty Images (Royalty-free); vi Ryan McVay/Photodisc green/Getty Images; viii Phillip Colla Natural History Photography; x Tim Fitzharris/Minden Pictures; xii Photodisc/ age fotostock; xiv Carlos S. Pereyra/age fotostock; xvi Tim Fitzharris/Minden Pictures; xviii Gary Crabbe/ Enlightened Images; xx–xxi Bill Ross/CORBIS.

Unit 1: 1 (t) The futures Channel; 1 (c) The Futures Channel; 1 (b) The Futures Channel; 2 Alanie/Life File/Getty Images ; 10 Douglas Plasencia/Courtesy American Numismatic Rarities; 11 James Porto/Getty Images; 12 Gail Mooney/Masterfile; 19 (bg) Craig Tuttle/Corbis; 20 SuperStock/Alamy; 21 Streeter Lecka/ Getty Images; 22 Bill Aron/Photo Edit; 24 Photo courtesy of Six Flags Magic Mountain; 29 Alanie/Life File/ Getty Images ; 33 (tr) Robert Warren/Taxi/Getty Images; 36 Charles O'Rear/CORBIS; 38 Bettmann/CORBIS; 39 Brooklyn Museum/Corbis; 42 Kathy Willens/ASSOCIATED PRESS; 43 Paul Wayne Wilson/PhotoStockFile/ Alamy; 44 David Madison/Getty Images; 46 WoodyStock/Alamy; 47 (br) Michael & Patricia Fogden/Corbis; 49 Mark E. Gibson/Ambient Images; 50 Tom Brakefield/ Corbis; 51 Alan Schein Photography/ Corbis; 55 (bg) Comstock Images/Alamy; 55 (tr) Robert Warren/Taxi/Getty Images; 55 (tr) (inset) Courtesy of the Santa Barbara Museum of Natural History; 58 Randy Wells/Corbis; 60 Juniors Bildarchiv/Alamy; 61 Flip Nicklin/ Minden Pictures; 62 Royalty-Free/Corbis; 63 Ken Reid/Getty Images; 66 Gerolf Kalt/zefa/Corbis; 68 Peter Titmuss/Alamy; 69 (tr) akg-images; 69 (cr) PhotoSpin, Inc/Alamy; 70 RNT Productions/Corbis; 72 Theo Allofs/ zefa/Corbis; 73 Klein/Peter Arnold, Inc.; 75 Jerry Millevoi/age fotostock; 76 Nick Hanna/Alamy; 77 Ariel Skelley/Corbis; 81 (tr) Getty Images/PhotoDisc/Harcourt; 84 Larry Brownstein/Ambient Images; 86 Jermy Walker/Getty Images; 87 Michael S. Yamashita/Corbis; 88 Corbis; 90 Matthis Kulla/Corbis; 94 Tim Street-Porter/Corbis; 96 Atlantide Phototravel/Corbis; 97 Envision/Corbis; 98 Envision/Corbis; 99 Jan Butchofsky-Houser/Corbis; 100 Garry Gay/Alamy; 103 Veer; 104 David Muench/Corbis; 105 Skip Brown/Getty Images (RM); 106 The Photolibrary Wales/Alamy; 111 (tr) PhotoSpin, Inc/Alamy; 114 (tr) John Pyle/Icon SMI/ NewsCom; 114–115 (bg) John Pyle/Icon SMI/NewsCom; 115 (tr) Ai Wire-Alan Smith/NewsCom.

Unit 2: 117 (t) The Futures Channel; 117 (c) The Futures Channel; 117 (b) The Futures Channel; 118 Ryan McVay/Photodisc green/Getty Images; 126 Scott Halleran/Getty Images; 128 John & Lisa Merrill-Getty Images; 129 Janet Horton/AG Pix; 130 Kim Taylor & Jane Burton/Getty Images; 131 Nancy Louie/iStockPhoto; 135 Royalty free/Corbis; 139 NASA; 142 AP Photo/Matt Sayles; 152 Ambient Images Inc./Alamy; 153 Masterfile; 155 (bg) Lee Cohen/Corbis; 158 (cr) Mike Powell/ Getty Images; 160 Banana Stock/age fotostock; 162 Corbis; 170 (tr) AP Photo/Nick Ut; 170 (br) Getty Images; 170–171 (bg) Getty Images.

Unit 3: 173 (t) The Futures Channel; 173 (c) The Futures Channel; 173 (b) The Futures Channel; 174 (t) Ed Young/AGSTOCK/Science Photo Library; 174 (br) Thomas Firak/JupiterImages; 178 2007 Mark Stadsklev/ AlaskaStock.com; 179 Ben Barden/Alamy; 180 Enigma/Alamy; 181 Royalty-Free/Corbis; 189 Jim Sugar/Corbis; 193 (tr) Stockdisc/Getty Images; 196 Robert Houser/Index Stock Imagery; 203 Royalty-Free/Corbis; 204 The Bridgeman Art Library; 207 (all) Marilyn Angel Wynn/NativeStock.com; 208 Jeffery L. Rotman/Corbis; 209 Bruce Coleman, USA; 215 (bg) Corbis/Harcourt; 218 (t) Johner/Getty Images; 224 Royalty-Free/Corbis; 227 JupiterImages; 229 (t) Sean Justice/Corbis; 229 (b) Monserrat J. Schwartz/Alamy; 233 (tr) Corbis/Harcourt; 233 (bg) Getty Images/PhotoDisc/Harcourt; 236 Phillip Colla Natural History Photography; 240 Brand X Picture/Alamy; 241 Robert White/zefa/Corbis; 242 Pornchai Mittongtare/JupiterImages; 246 Sabine Fritsch/Getty; 247 Darrell Gullin/Corbis; 254 Photofusion Picture Library/Alamy; 258 Robert Landau/Corbis; 259 Derick A. Thomas, Dat's JAzz/Corbis; 263 (tr) ©Bettmann/CORBIS; 266 (tr) Roger Ressmeyer/CORBIS; 266 (cr) Roger Ressmeyer/CORBIS; 266–267 (bg) NASA/JPL; 267 (tr) CORBIS.

Unit 4: 269 (t) Motorola Inc. Reproduced with Permission; 269 (c) The Futures Channel; 269 (b) The Futures Channel; 270 SuperStock/age fotostock; 274 Christian Forcher/epa/Corbis; 275 AP Photo/David J. Phillip; 277 Clive Rose/Getty Images; 279 Royalty-Free/Corbis; 280 David Sanger photography/Alamy; 282 David Young-Wolff/Photo Edit; 290 Tim Fitzharris/Minden Pictures; 294 Detlev van Ravenswaay/Photo Researchers, Inc.; 295 NASA; 298 Konrad Wothe/Minden Pictures; 299 Eva Momatiuk/John Eastcott/Minden Pictures; 300 Graham Robertson/Ardea.com; 302 Gerry Ellis/Minden Pictures; 303 (tl) P. Wilson/zefa/Corbis; 303 (tr) Digital Vision Ltd./SuperStock; 303 (br) Royalty Free/Corbis; 304 SuperStock; 305 John Harrison/Photographers Direct; 306 NHPA/Rich Kirchner; 311 (tr) Alistair Berg/Taxi/Getty Images; 311 (bg) Corbis/Harcourt.

314 Michio Hoshino/Minden Pictures; 318 Jonathan Nourok/Photo Edit; 319 britishcolumbiaphotos.com/Alamy; 320 BananaStock/Alamy; 322 Masterfile (Royalty-Free Div.); 323 Bill Bachmann/Alamy; 328 John Kelly/ Getty Images; 330 Foodfolio/Alamy; 332 (tr) Corbis; 333 Royalty-Free/Corbis; 337 (bg) PhotoDisc/Getty Images/Harcourt; 337 (r) Richard Hutchings/Corbis; 340 AP Photo/Lionel Cironneau; 340–341 (bg) Prisma/SuperStock; 341 (tr) Mike Blake/Reuters/Corbis.

Unit 5: 343 (t) The Futures Channel; 343 (c) The Futures Channel; 343 (b) The Futures Channel; 344 Photodisc/age fotostock; 346 Mark Raycroft/ Minden Pictures; 348 (cr) John Foxx/ImageState Stock Photography/Harcourt; 350 (t) Hemera Technologies/ JupiterImages; 350 (c) John Foxx/ImageState Stock Photography/Harcourt; 351 iStockPhoto; 354 Peter Weimann/Animals Animals-Earth Scenes; 356 Peter Weimann/Animals Animals-Earth Scenes; 357 ImageSource/age fotostock; 359 Robert E. Barber/Alamy; 360 Gerry Ellis/Minden Pictures; 362 Arco Images/Alamy; 363 David Fleetham/Alamy; 364 Paul Springett/Alamy; 365 NASA/Roger Ressmeyer/CORBIS; 366 Topham/The Image Works; 367 NASA/Photo Researchers, Inc.; 374 Flip Nicklin/Minden Pictures; 376 Galen Rowell/Corbis; 377 Royalty-Free/Corbis; 379 NASA; 380 Albaimages/Alamy; 381 Grant Heilman Photography, Inc.; 382 Peter Barrett/Masterfile; 383 Mark E. Gibson/Corbis; 386 NASA/Media Service; 387 Craig Lovell/Eagle Visions Photography/Alamy; 390 (b) Phototake/Alamy; 391 Michael Durham/Minden Pictures; 392 Gibson Stock Photography; 394 Royalty-Free/Corbis; 395 (t) Skyscan/Corbis; 402 Mark Gibson Stock Photography; 409 Denis Felix/ Getty Images; 410 Imagebroker/Alamy; 414 Sean Justice/Getty Images; 415 Royalty Free/Veer; 417 (bg) Duomo/Corbis; 419 Royalty-Free/Corbis; 421 (bg) Corbis; 427 (tr) David Young-Wolff/PhotoEdit; 430 (tr) Kim Kulish/Corbis; 430 (cr) AP Photo/University of Florida, Ron Franklin; 430–431 (bg) Getty/Harcourt; 431 (tr) Gene Blevins/Reuters/Corbis; 431 (cr) PRNewsFoto/NewsCom.

Unit 6: 433 (t) The Futures Channel; 433 (c) The Futures Channel; 433 (b) The Futures Channel; 434 Carlos S. Pereyra/age fotostock; 437 Art on File/Corbis; 440 Jon Gray/Getty Images; 446 (c) Bildarchiv Monheim GmbH/Alamy; 446 (cr) allOver Photography/Alamy; 450 Rob Lacey/Vividstock.net/Alamy; 452 Bettmann/Corbis; 463 Corbis/Harcourt; 456 Emiliano and Ada Martinez; 466 Jeremy Woodhouse/Masterfile; 468 Reuters/Corbis; 472 The Granger Collection, New York; 475 Royalty-Free/Corbis; 478 Kevin Fleming/Corbis; 479 Hubert Stadler/Corbis; 480 Ilene MacDonald/Alamy; 481 Al Greenberg; 482 William Milner/Shutterstock; 487 Danita Delimont/Alamy; 496 REUTERS/NASA; 498 Bill Ross/Corbis; 500 Panoramic Images/Getty Images; 504 David De Lossy/Getty Images; 509 Robert Holmes/Corbis; 510 Gibson Stock Photography; 511 Perfect Picture Parts/Alamy; 518 GC Minerals/Alamy; 518–519 (bg) Albert J.Copley/Visuals Unlimited; 519 Mark A. Schneider/Visuals Unlimited.

Unit 7: 521 (t) The Futures Channel; 521 (c) The Futures Channel; 521 (b) NASA; 522 Tim Fitzharris/Minden Pictures; 524 Photofusion Picture/Alamy; 526 Peder Bjorkegren/Etsa/Corbis; 530 PCL/Alamy; 532 Glow Images/Alamy; 534 Royalty Free/Corbis; 536 (t) Lee Snider/Photo Images/CORBIS; 536 (b) Vitali Ogorodnikov/Emporis; 537 (bl) AAD Worldwide Travel Images/Alamy; 537 (bc) Sandro Vannini/Corbis; 537 (br) Alamy; 541 (bg) Glowimages/Getty Images; 544 Tony Hertz/AGStockUSA; 562 Renzo Mancini/Getty Images; 569 (tr) Barros & Barros/Getty Images; 569 (bg) Pixoi Ltd/Alamy; 572 Jim Corwin/Photo Researchers, Inc.; 583 (t) Acco Engineered Systems; 583 (b) Craig Lovell/Eagle Visions Photography/Alamy; 592 (tr) LHB Photo/Alamy; 592–593 (bg) Geauga Lake, Aurora, Ohio; 593 (tr) LHB Photo/Alamy; 593 (bl) Yann Layma/Getty Images.

Unit 8: 595 (t) National Oceanic and Atmospheric Administration/Department of Commerce; 595 (c) University Corporation for Atmospheric Research; 595 (b) University Corporation for Atmospheric Research,; 596 Rob Gilley/Imagestate; 598 Jim Brandenburg/Minden Pictures; 600 (cr) John Watkins/Corbis; 600 (br) Ashley Cooper/Corbis; 602 Ronald C. Saari; 604 Royalty-Free/Corbis; 606 Mathias Kulka/Corbis; 608 Imagebroker/Alamy; 609 Royalty Free/Corbis; 613 Creatas/SuperStock; 622 Gary Crabbe/Enlightened Images; 624 John Neubauer/Photo Edit; 625 David R. Frazier/Photo Researchers, Inc.; 626 Mike Kipling Photography/Alamy; 628 Joeseph Sohm-Visions of America/Getty Images; 629 Richard Cummins/Corbis; 632 White Cross Productions/Getty Images; 637 Lee F. Snyder/Photo Researchers, Inc.; 641 (bg) Royalty-Free/Corbis; 644 (tr) ImageGap/Alamy; 644 (cr) Getty Images; 644–645 (bg) Andersen Ross/age fotostock; 645 (t) San Francisco History Center, San Francisco Public Library; 645 (b) AP Photo/Susan Ragan.

Student Handbook: Page H, GK Hart/Vikki Hart/Getty Images (Royalty-free); H1 Jim Brandenburg/Minden Pictures.